THE OXFORD HANDBOOK OF

THE MACROECONOMICS OF GLOBAL WARMING

THE OXFORD HANDBOOK OF

THE MACROECONOMICS OF GLOBAL WARMING

Edited by

LUCAS BERNARD

and

WILLI SEMMLER

OXFORD
UNIVERSITY PRESS

OXFORD
UNIVERSITY PRESS

Oxford University Press is a department of the University of Oxford.
It furthers the University's objective of excellence in research, scholarship,
and education by publishing worldwide.

Oxford New York
Auckland Cape Town Dar es Salaam Hong Kong Karachi
Kuala Lumpur Madrid Melbourne Mexico City Nairobi
New Delhi Shanghai Taipei Toronto

With offices in
Argentina Austria Brazil Chile Czech Republic France Greece
Guatemala Hungary Italy Japan Poland Portugal Singapore
South Korea Switzerland Thailand Turkey Ukraine Vietnam

Oxford is a registered trade mark of Oxford University Press
in the UK and in certain other countries.

Published in the United States of America by
Oxford University Press
198 Madison Avenue, New York, NY 10016,

Library of Congress Cataloging-in-Publication Data
CIP data is on file at the Library of Congress
ISBN 978–0–19–985697–8

1 3 5 7 9 8 6 4 2
Printed in the United States of America
on acid-free paper

Contents

PART IV ECONOMIC EFFECTS OF MITIGATION AND ADAPTATION

PART V INTERNATIONAL PERSPECTIVES

PART VI DIRECTIONS IN MITIGATION POLICY DESIGN

List of Contributors

Frank Ackerman is a Lecturer in climate and energy policy at Massachusetts Institute of Technology, and Senior Economist at Synapse Energy Economics.

Askar Akaev is Professor and Senior Researcher at Prigogine Institute for Mathematical Investigations of Complex Systems at Moscow State University and Co-Coordinator of the Russian Academy of Sciences Program "System Analysis and Mathematical Modeling of World Dynamics." He is former President of Kyrgyztan.

Angelo Antoci is Professor of Mathematical Economics in the Department of Economics and Business at the University of Sassari, Italy.

Frédéric Babonneau is vice president at ORDECSYS and Researcher at the Laboratory of Environmental and Urban Economics Laboratory (LEURE) at Swiss Federal Institute of Technology, Lausanne, Switzerland.

Lopamudra Banerjee is Assistant Professor of Economics at The New School for Social Research, New York City.

Lucas Bernard is Professor of Business at The New York City College of Technology of The City University of New York.

Simone Borghesi is Assistant Professor of Environmental Economics in the Department of Political and International Sciences at the University of Siena, Italy.

Thierry Bréchet is Professor at the Université catholique de Louvain, Center for Operations Research & Econometrics (CORE), and Holder of the Lhoist Berghmans Chair in Environmental Economics and Management, Belgium.

William Brock is Vilas Research Professor, Emeritus at University of Wisconsin and Research Professor at University of Missouri, Columbia.

Francisco Cabo is a researcher at IMUVA, Institute of Mathematics of the Universidad de Valladolid, and Associate Professor in the Faculty of Economics and Business at Universidad de Valladolid, Spain.

Carmen Camacho is a CNRS Researcher at the Centre d'Economie de la Sorbonne at Université Paris 1 Panthéon-Sorbonne, France.

Raphaële Chappe is a PhD candidate in the Department of Economics at The New School for Social Research, New York City.

Graciela Chichilnisky is Professor of Economics and Statistics and Director of the Columbia Consortium for Risk Management at Columbia University.

Ottmar Edenhofer is Professor of the Economics of Climate Change at Technische Universität Berlin and Co-Chair of Working Group III of the Intergovernmental Panel on Climate Change (IPCC, winner of the 2007 Nobel Peace Prize). He is also Deputy Director and Chief Economist at the Potsdam Institute for Climate Impact Research (PIK) and Director of the Mercator Research Institute on Global Commons and Climate Change (MCC), Berlin, Germany.

Neil Edwards is Reader in Earth Systems Science at The Open University, UK.

Gustav Engström is a Researcher at The Beijer Institute of Ecological Economics and Stockholm Resilience Centre, Stockholm University, Sweden.

Jacob Engwerda is Associate Professor in the Department of Econometrics and Operations Research at Tilburg University, Netherlands.

Christian Flachsland is Group Leader at the Mercator Research Institute on Global Commons and Climate Change (MCC), Berlin, Germany.

Alfred Greiner is in the Faculty of Economics at Bielefeld University, Germany.

James E. Hansen is Adjunct Professor and Director of the Climate Science, Awareness and Solutions Program at The Earth Institute at Columbia University.

Wolfgang Karl Härdle is Ladislaus von Bortkiewicz Chair of Statistics in the School of Business and Economics and Director of the Center for Applied Statistics and Economics at Humboldt University, Germany. He is visiting professor at School of Business, Singapore Management University, 50 Stamford Road, Singapore 178899.

Alain Haurie is Director and Co-Founder at ORDECSYS, Switzerland.

Phil Holden is Research Investment Fellow in the Faculty of Science of the Centre for Earth, Planetary, Space and Astronomical Research at The Open University, UK.

Michael Jakob is Researcher / Fellow at the Mercator Research Institute on Global Commons and Climate Change (MCC), Berlin, Germany.

Amit Kanudia is Founder and Partner at KanORS-EMR, India.

Mika Kato is Associate Professor in the Department of Economics at Howard University.

Klaus Keller is an Associate Professor in the Department of Geosciences at the Pennsylvania State University and an Adjunct Professor in the Department of Engineering and Public Policy at the Carnegie Mellon University.

Maryse Labriet is Researcher and Consultant at Eneris Environment and Energy Consultants, Spain.

Ulrike Lehr is Senior Expert at Gesellschaft für Wirtschaftliche Strukturforschung, Germany.

Kai Lessmann is Group Leader at the Potsdam Institute for Climate Impact Research (PIK), Germany.

Brenda López Cabrera is Professor "Weather, Climate and Energy Analysis" at the Ladislaus von Bortkiewicz Chair of Statistics in the School of Business and Economics at Humboldt Universität Berlin, Germany.

Christian Lutz is Managing Director at Gesellschaft für Wirtschaftliche Strukturforschung, Germany.

Zhong Maochu is Professor at the School of Economics at Nankai University, China.

Guiomar Martín-Herrán is a researcher at IMUVA, Institute of Mathematics of the Universidad de Valladolid and Full Professor in the Faculty of Economics and Business at Universidad de Valladolid, Spain.

María Pilar Martínez-García is Associate Professor in the Faculty of Economics and Business at Universidad de Murcia, Spain.

Helmut Maurer is Professor in the Institute for Computational and Applied Mathematics at Universität Muenster, Germany.

Kozo Mayumi is Professor of Economics in the Faculty of IAS at the University Tokushima, Japan.

Stefan Mittnik is Full Professor and Chair of Financial Econometrics at Ludwig Maximilian University, Munich, Germany.

Robert Nicholas is Managing Director of the Network for Sustainable Climate Risk Management (SCRiM) and Research Associate in the Earth and Environmental Systems Institute at Pennsylvania State University.

Barbara Pizzileo is Project Manager of the Faculty of Science in the Department of Environment, Earth and Ecosystems at The Open University, UK.

John M. Polimeni is Associate Professor of Economics at Albany College of Pharmacy and Health Sciences.

David Popp is Professor of Public Administration and International Affairs at The Maxwell School of Citizenship and Public Affairs at Syracuse University and a Research Associate at the National Bureau of Economic Research.

Johann Jakob Preuß was a student at the Institute for Computational and Applied Mathematics at the Universität Muenster, Germany.

Matthias Ritter is a Research Associate at the Department of Agricultural Economics, Farm Management Group, at Humboldt University Berlin, Germany.

Jeffrey D. Sachs is Director of the Earth Institute at Columbia University.

Daniel Samaan is Researcher at the International Institute for Labour Studies, International Labour Organization (ILO), Switzerland.

Willi Semmler is Henry Arnhold Professor of Economics at The New School for Social Research, New York City.

Mauro Sodini is Researcher in the Department of Economics and Management at University of Pisa, Italy.

Elizabeth A. Stanton is Senior Economist at Synapse Energy Economics.

Richard S. J. Tol is Professor in the Department of Economics at the University of Sussex, UK, and in the Institute for Environmental Studies and Department of Spatial Economics at Vrije Universiteit, Netherlands.

Vladimir M. Veliov is Professor and Head of the Research Unit ORCOS in the Institute of Mathematical Methods in Economics at Vienna University of Technology, Austria.

Marc Vielle is a Researcher in the REME Laboratory at Swiss Federal Institute of Technology at Lausanne, Switzerland.

Florian Wagener is Associate Professor in the Center for Nonlinear Dynamics in Economics and Finance (CeNDEF) at the University of Amsterdam, Netherlands.

Franz Wirl is Professor and Chair of Industry, Energy, and the Environment in the Department of Business Administration at the University of Vienna, Austria.

Anastasios Xepapadeas is Professor of Economic Theory and Policy in the Department of International and European Economic Studies at the Athens University of Economics and Business, Greece.

Shi Yadong is lecturer in the Department of International Economics at the University of International Relations, China.

Yuri Yegorov is senior researcher at th Faculty of Business, Economics, and Statistics at the University of Vienna, Austria.

CHAPTER 1

THE MACROECONOMICS OF GLOBAL WARMING

LUCAS BERNARD AND WILLI SEMMLER

THE year 1896 was a memorable one for two reasons. First, Henry Ford introduced the gasoline-powered automobile to the United States and second, a Swedish scientist, Svante Arrhenius, proposed that a greenhouse effect could result from increased atmospheric CO_2. So, the collision course between the Industrial Revolution and the environment began to develop.

More than 100 years have passed since then; research has demonstrated that the externalities stemming from industrial production and the use of fossil fuels has led to levels of CO_2 emission so high that the current course may be hard to reverse. As many argue, temperatures have probably reached a critical point, beyond which a return to preindustrial levels will be enormously difficult to achieve. Such a position has been put forward, largely owing to the enormous efforts of the Intergovernmental Panel on Climate Change (IPCC),[1] and may be read in numerous books[2] and academic papers. As climate researchers and geoscientists have been predicting for quite some time,[3] from the devastation of storms, for example, hurricanes Katrina and Sandy, flooding coastal regions and riverbanks, to heat waves and new desert formation, to the disappearance of island nations in the southern sections of the Pacific Ocean, the effects of global warming are making themselves felt and have begun to demand urgent action.

Academic work and particular policy proposals to combat climate change have emerged from a series of important international policy meetings. Beginning with the Kyoto Protocol (1997) and the associated conference at which it was proposed, then continuing through the meetings in, for example, Copenhagen (2009), Cancun (2010), Durban (2011), and, more recently, in Doha (2012) and at the IPCC meetings in September 2013, March 2014, and April 2014 (Working Groups I, II, and III, respectively), a dialog concerning the urgency of action against climate change is well underway. Geoscience researchers and the lead investigators of the IPCC have supported CO_2 emission reduction pledges with the view that the goal should be either to cap CO_2 emissions (the Kyoto Agreement) or to maintain the increase in temperature below 2°C (Copenhagen), either of which should be achieved through international coordination.

Yet, international cooperation on this matter faces severe challenges. The Europeans appear to be ready to move ahead with further agreements after Copenhagen, Cancun, Durban, and Doha, exhibiting a more optimistic view with respect to an agreement regarding the achievability of the 2°C limit to the increase in global temperatures.[4] However, this stands in stark contrast to the evaluations of the US Congress, which, for reasons of policy, does not appear to be ready to implement the Copenhagen CO_2 reduction commitments any time soon. On the other hand, developing countries are highly alarmed, as it is expected that climate change will hit the developing world the hardest. The developed world can protect itself against climate change through infrastructure improvement and will use more energy to adapt to climate change effects, but it is in developing countries where some of the most dangerous consequences of climate change will be concentrated.

In our view, it is timely that a comprehensive overview of these issues and challenges be presented in an academic handbook, one covering the many aspects of global warming. This Handbook presents material of interest to academics in different disciplines, researchers, practitioners, policymakers, and to those taking part in the worldwide discussions on this issue. Although this Handbook focuses on the *macroeconomics* of global warming, we include updates on climate research by geoscientists, geophysicists, and earth scientists. This has been done, however, through an economic "lens." Thus, we address broad issues, but from the perspective of macroeconomics.

In Part I, climate change is related to global economic growth. Some of the topics addressed in this section include improving climate projections, the economic consequences of sudden shifts in the environment, and analysis of sustainable growth that takes climate change into account. We are very happy to have on board climate scientists who can elaborate on the trends in climate change as well as its connection to economic growth.

We launch this section with the work of Klaus Keller and Robert Nicholas, who discuss research results pertaining to the projections of environmental scientists, and how these projections might be made more useful for mitigation and adaptation policies when tipping points are allowed for. William Brock, Gustav Engström, and Anastasios Xepapadeas make these concerns relating to tipping points and regime changes more specific in their modeling of the interaction of ice cap melting, energy balance, and economic growth. General mitigation policies are not likely to be as useful as those which are tailored to the dynamics of energy balance and latitudinal-dependent energy absorption—resulting from the ratio of incoming to outgoing solar energy. In doing so, they add a special dimension, that of the global distribution of damage, to climate research. Florian Wagener continues this type of analysis by highlighting the way in which the environment can undergo sudden regime change. Those regime shifts are a critical aspect of the modeling of the interaction of human activities with the environment. Helmut Maurer, Johann Jakob Preuß, and Willi Semmler also present a model with multiple regimes, but they focus on particular policy options. Beginning with the

Nordhaus canonical growth model, which includes economic growth, CO_2 emission, and climate change—and damages from climate change—important options as to how mitigation policies could be pursued are modeled and evaluated. The last contribution to this section is a chapter by Thierry Bréchet, Carmen Camacho, and Vladimir M. Veliov. Employing techniques from the theory of differential games, they build a model with heterogeneous agents interacting with the environment; however, their agents do not have perfect foresight. The authors incorporate predictive control, learning, and adaptive behavior, which results in more robust guidance for policy designers.

Part II is devoted specifically to mitigation policy modeling within the context of environmental games. Broadly speaking, mitigation policies include subjects such as cap-and-trade, carbon tax, increasing energy efficiency, land/forest use policies, technological change and more extensive development of renewable energy resources, and policies to reduce ocean acidification. In this way, the perspective is broadened beyond solely CO_2 reduction. The question as to whether there should be a single global solution or, rather, country-specific mitigation policies, as well as the topic of whether policies are compatible with the incentives of agents and countries are also addressed. This framework, one of cooperative and noncooperative environmental games, provides a natural perspective in which these issues can be studied.

Part II begins with two complementary papers; while Jacob Engwerda gives a comprehensive survey of the use of game theory to study cooperation and noncooperation between countries in the context of climate control policies, Alain Haurie and his team[5] present a game-theoretic analysis of how sharing the effort of controlling climate change might be made fair. Alfred Greiner, also using a cooperative and noncooperative game-theoretic approach, focuses attention on the interaction of pollution and abatement efforts for advanced and less developed countries on the international level. The chapter by Francisco Cabo, Guiomar Martín-Herrán, and María Pilar Martínez-García uses a dynamic model to investigate changes in trade between regions that have been affected differently by global warming. Employing overlapping-generations models, Jeffrey Sachs highlights the point that mitigation policy should be discussed side by side with intergenerational public finance. Ottmar Edenhofer and his team[6] provide a contribution that views the atmosphere as a common resource. They discuss the policymaking challenges for implementing global governance. Finally, Richard Toll gives a comprehensive review of the studies on how to assess damages from climate change, both the economic and social costs of it, and he evaluates those studies critically.

Part III focuses on technology and energy policies. Here, chapters concerning energy policies and issues connected with specific technologies, for example, nuclear power, especially important after the Fukushima event, are presented. Climate-friendly technological change and renewable sources of energy are also discussed in this part. To begin this part, David C. Popp reviews the existing literature on environmentally related technological change and derives important implications for developing countries. This meta-study is important because it describes the setting in which research is taking place. Next, Franz Wirl and Yuri Yegorov extensively discuss the challenges to a rapid phasing-in of renewable energy. They do this in the context of optimal control models to show that, among other things, industries and sectors will not adjust fast enough. Given typical business incentives, they evaluate to what extent government intervention may be necessary to stimulate needed research and development (R&D) in renewable energies and related technologies. Also in Part III is a contribution from Angelo Antoci, Simone Borghesi, and Mauro Sodini, who use methods from the theory of evolutionary games to study carbon trading systems. Finally, we have the chapter by Kozo Mayumi and John M. Polimeni. These authors critically elaborate on the possible role of nuclear technology in providing future energy needs. In particular, they discuss the lessons learned from the Fukushima disaster.

Part IV expands on the expected macroeconomic impact of the various technological, energy-related, and mitigation and adaptation strategies that have been proposed. These contributions study the interaction between and the impact of various policies, for example, cap-and-trade, carbon tax, renewable energies, and their effects, on employment and output. One emerging view seems to be that there need to be multiple policies. A neutral policy, with respect to output and employment, can be achieved only if the income from carbon tax and cap-and-trade is used to subsidize less carbon-intensive industries or to develop renewable energy. Another important consideration is that some research has demonstrated that cap-and-trade will probably unfairly burden developing countries, as the dollar price of a ton of carbon will mean a much larger penalty, in percentage terms, for low-income economies. Thus, it is argued, a carbon tax proportional to income should be implemented and a compensatory policy, an international financial fund, should be set up to help developing countries to adopt policies connected with climate change. Another aspect of multiple and complementary policies to mitigation policies are those connected to adaptation, that is, what needs to be done if the mitigation policies do not work or come too late.

An important aspect of the macroeconomics of climate change is the study of how financial markets can be used to complement climate policies. Wolfgang Karl Härdle, Brenda López-Cabrera, and Matthias Ritter begin Part IV with their work on weather derivatives. They propose two approaches: first, by studying the stochastic behavior of climate and second, by filtration of information sets and using these in the design of such derivatives. Mika Kato, Stefan Mittnik, Daniel Samaan, and Willi Semmler study double-sided climate policies in which some energy and carbon intensive sectors are financially penalized, the revenues being used to support less energy or carbon-intensive sectors. Here, the method of double-sided vector autoregression (VAR) is used to assess of how carbon tax strategies, on the one side, and subsidies, on the other side, can have neutral effects with respect to aggregate output and employment. Results from a multicountry study are shown. Finally, this section concludes with work by Christian Lutz and Ulrike Lehr, who use the recently developed economy–energy–environment model PANTA RHEI to analyze the macroeconomic effects of climate change policies.

In Part V, the Handbook includes contributions that are of region-specific importance. Some studies suggest that, in certain countries and regions, particular mitigation and adaptation policies might be needed. As there will be differences between countries and regions with regard to actual implementation costs and the benefits of CO_2 reduction policies, a collective discussion is required to take regional effects into account within the context of global goals. Given the regional differences, the question is: how can progress be made on global goals?

This section topic starts with the work of climate scientist Askar Akaev, from the Russian Academy of Sciences. His contribution is framed in a quantitative model that describes demographic dynamics with stabilization near stationary populations. Making use of modern modeling methods, with reference to Russia, various scenarios of demographic dynamics are developed alongside a corresponding energy dynamics. Next, Zhong Maochu and Shi Yadong ask the question: does the Kyoto Protocol intensify carbon leakage to China? The authors discuss the issue from the perspective of China and provide analysis using econometric methods. No discussion of "international perspectives" would be complete without some discussion of the regional concentration of climate-related catastrophes. Lopamudra Banerjee considers what we actually know about the economic and social costs of climate-related disasters. Specifically, she studies disaster events that are particularly related to regional concentrations of global climate change effects. To conclude Part V, Frank Ackerman and Elizabeth A. Stanton present important evidence from the Free-Air CO_2 Enrichment (FACE) experiments; this seems to indicate that climate change can be devastating for agriculture in developing economies.

In conclusion, Part VI presents broader views by focusing on past and future global climate policies. It also indicates new directions in mitigation policy design. Clearly the rules and regulations that have come out of international negotiations will be crucial to the success or failure of policy agreements. Thus, this section critically evaluates climate change negotiations and international agreements, and to what extent they represent only soft rules. Lastly, also in Part VI, broader long-run implications of the "business-as-usual" policy, as well as long-run alternatives are discussed.

Raphaele Chappe turns an attorney's eye toward the plethora of international agreements, protocols, and treaties that constitute modern international environmental governance. As is often noted, climate research and policies without a stricter regulatory and legal structure to enforce them will be insufficient. James E. Hansen discusses flaws in the Kyoto approach and other difficulties in handling released carbon. He proposes one major instrument to achieve significant changes, a more general carbon tax. On the other hand, Graciela Chichilnisky, who was involved in the initial crafting of the Kyoto agreements on the strategy of cap-and-trade, defends her position; she also sums up the volume nicely with her aptly entitled essay, "Avoiding Extinction."

Many friends, colleagues, and assistants were involved in the production of this Handbook. We would specifically like to express our gratitude, in alphabetical order, to Aleksandra Kotlyar, Unurjargal Nyambuu, and André Semmler, and to Scott Parris, Catherine Rae, Jennifer Vafidis, Cathryn Vaulman, and Terry Vaughn from

Oxford University Press; without their assistance, this project would never have been completed.

Notes

1. IPCC reports may be found on their website: http://www.ipcc.ch/publications_and_data/publications_and_data_reports.shtml
2. See, for example, Nordhaus, W. (2008) *A Question of Balance: Weighing the Options on Global Warming Policies* (New Haven, CT: Yale University Press).
3. See Chapter 2 by Keller and Nicholas and Chapter 26 by Hansen in this volume.
4. On the status of international negotiations and their achievements, see Chapter 25 by Chappe in this volume.
5. The full team consists of Alain Haurie, Frédéric Babonneau, Neil Edwards, Phil Holden, Amit Kanudia, Maryse Labriet, Barbara Pizzileo, and Marc Vielle.
6. The entire team consists of Ottmar Edenhofer, Christian Flachsland, Michael Jakob, and Kai Lessmann.

PART I

GROWTH AND CLIMATE CHANGE

CHAPTER 2

IMPROVING CLIMATE PROJECTIONS TO BETTER INFORM CLIMATE RISK MANAGEMENT

KLAUS KELLER AND ROBERT NICHOLAS

2.1 Introduction

Human activities have changed the Earth's climate (Alley et al., 2007). These anthropogenic climate changes impose considerable risks on current and future generations (Adger et al., 2007). What are sound strategies to manage these risks? On global and long-term scales, the United Nations Framework Convention on Climate Change (UNFCCC) calls for mitigation of greenhouse gas (GHG) emissions to "prevent dangerous anthropogenic interference with the climate system" (UNFCCC, 1992). Interpreting this phrase requires a value judgment (Oppenheimer and Petsonk, 2005). One common interpretation is that the triggering of large-scale, persistent discontinuities in the Earth system should be avoided (Keller et al., 2005, Schneider et al., 2007). Examples of such discontinuities or "tipping points" include disintegration of the Greenland and/or West Antarctic ice sheets, collapse of the North Atlantic thermohaline circulation, and weakening of the South Asian monsoon (Figure 2.1). A more recently discussed instrument for climate risk management is the deliberate engineering of the Earth's climate system, so-called geoengineering, for example, through injection of aerosol precursors into the stratosphere to reflect incoming sunlight back to space (Schelling, 1996; Crutzen, 2006; Bonnheim, 2011). On local and shorter time scales, risk management options focus on adapting to changing climates, for example, by increasing the height of coastal defenses (Figure 2.2).

Climate projections represent an important input to the design of risk management strategies. Climate projections are used, for example, to (1) characterize the probability associated with different future sea level rise scenarios (Meehl et al., 2007), (2) project impacts and risks (van Dantzig, 1956; Lempert et al., 2012; Tebaldi et al., 2012),

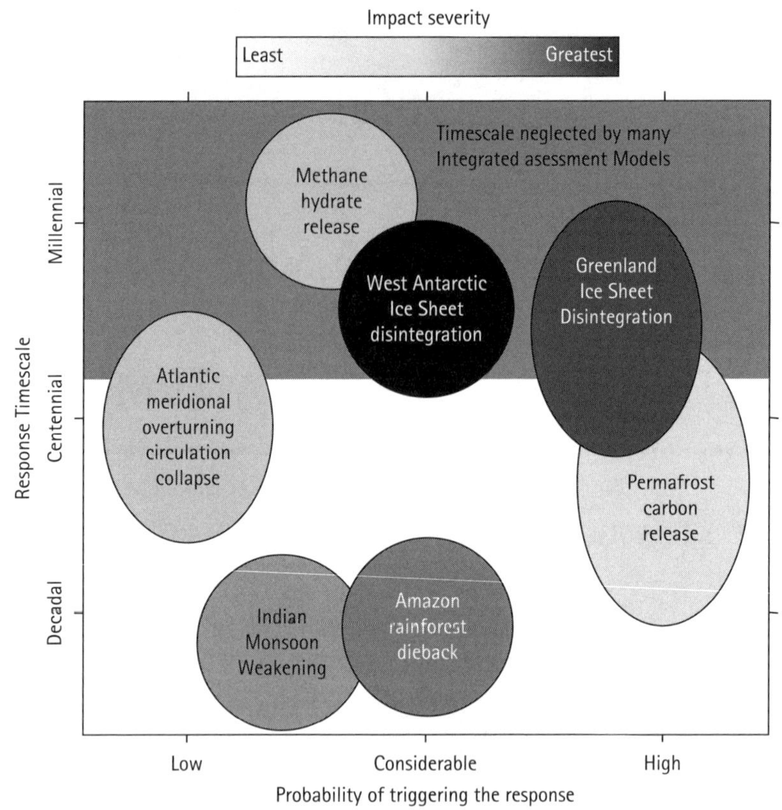

FIGURE 2.1 Categorization of selected potential climate-threshold responses by probability of triggering them following a business-as-usual climate strategy, the response time scale, and the severity of the projected impacts. (The transition in the background shading for the threshold responses from light to dark grey represents increasing severity) (Schneider et al., 2007; Keller et al., 2008; Lenton et al., 2008; Kriegler et al., 2009; Lenton, 2011). The rectangular grey area represents the timescale neglected by many Integrated Assessment Models. This literature synthesis neglects many important uncertainties and problem dimensions.

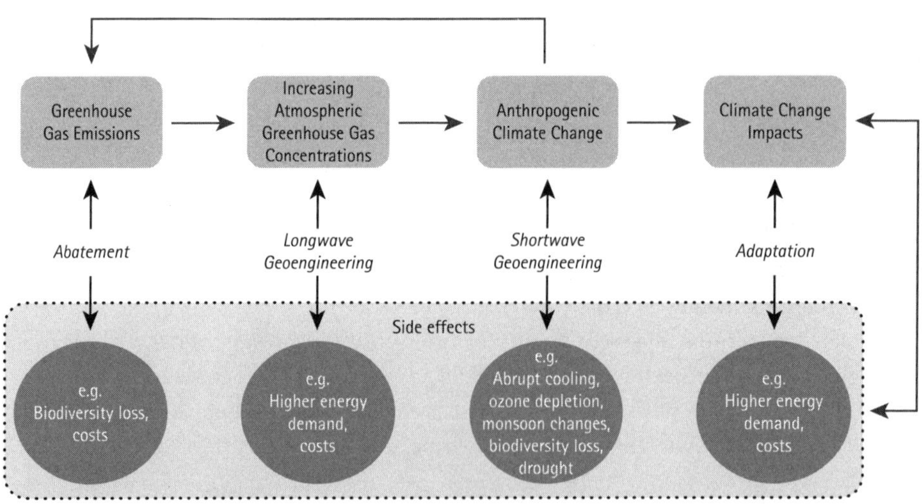

FIGURE 2.2 Overview of key climate risk management instruments (middle row)

(3) assess how quickly current uncertainties might be resolved (Keller and McInerney, 2008), and (4) assess tradeoffs among different strategies (Goes et al., 2011; Lempert et al., 2012).

2.2 What Are Decision-Relevant Climate Properties, Time Scales, and Uncertainties?

Climate change decision problems differ in the relative importance of climate properties, time scales, and uncertainties. We discuss these differences for two example decision problems: (1) adapting a coastal infrastructure to future sea level changes and (2) designing a global mitigation strategy.

Climate quantities relevant to decisions about adapting a coastal infrastructure to future sea level changes include (1) changes in local sea level, (2) short-term variability (e.g., the properties of storm surges), and (3) the rate at which uncertainties can be reduced (cf. van Dantzig, 1956; Lempert et al., 2012). The relevant time scales are determined by the lifetime of the infrastructure (accounting for potential lock-in effects) and the time horizon of private decision makers (van Dantzig, 1956; Lempert et al., 2012). These considerations suggest that a decadal time scale is most relevant. Sea level rise (SLR) adaptation decisions are an example of low-probability/high-impact events being considered as key drivers of climate risk management strategies (van Dantzig, 1956). For example, infrequent but highly damaging flooding events are of obvious importance for such decisions. Probabilistic estimates of these events are often complicated by disagreements among experts and decision makers as to the likelihood of floods of particular magnitudes; that is, there exist several probability density functions. This situation is often described as deep, Knightian, or second-order uncertainty (Knight, 1921; Lempert, 2002; Knutti and Hegerl, 2008).

Compared to local adaptation decisions, the design of global-scale climate risk management strategies through mitigation requires climate projections covering longer time scales, larger spatial scales, and including additional climate characteristics. One key policy-relevant question is the probability of triggering a dangerous anthropogenic interference with the climate system in the UNFCCC sense (UNFCCC, 1992; Urban and Keller, 2010). The very long time scales (centuries to millennia) that must be considered for mitigation decisions are sometimes characterized as "ethically relevant" (Lenton et al., 2008). Many integrated assessment models of the coupled human–natural system that are used to analyze mitigation decisions are silent on these very long time scales (cf. Keller et al., 2004; Nordhaus 2008).

2.3 How Well Do Current Climate Projections Cover These Decision-Relevant Climate Properties, Time Scales, and Uncertainties?

Current climate projections cover important aspects of these decision-relevant properties, time scales, and uncertainties, but there are still large gaps. Projections generally cover the decadal time scale reasonably well (Church et al., 2011), but projections of short-term (intra-annual) variability (e.g., through changes in storm surges) are still in the early stages (Bromirski et al., 2003; Mousavi et al., 2011; Tebaldi et al., 2012).

For the design of global scale mitigation strategies, the projections (or the way they are communicated) are often silent on the ethically relevant, and very long, time scale over which current GHG emissions affect future welfare (Figure 2.1). Consider, for example, the possibility that GHG emissions might trigger collapse of the Atlantic meridional overturning circulation or disintegration of the Greenland ice sheet (Keller et al., 2005, 2008; Lenton et al., 2008). For example, the previous report from the Intergovernmental Panel on Climate Change (IPCC) (Alley et al., 2007) states that: "it is very unlikely [the meridional overturning circulation] will undergo a large abrupt transition during the 21st century." Note that this statement is silent on the question whether such an event would be triggered in this century. Owing to the potential sizeable delays between triggering and experiencing climate threshold responses, the probability of triggering a threshold event in the 21st century may far exceed the probability of experiencing it (Alley et al., 2003; Urban and Keller, 2010).

Current climate projections have drastically improved in characterizing decision-relevant uncertainties, but they still neglect many potentially important uncertainties (O'Neill et al., 2006; Alley et al., 2007; Keller et al., 2008; Liverman et al., 2010). The resulting overconfidence can lead to risk estimates that are biased toward smaller values and, as a result, too-small investments in risk management (cf. Sriver et al., 2012).

The flooding risk estimate of Purvis et al. (2008) helps demonstrate this effect (Figure 2.3). Purvis et al. (2008) fit a triangular probability density function to the range of SLR projections in 2100 from the third IPCC assessment report (Church and Gregory, 2001) (0.09 to 0.8 m; Figure 2.3). As stated by Purvis et al. (2008), there is a "low but poorly determined probability that (an) ice sheet collapse may result in SLR of >0.88 m by 2100," but this deeply uncertain possibility is neglected. Accounting for the possibility of rapid ice sheet changes increases projected SLR to approximately 0.8 to 2 m (Pfeffer et al., 2008), and likely even wider (Sriver et al., 2012) (Figure 2.3). The overlap between these SLR probability density functions is minimal, and the most probable value from the Purvis et al. (2008) probability density function is outside the range given by the projections of Pfeffer et al.

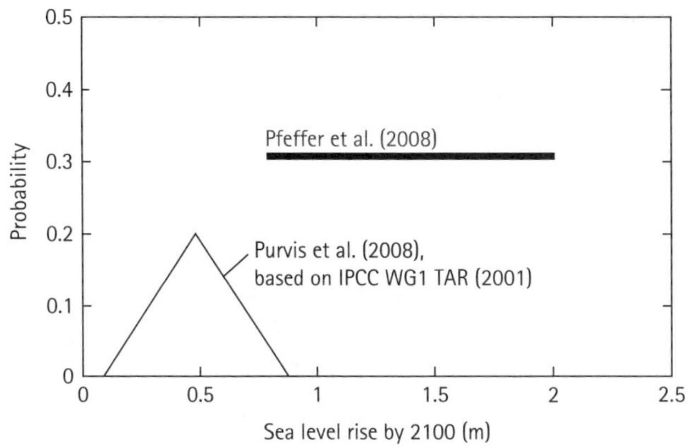

FIGURE 2.3 Comparison of sea level rise projections for the year 2100 adopted by Purvis et al. (2008) for a risk estimate and a more recent range of projections provided by Pfeffer et al. (2008).

(2008). For vulnerable areas, even a small increase in the upper bound of SLR can result in a substantial change in the probability of damaging floods (Sriver et al., 2012).

Thus, risk analyses based on overconfident projections that cut off plausible values (e.g., Purvis et al., 2008) can underestimate the risks of negative outcomes. Factors that can cause this overconfidence include (1) limited knowledge about processes and parameters, (2) limited computational resources that cause neglect of potentially important uncertainties, and (3) information loss in the use of climate projections to inform analyses of risk and decision making (cf. Hammitt and Shlyakhter, 1999; Oppenheimer et al., 2008; Ricciuto et al., 2008). The errors due to overconfidence are relevant, for example, for the design of flooding protection infrastructure that aims to limit the flooding probability to low values. One design criterion is, for example, to reduce the flooding frequency to one flood in a 10,000-year time span (Vrijling, 2001; Eijgenraam, 2007).

2.4 Research Needs

Promising avenues for improving the utility of climate projections to inform decision making include (1) a tighter collaboration between the producers and users of climate projections, (2) an improved characterization of deeply uncertain tails of the projection probability density functions, and (3) an expanded focus on the dynamics of learning and its effect on sequential decision making. We discuss these research avenues and point to relevant literature.

First, the analysis of climate risk management strategies requires an integrated and transdisciplinary approach linking disciplines such as decision science, Earth sciences, economics, philosophy, and statistics (Figure 2.4). This integrated approach is important because many decision-relevant questions span academic disciplines and because the transdisciplinary collaborations help reduce communication errors (Keller et al., 2008; Budescu et al., 2009; Lempert et al., 2012). Second, the characterization of decision-relevant tails of the projection probability density function needs to be improved to reduce biases in risk and decision analyses (cf. Figure 2.3). Approaches such as model emulation, nonparametric Bayesian inversion, and expert elicitation have broken new ground in these areas (Raper and Cubasch, 1996; Hankin, 2005; Tomassini et al., 2007; Kriegler et al., 2009; Urban and Fricker, 2010; Urban and Keller, 2010; Zickfeld et al., 2010). Note that characterizing the decision relevance of tails in a multivariate probability density function for climate projections requires the integrated approach discussed earlier (Lempert et al., 2012). Third, interactions between the dynamics of learning and sequential decision making can be important but thus far are largely underexplored. Typical approaches include observation system simulation experiments, scenario analyses, and optimal control methods. However, these analyses typically consider highly stylized decision problems, observation systems, or interactions between learning and decision making (cf. Kelly and Kolstad, 1999; Peterson et al., 2003; Keller et al., 2004; Keller and McInerney, 2008; Lempert et al., 2012). The nexus of relatively recent methodological advances such as approximate dynamic

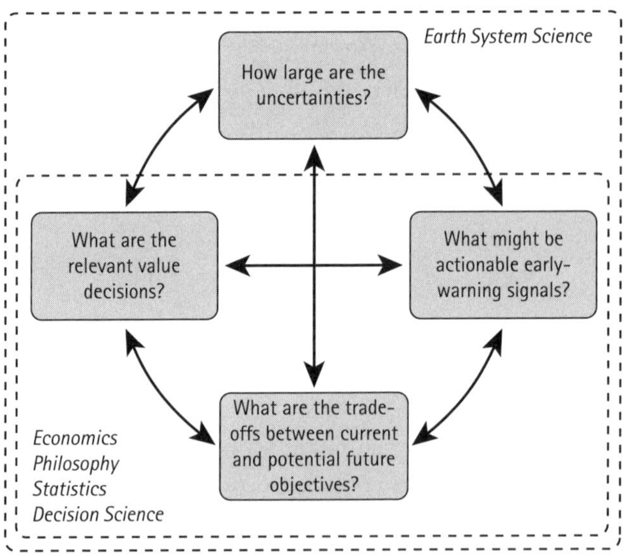

FIGURE 2.4 A subset of the relevant academic fields, research questions, and transdisciplinary interactions in climate risk management.

programming (Powell, 2011; Pena-Alcaraz et al., 2011; Webster et al., 2012), combined with emulators and the increasing availability of high-performance computation environments, may enable new insights in this area.

Acknowledgments

Insightful discussions with Richard Alley, Patrick Applegate, David Budescu, Chris Forest, Jim Kasting, Robert Lempert, Nancy Tuana, and Karen Fisher-Vanden improved the chapter. This work was partially supported by the National Science Foundation through the Network for Sustainable Climate Risk Management (SCRiM) under NSF cooperative agreement GEO-1240507 and the Penn State Center for Climate Risk Management. Any opinions, findings, and conclusions or recommendations expressed in this material are those of the author(s) and do not necessarily reflect the views of the National Science Foundation.

References

Adger, N., Aggarwal, P., Agrawala, S., Alcamo, J., Allali, A., Anisimov, O., Arnell, N., Boko, M., Canziani, O., Carter, T., Casassa, G., Confalonieri, U., Cruz, R. V., Alcaraz, E. d. A., Easterling, W., Field, C., Fischlin, A., Fitzharris, B. B., García, C. G., Hanson, C., Harasawa, H., Hennessy, K., Huq, S., Jones, R., Bogataj, L. K., Karoly, D., Klein, R., Kundzewicz, Z., Lal, M., Lasco, R., Love, G., Lu, X., Magrín, G., Mata, L. J., McLean, R., Menne, B., Midgley, G., Mimura, N., Mirza, M. Q., Moreno, J., Mortsch, L., Niang-Diop, I., Nicholls, R., Nováky, B., Nurse, L., Nyong, A., Oppenheimer, M., Palutikof, J., Parry, M., Patwardhan, A., Lankao, P. R., Rosenzweig, C., Schneider, S., Semenov, S., Smith, J., Stone, J., Ypersele, J.-P. v., Vaughan, D., Vogel, C., Wilbanks, T., Wong, P. P., Wu, S., and Yohe, G. (2007). Summary for Policymakers. In *Climate Change 2007: Impacts, Adaptation and Vulnerability. Contribution of Working Group II to the Fourth Assessment Report of the Intergovernmental Panel on Climate Change (IPCC)*. [Solomon, S., D. Qin, M. Manning, Z. Chen, M. Marquis, K. B. Averyt, M. Tignor and H. L. Miller (eds.)].Cambridge University Press, Cambridge, United Kingdom and New York, NY, USA, pp. 7–22.

Alley, R., Berntsen, T., Bindoff, N. L., Chen, Z., Chidthaisong, A., Friedlingstein, P., Gregory, J., Hegerl, G., Heimann, M., Hewitson, B., Hoskins, B., Joos, F., Jouzel, J., Kattsov, V., Lohmann, U., Manning, M., Matsuno, T., Molina, M., Nicholls, N., Overpeck, J., Qin, D., Raga, G., Ramaswamy, V., Ren, J., Rusticucci, M., Solomon, S., Somerville, R., Stocker, T. F., Stott, P., Stouffer, R. J., Whetton, P., Wood, R. A., and Wratt, D. (2007). Summary for Policymakers. In *Climate Change 2007: The Physical Science Basis. Contribution of Working Group I to the Fourth Assessment Report of the Intergovernmental Panel on Climate Change* [Solomon, S., D. Qin, M. Manning, Z. Chen, M. Marquis, K. B. Averyt, M. Tignor and H. L. Miller (eds.)] Cambridge University Press, Cambridge, United Kingdom and New York, NY, USA, pp. 1–18.

Alley, R. B., Marotzke, J., Nordhaus, W. D., Overpeck, J. T., Peteet, D. M., Pielke, R. A., Pierrehumbert, R. T., Rhines, P. B., Stocker, T. F., Talley, L. D., and Wallace, J. M. (2003). Abrupt climate change. *Science, 299*(5615), 2005–2010.

Bonnheim, N. B. (2011). History of climate engineering. *Wiley Interdisciplinary Reviews-Climate Change, 1*(6), 891–897.

Bromirski, P. D., Flick, R. E., and Cayan, D. R. (2003). Storminess variability along the California coast: 1858–2000. *Journal of Climate, 16*(6), 982–993.

Budescu, D. V., Broomell, S., and Por, H. H. (2009). Improving communication of uncertainty in the Reports of the Intergovernmental Panel on Climate Change. *Psychological Science, 20*(3), 299–308.

Church, J. A., and Gregory, J. M. (2001). Changes in sea level. In *Climate Change 2001: The Scientific Basis. Contribution of Working Group I to the Third Assessment Report of the Intergovernmental Panel on Climate Change* [J. T. Houghton, Y. Ding, D. J. Griggs, M. Noquer, P. J. van der Linden, X. Dai, K. Maskell and C. A. Johnson (eds.)]. Cambridge University Press, Cambridge, United Kingdom and New York, NY, USA, pp. 639–693.

Church, J. A., Gregory, J. M., White, N. J., Platten, S. M., and Mitrovica, J. X. (2011). Understanding and projecting sea level change. *Oceanography, 24*(2), 130–143.

Crutzen, P. J. (2006). Albedo enhancement by stratospheric sulfur injections: A contribution to resolve a policy dilemma? *Climatic Change, 77*(3–4), 211–219.

Eijgenraam, C. J. J. (2007). From optimal to practical safety standards for dike-ring areas. *Water Science and Technology, 56*(4), 113–124.

Goes, M., Tuana, N., and Keller, K. (2011). The economics (or lack thereof) of aerosol geoengineering. *Climatic Change, 109*(3), 719–744.

Hammitt, J. K., and Shlyakhter, A. I. (1999). The expected value of information and the probability of surprise. *Risk Analysis, 19*(1), 135–152.

Hankin, R. K. S. (2005). Introducing BACCO, an R bundle for Bayesian analysis of computer code output. *Journal of Statistical Software, 14*(16).

Keller, K., and McInerney, D. (2008). The dynamics of learning about a climate threshold. *Climate Dynamics, 30*, 321–332.

Keller, K., Bolker, B. M., and Bradford, D. F. (2004). Uncertain climate thresholds and optimal economic growth. *Journal of Environmental Economics and Management, 48*(1), 723–741.

Keller, K., Hall, M., Kim, S.-R., Bradford, D. F., and Oppenheimer, M. (2005). Avoiding dangerous anthropogenic interference with the climate system. *Climatic Change, 73*, 227–238.

Keller, K., Yohe, G., and Schlesinger, M. (2008). Managing the risks of climate thresholds: Uncertainties and information needs. *Climatic Change, 91*(1–2), 5–10.

Kelly, D. L., and Kolstad, C. D. (1999). Bayesian learning, growth and pollution. *Journal of Economic Dynamics and Control, 23*, 491–518.

Knight, F. H. (1921). *Risk, Uncertainty, and Profit.* Boston: Hart, Schaffner & Marx; Houghton Mifflin Company.

Knutti, R., and Hegerl, G. (2008). The equilibrium sensitivity of the Earth's temperature to radiation changes. *Nature Geosciences, 1*, 735–743.

Kriegler, E., Hall, J. W., Held, H., Dawson, R., and Schellnhuber, H. J. (2009). Imprecise probability assessment of tipping points in the climate system. *Proceedings of the National Academy of Sciences of the USA, 106*(13), 5041–5046.

Lempert, R., Sriver, R., and Keller, K. (2012). Characterizing Uncertain Sea Level Rise Projections to Support Infrastructure Investment Decisions. California Energy Commission,

Publication No. CEC-500-2012-056. http://www.energy.ca.gov/2012publications/CEC-500-2012-056/CEC-500-2012-056.pdf.

Lempert, R. J. (2002). A new decision sciences for complex systems. *Proceedings of the National Academy of Sciences of the USA 99*, 7309–7313.

Lenton, T. M. (2011). Early warning of climate tipping points. *Nature Climate Change, 1*(4), 201–209.

Lenton, T. M., Held, H., Kriegler, E., Hall, J. W., Lucht, W., Rahmstorf, S., and Schellnhuber, H. J. (2008). Tipping elements in the Earth's climate system. *Proceedings of the National Academy of Sciences of the USA, 105*(6), 1786–1793.

Liverman, D., Raven, P., Barstow, D., Bierbaum, R. M., Leiserowitz, A., Lempert, R., Lopez, J., Miles, E. L., Moore, B. I., Newton, M. D., Ramaswarmy, V., Richels, R., Scott, D. P., Tierney, K. L., Walker, C., and Wilson, S. T. (2010). *Informing an Effective Response to Climate Change*, p. 325. Washington, DC: "National Research Council" The National Academies Press. http://www.nap.edu/catalog.php?record_id=12784.

Meehl, G. A., Stocker, T. F., Collins, W. D., Friedlingstein, P., Gaye, A. T., JGregory, J. M., Kitoh, A., Knutti, R., Murphy, J. M., Noda, A., Raper, S. C. B., Watterson, I. G., Weaver, A. J., and Zhao, Z.-C. (2007). Global climate projections. In *Climate Change 2007: The Physical Science Basis. Contribution of Working Group I to the Fourth Assessment Report of the Intergovernmental Panel on Climate Change* [Solomon, S., D. Qin, M. Manning, Z. Chen, M. Marquis, K. B. Averyt, M. Tignor and H. L. Miller (eds.)] Cambridge University Press, Cambridge, United Kingdom and New York, NY, USA, pp. 747–845.

Mousavi, M. E., Irish, J. L., Frey, A. E., Olivera, F., and Edge, B. L. (2011). Global warming and hurricanes: The potential impact of hurricane intensification and sea level rise on coastal flooding. *Climatic Change, 104*(3–4), 575–597.

Nordhaus, W. (2008). *A Question of Balance.* New Haven, CT and London: Yale University Press.

O'Neill, B. C., Crutzen, P., Grubler, A., Duong, M. H., Keller, K., Kolstad, C., Koomey, J., Lange, A., Obersteiner, M., Oppenheimer, M., Pepper, W., Sanderson, W., Schlesinger, M., Treich, N., Ulph, A., Webster, M., and Wilson, C. (2006). Learning and climate change. *Climate Policy, 6*(5), 585–589.

Oppenheimer, M., and Petsonk, A. (2005). Article 2 of the UNFCCC: Historical origins, recent interpretations. *Climatic Change, 73*, 195–226.

Oppenheimer, M., O'Neill, B. C., and Webster, M. (2008). Negative learning. *Climatic Change, 89*(1–2), 155–172.

Pena-Alcaraz, M., Webster, M., and Ramos, A. (2011). An approximate dynamic programming approach for designing train timetables. MIT ESD working paper, http://esd.mit.edu/WPS/2011/esd-wp-2011-11.pdf.

Peterson, G. D., Carpenter, S. R., and Brock, W. A. (2003). Uncertainty and the management of multistate ecosystems: An apparently rational route to collapse. *Ecology, 84*(6), 1403–1411.

Pfeffer, W. T., Harper, J. T., and O'Neel, S. (2008). Kinematic constraints on glacier contributions to 21st-century sea level rise. *Science, 321*, 1340–1343.

Powell, W. B. (2011). *Approximate Dynamic Programming: Solving the Curses of Dimensionality*, 2nd ed. Hoboken, NJ: John Wiley & Sons.

Purvis, M. J., Bates, P. D., and Hayes, C. M. (2008). A probabilistic methodology to estimate future coastal flood risk due to sea level rise. *Coastal Engineering, 55*(12), 1062–1073.

Raper, S. C. B., and Cubasch, U. (1996). Emulation of the results from a coupled general circulation model using a simple climate model. *Geophysical Research Letters, 23*(10), 1107–1110.

Ricciuto, D. M., Davis, K. J., and Keller, K. (2008). A Bayesian calibration of a simple carbon cycle model: The role of observations in estimating and reducing uncertainty. *Global Biogeochemical Cycles, 22*(2).

Schelling, T. C. (1996). The economic diplomacy of geoengineering. *Climatic Change, 33*, 303–307.

Schneider, S. H., Semenov, S., Patwardhan, A., Burton, I., Magadza, C. H. D., Oppenheimer, M., Pittock, A. B., Rahman, A., Smith, J. B., Suarez, A., Yamin, F., Corfee-Morlot, J., Finkel, A., Füssel, H.-M., Keller, K., MacMynowski, D., Mastrandrea, M. D., Todorov, A., Sukumar, R., Ypersele, J.-P. v., and Zillman, J. (2007). Assessing key vulnerabilities and the risk from climate change. In *Climate Change 2007: Impacts, Adaptation and Vulnerability. Contribution of Working Group II to the Fourth Assessment Report of the Intergovernmental Panel on Climate Change* [Solomon, S., D. Qin, M. Manning, Z. Chen, M. Marquis, K. B. Averyt, M. Tignor and H. L. Miller (eds.)].Cambridge University Press, Cambridge, United Kingdom and New York, NY, USA, pp. 779–810.

Sriver, R.L, N. M. Urban, R Olson, and K. Keller: Towards a physically plausible upper bound of sea-level rise projections. *Climatic Change Letters*, DOI 10.1007/s10584-012-0610 (2012).

Stott, P. A., Stone, D. A., and Allen, M. R. (2004). Human contribution to the European heatwave of 2003. *Nature, 432*(7017), 610–614.

Tebaldi, C., Strauss, B. H., and Zervas, C. E. (2012). Modelling sea level rise impacts on storm surges along US coasts. *Environmental Research Letters, 7*(1).

Tomassini, L., Reichert, P., Knutti, R., Stocker, T. F., and Borsuk, M. E. (2007). Robust Bayesian uncertainty analysis of climate system properties using Markov Chain Monte Carlo methods. *Journal of Climate, 20*, 1239–1254.

UNFCCC. (1992). *UN Framework Convention on Climate Change.* Palais des Nations, Geneva, Switzerland. http://www.unfccc.de/index.html.

Urban, N. M., and Fricker, T. F. (2010). A comparison of Latin hypercube and grid ensemble designs for the multivariate emulation of a climate model. *Computers and Geosciences, 36*, 746–755.

Urban, N. M., and Keller, K. (2010). Probabilistic hindcasts and projections of the coupled climate, carbon cycle and Atlantic meridional overturning circulation system: A Bayesian fusion of century-scale observations with a simple model. *Tellus Series A-Dynamic Meteorology and Oceanography, 62*(5), 737–750.

van Dantzig, D. (1956). Economic decision problems for flood prevention. *Econometrica, 24*(3), 276–287.

Vrijling, J. K. (2001). Probabilistic design of water defense systems in The Netherlands. *Reliability Engineering & System Safety, 74*(3), 337–344.

Webster, M. D., Santen, N. R., and Parpas, P. (2012). An approximate dynamic programming framework for modeling global climate policy under decision-dependent uncertainty, *Computational Management Sciences, 9*, 339–362. DOI 10.1007/s10287-012-0147-1

Zickfeld, K., Morgan, M. G., Frame, D. J., and Keith, D. W. (2010). Expert judgments about transient climate response to alternative future trajectories of radiative forcing. *Proceedings of the National Academy of Sciences of the USA, 107*(28), 12451–12456.

CHAPTER 3

ENERGY BALANCE CLIMATE MODELS, DAMAGE RESERVOIRS, AND THE TIME PROFILE OF CLIMATE CHANGE POLICY

WILLIAM BROCK, GUSTAV ENGSTRÖM, AND ANASTASIOS XEPAPADEAS

3.1 Introduction

Energy balance climate models (EBCMs) have been extensively used to study Earth's climate (e.g., Budyko, 1969; Sellers, 1969; North, 1975a,b; North et al., 1981; Wu and North, 2007). The basic components of these models are incoming solar radiation, outgoing infrared radiation, transportation of heat across the globe, and the presence of an endogenous ice line where latitudes north (south) of the ice line are solid ice and latitudes south (north) of the ice line are ice free. The ice line has the important property of regulating the energy heat budget where the location of the ice line determines how much of the incoming solar radiation is reflected back out to space. Ice-covered areas have a higher albedo, implying that they absorb less of the incoming solar radiation, thus contributing less to planetary warming.

In the economics literature, climate change is often studied in the framework of Integrated Assessment Models (IAMs) featuring carbon cycles and temperature dynamics (e.g. Nordhaus, 1994; Tol, 1997; Nordhaus and Boyer, 2000; Hope, 2006; Nordhaus, 2007). These models typically feature empirically calibrated, for the most part linear, climate modules capturing global average estimates of, for example, atmospheric temperature levels. This approach tends to ignore the complexities associated with heat transportation across latitudes and ice-albedo feedback effects that lie at the heart of the Energy Balance Climate Model (EBCM) literature.[1] The importance of ice-albedo feedback effects and latitudinal heat transportation in regulating the climate was recognized early in efforts to represent the Earth's climate with EBCM's that uncovered the disconcerting possibility that a relatively small decrease in the solar input could lead to catastrophic global glaciation, the result of a runaway ice albedo feedback (North, 1984). Similarly it was also shown that the ice-albedo feedback effect could have an equally strong amplifying effect on the climate when driven by increasing concentrations of atmospheric carbon dioxide (Wang and Stone, 1980). This showed how something happening at one particular latitude, the albedo changing due to ice line movements, could act to affect the global mean climate. Such feedback effects have also been associated with the notion of climate "tipping points," defined as points where a small forcing is enough to set of a chain of interactions causing a major change in behavior of the system (Roe and Baker, 2010). The potential threats associated with such tipping points has raised much concern within the climate science community in recent years (see e.g., Kerr, 2008; Lenton et al., 2008; Smith et al., 2009).

In the present chapter we couple a latitude-dependent EBCM with an endogenous ice line based on the model by North (1975a,b) with a simplified economic growth model. This allows us to investigate what new insights might be gained regarding the time profile of mitigation policy and distribution of damages when accounting for increased complexitity in terms of the ice-albedo feedback and latitudinal heat transport. The explicit presence of a spatial dimension and an ice line, whose latitude is determined endogenously, also suggests a different damage profile for sources of damages connected to the movement of the ice line. This does not appear in traditional IAMs. In particular, we differentiate between two types of damages from climate change, traditional gradually increasing damages and a damage reservoir type, where the latter represents a finite source of economic damage associated with the movement of the ice line. Damage reservoirs in the context of climate change can be regarded as sources of damage that eventually will cease to exist when the source of the damage has been depleted. We identify ice caps and permafrost as typical damage reservoirs, where the state of the reservoir is connected to the latitudinal position of the ice line.

Concerning the ice caps, the movement of the ice line closer to the poles is clearly connected to shrinking ice caps. We consider the implied damages caused by sea level rise due to the release of water from melting glacial ice sheets. We might expect that marginal damages from melting ice caps will increase slowly at first, accelerating to a peak but then eventually diminishing as the ice line approaches the Poles. When there is no ice left on the Poles this damage reservoir will have been exhausted. The exact shape of an ice cap specific damage function is of course unknown; it might as well be that damages are proportional to the size of the ice caps so that marginal damages are initially high but diminish as more ice is melted.[2] However, regardless of the intermediate behavior, claiming that marginal damages due to ice melting must eventually be zero when all ice has melted is hardly controversial. Thus as human activities move the ice line toward the North Pole the ice area lost diminishes and marginal damages diminish also. The presence of an endogenous ice line in the EBCM allows us to model these types of damages explicitly given the relevant information.[3]

Permafrost is also related to damage reservoirs. Permafrost or permafrost soil is soil at or below the freezing point of water (0°C or 32°F) for two or more years. Permafrost regions occupy approximately 22.79 million square kilometers (about 24% of the exposed land surface) of the Northern Hemisphere (Zhang et al., 2003). Permafrost occurs as far north as 84°N in northern Greenland, and as far south as 26°N in the Himalayas, but most permafrost in the Northern Hemisphere occurs between latitudes of 60°N and 68°N. (North of 67°N, permafrost declines sharply, as the exposed land surface gives way to the Arctic Ocean.) Recent work investigating the permafrost carbon pool size estimates that 1400–1700 Gt of carbon is stored in permafrost soils worldwide. This large carbon pool represents more carbon than currently exists in all living things and twice as much carbon as exists in the atmosphere (Tarnocai et al., 2009). The thawing of permafrost as high latitudes become warmer can also be modeled in this context. Thawing of permafrost is expected to bring widespread changes in ecosystems; increase erosion; harm subsistence livelihoods; and damage buildings, roads, and other infrastructure. Loss of permafrost will also cause release of greenhouse gases (GHGs) methane in wetter areas and CO_2 in dryer areas. Furthermore, permafrost damages are related to damage reservoirs since when permafrost is gone they will vanish provided appropriate adaptation has been implemented.[4] Once again the exact shape of the damage function in the intermediate is unknown, but it is clear that damages must eventually diminish once all GHGs trapped in the soil has been released. The permafrost feedback also suggests that permafrost carbon emissions could affect long-term projections of future temperature change. An increase in Arctic temperatures could release a large fraction of the carbon stored in permafrost soils. Studies indicate that up to 22% of permafrost could be thawed already by 2100. Once unlocked under strong warming, thawing and decomposition of permafrost can release amounts of carbon until 2300 comparable to the historical anthropogenic emissions up to 2000 (approximately 440 GtC) (von Deimling et al., 2011).

To the best of our knowledge, we believe this to be the first attempt at introducing an explicit spatial dimension to the climate module of a climate-economy model that also connects the spatial aspects to the temporal profile of climate damages. This helps in understanding how latitude-dependent damages might affect decision making related to climate change. To be more precise, by allowing for damage reservoirs, as described above, we explicitly introduce two types of damage functions having different temporal profiles. These are the traditional damage function used in most IAMs, in which damages increase monotonically with temperature, and a damage function associated with damage reservoirs. The damage reservoir function is given a similar form as the traditional damage function with the exception that there exists a point where marginal damages will start to decline and eventually become zero, implying that damages are bounded from above. This is related to the idea that once the ice caps are gone and the thawed permafrost has released most of its carbon, then reservoir damages will be exhausted. Our results suggest that endogenous ice lines and damage reservoirs introduce non convexities that induce multiple steady states and Skiba points. The policy implication of these results is that when damage reservoirs are ignored we have a unique steady state and the policy ramp is monotonically increasing. That is, carbon taxes start at low levels and increase with time, which is the "gradualist approach" to climate policy (Nordhaus, 2007, 2010, 2011). On the other hand, the existence of damage reservoirs and multiple steady states induced by endogenous ice lines results in policy ramps, which suggests increased mitigation now, the opposite of what is advocated by the gradualist approach. Furthermore, by incorporating damage reservoirs into a DICE type model, our simulations suggest a U-shaped policy ramp with high mitigation now.[5]

The rest of the chapter is structured as follows. Since EBCMs are new in economics we proceed in steps that we believe make this methodology accessible to economists. In Section 3.2 we present a basic energy balance climate model[6] that incorporates human impacts on climate that result from carbon dioxide (CO_2) emissions that eventually block outgoing radiation. In developing the model we follow (North, 1975a, b) and use his notation. Section 3.3 couples the spatial EBCM with an economic growth model characterized by both traditional and reservoir damages. We show that nonlinearities induced by endogenous ice lines and reservoir damages result in multiple steady states and Skiba points. Section 3.4 derives similar results in a model more similar in struc ture to most IAM's. Finally, in Section 3.5 we simulate the well known DICE model allowing for damage reservoirs and derive a U-shaped policy ramp. The last section concludes the chapter.

3.2 A Simplified One-Dimensional Energy Balance Climate Model

In this section we present a simplified integrated model of economy and climate, with the climate part motivated by the one-dimensional energy balance models described in the introduction. The term "one-dimensional" means that there is an explicit spatial dimension in the model, measured in terms of latitudes. The important feature of these models is that they allow for heat diffusion or transportation across latitudes which increases the relevance of the models in describing climate dynamics. Let $T(x,t)$ denote the surface temperature at location (or latitude) x and time t measured in °C. Climate dynamics in the context of the ECBM (e.g., North, 1975a, b; North et al., 1981) are defined as:

$$C_c \frac{\partial T(x,t)}{\partial t} = QS(x)\alpha(x,x_s) - [A + BT(x,t) - g(M(t))] + D\frac{\partial}{\partial x}\left[(1-x^2)\frac{\partial T(x,t)}{\partial x}\right] \tag{3.1}$$

$$T_s = T(x_s(t),t) \tag{3.2}$$

where x denotes the sine of the latitude "x," where units of x are chosen so that $x = 0$ denotes the Equator, $x = 1$ denotes the North Pole[7] and to simplify we just refer to x as "latitude." C_c denotes the effective heat capacity per unit area of the earth.[8] A and B are empirically determined constants that are used to relate the outgoing longwave infrared radiation flux $I(x,t)$ measured in W/m^2 at latitude x at time t with the corresponding surface temperature $T(x,t)$ through the following formula,[9]

$$I(x,t) = A + BT(x,t) \tag{3.3}$$

where $g(M(t)$ denotes forcing induced by the atmospheric CO_2 concentration given by $M(t)$. A common form for $g(M(t)$ is a logarithmic form identifying the amount of global warming that can be induced from a doubling CO_2 levels.[10] For the qualitative exercise we pursue in this chapter we will, however, assume a simple linear form in order to keep technicalities to a minimum. More about this below. Q is the solar constant divided by 4.[11] As pointed out by North (1975b), in equilibrium at a given latitude the incoming absorbed radiant heat is not matched by the net outgoing radiation and the difference is made up by the meridional divergence of heat flux, which is modeled by the term $D\frac{\partial}{\partial x}\left[(1-x^2)\frac{\partial T(x,t)}{\partial x}\right]$. Several forms are possible here; the seminal contributions by Budyko (1969) and Sellers (1969) both differ in their parameterizations and structure of heat diffusion. Our form follows that of North (1975a,b) featuring a single thermal diffusion coefficient D which is a calibration parameter determining both heat diffusion and temperature anomalies across latitudes.[12] $S(x,t)$ is the mean annual meridional distribution of solar radiation, which is determined from astronomical calculations and ban be uniformly approximated within 2% by

$$S(x) = 1 + S_2P_2(x) \tag{3.4}$$

with $S_2 = -0.482$ and where $P_2(x) = (3x^2 - 1)/2$ is the second Legendre polynomial (North, 1975a). Note that $S(x)$ has been normalized so that its integral from 0 to 1 is unity, which implies that the integral of incoming radiation reaching the Earth is given by Q. $\alpha(x, x_s(t))$ is the absorption coefficient which equals one minus the albedo of the Earth–atmosphere system, with $x_s(t)$ being the latitude of the ice line at time t. In equation (3.5) below the ice line absorption drops discontinuously because the albedo jumps discontinuously. North (1975b), page 2034, equation (3) specifies this co-albedo function as:[12]

$$\alpha(x,x_s) = \begin{cases} b_0 = 0.38 & x > x_s \\ \alpha_0 + \alpha_2 P_2(x) & x < x_s \end{cases}, \quad \begin{matrix} \alpha_0 = 0.697 \\ \alpha_2 = -0.0779. \end{matrix} \tag{3.5}$$

where $P_2(x) = (3x^2 - 1)/2$ represents the second Legendre polynomial. In this set-up the ice line is determined dynamically by the following condition from (Budyko (1969), North (1975a,b)):

$$\begin{matrix} T > -10°\text{C} & \text{no ice line present} \\ T < -10°\text{C} & \text{ice present} \end{matrix} \tag{3.6}$$

finally equation (3.2) determines the location of the ice line ($x_s(t)$). Given the above specification the temperature (T_s) constitutes a break even temperature where temperatures below this level are assumed to be ice covered over the whole year and vice versa. Hence, by setting $T_s = -10$ as in Budyko and North we can solve the equation $T_s = T(x_s(t), t)$ for $x_s(t)$ which is needed in order to determine the solution to (3.1) for given levels of atmospheric carbon dioxide $M(t)$. Equation (3.1) thus states that the temperature at any given latitude is determined by the difference in incoming solar radiation $QS(x)\alpha(x, x_s)$ and outgoing radiation heat radiation $I(x, t)$ adjusted for latitudinal heat flux $D\frac{\partial}{\partial x}[\ldots]$.

Although the introduction of heat diffusion adds extra complexity, since it defined through the use of partial differential equations, a more simplified approach is available through the use of Legendre approximation methods as introduced by (North, 1975b). The solution can then be approximated by

$$T(x,t) = \sum_{nEven} T_n(t)P_n(x) \tag{3.7}$$

where $T_n(t)$ are solutions to appropriately defined ordinary differential equations (ODEs) and $P_n(x)$ are even numbered Legendre polynomials. A satisfactory approximation of the solution for (3.1) and (3.2) within a few percent, can be obtained by the so-called two-mode solution where $n = \{0, 2\}$ (North, 1975b).[13] The two-mode approximation is thus defined as $T(x,t) = T_0(t) + T_2(t)P_2(x)$ where $T_0(t)$, is the first mode, and $T_2(t)$, the second mode. Hence, a two-mode approximation to the system (3.1) and (3.2) can be obtained from the solution to the following system of differential algebraic equations:

$$C_c \frac{dT_0}{dt} = -(A + BT_0(t)) + \int_0^1 QS(x)\alpha(x, x_s(t))dx + g(M(t)) \tag{3.8}$$

$$C_c \frac{dT_2}{dt} = -(B + 6D)T_2(t) + 5\int_0^1 QS(x)\alpha(x, x_s(t))P_2(x)dx \tag{3.9}$$

$$T(x,t) = T_0(t) + T_2(t)P_2(x) \tag{3.10}$$

$$T(x_s, t) = T_s \tag{3.11}$$

where $P_2(x) = (3x^2 - 1)/2$ is the second Legendre polynomial that provides the spatial dimension to the solution. Note that the constant ice line temperature $T_s = -10$ is needed in order to determine the position of the ice line x_s and hence the co-albedo $\alpha(x, x_s(t))$ of (3.8) and (3.9).

From the two-mode approximation of the temperature, we obtain the global mean temperature $T_0(t)$, which is just the integral of $T(x,t)$ over x from zero to one. The variance of the temperature can be defined as

$$V_T = \int_0^1 [T(x,t) - T_0(t)]^2\, dx = \int_0^1 (T_2(t)P_2(x))^2 dx = \frac{(T_2(t))^2}{5} \tag{3.12}$$

Likewise, local temperature means at specific latitudes $(x, x + dx)$ are given by $[T_0(t) + T_2(t)P_2(x)]\, dx$, so that the mean temperature over a set of latitudes, $Z = [a, b]$, can thus be defined as

$$m[a,b] = \int_a^b [T_0(t) + T_2(t)P_2(x)]\, dx \tag{3.13}$$

while the variance of temperature over the set of latitudes $Z = [a, b]$ is

$$V[a,b] = \int_a^b [T_0(t) + T_2(t)P_2(x) - m[a,b;t]]^2\, dx. \tag{3.14}$$

When the area $Z = [a, b]$ is introduced, it is plausible to assume that utility in each area $[a, b]$ depends on both the mean temperature and the variance of temperature in that area. For example, we may expect increases in mean temperature and variance to have negative impacts on output in any area Z, if it is located in tropical latitudes. In contrast, mean temperature increases in some areas Z (e.g., Siberia) may increase rather than decrease utility.[14] Existing dynamic IAMs cannot deal with these kinds of spatial elements, such as impacts of changes in temperature variance, generated by climate dynamics over an area Z.

In the climate model $M(t)$ is the stock of the atmospheric CO_2. This stock affects the evolution of the temperature through the function g, and evolves through time under the forcing of human inputs in the form of emissions of Greenhouse gases (GHGs) $h(x, t)$ emitted at latitude x and time t.

For the human input we assume that emissions $h(x, t)$ relate to $M(t)$ by the simple equation

$$\dot{M}(t) = h(t) - mM(t) \tag{3.15}$$

where $h(t) = \int_0^1 h(x, t)dx$ and m is the carbon decay rate. To simplify the exposition we reduce the number of state variables in the problem by assuming that $M(t)$ has relaxed to a steady state and it relates to $h(t)$ through the simple linear relation $M(t) = (1/m)h(t)$. Thus we approximate $g(M(t))$ by a simple linear relation $\gamma h(t)$.[15] In this model the latitude of the ice line can move in time in response to changes in human input since the ice line solution depends on $h(t)$. Moving of the ice line toward the poles generates the damages related to damage reservoirs.

The climate model (3.8)–(3.11) that incorporates human input, which affects the evolution of temperature can be further simplified by following simplifications proposed by Wang and Stone (1980) which suggest that an approximation for the solution equation $T(x, t) = T_0(t) + T_2(t)P_2(x)$ can be achieved by replacing $T_2(t)$ by an appropriate constant. Then $dT(x, t)/dt = dT_0(t)/dt$, where $T_0(t)$, is global mean surface (sea level) temperature. Writing $T(t) = T_0(t)$ the evolution of the global mean temperature can be approximated by:

$$C_c \frac{dT(t)}{dt} = -A - BT(t) + \int_0^1 [QS(x)\alpha(x, x_s(t))]\, dx + g(M(t)). \tag{3.16}$$

Thus the Wang and Stone (1980) approximation reduces the model to one whose evolution is described by (3.16). Wang and Stone (1980) (equation 3.3) calibrate the model to get a simple equation for the ice line

$$x_s(t) = (a_{ice} + b_{ice}T(t))^{1/2}, a_{ice} = 0.6035, b_{ice} = 0.02078. \tag{3.17}$$

3.3 The Economic-Climate Model: Damage Reservoirs and Multiple Steady States

We introduce the two types of damages due to climate change mentioned earlier. Let us define these damages by two functions $D_1(T(t))$ and $D_2(x_s(t))$, where 1 denotes the traditional damages due to temperature rise, and 2 denotes damages due to reservoir damages from movement of the ice line toward the north and permafrost melting. A simplified integrated EBCM can be developed along the following lines.

We consider a simplified economy with aggregate capital stock K. An amount K_2 from this capital stock is diverted to alternative "clean technologies." Output in the economy is produced by capital and emissions h according to a standard production function $F(K - K_2, h + \phi K_2)$, where ϕ is an efficiency parameter for clean technologies.[16] The cost of using a unit of h is $C_h(h)$, with $C_h(0) = 0$, $C_h^{'} > 0, C_h^{''} > 0$. The use of emissions can be reduced by employing clean technologies at an effective rate ϕK_2. Denoting consumption by C, net capital formation in our simplified economy is described by

$$\frac{dK}{dt} = F(K - K_2, h + \phi K_2) - C - C_h(h) - \delta K \tag{3.18}$$

where δ is the depreciation rate on the capital stock. Assuming a linear utility function or $U(C) = C$, we consider the problem of a social planner that seeks to maximize discounted lifetime consumption less damages from climate change subject to (3.16), (3.17), and (3.18).

In this set-up the problem of the social planner can be described, in terms of the following Most Rapid Approach Problem (MRAP) problem,[17]

$$V(T(0)) = \max \int_0^{\infty} \mathrm{e}^{-\rho t} [F(K - K_2, h + \phi K_2) - C_h(h) - (\delta + \rho)K \tag{3.19}$$

$$-D_1(T(t)) - D_2(x_s(t))]\, dt$$

subject to (3.17) and

$$C_c \frac{dT(t)}{dt} = -A - BT(t) + \gamma h(t) + \Psi(T(t)), \tag{3.20}$$

$$\Psi(T(t)) = \int_0^1 [QS_2(x)\alpha(x, x_s(t))]\, dx\, , T(0) = T_0, \tag{3.21}$$

where $V(T(0))$ is the current value state valuation function, ρ is the subjective rate of discount on future utility, and the nonlinear function $\Psi(T(t))$ is an increasing function of T (North, 1975a). Problem (3.19)–(3.21), after the successive approximations have been made, has practically been reduced, regarding the climate part, to a zero-dimensional model as found in North et al. (1981). We believe that this exercise is of value because it outlines a pathway to extensions to one-dimensional models and is even suggestive via the Legendre basis method of how one might potentially extend the work to two-dimensional models on the sphere.[18] Problem (3.19)–(3.21) is in principle tractable to phase diagram methods with the costate variable on the vertical axis and the state variable on the horizontal axis.

At this point, it should be noted that technical change and population growth could also have been introduced in the form of Harrod neutral (labor augmenting) technical change, a formulation that is required for consistency with balanced growth in the neoclassical context. Balanced growth formulations allow us to conduct phase diagram analysis as in the text below. In this case the production function might be written as $F(K-K_2, h+\phi K_2, AL)$, where F is a constant returns to scale production function and $dA/dt = gA$, $dL/dt = nL$, where g is the rate of exogenous labor augmenting technical change and n is the population rate of growth. Output, capital, consumption, emissions, and the capital accumulation equation (3.18) can thus be defined in per effective worker (AL) terms. However, the temperature dynamics (3.21) and (3.23) now have a non-autonomous term due to exponentially growing emissions. Dealing with this problem while staying within a framework of autonomous dynamics, requires introduction of emission reducing technological progress at an appropriate rate in order to be able to transform the temperature dynamics into a stationary form so that phase diagram techniques of analysis of autonomous systems can still be applied. However, this is beyond the scope of the current chapter. In the current chapter we wish to show how spatial EBCMs can be integrated with capital accumulation models in economics while preserving analytical tractability. The time stationary analysis developed here indicates that a full analysis of more realistic non stationary systems is potentially tractable now that we have pointed the way in this chapter.

Returning to our time stationary framework, we feel that insights are gained more rapidly by analyzing the following qualitatively similar problem that is strongly motivated by the problem (3.19)–(3.21):

$$V(T(0)) = \max \int_0^{\infty} e^{-\rho t} [F(K-K_2, h+\phi K_2) - C_h(h) - (\delta+\rho)K \quad (3.22)$$

$$-D_1(T) - D_2(T)]\, dt$$

$$\text{s.t. } \frac{dT}{dt} = a_T - b_T T + c_T h\,, (a_T, b_T, c_T) > (0,0,0) \quad (3.23)$$

where $D_1^{'}(T) = a_1 T$, implying increasing marginal damages due to temperature increase, while $D_2^{'}(T)$ is a function increasing at low T reaching a maximum and then decreasing gradually to zero. The shape of $D_2(T)$ is intended to capture initially increasing marginal damages associated with damage reservoirs that reach a maximum as temperature increases, and eventually vanish once the polar ice caps are gone.

The exposition of a number of issues related to damages functions is useful at this point. Assuming a quadratic or a higher degree power function for damages $D_1(T)$ due to temperature increase is consistent with damages related to falling crop yields or reduction to ecosystem services, and this has been the shape adopted in many IAMs. To consider a plausible shape for $D_2(T)$ we have argued in the introduction that as the ice line moves toward the north, marginal damages must eventually tend to zero when the ice cap disappears. Similar behavior is expected by permafrost. Once permafrost is gone further damages associated with permafrost thawing should vanish. A potential damage function invoking these properties is the S-shaped function used in Brock and Starrett (2003) to describe internal loading of phosphorus in a lake system. This functional form has similar qualitative properties as the traditional damage function up to a certain point where marginal damages starts to decline eventually approaching zero. Furthermore, we argue that the combination of these two damage functions, $D_1(T)$ and $D_2(T)$, each one associated with climate change impacts having different time profiles and being disciplined by scientific evidence, provides a more comprehensive description of the problem.

To further analyze the economic part of the problem, define

$$\pi(h) = \max_{K \geq 0, K_2 \geq 0} \{F(K - K_2, h + \phi K_2) - (\delta + \rho)K\}. \quad (3.24)$$

Since we assume that $F(\cdot,\cdot)$ is concave increasing, $\pi(h)$ is an increasing concave function of h.[19] We may now write down the current value Hamiltonian and the first-order necessary conditions for an optimum,

$$\mathcal{H}(h, T, \lambda_T) = \pi(h) - C_h(h) - D_1(T) - D_2(T) + \lambda_T(a_T - b_T T + c_T h) \quad (3.25)$$

$$\pi'(h) = C_h' - \lambda_T c_T \Rightarrow h = h^*(\lambda_T),\ h^{*'}(\lambda_T) > 0, \quad (3.26)$$

where it is understood in (3.26) that the inequality conditions of boundary solutions are included, and

$$\frac{dT}{dt} = a_T - b_T T + c_T h^*(\lambda_T),\ T(0) = T_0 \quad (3.27)$$

$$\frac{d\lambda_T}{dt} = (\rho + b_T)\lambda_T + a_1 T + D_2'(T). \quad (3.28)$$

We know that since $\lambda_T(t) = \frac{\partial V(T(t))}{\partial T(t)} := V'(T(t)) < 0$, the costate variable can be interpreted as the shadow cost of temperature. We also know that if a decentralized representative firm pays an emission tax, then the path of the optimal emission tax is $-\lambda_T(t)$. We can study properties of steady states of the problem (3.19)–(3.21) by analyzing the phase portrait implied by (3.27)–(3.28). The isocline $dT/dt = 0$ is easy to draw for (3.27). Along this isocline we have $\frac{d\lambda_T}{dT} = \frac{b_T}{c_T h^{*'}} > 0$, by using (3.26), thus along this isocline λ_T is increasing in T. There is a value λ_{Tc} such that if $\lambda_T(t) < \lambda_{Tc}$ then

$h^* = 0$ and $a_T/b_T = T$. If there are no ice line damages, the $d\lambda_T/dt$ isocline is just a linear decreasing function of T that is zero at $T = 0$, or $\lambda_T = -\frac{a_1}{(\rho+b_T)}T$, which implies that $\lambda_T < 0$ for all $T > 0$. Now add the damages emerging from the damage reservoir to this function. The isocline is defined as

$$\lambda_T|_{\frac{d\lambda_T}{dt}=0} = -\frac{a_1 T + D_2'(T)}{(\rho + b_T)}, \quad \frac{d\lambda_T}{dT} = -\frac{a_1 + D_2''(T)}{(\rho + b_T)}$$

With an S-shaped function representation of $D_2(T)$, $D_2''(T)$ is positive and decreasing, it becomes negative, reaches a minimum, increases, and then approaches zero. This induces a nonlinearity to the $d\lambda_T/dt = 0$ isocline. In general it is expected that this isocline will have an inverted N-shape, which means that with an increasing $dT/dt = 0$ isocline if a steady state $(\bar{T}, \bar{\lambda}_T)$ exists, there will be either one or three steady states. To study the stability properties of these steady states we form the Jacobian matrix of (3.27)–(3.28),

$$J(\bar{T}, \bar{\lambda}_T) = \begin{bmatrix} -b_T & c_T h^{*'}(\bar{\lambda}_T) \\ a_1 + D_2''(\bar{T}) & b_T + \rho \end{bmatrix}. \tag{3.29}$$

If at a steady state $a_1 + D_2''(\bar{T}) > 0$ so that the $d\lambda_T/dt = 0$ isocline is decreasing then $\det J(\bar{T}, \bar{\lambda}_T) < 0$ and the steady state is a local saddle point. If $a_1 + D_2''(\bar{T}) < 0$ so that the $d\lambda_T/dt = 0$ isocline is increasing, the steady state is an unstable spiral.[20] Thus when a unique steady state exists it will be a saddle point. The case of three candidate optimal steady states $\bar{T}_1 < \bar{T}_2 < \bar{T}_3$ is of particular interest. In this case, given the shapes of the two isoclines, the smallest one and the largest one are saddles and the middle one is an unstable spiral. Thus we have a problem much like the lake problem analyzed by Brock and Starrett (2003), and following a similar argument, it can be shown (under modest regularity conditions so that the Hamiltonian is concave–convex in T) that there are two value functions, call them, $V_{\text{mitigate}}(T)$ and $V_{\text{adapt}}(T)$, and a "Skiba" point $T_s \in (\bar{T}_1, \bar{T}_3)$ such that $V_{\text{mitigate}}(T_s) = V_{\text{adapt}}(T_s)$. For $T_0 < T_s$, it is optimal to follow the costate/state equations associated with $V_{\text{mitigate}}(T)$ and converge to $\bar{T}_1$, while for $T_0 > T_s$ it is optimal to follow the costate/state equations associated with $V_{\text{adapt}}(T)$ and converge to $\bar{T}_3$. In Figure 3.1 we present this situation for an appropriate choice of functional forms and parameters.[21] Besides the solution path the figure also plots the isoclines both with and without ice line damages. Without ice line damages we have the case when the $\dot{\lambda}_T$-isocline is a linear decreasing function of T, implying that we get a unique global saddle point at the crossing of the $\dot{\lambda}_T = 0$, $\dot{T} = 0$ isoclines denoted by $\bar{T}_n$. For the case with ice line damages, on the other hand, we get the inverted N-shaped $\dot{\lambda}_T$, isocline giving us a "Skiba" point T_s lying just between the unstable spiral $\bar{T}_2$ and the local saddle point $\bar{T}_3$. Hence, for low initial $T_0 < \bar{T}_1$, it will be optimal to levy a low initial carbon tax even though there is a polar ice cap threat and then gradually increase the carbon tax along a gradualist policy ramp. However, if $T_0 \in (\bar{T}_1, T_s)$, it is optimal to tax carbon higher at T_0 and let the tax gradually fall. But if the initial temperature is large enough, the ice caps are essentially already gone and damage reservoirs have been

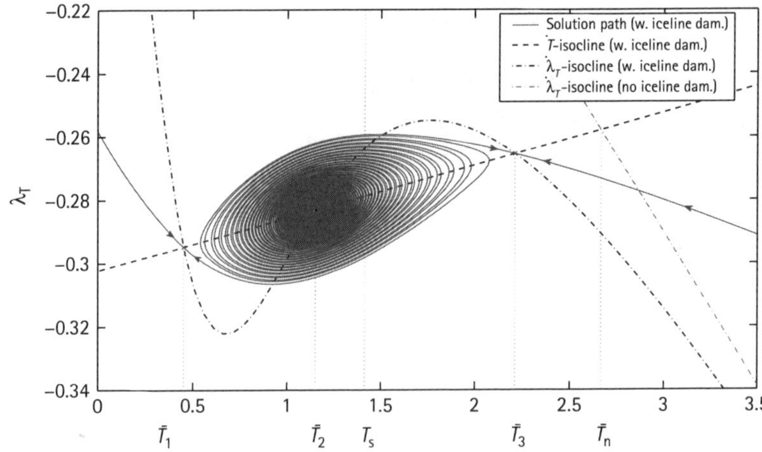

FIGURE 3.1 Phase diagram for the system (3.27)–(3.28). See appendix B for details on the numerical procedure. Parameter estimates can be found in table 3.1.

exhausted. Then the optimal thing to do is to tax carbon initially quite modestly but along an increasing schedule through time to deal with the rising marginal damages due to temperature rise. Figure 3.1 thus shows how the qualitative picture changes completely when a different shape for the ice line damage function is considered. In particular, the area $T \in (\bar{T}_1, T_s)$ is of interest since, if ice line damages go unaccounted for, the optimal strategy will be to levy a low carbon tax which eventually will raise temperature to $\bar{T}_n$, while in a model with ice line damages included the exact opposite will be true, implying a decrease in temperature to $\bar{T}_1$.

It is important to note that this stationary model is not rich enough to capture the eventual rather sharp increase along the "gradualist" policy ramp of (Nordhaus, 2007, 2010) because in Nordhaus's case the business-as-usual (BAU) emissions path would be growing because of economic growth. Thus the damages from temperature rise alone, growing quadratically as the quantity of emissions grows, would lead to the gradualist path of carbon taxes "taking off" in the future. However, this simple stationary model does expose the new behavior of a higher initial carbon tax for $T_0 \in (\bar{T}_1, T_s)$.

3.4 Energy Balance Integrated Assessment Models with Damage Reservoirs

In this section we incorporate the framework of the simplified energy balance models developed above into a framework similar to well established IAMs such as the

DICE/RICE models proposed by Nordhaus. We use notation close to that of Nordhaus for the DICE/RICE part of the model. Consider the continuous time spatial analog of Nordhaus's equations (Nordhaus, 2007 Appendix 1 or Nordhaus, 2010 A.1-A.20) where we have made some changes to be consistent with our notation and have suppressed (x,t) arguments to ease typing, unless (x,t) is needed for clarity,

$$W = \int_0^\infty e^{-\rho t} \int_0^1 \upsilon(x) U(C) dx dt, \tag{3.30}$$

where $U(C)$ is utility and C is aggregate consumption at (x,t), and $\upsilon(x)$ is a welfare weight assigned to latitude x.[22] Furthermore,

$$Y_n = C + \frac{dK}{dt} + \delta K \tag{3.31}$$

$$Y_n = \Omega(1-\Lambda)Y, \; Y = F(K) \tag{3.32}$$

where, $Y_n(x,t)$ is output of goods and services at latitude x and time t, net of abatement and damages; $\Omega(T(x,t))$ is the damage function (climate damages as fraction of output) as a function of temperature at (x,t); $\Lambda(x,t)$ is the abatement cost function (abatement costs as fraction of output)[23] at (x,t); and $F(K(x,t))$ is a concave production function of capital. δ is the usual depreciation rate of capital. As explained in the previous section, technology and labor have been removed from the production function in order to avoid problems of non-stationarity in the temperature equation.

Aggregate emissions at time t are defined as:

$$E(t) = \int_0^1 \sigma(1-\mu(x,t))Y(x,t)dx \tag{3.33}$$

where σ is ratio of industrial emissions to output (metric tons carbon per output at a base year prices), and $\mu(x,t)$ is the emissions-control rate at (x,t). Climate dynamics in the context of the ECBM are given by (3.1) and (3.2). Notice that we have replaced Nordhaus's climate equations Nordhaus (2010), equations A.14-A.20) with the spatial climate dynamics, (3.1) and (3.2).

Maximization of objective (3.30) subject to the constraints above is a very complicated and difficult optimal control problem of the partial differential equation (3.1) on an infinite dimensional space $x \in [0,1]$. We reduce this problem to a much simpler approximate problem of the optimal control of a finite number of "modes" using the two-mode approach described earlier.

For the two-mode approximation equations $T(x,t) = T_0(t) + T_2(t)P_2(x)$, (3.1) and (3.2) reduce to the pair of differential algebraic

$$C_c \frac{dT_0}{dt} = -(A + BT_0) + \int_0^1 QS(x)\alpha(x, x_s(t))dx + \gamma E(t) \tag{3.34}$$

$$C_c \frac{dT_2}{dt} = -(B+6D)T_2 + 5\int_0^1 QS(x)\alpha(x,x_s(t))P_2(x)dx \tag{3.35}$$

$$T_0(t) + T_2(t)P_2(x_s(t)) = T_s,\ T_s = -10°\text{C}. \tag{3.36}$$

Once again we have assumed emissions affect temperature in a linear fashion which is sufficient for the qualitative exercise we are pursuing here. A more accurate representation can be found in Table 6.2 of the IPCC (2001) report. Further, since γ adds nothing qualitatively we set $\gamma = 1$ and interpret σ as the product of these two parameters in what follows.

Before continuing notice that North's two-mode approximation has reduced a problem with a continuum of state variables indexed by $x \in [0,1]$ to a problem where the climate part has only two state variables. We can make yet a further simplification by assuming, as in Section 3.3, that the utility function is linear, i.e. $U(C) = C$. This will allow us to write (3.30) as the MRAP problem:

$$W = \int_0^\infty e^{-\rho t}\int_0^1 \upsilon C dx dt = \int_0^\infty e^{-\rho t}\int_0^1 \upsilon\left[\Omega(1-\Lambda)F - (\rho+\delta)K\right]dxdt. \tag{3.37}$$

Note that for the two mode approximation, the damage function should be defined as:

$$\Omega(T(x,t)) = \Omega(T_0(t) + T_2(t)P_2(x)). \tag{3.38}$$

To ease notation we introduce the inner product notation $\langle f,g\rangle = \int_0^1 f(x)g(x)dx$. We may now write the current value Hamiltonian for the optimal control problem (3.37) and show how we have drastically simplified the problem by using a two-mode approximation,[24]

$$\mathcal{H} = \int_0^1 \upsilon\left[\Omega(1-\Lambda)F - (\rho+\delta)K + \frac{\lambda_0}{C_c}\sigma(1-\mu)F\right]dx$$
$$\frac{\lambda_0}{C_c}\left[\langle QS\alpha, 1\rangle - A - BT_0\right] + \frac{\lambda_2}{C_c}\left[5\langle QS\alpha, P_2\rangle - (B+6D)T_2\right]. \tag{3.39}$$

For the simplified problem (3.37), the capital stock and the emissions control rate $K^*(x,t), \mu^*(x,t)$ are chosen to maximize $\mathcal{H}$ for each (x,t), which is a relatively simple problem. However, there is one complication to be addressed. The absorption function $\alpha(x,x_s(t))$ depends on the ice line $x_s(t)$ where the ice line is given by a solution of (3.36), that is,

$$x_s(t) = P_+^{-1}\left(\frac{T_s - T_0(t)}{T_2(t)}\right) \tag{3.40}$$

where the subscript "+" denotes the largest inverse function of the quadratic function $P_2(x) = (1/2)(3x^2 - 1)$. Notice that the inverse function is unique and is the largest one on the set of latitudes $[0,1]$. Equation (3.40) induces a nonlinear dependence of equations (3.34) and (3.35) through the absorption function, but no new state variables are introduced by this dependence. An additional dependence induced by equations (3.34) and (3.35) as well as equation (3.40) is on the damage function, which we parameterize as:

$$\Omega = \Omega(T_0(t), T_2^2(t)P_2^2(x); x_s(t), x) \tag{3.41}$$

The first term in (3.41) represents damages to output at latitude x as a function of average planetary temperature as in (Nordhaus, 2007, 2010) and the second term is an attempt to capture extra damages due to climate "variance". Note that the component $P_2^2(x)$ is larger at $x = 0$ and $x = 1$ than it is at the "temperate" latitude $x = (1/3)^{1/2}$ where $P_2^2(x) = 0$. This is an admittedly crude attempt to capture the component of damages due to "wetter places getting wetter" and "drier places getting drier" as well as damages to arctic latitudes compared to temperate latitudes. But some of this dependence can be captured also in the "x" term in the parameterization (3.41). Finally the impact on damages at latitude x due to shifts in the ice line is captured by inclusion of the ice line in (3.41). This is a fairly flexible parameterization of spatial effects (i.e., latitude specific effects) that are not captured in the traditional non spatial formulations of integrated assessment models.

3.4.1 Optimal Mitigation and Location Specific Policy Ramp

Let us first illustrate optimal mitigation using our two-mode simplification of our original "infinite mode" problem with linear utility by considering a version of the problem where the impact of policy $\{\mu(x,t)\}$ on the location of the ice line $x_s(t)$ is ignored. That is there is no ice line dependence of any functions of the problem including the absorption function. In this simplified case the albedo function depends only on x and thus the terms $\langle QS\alpha, 1\rangle, \langle QS\alpha, P_2\rangle$ do not depend on $T_0(t), T_2(t)$ in (3.34) and (3.35). We also start of by assuming that abatement costs are linear and given by $\Lambda = \psi\mu,\ \psi > 0$, implying that the solution is of the bang-bang type. In Section 3.4.2 we will consider a nonlinear version of abatement costs. Hence the two costate differential equations become

$$\begin{aligned}\frac{d\lambda_0}{dt} &= \rho\lambda_0 - \frac{\partial \mathcal{H}}{\partial T_0} = \left(\rho + \frac{B}{C_c}\right)\lambda_0 - \int_0^1 v\frac{\partial\Omega}{\partial T_0}(1-\Lambda)Fdx \\ \frac{d\lambda_2}{dt} &= \rho\lambda_2 - \frac{\partial \mathcal{H}}{\partial T_2} = \left(\rho + \frac{B+6D}{C_c}\right)\lambda_2 - \int_0^1 v\frac{\partial\Omega}{\partial T_2}(1-\Lambda)Fdx\end{aligned} \tag{3.42}$$

Wang and Stone (1980) argue that one can even get a fairly good approximation of T_2 by exploiting how fast mode 2 converges relative to mode zero in equation (3.35) as compared to (3.34). Hence we can further simplify the problem by assuming that T_2 has already converged to:

$$T_2 = \frac{5\langle QS\alpha, P_2\rangle}{(B+6D)} \tag{3.43}$$

for each $T(t)$.[25] The Hamiltonian (3.39) for the case when the absorption function and T_2 are constant can thus be written as[26]

$$\mathcal{H} = \int_0^1 \left[\upsilon(\Omega(1-\psi\mu)F - (\rho+\delta)K) + \frac{\lambda_0}{C_c}\sigma(1-\mu)F \right] dx \tag{3.44}$$

$$+ \frac{\lambda_0}{C_c}\left[Q\alpha - A - BT_0\right]. \tag{3.45}$$

In this case we obtain the following switching decision rule for $\mu^*(x,t)$

$$\mu^*(x,t) \begin{Bmatrix} = 0 \\ \in [0,1] \\ = 1 \end{Bmatrix} \text{ for } -\lambda_0(t) \begin{Bmatrix} < \\ = \\ > \end{Bmatrix} \frac{\upsilon(x)\psi C_c}{\sigma}\Omega \tag{3.46}$$

$$\Omega = \Omega(T_0(t), (T_2 P_2(x))^2, x) \tag{3.47}$$

$$\lambda_0(t) = \int_{s=t}^{\infty} e^{-\left(\rho + \frac{B}{C_c}\right)(s-t)} \left[\int_0^1 \upsilon(x)\Omega(1-\psi\mu^*)F\frac{\partial \Omega}{\partial T_0}dx \right] ds. \tag{3.48}$$

Suppose some type of institution wanted to implement this social optimum. One way to do it would be to impose a tax $\tau(\lambda) \equiv \frac{-\lambda_0(t)}{C_c}$ on emissions when individual agents solve the static problems

$$\max_{\{\mu \in [0,1], K \geq 0\}} \{\Omega(1-\psi\mu)F - (\rho+\delta)K - \tau(\lambda)\sigma(1-\mu)F\}. \tag{3.49}$$

We see right away that the first-order necessary conditions for the problem (3.49) are the same with those resulting from the Hamiltonian function (3.44). Since $F(K)$ is a concave increasing function, then setting $\tau(\lambda) = \frac{-\lambda_0(t)}{C_c}$ implements the social optimum. Note that the socially optimal emissions tax is uniform across all locations as one would expect from (Nordhaus, 2007, 2010). There are, however, exceptions to a uniform tax policy. In an accompanying paper, Brock et al. (2012b), we argue that if the institutional infra structure is not in place to implement transfers from the rest of the world to a heavily damaged latitude, then "income effects" argue that the heavily damaged poor latitudes should pay less per unit carbon than heavily damaged, but rich latitudes.

An important question arises at this point: What substantive difference does the spatial climate model coupled to the economic model add that is not already captured by nonspatial climate models? There are several important differences regarding policy implications.

The emission reduction policy ramp $\mu^*(x,t)$ is location specific and dictates $\mu^*(x,t) = 1$ for all (x,t) where the relative welfare weight $\upsilon(x)$ on welfare at that location is small (recall that $\int_0^1 \upsilon(x)dx = 1$ by normalization). Assume that the damage function $\Omega = \Omega(T_0(t), (T_2P_2(x))^2, x) = \Omega(T_0(t), (T_2P_2(x))^2)$ is decreasing in both arguments.[28] This crudely captures the idea that damages increase at each latitude as average planetary temperature, $T_0(t)$, increases and as a measure of local climate "variance" $(T_2P_2(x))^2$ increases. Let R denote a set of "at risk latitudes" with low values of $\Omega(T_0(t),(T_2P_2(x))^2)$, that is, with high values of the arguments. The set R is a crude attempt to capture latitudes that would be relatively most damaged by climate change. A plausible type of objective would be to solve the social problem above but with $\upsilon(x)>0, x\in R$, $\upsilon(x)\simeq 0, x\notin R$. We see right away that this social problem would require all xs not in R to reduce all emissions immediately. In general we have,

$$\mu^*(x,t)=1,\ for\ -\lambda_0(t)>\frac{\upsilon(x)\psi C_c}{\sigma}\Omega \tag{3.50}$$

and vice versa. This makes good economic sense. The marginal social burden on the planet as a whole of a unit of emissions at date t, no matter from which x it emanates is, $-\lambda_0(t)$. Locations x where the welfare weight on the location is small, where emissions per unit of output are relatively large (relatively large $\sigma(x)$), and that are already relatively heavily damaged $(\Omega(T_0(t),(T_2P_2(x))^2,x)$ is high) are ordered to stop emitting. Thus our modeling allows plausible specifications of the economic justice argument stemming from geography to shape policy rules.

In the following section, we use this framework to extend our results in the presence of an discontinuous absorption function that changes at the ice line. This is a more realistic model which introduces ice line damages which we develop in the context of a DICE/RICE-type integrated assessment model.

3.4.2 Optimal Mitigation in an IAM-Type Model with Damage Reservoirs

We now introduce as the absorption function the version proposed in North (1975a) where

$$\alpha(x,x_s)=1-\alpha(x)=\begin{cases}\alpha_1=0.38 & x>x_s\\ \alpha_0=0.68 & x<x_s\end{cases}, \tag{3.51}$$

where $\alpha(x)$ is the albedo. With this absorption function, the dynamics $T_0(t)$ in (3.34) and the T_2 approximation in (3.43) become respectively

$$\frac{dT_0}{dt}=\frac{1}{C_c}\left[-(A+BT_0)+Q(\alpha_0-\alpha_1)\int_{x=0}^{x=x_s(t)}(1+S_2P_2(x))dx+E+Q\alpha_1\right] \tag{3.52}$$

$$T_2=\frac{1}{(B+6D)}\left[5Q(\alpha_0-\alpha_1)\int_{x=0}^{x=x_s(t)}(1+S_2P_2(x))P_2(x)dx+Q\alpha_1S_2\right], \tag{3.53}$$

where the equation for the ice line is, using (3.40),

$$x_s(t)=\left[\frac{2}{3}\frac{T_s-T_0}{T_2}+\frac{1}{3}\right]^{\frac{1}{2}}. \tag{3.54}$$

The objective (3.30) and the constraints (3.51)–(3.54) determine optimal mitigation over time and latitude. The discontinuous absorption function can create a strong nonlinearity where a small change in T_0 can cause a large change in damages at some latitudes. However this nonlinearity makes it difficult to proceed with analytical solutions. To obtain a qualitative idea of the impact of the nonlinearity due to the absorption function and the ice line, we use the climate parametrization used by North (1975a) ($\alpha_0 = 0.68, \alpha_1 = 0.38, A = 201.4, B = 1.45, S_2 = -0.483, T_s = -10, Q = 334.4$). The heat transport coefficient D is found to be approximately 0.321 by calibrating the ice line function to the current ice line estimate ($x_s = 0.95$).[29]

The system (3.52)–(3.54) is highly nonlinear and can be simplified by deriving a polynomial approximation of x_s as a function of $T_0(t)$. We proceed in the following way. If we substitute $x_s(t)$ from (3.54) into (3.53), then T_2 is a fixed point of (3.53). We solve numerically the fixed point problem (3.53) for values of $T_0 \in [-\bar{T}_0, \bar{T}_0]$, obtaining the solution $\hat{T}_2(T_0)$. Substituting this back into equation (3.54) gives us the $\hat{x}_s(\hat{T}_2(T_0), T_0)$ which is then used to fit a quadratic curve on $(T_0, \hat{x}_s)$ by using least squares. Thus $\hat{x}_s$ is approximated by a convex curve $\hat{x}_s = \zeta_0 + \zeta_1 T_0 + \zeta_2 T_0^2 = \zeta(T_0)$, $(\zeta_0, \zeta_1, \zeta_2) > 0$.[30] Making use of this approximation, the system (3.52)–(3.54) can thus be written as:

$$\frac{dT_0}{dt} = \frac{1}{C_c}[-(A + BT_0) + Q(\alpha_0 - \alpha_1)\theta(T_0) + E + Q\alpha_1] \tag{3.55}$$

$$\text{where } \theta(T_0) := \left[\hat{x}_s + \frac{S_2}{2}(\hat{x}_s^3 - \hat{x}_s)\right] \text{ with } \hat{x}_s := \zeta_0 + \zeta_1 T_0 + \zeta_2 T_0^2$$

Assuming linear utility once again, the Hamiltonian can be written as:

$$\mathcal{H} = \int_0^1 \left[\upsilon[K^\beta \Omega(T_0)(1 - \Lambda) - (\rho + \delta)K] + \frac{\lambda_0}{C_c}\sigma(1 - \mu)K^\beta \right] dx$$
$$+ \frac{\lambda_0}{C_c}[-A - BT_0 + Q(\alpha_0 - \alpha_1)\theta(T_0) + Q\alpha_1]. \tag{3.56}$$

We now assume that abatement costs are increasing in abatement activities, $\Lambda = \psi\mu^2$. The optimal μ and K will thus be defined as:

$$\mu^*(x,t) = -\frac{\lambda_0 \sigma}{2C_c \upsilon \psi \Omega(T_0)}, \forall x \in [0,1] \tag{3.57}$$

$$K^*(x,t) = \left(\frac{\rho + \delta}{\beta}\right)^{\frac{1}{\beta - 1}} \left[\Omega(T_0)(1 - \psi\mu^{*2}) - \frac{\lambda_0}{\upsilon C_c}\sigma(1 - \mu^*)\right]^{\frac{-1}{\beta - 1}}. \tag{3.58}$$

and the canonical system becomes:

$$\frac{dT_0}{dt} = \frac{1}{C_c}\left[-A - BT_0 + Q(\alpha_0 - \alpha_1)\theta(T_0) + \int_0^1 \sigma(1 - \mu^*)K^{*\beta} dx\right] \tag{3.59}$$

$$\frac{d\lambda_0}{dt} = \left(\rho + \frac{B}{C_c} - \frac{Q}{C_c}(\alpha_0 - \alpha_1)\theta'(T_0)\right)\lambda_0 - \int_0^1 \upsilon\left[K^{*\beta}\Omega'(T_0)(1-\psi\mu^{*2})\right]dx \tag{3.60}$$

which can be solved numerically given a specific shape of $\upsilon(x)$.

To proceed further we need a more detailed specification for the damage function, which as explained above should contain a temperature component denoted by $D_1(T_0)$ and an ice line component, denoted by $D_2(T_0)$.[31] We specify the damage function in the following way. Lost output from temperature induced damages is: $Y - \frac{Y}{1+D_1(T_0)} = \frac{YD_1(T_0)}{1+D_1(T_0)} := Yd_1(T_0)$. Lost output from ice line movement toward the poles written as a function of T_0 is: $Y - \frac{Y}{1+D_2(T_0)} = \frac{YD_2(T_0)}{1+D_2(T_0)} := Yd_2(T_0)$. The sum of lost output from both sources is: $\text{Lost}Y = Yd_1(T_0) + Yd_2(T_0)$. Thus net output available for consumption and mitigation is: $Y - \text{Lost}Y = (1 - d_1(T_0) - d_2(T_0))Y$.

If we define $\Omega_i(T_0) = \frac{1}{1+D_i(T_0)}, i = 1,2$, then the term $(1 - d_1(T_0) - d_2(T_0))$ can be written as the damage function Ω of the system (3.57)–(3.60) in the form

$$\Omega(T_0) = \Omega_1(T_0) + \Omega_2(T_0) - 1. \tag{3.61}$$

As the global warming problem concerns damages resulting from temperature increases rather than decreases, we restrict the state space to include only temperatures $T_0 > 15°C$, that is, in the vicinity of the present average global temperature level.[32] In the spatial model used in this section, this temperature level is found by setting $E = 0$ and solving (3.55), which gives us $T_0 \approx 15.27$. Hence, 15°C can be viewed as a rough ballpark estimate of the preindustrial global temperature average. Damages are assumed to start at 15°C and we thus write our normalized damage function as $\Omega(T_0 - 15)$. Furthermore, we will use the same functional forms for the damage functions as used in Section 3.3 (see Appendix 3.7).[33]

The EBCM that we presented in this section, resulting from the concepts developed in the earlier part of the chapter, has many similarities to the traditional IAMs but also two potentially important differences. The first is the discontinuous absorption function and the second is an alternative shape for ice line damages as opposed to other temperature related damages. Together they introduce complex nonlinearities into the temperature dynamics. The question of whether these differences imply significant deviations from the model's predictions, cannot be answered analytically owing to the high complexity of the models. So we resort to numerical simulations.

Figure 3.2 shows the results for the spatial climate model presented in this section. As in Section 3.2 this model also gives us three candidate optimal steady states, $\bar{T}_{01} < \bar{T}_{02} < \bar{T}_{03}$, where the largest and the smallest ones are saddles while the middle one is an unstable spiral.[34] Between the unstable spiral $\bar{T}_2$ and the saddle $\bar{T}_1$ we have a Skiba point $\bar{T}_s$ similar to that of Section 3.2.[35] Hence, defining the carbon tax as above that is, $\tau = -\lambda_0(t)/C_c$, for low initial temperatures $T_{00} < \bar{T}_1$ a low but gradually increasing carbon tax will be optimal, while for $\bar{T}_1 < T_{00} < T_s$ the optimal carbon tax an inverted U-shape and is increasing close to T_s but starts decreasing as $\bar{T}_1$ is approached. In

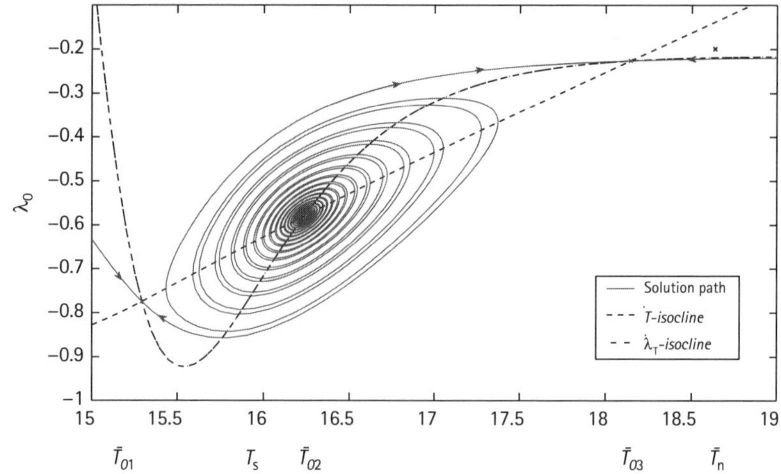

FIGURE 3.2 Phase diagram for the system (3.59)–(3.60). Parameter estimates can be found in table 3.2.

the region $T_s < T_{00} < \bar{T}_3$ on the other hand optimal tax policy is U-shaped where initially in the vicinity of T_s it is optimal to levy a high carbon tax which then gradually will decrease. Furthermore, figure 3.2 also depicts the case when ice line damages are omitted, $\bar{T}_n$. In contrast to Section 3.2, both of the isoclines are now affected and in order to keep the figure from becoming too messy, we have chosen to plot only the single equilibrium at the crossing of these isoclines, which is denoted by the black dot at $\bar{T}_n$ in figure 3.3. The qualitative behavior is, however, the same as in section 3.2, i.e. the "damage reservoir – no ice line damage equilibrium" is a saddle having a positive slope for the $\dot{T}$-isocline and a negative slope for the $\dot{\lambda}$-isocline.

3.5 The DICE Model with Damage Reservoirs

Both the relatively simple model of Section 3.2 and the more complex model of Section 3.4 strongly suggest that the explicit modeling of ice line damages shows the need for strong mitigation now. To further demonstrate that this result is robust to the choice of model, we now turn to the DICE model. The purpose of this exercise is to show how the introduction of ice line damages into the damage function, along the lines suggested by the EBCMs, will affect the optimal emission policy implied by DICE. The DICE model, probably the most well known of the IAMs, assumes that all damages to the economy evolve according to the quadratic equation (A.5) in Nordhaus (2007). The calibrated version of this damage function is plotted on page 51 of Nordhaus (2007). Based on this calibration we can see that a 4°C warming results in approximately a 5% loss of

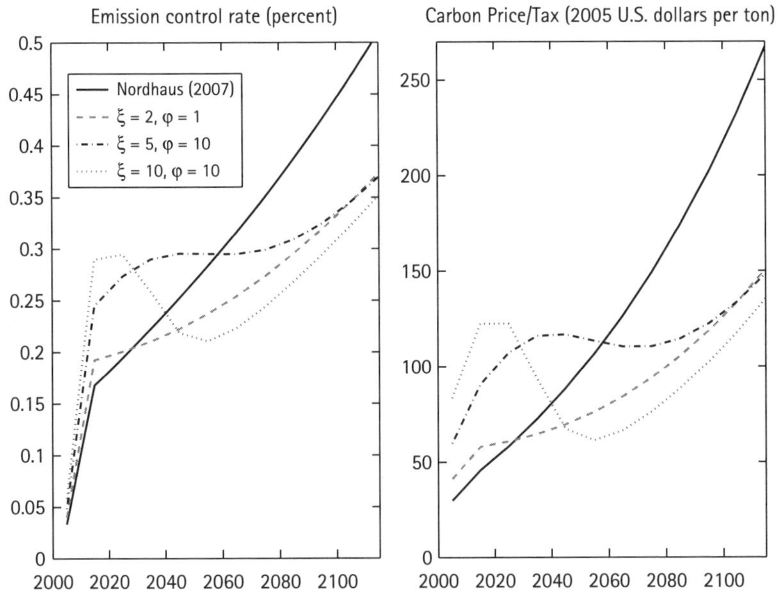

FIGURE 3.3 Optimal emission control rate and carbon prices *without* iceline damages (solid lines) corresponding to the Nordhaus (2007) and *with* iceline damages (dashed/dash-dotted/dotted) for the three sets of iceline damage coefficients with corresponding damage functions found in figure 3.4 of the Appendix B between the years 2000–2115.

output. We proceed by calibrating our disaggregated damage function in the following way. First, in order to separate out the ice line component from the total amount of damages, we follow the procedure shown in Section 3.4.2. We thus replace (A.5) of Nordhaus (2007) with equation (3.61) from Section 3.4.2. Hence, we have two separate damage components, $D_1(T)$ and $D_2(T)$, which can be calibrated independently. Next, we use the Nordhaus (2007) impact estimate of 5% loss of output for a 4°C warming and make a rough assumption that exactly half of these damages should be attributed to the melting of ice sheets causing sea level rises, flooding, changes in ocean currents, etc. Finally, using the same shapes for the temperature and ice line specific components as in previous sections, that is, $D_1(T) = \frac{a_1}{2}T^2$ and $D_2(T) = a_2\frac{T^\xi}{\varphi+T^\xi}$, we proceed by calibrating the damage parameters a_1 and a_2 so that $D_1(4) = D_2(4) = 0.025$. In this way our new damage function produces an amount of damage at a 4°C warming which is equivalent to that of the original model but with differing damage estimates for other temperature levels. For $D_1(T)$ this gives us an estimate of $a_1 = 0.0007813$. To calibrate $D_2(T)$ we however, also need to know the values of ξ and φ. The S-shaped function is usually used in models trying to capture thresholds or tipping points. Here, the parameters ξ and φ will have an effect on the steepness and level at which temperature crosses such a threshold. We provide estimates for three different assumptions regarding these parameters in order to highlight how they impact on optimal trajectories.

Figure 3.3 plots the optimal emission control rate and carbon price resulting from the DICE-2007 model for three different sets of estimates for ξ and φ. First, for comparison we provide the trajectories for the original model without iceline damages that is, $a_2 = 0$, which are depicted as solid lines in both graphs. These trajectories are thus based on the Nordhaus (2007) quadratic damage function calibrated as $D(4) = 0.05$ thus yielding a 5% drop in output at a warming of 4°C. This provides a good benchmark for comparison since both simulations with and without iceline specific damages in this way yield the same damage estimate for a 4°C rise in temperature.

As can be seen from this graph, the separation of different damage structures gives us U-shaped type policies where it is optimal to mitigate more initially as opposed to the normal gradualist policy ramp. Look first at the dashed lines which depart the least from the original quadratic damage function of Nordhaus. These paths were produced analogous to the calibration in the previous sections with $\xi = 2$ and $\varphi = 1$. The effect that ξ has on the shape of the damage function is that it increases the steepness of the function creating an almost discontinuous jump for very large values while φ is more of a shift parameter moving the location of the threshold. Figure 3.4 in the appendix depicts the iceline damage functions for the three sets of estimates we considered when generating the paths corresponding to Figure 3.3.[36] As can be seen for the case when $\xi = 2$ and $\varphi = 1$ this produces only a modest increase in the slope of the damage function when temperature is increased and thereby also logically generates paths similar to those of the original Nordhaus simulation. For higher values, however, $\xi = 5$ and $\varphi = 10$, we begin to see an increasingly clear U-shape depicted by the dash-dotted lines in Figure 3.3. The steepness of the iceline damage function thus seems to be have a large effect on the emission policy calling for more mitigation now. Finally, the dotted line depicts the most extreme case when ξ is raised to 10. As can be seen from Figure 3.4

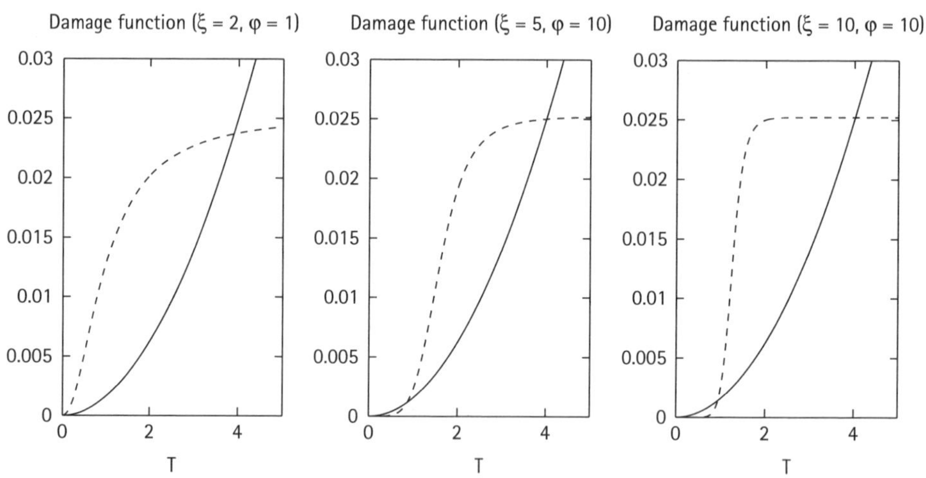

FIGURE 3.4 Calibrated damage functions D_1 (solid) and D_2 (dashed) for the three sets of estimates for ξ and φ.

in appendix this gives us a steep threshold type function for iceline damages where damages remain small up to a little over 1°C and then increase rapidly. This produces a clear U-shaped tax and emission policy as can be seen in Figure 3.3.

The results above thus show off how a U-shaped policy might arise with heavy mitigation now and less later when damages from climate change arrive in a more threshold specific manner as opposed to the more gradual increase, common in contemporary damage functions. Although these results remain specific to our assumptions regarding the shape of the damage function for the ice line as well as the temperature component, we still believe they are valuable since they show off the sensitivity of climate-economy models to structural changes in the damage function.

3.6 Summary, Conclusions, and Suggestions for Future Research

In this chapter we introduce the economics profession to spatial Energy Balance Climate Models (EBCMs) and show how to couple them to economic models while deriving analytical results of interest to economists and policy makers. Although we believe this contribution is of importance in its own right, we also show how introduction of the spatial dimension incorporated into the EBCMs leads to new ways of looking at climate policy.

In particular, by accounting for an endogenous ice line and paying attention to the associated damage reservoirs and albedo effects we show that due to nonlinearities even simple economic-EBCMs generated multiple steady states and policy ramps that do not in general follow the "gradualist" predictions. These results carry over to more complex models where the economic module has an IAM structure. The interesting issue from the emergence of multiple steady states, is that when the endogenous ice line and discontinuous albedo are ignored, as in traditional IAMs, the policy prescription of these models could be the opposite of the policy dictated by the economic-EBCMs. Furthermore the spatial aspect of the EBCMs allows arguments associated with the spatial structure of climate change damages to shape policy rules. When we applied the damage function implied by the EBCMs and calibrated appropriately simulations in the DICE model gave results interpretable as a U-shaped policy ramp indicating an important deviation from the gradualist policy ramp derived from the standard DICE model. Thus a rapid mitigation policy can be justified on the new insights obtained by coupling the economy with the EBCMs.

Areas for further research could range from making the economics more sophisticated by abandoning the simplifying assumption of linear utility; allowing for technical change and knowledge spillovers across latitudes; or introducing strategic interactions among regions and extensions of the EBCMs. It is thus also of importance to extend our Skiba type analysis to include (exogenous) growth. This could give rise to a dynamic set of Skiba points with a value function of both state and time, thus determining the optimal policy separately at each given point in time.[37] Other extensions might also consider how emissions arise more explicitly from the use of fossil fuels (see, e.g., Golosov et al., 2011). Future work also needs to be done regarding the extension of EBCMs to a two-dimensional spherical EBCM, because Earth is a sphere, not a line. Brock and Judd (2010) are attempting to make a dent in this problem. They frame the problem as a recursive dynamic programming problem where the state vector includes a number of "spherical modes" that are analogs of the modes in this chapter as well as economic state variables. Another possible extension could be the consideration of new policy instruments. Emissions reduction acts on the outgoing radiation in the sense that by reducing emissions the outgoing radiation increases through the second term of the right-hand side of (3.1). Another kind of policy could act on the first term of the right-hand side of (3.1) in the sense of reducing the incoming radiation. This type of policy might be associated with geoengineering options. Finally a policy that acts on the damage function in the sense of reducing damages for any given level of temperature and radiation balance might be associated with adaptation options. Unified economic-EBCMs might be a useful vehicle for analyzing the structure and the trade offs among these different policy options.

Appendix A: The Two-Mode Solution

In this appendix we show how to derive the two mode solution (3.8)–(3.11). We start with the basic partial differential equation

$$\begin{aligned} C_c \frac{\partial T(x,t)}{\partial t} &= QS(x)\alpha(x,x_s) - [A + BT(x,t) - g(M(t))] \\ &\quad + D\frac{\partial}{\partial x}\left[(1-x^2)\frac{\partial T(x,t)}{\partial x}\right] \end{aligned} \tag{3.62}$$

The two-mode solution is defined as:

$$T(x,t) = T_0(t) + T_2(t)P_2(x), \ P_2(x) = \frac{(3x^2-1)}{2} \tag{3.63}$$

then

$$\frac{\partial T(x,t)}{\partial t} = \frac{dT_0(t)}{dt} + \frac{dT_2(t)}{dt}P_2(x) \tag{3.64}$$

$$\frac{\partial T(x,t)}{\partial x} = T_2(t)\frac{dP_2(x)}{dx} = T_2(t)3x \tag{3.65}$$

Substitute the above derivatives into (3.62) to obtain:

$$C_c \frac{dT_0(t)}{dt} + C_c \frac{dT_2(t)}{dt} P_2(x) = QS(x)\alpha(x, x_s(t))$$
$$- \left[A + B(T_0(t) + T_2(t)P_2(x)) - g(M(t))\right] + D\frac{\partial}{\partial x}\left[(1-x^2)T_2(t)3x\right]$$

which can be written as

$$C_c \frac{dT_0(t)}{dt} + C_c \frac{dT_2(t)}{dt} P_2(x) = QS(x)\alpha(x, x_s(t)) - A - \tag{3.66}$$
$$BT_0(t) - BT_2(t)P_2(x) - g(M(t)) - 6T_2(t)P_2(x)$$

The following properties apply to Legendre polynomials:

$$\int_0^1 P_n(x)P_m(x)dx = \frac{\delta_{nm}}{2n+1}$$
$$\delta_{nm} = 0 \text{ for } n \neq m, \delta_{nm} = 1 \text{ for } n = 1$$

where we note that $P_0(x) = 1$, $P_2(x) = \frac{(3x^2-1)}{2}$

Multiply (3.66) by $P_0(x)$ and integrate from 0 to 1 to obtain

$$C_c \frac{dT_0(t)}{dt} = \int_0^1 \left[QS(x)\alpha(x, x_s(t))\right] dx - \left[A + BT_0(t)\right] + g(M(t)) \tag{3.67}$$

Multiply (3.66) by $P_2(x)$ and integrate from 0 to 1 noting that $\int_0^1 P_2(x)dx = 0$, and $\int_0^1 P_2(x)P_2(x)dx = \frac{1}{5}$ to obtain

$$C_c \frac{dT_2(t)}{dt} = 5\int_0^1 \left[QS(x)\alpha(x, x_s(t))P_2(x)\right] dx - (B + 6D)T_2(t) \tag{3.68}$$

where (3.67) and (3.68) are the ODEs of the two mode approximation given by (3.8)–(3.11).

3.7 Appendix B: Analytics and Calibration Results for Section 3.3 and 3.4

The production function in (3.24) is assumed to take the following form:

$$F(K - K_2, h + \phi K_2) = (K - K_2)^{\beta_1}(h + \phi K_2))^{\beta_2} \tag{3.69}$$

with $\beta_1 > 0, \beta_2 > 0$. The solution to problem (3.24) is derived from the first order conditions:

$$\frac{\partial F}{\partial K} = \beta_1 (K - K_2)^{\beta_1 - 1}(h + \phi K_2))^{\beta_2} - (\delta + \rho) = 0 \tag{3.70}$$

$$\frac{\partial F}{\partial K_2} = -\beta_1 (K - K_2)^{\beta_1 - 1}(h + \phi K_2))^{\beta_2} + \beta_2 \phi (K - K_2)^{\beta_1}(h + \phi K_2))^{\beta_2 - 1} = 0 \tag{3.71}$$

Solving the system (3.70) and (3.71) for K and K_2 gives the solution to problem (3.24).

$$K_2^*(h) = \frac{1}{\phi}\left(\frac{(\delta+\rho)}{\beta_1}\left(\frac{\beta_1}{\phi\beta_2}\right)^{1-\beta_1}\right)^{\frac{1}{\beta_1 - 1 + \beta_2}} - \frac{h}{\phi}$$

$$K^*(h) = \frac{\beta_1}{\phi\beta_2} h + \left(1 + \frac{\beta_1}{\beta_2}\right) K_2^*(h)$$

Plugging these values back into (3.24) allows us to write $\pi(h)$ as a linear function of h, i.e. $\pi(h) = \ddot{A} + \ddot{B}h$ with

$$\begin{aligned}\tilde{A} :=& \left(\frac{\beta_1}{\phi\beta_2}\right)^{\beta_1}\left(\frac{(\delta+\rho)}{\beta_1}\left(\frac{\beta_1}{\phi\beta_2}\right)^{1-\beta_1}\right)^{\frac{\beta_1+\beta_2}{\beta_1-1+\beta_2}} \\ & - (\delta+\rho)\frac{(1+\phi)}{\phi}\left(\frac{(\delta+\rho)}{\beta_1}\left(\frac{\beta_1}{\phi\beta_2}\right)^{1-\beta_1}\right)^{\frac{1}{\beta_1-1+\beta_2}} \\ \tilde{B} :=& -(\delta+\rho)\left(\frac{\beta_1}{\phi\beta_2} - \frac{(1+\phi)}{\phi}\right)\end{aligned}$$

which is increasing in h given that $\beta_1/\beta_2 < (1+\phi)$. Assuming also that $D_1(T) = \frac{a_1}{2}T^2$, $D_2(T) = a_2 \frac{T^\xi}{\varphi + T^\xi}$ and $C_h(h) = c_h h^2$.[38] Substituting this into (3.25), using the first order condition we can thus derive the function specific canonical system corresponding to (3.28)–(3.27) as:

$$\frac{dT}{dt} = a_T - b_T T + c_T \frac{\tilde{B} + \lambda_T c_T}{2c_h}, \; T(0) = T_0 \tag{3.72}$$

$$\frac{d\lambda_T}{dt} = (\rho + b_T)\lambda_T + a_2 \xi \left(\frac{T^{\xi-1}}{\varphi + T^\xi} - \frac{T^{2\xi-1}}{(\varphi + T^\xi)^2}\right) \tag{3.73}$$

From (3.72) and (3.73) it is easy to confirm the shape of the isoclines depicted in Figure 3.1. For the numerical calculations of the solution paths and the Skiba point we used numerical methods described in Grass et al. (2008), Grass (2010). The parameter values used for the numerical calculations are

Table 3.1 The Parameter Estimates Used to Generate Figure 3.1.

Parameter	Value	Description
ρ	0.02	Discount rate
β_1	0.3	Capital income share
β_2	0.5	Energy income share
δ	0.1	Depreciation rate of capital
ϕ	0.42	Efficiency parameter of clean energy
a_1	0.06	Damage parameter of $D_1(T)$
a_2	0.25	Damage parameter of $D_2(T)$
a_T	0.8	Parameter of temperature equation
b_T	0.6	Parameter of temperature equation
c_T	0.85	Parameter of temperature equation
c_h	0.01	Parameter of cost function
ξ	2	Parameter of $D_2(T)$ function
φ	1	Parameter of $D_2(T)$ function

Table 3.2 The Parameter Estimates Used to Generate Figure 3.2.

Parameter	Value	Description
ρ	0.02	Discount rate
A	201.4	Empirical coefficient outgoing radiation
B	1.45	Empirical coefficient outgoing radiation
α_0	0.68	Solar absorption coefficient for $x < x_s$
α_1	0.38	Solar absorption coefficient for $x > x_s$
ζ_1	0.7126	Estimated coefficient of iceline function
ζ_2	0.0098	Estimated coefficient of iceline function
ζ_3	0.0003	Estimated coefficient of iceline function
Q	334.4	Incoming solar radiation divided by 4
S_2	−0.482	Temperature distribution parameter
σ	0.01	Ratio of industrial emissions to output
T_0	15	Initial temperature
δ	0.1	Depreciation rate of capital
β	0.5	Capital income share
$\phi(x)$	1	Welfare weights for x
a_1	0.002	Damage function parameter for $D_1(T)$
a_2	0.1	Damage function parameter for $D_2(T)$
ξ	2	Parameter of $D_2(T)$ function
φ	1	Parameter of $D_2(T)$ function

ACKNOWLEDGMENTS

William Brock is a Vilas Research Professor, Emeritus, University of Wisconsin and Research Professor, University of Missouri, Columbia (wbrock@ssc.wisc.edu). W. Brock is grateful for financial and scientific support received from The Center for Robust Decision Making on Climate and Energy Policy (RDCEP) which is funded by a grant from the National Science Foundation (NSF) through the Decision Making Under Uncertainty (DMUU) program. He is also grateful to the Vilas Trust for financial support. None of the above are responsible for any errors, opinions, or shortcomings in this chapter. Gustav Engström is a reseacher at the Beijer Institute of Ecological Economics, G. Engström acknowledges research support from a 'European Project supported within the Ocean of Tomorrow call of the European Commission Seventh Framework Programme'. Anastasios Xepapadeas is a Professor at Athens University of Economics and Business, xepapad@aueb.gr. A. Xepapadeas acknowledges that his research has been co-financed by the European Union (European Social Fund ÃŘ ESF) and Greek national funds through the Operational Program "Education and Lifelong Learning" of the National Strategic Reference Framework (NSRF) - Research Funding Program: Thalis ÃŘ Athens University of Economics and Business - Optimal Management of Dynamical Systems of the Economy and the Environment.

NOTES

1. In this context, the ice-albedo feedback refers to a process allowing the surface albedo to vary with the climate state.
2. Damages due to sea level rise also depend on the shape of the shoreline which will determine the amount of land to be covered by water due to melting ice caps (see, e.g., the study by Li et al. (2009)). Further sea level rise can also be caused by thermal expansion of warming oceans, as a direct result of a rising global temperature. Which of these effects dominate depends upon the time scale studied. For example, the Intergovernmental Panel on Climate Change's Fourth Assessment Report (IPCC (2007)) concluded that thermal expansion can explain about 25% of observed sea-level rise for 1961–2003 and 50% for 1993–2003, but with considerable uncertainty. There may of course also be other damages caused by the increasing loss of the ice caps and their role in regulating the climate.
3. Scientific evidence seems to support the argument that ice sheets might be seriously affected by relatively low increases in temperature. Oppenheimer (2005) reports a number of results suggesting that both the Greenland Ice Sheet (GIS) and the West Antarctic Ice Sheet (WAIS) could be highly vulnerable to temperature rise within the range studied by the current IAMs. Oppenheimer and Alley (2004) report that a 2–4°C global mean warming could be justified for WAIS. Carlson et al. (2008) conclude that geologic evidence for a rapid retreat of the Laurentide ice sheet, which is the most recent (early Holocene epoch) and best documented disappearance of a large ice sheet in the Northern

Hemisphere, may describe a prehistoric precedent for mass balance changes of the Greenland Ice Sheet over the coming century. In a recent report from the European Energy Agency Agency (2010), it was stated that one of the potential large-scale changes likely to affect Europe is the deglaciation of the WAIS and the GIS and that there is already evidence of accelerated melting of the GIS. Further, a sustained global warming in the range of 1–5°C above 1990 temperatures, could generate tipping points leading to at least partial deglaciation of the GIS and WAIS, thus implying a significant rise in sea levels. See also Lindsay and Zhang (2005).

4. For more details see for example Zhang et al. (2003), Zimov et al. (2006), Schaefer et al. (2011).
5. Multiple equilibria and high current mitigation are also suggested by models incorporating uncertain climate thresholds into DICE (Keller et al., 2004; Lempert et al., 2006). See also Nævdal (2006) for an optimal control version featuring uncertain thresholds. More recently Judd and Lontzek (2011) have formulated a dynamic stochastic version of DICE which they call DSICE. They also extend their model to include stochastic tipping point possibilities. They show how this additional real world complexity substantially affects the optimal policy results in comparison to DICE.
6. For more on EBCMs, see for example Pierrehumbert (2011).
7. Symmetry for the part $x \in [-1,0]$ is assumed. This assumption is common in EBCMs.
8. Here, C_c is the average heat capacity of the Earth. This parameter may also be made spatially dependent and determined by the distribution of continents and ocean masses among other things. See, for example, North et al. (1981).
9. This empirical approximation of the true underlying physical system, was first derived in Budyko (1969) based on monthly data from 260 independent weather stations. It is important to note that the original Budyko (1969) formulation cited by North parameterizes A, B as functions of fraction cloud cover and other parameters of the climate system. North (1975b) points out that due to nonhomogeneous cloudiness A and B should be functions of x. There is apparently a lot of uncertainty involving the impact of cloud dynamics (e.g., Trenberth et al. (2010) versus Lindzen and Choi, 2009). Hence robust control in which A, B are treated as uncertain may be called for but this is left for further research. Example, of values used by North (1975a) are $A = 201.4\,\mathrm{W/m^2}$, $B = 1.45\,\mathrm{W/m^2}$.
10. See for example table 6.2 of the IPCC (2001) report.
11. The solar constant includes all types of solar radiation, not just the visible light. It is measured by satellite to be roughly 1.366 kilowatts per square meter ($\mathrm{kW/m^2}$).
12. As an example of the magnitude of D, North et al. (1981) pick a value of $D = 0.649$.
13. A smoothed version of a co-albedo function is equation (38) of North et al. (1981).
14. The complete derivation of the two-mode solution is provided in Appendix 3.6. For more details regarding the use of approximation methods see chapter 6 of Judd (1998).
15. Here, we are referring to variance across latitudes. In a stochastic generalization of our model, we could introduce a stochastic process to represent "weather," i.e. very high frequency fluctuations relative to the time scales we are modeling here. Here the "local variance" of high frequency phenomena like "weather" may change with changes in lower frequency phenomena such as mean area Z temperature and area Z temperature variance. See North et al. (1981) for an example of how stochastic forcing can be modeled in an EBM framework. We leave this task to future research.

16. More complicated and probably more realistic approximations will not affect our qualitative results regarding the multiplicity of steady states and the emergence of Skiba points.
17. See Xepapadeas (2005) for different ways in which emissions and environment can be modeled as production factors.
18. The assumption of linear utility allows the capital accumulation problem too be written as a MRAP problem. Problem (3.19) is an approximation of the MRAP problem for very large W and $-W \leq \frac{dK}{dt} \leq W$. In problem (3.19) capital, K, can thus be eliminated as a state variable. It should also be noted that in this section, damages are modeled using an additive functional form as explained in Weitzman (2010). In Section 3.4 we will revert to the more common multiplicative form. The main qualitative results hold for both these forms.
19. Research in progress Brock and Judd (2010) focuses on the development of a two-dimensional spherical coupled climate/economic dynamics model by using a basis of spherical harmonics as in Wu and North (2007). This approach, as well as the Legendre basis approach we are using in this chapter for one-dimensional models, fits in nicely with the general approach to approximation methods in (Judd, 1998, Chapter 6).
20. Note that $\pi'(0) < \infty$ if $\phi > 0$ for the alternative "clean" technology.
21. The eigenvalues of J are: $\frac{1}{2}(\rho \pm \sqrt{\Delta})$, where $\Delta = \rho^2 + 4\left[(a_1 + D_2''(\bar{T}))c_T h^{*'} + b_T(b_T + \rho)\right]$. When $a_1 + D_2''(\bar{T}) > 0$ then $\Delta < 0$ and we have two complex eigenvalues with positive real parts which implies an unstable spiral.
22. The assumed functions, parameters, and calculations used in Figure 3.3 are provided in Appendix 3.7.
23. The maximization of objective (3.30) with the welfare weight $\upsilon(x)$ set equal to the inverse of marginal utility of consumption, is a way of computing a Pareto Optimum competitive equilibrium allocation across latitudes as in Nordhaus (2010) discrete time non-spatial formalization. This is usually referred to as Negishi weighting. For a presentation of the use of the Negishi weights in IAMs, see Stanton (2010).
24. With our spatial approach abatement costs could be made site specific, which would enable a more comprehensive analysis of issues concerning, for example, geoengineering. However, this goes beyond the scope of the current chapter and is left for future research.
25. The important thing to note about this Hamiltonian compared to the Hamiltonian of the original problem (3.30) is this. The original problem would generate a Hamiltonian with a continuum of costate variables, one for each $x \in [0,1]$. The two-mode approximation approach developed could be quite easily extended to an n-mode approximation approach. Since, however, North argues that a two-mode approximation is quite good, we continue with a two-mode approximation here.
26. Note that in the case where the absorption function does not depend upon $x_s(t)$ the RHS of (3.43) is constant.
27. Note that with a constant absorption function, $\langle QS\alpha, 1\rangle = \langle Q(1 + S_2P_2(x))\alpha, 1\rangle = \langle Q\alpha + QS_2\alpha P_2(x), 1\rangle = \langle Q\alpha, 1\rangle = Q\alpha$, since $\langle QS_2\alpha P_2(x), 1\rangle = 0$.
28. $(T_2P_2(x))^2$ denotes the variance of the average temperature at location x.
29. The calibration procedure is explained in detail by North (1975b) (p. 2035–2037).
30. The estimated quadratic function was

$$\hat{x}_s = 0.7126 + 0.0098\,T_0 + 0.0003\,T_0^2\,,\; R^2 = 0.99.$$

31. To simplify the formulation we consider damages that depend only on the average global temperature, so that we can concentrate on the impact of damage reservoirs. For latitude specific damage functions see Brock et al. (2012b).
32. During the development of many energy balance models in the 1960s and 1970s the main concern was usually not that of global warming, but rather that of drastic global cooling that could result due to a slight decrease in the solar constant. This hypothesis was later coined “Snowball earth” by Kirschvink (1992).
33. The parameters estimates used in deriving Figure 3.2 can be found in Table 3.2 in the appendix.
34. The corresponding eigenvalues are approximated numerically as $e_{01} = [-0.7037, 0.7237]$, $e_{02} = [0.01 \pm 0.3302i]$ and $e_{03} = [-0.2355, 0.2555]$.
35. Greiner et al. (2009) find multiple equilibria in a zero-dimensional EBCM, where albedo is modeled by a continuous S-shaped function of temperature. The derived multiple-equilibria and Skiba planes, however, only apply for fixed levels of abatement, that is, there is just a single control variable (consumption). If, however, the social planner can control both consumption and abatement then there exists only a single stable saddle. Our approach, apart from explicitly addressing the more appropriate one-dimensional model also differs in the sense that we obtain multiple equilibria and Skiba points when controlling both consumption and abatement.
36. As we mention in the introduction, Oppenheimer and Alley (2004) report that a 2–4°C global mean warming could be justified for destabilization of the WAIS. Hence, if one confides in this study, the iceline damage function should be calibrated so that marginal damages become zero for temperatures above 4°C. This is met for varying degrees of approximation of the damage function parametrization adopted here as can be seen by inspection of Figure 3.4 in appendix.
37. These extensions will undoubtedly increase the complexity and the computational needs for solving the economic-EBCMs.
38. The shape of $D_1(T)$ has become fairly standard in the literature. Still, in a recent review by Weitzman M.L., 2010, they uncovered no rationale, whether empirical or theoretical, for adopting a quadratic form for the damage function. $D_2(T)$ follows the s-shape found in, for example, Brock and Starrett (2003).

References

Agency, E. E. (2010). *The European environment—state and outlook 2010: synthesis*, EEA, Copenhagen.

Brock W.A. and Judd, K.L. (2010). Coupling climate models and forward-looking economic models. In *Fall 2010 American Geophysical Union meeting in San Francisco (December 13–17) on “Climate Modeling in Support of Policy Decision-making: Needs and Limitations”.*, department of Economics, University of Wisconsin, Madison and Hoover Institution, Stanford University (Abstract).

Brock, W.A. and Starrett, D. (2003). Managing systems with non-convex positive feedback, *Environmental and Resource Economics*, *26*(4), 575–602.

Brock, W., Engström, G. and Xepapadeas, A. (2012b). Spatial climate-economic models in the design of optimal climate policies across locations. Beijer Discussion Chapter. The Beijer Institute of Ecological Economics.

Budyko, M. I. (1969). The effect of solar radiation variations on the climate of the earth. *Tellus, 21*, 611–619.

Carlson, A. E., LeGrande, A. N., Oppo, D. W., Came, R. E., Schmidt, G. A., Anslow, F. S., Licciardi, J. M. and Obbink, E. A. (2008). Rapid early Holocene deglaciation of the Laurentide ice sheet. *Nature Geoscience, 1*(9), 620–624.

Golosov, M., Hassler, J., Krusell, P. and Aleh, T. (2011). Optimal taxes on fossil fuel in general equilibrium. Working Paper 17348. Cambridge, MA: National Bureau of Economic Research.

Grass, D. (2010). Numerical computation of the optimal vector field in a fishery model. Technical Report. ORCOS, Institute of Mathematical Methods in Economics, Vienna University of Technology.

Grass, D. Caulkins, J. P., Feichtinger, G., Gernot T. and Behrens, D.A. (2008). *Optimal Control of Nonlinear Processes: With Applications in Drugs, Corruption, and Terror.* Berlin: Springer Verlag.

Greiner, A., Grüne, L. and Semmler, W. (2009). Growth and climate change: threshold and multiple equilibria. Schwartz Center for Economic Policy Analysis, New York Working Paper 2009-7.

Hope, C. (2006). The marginal impact of CO_2 from PAGE2002: An integrated assessment model incorporating the IPCC's five reasons for concern. *Integrated Assessment Journal*, 6(1), 566–577.

IPCC (2001). *Climate Change 2001: The Third Assessment Report of the Intergovernmental Panel on Climate Change.* UK: Press, Cambridge.

IPCC, 2001: Climate Change 2001: The Scientific Basis. Contribution of Working Group I to the Third Assessment Report of the Intergovernmental Panel on Climate Change [Houghton, J.T., Y. Ding, D.J. Griggs, M. Noguer, P.J. van der Linden, X. Dai, K. Maskell, and C.A. Johnson (eds.)]. Cambridge University Press, Cambridge, United Kingdom and New York, NY, USA, 881 pp.

IPCC, 2007: Climate Change 2007: The Physical Science Basis. Contribution of Working Group I to the Fourth Assessment Report of the Intergovernmental Panel on Climate Change [Solomon, S., D. Qin, M. Manning, Z. Chen, M. Marquis, K.B. Averyt, M. Tignor and H.L. Miller (eds.)]. Cambridge University Press, Cambridge, United Kingdom and New York, NY, USA, 996 pp.

IPCC (2007). *Climate Change 2007: The Fourth Assessment Report of the Intergovernmental Panel on Climate Change.* Cambridge, UK: Press, Cambridge.

Judd, K. L. (1998). *Numerical Methods in Economics*, Vol. 2. Cambridge, MA: MIT Press.

Judd, K. L., and Lontzek, T. S. (2011). Dynamic stochastic general equilibrium analysis of climate change policies. Conference presentation at INFORMS Annual Meeting, Austin, Texas.

Keller, K. Bolker, B. M., and Bradford, D. F. (2004). Uncertain climate thresholds and economic optimal growth. *Journal of Environmental Economics and Management, 48*, 723–741.

Kerr, R. A. (2008). Climate tipping points come in from the Cold. *Science, 319*, 153.

Kirschvink, J. (1992). Late Proterozoic low-latitude global glaciation: The snowball Earth. In W.J. Schopf and C. Klein, (eds.), *The Proterozoic Biosphere: A Multidisciplinary Study*, pp. 51–52. Cambridge, MA: Cambridge University Press.

Lempert, R. Sanstad, A. and Schlesinger, M. (2006). Multiple equilibria in a stochastic implementation of DICE with abrupt climate change. *Energy Economics, 28*, 677–689.

Lenton, T. M., Held, H. Kriegler, E., Hall, J. W., Lucht, W., Rahmstorf, S., and Schellnhuber, H. J. (2008). Tipping elements in the Earth's climate system. *Proceedings of the National Academy of Sciences of the USA, 105*, 1786–1793.

Li, X., Rowley, R. J., Kostelnick, J. C., Braaten, D., Meisel, J., and Hulbutta, K. (2009). GIS Analysis of global impacts from sea level rise. *Photogrammetric Engineering & Remote Sensing, 75*(7), 807–818.

Lindsay, R. W. and Zhang, J. (2005). The thinning of arctic sea ice, 1988–2003: Have we passed a tipping point?. *Journal of Climate, 18*, 4879–4894.

Lindzen, R. S. and Choi, Y. S. (2009). On the determination of climate feedbacks from ERBE data. *Geophysical Research Letters, 36*(16), 1–6.

Nævdal, E. (2006). Dynamic optimisation in the presence of threshold effects when the location of the threshold is uncertain with an application to a possible disintegration of the Western Antarctic Ice Sheet. *Journal of Economic Dynamics and Control, 30*(7), 1131–1158.

Nordhaus, W. D. (1994). *Managing The Global Commons: The economics of the greenhouse effect.* Cambridge, MA: MIT Press.

Nordhaus, W. D. (2007). *A Question of Balance.* New Haven, CT & London: Yale University Press.

Nordhaus, W. D. (2010). Economic aspects of global warming in a post-Copenhagen environment. *Proceedings of the National Academy of Sciences of the USA. 107*(26), 11721–11726.

Nordhaus, W. D. (2011). The architecture of climate economics: Designing a global agreement on global warming. *Bulletin of the Atomic Scientists, 67*(1), 9–18.

Nordhaus, W. D. and Boyer, J. (2000). *Warming the World: Economic Models of Global Warming.* Cambridge, MA: MIT Press.

North, G. R. (1975a). Analytical solution to a simple climate model with diffusive heat, *Journal of Atmospheric Sciences, 32*, 1301–1307.

North, G. R. (1975b). Theory of energy-balance climate models, *Journal of Atmospheric Sciences, 32*(11), 2033–2043.

North, G. R. (1984). The small ice cap instability in diffusive climate models, *Journal of Atmospheric Sciences, 41*(23), 3390–3395.

North, G. R., Cahalan, R. F., and Coakley, J. A. (1981). Energy balance climate models. *Reviews of Geophysics and Space Physics, 19*(1), 91–121.

Oppenheimer, M. (2005). Ice sheets, global warming, and Article 2 of the UNFCCC: An editorial essay. *Climatic Change, 68*, 257–67.

Oppenheimer, M., and Alley, R. B. (2004). The West Antarctic Ice Sheet and long term climate policy. *Climatic Change, 64*(1/2), 1–10.

Pierrehumbert, R. (2011). *Principles of Planetary Climate.* Cambridge UK: Cambridge University Press.

Roe, G. H., and Baker, M. B. (2010). Notes on a catastrophe: A feedback analysis of snowball Earth. *Journal of Climate, 23*(17), 4694–4703.

Schaefer, K., Zhang, T., Bruhwiler, L., and Barrett, A. (2011). Amount and timing of permafrost carbon release in response to climate warming. *Tellus B. 63*(2), 165–180.

Sellers, W. (1969). A global climatic model based on the energy balance of the earth-atmosphere system. *Journal of Applied Meteorology, 8*, 392–400.

Smith, J. B., Schneider, S. H., Oppenheimer, M., Yohe, G. W., Hare, W., Mastrandrea, M. D., Patwardhan, A., Burton, I., Corfee-Morlot, J., Magadza, C. H. D., Fussel, H., Pittock, A. B., Rahman, A., Suarez, A., and Van Ypersele, J. (2009). Assessing dangerous climate change through an update of the Intergovernmental Panel on Climate Change (IPCC) "reasons for concern", *Proceedings of the National Academy of Sciences, 106*, 4133–4137.

Stanton, E. A. (2011). Negishi welfare weights in integrated assessment models: The mathematics of global inequality. *Climatic Change, 107*(3–4), 417–432.

Tarnocai, C., Canadell, J., Schuur, E., Kuhry, P., Mazhitova, G. and Zimov, S. (2009). Soil organic carbon pools in the northern circumpolar permafrost region. *Global Biogeochemical Cycles, 23*(2), GB2023.

Tol, R. S. J. (1997). On the optimal control of carbon dioxide emissions: An application of FUND. *Environmental Modeling and Assessment, 2*, 151–163.

Trenberth, K. E., Fasullo, J. T., O'Dell, C., and Wong, T. (2010). Relationships between tropical sea surface temperature and top-of-atmosphere radiation. *Geophysical Research Letters, 37*(3), 1–5.

von Deimling, T., Meinshausen, M., Levermann, A., Huber, V., Frieler, K., Lawrence, D., and Brovkin, V. (2012). Estimating the permafrost-carbon feedback on global warming. *Biogeosciences Discussions, 89*, 649–665

Wang, W. C., and Stone, P. H. (1980). Effect of ice-albedo feedback on global sensitivity in a one-dimensional radiative-convective climate model. *Journal of the Atmospheric Sciences, 37*(5), 545–552.

Weitzman, M. L. (2010). What Is The "Damages function" for global warming? – and what difference might it make?. *Climate Change Economics, 1*(1), 56–79.

Wu, W., and North, G. R. (2007). Thermal decay modes of a 2-D energy balance climate model. *Tellus A, 59*(5), 618–626.

Xepapadeas, A. (2005). Economic growth and the environment. in K. G. Mäler, and J. R. Vincent, (eds.), *Handbook of Environmental Economics*, Vol.3, pp. 1219–1271. Philadelphia: Elsevier.

Zhang, T., Barry, R., Knowles, K., Ling, F. and Armstrong, R. (2003). Distribution of seasonally and perennially frozen ground in the northern hemisphere. In *Proceedings of the 8th International Conference on Permafrost, July 21–25 2003, Zurich, Switzerland*, pp. 1289–1294, Lisse, The Netherlands: A. A. Balkema.

Zimov, S., Schuur, E., and Chapin F. III. (2006). Permafrost and the global carbon budget. *Science, 312*(5780), 1612–1613.

CHAPTER 4

ECONOMICS OF ENVIRONMENTAL REGIME SHIFTS

FLORIAN WAGENER

4.1 Introduction

Many systems can exhibit several qualitatively different kinds of behaviour; which of these is selected is a function of the history of the system. This phenomenon is common in economics: we talk of societies languishing in poverty traps; evolutionary game theory explains why in a given country all cars drive on the same side of the road, though it does not make predictions about which side this will be; and archaeologists tell us that 6000 years ago, the Sahara desert was a pleasant place to stay. All of these are examples of systems that can be in qualitatively different regimes.

A regime is a collection of states with similar characteristics. Of course, big external shocks can transport a system from one regime to another. More usually, regime shifts are caused by accumulating processes driven by positive feedbacks. In economics, an early documented instance of such a feedback mechanism is the phenomenon of increasing returns to scale, perspicaciously described by Adam Smith in his discussion of the pin factory. This mechanism effected one of the most far-reaching regime shifts, transporting Western society from the agricultural-manufactural state to the industrial state.

The overriding interest of the problem of the existence of a general equilibrium, and the related hope that this equilibrium might be stable under some general conditions, has over time fostered a huge research effort in mechanisms that ensure stability, putting emphasis on static rather than dynamic aspects of economic systems. The literature on destabilizing mechanisms is in comparison much smaller, but typically in times of actual or impending economic crisis, interest in the dynamic aspects of economies has a tendency to return to the fore.

In these days, there is ample evidence that the mean temperature of the Earth's atmosphere and oceans is rising, and moreover that this is a consequence of human actions.

This temperature rise changes the living conditions of plant and animal species, and by itself it may have serious consequences for man's economic activities.

Moreover, ecological systems may respond to an incremental increase of environmental pressure with sudden regime shifts, which have short-term and long-term economic consequences. A body of important research on the economics of ecological systems with nonconvexities has been collected in Dasgupta and Mäler (2004). This chapter discusses economic set-ups in which regime shifts may occur that have been developed since, techniques to analyze them, and lessons that can be learned from them. Special emphasis is put on the so-called lake or shallow lake model, as it is in a sense the simplest dynamic economic model featuring a regime shift; this occupies the first part of the chapter. Other approaches treat the shift to a different dynamics as occurring with a certain probability. For a recent overview of literature treating the management aspects of regime shifts, we refer readers to Crépin et al. (2012).

4.2 Certain Regime Shifts: The Lake Model

The "lake" or "shallow lake" model was originally introduced to analyze the tragedy of the commons in the situation of a lake polluted by agricultural waste. Its simplicity makes it a prototypical study object for the ramifications of optimal management decisions when dealing with a system that features positive feedback.

Lakes host intricate ecosystems; for the present purposes, a simplified description is sufficient, but the real object is much more complicated (Scheffer, 1998).

The bottom of a lake is formed by the sediment; the root systems of water plants hold it in place. In a clear, "oligotrophic" state, the sunlight, which these plants need to live, filters through the water column above them. If artificial fertilizers are used on the fields around the lake, rainfall washes some of the phosphorus they contain into the lake. There it increases phytoplankton biomass in the water column as well as the periphyton layers on the water plants. Both deprive the plants of light.

When water plants die, they release the lake sediment as well as the phosphorus contained in the sediment. This initiates a positive feedback loop, as the resuspended phosphorus increases the phytoplankton biomass in turn: the lake becomes turbid or "eutrophic." Depending on the characteristics of the lake, a return to the oligotrophic state, if at all possible, necessitates a large reduction of inflow of phosphorus.

Denote by $x = x(t)$ the amount of phosphorus suspended in the water column of the lake, by $u = u(t)$ the inflow, per unit time, of phosphorus resulting from agricultural activities, and by b the sedimentation and outflow rate of phosphorus out of the water column. The following differential equation provides a model for the phosphorus concentration x in the lake (cf. Mäler et al., 2003):

$$\dot{x} = u - g(x). \tag{4.1}$$

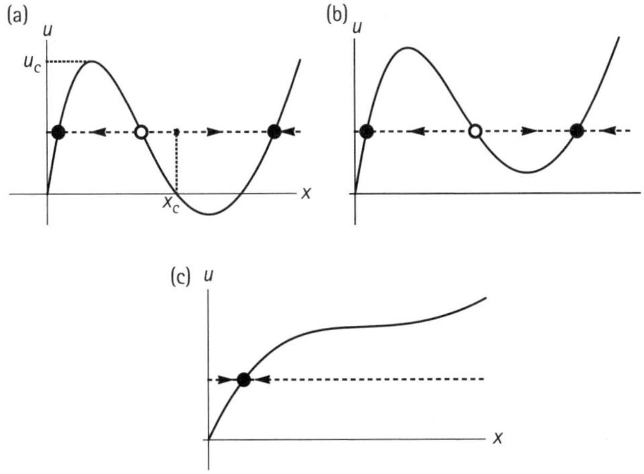

FIGURE 4.1 The lake dynamics for a fragile lake ($b = 0.49$), a reversible lake ($b = 0.51$) and a robust lake ($b = 0.66$). The point x_c indicates the point of no return of the fragile lake.

In particular, the natural dynamics g of the lake is often taken to be of the form

$$g(x) = bx - \frac{x^2}{x^2 + 1}. \tag{4.2}$$

Figure 4.1 illustrates the resulting dynamics for constant loadings u and three different values of the sedimentation rate b.

The arrows indicate the direction of the dynamics. Taking u for the moment to be a constant system parameter, it appears from Figure 4.1 that for some combinations (b, u) the lake dynamics (4.1) has a single steady state, whereas for others there are three steady states. Figure 4.2 indicates the precise parameter regions.

Increasing the value of the parameter u in, for instance, Figure 4.1a destabilizes the oligotrophic (left) steady state at a critical value u_c, and the system shifts to the eutrophic (right) steady state. Decreasing the value of u slowly, will not shift the system back. A fragile lake cannot be restored to an oligotrophic situation at all: if the state $x(t)$ reaches the level x_c (see Figure 4.1a for the location of x_c) for some time $t = t'$, it cannot decrease past x_c for any future time $t > t'$ again: the regime shift is irreversible. But even if the regime shift is reversible, as in Figure 4.1b, the phosphorus inflow has to be decreased to much lower levels than u_c before the reverse regime shift occurs.

Equation (4.1), with x as a negative capital and u as a negative investment, has similar properties to capital dynamics with increasing returns to scale, that is, with nonconcave production functions, which have been considered in the literature on optimal growth since the late 1960s (Treadway, 1969; Sethi, 1977; Skiba, 1978; Majumdar and Mitra, 1982; Dechert and Nishimura, 1983; Romer, 1986; Krugman, 1991). Pollution models with nonconcavities were studied by Tahvonen and Salo (1996) and Brock and Starrett (2003).

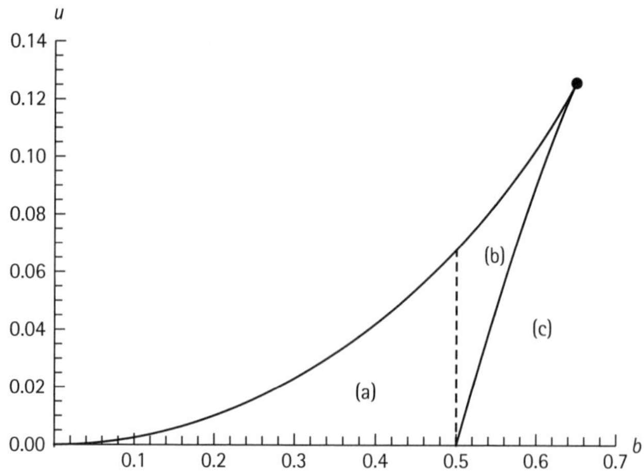

FIGURE 4.2 Bifurcation diagram for the lake dynamics (4.1). The labels refer back to the three typical situations depicted in Figure 4.1: region (a) corresponds to a fragile lake with three steady states, region (b) to a reversible lake with three steady states, and region (c) to a robust lake with only a single steady state. Two saddle-node bifurcation curves (solid), coalescing in a cusp point, bound the union of the regions (a) and (b) where there are three steady states. The line $b = \frac{1}{2}$ (dashed) divides these two regions.

4.3 Optimal Management

4.3.1 Affectors and Enjoyers

Equation (4.1) describes the ecological dynamics of the lake. An economic component enters if there are agents that use the lake. This may be direct use, by fishermen for fishing, by tourists for recreation, by a water company for freshwater, or indirect use, by farmers that use artificial fertilizer. In the terminology of Brock and Starrett (2003), the former agents are enjoyers of the lake, while the latter are affectors. The shallow lake literature assumes that the social stream of benefits β_s is of the form

$$\beta_s(x, u) = \beta_a(u) + c\beta_e(x). \tag{4.3}$$

The benefit stream $\beta_a(u)$ of the affectors is increasing and strictly concave in the use u of phosphorus, whereas the benefit stream $\beta_e(x)$ of the enjoyers is decreasing and strictly concave in the amount of phosphorus x in the water column of the lake. The parameter c is a weighting parameter, expressing the relative economic importance of the enjoyers relative to the affectors of the lake.

Mäler et al. (2003), who introduced the economic lake model, made the specific choices

$$\beta_a(u) = \log u, \qquad \beta_e(x) = -x^2. \tag{4.4}$$

In the shallow lake optimal control problem, a manager maximizes the integral I of the discounted stream of benefits over an infinite time horizon

$$I = \int_0^\infty e^{-\rho t} \beta_s(x,u)\, dt = \int_0^\infty e^{-\rho t} \left(\beta_a(u) + c\,\beta_e(x)\right) dt, \tag{4.5}$$

subject to the dynamic constraint (4.1).

4.3.2 Analysis of Long-Term Steady States

The lake problem almost always reduces to a quasi-static problem if future benefits are not discounted. To make this statement precise, the concept of an optimal solution of the problem has to be specified, as the integral (4.5) usually diverges if $\rho = 0$. Rather than introducing notions like catching up or overtaking optimality (von Weizsäcker, 1965), the much simpler notion of average benefit stream is used here.

Define the finite-horizon average benefit stream

$$A_T = \frac{1}{T} \int_0^T \beta_s(x,u)\, dt,$$

which compares the integrated undiscounted benefit stream with a constant benefit stream. The infinite-horizon average benefit stream is then

$$A = \lim_{T\to\infty} A_T.$$

For trajectories tending to a steady state, the value of A reduces to the value of β_s at the steady state, as the details of the transient dynamics do not influence the value of the limit. Only if there are several steady states with equal values of A, a more precise optimality criterion, like catching up or overtaking, is relevant. In the present context, this, however, constitutes a nongeneric "hairline" case.

In the situation without discounting, a manager has to maximize the benefit stream

$$\beta_s(x,u) = \beta_a(u) + \beta_e(x),$$

subject to the steady-state condition

$$u - g(x) = 0; \tag{4.6}$$

compare Mäler et al. (2003; Section 3). Substitution of the latter equation into the former yields the benefit stream as a function of the state

$$\beta(x) = \beta_a(g(x)) + \beta_e(x).$$

If this is maximal, then

$$\beta_e'(x) + \beta_a'(g(x))g'(x) = 0.$$

That is, the sum of the marginal benefits that the enjoyers and the affectors derive from the lake is zero.

For the specification (4.2) of the lake dynamics and (4.4) of the benefit streams, Figure 4.3 shows the graph of β.

It appears that the function β can have several local maxima. To find the parameter values for which one of these, say the left local maximum, is global, it suffices to determine those parameter values that are in the boundary of this set; these correspond to the bifurcating cases. For the situation that there are two local maxima, and the left one is global, there are two bifurcations: either the right local maximum is about to disappear in a degenerate critical point, or the two local maxima are both global. The numerical condition for the first case is that there are two points $x_1 < x_2$, such that

$$\begin{aligned} \beta'(x_1) &= 0, & \beta''(x_1) &< 0, \\ \beta'(x_2) &= \beta''(x_2) = 0, & \beta'''(x_2) &\neq 0, \end{aligned}$$

and for the second

$$\begin{aligned} &\beta'(x_1) = \beta'(x_2) = 0, \quad \beta''(x_1) < 0, \quad \beta''(x_2) < 0, \\ &\beta(x_1) = \beta(x_2). \end{aligned}$$

Figure 4.4 depicts the curves in the (b, c)-parameter plane determined by these conditions, as well as analogous conditions for the case that the right local maximum is global.

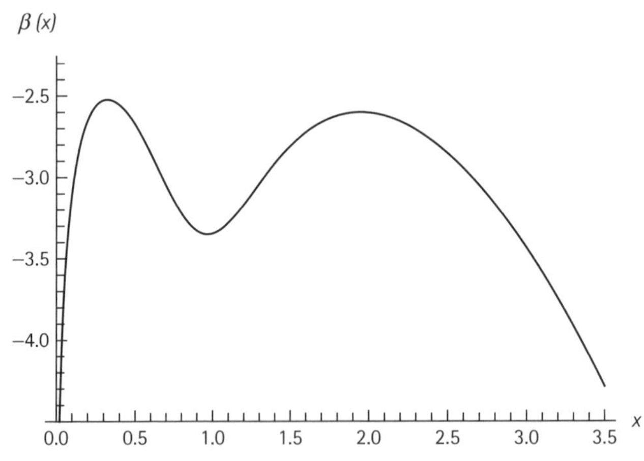

FIGURE 4.3 Total benefit stream in steady state: $b = 0.55$, $c = 0.35$.

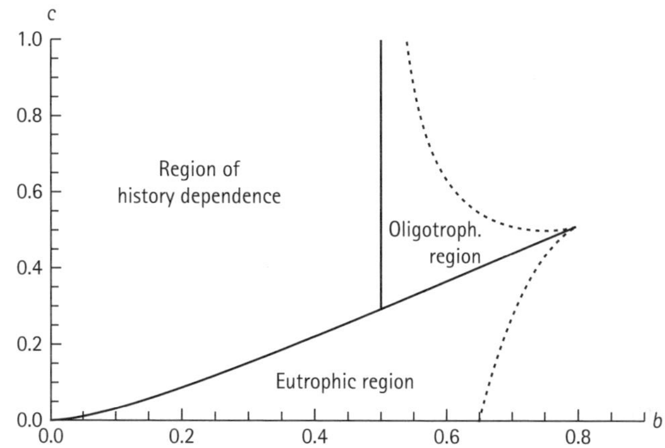

FIGURE 4.4 Bifurcation diagram of the quasi-static optimally managed lake.

There is a peculiarity in this figure, related to the line $b = \frac{1}{2}$. Recall that if $b \leq \frac{1}{2}$, the lake is irreversible, once it has reached an eutrophic state. The region where the oligotrophic steady state is optimal has therefore to be divided into two subregions, according to whether the oligotrophic maximum can be realised from all initial states, or whether it can be realized only from sufficiently unpolluted initial states.

Note that the interval of eutrophic c-values increases as b increases: this reflects the fact that for robust lakes, the eutrophic states are less damaging than for fragile lakes, and therefore it is less imperative to avoid them. Optimal management gives the highest priority to conserve the most fragile ecosystems.

4.3.3 Analysis of Dynamic Solutions

For positive discount rates, the details of the transient dynamics are not negligible any more. Solutions to the optimal management problem are computed using the Pontryagin maximum principle (see Seierstad and Sydsaeter, 1987). For this, introduce the (current-value) Pontryagin function

$$P(x, y, u) = \beta_a(u) + \beta_e(x) + y(u - g(x));$$

here y is the shadow cost of pollution. The function P is often called the (current-value) Hamilton function or the unmaximized Hamilton function. The maximum principle requires that for given x and y, the action u maximizes the value of P.

Let $u = u^*(y) = (\beta_a')^{-1}(-y)$ be this maximizer. The (current-value) Hamilton function of the problem, also called the maximized current-value Hamilton function, is then

$$H(x, y) = \beta_a(u^*(y)) + \beta_e(x) + y(u^*(y) - g(x)).$$

The maximum principle then further requires $(x,y) = (x(t), y(t))$ to satisfy the system of differential equations

$$\dot{x} = \frac{\partial H}{\partial y}(x,y) = u^*(y) - g(x), \tag{4.7}$$

$$\dot{y} = \rho y - \frac{\partial H}{\partial x}(x,y) = \rho y - \beta_e'(x) + y g'(x), \tag{4.8}$$

together with two additional boundary conditions in the time domain. The first of these

$$x(0) = x_0 \tag{4.9}$$

just expresses that at $t = 0$, the state trajectory is at the initial state x_0. The second is the transversality condition, which requires that

$$\lim_{t\to\infty} e^{-\rho t} y(t) = 0 \tag{4.10}$$

if the state trajectory is eventually bounded away from the state boundary point $x = 0$; that is, if there is some $\delta > 0$ and some $T > 0$ such that $x(t) > \delta$ for all $t > T$. If the state trajectory is not eventually bounded away from the state boundary, then the transversality condition requires that

$$\limsup_{t\to\infty} e^{-\rho t} y(t) \leq 0. \tag{4.11}$$

Equations (4.7), (4.8), (4.9) and (4.10), or (4.11) constitute necessary conditions for any optimal solution. These conditions take the form of a boundary value problem of a system of differential equations. The typical outcome of the maximum principle is a diagram as shown in Figure 4.5.

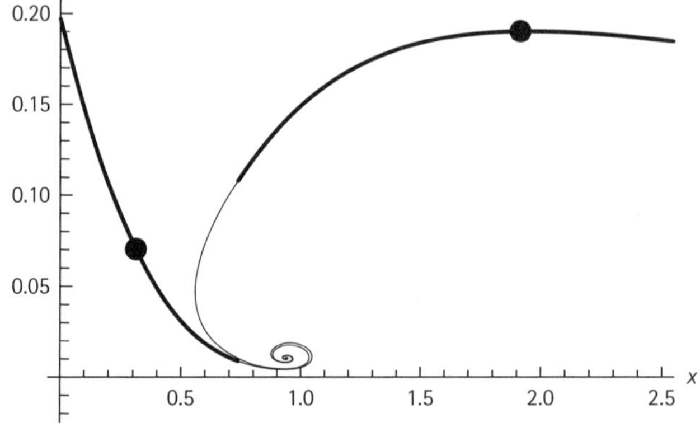

FIGURE 4.5 Candidate solutions found with the maximum principle. Parameters: $b = 0.51$, $c = 0.5$, $\rho = 0.03$.

The figure shows two curves in the (x, u)-plane that have the property that the graph of the optimal policy function, denoted by a thick line in the figure, is necessarily a part of the union of these curves. The two curves are the union of the orbits that approach the saddle equilibria of the state-costate system, indicated by dots in the figure, as t tends to infinity. The curves do not fully specify the optimal policy function, as there is a region, roughly between $x = 0.6$ and $x = 1.1$, where the graph of the optimal policy function could coincide with either of the curves.

To resolve this ambiguity, the value of the integral I has to be computed on all points of the two curves in the overlapping interval; this is usually done using numerical methods. It can be shown (Wagener, 2003) that there is exactly one point x_i in the ambiguous interval such that for all $x \leq x_i$, the curve through the left saddle point coincides with the graph of the optimal policy function, while for $x \geq x_i$, the same holds for the curve through the right saddle point. At x_i, the policymaker is indifferent between the two branches of the policy function; the point is therefore called an *indifference threshold*. Readers should note that there are many names used in the literature for this concept: for example, tie point, shock point, Maxwell point, Skiba point, Dechert-Nishimura(-Sethi)-Skiba point.

The result of the analysis is the optimal policy function, illustrated in Figure 4.6. In the figure the dashed line indicates the locus of the stabilizing levels of u; those are the levels of u which stabilize x at the given value. For the left steady state x_o, the optimal pollution policy is above the stabilizing level if $0 \leq x < x_o$, while it is below that level if $x_o < x \leq x_i$. This pushes the system towards x_o for all initial states below the indifference threshold—arrows on the horizontal axis indicate the dynamics under

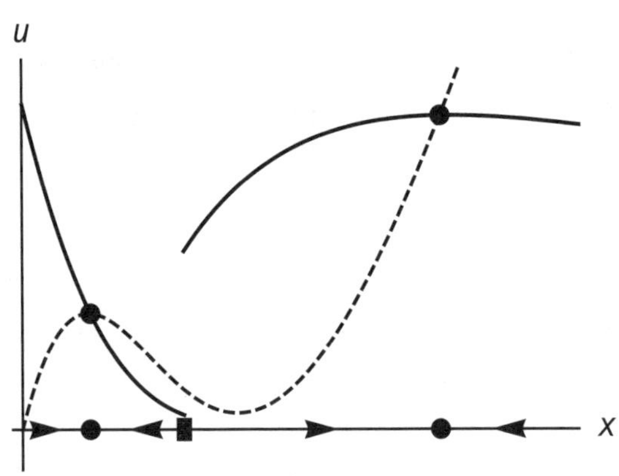

FIGURE 4.6 Optimal policy function and optimal dynamics. Intersections of the graph of the optimal policy function (solid) and the $\dot{x} = 0$ isocline (dashed) give the steady states under optimal management (black circles). The resulting dynamics under optimal policy is indicated on the horizontal axis: the circles indicate the stable steady states, whereas the square indicates the indifference threshold. Same parameters as in Figure 4.5.

the optimal policy. Analogously, for all initial states above x_i, the optimal policy pushes the state to the right steady state x_e.

Note also the gradient of the optimal policy function: at the oligotrophic steady state, it is strongly negative, implementing a strong negative feedback that stabilizes the lake at the tipping point, whereas at the eutrophic steady state the policy function is almost constant and the natural dynamics of the lake effect its stabilization.

The shallow lake problem depends on two additional parameters, the weight parameter c introduced above, and the discount rate ρ, which determines the relative weight of future benefits relative to present benefits. Depending on the values of the parameters b, c, and ρ, there are three structurally stable qualitatively different types of the dynamics of the lake under optimal policy.

In this context, "structural stability" of a type means that by slightly changing the problem, the type of the dynamics under optimal management of the changed problem is the same as of the original problem. In a parameter diagram, a structurally stable type corresponds therefore to an open set of parameter values, as small parameter changes cannot change the type of the dynamics. The structurally stable types are the "typical" configurations of the system dynamics.

Figure 4.6 shows a typical configuration: two attracting long-term steady states, separated by an indifference point. Figure 4.7 gives the other two: a single, globally attracting steady state, and two attracting steady states separated by a repelling steady state. In the latter configuration, the optimal values of u are close to the stabilizing values of u, for which $\dot{x} = 0$; this implies that for that configuration, the state $x(t)$ is changing only slowly over time.

4.3.4 Classification of Solutions

Systems that are not structurally stable are called bifurcating. Determining parameter values of bifurcating systems consequently yields the boundaries of the parameter regions that correspond to the various structurally stable types. Kiseleva and

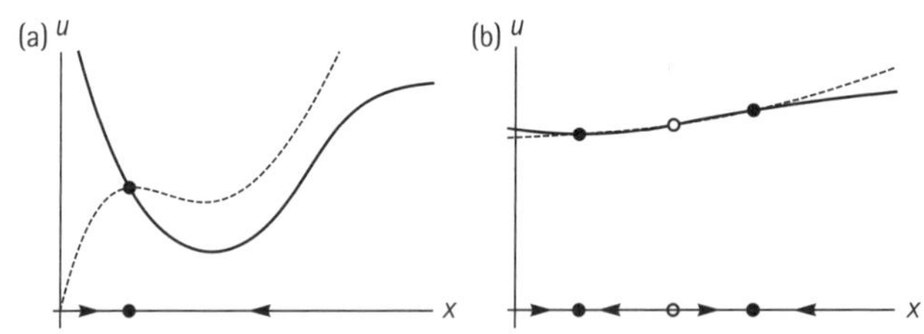

FIGURE 4.7 Two types of typical state dynamics under optimal management. Left: globally asymptotically stable attracting steady state. Parameters: $b = 0.6$, $c = 0.6$, $\rho = 0.03$. Right: two attracting steady states, separated by a repelling steady state. Parameters: $b = 0.675$, $c = 0.92$, $\rho = 0.16$. The open circle indicates a repeller; other symbols are as in Figure 4.6.

Wagener (2014) give a classification of the possible bifurcating systems for optimal control problems with one-dimensional state spaces.

The so-called codimension expresses the relative importance of a bifurcation. The main bifurcations are the bifurcations of codimension one: the parameter sets corresponding to systems at these bifurcations are composed of unions of manifolds whose dimensions are one less than the dimension of the parameter space. Higher codimensions are defined similarly. For instance, if the parameter space is two-dimensional, codimension one bifurcations trace out one-dimensional curves, codimension two bifurcations correspond to isolated points, and codimension three bifurcations do usually not occur in a two-parameter diagram.

There are three types of codimension one bifurcations for the dynamics under optimal management: a saddle-node (SN) bifurcation, where a repeller and an attracting steady state are created or destroyed; an indifference-attractor (IA) bifurcation, where an indifference threshold and an attracting steady state are created or destroyed, and an indifference-repeller (IR) bifurcation, where an indifference threshold turns in to a repeller or vice versa. For the shallow lake model, Figure 4.8 illustrates the regions of structural stability, as well as the codimension one bifurcation curves, for the (b, c)-parameter plane with $\rho = 0.03$, and for the (c, ρ)-parameter plane given by $b = 0.65$.

In the lake model, the parameter b is like a technology parameter: it is a typical physical feature of a given lake. In contrast to this, the parameters c and ρ describe economic preferences. Figure 4.8b is interesting, as it shows the dependency of the lake dynamics on the preferences of the decision maker. In particular, note that increasing ρ always eventually leads to the lake eutrophicating.

4.4 Game

Mäler et al. (2003) also considered a noncooperative game associated to the shallow lake system. In this game, a number of decision makers or "players," say n, where $n \geq 2$, use the lake. An example would be communes or states bordering the lake. Player i derives benefits from agricultural activities, causing a phosphorus inflow $u_i = u_i(t)$ into the lake. The amount of phosphorus in the lake is then described by

$$\dot{x} = \sum_{i=1}^{n} u_i - g(x). \tag{4.12}$$

All players suffer from the pollution in the lake; that is, the benefits of player i are given by the integral

$$I_i = \int_0^\infty \mathrm{e}^{-\rho t} \beta_{s,i}(x, u_i)\, dt = \int_0^\infty \mathrm{e}^{-\rho t} \left(\beta_{a,i}(u_i) + \beta_{e,i}(x)\right) dt.$$

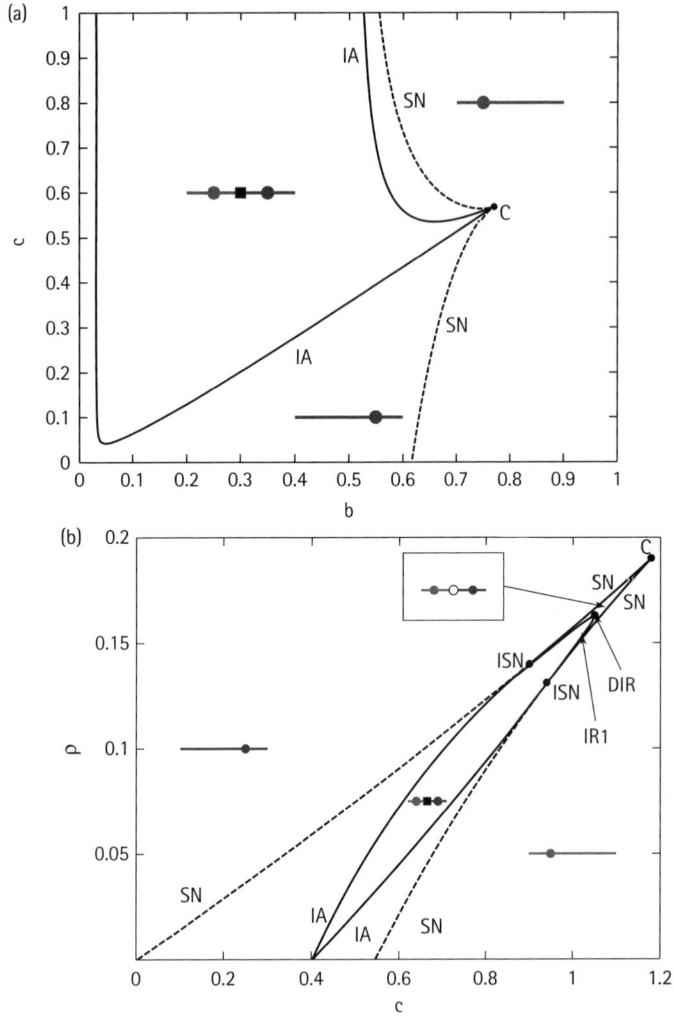

FIGURE 4.8 Bifurcation diagrams. Left: the (b, c)-diagram for $\rho = 0.03$. Right: the (c, ρ)-diagram for $b = 0.65$. Solid curves border regions of structural stable dynamics under optimal management. Dashed curves correspond to bifurcations of the state-costate system that do not correspond to bifurcations of the state dynamics under optimal management. The abbreviations ISN, DIR, C refer to codimension two bifurcation points not discussed in the text. (After Kiseleva and Wagener, 2010).

An action schedule that determines at each point in the game the pollution amount u_i of player i is called the strategy of player i. Strategies that consist of actions that are only conditioned on time, that is, for which $u_i = u_i(t)$, are said to be of "open-loop" type. Other types of strategies are considered below.

The optimal pollution rate of player i will depend, through the lake dynamics (4.12), on the choices of

$$u_{-i} = u_{-i}(t) = (u_1(t), \cdots, u_{i-1}(t), u_{i+1}(t), \cdots, u_n(t))$$

of the other players. The strategies u_j, $j = 1, \ldots, n$ form a Nash equilibrium if player i's strategy is optimal given the strategies of the other players.

For the specifications (4.4), Mäler et al. (2003) have investigated symmetric open-loop Nash equilibrium strategies in a game with n players; that is, in equilibrium, each player uses the same strategy $u_i(t) = u_{\mathrm{nc}}(t)$ (for noncooperative).

4.4.1 Steady-State Analysis

As for the optimal management case, a steady-state analysis can be performed. Again this corresponds, except for hairline cases, to the dynamic analysis of the situation for $\rho = 0$, that is, for vanishing discount rates. For the sake of simplicity, only the two-player situation $n = 2$ is considered.

Given that player 2 plays the time-constant strategy u_2, player 1 maximizes

$$\beta_1(u_1) = \beta_{\mathrm{a},1}(u_1) + \beta_{\mathrm{e},1}(x),$$

subject to the condition

$$u_1 + u_2 - g(x) = 0.$$

Eliminating u_1, the benefit stream β_1 as function of the steady state x takes the form

$$\beta_1(x) = \beta_{\mathrm{a},1}(g(x) - u_2) + \beta_{\mathrm{e},1}(x).$$

The condition for a maximizing steady state reads as

$$0 = \beta'_{\mathrm{a},1}(g(x) - u_2)g'(x) + \beta'_{\mathrm{e},1}(x),$$

and it has the same interpretation as before.

The symmetry condition requires that $u_1 = u_2$; if the lake is to be in steady state, then

$$u_1 = u_2 = \frac{1}{2}g(x),$$

leading to the eventual condition that

$$0 = \beta'_{\mathrm{a},1}\left(g(x)/2\right)g'(x) + \beta'_{\mathrm{e},1}(x). \tag{4.13}$$

As usual, this condition is necessary for a Nash equilibrium, but not sufficient. For, let $x = x^*$ be a state that satisfies (4.13); the implied actions of the players are then

$$u_1^* = u_2^* = \frac{1}{2}g(x^*).$$

The pair $(u_1, u_2) = (u_1^*, u_2^*)$ only defines a Nash strategy equilibrium if $x = x^*$ is a maximiser of the benefit stream of player 1 when $u_2 = u_2^*$. There are situations where that is not true.

Identifying the bifurcations in an analogous manner as in the optimal management problem, Figure 4.9 shows the regions corresponding to typical situations.

The dashed curve on the right bounds the region for which there is a unique solution of equation (4.13), which gives the Nash equilibrium steady state, from the region for which there are three solutions, two of which, corresponding to local maxima of $\beta_i(x)$, are candidate Nash equilibria. Both correspond to a Nash equilibrium in the regions marked "#NE = 2" and "#NE = 1 or = 2"; in the latter region, the oligotrophic Nash equilibrium may not be reachable due to irreversibility of the lake dynamics, if the initial steady state of the lake is too far in the eutrophic region. In the regions marked "oligotrophic NE" and "eutrophic NE," only one of the two local maxima of $\beta_i(x)$ corresponds to a Nash equilibrium, the other being not stable under nonsymmetric deviations.

Computing the payoffs V_{oligo} and V_{eutr} at the candidate Nash equilibria, it turns out that these are higher in the oligotrophic candidate whenever (b, c) is above the dotted curve in the region marked "eutrophic NE." That means that in the intersection of the region where $V_{\text{oligo}} > V_{\text{eutr}}$ with the "eutrophic NE" region, the game has the structure of the prisoner's dilemma, whereas in the region "#NE = 2," it is a stag-hunt game.

4.4.2 Dynamics: Open-Loop Nash

Mäler et al. (2003) show that symmetric open-loop Nash equilibrium strategies $u_i(t) = u_{\text{nc}}(t)$, $i = 1, \ldots, n$ of the n-player game with parameters (b, c, ρ) also are maximizers

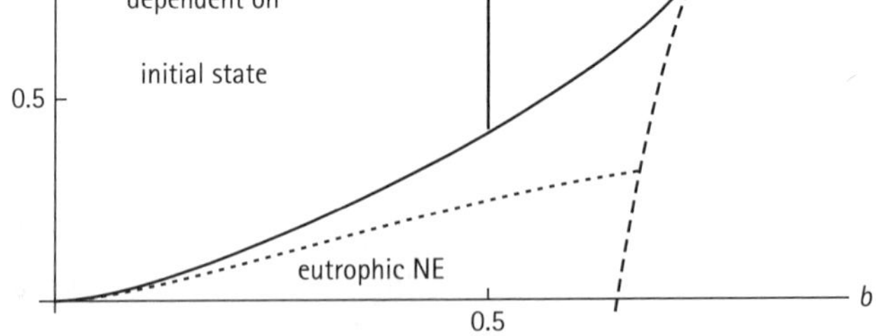

FIGURE 4.9 Steady-state Nash equilibria of the lake pollution game. (After Wagener (2013).)

of the optimal management problem with parameters $(b, c/n, \rho)$. It follows that if n is sufficiently large, the lake is always allowed to eutrophicate. In contrast to this, the symmetric cooperative strategies $u_i(t) = u_c(t)$, $i = 1, \ldots, n$, have the property that $nu_c(t)$ is a maximizer of the optimal management problem with parameters (b, c, ρ). That is, if there are too many players, the lake eutrophicates, while the optimal cooperative solution would be to conserve the lake in an oligotrophic state. Put differently, the lake problem is another instance of Hardin's tragedy of the commons (Hardin, 1968).

It does, however, not necessarily follow that the bifurcation diagram in Figure 4.8a, with c replaced by c/n, gives the structure of the open-loop Nash equilibria. As showed in Section 4.4.1, for $\rho = 0$ some candidate Nash equilibrium strategies may be unstable under nonsymmetric deviations. A bifurcation diagram for $\rho > 0$ where the possibility of unsymmetric deviations is taken into account has not yet been given in the literature.

4.4.3 Dynamics: Closed-Loop Nash

In contrast to open-loop strategies, closed-loop strategies condition actions on time as well as on the state of the system. That is $u_i = u_i(t, x)$. A subclass of closed-loop strategies are the feedback strategies, where the actions are exclusively conditioned on the state: $u_i = u_i(x)$. In infinite horizon games with exponential discounting, the optimisation problem is essentially time-invariant, and closed-loop strategies reduce to feedback strategies.

Kossioris et al. (2008) and Dockner and Wagener (2014) have found symmetric feedback strategies for the lake game numerically. To sketch the method, assume that feedback strategies $u_{-i}(x)$ of all players except player i are given. Introduce the value function V_i of player i as

$$V_i(x_0) = \sup \int_0^\infty e^{-\rho t}(\beta_{a,i}(u_i) + \beta_{e,i}(x))\, dt,$$

where the supremum is taken over all pollution schedules u_i, subject to the lake dynamics (4.12) as well as the initial condition $x(0) = x_0$. The Pontryagin function of player i reads as

$$P_i(x, y_i, u_i) = \beta_{a,i}(u_i) + \beta_{e,i}(x) + y_i\left(u_i + \sum_{j\neq i} u_j(x) - g(x)\right).$$

Then the value function V_i satisfies the Hamilton-Jacobi-Bellman equation

$$\rho V_i(x) = \max_{u_i} P\left(x, V_i'(x), u_i; u_{-i}(x)\right). \tag{4.14}$$

It can be shown that V_i is continuous for all x; at points where the value function is nondifferentiable, the Hamilton-Jacobi-Bellman equation is satisfied in the sense of viscosity solutions. In the present context, points of nondifferentiability are generically isolated. The notion of viscosity solution prescribes precisely in which way V_i' can jump at a point of nondifferentiability between the values of V_i' that yield the same value $\rho V_i(x)$ of the right-hand side of (4.14). In practice, these are the natural jump conditions.

Analogously to the optimal management case, the maximization in (4.14) yields a relation

$$u_i = u_i^*(V_i'(x)),$$

where $u_i^*(y_i) = (\beta_{a,i}')^{-1}(-y_i)$. These relations hold for every $i = 1, \cdots, n$. Substitution back into (4.14) yields

$$\rho V_i = H_i(x, V_1'(x), \cdots, V_n'(x)), \tag{4.15}$$

where

$$H_i(x, y_1, \cdots, y_n) = \beta_{a,i}(u_i^*(y_i)) + \beta_{e,i}(x) + y_i \left(\sum_{j \neq i} u_j^*(y_j) - g(x) \right) \tag{4.16}$$

is the Hamilton function of player i in the game. Taking equation (4.15) repeatedly for $i = 1, \cdots, n$ yields the system of Hamilton-Jacobi equations for the value functions of the players in a Nash equilibrium of feedback strategies.

In the symmetric situation, where the benefit streams are equal for all players, it is possible that the feedback strategies, the Hamilton functions and the associated value functions are also the same for all players. Then the system of Hamilton-Jacobi equations reduces to the single equation

$$\rho V = H_{\text{symm}}(x, V'(x)), \tag{4.17}$$

with

$$H_{\text{symm}}(x, y) = \beta_a(u^*(y)) + \beta_e(x) + y\big((n-1)u^*(y) - g(x)\big).$$

For the specifications (4.2) and (4.4) of the lake problem, equation (4.17) reads as

$$\rho V(x) = -\log\big(-V'(x)\big) - cx^2 - V'(x)g(x) - (n-1). \tag{4.18}$$

Equation (4.17) is an implicit differential equation for V; there is no initial condition. To solve the equation, introduce $y(x) = V'(x)$, differentiate both sides once with respect to x, and rearrange terms to obtain

$$\frac{\partial H_{\text{symm}}}{\partial y}(x, y(x))y'(x) = \rho y(x) - \frac{\partial H_{\text{symm}}}{\partial x}(x, y(x)). \tag{4.19}$$

This is sometimes called the shadow price equation (see Case, 1979; Tsutsui and Mino, 1990; Dockner and Van Long, 1994; Wirl, 1996; Rincón-Zapatero et al., 1998). Dockner and Wagener analyze this equation by remarking that a curve $(x(s), y(s))$ traces out the graph of $y = y(x)$ around a point where $y(x)$ is differentiable, if

$$x'(s) = \frac{\partial H_{\text{symm}}}{\partial y}(x(s), y(s)), \qquad y'(s) = \rho y - \frac{\partial H_{\text{symm}}}{\partial x}(x(s), y(s)). \tag{4.20}$$

Unlike the situation of the optimal management problem, the curve parameter s has not an interpretation in terms of time; it is a purely auxiliary quantity. For the lake game, this yields

$$x'(s) = u - g(x), \qquad y'(s) = \rho y + 2cx + yg'(x). \tag{4.21}$$

Since there is no initial condition, all integral curves of the system (4.20) that satisfy the transversality condition are candidates to generate Nash feedback equilibrium strategies.

Kossioris et al. (2008) report graphs generated by such families of integral curves as Nash feedback equilibria. However, the reported graphs are only defined on subintervals U of the state space $X = [0, \infty)$. To be a Nash equilibrium, no deviation from the equilibrium strategy should generate a higher payoff. But as it is possible to construct a strategy that takes the state out of the interval U, the payoff for the players that play a strategy only defined in U becomes undefined. To make such strategies admissible, the game has to be changed in such a way that no player can play an action taking the system out of U. But for the unrestricted game, these strategies cannot be admitted as solutions. Only those integral curves can constitute Nash equilibrium strategies that are defined on the whole state space.

For the lake game, the equations (4.20) coincide with the system (4.7)–(4.8); the optimal policy function given in Figure 4.6 is therefore also the Nash feedback strategy of a player in the game. However, as there are now several players, the resulting steady state will be lower. Figure 4.10 illustrates two situations.

Consider first Figure 4.10a, where the lake is reversible, but close to fragile. Under cooperation, the joint action of the cooperators is equal to optimal management, as illustrated in Figure 4.6. As noted before, the oligotrophic steady state is close to the tipping point of the lake dynamics, and the strong negative feedback provided by the optimal policy function stabilizes it. Under cooperation, each of the players are allowed half of the pollution level of the optimal pollution level; in Figure 4.10a this level is equal to the value of the vertical coordinate of the white circles.

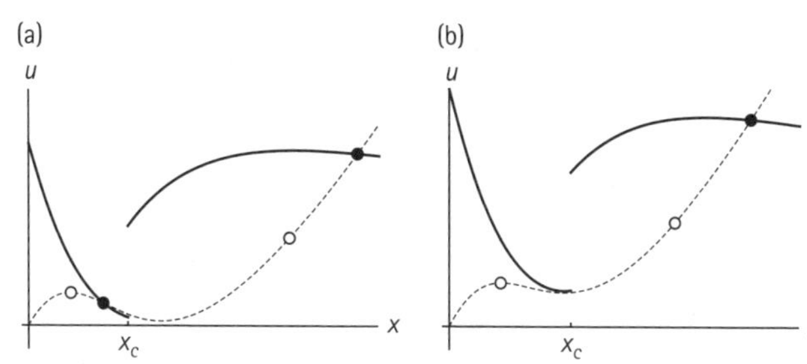

FIGURE 4.10 Two-player symmetric Nash equilibrium feedback strategies for the lake game (solid), as well as the associated long-term steady-state condition $2u = g(x)$ (dashed). The circles indicate long-term steady states under cooperation (white) and noncooperation (black). Parameters: $n = 2$, $\rho = 0.03$.

The cooperative level is much lower than the pollution level of the noncooperative feedback strategy at the tipping point. On the other hand, noncooperation results in an oligotrophic steady state that is past the tipping point, the left black circle in Figure 4.10a, where both the pollution level in the lake is higher, and the pollution stream allowance of the players is lower, than in the cooperative steady state. Moreover, the stabilizing feedback is much weaker: the graph of the feedback strategy runs close to that of the steady-state condition $u=g(x)/2$ of the lake, indicating that time-relaxation toward the steady state will be slow.

The relative locations of the eutrophic steady state under cooperation and noncooperation show a trade-off: under noncooperation, a worse state of the environment sets off higher production.

If the lake is more robust, as in Figure 4.10b, the eventual outcome of the economic interactions deteriorates: under noncooperation, the oligotrophic steady state disappears, and instead there is a discontinuity in the strategies of the players at a critical state $x = x_c$. The low values of the pollution stream for state values lower than but close to the critical state imply that the lake will remain for a long time still at low pollution levels; then, when the critical state is crossed, the lake deteriorates rapidly towards the eutrophic steady state.

Apparently, if the lake is robust and therefore can sustain more pollution, the danger of an environmental regime shift is not sufficiently pressing for it to be prevented; it is the fragile lake that more easily survives, because ending up in the eutrophic domain is much more costly in the long run.

4.5 Taxes

A possible way to alleviate the effects of the prisoner's dilemma in the shallow lake problem, or more generally in problems where different agents use a common pool resource, is to impose taxes that correct the shadow value of the stock. Mäler et al. (2003) and Kossioris et al. (2011) consider such tax schemes for the lake problem sketched above; Heijnen and Wagener (2013) model the pollution stream as an output of a capital-intensive industry and they consider taxes for this situation. Heijdra and Heijnen (2012) show that in presence of hysteresis, a policy of finite duration can have lasting beneficial effects.

4.5.1 Time-Dependent Tax Rates in the Lake Problem

A proportional tax $\tau = \tau(t)$ on the pollution stream, imposed on players using open-loop strategies, changes the total benefits of player i to

$$I_i = \int_0^\infty e^{-\rho t}\,(\beta_a(u_i) + \beta_e(x) + \tau\, u_i)\; dt.$$

Given the pollution streams of the other players, the dynamic optimization problem of player i then requires maximizing the Pontryagin function

$$P = \beta_a(u_i) + \beta_e(x) + \tau\, u_i + y_i \left(\sum_{j=1}^{n} u_j - g(x) \right),$$

which leads to

$$\beta_a'(u_i) + \tau + y_i = 0.$$

Let $u_c(t) = \frac{1}{n} u_o(t)$ be the optimal pollution stream allowance for each player under cooperation, which is the nth fraction of the optimal pollution stream u_o of a single player. For $u_i = u_c$, the corresponding shadow value of the lake for player i equals

$$y_{c,i} = -\beta_a(u_c).$$

In order that the optimal choice of u_i in an open-loop Nash equilibrium coincides with u_c, it is necessary that

$$\tau = y_{c,i} - y_i.$$

"The tax bridges the gap between the social shadow cost of the accumulated phosphorus [...] and the private shadow cost of the accumulated phosphorus" (Mäler et al., 2003, p. 615). However, a time-varying tax rate is in practice difficult to implement. In Mäler et al. (2003), the authors therefore turn to a constant tax rate that changes the dynamics in such a way that the oligotrophic steady state coincides with the steady state under cooperation.

4.5.2 State-Dependent Tax Rates in the Lake Problem

Kossioris et al. (2011), considering the situation that players use feedback strategies $u_i = u_i(x)$, investigate the effect of state-dependent tax rates $\tau = \tau(x)$ given by low-order polynomials: a constant rate is the simplest example in this class. Using a numerical algorithm to choose the tax rate optimally, they show that for a given initial value, a cubic state dependent tax rule can bridge almost two thirds of the gap between the payoffs per player in the noncooperative and the cooperative cases.

4.5.3 Time-Dependent Tax Rates in a Global Warming Model

Models where an industry affects a natural resource, and which can sustain multiple equilibria, have been studied by Greiner and Semmler (2005), Greiner et al. (2010), and Janmaat (2012). The latter author considers the fish stock in a lake as productive capital; naturally, the state of the lake affects the capital stock.

Greiner et al., slightly modifying the model of Greiner and Semmler, study global warming caused by the emission of greenhouse gases (GHGs): mean atmospheric temperature T and the concentration of GHGs M, expressed as a multiple of the preindustrial level, evolve according to

$$\dot{T} = g(T) + \log M,$$
$$\dot{M} = E - \mu M;$$

here g is a nonlinear relation deriving from the Earth's radiative energy balance, and E are industry emissions, taken to be proportional to the ratio of capital K to abatement activities A, or per capita capital k to per capita abatement a:

$$E \propto \frac{K}{A} = \frac{k}{a}.$$

The labor supply L is assumed to grow at a rate n. Expressing everything in per capita units, per capita output takes the form

$$y = bk^{\alpha} D(T);$$

the damage function D is decreasing, taking the value 1 for the preindustrial mean temperature T_0. Output is spent on consumption c, abatement a, replacement of old capital, and income tax and emission tax, at rates τ and τ_E respectively:

$$\dot{k} = (1 - \tau)y - c - a - \tau_E \frac{E}{L} - (\delta + n)k.$$

Optimizing total welfare

$$I = \int_0^{\infty} e^{-\rho t} L \log c \, dt,$$

they find, for a certain parameter combination, a surface of indifference threshold points in the three-dimensional state space (see Figure 4.11).

There are two attracting steady states under optimal management, "warm" and "cool": the warm steady state has both higher values of the mean temperature and of the steady state level of capital. For given values of K, the indifference thresholds are almost independent of T, except for a small interval around $T_c \approx 293$, where they decrease from $M \approx 2.1$ to $M \approx 1.8$.

Note the shape of the trajectories: for most initial points, first temperature is steered toward values around $T \approx 290$, that is about 17°C, in the cool regime, or around $T \approx 296$, about 23°C, in the warm regime. Only then are significant changes to the capital and the pollution levels effected by the optimal policy. In both situations, the asymptotic value of M is about 2, that is, twice the preindustrial level of GHGs.

Greiner and Semmler (2005) discuss also a competitive economy, where the impact of the decisions of indiviual agents on the state of the environment is negligible. As

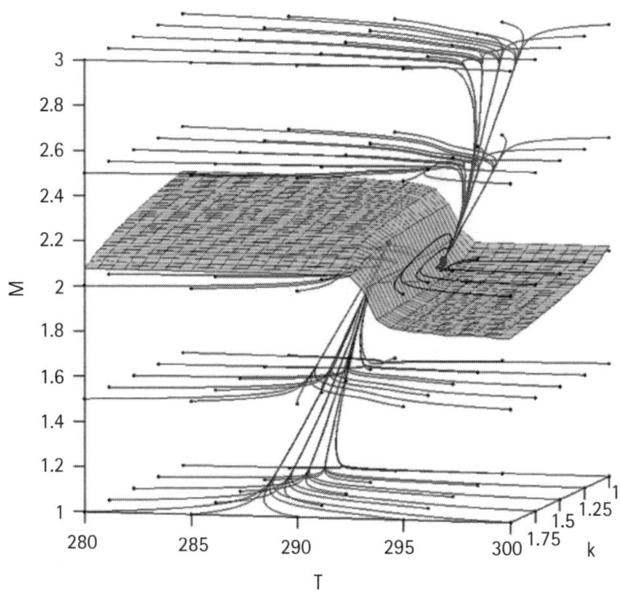

FIGURE 4.11 Indifference surface in the state space of the Greiner-Grüne-Semmler model. (After Greiner et al., 2010).

in the situation of the lake problem, imposing the tax τ_E on emissions to correct the shadow value of the environment lets the agents internalise the negative externality.

4.5.4 Constant Tax Rates in an Extended Lake Problem

Heijnen and Wagener (2013) extend the lake model by adding a capital-intensive industry with a fixed amount of labor and a variable amount of capital k; in the model, the state of the lake has no impact on the industry. As time-dependent taxes, like those considered above (Mäler et al., 2003; Greiner and Semmler, 2005) are hard to implement in practice, they investigate how well constant tax rates can reduce the pollution externality.

In their model, industry per capita output $y = f(k)$ is spent on investment in new capital, consumption κ, or taxes, which in the model take the form of mandatory contributions to pollution abatement. Capital dynamics then take the form

$$\dot{k} = f(k) - \kappa - (\delta + \tau\pi\eta)k; \tag{4.22}$$

here δ is the rate of depreciation of capital; η the amount of pollutant per unit time generated by the use of a single unit of capital; π the price of removing a unit of pollutant per unit time; and finally τ the imposed abatement level. The pollutant dynamics in the lake takes the form

$$\dot{x} = (1 - \tau\eta)k - g(x). \tag{4.23}$$

Two situations are compared: in the first, a social planner tries to maximize

$$I = \int_0^\infty \left(\log\kappa - cx^2\right) \mathrm{e}^{-\rho t}\, dt$$

by choosing the consumption level κ optimally. The maximum principle then yields the following set of equations, after eliminating the shadow price of capital in terms of consumption:

$$\dot{\kappa} = \big(f'(k) - (\rho + \delta + \tau\pi\eta)\big)\kappa + (1 - \tau)\eta q\kappa^2, \tag{4.24}$$

$$\dot{q} = (\rho + g'(x)) + 2cx; \tag{4.25}$$

here q is the shadow value of the lake.

In the second "competitive" situation, there is a continuum of identical consumers, supplying their labour to the industry at the prevailing wage rate $w = w(t)$. Wages are either spent on consumption or put in a bank account at an interest rate $r = r(t)$, which, in turn, is determined by the marginal productivity of capital:

$$f'(k) = r(t) + \delta + \tau\pi\eta.$$

The bank balances evolve as

$$\dot{b} = rb - \kappa + w,$$

subject to the condition that the discounted value of the bank balances are bounded away from $-\infty$; this is a "No Ponzi" condition. As actions of each individual consumer have negligible effects on the total amount of pollution, every consumer maximizes just discounted utility from individual consumption

$$\int_0^\infty \log(\kappa)\mathrm{e}^{-\rho t}\, dt.$$

Applying the maximum principle to this dynamic optimisation problem, and expressing the costate variable in terms of the consumption yields eventually that

$$\dot{\kappa} = (r(t) - \rho)\kappa.$$

As the industry is perfectly competitive, the marginal productivity of capital equals the price of capital, that is

$$r(t) = f'(k) - \delta - \tau\pi\eta.$$

This yields eventually

$$\dot{\kappa} = \big(f'(k) - (\rho + \delta + \tau\pi\eta)\big)\kappa. \tag{4.26}$$

Comparing this with (4.24) shows that here the consumers do not take the state of the lake into account in their consumption decisions.

Heijnen and Wagener investigate a parameter configuration for which, without abatement, the social planner keeps the lake in the oligotrophic state by the social planner, whereas it flips to the eutrophic state under competition. This is driven by consumption: while the social planner imposes low pollution streams, and implicitly low consumption levels, in the competitive case there is overconsumption and overpollution.

Increasing the abatement rate τ improves the social planner case somewhat: pollution abatement actually allows the industrial production to increase, as pollution effects are compensated for, which leads to higher consumption levels. When the abatement tax increases past a certain level, abatement becomes so costly that consumption starts to decrease again. However, the effects on the total welfare level are modest.

This is in sharp contrast to the competitive case: here the total welfare level increases quickly, though consumption decreases somewhat, until the lake no longer enters the eutrophic region. When that is the case, the welfare level of the competitive case is almost equal to that of the social planner case, and it follows the same pattern. Put differently, the external pollution costs can be largely avoided by imposing a tax whose proceeds are earmarked for abatement.

4.6 Uncertain Regime Shifts

The shallow lake system models a system that can exhibit a regime shift for which the dynamics are deterministic and fully known. This section will discuss a number of articles where a regime shift may occur with a given probability that may or may not depend on the actions of the agents. In the 1980s, Reed considered regime shifts occurring with a natural hazard rate for resource extraction problems, more precisely for forests in the presence of fire risk (Reed, 1984) and the catastrophic collapse of fisheries (Reed, 1988). Clarke and Reed (1994) (see also Tsur and Zemel, 1998) extended this to hazard rates that depended on pollution concentration, and thus indirectly on the actions of the agents in the problem. They found that if the hazard rate of a regime shift increased sufficiently quickly with pollution, optimal pollution levels and consumption levels are lower than in the case where there is no possibility of a regime shift. If this kind of precautionary behavior on the part of the agents is optimal, a "precautionary principle" is said to hold. What is puzzling about these results, however, is that in some situations, the optimal behavior of agents is ambiguous. That is, even in the presence of pollution-induced risk of regime shifts, it may be optimal to consume more, rather than less, than in the situation without risk.

To understand the underlying mechanisms, consider the following optimal harvesting problem discussed by Polasky et al. (2011). A manager is to maximize discounted revenues from harvesting

$$I = \int_0^\infty e^{-\rho t} pu\, dt, \tag{4.27}$$

with p the unit price of the harvested good, subject to stock dynamics

$$\dot{x} = G(x) - u, \tag{4.28}$$

as well as the requirements that $x \geq 0$, $u \geq 0$ for all t. There is a (stochastic) time τ such that for $0 \leq t \leq \tau$, stock growth is given by $G(x) = G_1(x)$, whereas for $t > \tau$, the stock dynamics satisfy $G(x) = G_2(x)$. It is possible that the regime shift from G_1 to G_2 never takes place. Both functions are strictly concave, take a maximum for some positive stock value, and satisfy $G_i(0) = 0$ $(i = 1, 2)$. Deterioration of the system after the regime shift is expressed by the assumptions that $G_1(x) \geq G_2(x)$ and $G_1'(x) \geq G_2'(x)$ for all $x \geq 0$.

The optimization problem is most conveniently stated and solved in terms of two Hamilton-Jacobi-Bellman equations: the first for the value V_1 of the stock before the shift, and the second for the value V_2 after the shift. The solution is sketched for the, simpler, second case, after which the Hamilton-Jacobi-Bellman equation and the result for the first case are stated.

After the regime shift, the natural growth function of the stock is $G_2(x)$. The Hamilton-Jacobi-Bellman equation for V_2 reads as

$$\rho V_2(x) = \max_{u \geq 0} \left\{ pu + V_2'(x)\,(G_2(x) - u) \right\}. \tag{4.29}$$

As the integrand of the revenue I is linear in the harvest rate u, maximizing over u results in a so-called bang-bang harvesting policy:

$$u = \begin{cases} 0 & \text{if } V_2'(x) > p, \\ \text{indeterminate} & \text{if } V_2'(x) = p, \\ \infty & \text{if } V_2'(x) < p. \end{cases} \tag{4.30}$$

That is, the stock grows at the natural rate as long as its shadow value is above the market price for the harvest; if it is below the market price, it is harvested at the maximal rate.

The solution of equation (4.29) is

$$V_2(x) = \begin{cases} e^{-\rho\theta(x)} \frac{pG_2(x_2)}{\rho} & \text{for } 0 \leq x \leq x_2, \\ p(x - x_2) + \frac{pG_2(x_2)}{\rho} & \text{for } x > x_2; \end{cases}$$

here x_2 is the unique solution of the "golden rule"

$$G_2'(x_2) = \rho, \tag{4.31}$$

and $\theta(x)$ is the time needed by the stock to reach the equilibrium level x_2, starting from the initial level x. That is, when starting below x_2, the optimal harvesting policy does not harvest until the stock level reaches x_2, after which it harvests at the equilibrium rate $G_2(x_2)$. When the initial stock is larger than x_2, the excess stock $x - x_2$ is harvested and sold instantly, after which harvest proceeds as before at the equilibrium rate.

Consider now the situation before the regime shift. Recall that τ denotes the stochastic time at which the shift occurs. The probability that the shift occurs in a time interval $[t, t+h)$, conditional on the fact that it did not occur before time t, satisfies

$$\lim_{h\to 0} \frac{P(\tau \in [t,t+h) | \tau \geq t)}{h} = \lambda(x(t)),$$

where the limit $\lambda(x)$ is the "hazard rate" at state x. The Hamilton-Jacobi-Bellman equation for the stock value in the first regime is then of the form

$$\rho V_1(x) = \max_{u\geq 0} \left\{ pu + V_1'(G_1(x) - u) + \lambda(x)(V_2(x) - V_1(x)) \right\}.$$

If the rate of stock growth deteriorates after the shift, it follows that $V_2(x) \leq V_1(x)$; the last term in the equation then models the penalty incurred if the regime shift occurs.

The golden rule for the situation before the shift, which is analogous to condition (4.31) for the steady state after the shift, states that a steady state x_1 under optimal harvesting satisfies

$$G_1'(x_1) = \rho + \lambda(x_1)\left(1 - \frac{V_2'(x_1)}{p}\right) + \frac{\lambda'(x_1)}{\rho + \lambda(x_1)}\left(G_1(x_1) - \frac{\rho V_2(x_1)}{p}\right). \qquad (4.32)$$

This equation furnishes information both if the shift probability is independent of the stock level (exogenous shift) or dependent (endogenous shift), and both if the stock collapses after the shift ($V_2(x) = 0$ for all x), or if only the growth dynamics changes. There are four combinations in total.

First, consider the exogenous shifts, for which λ is constant. With stock collapse, equation (4.32) reads as

$$G_1'(x_1) = \rho + \lambda.$$

As G_1' is a decreasing function, it follows that the steady state x_1 decreases relative to the situation without the possibility of a regime shift: the optimal harvest rate increases, as the expected time interval over which harvesting is possible decreases: the planner is more impatient.

If, however, only the growth dynamics deteriorates, the steady state x_2 after the shift is lower than x_1, and the excess stock is harvested immediately. This implies that the second term on the right-hand side of equation (4.32) vanishes. The third term vanishes as $\lambda'(x) = 0$ for a constant hazard rate, and the equation takes the form

$$G_1'(x_1) = \rho.$$

In this situation, the steady state under optimal harvesting is independent on the natural hazard rate.

Endogenous shifts with total stock collapse lead to

$$G_1'(x_1) = \rho + \lambda(x_1) + \frac{\lambda'(x_1)}{\rho + \lambda(x_1)} G_1(x_1). \tag{4.33}$$

Viewing the stock level as environmental quality, the hazard rate is expected to decrease as the stock level increases. If the decrease is sufficiently rapid, the result of Clarke and Reed is recovered that the right-hand side of (4.33) is smaller than ρ, and the steady state value x_1 is larger than in the case without risk of collapse. On the other hand, for marginal hazard rates that are small in absolute value, impatience of the planner leads to a decrease of the steady state stock, much like in the case of exogenous risk of stock collapse.

Finally, for endogenous shifts with deteriorating growth dynamics, and for decreasing hazard rates, the last term on the right-hand side of (4.32) is negative; this involves some reasoning. As the second term in the expression is again equal to 0, it follows that here the steady-state stock is always greater than in the situation without regime shifts. Put differently: if the hazard rate decreases with the stock, and if the planner does not lose stock at the moment of collapse, the optimal harvesting rate is precautionary compared with the situation without risk of collapse.

4.7 Conclusion

Negative feedbacks generate stable regimes; positive feedbacks differentiate between regimes. Natural systems under stress can have several regimes; if the stresses are too large, a regime may lose stability and the system shifts to a different regime (Figure 4.1). Management improves the robustness of systems by strengthening the negative feedback: the oligotrophic steady state of Figure 4.6 and the steady state of Figure 4.7a, both marginally stable under constant loading, are robustly stable under optimal management.

If the use of the natural system is shared between agents, the situation deteriorates, as is usual with common pool problems. There are generally various situations, depending on the precise specifications of the system, classified for the quasi-static situation in the bifurcation diagram of Figure 4.9. In the prototypical lake system, there is a large parameter region for which there are either two candidate steady-state outcomes. Though for most of this region, the oligotrophic steady state maximizes the player's welfare, only for a small subregion this steady state is the unique outcome of a Nash equilibrium in loading strategies. The other possibilities are that it is a welfare-preferred outcome of two Nash equilibria, or that it is dominated by a Nash equilibrium resulting in the eutrophic steady state. A final possibility, which is uncommon and which derives from the fact that this game is dependent on initial states, is that the welfare-preferred steady state is not reachable if the initial state is outside a certain region.

In the situation with discounted future benefit streams, the whole time-evolution determines the resulting outcome, not only the steady states. Modelling the behavior of the agents in terms of strategies, taken from certain strategy classes, tax rules can be devised that sustain the cooperative outcome. This may result in vastly better long-term economic performance of the system (Figure 4.10b).

All this analysis presupposes knowledge of the response of the natural system. If the occurrence of a regime shift is uncertain, but the actions of the agents influence the probability of the shift occurring, one strand of thought advises to increase consumption, implicitly stressing the environment, in order to make optimal use of the time before the collapse—"Après nous, le déluge." The precautionary principle, which advises to reduce stress on the environment in order to retard the moment of collapse, embodies the opposite stance. It turns out that, depending on particulars, both situations may be optimal if the collapse of the environmental system also entails the collapse of the natural resources sustained by the system. If there is, however, only a regime shift of the system, but no instantaneous deterioration of the stock, then precautionary behavior is unambiguously to be preferred.

The analysis of uncertain regime shifts suggests that it may be of interest to consider learning models in the future: as the system moves to—"explores"—regions of the state space not visited previously, the agents learn about the dynamics there, and modify their behavior accordingly. Also, the assumptions of fully rational behaviour of agents might have to be relaxed. Finally, the institutional problem remains challenging: how to decentralise the decision problem such that the negative externalities from environmental degradation are, at least partly, internalized (cf. Starrett, 1972), and how to do this in a practicable way.

References

Brock, W. A., and Starrett, D. (2003). Nonconvexities in ecological managment problems. *Environmental and Resource Economics, 26*(4), 575–624.

Case, J. H. (1979). *Economics and the Competitive Process.* New York: New York University Press.

Clarke, H. R., and Reed, W. J. (1994). Consumption/pollution tradeoffs in an environment vulnerable to pollution-related catastrophic collapse. *Journal of Economic Dynamics and Control, 18*(5), 991–1010.

Crépin, A. S., Biggs, R., Polasky, S., Troell, M., and de Zeeuw, A. (2012). Regime shifts and management. *Ecological Economics, 84,* 15–22.

Dasgupta, P., and Mäler, K.-G., eds. (2004). *The Economics of Non-convex Ecosystems.* Dordrecht, The Netherlands: Kluwer.

Dechert, W. D., and Nishimura, K. (1983). A complete characterization of optimal growth paths in an aggregated model with a non-concave production function. *Journal of Economic Theory, 31,* 332–354.

Dockner, E. J., and Van Long, N. (1994). International pollution control: Cooperative versus non-cooperative strategies. *Journal of Environmental Economics and Management, 24*, 13–29.

Dockner, E. J., and Wagener, F. O. O. (2014). Markov perfect Nash equilibria in models with a single capital stock. *Economic Theory, 56*, 585–625.

Greiner, A., and Semmler, W. (2005). Economic growth and global warming: A model of multiple equilibria and thresholds. *Journal of Economic Behavior & Organization, 57*, 430–447.

Greiner, A., Grüne, L., and Semmler, W. (2010). Growth and climate change: Threshold and multiple equilibria. In J. C. Cuaresma, T. Palokangas, and A. Tarasyev (eds.), *Dynamic Modeling and Econometrics in Economics and Finance, Dynamic Systems, Economic Growth, and the Environment*, Vol. 12: pp. 63–78. New York: Springer Science & Business Media.

Hardin, G. (1968). The tragedy of the commons. *Science, 162*(3859), 1243–1248.

Heijdra, B. J., and Heijnen, P. (2013). Environmental abatement and the macroeconomy in the presence of ecological thresholds. *Environmental and Resource Economics, 55*, 47–70.

Heijnen, P., and Wagener, F. O. O. (2013). Avoiding an ecological regime shift is sound economic policy. *Journal of Economic Dynamics & Control, 37*, 1322–1341.

Janmaat, J. A. (2012). Fishing in a shallow lake: Exploring a classic fishery model in a habitat with shallow lake dynamics. *Environmental & Resource Economics, 51*, 215–239.

Kiseleva, T., and Wagener, F. O. O. (2010). Bifurcations of one-dimensional optimal vector fields in the shallow lake system. *Journal of Economic Dynamics & Control, 34*, 825–843.

Kiseleva, T., and Wagener, F. O. O. (2014). Bifurcations of optimal vector fields. *Mathematics of Operations Research* (in press).

Kossioris, G., Plexousakis, M., Xepapadeas, A., and de Zeeuw, A. (2011). On the optimal taxation of common-pool resources. *Journal of Economic Dynamics and Control, 35*, 1868–1879.

Kossioris, G., Plexousakis, M., Xepapadeas, A., de Zeeuw, A., and Mäler, K.-G. (2008). Feedback Nash equilibria for non-linear differential games in pollution control. *Journal of Economic Dynamics and Control, 32*, 1312–1331.

Krugman, P. (1991). Increasing returns and economic geography. *The Journal of Political Economy, 99*(3), 483–499.

Majumdar, M., and Mitra, T. (1982). Intertemporal allocation with a non-convex technology: The aggregative framework. *Journal of Economic Theory, 27*(1), 101–136.

Mäler, K.-G., Xepapadeas, A., and de Zeeuw, A. (2003). The economics of shallow lakes. *Environmental and Resource Economics, 26*(4), 105–126.

Polasky, S., de Zeeuw, A., and Wagener, F. O. O. (2011). Optimal management with potential regime shifts. *Journal of Environmental Economics and Management, 62*, 229–240.

Reed, W. J. (1984). The effects of the risk of fire on the optimal rotation of a forest. *Journal of Environmental Economics and Management, 11*(2), 180–190.

Reed, W. J. (1988). Optimal harvesting of a fishery subject to random catastrophic collapse. *IMA Journal of Mathematics Applied in Medicine & Biology, 5*(3), 215–235.

Rincón-Zapatero, J. P., Martínez, J., and Martín-Herrán, G. (1998). New method to characterize subgame perfect Nash equilibria in differential games. *Journal of Optimization Theory and Applications, 96*(2), 377–395.

Romer, P. M. (1986). Increasing returns and long-run growth. *The Journal of Political Economy, 94*(5), 1002–1037.

Scheffer, M. (1998). *Ecology of Shallow Lakes.* London: Chapman & Hall.

Seierstad, A., and Sydsaeter, K. (1987). Optimal control with economic applications. Amsterdam: North-Holland.

Sethi, S. P. (1977). Nearest feasible paths in optimal control problems: Theory, examples, and counterexamples. *Journal of Optimization Theory and Applications, 23*(4), 563–579.

Skiba, A. K. (1978). Optimal growth with a convex–concave production function. *Econometrica, 46*, 527–539.

Starrett, D. A. (1972). Fundamental nonconvexities in the theory of externalities. *Journal of Economic Theory, 4*(2), 180–199.

Tahvonen, O., and Salo, S. (1996). Nonconvexities in optimal pollution accumulation. *Journal of Environmental Economics and Management, 31*(2), 160–177.

Treadway, A. B. (1969). On rational entrepreneurial behaviour and the demand for investment. *The Review of Economic Studies, 36*(2), 227–239.

Tsur, Y., and Zemel, A. (1998). Pollution control in an uncertain environment. *Journal of Economic Dynamics and Control, 22*, 967–975.

Tsutsui, S., and Mino, K. (1990). Nonlinear strategies in dynamic duopolistic competition with sticky prices. *Journal of Economic Theory, 52*, 136–161.

von Weizsäcker, C. (1965). Existence of optimal programs of accumulation for an infinite time horizon. *Review of Economic Studies, 32*, 85–104.

Wagener, F. O. O. (2003). Skiba points and heteroclinic bifurcations, with applications to the shallow lake system. *Journal of Economic Dynamics and Control, 27*, 1533–1561.

Wagener, F. O. O. (2013). Shallow lake economics run deep: Nonlinear aspects of an economic-ecological interest conflict. *Computational Management Science, 10*(4), 423–450.

Wirl, F. (1996). Dynamic voluntary provision of public goods: Extension to nonlinear strategies. *European Journal of Political Economy, 12*, 555–560.

CHAPTER 5

POLICY SCENARIOS IN A MODEL OF OPTIMAL ECONOMIC GROWTH AND CLIMATE CHANGE

HELMUT MAURER, JOHANN JAKOB PREUSS, AND WILLI SEMMLER

5.1 Introduction

NORDHAUS, (Nordhaus and Boyer, 2000; Nordhaus, 2008) has developed a dynamical model linking economic growth with climate change. This model represents the core of the DICE (Dynamic Integrated model of Climate and the Economy) climate model which is extensively calibrated in his book (Nordhaus, 2008). This canonical model has by now become a workhorse of the research on the economics of climate change. The model variants presented here focus only on the core dynamic equations of the canonical model of growth and climate change. Though we refer to the Nordhaus DICE model as a point of reference, we work with a lower dimensional system. We have fewer equations but a more realistic modeling of the temperature dynamics. This simpler model variant allows us to explore in a transparent way policy options and permits to suggest some directions of future research.

The model considered here builds on the dynamical model developed by Greiner et al. (2010), who discuss multiple equilibria and thresholds in a canonical optimal control problem with infinite horizon. In this chapter, we study various extensions of the basic optimal control problem and compare the solutions for finite horizon and infinite horizon. We admit terminal constraints for the state variable, consider the impacts of constraints (such as CO_2 and temperature constraints) on abatement policies and consumption, and try to adjust the preferences by suitable penalties from

This chapter is based on a previous paper by the authors which is, however, extensively revised and further policy scenarios are added. The previous paper is published as Maurer et al. (2013).

temperature by suitable penalties on the temperature. Such constraints allow to explore the implications for mitigation policies arising from the Kyoto treaty (CO_2 constraint) and the Copenhagen agreement (temperature constraint). Overall, we understand the exploration of our different scenarios as guidance to different policy options.

The chapter is organized as follows. Section 5.2 introduces the dynamic model of growth and climate change that will be called the canonical model. Delays are admitted in the dynamic equation of the temperature. In Section 5.3, we formulate the basic optimal control problem associated with the canonical model. We consider several extensions of the basic control problem incorporating terminal conditions, a penalty functional on the temperature as well as control and state constraints. Section 5.4 discusses the evaluation of the necessary optimality conditions (Pontryagin Maximum Principle) for the different optimal control problems in Section 5.3. In particular, the adjoint equations allow us to compute the stationary points (steady states) of the canonical system which determine the behavior of the infinite-horizon optimal solution. Finally, in Section 5.5 we present a number of case studies illustrating the various types of optimal control problems in Section 5.3. We focus first on business-as-usual (BAU) strategies with a low and constant rate of abatement and then discuss the so-called Social Optimum solutions, where both consumption and abatement are used as control variables. Optimal control and state trajectories of infinite-horizon control problems are computed by the routine OPTTRJ, whereas solutions of finite-horizon control problems with control and state constraints are obtained by discretization and nonlinear programming methods (Büskens and Maurer, 2000; Wächter and Biegler, 2006; Betts, 2010).

5.2 Dynamic Model of Growth and Climate Change

Our model starts with a basic growth model which includes a simplified dynamics of the link between economic growth and the Earth's climate. For details of the model the reader can be referred to the model description in Nordhaus (2008) and Greiner et al. (2010). For basic facts on climate change, as much as it is caused by economic activity, we refer readers to the work by Keller, et al. (2000, 2004). In the basic model the economy is represented by a decision making household. Its consumption is chosen optimally over time. Greiner et al. (2010) treat only the case of discounted utility that is maximized over an infinite time horizon. In this chapter also the case of a finite horizon will be treated. In contrast to Nordhaus and Greiner et al., the case of how damages affect the household's welfare will also be studied as well as the cases of state constraints, for example, temperature and CO_2 constraints.

5.2.1 Capital

The dynamics of the per capita capital is described by the following differential equation:

$$\dot{K}(t) = Y(t) - C(t) - A(t) - \delta K(t), \quad K(0) = K_0, \tag{5.1}$$

where Y is the per capita production, K the per capita capital, A the per capita abatement measure, and δ the depreciation of capital. In contrast to our recent paper (Maurer et al., 2012), the input of labor, L, is kept constant and does not grow at a rate n. The per capita production Y is defined by the production function

$$Y = BK^{\alpha} D(T), \tag{5.2}$$

where $\alpha \in (0,1)$ is the capital share and B a positive constant. The function $D(T)$ denotes the inverse of the damage that results from an increase of the temperature T above the preindustrial temperature T_o, and has the form

$$D(T) = \left(a_1(T - T_o)^2 + 1\right)^{-\psi} \tag{5.3}$$

with $a_1 > 0$ and $\psi > 0$. This is called the *damage function* and its effect can be characterized as follows: The greater the deviation of the current temperature T from the preindustrial temperature T_o, the smaller the function value $D(T)$ and accordingly the smaller the value of the per capita production Y.

5.2.2 Emission and CO_2 Concentration

It is assumed that economic activity emits greenhouse gases (GHGs), which depend on the capital that is used for production and which are here given in CO_2 equivalents. Thus they can be understood as a function of the per capita capital K, relative to the per capita abatement measure A. A larger capital goes along with higher emissions. Formally, this results in the expression

$$E = \left(a\frac{LK}{LA}\right)^{\gamma} = (aK/A)^{\gamma} \tag{5.4}$$

for the emission, where L is the labor input and $\gamma > 0$ and $a > 0$ are constants. The bigger a, the bigger the emission for given K and A and accordingly the worse the corresponding technology for the environment.

Emission causes an increase of the GHG (CO_2 concentration) in the atmosphere. It develops according to the differential equation

$$\dot{M}(t) = \beta_1 E(t) - \mu M(t), \quad M(0) = M_0. \tag{5.5}$$

Here, μ is the inverse of the atmospheric lifetime of CO_2 and β_1 highlights the fact that a certain part of the GHG emission is captured by the oceans and does not reach the atmosphere.

5.2.3 Temperature

To model the climate system of the Earth, an *energy balance model* is used; cf. Roedel and Wagner (2011). Some parameters in the following equations have been improved by discussions with W. Roedel (2011). The change of the average surface temperature T is given by the equation

$$c_h \frac{dT}{dt} = S_E - H - F_N, \quad T(0) = T_0. \tag{5.6}$$

All magnitudes on the right side indicate annual averages, so each time step has to include exactly one year, hence $\Delta t = 365 \cdot 24 \cdot 60 \cdot 60\,\text{s} = 31{,}536{,}000\,\text{s}$ is assumed. Because of that the differential equation changes to

$$\dot{T} \equiv \frac{dT}{dt} = \frac{\Delta t}{c_h}(S_E - H - F_N), \quad T(0) = T_0. \tag{5.7}$$

The Earth's surface is greatly covered by oceans. Its heat capacity is given by the numerical value $c_h = 210652078\,\text{J}/(\text{m}^2\text{K})$, that follows from the identity $c_h = 0.7\rho_w c_w d$, where $\rho_w = 1027\,\text{kg}/\text{m}^3$ is the density and $c_w = 4186\,\text{J}/(\text{kgK})$ the specific heat capacity of the sea water and $d = 70\,\text{m}$ describes the depth of the oceanic top layer where a mixing and thus a heat transport takes place. The factor 0.7 represents the proportion of sea water in the total surface of the Earth. The unit of $\frac{\Delta t}{c_h}$ is given by

$$\frac{\text{s}}{\text{J}/(\text{m}^2\text{K})} = \text{s}\,\text{m}^2\text{K}/\text{J} = \text{m}^2\text{K}/\text{W},$$

from which it follows that $\frac{\Delta t}{c_h} \approx 0{,}149707\,\text{m}^2\text{K}/\text{W}$.

S_E is the supplied sun energy, H the nonradiative energy flux and $F_N = F_\uparrow - F_\downarrow$ the net flux of the terrestrial radiation. $F_\uparrow$ complies with the Stefan Boltzmann law, which has the form

$$F_\uparrow = \varepsilon\sigma T^4 \tag{5.8}$$

with the relative emissivity $\varepsilon = 0.95$ and the Stefan Boltzmann constant $\sigma = 5.67 \cdot 10^{-8}\text{W}/(\text{m}^2\text{K}^4)$. Furthermore, the flux ratio is $F_\uparrow/F_\downarrow = 116/97$ and the difference is $S_E - H = (1 - \alpha_1(T))\,\frac{Q}{4}$ with the solar constant $Q = 1367\,\text{W}/\text{m}^2$ and the planetary albedo α_1, which indicates how much energy is reflected back to space. The factor $\frac{1}{4}$ is the ratio between the cross-sectional area πr^2_{Earth} and the surface area $4\pi r^2_{\text{Earth}}$ of the Earth, because it receives the sun's radiation flux only on a hemisphere. The share of non-reflected sun energy is given by the differentiable function

$$1-\alpha_1(T)=k_1\frac{2}{\pi}\arctan\left(\frac{\pi(T-293)}{2}\right)+k_2, \tag{5.9}$$

in which $k_1=5.6\times10^{-3}$ and $k_2=0.1795$ should apply.

A high concentration of GHGs affects the temperature through the so-called radiative forcing, which describes the change of incoming and outgoing energy in the atmosphere. For carbon dioxide (CO_2) we have

$$F=5.35\ln\left(\frac{M(t-d)}{M_o}\right)\ [\mathrm{W/m^2}] \tag{5.10}$$

with the preindustrial CO_2 concentration M_o. Here, we allow for *delays* $d\geq 0$, since a change in the concentration of (CO_2) may not immediately affect a change in the temperature. We shall compare non-delayed solutions ($d=0$) with delayed solutions for $d=5$ or $d=10$ years.

In summary, we obtain the following differential equation for the average surface temperature T,

$$\dot{T}(t)=\frac{\Delta t}{c_h}\left((1-\alpha_1(T(t)))\frac{Q}{4}-\frac{19}{116}\varepsilon\sigma T(t)^4+5.35\ln\left(\frac{M(t-d)}{M_o}\right)\right),\quad T(0)=T_0, \tag{5.11}$$

where the unit on the right-hand side is given by $\mathrm{m^2K/W\cdot W/m^2=K}$.

5.3 Optimal Control Problems

We present several versions of optimal control problems associated with the dynamics (5.1), (5.5) and (5.7) which is considered on a time interval $[0,t_f]$ with terminal time $0<t_f\leq\infty$. The state variable is the vector $X=(K,M,T)\in\mathbb{R}^3$, the control variable is given by $u=(C,A)\in\mathbb{R}^2$. Since the input of labor L, that is, the number of households, is kept constant, we can normalize it to $L(t)\equiv 1$. Then the *basic optimal control problem* is defined as follows: determine a (piecewise continuous) control function $u=(C,A):[0,t_f]\to\mathbb{R}^2$ that *maximizes* the objective (cost functional),

$$\max\quad J(X,u)=\int_0^{t_f}\mathrm{e}^{-\rho t}\ln C(t)\,dt, \tag{5.12}$$

subject to the differential equations (5.1), (5.5), (5.7),

$$\begin{aligned}\dot{K}(t)&=BK(t)^{\alpha}D(T(t))-C(t)-A(t)-\delta K(t),\\ \dot{M}(t)&=\beta_1(aK(t)/A(t))^{\gamma}-\mu M(t),\\ \dot{T}(t)&=\tfrac{\Delta t}{c_h}\left((1-\alpha_1(T(t)))\tfrac{Q}{4}-\tfrac{19}{116}\varepsilon\sigma T(t)^4\right)+5.35\ln\left(\tfrac{M(t-d)}{M_o}\right),\end{aligned} \tag{5.13}$$

with initial conditions

$$K(0) = K_0, \quad M(0) = M_0, \quad T(0) = T_0. \tag{5.14}$$

Recall the damage function (5.3) and albedo function (5.9):

$$D(T) = (a_1(T - T_o)^2 + 1)^{-\psi},$$
$$1 - \alpha_1(T) = k_1 \tfrac{2}{\pi} \arctan\left(\tfrac{\pi(T-293)}{2}\right) + k_2.$$

A complete list of parameters can be found in Table 5.1; recall that the number of households is normalized to $L \equiv 1$.

The problem (5.12)–(5.14) is called a *finite-horizon* optimal control problem if the terminal time is *finite*, $0 < t_f < \infty$; otherwise for $t_f = \infty$ it is called an *infinite-horizon* control problem.

Now we present some variants and extensions of the basic control problem. A simplified version of the control problem arises, when the abatement control is kept constant,

$$A(t) \equiv A_c \quad \text{for} \quad 0 \le t \le t_f. \tag{5.15}$$

Then the consumption C is the only control variable. We shall also study terminal constraints for the state variable given by

$$K(t_f) \ge K_f, \quad M(t_f) \le M_f, \quad T(t_f) \le T_f, \tag{5.16}$$

with appropriate values K_f, M_f, T_f. In particular, a positive value $K_f > 0$ will prevent the capital from approaching zero. It is also of interest to impose *control constraints* of the form

$$C_{\min} \le C(t) \le C_{\max}, \quad A_{\min} \le A(t) \le A_{\max} \quad 0 \le t \le t_f, \tag{5.17}$$

with suitable bounds $C_{\min} < C_{\max}$ and $A_{\min} < A_{\max}$. Another variant of the control problem is obtained when the objective functional (5.12) is modified by subtracting a penalty term that measures the quadratic deviation of the temperature $T(t)$ from a desirable temperature T_c,

$$\max \quad J_T(X, u) = J(X, u) - c_T \int_0^{t_f} (T(t) - T_c)^2 dt \quad (c_T > 0). \tag{5.18}$$

Table 5.1 Parameter Values in the Order of Appearance in (5.12) and (5.13).

$\rho = 0.035$,	$B = 1$,	$\alpha = 0.18$,	$a_1 = 0.025$,	$T_0 = 288$,
$\psi = 0.025$,	$\delta = 0.075$,	$\beta_1 = 0.49$,	$a = 3.5 \times 10^{-4}$,	$\gamma = 1$,
$\mu = 0.1$,	$\Delta t = 31\,536\,000$,	$c_h = 210\,652\,078$,	$k_1 = 5.6 \times 10^{-3}$,	$k_2 = 0.1795$,
$Q = 1367$,	$\varepsilon = 0.95$,	$\sigma = 5.67 \times 10^{-8}$,	$M_0 = 1$.	

Here, the negative sign of the penalty appears in the modified functional, since the penalty term will be minimized. Note that the penalty term does not involve a discount factor. The penalty term in the extended functional can be viewed as a so-called *soft state constraint.* From a practical point of view, it is more important to consider explicit *state constraints* of the form

$$S(X(t)) = S(K(t), M(t), T(t)) \geq 0 \quad \forall\, 0 \leq t_s \leq t \leq t_f, \tag{5.19}$$

where the function $S : \mathbb{R}^3 \to \mathbb{R}$ is assumed to be sufficiently often differentiable. The starting time t_s for the state constraint can be positive, $t_s > 0$, to account for the fact that the state constraint may not be feasible at the initial time but should be satisfied on a terminal interval $[t_s, t_f]$.

We briefly review some basic notions for *non-delayed* control problems with state constraints and refer the readers to Hartl et al. (1995) and Maurer (1979) for a thorough theoretical discussion. A *boundary arc* is a subinterval $[t_1, t_2] \subset [t_s, t_f]$ with $S(X(t)) = 0$ for $t_1 \leq t \leq t_2$. If the interval $[t_1, t_2]$ is maximal with this property, then t_1 is called the *entry-time* and t_2 is called the *exit-time* of the boundary arc; t_1 and t_2 are also called *junction times.* A *contact point* $t_c \in (t_s, t_f)$ is defined by the condition that there exists $\varepsilon > 0$ such that

$$S(X(t_c)) = 0, \quad S(X(t)) > 0 \quad \text{for} \quad t_c - \varepsilon \leq t < t_c \text{ and } t_c < t \leq t_c + \varepsilon.$$

The occurrence of boundary arcs and contact points is closely related to the notion of the *order* $q \in \mathbb{N}_+$ *of a state constraint.* The index $q \in \mathbb{N}_+$ is defined as the lowest order time derivative of $S(X(T))$ that contains the control variable explicitly (Maurer, 1979; Hartl et al., 1995). Specifically, we consider the following state constraints for K, M and T, which should hold jointly or separately:

$$S(X(t)) = K(t) - K_{\min} \geq 0 \quad \forall\, t_s \leq t \leq t_f, \tag{5.20}$$

$$S(X(t)) = M_{\max} - M(t) \geq 0 \quad \forall\, t_s \leq t \leq t_f, \tag{5.21}$$

$$S(X(t)) = T_{\max} - T(t) \geq 0 \quad \forall\, t_s \leq t \leq t_f. \tag{5.22}$$

It is straightforward to show that the state constraint (5.20) for K has the order $q = 1$, the constraint (5.21) for M has the order $q = 2$, and the constraint (5.22) for T has the order $q = 3$. State constraints of order $q = 1$ usually exhibit only boundary arcs and no contact points, whereas state constraints of order $q = 2$ can have both boundary arcs and contact points. For $q = 3$, there are no boundary arcs with an analytic junction, that is, every junction with a boundary arc exhibits some kind of chattering. Examples for boundary arcs and contact points and the phenomenon of a non-analytic junction with a boundary arc $T(t) = T_{\max}$ will be discussed in Section 5.5.

5.4 Maximum Principle: Necessary Optimality Conditions

In this section, we discuss necessary optimality conditions only for *non-delayed* control problems with $d = 0$ in the temperature dynamics (5.11). For delayed control problems, necessary optimality conditions have been derived, for example, in Göllmann et al. (2009). The celebrated Pontryagin Maximum Principle (Pontryagin et al., 1964; Hestenes, 1966; Sethi and Thompson, 2000) furnishes the necessary optimality conditions for the *finite-horizon* control problem (5.12)–(5.16). Maximum Principles for state constrained optimal control problems were discussed in Maurer (1979) and Hartl et al. (1995). The Maximum Principle for *infinite-horizon* control problems is presented in Aseev and Kryazhimskiy (2004, 2007), Michel (1982) and Seierstadt and Sydsaeter (1987). For a modern theory of infinite-horizon control problems we refer to Lykina et al. (2008, 2010). To date, a theory of infinite-horizon *delayed* control problems does not exist.

5.4.1 Basic Control Problem

5.4.1.1 *Steady States for Constant Abatement $A(t) = A_c$*

First, we consider the case of a constant abatement control (5.15) with $A(t) \equiv A_c = 1.21 \times 10^{-3}$ for $0 \leq t \leq t_f$. Here, the consumption C is the only control variable. The current-value Hamiltonian (Pontryagin function) (cf. Seierstadt and Sydsaeter, 1987; Sethi and Thompson, 2000; Aseev and Kryazhimskiy, 2007) is given by

$$\begin{aligned} H(X,\lambda,C) = {} & \ln C + \lambda_K \left(BK^{\alpha} D(T) - C - A_c - (\delta + n)K\right) \\ & + \lambda_M \left(\beta_1 a^{\gamma} K^{\gamma} A_c^{-\gamma} - \mu M\right) \\ & + \lambda_T \frac{\Delta t}{c_h} \left((1 - \alpha_1(T))\frac{Q}{4} - \frac{19}{116}\varepsilon\sigma T^4 + 5.35 \ln\left(\frac{M}{M_o}\right)\right), \end{aligned} \tag{5.23}$$

where $\lambda = (\lambda_K, \lambda_M, \lambda_T)$ is the vector of adjoint variables (shadow prices). The adjoint differential equations $\dot{\lambda} = (\rho - n)\lambda - H_X$ read explicitly:

$$\begin{aligned} \dot{\lambda}_K &= (\rho + \delta)\lambda_K - \lambda_K \alpha K^{\alpha-1} BD(T) - \lambda_M \beta_1 \gamma a^{\gamma} K^{\gamma-1} A^{-\gamma}, \\ \dot{\lambda}_M &= \rho\,\lambda_M + \lambda_M \mu - \lambda_T \frac{\Delta t}{c_h} 5.35 \frac{1}{M}, \\ \dot{\lambda}_T &= \rho\,\lambda_T - \lambda_K BK^{\alpha} D'(T) + \lambda_T \frac{\Delta t}{c_h}\left(\frac{Q}{4}\alpha_1'(T) + \frac{19}{116}\varepsilon\sigma 4T^3\right). \end{aligned} \tag{5.24}$$

The derivatives of the albedo function $\alpha_1(T)$ and the damage function $D(T)$ are

$$\begin{aligned} \alpha_1'(T) &= -5.6 \times 10^{-3}\left(1+0.25\pi^2(T-293)^2\right)^{-1}, \\ D'(T) &= -2a_1\psi(T-T_o)\left(a_1(T-T_o)^2+1\right)^{-\psi-1}. \end{aligned} \tag{5.25}$$

The control C maximizes the Hamiltonian (5.23). Since no control constraints are imposed, we get the condition $H_C = 1/C - \lambda_K = 0$ implying

$$C = \frac{1}{\lambda_K} \quad \text{or} \quad \lambda_K = \frac{1}{C}. \tag{5.26}$$

Note that the *strict Legendre-Clebsch condition* is satisfied in view of

$$H_{CC} = -1/C^2 < 0.$$

The two expressions in (5.26) lead to two different systems of differential equations that contain either the control C or the Adjoint variable λ_K. In this chapter, we use the expression $C = 1/\lambda_K$ and work with the adjoint equations (5.24), whereas Greiner et al. (2010) choose $\lambda_K = 1/C$ to eliminate λ_K.

Thus with $C = 1/\lambda_K$, the state equations (5.13) and the adjoint equations (5.24) constitute a system of six differential equations. To calculate the steady states (stationary points) of this system, we consider the nonlinear equation of order 6,

$$F(X,\lambda)^* = (\dot{X}^*, \dot{\lambda}) = 0 \in \mathbb{R}^6, \tag{5.27}$$

where * denotes the transpose. To solve this equation we proceed as follows

1. $\dot{\lambda}_M = 0$ is solved for $M = M(\lambda_M, \lambda_T, \cdot)$,
2. $\dot{M} = 0$ is solved for $\lambda_T = \lambda_T(K, T, \lambda_M, \cdot)$,
3. $\dot{\lambda}_K = 0$ is solved for $\lambda_K = \lambda_K(K, T, \lambda_M, \cdot)$ and finally
4. $\dot{K} = 0$ is solved for $\lambda_M = \lambda_M(K, T, \cdot)$.

In this way, we eliminate the variables M and λ in the equation (5.27) and are left with two equations for $\dot{T}$ and $\dot{\lambda}_K$ that depend only on the variables T and K. Figure 5.1a shows that the isoclines $\dot{T} = 0$ and $\dot{\lambda}_K = 0$ have three intersection points, each of them corresponding to a steady state. Numerical values of the three steady states are found in Table 5.2.

Stability properties of the three steady states are determined by the eigenvalues of the Jacobian of the function $F(X,\lambda)$ in (5.27) evaluated at the steady states. The Jacobian has six eigenvalues that are listed in Table 5.3. Since the real parts of the eigenvalues are nonzero, every steady state is *hyperbolic*. The first and third steady state have three eigenvalues with a positive and three eigenvalues with a negative real part, which implies that they are *saddle points*. However, the second steady state has only two eigenvalues with a negative real part, hence, it is unstable but has a two-dimensional stable manifold.

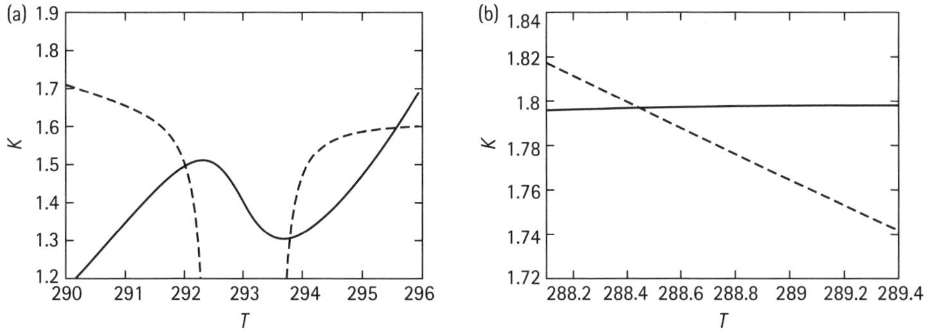

FIGURE 5.1 Isoclines for $\dot{T} = 0$ (solid) and $\dot{\lambda}_T = 0$ (dashed). (a) Constant abatement $A(t) \equiv 1.21 \times 10^{-3}$. (b) Social optimum for control $u = (C, A)$.

Table 5.2 Steady States for Abatement $A(t) \equiv 1.21 \times 10^{-3}$

	Steady state I	Steady state II	Steady state III
K	1.4964721	1.3067125	1.5968889
M	2.1210328	1.8520760	2.2633592
T	292.00933	293.79535	295.56599
λ_K	1.0495720	1.0703803	1.0604116
λ_M	−0.13512451	−0.24437749	−0.074322059
λ_T	−0.048308205	−0.076288513	−0.028353739
C	0.95276933	0.93424738	0.94303002

Table 5.3 Eigenvalues of the Jacobian of F, $A = 1.21 \times 10^{-3}$

Steady state I	Steady state II	Steady state III
−0.258501	−0.273678	−0.235612
0.293501	−0.161043	0.270612
−0.0851921 + 0.0740369i	0.196043	−0.101029 + 0.0183800i
−0.0851921 − 0.0740369i	0.318678	−0.101029 − 0.0183800i
−0.1201920 + 0.0740369i	0.0174999 + 0.123860i	−0.136029 + 0.0183800i
−0.1201920 − 0.0740369i	0.0174999 − 0.123860i	−0.136029 − 0.0183800i

5.4.1.2 *Social Optimum for Control $u = (C, A)$*

The current-value Hamiltonian for the optimal control problem with two control variables (C, A) agrees with that in (5.23) except that now the abatement A is an optimization variable,

$$H(X,\lambda,C,A) = \ln C + \lambda_K\left(BK^\alpha D(T) - C - A - (\delta+n)K\right) + \lambda_M\left(\beta_1 a^\gamma K^\gamma A^{-\gamma} - \mu M\right) + \lambda_T \frac{\Delta t}{c_h}\left((1-\alpha_1(T))\frac{Q}{4} + \frac{19}{116}\varepsilon\sigma T^4 + 5.35\ln\left(\frac{M}{M_o}\right)\right), \quad (5.28)$$

The adjoint equations $\dot{\lambda} = (\rho - n)\lambda - H_X$ are identical with (5.23). The controls C and A that maximize the Hamiltonian are determined by the conditions

$$H_C = 1/C - \lambda_K = 0, \quad H_A = -\gamma\lambda_M\beta_1 a^\gamma K^\gamma A^{-\gamma-1} - \lambda_K = 0,$$

which implies

$$C = \frac{1}{\lambda_K}, \quad A = \left(-\gamma\frac{\lambda_M}{\lambda_K}\beta_1 a^\gamma K^\gamma\right)^{1/(1+\gamma)}. \quad (5.29)$$

The second derivatives of H are given by $H_{CA} = 0$ and

$$H_{CC} = -\frac{1}{C^2} < 0, \quad H_{AA} = \gamma(\gamma+1)\lambda_M\beta_1 a^\gamma K^\gamma A^{-\gamma-2} < 0 \quad \text{for} \quad \lambda_M < 0. \quad (5.30)$$

Note that the strict Legendre-Clebsch condition $H_{uu} < 0$ is only satisfied if $\lambda_M < 0$ holds. This sign condition will be verified in all examples in the next section. It follows from the control representation (5.29) that the optimal control $u = (C,A)$ is a *continuous* and even an analytic function.

The steady state calculation proceeds as above. Here, one substitutes the control terms (5.29) into the state equation (5.13) and adjoint equation (5.24), and thus obtains as in (5.27) a six-dimensional equation

$$F(X,\lambda)^* = (\dot{X}^*, \dot{\lambda}) = 0 \in \mathbb{R}^6.$$

In this case, one finds only a single steady state; see Figure 5.1b and Table 5.4. The six eigenvalues of the Jacobian of $F(X,\lambda)$ at the steady state are computed as

$$-0.205\,599, \quad 0.240\,599, \quad -0.152\,695 \pm 0.126\,248i, \quad 0.187\,695 \pm 0.126\,248i.$$

There are three eigenvalues with a positive and three eigenvalues with a negative real part. Therefore, the steady state is a *saddle point.*

Table 5.4 Steady State for Control (C,A): Social Optimum

K	1.7969353	λ_K	1.0266800
M	1.3174399	λ_M	−0.0182292301
T	288.44591	λ_T	−0.0040479951
C	0.97401332	A	0.0023391909

5.4.1.3 Parametric Sensitivity Analysis of Steady States

Table 5.1 lists the *nominal parameters* that will be used for all computations in Section 5.5. It is clear that some parameters are subject to stochastic uncertainty and cannot be determined precisely.[1] Hence, it is of interest to perform a parametric sensitivity analysis of the steady states and optimal solutions. Here, we restrict the analysis to the sensitivity analysis of the steady state I and the social optimum and choose as a typical parameter the parameter μ in the dynamic equation (5.5) for the M,

$$\dot{M}(t) = \beta_1 E(t) - \mu M(t).$$

The following table summarizes the numerical results.

The table clearly indicates the fact that the CO_2 concentration M and the temperature T are mildly *increasing* and the capital K is strongly *decreasing*, when the parameter μ is *decreasing*.

5.4.2 Transversality Conditions for Adjoint Variables

In the basic control problem, no terminal state conditions were prescribed. In the *finite-horizon* case, the transversality for the adjoint variables is

$$\lambda(t_f) = (\lambda_K(t_f), \lambda_M(t_f), \lambda_T(t_f)) = (0,0,0).$$

Note that the condition $\lambda_K(t_f) = 0$ is incompatible with the control law $C(t) = 1/\lambda_K(t)$. As consequence, in order to get a well-defined solution one has to impose either a terminal constraint $K(t_f) \geq K_f > 0$ or a control constraint $C(t) \leq C_{\max}$; cf. Section 5.5.5.

Table 5.5 Steady State I and Social Optimum for Some Values of the Parameter μ in Equation (5.5)

μ	0.1	0.09	0.08	0.07
Steady State I for constant abatement $A = A_c = 1.21 \times 10^{-3}$				
K	1.49647211	1.35800143	1.20888529	1.05782773
M	2.12103278	2.13863402	2.14177508	2.14188259
T	292.00932611	292.19677297	292.28268749	292.33071644
Social Optimum				
K	1.79693533	1.79426843	1.79100604	1.78692706
M	1.32929638	1.32929638	1.34473027	1.36556701
T	288.50508537	288.50508537	288.58137500	288.68308854

This is not relevant when studying *infinite-horizon* optimal control problems. Here, the adjoint variable $\lambda(t)$ converges to one of the steady states. The transversality condition at infinity then takes the form (Michel, 1982; Sethi and Thompson, 2000; Aseev and Kryazhimskiy, 2004, 2007),

$$\lim_{t\to\infty} e^{-(\rho-n)t}\lambda(t) = 0. \tag{5.31}$$

When the terminal constraints (5.16)

$$K(t_f) \geq K_f, \quad M(t_f) \leq M_f, \quad T(t_f) \leq T_f,$$

are imposed in the *finite-horizon* control problem, the transversality condition for adjoint variables asserts that there exist multipliers $\nu_K, \nu_M, \nu_T \in \mathbb{R}$ with

$$\begin{aligned} \lambda_K(t_f) = \nu_K &\geq 0, & \nu_K(K(t_f) - K_f) &= 0, \\ \lambda_M(t_f) = \nu_M &\leq 0, & \nu_M(M(t_f) - M_f) &= 0, \\ \lambda_T(t_f) = \nu_T &\leq 0, & \nu_T(T(t_f) - T_f) &= 0. \end{aligned} \tag{5.32}$$

Recall that in the *infinite-horizon* case we can not prescribe terminal conditions, since the trajectory converges to one of the steady states.

5.4.3 Control Constraints

In the case of the control constraints (5.17),

$$C_{\min} \leq C(t) \leq C_{\max}, \quad A_{\min} \leq A(t) \leq A_{\max} \quad \forall\, t \in [0, t_f],$$

the control expressions (5.17) have to be replaced by the projections onto the control sets,

$$C = \text{proj}_{[C_{\min}, C_{\max}]}(1/\lambda_K), \quad A = \text{proj}_{[A_{\min}, A_{\max}]}\left(-\gamma \frac{\lambda_M}{\lambda_K}\beta_1 a^\gamma\right). \tag{5.33}$$

5.4.4 State Constraints

In (5.19), we considered the general state constraint

$$S(X(t)) = S(K(t), M(T), T(t)) \geq 0 \quad \forall\, 0 \leq t_s \leq t \leq t_f,$$

Practically relevant state constraints were considered in (5.20)–(5.22),

$$\begin{aligned} S(X(t)) &= K(t) - K_{\min} & \geq 0 \quad \forall\, t_s \leq t \leq t_f, \\ S(X(t)) &= M_{\max} - M(t) & \geq 0 \quad \forall\, t_s \leq t \leq t_f, \\ S(X(t)) &= T_{\max} - T(t) & \geq 0 \quad \forall\, t_s \leq t \leq t_f. \end{aligned} \tag{5.34}$$

To evaluate necessary optimality conditions, we use the *direct adjoining approach* described in Maurer (1979) and Hartl et al. (1995), where the state constraint is directly adjoined to the Hamiltonian by a multiplier μ which defines the *augmented Hamiltonian*

$$\mathcal{H}(X,\lambda,\mu,C,A) = H(X,\lambda,C,A) + \mu S(X)$$

Under some additional regularity conditions, the Maximum Principle (Maurer, 1979; Hartl et al. (1995) asserts that there exists a multiplier function $\mu : [0,t_f] \to \mathbb{R}_+$ such that the adjoint variables λ satisfies the adjoint equation

$$\dot{\lambda} = (\rho - n)\lambda - \mathcal{H}_X = (\rho - n)\lambda - H_X - \mu S_X \tag{5.35}$$

and the complementarity condition $\mu(t)S(X(t)) = 0 \forall\ t \in [0,t_f]$ holds. Moreover, at every contact or junction point t_1, the adjoint variable may have a jump according to

$$\lambda(t_1^+) = \lambda(t_1^-) - \nu_1 S_X(X(t_1)), \quad \nu_1 \geq 0. \tag{5.36}$$

For the state constraints (5.34), we get the jump conditions

$$\begin{array}{rcll} \lambda_K(t_1^+) & = & \lambda_K(t_1^-) - \nu_K, & \nu_K \geq 0, \\ \lambda_M(t_1^+) & = & \lambda_M(t_1^-) - \nu_M, & \nu_M \geq 0, \\ \lambda_T(t_1^+) & = & \lambda_T(t_1^-) - \nu_T, & \nu_T \geq 0. \end{array} \tag{5.37}$$

5.5 Numerical Case Studies

5.5.1 Numerical Methods

We use direct optimization methods for solving the *finite-horizon* basic optimal control problem (5.12)–(5.14) and its extension incorporating the control and state constraints or a modified functional (5.16)–(5.22). The direct optimization approach is based on a suitable discretization of the control problem by which the control problem is transcribed into a (large-scale) nonlinear programming problem (NLP). Such NLP can efficiently be solved either by Sequential Quadratic Programming (SQP) methods (cf. Büskens and Maurer, 2000; Betts, 2010) or by an Interior-Point method like IPOPT (cf. Wächter and Biegler, 2006). It is very convenient to formulate the discretized control problem by means of the modeling language AMPL developed by Fourer et al. (1993). It can be shown that the Lagrange multipliers of the NLP represent the adjoint variables $\tilde{\lambda}(t)$ for the discounted objective (5.12). Then the adjoint variables in the current-value formulation are obtained as $\lambda(t) = \exp(\rho t)\tilde{\lambda}(t)$. Similar discretization and NLP methods can be used to solve *delayed* optimal control problems: cf. Göllmann, et al. (2009). In all cases presented below, we shall use $N = 10,000$ gridpoints and the Implicit Euler integration scheme.

To obtain solutions the *infinite-horizon* optimal control problem we implemented the solver TRJ developed by Kunkel and von dem Hagen (2000). In this approach, a boundary value problem for the state and adjoint variable $(X, \lambda) \in \mathbb{R}^6$ is solved, where the dynamic equations are given by (5.13) and (5.23) and the control variables are substituted by the expressions (5.26) or (5.29). By a suitable time transformation, the infinite time interval $[0, \infty)$ is transformed into the finite time interval $[0, 1]$. Terminal conditions for state and adjoint variables are determined by the eigenvalues of the Jacobian of the mapping $F(X, \lambda)$ in (5.27) evaluated at the steady states.

The following numerical analysis explores two main cases: (1) the BAU strategies with a low and constant abatement $A(t) \equiv A_c = 1.21 \times 10^{-3}$; (2) the Social Optimum using the full power of the two control variables C and A. The focus is on finding feasible and optimal strategies by which the initial temperature or CO_2 concentration can be considerable decreased while keeping the consumption and capital at acceptable levels. To achieve this aim we shall incorporate various control and state constraints.

5.5.2 BAU Strategies with Low Abatement $A(t) \equiv A_c = 1.21 \times 10^{-3}$

5.5.2.1 *Infinite Horizon:* $T(0) = 290$

For the initial condition

$$T(0) = 290,\ K(0) = 1.4,\ M(0) = 2.0,$$

the infinite horizon solution converges to the steady state I in Table 5.2.

The control and state and adjoint variables are shown in Figures 5.2 and 5.3 on the time interval $[0, 500]$. The code OPTTRJ Kunkel and von dem Hagen (2000) yields the

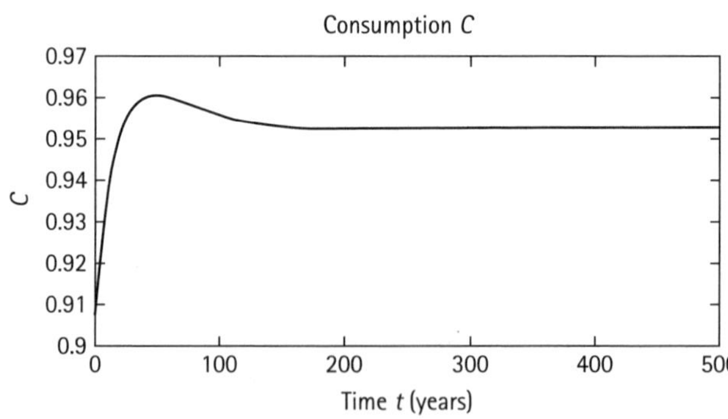

FIGURE 5.2 Infinite horizon, abatement $A_c = 1.21 \times 10^{-3}$, $T(0) = 290$. Consumption C.

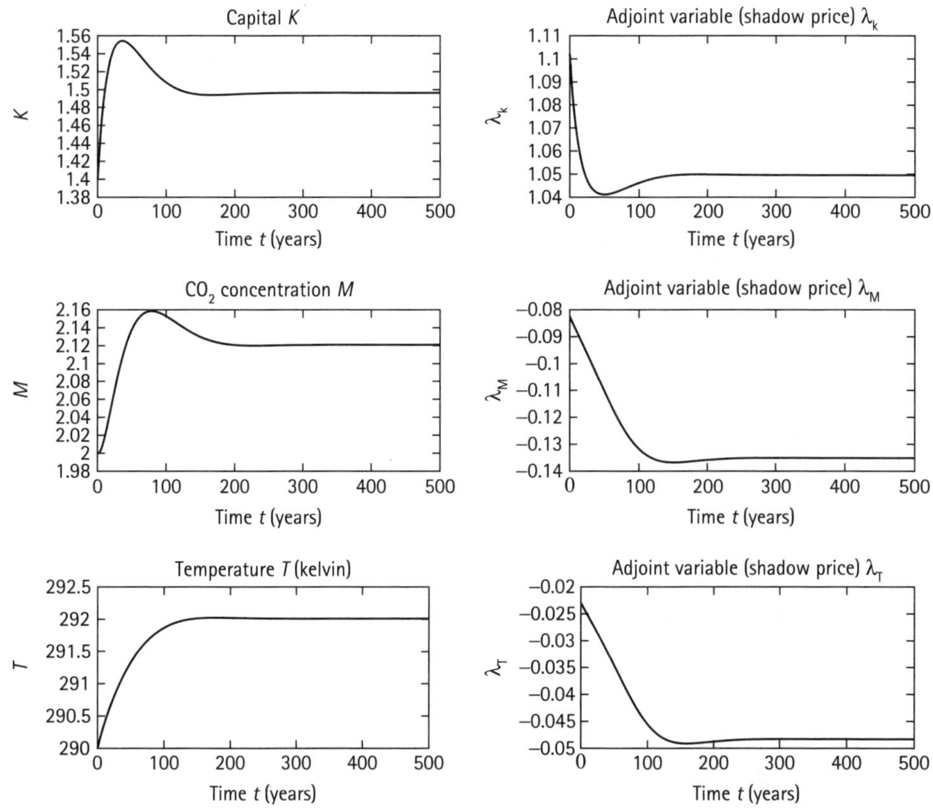

FIGURE 5.3 Infinite horizon, abatement $A_c = 1.21 \times 10^{-3}$, $T(0) = 290$. *Top row*: capital K and adjoint variable λ_K. *Middle row*: CO_2 concentration M and adjoint variable λ_M. *Bottom row*: temperature T and adjoint variable λ_T.

following numerical results

$$\begin{aligned} X(\infty) &= (1.4964729, 2.1210329, 292.00933), \\ \lambda(0) &= (1.1022577, -0.082505060, -0.022939734), \\ \lambda(\infty) &= (1.04957199, -0.13512455, -0.048309243). \end{aligned}$$

5.5.2.2 *Infinite Horizon:* $T(0) = 293$

We chose the initial condition

$$T(0) = 293,\ K(0) = 1.4,\ M(0) = 2.0$$

with a rather high initial temperature. Even in this case, the infinite horizon solution converges to the steady state I in Table 5.2. The control and state variables are shown in Figure 5.4 on the time interval $[0, 500]$. The code OPTTRJ (Kunkel and von dem Hagen, 2000) gives the numerical results

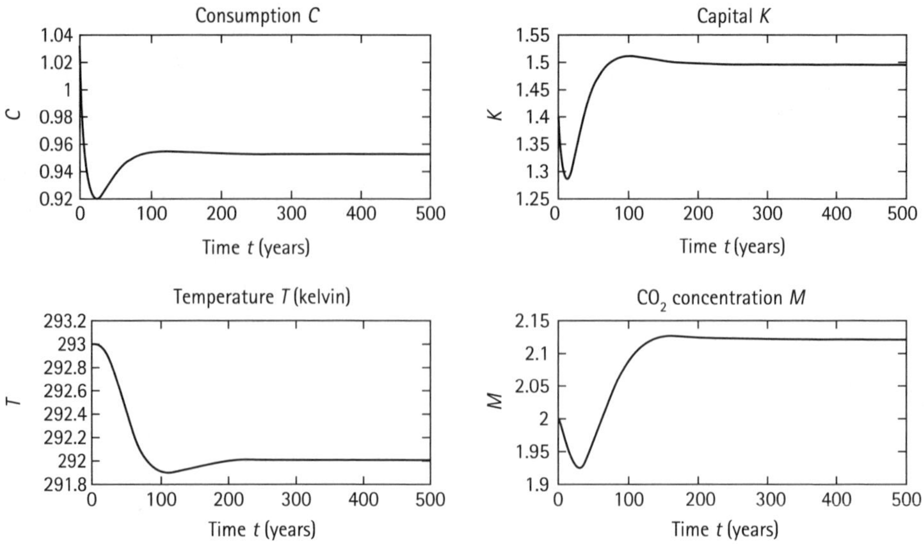

FIGURE 5.4 Infinite horizon, abatement $A_c = 1.21 \times 10^{-3}$, $T(0) = 293$. *Top row*: consumption C and capital K. *Bottom row*: temperature T and CO_2 concentration M.

$$\begin{aligned} X(\infty) &= (1.4964729, 2.1210329, 292.00933), \\ \lambda(0) &= (0.96880108, -0.53992408, -0.35185121), \\ \lambda(\infty) &= (1.04957199, -0.13512455, -0.048309243). \end{aligned}$$

It is noteworthy that even for the higher initial temperature $T(0) = 294$ the optimal trajectories converge to the steady state I and are similar to those in Figure 5.4. Thus, despite high initial temperatures there exist infinite-horizon solutions that are not doomed to converge to the steady state III in Table 5.2 with the high final temperature $T = 294.969$.

5.5.2.3 Finite Horizon: Basic Control Problem

The initial condition are

$$T(0) = 290, \ K(0) = 1.4, \ M(0) = 2.0.$$

Since no terminal conditions are prescribed, a control constraint has to be imposed. Otherwise the control law $C = 1/\lambda_K$ can not be applied due to $\lambda_K(t_f) = 0$. We choose the control constraint

$$C(t) \leq 1 \quad \forall \, 0 \leq t \leq t_f.$$

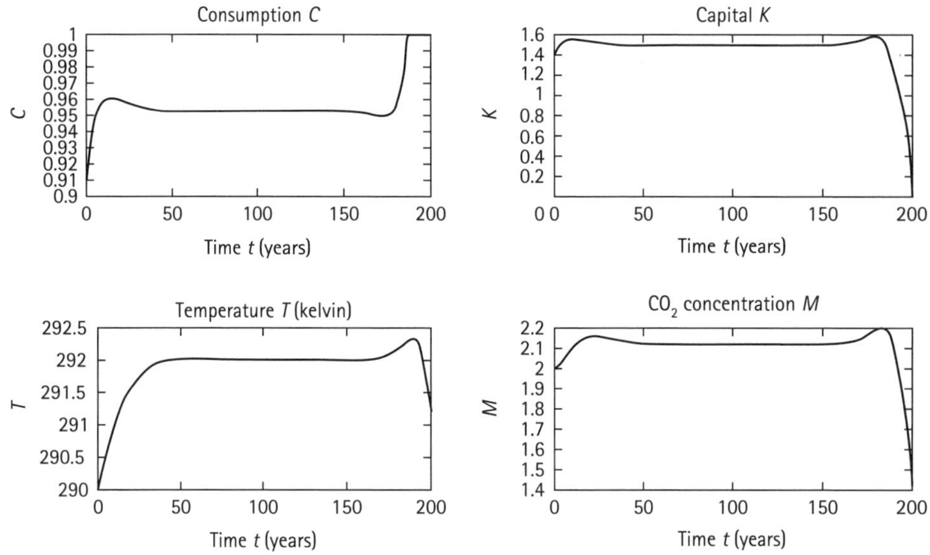

FIGURE 5.5 Finite horizon $t_f = 200$, abatement $A_c = 1.21 \times 10^{-3}$, $T(0) = 290$. *Top row*: consumption C and capital K. *Bottom row*: temperature T and CO_2 concentration M.

The code IPOPT provides the control C and state variables displayed in Figure 5.5 and the numerical results

$$\begin{aligned} J(X,u) &= -1.40981, \\ X(t_f) &= (0.000446022, 1.41677, 291.200), \\ \lambda(0) &= (1.10226, -0.0825050, -0.0229397), \\ \lambda(t_f) &= (0.138543, 0.0, 0.0). \end{aligned}$$

5.5.2.4 *Finite Horizon: Steady State I as Terminal Condition* $X(t_f) = X_{s,1}$

To avoid the strong decrease of capital and increase of consumption in Figure 5.5 the basic control problem, we prescribe the steady state I in Table 5.2 as a terminal condition and choose the boundary conditions

$$T(0) = 292,\ K(0) = 1.4,\ M(0) = 2,\ X(t_f) = X_{s1} = (1.4471998, 2.0511964, 291.60713)$$

The solution is displayed in Figures 5.6 and 5.7. The code IPOPT gives the results

$$\begin{aligned} J(X,u) &= -1.46910, \\ \lambda(0) &= (1.09275, -0.114479, -0.0399786), \\ \lambda(t_f) &= (1.04957, -0.135139, -0.0483026). \end{aligned}$$

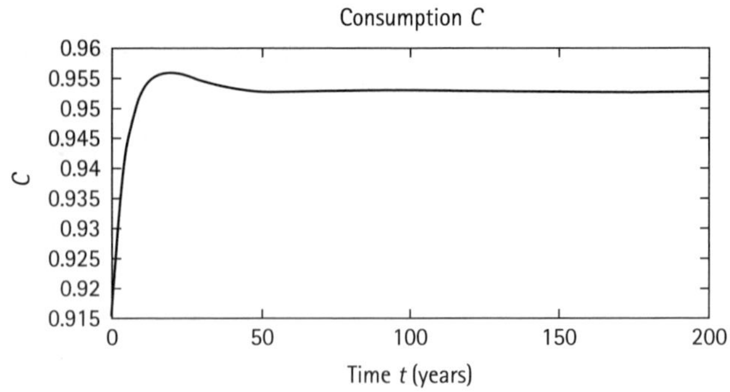

FIGURE 5.6 Finite horizon $t_f = 200$: abatement $A_c = 1.21 \times 10^{-3}$, $T(0) = 292$, terminal constraint $X(t_f) = X_{s1}$. Consumption C.

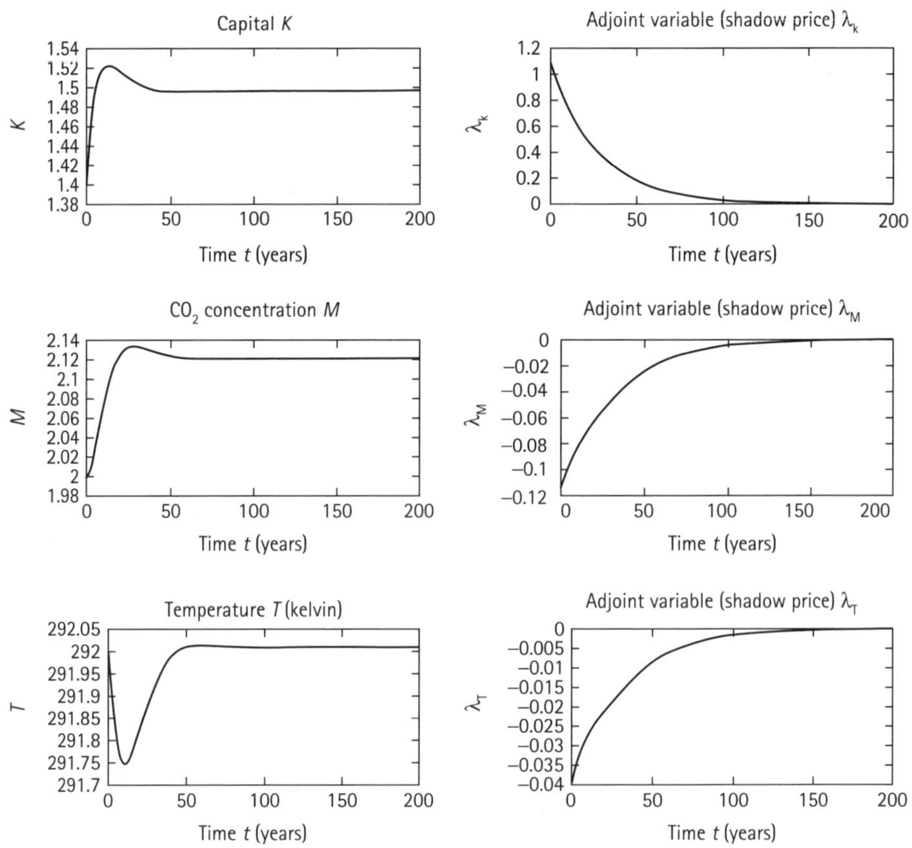

FIGURE 5.7 Finite horizon $t_f = 200$, abatement $A_c = 1.21 \times 10^{-3}$, $T(0) = 292$, terminal constraint $X(t_f) = X_{s1}$. *Top row*: capital K and adjoint variable λ_K. *Middle row*: CO_2 concentration M and adjoint variable λ_M. *Bottom row*: temperature T and adjoint variable λ_T.

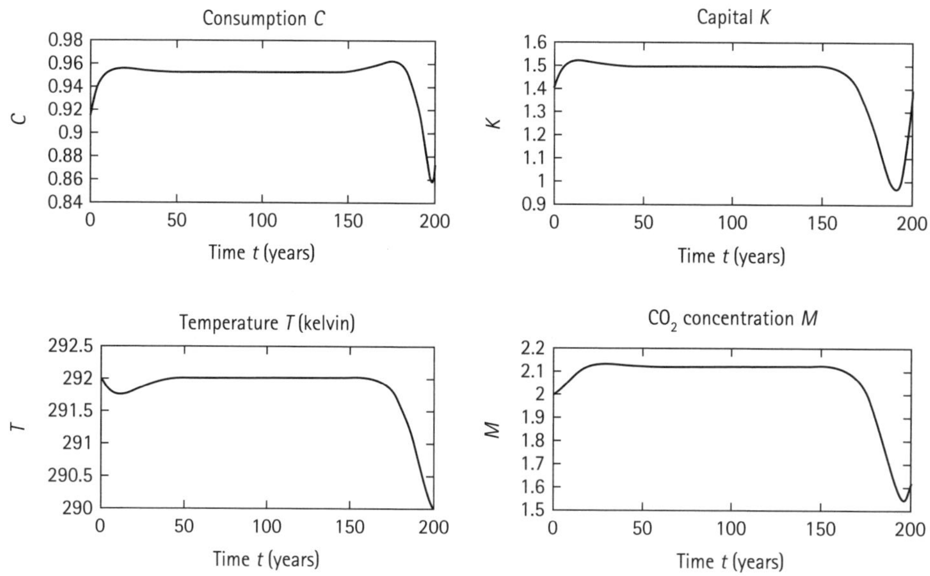

FIGURE 5.8 Finite horizon $t_f = 200$, abatement $A_c = 1.21 \times 10^{-3}$, $T(0) = 292$, terminal temperature $T(t_f) = 290$. *Top row*: consumption C and capital K. *Bottom row*: temperature T and CO_2 concentration M.

5.5.2.5 *Finite Horizon:* $T(0) = 292, T(t_f) = 290$

It is desirable to reach a smaller terminal temperature than the steady state temperature $T(t_f) = 291.607$ in the preceding case and attain a smaller CO_2 concentration M. Here, we choose the boundary conditions

$$T(0) = 292,\ K(0) = 1.4,\ M(0) = 2, \quad T(t_f) = 290, K(t_f) = 1.4, M(t_f) = 1.8.$$

The optimal trajectories computed by IPOPT are shown in Figure 5.8. Numerical results of the functional value and the adjoint variables are

$$\begin{aligned} J(X,u) &= -1.46950, \\ X(t_f) &= (1.4, 1.61636, 290.0), \\ \lambda(0) &= (1.09275, -0.114479, -0.0399786), \\ \lambda(t_f) &= (1.14376, 0.0, -0.476751). \end{aligned}$$

The solution shows a strong decrease in capital and consumption. This effect can be avoided by imposing suitable control and state constraints; cf. the following scenario.

5.5.2.6 *Finite Horizon: Control and State Constraints*

This scenario treats the boundary conditions

$$T(0) = 292,\ K(0) = 1.4,\ M(0) = 2; \quad T(t_f) = 290,\ K(t_f) = 1.3.$$

Motivated by Figure 5.8, we impose control and state constraints,

$$0.895 \leq C(t) \leq 0.95, \; K(t) \geq 1.1, \; M(t) \leq 1.8, \quad t_s = 10 \leq t \leq t_f,$$

for which we obtain the numerical results

$$\begin{array}{lcl} J(X,u) & = & -1.60049, \\ X(t_f) & = & (1.3, 1.65261, 290.0), \\ \lambda(0) & = & (0.992006, -0.254613, -0.0320533), \\ \lambda(t_f) & = & (1.12260, 0.0, -0.511674). \end{array}$$

The consumption C displayed in Figure 5.9 has three boundary arcs, where the constraints $0.895 \leq C(t) \leq 0.95$ become active. The constraint $K(t) \geq 1.1$ is binding towards the end of the planning period. The associated adjoint variable λ_K is continuous though jumps are permitted according to the jump condition (5.37). This is due to the fact that this state constraint is of order $q = 1$, cf. Hartl, et al. (1995). The state constraint $M(t) \leq 1.8$, $t \geq 10$, of order $q = 2$ becomes active at $t = t_s = 10$ and has a boundary arc in an intermediate interval $[t_1, t_2]$. Note that the adjoint variable $\lambda_K(t)$ has jumps at t_s and t_1, t_2.

5.5.2.7 Finite Horizon: State Constraint for T

We take the boundary conditions

$$T(0) = 292, \; K(0) = 1.4, \; M(0) = 2.0; \quad K(t_f) = 1.3$$

and try to substantially decrease the initial temperature $T(0) = 292$ by imposing the state constraint

$$T(t) \leq 289 \quad \text{for} \quad t_s = 10 \leq t \leq t_f.$$

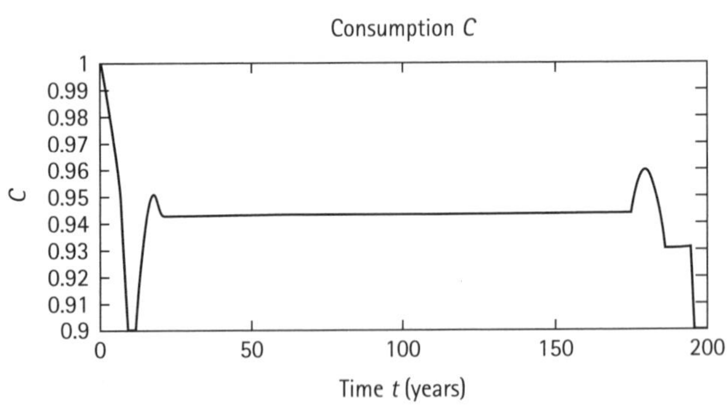

FIGURE 5.9 Finite horizon $t_f = 200$: abatement $A_c = 1.21 \times 10^{-3}$, $T(0) = 292$, $T(t_f) = 290$, constraints $M(t) \leq 1.8$, $K(t) \geq 1.1$ and $0.895 \leq C(t) \leq 0.95$ for $t \geq 10$. Consumption C.

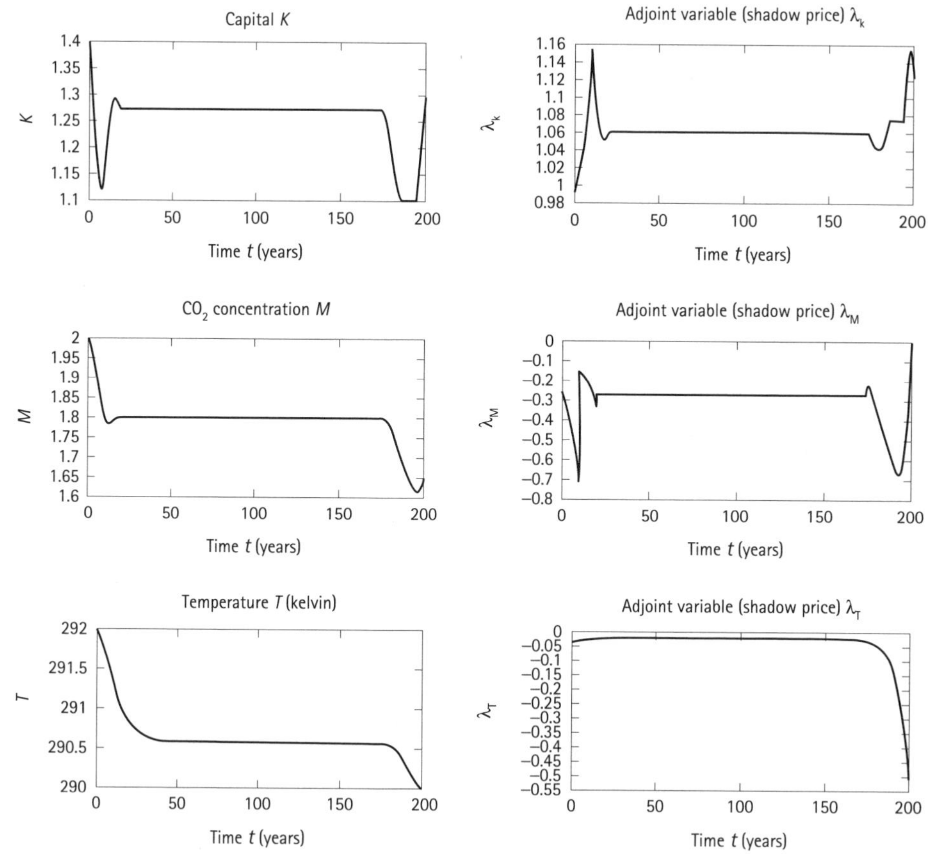

FIGURE 5.10 Finite horizon $t_f = 200$, abatement $A_c = 1.21 \times 10^{-3}$, $T(0) = 292$, $T(t_f) = 290$, constraints $M(t) \le 1.8$, $K(t) \ge 1.1$ and $0.895 \le C(t) \le 0.95$ for $t \ge 10$. *Top row*: capital K and adjoint λ_K. *Middle row*: CO_2 concentration M and adjoint λ_M. *Bottom row*: temperature T and adjoint λ_T.

We find the numerical results

$$\begin{aligned} J(X,u) &= -2.21118, \\ X(t_f) &= (1.3, 1.50412, 289.0), \\ \lambda(0) &= (-0.865165, -0.563912, -0.0788248), \\ \lambda(t_f) &= (1.10595, 0.0, -0.432660). \end{aligned}$$

Figure 5.12 shows that the state constraint for T becomes active at $t = t_s = 10$ and on a boundary arc $[t_1, t_2]$. The adjoint variable $\lambda_K(t)$ has jumps at $t = 10, t_1, t_2$ in agreement with the jump condition (5.37). Since the state constraint has order $q = 3$, the junctions to the boundary arc are non-analytic which, however, can hardly be detected from the numerical solution.

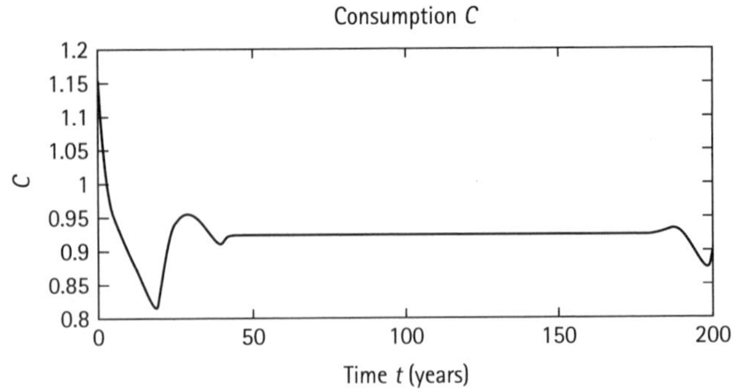

FIGURE 5.11 Finite horizon $t_f = 200$, abatement $A_c = 1.21 \times 10^{-3}$ and state constraint $T(t) \leq 289$ for $t \geq t_s = 10$. Consumption C.

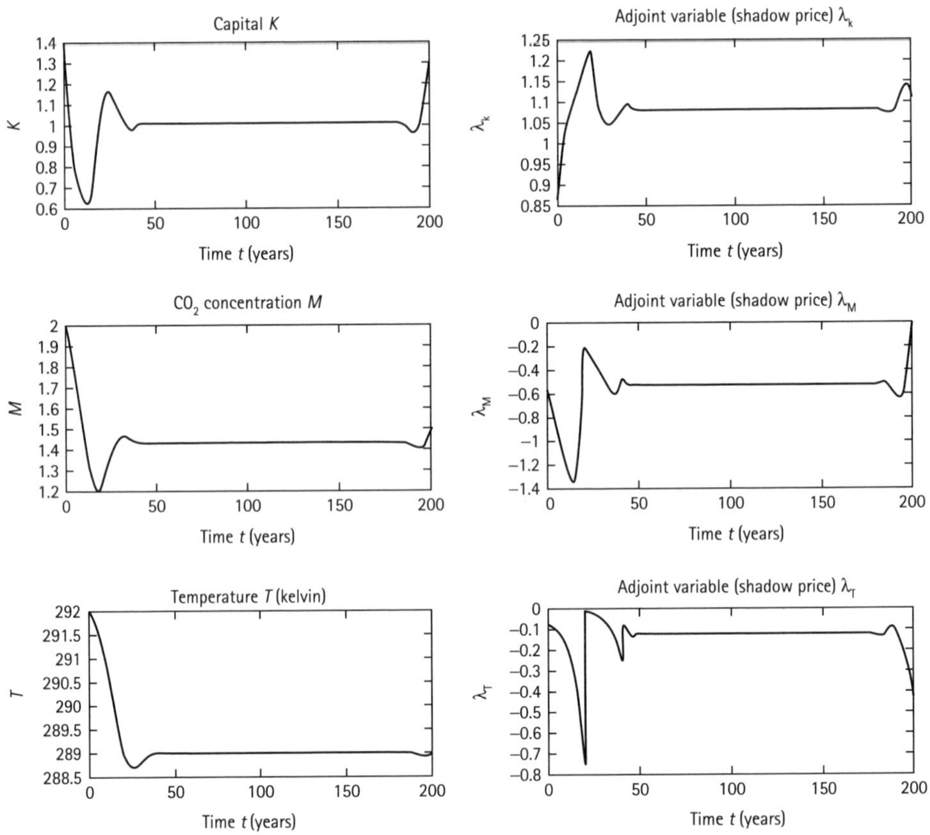

FIGURE 5.12 Finite horizon $t_f = 200$, abatement $A_c = 1.21 \times 10^{-3}$ and state constraint $T(t) \leq 289 \forall\ t \geq 10$. *Top row*: capital K and adjoint variable λ_K. *Middle row*: CO_2 concentration M adjoint variable λ_M. *Bottom row*: temperature T and adjoint variable λ_T.

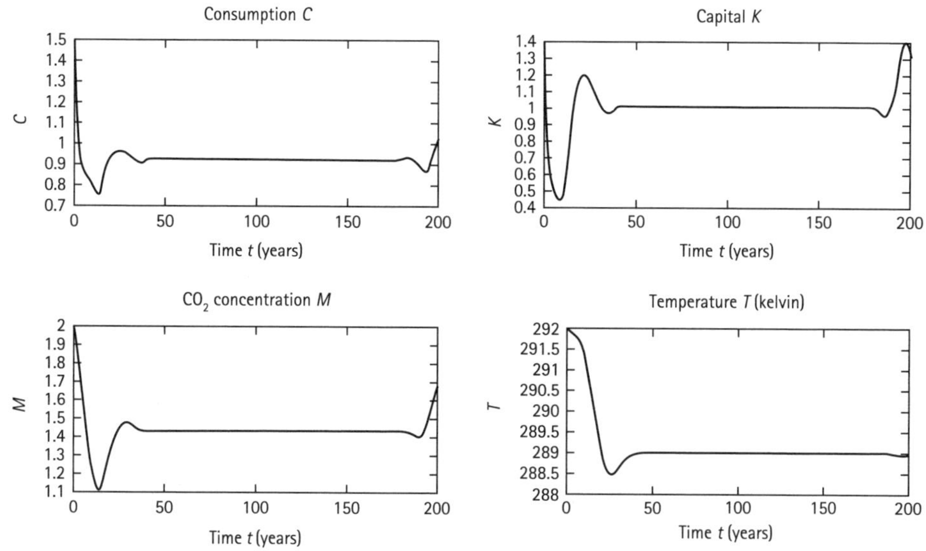

FIGURE 5.13 Finite horizon $t_f = 200$, abatement $A_c = 1.21 \times 10^{-3}$, state constraint $T(t) \leq 289 \; \forall \, t \geq 10$ and delay $d = 5$ in (5.11). *Top row*: consumption C and capital K. *Bottom row*: CO_2 concentration M and temperature T.

5.5.2.8 Finite Horizon: State Constraint for T and Delay d = 5

Now consider the delay $d = 5$ (years) in the dynamic equation (5.11) of the temperature. The discretization approach in Göllmann, et al. (2009) yields the numerical results

$$
\begin{aligned}
J(X,u) &= -2.61229, \\
X(t_f) &= (1.3, 1.67948, 289.0), \\
\lambda(0) &= (0.667956, -1.29567, -0.141026), \\
\lambda(t_f) &= (0.969177, 0.0, -0.538238).
\end{aligned}
$$

The solution is very similar to that in Figure 5.12; the delayed solution exhibits a smaller initial decrease in temperature and large increase of M at the end of the planning period.

5.5.2.9 Finite Horizon: Penalty Functional

We make an attempt for adjusting the temperature during the control process by maximizing the penalty functional (5.18):

$$
\max J_T(X,u) = \int_0^{t_f} e^{-(\rho-n)t} \ln C \, dt - c_T \int_0^{t_f} (T(t) - T_c)^2 \, dt \quad (c_T > 0).
$$

We have to impose a lower bound for the capital; otherwise the capital tends to zero. For convenience, we also consider an upper bound for the consumption and thus

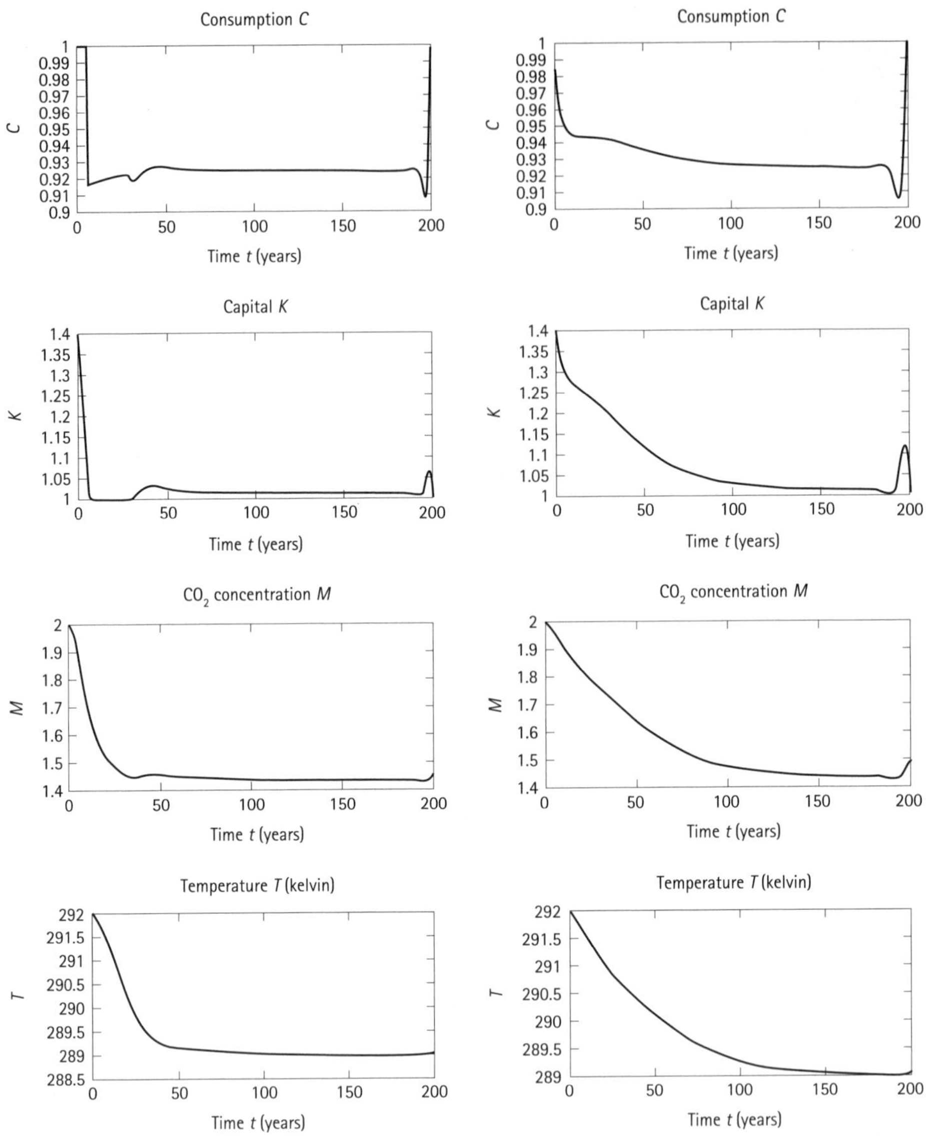

FIGURE 5.14 Finite horizon $t_f = 200$, abatement $A_c = 1.21 \times 10^{-3}$, $T(0) = 292$ and penalty (5.18). *Left column*: penalty $c_T = 0.01$. *Right column*: penalty $c_T = 0.001$. Consumption C, capital K, CO_2 concentration M and temperature T.

impose the constraints

$$C(t) \leq 1, \quad K(t) \geq 1 \quad \text{for all } t \in [0, t_f].$$

We choose the initial temperature $T(0) = 292$ and try to get near the desired temperature $T_c = 289$ by choosing suitable penalty parameters c_T. In Figure 5.14, the solutions for the penalty parameters $c_T = 0.01$ (left column) and $c_T = 0.001$ (right column) are compared. The left column in Figure 5.14 shows that the aim of reaching the desired temperature $T_c = 289$ is quite well attained but goes at the expense of a decreasing consumption and capital level. A larger penalty does not significantly improve on this result, since the state constraint $K(t) \geq 1$ is an obstacle to further improvement.

The values of the cost functionals are

$$\begin{array}{lcll} c_T = 0.01 & : & J(X,u) = -1.87843, & J_T(X,u) = -3.00250, \\ c_T = 0.001 & : & J(X,u) = -1.64061, & J_T(X,u) = -1.86391. \end{array}$$

5.5.3 Social Optimum with Control *u*=(*C*,*A*)

5.5.3.1 *Infinite Horizon:* $T(0) = 292$

Again, we consider the initial condition

$$T(0) = 292,\ K(0) = 1.4,\ M(0) = 2.0.$$

Using both controls C and A the infinite horizon solution converges to the steady state in Table 5.3 and thus terminates slightly above the pre-industrial temperature $T_o = 288$.

The controls C and A are shown in Figure 5.16, while the state and adjoint variables are depicted in Figure 5.15. We obtain the numerical results

$$\begin{array}{rcl} X(\infty) & = & (1.7969353, 1.3174399, 288.445913), \\ \lambda(0) & = & (1.0547562, -0.059005094, -0.025764200), \\ \lambda(\infty) & = & (1.0266800, -0.018229301, -0.0040479951). \end{array}$$

5.5.3.2 *Finite Horizon:* $T(0) = 292$ *and Terminal Constraint* $X(t_f) = X_s$

Finally, we study the case of a social optimum using both controls $u = (C, A)$. We prescribe the steady state in Table 5.4 as terminal state. Hence, we choose the initial and terminal conditions

$$T(0) = 292,\ K(0) = 1.4,\ M(0) = 2.0; \quad X(t_f) = (1.7996353, 1.3774399, 288.44591).$$

Moreover, the following upper bound is imposed on the abatement control:

$$A(t) \leq 0.003, \quad \forall\, 0 \leq t \leq t_f.$$

We obtain the following numerical results:

$$\begin{array}{lcl} J(X,u) & = & -1.2601348, \\ \lambda(0) & = & (1.14549, -0.0612496, -0.0268832), \\ \lambda(t_f) & = & (-1.02668, -0.0182325, -0.00404918). \end{array}$$

Figure 5.17 displays the control and state variables for the initial temperature $T(0) = 292$; it clearly reflects the fact that the maximum abatement is needed for at least 13

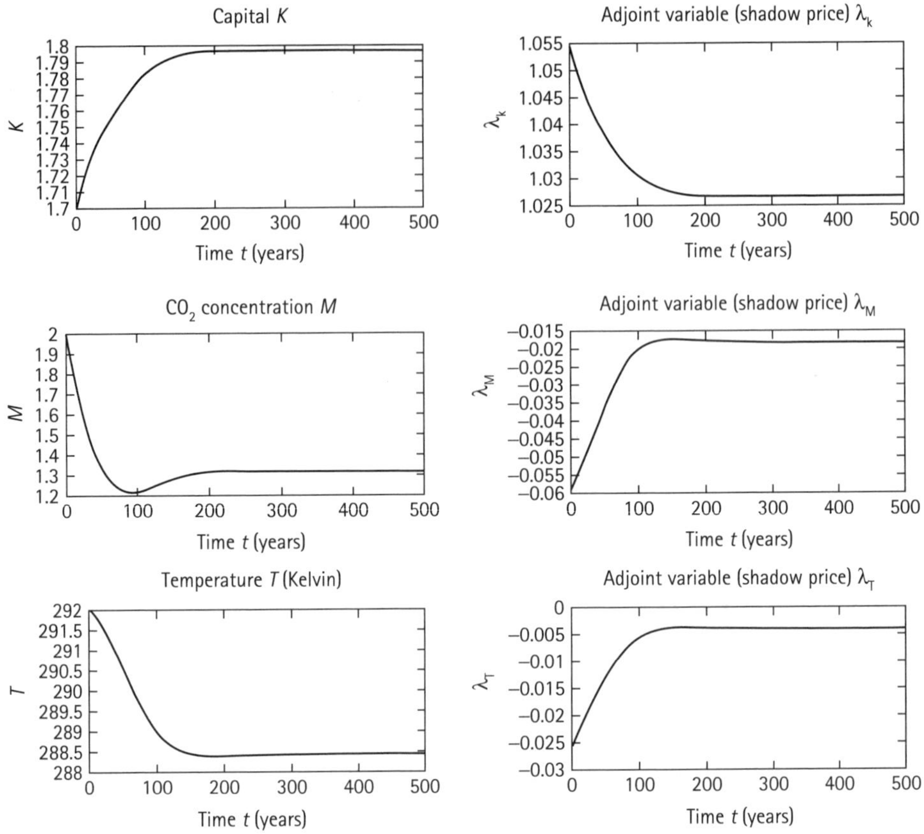

FIGURE 5.15 Infinite horizon, social optimum, $T(0) = 292$. *Top row*: capital K and adjoint variable λ_K. *Middle row*: CO_2 concentration M and adjoint variable λ_M. *Bottom row*: temperature T and adjoint variable λ_T.

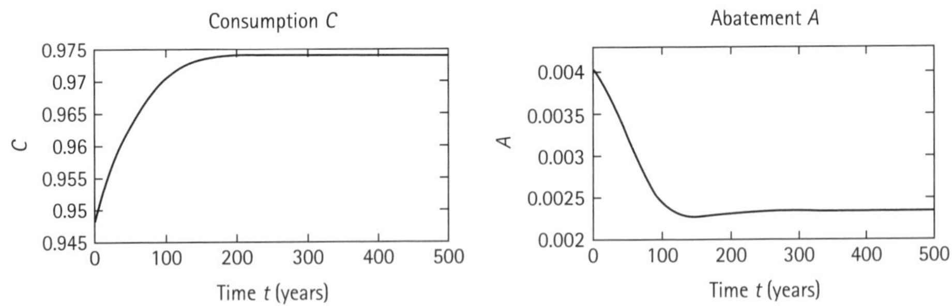

FIGURE 5.16 Infinite horizon, social optimum, $T(0) = 292$. Consumption C and abatement A

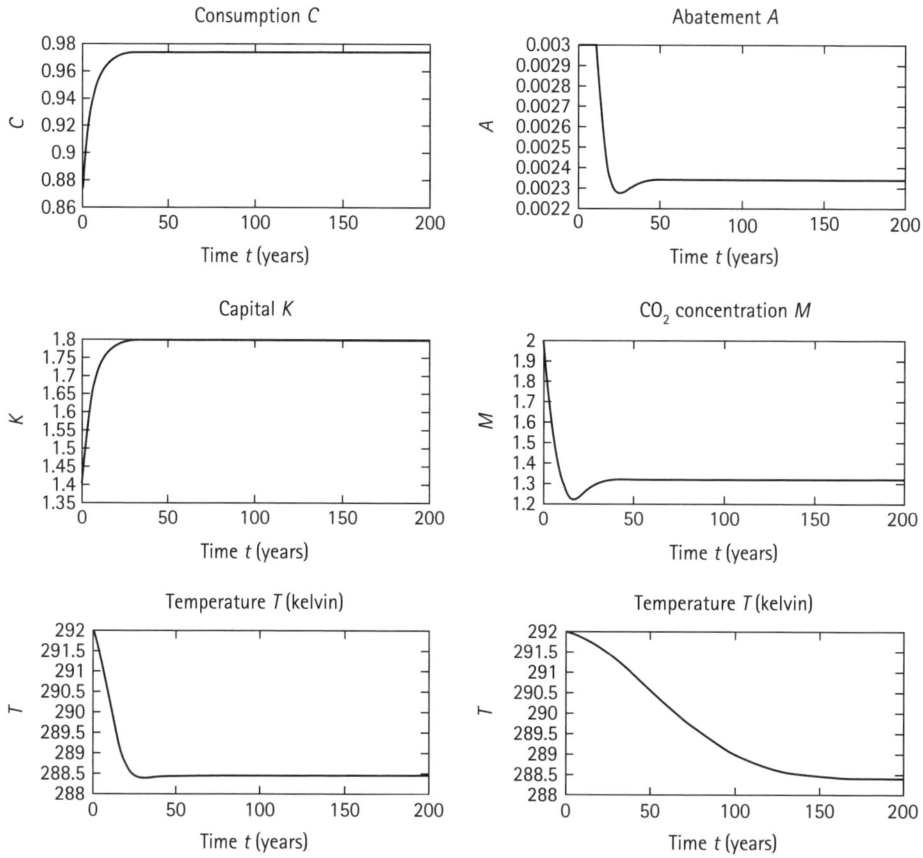

FIGURE 5.17 Finite horizon $t_f = 200$, social optimum with control $u = (C, A)$. *Top row*: consumption C and abatement A. *Middle row*: capital K and CO_2 concentration M. *Bottom row*: (a) temperature T, (b) temperature T in infinite-horizon solution.

years to substantially decrease the temperature T and CO_2 concentration M. However, it is remarkable that the decrease in temperature is more pronounced in the finite-horizon solution than in the infinite-horizon solution displayed in Figure 5.17, bottom row (b).

5.5.3.3 Finite Horizon: Terminal Constraint $X(t_f) = X_s$ and Delay $d = 5$

Now we introduce the delay $d = 5$ (years) into the dynamic equation (5.11) of the temperature T. Moreover, a more stringent constraint for the consumption C is imposed:

$$0.95 \leq C(t) \leq 0.975 \quad \forall\, 0 \leq t \leq t_f.$$

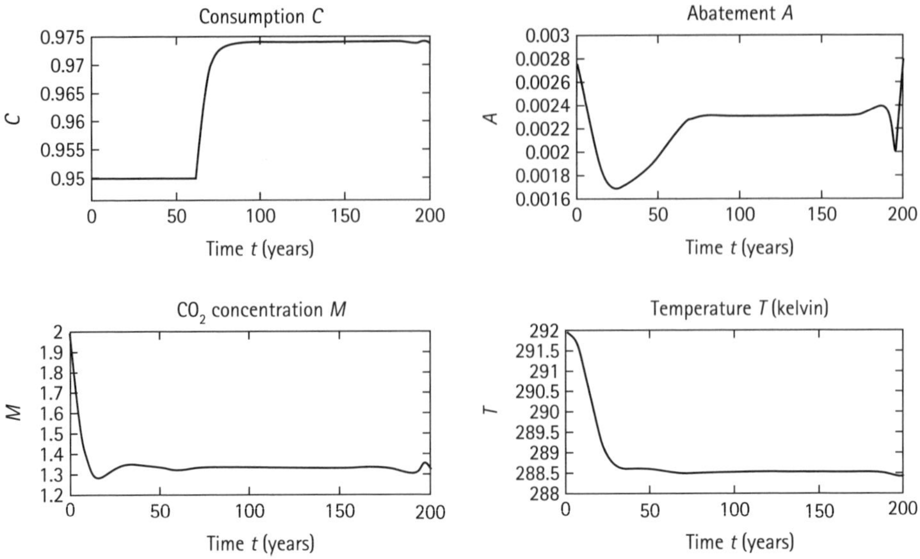

FIGURE 5.18 Finite horizon $t_f = 200$, social optimum with control $u = (C, A)$ and delay $d = 5$. *Top row*: consumption C and abatement A. *Bottom row*: CO_2 concentration M and temperature T.

We get the following numerical results:

$$
\begin{aligned}
J(X,u) &= -1.395618, \\
\lambda(0) &= (4.45221, -0.142163, -0.111959), \\
\lambda(t_f) &= (1.02688, -0.0264435, -0.00746241).
\end{aligned}
$$

Figure 5.18 displays the two control and state variables M, T for the initial temperature $T(0) = 292$. Due to the more restrictive lower bound for the consumption C, this bound becomes active for a rather large initial interval. It is remarkable that a feasible solutions exist that keep the consumption at a high level while achieving the terminal low temperature $T(t_f) = 288.446$. The abatement control A takes smaller values than the non-delayed abatement control in Figure 5.17.

5.6 Conclusion

In this chapter, we study the canonical model of growth and climate change as put forward by Nordhaus' work (Nordhaus and Boyer, 2000; Nordhaus, 2008) and explore extensions of the basic model with respect to different scenarios. Policy options to mitigate climate change are often constrained by political events, lack of coalition formation, and the countries' political and economic means. In our paper, we explore a large number of scenarios of how mitigation policies could be pursued. We study the implication of infinite and finite horizon models, investigate the BAU scenario (business as usual scenario with low level abatement), and contrast it with an optimal abatement policy for infinite and finite horizon. In all scenarios, we have computed control, state and adjoint variables, the latter being used for the verification of the Maximum Principle.

In finite-horizon scenarios, we explore the implications of terminal constraints of the state variable and consider the impacts of state constraints (such as CO_2 and temperature constraints) on abatement policies and consumption. Imposing such constraints allows us to find feasible control strategies for keeping the temperature and CO_2 concentration at low levels while preserving acceptable levels of consumption and capital. We also study another approach of keeping the temperature at a desirable level by putting suitable quadratic penalties on temperature deviations. The numerical analysis of these scenarios takes advantage of modern numerical techniques for solving constrained optimal control problems. In particular, the constrained scenarios allow us to explore the implications for mitigation policies arising from the Kyoto Protocol (CO_2 constraint) and the Copenhagen agreement (temperature constraint). It is in this sense that we want to understand the exploration of our suggested different scenarios as guidance for different policy options.

Notes

1. The issue of parameter uncertainty in such models is extensively explored by Bréchet, Camacho, and Veliov in this volume.

References

Aseev, S. M., and Kryazhimskiy, A. V. (2004). The Pontryagin maximum principle and transversality condition for a class of optimal control problems with infinite time horizons. *SIAM Journal of Control Optimization*, 43, 1094–1119.

Aseev, S. M., and Kryazhimskiy, A. V. (2007). The Pontryagin maximum principle and economic growth. *Proceedings of the Steklov Institute of Mathematics*, 257(1), 1–255.

Betts, J. T. (2010). *Practical Methods for Optimal Control and Estimation Using Nonlinear Programming*, 2nd ed. Advances in Design and Control. Philadelphia: SIAM.

Bréchet, T., Camacho, C., and Veliov, V. M. (2014). Adaptive model-predictive climate policies in a multi-country setting, this volume.

Büskens, C., and Maurer, H. (2010). SQP-methods for solving optimal control problems with control and state constraints: Adjoint variables, sensitivity analysis and real-time control. *Journal of Computational and Applied Mathematics*, 120, 85–108.

Crespo Cuaresma, J., Palokangas, T., and Tarasyev, A. (2010). *Dynamic Systems, Economic Growth, and the Environment*. Heidelberg and New York: Springer.

Deutsch, C., Hall, M. G., Bradford, D. F., and Keller, K. (2002). Detecting a potential collapse of the north atlantic thermohaline circulation: Implications for the design of an ocean observation system. Mimeo, Princeton University.

Fourer, R., Gay, D. M., and Kernighan, B. W. (1993). *AMPL: A Modeling Language for Mathematical Programming*. Independence, KY: Duxbury Press, Brooks-Cole.

Göllmann, L., Kern, D., and Maurer, H. (2009). Optimal control problems with delays in state and control and mixed control-state constraints. *Optimal Control Applications and Methods*, 30, 341–365.

Greiner, A., Gruene, L., and Semmler, W. (2010). Growth and climate change: Threshold and multiple equilibria. In J. Crespo Cuaresma, T. Palokangas, and A. Tarasyev (eds.), *Dynamic Systems, Economic Growth, and the Environment*, pp. 63–78. Heidelberg and New York: Springer.

Hartl, R. F., Sethi, S. P., and Vickson, R. G. (1995). A survey of the maximum principles for optimal control problems with state constraints. *SIAM Review*, 37, 181–218.

Hestenes, M. (1966). *Calculus of Variations and Optimal Control Theory*. New York: John Wiley & Sons.

Keller, K., Bolkerb, M. B., and Bradford, D. F. (2004). Uncertain climate thresholds and optimal economic growth. *Journal of Environmental Economics and Management*, 48(1), 723–741.

Keller, K., Tan, K., Morel, F. M., and Bradford, D. F. (2000). Preserving the ocean circulation: Implications for the climate policy. *Climate Change*, 47, 17–43.

Kunkel, P., and von dem Hagen, O. (2000). Numerical solution of infinite-horizon optimal control problems. *Computational Economics*, 16, 189–205.

Lykina, V. (2010). *Beiträge zur Theorie der Optimalsteuerungsprobleme mit unendlichem Zeithorizont*. Dissertation, Bandenburgische Technische Universität Cottbus, Cottbus, Germany.

Lykina, V., Pickenhain, S., and Wagner, M. (2008). Different interpretations of the improper integral objective in an infinite horizon control problem. *Journal of Mathematical Analysis and Applications, 340*, 498–510.

Maurer, H. (1979). On the minimum principle for optimal control problems with state constraints. Rechenzentrum der Universität Münster, Report no. 41, Münster, Germany.

Maurer, H., Preuss, J. J., and Semmler, W. (2013). Optimal control of growth and climate change—Exploration of scenarios. In J. Crespo Cuaresma, T. Palokangas, and A. Tarasyev (eds.), *Green Growth and Sustainable Development*, pp. 113–139. Berlin: Springer.

Michel, P. (1982). On the transversality conditions in infinite horizon optimal control problems. *Econometrica*, 50, 975–985.

Nordhaus, W. (2008). *The Question of Balance*. New Haven, CT: Yale University Press.

Nordhaus, W. D., and Boyer, J. (2010). *Warming the World. Economic Models of Global Warming*. Cambridge, MA: MIT Press.

Pontryagin, L. S., Boltyanski, V. G., Gramkrelidze, R. V., and Miscenko, E. F. (1964). *The Mathematical Theory of Optimal Processes*. Moscow: Fitzmatgiz. English translation: New York: Pergamon Press.

Preuss, J. J. (2011). *Optimale Steuerung eines ökonomischen Modells des Klimawandels*. Diploma Thesis, Universität Münster, Institut für Numerische und Angewandte Mathematik.

Roedel, W. (2011). *Private communication*.

Roedel, W., and Wagner, T. (2011). *Physik unserer Umwelt: Die Atmosphäre.* Berlin, Heidelberg: Springer.

Sethi, S. P., and Thompson, G. L. (2000). *Optimal Control Theory: Applications to Management Science and Economics*, 2nd ed., New York: Kluwer Academic.

Wächter, A., and Biegler, L. T. (2006). On the Implementation of an Interior-Point Filter Line-Search Algorithm for Large-Scale Nonlinear Programming. *Mathematical Programming, 106*(1), 25–57; cf. Ipopt home page (C. Laird and A. Wächter): https://projects.coin-or.org/Ipopt.

CHAPTER 6

ADAPTIVE MODEL-PREDICTIVE CLIMATE POLICIES IN A MULTICOUNTRY SETTING

THIERRY BRÉCHET, CARMEN CAMACHO, AND VLADIMIR M. VELIOV

6.1 Introduction

Once upon a time there was a world in which people were refusing to see that their world was changing–let's say because of global warming. The main wish of these many people was to keep on doing their business-as-usual (BAU). For sure, the best strategy in the changing world would be for them to learn as much as possible about the expected changes (all of them) and to adopt the optimal behavior with respect to this large set of knowledge. But implementing this optimal strategy was beyond their force or skill. The question we raise in this chapter is not to define what would be the optimal strategy from the whole society's standpoint (which is already widely explored in the literature) but to highlight possible alternative trajectories, considering that agents are always rational, but sometimes stubborn, lazy, or myopic. Stubborn because they always refuse to change their view. Lazy because they revise their view but only after a while (or after some evidence). Myopic because they are more or less short-sighted about how the world will look like in the future. The objective of this chapter is to explore the consequences of such behaviors in the context of global warming. In this purpose, we develop an innovative theoretical framework to redefine more realistic trajectories of the economies that are fully rational, in contrast with the BAU scenario defined in integrated assessment models in the current literature.

Our contribution relies on the integrated assessment modeling of the economy and the climate. Integrated means that feedbacks in both ways are considered: economic activity generates greenhouse gases emissions that cause global warming, and global warming affects the economy with productivity and welfare losses. Integrated assessment models (IAMs) allow to implement a dynamic cost–benefit analysis and to determine the optimal policies. Basically, policies in IAMs consist in choosing the path for productive investment and emission abatement that maximize some objective function, like country's welfare. It is important to stress that welfare, in IAMs, is expressed as consumption net of climate damages. It is indeed *green consumption* that is maximized.

To to develop this new framework we use the concepts of *model predictive control* and *adaptive behavior*, and we combine them into the IAM framework. Ideas from the *model predictive control* (see, e.g., Grüne and Pannek, 2011) are employed owing to the uncertainties about the future environment and its impact on the economy that the agents persistently face. Adaptive learning is involved to take into account the improvement (with time and/or experience) in the measurements quality and in the agents' knowledge about the environmental-economic dynamics.

The chapter is organized as follows. In Section 6.2, integrated assessment modeling and how it is used for the climate change analysis is presented with some details. This section gathers a condensed explanation of the very concept of IAM, a benchmark model, and a survey of the many uses of IMAs in the literature. In Section 6.3 we present the general model describing the dynamics of a multiagent economic-environmental system that will be used in the chapter. The concepts of "model predictive rational behavior" and "adaptive behavior" are presented in Sections 6.4 and 6.5. The adaptive behaviors considered in this chapter will concern the knowledge about climate damages (a better knowledge with evidence for climate change) and the discount factor (a decrease in the discount factor as wealth increases). Some numerical experiments are provided in Section 6.6 with a two-country setting (the world is roughly divided into Organisation for Economic Co-operation and Development [OECD] and non-OECD countries).

6.2 Integrated Assessment of Global Warming

The purpose of this first section is threefold: (1) to provide the reader with some elements on the history of applied IAMs and its economic rationale, (2) to sketch a benchmark model, and (3) to survey the wide variety of uses of applied integrated assessment models in the literature. This will allow us to better gauge the importance of each contribution we shall introduce later in the chapter.

6.2.1 What Is Integrated Assessment?

Although the IPCC reports (1990, 1995, 2001, 2007) had been repeatedly calling for sharp cuts in greenhouse gas (GHG) emissions (minus 50 to 80 % at the world level, immediately), they never attempted to balance the costs and benefits of such policies, as initially suggested by Nordhaus in 1984.[1] Nonetheless, balancing costs and benefit has been a prominent methodological and normative contribution of economics for many years. Why not for climate change? Although cost–benefit raises several methodological and theoretical challenges (and it is far beyond the scope of this chapter to tackle them; see Pearce et al. (2006) for a comprehensive analysis of CBA analysis and policy applications) it remains a comprehensive framework to understand what *should* be done, and what *could* be achieved.

Starting in the early 1990s, some aggregative models were developed to analyze the consequences of economic activity on GHGs concentration and how this concentration may harm the economy (see Rotmans, 1990; Nordhaus, 1992, 1993a; Gaskins et al., 1993; Manne and Richels, 1992; Yang, 1993). These are the very first IAMs, so called because they model the economy and its interplay with climate. Economic activity generates GHGs that cause global warming, and global warming provokes physical damages that have an economic cost. IAMs seek at maximizing intertemporal welfare by taking these two components into account. Indeed, it boils down to a standard cost–benefit analysis, but applied to a worldwide and long-term issue.

Basically, the economic part of IAMs is made of a dynamic general equilibrium model of the economy. A policymaker is assumed to optimally choose consumption/saving path that maximizes the discounted sum of the utility, taking into account how physical capital evolves with time and taking the adverse impacts of climate change into account. Toward this purpose, IAMs make use of damage functions that translate temperature increase into economic losses. Besides, the policymaker knows the flow of GHGs emissions due to economic activity, how they convert into concentration in the atmosphere, and how this concentration affects the average temperature of Earth.

In sum, there exists a closed loop between polluting economic human activities, how these affect the climate, and how climate change impacts on the economy. What causes global warming is not the flow of GHGs but their accumulation in the atmosphere at a stock. So IAMs are necessarily intertermporal optimization models. They endogenously determine not only the flow of GHGs but also emission abatement efforts and the path of productive investment.

6.2.2 A Benchmark IAM

The benchmark IAM is based on the DICE model (Dynamic Integrated Climate-Economy model) built up by Nordhaus (1993a, 1993b). DICE is a stylized cost–benefit analysis framework to optimally decide on the trajectory of GHG emissions and capital accumulation at the world level. The model represents a central-planner problem that maximizes the discounted utility taking into account economic and climatic constraints and their interconnection. The economic constraints are those of the Ramsey model.[2] Output is given by a Cobb-Douglas production function, with the peculiarity that a damage function enters multiplying the formulation:

$$Q(t) = \Omega(\tau)A(t)K(t)^{\gamma}P(t)^{1-\gamma},$$

where A is a technology index, K physical capital, and P population. γ is the elasticity of output to capital and Ω is the aforementioned damage function. Damage is a function of average temperature τ, and $1-\Omega$ is the percentage of foregone production.

Emissions of GHGs flow from the global economic activity (Q) with an exogenous emission factor intensity $(\sigma(t))$, but taking into account emission abatement efforts, denoted by $\mu \in (0,1)$. Actual emissions are thus given by:

$$E(t) = (1-\mu(t))\sigma(t)Q(t),$$

The concentration of GHGs in the atmosphere (M) is given by past concentration plus new emissions net of the natural decay rate:

$$M(t) = \beta E(t) + (1-\delta_M)M(t-1),$$

with β the atmospheric retention ratio and δ_M the rate of GHGs absorbed in deep ocean. Then, an equation is added to give the temperature increase. Nordhaus considers three different layers: the atmosphere, the mixed layer of the oceans, and the deep oceans. The main link is the damage function, with makes the retroaction between climate and the economy. The damage function represents the economic losses for a given a temperature increase. It is an increasing convex function of global temperature increase:

$$D(t) = \alpha_1 (T(t)/3)^{\alpha_2},$$

with $\alpha_1, \alpha_2 \in \mathbb{R}^+$. The last piece of the model is the abatement cost function. Abatement costs have been extensively studied. This function is thus deemed as more reliable. A 50% decrease in GHGs intensity would cost 1% of the world output. The total abatement cost function is:

$$C(t) = \beta_1 \mu(t)^{\beta_2} Q(t).$$

where $\mu(t) \in (0,1)$ is the abatement rate and β_1, β_2 are positive constants. Nordhaus uses the DICE model to compare BAU (defined as $\mu(t) = 0, \forall t$) with different emission stabilization scenarios and the optimal policy. The optimal policy leads to a 10% reduction of carbon emissions from 2005, inducing a temperature decrease of 0.2°C by 2100 with respect to the BAU scenario.

6.2.3 On the Many Uses of Applied IAMs

Starting from Nordhaus, IAMs have evolved introducing more realistic economic behaviors or outcomes, trying to escape from the basic comparison between BAU (no climate policy, myopic agent) and the socially optimal solution (perfect foresight), because none of them is realistic. In this section, our objective is not to provide an exhaustive survey of IAMs but to review some examples of interesting extensions such as the inclusion of the regional dimension, models with a better description of the power sector, research and development (R&D) behaviors, and coalition formation issues. A recent survey of these approaches is provided by Stanton et al. (2009).

A direction along that IAMs were developed was geography, and depending on the paper, geography is understood as space or as the union of economic regions. Let us first mention the Integrated Model to Assess the Greenhouse Effect (IMAGE) by Rotmans (1990). In its first version, IMAGE was a model integrating three clusters: the energy system, the terrestrial environment system, and the atmosphere–ocean system. The second version of the model included a geographical scale, rare at that time. Geography was a grid of 0.5 by 0.5 degrees, making possible the biophysical modeling of land cover, its history, carbon cycle, nutrients, climate, etc. Still, all macroeconomic drivers were exogenous inputs to the model.

In 1996, Nordhaus and Yang extended the DICE model by producing a regional model, RICE (Regional Integrated Climate-economic Model). In this model, the decision is taken at the national level, and the authors consider different levels of coordination among nations. They propose three different scenarios to study how nations could deal with climate change: market policies (i.e., no-control on emission), cooperative policies (countries act as a unique decision maker), and non-cooperative policies (in that countries act in their own interests ignoring the externality create on the other countries). These scenarios were labeled "Business-as Usual," "Cooperative" and "Nash equilibrium" scenarios, respectively. This terminology will be widely used later on in the literature.

Taking DICE or RICE as benchmarks, many authors searched to refine their modeling by incorporating detailed descriptions of the energy sector, allowing for a plethora of mitigation policies, etc. Edenhofer et al. (2005) introduce learning by doing in R&D, allowing for investment in R&D in different sectors. In the long term, improving energy efficiency of existing technologies becomes too costly to be kept as the major mitigation policy. Instead, they find that a backstop technology with the potential of learning by doings the best option to protect climate at a lesser cost. They put forward Carbon Capturing and Sequestration (CCS) techniques to reduce the cost of the transition from a fossil-fuel based system to a system based on renewable resources.

Bosetti et al. (2006) build the WITCH model (World Induced Technical Change Hybrid Model). WITCH is a multiregional neoclassical growth model in that technological progress is endogenous that is, the price of new vintage of capital and R&D investment are endogenous. The model is hybrid because the energy sector (a key sector) is modeled in great detail, separating electric and non-electric uses of energy, with seven power generation technologies and allowing the use of multiple fuels. The authors account for seven channels for regional interaction. Let us mention among them the first, that is the fact that both R&D and consumption decisions are affected by energy prices worldwide. Other interactions are learning by doing, R&D spillovers, international trade of oil and gas, and emissions trading.

The MARKAL-TIMES family of models aims at better describing the technology options, in particular in the power and industry sectors. They are technico-economic models. The modeler needs to introduce technology characterizations and costs, resource availability, environmental constraints, services demands and macroeconomic indicators. In this sense, MARKAL-TIMES is much more detailed than other IAMs. In TIMES, the quantities and prices of the various commodities are in equilibrium, that is, their prices and quantities in each time period are such that the suppliers produce exactly the quantities demanded by the consumers. This equilibrium has the property that the total surplus (consumers plus producers surpluses) is maximized. There also exists a World multi regional Markal-Times model (Kanudia et al., 2005). Notice that MARKAL models can be developed at all decision levels from wide regions of the world with several countries, to single countries, regions, counties, cities or even villages.

Another kind of model is MERGE (Manne and Richels, 2005). MERGE is a model for estimating the regional and global effects of GHG reductions. The model is flexible enough to explore alternative views on a wide range of contentious issues, such as costs of abatement, damages from climate change, valuation, and discounting. The model covers the domestic and international economy, energy-related emissions of GHGs, non-energy emissions of GHGs, global climate change, and market and nonmarket damages. Each region's domestic economy is viewed as a Ramsey-Solow model of optimal long-term economic growth. Price-responsiveness is introduced through a top-down production function where output depends upon the inputs of capital, labor, and energy bundle. Separate technologies are defined for each source of electric and nonelectric energy.

Two specific problems in the climate issue are that, first, there exists no supranational authority entitled to implement the optimal policy and, second, emission reduction must be worldwide to be effective against global warming. As a result, a wide international agreement among the countries is required, and such an agreement can be found only on a voluntary basis. This is the issue of coalition formation raised by Eyckmans and Tulkens (2003) with the CWS integrated assessment model: that international agreements are feasible, and how to implement them? In other words, between Nash and the socially optimal solution, what international agreement could be achieved? Bréchet et al. (2011) extend this analysis by comparing the policy implications of the two competing theoretical streams available to date, namely, the cooperative and non-cooperative settings.[3]

DICE has also been developed in another direction. Rather than pursuing the perfection of climate modeling, the power sector, etc., Greiner et al. (2010), Maurer et al. (2012), or Brechet et al. (2011) opt for a canonical DICE. In these canonical models, the link between economic activity and the earth's climate is simpler than in the full version of DICE. Although this link is weakened, other pieces of the model are reinforced: Maurer et al. (2012) improve the description of the temperature dynamics, that is crucial to study the effect of terminal constraints on temperature and concentration on optimal decisions on abatement and consumption. On the other hand, Brechet et al. (2011) diversify the type of policymakers, that ranges from optimal planners to planners who neglect any environmental change.

The quest for precision and realism is necessary and still has many venues for future research. Indeed, many processes involved in climate change are uncertain at best. Nevertheless, the climate projections, predictions and policy recommendations issued from IAMs need to be as precise as possible to guide risk managers and policymakers (for a survey on this issue, see Keller and Nicholas, 2012).

6.3 The Dynamics of a Multiagent Economic-Environmental System

Let the global economy consists of n agents (regions, countries, or groups of countries) and let $x_i(t)$ denote the economic state of the ith agent at time t (this may include physical capital, human capital, and other dynamic stock-variables, so that x_i is a single or multidimensional vector). Let $v_i(t)$ be the policy vector of the ith agent at time t, that may include investments, abatement, and other components. The economic agents operate in a common environment, the state of that may influence the productivity or the utility of the agents. The state of the environment at time t will be represented by a vector $y(t)$, whose components can be the concentrations of GHGs in different sectors of the environment and the average world temperature. Let the economy of the ith agent be driven by the equation

$$\dot{x}_i(t) = f_i(t, x_i(t), v_i(t), y(t)),$$

where $v_i(\cdot)$ is the chosen by this agent policy (control) function. (Everywhere in this chapter $\dot{x}$ denotes the derivative with respect to the time.) Then the overall dynamics of the world economy is described by the equation

$$\dot{x}(t) = f(t, x(t), v(t), y(t)),$$

where $x = (x_1, \ldots, x_n)$, $v = (v_1, \ldots, v_m)$, $f = (f_1, \ldots, f_n)$.

On the other hand, the economic activities have impact on the evolution of the environment, say due to emission of GHGs. Let $e(t, x, v, y)$ represents the instantaneous impact vector resulting from global economic state x, control v and environmental state y at time t.

Because GHGs are fungible (they melt in the upper atmosphere irrespective to the country of origin), the impact vector is represented by the aggregate emissions

$$e(t,x,v,y) = \sum_{i=1}^{n} e_i(t,x_i,v_i,y), \tag{6.1}$$

where $e_i(t,x_i,v_i,y)$ is the emission of agent i at time t, determined by her economic state, control, and the environmental state at this time.

We assume that the dynamics of the environment can be represented by an equation of the form

$$\dot{y}(t) = h(t,e(t,x(t),v(t),y(t)),y(t)).$$

Thus, given the control function $v(\cdot)$ chosen by the agents, the overall economic-environment system is described by the equations

$$\dot{x}(t) = f(t,x(t),y(t),v(t)), \qquad x(0) = x^0, \tag{6.2}$$

$$\dot{y}(t) = h(t,e(t,x(t),v(t),y(t)),y(t)), \quad y(0) = y^0, \tag{6.3}$$

where x^0 and y^0 are initial data.

In the numerical analysis in this chapter we use one simple version of the IAM as described below.

In the benchmark model we specify $x_{i(t)} = k_{i(t)}$ – the physical capital stock of the i-th agent, $v_{i(t)} = (u_{i(t)}, a_{i(t)})$ – the investment intensity and the abatement effort, $y(t) = (\tau(t), m(t))$ – the average atmospheric temperature at the Earth surface and the concentration of GHG (measured in the CO_2 equivalent units in the warming context). Equations (6.2), (6.3) are specified as

$$\dot{k}_i(t) = -\delta_i k_i(t) + [1 - u_i(t) - c_i(a_i(t))]\,\pi_i(t)\,\varphi_i(\tau(t))\,(k_i(t))^{\gamma_i}(l_i(t))^{1-\gamma_i},$$

$$k_i(0) = k_i^0, \tag{6.4}$$

$$\dot{\tau}(t) = -\lambda(m(t))\,\tau(t) + d(m(t)), \quad \tau(0) = \tau^0, \tag{6.5}$$

$$\dot{m}(t) = -\mu m(t) + \sum_{i=1}^{n} e_i(t,k_i(t),a_i(t),\tau(t)) + \nu(t,\tau(t)), \quad m(0) = m^0, \tag{6.6}$$

with

$$e_i(t,k_i,a_i,\tau) = (1 - a_i)\,\eta_i(t)\pi_i(t)\varphi_i(\tau)k_i^{\gamma_i} l_i^{1-\gamma_i}.$$

Since versions of the above most simple IAM are widely used in the literature (see the literature review in Section 6.2.3) we only shortly explain the appearing notations.

Physical capital accumulation is described by equation (6.4). The depreciation rate of the physical capital of agent i is $\delta_i > 0$. The labor supply of agent i is $l_i(t)$ and the production function is of Cobb-Douglas type with elasticity of substitution $\gamma_i \in (0,1)$. The productivity of the i-th agent is $\pi_i(t)$ and $\varphi_i(\tau)$ is a correction factor for the productivity depending on the current temperature τ. Thus

$Y_i(t) = \pi_i(t)\varphi_i(\tau(t))(k_i(t))^{\gamma_i}(l_i(t))^{1-\gamma_i}$ is the economic output of agent i. It is assumed that the emission (without any costly abatement) is proportional to the output Y_i, namely equals $\eta_i(t)Y_i(t)$, where $\eta_i(t)$ takes into account the change of emission per output due to technological change.

A fraction $u_i(t)$ of the output is consumed and another fraction, $c(a_i)$, is devoted to CO_2 abatement at rate a_i, the rest is invested, as seen in equation (6.4). Abatement at rate a_i reduces the emission by a factor a_i: $e_i = (1 - a_i)\eta_i Y_i$ and costs a fraction $c_i(a_i)$ of the total product.

The evolution of the CO_2 concentration is described by equation (6.6), where μ is the natural absorption rate, $\nu(t,\tau)$ is the non-industrial emission at temperature τ. Finally, (6.5) establishes the link between CO_2 concentration and temperature change. The CO_2 concentration increases the atmospheric temperature through d but also may affect the cooling rate λ. The initial values k^0, τ^0, m^0 are given.

The control functions $v_i = (u_i, a_i)$ chosen by the agents should satisfy the constraints

$$u_i(t),\ a_i(t) \geq 0, \quad u_i(t) + a_i(t) \leq 1. \tag{6.7}$$

These inequalities define a constraining set V for (u_i, a_i), that imply in particular that no transformation of existing capital into consumption or abatement is possible.

The particular specifications used in the numerical simulations is given below. The main trouble with the above model and its extensions is that most of the model components are actually not known with certainty. In fact this applies to all of the involved in the benchmark model exogenous functions.

Since the economic agents have to make their policy decisions, $v_i(t)$, in conditions of uncertainty about the future changes of the data, these decisions have to be made on the basis of predictions. Therefore in the next section we develop the concept of prediction-based rational behavior of an individual agent.

In the following two sections we define the two concepts we shall introduce in the IA framework: model predictive Nash equilibrium and adaptive behavior. The methodology presented below is not restricted to a specific model. Therefore the exposition is carried out for the general model (6.2), (6.3), while we refer to the benchmark case (6.4)–(6.6) only for clarification, and in Section 6.6 – for numerical simulations.

6.4 Model Predictive Rational Behavior

Even if the model (6.2), (6.3) provides a reasonable description of the dynamics of the real global economic-environment system, it is not exactly known to the agents due to imperfection of the modeling and due to uncertainties in its parameters. That is, at time s agent j chooses her future control policy based on a model that may differ from the "true" one. At any time instant s agent j models her economy in her own way, including the impact of the environment on the economy and her own input to the environment. Moreover, the performance criterion of each individual agent may depend on the time at that the control decision has to be made. Thus at any time s agent j maximizes an individual objective function representing the total (possibly discounted) utility

$$\int_s^{\infty} g_j^s(t, x_j(t), v_j(t), y(t))\, \mathrm{d}t \tag{6.8}$$

subject to the controlled dynamics

$$\dot{x}_j(t) = f_j^s(t, x_j(t), v_j(t), y(t)), \qquad x_j(s) = x^s - \text{known at time } s,\ t \geq s, \tag{6.9}$$

$$\dot{y}(t) = h^s(t, e_j(t, x_j(t), v_j(t), y(t)) + \bar{e}_j(t), y(t))$$
$$y(s) = y^s - \text{known at time } s \tag{6.10}$$

and the control constraint (see (6.7) for the benchmark constraints)

$$v_j(t) \in V. \tag{6.11}$$

Here g_j^s is the function that agent j uses at time s for evaluation of the future (discounted) utility, f_j^s represents the model that agent j employs at time s for predicting the evolution of her economic state $x_j(t)$ (for any given future control policy $v_j(t)$ and future environmental state $y(t)$, $t \geq s$), h^s is the model that all agents use at time s for predicting the evolution of the environmental state $y(t)$, $t \geq s$ (given the future total emission $e(t)$). From the point of view of agent j the total emission $e(t)$ consists of own emission $e_j(t, x_j(t), v_j(t), y(t))$ depending on the own control and economic state and on the environmental state $y(t)$, and of the emission of the rest of the agents, $\bar{e}_j(t)$, that is not a priori known to agent j. The environmental dynamics h^s employed at time s is the same for all agents.[4]

As it will be argued at the end of this and in the next section, this assumption is not too restrictive, since the agents may use the predictions obtained by the environmental model in diverse ways, varying between total ignorance and complete trust.

The interconnected problems (6.8)–(6.11) of the n agents at time s are regarded as defining a differential game in that the players (that is, the agents) implement (an open-loop) Nash equilibrium solution. In the next lines we clarify what is the meaning of the Nash equilibrium solution in the present context.

A specific feature of this context is the information pattern. In solving her optimization problem agent j is not necessarily aware of the models f_i^s that agents $i \neq j$ use at time s (as we see below these models may change with s due to agent-specific adaptive learning). Instead, it is assumed that agent j solves the problem (6.8)–(6.11) if the emission $\bar{e}_j(t)$ of the rest of the agent is given. Let $(x_j^s[\bar{e}_j](t), v_j^s[\bar{e}_j](t), y_j^s[\bar{e}_j](t)))$, $t \geq s$, be a solution of problem (6.8)–(6.11) for the given function $\bar{e}_j(t)$, $t \geq s$.[5] The resulting emission of agent j is

$$e_j^s[\bar{e}_j](t) := e_j\left(t, x_j^s[\bar{e}_j](t),\ v_j^s[\bar{e}_j](t), y_j^s[\bar{e}_j](t)\right).$$

In the definition of Nash equilibrium it is enough to assume that (instead of the dynamics f_i^s of all other agents) the emission functional

$$\bar{e}_j(\cdot) \longrightarrow e_j^s[\bar{e}_j](\cdot) \tag{6.12}$$

of each agent is known to the rest of the agents. That is, each agent gives a correct information about her future emissions, given any scenario for the cumulated future emission of the rest of the agents. (This information would be automatically available if the models f_i^s on that the agent's decisions are based were known to all agents.) Then the Nash solution consists of an n-tuple of control policies $\{v_i^s(t)\}$, trajectories $\{x_i^s(t)\}$ of the economies, and emissions $\{e_j^s(t)\}$, $t \geq s$, such that following equilibrium conditions hold for $j = 1,\ldots,n$ and $t \geq s$:

$$v_j^s[\bar{e}_j^s](t) = v_j^s(t) \quad \text{with} \quad \bar{e}_j^s(\cdot) := \sum_{i \neq j} e_i^s(t), \tag{6.13}$$

$$x_j^s[\bar{e}_j^s](t) = x_j^s(t), \tag{6.14}$$

$$e_j^s(t, x_j^s(t), v_j^s(t), y^s(t)) = e_j^s(t), \tag{6.15}$$

where y^s is the solution of the equation

$$\dot{y}(t) = h^s(t, e^s(t), y(t)), \quad y(s) = y^s, \quad \text{with} \quad e^s(t) := \sum_{i=1}^{n} e_i^s(t). \tag{6.16}$$

The meaning of the above equalities is the following. Equations (6.13) and (6.14) means that for the cumulated emission $\bar{e}_j^s(t)$ of the rest of the agents, agent j will have (x_j^s, v_j^s) as an optimal solution. Equation (6.15) means that the optimal emission of each agent j would equal $e_j^s(t)$, provided that the trajectory of the environmental state is $y^s(\cdot)$.

It remains to notice that due to (6.15) the equalities

$$y_j[\bar{e}_j^s](t) = y^s(t), \quad j = 1,\ldots,n$$

are automatically fulfilled. That is, at the Nash equilibrium solution each agent evaluates the future environmental state in the same way.

The numerical calculation consists of iterating the fixed point system (6.13)–(6.16). Between three and seven iterations give enough accuracy in the numerical investigation in Section 6.6.

Now we continue with the definition of the model predictive rational behavior of the economic agents. Let us fix a time-step $\epsilon > 0$ and set $s_k := i\epsilon$, $k = 0, 1, \ldots$.

At time $s = s_0 = 0$ the agents determine the Nash equilibrium controls $\{v_i^{s_0}(t)\}$ resulting from the models $f_j^{s_0}$, $g_j^{s_0}$, h^{s_0} that the agents use at time s_0, and from the measurements $x_j^{s_0}$, y^{s_0} of the states. The so obtained controls are implemented, however, only in the time-interval $[s_0, s_1]$. Then the agents update their models and measure the actual state $x_j^{s_1}$, y^{s_1}. The agents determine the Nash equilibrium controls $\{v_i^{s_1}(t)\}$ resulting from the updated models $f_j^{s_1}$, $g_j^{s_1}$, h^{s_1} and implement them in the time interval $[s_1, s_2]$. The same procedure repeats further on. The resulting control policies are

$$\hat{v}_j^{\epsilon}(t) := v_j^{s_k}(t) \quad \text{for } t \in [s_k, s_{k+1}],\ k = 0, 1 \ldots.$$

The time-step ϵ can be viewed as the length of the commitment periods defined under a legally binding international agreement, such as the Kyoto protocol. However, both for mathematical convenience and due to the continual and non-synchronized adjustment of the policies of the agents at micro level, we eliminate the dependence of the control policies on the choice of ϵ letting it tend to zero.

Definition 1. Every limit point of any sequence $\hat{v}_j^{\epsilon}$ defined as above in the space $L_1^{\text{loc}}(0,\infty)$ when $\epsilon \longrightarrow 0$ (if such exists) will be called *Model Predictive Nash Equilibrium (MPNE)* policy.

In practice the time-step at that the actual state of the environment is updated may be many years long owing to the slow change of the environment and the relatively high fluctuations from the trend. However, the model updates may take place more frequently due to the relatively faster change of the economic states and the progress in the modeling methodologies.

We outline the particular case in that an agent j chooses her model f_j^s, g_j^s independent of the environmental state y. That is, in her current control policy agent j does not take into account the influence of the future changes in the environmental state on her economy. Accordingly, such an agent disregards the impact of her economic activities on the environment; hence the environmental component (6.10) is irrelevant for her decisions. In Bréchet et al. (2014) we interpret such an agent as doing business as usual (BAU). A BAU agent disregards her interconnections with the environment and, consequently does not abate emissions. We stress that the above notion of BAU differs from the one used in the literature (see, e.g., Nordhaus and Yang, 1996), where BAU is an agent who does not abate, although having a foresight about the influence of the future environmental changes on the economy.

In the above consideration the models of the individual economic dynamics and objectives of the agents, as well as the model of the environment, are considered as given, although changing with the time in a non-anticipative way (the future changes in the models are not known, hence not involved in the formation of the current control policies). In the next section we partly endogenize the evolution of the models that agents employ by using a simple version of *adaptive learning.*

6.5 Adaptive Behavior

At any time s the agents use models (given by the triplet (f_j^s, g_j^s, h^s)) to determine their policy for some period of time after s, as described in the previous subsection.

In this subsection we address the following question: how the agents change the models that they use, depending on the newly available measurements of the actual economic and environmental states?

A variety of data assimilation techniques can employed for this purpose, out of that a simple adaptive learning is chosen in this chapter.

For the sake of clarity and for numerical simulations we consider here only the benchmark model. The environment is assumed to be relevantly described by equations (6.5), (6.6), thus in this case $h^s = h$ for all s. Moreover, we apply adaptive learning to only two crucial uncertain factors that may vary with the time at that the control decisions are taken and that essentially influence the behavior of the agents: the damage function that represents the effect of the climate change on the economy, and the discount rate used by the agents in the formulation of their future objectives. It is reasonable to apply adaptive learning to many other economic factors, such as future productivity, $\pi_i(t)$, future labor $l_i(t)$, future emission per output, $\eta_j(t)$, future natural emission, $\nu(t)$, etc., but here we assume a perfect knowledge for their evolution.

In the benchmark case the model (6.9)–(6.11) that agent j uses at time s reads as

$$\dot{k}_j = -\delta_j k_j + [1 - u_j - c_j(a_j)]\, \pi_j \varphi_j^s(\tau)\, k_j^{\gamma_j} l_i^{1-\gamma_j}, \quad k_j(s) = k_j^s, \tag{6.17}$$

$$\dot{\tau} = -\lambda(m)\,\tau + d(m), \quad \tau(s) = \tau^s, \tag{6.18}$$

$$\dot{m} = -\mu\, m + (1 - a_j)\, \eta_j \pi_j \varphi_j^s(\tau)\, k_j^{\gamma_j} l_i^{1-\gamma_j} + \bar{e}_j + \nu(\tau), \quad m(s) = m^s, \tag{6.19}$$

$$u_j(t),\ a_j(t) \geq 0, \quad u_j(t) + a_j(t) \leq 1. \tag{6.20}$$

To complete the benchmark agent's model we consider a particular objective function g_j^s in (6.8) defined as

$$\int_s^\infty e^{-r_j^s t} \left[u_j(t)\, \pi_j(t)\, \varphi_j^s(\tau(t))\, (k_j(t))^{\gamma_j} (l_j(t))^{1-\gamma_j} \right]^{1-\alpha} dt, \tag{6.21}$$

where r_j^s is the discount rate used by agent j at time s.

As already said, the model components that the agent j updates at time s (based on the available measurements for $k_j(t)$ and $\tau(t)$ till time s) are the damage function $\varphi_j^s(\tau)$ the discount rate r_j^s.

6.5.1 Updating the Damage Function

In the next paragraphs we analyze how agents with diverse level of knowledge and concerns or with diverse opinion about the reliability of the presently used environmental models and monitoring (in our case (6.18), (6.19)) may build their formal estimates about the influence of the global warming on their regional economic efficiency.

Below it will be assumed that the true damage on the productivity in the region of agent j caused by a temperature increase τ above the preindustrial level is given by the formula

$$\varphi(\tau) = \frac{1}{1 + \theta_* \tau^\kappa}, \tag{6.22}$$

where κ is a known constant and the value of θ_* is not known to the agent (considering also κ or more parameters as unknown does not bring principal difference). The above constants are agent-specific, but we skip the index j in the notations since the considerations below apply to an individual agent.

As a specification of the benchmark model we assume that at any time s instead of the "true" damage function (6.22) for her region agent j uses the following one:

$$\varphi^s(\tau) = \frac{1}{1 + \theta_s(\beta_s \tau^s + (1-\beta_s)\tau)^\kappa}, \tag{6.23}$$

where θ_s represents the current estimate of the true value θ_*, τ^s is the measured average temperature at time s, and $\beta_s \in [0,1]$ is an additional parameter chosen by the agent at the current time s. As argued below, this parameter reflects the level of confidence in the environmental model (6.18), (6.19). Notice that at the current time s the temperature is $\tau(s) = \tau^s$, hence the evaluation of the damage function gives

$$\varphi^s(\tau(s)) = \frac{1}{1 + \theta_s \tau(s)^\kappa}. \tag{6.24}$$

Since the true value of the damage is measurable, the agent may calculate the value $\tilde{\theta}_s$ that fits to the current measurements of $\tau(s)$ and $\varphi(\tau(s))$. Owing to the uncertainties in the measurements the agent evaluates the parameter θ_s to be used in her current model as

$$\theta_s = \theta_{s-} + \varepsilon\rho_s(\tilde{\theta}_s - \theta_{s-}),$$

where θ_{s-} is the agent's estimation of θ prior to time s (that depends on past measurements). The parameter $\rho_s \in [0,1]$ reflects the agent's uncertainty about the currently estimated factors: temperature, capital stock, economic output: the lower is the confidence of the agent, the smaller is ρ_s. The parameter $\varepsilon > 0$ is the time step for updating the damage function, as in the preceding subsection. In the limit case with $\varepsilon \to 0$ and $\rho_s = \rho$ the value ρ can be interpreted as the exponential decay rate of the error: $\theta_* - \theta_s = e^{-\rho s}(\theta_* - \theta_0)$.

On the other hand, at time s the agent employs the damage function in her long-run investment/abatement planning model (6.17)–(6.21), as described in the previous subsection. Since the temperature τ may change in the future and the agent uses the environmental model (6.18), (6.19) to predict this change, the anticipated error in τ produced by the model may distort the predicted damage rate. To take into account these uncertainties the agent modifies the damage function (6.24) in the way given by (6.23). The argument for choosing a damage function in the form of (6.23) is shortly explained below, taking for simplicity the value $\kappa = 2$.

At time s the agent has updated her damage function φ^s by choosing the new parameter θ_s in (6.24) as described above. However, the agent realizes that the true temperature at time $t > s$ may be different from the one resulting from the model (6.18), (6.19), with an error $\xi = \xi(t)$. Then the anticipated value of the damage function, when using (6.23) at time t and with the true temperature $\tau = \tau(t)$ will be

$$\frac{1}{1+\theta_s(\beta\tau^s + (1-\beta)(\tau+\xi)^2)}.$$

Since ξ can be viewed as a random variable (although its distribution is unknown), the rational agent would try to minimize by choosing the parameter $\beta \in [0,1]$ the expectation

$$\mathcal{E}\left(\left(\frac{1}{1+\theta_s\tau^2} - \frac{1}{1+\theta_s(\beta\tau^s + (1-\beta)(\tau+\xi)^2)}\right)^2\right).$$

Having in mind that θ_*, hence also θ, is a small number ($\theta_* = 0.0054$ according to Nordhaus, 2007), one can reasonably represent the above expression as

$$\theta_s^2\mathcal{E}\left(\left(\beta\Delta(\beta\Delta+2\tau) + 2(\beta\Delta+\tau)(1-\beta)\xi + (1-\beta)^2\xi^2\right)^2\right) + O(\theta_s^3), \qquad (6.25)$$

where $\Delta = \tau^s - \tau$ and $O(\varepsilon)/\varepsilon$ is bounded when $\varepsilon \to 0$. From here one can make the following essential observation:

(i) if the agent trusts the employed environmental model (hence $\xi = 0$), then this agent would choose $\beta = 0$, that gives value zero in the error-expectation formula (6.25);

(ii) if the agent does not believe in the long run trend of the temperature change (assuming $\Delta = 0$) and anticipates an error $\xi \neq 0$ of the model-base prediction for the temperature, then this agent would choose $\beta = 1$.

The analysis may be continued by considering the optimal choice of the parameter β, that is, choosing the β that minimizes the expression in (6.25). We skip this technical (and not very precise) consideration, that suggests that an agent whose opinion about the accuracy of the environmental model (6.18), (6.19) measured by $\sum_{n=1}^{4} |\mathcal{E}(\xi^n)|$ is large relative to the expected by the agent temperature change $\Delta = \tau - \tau^s$ (a "skeptical" agent), then this agent would choose β closer to 1, while an agent who trusts more the model and anticipates a temperature increase would choose

β closer to zero. Of course, the same learning procedure as for θ can be applied also for β.

Summarizing, one may say that the choice of the predictor for the future damage caused by the global warming is a subjective decision of the agent, that can be formally characterized by the following statement in terms of the parameters ρ_s and β_s in the update of the damage function: agents who are skeptical about the measurements (and the model) of the economy and about the measurement of the current temperature choose lower value of ρ_s; agents who are skeptical about the credibility of the employed environmental model choose a higher value for the parameter $\beta_s \in [0,1]$.

We note that an agent choosing $\beta = 1$ makes no use of the environmental model at all, since this agent always takes the current temperature as a proxy for the future one. Thus $\beta = 1$ represents a BAU agent. In the present framework the agents are distinguished by their parameters ρ^s and β^s and the BAU agent is an extreme case in a continuous variety of agents.

6.5.2 Updating the Discount Rate

The discount rate r_j^s chosen by agent j at time s in its utility function represents her opinion about the value of the present utility relative to a future one. Of course, the discount rate r_j^s depends on the agent's view on the future uncertainty, but in the context of the environmental concerns it depends also on the agent's per capita wealth. As one can clearly see from the daily practice, a rich country tends to be more farsighted than a poor country in that the political and the economic policies are more myopic. Similar suggestions are given in the economic literature (see, e.g., Lawrence, 1991; Samwick, 1998). Therefore, it is reasonable to assume that the discount rate of agent j depends on her per capita wealth measured at time s by $k_j(s)/l_j(s) = k_j^s/l_j(s)$ (where labor is proportional to the population size). Thus, at time s the agent would have an endogenous discount rate $r_j^s = R(k_j^s/l_j(s))$. The particular specification of the function R used in the subsequent numerical analyses is given in Section 6.6.

6.6 Some Simulation Results

The agents in the benchmark model (6.17)–(6.21) are heterogeneous with respect to all involved parameters. However, we shall focus on the heterogeneity with respect to their behavioral features, represented by the damage function $\varphi_j^s(\tau)$ and the discount rate r_j^s used at time s by agent j.

6.6.1 Model Calibration

The individual damage function used by an agent at time s is characterized in the previous section by three parameters: the knowledge about the "true" damage function prior to s, denoted by θ_{s-}, the learning parameter ρ_s, and the "trust" parameter β_s. Diverse values of these parameters and of the discount rate r_j^s allow to cover agents with rather different behavior, including such doing BAU (see the end of Section 6.4), myopic versus far-sighted agents, skeptical about the accuracy of the climate predictions versus "believers," etc. Given any configuration of agents, their (interconnected) economic behavior is defined in Section 6.4 by the Model Predictive Nash Equilibrium (MPNE).

Although the concept of MPNE applies to any number of agents, in the simulation results below we consider for more transparency only two agents. The first agent, named agent R (from "Rich"), is presumably richer, hence less discounting the future, has better knowledge on the damage function and trusts more the predictions for the climate change. The second one, agent P (from "Poor"), is presumably poorer, hence more myopic, has bad knowledge on the damage function but may learn with experience, and is skeptical about the predictions for the climate change. In the benchmark model agents R and P are indexed by $i = 1$ and $i = 2$, respectively.

The prototypes of these two agents in some of the simulations below are the OECD and the non-OECD countries, respectively. Therefore in all simulations 74.7% of the world physical capital stock (estimated as 733.2 trillion USD in 2005) belongs to agent R, while the rest of 25.3% belongs to agent P. Thus the initial data for the economy are $k_1^0 = 547.7004$ and $k_2^0 = 185.4996$ trillion USD. On the other hand, the population of agent R is 18.2% of the total, that gives $l_1 = 0.184L$, $l_2 = 0.816L$ with the total population $L = 6464.75$ million. The initial data for the environment are $m^0 = 808.9$ and $\tau^0 = 0.7307$, representing the concentration of CO_2 in GtC and the increase of temperature above the pre-industrial level in 2005, respectively.

The constant parameters of the benchmark model are given on Table 6.1. The calibration year is 2005.

The functional parameters in the benchmark model are specified as follows.

Due to technological progress the productivity $\pi_i(t)$ is assumed linearly increasing with time so that technology is 25% more efficient after 175 years, that is, $\pi_i(175) = 1.25\pi_i(0)$ for $i = R, P$.

The technological progress reduces the emission per unit of output (without abatement) at an exponential rate 0.00384, that corresponds to a decrease by 25% in 75 years: $\eta_i(t) = e^{-0.00384t}\eta_i(0)$. The cost-of-abatement function $c_i(a) = c(a)$ is specified as $c(a) = 0.01a/(1-a)$, that implies that reducing emission by 50% incurs cost of 1% of GDP. The true damage function for all agents is assumed to be

$$\varphi^*(\tau) = \frac{1}{1+\theta_*\tau^2}, \quad \text{with } \theta_* = 0.0057$$

(of course it is not assumed to be known to the agents).

Table 6.1 Values of stationary parameters

Economic parameters		
intertemporal elasticity of substitution	α	0.5
depreciation rate	δ_i	0.1
capital elasticity	γ_i	0.75
initial productivity of R	$\pi_1(0)$	1.75
initial productivity of P	$\pi_2(0)$	1.17
initial emission rate	$\eta_i(0)$	0.0427
Climate parameters		
temperature stability rate	λ	0.11
CO_2 absorption rate	μ	0.0054
natural emission	ν	3.211

Finally, the effect of CO_2 concentration on the average temperature increase is captured by the standard function $d(m) = 0.5915 \ln(m/m_0^*)$, where $m_0^* = 596.4$ GtC is the preindustrial CO_2 concentration in the atmosphere. All the specifications are within usually suggested ranges.

6.6.2 Scenarios Description

For the behavioral parameters $\varphi_j^s(\cdot)$ in (6.23) and the discount rate r_j^s we consider several scenarios as described below.

Scenarios 1 and 2. These are two "extreme" scenarios. In Scenario 1 both agents are myopic and totally neglect the environmental dynamics in their decisions, adapting to the temperature change only post factum (this is what we called BAU agent in the end of Section 6.4). Precisely, agent R has the parameters $r_1^s = r_1 = 0.02$ (myopic), $\theta_s = \theta_*$ (evaluates correctly her damage at the current temperature τ^s), $\beta = 1$ (ignores the prediction for future change of temperature), ρ is irrelevant. Agent P has the same parameters with the only difference that $\theta_s = \theta_*/6$ and $\rho = 0$ (underestimates the damage of the current temperature and does not learn).

In Scenario 2 we consider that both agents as far-sighted, perfectly informed about the environmental dynamics and the damage function. Precisely, for both agents $r_i^s = 0.005$, $\theta_s = \theta_*$, $\beta_s = 0$. In fact, in this case the MPNE coincides with the usual Nash equilibrium due to the perfect foresight of both agents.

Scenario 3. In the third scenario we take into account that agent P may learn and may become less skeptical with experience, still remaining myopic. The role of this scenario is to exhibit the effect of learning. Formally, agent R is exactly as in Scenario 2, while agent P has $r_2^s = 0.02$, $\theta_s = \theta_* - e^{-\rho s}(\theta_* - \theta_0)$, with $\theta_0 = \theta_*/6$, $\rho = 0.03465$, and $\beta_s = e^{-\rho s}$. The chosen value of ρ means that agent P reduces the error in θ by half and the value of the distrust parameter β from 1 to 0.5 in 20 years.

Scenario 4. This last scenario involves endogenous discount for agent P, all the rest is as Scenario 3. Agent P is initially myopic ($r_2^0 = 0.02$), but her discount rate decreases quadratically with the per capita stock of capital till the value $r = 0.005$ is achieved when the capital stock reaches the initial value of the initial capital stock of agent R. That is, at this point agent P starts discounting as low as agent R, who has $r_1 = 0.005$ all the time.

In all scenarios the agents use the investment and the abatement rates, $u_i(t)$ and $a_i(t)$, as policy instruments. Of course, in Scenario 1 the agents have no reasons to abate (hence $a_j(t) = 0$).

6.6.3 Simulation Results

The four scenarios are graphically depicted in figures 6.1 to 6.3. Our results support the intuitive idea that the more you know the better you do. Indeed, Scenario 2 represents the economy with the best informed individuals who care the most about the future. On the other side, agents in Scenario 1 are myopic about global warming and do not care much about the future. On top of this, they are unable to learn. This implies that they never revise their vision about global warming nor do they increase their concern about the future. They are stubborn and short-sighted, that are rather common psychological features in the the real word. As a result, in short, Scenario 2 provides the highest consumption and GDP per capita in the long-term, incurring in the lowest increase in temperature while Scenario 1 provides the worst results.

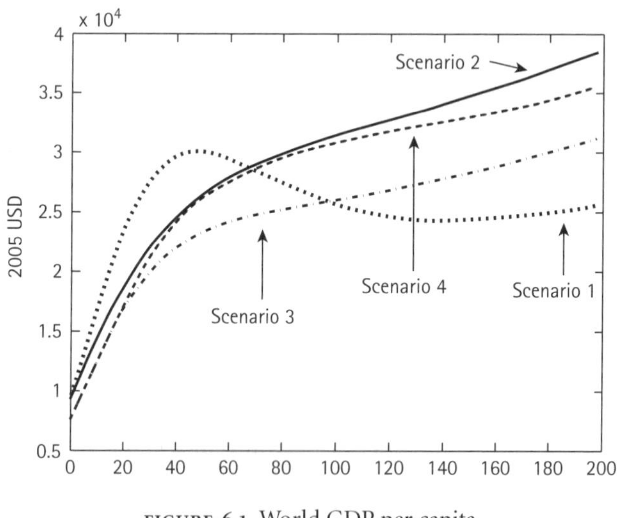

FIGURE 6.1 World GDP per capita

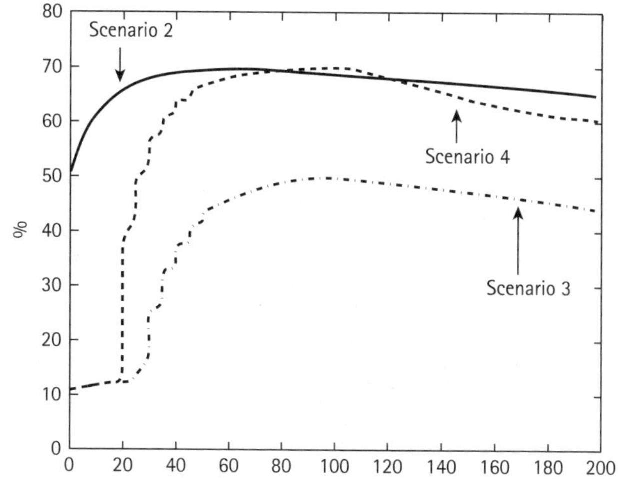

FIGURE 6.2 Average abatement rate

A striking result to be mentioned about these two scenarios is the shape of GDP (or consumption) over time. After an increase in GDP per capita at the beginning of the simulation period, Scenario 1 displays a shrink in the level of the world GDP by 25% in 90 years. This reflects the economic consequences of neglecting climate change. Actually, in Scenario 1 World GDP declines by 0.3% per year between time 50 and 140. In the same period of time world GDP increases by 0.3% per year on average in Scenario 2. This shows how a more realistic definition of a BAU translates into climate costs on the economy. Let us remind that we use the same calibration parameter values as Nordhaus (2007). What makes the difference is the rational behind the scenarios. Clearly, this result sheds a new light on the potential costs of no-action against global warming. Most people agree that emission abatement is costly but forget that climate change itself is costly to the economy. This simulation reveals that these costs may be much higher than usually appraised with IAMs because they ill-define what is business-as-usual.

After 100 years, Scenario 2 induces a temperature increase of less than 3°C, providing a GDP of US$30,000 per capita. Scenario 1 provides higher consumption during the first 90 years, given that agents do not abate. Nevertheless, because they incur in the largest emissions, their productivity is harmed the most. To preserve a high level of consumption during the entire period, agents in Scenario 2 abate more than 50% of their emissions, attaining up to 70% after 50 years. Given that agents do not abate at all in Scenario 1, temperature increases by more than 6.5°C after 100 years, that dampens their productivity and hence their income.

Naturally, Scenarios 3 and 4 provide results that lie in between Scenario 1 and 2, getting closer to Scenario 2 as the amount of information and concern about the future increase. Scenarios 3 and 4 are similar during the first 20 years. Differences arise after

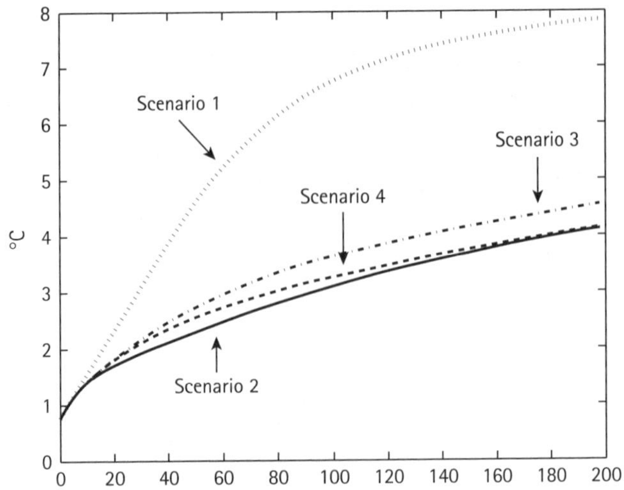

FIGURE 6.3 Temperature increase

and one can observe the behavioral differences between agents who update their discount rate, and those who do not. In Scenario 3, agent R knows exactly the damages induced by global warming, and she discounts future at at a higher rate. On the other side, agent P, who does not abate at the beginning, starts soon doing so, adding her effort to agent R's. However, agent P's lack of care about the future impedes larger abatement efforts. Consequently, GDP per capita and consumption are larger than in Scenario 1, and temperature increase after 100 years is 3.75°C above the preindustrial level. Therefore, although this economy starts abating a 10% of their emissions on the average, it gradually increases abatement efforts until 50% after one century.

Finally, building on Scenario 3, we allow agent P in Scenario 4 to become more patient as she becomes wealthier. Hence, as agent P accumulates wealth with time, she starts caring more about its future and increases her abatement effort accordingly. We can see in figure 6.2 that the average abatement rate equalizes Scenario 2's after 70 years and then over-reach it for some decades. Agents get very close to Scenario 2 in terms of consumption and GDP as well, but they cannot catch them because of the damages accumulated on productivity during the first 60 years.

It is interesting to notice that, although Scenario 2, 3, and 4 are relatively close in terms of temperature increase, they display contrasting profiles regarding GDP, consumption, and abatement policies. For example, in Scenario 4 abatement efforts are stronger than in the "optimistic" Scenario 2 for most time periods because of the delay incurred by the endogenous discounting. It shows that the idea of relying on endogenous discounting (driven by economic development) to cope with global warming is inadequate because it takes too long.

It is interesting to compare the aggregated discounted utility of agent R (given by (6.21) on a 200 years long horizon) in Scenarios 2 and 4. The discount factor of agent

R is $r = 0.005$ in each of these scenarios, therefore the results are comparable: the values are 52,995 in Scenario 2 and 37,022 in Scenario 4. Since agent R has exactly the same parameters in the two scenarios, the reason for the large difference of her welfare is caused by agent P. Notice that due to learning and due to the endogenous discount, after 100 years agent P in Scenario 4 behaves exactly as agent P in Scenario 2: has a perfect knowledge and discounts with $r = 0.005$. However, due to the delay in the evolution of agent P from a myopic ignorant to a far-sighted knowledgeable agent (as R is from the very beginning), agent R loses about 30% of her 200-years utility. This result shows how important it is for the rich country to help the poor one to develop, because both share the same common good, climate.

6.7 Conclusion

The purpose of this chapter was to extend the standard integrated assessment framework applied to climate change by incorporating model predictive control and adaptive behavior. Model predictive control is employed owing to the uncertainties about the future environment. It allows agents to redefine their optimal strategy on a regular basis, on the grounds of the observed changes in the world or in the agents' time preferences (endogenous discounting in our model). With this setting, agents are rational (they adopt the optimal policy) but revise it (with some inertia) as the word changes. Adaptive behavior (or learning) is involved since the agents gradually improve their knowledge about the world (the interconnection between environment and economy, in our model). These ingredients are particularly relevant in the context of global warming. We provide a generic theoretical model encompassing all elements of an integrated assessment model. In particular, we define an innovative concept of Model Productive Nash Equilibrium (MPNE) to characterize an economy with many countries. Simulations show, among other results, how the trajectory of the economy can be affected by the adaptive configuration. In particular, a pessimistic configuration (pessimistic, but maybe not so far from reality) displays a shrink in the world GDP due to the adverse effects of climate change and the persistent agent's will to disregard them. This new framework would deserve to be extended in several directions. A first natural one would be to split the word in many countries or regions. In this case, strategic interactions among countries would become a new ingredient of the framework.

Acknowledgments

This research was initially supported by the Belgian Science Policy under the CLIMNEG III Project (SD/CP/05A). The third author was partly financed by the Austrian Science Foundation (FWF) under grant No I 476-N13. The chapter was finalized while Th. Bréchet was visiting research fellow at the Grantham Institute for Climate Change at Imperial College London, and visiting professor at the European University at St Petersburg, Russia.

Notes

1. Twenty-three years later, Nordhaus publishes a new book entitled "*A Question of Balance*." Is it a new illustration of the slow pace between science and policy?
2. We reproduce here the DICE equations taken from Nordhaus (1992), respecting notation, calibration, and interpretation.
3. See also Bréchet and Eyckmans (2012) for a survey on the use of game theory with IAMs, or Yang (2008) for an application with the RICE model.
4. The assumption that all agents use the same environmental model is made only for the sake of simplicity. An additional comment on this is given in Endnote 6..
5. In this chapter we ignore the issues of existence and uniqueness. Some comments on these issues in a slightly different framework are given in Bréchet et al. (2014). In the economic-environmental model in Greiner et al. (2010), for example, the solution does not need to be unique.
6. This is the place where the assumption that all agents use the same environmental model h^s at any given instant s plays a role. If each agent uses its own model h_j^s for the environment, then the definition of the Nash equilibrium solution becomes more complicated and depends on the information pattern: do the rest of the agents know what is the environmental model used by the agent j, or do they know only the emission mapping (6.12)?. In the latter case only a slight modification of the above definition of Nash equilibrium is needed. In the former case the definition of a Nash solution is more complicated.
7. A sequence v^ϵ converges to v in $L_1^{\text{loc}}(0,\infty)$ if $\int_0^T |v^\epsilon(t) - v(t)|\,dt$ converges to zero for every $T > 0$.
8. The adjective "behavioral" indicates dependence on subjective attitude of the agent. Moreover, the agents have no foresight about the damage function and the interest rate that they will use in the future.
9. See the IPCC (2007), Nordhaus (2008), Stern (2008), and Yang (2009).

References

Bosetti V., C. Carraro, M. Galeotti, E. Massetti, M. Tavoni (2006). "WITCH: A World Induced Technical Change Hybrid Model", *The Energy Journal*, Special Issue 2, 13–38.

Bréchet V., Camacho C. and Veliov V. (2014). "Model predictive control, the economy, and the issue of global warming", *Annals of Operations Research*, 220, 25–48.

Bréchet T., Gérard F. and Tulkens H. (2011). "Efficiency vs. stability of climate coalitions: a conceptual and computational appraisal" *The Energy Journal* 32(1), 49–76.

Bréchet T. and Eyckmans J. (2012). "Coalition Theory and Integrated Assessment Modeling: Lessons for Climate Governance", in E. Brousseau, P.A. Jouvet and T. Dedeurwareder (eds). *Governing Global Environmental Commons: Institutions, Markets, Social Preferences and Political Games*, Oxford University Press, forthcoming, 2012.

Edenhofer O., N. Bauer, E. Kriegler (2005). "The impact of technological change on climate protection and welfare: Insights from the model MIND", *Ecological Economics*, 54, 277–292.

Eyckmans J. and Tulkens H. (2003). "Simulating coalitionally stable burden sharing agreements for the climate change problem", *Resource and Energy Economics*, 25, pp. 299–327.

Gaskins, D.W. Jr. and J. P. Weyant (1993). "Model Comparisons of the Costs of Reducing CO2 Emissions", *The American Economic Review*, Vol. 83, No. 2, 318–323.

Greiner, A., L. Gruene and W. Semmler (2010). "Growth and climate change: threshold and multiple equilibria", in J. Crespo Cuaresma, T.P. Palokangas and A. Tarasyev (eds), *Dynamic Systems, Economic Growth, and the Environment*, Springer-Verlag, pp. 63–79.

Grüne, L. and J. Pannek (2011). *Nonlinear model predictive control*, Springer, London.

Kanudia A., Labriet M., Loulou R., Vaillancourt K. and Waaub J-Ph. (2005). "The World-Markal Model and Its Application to Cost-Effectiveness, Permit Sharing, and Cost-Benefit Analyses " *Energy and Environment*, pp. 111–148.

Keller K. and R. Nicholas (2012). "Improving climate projections to better inform climate risk management", this volume.

Keller E., M. Spence and R. Zeckhauser (1971). "The Optimal Control of Pollution", *Journal of Economic Theory*, 4, 19–34.

Lawrence, E. C. (1991). "Poverty and the rate of time preference: evidence from panel data", *Journal of Political Economy*, 99, 54–75.

Manne, A.S., R. Richels (1996). "*Buying greenhouse insurance: The economic costs of CO_2 emission limits*, MIT Press.

Manne, A.S., R. Richels (2005). "Merge: An Integrated Assessment Model for Global Climate Change", Energy and Environment pp. 175–189.

Maurer H., Preuss J.J. and W. Semmler (2012), "Policy Scnearios in a Model of Optimal Economic Growth and Climate Change", this volume.

Nordhaus W. (1977). "Economic Growth and Climate: The Case of Carbon Dioxide", *The American Economic Review*, Vol. 67, No. 1, pp. 341–346.

Nordhaus, W.D. (1992). "An Optimal Transition Path for Controlling Greenhouse Gases", *Science*, 258, 1315–1319.

Nordhaus W. (1984). "CO_2 Forecasting and Control: A Mathematical Programming Approach" with T. A. Daly, N. Goto, and R. F. Kosobud, in John Weyant, ed., The Energy Industries in Transition, Part I, International Association of Energy Economists, Washington, D.C., pp. 547–561.

Nordhaus, W.D. and Z. Yang (1996). "A Regional Dynamic General-Equilibrium Model of Alternative Climate-Change Strategies", *The American Economic Review*, Vol. 86, No. 4, pp. 741–765

Nordhaus W. (1993a). "Rolling the DICE: An Optimal Transition Path for Controlling Greenhouse Gases", *Resource and Energy Economics*, 15, pp. 27–50

Nordhaus W. (1993b). "Optimal Greenhouse-Gas Reductions and Tax Policy in the DICE Model", *American Economic Review*, Vol. 83, No. 2, pp. 313–317.

Nordhaus W. (2007). "A Review of the Stern Review on the Economics of Climate Change," *Journal of Economic Literature, American Economic Association*, vol. 45(3), pp. 686–702.

Pearce D., Atkinson G., Mourato S. (2006). *Cost-Benefit Analysis and the Environment: Recent Developments* OECD, Paris.

Rotmans, J. (1990). *IMAGE: an integrated model to assess the greenhouse effect*, Springer.

Samwick, A. (1998). " Discount rate homogeneity and social security re- form", *Journal of Development Economics*, 57, 117–146.

Stanton E.A, Ackerman F. and Kartha S. (2009). "Inside the integrated assessment models: Four issues in climate economics", *Climate and Development*, 1(2), pp. 166–184.

Stern N. (2006). *The Economics of Climate Change: The Stern Review*, Cambridge, UK: Cambridge University Press.

Yang Z. (1993). "Essays on the International Aspects of Resource and Environmental Economics", Ph.D. dissertation, Yale University.

Yang Z. (2008). *Strategic Bargaining and Cooperation in Greenhouse Gas Mitigations - An Integrated assessment Modeling Approach*, MIT Press.

PART II

MITIGATION POLICY MODELING

CHAPTER 7

PROSPECTS OF TOOLS FROM DIFFERENTIAL GAMES IN THE STUDY OF MACROECONOMICS OF CLIMATE CHANGE

JACOB ENGWERDA

7.1 Introduction

Writing a chapter for this Handbook is quite a challenging task. According the guidelines this chapter should make on the one hand new and original arguments and on the other hand survey what are the essential issues and questions in the field of research the author is supposed to address. Further, though the author should aim to present the theories and opinions of all sides fairly and accurately, the coverage may and should advocate the specific opinion and standpoint of the author. As a mathematician, who is trained to think in terms of definitions and resulting theorems, this is a hard job. After some lengthy thoughts I decided to sketch a framework within which the discussion on the macro economic effects of climate change take place. Section 7.2 argues that the problem setting is characterized by scientific uncertainties about the development of climate, potential large losses and human beings having their specific features. The section provides some considerations about climate change, macroeconomics and their relationship. A characteristic feature of the problem setting is that there are multiple decision makers interacting in a dynamic world with large uncertainties. Problems of this type have been studied extensively by (dynamic) game theory. Section 7.3 starts with an introductory section on what (dynamic) game theory is about, followed by an overview of tools that have been developed in this area and that (may) play a role in the analysis of macroeconomics of climate change. An important aspect in this analysis is whether and when countries will engage in "green energy" and its technology.

Section 7.4 illustrates some issues that occur when one likes to tackle this question. Using some simple well-known game theoretic modeling tools, it is illustrated how coordination problems occur that may lead to suboptimal policies. A literature review suggests that, though there has been done already quite some work to better understand and solve the resulting problems, the current game theoretic tools can only partially address these problems. An extensive list of "to do" items concludes this section. The chapter concludes with some general observations.

This chapter is based on an extensive literature and it is, therefore, impossible to list all adequate references. For that reason a number of survey articles and books are referenced where one can find extensive lists of relevant literature.

7.2 Some Private Considerations

7.2.1 Considerations about Climate Change

The main reason to include this section is twofold. First we hope to give readers who are not too familiar with the subject some basic insights into the complex material. Second, we hope that this (far from complete) outline may help to better understand some issues dealt with in the next sections.

Going through the literature to find an explanation of that factors basically determine the climate (average weather conditions and the distribution of events around that average) one gets puzzled. Below we give some considerations that can be traced in literature about climate change. They are mainly based on the Intergovernmental Panel on Climate Change report 2007 (IPCC, 2007), where one can find many references to scientific studies that lead to these considerations. Unfortunately, however, there are also studies that question the accuracy or even conclusions of this report, see, for example, Christy et al. (2010), Scafetta (2009), Inter Academy Council (IAC, 2010). As a scientist, and layman in this field, the overall impression is that we start to see some global contours and factors impacting each other, but that an in-depth understanding of the material is far from complete.

Studies on deep sea sediments, continental deposits of flora, fauna and loess, and ice cores show that during the last one million years series of large glacial-interglacial changes occurred with cycles of about 100,000 years (see e.g. Imbrie et al. (1992), Tzedakis et al. (1997)). This implies that climate in the past was not fixed.

From a physics point of view temperature changes are due to changes in the global energy balance on earth. At this time there is no reasonable doubt to believe that the main source of energy is the sun and that energy is lost to space. If either the input from the sun and/or the output to space changes and these changes do not outweigh each other the total energy that is available on earth changes. Energy is distributed around the globe by winds, ocean currents, and other mechanisms and determines the climate of different regions. So, if there is a change in the amount of energy to be distributed, climate will change in at least some regions.

Looking for an explanation for these large glacial-interglacial changes Milankovith (1941) came up with the idea to relate local changes in solar radiation to long-term variations in Earth's orbital variations. Slight variations in Earth's orbit lead to changes in the seasonal distribution of sunlight reaching the Earth's surface and how it is distributed across the globe. Milankovith (1941) and later on Berger (1977) show that there is a high correlation between the Earth's orbital variations and the occurrence of glacial and interglacial periods. A model of future climate solely based on the observed orbital–climate relationships predicts that the long-term trend over the next seven thousand years is toward extensive Northern Hemisphere glaciation (see Hays et al. (1976)).

Other factors that impact climate on a long term basis are, for example, mountain building and continental drift.

A factor that one expects to affect the energy balance on a more short-term basis is the amount of solar radiation produced by the sun. Sunspots, indicating lower sun temperatures, are an indicator for a change in the solar radiation. They have a cycle of approximately 11 years and they are reported already in ancient times. Also studies of rock layers and layering show repeating peaks in layer thickness, with a pattern approximately repeating every 11 layers. This suggests that solar cycles have been active for hundreds of millions of years. From 1978 on there are measurements on the total solar irradiation obtained by satellites. Since the observed changes in solar radiation over the last decades are quite small the common conclusion of a wide range of studies (see, e.g., the third assessment report of IPCC) is that the changes in solar irradiance are not the major cause of the temperature changes in the second half of the 20th century unless those changes can induce unknown large feedbacks in the climate system. This reservation is made because the exact relationships between solar irradiance and long-term climatological changes, such as global warming, are not well understood yet.

Statistics show that in the last 100 years, Earth's average surface temperature increased by about 0.8°C (1.4°F) with about two thirds of the increase occurring over just the last three decades. Physicists have produced a model that relates the incoming sun radiation to the Earth temperature. An important point in this model is that thermal radiation that is reflected by the Earth into space is partially reflected to Earth again due to, so-called, greenhouse gases (GHGs) in the atmosphere. One of these gases is carbon dioxide (CO_2). An important property of CO_2 is that once it is in the atmosphere, it stays there for a long time (estimates range from 30 to 95 years). Since due to fossil burning and deforestation CO_2 concentrations have increased exponentially over the last 150 years (and as such have a strong correlation with the increase of temperature during these years), and given the above mentioned greenhouse effect of CO_2, it seems at least plausible that this increase in CO_2 has caused part of the increases in global average temperatures. However, the above temperature model is just an approximation of reality and there are, separate from a complete understanding of the relationship between more CO_2 concentration in the atmosphere and its impact on the amount of thermal reflection, also other factors that (might) affect the transfer of solar energy into the temperature on Earth.

An important factor are the feedbacks induced by a change in temperature. In case temperature increases, for example, the composition and formation of clouds will change too. This has both negative (e.g., sun blocking) and positive effects (increase of greenhouse effect) on the thermal radiation. The balance of it is unclear. An extensive list of potential feedbacks can be found in the IPCC reports. An important point is that quite a number of these feedbacks induce transitions that last for long time horizons and as such cannot be redirected within a short time span.

From the above considerations it will be clear that, with no spare Earth with that to experiment, the question whether a climate change occurs that can be attributed to human behavior is far from easy. Models have to be used to make projections of possible future changes over time scales of many decades and for that there are no precise past analogues. To deal with this issue the IPCC working group I pursued the following: (1) detect whether the climate has changed; (2) demonstrate that the detected change is consistent with computer model simulations of the climate change signal that is calculated to occur in response to human behavior; and (3) demonstrate that the detected change is not consistent with alternative, physically plausible explanations of recent climate change that exclude important human behavior.

Using this set up the fourth IPCC reports that the global mean equilibrium warming for doubling (relative to the year 2000) CO_2 is likely (probability larger than 66%) to lie in the range 2°C to 4.5°C, with a most likely value of about 3°C. With a probability of 90% the impact of such a doubling will be at least 1.5°C.

So, in short, there is a trend that average surface temperature rises on Earth, and if we extrapolate this trend the temperature will rise considerably in the nearby future. Furthermore, if indeed the CO_2 concentration is responsible for this increase (as expected by the IPCC reports), this effect will impact for a long period of time.

7.2.2 Considerations about Macroeconomics

7.2.2.1 Growth Prospects

The last decades have shown a large increase of international economic integration (i.e., international trade, finance, investment and migration). As a consequence countries/people have become increasingly interdependent on issues such as, for example, employment, production of goods and income spent abroad. As a consequence economic growth in a single country has become much more vulnerable to developments of growth in other parts of the world. Examples illustrating this are the Asian financial crisis in 1997–1998 that arose due to weaknesses in financial and monetary systems in Asian countries and, more recently, the collapse of the US subprime mortgages, and the Eurozone crisis. Asia's recovery from its financial crisis was supported by healthy growth and demand conditions in the developed world. The financial crisis originating in the United States, however, had an impact on loans of banks worldwide. In Europe, for example, generous bank rescue operations were implemented to counteract the serious threat of a negative spiral of an increasing number of banks having solvency problems. Since banks had solvency problems they were very reluctant to provide new loans for any risky investment (that included lending to each other). For that reason governments also engaged in recovery programs. The Eurozone crisis has its roots back in the 1990's . In that time the deregulation of financial markets (enhancing too much and/or bad private and government loans) was initiated and, together with a bad monitoring of government debt by the European Union, this led to an increase of government debt in, for example, Greece. Since there was a distrust in financial markets whether Greece would be able to meet its future obligations in 2009 and the European Central Bank (ECB) was forbidden by the Lisbon treaty to buy bonds of its member states, the Greek could not refinance their debts and the Eurozone crisis occurred. Not completely accidently, this happened at the time Europe was just recovering from the US-induced financial crisis. Due to the solvency problems of private banks[1], the ECB regulations and the fact that debts in the northern EU countries were also beyond the limits set by the European Monetary Union (EMU) treaty, particularly, in Greece, Italy, Portugal, Spain, and Ireland a period of hard budget constraints and belt-tightening has set in, that reverses the growth patterns of the past. The experience of the great depression in the 1930's shows that it is questionable whether in this way the debt ratio of these countries will improve and that the social consequences of such policies can be quite severe. For that reason Article 103 of the Maastricht Treaty that explicitly rules out member state liability for the debts of other EMU member countries is now under revision. The European Union that has intervened from mid 2010 onwards with sometimes rather hastily constructed rescue packages is bracing now for a major reform of the European economic governance system, attempting to blend solidarity with market discipline. This should also become visible in the ECB's regulations concerning the buying/selling of member states's bonds. European banks used to finance a large part of economic activities worldwide. From a world wide economic growth perspective it is therefore important to find a solution for their solvency problems so that European banks can take on this job again.

For the nearby future another problem is the structural trade deficit of the United States versus the trade surplus of China, together with the increasing US deficit. In the long end this situation is not sustainable. The standard way out of this would be for the United States either to devaluate the dollar and/or to decrease the rate of consumption, whereas China should increase the value of the yuan and/or increase its rate of consumption. Given these conditions and (a further expected) increase of the debt ratio in the United States may, however, result in investors to demand higher interest rates since they anticipate a dollar depreciation. Paying these higher interest rates may slow down domestic US growth again.

So, the general perception is that the main economic growth stimulus in the nearby future is to come from the new developing countries like China and Brazil.

7.2.2.2 GDP versus Quality of Life

A confusion that frequently occurs in people's mind is that maximization of economic growth is synonymous with maximization of quality of life (QOL). In fact, economic growth (standard of living/economic wealth/GDP) is just one entry of QOL. QOL has many more entries like, for example, the built environment, physical and mental health, education, recreation and leisure time, and social belonging (Gregory and Johnston (2009)). Probably confusion arises since, often, by using additional money the value of an entry of QOL can be increased. This additional amount of money is then aligned with the additional value of the entry. But, clearly, every entry of QOL has its own dimension and scale of measurement. So, in fact, the above statement of maximizing QOL does not make any sense. Looking for solutions that cannot be improved simultaneously by a better use of the inputs (like, e.g., money) is then all one can do. Usually there is more than one QOL vector satisfying this property. It remains then to the decision maker to choose somehow one solution from this set. This was already formalized by the Italian economist/sociologist Pareto at the end of the 19th century (Pareto (1896)). Notice that increasing the value of one entry of QOL may sometimes have a positive effect on some other entries (positive externalities) too but also, on the contrary, sometimes have a negative effect on some other entries (negative externalities). For instance, if unemployment decreases probably not only GDP increases but also social belonging may increase; in case unemployment decreases the recreation and leisure time decreases too.

In particular one should keep in mind that improving the standard of living may sometimes have quite a large negative impact on other entries of QOL, like environment, recreation, and leisure time. A fact that often is under exposed, particularly in those situations where the standard of living is already high. So, using additional money/input just to improve the standard of living probably does not lead in those cases to a better (let alone optimal) Pareto solution. Or, stated differently, a complete fixation on increasing the standard of living will, usually, not yield a Pareto efficient point within the set of QOL vectors.

Since thinking in more dimensional terms is difficult there have been formulated functions of QOL like, for example, the Human Development Index (HDI), to compare living standards in different countries.

To be able to shrink, or even make a specific choice within, the set of Pareto efficient points additional preference information of the involved person is required. This, however, presumes that QOL variables can somehow be quantified. To measure QOL variables and compare them is not a trivial job. Most of them are measured in different units. To make them comparable one can normalize these numbers by, for example, division by the goal target value of the corresponding objective (hence turning all deviations into percentages) or division by the range of the corresponding objective (between the best and the worst possible values, hence mapping all deviations onto a zero to one range). But notice that the effect of this normalization is just that to each variable a real number is attached. How to value the distance between these numbers for variables relative to each other is then still another issue that has to be tackled. Provided with a measure of QOL variables would probably better inform a decision maker about the choices and the directions where to go.

7.2.2.3 (Socio)Economic Factors Affecting (Macro)Economic Behavior

Every human being has one certainty, namely that he will die (at least physically). Time and what happens after that are uncertain. To cope with this uncertainty is not an easy job. Probably this, together with his instinct to survive, is a drive that makes that (see also Seabright (2010)) humans look for new challenges (that maybe could lead to at least a partial answer to the uncertainties); they look for (at least some) rest points during their life time; they act according to their own individual preferences, without regard for the consequences of this for the group as a whole; their willingness to repay kindness with kindness and betrayal with revenge; and they show short run behavior. This might clarify, for example, the constant drive to change things; herding behavior by people and the current level of international economic integration. Herding behavior is explained from this by the observation that joining a group is a relatively mentally easy job, furthermore it makes the chance that you are doing things wrong small, and if things are wrong, you have the certainty that you are not the only one who went the wrong way. In economics this herding behavior is cleverly manipulated by, for example, the fashion industry.

Seabright explains the current level of international economic integration in Seabright (2010) from the optimizing human behavior's point of view. To clarify his point of view we first recall some other basic facts of life, that is, in order to live one has to eat. To eat one has to grow food. To grow food one has to seed, work on the crop and harvest. This can be done either in isolation or in cooperation with others. Seabright points out three fundamental advantages (and their mutual accumulating effects) that may occur due to cooperation. That is, (1) higher levels of specialization (and as a result production levels); (2) reduction of individual risks and uncertainty from unpredictable adverse outcomes; and (3) an increase in the speed of accumulation of knowledge and technological change. According Seabright (see also Berg (2010)) the current setting of international economic integration might be explained by human beings' optimization drive to exploit these advantages and could be established due to humans' exceptional capacity to engage in abstract reasoning. This enabled them to design social and economic institutions based on trust that effectively enable total strangers to behave routinely in a cooperative manner despite their instinctive fears of exploitation and personal harm.

7.2.2.4 *Considerations about Some Growth Factors*

A number of QOL variables, like environment, cannot be changed instantaneously. They are determined by what happened "long" ago, where the phrase "long" can be either years (litter), decades (CO_2 emissions), centuries or even millennia (nuclear waste). Clearly we cannot judge whether and how these QOL variables will be valued by future generations, or whether future generations will be able to affect these variables at short notice. The short run and optimizing behavior makes that there is a constant pressure not to worry too much about these variables in the future.

Another consequence of optimizing behavior is that if people have a longer-term view of life this longer time perspective enhances investment, innovation, and learning, as all of these activities require some form of short-run sacrifice in exchange for potential future gains.

From an economic point of view, the opportunity cost of global poverty are high due to missed potential contribution to the economic process, migration cost, cost from (prevention of) terrorism, and potential destabilization cost of social networks in developed countries. So an important issue is how to improve on this situation. Probably most human beings would like to assist (everyone in his own way) to help people out of their misery if they cannot be blamed they got into it. The past sad African experience where on a regular basis aid has been provided followed by civil wars again, however, gives people the impression they contribute to a vicious circle. Maybe a way out of this circle is to make aid conditional on progress that has been made on previous projects aimed at welfare improvement ("stepped lending"). Furthermore it may be wise to let countries come up with proposals themselves. This, because they can better judge the local situation. Furthermore, in this way it makes them better accountable for the projects and it makes it possible to better coordinate the help among potential providers. Some main starting points to improve QOL variables in developing countries are clean water supply, sanitation, basic health care, education, and building an infrastructure (including a formal and informal (like a stepped lending microfinancing) economic infrastructure).

Free trade is the perfect solution in a perfect world, since everybody can specialize on those issues at that he is best. This creates dependency amongst people and people must therefore be able to trust each other. Particularly in stressful situations. However, most people want to be able to take their own decisions, to control their own life, and have the natural reaction to choose for their own interest first in stress situations. Consequently, in a non-perfect world with many stress situations, for aggregations of people grouped into countries free trade is probably not optimal from their welfare point of view (for simplicity we identify welfare here with the set of QOL variables). Particularly concerning some basic living conditions (agricultural, energy, security) point of view, the situation where they are up to (at least) some level self supporting seems to be more comfortable and welfare improving.

As previously mentioned, reducing the level of unemployment usually not only positively affects GDP but impacts other entries of QOL too. In case there is large unemployment due to a saturated economy, there are two possibilities to deal with this. One way is to divide the work more equally among everyone. This implies that the employed people would have to substitute income for leisure time. In case this option is not feasible/disliked this option seems to be not welfare improving and there is clearly a need for new employment initiatives. In those situations it seems good to look for initiatives that could improve QOL on other than GDP variables as well. Within the current context of a potential drastic climate change, one could think, for example, of initiatives that make a better use of/find substitutes for current energy or to invest in new infrastructure to deal with changed weather conditions.

Ideally this should be financed from saved budgets when economic times are fine. This requires a strict execution of policy rules in economic good times. Unfortunately, as the Euro crises illustrates, this is not always as easy as it looks like. Particularly if there are no strict sanctioned policy rules there are always people/countries who want to have their dinner paid by their neighbor. Moreover in most of the cases politicians are driven by election scores that depend on public opinion. Again, since many people like to have their dinner paid by their neighbor, and the government is presumed to be one of them, there is a constant pressure on politicians to spend at least all of the government budget. Given all these considerations it seems good to reflect on the establishment of funds like, for example, a recession unemployment fund, governed by some independent institution, that is fed by a fixed percentage of economic growth of government income during good times and that conducts the afore mentioned unemployment policy during recession times. Given such a fixed policy rule there is maybe some automatism to reintegrate unemployed people into the economic process again mitigating the negative effects of large unemployment.

Debt in one country are assets for another party. In case those parties doubt whether the country will meet its future obligations and the central bank of the country does not want to provide the government with additional money too to finance the debt the government has to find other political unpopular ways (like raising taxes, cutting social security funds, privatizing publicly owned undertaking). If a country has large foreign debts and a large number of privatized undertaking are owned by foreign companies it will be difficult for a government to conduct a private economic policy. The economy of the country is out of its government control, that usually is disliked by the people for reasons mentioned earlier. This may lead to stress between countries, usually, resulting in a worse realization of welfare in both countries.

7.2.3 Considerations about Macroeconomics of Climate Change

An increase in global temperature will cause sea levels to rise and will change the amount and pattern of precipitation. Warming is expected to be strongest in the Arctic and implies a continuing retreat of glaciers, permafrost and sea ice. Other likely effects of the warming include more frequent occurrence of extreme weather events including heatwaves, droughts and heavy rainfall events, expansion of subtropical deserts, changes in flora and fauna, and changes in agricultural yields. Warming and related changes will vary from region to region around the globe, with projections being more robust in some areas than others (see IPCC reports). The IPCC reports show that not all countries are hit in the same way. In fact some countries may incur better environmental living conditions. According to reports the Northern Hemisphere in particular will incur the largest rises in temperatures.

So there are large changes to be expected in important QOL variables if temperature increases by some degrees. As previously mentioned, according the IPCC reports an increase of 1.5°C will occur with a probability of 90% if a doubling (compared to its value in the year 2000) or more of CO_2 concentration occurs.

Going through the scientific literature it is striking to see that there are relatively few papers dealing with the impact of climate change on economics. Tol (2010) provides in Tol (2010) a literature review. Based on a partial assessment of some important variables (agriculture and forestry, water resources, coastal zones, energy consumption, health) his main findings are that, although climate change has both positive and negative effects, the negative effects dominate. In particular when temperature rises by more than 1°C. He reports, for example, that an increase of temperature by 2.5°C will have an estimated negative impact on global GDP of −1%. The corresponding 95% confidence interval is, however, ranging from +4% to −11%. In his overview Tol also mentions a number of variables that have not been considered in the analysis and a number of other shortcomings/points that need additional research. However, his impression is that all these points will not reverse the direction of the line of outcome. A second conclusion is that climate change primarily impacts poorer countries, and poverty is one of the main causes for this vulnerability.

Since the risks worldwide associated with the option to do nothing can be quite large, whereas the costs involved with an "overly ambitious" policy are moderate (one can always reverse these policies, if needed) it seems from a risk management point of view for the developed countries best to try to reduce GHG emissions substantially within a not too long time span. Since, also due to an increasing population's demand, fossils are getting more and more scarce, it seems also from a long-term energy supply point of view good for them to look for GHG friendly energy. The perspective that they might be self-supporting with respect to the supply of energy to a certain extent will probably also have a positive effect on the engagement in "green energy" (and technology). Furthermore the potential smaller loss in value of a number of QOL variables might outweigh the potential drop in increase of GDP. Clearly, the more self-supporting a developed country is projected to be w.r.t. its supply of energy, the less risks it experiences.

It is expected that developing countries will be hit the hardest if temperature increases. This, since they are more exposed to the most additional dangerous consequences of changes in precipitation patterns, rising sea levels, and more frequent weather-related disasters posed risks for agriculture, food, water supplies and health. This assessment is confirmed by Tol's review, where one of his conclusions is that climate change primarily impacts poorer countries, and poverty is one of the main causes for this vulnerability. So poorer countries seem to be trapped. A climate policy that negatively affects economic development may harm them most, whereas a development policy aiming to improve living standards using conventional production technologies may drastically increase CO_2 emissions leading to a probably additional increase of temperature. From the developing aid providing countries' point of view it is to be expected that they will condition economic aid on whether poor countries pursue CO_2 emission friendly policies. This is illustrated, for example by the request in 2005 of the industrialized G-8 countries who asked the World Bank to develop a plan for more investments in clean energy in the developing world, in cooperation with other international financial institutions. According the 2010 edition of the World Development Report of the World Bank (2010) there is now a focus on development in a changing climate. Climate change adaptation considerations are being integrated into Country Assistance Strategies. The bank is also piloting innovative climate risk insurance possibilities to help countries integrate disaster planning into their development strategies. An increasing interest in trying to improve the identification, quantification, pricing, and mitigation of the risks involved is also shown by large insurance companies (see, e.g., Allianz (2010)).

A number of the new industrializing countries like Russia and Brazil are projected to be major providers of fossil fuel energy over the coming decades (WEO (2011)). So they may expect a substantial increase in GDP that potentially can lever a substantial increase of various other QOL variables too.

So, we may conclude that different types of countries have different perceptions about the need to engage in "green energy/technology".

7.3 What Is (Dynamic) Game Theory About[2]

Game theory studies the interactive decision-making process between persons (or more abstract: decision-making entities) with (at least partial) conflicting interests in situations where decisions by one person affect the decision made by another person. This decision making can be done in either a cooperative setting or a non cooperative setting. It is used to describe, predict, explain, and enforce desired behavior.

Most research in game theory has been done on, so-called, static games (see e.g., Osborne and Rubinstein (1994) or Osborne (2004) for an elementary introduction). In static games one concentrates on the normal form of a game. In this form all possible sequences of decisions of each player are set out against each other. So, for example, for a two-player game this results in a matrix structure. The information agents have about the game is crucial for the outcome of the decision making. A distinction is made between complete and incomplete information games. In a complete information game, agents know not only their own payoffs, but also the payoffs and strategies of all the other agents. Characteristic for a static game is that it takes place in one moment of time: all players make their choice once and simultaneously and, dependent on the choices made, each player receives his payoff. In such a formulation important issues such as the order of play in the decision process, information available to the players at the time of their decisions, and the evolution of the game are suppressed, and this is the reason why this branch of game theory is usually classified as "static."

To capture information aspects in a static game one uses the so-called extensive form of the game. Basically this involves a tree structure with several nodes and branches, providing an explicit description of the order of play and the information available to each agent at the time of his decision. In case at least one of the agents has an infinite number of actions to choose from it is impossible to use the tree structure to describe the game. In those cases the extensive form involves the description of the evolution of the underlying decision process using a set of difference or differential equations.

Games in which a noncooperative static game is played repeatedly are known as repeated games. Aumann and Maschler (1995) studies repeated games with incomplete information. Formally the basic model here is a finite family of games with an initial probability that determines that one of these games will be played. In this set-up, after each stage, the players receive information on their opponents' moves and/or on the game chosen.

In case the agent's act in a dynamic environment, strategic behavior and interdependencies over time play a crucial role and need to be properly specified before one can infer what the outcome of the game will be. This is typically the case in macroeconomic modeling. Games dealing with these aspects are called dynamic games. Dynamic game theory brings together four features that are key to many situations in economy, ecology, and elsewhere: optimizing behavior, presence of multiple agents/players, enduring consequences of decisions, and robustness with respect to variability in the environment.

To deal with problems bearing these four features the dynamic game theory methodology splits the modeling of the problem into three parts.

One part is the modeling of the environment in that the agents act. To obtain a mathematical model of the agents' environment, usually a set of differential or difference equations is specified describing the change over time of the set of variables of interest (usually represented in one vector the, so-called, state vector of the considered system). These equations are assumed to capture the main (dynamical) features of the environment. A characteristic property of this specification is that these dynamic equations mostly contain a set of so-called "input" functions. These input functions model the effect of the actions taken by the agents on the environment during the course of the game. In particular, by viewing "nature" as a separate player in the game who can choose an input functional that works against the other player(s) one can model worst case scenarios and, consequently, analyze the robustness of the "undisturbed" game solution.

A second part is the modeling of the agents' objectives. Usually the agents' objectives are formalized as cost/utility functionals that have to be minimized. Since this minimization has to be performed subject to the specified dynamic model of the environment, techniques developed in optimal control theory play an important role in solving dynamic
games.

The third part is then the formalization of the the order of play in the decision process and information available to the players at the time of their decisions (so, in particular, will learning take place over time).

A branch of dynamic games that is frequently analyzed in the literature is where the system dynamics are modeled by a set of differential equations, the so-called differential games. But many other mathematical models to describe systems that change over time (or sequentially) such as, for example, difference equations, partial differential equations, differential and algebraic equations, time-delay equations where either stochastic uncertainty is added or not, are considered too. All of these give rise to different classes of dynamic games that have their own specific model features.

To realize his objective an agent can either cooperate with one or more agents in the game or not. In case all agents cooperate we speak about a cooperative game. In case none of the agents cooperates with someone else the game is called a noncooperative game. The intermediate case that groups of agents cooperate in coalitions against each other in a noncooperative way is called a coalitional game.

In some situations where agents cooperate it is possible that agents can transfer (part of) their revenues/cost to another agent. If this is the case the game is called a transferable utility (TU) game. Otherwise it is called a nontransferable utility (NTU) game.

An important issue that affects the outcome of the game is the organization of the decision-making process. In case there is one agent who has a leading position in the decision-making process the game is called a Hierarchical or Stackelberg game (after H. von Stackelberg (1934)). So in this case there is a vertical structure in the decision-making process. In case there does not exist such a dependency we talk about a horizontal decision-making structure.

Two popular decision rules in dynamic games are the so-called open-loop and feedback strategy. In the open-loop strategy players determine their plans for the entire planning horizon of the game at the start of the game. Next they submit these plans to some authority, who then enforces these plans as binding commitments for the whole planning period. If feedback strategies are used it is assumed that players determine their actions at any point in time as a function of the state of the system at that time. This strategy sets out of course that players can actually implement this strategy at every point in time.

7.3.1 Choice of Actions

From the previous section it will be clear that the actions played by the agents in a dynamic game depend on the coordination structure, organizational structure, information structure and decision rule (or strategy) followed by the agents. Assuming that every agent likes to minimize his cost the problem as stated so far, however, is not well defined yet. Depending on the coordination structure and organizational structure different solution concepts can be considered.

If a static noncooperative game is played repeatedly, the notion of mixed strategies is often used. In a mixed strategy the agents choose their actions based on a probability distribution. The probability distribution chosen by the agents might be such that, for example, their average value of the game is optimized.

In a Stackelberg game (see, e.g., He et al. (2007) for a review of its use in supply chain and marketing models) it is assumed that the leader announces his decision u_L, that is subsequently made known to the other player, the follower. With this knowledge, the follower chooses his decision u_F by minimizing his cost for this choice of u_L. So, the optimal reaction of the follower u_F is a function of u_L. The leader takes this optimal reaction function of the follower into account to determine his action as the argument that minimizes his cost $J_L(u_L, u_F(u_L))$. Notice that in this solution concept it is assumed that the leader has a complete knowledge about the follower's preferences and strategy. Other solution concepts have been studied too, such as, for example, the so-called inverse Stackelberg equilibrium, where the leader does not announce his action u_L, but his reaction function $\gamma_L(u_F)$. This concept can be used to enforce by the leader a desired behavior of the follower (see Olsder (2009),Olsder (2009)). Closely related to this are games of mechanism design in, so-called, Bayesian games (i.e., games in that information about the other players payoffs is incomplete see, e.g., Myerson (2008)). Within these kinds of games there is a leader who chooses the payoff structure of the game. The idea is that this leader sets the rules so as to motivate followers to disclose private information (see also Salanie (2002)). Consistent conjectural variations equilibria are equilibria that can be viewed as "double sided Stackelberg" equilibria. Here it is assumed that both players conjecture a reaction function $\gamma_i(u_j)$ of their opponent in function of their own decision. If the resulting best responses u_i^* and conjectured reactions coincide these responses are called a consistent conjectural variations equilibrium (see Basar and Olsder (1999) or Figuières (2004)).

In a noncooperative game one of the most frequent used solutions is the *Nash equilibrium*. As the name suggests, this is an equilibrium concept. It is assumed that ultimately those actions will be played by the agents that have the property that none of the agents can unilaterally improve by playing a different action. One of the main references that documents the theoretical developments on this issue in dynamic games is the seminal book Basar and Olsder (1999). Furthermore, uncertainty can be dealt within this framework by assuming that the player "nature" always selects a worst-case scenario (see, e.g., Basar and Bernhard (1995), Kun (2001), Broek, et al. (2003), Engwerda (2005) and Azevedo-Perdicolis and Jank (2011)). Another minimax approach to model uncertainty that has been used in finance are so-called interval models (Bernhard, et al. (2012)). Here it is assumed that a compact set is known that contains the new state vector. Furthermore, in case one views uncertainty as some separate vector entering the system, approaches to isolate this "disturbance" in a multiplayer context have been formulated in, for example, Broek and Schumacher (2000).

Since the Nash equilibrium is an equilibrium concept, in many applications an important issue is how this equilibrium is attained. Two of the approaches that try to answer this question, particularly in the context with a large number of agents, are evolutionary game theory and coordination games. Using, for example, learning models they try to predict the road toward the equilibrium (see, for example, Fudenberg and Levine (1998), Hart (2005), Sandholm (2010), Chasparis and Shamma (2012)).

In a cooperative setting it seems reasonable to look for those combinations of control actions that have the property that the resulting cost incurred by the different players cannot be improved for all players simultaneously by choosing a different set of control actions. Formally, a set of control actions $\hat{u}$ is called *Pareto efficient* if the set of inequalities $J_i(u) \leq J_i(\hat{u})$, $i = 1, \cdots, N$, where at least one of the inequalities is strict, does not allow for any solution $u \in \mathcal{U}$. The corresponding point $(J_1(\hat{u}), \cdots, J_N(\hat{u}))$ is called a *Pareto solution.* Usually there is more than one Pareto solution. The set of all Pareto solutions is called the *Pareto frontier.* In particular this implies that this Pareto efficiency concept in general does not suffice to conclude that action is optimal for an agent in a cooperative setting.

In a NTU game the cost of the agents are fixed once the actions of the agents are fixed. So, the question is then that point is reasonable to select on the Pareto frontier. Bargaining theory may help then to select a point on the Pareto frontier.

Bargaining theory has its origin in two papers by Nash (1950) and Nash (1953). In these papers a bargaining problem is defined as a situation in that two (or more) individuals or organizations have to agree on the choice of one specific alternative from a set of alternatives available to them, while having conflicting interests over this set of alternatives. Nash proposes in Nash (1953) two different approaches to the bargaining problem, namely the *axiomatic* and the *strategic* approach. The axiomatic approach lists a number of desirable properties the solution must have, called the *axioms.* The strategic approach, on the other hand, sets out a particular bargaining procedure and asks what outcomes would result from rational behavior by the individual players.

So, bargaining theory deals with the situation in that players can realize—through cooperation—other (and better) outcomes than the one that becomes effective when they do not cooperate. This noncooperative outcome is called the *threatpoint.* The question is to that outcome the players may possibly agree.

In Figure 7.1 a typical bargaining game is sketched. The ellipse marks out the set of possible outcomes, the *feasible set* S, of the game. The point d is the threatpoint. The edge P is the Pareto frontier.

Three well-known solutions are the Nash bargaining solution, N, the Kalai-Smorodinsky solution, K, and the Egalitarian solution, E. The *Nash bargaining solution* selects the point of S at that the product of utility gains from d is maximal. The Kalai-Smorodinsky solution divides utility gains from the threatpoint proportional to the

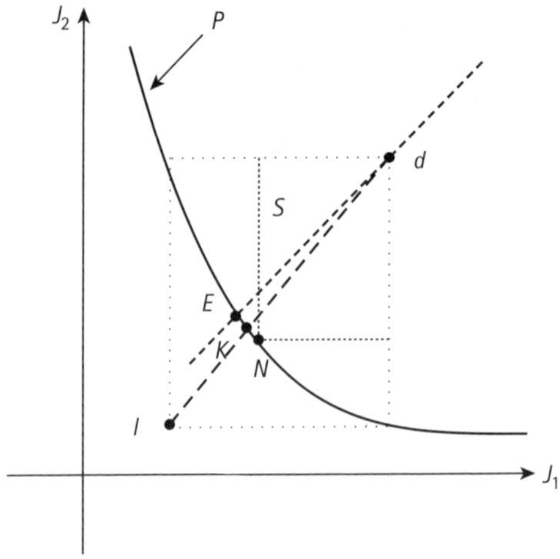

FIGURE 7.1 The bargaining game.

player's most optimistic expectations, *I*. For each agent, the most optimistic expectation is defined as the lowest cost he can attain in the feasible set subject to the constraint that no agent incurs a cost higher than his coordinate of the threatpoint. Finally, the *Egalitarian solution* represents the idea that gains should be equal divided between the players. For more background and other axiomatic bargaining solutions we refer to Thomson (1994).

In transferable utility games it may happen that it is less clear-cut how the gains of cooperation should be divided. Consider, for example, the case that agents are involved in a joint project and the joint benefits of this cooperation have to be shared. In those cases an agreement in the cooperative dynamic game, or *solution* of the cooperative dynamic game, involves both an agreement on the allocation rule and an agreement on the set of strategies/controls. Again, in this case the allocation rule is required to be individually rational in the sense that no agent should be worse off than before his decision to cooperate.

In differential games an important issue is then at what point in time the "payments" occur. Is this at the beginning of the planning horizon of the game, at the end of the planning horizon of the game, at some a priori determined fixed points in time of the game, or is every agent paid continuously during the length of the game? Particularly in the last case it seems reasonable to demand from the allocation rule that it is consistent over time. That is, the allocation rule is such that the allocation at any point in time is optimal for the remaining part of the game? along the optimal state trajectory. So in particular at any point in time the payment should be individually rational for every player. An allocation rule that has this property is called subgame-consistent. Of course in a dynamic cooperative game not only the payment allocation rule is important but, like for all dynamic games, also the time-consistency of the strategies is important from a robustness point of view. A solution is called *subgame-consistent* if the allocation rule is subgame-consistent and the cooperative strategies are strongly time consistent. Yeung and Petrosyan (2006) give a rigorous framework for the study of subgame-consistent solutions in cooperative stochastic differential games (see also Yeung (2011) for an extension of this theory).

7.3.2 Coalitional Games

The bargaining approach presented in the previous section does not consider the formation of coalitions. In the presence of nonbinding agreements, even if the players agree on a cooperative outcome, situations arise where the grand coalition could break down. Classical coalitional games are casted in characteristic function form. When the utilities are transferable a *characteristic function* $v(.)$ assigns to every coalition a real number (*worth*), representing the total payoff of this coalition of players when they cooperate. Stated differently, it denotes the power structure of the game, that is, the players in a coalition collectively demand a payoff $v(S)$ to stay in the grand coalition. In the bargaining problem the coordinates of the threat point d_i represent the payoff each player receives by acting on their own. Similarly $v(S)$ represents the collective payoff that a coalition $S \subset N$ can receive when the left out players in the coalition $N \backslash S$ act against S. In a nontransferable utility setting, however, two distinct set valued characteristic functions have been proposed, see Aumann (1961), as the α and β characteristic functions. The main difference originates from the functional rules used in deriving them from the normal form game.

Under the α notion, the characteristic function indicates those payoffs that coalition S can secure for its members even if the left out players in $N \backslash S$ strive to act against S. Here, players in S first announce their joint correlated strategy before the joint correlated strategy of the players in $N \backslash S$ is chosen. So, this is an assurable representation. Under the β notion, the characteristic function indicates those payoffs that the left out players in $N \backslash S$ cannot prevent S from getting. Here, players in S choose their joint correlated strategy after the joint correlated strategy of the players in $N \backslash S$ is announced. So, this is an unpreventable representation.

An *imputation* is a set of allocations that are individually rational, that is, every allocation is such that it guarantees the involved player a payoff more than what he could achieve on his own. A set of allocations is in the *core* when it is coalitionally rational. That is, the core consists of those imputations for that no coalition would be better off if it would separate itself and get its coalitional worth. Or, stated differently, a set of allocations belongs to the core if there is no incentive to any coalition to break off from the grand coalition. Clearly, the core is a subset of the Pareto frontier. The core is obtained by solving a linear programming problem. It can be empty. There are other solution concepts based on axioms such as Shapley value and nucleolus.

(Endogenous) coalition formation theory studies rules (like coalition membership, voting, structure of the negotiation process) of coalition formation. These rules can be interpreted as different institutional designs where the negotiations take place. Different rules will generally lead to different equilibrium coalition structures. The phrase equilibrium within this context means, for example, that no player can increase his payoff unilaterally by joining a different coalition. In particular, the effect of the rules on the efficiency of the resulting equilibrium coalition structure is analyzed (see, e.g., Bloch (1997), Carraro (1999), Finus (2005), Plasmans et al. (2006), Ray (2008)).

The cooperative solutions mentioned above are static concepts. Introducing dynamics in a coalitional setting raises new conceptual questions. It is not straightforward as to how one can extend the classical definition of core in a dynamic setting since there exist many notions of a profitable deviation. As a result, a unifying theory of dynamic coalitional games, at present, seems too ambitious. However, intuitively, in this context one expects the definition of core should capture those situations in that at each stage the grand coalition is formed no coalition has a profitable deviation, that is, dynamic stability, taking into account the possibility of future profitable deviations of subcoalitions. In an environment with nonbinding agreements only self-enforcing allocations are deemed to be stable. The main difference between static and dynamic setting is the credibility Ray (2008) of a deviation. A deviation of a coalition S is *credible* if there is no incentive for a subcoalition $T \subset S$ to deviate from S. The set of deviations and credible deviations coincide for a static game but differ in a dynamic setting. Kranich et al. (2005) suggest new formulations of the core in dynamic cooperative games using credible deviations. For instance, if one makes an assumption that once a coalition deviates players cannot return to cooperation later, results in a core concept called strong sequential core. This allows for further splitting of the deviating coalition in the future. They also introduce a notion of weak sequential core that is a set of allocations for the grand coalition from that no coalition has ever a credible deviation. See, Habis (2011) for more details.

We review some work done toward extending the idea of a core in a differential game setting. Haurie (1975) constructs an α characteristic function assuming the behavior of left out players is modeled as unknown bounded disturbances. Using this construction he introduces in Haurie and Delfour (1974) collectively rational Pareto-optimal trajectories with an intent to extend the concept of core to dynamic multistage games. Analogously, a Pareto equilibrium is called collectively optimal (C-optimal) when, at any stage, no coalition of a subset of the decision-makers can assure each of its members a higher gain than what he can get by full cooperation with all the other decision-makers. It is shown that if the game evolves on these trajectories any coalition does not have an incentive to deviate from the grand coalition in the later stages.

Time consistency, as introduced by Petrosjan et al. (2005), in a dynamic cooperative game means that when the game evolves along the cooperative trajectory generated by a solution concept (that can be any solution concept such as core, Shapley value, and nucleolus) then no player has an incentive to deviate from the actions prescribed by that solution. The notion of strong sequential core introduced in Kranich et al. (2005) is the same as time consistency. Zaccour (2003) studies the computational aspects of characteristic functions for linear state differential games. Evaluation of the characteristic function involves $2^N - 2$ equilibrium problems and one optimization problem (for the grand coalition), that is computationally expensive with a large number of players. Therefore, instead, they propose an approach by optimizing the joint strategies of the coalition players while the left out players use their Nash equilibrium strategies. This modification involves solving one equilibrium problem and $2^N - 2$ optimization problems. Further, they characterize a class of games where this modified approach provides the same characteristic function values.

Assuming that players at each period/instant of time consider alternatives "cooperate" and "do not cooperate," Klompstra (1992) studies a linear quadratic differential game. It is shown that for a three-player game, there exists time-dependent switching between different modes, namely the grand coalition, formation of subcoalitions, and total noncooperation. Assuming similar behavior of players, that is, to "cooperate" or "do not cooperate" at each time instant, Germain et al. (2003) introduce a rational expectations core concept. They use the γ characteristic function Chander and Tulkens (1997) where the left out players act individually against the coalition instead of forming a counter coalition. They show, using an environmental pollution game, that if each period of time players show interest in continued cooperation then, based on the rational expectations criterion, there exists a transfer scheme that induces core-theoretic cooperation at each period of time. Recently, Jørgensen (2010) studies a differential game of waste management and proposes a transfer scheme that sustains intertemporal core-theoretic cooperation.

7.3.3 Decentralization

In a cooperative setting, agents coordinate their strategies and it is not always feasible to maintain communication to implement their coordinated actions. Further, problems can arise due to lack of stability in the cooperative agreement. Threats and deterrence are some of the common stability inducing mechanisms used to enforce cooperation, such as, for instance, trigger strategies where a player using a trigger strategy initially cooperates but punishes the opponent if a certain level of defection (i.e., the trigger) is observed. In the context of differential games, see Section 6.2 of Dockner et al. (2000) for more details on such strategies. In his seminal paper, Rosen (1965) introduces a concept of normalized equilibrium that deals with a class of noncooperative games in that the constraints as well as the payoffs may depend on the strategies of all players. Using this approach Tidball and Zaccour (2009) show in a static game that a cooperative solution can be attained by a suitable choice of the normalized equilibrium. Further, they show, in a dynamic context, that only by introducing a tax mechanism it is possible to attain cooperation in a decentralized manner. Rosenthal (1973) introduced a class of games that admit pure strategy Nash equilibria, that were later studied in a more general setting by Monderer and Shapley (1996) as potential games. A strategic game is a potential game if it admits a potential function. A potential function is a real valued function, defined globally on the strategies of the players, such that its local optimizers are precisely the equilibria of the game. So, these games enable the use of optimization methods to find equilibria in a game instead of fixed point techniques. If, the social objective of the game coincides with the potential function then we see that the social optimum can be implemented in a non-cooperative manner. Dragone et al. (2009) present some preliminary work toward the extension of potential games in a differential game setting and study games that arise in advertising.

7.4 Differential Games and Macroeconomics of Climate Change

7.4.1 An Illustration

In the previous chapter we flashed some major concepts used in game theory to model situations with players that have different interests. In this section we indicate how these concepts can be/have been used in modeling impacts of climate change on macroeconomic developments. As a first simple illustration of a static single-act matrix game consider the conflict of interest of the developed countries versus the new industrialized countries on the implementation speed of green energy production. Table 7.1 provides some fictive numbers representing a measure of realized QOL variables using either a laissez faire (LF) (mainly use of fossil fuel) or a green orientated (GO) (more use of "green energy") strategy on a short (S, 5 years), medium (M, 15 years), and longer (L, 30 years) horizon.

Table 7.1 Gains of LF versus Go strategy. First entries denote gains DC countries, second entries denote gains NDC countries

S	NDC		M	NDC		M/L	NDC		L	NDC	
DC	GO	LF	DC	GO	LF	DC	GO	LF	DC	GO	LF
GO	100,50	95,60	GO	110,70	105,75	GO	120,95	115,83	GO	130,100	120,87
LF	105,55	110,65	LF	115,60	115,78	LF	123,70	116,82	LF	125,75	117,85

First consider the short horizon case. From the S table we see that if the policy of the DC is GO, the best strategy for the NDC is LF. If the DC choose for LF, LF is also the best strategy for the NDC. So the NDC will always choose for LF irrespective of the DC's choice. Therefore the equilibrium outcome will be LF for both the NDC and DC countries. This equilibrium is enforced by the NDC's choice. For the long horizon case things are reversed. Here the equilibrium GO is chosen by both the NDC and DC countries and is enforced by the DC countries because irrespective of the choice of the NDC's choice the DC countries choose for the GO option. In the intermediate horizon case both the DC and NDC choose the LF strategy.

We also included a situation M/L that might occur in between the medium and long horizon case. In that case we see that the DC countries always choose for LF, with as a consequence that the NDC will choose for that option too. This solution is, however, suboptimal. If both the DC and NDC countries choose for GO they both can achieve a better outcome. The reason why this does not occur is the lack of coordination (see also Plasmans et al. (2006), where policy cooperation as a prisoners' dilemma is described). This example describes a case of pure discretionary coordination. The DC and NDC countries decide on a case-by-case basis to internalize the economic externalities resulting from macroeconomic interdependence and each country may gain without giving up anything of its sovereignty.

In the above example it was assumed that both DC and NDC countries could choose from just two strategies, that is, GO or LF. A more realistic assumption is that they can opt for any mix of both strategies too. In that case, assuming some fixed strategy is played by the NDC countries, the DC can determine their optimal strategy (response) given that choice. By considering all potential strategies from the NDC countries the DC countries obtain then an optimal response set (reaction curve). In a similar way the NDC countries arrive at their reaction curve. Figure 7.2 visualizes this case. On the axis the policies, u_D and u_N, of the DC and NDC countries are displaced. Each combination of policies yields a realization (Q_D, Q_N) of the measure of QOL variables for both countries, like in Table 7.2. Indifference curves for policies yielding the same value for the DC and NDC countries are drawn, respectively. I_D (I_N) represents the point at that the Q_D (Q_N) value for the DC (NDC) countries is maximal. So, a curve further away from I_D (I_N) indicates a lower value for Q_D (Q_N). The non cooperative equilibrium of the game is given by point N, where both reaction curves intersect. Clearly in N both the DC and NDC countries have no incentive to deviate from their policy. From the plot we see that by moving north east it is possible to increase for both DC and NDC countries their Q_i value. Pareto-efficient equilibria, like point C, are represented by the contract curve $I_D - I_N$. All points on this curve can be implemented as the result of a cooperative agreement. Of course, any of these agreement should be binding since points as C are not located on the reaction curves. So they imply an expost incentive for both the DC and NDC countries to deviate from them.

We also indicated the Stackelberg solution S if the NDC countries are the leader. Clearly for the NDC countries S is a better outcome than the N solution. Finally we

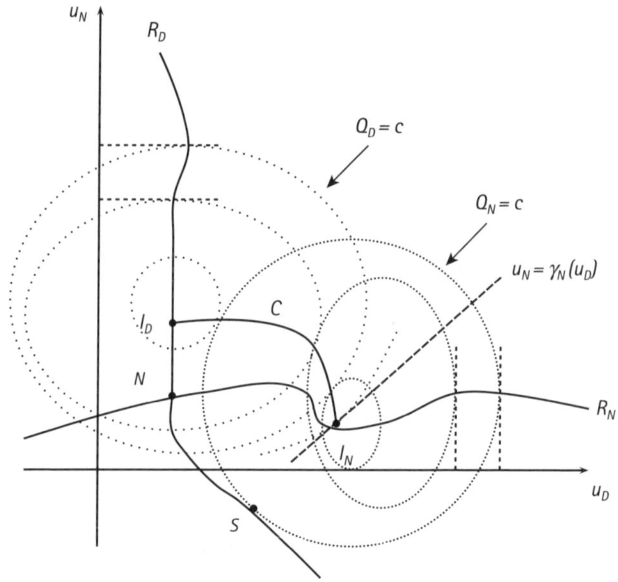

FIGURE 7.2 Hamada's diagram. *N*: Nash; *S*: Stackelberg (leader NDC); *C*: Cooperative solutions; I_i: Ideal point player *i*; R_i: Reaction curve player *i*; $\gamma_N(u_D)$: Optimal reaction function Stackelberg leader NDC; $Q_i = c$: indifference curves.

illustrated a reaction function for the NDC countries that would provide them with their maximum Q_N value at the point I_N.

As noticed above cooperation will become nonsustainable if countries do not stick to their commitment and cheat by deviating in their policies from the agreed policy stance. The cooperation problem is closely related to the reputation issue and the international institutional design like, for example, the existence of a supranational authority that enforces international cooperation agreements (see Plasmans et al. (2006)). If countries face the same international coordination problem in the future, that is, the game is repeated each period, it must be possible to achieve efficient outcomes by a reputation mechanism. If a country comes to a decision node where there is an incentive to renege on the cooperative outcome, such a cooperative agreement will clearly lack credibility and rational policymakers will not enter into such an agreement and, by symmetry, no cooperation is the outcome. The folk theorem of repeated games stresses that even if countries have an incentive to renege they will not do so because they fear to lose payoffs when other countries can punish them in the subsequent periods. The reason why trigger strategies can support repeated games, consistent with efficient policies, is that for each country the value of deviating from the efficient policy in each period is outweighed by the discounted value of having efficient policies played in the future. Therefore, for trigger strategies to work, payoffs in the future must not be discounted too heavily. As suggested by the example, within the current context of taking a decision whether and when to engage in more "green" (energy) production this may be an issue. If future realizations of QOL variables are discounted, many of the future gains of engaging in an early "green" strategy might be undervalued.

Another way to restore sustainability is to develop an incentive mechanism through sanctions against reneging. If there are supranational institutions that can legally enforce the coordinated solution, then policies will be credible. Such an institution will reduce the likelihood that countries renege upon their commitments. The supranational enforcement implies a loss of sovereignty (see Canzoneri Henderson (1991)) in comparison with a sovereign policymaking process (with countries coordinating on an agreed outcome and employing a trigger mechanism to enforce it). Other pros and cons of institutionalized rule-based cooperation can be found, for example, in Plasmans et al. (2006)[p.10].

More recently, the idea of issue linkage has been introduced as a device supporting cooperation. This is basically an agreement designed in which participants do not negotiate on only one issue, but on two or more issues. The intuition is that by adopting cooperative behavior, some agents gain in a given issue, whereas other agents gain in another. By linking the two issues, the agreement in that agents decide to cooperate on both issues may become profitable to all of them. Issue linkage is a way to increase cooperation on issues where the incentives to free ride are particularly strong. The goal is to determine under that conditions players actually prefer to link the negotiations on two different issues rather than negotiating on the two issues separately in the context of endogenous coalition formation Carraro and Marchiori (2003).

7.4.2 Literature Review and Open Ends

Recently two review papers have been published that give a good impression of what has been achieved the last few decades in modeling environmental and optimal resource extraction problems within a (macro) economic setting using game theoretic tools. We briefly indicate the subjects dealt with in these papers below. Readers can consult then either one of both papers for references concerning their favorite subject. We conclude this section by listing a number of subjects that need additional attention.

Jørgensen et al. (2010) provide a survey of the literature that utilizes dynamic state-space games to formulate and analyze intertemporal, many decision-maker problems in the economics and management of pollution. In particular Jørgensen (2010) surveys the literature devoted to the analysis of various macroeconomic problems using a dynamic game framework. Studies about the interaction between growth and environmental problems, economic-environmental problems of climate change, the effect of population growth and mitigation on macroeconomic policies, the use of income transfers as a mechanism to improve environmental quality, and sustainable development are reviewed.

Van Long (2011) provides a survey of the use of dynamic games in the exploitation of renewable and exhaustible resources. It includes dynamic games at the industry level (oligopoly, cartel versus fringe, tragedy of the commons) and at the international level (tariffs on exhaustible resources, fish wars, entry deterrence). Among other things, international strategic issues involving the link between resource uses and transboundary pollution, the design of taxation to ensure efficient outcomes under symmetric and asymmetric information, and the rivalry among factions in countries where property rights on natural resources are not well established are discussed. Outcomes under Nash equilibria and Stackelberg equilibria are compared.

The general impression from the literature is that a great deal of work has been done predominantly using an analytic approach. This has improved the understanding of macroeconomic relationships in a strategic and dynamic setting. However, these results are obtained under rather simplifying assumptions. This is an inherent property of dealing with analytic models. Only models having a simple structure are tractable (see Turnovsky (2011) for a discussion on the use of small macromodels). To present dynamic games as a relevant decision support tool to better understand macroeconomic processes and more in particular the consequences of climate change on it requires still a lot of work. Extensions as well in the development of more analytic models, numerical simulation models, and dynamic game theory are required. In particular it seems that not much progress has been made in developing numerical multicountry dynamic macroeconomic simulation models that contain strategic elements to analyze potential effects of climate change on key macroeconomic variables (as have been developed for studying macroeconomic policy problems elsewhere (see e.g., Behrens and Neck (2007), Plasmans et al. (2006))). Some important topics that need further attention are modeling more general environments of interaction; the integration of learning dynamics, including intertemporal budget constraints; the endogeneization of (energy) prices; and including demographic structures (in particular modeling population growth and migration). Further issues concern the use of different information structures by different players (e.g., different time horizons with different discounting, different philosophies about common property resources) and the use of different solution concepts. An important point is also to achieve a better understanding on how uncertainty affects human response on, for example, their engagement in innovation strategies. Finally there is a need to develop within this context further models of dynamic decision making, enforcement rules, and satisficing strategies Bearden and Connolly (2008).

7.5 Concluding Remarks

Modeling climate change is an intricate job that involves the modeling of many complex processes that affect each other. Since quite a number of these processes are not completely understood this brings on uncertainty if one uses models of these processes to predict the future development of climate. The IPCC reports have been produced to reflect the current knowledge on this. Through its assessment reports, the IPCC has gained enormous respect. However, as noticed in the IAC 2010 report IAC (2010), the reports can be improved in particular w.r.t. the presentation of (uncertainty in) results. Expecting that these key recommendations by the IAC will be taken into account one just can hope that the 2013 IPCC report will provide a better insight into the various involved uncertainties.

The historical development of human beings behavior (with optimizing behavior w.r.t. a relatively short time horizon), the potential long-term effects of CO_2 increases on temperature and the increase of a large number of people asking for energy will (at some point in time) lead to an increase of demand for "green energy" by many countries. This due to the increase of (taxed) prices of fossil fuels and the desire to be more independent w.r.t. its energy supply. This adaptation will most likely first be carried out by the developed countries, since quite a number of the new developing countries possess large amounts of fossil fuels, and therefore have a preference to use old fossil fuel consuming production strategies, and the developing countries cannot pay this investment. A positive aspect of such an adaptation is that it may give a boost to the development of new technology. Since for the (new) developing countries the (much less taxed) prices of fossil fuels are much lower they will continue using them, leading to a boost of CO_2 emissions due to the large number of population involved. Given the expected extension of life expectancy, population growth will perhaps stop. However, such a scenario will take quite some years before it reaches a plateau and by that time a huge increase of CO_2 emissions will have occurred. One way out of this trap seems to make the developing countries use the "green energy" production technology too. Given the vulnerability of poor countries for temperature rises and the help provided by the developed countries, the implementation of such production technologies is probably feasible in those countries. In particular there is a large potential for developing countries to cooperate with the developed countries in the realization of, for example, more solar energy. However, the political instability of developing countries is a serious obstacle here. So, from this perspective, the major problem seems whether the developed countries and the newly industrialized countries can engage in a binding settlement to switch toward societies that depend to a large extent on green energy production. Two major questions here are, first, how countries can be supported in their vast increasing demand for energy. Or, stated differently, how fast can the production of green energy be increased? Second, countries such as Russia and Brazil are projected to be a major provider of energy over the coming decades (WEO (2011)) and will probably experience growth rates in GDP that exceed those of the developed countries. The question is how to compensate them for the involved short-term opportunity cost.

Can dynamic game theory contribute to the solution of these problems? We illustrated, using a fictive example, how dynamic game theory helps to better understand the arising conflict situations. In particular the example illustrated that without any form of international binding agreements it is hard to expect that Pareto-efficient solutions will be obtained. Further, we showed in this chapter that there are many facets and kinds of risk involved in modeling the effect of climate change on QOL variables and in particular GDP. In the previous section we already mentioned that using mainly analytic models insights have been obtained in various directions and we indicated a number of issues that need further exploration. On the other hand, it should be clear from the sketched framework that a basic deterministic mathematical modeling of reality is not possible. Uncertainties are present at all levels and (dynamic) game theory cannot solve these uncertainties. What it is able to do, or at least tries to do, is to provide a better understanding of interacting systems (where systems should be interpreted in a broad sense) and to provide mechanisms that after implementation imply a more smooth behavior of the complete system.

Notes

1. In the Netherlands these solvency problems are even increased by the fact that pension funds must value their assets at the current interest rate. This implies that at the current low interest rates they are underfunded and cannot invest too.
2. Parts of this section were presented in Engwerda and Reddy (2011).

References

Allianz, (2010). Allianz Group Portal: Strategy and management, climate change. https://www.allianz.com/en/responsibility/global_issues/climate_change/index.html

Aumann, R. J. (1961). The core of a cooperative game without sidepayments. *Transactions of the American Mathematical Society, 98*, 539–552.

Aumann, R. J., and Maschler, M. (1995). *Repeated Games with Incomplete Information.* Cambridge, MA: MIT Press.

Azevedo-Perdicolis, T.-P., and Jank, G. (2011). Existence and uniqueness of disturbed open-loop nash equilibria for affine-quadratic differential games. *Advances in Dynamic Games, 11*, 25–39.

Basar, T., and Bernhard, P. (1995). *H^∞-Optimal Control and Related Minimax Design Problems.* Boston: Birkhäuser.

Basar, T., and Olsder, G. J. (1999). *Dynamic Noncooperative Game Theory.* Philadelphia: SIAM.

Bearden, J. N., and Connolly, T. (2008). On optimal satisficing: How simple strategies can achieve excellent results. In T. Kugler, et al. (eds.), *Decision Modeling and Behavior in Complex and Uncertain Environments*, pp. 79–97. Berlin: Springer.

Behrens, D. A., and Neck, R. (2007). OPTGAME: An algorithm approximating solutions for multi-player difference games. In K. Elleithy (ed.), *Advances and Innovations in Systems, Computing Sciences and Software Engineering*, pp. 93–98. Dordrecht, The Netherlands: Springer.

Berg, H. van den. (2010). *International Economics. A Heterodox Approach.* London: M.E. Sharpe.

Berger, A. (1977). Support for the astronomical theory of climatic change. *Nature, 269*, 44–45.

Bernhard, P., et al. (2012). *The Interval Market Model in Mathematical Finance: Game Theoretic Models.* Berlin: Springer.

Bloch, F. (1997). Non-cooperative models of coalition formation in games with spillovers. In C. Carraro and D. Siniscalco (eds.), *New Directions in the Economic Theory of the Environment.* Cambridge, UK: Cambridge University Press.

Broek, W. A. van den, and Schumacher, J. M. (2000). Noncooperative disturbance decoupling. *Systems and Control Letters, 41*, 361–365.

Broek, W. A. van den, Engwerda, J. C., and Schumacher, J. M. (2003). Robust equilibria in indefinite linear-quadratic differential games. *Journal of Optimization Theory and Applications, 119*, 565–595.

Canzoneri, M. B., and Henderson, D. W. (1991). *Monetary Policy in Interdependent Economies: A Game Theoretic Approach.* Cambridge, UK: Cambridge University Press.

Carraro, C. (1999). *The Structure of International Agreements on Climate Change.* Dordrecht, The Netherlands: Kluwer.

Carraro, C., and Marchiori, C. (2003). Stable coalitions. In C. Carraro (ed.), *The Endogenous Formation of Economic Coalitions.* Cheltenham, UK: Elgar.

Chander, P., and Tulkens, H. (1997). The core of an economy with multilateral environmental externalities. *International Journal of Game Theory, 26*, 379–401.

Chasparis, G. C., and Shamma, J. S. (2012). Distributed dynamic reinforcement of efficient outcomes in multiagent coordination and network formation. *Dynamic Games and its Applications, 2*, 18–50.

Christy, J. R., et al. (2010). What do observational datasets say about modeled tropospheric temperature trends since 1979? *Remote Sensing, 2*(9), 2148–2169.

Dockner, E., Jørgensen, S., Long, N. van, and Sorger, G. (2000). *Differential Games in Economics and Management Science.* Cambridge, UK: Cambridge University Press.

Dragone, D., Lambertini, L., Leitmann, G., and Palestini, A. (2009). Hamiltonian Potential Functions for Differential Games. *Proceedings of IFAC CAO'09, Yvskyl (Finland)*, May 6–8.

Engwerda, J. C., (2005). *LQ Dynamic Optimization and Differential Games.* New York: John Wiley & Sons.

Engwerda, J. C., and Reddy, P. V. (2011). A positioning of cooperative differential games. In *Proceedings of the International Conference on Performance Evaluation Methodologies and Tools (ValueTools)*, Paris, May, 16–20, 2011.

Figuières, C., Jean-Marie, A., Quérou, N., and Tidball, M. (2004). *Theory of Conjectural Variations.* Singapore: World Scientific.

Finus, M., Altamirano-Cabrera, J.-C., and Ierland, E. C. van. (2005). The effect of membership rules and voting schemes on the success of international climate agreements. *Public Choice, 125*, 95–127.

Fudenberg, D., and Levine, D. K. (1998). *The Theory of Learning in Games.* Cambridge, MA: MIT Press.

Germain, M., Toint, P., Tulkens, H., and Zeeuw, A. de. (2003). Transfers to sustain dynamic core-theoretic cooperation in international stock pollutant control. *Journal of Economic Dynamics and Control, 28*, 79–99.

Gregory, D., and Johnston, R. (2009). Quality of life. In G. Pratt, et al. (eds.), *Dictionary of Human Geography*, 5th ed. Oxford: Wiley-Blackwell.

Habis, H. (2011). *Dynamic Cooperation.* PhD thesis. The Netherlands: Maastricht University.

Haigh, J. D., Winning, A. R., Toumi, R., and Harder, J. W. (2010). An influence of solar spectral variations on radiative forcing of climate. *Nature, 467*, 696–699.

Hart, S. (2005). Adaptive heuristics. *Economcetrica, 73*, 1401–1430.

Haurie, A. (1975). On some properties of the characteristic function and the core of a multistage game of coalitions. *IEEE Transactions on Automatic Control, 20*, 238–241.

Haurie, A., and Delfour, M. C. (1974). Individual and collective rationality in a dynamic Pareto equilibrium. *Journal of Optimization Theory and Aplications, 13*, 290–302.

Hays, J. D., Imbrie, J., and Shackleton, N. J. (1976). Variations in the earth's orbit: Pacemaker of the ice ages. *Science, 194*, 1121–1132.

He, X., Prasad, A., Sethi, S., and Gutierrez, G. (2007). A survey of Stackelberg differential game models in supply and marketing channels. *Journal of Systems Science and Engineering, 16*, 385–413.

Inter Academy Council. (2010). Interacademy Council Review of the IPCC. http://reviewipcc.interacademycouncil.net/report.html.

Imbrie, J., et al. (1992). On the structure and origin of major glaciation cycles. 1. Linear responses to Milankovich forcing. *Paleoceanography, 7*, 701–738.

Jørgensen, S. (2010). A dynamic game of waste management. *Journal of Economics Dynamics and Control, 34*, 258–265.

Jørgensen, S., Martìn-Herràn, G., and Zaccour, G. (2010). Dynamic games in the economics and management of pollution. *Environmental Modeling and Assessment, 15*, 433–467.

Kirkby, J., et al., (2011). Role of sulphuric acid, ammonia and galactic cosmic rays in atmospheric aerosol nucleation. *Nature, 476*, 429–433.

Klompstra, M. (1992). *Time Aspects in Games and in Optimal Control.* PhD. Thesis, The Netherlands: Delft University.

Köksalan, M., Wallenius, J., and Zionts, S. (2011). *Multiple Criteria Decision Making: From Early History to the 21st Century.* Singapore: World Scientific.

Kranich, L., Perea, A., and Peters, H. (2005). Core concepts for dynamic TU games. *International Game Theory Review, 7*, 43–61.

Kun, G. (2001). *Stabilizability, Controllability, and Optimal Strategies of Linear and Nonlinear Dynamical Games.* PhD thesis. Germany: RWTH-Aachen.

Long, N. Van. (2011). Dynamic games in the economics of natural resources: A survey. *Dynamic Games and its Applications, 1*, 115–148.

Milankovith, M. M. (1941). *Canon of Insolation and the Ice-Age Problem.* Beograd: Köninglich Serbische Akademie.

Monderer, D. and Shapley, L. S. (1996). Potential games. *Games and Economic Behavior, 14*, 124–143.

Myerson, R. B. (2008). Mechanism design. In S. N. Durlauf and L. E. Blume (eds.), *The New Palgrave Dictionary of Economics* (2nd ed.). Palgrave Macmillan. http://www.dictionaryofeconomics. com/article?id=pde2008_M000132.

Nash, J. (1950). The bargaining problem. *Econometrica, 18*, 155–162.

Nash, J. (1953). Two-person cooperative games. *Econometrica, 21*, 128–140.

Olsder, G. J. (2009). Phenomena in inverse Stackelberg games, part 1: static problems. *Journal of Optimization Theory and Application, 143*, 589–600.

Olsder, G. J. (2009). Phenomena in inverse Stackelberg games, part 2: dynamic problems. *Journal of Optimization Theory and Application, 143*, 601–618.

Osborne, M. J., and Rubinstein, A. (1994). *A Course in Game Theory.* Cambridge, MA: MIT Press.

Osborne, M. J. (2004). *An Introduction to Game Theory.* Oxford: Oxford University Press.

Pareto, V. (1896). *Cours d'economie politique.* Lausanne: F. Rouge.

Petit, R. A. et al., (1999). Climate and atmospheric history of the past 420,000 years from the Vostok ice core, Antarctica. *Nature, 399*, 429–436.

Petrosjan, L. A. (2005). Cooperative differential games. *Advances in Dynamic Games* 7, pp. 183–200. Boston, MA: Birkhuser.

Plasmans, J., Engwerda, J., Aarle, B. van, Bartolomeo, G. di, and Michalak, T. (2006). *Dynamic Modeling of Monetary and Fiscal Cooperation among Nations.* Berlin: Springer.

Ray, D. (2008). *A Game-Theoretic Perspective on Coalition Formation.* New York: Oxford University Press.

Rosen, J. B. (1965). Existence and uniqueness of equilibrium points for concave N-person games. *Econometrica, 33*, 520–534.

Rosenthal, R. W. (1973). A class of games possessing pure-strategy Nash equilibria. *International Journal of Game Theory, 2*, 65–67.

Salanie, B. (2002). *The Economics of Contracts.* Cambridge, MA: MIT Press.

Sandholm, W. H. (2010). *Population Games and Evolutionary Dynamics.* Cambridge, MA: MIT Press.

Scafetta, N. (2009). Empirical analysis of the solar contribution to global mean air surface temperature change. *Journal of Atmospheric and Solar-Terrestrial Physics, 71*, 1916–1923.

Seabright, P. (2010). *The Company of Strangers: A Natural History of Economic Life.* Princeton, NJ: Princeton University Press.

Solomon, S., et al., (2007). *Climate Change 2007: The Physical Science Basis, Contribution of Working Group I to the Fourth Assessment Report of the Intergovernmental Panel on Climate Change.* Solomon, S. D. Qin, M. Manning, Z. Cheng, M. Marquis, K.B. Avert, M. Tignor, and H.L. Mille (eds.), Cambridge, UK: Cambridge University Press.

Von Stackelberg, H. (1934). *Marktform und Gleichgewicht.* Berlin: Springer-Verlag.

Thomson, W. (1994). Cooperative models of bargaining. In R. J. Aumann and S. Hart (eds.), *Handbook of Game Theory* 2. Amsterdam: Elsevier Science, pp. 1238–1277.

Tidball, M., and Zaccour, G. (2009). A differential environmental game with coupling constraints. *Optimal Control Applications and Methods*, 121–221.

Tol, R. S. J. (2010). The economic impact of climate change. *Perspektiven der Wirtschaftspolitik, 11*, 13–37.

Turnovsky, S. J. (2011). On the role of small models in macrodynamics. *Journal of Economic Dynamics and Control, 35*, 1605–1613.

Tzedakis, P. C., et al., (1997). Comparison of terrestrial and marine records of changing climate of the last 500,000 years. *Earth and Planetery Science Letters, 150*, 171–176.

World Development Report. (2010). World Bank. http://go.worldbank.org/ZXULQ9SCC0.

World Energy Outlook. (2011). Internatial Energy Agency. http://www.worldenergyoutlook.org/

Yeung, D. W. K., and Petrosyan, L. A. (2006). *Cooperative Stochastic Differential Games.* Berlin: Springer-Verlag.

Yeung, D. W. K. (2011). Dynamically consistent cooperative solutions in differential games. *Advances in Dynamic Games* 11, pp. 375–395. The Netherlands: Springer, Dordrecht.

Zaccour, G. (2003). Computation of characteristic function values for linear-state differential games. *Journal of Optimization Theory and Application, 117*, 183–194.

CHAPTER 8

FAIRNESS IN CLIMATE NEGOTIATIONS: A META-GAME ANALYSIS BASED ON COMMUNITY INTEGRATED ASSESSMENT

ALAIN HAURIE, FRÉDÉRIC BABONNEAU, NEIL EDWARDS, PHIL HOLDEN, AMIT KANUDIA, MARYSE LABRIET, BARBARA PIZZILEO AND MARC VIELLE

8.1 Introduction and Motivation

Just under a century after Arrhenius' first attempt to calculate the climatic warming effect of CO_2 in 1896 Arrhenius (1896), growing levels of concern over human greenhouse gas emissions prompted the international community, through the United Nations Framework Convention on Climate Change (UNFCCC) in 1992, to commit to avoiding 'dangerous anthropogenic interference with the climate system'. In practice, however, the lack of any cheap and ready substitute for carbon-intensive energy forms to drive continued economic development, has meant two more decades of rapid growth in CO_2 emissions while scientists and states have debated the precise interpretation of the UNFCCC declaration and possible political and legal instruments to effect its aims. The CO_2 problem is a quintessential tragedy of the global commons in that emissions from all nations contribute equally to long-lasting environmental damage that is experienced by all. In economic terms damages are separated temporally and geographically from benefits of emissions in a colossal market failure. According to Lord Stern's highly influential report to the UK government Stern (2007) a failure that obscures substantial net economic gains of concerted emission reduction, at least if the societal imperative to protect environmental goods for which there is no market is represented with appropriately low discount rates. More recent large-scale synthesis work on impacts Arnell (2013) has reinforced the potential economic benefits of avoiding damages by reducing greenhouse gas emissions, and even highlighted potentially large co-benefits for health at EU level as a result of improved air quality Watkiss (2011).

Meanwhile, emissions have carried on rising, but important steps towards global agreement have nevertheless been taken, both within the United Nations framework and outside. Within the framework, a critical level of 2°C global mean surface temperature increase above pre-industrial levels was recognised by the 15th conference of the parties (COP) in Copenhagen in 2009 as a threshold to be avoided, while the Durban Platform negotiated at COP17 established the long-awaited basis for an agreement 'with legal force' applicable to all parties to be agreed by 2015 and implemented from 2020. At national level, the GLOBE international report Townshend et al. (2013) documents progress on related climate or energy legislation in 32 out of 33 major economies.

The need to agree global limits on emissions by 2015 will necessarily invoke further rounds of protracted discussions on the complex issues of entitlement and responsibility surrounding fair allocation of emission allowances between states. The analytical debate on these burden-sharing issues, while essentially driven by ethical and development concerns, must nevertheless be underpinned by detailed, quantitative analysis of the distribution of costs and benefits incurred by proposed trading or taxation regimes. Furthermore, realistic analyses must recognise a further essential factor of real-world negotiations, namely that as soon as any particular emission-restriction or trading scheme is implemented (or even mooted) in the context of an international framework, individual signatories are liable to modify their actions in a competitive way to obtain the maximum benefit within the constraints of the imposed regime. In other words, once an agreement is proposed, the responses of individual countries and groups of countries to the terms of the agreement can be represented as a non-cooperative game to optimise their payoff in welfare terms to the responses of the other states or groups. In the language of game theory, the resulting problem can be represented as game in which the solutions most likely to be realised in practice correspond to the set of stable Nash equilibria of the game.

Realistic analysis of possible emissions trading regimes therefore demands the application of detailed integrated assessment models, incorporating faithful representations of the energy system and macro-economic feedbacks, as well as regionalised climate damages, be used to calculate the payoffs corresponding to potential strategies in the game resulting from any proposed emissions trading regime. In this article we present the results of work carried out in the EU seventh framework project 'Enhancing robustness and model integration for the assessment of global environmental change' (ERMITAGE), which aims to facilitate such analyses by coupling intermediate complexity climate models with environmental impact models and detailed energy technology and macroeconomic models and using the resulting analyses to inform game-theoretic analyses of possible international environmental agreements (IEAs). In doing so, we build on the results of a series of previous works that have used simplified integrated assessment frameworks as a basis for game-theoretic analyses of IEAs.

The issue of fairness in the design of international environmental agreements (IEA) like those that are discussed in the recurrent COP meetings must be dealt with efficiently if one wants to create a successful IEA. A community integrated assessment system Warren et al. (2008) (CIAS), which brings together different numerical models and climate-related datasets into a common framework can provide interesting insight concerning the possibility to reach a fair IEA that will encourage participation, achieve abatement efficiently and create incentives for compliance. Enhancement and extension of the CIAS concept is one of the main goals of the EU-FP7 research project ERMITAGE http://ermitage.cs.man.ac.uk/.

To characterize a fair IEA we will formulate a multilevel game of fair division of a global "safety budget" of cumulative emissions that remains compatible with a twenty-first century warming that will remain below 2°C above preindustrial with sufficiently high probability.[1] To reach efficiency and to distribute the benefits of the permit allowances, we assume that an international emissions trading market will be implemented. Finally, we adopt as a criterion of fairness the Rawlsian view that we should minimize the maximum loss of welfare, relative to a business as usual situation. The effect of allowing for non-cooperative behaviour is addressed by comparing the game-theoretic approach with analagous solutions from a partial equilibrium bottom-up modelling framework that utilises a linear programme to derive globally balanced solutions.

In the game-theoretic approach, we suppose that a fair and efficient IEA is reached through the following steps:

First, through international negotiations, several groups of countries, each sharing among its member states a similar level of economic development and exposure to climate risks, agree on: (a) the total level of cumulative GHG emissions allowed over the period 2010-2050, to remain compatible with a 2°C temperature increase at the end of the twenty-first century; (b) a distribution of this cumulative emission budget among the different groups, for instance using some concepts of equity such as an egalitarian principle à la Rawls (1971).

Then, an international emission trading scheme is implemented, with a strategic allocation of allowances to different groups of countries. The different groups of countries play a game of timing, where each group of countries allocates its share of the global allowance over time in order to reach an optimum, if the game is played cooperatively, or an equilibrium, if the game is played non-cooperatively. The payoffs are expressed in terms of variation of surplus with respect to a BAU or reference situation where no climate constraint applies.

To formulate the optimization problem describing a fully cooperative solution to the game we use the bottom-up partial equilibrium model TIAM-WORLD. To formulate a non-cooperative game of emission quotas supply we extend the model proposed by C. Helm et al. (2003; 2008; 2009) to a framework where the players' payoffs are computed through statistical emulation of a general equilibrium model, GEMINI-E3 Bernard

(2003). By proposing that the structure of the IEA involves a fixed emissions budget that is shared in a given proportion between states, which can distribute their emissions freely, in a competitive response to market conditions, across a given time horizon, we are recognising the result of Meinshausen and others Malte et al. (2009) that, to first order, the level of environmental damage depends on the integrated global emissions up to a given time independent of the time-profile of emissions.

It is beyond the scope of the present article to address the political challenge of negotiating appropriate safety budgets and equity rules. Instead, the focus of the present article is to address the consequences of allowing for non-cooperation between players in their implementation of the envisaged burden-sharing regime, using the most detailed economic and climate modelling practicable to quantify the gains and losses involved. In this way we aim to provide a more realistic basis for addressing the costs and benefits of various burden-sharing possibilities.

In Malte et al. (2009) Meinshausen et al. claimed that for a class of emission scenarios, "*both cumulative emissions up to 2050 and emission levels in 2050 are robust indicators of the probability that twenty-first century warming will not exceed 2°C relative to pre-industrial temperatures. Limiting cumulative CO_2 emissions over 2000—50 to 1,000 $GtCO_2$ yields a 25% probability of warming exceeding 2°C—and a limit of 1,440 $GtCO_2$ yields a 50% probability—given a representative estimate of the distribution of climate system properties.*[2] This observation has important consequences in the way one can envision international negotiations on climate policy.

However a large uncertainty remains on the safe cumulative emissions limit. Based on recent IEA scenarios Moss et al. (2010); van Vuuren et al. (2011) Schaeffer and van Vuuren (2012) have proposed new global cumulative emissions budget for 2000-2050 around 1260 $GtCO_2$ (342 GtC), i.e. 26% higher than the estimate made in Malte et al. (2009).

In Ref. England et al. (2010), four institutes of climate research explored different emission pathways that would remain compatible with a global emission budget for 2050 and showed the difficulty to obtain equity in the treatment of developing countries. They noticed, however that a transformation of the world energy system in order to remain compatible with the global cumulative emissions target, is feasible at a cost of less than 2.5 % of GDP. One important insight of the research reported here concerns the possibility to obtain equity through a fair sharing of the cumulative emission budget among different groups of countries, associated with the introduction of an international emissions trading system with full banking and borrowing.[3]

The global cumulative emissions budget approach could be linked with the contraction and convergence proposal, which has attracted considerable attention in recent years, see Ref. Broad (1999), in which global emissions are assumed to reduce through time while convergent economic development simultaneously reduces the disparity in per-capita emissions between countries.

The chapter is organized as follows: in Section 8.2 we present the use of a statistical emulation of the climate model PLASIM-ENTS to permit a coupling with techno-economic models and obtain an evaluation of a safe cumulative emissions limit, over the period 2010–2050, compatible with a 2°C warming in 2100; in Section 8.3 we use a scenario built with the integrated assessment energy-climate model TIAM-WORLD, coupled with PLASIM-ENTS to assess the optimal abatement strategies and propose a regional allocation of emission quotas based on cost criteria; in Section 8.4 we use GEMINI-E3 scenarios to identify the effect of strategic play of countries in an international emissions trading market with full banking and borrowing; we show how to design a meta-game for the fair sharing of the global cumulative emissions budget. Each of the two approaches has its own limits and specific advantages. In Section 8.5 we conclude with a comparison of these results and an interpretation in terms of the possible forthcoming IEA.

8.2 Statistical Emulation of PLASIM-ENTS

One of the principal obstacles to coupling complex climate models to impacts models is their high computational expense. Replacing the climate model with an emulated version of its input-output response function circumvents this problem without compromising the possibility of including feedbacks and non-linear responses Holden and Edwards (2010). This approach yields two further benefits in the field of integrated assessment. First, the emulation can allow for the construction of gradients of the response function. These may be required, for instance, in an optimisation-based application. Second, a calibrated statistical emulation, based on ensembles of simulations, also provides a quantification of uncertainty and modelling errors.

The climate model we apply here is PLASIM-ENTS, the Planet Simulator Fraedrich et al. (2005) coupled to the ENTS land surface model Williamson et al. (2006). The resulting model has a 3D dynamic atmosphere, flux-corrected slab ocean and slab sea ice, and dynamic coupled vegetation. We run this model at T21 resolution. As a result of stability issues in the sea ice that have not yet been resolved, all simulations were performed with fixed sea ice. An important consequence is that the modelled climate sensitivity is inevitably reduced, leading to an increased estimate of allowable cumulative emissions in the analysis that follows (i.e. constrained by 2° global warming).

A 564-member PLASIM-ENTS ensemble was performed varying 22 key model parameters and constrained to generate plausible preindustrial states, following Holden et al. (2010). Each simulation was continued from 1765 to 2105, applying transient historical radiative forcing (1765 to 2005) and a wide range of possible future forcing (2005 to 2105). Globally averaged radiative forcing was expressed as effective CO_2 concentration (CO_2e), together with actual CO_2 concentration (required by the vegetation model). Future radiative forcing has a temporal profile described by a linear decomposition of the 1st three Chebyshev polynomials:

$$CO_{2e} = CO_{0e} + 0.5\{A_{1e}(t+1) + A_{2e}(2t^2-2) + A_{3e}(4t^3-4t)\}$$

where CO_{0e} is CO_2e in 2005 (393 ppm), t is time (2005 to 2105) normalised onto the range $(-1, 1)$ and the three coefficients which describe the concentration profile (A_{1e}, A_{2e} and A_{1e}) take values which allow for a wide range of possible future emissions profiles. The same approach was taken to describe the temporal profile of actual CO_2:

$$CO_2 = CO_0 + 0.5\{A_1(t+1) + A_2(2t^2 - 2) + A_3(4t^3 - 4t)\}$$

The resulting ensemble of 564 transient simulations of future climate thus incorporates both parametric and forcing uncertainty. We note that the 564 simulations comprise 188 model parameterisations, each reproduced three times and combined with 564 combinations of the six Chebyshev coefficients.

For coupling applications we require an emulator that will generate spatial patterns of climate through time for an arbitrary future forcing, although note that the coupling described here is constrained only by global warming, and hence does not fully utilise this spatio-temporal information. To achieve this, ten decadally averaged output fields (here we consider only surface warming) from 2010 to 2100 were generated for each ensemble member and combined into a single 20480-element vector where, for instance, the first 2,048 elements describe the 64×32 (T21) warming field over the first averaging period. This vector thus represents a self-consistent description of the temporal and spatial dependence of the warming of the respective ensemble member. These vectors were combined into a $20,480 \times 564$ matrix describing the entire ensemble output of warming.

Singular vector decomposition (SVD) was performed on this matrix to decompose the ensemble warming patterns into Empirical Orthogonal Functions (EOFs). The physics of the climate system results in spatio-temporal correlations between ensemble members, patterns of change that are a function of the climate model itself rather than of parameter choices. As a consequence, it is generally the case that a small subset of the 564 EOFs is sufficient to describe most of the variance across the ensemble. The simpler approach of pattern scaling utilises these correlations by assuming that a single pattern (equivalent to the first EOF) can be applied to approximate the pattern from any simulation. Here we retain the first ten EOFs.

Each individual simulated warming field can be approximated as a linear combination of the first ten EOFs, scaled by their respective Principal Components (PCs). As each simulated field is a function of the input parameters, so are the PCs, which are thus scalar quantities that can be emulated as a function of the input parameters. PC emulators of the first ten EOFs were derived as functions of the 22 model parameters and the 6 concentration profile coefficients. The simplest possible emulator was considered here, constructed as a linear function of the 28 inputs.

In order to apply the emulator, we provide the six Chebyshev coefficients that together describe some future concentration pathway of CO_2e and CO_2 as inputs. The emulator generates a 188-member ensemble of the ten PCs (i.e. using each of the 188 parametrisation to make a separate prediction). The ten PCs for each prediction are combined with the ten EOFs to generate patterns of warming over the period (2005-2105). An important aspect of the emulator is its potential to propagate model error through a coupling.

8.3 A Cooperative Approach based on TIAM-WORLD Coupled with PLASIM-ENTS

In this first approach we use a bottom-up partial equilibrium model, focussing on the evolution of the energy system in different world regions. We couple it with the PLASIM-ENTS emulator to obtain a scenario that satisfies the target of keeping surface air temperature (SAT) below 2°C in year 2100. From this scenario we derive a cumulative emissions budget for the 2010–2050 time interval and also an emission profile for each of the eight regions modelled. Now, for each period 2020, 2030, 2040, 2050 we define an international emissions trading scheme which allocates the total emissions of the period to each region, in the form of quotas, in such a way that the different regions end up paying the same share of their GDP as net abatement cost (including buying or selling permits). From the shares of emission budget given to each region at each period, we deduce the share of the cumulative safety budget allocated to each region.

8.3.1 Presentation of TIAM-WORLD

The TIMES Integrated Assessment Model (TIAM-WORLD) is a technology-rich model of the entire energy/emission system of the World split into 16 regions, providing a detailed representation of the procurement, transformation, trade, and consumption of a large number of energy forms (see Loulou 2008; Loulou and Labriet 2008). It computes an inter-temporal dynamic partial equilibrium on energy and emission markets based on the maximization of total surplus, defined as the sum of suppliers and consumers surpluses. The model is set up to explore the development of the World energy system until 2100.

The model contains explicit detailed descriptions of more than 1500 technologies and several hundreds of energy, emission and demand flows in each region, logically interconnected to form a Reference Energy System. Such technological detail allows precise tracking of optimal capital turnover and provides a precise description of technology and fuel competition.

TIAM-WORLD is driven by demands for energy services in each sector of the economy, which are specified by the user for the Reference scenario, and have each an own price elasticity. Each demand may vary endogenously in alternate scenarios, in response to endogenous price changes. Although the model does not include macroeconomic variables beyond the energy sector, there is evidence that accounting for price elasticity of demands captures a preponderant part of feedback effects from the economy to the energy system (Bataille 2005; Labriet et al. 2010).

TIAM-WORLD integrates a climate module permitting the computation and modeling of global changes related to greenhouse gas concentrations, radiative forcing and temperature increase, resulting from the greenhouse gas emissions endogenously computed (Loulou et al. 2009).

In the recent years, TIAM-WORLD has been used to assess future climate and energy strategies at global and region levels in full or partial climate agreements and uncertain contexts (see Labriet et al. 2012; Loulou et al. 2009; Kanudia et al. 2014; Labriet and Loulou 2008).

8.3.2 Coupling of TIAM-WORLD and PLASIM-ENTS

Although TIAM-WORLD, as any integrated assessment model, can be run with temperature constraint, the climate module of TIAM-WORLD does not compute the regional or seasonal temperature changes as needed for a relevant representation of the possible heating and cooling adjustments due to climate change. Hence the need for a more detailed climate model like PLASIM-ENTS, or more precisely its emulator permitting a rapid evaluation of scenarios.

In essence, there is an iterative exchange of data between the two models, whereby TIAM-WORLD sends to the climate emulator a set of total greenhouse gas concentrations for the entire 21st century, and the climate emulator sends to TIAM-WORLD the seasonal and regional temperatures, converted in heating and cooling degree-days, and used to compute new seasonal and regional heating and cooling demands in TIAM-WORLD. Iteration continues until the global temperature computed by PLASIM-ENTS reaches the desired value. In cases with temperature limit from 2 to 3°C in 2100, convergence is obtained in 2 to 13 iterations, with a precision of 0.01°C.

The cumulative emission budget over 2010–2050, including carbon dioxide (CO_2), methane (CH_4), and nitrous oxide (N_2O), reduces from 598 in the Reference case to 484 Gt carbon-equivalent (C-eq) in the case with a temperature limit of 2°C in 2100 (Table 8.1). The emission budget does not change a lot in the intermediate cases with 2.5 and 3.0°C temperature limit in 2100 compared to the reference case. Indeed, most of the optimal emission reductions occur after 2050 in these not tight and considered unsafe climate cases. The 2°C target remains the focus of this paper.

The resulting carbon marginal abatement cost remains moderate until 2050 (Table 8.2) reflecting the fact that the 2°C limit was imposed in 2100 without any intermediate constraint; although temperature did not overshoot the imposed limit in the intermediate years, the resulting radiative forcing increased up to 3.8 W/m^2 before decreasing at the end of the horizon.

Table 8.1 Cumulative emission budget 2010-2050 and 2100 radiative forcing

Scenario	GtC-eq	RF_{2100} (W/m^2)
2°C	484	3.7
2.5°C	572	4.6
3°C	591	5.7
Ref	595	6.3

Table 8.2 Marginal abatement cost (Price of carbon)

	2020	2030	2040	2050
$/tC	95	135	189	261

Table 8.3 Aggregation of regions

USA	United States of America
EUR	Europe of 27 + Switzerland, Iceland and Norway
CHI	China
IND	India
RUS	Russia
OEC	Other OECD countries (Japan, Canada, Australia and New-Zeland, Mexico, South Korea)
OPE	Middle-East
ROW	Africa + Central and South America + Central Asia and Caucase (such as Kazakhstan, Turkmenistan, etc.) + Other Developing Asia (such as Indonesia)

Although TIAM-WORLD includes 16 different regions, the regional emission results were aggregated according to the definition of players used and are presented in Table 8.4 (reference case) and Table 8.5 (2°C case). These regions described in Table 8.3 have been selected to simplify the development of a game theoretic analysis in forthcoming Section 8.4 and so, a comparison of results will be possible.

Notice that China contributes almost one third of global emissions by 2050 in the Reference case. In other words, any partial climate agreement without China may jeopardize the capacity of the climate system to remain in a safe window on the longer term.

Table 8.4 Annual emissions (GtC-eq) in the reference case

	2010	2020	2030	2040	2050
USA	1.93	1.82	1.84	1.72	1.72
EUR	1.23	1.26	1.29	1.25	1.36
OEC	1.08	1.17	1.18	1.18	1.26
CHI	2.57	3.13	3.90	4.69	5.54
IND	0.62	0.77	0.99	1.28	1.39
RUS	0.62	0.74	0.94	1.00	1.09
OPE	0.61	0.72	0.84	0.96	1.07
ROW	3.07	3.34	3.66	3.89	4.22
World	11.72	12.94	14.64	15.98	17.64

Table 8.5 Annual emissions (GtC-eq) for the 2° C scenario

	2010	2020	2030	2040	2050
USA	1.93	1.74	1.65	1.45	1.07
EUR	1.23	1.17	1.11	0.99	0.83
OEC	1.08	1.07	1.01	0.91	0.77
CHI	2.57	2.81	3.14	3.12	2.86
IND	0.62	0.70	0.78	0.77	0.82
RUS	0.62	0.71	0.82	0.81	0.77
OPE	0.61	0.69	0.78	0.76	0.73
ROW	3.07	2.98	3.09	2.93	2.87
World	11.72	11.88	12.38	11.74	10.72

8.3.3 Computation of Fair Side-payments

In Vaillancourt et al. (2007) Vaillancourt et al. (2007) have shown how to use a bottom-up world model (MARKAL-WORLD) to compute dynamic permit allocations having cost-related fairness properties. The proposed equity criterion was defined as the equalization of the net abatement costs of each region per unit of GDP at each period. We repeat this calculation with TIAM-WORLD, coupled to the emulator of PLASIM-ENTS.

For this purpose, TIAM-WORLD, coupled to the emulator of PLASIM-ENTS, is first run without climate constraint, to obtain the global and regional costs in the reference case, and then run with a global constraint on temperature in 2100 to obtain the optimal (efficient) emission levels $E_j(t)$ in each region j, and the new system costs. The gross abatement cost $C_j(t)$ of region j is the difference between the corresponding two system costs. The net abatement cost $x_j(t)$ is defined as the gross abatement cost $C_j(t)$ plus the cost of buying permits/minus the revenue of selling permits, i.e.:

$$x_j(t) = C_j(t) + y_j(t)P_w(t) \tag{8.1}$$

where $y_j(t)$ is the quantity of permits purchased (if positive) / sold (if negative) by region j, and $P_w(t)$ is the price of permits (computed by the model in the dual solution of the linear program). The equalization of the net abatement costs per GDP across regions means that, for each region j and each period t:

$$\frac{x_j(t)}{GDP_j(t)} = \frac{\sum_i x_i(t)}{\sum_i GDP_i(t)} = \frac{C_w(t)}{GDP_w(t)} = K(t), \tag{8.2}$$

Where $C_w(t)$ is the global net abatement cost (equal to the global gross abatement cost) provided by the model. Equations (8.2) are equivalent to

$$x_j(t) = K(t)\, GDP_j(t) \tag{8.3}$$

or, using (8.1) above

$$y_j(t) = \frac{1}{P_w(t)} \left[K(t)\, GDP_j(t) - C_j(t)\right] \quad \forall j \quad \forall t. \tag{8.4}$$

Finally, the allocation of quotas $a_j(t)$ to region j is equal to the emissions obtained in the optimal solution minus permits purchased

$$a_j(t) = E_j(t) - y_j(t) \quad \forall j \quad \forall t. \tag{8.5}$$

8.3.4 Proposed Sharing of a Safety Budget and Distribution of Quotas

Running TIAM-WORLD coupled with PLASIM-ENTS, a safety budget of 484 GtC-eq has been obtained for the time interval 2010-2050 with a temperature change constraint of 2°C increase of SAT in 2100 (Table 8.1). This budget corresponds to the optimal emissions computed by TIAM-WORLD to maximize the total surplus of the system over 2005-2100, as defined as the sum of suppliers and consumers surpluses (see Section 8.3.1). In other words, the optimal solution computed by TIAM-WORLD informs us about the optimal location of emission reductions, but it does not answer the question of "who should pay" for these reductions.

As an answer to this latter question, the emission budget was allocated to the 8 regions in order to equalize, at each period, the abatement costs supported by each region as a share of the regional GDP, as proposed by Vaillancourt et al. (2007) and described in Section 8.3.3.

Regional allocations of quotas (Tables 8.6, 8.7 and 8.9) and the resulting permit trading (Table 8.10) indicate that industrialized countries (USA, EUR and OEC) would

Table 8.6 Allocation of emission quotas (GtC-eq) to equalize regional abatement costs per GDP

	2020	2030	2040	2050
USA	1.48	1.27	0.99	0.72
EUR	0.93	0.72	0.53	0.45
OEC	1.04	0.90	0.76	0.69
CHI	2.97	3.53	3.63	3.51
IND	0.75	0.91	0.81	0.78
RUS	0.66	0.86	0.90	0.89
OPE	0.90	0.86	0.97	0.90
ROW	3.14	3.31	3.13	2.78
World	11.87	12.38	11.74	10.72

Table 8.7 Allocation of emission quotas (%) to equalize regional abatement costs per GDP

	2020	2030	2040	2050
USA	13%	10%	8%	7%
EUR	8%	6%	5%	4%
OEC	9%	7%	7%	6%
CHI	25%	28%	31%	33%
IND	6%	7%	7%	7%
RUS	6%	7%	8%	8%
OPE	8%	7%	8%	8%
ROW	26%	27%	27%	26%
World	100%	100%	100%	100%

receive lower quotas than the optimal emissions as computed by TIAM-WORLD (Table 8.8) and would therefore buy permits from the other regions of the World, and more particularly from China. In other words, USA, EUR and OEC will pay for abatement to be done in these regions, in order to keep regional abatement costs per GDP equal across regions. This reflects both the stronger economic capacity of industrialized countries (higher GDP) to pay for abatement, and the opportunities of abatement available in the different countries. More particularly, given the high contribution of China to global emissions, any climate strategy requires deep changes in the energy system of country to guarantee the reduction of the global emissions, hence higher costs.

The annual transactions (buying or selling permits) are shown in Table 8.10 (MtC-eq).

As indicated above, the definition of the quotas allocations equalizes the abatement cost per unit of GDP at each period, as shown in Table 8.11.

Table 8.8 Allocation of emission quotas (%) in the optimal solution

	2020	2030	2040	2050
USA	15%	13%	12%	10%
EUR	10%	9%	8%	8%
OEC	9%	8%	8%	7%
CHI	24%	25%	27%	27%
IND	6%	6%	7%	8%
RUS	6%	7%	7%	7%
OPE	6%	6%	7%	7%
ROW	25%	25%	25%	27%
World	100%	100%	100%	100%

Table 8.9 Cumulative regional budgets over 2010–2050 to equalize regional abatement costs per GDP

Region	GtC-eq	%
USA	52.6	11%
EUR	31.3	7%
OEC	37.1	8%
CHI	134.3	28%
IND	32.4	7%
RUS	32.4	7%
OPE	35.4	7%
ROW	128.1	26%
World	483.7	100%

8.3.5 Interpretation of the Results Obtained

The approach proposed with TIAM-WORLD involves the endogenous computation of the optimal emission trajectory over the 2005–2100 horizon to satisfy the 2°C target imposed in 2100 in the PLASIM-ENTS emulator coupled with TIAM-WORLD. Carbon prices in the first part of the horizon appear moderate, which could be interpreted as making feasible an international agreement on climate change over this time horizon, under the condition that countries pursue emission abatement after 2050 to keep temperature increase below the desired target. The costs and carbon prices obtained in the current application are slightly smaller than the ones obtained with TIAM-WORLD

Table 8.10 Buying (−) and selling (+) of quotas (MtC-eq)

	2020	2030	2040	2050
USA	−254	−373	−454	−346
EUR	−243	−391	−460	−375
OEC	−33	−103	−141	−79
CHI	162	382	508	645
IND	48	135	46	−37
RUS	−46	39	89	118
OPE	211	84	204	161
ROW	156	228	208	−87
World	0	0	0	0

Table 8.11 Equalized abatement cost per unit of GDP at each period

	2020	2030	2040	2050
Abatement cost / GDP	0.06%	0.15%	0.28%	0.35%

in its most recent applications for the Energy Modeling Forum, Kanudia et al. (2014). Two reasons contribute to this situation: first, the climate target used in the current paper is not as severe, especially as regards intermediate years where no constraint was considered here; second, the global temperature increase computed by PLASIM-ENTS is slightly lower than the one obtained with the simplified climate module of TIAM-WORLD for the same emission trajectory (increase of global temperature of 2.18°C in 2100 obtained with TIAM-WORLD when the target of 2°C is reached in PLASIM-ENTS); in other words, slightly less emission reductions are needed when using TIAM-WORLD coupled with PLASIM-ENTS than TIAM-WORLD in a standalone manner.

The success of international negotiations is however more directly related to regional costs than to the minimization of the global cost of the climate strategies, hence the proposal of a fairness rule to equalize the abatement costs supported by each region given as a proportion of the regional GDP. This simple rule, respecting horizontality principles since it equalizes the net costs across regions as a percent of GDP, results in industrialized countries paying for abatement to be done in developing or emerging countries, given both the economic power of the countries and the regional optimal abatements assessed by TIAM-WORLD. In other words, in this application, TIAM-WORLD is used to identify what to do (optimal abatement over the entire horizon), while the proposed equity rule serves to assess who should pay for this abatement. Of course, other rules may be applied, as illustrated by Vaillancourt et al. (2007), and partial agreements could be assessed with the model. Moreover, given the global nature of the climate change issue, there is of course no guarantee that the proposed allocation of emission permits would prevent countries from rejecting any international agreement, hence the interest for the analysis of Nash games, as illustrated by Labriet and Loulou (2008) with a global model close to TIAM-WORLD. The following analysis with GEMINI-E3 helps to deeper assess the insights learnt with such games.

8.4 A Game Theoretic Approach based on an Ensemble of Scenarios Provided by GEMINI-E3 Coupled with PLASIM-ENTS

In this section we propose a different approach to identify a fair sharing of the safety emissions budget. The sharing itself is obtained as the solution of a game design problem. The game is an adaptation of C. Helm modelling of international emissions trading with endogenous allowance choices Helm (2003). The design parameters are the shares of the safety emissions budget given to the different regions. The use of these shares by the regions is determined by a Nash equilibrium for this game. The rules of the game, i.e. payoffs as functions of strategy choices are obtained from statistical emulations of the general computable equilibrium model GEMINI-E3. This consists in generating a large sample of scenarios corresponding to different strategy choices and identifying through regression analysis the functions describing the regions' costs and benefits that enter into the payoff definition. In fact we should call the resulting model a "meta-game" model defined from statistical emulations of the general computable equilibrium model GEMINI-E3.

In this second approach the fair sharing will be defined according to a Rawlsian principle. We look for the sharing that maximizes the worst ratio of discounted sum of surplus variation over the discounted sum of household consumption in the reference (BAU) case, for the time interval under consideration, 2010–2050.

8.4.1 Presentation of GEMINI-E3

GEMINI-E3 Bernard and Vielle (2008)[4] is a multi-country, multi-sector, recursive computable general equilibrium model comparable to the other CGE models (EPPA, ENV-Linkage, etc) built and implemented by other modeling teams and institutions, and sharing the same long experience in the design of this class of economic models. The standard model is based on the assumption of total flexibility in all markets, both macroeconomic markets such as the capital and the exchange markets (with the associated prices being the real rate of interest and the real exchange rate, which are then endogenous), and microeconomic or sector markets (goods, factors of production).

The GEMINI-E3 model is now built on a comprehensive energy-economy dataset, the GTAP-8 database Narayanan et al. (2012). This database incorporates a consistent representation of energy markets in physical units, social accounting matrices for each individualized country/region, and the whole set of bilateral trade flows. Additional statistical information accrues from OECD national accounts, IEA energy balances and energy prices/taxes and IMF Statistics. We use an aggregated version of GEMINI-E3 that described 11 sectors/goods and 8 regions. Table 8.12 gives the definition of the classifications used.

Reference scenarios in CGE models are built from i) forecasts or assumptions on population and economic growth in the various countries/regions, ii) prices of energy in world markets, in particular the oil price and iii) national (energy) policies. We build a reference baseline on the period 2007-2050 with yearly timesteps. Assumptions on population are based on the last forecast done by United Nations (2010), we use *the median-fertility* variant. In 2050 the World population will reach 9.27 billions of inhabitants. We use an harmonized set of common economic assumptions with the TIAM-WORLD model and check that our GDP growths are also in line with the last *International Energy Outlook* published by the U.S. Department of Energy (2011). Global GDP growth decreases slightly over the period from 3% annually to 2.5% at the end of our simulation. Prices of energy in the World markets used by GEMINI-E3 are calibrated on those computed by the TIAM-WORLD model.

Table 8.12 Dimensions of the GEMINI-E3 model

Regions		Sectors
United States of America	USA	*Energy*
European Union	EUR	01 Coal
Other OECD countries	OEC	02 Crude Oil
China	CHI	03 Natural Gas
India	IND	04 Refined Petroleum
Russia	RUS	05 Electricity
OPEC	OPE	*Non-Energy*
Rest of the World	ROW	06 Agriculture
		07 Energy intensive industries
		08 Other goods and services
		09 Land Transport
		10 Sea Transport
		11 Air Transport

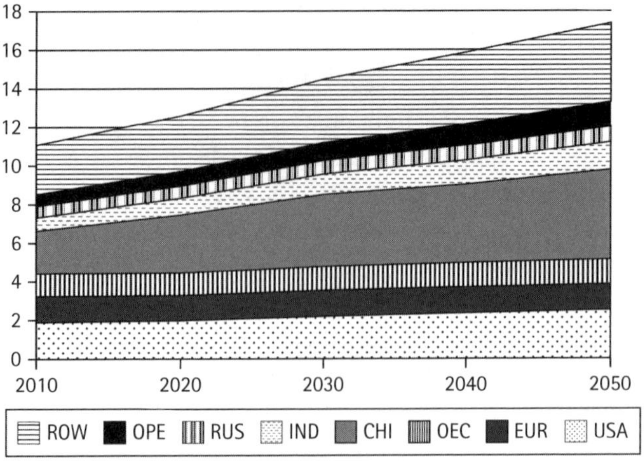

FIGURE 8.1 GHG emissions in GtC-eq for the reference case

GHG emissions computed by GEMINI-E3 are presented by regions in Figure 8.1. These emissions include CO_2 emissions from energy combustion and non-CO_2 greenhouse gases from anthropogenic sources. The non-CO_2 greenhouse gases included in GEMINI-E3 are the direct non-CO_2 GHGs covered by the UNFCCC: methane (CH_4), nitrous oxide (N_2O), and the high global warming potential (high-GWP) gases. In 2050, total GHG emissions reaches 17.4 GtC-eq. The CO_2 emissions profile is in line with RCP 6.0 published recently by van Vuuren et al. (2011) and close to those computed by the TIAM-WORLD, these emissions will generate a cumulative emissions budget of 586 GtC-eq over the period 2010–2050.

8.4.2 Coupling GEMINI-E3 with the Emulator of PLASIM-ENTS

The objective of the present coupling is to use the emulator of PLASIM-ENTS to set up emissions constraints into GEMINI-E3 in order to assess climate policy scenarios compatible with a given temperature increase in 2050. As GEMINI-E3 is a time-step optimization model, one can not build a coupled model that would compute endogenously an optimal emissions path with respect to the economy, as done with TIAM-WORLD. For this reason, we opt for a soft coupling approach producing acceptable and realistic emission profiles. These emission profiles are then used in GEMINI-E3 as an upper bound vector on the emissions of CO_2 equivalent. In other words, the coupling of GEMINI-E3 with PLASIM-ENTS has not exactly the same meaning as the coupling of TIAM-WORLD with PLASIM-ENTS. This illustrates how different techno-economic models can be used in a coordinated manner with a climate model: the coupling implemented with TIAM-WORLD aims the detailed representation of temperature to assess the impacts of climate change on the energy system, while the coupling implemented with GEMINI-E3 aims the computation of emission profiles to respect upper climate constraints.

As the number of emissions trajectories satisfying a given warming target is potentially unlimited, the coupling procedure restricts its search to a subset of trajectories. We assume that CO_2 emissions E_{CO_2} have a temporal profile on the range [2000, 2050] described by a linear decomposition of the 1st three Chebyshev polynomials:

$$E_{CO_2}(t) = \alpha_1(t+1) + \alpha_2(2t^2 - 2) + \alpha_3(4t^3 - 4t), \quad \forall t \in [2000, 2050].$$

To build such functions, the coefficients α_i, $i = 1, 2, 3$, are calibrated on the observed emissions between 2000 and 2010 and on an emission objective in 2050. By changing the latter, one obtains different trajectories that are converted into concentrations to be evaluated by PLASIM-ENTS's emulator. We thus use an interval-halving technique on the emissions target in 2050 to find the emission trajectory satisfying the temperature rise limit.

For the present study, the definition of the safety emission budget for the time period 2010-2050 is crucial as one has to select an appropriate warming target in 2050 that remains compatible with the objective of 2°C warming in 2100. Here we refer to the RCP2.6 concentration pathway which according to van Vuuren et al. (2011) *is representative of the literature on mitigation scenarios aiming to limit the increase of global mean temperature to 2°C*. PLASIM-ENTS's emulator computes for this RCP2.6 concentration pathway a warming of 1.45°C in 2050, so we use this target in our coupling and we derive a safety budget of 424 GtC-eq.

Notice that that all this coupling exercise is used to obtain an evaluation of the safety budget. The emission profile that will be implemented under an international agreement will have to satisfy this global budget. The emissions, for each period, will be determined by the regions using strategically their shares of the safety budget to supply permits on an international emissions trading system, at each period. This game structure is described in the following subsections.

8.4.3 Statistical Analysis of a Sample of GEMINI-E3 Numerical Simulations to Define a Meta-game of Climate Negotiations

We apply regression analysis to identify the payoff functions of a game where the strategic variables are the quota supplies by the different regions, at different periods.

The statistical analxsis is based on a sample of 200 numerical simulations of different possible world climate policy scenarios performed with GEMINI-E3. In each scenario, we suppose that a carbon tax is implemented at the world level without emissions trading. We suppose that all greenhouse gases are taxed including CH_4, N_2O and high-GWP. We compute for each group of countries:

- The abatement level relative to the BAU emissions reported in Figure 8.1 expressed in million ton of carbon equivalent;
- The welfare cost measured by the households' surplus, and represented by the Compensative Variation of Income (CVI) expressed in US $ Bernard (2003);
- The Gains or losses from the Terms of Trade (GTT) representing the spill-over effects through change in international prices. In a climate change policy these gains or losses from the terms of trade come mainly from the drop in fossil energy prices due to the decrease of world energy demand. The GTT are expressed in US $.

By subtracting the GTT from the surplus we obtain the Deadweight Loss of Taxation (DWL) i.e. the domestic cost that would occur in a closed economy and which only depends on the abatement done within the country. The GTT represents the imported cost: negative for energy exporting countries such as OPEC and positive for net energy importing countries like Europe and Japan Böhringer and Rutherford (2002). This imported cost/benefit is function of the world GHG abatement.

Using linear regression techniques, we estimate the abatement cost function (8.12) (i.e. the parameters $\alpha_j^0(t)$, $\alpha_j^1(t)$, $\alpha_j^2(t)$, $\alpha_j^3(t)$ and $\alpha_j^4(t)$) of player j and period t as a polynomial of degree 4 in the country abatement level. The time periods (t) are 2020, 2030, 2040, 2050 with $n(t)$=10 years for each period. Figure 8.2 presents the marginal abatement cost (MAC) curves (i.e. the derivative of the abatement cost function with respect to the abatement, see Equation (8.14)) estimated for the year 2030. It shows where it is the cheapest to abate GHG emissions (Russia, India and China) and where it is the most expensive (EU and ROW).

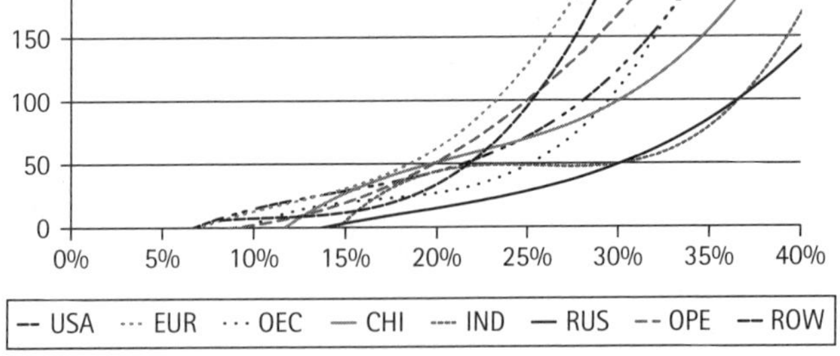

FIGURE 8.2 Marginal abatement costs by region in US $ per CO_2 equivalent for the year 2030, proportional abatement

The gains from the terms of trade of player j is assumed to be an affine function of the global abatement in a given period (see Equation (8.15)).

8.4.4 Formulation of the Game Design Problem, based on GEMINI-E3 Statistical Emulation

Design variables:

θ_j, share of the safety emission budget given to player j.

These variables define the key element of the negotiations, namely the sharing of the safety emission budget.

Strategic variables:

$\omega_j(t)$, supply of quotas by player j during period t.

We assume that once a player (group of countries) has been given a share of the emission budget, it can supply this amount of quotas (emission rights) on the emissions trading markets organized in the four different decades of the planning horizon. These supplies are strategic variables. They influence the market structure, determining price of carbon, then emission levels by each player, and, finally the transfers (buying and selling of permits) and the net surplus variations.

Secondary (passive) variables:

These are variables that will be computed from the values given to the strategic variables. They will be used to describe the permits market functioning. The abatements realized w.r.t. the BAU scenario are the argument of the abatement cost and of the gains from the terms of trade functions that have been identified through regression analysis of a sample of GEMINI-E3 numerical simulations.

$e_j(t)$: emission level for player j in period t;
$q_j(t)$: abatement level for player j in period t;
$p(t)$: carbon price in period t;
$AC_j(t)$: abatement cost for player j in period t;
$MAC_j(t)$: marginal abatement cost for player j in period t;
$GTT_j(t)$: gains from the terms of trade for player j in period t;
ν_j: multiplier associated with the share of budget given to player j.

parameters

safety_budget: global safety emission budget;
$\text{bce}_j(t)$: BAU emissions for player j in period t;
ny(t): number of years in period t;
n(t): number of years in time interval $[1, t]$;
$\alpha_j^0(t), \alpha_j^1(t), \alpha_j^2(t), \alpha_j^3(t), \alpha_j^4(t)$: coefficients in the abatement cost function;

$\mu_j^0(t)$, $\mu_j^1(t)$: coefficients in the gain from the terms of trade function;
β: discount factor;
hc_j: discounted household consumption in BAU over the planning horizon.

Payoffs for the game of quotas supply:
The players try to minimize the discounted sum of net surplus losses, W, which is the discounted sum of the gains from the terms of trade plus the gains from the permit trading (can be negative) minus the abatement cost, given the actions taken by the other players.

$$W_j(t) = -\sum_t \beta^{\mathrm{n}(t)}\mathrm{ny}(t)\left\{AC_j(t) - p(t)(\omega_j(t) - e_j(t)) - GTT_j(t)\right\} \tag{8.6}$$

Notice here that we define the payoffs in terms of surplus gains instead of losses.

Objective of the game design problem:
At the upper level where one negotiates the sharing of the safety emissions budget, one may apply a criterion of fairness inspired from the Rawlsian theory of justice:

$$z = \max_\theta \min_j \frac{W_j^\star(t)}{\mathrm{hc}_j}, \tag{8.7}$$

where $W_j^\star(t)$ is the equilibrium payoff for the game designed by the choice of θ. So we select the sharing which, in the Nash equilibrium solution of the game of quotas supply, maximizes the worst surplus gain among the players.

Constraints and functions:
They link the passive variables to the strategic variables, define the cost and profit functions, limit the choices for the strategic variables.

Shares of safety budget: The total supply of quotas by each player is equal to its share of the safety budget:

$$\sum_\tau \omega_j(\tau) = \theta_j\,\mathrm{safety\_budget}. \tag{8.8}$$

Price of carbon equal marginal abatement cost: In a competitive emission permits market, each player will abate at a level where the price of permit equals the marginal abatement cost:

$$p(t) = MAC_j(t), \forall t, j. \tag{8.9}$$

Permit market clears: In this market, the price is set at such a level that the total emission equals the total supply of quotas:

$$\sum_j \omega_j(t) = \sum_j e_j(t), \forall t. \tag{8.10}$$

Define emissions from abatements: One must compute abatement level to evaluate abatement costs:

$$e_j(t) + q_j(t) = \mathrm{bce_j(t)}. \tag{8.11}$$

Abatement cost: The abatement cost is a polynomial of degree 4 in the abatement variable:

$$AC_j(t) = \alpha_j^0(t) + \alpha_j^1(t)\, q_j(t) + \alpha_j^2\, q_j(t)^2 + \alpha_j^3(t)\, q_j(t)^3 + \alpha_j^4(t)\, q_j(t)^4. \tag{8.12}$$

Marginal abatement cost: The marginal abatement cost is obtained through derivation of the abatement cost:

$$MAC_j(t) = \alpha_j^1(t) + 2\alpha_j^2(t)\, q_j(t) + 3\alpha_j^3(t)\, q_j(t)^2 + 4\alpha_j^4(t)\, q_j(t)^3. \tag{8.13}$$

Derivative of marginal abatement cost: One also needs to compute the derivative of the marginal cost function:

$$DMAC_j(t) = 2\alpha_j^2(t) + 6\alpha_j^3(t)\, q_j(t) + 12\alpha_j^4(t)\, q_j(t)^2. \tag{8.14}$$

Gains from the terms of trade: The gains from the term of trade are expressed as a linear function of the sum of the abatements decided by all the players:

$$GTT_j(t) = \mu_j^0(t) + \mu_j^1(t) \sum_i q_i(t). \tag{8.15}$$

Derivative of carbon price: One has to compute the derivative of the carbon price w.r.t. any supply $\omega(t)$ which is given by (see Helm 2003):

$$DP(t) = \frac{-1}{\sum_j \frac{1}{DMAC_j(t)}}. \tag{8.16}$$

Pseudo-gradient of payoffs: We can now write pseudo-gradient of the payoffs w.r.t. the strategic variables

$$PSGRAD_j(t) = -\beta^{\mathrm{n(t)}}\mathrm{ny(t)}\left\{MAC_j(t) - DP(t)\,(\omega_j(t) - e_j(t)) - \mu_j^1(t)\right\} + \nu_j. \tag{8.17}$$

The first order conditions for a Nash equilibrium are then

$$\nu_j \geq 0$$

$$\theta_j\,\mathrm{safety\_budget} - \sum_\tau \omega_j(\tau) \geq 0$$

$$\nu_j \theta_j\,\mathrm{safety\_budget} - \sum_\tau \omega_j(\tau) = 0$$

$$\forall j$$

$$
\begin{aligned}
-PSGRAD_j(t) &\geq 0 \\
\omega_j(t) &\geq 0 \\
\omega_j(t)\, PSGRAD_j(t) &= 0 \\
& \qquad \forall j, \forall t.
\end{aligned}
$$

8.4.5 A Solution to the Game Design Problem

We use a safety budget equal to 424 GtC-eq as defined in section 8.4.2, the discount factor β is 3% per year. We start with the sharing of the safety budget computed by TIAM-WORLD, we also simulate other options that have been proposed for designing a global agreement on climate change Baumert (2002). The first one is based on an egalitarian rule that supposes that each individual has the right to emit an equal amount of greenhouse gases, in our case the budget share is proportional to the population over the period 2010–2050. The second rule considers that the allocation of quotas is proportional to emissions in the BAU simulation. This sovereignty principle is usually proposed as a starting point in environmental negotiations taking into account the existing situations. Finally we also present a solution corresponding to the max min of the surplus losses expressed in % of BAU consumption, computed from a sample of simulations that we have tested.[5] In this solution the maximum loss, among the eight groups of countries, expressed as a percentage of the discounted total consumption in the BAU case, is minimal. This max min solution tends to equalize welfare costs as a percentage of GDP. One notices that the max min is close to the equity solution computed with the TIAM-WORLD except for China and USA. TIAM-WORLD gives less to USA (−0.4) and more to China (+0.3).

Experience shows that negotiators do not put forward a single allocation rule based on a clearly identified value judgment on equity but a mix that takes into account their own features and situation. Table 8.13 gives the different distributions of the total budget that have been tested.

In each case we have computed the Nash equilibrium for the game of quota supply defined above and we have obtained the following evaluations of the surplus loss,

Table 8.13 Different sharings tested (θ_j)

	USA	EUR	OEC	CHI	IND	RUS	OPE	ROW
TIAM-WORLD equity solution	0.11	0.07	0.08	0.28	0.07	0.07	0.07	0.26
Egalitarian rule	0.04	0.06	0.06	0.17	0.18	0.02	0.07	0.40
Sovereignty rule	0.15	0.09	0.09	0.25	0.07	0.05	0.07	0.23
max min solution	0.15	0.07	0.075	0.25	0.07	0.05	0.085	0.25

Table 8.14 Corresponding surplus losses (% of BAU discounted household consumption)

	USA	EUR	OEC	CHI	IND	RUS	OPE	ROW	Max loss
TIAM-WORLD equity solution	1.66	0.81	0.62	-1.69	1.01	-5.44	3.42	0.15	3.42
Egalitarian rule	4.81	1.64	2.02	10.63	-34.51	13.65	3.97	-7.74	13.65
Sovereignty rule	0.79	0.33	0.18	0.64	0.87	0.26	4.51	1.70	4.51
max min solution	0.78	0.87	0.86	0.75	0.93	0.33	0.23	0.62	0.93

expressed as a percentage of discounted total consumption over the 2010–2050 period. The results are shown in Table 8.14. The equalitarian rule gives a large number of extreme welfare impacts, where Russia, China and USA would support a very high burden whereas the ROW and India would largely benefit from climate protection. In contrary the sovereignty rule would have a more concentrated range of welfare costs, but would impose a high burden on OPEC and ROW.

8.4.6 Equilibrium for the max min allocation

We examine the equilibrium solution corresponding to the sharing of the safety budget shown in Table 8.15.

It is interesting to compare this budget allocation with the emissions reduction target defined by the countries. The EU climate change policy aims to reducing by 20%

Table 8.15 Allocation and equilibrium solution expressed in surplus loss ratios

Countries	GtC-eq	% safety budget
USA	63.6	15.0%
EUR	29.7	7.0%
OEC	31.8	7.5%
CHI	106.0	25.0%
IND	29.7	7.0%
RUS	21.2	5.0%
OPE	36.4	8.5%
ROW	106.0	25.0%
World	424.0	100.0

Table 8.16 Quotas supplied by countries at each decade in GtC-eq

	2011-2020	2021-2030	2031-2040	2041-2050	2011-2050
USA	14.7	15.6	16.3	17.0	63.6
EUR	7.9	7.7	7.3	6.8	29.7
OEC	8.1	8.1	7.9	7.8	31.8
CHI	21.5	26.0	27.8	30.7	106.0
IND	6.0	6.9	7.9	8.8	29.7
RUS	4.7	5.1	5.6	5.8	21.2
OPE	6.9	8.3	9.8	11.1	36.0
ROW	22.6	25.0	28.0	30.4	106.0
Total decade	92.6	102.6	110.5	118.4	424.0

in 2020 and 75% in 2050 the GHG emissions from the 1990 levels, this gives a budget equal to 35 GtC-eq for the next 40 years. This budget is 17% higher than the one computed in our equilibrium. The US climate targets is more uncertain in the long term. At the Cancún UN climate summit in December 2010 the U.S. delegation confirmed the target of reducing GHG emissions by 17% in 2020 compared to 2005 levels. But nothing was enacted concerning long term target like 2050. In Palsey et al. (2009) the authors developed three paths of emissions control spanning the range of Congressional proposals, the cumulative allowance allocations between 2012 and 2050 of the policy are 78.4, 55.5 and 45.6 GtC. The three climate policies are based on allowance allocations that through 2050 are: 1) constant at 2008 emissions levels, 2) linearly reduced to 50% below 2008 levels, 3) linearly reduce emissions to 80% below 2008 levels. Our allocation for USA is close the -50% target even if our budget is 8 GtC-eq more generous. Concerning developing countries, we can translate their cumulative emissions budget in a target for the year 2050 that would be required to reach if we suppose that this climate target is achieved through a linear decrease of GHG emissions. We compute the target in comparison with the 2010 emissions levels. These objective are for China, India, Russia, OPEC and ROW respectively +38%, +17%, −16%, +155% and +18%. Our target for China gives in 2020 a reduction in Chinese GHG intensity (i.e. GHG emissions divided by GDP) in 2020 with respect to 2007 levels by −52% which is in line with the target defined by the Chinese government. In 2009, the Chinese government committed to cut its CO_2 emissions per unit of GDP by 40–45% of the 2005 levels by 2020 Yi et al. (2011). The allocation given to OPEC is necessary to compensate the loss of energy exporting revenue and is close to the cumulative BAU emissions that are equal to 40 GtC-eq.

The prices of permits are shown in Table 8.17.

Figure 8.3 below shows how the distribution of quota supplies by each group of countries changes over the periods. One notices a relative stability of these ratios.

Table 8.17 CO_2 price in US$ per ton of CO_2-equivalent

2020	61
2030	81
2040	108
2050	145

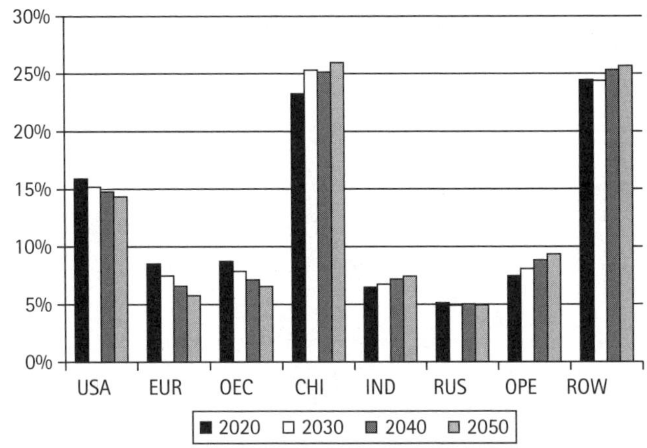

FIGURE 8.3 Quotas supplied by countries in % at each decade

Comparing quotas and emissions we obtain the yearly transfers of emission rights (positive means Sale, negative means Buy) shown in Table 8.18, OECD countries (USA, EUR and OEC) are net buyers of permits, in contrary emerging and developing countries sale quotas. The main buyers of permits is the European Union whose GHG abatement costs are high. Concerning the sellers side, China and OPEC are the main actors. China benefits from large possibilities of reduction associated with limited abatement costs and OPEC can sell its generous allocations that have been given to overcompensate the losses of energy exporting revenue.

For comparison we give in Table 8.19 the similar transfer values that have been obtained in the "equity" solution based on TIAM-WORLD scenarios.

The costs borne by regions presented in Table 8.14 can be decomposed in three components 1) the domestic cost of abatement, 2) the gains or losses coming from the terms of trade (i.e. the imported cost/gain), 3) the buying or selling of permits. This decomposition is displayed in Figure 8.4, it shows that for India and Russia large positive transfers of permits are required to compensate the abatement cost of GHG. In the case of OPEC the selling of permits allows also a reduction of the important losses of

Table 8.18 Net selling (+) or buying (-) of quotas by countries at each decade in GtC-eq

	2011-2020	2021-2030	2031-2040	2041-2050	2011-2050
USA	−0.58	−0.53	−0.59	−0.69	−2.39
EUR	−2.84	−2.98	−3.26	−3.56	−12.64
OEC	−0.94	−0.96	−1.02	−1.12	−4.04
CHI	2.25	1.92	1.85	1.93	7.94
IND	0.47	0.52	0.55	0.58	2.12
RUS	0.36	0.45	0.55	0.63	1.98
OPE	0.92	1.16	1.43	1.66	5.17
ROW	0.36	0.43	0.50	0.57	1.85
World	0.00	0.00	0.00	0.00	0.00

Table 8.19 Net selling (+) or buying (-) of quotas by countries at each decade in GtC-eq, in TIAM-WORLD equity solution

	2020	2030	2040	2050
USA	−0.66	−1.37	−2.34	−2.46
EUR	−0.63	−1.44	−2.38	−2.67
OEC	−0.09	−0.38	−0.73	−0.56
CHI	0.42	1.40	2.62	4.59
IND	0.12	0.50	0.24	−0.26
RUS	−0.12	0.14	0.46	0.84
OPE	0.55	0.31	1.06	1.15
ROW	0.41	0.84	1.07	−0.62

energy export revenues. China is the only region where the gains from terms of trade represent an important share in the aggregated cost. In industrialized regions the trade of permits represents a cost. This cost is significant for European Union and Other OECD regions. In contrary, the buying of quotas represents a small share of the total cost borne by USA.

8.4.7 Interpretation of the Results Obtained in this Game Theoretic Approach

The optimisation based approach implemented with the TIAM-WORLD / PLASIM-ENTS coupling and the game design approach implemented with the GEMINI-E3 /

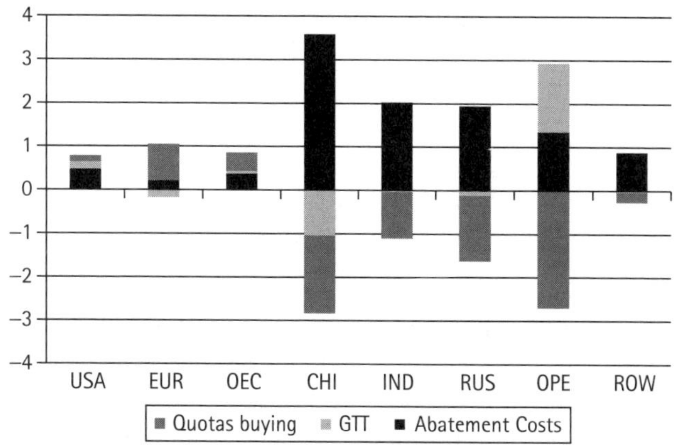

FIGURE 8.4 Decomposition of the surplus losses in % of BAU discounted household consumption

PLASIM-ENTS coupling are not directly comparable. Indeed, even the way one computes the safety budget is different in each approach. In the first case one optimizes the energy model over a time horizon reaching 2100 and one imposes a radiative forcing constraint on that final time, whereas in the second case one imposes a temperature change limit in 2050, temperature change which is considered as compatible with an increase of SAT less than 2°C in 2100. We see that this second approach led to a lower global budget. The energy technology options are less efficient in GEMINI-E3. For example, production of electricity from biomass with carbon capture and sequestration is very present in TIAM-WORLD and used in many regions, whereas this option does not exist in GEMINI-E3. This means that the abatement costs are much higher in the second case.

In addition, the emission trajectory used in GEMINI-E3 considers higher emission abatement at the beginning of the horizon compared to the optimal trajectory computed in TIAM-WORLD. Although expensive, these reductions raise the question of "when" abatement should occur. While early abatement is expensive, hence the trend to delay emission reductions in optimal strategies, early abatement might be also considered as safer than late abatement given the uncertainties in both the long term commitments of the countries and the impacts of climate change.

The consideration of a Nash equilibrium for the game of allocation of quotas should make this approach more acceptable to the parties in the negotiation. The ratios are higher in this second approach; they have not been computed in exactly the same way. The household consumption is not very different from GDP; however the game includes in the payoffs the gains from the terms of trade and this, with the higher abatement cost, could explain the larger values of the ratios that serve to find the optimal solution (max min sharing). With all these differences the proximity in the sharings proposed in the two approaches is interesting to observe.

8.5 Conclusion

In this study we have used two complementary approaches to evaluate a possible fair sharing of the burden of keeping climate change inside a tolerable region. The outcome of negotiation is assumed to be reduced to the definition of a fair sharing of a safety emission budget. To evaluate this budget we have used first an emulator of a complex climate model, PLASIM-ENTS coupled with either a bottom-up energy model, TIAM-WORLD, or a top-down general equilibrium model GEMINI-E3. Using these different models we have defined two ways to assess the net benefit, expressed in terms of a ratio of surplus over GDP or household consumption. The surplus is computed after the establishment of an "optimal international emissions trading market". Then we were able to find the sharing of the safety emissions budget that would maximize the minimum of these ratios. In the case of TIAM-WORLD we could allocate the quotas of each player, in each period so that all these ratios are equal, in each period. In the second approach, we used statistical analysis of a sample of numerical simulations performed with GEMINI-E3 to define the payoff functions of the players/regions in a non-cooperative game of strategic allocation of their shares of the safety emission budget, as quotas for each period in the international emissions trading system. This second way of organizing the market has the advantage of avoiding the (restrictive) assumption that a benevolent planner determines the allocation of quotas for each player at each period; it should therefore be more acceptable in the negotiation process.

Doing this analysis with two large-scale techno-economic models coupled with an emulator of an advanced moderate complexity climate model we made the following observations that could be important for the forthcoming climate negotiations:

(i) The mid-term (2010-2050) costs of the climate abatement strategies to keep the long term temperature increase below 2°C remain moderate: at the worldwide level, the cumulative discounted abatement cost in percentage of cumulative and discounted GDP is equal to 0.16% with TIAM-WORLD and 0.46% with GEMINI-E3. The difference between bottom-up and top-down, the latter indicating a larger cost for a same mitigation policy, is well established and documented Wilson and Swisher (1993). A possible factor explaining this difference is the inclusion in bottom-up models of very low cost emission reduction possibilities IPCC (2001). In fact the mitigation policies are different in the two approaches. The 2°C PLASIM-ENTS temperature constraint in 2100 is applied in TIAM-WORLD, giving an emissions budget of 484 GTC; whereas in GEMINI-E3, RCP2.6 is assumed (which gives 1.45°C PLASIM-ENTS warming in 2050), and provides emissions budget of 424 GTC. Notice that the RCP2.6 emissions profile was only used to evaluate the safety budget. The actual emissions will be the result of the negotiation, i.e. the result of the Nash equilibrium in the game of quotas. Running the same game model with an emission budget of 484 GTC would give abatement costs with GEMINI-E3 that are much closer to those evaluated by TIAM-WORLD. So the GEMINI-E3 / PLASIM-ENTS assessment was more conservative and cautious given the low climate sensitivity of PLASIM-ENTS. However these two approaches show that to reach the 2°C target as defined by EU seems feasible with reasonable economic costs over the time horizon 2050. It is important to remember that these costs, over 2010-2050, represent only one part of the total abatement costs needed to respect the 2°C target. Indeed, abatement must be pursued after 2050, with corresponding costs to be considered.

(ii) A crucial issue is to identify the distribution of the burden that equalizes and limits high costs of implementation; we have shown that the models currently available can provide some valuable insights when they are associated with some optimization or game design meta-models. We also demonstrate that the implementation of a global market of tradable permits is a relevant economic instrument that could help to achieve the burden sharing. The first steps of the The EU Emissions Trading System and its extension to new partners could be the presages of a worldwide trading scheme.

(iii) In the two approaches developed in this paper the models TIAM-WORLD and GEMINI-E3 coupled with PLASIM-ENTS give some common conclusions: (a) OECD countries are net buyers of permits and the contributions computed by our models are close to the existing commitments or propositions made by OECD countries; (b) Emerging and developing countries are net sellers; they will be helped by the organization of international emissions trading systems, on which they can play strategically with their shares of the safety emissions budget; (c) China is an essential player as it received more than 25% of the budget in all cases.

(iv) The agreements analyzed in this paper considered a limited number of players, compared to the 197 countries involved in the UNFCCC negotiations. The need to define a more limited forum to discuss the type of agreement architecture proposed in this paper might deserve some more attention. The Group of Twenty (G20) might be a possibility: in 2010, the G20 members represent 76% of global GHG emissions and almost 90% of global GDP.

Finally, our analysis demonstrates the potential for using statistical emulation and meta-modelling techniques to derive more realistic representations of the potential costs and benefits associated with various possible international environmental agreements, including the effects of non-cooperative behaviour of agents. The construction of statistical emulators from large ensembles of model simulations to cover a wider range of possibilities, and comparison between models of different structures, can play an essential role in assessing the multitude of related uncertainties. Further work is needed in this area to identify the most robust forms of agreements.

Acknowledgments

The research leading to these results has received funding from the EU Seventh Framework Programme (ERMITAGE FP7/2007-2013) under Grant Agreement n°265170.

Notes

1. We assume that this corresponds to a 3.75 W/m^2 radiative forcing.
2. Using the conversion factor of 3.67 t CO_2 per t C, the cumulative emissions are 272 GtC and 391 GtC respectively.
3. At the Durban Climate Change Conference - November/December 2011 - the importance of emissions trading and project-based mechanisms in continuation of the Kyoto Protocol. See http://unfccc.int/resource/docs/2011/cmp7/eng/ 10a01.pdf
4. All information about the model can be found at http://gemini-e3.epfl.ch, including its complete description.
5. We test the local stability of this equilibrium (called $\theta_j^\star$) by varying the θ_j around this equilibrium. We simulate all the solutions in the range $[\theta_j^\star$-0.02; $\theta_j^\star$+0.02] with a step of 0.01. It gives 5^7 (78125) runs with $\theta_{row} = 1 - \sum \theta_i$.

References

Aghassi, M., and Bertsimas, D. (2006). Robust game theory. *Mathematical Programming B, 107*, 231–273.

Arnell, N. W., Lowe, J. A., Brown, S., Gosling, S. N., Gottschalk, P., Hinkel, J., Lloyd-Hughes, B., Nicholls, R. J., Osborn, T. J., Osborne, T. M., Rose, G. A., Smith, P., and Warren, R. F. (2013). A global assessment of the effects of climate policy on the impacts of climate change. *Nature Climate Change, 3*, 512–519.

Arrhenius, S. (April 1896). On the Influence of Carbonic Acid in the Air upon the Temperature of the Ground. London, Edinburgh, and Dublin Philosophical Magazine and Journal of Science (fifth series), 41:237–275.

Bataille, C. (2005). Design & Application of a Technologically Explicit Hybrid Energy-Economy Policy Model with Micro and Macro Economic Dynamics. Ph.D. Thesis, Simon Fraser University, p. 294.

Baumert, K. A., Blanchard, O., Llosa, S., and Perkaus, J.F. (Ed.). (2002). Building on the Kyoto Protocol: Options for Protecting the Climate, World Resources Institute, Washington D.C..

Bernard, A., and M. (2003). GEMINI-E3, a general equilibrium model of international–national interactions between economy, energy and the environment. *Environmental Modeling & Assessment, 8*, 199–217.

Bernard, A., and Vielle, M. (2008). GEMINI-E3, a general equilibrium model of international-national interactions between economy, energy and the environment. *Computational Management Science, 5*, 173–206.

Böhringer, C., and Rutherford, T. F. (2002). Carbon abatement and international spillovers. *Environmental and Resource Economics, 22*, 391–417.

Böhringer, C., and Helm, C. (2008). On the fair division of greenhouse gas abatement cost. *Resource and Energy Economics, 30*(2), 260–276.

Broad, J. (1999). Contraction and Convergence. *Ecologist, 29*(2), 141.

Carbone, J. C., Helm, C., and Rutherford, T. F. (2009). The case for international emission trade in the absence of cooperative climate policy. *Journal of Environmental Economics and Management, 58*(3), 266–280.

Energy Information Administration, International Energy Outlook U.S., Department of Energy, 2011.

England, M., Kartha, S., Siebert, C. K., Mathur, R., McCarthy, J., Messner, D., Nakicenovic, N., Ramanathan, V., Rockström, J., Schellnhuber, J., and Srivastava, L. (2010). A Copenhagen Prognosis: Towards a Safe Climate Future. Technical Report by the Potsdam Institute for Climate Impact Research, Stockholm Environment Institute, and The Energy and Resources Institute.

Ferris, M., and Munson, T. (2000). Complementarity Problems in GAMS and the PATH Solver. *Journal of Economic Dynamics and Control, 24*, 165–188.

Fraedrich, K., Jansen, H., Kirk, E., Luksch, U., and Lunkeit, F. (2005). The Planet Simulator: Towards a user friendly model. *Meteorologische Zeitschrift, 14*, 299–304. doi: http://dx.doi.org/10.1127/0941-2948/2005/0043

Townshend, T., Fankhauser, S., Aybar, R., Collins, M., Landesman, T., Nachmanyand, M., and Pavese, C. (2013). Climate Legislation Study: A Review of Climate Change Legislation in 33 Countries. Third Edition Globe International.

Helm, C. (2003). International emissions trading with endogenous allowance choices. *Journal of Public Economics, 87*(12), 2737–2747.

Holden, P. B., and Edwards, N. R. (2010). Dimensionally reduced emulation of an AOGCM for application to integrated assessment modelling. *Geophysical Research Letters, L21707.* doi:10.1029/2010GL045137

Holden, P. B., Edwards, N. R., Oliver, K. I. C., Lenton, T. M., and Wilkinson, R. D. (2010). A probabilistic calibration of climate sensitivity and terrestrial carbon change in GENIE-1. *Climate Dynamics, 35*, 785–806. doi: 10.1007/s00382-009-0630-8.

IPCC Climate Change; Watson, R. T.; and the Core Writing Team, ed. (2001). *Mitigation, A report of the Working Group III of the Intergovernmental Panel on Climate Change.* Cambridge University Press, 2001.

Kanudia, A., Labriet, M., and Loulou, R. (2014). Effectiveness and efficiency of climate change mitigation in a technologically uncertain World. *Climatic change, 123*, 3–4, Special Issue on "The EMF27 Study on Global Technology and Climate Policy." 543–558.

Labriet, M., Kanudia, A., and Loulou, R. (2012). Climate mitigation under an uncertain technology future: A TIAM-WORLD analysis. *Energy Economics, 34*(Supplement 3), S366–377.

Labriet, M., Drouet, L., Vielle, M., Haurie, A., Kanudia, A., and Loulou, R. (2010). Coupled bottom-up and top-down modelling to investigate cooperative climate policies. Les Cahiers du GERAD, G-2010-30.

Labriet, M., and Loulou, R. (2008). How Crucial is Cooperation in Mitigating World Climate? Analysis with World-MARKAL. Computational Management Science, Special issue *Managing Energy and the Environment, 5*(1), 67–94.

Loulou, R., Labriet, M., and Kanudia, A. (2009). Deterministic and Stochastic Analysis of alternative climate targets under differentiated cooperation regimes. *Energy Economics, 31*(Suppl. 2), S131–143.

Loulou, R., and Labriet, M. (2008). ETSAP-TIAM: the TIMES integrated assessment model Part I: Model structure. Computational Management Science, Special issue *Managing Energy and the Environment, 5*(1), 7–40.

Loulou, R. (2008). ETSAP-TIAM: the TIMES integrated assessment model Part II: Mathematical formulation. Computational Management Science, Special issue *Managing Energy and the Environment, 5*(1–2), 41–66.

Maurer, H., Preuss, J. J., and Semmler, W. (2013). Policy Scenarios in a Model of Optimal Economic Growth and Climate Change, In this handbook.

Malte, M., Nicolai, M., William, H., Sarah, C. B. Raper, Katja, F., Reto, K., David, J. F., and Myles, R. A. (2009). Greenhouse-gas emission targets for limiting global warming to 2°C. *Nature, 458*, 1158–1163.

Moss, R. H., Edmonds, J. A., Hibbard, K. A., Manning, M. R., Rose, S. K., van Vuuren, D. P., Carter, T. R., Emori, S., Kainuma, M., Kram, T., et al. (2010). The next generation of scenarios for climate change research and assessment. *Nature, 463*, 747–756.

Narayanan, B., Aguiar, A., and McDougall, R. (Eds.). (2012). Global Trade, Assistance, and Production: The GTAP 8 Data Base.Center for Global Trade Analysis, Purdue University.

Ordás Criado, C., and Grether, J.-M. (2010). Convergence in per capita CO_2 emissions: A robust distributional approach. CEPE Working Paper No. 70. CEPE. Zurichbergstrasse 18 (ZUE E) CH-8032 Zurich.

Palsey, S., Reilly, J. M., Jacoby, H. D., and Morris, J. F. (2009). The cost of climate policy in the United States. *Energy Economics, 31*(2), S235–S243.

Rawls, J. (1971). *A Theory of Justice.* Harvard University Press, p. 623.

Schaeffer, M., and van Vuuren, D. (2012). Evaluation of IEA ETP 2012 emission scenarios. Climate Analytics Working Paper 201281. Karl-Liebknecht-Strasse 5, 10178 Berlin, Germany.

Stern, N. (2007). *The Economics of Climate Change.* The Stern Review, Cambridge University Press, p.712.

United Nations, Department of Economic and Social Affairs, Population Division, World Population Prospects: The 2010 Revision, 2011.

Vaillancourt, K., Loulou, R., and Kanudia, A. (2007). The Role of Abatement Costs in GHG Permit Allocations: A Global Stabilization Scenario Analysis. *Environmental Modeling & Assessment, 13*(2), 169–179.

van Vuuren, D. P., Edmonds, J., Kainuma, M., Riahi, K., Thomson, A., Hibbard, K., Hurtt, G. C., Kram, T., Krey, V., Lamarque, J.-F., Masui, T., Meinshausen, M., Nakicenovic, N., Smith, N. S. J., and Rose, S. K. (2011). The representative concentration pathways: An overview. *Climatic Change, 109*, 5–31.

van Vuuren, D. P., Stehfest, E., den Elzen, M. G. J., Kram, T., van Vliet, J., Deetman, S., Isaac, M., Klein Goldewijk, K., Hof, A., Mendoza Beltran, A., Oostenrijk, R., and van Ruijven, B.

(2011). RCP2.6: Exploring the possibility to keep global mean temperature increase below 2°C, *Climatic Change, 109*(1–2), 95–116.

Warren, R., de la Nava Santos, S., Arnell, N. W., Bane, M., Barker, T., Barton, C., Ford, R., Fuessel, H.-M., Hankin, R. K. S., Hinkel, J., Klein, R., Linstead, C., Kohler, J., Mitchell, T. D., Osborn, T. J., Pan, H., Raper, S. C. B., Riley, G., Schellnhueber, H. J., Winne, S., and Anderson, D. (2008). Development and illustrative outputs of the Community Integrated Assessment System (CIAS), a multi-institutional modular integrated assessment approach for modelling climate change, *Environ. Model. Software, 23*(5), 592–610.

Watkiss, P. (Ed.). (2011). The ClimateCost Project, Final Report, Vol. 1. Sweden: Europe, Stockholm Environment Institute.

Williamson, M. S., Lenton, T. M., Shepherd, J. G., and Edwards, N. R. (2006). An efficient numerical terrestrial scheme (ENTS) for Earth system modelling. *Ecological Modelling, 198*, 362–374.

Wilson, D., and Swisher, J. (1993). Exploring the gap. Top-down versus bottom-up analyses of the cost of mitigating global warming. *Energy Policy, 21*, 249–263.

Yi, W.-J., Zou, L.-L., Guo, J., Wang, K., and Wei, Y.-M. (2011). How can China reach its CO_2 intensity reduction targets by 2020? A regional allocation based on equity and development. *Energy Policy, 39*, 2407–2415.

CHAPTER 9

CLIMATE CHANGE AND SECOND-BEST ABATEMENT IN A MULTIREGION WORLD WITH ENDOGENOUS GROWTH

ALFRED GREINER

9.1 Introduction

The Intergovernmental Panel on Climate Change (IPCC) estimates that the global average surface temperature has increased by $0.6 \pm 0.2\,^\circ$C over the 20th century. It is very likely[1] that the 1990s was the warmest decade since 1861 (IPCC, 2001, p. 26). Looking at the period 1995–2006, one realizes that 11 years out of that time frame were among the 12 warmest years since 1850 (IPCC, 2007). According to NASA data the year 2010 was the warmest year ever since mankind began to record the average surface temperature on Earth (see also Hansen et al., 2010). Besides the rise of the surface temperature, it is likely that statistically significant increases in heavy and extreme weather events have occurred in many mid- and high-latitude areas, especially in the Northern Hemisphere.[2] Changes in the climate system occur as a result of both internal variability within the system and as a result of external factors that can be either natural or anthropogenic. But natural factors have made little contributions to the climate change that has been observed over the past century. Instead, there is strong evidence that most of the warming observed over the last 50 years is the result of human activities. In particular, the emission of greenhouse gases (GHGs), such as carbon dioxide (CO_2) or methane (CH_4) just to mention two, are considered as the cause of global warming and these emissions continue to change the atmosphere in ways that will affect climate on Earth.

In the environmental economics literature there exist numerous contributions that study the interrelation between economic growth and environmental degradation (for a survey see, e.g., Smulders, 1995; Hettich, 2000). These studies are rather abstract because they intend to derive general results in analytical models. It is assumed that economic activities lead to environmental degradation and, as a consequence, reduce utility and/or production possibilities. The question then arises how government policies can improve the environment and how such measures affect the growth rate and welfare of economies.

On the other hand, there exist studies that try to evaluate the effects of global warming (see, e.g., Nordhaus, 1994; Nordhaus and Boyer, 2000; Deke et al., 2001; Kemfert, 2001; Tol, 2003; Stern, 2006; and for a survey IPCC, 1996, 2007; Tol, 2008). For example, in Nordhaus and Boyer (2000) different abatement scenarios are analyzed where the growth rate of the economy is assumed to be an exogenous variable and the results are compared with the social optimum. In this study it is shown, among others, that in all scenarios carbon taxes rise over time. Other studies dealing with global warming are cost–benefit analysis, which also take the growth rate of economies as an exogenous variable. These studies, then, compute the discounted cost of reducing GHG emissions and confront them with the discounted benefit of a lower increase in the GHG concentration. Examples of such studies are Tol (2001) and Hackl and Pruckner (2002).

A great problem arising when one intends to study the economic consequences of global warming is the uncertainty concerning the damages caused by a change of the Earth climate. The IPCC estimates that a doubling of CO_2, which goes along with an increase of global average surface temperature between 1.5 and 4.5 °C, reduces world GDP by 1.5 to 2% (see IPCC, 1996, p. 218). This damage is obtained for the economy in steady state and comprises both market and nonmarket impacts. Nonmarket impacts are direct reductions of people's welfare resulting from a climate change. But, of course, it must be repeated that there is great uncertainty in social cost estimates, especially as concerns the direct impact of climate change on individuals' utility. Tol (2008) presents a meta-study that summarizes about 200 studies that deal with climate change and compares the social cost of climate change in these contributions.

In this chapter we intend to bring together models of endogenous growth and models dealing with changes in the climate on Earth. The difference between our chapter and many contributions on economic growth and the environment is that we use insights from physics to model the environment, where we focus on the problem of global warming. Further, we resort to a reduced type of endogenous growth model with a constant marginal product of capital (AK approach). Starting point of our contribution is the approach by Greiner (2004), where optimal abatement ratios are derived assuming that the world is composed of one country. That model is extended by allowing for different regions where we closely follow Greiner (2005).

The rest of our contribution is organized as follows. In the next section we give a brief survey of macroeconomic models featuring climate change where the interaction of different countries is taken into account. In Section 9.3 we describe the interrelation between the economic system and the climate system, where we first describe the climate module that is integrated into an endogenous growth model and then describe the economic framework. Section 9.4 analyzes the open-loop equilibrium for the non-cooperative case and Section 9.5 gives the second-best solution when the world cooperates. Section 9.6 summarizes the main conclusions.

9.2 Climate Change in Macroeconomic Models of Interacting Countries

A good and exhaustive survey of dynamic games in economic models dealing with environmental degradation is given by Jorgensen et al. (2010). Most game theoretic approaches in economics, however, are microeconomic models that analyze the interrelation of several heterogeneous agents. Nevertheless, there also exist macroeconomic approaches with heterogeneous countries that study the impact of different environmental policies in the economies under consideration. In this section we give a brief survey of macro models that deal with climate change taking into account that economies are heterogeneous as regards their output, their contribution to worldwide GHG emissions, and with respect to the damages they suffer from global warming.

The models that analyze the evolution of economic variables taking into account global warming are rather complex. Often, many players are involved in generating a high-dimensional dynamic system to be analyzed. Therefore, numerical techniques are frequently resorted to in order to gain insight into the evolution of economies. The goal is to detect cooperative and noncooperative solutions and to compare the outcome of these two strategies in terms of economic output, consumption, and welfare and as regards emission of GHGs.

An early approach by Scheffran and Pickl (2000) sets up a game theoretic model where they study a Joint Implementation program to find how cooperation between industrialized and developing economies affects output and GHG emissions. The paper derives conditions such that cooperation between industrialized and developing countries reduces costs compared to noncooperation, where the goal of the industrialized countries is to reduce emissions to a certain degree while developing countries aim to raise their output. Both economies have different technologies as regards their emissions of GHGs and with respect to their costs. Cooperation is measured through transfers of technology and through capital flows from the industrialized to the developing economy. In two other papers, Scheffran (2000, 2000a) analyzes effects of transferring a reduced-emission technology in the developing country with financial support from the industrialized economy. The model is then solved with the help of simulations to derive energy consumption, economic output, emissions, investment, and technological progress.

The effects of international treaties on climate change, such as the Kyoto Protocol, for example, have been analyzed in Bosello et al. (2003). These authors study how the equity criterion affects the decision of developing countries to participate in an international treaty on GHG reduction. One criterion is equal average abatement costs, another is equal per capita abatement, and the last is equal abatement costs per unit of output. The analysis of that model demonstrates that the adoption of any of the three criteria increases profitability of a climate agreement but not its stability. A Pareto-optimal transfer mechanism is also proposed that, however, does not lead to a global agreement on global warming.

New technologies that result from research and development (R&D) play an important role in reducing GHG emissions and the cost to do so. Bosetti et al. (2006, 2008) developed the so-called World Induced Technical Change Hybrid (WITCH) model to evaluate the effects of international knowledge flows as concerns the R&D sectors as well as with respect to other economic and environmental variables. Technological change is endogenous and depends on climate policy and on international spillovers among other factors, where learning by doing is an important driver of technical change. Computing open-loop noncooperative solutions, it has been demonstrated that there exist incentives to free ride on carbon-free investment which leads to a delay in the introduction of GHG reducing technologies. As investment costs decline, due to learning by doing, new technologies are introduced faster. The chapter demonstrates that emissions in the cooperative situation are drastically smaller compared to the noncooperative situation.

The role of international technology transmission concerning new and more efficient technologies to produce energy has also been studied by Bosetti et al. (2008) with the help of the WITCH model. There are international knowledge spillovers that allow to analyze the cost reductions that result from a rise in the diffusion of knowledge. The analysis shows that the endogenization of international energy R&D spillovers raises the incentives to free ride and leads to less R&D in new energy-producing technologies. Consequently, neither the overall domestic knowledge nor the cost of stabilizing the world GHG concentration in the atmosphere are greatly affected. But the cost of stabilizing the GHG emissions can be reduced to a great degree by implementing a stabilization policy that should use a global permit market that should be combined with a technology policy that helps to disseminate knowledge, in particular to economies with low incomes.

In the next section we present a simple model of endogenous growth with heterogeneous economies where we integrate a simple energy balance model to allow for climate change.

9.3 Global Warming in a Simple Endogenous Growth Model

In this section we present our model where we first describe the climate module and then the economic framework into which this module is integrated.

9.3.1 The Climate Module

As regards the change in the average global surface temperature we adopt the simplest climate module where the climate system of the Earth is modeled in terms of its global energy balance, which is done by so-called energy balance models (EBMs). Here, we follow Roedel (2001), Chapter 10.2.1 and Chapter 1 (see also Henderson-Sellers and McGuffie, 1987, or Gassmann, 1992; a more complex presentation can be found in Harvey, 2000).

According to an EBM the change in the average surface temperature on Earth can be described by the following equation:

$$\frac{dT(t)}{dt}\,c_h := \dot{T}(t)\,c_h = S_E - H_E(t) - F_N(t) + \beta_2\,(1-\xi)\,6.3\ln\frac{M(t)}{M_o},\quad T(0)=T_0, \tag{9.1}$$

with $T(t)$ the average global surface temperature measured in Kelvin, with 273 Kelvin equal to 0 °C, and c_h the constant heat capacity of the Earth with dimension $\mathrm{J\,m^{-2}\,K^{-1}}$ (Joules per square meter per Kelvin, where 1 Watt is 1 Joule per second). Note that the heat capacity is the amount of heat that needs to be added per square meter of horizontal area to raise the surface temperature of the reservoir by 1 Kelvin. S_E is the solar input, $H_E(t)$ is the nonradiative energy flow, and $F_N(t) = F\uparrow(t) - F\downarrow(t)$ is the difference between the outgoing radiative flux and the incoming radiative flux. The variable $M(t)$ denotes the concentration of GHGs in the atmosphere and M_o is the preindustrial level of GHGs.

S_E, $H_E(t)$, and $F_N(t)$ have the dimension Watt per square meter ($\mathrm{Wm^{-2}}$). $F\uparrow$ follows the Stefan-Boltzmann equation, which is[3]

$$F\uparrow = \epsilon\,\sigma_T\,T^4, \tag{9.2}$$

with ϵ the emissivity, which gives the ratio of actual emission to blackbody emission. Blackbodies are objects that emit the maximum amount of radiation and that have $\epsilon = 1$. For the Earth ϵ can be set to $\epsilon = 0.95$. σ_T is the Stefan-Boltzmann constant, which is given by $\sigma_T = 5.67\,10^{-8}\,\mathrm{Wm^{-2}K^{-4}}$. Further, the ratio $F\uparrow/F\downarrow$ is given by $F\uparrow/F\downarrow = 109/88$. The difference $S_E - H_E$ can be written as $S_E - H_E = Q(1-\alpha_1)\alpha_2/4$, with $Q = 1367.5\ Wm^{-2}$ the solar constant, $\alpha_1 = 0.3$ the planetary albedo, determining how much of the incoming energy is reflected by the atmosphere, and $\alpha_2 = 0.3$ captures the fact that a part of the energy is absorbed by the surface of the Earth.

A rise in the emissions of GHGs results in an increase in the concentration of GHGs in the atmosphere which leads to the greenhouse effect of the Earth. The effect is obtained by calculating the so-called radiative forcing, which is a measure of the influence a GHG, such as CO_2 or CH_4, has on changing the balance of incoming and outgoing energy in the Earth–atmosphere system. The dimension of the radiative forcing is $\mathrm{Wm^{-2}}$. For example, for CO_2 the radiative forcing, which we denote as F, is given by

$$F \equiv 6.3\ln(M/M_o), \tag{9.3}$$

with M the actual CO_2 concentration, M_o the preindustrial CO_2 concentration and ln the natural logarithm (see IPCC, 2001, pp. 52–53). The chapter of CO_2 is given in parts per million (ppm). For other GHGs other formulas can be given describing their respective radiative forcing and these values can be converted in CO_2 equivalents. In this chapter we assume that all GHGs have been converted into CO_2 equivalents so that the term $6.3\ln(M/M_o)$ in equation (9.1) captures the effect of all GHGs in the atmosphere.

The parameter β_2 in (9.1) is a feedback factor that captures the fact that a higher CO_2 concentration affects, for example, atmospheric water vapor, which has effects for the surface temperature on Earth. β_2 is assumed to take values between 1.1 and 3.4. The parameter ξ, finally, takes into account that $\xi = 0.3$ of the warmth generated by the greenhouse effect is absorbed by the oceans, which transport the heat from upper layers to the deep sea. In equilibrium, that is, for $\dot{T} = 0$, (9.1) gives a surface temperature of about 288.4 Kelvin which is about 15 °C for the preindustrial GHG concentration, i.e., for $M = M_o$.

The heat capacity of the Earth, c_h, is largely determined by the oceans since most of the Earth's surface is covered by seawater. Consequently, the heat capacity of the oceans can be used as a proxy for that of the Earth. Thus, c_h is given by $c_h = \rho_w c_w d 0.7$, with ρ_w the density of seawater ($1027\,\mathrm{m}^{-3}\,\mathrm{kg}$), c_w the specific heat of water ($4186\,\mathrm{J\,kg}^{-1}\,\mathrm{K}^{-1}$), and d the depth of the mixed layer which is set to 70 meters. The constant 0.7 results from the fact that 70% of the Earth are covered with seawater. Inserting the numerical values, assuming a depth of 70 meters and dividing by the surface of the Earth gives $c_h = 0.1497$.

When we set $\beta_2 = 1.1$ and assume a doubling of CO_2 we get that in equilibrium the average surface temperature rises from 288.4 to 291.7 Kelvin, causing a temperature increase of about 3.3 °C. This is in the range of IPCC estimates, which however, are obtained with more sophisticated Atmosphere–Ocean General Circulation Models and that yield increases between 1.5 and 4.5 °C as a consequence of a doubling of the GHG concentration on Earth (IPCC, 2001, p. 67).

To summarize this discussion we can rewrite the EBM as

$$\dot{T}(t)\,c_h = \frac{1367.5}{4}\,0.21 - 0.95\,\left(5.67\,10^{-8}\right)(21/109)\,T^4 + 4.851\ln\frac{M}{M_o},\ T(0) = T_0. \quad (9.4)$$

Next, we describe the interrelation between economic activities and the change in the average global surface temperature.

9.3.2 The Economic Framework

As regards the economic system we consider different regions i, $i = 1, \ldots, n$, where aggregate per capita production in each region takes place according to the following function:

$$Y_i = A_i K_i D_i (T - T_o), \quad (9.5)$$

with Y_i per capita production in region i, A_i a positive constants, and K_i a composite of human and physical capital. $D_i(T - T_o)$ is the damage function giving the decline in aggregate per capita production in country i as a result from deviations of the actual temperature from the preindustrial temperature, T_o. Note that, strictly speaking, the damage of the temperature increase is given by $1 - D_i(\cdot)$. The assumption of a continuous function $D_i(T - T_o)$ is justified only provided the increase in the average surface temperature does not exceed a certain threshold because for higher temperature increases catastrophic events may occur, going along with extremely high economic costs which are difficult to estimate. An example would be the break down of the Gulf Stream, which would dramatically change the climate in Europe. Therefore, one should keep in mind that the analysis assuming a function like $D_i(\cdot)$ makes sense for temperature increases only within certain bounds.

Further, we should also like to point out that AK models are very sensitive with respect to the parameters. We do not intend to make calibrations but we intend to get insight into the structure of the model and to see how certain climate policies affect economies qualitatively. This should be kept in mind in the interpretation of the results derived in the next sections.

As regards the function $D_i(T - T_o)$ we posit that it is continuously differentiable and that it satisfies

$$D_i(T - T_o)\begin{cases} = 1, & \text{for } T = T_o \\ < 1, & \text{for } T > T_o, \end{cases} \tag{9.6}$$

where

$$\frac{\partial\, D_i(\cdot)}{\partial\, T} := D_i'(\cdot) < 0. \tag{9.7}$$

Accumulation of per capita capital is given by

$$\frac{\partial K}{\partial t} := \dot{K}_i = A_i K_i D_i(\cdot)(1 - c_i - \tau_{B,i}) - (\delta_i + n_i)K_i, \tag{9.8}$$

where c_i denotes the consumption share in region i and $\tau_{B,i}$ is the abatement share. The population growth rate in region i is given by $n_i \in (0,1)$ and $\delta_i \in (0,1)$ is the depreciation rate of capital.

We take as a starting point the Solow-Swan approach with a given consumption and saving share because we want to focus on effects resulting from climate changes that affect production as modeled in equations (9.5)–(9.7) and therefore neglect effects resulting from different preferences. From equations (9.5) and (9.8) we see that the gross marginal product of private capital, which equals the interest rate in our economy, is equal to $A_i D_i(\cdot)$ and that the climate change that leads to deviations from the preindustrial temperature affects the level of production as well as the growth rate of capital and production.

With respect to GHG emissions we suppose that these are a by-product of production. In addition all emissions are expressed in CO_2 equivalents. Thus, emissions are a function of per capita output relative to per capita abatement activities. This implies that more production goes along with higher emissions for a given level of abatement spending. This assumption is frequently encountered in environmental economics (see, e.g., Smulders, 1995). It should also be pointed out that the emission of GHGs does not affect production directly but only indirectly by raising the concentration of GHGs in the atmosphere, which affects the climate of the Earth and which leads to a higher surface temperature and to more extreme weather situations.

Emissions in region i are given in our model by

$$E_i = \left(\frac{a_i Y_i}{B_i}\right)^{\gamma_i} = \left(\frac{a_i}{\tau_{B,i}}\right)^{\gamma_i}, \tag{9.9}$$

with B_i per capita abatement, where $B_i = \tau_{B,i} Y_i$, and $\gamma_i > 0$ and $a_i > 0$ positive constants. The parameter a_i gives a technology index that shows how polluting a given technology is. For large values of a_i a certain level of production and abatement go along with high emissions implying a relatively polluting technology and vice versa.

Concentration of GHGs, M, evolves according to the following differential equation

$$\dot{M} = \beta_1 \sum_{j=1}^{n} E_j - \mu M, M(0) = M_0. \tag{9.10}$$

where μ is the inverse of the atmospheric lifetime of CO_2. As to the parameter μ we assume a value of $\mu = 0.1$ which is in the range given by the IPCC, who consider $\mu \in (0.005, 0.2)$ (see IPCC, 2001, p. 38). β_1 captures the fact that a certain part of GHG emissions are taken up by oceans and do not enter the atmosphere. According to IPCC the parameter β_1 can be set to $\beta_1 = 0.49$ for the time period 1990–1999 for CO_2 emissions (IPCC, 2001, p. 39). Thus, our model economy is completely described by equations (9.4), (9.8), and (9.10), with emissions given by (9.9).

In the next section we first analyze the noncooperative world where we compute the open-loop Nash equilibrium.

9.4 The Open-Loop Equilibrium in Case of Noncooperation

The Starting point of our analysis is the assumption that each region maximizes intertemporal utility resulting from per capita consumption where we assume a logarithmic utility function. This leads to the following optimization problem in each region $i = 1, \ldots, n$:

$$\max_{\tau_{B,i}} \int_0^\infty e^{-\rho_i t} \ln(c_i A_i K_i D_i(\cdot))dt \tag{9.11}$$

subject to (9.4), (9.8) and (9.10) with $c_i A_i K_i D_i(\cdot) = C_i$ per capita consumption. ln denotes the natural logarithm and ρ_i is the discount rate.

The current-value Hamiltonian for this problem is given by

$$H_i(\cdot) = \ln(c_i A_i K_i D_i(\cdot)) + \lambda_{1,i}\left(\beta_1 \sum_{j=1}^{n}\left(\frac{a_j}{\tau_{B,j}}\right)^{\gamma_j} - \mu M\right) + \lambda_{2,i}\left(k_1 - k_2 T^4 + k_3 \ln\frac{M}{M_o}\right)$$

$$+\lambda_{3,i}(A_i K_i D_i(\cdot)(1 - c_i - \tau_{B,i}) - (\delta_i + n_i)K_i), \tag{9.12}$$

with $k_1 \equiv c_h^{-1} 0.21 \cdot 1367.5/4$, $k_2 \equiv c_h^{-1} 0.95\,(5.67\,10^{-8})\,(21/109)$, and $k_3 \equiv 4.851 c_h^{-1}$. $\lambda_{k,i}$, $i = 1,2,3$, denote the shadow prices of M, T, and K_i in region i respectively and $E_i = a_i^{\gamma_i} Y_i^{\gamma_i} B_i^{-\gamma_i}$ are emissions.

It should be noted that the shadow prices $\lambda_{1,i}$ and $\lambda_{2,i}$ are negative while $\lambda_{3,i}$ are positive. Necessary optimality conditions are obtained as

$$\frac{\partial H_i(\cdot)}{\partial \tau_{B,i}} = \lambda_{1,i}\beta_1(-\gamma_i) a_i^{\gamma_i} \tau_{B,i}^{-\gamma_i - 1} - \lambda_{3,i} A_i K_i D_i(\cdot) = 0, \tag{9.13}$$

$$\dot{\lambda}_{1,i} = (\rho_i + \mu)\lambda_{1,i} - \lambda_{2,i} k_3 M^{-1} \tag{9.14}$$

$$\dot{\lambda}_{2,i} = \rho_i \lambda_{2,i} - D_i'(\cdot)/D_i + \lambda_{2,i} k_2\, 4\, T^3 - \lambda_{3,i} A_i K_i D_i'(\cdot)(1 - c_i - \tau_{B,i}) \tag{9.15}$$

$$\dot{\lambda}_{3,i} = (\rho_i + \delta_i + n_i)\lambda_{3,i} - K_i^{-1} - \lambda_{3,i} A_i D_i(\cdot)(1 - c_i - \tau_{B,i}). \tag{9.16}$$

In addition, the limiting transversality condition $\lim_{t\to\infty} e^{-\rho_i t}(\lambda_{1,i} M + \lambda_{2,i} T + \lambda_{3,i} K_i) = 0$ must hold, too.

The optimal abatement activities (as a ratio to GDP) in each region are obtained from equation (9.13) as

$$\tau_{B,i}^{o} = \left(\frac{\beta_1(-\lambda_{1,i})\gamma_i a_i^{\gamma_i}}{\lambda_{3,i} A_i K_i D_i(\cdot)}\right)^{1/(1+\gamma_i)} \tag{9.17}$$

Equation (9.17) demonstrates that $\tau_{B,i}^{o}$ is higher the more polluting the technology in use is, which is modeled in our framework by the coefficient a_i. Consequently, economies with more polluting production technologies have higher optimal abatement shares than those economies that produce with cleaner technologies. However, this does not mean that economies with cleaner technologies have more emissions. This is the case because, on the one hand, the higher abatement share may not be sufficiently high to compensate for the more polluting technology. On the other hand, the second-best abatement share also depends on $\lambda_{1,i}$, $\lambda_{3,i}$ and the level of physical capital K_i. In addition, from the expression for $\tau_{B,i}^{o}$ we also realize that the higher the absolute value of the shadow price of the GHG concentration, $|\lambda_{1;i}|$, the higher the abatement share will be set in optimum.

In the following we confine our analysis to the steady state or balanced growth path (BGP), which is defined as a path such that $\dot{T} = \dot{M} = 0$ and $\dot{K}/K = C_1$, with $M \geq M_o$ and $C_1 > 0$ a positive constant. This definition contains several aspects. First, we require that the GHG concentration and the temperature must be constant along a BGP which is to be seen as a sustainability aspect. Second, there is ongoing growth with a constant growth rate of per capita capital over time, which implies that all other economic variables, such as GDP and consumption, also grow at constant rates that are equal to those of capital. Third, we consider only balanced growth paths with a GHG concentration that is larger than or equal to the preindustrial level. This requirement is made for reasons of realism because the GHG concentration has been rising monotonically over the last decades so that it is not necessary to consider a situation with a declining GHG concentration.

Our model is relatively complex. Therefore, to gain insight into the structure of our model we use numerical simulations and we limit our considerations to three regions. We consider two relatively highly developed regions where one region is producing with a relatively clean technology and the other uses a relatively polluting technology. As an example, one may think of the European Organisation for Economic Co-operation and Development (OECD) countries as the first region and of the United States as the second region. The third region is given by low-income countries with a technology that is more polluting than the other two regions. We set $a_1 = 3.75\,10^{-4}$. a_2 is double as large as a_1, that is, $a_1 = 7.5\,10^{-4}$, and a_3 is four times as large as a_1, that is, $a_3 = 0.003$. These relations roughly reflect the situation in European OECD countries relative to the United States and relative to low-income countries in 1995 (see Nordhaus and Boyer, 2000, Table 3.1). The parameter γ_i, $i = 1,2,3$, is set to one in all three regions, that is, $\gamma_i = 1$, $i = 1,2,3$.

With respect to the damage function $D_i(T(t) - T_o)$ we assume the following function

$$D_i = \left(1 + m_i(T - T_o)^2\right)^{-b_i}, \; m_i, b_i > 0, \qquad (9.18)$$

which fulfills the requirements of (9.6). The damage caused by a higher GHG concentration is assumed to be the same for the first and second regions and about three times as high in the third region for a doubling of GHGs which is achieved by setting the parameter values to the following numerical values: $m_1 = m_2 = 0.0013$, $b_1 = b_2 = 1$ and $m_3 = 0.0087$, $b_3 = 0.5$. These values imply that an increase of the average surface temperature by 3 °C as a result of a doubling of GHGs goes along with a damage of about 1.2% in regions 1 and 2. A rise of the temperature by about 6 °C implies a damage of roughly 4.5%. As regards the third region the damage is assumed to be 4% for an increase of the temperature of 3 °C and it amounts to about 13% when the temperature rises by 6 °C. It can be stated that these values roughly reflect the situation in European OECD countries, in the United States and in low-income countries (see Table 1 in Hackl and Pruckner, 2003).

We also posit that the damages are not the same in the regions because of differences in the state of development. For example, in developing countries people are less prepared for possible catastrophes than in developed countries because they cannot afford to invest in preventive measures. In addition, poor countries depend more heavily on agricultural production and have fewer means to compensate losses in agriculture compared to highly developed countries. Therefore, the consequences of climatic changes are more dramatic in less developed countries.

The subjective discount rate is assumed to be the same in the three regions and we set it to 3%, that is, $\rho_i = 0.03$, $i = 1,2,3$. We assume that the discount rates are identical in all regions because we want to focus on growth effects resulting from the supply side which is affected by a temperature increase and because we are not interested in differences resulting from different preferences. If the discount rates were different this would lead to differences in growth rates even if the effects of the temperature increase in the regions were the same, which would complicate the analysis. The growth rates of the population are assumed to be zero in the first two regions, $n_1 = n_2 = 0$, and 2% in the third less developed region, $n_3 = 0.02$.

Finally, the marginal propensity to consume is set to 80% in all three regions, $c_i = 0.8$, $i = 1,2,3$. The marginal product of capital in the second region is assumed to be larger than in the first region and the latter is larger than in the third region and we set $A_1 = 0.35$, $A_2 = 0.5$, and $A_3 = 0.25$. This implies a higher marginal product of capital in the second region compared to the first and third. Depreciation rates are set to $\delta_1 = \delta_2 = 0.04$ in regions 1 and 2 and $\delta_3 = 0.01$ in region 3. With this, we acknowledge that depreciation of capital is higher in those regions with higher income.

Setting $\phi_i := \lambda_{3,i} \cdot K_i$, a BGP is given by the solution of the following equations:

$$\beta_1 \sum_{j=1}^{3} \left(\frac{a_j}{\tau_{B,j}^o} \right) - \mu M = 0 \tag{9.19}$$

$$k_1 - k_2 T^4 + k_3 \ln \frac{M}{M_o} = 0 \tag{9.20}$$

$$\phi_i \left(\dot{K}_i / K_i + \dot{\lambda}_{3,i} / \lambda_{3,i} \right) = 0 \tag{9.21}$$

$$(\rho_i + \mu) \lambda_{1,i} - \lambda_{2,i} k_3 M^{-1} = 0 \tag{9.22}$$

$$\rho_i \lambda_{2,i} - D_i'(\cdot)/D_i + \lambda_{2,i} k_2 4T^3 - \phi_i A_i D_i'(\cdot)(1 - c_i - \tau_{B,i}) = 0, \tag{9.23}$$

where $\tau_{B,i}^o = \left((\beta_1(-\lambda_{1,i})a_i)/(\lambda_{3,i} A_i K_i D_i(\cdot)) \right)^{0.5}$, $i = 1,2,3$. Equation (9.19) follows from (9.10) and (9.20) follows from (9.4) and equation (9.21) is obtained by combining (9.8) and (9.16) and (9.22) and (9.23), finally, are obtained from the two equations (9.14) and (9.15). It should be noted that a constantly rising capital stock goes along with a constantly declining (shadow) price of capital so that ϕ_i is constant on a BGP. Solving equations (9.19)–(9.23) gives steady state values for the level of GHGs ($M^\star$), for the temperature ($T^\star$), for the product of the capital stock and its shadow price ($\phi^\star$), and for the shadow prices of GHGs ($\lambda_1^\star$), and of temperature ($\lambda_2^\star$), where we denote steady-state values by a $\star$. These variables, then, determine the balanced growth rate in region i, which is given by $g_i \equiv A_i D_i(\cdot)(1 - c_i - \tau_{B,i}) - (\delta_i + n_i)$, with $\tau_{B,i}^o$ as above. In Table 9.4.1 we give the result of our calculations for the three regions.

Table 9.1 Average temperature, optimal abatement, GHG emissions and balanced growth rates for region 1,2,3 (non-cooperative case).

$T^\star$	$\tau^o_{B,1}$	E_1	g_1	$\tau^o_{B,2}$	E_2	g_2	$\tau^o_{B,3}$	E_3	g_3
293.1	0.29%	0.131	2.69%	0.38%	0.1949	5.51%	1.36%	0.2214	1.27%

Table 9.1 demonstrates that the region with the more polluting production technology (region 2 in our model economy) has a higher abatement share than the region with the cleaner production technology (region 1 in our model economy) if damages caused by a rise in the average surface temperature are identical in the two regions. But this does not mean that emissions in the region 2 are smaller than in region 1. Hence, region 1 has fewer emissions than region 2, which demonstrates that the higher abatement share cannot compensate for the less clean production technology.

When we take into account that both the production technology and the damages caused by a rise in GHGs are different (comparing regions 2 and 3 of our model) one can see that region 2 spends relatively less for abatement than region 3 (0.4% versus 1.4% in our example). In addition, region 3 has more emissions than region 2 although the first spends a higher share of GDP for abatement.

As regards the increase in GHGs, we can state that with no cooperation GHGs rise by about the factor 2.7 of the preindustrial level, implying an increase in the average global surface temperature of 4.7 °C for the parameter values we assume.[4]

9.5 Optimal Solution in the Cooperative World

In this section we compare the results of the last noncooperative world to the outcome in the cooperative world.

The difference between the noncooperative world and the cooperative world is that in the latter the planner maximizes joint welfare in all regions simultaneously. Thus, in the cooperative world the optimization problem of the planner is given by

$$\max_{\tau_{B,i}} \int_0^\infty e^{-\rho t} \sum_{j=1}^n w_j \ln (c_j A_j K_j D_j(\,\cdot\,))dt \tag{9.24}$$

subject to (9.8) and (9.10) with $c_i A_i K_i D_i(\,\cdot\,) = C_i$ per capita consumption in region i. ln again denotes the natural logarithm and ρ is the discount rate. w_i gives the weight given to region i. It should also be mentioned that we do not call this situation a Pareto optimum because in the Pareto optimum the social planner would also determine the savings rate, which is exogenous in our context. Therefore, this solution is to be seen as a second-best solution.

To find the optimum we construct the current-value Hamiltonian which is now written as

$$H(\cdot) = \sum_{j=1}^{n} w_j \ln (c_j A_j K_j D_j(\cdot)) + \lambda_4 \left(\beta_1 \sum_{j=1}^{n} \left(\frac{a_j}{\tau_{B,j}} \right)^{\gamma_j} - \mu M \right)$$
$$+ \lambda_5 \left(k_1 - k_2 T^4 + k_3 \ln \frac{M}{M_o} \right)$$
$$+ \sum_{j=1}^{n} \lambda_{6,j} (A_j K_j D_j(\cdot)(1 - c_j - \tau_{B,j}) - (\delta_j + n_j) K_j), \qquad (9.25)$$

with λ_4, λ_5 the shadow prices of M and T and $\lambda_{6,i}$ the shadow prices of K_i. Again, λ_4 and λ_5 are negative while $\lambda_{6,i}$ are positive.

The necessary optimality conditions are obtained as

$$\frac{\partial H(\cdot)}{\partial \tau_{B,i}} = \lambda_4 \beta_1 (-\gamma_i) a_i^{\gamma_i} \tau_{B,i}^{-\gamma_i - 1} - \lambda_{6,i} A_i K_i D_i(\cdot) = 0, \qquad (9.26)$$

$$\dot{\lambda}_4 = (\rho + \mu) \lambda_4 - \lambda_5 k_3 M^{-1} \qquad (9.27)$$

$$\dot{\lambda}_5 = \lambda_5 \rho + \lambda_5 k_2 4 T^3 - \sum_{j=1}^{n} w_j D_j'(\cdot)/D_j$$
$$- \sum_{j=1}^{n} \lambda_{6,j} A_j K_j D_j'(\cdot)(1 - c_j - \tau_{B,j}) \qquad (9.28)$$

$$\dot{\lambda}_{6,i} = (\rho + \delta_i + n_i) \lambda_{6,i} - w_i K_i^{-1} - \lambda_{6,i} A_i D_i(\cdot)(1 - c_i - \tau_{B,i}). \qquad (9.29)$$

Further, the limiting transversality condition $\lim_{t\to\infty} e^{-\rho t}(\lambda_4 M + \lambda_5 T + \sum_{j=1}^{n} \lambda_{6,j} K_j) = 0$ must hold.

The optimal abatement ratios are obtained from equation (9.26) as

$$\tau_{B,i}^{o} = \left(\frac{\beta_1 (-\lambda_4) \gamma_i a_i^{\gamma_i}}{\lambda_{6,i} A_i K_i D_i(\cdot)} \right)^{1/(1+\gamma_i)} \qquad (9.30)$$

One realizes that equation (9.30) is basically equivalent to (9.17) with the exception that the shadow prices are different because the regions do not optimize separately in the cooperative world.

Next, we proceed as in the last section to get further insight. That is, we consider three regions; insert numerical values for the parameters; and then calculate the corresponding optimal abatement shares, GHG emissions, balanced growth rates as well as the rise in GHG concentration and in the average global surface temperature. The parameter values are as in the last section, with $\rho = 0.03$.

Table 9.2 Average temperature, optimal abatement, GHG emissions and balanced growth rates for region 1,2,3 (cooperative case).

T^*	$\tau^o_{B,1}$	E_1	g_1	$\tau^o_{B,2}$	E_2	g_2	$\tau^o_{B,3}$	E_3	g_3
290.7	0.57%	0.065	2.75%	0.68%	0.11	5.59%	1.9%	0.155	1.41%

Again defining $\phi_i := \lambda_{6,i} \cdot K_i$ a BGP is given by the solution of the following system of equations:

$$\beta_1 \sum_{j=1}^{3} \left(\frac{a_j}{\tau^o_{B,j}} \right) - \mu M = 0 \quad (9.31)$$

$$k_1 - k_2 T^4 + k_3 \ln \frac{M}{M_o} = 0 \quad (9.32)$$

$$\phi_i \left(\dot{K}_i / K_i + \dot{\lambda}_{6,i} / \lambda_{6,i} \right) = 0 \quad (9.33)$$

$$(\rho + \mu) \lambda_4 - \lambda_5 k_3 M^{-1} = 0 \quad (9.34)$$

$$\lambda_5 \rho + \lambda_5 k_2 4 T^3 - \sum_{j=1}^{n} w_j D_j'(\cdot)/D_j - \sum_{j=1}^{n} \phi_j A_j D_j'(\cdot)(1 - c_j - \tau_{B,j}) = 0, \quad (9.35)$$

where $\tau^o_{B,j}$ is given by equation (9.30). Table 9.1 shows the result with equal weight to each region ($w_1 = w_2 = w_3 = 1$).

Comparing the outcome of the cooperative case with the noncooperative one, it can be realized that the increase in the GHG concentration is smaller and, consequently, the rise in the temperature is smaller. The GHGs rise by about the factor 1.6, giving an increase in temperature of 2.3 °C. This is the result of higher abatement shares in the cooperative world which leads to smaller emissions in all regions.

One can also realize that GHG emissions are clearly smaller than in the noncooperative case. In the region 1 emissions are 50% lower, in the region 2 44% lower and in region 3 there are 37% fewer emissions compared to the noncooperative world. The reason why emissions in regions 1 and 2 in the cooperative case are much smaller than in the noncooperative case compared to region 3 is that shadow price of emissions for the regions 1 and 2 in the cooperative case is much higher in absolute values than in the noncooperative world because in the cooperative case regions 1 and 2 take into account not only their own damages but also the damages caused region 3. In addition, growth rates tend to be larger in the cooperative world where the highest increase is given for the poor region. The higher growth rates are the result of the smaller increase in the average surface temperature compared to the noncooperative world.

Table 9.3 Average temperature, optimal abatement, GHG emissions and balanced growth rates for region 1,2,3, with $w_3 = 2w_1 = 2w_2 = 2$.

$T^\star$	$\tau^o_{B,1}$	E_1	g_1	$\tau^o_{B,2}$	E_2	g_2	$\tau^o_{B,3}$	E_3	g_3
290.9	0.66%	0.057	2.71%	0.78%	0.096	5.53%	1.6%	0.19	1.49%

Next, we analyze our model assuming that the welfare of the poor region receives a higher weight than welfare of the rich countries. A possible justification for higher weights of poor countries can be seen by applying the Rawls criterion according to which welfare in an economy is determined by the poorest. Then, one can argue that welfare in the poorest region should receive a higher weight. But of course, a strict application of the Rawls criterion would require to maximize welfare of only the poorest region which, however, would not be a cooperative solution. In Table 9.2 we analyze our model assuming that welfare in region 3 gets a weight that is double the weight given to welfare in regions 1 and 2, that is, $w_3 = 2w_1 = 2w_2 = 2$.

Now, region 3 has a smaller optimal abatement share and higher emissions if welfare of that region gets a higher weight, compared to the case where all three regions get the same weight as Table 9.2 shows. As regards the other two regions one can see that they have higher optimal abatement shares and smaller GHG emissions. As a consequence, the growth rates in regions 1 and 2 tend to fall while that in region 3 tends to rise.

9.6 Conclusion

In this chapter we have integrated a simple climate module into a basic endogenous growth framework to highlight the interaction between climate change and economic growth.

Analyzing our model we found, among other things, that countries with more polluting technologies and higher damages resulting from climate change should spend a higher share of GDP for abatement. But, nevertheless, these countries may still emit more GHG emissions than countries with cleaner technologies and smaller damages from a change in the average global surface temperature. The outcome could be derived both for the noncooperative as well as for the cooperative world when abatement ratios are second-best. This implies that economies with more polluting technologies should invest relatively more in abatement spending but not so much that their emissions attain that level of those countries with a cleaner production technology. The reason is simply that more abatement leads to smaller growth, which has negative welfare effects. Hence, for example, countries such as China or India should invest in abatement but their GHG emissions should not be as small as those of developed economies with cleaner technologies. In addition, we could show that poor regions in our model economy profit most from cooperation compared to the noncooperative case.

As regards the methodology, we used dynamic games where we computed open-loop strategies. This implies that countries commit to a certain strategy at the initial point of time, which may indeed be unrealistic. In fact, closed-loop strategies where countries make their decisions as regards abatement policies dependent on the state seem to be more realistic. Nevertheless, the qualitative results would not differ much from the outcome obtained in this contribution so that the open-loop scenario can should not be discarded as irrelevant. Further, there are other promising lines of research that would give interesting insight into optimal strategies of countries such as the approach by Brechet et al. (2011). There, it is assumed that countries stick to a fixed abatement strategy for a certain period of time that is revised after that period depending on the state of the environment at the end of the planning period.

Notes

1. Very likely (likely) means that the level of confidence is between 90 and 99 (66 – 90)%.
2. More climate changes are documented in IPCC (2001), p. 34.
3. In the following we delete the time argument t as long as no ambiguity arises.
4. Setting μ to a different value does not change the qualitative results; cf. Greiner (2005).

References

Bosello, F., Buchner, B., and Carraro, C. (2003). Equity, development, and climate change control. *Journal of the European Economic Association 1*, 601–611.

Bosetti, V., Carraro, C., Galeotti, M., Massetti, E., and Tavoni, M. (2006). WITCH — a world induced technical change hybrid model. *Energy Journal, 2*, 13–37.

Bosetti, V., Carraro, C., Massetti, E., and Tavoni, M. (2008). International energy R&D spillovers and the economics of greenhouse gas atmospheric stabilization. *Energy Economics, 30*, 2912–2929.

Brechet, T., Camacho, C., and Veliov, V. M. (2011). Model predictive control, the economy, and the issue of global warming. *Annals of Operations Research*, DOI 10.1007/s10479-011-0881-8.

Deke O., Hooss, K. G., Kasten, C., Klepper, G., and Springer, K. (2001). Economic impact of climate change: Simulations with a regionalized climate-economy model. Kiel Working Paper, No. 1065, Kiel.

Gassmann, F. (1992). Die wichtigsten Erkenntnisse zum Treibhaus-Problem. In Schweizerische Fachvereeinigung für Energiewirtschaft (ed.), *Wege in eine CO_2 — arme Zukunft*, pp. 11–26. Zürich: Verlag der Fachvereine.

Greiner, A. (2004). Anthropogenic climate change in a descriptive growth model. *Environment and Development Economics, 9*, 645–662.

Greiner, A. (2005). Anthropogenic climate change and abatement in a multi-region world with endogenous growth. *Ecological Economics, 55*, 224–234.

Hackl, F., and Pruckner, G. J. (2003). How global is the solution to global warming? *Economic Modelling, 20*, 93–117.

Hansen, J., Ruedy, R., Sato, M., and Lo, K. (2010). Global surface temperature change. *Review of Geophysics, 48*, RG4004, DOI:10.1029/2010RG000345.

Harvey, D. L. D. (2000). *Global Warming — The Hard Science.* Harlow UK: Prentice Hall.

Henderson-Sellers, A., and McGuffie, K. (1987). *A Climate Modelling Primer*, Chichester, UK: John Wiley & Sons.

Hettich, F. (2000). *Economic Growth and Environmental Policy.* Cheltenham, UK: Edward Elgar.

IPCC. (1996). *Climate Change 1995: Economic and Social Dimensions of Climate Change, Contribution of Working Group III to the Second Assessment Report of the IPCC.* Cambridge, United Kingdom and New York: Cambridge University Press (available at http://www.ipcc.ch).

IPCC. (2001). *Climate Change 2001: The Scientific Basis, IPCC Third Assessment Report of Working Group I* (available at http://www.ipcc.ch).

IPCC. (2007). *Fourth Assessment Report, Working Group I, II, and III* (available at http://www.ipcc.ch).

Jorgensen, S., Martin-Herran, G., and Zaccour, G. (2010). Dynamic games in the economics and management of pollution. *Environmental Modeling and Assessment*, 15, 433–467.

Kemfert, C. (2001). Economy-energy-climate interaction: The model WIAGEM. *Fondazione Eni Enrico Mattei, Nota Di Lavora 71.2001.*

OECD (1995). *Global Warming – Economic Dimensions and Policy Responses.* Paris for Economic: Organisation Cooperation and Development.

NASA (2011) NASA Research Finds 2010 Tied for Warmest Year on Record. *NASA Goddard Institute for Space Studies.* News release from GISS Surface Temperature Analysis (GISTEMP), 2011-01-12, http://www.giss.nasa.gov/research/news/20110112/

Nordhaus W. D. (1994) *Managing the Global Commons: The Economics of Climate Change.* Cambridge, MA: MIT Press.

Nordhaus, W. D. and Boyer J. (2000). *Warming the World. Economic Models of Global Warming,* Cambridge, MA: The MIT-Press.

Roedel, W. (2001), *Physik unserer Umwelt – Die Atmosphäre.* Berlin: Springer-Verlag.

Scheffran, J. (2002). Economic growth, emission reduction and the choice of energy technology in a dynamic game framework. In P. Chamoni, R. Leisten, A. Martin, J. Minnemann, and H. Stadtler (eds.) *Operations Research Proceedings*, pp. 329–333. Berlin: Springer.

Scheffran, J. (2002a) Conflict and cooperation in energy and climate change: The framework of a dynamic game of power-value interaction. In M. J. Holer, H. Kliemt, D. Schmidtchen, and M. Streit (eds.), *Power and Fairness, Yearbook New Political Economy, 20,* 229–254. Tübingen Germany: Mohr Siebeck.

Scheffran, J. and Pickl, S. (2000). Control and game-theoretic assessment of climate change: Options for joint implementation. *Annals of Operations Research, 97*, 203–212.

Smulders, S. (1995). Entropy, environment, and endogenous growth. *International Tax and Public Finance, 2*, 319–340.

Stern, N. (2006, 2007). What is the economic impact of climate change? Stern Review on the Economics of Climate Change. Discussion Paper. http://www.hm-treasury.gov.uk (Printed version, 2007, Cambridge, UK: Cambridge University Press.

Tol, R. S. J. (2001). Equitable cost-benefit analysis of climate change. *Ecological Economics, 36*, 71–85.

Tol, R. S. J. (2003). Is the uncertainty about climate change too large for expected cost-benefit analysis.? *Climatic Change, 56*, 265–289.

Tol, R. S. J. (2008). The social cost of carbon: Trends, outliers and catastrophes. *Economics: The Open-Access, Open-Assessment E-Journal, 2*, 2008–2025.

CHAPTER 10

GLOBAL WARMING AND R&D-BASED GROWTH IN A TRADE MODEL BETWEEN ENVIRONMENTALLY SENSITIVE AND ENVIRONMENTALLY NEGLECTFUL COUNTRIES

FRANCISCO CABO, GUIOMAR MARTÍN-HERRÁN, AND MARÍA PILAR MARTÍNEZ-GARCÍA

10.1 Introduction

FULL cooperation in a global environmental problem like global warming has proved difficult to achieve both theoretically and in practice (see, e.g., Finus, 2001 and Barrett, 2003 for excellent books summarizing the literature on International Environmental Agreement). Currently a group of countries is engaged in active policies to reduce greenhouse gas (GHG) emissions, while the rest of the world's countries are not committed to any abatement activities. This dichotomy between abating and non-abating countries does not seem easy to overcome, at least in the foreseeable future. While all abating countries are developed countries, the vast majority of non-abating countries are developing or underdeveloped countries, although the reluctance of some developed countries (notoriously United States) to ratify the Kyoto Protocol is well known.

Considering that the two regions in question confront the problem of global warming differently, an immediate question arises: If the abating region reduces its emissions of pollutants, would the non-abating region not have an incentive to increase its own? Typically, considering carbon emissions as stemming from the use of a nonrenewable fossil fuel, a decrease in the demand for this fossil fuel by the abating region would reduce its price, so creating an incentive for the non-abating region to increase its use of this resource, and hence increasing carbon emissions (carbon leakage). Leaving aside the link between fossil fuels and emissions, this chapter finds conditions to reverse the carbon leakage hypothesis.

Emissions are linked to the production of final output, which uses a renewable natural resource, timber, as an input. Specialization in timber harvesting is more common in developing countries, which usually are less inclined to acknowledge global warming when taking production decisions. As stated in (Barbier, 2001), developing countries (e.g., Indonesia, Malaysia, Brazil, Chile) are leading exporters in the international market of forest products. The exports of most forest products (wood pulp and chapter, wood-based panels and furniture) have expanded considerably over the last quarter of the 20th century (Bulte and Barbier, 2005). For simplicity, this chapter considers that timber is exclusively harvested in countries that ignore global warming, although it is used as an input to produce final output in both regions. Therefore, part of this harvesting is traded from the countries that neglect to the countries that acknowledge global warming.

The effect of the forests on climate change comes mainly from their ability to remove carbon dioxide from the atmosphere and store it in wood, leaves, and soil. It is estimated that forests store more carbon than the entire atmosphere.[1] In addition, forest products are considered in this chapter as an input in the production of final goods. Because forests contribute to the fight against global warming, they provide a double dividend on the economy. First, they enhance the well-being of the individuals in both regions by improving environmental quality. Second, forests help to alleviate the highly uncertain although undeniable effect of temperature rising on the productive sector. In consequence, the forests can be regarded as a key element for the sustainability of economic growth. In this chapter a sustainable growth path is defined as an equilibrium where final output production and consumption grow at constant rates, while the extent of forest resources, the emission of pollutants, and the quality of the environment remain unchanged. This definition is in contrast with the habitual requirement of a continuous decrease in emissions of pollutants along a sustainable growth path, when these emissions are linked to the use of exhaustible fossil fuels.

Because the emission of pollutants is a by-product of the economic activity, technological progress in goods production usually increases emissions (scale effect). In consequence, sustainability further requires a parallel technological progress in abatement, that is, a pure technique effect to reduce emissions (Brock and Taylor, 2006). In this chapter technology takes the form of an expansion in the number of varieties of intermediate goods (see, e.g., Barro and Sala-i-Martin, 1999). The continuous increment in the number of these inputs enhances the production of final goods. Furthermore, it is assumed that new intermediate inputs allow for higher production without increasing emissions. It may be assumed that new inputs either increase production causing no ulterior emissions or that they reduce the emissions generated by previously existing intermediate inputs in exactly the same amount as emissions linked to a higher production rise (scale effect). Thus, the scale and technique effects exactly cancel out and sustainable growth becomes feasible. Bovenberg and Smulders (1995) also attain an unbounded constant growth in consumption while keeping emissions and the environmental quality unchanged when they consider a "pollution-augmenting technological progress."

Trade relationships are rarely taken into account in the literature on endogenous growth and the environment. An exception is Elíasson and Turnovsky (2004), who consider a country endowed with a renewable resource that is traded in exchange for a consumption good. They study the resource curse for an endogenous AK model with no innovative activities and no environmental problem. Cabo et al. (2006) studied the gains from cooperation for two regions related by a unidirectional trade of an intermediate good and considered a global pollution problem. An analysis of how technology diffusion through trade may influence economic growth can be found in Cabo et al. (2008, 2012, 2013) for a renewable and an exhaustible natural resource, respectively.

This chapter studies research and development (R&D)-based endogenous growth in a two-region fully specialized trade model. Timber harvested in the region that ignores global warming is traded in exchange for the new intermediate inputs discovered in the region that acknowledges this phenomenon (this would be an extreme à la Chichilnisky, 1994 North–South specialization). Trade is the transmission channel of new technology from the region that disregards to the region that acknowledges global warming. It is due to this trade that R&D activities in the innovative region are sufficient to hold pollution in check and drive long-run growth, not only in this region, but also in forest-endowed countries. The repercussion of this bilateral trade on the growth rate of the two trading economies, their emissions of pollutants, and the environmental quality are analyzed.

Two scenarios are compared. In a business-as-usual (BAU) scenario, no region acknowledges the problem of global warming. This is a decentralized scenario characterized by monopolistic producers in leading research countries that sell intermediate goods both within these countries and abroad. In a second scenario, innovative countries are aware of how their decisions affect and are affected by global warming. These countries are also aware of the inefficiency of monopolistic competition, and also commit themselves to charging two differentiated prices for the intermediate goods sold to final output producers: a competitive price to domestic producers and a monopolistic price to producers located in forest countries that neglect the effect of their production on the accumulation of pollutants in the atmosphere.

For the bipolar trade model described in this chapter interregional trade serves as the transmission channel through that the concern about lower emissions is transferred from the region that commits itself to acknowledging global warming to the forest region. Interestingly, owing to this trade the willingness to reduce emissions is greater in the forest region, that initially disregards global warming, than in the innovative region that acknowledges this problem. Thus the carbon leakage hypothesis is reversed. The mechanism that grants this reversal is the agreement of R&D

leading countries to settle a higher price for the intermediate good traded to the forest countries. These economies will utilize intermediate goods less intensively, leading to lower emission of pollutants. However, although each intermediate good is used less intensively, the speed at that new intermediate goods are invented does not necessarily shrink. Technology, and consequently the economies, might grow even faster if supported by a more efficient internal market for intermediate goods that lacks monopolistic competition in the countries committed to acknowledging global warming.

The chapter is organized as follows. Section 10.2 presents the model in a decentralized scenario and characterizes the steady-state equilibrium and the growth rate of the economies along the balanced path. Section 10.3 presents the results in a second scenario with commitment to acknowledging global warming. Section 10.4 compares the emissions and the growth rates under both scenarios. The main results are summarized in Section 10.5.

10.2 The Model

The chapter considers a bipolar world with two trading regions. This section describes the market approach or the BAU scenario in that the two regions differ in terms of resource endowments and sectorial specialization. However, none of the regions is concerned about the emissions of GHGs but, conversely, they ignore the effect of their actions on global warming. It is assumed that the world is divided between industrialized countries that carry out innovative activities and developing countries endowed with forest resources. In what follows, the former will be denoted the technologically leading region, while the supplier of timber will be the forest region.

The optimal path for consumption and emissions when production requires the use of non-renewable fossil fuel has been extensively analyzed in the literature. Here the concern is about the role of the forest from a double perspective: providing productive inputs and playing a critical part in the carbon cycle. Timber harvested in developing forest countries is used as an essential input in the production of final output both in industrialized (technologically leading) and in developing (forest) countries, combined with labor and intermediate nondurable goods. The total labor force in a representative forest country is allocated between the harvesting of the renewable natural resource (forest) and the production of final output. In contrast, innovation occurs in developed, technologically leading economies. It comes as an increment in the number of intermediate goods, that are produced by monopolistic entrepreneurs also located in these industrialized countries. New intermediate goods produced in the technologically leading region are traded in exchange for timber harvested in the developing forest region. The economies in forest and technologically leading regions are described below.

10.2.1 Forest Region

Population is assumed constant, L_F, in this region. In the resource sector, the property rights associated with the natural resource are equally distributed among identical consumer-owner agents. Each agent initially owns a portion s_0 of the natural resource.[2] The time evolution of each agent's resource share is given by its natural reproduction minus harvesting, that is,[3]

$$\dot{s} = g(s) - h = gs(1 - s/\kappa) - h, \quad s(0) = s_0, \tag{10.1}$$

where s is the stock of the consumer-owned natural resource; $g(s)$ describes its gross reproduction rate, that is assumed to be of the logistic or Verlhust type (see, e.g., Clark, 1990); and h is the rate of harvest. The parameters g and κ denote the intrinsic growth rate and the carrying capacity or saturation level of each agent's forest share.

In addition to the natural resource, a representative consumer is endowed with one unit of labor per unit of time. At each time, the consumer supplies a fraction v of his labor to producing final output and a fraction $1 - v$ to harvesting his natural resource share, with $v \in (0, 1)$. The harvesting function presents decreasing marginal returns to the effort (identified by labor). Thus, the per-capita harvest rate can be represented by:

$$h(v) = b(1 - v)^{1-\varphi}, \quad b > 0, \quad 0 < \varphi < 1. \tag{10.2}$$

The decreasing marginal return to labor is a consequence of ultimate gear saturation. As Elíasson and Turnovsky (2004) argue, the assumption of harvesting as independent of the stock size is appropriate for a resource like the forest. In what follows we shall call the harvest flow h, omitting the argument v.

From (10.1), the dynamics of the global stock of forest in this region can be written as[4]:

$$\dot{S} = G(S) - H = gS(1 - S/C) - H, \quad S(0) = S_0,$$

where $S = sL_F$, $H = hL_F$, $C = \kappa L_F$, $S_0 = s_0 L_F$.

The extracted natural resource (timber) is sold to final output producers in the technologically leading and the forest regions, who use it as a productive input. A representative consumer receives the income derived from the exploitation of the forest, that is sold at a price p_h, and the wage income derived from his labor services in the final output sector, where the wage rate is denoted by w_F. This economy does not carry out investment activities; neither does it trade financial assets internationally. Then consumers from region F do not accumulate assets in the form of ownership claims on innovative firms and, they do not receive financial interest income from them. Thus, the per-capita budget constraint for a representative consumer is:

$$c_F = vw_F + p_h h = vw_F + p_h b(1 - v)^{1-\varphi}, \tag{10.3}$$

where c_F is per-capita consumption in country F, and $h = h_L + h_F$ is the timber used in the production of final output in leader and forest regions (per harvester in the forest region).

A representative consumer has to decide the consumption c_F, or equivalently the fraction of labor employed in either the final-output sector, v, or in forestry, $1 - v$, to maximize utility. This utility depends on consumption, but also on the stock of pollution accumulated in the atmosphere, Z. The separable instantaneous utility function used by Aghion and Howitt (1998, Chapter 5) is considered here[5]:

$$U(c_F, Z) = \frac{c_F^{1-\tilde{\varepsilon}}}{1-\tilde{\varepsilon}} - \tilde{\theta}\frac{Z^{1+\tilde{\mu}}}{1+\tilde{\mu}}, \quad \tilde{\varepsilon}, \tilde{\mu}, \tilde{\theta} > 0, \tag{10.4}$$

with a constant elasticity of intertemporal substitution in consumption, $1/\tilde{\varepsilon}$. A higher $\tilde{\mu}$ reflects a higher concern for the quality of the environment. Thus, the maximization problem for the representative consumer reads:

$$\max_{v} \left\{ \frac{c_F^{1-\tilde{\varepsilon}}}{1-\tilde{\varepsilon}} - \tilde{\theta}\frac{Z^{1+\tilde{\mu}}}{1+\tilde{\mu}} \right\}, \tag{10.5}$$

subject to (10.2) and (10.3).

The stock of pollution increases with the total emissions in both regions, $E_L + E_F$, and decreases with the absorption capacity of the environment. The absorption capacity, $\delta(Z, S)$, can be viewed as a function of the accumulated stock of pollution, Z, but also of the existing stock of forest in the forest economy, S:

$$\dot{Z} = E_L + E_F - \delta(S, Z) = E_L + E_F - \delta_1 Z - \delta_2 S, \quad Z(0) = Z_0, \quad \delta_1, \delta_2 > 0. \tag{10.6}$$

In the equation above, the simplest assumption for the absorption capacity function, a linear function, is considered.

The final output sector comprises a large number of identical firms. The producers of final output demand labor, timber, and intermediate goods. Furthermore, the production of final output is negatively affected by the stock of accumulated pollution, reflecting the negative effect of global warming on the productive sector. Thus, the output-production function of a representative firm is given by

$$Y_F = \tilde{A}Z^{-\phi}(vL_F)^{1-\alpha-\beta}\sum_{j=1}^{N} X_{Fj}^{\alpha} H_F^{\beta}, \quad \tilde{A}, \phi > 0, \quad 0 < \alpha, \beta, \alpha + \beta < 1, \tag{10.7}$$

where N is the number of intermediate good varieties and X_{Fj} is the amount of the jth type of intermediate good, $j \in \{1, \ldots, N\}$. Based on the production function in Spence (1976), Dixit and Stiglitz (1997) and Ethier (1982), here, in (10.7) the natural resource (timber), $H_F = h_F L_F$, is considered a necessary factor for production. Output production has diminishing marginal productivity for each input (vL_F, X_{Fj}, H_F), and constant returns to scale for all inputs taken together. The final good sector is competitive and firms take prices as given. Therefore, the problem of a representative firm in the final-good sector is given by

$$\max_{v, H_F, X_{Fj}} p_F \tilde{A} Z^{-\phi} (vL_F)^{1-\alpha-\beta} \sum_{j=1}^{N} X_{Fj}^{\alpha} H_F^{\beta} - w_F(vL_F) - \sum_{j=1}^{N} p_j X_{Fj} - p_h H_F, \qquad (10.8)$$

where p_F is the price of the final output; p_j is the price of the intermediate good j that producers of final output in F pay to producers of this intermediate in L; and p_h is the price of timber paid to harvesters in the forest region.

10.2.2 Technologically Leading Region

Population is also considered constant in this region, L_L. Assuming no forest in this region, labor is used exclusively in the production of output. Furthermore, because innovation takes place in this region, consumers can accumulate assets and receive financial interest income from them. Thus, the per-capita budget constraint for a representative consumer in this region reads:

$$\dot{a}_L = ra_L + w_L - c_L, \quad a_L(0) = a_{L0}, \qquad (10.9)$$

where a_L are the per capita assets, r is the rate of return on assets, and c_L is the per capita consumption of final good. The initial amount of per capita assets is denoted by a_{L0}.

A representative consumer has to decide consumption, c_L, and therefore savings, in order to solve

$$\max_{c_L} \int_0^{\infty} \left[\frac{c_L^{1-\varepsilon}}{1-\varepsilon} - \theta \frac{Z^{1+\mu}}{1+\mu} \right] e^{-\rho t} dt, \qquad \rho, \varepsilon, \mu, \theta > 0, \qquad (10.10)$$

subject to (10.9). Parameter ρ denotes the constant rate of time preference.[6]

Production of final output by a representative firm in region L is described by:

$$Y_L = AZ^{-\phi} L_L^{1-\alpha-\beta} \sum_{j=1}^{N} X_{Lj}^{\alpha} H_L^{\beta}, \qquad (10.11)$$

where $H_L = h_L L_F$. Producers of final output buy timber, H_L, from consumers-harvesters in the forest region, and the intermediate goods, X_{Fj}, from the producers of these varieties located in the technologically leading region. The problem of a representative firm in the final-good sector is given by:

$$\max_{H_L, X_{Lj}} AZ^{-\phi} L_L^{1-\alpha-\beta} \sum_{j=1}^{N} X_{Lj}^{\alpha} H_L^{\beta} - w_L L_L - \sum_{j=1}^{N} p_j X_{Lj} - p_h H_L. \qquad (10.12)$$

The price of the final output in this region is normalized to one. Thus, p_F can be interpreted as the units of Y_L for one unit of Y_F, that is, it represents the terms of trade.

Technological progress takes place in an innovative sector in region L. At a given point in time there is a number, N, of firms in this sector, each of that monopolizes the production of a specific intermediate good. Technological progress takes the form of an expansion in the number of varieties of intermediate goods as it does in (Barro and Sala-i-Martin 1999, Chapter 6).[7] This situation applies as long as intellectual property rights are protected both domestically and internationally. Once invented, one unit of an intermediate good of type j costs σ_L units of Y_L (the numeraire) to produce, while the innovator who produces this intermediate good obtains p_j unit of Y_L. Parameter σ_L is normalized to one for simplicity. The monopolist decides the price p_j to maximize instantaneous profits from sales to final-output producers in L and F, given by $\pi_j = (p_j - 1)\left(X_{Lj} + X_{Fj}\right)$, where X_{Lj} and X_{Fj} are the demand functions of intermediate good j in regions L and F, respectively.

The cost of creating a new intermediate is supposed to be η times the cost of producing it, that is, η units of Y_L. Moreover, an innovator must pay a cost beyond the initial R&D outlay to transfer and adapt his product for use in region F. This cost is represented by ν and is lower than η because it is assumed that the innovator is better suited than other entrepreneurs to the process of adapting a discovery for use in the other region. It is also assumed that the cost ν is low enough to ensure this adaptation is immediately worthwhile. The free-entry assumption equates the present value of the profits for each intermediate to $\eta + \nu$, that is,

$$\eta + \nu = \int_t^{\infty} \pi_j e^{-\bar{r}(s,t)(s-t)} ds, \tag{10.13}$$

where $\bar{r}(s,t) = [1/(s-t)] \int_t^s r(w)dw$ is the average interest rate between times t and s.

10.2.3 Equilibrium

Firms in the final output sector maximize benefits by equalizing net marginal products to factor prices. In the leader economy:

$$w_L = (1-\alpha-\beta)\frac{Y_L}{L_L}, \qquad p_h = \beta\frac{Y_L}{H_L}, \tag{10.14}$$

$$X_{Lj} = \left(\frac{\alpha A}{p_j}\right)^{\frac{1}{1-\alpha}} Z^{-\frac{\phi}{1-\alpha}} L_L^{\frac{1-\alpha-\beta}{1-\alpha}} H_L^{\frac{\beta}{1-\alpha}}; \tag{10.15}$$

and in the forest region:

$$w_F = p_F(1-\alpha-\beta)\frac{Y_F}{\nu L_F}, \qquad p_h = p_F\beta\frac{Y_F}{H_F}, \tag{10.16}$$

$$X_{Fj} = \left(\frac{\alpha \tilde{A} p_F}{p_j}\right)^{\frac{1}{1-\alpha}} Z^{-\frac{\phi}{1-\alpha}} (\nu L_F)^{\frac{1-\alpha-\beta}{1-\alpha}} H_F^{\frac{\beta}{1-\alpha}}. \tag{10.17}$$

Taking the demand functions for an intermediate good j as given in (10.15) and (10.17), the monopolistic producer maximizes profits at price $p_j = 1/\alpha > 1$. Using this price in (10.15) and (10.17) it follows that:

$$X_{Lj} = X_L = A^{\frac{1}{1-\alpha}} \alpha^{\frac{2}{1-\alpha}} Z^{-\frac{\phi}{1-\alpha}} L_L^{\frac{1-\alpha-\beta}{1-\alpha}} H_L^{\frac{\beta}{1-\alpha}}, \tag{10.18}$$

$$Y_L = ANZ^{-\phi} L_L^{1-\alpha-\beta} X_L^{\alpha} H_L^{\beta} = \frac{NX_L}{\alpha^2}, \tag{10.19}$$

$$X_{Fj} = X_F = \tilde{A}^{\frac{1}{1-\alpha}} (\alpha^2 p_F)^{\frac{1}{1-\alpha}} Z^{-\frac{\phi}{1-\alpha}} (\nu L_F)^{\frac{1-\alpha-\beta}{1-\alpha}} H_F^{\frac{\beta}{1-\alpha}}, \tag{10.20}$$

$$Y_F = \tilde{A} NZ^{-\phi} (\nu L_F)^{1-\alpha-\beta} X_F^{\alpha} H_F^{\beta} = \frac{NX_F}{\alpha^2 p_F}. \tag{10.21}$$

Note that the amounts of the intermediate good X_{Lj} and X_{Fj} are not dependent on the type $j \in \{1, \ldots, N\}$. Now, the production of final output in both economies can be written as an homogeneous function of degree one in the three inputs: labor, intermediate goods, and timber. Furthermore, a linear externality is associated to the technology, defined as the number of new intermediate goods, N.

It is further assumed that the technology reduces the ratio of emissions per unit of output, hence: $E_i/Y_i = g_i(N)$, with $g_i'(N) < 0$, $i \in \{L, F\}$. For simplicity it is assumed that $g_L(N) = \tau/N$ and $g_F(N) = \tilde{\tau}/N$, therefore, $E_L = \tau Y_L/N$ and $E_F = \tilde{\tau} Y_F/N$. This definition, together with equations (10.19) and (10.21), implies that the emission of pollutants in the technologically leading and the forest regions are proportional to the share of output that each intermediate good is worth for the producer of final output:

$$E_L = \frac{\tau}{\alpha}(p_j X_L) = \frac{\tau}{\alpha^2} X_L, \qquad E_F = \frac{\tilde{\tau}}{\alpha}\left(\frac{p_j}{p_F} X_F\right) = \frac{\tilde{\tau}}{\alpha^2 p_F} X_F. \tag{10.22}$$

Notice that although the stock of pollution affects the production of final output and consumers' utility in both regions, in this BAU regime none of the economic agents takes into account the effect of his decisions on the evolution of this variable.

10.2.4 Maximization Problem for Consumers in the Forest Region

Consumers in this region solve the following static maximization problem:

$$\max_{\nu} \left\{ \frac{\left(\nu w_F + p_h b(1-\nu)^{1-\varphi}\right)^{1-\tilde{\varepsilon}}}{1-\tilde{\varepsilon}} - \tilde{\theta} \frac{Z^{1+\tilde{\mu}}}{1+\tilde{\mu}} \right\}.$$

The optimality condition is given by:

$$U'_{c_F}\left[w_F + p_h\frac{\partial h}{\partial v}\right] = 0,$$

with $U'_{c_F} = \partial U(c_F, Z)/\partial c_F$, where $U(c_F, Z)$ is defined in (10.4). From this equation it follows that:

$$v = \bar{v} = \frac{1-\alpha-\beta}{1-\varphi(\alpha+\beta)} \in (0,1), \tag{10.23}$$

and therefore,

$$\bar{h} = h(\bar{v}) = b\left[\frac{(\alpha+\beta)(1-\varphi)}{1-\varphi(\alpha+\beta)}\right].$$

10.2.5 Maximization Problem for Consumers in the Technologically Leading Region

Necessary conditions for the maximization problem in (10.10) subject to (10.9) lead to the Ramsey rule:

$$\frac{\dot{c}_L}{c_L} = \frac{1}{\varepsilon}(r-\rho).$$

By differentiating (10.13) with respect to t, the rate of return reads:

$$r = \frac{1-\alpha}{\alpha(\eta+v)}(X_L + X_F) = \frac{\alpha(1-\alpha)}{\eta+v}\left(\frac{E_L}{\tau} + p_F\frac{E_F}{\tilde{\tau}}\right). \tag{10.24}$$

Hence:

$$\frac{\dot{c}_L}{c_L} = \frac{1}{\varepsilon}\left[\frac{\alpha(1-\alpha)}{\eta+v}\left(\frac{E_L}{\tau} + p_F\frac{E_F}{\tilde{\tau}}\right) - \rho\right]. \tag{10.25}$$

Trade between the two regions is defined as the exchange of timber for intermediate goods. The balanced trade equation can be written by equating the value of the timber traded in exchange for the intermediate goods:

$$p_h H_L = p_j N X_F. \tag{10.26}$$

This equation, together with (10.14), (10.19) and (10.21), leads to

$$p_F = \frac{\beta Y_L}{\alpha Y_F} = \frac{\beta\tilde{\tau}E_L}{\alpha\tau E_F} \quad\Leftrightarrow\quad \alpha X_F = \beta X_L. \tag{10.27}$$

Investment returns in the technologically leading region are linked to the monopolistic benefits in the intermediate-goods sector. Since the economy is closed to international asset exchange, total households' assets, $a_L L_L$, are equal to the market value of the firms that produce these intermediate goods, $(\eta+v)N$. The dynamic of N is obtained from the equality $a_L L_L = (\eta+v)N$, the dynamics of the assets in (10.9), the equilibrium equations in (10.14), the relationships $\alpha^2 Y_L = NX_L$, and $\alpha^2 Y_F p_F = NX_F$, and the balanced trade equation (10.26):

$$\dot{N} = \frac{1}{\eta+\nu}\left[Y_L - N(X_L + X_F) - c_L L_L\right], \quad N(0) = N_0.$$

Taking into account equation (10.27), the rate of return on assets can be written as:

$$r = \frac{(1-\alpha)(\alpha+\beta)}{(\eta+\nu)\alpha^2} X_L = \frac{(1-\alpha)(\alpha+\beta)}{(\eta+\nu)\tau} E_L. \tag{10.28}$$

Considering the expression for the rate of return in (10.24), together with (10.27), the dynamics of N can be rewritten as:

$$\frac{\dot{N}}{N} = \frac{1}{\eta+\nu}\left[\frac{1-\alpha(\alpha+\beta)}{\tau} E_L - \frac{c_L}{N} L_L\right], \quad N(0) = N_0. \tag{10.29}$$

Notice that from (10.16), (10.17), (10.26) and taking into account that $X_{Fj} = X_F$, $\forall j$, the total harvested amount, $\overline{H}$, can be split between the timber used in the leader and in the forest economies as:

$$\overline{H}_L = \frac{\alpha}{\alpha+\beta}\overline{H}, \qquad \overline{H}_F = \frac{\beta}{\alpha+\beta}\overline{H}, \tag{10.30}$$

and hence,

$$\beta \overline{H}_L = \alpha \overline{H}_F. \tag{10.31}$$

Emissions in each region can now be written as:

$$E_L = \tau \Lambda L_L \overline{H}^{\frac{\beta}{1-\alpha}} Z^{-\frac{\phi}{1-\alpha}}, \qquad E_F = \frac{\tilde{\tau}\beta}{\alpha \overline{p}_F} \Lambda L_L \overline{H}^{\frac{\beta}{1-\alpha}} Z^{-\frac{\phi}{1-\alpha}}, \tag{10.32}$$

where $\Lambda = \alpha^{\frac{2\alpha}{1-\alpha}} A^{\frac{1}{1-\alpha}} \left(\frac{\alpha}{(\alpha+\beta)L_L}\right)^{\frac{\beta}{1-\alpha}}$. Finally, from (10.27) and (10.31), the terms of trade can be obtained:

$$\overline{p}_F = \left(\frac{\beta}{\alpha}\right)^{1-\alpha-\beta} \left(\frac{L_L}{\overline{\nu} L_F}\right)^{1-\alpha-\beta} \frac{A}{\tilde{A}}. \tag{10.33}$$

10.2.6 Steady-State Equilibrium under the BAU Scenario

In this section the focus is on the existence and the stability of a balanced growth path. Here a steady-state equilibrium or a balanced growth path is defined as an equilibrium where all variables either grow at constant rates or remain constant. If γ_x denotes the growth rate of variable x, along the balanced growth path, γ_N must be constant. From (10.29) a necessary condition is a constant E_L and $\gamma_{c_L} = \gamma_N$. Moreover, from (10.18), and since H_{L} is constant, Z must also be constant. Because a balanced growth path requires a constant X_{L}, then expression (10.28) immediately implies a constant rate of return, r. In consequence, the consumption in the leader economy grows at the constant rate in (10.25).

Given the definition of emissions and provided that E_{L} remains constant on the steady-state equilibrium, the production of output in the technologically leading economy grows at the same rate as N. Since the emissions in the technologically leading economy are constant, a stationary stock of pollution is feasible only if emissions in the forest region, E_{F}, also keep constant. Likewise, from (10.21), because $v, X_{\mathrm{F}}, Z, H_{\mathrm{F}}$ remain constant along the steady-state equilibrium, Y_{F} grows at the same rate as N. Notice finally that factor prices $w_{\mathrm{L}}, w_{\mathrm{F}}, p_h$ in (10.14) and (10.16) grow at the same rate as $Y_{\mathrm{L}}, Y_{\mathrm{F}}$ and N. In consequence, emission of pollutants in technologically leading and forest countries remain unchanged.

Proposition 1. *Any steady-state equilibrium*[8] $(\tilde{c}_{\mathrm{L}}^*, Z^*, S^*)$ *under the BAU scenario corresponds to a steady state of the following system of three differential equations:*

$$\dot{\tilde{c}}_{\mathrm{L}} = \tilde{c}_{\mathrm{L}} \left\{ \frac{L_{\mathrm{L}}}{\eta + \nu} \left[\tilde{c}_{\mathrm{L}} + \frac{(1-\varepsilon)[1-\alpha(\alpha+\beta)] - (1-\alpha-\beta)}{\varepsilon} \Lambda Z^{-\frac{\phi}{1-\alpha}} \overline{H}^{\frac{\beta}{1-\alpha}} \right] - \frac{\rho}{\varepsilon} \right\}, \tag{10.34}$$

$$\dot{Z} = \Lambda Z^{-\frac{\phi}{1-\alpha}} \overline{H}^{\frac{\beta}{1-\alpha}} L_{\mathrm{L}} \left(\tau + \frac{\tilde{\tau}\beta}{\alpha \bar{p}_{\mathrm{F}}} \right) - \delta_1 Z - \delta_2 S, \tag{10.35}$$

$$\dot{S} = G(S) - \overline{H}, \tag{10.36}$$

where $\tilde{c}_{\mathrm{L}} = c_{\mathrm{L}}/N$, $Z(0) = Z_0$ *and* $S(0) = S_0$.

Proof. Equation (10.34) immediately follows from (10.25) and (10.29) taking into account (10.32). On inserting this last expression in equation (10.6), equation (10.35) follows. ∎

Proposition 2. *There is a unique saddle-path stable steady-state equilibrium.*

Proof. In general the solution for Z of equation $\dot{Z} = 0$ cannot be explicitly found because of owing to the nonlinearity of equation (10.35). Rewriting this equation as $\dot{Z} = g^Z(\tilde{c}_{\mathrm{L}}, Z, S)$, it can be easily seen that:

$$\frac{\partial g^Z}{\partial Z} = -\frac{\phi}{(1-\alpha)Z} \Lambda Z^{-\frac{\phi}{1-\alpha}} \overline{H}^{\frac{\beta}{1-\alpha}} L_{\mathrm{L}} \left(\tau + \frac{\tilde{\tau}\beta}{\alpha \bar{p}_{\mathrm{F}}} \right) - \delta_1 < 0,$$

and

$$\lim_{Z \to \infty} g^Z = -\infty, \qquad \lim_{Z \to -\infty} g^Z = +\infty.$$

Hence a unique steady state Z^* exists. Thus, from (10.34), the steady-state value for $\tilde{c}_L$ follows:

$$\tilde{c}_L^* = \frac{\rho(\eta+\nu)}{L_L} + (1-\alpha-\beta)\Lambda(Z^*)^{-\frac{\phi}{1-\alpha}}\overline{H}^{\frac{\beta}{1-\alpha}}.$$

Under the assumption $gC - 4\overline{H} > 0$, two steady-state values exist for equation (10.36). Nevertheless, since the dynamics of this variable only depends on S, the unique valid solution is the stable one:

$$S^* = \frac{gC + \sqrt{gC(gC - 4\overline{H})}}{2g} > \frac{C}{2}. \tag{10.37}$$

The Jacobian matrix for the system of differential equations (10.34)–(10.36) evaluated at the steady state has one positive and two negative eigenvalues. This proves saddle-path stability of dimension two for a system with two states (Z and S) and one control variable $\tilde{c}_L$. ■

Proposition 3. *The growth rate along the balanced path (equal for the two economies) can be written as a weighted sum of the emissions in the technologically leading and the forest regions:*

$$\gamma^* = \frac{1}{\varepsilon}\left[\frac{\alpha(1-\alpha)}{\eta+\nu}\left\{\frac{1}{\tau}E_L^* + \frac{\overline{p}_F}{\tilde{\tau}}E_F^*\right\} - \rho\right].$$

Or equivalently, as a function of the stock of pollution at the steady state:

$$\gamma^* = \frac{1}{\varepsilon}\left[\frac{(1-\alpha)(\alpha+\beta)}{\eta+\nu}\frac{E_L^*}{\tau} - \rho\right], \quad \textit{where} \quad E_L^* = \tau\Lambda L_L\overline{H}^{\frac{\beta}{1-\alpha}}(Z^*)^{-\frac{\phi}{1-\alpha}}. \tag{10.38}$$

Proof. Straightforward from expression (10.25). ■

10.3 Commitment to Acknowledging Global Warming

In this section forest countries behave as in the BAU scenario, acting as if their decisions on production neither affect nor are affected by global warming. In contrast, technologically leading countries stop ignoring global warming and commit themselves to incorporating the knowledge about the economics of climate change in their decision making process, that is, the time evolution of the stock of pollutants and its effect on production and welfare. At the same time, countries in this region agree to fix the price of the intermediate goods invented in this region and traded to forest countries. This agreement allows the environmentally concerned region to transfer this concern to forest countries.

This is equivalent to considering a central planner in the technologically leading region who does not only decide consumption and final output production, but also the price of the technology sold abroad. Furthermore, the condition of a same quantity for every intermediate input j is imposed (see Barro and Sala-i-Martin, 1999). When choosing the price of the intermediate good of type j, the agent acting as a central planner in the technologically leading region knows the demand made by output producers in the forest region, $X_F(p_j)$ given in (10.17):

$$\max_{c_L, H_L, X_L, p_j} \int_0^\infty \left(\frac{c_L^{1-\varepsilon}}{1-\varepsilon} - \theta \frac{Z^{1+\mu}}{1+\mu} \right) e^{-\rho t} dt,$$

$$\text{s.t.} \quad \dot{N} = \frac{1}{\eta + \nu} \left[Y_L + N(p_j - 1) X_F(p_j) - N X_L - p_h H_L - c_L L_L \right], \quad N(0) = N_0 > 0,$$

$$\dot{Z} = \tau \frac{Y_L}{N} + \tilde{\tau} \frac{Y_F}{N} - \delta_1 Z - \delta_2 S, \quad Z(0) = Z_0 > 0,$$

$$\dot{S} = gS \left(1 - \frac{S}{C} \right) - (H_L + H_F), \quad S(0) = S_0 > 0,$$

with $Y_L = ANZ^{-\phi} L_L^{1-\alpha-\beta} X_L^\alpha H_L^\beta$, $\quad Y_F = \tilde{A} N Z^{-\phi} (\nu L_F)^{1-\alpha-\beta} (X_F(p_j))^\alpha H_F^\beta$.

From Pontryagin's Maximum Principle, first-order optimality conditions include:

$$c_L^{-\varepsilon} = \frac{\lambda_N L_L}{\eta + \nu}, \tag{10.39}$$

$$\left(\frac{\lambda_N N}{\eta + \nu} + \tau \lambda_Z \right) A \alpha X_{Lj}^{\alpha - 1} L_L^{1-\alpha-\beta} H_L^\beta Z^{-\phi} = \frac{\lambda_N N}{\eta + \nu}, \tag{10.40}$$

$$X_F (1 - \alpha p_j) = \alpha \tilde{\tau} \frac{\lambda_Z (\eta + \nu)}{\lambda_N N} \frac{Y_F}{N}, \tag{10.41}$$

$$\left(\frac{\lambda_N N}{\eta + \nu} + \tau \lambda_Z \right) A \beta X_{Lj}^\alpha L_L^{1-\alpha-\beta} H_L^{\beta - 1} Z^{-\phi} = \lambda_S + \frac{\lambda_N}{\eta + \nu} p_h, \tag{10.42}$$

where λ_N, λ_Z, and λ_S denote the co-state variables associated with the state variables N, Z, and S, respectively.

The dynamic efficiency conditions can be written as:

$$\dot{\lambda}_N = \lambda_N \left[\rho - \frac{Y_L + N p_j X_F - N(X_L + X_F)}{N(\eta + \nu)} \right], \tag{10.43}$$

$$\dot{\lambda}_Z = \left[\rho + \delta_1 + \frac{\phi}{NZ} \left(\tau Y_L + \tilde{\tau} \frac{Y_F}{1 - \alpha} \right) \right] \lambda_Z + \frac{\phi \lambda_N}{(\eta + \nu) Z} \left[Y_L + \frac{N(p_j - 1) X_F}{1 - \alpha} \right] + \theta Z^\mu, \tag{10.44}$$

$$\dot{\lambda}_S = \left[\rho - g \left(1 - 2 \frac{S}{C} \right) \right] \lambda_S + \delta_2 \lambda_Z. \tag{10.45}$$

Proposition 4. *A balanced path with a positive growth rate of consumption requires* $\varepsilon = 1$.

Proof. From (10.39) a balanced growth path requires $-\varepsilon\gamma_{c_L} = \gamma_{\lambda_N}$. Furthermore, from (10.40), $\lambda_N N$ should remain constant. But from the definition of $\dot{N}$ and $\dot{\lambda}_N$ this is possible only if:

$$\frac{p_h}{N}H_L + \frac{c_L L_L}{N} = \rho(\eta + \nu).$$

For this to be so it is necessary that $\gamma_{c_L} = -\gamma_{\lambda_N}$. But this is possible only if either $\gamma_{c_L} = 0$ or $\varepsilon = 1$. In consequence, a balanced growth path with a positive growth rate of consumption would only be feasible under the assumption considered hereinafter $\varepsilon = 1$ (see, e.g., Smulders and Gradus, 1996). ∎

10.3.1 Equilibrium

From the production function, Y_L, and the optimality condition (10.40), the optimal emissions in the technologically leading region can be written as:

$$E_L = \frac{\tau X_L}{\alpha(1+\tau\Psi)} = \tau\Lambda L_L\left[\left(\frac{1+\tau\Psi}{\alpha}\right)^{\alpha}\overline{H}^{\beta}Z^{-\phi}\right]^{\frac{1}{1-\alpha}}, \tag{10.46}$$

where $\Psi = \lambda_Z \tilde{c}_L L_L$, represents the total consumption per unit of intermediate good valued at the (negative) shadow value of pollution.

On the other hand, given the demand for an intermediate good of type j in (10.17) and expression (10.30), then from the optimality condition in (10.41) the relationship between the terms of trade, p_F, and the price of this intermediate good, p_j, follows:

$$p_j = \frac{p_F}{\alpha p_F + \tilde{\tau}\Psi}. \tag{10.47}$$

Moreover, since $\nu = \overline{\nu}$ and (10.31) is satisfied, the amount of intermediate good sold to the forest economies, and hence emissions in this region, is given by:

$$E_F = \frac{\tilde{\tau} X_F}{\alpha\left(\alpha p_F + \tilde{\tau}\Psi\right)} = \tilde{\tau}\beta\Lambda L_L\left[\frac{\left(\alpha p_F + \tilde{\tau}\Psi\right)^{\alpha}}{\alpha\overline{p}_F}\overline{H}^{\beta}Z^{-\phi}\right]^{\frac{1}{1-\alpha}}. \tag{10.48}$$

The proportionality factor between emissions in the technologically leading and the forest region is then immediately obvious:

$$E_F = \frac{\tilde{\tau}\beta}{\tau\alpha}\left(\frac{\alpha p_F + \tilde{\tau}\Psi}{1+\tau\Psi}\right)^{\frac{\alpha}{1-\alpha}}\frac{1}{\left(\overline{p}_F\right)^{\frac{1}{1-\alpha}}}E_L. \tag{10.49}$$

Given the definition of Ψ, from (10.46) and (10.48), E_L and E_F are functions of variables λ_Z, $\tilde{c}_L$, and p_F. Moreover, from condition (10.42) and the balanced trade equation given in (10.26), p_F can be defined as dependent on the first two variables and λ_S:

$$p_F\left(\alpha p_F+\tilde{\tau}\Psi\right)^{\frac{\alpha}{1-\alpha}}=\left(\overline{p}_F\right)^{\frac{1}{1-\alpha}}\left[(1+\tau\Psi)^{\frac{1}{1-\alpha}}-\lambda_S\frac{\tilde{c}_L\alpha^{\frac{1}{1-\alpha}}\overline{H}^{\frac{1-\alpha-\beta}{1-\alpha}}}{\Lambda\beta(\alpha+\beta)Z^{-\frac{\phi}{1-\alpha}}}\right]. \quad (10.50)$$

The equation above implicitly defines p_F as a function of variables λ_Z, $\tilde{c}_L$, λ_S, and Z. In this equation, constant $\overline{p}_F$ is given in (10.33) and denotes the terms of trade in the initial formulation when there is no commitment in the technologically leading countries with respect to the management of the intermediate goods industry and to the incorporation of the time evolution of the pollution stock in their decision-making process. The four variables λ_Z, $\tilde{c}_L$, λ_S, and Z, together with variable S, will define the system that characterizes the steady-state equilibrium for the model with commitment in the technologically leading countries.

10.3.2 Steady-State Equilibrium under Commitment

This section presents the system of differential equations that characterizes a balanced growth path or steady-state equilibrium. Following the same reasoning as in Subsection 10.2.6, the variables Z and S remain constant along the balanced growth path, while Y_F and Y_L grow at the same rate as N. Therefore, E_L and E_F also remain constant.

Proposition 5. *Any steady-state equilibrium for the model with commitment in technologically leading countries corresponds to a steady state of the following system of five differential equations:*

$$\frac{\dot{\tilde{c}}_L}{\tilde{c}_L}=\left[\frac{1}{\eta+\nu}\left(\alpha p_F\frac{E_F}{\tilde{\tau}}+\tilde{c}_L L_L\right)-\rho\right], \quad (10.51)$$

$$\dot{\lambda}_Z=\left\{\rho+\delta_1+\frac{\phi}{\Psi Z}\left[\frac{(1+\tau\Psi)E_L}{\tau}+\frac{(\alpha p_F+\tilde{\tau}\Psi)E_F}{\tilde{\tau}}\right]\right\}\lambda_Z+\theta Z^{\mu}. \quad (10.52)$$

$$\dot{\lambda}_S=\left[\rho-g\left(1-2\frac{S}{C}\right)\right]\lambda_S+\delta_2\lambda_Z, \quad (10.53)$$

$$\dot{Z}=E_L+E_F-\delta_1 Z-\delta_2 S,\quad Z(0)=Z_0>0, \quad (10.54)$$

$$\dot{S}=gS\left(1-\frac{S}{C}\right)-\overline{H},\quad S(0)=S_0>0, \quad (10.55)$$

where E_L and E_F are defined in (10.46) and (10.48).

Proof. Equation (10.51) is obtained from (10.39), taking into account that the balanced trade equation in (10.26) is satisfied at the equilibrium. On manipulating equation (10.44), equation (10.52) follows. ■

Because the distribution of labor in the forest region, ν, is the same as in the BAU scenario, the stock of forest at the stable steady state is also given by S^* in (10.37) as under BAU. Defining $\Theta = \rho - G'(S^*)$, then from equation (10.53) it follows that $\lambda_S^* = -\delta_2\lambda_Z^*/\Theta$. In consequence, the implicit equation that defines the terms of trade at the steady state can be rewritten as:

$$p_F^*\left(\alpha p_F^* + \tilde{\tau}\Psi^*\right)^{\frac{\alpha}{1-\alpha}} = \left(\overline{p}_F\right)^{\frac{1}{1-\alpha}}\left[\left(1+\tau\Psi^*\right)^{\frac{1}{1-\alpha}} + \delta_2\frac{\Psi^*\alpha^{\frac{1}{1-\alpha}}\overline{H}^{\frac{1-\alpha-\beta}{1-\alpha}}}{L_L\Theta\Lambda\beta(\alpha+\beta)(Z^*)^{-\frac{\phi}{1-\alpha}}}\right]. \tag{10.56}$$

Proposition 6. *As in the BAU scenario, the long-run growth rate (equal for the two economies) can be written as a weighted sum of the emissions in the technologically leading and the forest regions:*

$$\gamma^* = \frac{1}{(\eta+\nu)}\left\{\frac{1-\alpha(1+\tau\Psi^*)}{\tau}E_L^* + \alpha\frac{(1-\alpha)p_F^* - \tilde{\tau}\Psi^*}{\tilde{\tau}}E_F^*\right\} - \rho,$$

with E_L^* and E_F^* the steady-state values of the emissions given in (10.46) and (10.48).

Alternatively, it can be written as a function of the stock of the pollution at the steady state:

$$\gamma^* = \frac{B^C}{(\eta+\nu)}\frac{E_L^*}{\tau} - \rho, \quad \textit{where} \quad E_L^* = \tau\Lambda L_L\overline{H}^{\frac{\beta}{1-\alpha}}\left(\frac{1+\tau\Psi}{\alpha}\right)^{\frac{\alpha}{1-\alpha}}(Z^*)^{-\frac{\phi}{1-\alpha}}, \tag{10.57}$$

and

$$B^C = [1-\alpha(1+\tau\Psi^*)] + \beta\frac{(1-\alpha)p_F^* - \tilde{\tau}\Psi^*}{(\overline{p}_F)^{\frac{1}{1-\alpha}}}\left(\frac{\alpha p_F^* + \tilde{\tau}\Psi^*}{1+\tau\Psi^*}\right)^{\frac{\alpha}{1-\alpha}}.$$

Proof. The growth rate of the economy along the balanced growth path γ^* can be computed for $\varepsilon = 1$ when $\gamma_{c_L} = -\gamma_{\lambda_N}$, with this latter given in (10.43). ■

10.4 Comparison between Scenarios

This section compares the laissez-faire or BAU scenario with the scenario where technologically leading countries commit to acknowledging global warming and sign an agreement to cooperatively determine the price charged for the intermediate goods to noncommitted forest countries.[9] First, the emissions in leader and forest regions are compared with and without commitment in technologically leading countries. Second, attention is focused on the growth rate of the economies.

Emissions in this section are defined as the product of two terms, separating the effect of the stock of pollution (through its effect on production) from the global effect of other variables:

$$E_{\mathrm{L}} = \bar{E}_{\mathrm{L}} Z^{-\frac{\phi}{1-\alpha}}, \quad \bar{E}_{\mathrm{L}} = \tau \Lambda L_{\mathrm{L}} \overline{H}^{\frac{\beta}{1-\alpha}}; \quad E_{\mathrm{L}}^{\mathrm{C}} = \bar{E}_{\mathrm{L}}^{\mathrm{C}} Z^{-\frac{\phi}{1-\alpha}}, \quad \bar{E}_{\mathrm{L}}^{\mathrm{C}} = \bar{E}_{\mathrm{L}} \left(\frac{1+\tau\Psi}{\alpha} \right)^{\frac{\alpha}{1-\alpha}},$$

$$E_{\mathrm{F}} = \bar{E}_{\mathrm{F}} Z^{-\frac{\phi}{1-\alpha}}, \ \bar{E}_{\mathrm{F}} = \frac{\tilde{\tau}\beta}{\alpha \bar{p}_{\mathrm{F}}} \Lambda L_{\mathrm{L}} \overline{H}^{\frac{\beta}{1-\alpha}}; \quad E_{\mathrm{F}}^{\mathrm{C}} = \bar{E}_{\mathrm{F}}^{\mathrm{C}} Z^{-\frac{\phi}{1-\alpha}}, \quad \bar{E}_{\mathrm{F}}^{\mathrm{C}} = \bar{E}_{\mathrm{F}} \left(\frac{\alpha p_{\mathrm{F}}^{\mathrm{C}} + \tilde{\tau}\Psi}{\alpha \bar{p}_{\mathrm{F}}} \right)^{\frac{\alpha}{1-\alpha}}.$$

From these definitions, the next proposition compares the emissions in the forest and the technologically leading regions when the latter shifts from the BAU to the commitment scenario, provided that the stock of pollution remains unchanged.

Proposition 7. *The relative variation in emissions after a change from the BAU to the commitment scenario, assuming no change in the accumulated stock of pollution, is greater in the technologically leading region than in the forest region, that is:*

$$\frac{\Delta \bar{E}_{\mathrm{L}}}{\bar{E}_{\mathrm{L}}} > \frac{\Delta \bar{E}_{\mathrm{F}}}{\bar{E}_{\mathrm{F}}}, \tag{10.58}$$

with $\Delta \bar{E}_i = \bar{E}_i^{\mathrm{C}} - \bar{E}_i$, $i \in \{L, F\}$.

Proof. Expression (10.50) can be rewritten as:

$$p_{\mathrm{F}}^{\mathrm{C}} \left(\alpha p_{\mathrm{F}}^{\mathrm{C}} + \tilde{\tau}\Psi \right)^{\frac{\alpha}{1-\alpha}} = \left(\bar{p}_{\mathrm{F}} \right)^{\frac{1}{1-\alpha}} (1+\tau\Psi)^{\frac{1}{1-\alpha}} \left[1 - \lambda_S \frac{\tilde{c}_{\mathrm{L}}}{\Lambda\beta(\alpha+\beta)} \left(\frac{\alpha \overline{H}^{1-\alpha-\beta}}{(1+\tau\Psi) Z^{-\phi}} \right)^{\frac{1}{1-\alpha}} \right].$$

Taking into account that $\lambda_S > 0$, $\Psi < 0$ and hence $\alpha p_{\mathrm{F}}^{\mathrm{C}} + \tilde{\tau}\Psi < \alpha p_{\mathrm{F}}^{\mathrm{C}}$, the previous equation implies that:

$$\left(\alpha p_{\mathrm{F}}^{\mathrm{C}} + \tilde{\tau}\Psi \right)^{\frac{1}{1-\alpha}} < \alpha \left(\bar{p}_{\mathrm{F}} \right)^{\frac{1}{1-\alpha}} (1+\tau\Psi)^{\frac{1}{1-\alpha}},$$

and because $\alpha \in (0,1)$ implies $\alpha^{\alpha} > \alpha$, then,

$$\frac{\alpha p_{\mathrm{F}}^{\mathrm{C}} + \tilde{\tau}\Psi}{\alpha \bar{p}_{\mathrm{F}}} < \frac{1+\tau\Psi}{\alpha^{\alpha}} < \frac{1+\tau\Psi}{\alpha}. \tag{10.59}$$

Because the relative variation of emissions in each region is given by:

$$\frac{\Delta \bar{E}_{\mathrm{L}}}{\bar{E}_{\mathrm{L}}} = \left(\frac{1+\tau\Psi}{\alpha} \right)^{\frac{\alpha}{1-\alpha}} - 1, \qquad \frac{\Delta \bar{E}_{\mathrm{F}}}{\bar{E}_{\mathrm{F}}} = \left(\frac{\alpha p_{\mathrm{F}}^{\mathrm{C}} + \tilde{\tau}\Psi}{\alpha \bar{p}_{\mathrm{F}}} \right)^{\frac{\alpha}{1-\alpha}} - 1,$$

result (10.58) follows. ∎

According to Proposition 7, if a shift from BAU to commitment (assuming the same stock of pollutants) pushes the technologically leading region to reduce its emissions, then the forest region will reduce its emissions more intensively. Alternatively, even if emissions were increased in the former, emissions could be either reduced or increased to a lower extent in the latter. Which of these situations would arise crucially depends on the negative marginal valuation of a higher concentration of pollutants in the atmosphere by societies in technologically leading countries, λ_Z. Let us start by assuming that this negative value is sufficiently strong to guarantee that a commitment to acknowledge global warming reduces emissions in this region for a given stock of pollution.

Proposition 8. *Under assumption:*

$$\alpha > 1 + \tau\Psi, \tag{10.60}$$

and considering the same stock of pollutants in the BAU and the commitment scenarios, emissions in each region decrease if technologically leading countries commit to acknowledging global warming, that is:

$$\bar{E}_{\mathrm{L}}^{\mathrm{C}} < \bar{E}_{\mathrm{L}}, \qquad \bar{E}_{\mathrm{F}}^{\mathrm{C}} < \bar{E}_{\mathrm{F}}. \tag{10.61}$$

Proof. Assumption (10.60) is made to guarantee $\bar{E}_{\mathrm{L}}^{\mathrm{C}} < \bar{E}_{\mathrm{L}}$. Moreover, from (10.59) it is immediately obvious that

$$\frac{\alpha p_{\mathrm{F}}^{\mathrm{C}} + \tilde{\tau}\Psi}{\alpha \bar{p}_{\mathrm{F}}} < 1,$$

and therefore, $\bar{E}_{\mathrm{F}}^{\mathrm{C}} < \bar{E}_{\mathrm{F}}$. ■

Commitment to acknowledging global warming is linked to an agreement to fix the price paid by producers in forest countries for the intermediate goods. In consequence, this price is lower under the BAU regime than when the technologically leading countries commit themselves to the agreement, as is stated in the following proposition.

Proposition 9. *The price charged by the producers of intermediate goods to final output producers in the forest region is greater under the commitment than under the BAU scenario:*

$$p_j^{\mathrm{C}} > p_j.$$

The result is also valid when expressed in units of output in the forest region, since inequality $\bar{E}_{\mathrm{F}}^{\mathrm{C}} < \bar{E}_{\mathrm{F}}$ *holds (under sufficient condition (10.60)):*

$$\frac{p_j^{\mathrm{C}}}{p_{\mathrm{F}}^{\mathrm{C}}} > \frac{p_j}{\bar{p}_{\mathrm{F}}}.$$

Proof. Results immediately follow from expression (10.47) and assumption (10.60). ■

Thus, when the technologically leading countries commit themselves to acknowledging global warming they can induce forest countries to reduce their emissions. The incentive to reduce emissions in the forest region succeeds if the technologically leading region manages to charge a higher price to producers in forest countries (in units of Y_{F}) for the intermediate goods traded from the leader to the forest region. According to Proposition 8, if the technologically leading region reduces its own emissions it will also induce a reduction in the forest region. Moreover, the next corollary states that even if the technologically leading region does not reduce its emissions, it might succeed in forcing a reduction in the forest region by increasing the price of the traded intermediate good. A sufficient condition on the negative shadow value of pollution guarantees this type of solution.

Corollary 10. *Under a sufficient condition:*

$$\alpha < 1 + \tau\Psi < \alpha^{\alpha}, \tag{10.62}$$

and considering the same stock of pollutants in the two scenarios, emissions decrease in the forest region but increase in the technologically leading countries when these commit to acknowledging global warming, that is:

$$\bar{E}_{\mathrm{L}}^{\mathrm{C}} > \bar{E}_{\mathrm{L}}, \qquad \bar{E}_{\mathrm{F}}^{\mathrm{C}} < \bar{E}_{\mathrm{F}}. \tag{10.63}$$

Up until this point it has been analyzed how the emissions would vary as a consequence of commitment in the technologically leading region if the stock of pollutants under the two scenarios remains unchanged. But since emissions of GHGs diverge from one scenario to the other, the concentration of these gases in the atmosphere will also be different. In particular, the next lemma shows that the stock of pollutants in the atmosphere would decrease in the long run if global emissions (in the two regions taken together) are reduced when technologically leading countries shift from BAU to commitment.

Lemma 11. *If $\bar{E}_{\mathrm{L}}^{\mathrm{C}} + \bar{E}_{\mathrm{F}}^{\mathrm{C}} \equiv \bar{E}^{\mathrm{C}} < \bar{E} \equiv \bar{E}_{\mathrm{L}} + \bar{E}_{\mathrm{F}}$, then the concentration of pollutants in the atmosphere at the steady-state equilibrium is greater in the BAU than in the commitment scenario, that is:*

$$(Z^{\mathrm{C}})^{*} < Z^{*}.$$

Proof. The dynamics of the stock of pollutants in the BAU and the commitment scenarios can be rewritten as:

$$\dot{Z} = (\bar{E}_{\mathrm{L}} + \bar{E}_{\mathrm{F}})Z^{-\frac{\phi}{1-\alpha}} - \delta_1 Z - \delta_2 S = \bar{E}Z^{-\frac{\phi}{1-\alpha}} - \delta_1 Z - \delta_2 S = F(\bar{E}, Z). \tag{10.64}$$

At the steady state, equation $F(\bar{E}, Z^*) = 0$ defines Z^* as an implicit function of $\bar{E}$ in both scenarios, with

$$(Z^*)'(\bar{E}) = \frac{(Z^*)^{-\frac{\phi}{1-\alpha}}}{\delta_1 + \frac{\phi}{1-\alpha}\bar{E}\cdot(Z^*)^{-\frac{\phi}{1-\alpha}-1}} > 0.$$

Thus, if $\bar{E}^C < \bar{E}$, it immediately follows that $(Z^C)^* < Z^*$. ■

There exist two opposite forces when comparing long-run emissions under the BAU and the commitment scenarios. Defining global emissions as $E = \bar{E}Z^{-\frac{\phi}{1-\alpha}}$, if commitment in the technologically leading countries implies a reduction in the first factor, $\bar{E}^C < \bar{E}$, it would also lead to an increment in the second factor. The next proposition proves that the first effect is stronger.

Proposition 12. *At the steady-state equilibrium, if $(\bar{E}^C)^* < \bar{E}^*$, then global emissions decrease when technologically leading countries commit to acknowledge global warming, that is:*

$$\left(E^C\right)^* < E^*. \tag{10.65}$$

Proof. From the definition of global emissions and the implicit equation (10.64) the total derivative of global emissions at the steady state with respect to $\bar{E}$ reads:

$$\frac{dE^*}{d\bar{E}} = \frac{d(\bar{E}\cdot(Z^*)^{-\frac{\phi}{1-\alpha}})}{d\bar{E}} = \frac{\delta_1(Z^*)^{-\frac{\phi}{1-\alpha}}}{\delta_1 + \frac{\phi}{1-\alpha}\bar{E}\cdot(Z^*)^{-\frac{\phi}{1-\alpha}-1}} > 0,$$

and the result in the Proposition follows. ■

If $(\bar{E}^C)^* < \bar{E}^*$, global emissions at the steady state (in the two regions considered jointly) decrease when technologically leading countries move from BAU to the commitment scenario. However, as stated in Proposition 7 the reduction of emissions is stronger in the forest region than in the technologically leading region. Therefore, the reduction in long-run emissions could be owing to a reduction in each of the two regions. Interestingly, long-run emissions could increase in the technologically leading region while the forest region reduces its emissions counterbalancing the increment in the former. This latter type of behavior would appear if the sufficient condition (10.62) is fulfilled at the steady state and $(\bar{E}^C)^* < \bar{E}^*$ still holds.

10.4.1 Comparison of Long-run Growth Rates between Scenarios

The comparison of the long-run growth rates in the BAU and the commitment regimes is not completely determined. Growth rates in (10.38) and (10.57) are written as functions of the emissions in the leading country. However, the variation in these emissions when technologically leading countries commit to acknowledging global warming is not fully determined. Even if emissions decrease, this does not necessarily imply a reduction in the growth rate. It can be proved that the coefficient of E_L^* in the formulae that define growth rates is greater under the commitment than under the BAU regime.

From (10.38) and (10.57), considering $\varepsilon = 1$, the growth rates of the economies along the balanced growth path can be written as:

$$\gamma^* = \frac{(1-\alpha)(\alpha+\beta)}{(\eta+\nu)\tau} \bar{E}_L^*(Z^*)^{-\frac{\phi}{1-\alpha}} - \rho, \qquad (\gamma^C)^* = \frac{B^C}{(\eta+\nu)\tau}(\bar{E}_L^C)^*((Z^C)^*)^{-\frac{\phi}{1-\alpha}} - \rho.$$

Lemma 13. *If a steady-state equilibrium with non-negative emissions in both economies exists, then* $B^C > (1-\alpha)(\alpha+\beta)$.

Proof. The proof is straightforward, because the last term of B^C is positive and $1 - \alpha(1+\tau\Psi^*) > 1-\alpha > (1-\alpha)(\alpha+\beta)$. ■

Therefore, even if commitment implied a reduction of emissions in the leading and hence in the forest region, assuming that the concentration of pollutants had not change ($\bar{E}_L^C < \bar{E}_L$), from Lemma 11 the stock of pollutants would decrease in the long run $(Z^C)^* < Z^*$. Moreover, from Lemma 13 it becomes clear that $B^C\left((Z^C)^*\right)^{-\phi/(1-\alpha)} > (1-\alpha)(\alpha+\beta)(Z^*)^{-\phi/(1-\alpha)}$. In consequence, even if $\bar{E}_L^C < \bar{E}_L$, the growth rate of the two economies could be boosted when the innovative countries commit to acknowledging global warming and agree on the price charged to forest countries for the intermediate goods.

A numerical example showing this type of behavior is presented below: global emissions decrease while the growth rate of the two regions becomes larger. For illustration purposes we choose the following parameters values, that we do not consider unreasonable:

$$\alpha = 0.5,\ \beta = 0.2,\ \delta = 0.5,\ \rho = \tilde{\rho} = 0.01,\ \eta = 0.2,\ \nu = 0.1,\ \tau = \tilde{\tau} = 0.3,$$
$$\delta_1 = \delta_2 = 0.1,\ g = 4,\ A = \tilde{A} = b = L_L = L_F = \theta = \mu = C = 1.$$

Numerical results are obtained using Matlab. For two values of parameter ϕ, Table 1 presents the rates of change of the main variables when switching from the BAU to the commitment scenario: $\widehat{X} = (X^C - X)/X$. In both cases the price that final output producers have to pay for the intermediate goods increases when technologically leading countries commit to acknowledging global warming.

The first row ($\phi = 0.5$) gives an example where condition (10.60) is fulfilled. A change from BAU to commitment, keeping the stock of pollutants unchanged, leads both technologically leading and forest countries to reduce their emissions. Nevertheless, the concentration of pollutants in the atmosphere does not remain constant but decreases, so pushing up emissions. In this example, this latter effect is strong enough to enhance long-run emissions in the technologically leading region. This increment is

Table 10.1 Relative Variation with Commitment of the Technologically leading region

	$\widehat{p_j/p_F}$	$\widehat{E_L^*}$	$\widehat{E_F^*}$	$\widehat{E^*}$	$\widehat{E_L^*}$	$\widehat{E_F^*}$	$\widehat{E^*}$	$\widehat{Z^*}$	$\widehat{\gamma^*}$
$\phi=0.5$ $\alpha>1+\tau\Psi$	+	−	−	−	+	−	−	−	+
$\phi=0.3$ $\alpha<1+\tau\Psi<\alpha^\alpha$	+	+	−	−	+	−	−	−	+

counterbalanced by a stronger reduction of emissions in the forest region. Finally, even though global emissions are reduced, the long-run growth rate rises.

In the second row ($\phi = 0.3$), condition (10.60) is not fulfilled, but under condition (10.62) although the technologically leading region does not reduce its own emissions, it manages to induce the forest region to reduce its own. This reduction is strong enough to improve the environmental quality and to drive global emissions down in the long run. Again the growth rate of both economies increases.

10.5 Conclusions

The chapter analyzes the economic growth and the emissions of pollutants in a dynamic trade model between two differentiated regions threatened by global warming. Forests' products are considered a necessary input here to produce consumption goods. Furthermore, the forests' capacity to sequestrate and store carbon dioxide helps to keep the stock of pollution in check, hence affecting agents' utility as well as the productive process. These forests are located in developing countries that trade forest products in exchange for the technology developed abroad. The countries that invest in R&D may sign an agreement committing themselves to following the optimal policies that take into account the evolution of the stock of pollution and its connection with the economic activity. Furthermore, this agreement could include a perfectly competitive price for the technology within the signatory countries and a differentiated optimal price for the technology exported to forest countries.

Different scenarios may arise when technologically leading countries commit to acknowledging the problem of global warming and determine in a central manner the price of the intermediate goods traded to the forest countries. If the technologically leading region wishes to decrease its emissions this will induce an even stronger wish to reduce emissions in the forest region (see Proposition 7). Furthermore, even if the technologically leading countries wish to increase emissions, the forest region might reduce its emissions, and this reduction could be strong enough to pull global emissions down. International trade of technology for timber serves as the transmission mechanism of the engagement to reduce emissions from the technologically leading to the forest region. The former region fixes a higher price for the intermediate goods than in the BAU regime (in the units of the forest region's output). The terms of trade in this case are also higher. Being more expensive, the forest region reduces the demand for these inputs, which pushes emissions down. According to this mechanism, forest countries do not take advantage of the commitment in the technologically leading region (like models that show carbon leakage), but conversely they are induced to behave cooperatively.

Regardless of whether only the forest region or both regions aim to reduce emissions, if global emissions are reduced for a given stock of pollutants, the concentration of pollutants in the atmosphere decays in the long run, that represents an amelioration of the quality of the environment. Besides, global emissions also decrease in the steady-state equilibrium. Nevertheless, although this reduction in global long-run emissions always comes as a result of lower emissions in the forest region, the technologically leading region either experiences a lower reduction in emissions or may even increase its emission.

The price of intermediate goods paid by producers of final output in the forest region increases and, in consequence, forest countries utilize a lower amount of each intermediate good. However, this does not necessarily shrink the economies of the forest countries. The commitment of the technologically leading countries affects not only the amount but also the number of varieties of intermediate goods. Commitment is linked to a reduction in the inefficiencies in the market for intermediate goods. In particular, monopolistic markets do not apply for intermediate goods sold within the abating region. New intermediate goods might be discovered at a faster rate, that might induce a faster growth rate in both economies. We prove that a reduction in global emissions together with a faster economic growth is feasible and show some numerical examples.

To summarize, the chapter considers three main assumptions: emissions are linked to the intensity with that intermediate inputs are used but not to the number of varieties of these inputs; countries that commit to acknowledging global warming also agree to fix a differentiated price on the technology traded to noncommitted countries; and inefficiencies associated with the monopolistic power of innovative firms are reduced by the agreement. From these conditions, three results are derived: environmental concern can be transmitted from the technologically committed leading countries to the forest noncommitted countries through trade; if a reduction in global emissions exists it is always stronger in the forest region; and a reduction in emissions and the amelioration in the environmental quality can be accompanied with a faster economic growth.

Acknowledgments

The authors have been partially supported by MEC under projects ECO2008-01551/ECON, ECO2011-204352 and by JCYL under project VA001A10-1. All projects are co-financed by FEDER funds. The authors thank also the support of European RTD Framework Programme under project COST 4154/11.

Notes

1. GreenFacts. Facts on Health and the Environment. http://www.greenfacts.org
2. Historically, the distribution of communal resources among the users is one of the solutions that the economic literature has proposed to avoid the overexploitation of open-access resources. This approach relies on the action of an external central authority that distributes the property rights. However, researchers have recently proved that private property rights may emerge internally as a result of individual agents' desires to avoid cost externalities. See (Birdyshaw and Ellis, 2007) and the real examples therein. The distribution of property rights among users can be easily established in the case of forestry.
3. The time argument is eliminated when no confusion can arise.
4. Henceforth subscripts L/F denote variables corresponding to leader/forest country.
5. If $\tilde{\varepsilon} = 1$ the first component of this additive utility function would be logarithmic.
6. Again for $\varepsilon = 1$ consumption would enter utility as a logarithm.
7. Technology increases productivity in the final output sector of both economies. It does not, however, affect the forestry sector. New technologies could be used to improve harvesting, and they could also modify the natural reproduction function of the forest, increasing either the carrying capacity or the intrinsic growth rate. The analysis of sustainability under these assumptions is a subject for further research.
8. Henceforth the superscript star is used to denote the steady-state equilibrium of the corresponding variable.
9. Throughout this section superscript C refers to the commitment scenario and no superscript to BAU.

References

Aghion, P., and Howitt, P. (1998). *Endogenous Growth Theory.* Cambridge and London: MIT Press.

Barbier, E. (2001). International trade and sustainable forestry. In G. Schulze and H. Ursprung, *International Environmental Economics: A Survey of the Issues*, pp. 114–147. Oxford: Oxford University Press.

Barrett, S. (2003). *Environment and Statecraft: The Strategy of Environmental Treaty-making.* Oxford: Oxford University Press.

Barro, R., and Sala-i-Martin, X. (1999). *Economic Growth*. Cambridge and London: MIT Press.

Birdyshaw, E., and Ellis, C. (2007). Privatizing an open-access resource and environmental degradation. *Ecological Economics, 61*, 469–477.

Bovenberg, A. L., and Smulders, S. (1995). Environmental quality and pollution-augmenting technological change in a two-sector endogenous growth model. *Journal of Public Economics, 57*, 369–391.

Brock, W. A., and Taylor, M. S. (2006). Economic growth and the environment: A review of theory and empirics. In S. Durlauf and P. Aghion (eds.), *Handbook of Economic Growth*, pp. 1749–1821. Amsterdam: Elsevier.

Bulte, E., and Barbier, E. (2005). Trade and renewable resources in a second best world: An overview. *Environmental and Resource Economics, 30*, 423–463.

Cabo, F., Escudero, E., and Martín-Herrín, G. (2006). A time-consistent agreement in an interregional differential game on pollution and trade. *International Game Theory Review, 8*, 369–393.

Cabo, F., Martín-Herrín, G. and Martínez-García, M. P. (2008). Technological leadership and sustainable growth in a bilateral trade model. *International Game Theory Review, 10*, 73–100.

Cabo, F., Martín-Herrín, G. and Martínez-García, M. P. (2014). Can sustained growth be attained through trading exhaustible resources for foreign research? *The Journal of International Trade & Economic Development, 23*(2), 267–298.

Cabo, F., Martín-Herrín, G. and Martínez-García, M. P. (2014). On the effect of resource exploitation on growth: domestic innovation vs. technological diffusion through trade. In E. Moser, W. Semmler, G. Tragler, and V. M. Veliov (eds.), *Dynamic Optimization in Environmental Economics*, pp. 243–264. Berlin: Springer.

Chichilnisky, G. (1994). North-South trade and the global environment. *American Economic Review, 84*(4), 851–874.

Clark, C. W. (1990). *Mathematical Bioeconomics. The Optimal Management of Environmental Resources*. New York: John Wiley & Sons.

Dixit, A. K., and Stiglitz, J. E. (1977). Monopolistic competition and optimum product diversity. *American Economic Review, 67*, 297–308.

Elíasson, L., and Turnovsky, S. J. (2004). Renewable resources in an endogenous growing economy: Balanced growth and transitional dynamics. *Journal of Environmental Economics and Management, 48*, 1018–1049.

Ethier, W. J. (1982). National and international returns to scale. *American Economic Review, 72*, 389–405.

Finus, M. (2001). *Game Theory and International Environmental Cooperation*. Cheltenham, UK and Northampton, MA: Edward Elgar.

Spence, M. (1976). Product selection, fixed costs, and monopolistic competition. *Review of Economic Studies, 43*, 217–235.

Smulders, S., and Gradus, R. (1996). Pollution abatement and long-term growth. *European Journal of Political Economy, 12*, 505–532.

CHAPTER 11

CLIMATE CHANGE AND INTERGENERATIONAL WELL-BEING

JEFFREY D. SACHS

11.1 Introduction

The problem of climate change is typically discussed as a problem of intergenerational well-being. Current generations are called upon to make sacrifices today for the well-being of future generations. These sacrifices arise in the form of the increased costs of mobilizing low-carbon energy systems (such as renewable energy and carbon capture and sequestration) to cut carbon emissions and thereby reduce the buildup of climate change in the future.

The case for climate change mitigation is therefore dependent on how the well-being of today's generation is weighed against that of future generations. As usually discussed, this in turn hinges on the social discount rate, according to which the well-being of future generations is weighted relative to that of those alive today. If the discount rate is high, so that future well-being is not accorded much importance relative to that of the current generation, then the case for investing in climate change mitigation (i.e., the reduction of greenhouse gas [GHG] emissions) is thereby reduced. The paradox is that even if the social discount rate is as low as 3% per annum, the weight accorded 100 years in the future relative to today is a mere 5%, equal to 1 divided by (1.03) raised to the 100th power. This would seem not to give much importance to future well-being, and therefore not to give too much importance to the calls for climate control.

Of course we don't sit very comfortably with such a conclusion. Something isn't correct about the geometric discounting operation. It may be that 3% per annum is too high. Some ethicists call for much lower social discount rates, even zero, to reflect the moral symmetry of those living today with future generations. Some say that the discounting should really be represented as a kind of hyperbolic discounting, with just one step between "today" and the "future," rather than as continuous geometric discounting into the distant horizon. As just one example of this logic, we may care roughly the same about three generations in the future and six generations in the future, suggesting that we don't really discount the three extra generations using a factor such as 3% per annum between those two distant generations.

There is a wholly different reason for avoiding the overemphasis on a social discount factor to calibrate the interests of different generations. Society can use intergenerational fiscal transfers to allocate the burdens and benefits of climate change mitigation across generations without the need to trade off one generation's well-being for another's. This is an option too rarely considered in the current policy debate.

In the simplest terms, it comes down to this. If climate change is important for future generations, but costly action is needed today, then it may be possible to fund today's actions with public debt, so as to shift the ultimate costs of mitigation to later generations. In this way, climate change policy is not really a tradeoff of current well-being and future well-being. It is instead a tradeoff of climate change versus taxation facing future generations.

This chapter illustrates this proposition with two very simple overlapping generations models, designed to make a simple point. Climate change mitigation policy should be discussed alongside intergenerational public finance. In this way, it may be possible to construct mitigation policies that are Pareto improving for all generations relative to a business-as-usual (BAU) scenario of no climate change mitigation.

11.2 A Two-Period Illustration

Consider a simple two-period model, with periods indexed by $t = 1, 2$. A young generation today lives for periods 1 and 2. This young generation works in the first period and retires in the second. The current young generation saves part of its disposable wage income for consumption in the second period. Another young generation is born in period 2 and works and lives just in the second period. In each period, the young workers earn a pre-tax wage $w(t)$ and pay taxes $T(t)$. If $T(t) < 0$, the government is making a net transfer to the young workers of generation t.

The wage in the first period depends on climate policy. The economy emits GHGs. In the BAU scenario of no climate change control, emission are E. There is an emissions mitigation technology $M(1)$, with $0 \leq M(1) \leq 1$, so that emissions net of mitigation are $[1 - M(1)]E$. The government chooses the level of M through regulatory policies imposed on the private sector.

Because mitigation is costly, the market wage w_1 is reduced by the use of mitigation technology:

$$w(1) = W - \lambda M(1) \tag{11.1}$$

GHG concentrations in period 2 are determined by the emissions in period 1:

$$G(2) = [1 - M(1)]E \tag{11.2}$$

Wages of the young in the second period are reduced by climate change, which is proportional to the level of GHGs. Thus, as shorthand we can write that wages are directly dependent on the level of GHGs:

$$w(2) = W - \theta G(2) \tag{11.3}$$

The disposable labor income of each young generation is equal to the market wage net of taxes:

$$Y(t) = w(t) - T(t), \quad t = 1, 2 \tag{11.4}$$

Suppose that the government makes transfers to the young today, $T(1) < 0$, by selling bonds $B(2)$ and then redeems those bonds by taxing the youth of the second generation. Thus, $B(2) = -T(1)$ and $T(2) = (1 + r)B(2)$, where r is the rate of interest on the bonds. Clearly, the government's two-period budget constraint is:

$$T(1) + T(2)/(1 + r) = 0 \tag{11.5}$$

Note that we can write the second-period disposable labor income in terms of first-period mitigation and tax policies by collecting terms (11.2)–(11.5):

$$Y(2) = W - \theta[(1 - M(1)]E + T(1)(1 + r) \tag{11.6}$$

Finally, note that workers of the first generation consume $C1$ when they are young and $C2$ when they are old. They save part of their disposable labor income s in the form of bonds and claims to physical capital, with the saving rate presumably chosen to maximize lifetime utility. Therefore:

$$C1(1) = (1 - s)Y(1) \tag{11.7}$$

$$B(2) + K(2) = sY(1) \tag{11.8}$$

We assume that physical capital earns a constant net rate of return r and that government bonds must also therefore pay the same rate of return. Thus, the consumption of today's young when they are old in the second period is:

$$C2(2) = (1 + r)[B(2) + K(2)] \tag{11.9}$$

The young of the second period simply consume their disposable labor income:

$$C1(2) = Y(2) \tag{11.10}$$

Suppose that there are L workers in each generation. Total GDP in period 1 is therefore:

$$Q(1) = w(1)L \tag{11.11}$$

Total GDP in period 2 is the sum of labor income and net capital income:

$$Q(2) = w(2)L + rK(2) \tag{11.12}$$

Finally, let us specify the lifetime utility of each generation according to their lifetime consumption levels. For the first-period young, $U_1 = U_1[C1(1), C2(2)]$. For the second-period young, $U_2 = U_2[C1(2)]$. If these utility functions are well behaved, we can write the utility of each generation more simply as a function of their disposable labor income:

$$U_i = U_i[Y(t)] \tag{11.13}$$

Now, we are finally ready to make some basic observations about climate policy. Collecting terms, the well-being of the first-period young generation is given by:

$$U_1 = U_1[W - \lambda M(1) - T(1)] \tag{11.14}$$

The well-being of the second generation is:

$$U_2 = U[W - \theta[1 - M(1)] + T(1)(1 + r)] \tag{11.15}$$

Now let us turn to optimum climate policy. Let us start with the case of balanced budgets, $T_1 = T_2 = 0$. In this case, climate change poses a direct intergenerational conflict. The first generation wants $M(1) = 0$ while the second generation wants $M(1) = 1$. Suppose that the government must decide on $M(1)$. We can imagine two scenarios. In the case of a wise central planning government, the proper outcome is to maximize a Social Welfare Function (SWF) that is a function of the well-being of each generation:

$$\text{SWF} = V(U_1, U_2) \tag{11.16}$$

A utilitarian might represent this in additive form:

$$\text{SWF} = U_1 + U_2/(1 + \delta) \tag{11.17}$$

where δ is the pure rate of social discount in the SWF, with a value between -1 (all weight to the future) and infinity (all weight to the present). The social planner would then select $M(1)$ to balance the interests across the two generations. If δ is very high, the optimum $M(1)$ will be close to zero. If δ is just slightly greater than -1, then all of the weight is put on the future, and $M(1)$ will be close to 1.

An alternative view of government, at least in the electoral democracies, is that government represents the interests of the voters. If the voters vote to maximize their own well-being, today's young generation would vote for $M(1) = 0$. The unborn next generation does not vote in first-period elections. Thus, representative government would choose to have no mitigation, the so-called BAU trajectory.

There is a third possibility, however, that is typically ignored or underplayed. That is to use intergenerational fiscal transfers to improve upon the BAU trajectory. Suppose that we begin at BAU and ask whether there is some combination of taxes, transfers, and mitigation policies that can leave each generation better off than in the BAU trajectory. The answer is yes if climate change is sufficiently costly relative to the costs of mitigation. Consider a mitigation policy that is funded with debt, leaving the current generation with unchanged disposable income. Specifically, set $T(1) = -\lambda M(1)$ so that the young workers of the first generation receive transfer payments from the government that exactly offset the costs of mitigation. We see that $Y(1) = W$, the same as on the BAU trajectory when $M(1) = 0$.

Now consider the situation of the second generation. $Y(2) = W - \theta[1 - M(1)]E + T(1)(1+r) = W - \theta[(1 - M(1)]E - \lambda M(1)(1+r)$. We see that second-period disposable labor income $Y(2)$ is an increasing function of $M(1)$ if and only if $\theta E/(1+r) > \lambda$. That is, if the present value of the benefit of a unit of mitigation, given on the left-hand side, is greater than the marginal cost of mitigation, given on the right-hand side, then mitigation should be undertaken. In that case, given the linearity assumptions of this simple model, all emissions are abated, with $M(1) = 1$.

Let us assume that the fundamental case for climate change mitigation applies, that is, that $\theta E/(1+r) > \lambda$. Then the young generation can vote a mitigation strategy and transfer policy that is financed by government debt. The next generation will repay that debt by taxes on labor income. Today's young generation is left unharmed. The second-period young generation is made better off. Mitigation policy is Pareto improving across the two generations.

11.3 An Overlapping Generations Framework

Let us now generalize these results, by considering an overlapping generations (OLG) model in which every generation $t = 1, 2, 3, \ldots$ lives for two periods, working and paying taxes while young and consuming while old. The same principles apply as in the two-period model. Climate change would seem to pit today's young generation against future generations. An intergenerational tax-and-transfer policy, however, can eliminate the intergenerational conflict, and turn climate change mitigation into a Pareto improving strategy.

Individuals of generation t live for two periods, t and $t+1$. They consume $C1(t)$ when young and $C2(t+1)$ when old. The population is unchanging and normalized to be L in each generation.

The production function is:

$$Q(t) = w(t) + rK(t) \tag{11.18}$$

where $w(t) = W - \theta G(t) - \lambda M(t)$ and W is a fixed gross wage, $G(t)$ again stands for GHGs as of period t, and $M(t)$ again stands for the mitigation effort in period t, ranging from zero to 1. $K(t)$ is the capital stock in period t, owned by the old generation. We again assume that the net return on capital r is fixed.

As in the two-period model, $T(t)$ is the tax paid by members of the young generation at time t. If $T(t)$ is negative, the young in generation (t) receive a transfer from government. The government finances its taxes and transfers through sales of government bonds $B(t)$. All taxes and transfers, for simplicity, are assumed to occur in youth. Disposable income of the young is:

$$Y(t) = w(t) - T(t) \tag{11.19}$$

One-period government bonds $B(t)$ pay net interest r, which is the same as the net return on physical capital. The government's intertemporal budget constraint is

$$B(t+1) = (1+r)B(t) - T(t) \tag{11.20}$$

where $T(t)$ equals net taxes.

The government cannot borrow in a Ponzi scheme, meaning that the government's intertemporal budget constraint must be satisfied. This budget constraint states that the present discounted value of net taxes must be non-negative.

$$\sum_{t=0}^{\infty} (1+r)^{-t} T(t) \geq 0 \tag{11.21}$$

Let $Y(t)$ stand for $w(t)$ net of $T(t)$. The young household saves $Y(t) - C1(t)$ at time t, which goes into a portfolio of capital and bonds (which are perfect investment substitutes):

$$K(t+1) + B(t+1) = Y(t) - C1(t) \tag{11.22}$$

Second-period consumption is given by the value of wealth in the second period:

$$C2(t+1) = (1+r)[K(t+1) + B(t+1)] \tag{11.23}$$

The utility of generation t is given by

$$U(t) = U[C1(t), C2(t+1)]$$

We assume that $U(C1, C2)$ is a homothetic function, specifically the discounted sum of isoelastic utility functions:

$$U(t) = [C1(t)^{(1-\sigma)}]/(1-\sigma) + \beta[C2(t+1)^{(1-\sigma)}]/(1-\sigma) \tag{11.24}$$

The budget constraint of generation t is:

$$C1(t) + C2(t+1)/(1+r) = Y(t) \tag{11.25}$$

Because of homothetic tastes and constant r, $C1(t)$ and $C2(t)$ are fixed multiples of $Y1(t)$

$$C1(t) = (1-s)Y(t) \tag{11.26}$$

$$C2(t+1) = s(1+r)Y(t) \tag{11.27}$$

Because $U(t)$ is therefore proportional to $[Y(t)]^{(1-\sigma)}$ we can again take $Y(t)$ as an index of the lifetime utility of generation t as we did in the two-period model.

11.4 Climate Change

Now suppose that this economy is vulnerable to climate change, according to the following dynamics. Emissions in any period are at level $[1 - M(t)]E$ where $M(t)$ is the proportion of mitigation in period t, $0 \leq M(t) \leq 1$. Because there is no direct incentive for any individual firm to abate its emissions, mitigation control is set in a political process, voted by the currently alive generation.

GHGs accumulate according to

$$G(t+1) = (1-\delta)G(t) + [(1 - M(t)]E \tag{11.28}$$

Note that a fraction of GHGs δ naturally leaves the atmosphere each period to a long-term marine or terrestrial sink. In the absence of new emissions, therefore, the GHG concentration decays exponentially.

The losses each period associated with GHG concentration $G(t)$ is $\theta G(t)$, and these losses are assumed to come out of wages. The cost of mitigation is $\lambda M(t)$, which also is borne by wages. Thus, the net disposable income of the young is therefore:

$$Y(t) = W - \theta G(t) - \lambda M(t) - T(t) \tag{11.29}$$

Note that as in the two-period model, in the absence of intertemporal fiscal policy no generation has an incentive to support mitigation. Each young generation takes as given the prevailing GHGs at time t, and any mitigation cost would have to come out of contemporaneous wages. The older generation, which is living off of its savings, is assumed to be unaffected by $G(t)$ or $M(t)$ in a direct way, and is therefore indifferent to mitigation. Thus, if put to a vote by today's living generations, $M(t)$ would be set equal to 0 in each period t. $G(t)$ would grow over time, asymptotically approaching E/δ. This is an inefficient outcome if θ is high enough and λ is low enough to justify mitigation. Later generations end up *unnecessarily impoverished* by the lack of mitigation. The outcome is intergenerationally inefficient.

11.5 Intergenerational Fiscal Policy to the Rescue

A better approach is found as follows. We first calculate the no-mitigation path of $G(t)$, assuming (for notational simplicity but with no other implication) that $G(0) = 0$.

$$G(t) = E\sum_{0}^{t-1}(1-\delta)^{i} = E*(1/\delta)[1-(1-\delta)^{t}] \tag{11.30}$$

In the event of no mitigation and no fiscal transfers, income of the young is therefore:

$$Y^{NM(t)} = W - \theta E(1/\delta)[1-(1-\delta)^{t}] \tag{11.31}$$

In the event of full mitigation, $M(t) = 1$, and no fiscal transfers, income of the young is:

$$Y^{FM(t)} = W - \lambda \tag{11.32}$$

Now, suppose that the government proposes a policy of full mitigation, $M(t) = 1$ for all t, starting at $t = 0$ and proposes also to tax each generation in the amount

$$T(t) = Y^{\mathrm{FM}} - Y^{\mathrm{NM}} = \theta E(1/\delta)[1-(1-\delta)^{t}] - \lambda. \tag{11.33}$$

This policy compensates each generation for the full-mitigation program, in the sense that $Y(t)$ is the kept the same as in the *no-mitigation baseline*. It is feasible if the proposed discounted time path of taxes is indeed positive. In that case, the government would actually distribute part of the "excess taxation" to each generation, leaving every generation absolutely better off than in the BAU trajectory without mitigation.

Note that in the early periods, when t is small, the taxes are negative. The government subsidizes early generations to compensate for the up-front costs of mitigation. The taxes on later generations are positive, as those later generation would be willing to pay to avoid the high costs of climate change relative to a BAU path.

Thus, we need to check that the proposed policy $T(t)$ in (11.33) is indeed feasible in the sense of the inequality in (11.21). After some algebra, it's possible to show that the discounted value of net taxes $\Sigma(1+r)^{-t}T(t)$ is non-negative (and hence feasible) if and only if:

$$\theta E/(r+\delta) \geq \lambda \tag{11.34}$$

The left-hand side expression $\theta E/(r+\delta)$ is the discounted social cost of an increment of emission in the current period, taking into account the discount rate r and the natural rate of dissipation of GHGs δ. The right-hand side is the current cost of abating an increment E of emission. If (11.34) holds, it is indeed efficient (i.e., cost-effective for society in a discounted inter-temporal sense) to abate emissions. And if that is the case, fiscal policy can redistribute the burden so that all generations are at least as well off with mitigation as with no mitigation. If (11.34) is a strict inequality, then at least one generation can be made better off while leaving all other generations unchanged.

The conclusion is that if mitigation is intertemporally efficient, as in (11.34), then it is also possible to design an intertemporal fiscal scheme in which each generation is at least as well off with mitigation as without mitigation. Early generations get subsidized to undertake mitigation while later generations get taxed to service the debt on the early subsidies. Assuming a strict inequality in (11.34), all generations can indeed be made better off than in the non-mitigation baseline.

11.6 A Numerical Illustration

Consider the following parameter values, adopted for illustration and without any pretense of realism:

$$W = 100 \text{ (pretax wage of the young)}$$

$$E = 1 \text{ (emission level)}$$

$$r = 0.5 \text{ (one-period interest rate)}$$

$$\delta = 0.25 \text{ (one-period dissipation of GHGs)}$$

$$\theta = 10$$

$$\lambda = 5$$

Generational utility is $U(t) = \ln[C1(t) + 0.5\ln[C2(t+1)]$. The consumption function is then given by $C1(t) = (2/3)Y(t)$ and $K(t+1) + B(t+1) = (1/3) * Y(t)$.

In the event of no mitigation, GHG concentrations rise from 0 to 4, and damages rise from 0 to 40. The path of $Y(t)$ is shown as the declining path in Figure 11.1. If mitigation is undertaken starting in period 1, without intergenerational fiscal policy, the first generation bears the burden on behalf of later generations. This is shown in Figure 11.2, which shows $Y^{\text{FM}}(t)$ with mitigation minus $Y^{\text{NM}}(t)$.

We now introduce a feasible path of fiscal policy, with subsidies in the early periods enough to more than compensate for the cost of mitigation, financed by taxes in the later periods, such that the discounted value of net taxation as in (11.21) is exactly 0 and such that every generation is better off compared with the baseline. There is, of course, no unique tax path to select, as there is a choice of how to distribute the intergenerational benefits across time. The scenario is labeled FM, for the combination of fiscal policy and mitigation policy. The chosen tax path $T^{\text{FM}}(t)$ is shown in Figure 11.3. In Figure 11.4, we show the time path of

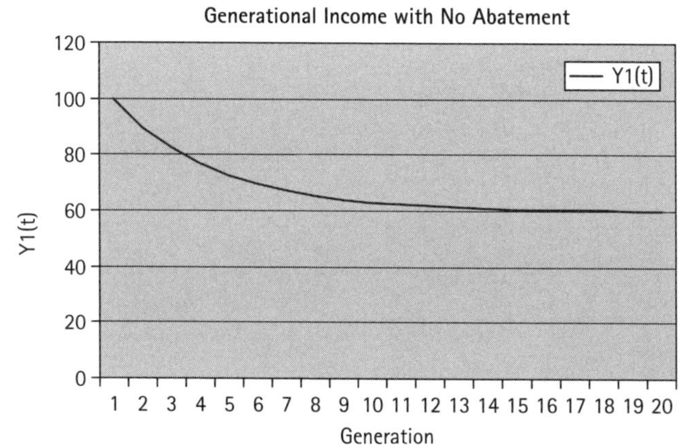

FIGURE 11.1 The baseline case (no mitigation, no intergenerational fiscal policy).

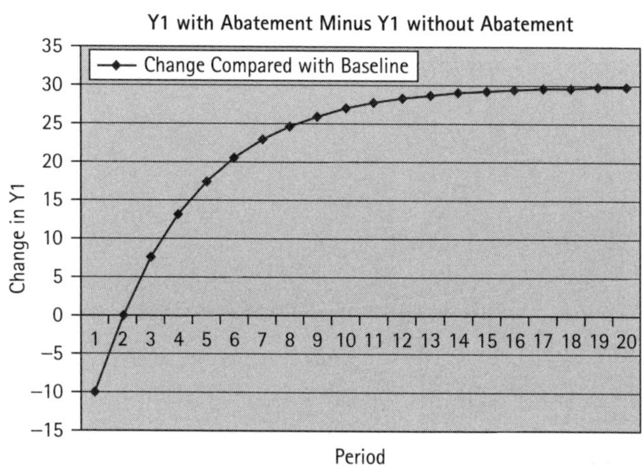

FIGURE 11.2 The change in generational income compared with baseline with mitigation and no fiscal policy.

$Y^{FM}(t) - Y^{NM}(t)$, demonstrating that every generation is better off than in the no-mitigation baseline.

Figure 11.5 illustrates the time paths of the capital stock in the baseline (NM) and mitigation (FM) scenarios, and the time path of government bonds $B^{FM}(t)$ in the full-mitigation scenario. Remember that $B^{NM}(t) = 0$ in the baseline. The fiscal policy is to run deficits in early periods, building up $B(t)$, and then to stabilize the stock of government bonds, servicing $B(t)$ through a constant level of taxation. Note that the rise of $B(t)$ partially crowds out the capital stock $K(g)$, but nonetheless leaves all generations with higher welfare than in the no-mitigation baseline.

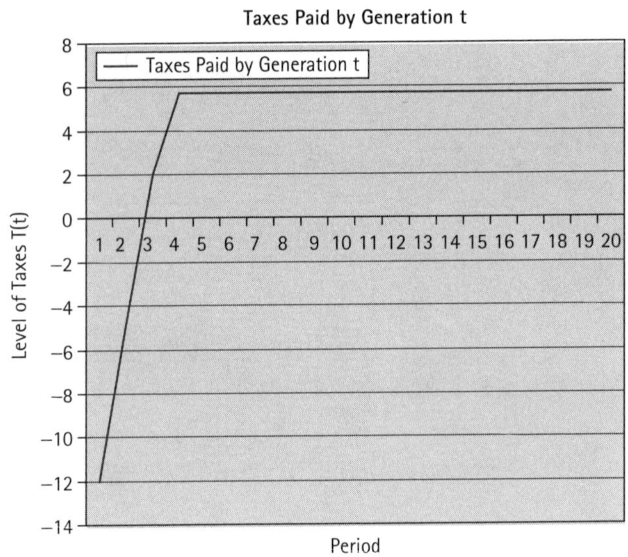

FIGURE 11.3 Time path of generational taxes to compensate for mitigation.

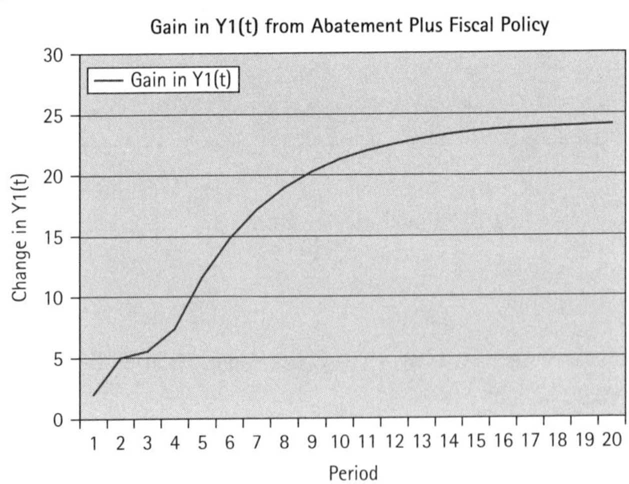

FIGURE 11.4 Rise in net generational income from mitigation with fiscal transfers.

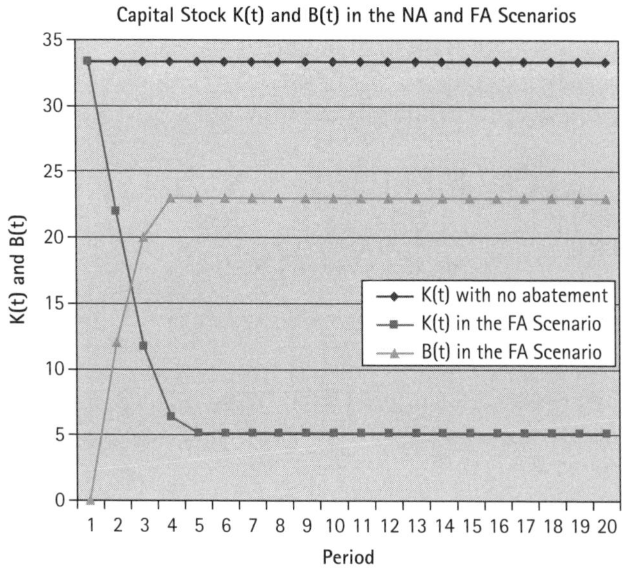

FIGURE 11.5 The time path of $K(t)$ and $B(t)$ in the NM and FM scenarios.

11.7 CONCLUSIONS AND NEXT STEPS

This chapter seeks to add an underexamined dimension to the climate change policy debate. The current debate tends to pit today's generation against the future, calling on the current generation to make sacrifices on behalf of future well-being. This chapter shows a different interpretation. The current generation can choose debt-financed mitigation to remain as well off as without mitigation, but to improve the well-being of future generations. In this sense, the current generation is acting like a steward for the future, not sacrificing for it, but still orienting public investments for the sake of future well-being.

Of course when the future arrives, later generations might not feel too happy by this scenario. They will be paying high taxes imposed on them by the choices of earlier generations. They may well resent these taxes as they would not feel clearly the benefits of avoided climate change. In the scenario depicted in the OLG example, future generations are indeed less well off than earlier generations in the full-mitigation scenario, though better off than they would have been in the no-mitigation scenario. Whether or not this wins the praise and thanks of the ancestors is hard to say!

Of course I have just sketched a simple example here without delving deeply into the intergenerational politics. Is the tax-transfer-mitigation system here indeed time consistent? Will later generations continue the policies selected by the preceding generations? Are these considerations empirically relevant if we look at the real time horizon of climate policies? These are all good questions for follow-up studies.

CHAPTER 12

THE ATMOSPHERE AS A GLOBAL COMMONS

OTTMAR EDENHOFER, CHRISTIAN FLACHSLAND, MICHAEL JAKOB, AND KAI LESSMANN

12.1 Introduction

This chapter analyzes global climate policy as the problem of transforming governance of the atmosphere from an open-access into a global commons regime. Establishing such a regime raises a series of challenges. First, specification of a limit for anthropogenic greenhouse gas (GHG) disposal in the atmosphere requires balancing the risks of unmitigated climate change with the risks of emission reductions. Section 12.2 investigates the difficulty of deriving a globally optimal stabilization target from a cost–benefit analysis and argues that emission reduction policies can be regarded as investments that reduce the likelihood of catastrophic climate change.

Section 12.3 reviews the literature on optimal policy instrument choice and explores the distributional challenges and options for governing the atmosphere as a global commons. This requires consideration of the supply-side dynamics in global fossil fuel resource markets and the transformation of the fossil resource rent into a climate rent due to climate policy.

Section 12.4 discusses the free-riding incentives in climate policy and provides an overview of the theoretical work on how these might be reduced. Rationales for unilateral action include co-benefits, cost reductions of low-carbon technologies, and signaling in the presence of asymmetric information. The problem of international cooperation might be alleviated when introducing such measures as international transfers, technology clubs, trade policy, repeated interactions, as well as assumptions about ethics.

Finally, Section 12.5 reviews the literature on (vertical) fiscal decentralization and (horizontal) fiscal federalism to investigate additional rationales for unilateral and local climate policy. One key hypothesis is that—under specific circumstances—local emission reduction efforts might facilitate the adoption of globally efficient policy. In this perspective, the effectiveness of local and national policies depends on efficient coordination of policy instruments between different levels of government. Another finding is that under very stylized conditions assuming mobile capital and population a global public good can be provided even in a decentralized governance setting. These findings might offer an interesting starting point for future research on the globally efficient and practically feasible polycentric management of global commons.

12.2 Climate Policy as Risk Management

12.2.1 Risks of Climate Change

The atmosphere is a global common pool resource in its function as a sink for CO_2 and other GHGs. Currently, it is an unregulated "no man's land" that is openly accessible and appropriated by everyone free of charge in most regions of the world, with the exception of the European Union and a select few others that have started to price carbon emissions (see Section 12.4.2). Oceans, forests, and other ecosystems are closely linked to the atmospheric sink and provide services by absorbing a fraction of the anthropogenic CO_2 emissions. In recent years, however, their sink capacity has begun to decline (Canadell et al., 2007). Congesting the atmosphere with GHG emissions leads to dangerous and potentially catastrophic climate change. Further increases of the global mean temperature may trigger irreversible tipping elements in the Earth system. These include melting of the Greenland Ice Sheet (GIS) over several centuries as well as melting of the West Antarctic Ice Sheet (WAIS), each containing enough ice to raise the global sea level by several meters (maximally 7 m from GIS, and 3 m from WAIS). Further, melting of the Siberian permafrost will lead to the release of methane, a potent GHG, and thus accelerate global warming. Other tipping elements include the breakdown of the thermohaline circulation in the northern Atlantic, triggering a drop in average temperatures in Europe, and a complete drying of the Amazon rainforest. Notably, tipping of any of these elements may severely damage or destroy the habitats mankind has populated since the Holocene epoch. The precise threshold values—less than 1.5°C, 2°C, 3°C or more—at which these and other tipping elements are triggered are subject to substantial uncertainty (Lenton et al., 2008). There are indicators that a disintegration process of parts of the WAIS implying 1.5 m sea level rise has already been initiated (Levermann et al., 2012). Notwithstanding these uncertainties concerning the precise threshold values of tipping elements, a recent assessment of impacts concludes that a rising global mean temperature would affect the frequency and intensity of extreme weather and climate events (IPCC, 2012).

In addition to the uncertainty over impacts, there is uncertainty regarding the climate system response in terms of warming for a given level of atmospheric GHG concentration (climate sensitivity). Given the unprecedented character of the experiment mankind is currently conducting with the Earth system, values for this parameter need to be derived from a combination of historical data and climate modeling. Meinshausen et al. (2009) apply a probabilistic analysis to scenario data obtained from climate modeling that takes into account the uncertainty over the warming triggered by a certain increase of the atmospheric GHG concentration. Their analysis indicates that a doubling of the atmospheric concentration of CO_2 corresponds to global warming of 2.3–4.5°C within the 68% confidence interval, and 2.1–7.1°C in the 90% confidence interval. This leaves open the possibility of surprises of even higher as well as lower climate sensitivity. Clearly, warming of 7°C or more within one century will impose severe impacts on human societies and the global economy.

Figure 12.1a, b shows two global emission scenarios and an assessment of concomitant global warming levels based on a probabilistic analysis of existing global warming models. The simulations are based on the so-called Representative Concentration Pathways (RCPs) (Meinshausen et al., 2011). RCP8.5 can be regarded as a business-as-usual (BAU) emission scenario leading to a radiative forcing (i.e., the balance of incoming and outgoing energy of planet Earth) of 8.5 W m^{-2} in the year 2100. Emissions are assumed to peak between 2100 and 2150 and decline thereafter. Figure 12.1b shows that there is a probability of at least 50% of global warming exceeding 6°C by 2150 in this scenario, rising continuously thereafter (the mean temperature increase is denoted by the solid line in the RCP8.5 distribution in Figure 12.1b). By contrast, reducing emissions as indicated by the RCP3-PD scenarios (radiative forcing peaking at 3 W m^{-2}) would provide considerable certainty of avoiding warming above 2°C. However, this scenario would require constant *net negative* global emissions after the year 2075. This requires a major global mitigation effort. Net negative global emissions could potentially be achieved by using biomass—with plants absorbing CO_2 from the atmosphere—in combination with carbon capture and sequestration (CCS) technology that separates CO_2 contained in the biomass to store it underground.

12.2.2 Risks of Mitigation

Some observers argue that limited supplies of coal, oil, and gas will soon lead to increasing resource prices, which will induce a rapid switch to renewable energy sources and increased energy efficiency even if the climate benefits of these technologies are not taken into account (e.g., UNEP, 2011). That is, they hope that green technologies can offer a means to foster rather than reduce economic growth, and yield environmental benefits at the same time.

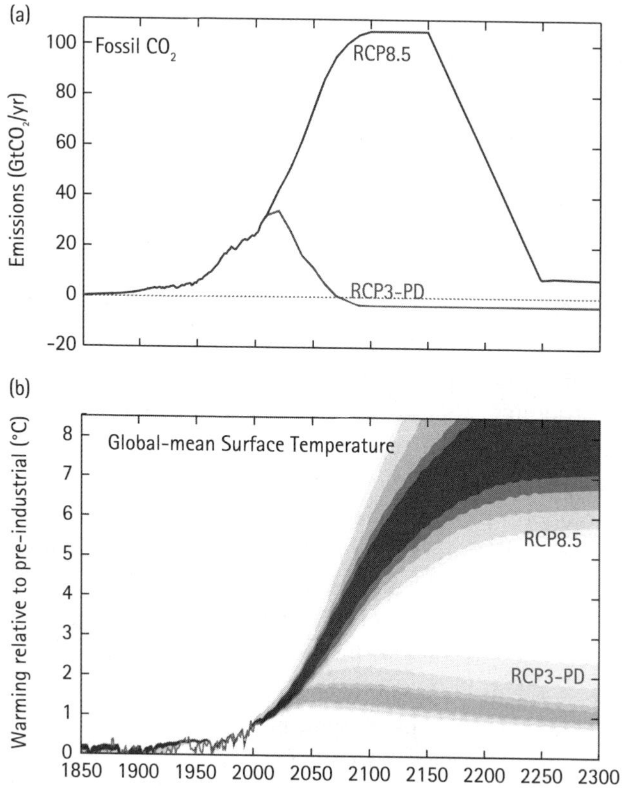

FIGURE 12.1 (a) Two anthropogenic CO_2 emission pathways (RCP8.5 and RCP3) and (b) global warming relative to preindustrial level associated with these pathways expressed in probabilistic terms.

Adapted from Figs 3 and 6 in Meinshausen et al. (2011).

This assertion, however, is likely to be an illusion. Up to 15.000 gigatons (Gt) of CO_2 are still stored underground, mostly in the form of coal, which can be used to generate electricity and even to produce transport fuels via coal-to-liquid processes (IPCC, 2011).

For those proposing ambitious atmospheric stabilization goals, hoping for a rapid autonomous cost decrease of renewables is a dangerous gamble because this expectation might deter further climate policy efforts. Renewables have indeed experienced large cost reductions in recent years, but their share in meeting global primary energy consumption is only about 13%, with half of that coming from traditional biomass, such as wood, charcoal, or animal dung (IPCC, 2011). Prices for fossil energy sources will rise at some point and costs of renewables will decrease. Thus, the question is: Will this structural change come about in time to prevent a significant rise in global mean temperature? The answer from almost all scenario calculations reviewed in the IPCC Special Report on Renewable Energy Sources and Climate Change Mitigation (IPCC, 2011) is: no. In fact, instead of decarbonization and a decline of emissions, the world energy system is currently experiencing a renaissance of coal leading to steeply rising CO_2 emissions, particularly due to rapid economic growth in China (Raupach et al., 2007; Steckel et al., 2011).

Emission scenarios for the 21st century generated by large-scale numerical economy–energy–climate models indicate that limiting global warming to 2°C with 100% certainty is highly challenging, if not practically impossible, by this point in time. Cumulated emissions of 1300 Gt CO_2 have already been emitted since 1850 (WRI, 2012), leaving little space for future atmospheric emission disposals if the ambitious 2°C goal is to be observed. Even attaining the 2°C goal with significant probability is highly challenging when considering that global net negative emissions are likely to be required by the end of this century (see Figure 12.1).

What are the economic costs of meeting specific "carbon budgets," that is, limits to cumulative emission disposal in the atmosphere until the year 2100? Table 12.1 summarizes the cost estimates from scenario calculations of the globally available climate–energy–economy models reviewed and synthesized by the IPCC Fifth Assessment Report (IPCC 2014). Assuming a cost-efficient transformation of the global energy system (lightest grey left columns in Table 12.1)—defined as immediate start of mitigation in all countries and a uniform global carbon price, without additional limitations on technology relative to the models' default technology assumptions—the loss in gross world product could be limited to a few percentage points. The costs of restricting atmospheric usage typically rise with the level of ambition. The costs of mitigation correspond to an annualized reduction of consumption growth by 0.04 to 0.14 (median: 0.06) percentage points over the century relative to annualized consumption growth which in the baseline lies between 1.6 % and 3 % per year. Estimates at the high end of these cost ranges are from models that are relatively inflexible to achieve the deep emissions reductions required in the long run to meet these goals and include assumptions about market imperfections that would raise costs.

Under the absence or limited availability of technologies, mitigation costs can increase substantially depending on the technology considered (middle segment in Table 12.1). This is of particular relevance for CCS and biomass use (the latter may also have an impact on food prices as a result of competing use of arable land). By contrast, limiting the availability of renewables (see text below Table 12.1 for definition) or phasing out nuclear power globally can be achieved at relatively low increases in costs, if all other technologies are available as substitutes.

Delaying additional mitigation further increases mitigation costs in the medium- to long-term (Table 12.1, dark grey segment). The background here is that already existing energy and transport infrastructures are estimated to account for a commitment of almost 500 billion tons of CO_2 over the next 50 years (Davis et al., 2010). Without climate policy, additional carbon-intensive infrastructure will be built up in the near future, which owing to this infrastructure's lifetime of several decades, would result in a lock-in of the associated emissions (Jakob et al., 2012). Many models cannot achieve

Table 12.1 Mitigation costs for different model scenarios

2100 Concentration (ppm CO_2eq)	Cumulative CO_2 emissions ($GtCO_2$) 2011–2100	Consumption losses in cost-effective scenarios				Increase in total discounted mitigation costs in scenarios with limited availability of technologies				Increase in medium- and long-term mitigation costs due to delayed additional mitigation until 2030			
		% reduction in consumption relative to baseline			Percentage point reduction in annualized consumption growth rate	% increase in total discounted mitigation costs (2015–2100) relative to default technology assumptions				% increase in mitigation costs relative to immediate mitigation			
										<55 $GtCO_2$eq		>55 $GtCO_2$eq	
		2030	2050	2100	2010–2100	No CCS	Nuclear phase out	Limited Solar/Wind	Limited Bioenergy	2030–2050	2050–2100	2030–2050	2050–2100
450 (430–480)	630–1180	1.7 (1.0–3.7) [N: 14]	3.4 (2.1–6.2)	4.8 (2.9–11.4)	0.06 (0.04–0.14)	138 (29–297) [N: 4]	7 (4–18) [N: 8]	6 (2–29) [N: 8]	64 (44–78) [N: 8]	28 (14–50) [N: 34]	15 (5–59)	44 (2–78) [N: 29]	37 (16–82)
500 (480–530)	990–1150	1.7 (0.6–2.1) [N: 32]	2.7 (1.5–4.2)	4.7 (2.4–10.6)	0.06 (0.03–0.13)								
550 (530–580)	1170–2100	0.6 (0.2–1.3) [N: 46]	1.7 (1.2–3.3)	3.8 (1.2–7.3)	0.04 (0.01–0.09)	39 (18–78) [N: 11]	13 (2–23) [N: 10]	8 (5–15) [N: 10]	18 (4–66) [N: 12]	3 (−5–16) [N: 14]	4 (−4–11)	15 (3–32) [N: 10]	16 (5–24)
580–650	1870–2440	0.3 (0–0.9) [N: 16]	1.3 (0.5–2.0)	2.3 (1.2–4.4)	0.03 (0.01–0.05)								

Global mitigation costs in cost-effective scenarios and estimated cost increases due to assumed limited availability of specific technologies and delayed additional mitigation (percentage increase of net present value of consumption losses in percent of baseline consumption (for scenarios from general equilibrium models) and abatement costs in percent of baseline GDP (for scenarios from partial equilibrium models) for the period 2015–2100, discounted at 5% per year). Cost estimates shown in this table do not consider the benefits of reduced climate change as well as co-benefits and adverse side-effects of mitigation.

The light grey columns to the left show consumption losses in the years 2030, 2050, and 2100 and annualized consumption growth reductions over the century in cost-effective scenarios relative to a baseline development without climate policy.

The darker grey columns in the middle show the percentage increase in discounted costs over the century, relative to cost-effective scenarios, in scenarios in which technology is constrained relative to default technology assumptions (No CCS: CCS is not included in these scenarios. Nuclear phase out: No addition of nuclear power plants beyond those under construction, and operation of existing plants until the end of their lifetime. Limited Solar / Wind: a maximum of 20 % global electricity generation from solar and wind power in any year of these scenarios. Limited Bioenergy: a maximum of 100 EJ / yr modern bioenergy supply globally (modern bioenergy used for heat, power, combinations, and industry was around 18 EJ / yr in 2008)).

The darkest grey columns to the right show the increase in mitigation costs over the periods 2030–2050 and 2050–2100, relative to scenarios with immediate mitigation, due to delayed additional mitigation through 2030. These scenarios with delayed additional mitigation are grouped by emission levels of less or more than 55 $GtCO_2$eq in 2030, and two concentration ranges in 2100 (430–530 ppm CO_2eq and 530–650 CO_2eq).

In all figures, the median of the scenario set is shown without parentheses, the range between the 16th and 84th percentile of the scenario set is shown in the parentheses, and the number of scenarios in the set is shown in square brackets.

Source: IPCC (2014).

atmospheric concentration levels of about 450 ppm CO_2eq by 2100 if additional mitigation is considerably delayed or under limited availability of key technologies, such as bioenergy, CCS, and their combination.

12.2.3 Choosing a Global Stabilization Target

As the preceding sections have shown, choosing a global stabilization target involves a tradeoff between reducing the risk of anthropogenic climate change and increasing the costs of mitigation. An often employed tool to perform an economic valuation of this kind of problem is cost–benefit analysis (CBA), which aims at determining the abatement level that maximizes the difference between the benefits from avoided climate damage and the associated mitigation costs. Pursuing this technique, different authors have come up with estimates of socially optimal carbon prices that differ by an order of magnitude, ranging from about US$10 per ton of CO_2 (Nordhaus, 2007) to US$100 per ton of CO_2 (Stern, 2007).

Detailed analysis of these divergent results reveals that—as the large brunt of climate damages are likely to manifest themselves in the far future—the optimal carbon price depends crucially on the discount rate that is employed to convert future damages into net present values (Weitzman, 2007). While Nordhaus (2007) uses a discount rate of 5% derived from observed market transactions, Stern (2007) applies a considerably lower rate of 1.4%, arguing that it represents first and foremost an ethical choice regarding the welfare of future generations that cannot be derived from market outcomes. This latter argument receives support by the point that—in contrast to the assumption of infinitely lived representative agents incorporated in models commonly used to study the economic implications of climate policy—a model with overlapping generations that are only mildly altruistic might provide a more realistic description of the relevant tradeoffs between foregoing current consumption and preventing future damages. In such a setting, there is no reason to expect that market interactions will yield the outcome that would seem mandated from an ethical perspective. In particular, a utilitarian social planner would employ a strictly lower discount rate than private agents to compare current costs with future benefits (Schneider et al., 2012).

The task of choosing a stabilization target is made even more difficult when uncertainty is taken into account. For instance, future increases of total factor productivity, and hence consumption growth, are impossible to predict with certainty. It is well known that future consumption growth has an important influence on the discount rate; the wealthier people are in the future, the less they will value any additional unit of consumption and the higher hence the discount rate. Consequently, with uncertain long-term growth prospects policymakers are confronted with a wide array of possible discount rates. In this situation the optimal discount rate displays a declining term structure, that is, the discount rate should be the lower depending on how far a project's payoff lies in the future. This is due to the fact that in the calculation of the (weighted) average over possible discount factors (which are convex functions of discount rates) to derive an expected discount factor, lower discount rates receive higher weights in the long term than in the short term (Freeman, 2010; Gollier and Weitzman, 2010).

In addition, the standard cost–benefit approach faces serious difficulties when considering low probability climate impacts that may yield catastrophic impacts *and if such destruction is to be avoided by all means* (Weitzman, 2009). Even though the question how to ascribe an economic value to catastrophic impacts raises serious ethical as well as empirical challenges (Millner, 2011), the rationale for such a precautionary approach appears pervasive in the climate change context because of the large-scale and indeed planetary stakes. According to Weitzman (2009), if the precautionary principle is applied, the marginal damage of a ton of CO_2 may rise to infinity and hence cannot be weighed against the marginal costs of mitigation. Even though this so-called "dismal theorem" only identifies marginal effects, it has been demonstrated to apply also for a nonmarginal analysis in cases in which current consumption can—as an insurance against catastrophic impacts—be transferred to the future only with uncertainty (Millner, 2011). As uncertainty about climate damages seems likely to affect also intertemporal transfers, this assumption seems realistic. From the aspect of the precautionary principle, then, climate change should be mitigated to a level that minimizes the risk of irreversible and potentially infinite damages.

Figure 12.2 summarizes this rationale in a stylized manner. The horizontal axis indicates the magnitude of damages from climate change, while the vertical axis denotes probability. Restricting the carbon budget relative to BAU tilts the aggregate probability density function—combining uncertainty about climate sensitivity and damages—and its "fat tail" to the left. In this framework, a more ambitious stabilization target can be regarded as an option to reduce the probability of catastrophic climate impacts. As new information on climate impacts or mitigation costs and risks will become available in the future, climate stabilization goals may be revised.

While formally deriving decision criteria on the optimal level of abatement in such an alternative framework remains a theoretical challenge that inevitably raises important value questions, it seems convincing to consider mitigation policy as an investment

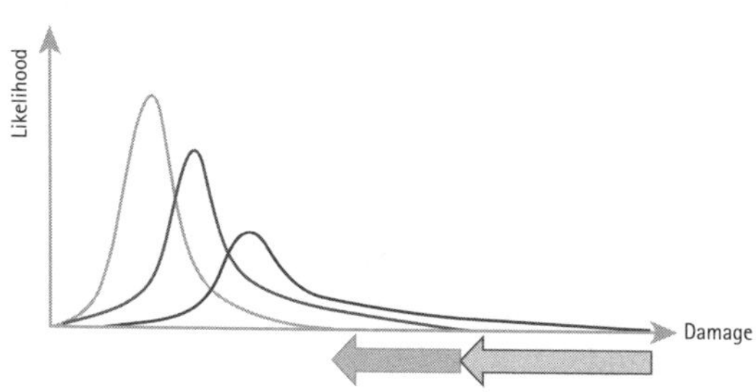

FIGURE 12.2 Climate policy can be regarded as reducing the probability of catastrophic climate change: A more stringent global carbon budget—as indicated by the arrows and the corresponding probability density functions—shifts the probability distribution to the left.

to reduce the probability of catastrophic climate change. Even if the future should reveal that dangerous climate change is less likely than feared, and the costs of mitigation higher than hoped, it is rational to invest into avoiding existential risk given the best available knowledge today. For this reason, the international community's agreement at Copenhagen (in 2009) and Cancún (in 2010) to limit global warming to 2°C above the preindustrial level should probably best be regarded as an attempt to reduce the risk of triggering the Earth system's "tipping-elements" (cf. Section 12.2.1), while at the same time keeping mitigation costs under control to minimize risks to prosperity and human well-being, rather than the outcome of a cost–benefit analysis.

Even if the global community agrees on a global stabilization goal such as 2°C and a corresponding global carbon budget, there are three major additional problems that must be overcome. First, appropriate policies to incentivize emission reduction are needed for implementation at national and subnational levels. Second, defining the scarcity of the atmospheric disposal space creates a novel climate rent and reduces the rents of fossil resource owners, thus raising distributional issues. Third, limiting the use of the atmosphere involves a collective action problem. These challenges are discussed in the following sections.

12.3 Governing the Atmospheric Commons

While the atmosphere meets the descriptive criterion of a *common pool resource* as exclusion from usage is costly and usage of sink capacity is subtractive, it is currently clearly not governed as a "commons," that is, there is no *common property regime* in place. Instead, in most world regions the atmosphere is de facto a "res nullius" with open access to anyone wishing to deposit carbon or other GHGs. One option to manage the atmosphere is to declare it a common property of mankind and regulate it accordingly. The following subsections analyze the climate problem as a problem of governing such a global commons and investigate options for implementing policy instruments (12.3.1) as well as the inescapable distributional issues (12.3.2).

12.3.1 Policy Instruments and Supply-Side Dynamics

The optimal policy to deal with a global environmental problem recommended by economic theory requires a globally uniform price equal to the marginal damage caused by the pollution (Baumol and Oates, 1975). This can be achieved by either taxing GHG emissions or by limiting the total amount that can be emitted by a cap and introducing tradable emission permits.

Though both approaches are fully equivalent in the deterministic case, they display important differences in the presence of uncertainty. As pointed out by Weitzman

(1974) in a static setting, the choice of an optimal instrument crucially depends on the slopes of the functions describing the marginal benefits of avoided emissions and the marginal costs of abatement. Based on this reasoning, a flat marginal benefit function would mandate a tax policy, while with a flat cost function a quantity instrument should be preferred. As carbon emissions have a relatively long atmospheric lifetime (Archer et al., 2009), they can be regarded as a "stock pollutant." Emissions in a single year or even decade have only a minor impact on the total amount of GHGs in the atmosphere, such that the marginal benefit function can be considered to be rather flat in this temporal perspective (Pizer, 1999). However, a more careful analysis reveals that for a dynamic problem possible serial correlation of mitigation costs also plays a crucial role (Newell and Pizer, 2003; Karp and Zhang, 2005). That is, if changes in the marginal abatement cost structure are not only transitory but also persistent (e.g., owing to a slowdown in the technological progress of low-carbon technologies, which leads to higher mitigation costs not only in the current time period, but also in future ones) the main advantage of a tax—namely to smooth costs by performing more (less) abatement in periods with lower (higher) costs—is severely reduced.

Taking these caveats into account, the respective literature has found that for a wide range of realistic parameter values a price instrument (i.e., a carbon tax) should be preferred to a quantity instrument (i.e., emissions trading) if the time path of the respective future policy is to be specified ex ante (Newell and Pizer, 2003; Karp and Zhang, 2005). However, introducing banking and borrowing of emission permits across trading periods provides greater flexibility for firms to react to higher (lower) costs in any single period by abating less (more) emissions, thus smoothing abatement costs over time and also reducing the costs of complying with a given climate target (Rubin, 1996). Given a correctly specified "trading ratio" at which emission permits originally issued for one trading period can be transferred to another one, emissions trading with banking and borrowing results in the socially optimal distribution of emissions over time even in the presence of uncertainty (Leiby and Rubin, 2001).

A further distinction between price and quantity instruments to put a price on emissions arises when taking into account the supply side of fossil fuels, or, more precisely, the resource suppliers' strategic reaction to climate policies (Kalkuhl and Edenhofer, 2010). That is, putting a tax on the use of fossil fuels that rises over time could in effect accelerate global warming, as resource owners anticipate higher future taxes and increase near-term extraction, even if these taxes are implemented globally to cover all countries (Sinn, 2008). This "green paradox" has been shown to arise only under some specific conditions (i.e., if the carbon tax rises at a rate that exceeds the effective discount rate of the resource owners), and assumes that the regulator implements and commits to a permanently maladjusted tax (Edenhofer and Kalkuhl, 2011). Nevertheless, the possibility of strategic resource supply-side reactions in conjunction with the regulator's informational requirement of setting the right tax (which would vary across resource owners as a function of their cumulative past extraction) and credibly committing to its policy schedule might mandate against a purely price-based regulation. The efficiency of a carbon trading scheme with banking and borrowing, however, depends on the availability of complete and efficient future commodities market which is a rather strong assumption (Kalkuhl and Edenhofer, 2010).

It should be noted that the choice between a price and a quantity instrument is not necessarily an exclusive decision for or against one of these policy instruments. In this vein, so-called "hybrid approaches" that combine price and quantity targets have been proposed (see Pizer, 2002 and Newell et al., 2005). These include, for example, price corridors to establish a "safety valve" against excessive price volatility by increasing (decreasing) the supply of permits if their price reaches a previously specified upper (lower) bound (Burtraw et al., 2009a).

Besides the environmental externality arising GHG emissions, the development of novel low-carbon technologies has been identified as an additional source of market failure in mitigation policy (Jaffe et al., 2005). From this perspective, the fact that the inventor is unable to fully appropriate the associated social benefits of a new technology results in their under-provision, hence mandating subsidies for technology development and deployment (Newell et al., 2006). While such technology market failures are widespread across the entire economy and not restricted to "green" technologies, they can be considered to be of special importance for the case of energy technologies. As highlighted by Kalkuhl et al. (2011), with a high degree of substitutability between fossil energy sources and low-carbon technologies in combination with potential future cost reductions by means of learning-by-doing for the latter, even small market imperfections can result in a "lock-in" in which the widespread adoption of the socially desirable technology option is delayed by several decades. Consequently, the optimal policy to address climate change is considered to include a portfolio of instruments targeted at emissions, learning-by-doing, as well as research and development (Fischer and Newell, 2008).

Obviously, it would also be conceivable to conduct climate policy without directly putting a price on carbon (for instance, if this is impossible owing to political constraints). Handing out subsidies to renewable energy sources that are high enough to render the latter competitive with fossil fuels would be such a "second-best" policy. Yet, by lowering the price of energy, this approach can be expected to significantly increase energy consumption and thus increase the costs of reaching a given climate target, at least in the long run. For transitory periods followed by carbon pricing in the not too distant future, renewable subsidies may be an intermediate "second-best" substitute to carbon pricing (Kalkuhl et al., 2011). For this reason, policies that avoid emissions without reducing fossil fuel demand (which would lead to lower energy prices)—such as subsidies for carbon capture and sequestration—are likely to carry the lowest costs in the presence of imperfect or missing carbon prices (Kalkuhl et al., 2012).

In addition to cost-efficiency considerations, the distributional impacts of climate policies are an issue of primordial importance for policymakers—at least in a realistic setting in which transfers to compensate those that bear over-proportional losses are

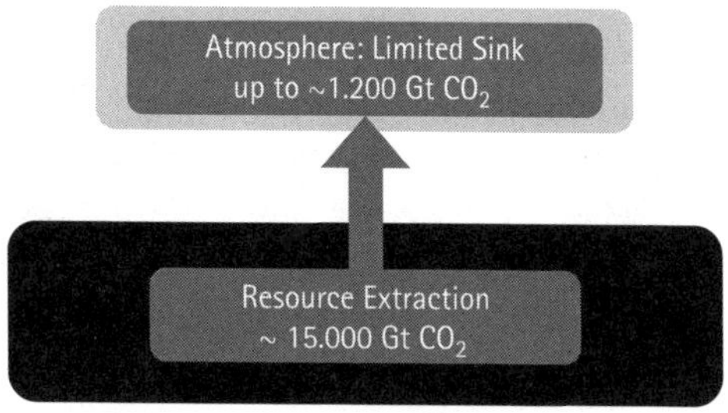

FIGURE 12.3 With an ambitious climate policy goal the atmospheric sink constraint is tighter than the constraint from fossil resource scarcity.

unavailable. Some studies find regressive effects of carbon pricing, as poorer households spend a larger share of their income on energy-intensive goods (e.g., Grainger and Kolstad, 2010), while others highlight that if associated changes in wages and returns to capital are properly taken into account, the effects of such policies might in fact be progressive (e.g., Rausch et al., 2010). In any case, the distributional effect of carbon pricing will crucially depend on how revenues from a carbon tax or auctioned permits will be employed, for example, to lower taxes on labor income (Burtraw et al., 2009b). Besides households, firms will also be affected by climate policies. That is, highly carbon-intensive activities are likely to be most severely impacted by a price on carbon, while less carbon-intensive ones could even increase their market share (Pahle et al., 2012). As a consequence, these distributional effects can provide incentives to engage in lobbying to strategically influence the formulation of climate policy (Habla and Winkler, 2011). Finally, climate policy does not only entail distributional effects within individual countries, but also between countries. This aspect is discussed in the following subsection.

12.3.2 Allocating the Climate Rent

Pricing CO_2 emissions to limit the use of the atmospheric sink has significant economic implications: in effect, novel atmospheric property rights are created and become subject to a distributional process. In a world without climate protection, everybody can use the atmosphere for free. With a binding limit such as a global carbon budget the disposal space is restricted and a novel scarcity rent, the "climate rent," is created. In a global emissions trading system, the net present value (NPV) of the total climate rent is equal to the intertemporal budget of emission permits times the carbon price. Equivalently, with a global carbon tax scheme ensuring compliance with a corresponding budget, the climate rent is equal to the cumulated NPV of the carbon tax revenue over time.

12.3.2.1 Transformation of Fossil Resource Rent into Climate Rent

In addition to creating a climate rent, restricting the use of the atmosphere as a carbon sink devalues the property titles of the owners of coal, oil, and gas, as depicted in Figure 12.3. Particularly coal extracted and deposited into the atmosphere in the BAU scenario needs to remain underground in case of ambitious global climate policy (IPCC, 2011). At the same time, restricting global demand for fossil fuels is conceptually equivalent to exerting market power on the international fossil resource market, thus lowering world fossil resource prices and reducing the scarcity rent of fossil resource owners (Leimbach et al., 2010).

Both effects combined imply shifting rents from fossil resource owners to the novel owners of the climate rent, with the latter needing yet to be defined (Kalkuhl and Edenhofer, 2010). This economic mechanism explains resistance against ambitious and uncompensated climate policy by fossil resource owners. It also indicates why international negotiations over regional emission reduction goals, which are equivalent to the allocation of valuable regional carbon budgets, are so contended.

From a libertarian perspective or from the point of view of the affected fossil resource owners, the following ethical argument against the legitimacy of these distributional effects of climate policy may be put forward: insofar as climate policy expropriates the owners of fossil resources, it can be regarded as an illegitimate attack against the institution of private property. This argument then requires showing why such "expropriation" might be ethically legitimate. We briefly consider four arguments.

First, it may be argued that climate policy does not lead to a redistribution of property titles in resource stocks, but only to a change in their value. Such changes in the value of property induced by policy or technological progress have occurred throughout history. Protection of property titles as such need not imply protecting their market values. On the other hand, setting a limit on global carbon extraction implies that not all fossil resource titles can be put to market use (unless CCS is adopted), so some element of expropriation appears to prevail. Further, claims for compensating "regulatory takings" (devaluation of assets due to public policy) are not uncommon (Miceli and Segerson, 2007). Second, even if fossil resource devaluation is considered genuine expropriation, the institution of "eminent domain" may be invoked, which justifies expropriation if it serves the public good—in this case a reduction of catastrophic climate risk. Eminent domain usually requires compensating expropriated value, which raises the question if fossil resource owners should be financially compensated under climate policy. Indeed, fossil resource rich countries in United Nations Framework Convention on Climate Change (UNFCCC) negotiations have demanded this (Depledge, 2008; Mouawad and Revkin, 2009). A third and related argument draws on the principle of the "social obligation of private property." This argument goes back to Thomas Aquinas (1265–1274; see also Chroust and Affeldt, 1951) and holds that the institution of private property in natural resource endowments is ethically justified only if it serves the common good more than the primordial concept of common property.

Summing up, it may be argued that even while the final verdict on the debate over compensatory claims of fossil resource owners will inevitably be subject to political negotiations, a rational exchange of ethical arguments pertaining the legitimacy of such claims is both feasible and useful to inform political negotiations, especially if questions of legitimacy beyond pure power politics are to play a role.

12.3.2.2 Distributing the Climate Rent

Deliberately creating a climate rent by limiting atmospheric usage via carbon pricing raises the question of how to distribute this rent. As international climate policy negotiations over regional emission reduction goals imply the distribution of regional climate rent endowments, a major and so far perhaps underappreciated challenge of climate policy negotiations is to deal with what may be largest distributional negotiations the global community has ever engaged in.

To illustrate the orders of magnitude, consider a simple back-of-the envelope calculation: With 33 billion tons global CO_2 emissions in the year 2010 (CDIAC, 2012), the potential global climate rent was US$ 330 billion assuming a carbon price of US$10/t$CO_2$ this year, or US$1.65 trillion assuming a carbon price of US$50/t$CO_2$ (omitting that such a carbon price would lower emissions for the sake of simplicity). With a global GDP of US$77 trillion in 2010 (CIA World Factbook, 2012), the latter climate rent volume implies 2% of global GDP being put on the UNFCCC negotiation table.

For identifying key conceptual issues, let us assume the global implementation of an ambitious carbon budget, for example, associated with the 2°C stabilization target by means of a global cap-and-trade scheme where permits (the value of which represents the climate rent) are freely tradable. In addition, we assume separability of permit allocation and efficiency. In such a stylized setting, the question of permit and concomitant rent distribution boils down to a zero-sum game (WBGU, 2009; Luderer et al., 2012). Different ethical proposals to address this distributional problem—usually framed in the context of allocating emission permits among countries or individuals—have been advanced. We briefly inspect three major approaches in this debate.

The so-called *grandfathering* rule foresees distribution of permits in proportion to countries' current emissions or GDP. It might be justified on libertarian grounds by arguing that current emission levels represent a legitimate property title constituted by an "atmospheric taking," or simply by invoking custom and practice. Grandfathering of emissions is the starting point for proposals by developed countries such as the United States and EU member states, combined with the offer to reduce the initial endowment over time. Caney (2009) states that no moral or political philosopher defends a pure grandfathering principle for emission permit distribution, as it is both insensitive to the legitimate needs and rights of non-emitters (usually poorer individuals and countries) and the concept of historical responsibility. This does not exclude the ethical argument to accept a grandfathering rule if it facilitates the adoption of a global climate policy that will reduce climate impacts and large-scale risks. Still, he argues that such acceptance does not render the grandfathering rule ethically convincing as such.

The proposal of distributing the climate rent according to *historical emissions* has in particular been put forward by developing countries (see most notably Brazil, 1997). It frames the atmosphere as a common-pool sink with finite capacity and distributes equal-per-capita ownership rights over time, for example, since 1850. As developed countries have emitted relatively more in the past, their remaining endowments shall be lower than those of developing countries. The claim of historical responsibility of industrialized countries appears convincing at first glance. However, on closer examination there are two key problems. First, people living today and in the future can hardly be directly held responsible for the past activities (e.g., emissions) of their ancestors. Second, earlier generations cannot be held responsible as they did and could not know about the harmful consequences of emissions. On the other hand, some argue that historical emissions are relevant for permit allocations insofar as citizens in developed countries today benefit from the significant capital stocks that have been accumulated using carbon emissions (Meyer and Roser, 2006).

Finally, the remaining carbon budget may be distributed according to an equal-per-capita rule. This principle may be derived from the theory suggested by Thomas Aquinas (1265–1274), who argues that the primordial ownership structure for natural endowments is communal, with legitimate private property titles (e.g., emission permits) being introduced for efficiency reasons. The equal-per-capita rule also resonates with Locke (2003[1689], Essay 2, Chapter V) and subsequently Nozick (1974, 174–182), who argue that unequal initial appropriation of natural resources is legitimate only if there is "...enough, and as good, left in common for others." This is clearly not the case with scarce emission permits, and thus an equal distribution of these endowments might constitute a more convincing approach.

An alternative perspective on concepts for distributing the climate rent is to consider the regional (or perhaps even individual) economic cost of attaining a certain stabilization goal and then consider the merits of different permit allocations in achieving an ethically convincing final distribution of the aggregate global costs of mitigation (Rose et al., 1998). Conceptually, in a comprehensive and efficient global carbon trading scheme and assuming perfect information on regional mitigation costs, any distribution of mitigation costs can be achieved using appropriate permit allocations. Those who value the ability to emit relatively highly—for example, because they have a carbon-intensive industrial infrastructure—will purchase permits from those who value them less, thus leading to financial transfers. In fact, in this perspective the equal per capita distribution may be considered less convincing as it can lead to windfall profits from mitigation policy in developing countries (e.g., Knopf et al., 2012). While such net transfers to developing countries may be considered desirable though a global equity perspective, a more intuitive—and politically realistic—rule may resort to a two-step argument: First, there could be a principle of "no negative costs," that is, no region derives net profits from mitigation policy, and second, total global mitigation costs could be shared according to a progressive "ability to pay" burden-sharing rule, reminiscent of standard UN arrangements for financing UN operations and peacekeeping missions (Barrett, 2007). Such an approach would also resonate with the UNFCCC principle of sharing mitigation costs according to "common but differentiated responsibilities and respective capabilities" (UNFCCC, 1992, Article 3.1).

The major conceptual problem of the cost-sharing approach is that the global and regional distribution of mitigation costs and permit prices that determine the value of international financial transfers in a permit trading scheme are uncertain. Also, a thorough adoption of this line of argument requires evaluating the costs of complementary climate policies such as technology support schemes, which raise significant complexities in monitoring and evaluating the costs of regional mitigation efforts. Nevertheless, it seems convincing that this outcome-based perspective should complement the negotiations over regional emission budgets and the initial allocation of climate rents.

While naturally the distributional debate can only be resolved in political negotiations, the arguments briefly outlined here shall illustrate that the rational exchange of arguments pertaining the ethical legitimacy of distributional rules for sharing the global climate rent may be useful to inform political negotiations, and that scientific and philosophical analysis can contribute productively to this discourse.

12.4 The Challenge of Global Cooperation

Efficient governance of the atmosphere requires global cooperation and coordination of climate policies. The slow progress of the climate policy negotiations under the UNFCCC has made it obvious that global cooperation is not achieved easily. This is matched by the game theoretic prediction of a "cooperation paradox." But game theory may also help to identify ways to overcome the dilemma: A better understanding of the motivations for unilateral climate policy as well as of ways to raise the level of cooperation might contribute to facilitating political negotiations. We briefly recapitulate the cooperation dilemma before discussing rationales for unilateral mitigation and options to improve global cooperation in turn.

12.4.1 The Paradox of International Environmental Agreements

When nation-states have the choice of contributing to a global effort to reduce GHG emissions, they face a strong collective action problem. This is because everybody can benefit from the abatement of one party without contributing to the associated cost of abatement, while the costs are borne by the abating state alone. There is no world government that might resolve this problem by devising and enforcing policies or contracts. Carbon leakage and the green paradox exacerbate the problem: reducing demand for fossil fuels in one region will lower their world market price, thus inducing increased consumption in other regions; further, announcing climate policies without deploying appropriate and globally coordinated instruments can shift the intertemporal fossil fuel extraction schedule toward the present, thus lowering prices, spurring demand, and increasing emissions (cf. Section 12.3.1). Hence, to game theorists, the game of climate change mitigation has the familiar incentive structure of public good provision.

Consequently, climate negotiations have been analyzed in terms of stylized games such as "Prisoners' Dilemma" or "Chicken Game" (Pittel and Rübbelke, 2012). It is well known that cooperation is not an equilibrium of these games. However, one should be weary of the conclusions drawn from these simple games—other than the obvious point that such incentives hamper cooperation—owing to their long list of strong assumptions. The standard prisoners' dilemma is a simultaneous, one-shot game with discrete choices. Among other things, the game abstracts from the fact that nations communicate, interact repeatedly in various matters, and can graduate their ambitions and sanctions.

One approach that has received broad attention in the game theory literature is the idea that introducing international environmental agreements (IEAs) may change the rules of the game and thereby give rise to a more cooperative outcome. Indeed, the seminal analyses show that agreements raise cooperation above the purely non-cooperative case (Hoel, 1992; Carraro and Siniscalco, 1993). Alas, the voluntary participation in such self-enforcing agreements remains low, especially when the gains from cooperation are large (Barrett, 1994).

Game theoretic analysis relies on CBA with continuous benefit and damage functions. Yet, as we have discussed above, CBA may not be the appropriate tool when the danger of catastrophic impacts, even at low probabilities, is taken into account (cf. discussion of Weitzman, 2009 in Section 12.2.3). One study that analyzes catastrophic impacts that occur at a certain climate threshold in the framework of coalition formation finds that the threat of disaster suffices to overcome the cooperation problem (Barrett, 2011). Intuitively, nature becomes the credible enforcer that is missing in the international climate policy domain. But the same study also shows that uncertainty about the threshold overturns this result, as uncertainty transforms the discontinuous disaster into its (smooth) expectation.

Given the reluctance of several world regions to coordinate a global climate agreement, are there any options to improve cooperation? What are sensible strategic choices for first movers? Should they wait for action by others, or are there good reasons for ambitious countries or cities to develop good examples? There are two basic arguments in favor of such action by first movers. First, a number of rationales and mechanisms make unilateral initiatives economically rational even in presence of free riding incentives. These include efficient policies, technological change, local co-benefits, international transfers, issue linking, and ethical considerations. Second, unilateral action can prepare the ground for more international cooperation in the future. The following two subsections discuss these in turn.

12.4.2 Rationales for Unilateral Action

While the standard game theory analysis predicts a climate policy cooperation failure and real-world negotiations on a meaningful international climate policy agreement succeeding the Kyoto Protocol have been stalled since the 2009 UNFCCC conference at Copenhagen, a number of regions are already adopting climate policies varying in scope and level of ambition. The European Union has adopted the most far-reaching package of climate policies and aims at reducing its GHG emissions by 20% in 2020 relative to the year 1990 (for an overview of recent EU climate policies, see Oberthür and Pallemaerts, 2011). The European Union also aims toward increasing the share of renewable energies to 20% of the primary energy mix in 2020. To achieve these goals, the EU emission trading scheme (EU ETS), a company-level cap-and-trade system covering roughly half of European GHG emissions was implemented in 2005 (Ellerman et al., 2010). Additional policies especially in the sectors not covered by the EU ETS include technology standards such as a fleet-level CO_2-intensity standard for cars and biofuel mandates (Creutzig et al., 2011), as well as national-level renewable energy targets and policies. Germany specifically aims at implementing a particularly ambitious climate policy with its "Energiewende," which was initiated after the 2011 Fukushima incident. The goal is to simultaneously phase out nuclear energy and reduce GHG emissions by 40% by 2020, and by 80–95% by 2050, relative to 1990.

Beyond the European Union, a number of policy initiatives for adopting GHG pricing by means of emissions trading are under way. New Zealand has introduced an ETS in 2010. Australia is implementing an ETS subject to fierce political contests (Jotzo, 2012), and South Korea plans to adopt of its ETS by 2015. On the subnational level, California envisages implementation of its regional cap-and-trade system for 2013, with the intention to link to the ETS in Quebec planned to commence operations in 2013, and perhaps also to the Regional Greenhouse Gas Initiative (RGGI) trading system in the northeastern United States operating since 2009. Perhaps most notably, in China five cities and two provinces are in the process of setting up pilot emission trading systems to inform a national cap-and-trade system envisaged to commence operations after 2015 (Petherick, 2012; World Bank, 2012).

In addition to carbon pricing policies, investments to renewables have expanded considerably in recent years, with 118 countries having adopted renewable energy targets in 2011. The most important support policies are feed-in tariffs and renewable quotas or portfolio standards, where a general trend of weakening these schemes was observable after 2009 as a result of the global economic crisis and austerity policies.

Total global net investment into renewable power capacity was US$262 billion in 2011, which was US$40 billion higher than the same figure for fossil power generation. China (US$52 billion) leads investment into renewables, closely followed by the United States (US$51 billion) and Germany (US$31 billion). Owing to the relatively low load factors of renewable power, however, the share of modern renewable power generation (excluding hydro) increased only from 5.1% in 2010 to 6% in 2011 (McCrone et al., 2012).

Despite these unilateral actions, in their analysis of 76 countries' emission reduction pledges made under the Copenhagen Accord, Rogelj et al. (2010) find that a conservative interpretation of these pledges implies virtually no difference to BAU emissions in the year 2020. A more optimistic interpretation assuming a closure of potential loopholes from land-use and forestry accounting and overallocation of permits under the Kyoto Protocol (especially to Russia), as well as pledges implemented at the upper end of their proposed range, would yield about 5 Gt of annual emission reductions compared to BAU in 2020. Freezing global emissions at the conservative 2020 estimate until 2050 and beyond would lead to global warming of 3–4°C above preindustrial levels by 2100 with 50–68% probability. It leaves a 5% likelihood of 5°C warming by 2100, with temperatures continuing to rise thereafter. This indicates a gap between the collective agreement to limit global warming to 2°C as endorsed in Copenhagen, and individual countries' actions (see also UNEP, 2011).

Can this situation be analyzed in terms of the standard game theory analyses outlined earlier? An obvious interpretation may be that the gap between collective ambition and individual reluctance of countries confirms the diagnosis of a dilemma situation. Countries unilaterally reducing emissions via carbon pricing and renewables policies take on the role of "chickens," with the rest of the world having a free ride on their reduction efforts. However, a thorough assessment of empirical climate policies in terms of game theory is not available, and both common sense and the available scientific literature suggest that there are additional rationales informing international climate negotiations and unilateral emission reduction activities that require an extension of the simple standard model.

12.4.2.1 *Co-Benefits*

It is sometimes argued that local and regional co-benefits from emission abatement, such as cleaner air and reduced energy imports, increase unilateral benefits of abatement and can thus motivate unilateral emission reductions (Pittel and Rübbelke, 2008; Ostrom, 2010). The argument is that including co-benefits in the cost–benefit calculus of mitigation reduces the effective costs of mitigation, thus motivating higher levels of unilateral emission reductions compared to the case where they are not accounted for (Bollen et al., 2009). Going further, some argue that there are many advantageous negative cost (or "win–win") options for reducing or adjusting energy consumption, which do not even require resorting to climate change mitigation benefits (e.g., Enkvist et al., 2007).

The critical question in this context is why welfare-improving policies in other issue areas such as local air pollution are not implemented in the first place. Conceptually, if all policy goals are addressed with first best instruments to balance marginal costs and benefits, it is not obvious that climate policy will induce any positive effects regarding additional policy goals. By definition, any reduction beyond those that are optimal will raise overall costs.

Clearly, where the introduction of climate policy enables improvement over previously second-best implementation of policies (e.g., due to limited government capacity), climate policies may induce local or regional co-benefits. Thus, careful examination is required whether co-benefits can actually be attributed to climate policy. Also, it needs to be considered if studies on low or negative cost abatement potentials have taken into account the full costs of abatement options, including institutional and transaction costs or intangible amenity values of certain technologies.

Finally, there can be nonmaterial co-benefits from unilateral climate policy. Some agents may have a preference for contributing to emission reductions that may be derived from their conviction of the ethical value of emission reductions. Such agents will derive benefits from contributing to the global public good of emission reductions or by sticking to unilaterally adopted permit budgets elicited through ethical reasoning, even in presence of the free-rider dilemma. This may be motivated by the hope for reciprocal behavior of other agents in other world regions (Ostrom, 2003), a "warm glow" sensation (Andreoni, 1990), or the nonmaterial internal reward from individually and collectively acting in a manner considered to be morally sound (see also 12.4.3.5).

12.4.2.2 Low-Carbon Technology Development

The costs of low-carbon technologies such as renewables have decreased significantly in recent years, driven by increased technology adoption and research and development (R&D) efforts (IPCC, 2011). To the extent that firms or countries face sufficient demand, for example, as secured by a long-term price on carbon and an expectation to be able to capture the scarcity rent of such novel low-cost low-emission technologies through viable patent protection, they face a market-based incentive to develop these technologies (Edenhofer et al., 2006). Combined with the expectation of network externalities and economy of scale agglomeration dynamics in green technology industries, as well as the regional benefits believed to be associated with these technologies such as "green jobs" in addition to enhanced competitiveness from technology leadership, this rationale has motivated first mover behavior at the national level expressed, for example, in "green industrial policies" in Germany in recent years (BMU/UBA, 2011). However, in presence of international spillover effects from technology learning (Jaffe et al., 2005), the magnitude of the technology development incentive for firms and the related national social benefits of green industrial policies remain unclear. In fact, despite its prominence in the public debate, little research is available to assess the validity of this rationale for unilateral action in low-carbon technology deployment and development.

Heal and Tarui (2010) demonstrate that in a Nash setting technology spillovers may reduce free-riding depending on the magnitude of these spillovers and the effect of R&D on marginal abatement costs. Heal (1999) points out that if the costs of low-carbon technologies can be reduced below the costs of competing emission-intensive technologies via learning effects, the climate stabilization game may in fact be a coordination game with two equilibria. The first is one where the world remains locked-in an emission-intensive energy system. In the other one collective investment into low-carbon technologies reduces their costs so much that they become universally adopted as a result of economic incentives and market forces. Clearly, the prospect for this promising avenue heavily depends on the cost reduction potentials for low-emission technologies compared to emission-intensive options. As noted previously, the 164 scenarios analyzed by IPCC (2011) indicate that within the 21st century such a dramatic large-scale shift in the relative costs of technologies cannot be expected. This is due to the ample availability of fossil energy carriers and technologies at low costs relative to carbon-free technologies.

12.4.2.3 Signaling

One explanation as to why international cooperation is seriously hampered might be the presence of "asymmetric information" (Afionis, 2011). For instance, it is well conceivable that negotiators are only imperfectly informed on their interlocutors' perceived benefits from climate change mitigation, which are not exclusively determined by physical climate damages, but also by political considerations as well as ethical judgments (Gardiner, 2004). With such informational asymmetries, actors may face uncertainty on whether they are actually confronted with a prisoners' dilemma, in which non-cooperation constitutes a dominant strategy, or rather a game of coordination, in which there is no incentive for any player to unilaterally deviate from the cooperative outcome (Caparrós et al., 2004). A pessimistic expectation of the benefits obtained by other actors' via climate change mitigation can then render cooperation impossible, even if it would be in both players' best interest. Unilateral action by an actor with high benefits as well as high mitigation costs can then act as a signal that his benefits are indeed high enough to mandate concluding a long-term agreement that includes side payments to finance abatement in other countries (Jakob and Lessmann, 2012).

An alternative, related incentive for unilateral action arises if all actors' abatement costs—even their own—are known only with uncertainty but display a positive correlation. An actor who discovers that he has low abatement costs may in this case engage in unilateral action in order to signal to other actors that their costs are likely to be low as well, and hence provide them with an incentive to increase their mitigation levels (Brandt, 2004).

12.4.3 Options to Improve Global Cooperation

Besides the first mover rationales that may enhance global cooperation outlined above, there are at least five further options that provide starting points for alleviating the global cooperation problem.

12.4.3.1 Burden-sharing and Financial Transfers

International transfers are an important tool to foster cooperation as they enable sharing the gains from improved cooperation: countries that are more willing to pay for mitigation can compensate other countries to reduce their emissions if they have cheaper mitigation options at their disposal. A number of studies have investigated the prospect of transfers using numerical models of coalition formation to factor in heterogeneity among countries. Two approaches frequently pursued are (1) burden sharing through emission permit allocations and (2) transfer rules aimed at coalition stability.

Examples of the former are found in the burden sharing literature (e.g., den Elzen and Lucas, 2005), but similar permit allocation schemes, ranging from equitable transfer schemes (e.g., following egalitarianism or historical responsibility) to pragmatic schemes such as "grandfathering" have been incorporated in the analysis of self-enforcing agreements (Altamirano-Cabrera and Finus, 2006). However, insofar as these allocations are not derived so as to induce strategic effects, they show little or no effect on cooperation. By contrast, Lessmann et al. (2010) demonstrate that strategic use of permit trading can facilitate the inclusion of nonsignatories via flexible mechanisms like the Kyoto Protocol's Clean Development Mechanism.

Surplus sharing schemes that are designed to favorably alter incentives show a stronger impact on coalition formation (Nagashima et al., 2009). In particular, under "optimal surplus sharing," that is, payoff transfers that stabilize coalitions (cf. Carraro et al., 2006; McGinty, 2007; Weikard, 2009), cooperation is much improved compared to the absence of transfers: 56% of the cooperation failure (difference in total welfare between the noncooperative Nash equilibrium and full cooperation case) is overcome. With a different model and the same idea of optimal transfers, only 5% of the initial cooperation failure remain (Carraro et al., 2006). Earlier studies in this strand of literature also find significant increases in participation as a result of strategic transfers (Botteon and Carraro, 2001; Eyckmans and Tulkens, 2003). Thus, as highlighted in Section 12.3.2, a strong conclusion that arises from these studies is that to be effective, strategic implications of transfers should be taken into account in addition to normative considerations of burden sharing.

In contrast to the models investigating permit allocation-based transfers, models analyzing transfers in aggregate payoff do not specify how transfers are implemented and when they occur empirically: In dynamic models, which often span several centuries, neither the beginning nor the end of the time horizon are realistic points in time for a one-time side payment. New institutions of climate finance to implement these transfers are therefore required. Obvious candidates are funds such as the Green

Climate Fund (UNFCCC, 2010). The volume of transfers that stabilize coalitions may, however, be large, and it is not obvious whether countries are willing to agree to such explicit transfers.

12.4.3.2 Technology (Clubs)

Development of low-carbon technologies can potentially reduce the cost of climate change mitigation and thus the costs of joining a climate agreement. But unless better technologies make abatement individually rational, the incentive to free ride will remain. Still, technology R&D offers at least two ways to enhance the incentive structure by either exploiting international knowledge spillovers associated with innovation, or by setting up a technology treaty rather than an environmental agreement. The former proposal links international emission reduction agreements to cooperative R&D efforts that are designed to restrict access to the fruits of these efforts—more efficient technologies—to the club of signatories. As joint R&D efforts generate a club good surplus to be allocated between the cooperating parties, the net costs from mitigation are reduced and the adoption of more stringent abatement targets is facilitated (Botteon and Carraro, 1998; Lessmann and Edenhofer, 2011). However, institutional arrangements need to ensure that the benefits from joint R&D are indeed restricted to the signatories, which is challenging.

Other studies explore treaties that are tailored to produce "breakthrough technologies." In this setup the prospect of cooperation only increases if there is a technology with increasing returns to adoption. In view of today's available technologies, however, there is no likely candidate exhibiting these features (Barrett, 2006). Conclusions regarding the potential for cooperation are more optimistic when R&D is conceptualized as reducing the costs of technology adoption (Hoel and de Zeeuw, 2010).

12.4.3.3 Trade Policies

Without full cooperation in climate change mitigation the existence of international trade will lead to carbon leakage. Moreover, abating countries are at a competitive disadvantage in international markets. One obvious option may therefore be to combine climate policy with trade policy such as carbon border tax adjustments which could reduce leakage and restore a level playing field (Stiglitz, 2006a, b). Furthermore, trade sanctions or trade bans against nonsignatories of a climate agreement can reduce the incentive to free ride to the extent where participation in the agreement increases (Barrett, 1997; Lessmann et al., 2009).

Implementing linked trade and climate policies, however, is riddled with problems (Barrett, 2010). The carbon footprint of traded goods, a prerequisite for meaningful border tax adjustments, is notoriously difficult to evaluate. The threat of punitive sanctions is often not credible, as the cost of limiting free trade cuts both ways. Moreover, it is quite possible that countries would retaliate; sanctions and countersanctions could escalate into trade wars. It is therefore important that carbon tariffs or trade sanctions are generally considered to be legitimate, which might reduce the risk of retaliation.

Finally, it is not obvious whether trade sanctions would conform to the rules of the World Trade Organization (WTO), even though the case that they can conform has been made (Perez, 2005), and it has been argued that, given a broad sense that sanctions are legitimate, conforming with WTO rules is not crucial (Barrett, 2010). Despite these complications, trade policies have the appeal of being the most obvious mechanisms to facilitate unilateral climate policy and to enforce an agreement; hence it seems likely that sanctions will be discussed in future climate policy negotiations (Barrett, 2010).

12.4.3.4 Repeated Interaction: Punishment, Reputation, and Norms

The one-shot perspective of the standard climate policy game neglects that interaction of nations is not restricted to a single time step and a single issue. Rather, nation states will negotiate contracts over a range of topics, and even an agreement on a single issue may have many commitment periods that require separate negotiations. Thus, one may argue that international climate agreements are more aptly described as repeated games, which have a distinctly richer strategy space. In particular, strategies can be contingent on the previous behavior of the opponent, and in turn must take into account the reactions of the opponent. Further, defectors may be punished, while cooperators may build a reputation, to name two prominent examples that we discuss in turn.

The threat of punishment can only effectively deter free riding if it is credible, that is, once defection has occurred it must be beneficial for the punisher to carry out the punishment. This makes punishment a tradeoff of being severe enough but not too expensive so as to become noncredible. For example, in Froyn and Hovi (2008) the threat becomes credible only when a fraction of the signatories carry out the punishment; the remaining signatories continue to "cooperate" and thus maintaining a high level of payoffs for all signatories. Asheim and Holtsmark (2009) generalize this idea for continuous strategies and find that as long as the discount rate is sufficiently low, a broad and deep treaty can always be implemented. In Heitzig et al. (2011) punishment takes the form of a higher future emission reduction burden for the defector (proportionally to her shortfall), and a correspondingly lower burden for the punishing parties, which makes the threat credible. These results not only show that the well-known result that the prisoners' dilemma can be overcome in its (unlimitedly) repeated extension also translates to the climate game, but they also suggest first ideas for practicable implementations.

Incorporating the effects of reputation reverses the burden of proof compared to punishment in the following sense: rather than avoiding punishment, cooperative behavior will establish the player as worthy, for example, to receive voluntary donations from others. Laboratory experiments show that reputation effects in alternating games of public good provision and indirect reciprocity increase cooperative behavior (Milinski et al., 2002, 2006). Such desire to build a good reputation may over time turn into societal norms of good behavior. In how far nation states value norms or their reputation, and how it compares to economic incentives to free ride is difficult to quantify.

The following paragraphs report studies that have made efforts to take genuine ethical considerations into account.

12.4.3.5 Ethics

Ethical considerations that impact the actual choices of people and nations can make a difference to the prospect for abatement, cooperation, and welfare. Previous literature on the provision of public goods has taken into account that contributing may be seen as a moral obligation (Sugden, 1984), or that at least "impure altruism" is at play, when players are not entirely selfless but receive a "warm glow" feeling from contributing (Andreoni, 1990), or that contribution signals information regarding wealth or income of players engaged in status competition (Glazer and Konrad, 1996). In the economic analysis of international environmental agreements it is obvious that if every player takes the benefits of its own abatement on others fully into account when determining their own behavior, the social optimum—that is, full cooperation—will emerge. But even when concern for others plays only a small role the effects on cooperation may be large. Introducing even a little altruism may give rise to a much higher participation in climate policy (van der Pol et al., 2012). Similarly, a preference for "fair burden sharing" of mitigation may stabilize full cooperation (Lange and Vogt, 2003).

The magnitude of people's willingness to take the fate of others into account in their decisions is an exogenous assumption in most economic analyses. It is usually assumed that this willingness is zero, that is, agents base their decisions on pure self-interest. However, the concern for climate impacts on others is an endogenous issue in the public debate about intertemporal and interregional impacts of climate change and fairness. In these debates various questions arise. For example: How does a citizen in the European Union or the United States value the risk of submergence of low-lying islands such as the Maldives, possibly prior to the end of the 21st century? In the terminology of Keohane (1984), to what degree do people adopt a cosmopolitan welfare function in making their decisions? Do rich countries accept the claim that their historically high emissions oblige them to adopt more stringent abatement efforts? Is there a "moral incentive" to refrain from free riding? Ultimately, the behavioral consequences from these normative considerations are empirical questions (notably, Lange et al. [2007] is a rare empirical inquiry into the normative principles of actors in international climate policy). An open societal discussion of ethical issues, where each individual and each community is free to make an informed decision on her ethical preferences, is the proper place to deal with these normative considerations in policy. It seems rational that societies where a majority of citizens are willing to take such considerations into account and aim to convince citizens in other regions to act similarly would signal their preference to these other regions by acting as good examples as to how a sensible climate policy portfolio may be deployed in their own backyards.

12.5 Think Globally, Act Locally? The Challenge of Polycentric Governance of Global Commons

The review of the standard game theory literature in the previous section indicated that there are certain incentives for regions to act as first movers in climate policy, and that transfers, sanctions, and in particular repeated interactions and ethical considerations can make a substantial difference to whether cooperative climate policy is feasible. Elinor Ostrom and the literature on fiscal decentralization and fiscal federalism offer additional perspectives indicating that the cooperation problem in climate policy may not be insurmountable. Arguing that local mitigation action can facilitate international cooperation, Ostrom (2010) challenges the conventional wisdom that free riding, carbon leakage, and the green paradox preclude options for unilateral action. She suggests that a polycentric governance approach that recognizes the existence of multiple political actors at different levels provides a more promising and realistic framework to analyze real word climate policy, as opposed to the standard view of centralized nation states as the key agents of policymaking.

The perspective suggested by Ostrom has analytically been developed to some extent in the literature on *vertical* fiscal decentralization on the one hand and *horizontal* fiscal federalism on the other (for an overview in the environmental policy context see Dalmazzone, 2006). In contrast to the literature on international environmental agreements, the literature on vertical fiscal decentralization does not assume a unitary government but acknowledges the dispersed allocation of power to adopt environmental policies at different levels (e.g., national, regional, and subregional) of governance. It explores the interactions between these different levels and the potential of decentralizing policy in order to reduce mitigation costs. Such reductions of mitigation costs might both enable more ambitious unilateral emission reductions and reduce the incentives for free riding at the international level. The literature on horizontal fiscal federalism, on the other hand, analyzes the interaction of unitary actors located on the same level of government, taking into account different degrees of mobility of capital and population. A prominent example is tax competition between countries or between individual regions within a country. For the case of transboundary environmental problems, this literature derives ideal conditions under which efficient internalization of externalities is feasible even without an explicit global environmental agreement (Hoel and Shapiro, 2003).

12.5.1 Vertical Fiscal Decentralization

The literature on *vertical fiscal decentralization* analyzes the optimal deployment and design of policy instruments at different levels of governance. Conceptually, efficiency gains from fiscal decentralization can result from the exploitation of asymmetric local and regional preferences for mitigation. In the climate policy context, the underlying reasons for diverse preferences among the population may be social norms or self-interested cost–benefit calculations, including co-benefits of climate policy on local air quality (see Section 12.4.2), or strategic behavior vis-à-vis higher levels of government. According to the so-called Oates theorem (Oates, 1999), vertical fiscal decentralization is welfare enhancing if it enables diverse preferences for mitigation (compared to the federal and global levels) to be taken into account in the policy instrument setup.

Indeed, the climate policy efforts of various states (e.g., California and the RGGI in the United States) and cities indicate that preferences at the local level might differ substantially from preferences at the international or national scale. A key aspect of the vertical fiscal decentralization perspective is that policy efficiency crucially hinges on the efficient division of responsibilities as well as policies and, correspondingly, on the transmission of incentives across different government levels (Dalmazzone, 2006). Recent case studies on vertical climate federalism argue that current climate policy structures within the United States and European Union are inefficient in this respect, as the best strategic response of decision makers located at lower level of governance to policies set at the top level could be insufficient to ensure full pass-through of the price signals to consumers (Shobe and Burtraw, 2012). That is, a carbon price might not pose the right incentive for local governments to adopt measures such as zoning laws, building codes, or road charges to target additional market failures. Likewise, Williams (2012) argues that for a pollutant that causes both local and transboundary damages, a federal-level pollution tax might lead to a more efficient outcome than federal command-and-control policy or a federal system of tradable permits, as the former poses the greatest incentives for governments on the local level to implement additional efficiency-enhancing measures. Also, states and municipalities can have an incentive to strategically withhold assent to ambitious national climate policy goals to receive a larger share of the national climate rent (Shobe and Burtraw, 2012), thus replicating some collective action and distributional challenges observed in international negotiations (see Sections 12.3 and 12.4) on the subnational level. One interesting avenue for future research in this field is to investigate the potential for improving coordination, for example, between EU-level and national member state policies such as the EU ETS and national renewable subsidy schemes to reduce mitigation costs below current levels.

A second promise offered by applying the fiscal decentralization perspective to climate policy is the possibility of local experiments leading to examples of best practices, which can be scaled up after their success has been proven. Decentralization might induce more policy innovation because a higher degree of heterogeneity of local governments can lead to multiple parallel experimental policies (Strumpf, 2002). Such learning-by-doing efforts to reduce cost uncertainty might also reduce aggregate mitigation costs substantially (Ostrom, 2012), but further conceptual work remains to be done.

In general, until now there are basically no quantitative estimates exploring the potential for mitigation cost reductions from a proper design of vertical incentives structures and policies. This appears to be an interesting field for future research (Shobe and Burtraw, 2012).

12.5.2 Horizontal Fiscal Federalism

Analyzing the circumstances under which independent jurisdictions can provide local or global public goods in absence of a central government, *horizontal fiscal federalism* offers a strand of research that is complementary to the literature on IEAs reviewed in Section 12.4. In contrast to the literature on IEAs, horizontal fiscal federalism assumes independent jurisdictions competing for mobile population and capital by means of policy instruments such as taxes, subsidies, and environmental standards. Some of the models developed in this field suggest that efficient regulation of transboundary pollution is possible even without explicit cooperative agreements, assuming that population is perfectly mobile and jurisdictions anticipate the migration response to their own policy choices (Hoel and Shapiro, 2003). Other models providing a more detailed description of the design of policy instruments (Wellisch, 1994, 1995, 2000) show that even a global environmental public good can be provided at a Pareto-optimal level if first, capital and population are mobile, and second if there is a fixed supply of land that is taxed or on which governments can impose a head tax to the residents. However, if migration of population entails costs, transfers between regions are required for Pareto-optimal provision.

To a certain extent these models can be regarded as extending the scope of the Henry George Theorem—well established in urban economics (Fujita and Thisse, 2002)—claiming that local public goods can be provided at an optimal level even without a central authority. If households are mobile their preferences for local public goods are capitalized in the land rent because competing jurisdictions supply local public goods in order to attract people. Increasing population increases land rents because of the fixed supply of land, which in turn decreases the attractiveness of the jurisdiction for mobile labor. In equilibrium taxing the land rent is sufficient to finance the optimal amount of the local public good. In this setting "voting with the feet" or "Tiebout sorting" (Tiebout, 1956) allows for an optimal revelation of preferences.

The intuition behind transferring this strand of literature to the climate context is that citizens will move to jurisdictions that provide local and global public goods according to their preferences. Governments take these preferences and the migration response of citizens into account when devising their policies. As a result, the mobility of capital and households combined with taxation of land rents substitutes for Coasian bargaining or a utilitarian policy by a central world government. Availability of sufficient policy instruments, the absence of market power and the perfect mobility of production factors results in a Nash equilibrium that is Pareto-optimal. Admittedly, these conditions are unlikely to be met in reality. However, the fiscal federalism literature illustrates that the assumption of immobile production factors used in the IEA literature is not innocent.

A second branch of the fiscal federalism literature adopts the more realistic assumption that only capital is mobile whereas population is immobile. In this setting the familiar result reappears with competition between jurisdictions precluding the efficient provision of even local public goods due to a so-called "race to the bottom" (Wilson, 1986; Zodrow and Mieszkowski, 1986). Without intergovernmental cooperation, the problem of local public good provision cannot be resolved. By contrast, Ogawa and Wildasin (2009) claim that in a setting with immobile households and mobile capital decentralized policymaking can indeed lead to efficient resource allocation and global public good provision. However, Eichner and Runkel (2012) challenge this result arguing that the Ogawa–Wildasin assumption of fixed capital supply (and thus aggregate global emissions) even in the presence of climate policy–induced changes in the net rate of return to capital is not very plausible. Eichner and Runkel demonstrate that if the capital supply elasticity with regard to the net rate of return to capital is—more plausibly so—strictly positive (i.e., capital stock dynamics are affected by climate policy), decentralized capital taxation and the provision of the global public good are inefficiently low. This analysis reconfirms the basic insight of this strand of literature in its argumentation that mobile capital and immobile households lead to suboptimal levels of public goods and capital taxes.

As an avenue for future research in this field, it seems interesting to combine the analysis of local climate policy choice with local public infrastructure investment decisions. Such infrastructure (local public good) investments, financed, for example, by a local carbon tax that simultaneously provides a global public good, will enhance local productivity, thus attracting foreign capital. This effect may counterbalance the negative impact of capital mobility on optimal local tax rates and the provision of local and global public goods at least to some extent.

12.5.3 Outlook for Theories of Polycentric Governance

To conclude, the quest for an efficient substitute for perfect global and intertemporal Coasian bargaining or a central world government is a difficult one. Still, the approaches developed by vertical fiscal decentralization and horizontal fiscal federalism may indicate interesting directions for further analysis for two reasons. First, in these settings national governments have more realistic taxation instruments at their disposal. As such, this enables analyzing potential linkages between climate policy and public finance considerations. Second, the broader scope of the policy instrument portfolio facilitates the understanding of second-best climate policies, for example, harnessing co-benefits from climate policy. Accounting for second-best settings will not automatically resolve social dilemma situations. However, it might indicate rationales and options that reduce the magnitude of the challenge for international climate negotiations. At the end of the day, national and subnational action can likely not fully substitute international cooperation. However, it seems worthwhile to explore options how international cooperation can be complemented and enhanced by polycentric governance of the planet's atmosphere.

References

Afionis, S. (2011). The European Union as a negotiator in the international climate change regime. *International Environmental Agreements: Politics, Law and Economics*, 11(4): 341–360.

Altamirano-Cabrera, J., and Finus, M. (2006). Permit trading and stability of international climate agreements. *Journal of Applied Economics*, 9, 19–47.

Andreoni, J. (1990). Impure altruism and donations to public goods: A theory of warm-glow giving? *Economic Journal, 100*(401), 464–477.

Aquinas, Thomas. (1265–1274). *Summa Theologiae* II/II, qu.66. http://www.newadvent.org/summa/3066.htm

Archer, D., Eby, M., Brovkin, V., Ridgwell, A., Cao, L., Mikolajewicz, U., Caldeira, K., Matsumoto, K., Munhoven, G., Montenegro, A., and Tokos, K. (2009). Atmospheric lifetime of fossil fuel carbon dioxide. *Annual Review of Earth and Planetary Sciences, 37*, 117–134.

Asheim, G., and Holtsmark, B. (2009). Renegotiation-proof climate agreements with full participation: Conditions for Pareto-efficiency. *Environmental and Resource Economics, 43*, 519–533.

Barrett, S. (1994). Self-enforcing international environmental agreements. *Oxford Economic Papers, 46*, 878–894.

Barrett, S. (1997). The strategy of trade sanctions in international environmental agreements. *Resource and Energy Economics, 19*, 345–361.

Barrett, S. (2006). Climate treaties and "breakthrough" technologies. *The American Economic Review, 96*(2), 22–25.

Barrett, S. (2007). *Why Cooperate? The Incentive to Provide Global Public Goods.* Oxford: Oxford University Press.

Barrett, S. (2010). Climate change and international trade: Lessons on their linkage from international environmental agreements. Working Paper prepared for Conference on Climate Change, Trade and Competitiveness: Issues for the WTO, World Trade Organization, Geneva, 16–18 June 2010.

Barrett, S. (2011). Rethinking climate change governance and its relationship to the world trading system. The World Economy. *Wiley Online Library, 34*, 1863–1882.

Baumol, W. J., and Oates, W. E. (1975). *The Theory of Environmental Policy.* Cambridge, UK: Cambridge University Press.

BMU/UBA (2011). Umweltwirtschaftsbericht 2011. Daten und Fakten für Deutschland.

Bollen, J., Guay, B., Jamet, S., Corfee-Morlot, J. (2009). Co-benefits of climate change mitigation policies: Literature review and new results. OECD Economics Department Working Papers, No. 693. Paris: OECD Publishing.

Botteon, M., and Carraro, C. (1998). Strategies for environmental negotiations: Issue linkage with heterogeneous countries. In C. Hanley and H. Folmer (eds.), *Game Theory and the Environment*, pp. 180–200. Cheltenham, UK: Edward Elgar.

Botteon, M., and Carraro, C. (2001). Environmental coalitions with heterogeneous countries: Burden sharing and carbon leakage. In A. Ulph (ed.), *Environmental Policy, International Agreements and International Trade*, pp. 26–55, Oxford: Oxford University Press.

Brandt, U. S. (2004). Unilateral actions, the case of international environmental problems. *Resource and Energy Economics, 26*(4), 373–391.

Brazil (1997). Proposed elements of a protocol to the United Nations Framework Convention on Climate Change. Presented by Brazil in response to the Berlin mandate. FCCC/AGBM/1997/MISC.1/Add.3.

Burtraw, D., Palmer, K. L., and Kahn, D. (2009a). A symmetric safety valve. Discussion Paper 09-06. Washington, DC: Resources for the Future.

Burtraw, D., Sweeney, R., and Walls, M. (2009b). The incidence of U.S. climate policy: Alternative uses of revenues from a cap-and-trade auction. Discussion Paper 09-17-REV. Washington, DC: Resources for the Future.

Canadell, J. G., Le Quéré, C., Raupach, M. R., Field, C. B., Buitenhuis, E. T., Ciais, P., Conway, T. J., Gillett, N. P., Houghton, R. A., and Marland, G. (2007). Contributions to accelerating atmospheric CO_2 growth from economic activity, carbon intensity, and efficiency of natural sinks. *Proceedings of the National Academy of Sciences of the USA, 104*, 18866–18870.

Caney, S. (2009). Justice and the distribution of greenhouse gas emissions. *Journal of Global Ethics, 5*(2), 125–146.

Caparrós A., Péreau J.-C., and Tazdaït, T. (2004). North-South climate change negotiations: A sequential game with asymmetric information. *Public Choice, 121*(3), 455–480.

Carbon Dioxide Analysis Information Center (CDIAC). (2012). Preliminary 2010 global & national estimates by extrapolation. http://cdiac.ornl.gov/trends/emis/prelim_2009_2010_estimates.html

Carraro, C., and Siniscalco, D. (1993). Strategies for the international protection of the environment. *Journal of Public Economics, 52*, 309–328.

Carraro, C., Eyckmans, J., and Finus, M. (2006). Optimal transfers and participation decisions in international environmental agreements. *Review of International Organizations, 1*, 379–396.

Chroust, A. H., and Affeldt, R. J. (1951). The problem of private property according to St. Thomas Aquinas. *Marquette Law Review, 34*(3), 151–182.

CIA World Factbook. (2012). Global economy. https://www.cia.gov/library/publications/the-world-factbook/geos/xx.html

Creutzig, F., McGlynn, E., Minx, J., and Edenhofer, O. (2011). Climate policies for road transport revisited (I): Evaluation of the current framework. *Energy Policy, 39*(5), 2396–2406.

Dalmazzone, S. (2006). Decentralization and the environment. In E. Ahmad and G. Brosio (eds.), *Handbook of Fiscal Federalism*, pp. 459–477. Cheltenham, UK: Edward Elgar.

Davis, S. J., Caldeira, K., and Matthews, H. D. (2010). Future CO_2 emissions and climate change from existing energy infrastructure. *Science, 10*(5997), 1330–1333.

den Elzen, M., and Lucas, P. (2005). The FAIR model: A tool to analyse environmental and costs implications of regimes of future commitments. *Environmental Modeling and Assessment, 10*, 115–134.

Depledge, J. (2008). Striving for no: Saudi Arabia in the climate change regime. *Global Environmental Politics, 8*(4), 9–35.

Edenhofer, O., and Kalkuhl, M. (2011). When do increasing carbon taxes accelerate global warming? A note on the green paradox. *Energy Policy, 39*, 2208–2212.

Edenhofer, O., Carraro, C., Koehler, J., and Grubb, M., eds. (2006). Endogenous technological change and the economics of atmospheric stabilisation. *The Energy Journal, 27* (Special Issue).

Eichner, T., and Runkel, M. (2012). Interjurisdictional spillovers, decentralized policymaking, and the elasticity of capital supply. *American Economic Review, 102*(5), 2349–2357.

Ellerman, A. D., Convery, F. J., and de Perthius, C. (2010). *Pricing Carbon: The European Union Emissions Trading Scheme.* Cambridge, UK: Cambridge University Press.

Enkvist, P.-A., Nauclér, T., and Rosander, J. (2007). A cost curve for greenhouse gas reduction. *McKinsey Quarterly*, February (1), 34–45.

Eyckmans, J., and Tulkens, H. (2003). Simulating coalitionally stable burden sharing agreements for the climate change problem. *Resource and Energy Economics, 25*, 299–327.

Fischer, C., and Newell, R. G. (2008). Environmental and technology policies for climate mitigation. *Journal of Environmental Economics and Management, 55*(2), 142–162.

Freeman, M. C. (2010). Yes, we should discount the far-distant future at its lowest possible rate: A resolution of the Weitzman-Gollier puzzle. *Economics* E-journal, *4*.

Froyn, C., and Hovi, J. (2008). A climate agreement with full participation. *Economics Letters, 99*, 317–319.

Fujita, M., and Thisse, J. F. (2002). *Economics of Agglomeration: Cities, Industrial Location, and Regional Growth.* Cambridge, UK: Cambridge University Press.

Gardiner, S. M. (2004). Ethics and global climate change. *Ethics, 114*(3), 555–598.

Glazer, A., and Konrad, K. A. (1996). A signaling explanation for charity. *American Economic Review, 86*(4), 1019–1028.

Gollier, C., and Weitzman, M. L. (2010). How should the distant future be discounted when discount rates are uncertain? *Economics Letters, 107*(3), 350–353.

Grainger, C., and Kolstad, C. (2010). Who pays a price on carbon? *Environmental & Resource Economics, 46*(3), 359–376.

Habla, W., and Winkler, R. (2011). Political influence on non-cooperative international climate policy. Working Paper No. 11-06. Bern, Switzerland: Department of Economics, University of Bern.

Heal, G. (1999). New strategies for the provision of global public goods: Learning from international environmental challenges. In I. Kaul, I. Grunberg, and M. A. Stern (eds.), *Global Public Goods: International Cooperation in the 21st Century*, pp. 220–239. Oxford: Oxford University Press.

Heal, G., Tarui, N. (2010): Investment and emission control under technology and pollution externalities. *Resource and Energy Economics, 32*(1), 1–14.

Heitzig, J., Lessmann, K., and Zou, Y. (2011). Self-enforcing strategies to deter free-riding in the climate change mitigation game and other repeated public good games. *Proceedings of the National Academy of Sciences of the USA, 108*, 15739–15744.

Hoel, M. (1992). International environment conventions: The case of uniform reductions of emissions. *Environmental and Resource Economics, 2*, 141–159.

Hoel, M., and De Zeeuw, A. (2010). Can a focus on breakthrough technologies improve the performance of international environmental agreements? *Environmental and Resource Economics, 47*, 395–406.

Hoel, M., and Shapiro, P. (2003). Population mobility and transboundary environmental problems. *Journal of Public Economics, 87*(5–6), 1013–1024.

IPCC. (2011). Summary for Policymakers. In IPCC Special Report on Renewable Energy Sources and Climate Change Mitigation [O. Edenhofer, R. Pichs-Madruga, Y. Sokona, K. Seyboth, P. Matschoss, S. Kadner, T. Zwickel, P. Eickemeier, G. Hansen, S. Schlomer, C. von Stechow (eds.)], Cambridge University Press, Cambridge, United Kingdom and New York, NY, USA, pp. 3–26.

IPCC. (2012). Managing the Risks of Extreme Events and Disasters to Advance Climate Change Adaptation. A Special Report of Working Groups I and II of the Intergovernmental Panel on Climate Change [Field, C.B., V. Barros, T.F. Stocker, D. Qin, D.J. Dokken, K.L. Ebi, M.D. Mastrandrea, K.J. Mach, G.-K. Plattner, S.K. Allen, M. Tignor, and P.M. Midgley (eds.)]. Cambridge University Press, Cambridge, UK, and New York, NY, USA, 582 pp.

IPCC, 2014: Summary for Policymakers, In: Climate Change 2014, Mitigation of Climate Change. Contribution of Working Group III to the Fifth Assessment Report of the Intergovernmental Panel on Climate Change [Edenhofer, O., R. Pichs-Madruga, Y. Sokona, E. Farahani, S. Kadner, K. Seyboth, A. Adler, I. Baum, S. Brunner, P. Eickemeier, B. Kriemann, J. Savolainen, S. Schlömer, C. von Stechow, T. Zwickel and J.C. Minx (eds.)]. Cambridge University Press, Cambridge, United Kingdom and New York, NY, USA.

Jaffe, A., Newell, R. G., and Stavins, R. N. (2005). A tale of two market failures: Technology and environmental policy. *Ecological Economics, 54*(2–3), 164–174.

Jakob, M., and Lessmann, K. (2012). Signaling in international environmental agreements: The case of early and delayed action. *International Environmental Agreements: Policy, Law, and Economics, 12*(4), 309–325.

Jakob, M., Luderer, G., Steckel, J., Tavoni, M., and Monjon, S. (2012). Time to act now? Assessing the costs of delaying climate measures and benefits of early action. *Climatic Change, 114*(1), 79–99.

Jotzo, F. (2012). Australia's carbon price. *Nature Climate Change, 2*, 475–476.

Kalkuhl, M., and Edenhofer, O. (2010). Prices vs. quantities and the intertemporal dynamics of the climate rent. CESifo Working Paper No. 3044.

Kalkuhl, M., Edenhofer, O., and Lessmann, K. (2011). Renewable energy subsidies: Second-best policy or fatal aberration for mitigation? FEEM Working Paper 48.2011.

Kalkuhl, M., Edenhofer, O., and Lessmann, K. (2012). Learning or lock-in: Optimal technology policies to support mitigation. *Resource and Energy Economics, 34*(1), 1–23.

Karp, L., and Zhang, J. (2005). Regulation of stock externalities with correlated costs. *Environmental and Resource Economics, 32*, 273–299.

Keohane, R. (1984). *After Hegemony: Cooperation and Discord in the World Political Economy.* Princeton, NJ: Princeton University Press.

Knopf, B., Kowarsch, M., Lüken, M., Edenhofer, O., and Luderer, G. (2012). A global carbon market and the allocation of emission rights. In O. Edenhofer, J. Wallacher, H. Lotze-Campen, M. Reder, B. Knopf, and J. Müller (eds.), *Climate Change, Justice and Sustainability*, pp. 269–286. New York: Springer Science+Business Media.

Knopf, B., Luderer, G., and Edenhofer, O. (2011). Exploring the feasibility of low stabilization targets. *Wiley Interdisciplinary Reviews of Climate Change, 2*(4), 617–626.

Lange, A., and Vogt, C. (2003): Cooperation in International Environmental Negotiations due to a Preference for Equity. *Journal of Public Economics, 87*, 2049–2067.

Lange, A., Vogt, C., and Ziegler, A. (2007). On the importance of equity in international climate policy: An empirical analysis. *Energy Economics, 29*(3), 545–562.

Leiby, P., and Rubin, J. (2001). Intertemporal permit trading for the control of greenhouse gas emissions. *Environmental and Resource Economics, 19*, 229–256.

Leimbach, M., Bauer, N., Baumstark, L., Lüken, M., and Edenhofer, O. (2010). Technological change and international trade: Insights from REMIND-R. *The Energy Journal, 31*, 109–136.

Lenton, T. M., Held, H., Kriegler, E., Hall, J. W., Lucht, W., Rahmstorf, S., and Schellnhuber, H. J. (2008). Tipping elements in the Earth's climate system. *Proceedings of the National Academy of Sciences of the USA, 105*, 1786–1793.

Lessmann, K., and Edenhofer, O. (2011). Research cooperation and international standards in a model of coalition stability. *Resource and Energy Economics, 33*, 36–54.

Lessmann, K., Marschinski, R., and Edenhofer, O. (2009). The effects of tariffs on coalition formation in a dynamic global warming game. *Economic Modeling*, 641–649.

Lessmann, K., Marschinski, R., Finus, M., and Edenhofer, O. (2010). Emission trading with non-signatories in a climate agreement. An analysis of coalition stability. The Manchester School. doi: 10.1111/manc.12045.

Levermann, A., Bamber, J., Drijfhout, S., Ganopolski, A., Haeberli, W., Harris, N. R. P., Huss, M., Krüger, K., Lenton, T., Lindsay, R. W., Notz, D., Wadhams, P., and Weber, S. (2012). Potential climatic transitions with profound impact on Europe—Review of the current state of six "tipping" elements of the climate system. *Climatic Change, 110*, 845–878.

Locke, J. (2003 [1689]). *Two Treatises on Government*. New Haven, CT: Yale University Press.

Luderer, G., Bosetti, V., Jakob, M., Leimbach, M., Steckel, J., Waisman, H., and Edenhofer, O. (2012). The economics of decarbonizing the energy system—Results and insights from the RECIPE model intercomparison. *Climatic Change, 114*(1), 9–37.

McCrone, A., Usher, E., Sonntag-O'Brien, V., Moslener, U., Grüning, C. (2012). Global trends in renewable energy investments 2012. Frankfurt School of Finance and Management, UNEP, and Bloomberg.

McGinty, M. (2007). International environmental agreements among asymmetric nations. *Oxford Economic Papers, 59*, 45–62.

Meinshausen, M., Meinshausen, N., Hare, W., Raper, S., Frieler, K., Knutti, R., Frame, D., and Allen, M. (2009). Greenhouse-gas emission targets for limiting global warming to 2°C. *Nature, 458*, 1158–1163.

Meinshausen, M., Smith, S., Calvin, K., Daniel, J., Kainuma, M., Lamarque, J. F., Matsumoto, K., Montzka, S., Raper, S., Riahi, K., Thomson, A., Velders, G., and van Vuuren, D. P. (2011). The RCP greenhouse gas concentrations and their extensions from 1765 to 2300. *Climatic Change, 109*(1), 213–241.

Meyer, L. H., and Roser, D. (2006). Distributive justice and climate change: The allocation of emission rights. *Analyse & Kritik, 28*, 223–249.

Miceli, T. J., and Segerson, K. (2007). The economics of eminent domain: Private property, public use, and just compensation. *Foundations and Trends in Macroeconomics, 3*(4), 275–329.

Milinski, M., Semmann, D., and Krambeck, H. (2002). Reputation helps solve the "tragedy of the commons." *Nature, 415*, 424–426.

Milinski, M., Semmann, D., Krambeck, H., and Marotzke, J. (2006). Stabilizing the Earth's climate is not a losing game: Supporting evidence from public goods experiments *Proceedings of the National Academy of Sciences of the USA, 103*, 3994–3998.

Millner, A. (2011). On welfare frameworks and catastrophic climate risks. http://are.berkeley.edu/~a.millner/Antony_Millner/Research.html

Mouawad, J., and Revkin, A. C. (2009). Saudis seek payments for any drop in oil revenues. *New York Times*, October 14, B1.

Nagashima, M., Dellink, R., Van Ierland, E., and Weikard, H. (2009). Stability of international climate coalitions—A comparison of transfer schemes. *Ecological Economics, 68*, 1476–1487.

Newell, G. R., and Pizer, W. A. (2003). Regulating stock externalities under uncertainty. *Journal of Environmental Economics and Management, 45*, 416–432.

Newell, R., Pizer, W., and Zhang, J. (2005). Managing permit markets to stabilize prices. *Environmental & Resource Economics, 31*(2), 133–157.

Newell, R. G., Jaffe, A. B., and Stavins, R. N. (2006). The effects of economic and policy incentives on carbon mitigation technologies. *Energy Economics, 28*(5–6), 563–578.

Nordhaus, W. D. (2007). A review of the Stern Review on the Economics of Climate Change. *Journal of Economic Literature, 45*(3), 686–702.

Nozick, R. (1974): *Anarchy, State and Utopia.* New York: Basic Books.

Oates, W. E. (1999). An essay on fiscal federalism. *Journal of Economic Literature, 37*(3), 1120–1149.

Oberthür, S., and Pallemaerts, M., eds. (2011). *The New Climate Policies of the European Union: Internal Legislation and Climate Diplomacy.* Brussels: VUB Press.

Ogawa, H., and Wildasin, D. E. (2009). Think locally, act locally: Spillovers, spillbacks, and efficient decentralized policymaking. *American Economic Review, 99*(4), 1206–1217.

Ostrom, E. (2003). Towards a behavioral theory linking trust, reciprocity and reputation. In E. Ostrom and S. Walker (eds.), *Trust and Reciprocity.* New York: Russell Sage Foundation.

Ostrom, E. (2010). Polycentric systems for coping with collective action and global environmental change. *Global Environmental Change, 20*, 550–557.

Ostrom, E. (2012). Nested externalities and polycentric institutions: Must we wait for global solutions to climate change before taking actions at other scales? *Economic Theory, 49*(2), 353–369.

Pahle, M., Lessmann, K., Edenhofer, O., and Bauer, N. (2012). Investments in imperfect power markets under carbon pricing: A case study based analysis. *The Energy Journal, 34*(4), 199–227.

Perez, O. (2005). Multiple regimes, issue linkage, and international cooperation: Exploring the role of the WTO. *University of Pennsylvania Journal of International Economic Law, 26*, 735–778.

Petherick, A. (2012). Sweetening the dragon's breath. *Nature Climate Change, 2*, 309–311.

Pittel, K., and Rübbelke, D. (2008). Climate policy and ancillary benefits: A survey and integration into the modelling of international negotiations on climate change. *Ecological Economics, 68*, 210–220.

Pittel, K., and Rübbelke, D. T. G. (2012). Transitions in the negotiations on climate change: From prisoner's dilemma to chicken and beyond. *International Environmental Agreements: Politics, Law and Economics, 12*, 23–39.

Pizer, W. A. (1999). The optimal choice of climate change policy in the presence of uncertainty. *Resource and Energy Economics, 21*(3–4), 255–287.

Pizer, W. A. (2002). Combining price and quantity controls to mitigate global climate change. *Journal of Public Economics, 85*(3), 409–434.

Raupach, M. R., Marland, G., Ciais, P., Le Quéré, C., Canadell, J. G., Klepper, G., and Field, C. B. (2007). Global and regional drivers of accelerating CO_2 emissions. *Proceedings of the National Academy of Sciences of the USA, 104*, 10288–10293.

Rausch, S., Metcalf, G. E., Reilly, J. M., and Paltsev, S. (2010). Distributional implications of alternative U.S. greenhouse gas control measures. NBER Working Paper 16053.

Rogelj, J., Nabel, J., Chen, C., Hare, W., Markmann, K., Meinshausen, M., Schaeffer, M., Macey, K., and Höhne, N. (2010). Copenhagen Accord pledges are paltry. *Nature, 464*(7292), 1126–1128.

Rose, A., Stevens, B., Edmonds, J., and Wise, M. (1998). International equity and differentiation in global warming policy. An application to tradeable emission permits. *Environmental and Resource Economics, 12*, 25–51.

Rubin, J. D. (1996). A model of intertemporal emission trading, banking, and borrowing. *Journal of Environmental Economics and Management, 31*(3), 269–286.

Schneider, M.T., Traeger, C., and Winkler, R. (2012). Trading off generations: Infinitely lived agent versus OLG. CESifo Working Paper Series 374.

Shobe, W. M., and Burtraw, D. (2012). Rethinking environmental federalism in a warming world. *Climate Change Economics, 3* (4), 1–33.

Sinn, H. W. (2008). Public policies against global warming: A supply side approach. *International Tax and Public Finance, 15*, 360–394.

Steckel, J., Jakob, M., Marschinski, R., and Luderer, G. (2011). From carbonization to decarbonization?—Past trends and future scenarios for China's CO_2 emissions. *Energy Policy, 39*(6), 3443–3455.

Stern, N. (2007). *The Economics of Climate Change.* Cambridge, UK: Cambridge University Press.

Stiglitz, J. E. (2006a). *Making Globalization Work.* New York: W.W. Norton.

Stiglitz, J. E. (2006b). A new agenda for global warming. *The Economists' Voice* 3(7): Art. 3. http://www.bepress.com/ev/vol3/iss7/art3.

Strumpf, K. S. (2002). Does government decentralization increase policy innovation? *Journal of Public Economic Theory, 4*(2), 207–241.

Sugden, R. (1984). Reciprocity: The supply of public goods through voluntary contributions. *Economic Journal, 94*(376), 772–787.

Tiebout, C. (1956). A pure theory of local expenditures. *Journal of Political Economy, 64*(5), 416–424.

UNEP. (2011). Towards a green economy: Pathways to sustainable development and poverty eradication. http://www.unep.org/greeneconomy/greeneconomyreport/tabid/29846/default. aspx

UNFCCC. (1992). United Nations Framework Convention on Climate Change.

UNFCCC. (2010). Ad Hoc Working Group on Long-term Cooperative Action, Thirteenth Session, Cancun, Mexico, November 29–December 10, 2010, Outcome of the Work of the Ad Hoc Working Group on Long-term Cooperative Action Under the Convention, UN Doc.FCCC/AWGLCA/2010/L.7 (December 10, 2010). http://unfccc.int/resource/docs/2010/awglca13/eng/l07.pdf

van der Pol, T.; Weikard, H., and van Ierland, E. (2012). Can altruism stabilise international climate agreements? *Ecological Economics, 81*, 112–120.

Weikard, H. (2009). Cartel stability under an optimal sharing rule: The Manchester School. *Wiley Online Library, 77*, 575–593.

Weitzman, M. L. (1974). Prices vs. quantities. *Review of Economic Studies, 41*(4), 477–491.

Weitzman, M. L. (2007). A review of the Stern Review on the Economics of Climate Change. *Journal of Economic Literature, 45*(3), 703–724.

Weitzman, M. L. (2009). On modeling and interpreting the economics of catastrophic climate change. *The Review of Economics and Statistics, 91*(1), 1–19.

Wellisch, D. (1994). Interregional spillovers in the presence of perfect and imperfect household mobility. *Journal of Public Economics, 55*, 167–184.

Wellisch, D. (1995). Can household mobility solve basic environmental problems? *International Tax and Public Finance, 2*, 245–260.

Wellisch, D. (2000). *Theory of Public Finance in a Federal State.* Cambridge, UK: Cambridge University Press.

WBGU. (2009). German Advisory Council on Global Change, "Solving the climate dilemma: The budget approach." Special Report, Berlin.

Williams, R.C. (2012). Growing state-federal conflicts in environmental policy: The role of market based regulation, *Journal of Public Economics, 96* (11–12), 1092–1099.

Wilson, J. D. (1986). A theory of interregional tax competition. *Journal of Urban Economics, 19*, 296–315.

World Bank. (2012). State and Trend of the Carbon Market 2012. http://siteresources.worldbank.org/INTCARBONFINANCE/Resources/State_and_Trends_2012_Web_Optimized_19035_Cvr&Txt_LR.pdf

WRI. (2012). Climate Analysis Indicators Tool. http://www.wri.org/publications/data-sets

Zodrow, G. R., and Mieszkowski, P. (1986). Pigou, Tiebout, property taxation, and the underprovision of local public goods. *Journal of Urban Economics*, 19(3), 356–370.

CHAPTER 13

THE SOCIAL COST OF CARBON

RICHARD S. J. TOL

13.1 Introduction

Climate policy is one of the controversial issues of our times. Some argue that climate change is not real, not human-made, or not a problem. Others argue that the end of world is nigh. Politicians have announced stringent targets for greenhouse gas (GHG) emission reduction, but have failed to put in policies that would achieve those aims. In this chapter, I take a step back and consider the optimal tax on carbon dioxide (CO_2).

First-best policy is a fiction, but provides a useful yardstick against which to measure more realistic policies. As I argue in the text that follows, the optimal course of action also proves to be a middle ground between policy rhetoric and policy action, and between those who favor drastic action and those who prefer no action.

The chapter proceeds as follows. Section 13.2 discusses estimates of the total impact of climate change. Section 13.3 treats the marginal impacts. Section 13.4 estimates growth rate of the marginal impact. Section 13.5 considers three key assumptions in the estimates of the marginal impact. Section 13.6 concludes the chapter.

13.2 The Impact of Climate Change on Welfare

There are 16 studies and 17 estimates of the *global* welfare impacts of climate change (see Table 13.1). These studies use a variety of methods. Nordhaus (1994a) interviewed a limited number of experts. Fankhauser (1994, 1995), Nordhaus (1994b, 2008), and Tol (1995, 2002a, 2002b) multiplied estimates of the "physical effects" of climate change with estimates of their price. Bosello et al. (2012) use similar estimates of the physical impacts but compute the general equilibrium effects on welfare.

Table 13.1 Estimates of the Welfare Loss Due to Climate Change (as equivalent income loss in percent)

Study	Warming (° C)	Impact (% GDP)
Nordhaus (1994b)	3.0	−1.3
Nordhaus (1994a)	3.0	−3.6
		(−30.0 to 0.0)
Fankhauser (1995)	2.5	−1.4
Tol (1995)	2.5	−1.9
Nordhaus and Yang (1996)[a]	2.5	−1.7
Plamberk and Hope (1996)[a]	2.5	−2.5
		(−0.5 to −11.4)
Mendelsohn et al. (2000a)[a,b,c]	2.5	0.0[b]
		0.1[b]
Nordhaus and Boyer (2000)	2.5	−1.5
Tol (2002a)	1.0	2.3
		(1.0)
Maddison (2003)[a,d]	2.5	−0.1
Rehdanz and Maddison (2005)[a,c]	1.0	−0.4
Hope (2006)[a,e]	2.5	−0.9
		(−2.7 to 0.2)
Nordhaus (2006)	2.5	−0.9
		(0.1)
Nordhaus (2008)	3.0	−2.5
Maddison and Rehdanz (2011)[a]	3.2	−11.5
Bosello et al. (2012)	1.9	−0.5

Estimates of the uncertainty are given in bracket as standard deviations or 95% confidence intervals.
[a]Note that the global results were aggregated by the current author.
[b]The top estimate is for the "experimental" model, the bottom estimate for the "cross-sectional" model.
[c]Mendelsohn et al. include only market impacts.
[d]Maddison considers only nonmarket impacts on households.
[e]The numbers used by Hope are averages of previous estimates by Fankhauser (1995) and Tol (2002a); Stern et al. (2006) adopt the work of Hope.

Mendelsohn et al. (2000a, 2000b), Maddison (2003), and Nordhaus (2006) use observed variations (across space) in prices and expenditures to discern the effect of climate. Rehdanz and Maddison (2005) and Maddison and Rehdanz (2011) use self-reported well-being.

There is broad agreement between these studies in four areas. First, the welfare effect of a doubling of the atmospheric concentration of GHG emissions on the current economy is relatively small—a few percentage points of gross domestic product (GDP). The impact of a century of climate change is roughly equivalent to a year's growth in the global economy.

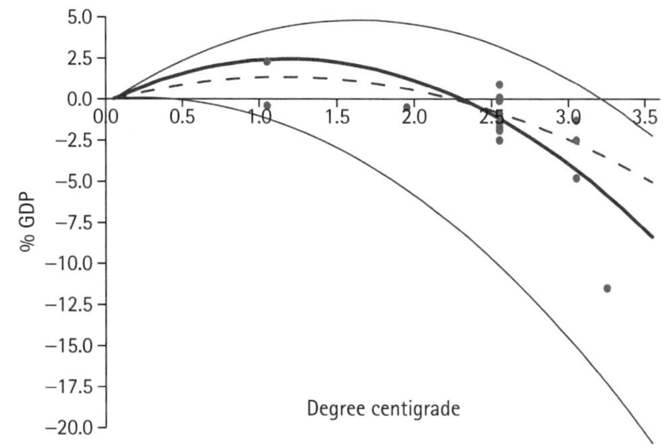

FIGURE 13.1 The 17 estimates of the global economic impact of climate change, expressed as the welfare-equivalent income loss, as a functions of the increase in global mean temperature relative to today. The blue dots represent the estimates. The central line is the least squares fit to the 14 observations: $D = 4.33(1.49)T - 1.92(0.56)T^2, R^2 = 0.62$, where D denotes impact and T denotes temperature. The dotted line is from (Tol, 2009), with the three most recent estimates omitted. The outer lines are the 95% confidence interval, where the standard deviation is the least squares fit to the five reported standard deviations or half confidence intervals (cf. Table 13.1): $S_{\text{optimistic}} = 0.87(0.28)T, R^2 = 0.70, S_{\text{pessimistic}} = 1.79(0.87)T, R^2 = 0.51$ where S is the standard deviation.

Second, the initial benefits of a modest increase in temperature are probably positive, followed by losses as temperatures increase further. Figure 13.1 illustrates this pattern. The initial benefits arise partly from CO_2 fertilization and partly from reduced heating costs and cold-related health problems in temperate zones. However, as the initial warming can no longer be avoided, these are sunk benefits.

Third, as illustrated in Figure 13.1, the uncertainty is vast and right-skewed. Undesirable surprises are more likely than desirable surprises of equal magnitude. For instance, the climate sensitivity—the equilibrium warming due to a doubling of the atmospheric concentration of CO_2—is bounded from below by the laws of physics but it is hard to put an upper bound on its value. It is relatively easy to paint disastrous pictures of the impacts of climate change—rapid sea level rise in the Bay of Bengal leading to mass migration and nuclear war—but difficult to imagine that climate change would make the world prosperous and peaceful. Estimates stop at 3° C of global warming, but climate change may well go beyond that. The uncertainties about the impacts beyond a 3° C warming are compounded by extrapolation (Tol, 2012c).

Fourth, not shown in Figure 13.1, poorer countries tend to be more vulnerable to climate change. Poorer countries have a large share of their economic activity in sectors, such as agriculture, that are directly exposed to the weather. Poorer countries tend to be in hotter places, and thus closer to their biophysical limits and with fewer technical and behavioral analogues. Poorer countries also tend to be worse at adaptation, lacking resources and capacity (Yohe and Tol, 2002).

The number of impact estimates is not commensurate with claims that climate change is the biggest (environmental) problem of humankind. Indeed, the results are not commensurate with such claims. New impact estimates are of a policy rather than an academic interest. Funders of policy-relevant research rarely seek to influence results, but frequently steer the questions asked. The empirical basis for climate change impact estimates is therefore narrow. This increases the uncertainty. The number of researchers involved is smaller still than the number of studies, and they are familiar with each other's work. The agreement on key points may not be a sign of robustness but rather of groupthink.

13.3 The Social Cost of Carbon

The marginal damage cost of CO_2 is defined as the net present value of the incremental damage due to a small increase in CO_2 emissions (Newbold et al., 2010). If evaluated along an arbitrary emissions trajectory, I refer to the marginal damage costs as the social cost of carbon. If evaluated along the optimal emission trajectory, it is of course the Pigou tax (Pigou, 1920).

There are 79 studies of the social cost of carbon, with 759 estimates.[1] The social cost of carbon depends on many things. The total welfare impact of climate change is but one input. Other parameters are the rate of pure time preference, the growth rate of per capita consumption, and the elasticity of marginal utility of consumption. Estimates also differ with regard to projections of CO_2 emissions, the carbon cycle, the rate of warming, and so on. Different studies may calibrate a different curve to the same benchmark estimate of the total impact. Alternative population and economic scenarios also yield different estimates, particularly if vulnerability to climate change is assumed to change with a country or region's degree of development and if forecasts about development patterns are different. Marginal cost estimates further vary with the way in which uncertainty is treated and with how regional effects of climate change are aggregated.

Figure 13.2 plots the 759 estimates as a function of the year of publication. Estimates of the social cost of carbon come in bursts. Six papers on the subject were published in 1996, following the controversies around the Second Assessment Report of the IPCC (Pearce et al., 1996). Only eight papers were published between 1997 and 2002. After that, more papers were published again. Since 2009, 27 papers appeared, mostly in the wake of the US regulation (EPA and NHTSA, 2009).

Besides the estimates, Figure 13.2 shows the mean of previously published estimates as well as the 95% confidence interval (assuming normality). Three features emerge. First, the range is quite large. Second, the range is narrowing over time. The mean of all published estimates is US\$165 per metric tonne of carbon (tC), with a standard deviation of US\$443/tC. The mean of estimates published before 1993 was US\$394/tC,

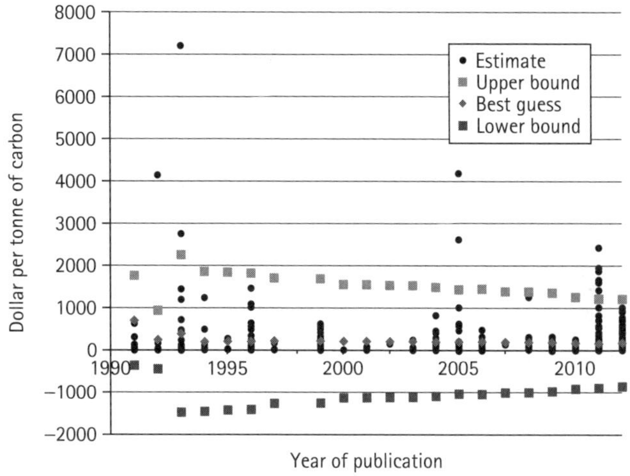

FIGURE 13.2 Estimates of the social cost of carbon (2010 dollar per tonne of carbon for emissions in 2010) as a function of the year of publication; best guesses and bounds are based on the publications in previous years.

with a standard deviation of US$933/tC. There appears to be convergence on an agreed, perhaps even a true value, but it is slow.

The third feature of Figure 13.2 is that there are numerous large positive deviations from the mean but few large negative deviations. New estimates regularly exceed the upper bound but never the lower bound. The assumption of normality, implicit in Figure 13.2, is violated.

I therefore applied a kernel density estimator to the 759 observations (expressed in 2010 US dollars, and pertaining to emissions in the year 2010). I use one parameter from each published estimate of the social cost of carbon (the mode) and the standard deviation of the entire sample[2]—and build up an overall distribution of the estimates and their surrounding uncertainty on this basis.[3]

Figure 13.3 shows the cumulative distribution function of the marginal damage costs of CO_2 emissions. Just looking at the distribution of the medians or modes of these studies is inadequate, because this does not give a fair sense of the uncertainty surrounding these estimates—it is particularly hard to discern the right tail of the distribution, which may dominate the policy analysis (Weitzman, 2009b).

Figure 13.3 reaffirms that uncertainty about the social costs of climate change is very large. Table 13.2 shows some characteristics. The mean estimate in these studies is a marginal cost of carbon of US$422/tC, but the modal estimate is only $91/tC. Of course, this divergence suggests that the mean estimate is driven by some very large estimates. This large divergence is partly explained by the use of different pure rates of time preference in these studies. Figure 13.3 extracts three subsamples from the complete list of studies, each using a different common pure rate of time preference. A higher rate of time preference means that the costs of climate change incurred in the

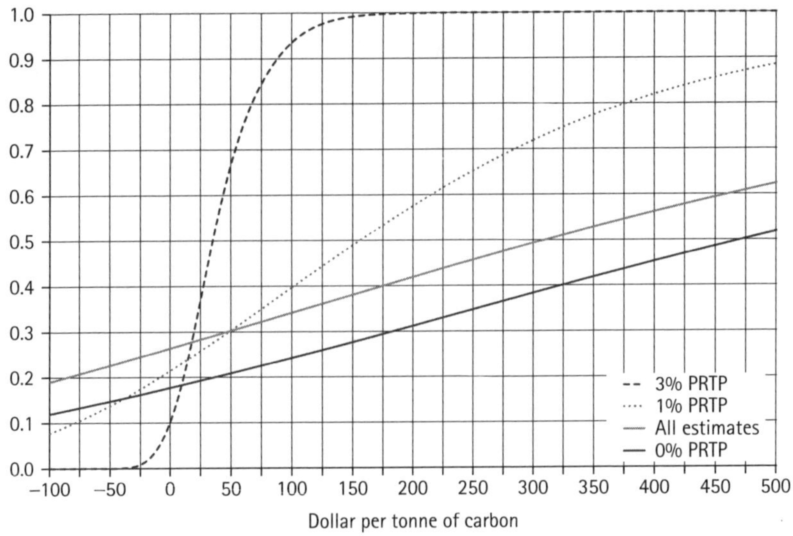

FIGURE 13.3 The cumulative density function of the marginal damage cost of CO_2 emissions for all estimates and for all estimates that use a particular pure rate of time preference (PRTP).

Table 13.2 Selected Characteristics of the 2010 Marginal Damage Cost, the Social Cost of Carbon (SCC) and the Pigou Tax on Carbon (PT)

	Unit	Marginal damage cost				SCC	PT
PRTP		–	3%	1%	0%	3%	3%
Mode	$/tC	91	27	87	240	31	24
Median	$/tC	310	35	156	471	43	30
Mean	$/tC	422	40	208	590	50	34
Standard deviation	$/tC	688	36	285	685	38	32
Skewness	–	2	1	2	2	1	1
Kurtosis	–	13	4	8	11	4	5

future have a lower present value, and so for example, the mean social cost of carbon for the studies with a 3% rate of time preference is US$27/tC, while it is US$240/tC for studies that choose a zero percent rate of time preference. But even when the same discount rate is used, the variation in estimates is large. The means are pulled up by some studies with very high estimated social costs. This effect is stronger for lower discount rates. Figure 13.3 shows that the estimates for the whole sample are dominated by the estimates based on lower discount rates.

Although Table 13.2 reveals a large estimated uncertainty about the social cost of carbon, there is reason to believe that the actual uncertainty is larger still. First of all, the

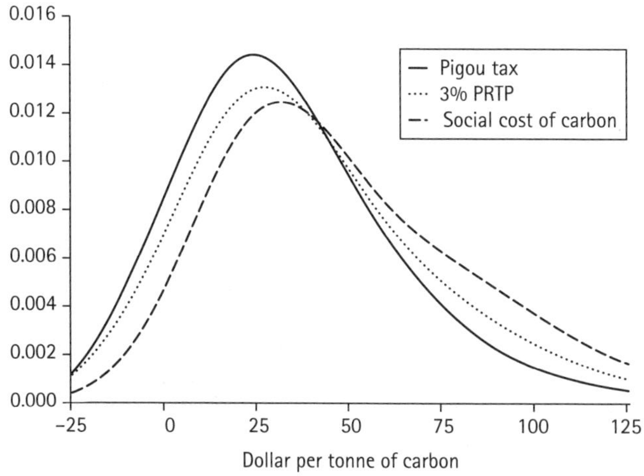

FIGURE 13.4 The probability density function of the marginal damage cost of CO_2 emissions for all estimates with 3% pure rate of time preference, for the estimates along an arbitrary trajectory (social cost of carbon), and for estimates along an optimal trajectory (Pigou tax).

social cost of carbon derives from the total economic impact estimates, of which there are few, incomplete estimates. Second, the researchers who published impact estimates are from a small and close-knit community, who may be subject to group-think, peer pressure, and self-censoring.

Figure 13.4 shows the kernel density, splitting the sample between those studies that use an arbitrary scenario and an optimal scenario. The sample is limited to a 3% pure rate of time preference, the common assumption in optimal control studies. As expected, the Pigou tax is lower than the social cost of carbon—for instance, the median Pigou tax is US$30/tC and the median social cost of carbon is US$43/tC—but the difference is not statistically significant. (Few studies report estimates in both, so we cannot match observations to compute the difference.) The Pigou tax is lower because imposing a carbon tax would reduce emissions and hence impacts as well as marginal impacts.

13.4 The Growth Rate of the Marginal Damage Cost

There are a number of studies of the evolution over time of the marginal damage costs of GHG emissions (see appendix). The results are displayed in Figure 13.5. As mentioned earlier, kernel density estimation is used, assuming a gamma distribution with the sample standard deviation and the estimate as mode.

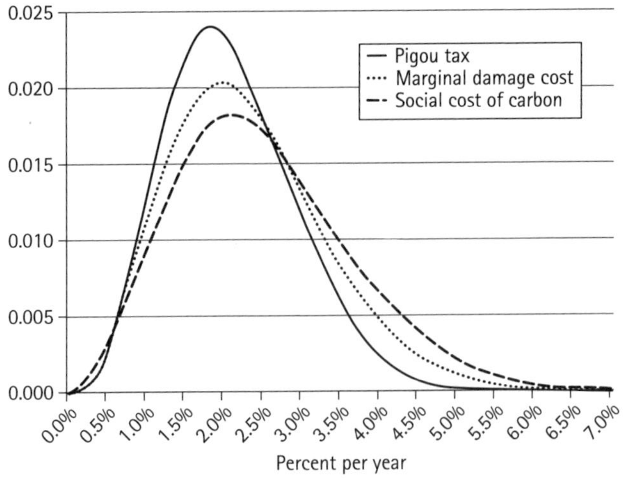

FIGURE 13.5 The kernel density of the annual growth rate of the marginal damage cost of CO_2 emissions, the Pigou tax, and the social cost of carbon.

If we take all studies, the mean growth rate of the marginal damage cost is 2.3% per year, with a standard deviation of 1.4%. If we take all studies that use a no-policy scenario, the mean growth rate of the social cost of carbon is 2.5% with a standard deviation of 1.8%. If we take all studies that use an optimal scenario, the mean growth rate of the Pigou tax is 2.1% with a standard deviation of 0.9%.

The reason for the difference in growth between the social cost of carbon and the Pigou tax is that climate policy affects climate change in the long run but not in the short run. The Pigou tax is therefore not only lower than the social cost of carbon (cf. Figure 13.4), but it also rises more slowly.

13.5 Time, Space, Uncertainty

13.5.1 The Discount Rate

The discount rate is one of economists' favorite topics for discussion. At an axiomatic level, however, things are relatively clear. With an infinite time horizon, an intertemporal welfare function cannot simultaneously satisfy two conditions: either one prefers a situation in which one generation is better off and none worse off (Pareto), or one is sensitive to a reordering of generations (anonymity) (van Liedekerke and Lauwers, 1997). Neither axiomatic violation is pretty, but because generations arrive in order, anonymity is rather artificial and discounted utilitarianism seems to be the better choice (Koopmans 1960, 1966, 1967). Asheim and Mitra (2010) and Zuber and Asheim

(2012) define welfare functions that satisfies anonymity (and hence violate Pareto). Dietz and Asheim (2012) explore the implications for climate policy (while assuming, incongruently, that discounted utility informs all other decisions) and find a modest acceleration of "optimal" emission control. Alvarez-Cuadrado and Van Long (2009) and Chichilnisky (1996) replace anonymity with weaker non-dictatorship axioms. Tol (2012a) applies the former and finds that it has little effect on climate policy and may even increase near-term emissions.

Most of the discussion, however, is focused on (1) the pure rate of time preference in the Ramsey (1928) discount rate and (2) hyperbolic discounting.

Figure 13.2 shows estimates of the marginal damage cost of CO_2 emissions for three alternative pure rates of time preference. Unsurprisingly, a lower pure rate of time preference implies a greater concern about a problem with slow dynamics like climate change. Some authors argue, on ethical grounds, for a low discount rate (Cline, 1992; Stern et al., 2006). Other authors argue, on ethical grounds, that the will of the people should be respected and that all empirical evidence has that people discount future utility (Bradford, 2001; Nordhaus, 2007).

So, there are good reasons to use a high discount rate and good reasons to use a low discount rate. Hyperbolic discounting allows one to use both. The standard discount rate is geometric. The discount factor falls by the same fraction per period. This implies that the relative difference between year 10 and year 11 is the same as the relative difference between year 100 and year 101. That is counterintuitive. Year 10 versus 11 is more like year 100 versus 110. Empirical evidence shows that people indeed use a hyperbolic discount factor (Cropper et al., 1992; Henderson and Bateman, 1995).[4] The discount rate falls as the time horizon expands.[5] The near future of climate policy is then discounted at a rate comparable to other short-term problems, while the far future is not discounted much further. This implies, obviously, that the social cost of carbon is higher (Newell and Pizer, 2003; Guo et al., 2006).

13.5.2 Uncertainty

Uncertainty is one of the key features of the climate problem, and it has played an important role in decision analysis of climate policy (Pindyck, 2012). Most economists would be aware of the standard certainty equivalences. In many cases, a cost–benefit analysis under uncertainty is tantamount to equating the *expected* marginal costs to the *expected* marginal benefits. Because climate change is a large-scale and long-term problem, things are not as simple.

For example, Weitzman (2001), Gollier (2002a, 2002b), and Gollier and Weitzman (2010) show that if there is uncertainty about the pure rate of time preference or future economic growth, then the certainty-equivalent consumption discount rate is not constant, but rather falls over time. One could apply a falling discount rate to the expected costs and benefits. However, a function of two certainty equivalents is not necessarily a certainty equivalent—and certainly not if climate change or climate policy affects the growth path of the economy. Analytical results on certainty equivalents can provide shortcuts in a numerical analysis, but some of the underlying assumptions may be violated. It is better, therefore, to do the full policy analysis under uncertainty and use the analytical results to help interpret the results.

Tol (1999) first showed that the Pigou tax on GHG emissions is larger under risk than under perfect information. This is because of a combination of risk aversion and asymmetric uncertainties (see earlier). Table 13.2 confirms that the mean social cost of carbon is indeed greater than the mode. Therefore, risk increases the desired ambition for GHG emission reduction.

Nordhaus (2008) suggests that the risk premium—the difference between (1) a conversion from utility to money followed by a risk analysis and (2) a risk analysis followed by a conversion to money—is negative because high climate change impact scenarios are more likely high-income, high-emission scenarios. It is unclear whether this result will hold if one assumes that richer countries are less vulnerable to climate change (Anthoff and Tol, 2012).

Besides the uncertainty about model parameters, there is the prospect of things going dramatically wrong because of the climate change. Analysts have used three approaches to incorporate such catastrophic risk. In the first, catastrophe is interpreted as zero utility (Tsur and Zemel, 1996; Gjerde et al., 1999; Baranzini et al., 2003; De Zeeuw and Zemel, 2012). The probability of a catastrophe then acts as a discount rate—and under particular assumptions about the probability density function, the probability of a catastrophe is simply added to the discount rate. This again calls for more stringent emission reduction. This is counterintuitive at first sight: a higher discount rate implying more concern for the future? The explanation is that GHG emission reduction would reduce the catastrophe probability, and hence the effective discount rate. This would increase the net present value.

Keller et al. (2000, 2004, 2005) show that the preceding is true as long as catastrophe can be avoided. If a catastrophe becomes inevitable, its impact is sunk and should not affect policy.

In the second approach to catastrophic risk, a premium is added to the impact of climate change (Stern et al., 2006; Nordhaus 2008), or a highly nonlinear term to the impact function (Manne et al., 1995; Weitzman 2012). The former has the effect of increasing the general level of policy stringency. The latter may imply that a particular degree of global warming is avoided at almost any cost. Both approaches are ad hoc.

Figure 13.6 illustrates the effect of replacing the parabola of Figure 13.1, $I = aT + bT^2$ as proposed by Tol (2009), with $I = aT^2 + bT^6$, as proposed by Weitzman (2012). According to this, initial warming has hardly any impact, intermediate warming is beneficial, and large warming is disastrous. The Weitzman function actually fits the observations better ($R^2 = 0.74$ vs. $R^2 = 0.62$ for the parabola). However, two (rather than one) of the observations are deemed outliers. More importantly, the out-of-sample behavior of the function is driven by a few observations only. Botzen and

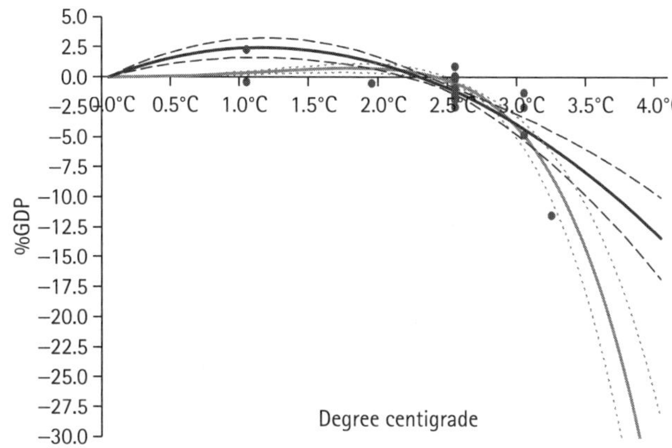

FIGURE 13.6 Estimates of the global economic impact of climate change (blue dots) and two fitted functions: $I = 4.33(1.49)T - 1.92(0.56)T^2$ (red line) and $I = 0.348(0.166)T^2 - 0.0109(0.0025)T^6$ (green line); the thin lines demarcate the 95% confidence interval based on the bootstrapped standard deviation.

van den Bergh (2012) find that a Weitzman damage function has a negligible effect on the Pigou tax in the near term, but that it rises much faster over the century.

The third approach to catastrophic risk is better founded. Weitzman (2009b) shows that, under relatively general assumptions, the expected value of the net present impact of climate change may not exist or be arbitrarily large (see also Tol, 2003; Tol and Yohe, 2006, 2007; Weitzman, 2007, 2009a; Nordhaus, 2011). This could be interpreted as a call for arbitrarily stringent climate policy. That would be wrong (Hennlock, 2009; Pindyck, 2011). Arbitrarily stringent climate policy means that we should stop burning fossil fuel now. Unfortunately, we cannot grow enough food without artificial fertilizers, and we cannot transport that food from the fields to the people without fossil fuels. Arbitrarily stringent climate policy would be a disaster: billions of people would starve to death.

In fact, Weitzman (2009b) shows that one cannot apply expected utility maximization to a problem like climate change. It follows that alternative decision criteria should be applied or perhaps developed. Lempert et al. (1996) and Anthoff and Tol (2010a) attempt to do this, and call for climate policy that is stringent but not arbitrarily so.

13.5.3 Equity Weighting

In Section 13.2, the impacts of climate change are measured in welfare-equivalent income losses. Care needs to be taken that the measure used is indeed a welfare-equivalent. In the older literature on the impacts of climate change, researchers estimated the impact in various regions of the world and added up the dollars to a world total. That is incorrect (Sandmo, 2011).

The starting point of an optimal climate policy is a global welfare function. The marginal damage cost of climate change is the first partial derivative of global welfare to emissions, divided by the marginal utility of consumption. Adding the dollar impacts on regions to a global total assumes that there is neither risk aversion nor inequity aversion—a rather debatable assumption.

The correct welfare equivalent uses so-called equity weights when adding impacts across regions (Azar and Sterner 1996; Fankhauser et al. 1997, 1998). Assuming a utilitarian welfare function—global welfare is the sum of regional utility—and a constant relative risk aversion (CRRA) utility function—regional utility is a power function of average consumption—equity weights equal global average per capita consumption over regional average per capita consumption raised to the power of the rate of risk aversion.

Equity weights are greater (smaller) than one for regions whose income falls below (above) the world average. Typically, impacts are found to be greater in poor countries, so equity weighing increases the global impacts of climate change.

This conclusion is not universal. Anthoff et al. (2009b) find substantial benefits from CO_2 fertilization of agriculture. These benefits are in the near future (because ocean heat diffusion is irrelevant, unlike for temperature) and fall disproportionally on the poor.

Anthoff et al. (2009a) and Anthoff and Tol (2010b) explore equity weights in the context of a regional decision maker. In the latter paper, equity weights vanish if impacts are compensated—that is, there are income transfers between regions. However, monetized impacts are then discounted at a different rate, namely the discount rate of the compensator rather than the compensated.

13.6 CONCLUSIONS

There are few estimates of the total welfare impact of climate change. These estimates suggest that climate change is a problem, but a relatively small problem. The uncertainty about the impact estimates is large, however, and the distribution is uneven. There are many estimates of the marginal damage costs of CO_2 emissions. The estimates span a large range, reflecting both uncertainties in the estimates and ethical choices in the evaluation of the impacts. Using values that are common in public policy, the optimal carbon tax would be about US$34/tC, and growth by 2.1% per year.

A carbon tax of US$34/tC would accelerate energy efficiency improvements and induce a switch from carbon-intensive to carbon-neutral fuel. However, as shown by Tol (2012b), such a carbon tax, if applied uniformly to all GHG emissions from all sectors in all countries, would imply a stabilization of GHG concentrations in excess of 550 ppm CO_2-eq, substantially higher than the declared goals.

Further research should focus on estimates of the total impact of climate change, particularly at higher levels of warming than previously studied. Hitherto omitted impacts should be included, such as energy supply, tourism, and ocean acidification. Current estimates ignore that population growth is endogenous, and the thorny implications for welfare have yet to be assessed.

Notes

1. The studies are listed in the appendix. The data are linked there.
2. In a conventional kernel density estimation, sometimes referred to as Laplacean mixing, the spread parameter is chosen so as to minimize the distance to some assumed density function. This may imply overconfidence. If both the kernels and the target density are Normal, for instance, then the spread parameter is 1.06 times the sample standard deviation over the number of observations to the power 0.2; $1.06 \times 588^{-0.2} = 0.3$.
3. I used the Fisher–Tippett distribution, the only two-parameter, right-skewed, fat-tailed distribution that is defined on the real line. A few published estimates are negative, and given the uncertainties about risk, thick-tailed distributions seem appropriate (Tol, 2003;Weitzman, 2009b). I use weights that reflect the age and quality of the study as well as the importance that the authors attach to the estimate—some estimates are presented as central estimates, others as sensitivity analyses or as upper and lower bounds.
4. A hyperbolic discount factor also emerges as the certainty equivalent of a geometric discount factor. See later.
5. This implies time-inconsistency: decisions are revised because of the mere passing of time.

References

Alvarez-Cuadrado, F., and Van Long, N. (2009). A mixed Bentham-Rawls criterion for intergenerational equity: Theory and implications. *Journal of Environmental Economics and Management, 58*(2), 154–168.

Anthoff, D., and Tol, R. S. J. (forthcoming). Climate Policy under Fat-tailed risk *Annals of Operations Research.*

Anthoff, D., and Tol, R. S. J. (2010b). On international equity weights and national decision making on climate change. *Journal of Environmental Economics and Management, 60*(1), 14–20.

Anthoff, D., and Tol, R. S. J. (2012). Schelling's conjecture on climate and development: A test. In R. W. Hahn and A. M. Ulph (eds.), *Climate Change and Common Sense—Essays in Honour of Tom Schelling*, pp. 260–274. Oxford: Oxford University Press.

Anthoff, D., Hepburn, C. J., and Tol, R. S. J. (2009a). Equity weighting and the marginal damage costs of climate change. *Ecological Economics, 68*(3), 836–849.

Anthoff, D., Tol, R. S. J., and Yohe, G. W. (2009b). Discounting for climate change. *Economics—the Open-Access, Open-Assessment E-Journal, 3*(2009-24), 1–24.

Asheim, G. B., and Mitra, T. (2010). Sustainability and discounted utilitarianism in models of economic growth. *Mathematical Social Sciences, 59*(2), 148–169.

Azar, C., and Sterner, T. (1996). Discounting and distributional considerations in the context of global warming. *Ecological Economics, 19*, 169–184.

Baranzini, A., Chesney, M., and Morisset, J. (2003). The impact of possible climate catastrophes on global warming policy. *Energy Policy, 31*, 691–701.

Bosello, F., Eboli, F., and Pierfederici, R. (2012). Assessing the economic impacts of climate change. *Review of Environment Energy and Economics*, 1–9.

Botzen, W. J. W., and van den Bergh, J. C. J. M. (2012). How sensitive is Nordhaus to Weitzman? Climate policy in DICE with an alternative damage function. *Economics Letters, 117*, 372–374.

Bradford, D. F. (2001). Time, money and tradeoffs. *Nature, 410*, 649–650.

Chichilnisky, G. (1996). An axiomatic approach to sustainable development. *Social Choice and Welfare, 13*(2), 219–248.

Cline, W. R. (1992). *The Economics of Global Warming.* Washington, DC: Institute for International Economics.

Cropper, M. L., Aydede, S. K., and Portney, P. R. (1992). Rates of time preference for saving lives. *American Economic Review, 82*(2), 469–472.

De Zeeuw, A., and Zemel, A. (2012). Regime shifts and uncertainty in pollution control. *Journal of Economic Dynamics and Control, 36*(7), 939–950.

Dietz, S., and Asheim, G. B. (2012). Climate policy under sustainable discounted utilitarianism. *Journal of Environmental Economics and Management, 63*(3), 321–335.

EPA and NHTSA. (2009). Proposed rulemaking to establish light-duty vehicle greenhouse gas emission standards and corporate average fuel efficiency standards. *Federal Register, 74*(187), 49454–49789.

Fankhauser, S. (1994). The economic costs of global warming damage: A survey. *Global Environmental Change, 4*(4), 301–309.

Fankhauser, S. (1995). *Valuing Climate Change—The Economics of the Greenhouse*, 1st ed. London: EarthScan.

Fankhauser, S., Tol, R. S. J., and Pearce, D. W. (1997). The aggregation of climate change damages: A welfare theoretic approach. *Environmental and Resource Economics, 10*(3), 249–266.

Fankhauser, S., Tol, R. S. J., and Pearce, D.W. (1998). Extensions and alternatives to climate change impact valuation: On the critique of IPCC Working Group III's impact estimates. *Environment and Development Economics, 3*, 59–81.

Gjerde, J., Grepperud, S., and Kverndokk, S. (1999). Optimal climate policy under the possibility of a catastrophe. *Resource and Energy Economics, 21*, 289–317.

Gollier, C. (2002a). Discounting an uncertain future. *Journal of Public Economics, 85*, 149–166.

Gollier, C. (2002b). Time horizon and the discount rate. *Journal of Economic Theory, 107*, 463–473.

Gollier, C., and Weitzman, M. L. (2010). 'How should the distant future be discounted when discount rates are uncertain? *Economics Letters, 107*(3), pp. 350–353.

Guo, J., Hepburn, C. J., Tol, R. S. J., and Anthoff, D. (2006). Discounting and the social cost of climate change: A closer look at uncertainty. *Environmental Science & Policy, 9*, 205–216.

Henderson, N., and Bateman, I. J. (1995). Empirical and public choice evidence for hyperbolic social discount rates and the implications for intergenerational discounting. *Environmental and Resource Economics, 5*, 413–423.

Hennlock, M. (2009). *Robust Control in Global Warming Management: An Analytical Dynamic Integrated Assessment.* Working Papers in Economics 354. Gothenburg: Department of Economics, University of Gothenburg.

Hope, C. W. (2006). The marginal impact of CO_2 from PAGE2002: An integrated assessment model incorporating the IPCC's five reasons for concern. *Integrated Assessment Journal, 6*(1), 19–56.

Keller, K., Bolker, B. M., and Bradford, D. F. (2004). Uncertain climate thresholds and optimal economic growth. *Journal of Environmental Economics and Management, 48,* 723–741.

Keller, K., Hall, M., Kim, S.-R., Bradford, D. F., and Oppenheimer, M. (2005). Avoiding dangerous anthropogenic interference with the climate system. *Climatic Change, 73,* 227–238.

Keller, K., Tan, K., Morel, F. M. M., and Bradford, D. F. (2000). Preserving the ocean circulation: Implications for climate policy. *Climatic Change, 47,* 17–43.

Koopmans, T. C. (1960). Stationary ordinal utility and impatience. *Econometrica, 28*(2), 287–309.

Koopmans, T. C. (1966). On the concept of optimal economic growth. In *The Econometric Approach to Development Planning,* pp. 225–300. Amsterdam: North Holland.

Koopmans, T. C. (1967). Objectives, constraints, and outcomes in optimal growth models. *Econometrica, 35,* 1–15.

Lempert, R. J., Schlesinger, M. E., and Bankes, S. C. (1996). When we don't know the costs or the benefits: Adaptive strategies for abating climate change. *Climatic Change, 33,* 235–274.

Maddison, D., and Rehdanz, K. (2011). The impact of climate on life satisfaction. *Ecological Economics, 70*(12), 2437–2445.

Maddison, D. J. (2003). The amenity value of the climate: The household production function approach. *Resource and Energy Economics, 25*(2), 155–175.

Manne, A. S., Mendelsohn, R. O., and Richels, R. G. (1995). MERGE—A model for evaluating regional and global effects of GHG reduction policies. *Energy Policy, 23*(1), 17–34.

Mendelsohn, R. O., Morrison, W. N., Schlesinger, M. E., and Andronova, N. G. (2000a). Country-specific market impacts of climate change. *Climatic Change, 45*(3–4), 553–569.

Mendelsohn, R. O., Schlesinger, M. E., and Williams, L. J. (2000b). Comparing impacts across climate models. *Integrated Assessment, 1*(1), 37–48.

Newbold, S., Griffiths, C., Moore, C. C., Wolverton, A., and Kopits, E. (2010). *The Social Cost of Carbon Made Simple.* Working Paper 2010-07. Washington, DC: National Center for Environmental Economics, Environmental Protection Agency.

Newell, R. G., and Pizer, W. A. (2003). Discounting the distant future: How much do uncertain rates increase valuations? *Journal of Environmental Economics and Management, 46,* 52–71.

Nordhaus, W. D. (1994a). Expert opinion on climate change. *American Scientist, 82*(1), 45–51.

Nordhaus, W. D. (1994b). *Managing the Global Commons: The Economics of Climate Change.* Cambridge, MA: MIT Press.

Nordhaus, W. D. (2006). Geography and macroeconomics: New data and new findings. *Proceedings of the National Academy of Sciences of the USA, 103*(10), 3510–3517.

Nordhaus, W. D. (2007). Critical assumptions in the Stern Review on Climate Change. *Science, 317,* 201–202.

Nordhaus, W. D. (2008). *A Question of Balance—Weighing the Options on Global Warming Policies.* New Haven, CT: Yale University Press.

Nordhaus, W. D. (2011). The economics of tail events with an application to climate change. *Review of Environmental Economics and Policy, 5*(2), 240–257.

Nordhaus, W. D., and Boyer, J. G. (2000). *Warming the World: Economic Models of Global Warming.* Cambridge, MA: MIT Press.

Nordhaus, W. D., and Yang, Z. (1996). RICE: A regional dynamic general equilibrium model of optimal climate-change policy. *American Economic Review, 86*(4), 741–765.

Pearce, D. W., Cline, W. R., Achanta, A. N., Fankhauser, S., Pachauri, R. K., Tol, R. S. J., and Vellinga, P. (1996). The social costs of climate change: Greenhouse damage and the benefits of control. In J. P. Bruce, H. Lee, and E. F. Haites (eds.), *Climate Change 1995: Economic and Social Dimensions—Contribution of Working Group III to the Second Assessment Report of the Intergovernmental Panel on Climate Change*, pp. 179–224. Cambridge, UK: Cambridge University Press.

Pigou, A. C. (1920). *The Economics of Welfare.* London: Macmillan.

Pindyck, R. S. (2011). Fat tails, thin tails, and climate change policy. *Review of Environmental Economics and Policy, 5*(2), 258–274.

Pindyck, R. S. (2012). Uncertain outcomes and climate change policy. *Journal of Environmental Economics and Management, 63*(3), 289–303.

Plamberk, E. L., and Hope, C. W. (1996). PAGE95—An updated valuation of the impacts of global warming. *Energy Policy, 24*(9), 783–793.

Ramsey, F. (1928). A mathematical theory of saving. *Economic Journal, 38*, 543–549.

Rehdanz, K., and Maddison, D. J. (2005). Climate and happiness. *Ecological Economics, 52*(1), 111–125.

Sandmo, A. (2011). Atmospheric externalities and environmental taxation. *Energy Economics, 33* (Suppl. 1), S4–S12.

Stern, N. H., Peters, S., Bakhski, V., Bowen, A., Cameron, C., Catovsky, S., Crane, D., Cruickshank, S., Dietz, S., Edmondson, N., Garbett, S.-L., Hamid, L., Hoffman, G., Ingram, D., Jones, B., Patmore, N., Radcliffe, H., Sathiyarajah, R., Stock, M., Taylor, C., Vernon, T., Wanjie, H., and Zenghelis, D. (2006). *Stern Review: The Economics of Climate Change.* Cambridge, UK: Cambridge University Press.

Tol, R. S. J. (1995). The damage costs of climate change toward more comprehensive calculations. *Environmental and Resource Economics, 5*(4), 353–374.

Tol, R. S. J. (1999). The Marginal Costs of Greenhouse Gas Emissions. *Energy Journal, 20*(1), 61–81.

Tol, R. S. J. (2002a). Estimates of the damage costs of climate change—Part 1: Benchmark estimates. *Environmental and Resource Economics, 21*(1), 47–73.

Tol, R. S. J. (2002b). Estimates of the damage costs of climate change—Part II: dynamic estimates. *Environmental and Resource Economics, 21*(2), 135–160.

Tol, R. S. J. (2003). Is the uncertainty about climate change too large for expected cost-benefit analysis? *Climatic Change, 56*(3), 265–289.

Tol, R. S. J. (2009). The economic effects of climate change. *Journal of Economic Perspectives, 23*(2), 29–51.

Tol, R. S. J. (2013a). Climate policy with Bentham-Rawls preferences. *Economics Letters, 118*, 424–428.

Tol, R. S. J. (2013b). Targets for global climate policy. *Journal of Economic Dynamics and Control, 37*, 911–928.

Tol, R. S. J. (2012c). The uncertainty about the total economic impact of climate change. *Environmental and Resource Economics, 53*, 97–116.

Tol, R. S. J., and Yohe, G. W. (2006). Of dangerous climate change and dangerous emission reduction. In H.-J. Schellnhuber et al. (eds.), *Avoiding Dangerous Climate Change*, pp. 291–298. Cambridge, UK: Cambridge University Press.

Tol, R. S. J., and Yohe, G. W. (2007). Infinite uncertainty, forgotten feedbacks, and cost-benefit analysis of climate change. *Climatic Change, 83*(4), 429–442.

Tsur, Y., and Zemel, A. (1996). Accounting for global warming risks: Resource management under event uncertainty. *Journal of Economic Dynamics & Control, 20*, 1289–1305.

van Liedekerke, L., and Lauwers, L. (1997). Sacrificing the patrol: Utilitarianism, future generations and infinity. *Economics and Philosophy, 13*, 159–174.

Weitzman, M. L. (2001). Gamma discounting. *American Economic Review, 91*(1), 260–271.

Weitzman, M. L. (2007). A review of the Stern Review on the Economics of Climate Change. *Journal of Economic Literature, 45*(3), 703–724.

Weitzman, M. L. (2009a). Additive damages, fat-tailed climate dynamics, and uncertain discounting. *Economics—the Open-Access, Open-Assessment E-Journal, 3*(2009-39), 1–23.

Weitzman, M. L. (2009b). On modelling and interpreting the economics of catastrophic climate change. *Review of Economics and Statistics, 91*(1), 1–19.

Weitzman, M. L. (2012). GHG targets as insurance against catastrophic climate damages. *Journal of Public Economic Theory, 14*, 221–244.

Yohe, G. W., and Tol, R. S. J. (2002). Indicators for social and economic coping capacity—Moving towards a working definition of adaptive capacity. *Global Environmental Change, 12*(1), 25–40.

Zuber, S., and Asheim, G. B. (2012). Justifying social discounting: The rank-discounted utilitarian approach. *Journal of Economic Theory, 147*(4), 1572–1601.

TARGETS FOR GLOBAL CLIMATE POLICY – APPENDIX

The database on the marginal damage costs of carbon dioxide emissions and its growth rate can be found at: http://www.sussex.ac.uk/Users/rt220/marginaldamagecost.xlsx

The following papers are included in the database on the marginal damage costs of carbon dioxide emissions: (Ackerman and Munitz 2012; Ackerman and Stanton 2012; Anthoff et al. 2009b; Anthoff et al. 2009a; Anthoff et al. 2009c; Anthoff et al. 2011a; Anthoff et al. 2011b; Anthoff and Tol 2010; Anthoff and Tol 2011; Ayres and Walter 1991; Azar 1994; Azar and Sterner 1996; Botzen and van den Bergh 2012; Cai et al. 2012; Ceronsky et al. 2006; Ceronsky et al. 2011; Clarkson and Deyes 2002; Cline 1992; Cline 1997; Cline 2004; Downing et al. 1996; Downing et al. 2005; EPA and NHTSA 2009; Eyre et al. 1999; Fankhauser 1994; Guo et al. 2006; Haraden 1992; Haraden 1993; Hohmeyer 1996; Hohmeyer 2004; Hohmeyer and Gaertner 1992; Hope 2005a; Hope 2005b; Hope 2006a; Hope 2006b; Hope 2008a; Hope 2008b; Hope 2011; Hope and Maul 1996; Johnson and Hope 2012; Kemfert and Schill 2010; Kopp et al. 2012; Link and Tol 2004; Maddison 1995; Manne 2024; Marten 2011; Mendelsohn 2004; Narita et al. 2009; Narita et al. 2010; Newell and Pizer 2003; Nordhaus 2010; Nordhaus 1982;

Nordhaus 1991; Nordhaus 1993; Nordhaus 1994; Nordhaus 2008; Nordhaus and Boyer 2000; Nordhaus and Popp 1997; Nordhaus and Yang 1996; Parry 1993; Pearce 2003; Peck and Teisberg 1993; Penner et al. 1992; Perrissin Fabert et al. 2012; Plambeck and Hope 1996; Pycroft et al. 2012; Reilly and Richards 1993; Roughgarden and Schneider 1999; Schauer 1995; Sohngen 2010; Stern et al. 2006; Stern and Taylor 2007; Tol 1999; Tol 2005; Tol 2010; Tol 2012; Uzawa 2003; Wahba and Hope 2006; Waldhoff et al. 2011)

The following papers are included in the database on the growth rate of the marginal damage costs of carbon dioxide emissions: (Ackerman and Stanton 2012; Anthoff et al. 2011a; Anthoff et al. 2011b; Botzen and van den Bergh 2012; Cai et al. 2012; Cline 1992; Cline 1997; Cline 2004; EPA and NHTSA 2009; Fankhauser 1994; Haraden 1992; Haraden 1993; Hope 2008b; Maddison 1995; Mendelsohn 2004; Nordhaus 2010; Nordhaus 1993; Nordhaus 1994; Nordhaus 2008; Nordhaus and Boyer 2000; Nordhaus and Popp 1997; Nordhaus and Yang 1996; Peck and Teisberg 1993; Perrissin Fabert et al. 2012; Roughgarden and Schneider 1999; Sohngen 2010; Tol 1999; Tol 2012; Wahba and Hope 2006)

References

Ackerman, F. and C.Munitz (2012), 'Climate damages in the FUND model: A disaggregated analysis', *Ecological Economics*, **77**, (0), pp. 219–224.

Ackerman, F. and E.A.Stanton (2012), 'Climate Risks and Carbon Prices: Revising the Social Cost of Carbon', *Economics – the Open-Access, Open-Assessment E-Journal*, **6**, (10), pp. 1–27.

Anthoff, D., C.J.Hepburn, and R.S.J.Tol (2009a), 'Equity weighting and the marginal damage costs of climate change', *Ecological Economics*, **68**, (3), pp. 836–849.

Anthoff, D., S.K.Rose, R.S.J.Tol, and S.Waldhoff (2011a), *Regional and sectoral estimates of the social cost of carbon: An application of FUND*, Working Paper **375**, Economic and Social Research Institute, Dublin.

Anthoff, D., S.K.Rose, R.S.J.Tol, and S.Waldhoff (2011b), *The Time Evolution of the Social Cost of Carbon: An Application of FUND*, Working Paper **405**, Economic and Social Research Institute, Dublin.

Anthoff, D. and R.S.J.Tol (2010), 'On international equity weights and national decision making on climate change', *Journal of Environmental Economics and Management*, **60**, (1), pp. 14–20.

Anthoff, D. and R.S.J.Tol (2011), *The uncertainty about the social cost of carbon: A decomposition analysis using FUND*, Working Paper **404**, Economic and Social Research Institute, Dublin.

Anthoff, D., R.S.J.Tol, and G.W.Yohe (2009b), 'Discounting for Climate Change', *Economics – the Open-Access, Open-Assessment E-Journal*, **3**, (2009–24), pp. 1–24.

Anthoff, D., R.S.J.Tol, and G.W.Yohe (2009c), 'Risk Aversion, Time Preference, and the Social Cost of Carbon', *Environmental Research Letters*, **4**, (2–2), 1–7.

Ayres, R.U. and J.Walter (1991), 'The Greenhouse Effect: Damages, Costs and Abatement', *Environmental and Resource Economics*, **1**, (3), 237–270.

Azar, C. (1994), 'The Marginal Cost of CO_2 Emissions', *Energy*, **19**, (12), 1255–1261.

Azar, C. and T.Sterner (1996), 'Discounting and Distributional Considerations in the Context of Global Warming', *Ecological Economics*, **19**, 169–184.

Botzen, W.J.W. and J.C.J.M.van den Bergh (2012), 'How sensitive is Nordhaus to Weitzman? Climate policy in DICE with an alternative damage function', *Economics Letters*, **117**, pp. 372–374.

Cai, Y., K.L.Judd, and T.S.Lontzek (2012), 'Open science is necessary', *Nature Climate Change*, **2**, (5), p. 299.

Ceronsky, M., D.Anthoff, C.J.Hepburn, and R.S.J.Tol (2006), *Checking the Price Tag on Catastrophe: The Social Cost of Carbon under Non-linear Climate Response*, Working Paper **87**, Research unit Sustainability and Global Change, Hamburg University and Centre for Marine and Atmospheric Science, Hamburg.

Ceronsky, M., D.Anthoff, C.J.Hepburn, and R.S.J.Tol (2011), *Checking the Price Tag on Catastrophe: The Social Cost of Carbon under Non-linear Climate Response*, Working Paper **392**, Economic and Social Research Institute, Dublin.

Clarkson, R. and K.Deyes (2002), *Estimating the Social Cost of Carbon Emissions*, Government Economic Service Working Papers **Working Paper 140**, The Public Enquiry Unit — HM Treasury, London.

Cline, W.R. (1992), *Optimal Carbon Emissions over Time: Experiments with the Nordhaus DICE Model*, Institute for International Economics, Washington, D.C.

Cline, W.R. (1997), 'Modelling Economically Efficient Abatement of Greenhouse Gases', in *Environment, Energy, and Economy*, Y. Kaya and K. Yokobori (eds.), United Nations University Press, Tokyo, pp. 99–122.

Cline, W.R. (2004), *Meeting the Challenge of Global Warming*, Copenhagen Consensus Challenge Paper ,National Environmental Assessment Institute, Copenhagen.

Downing, T.E., D.Anthoff, R.Butterfield, M.Ceronsky, M.J.Grubb, J.Guo, C.J.Hepburn, C.W.Hope, A.Hunt, A.Li, A.Markandya, S.Moss, A.Nyong, R.S.J.Tol, and P.Watkiss (2005), *Social Cost of Carbon: A Closer Look at Uncertainty*, Department of Environment, Food and Rural Affairs, London.

Downing, T.E., N.Eyre, R.Greener, and D.Blackwell (1996), *Full Fuel Cycle Study: Evaluation of the Global Warming Externality for Fossil Fuel Cycles with and without CO2 Abatament and for Two Reference Scenarios*, Environmental Change Unit, University of Oxford, Oxford.

EPA and NHTSA (2009), 'Proposed Rulemaking to Establish Light-Duty Vehicle Greenhouse Gas Emission Standards and Corporate Average Fuel Efficiency Standards', *Federal Register*, **74**, (187), 49454–49789.

Eyre, N., T.E.Downing, K.Rennings, and R.S.J.Tol (1999), 'Assessment of Global Warming Damages', in *Externalities of Energy, Vol. 7: Metholodogy and 1998 Update*, M.R. Holland, J. Berry, and D. Forster (eds.), Office for Official Publications of the European Communities, Luxembourg, pp. 101–112.

Fankhauser, S. (1994), 'The Social Costs of Greenhouse Gas Emissions: An Expected Value Approach', *Energy Journal*, **15**, (2), 157–184.

Guo, J., C.J.Hepburn, R.S.J.Tol, and D.Anthoff (2006), 'Discounting and the Social Cost of Climate Change: A Closer Look at Uncertainty', *Environmental Science & Policy*, **9**, 205–216.

Haraden, J. (1992), 'An improved shadow price for CO_2', *Energy*, **17**, (5), 419–426.

Haraden, J. (1993), 'An updated shadow price for CO_2', *Energy*, **18**, (3), 303–307.

Hohmeyer, O. (1996), 'Social Costs of Climate Change – Strong Sustainability and Social Costs', in *Social Costs and Sustainability – Valuation and Implementation in the Energy and*

Transport Sector, O. Hohmeyer, R.L. Ottinger, and K. Rennings (eds.), Springer, Berlin, pp. 61–83.

Hohmeyer, O. (2004), 'Verguetung nach dem EEG: Subvention oder fairer Ausgleich externer Kosten?', in *Externe Kosten in der Stromerzeugung*, H.-J. Ziesing (ed.), VWEW Energieverlag, Frankfurt, pp. 11–24.

Hohmeyer, O. and M.Gaertner (1992), *The Costs of Climate Change — A Rough Estimate of Orders of Magnitude*, Fraunhofer-Institut fur Systemtechnik und Innovationsforschung, Karlsruhe.

Hope, C.W. (2005a), *Exchange Rates and the Social Cost of Carbon* **WP05/2005**, Judge Institute of Management, Cambridge.

Hope, C.W. (2005b), 'The climate change benefits of reducing methane emissions', *Climatic Change*, **68**, 21–39.

Hope, C.W. (2006a), 'The Marginal Impact of CO2 from PAGE2002: An Integrated Assessment Model Incorporating the IPCC's Five Reasons for Concern', *Integrated Assessment Journal*, **6**, (1), 19–56.

Hope, C.W. (2006b), 'The Marginal Impacts of CO2, CH4 and SF6 Emissions', *Climate Policy*, **6**, (5), 537–544.

Hope, C.W. (2008a), 'Discount rates, equity weights and the social cost of carbon', *Energy Economics*, **30**, (3), 1011–1019.

Hope, C.W. (2008b), 'Optimal Carbon Emissions and the Social Cost of Carbon over Time under Uncertainty', *Integrated Assessment Journal*, **8**, (1), 107–122.

Hope, C.W. (2011), *The Social Cost of CO2 from the PAGE09 Model*, Discussion Papers **2011–39**, Economics — The Open Access, Open Assessment E-Journal, Kiel.

Hope, C.W. and P.Maul (1996), 'Valuing the Impact of CO_2 Emissions', *Energy Policy*, **24**, (3), 211–219.

Johnson, L.T. and C.W.Hope (2012), 'The social cost of carbon in the US regulatory impact analyses: An introduction and critique', *Journal of Environmental Studies and Science*, **2**, pp. 205–221.

Kemfert, C. and W.-P.Schill (2010), 'Methane Mitigation', in *Smart Solutions to Climate Change*, B. Lomborg (ed.), Cambridge University Press, Cambridge, pp. 172–197.

Kopp, R.E., A.Golub, N.O.Keohane, and C.Onda (2012), 'The influence of the specification of climate change damages on the social cost of carbon', *Economics – the Open-Access, Open-Assessment E-Journal*, **6**, pp. 1–42.

Link, P.M. and R.S.J.Tol (2004), 'Possible economic impacts of a shutdown of the thermohaline circulation: an application of FUND', *Portuguese Economic Journal*, **3**, (2), 99–114.

Maddison, D.J. (1995), 'A Cost-Benefit Analysis of Slowing Climate Change', *Energy Policy*, **23**, (4/5), 337–346.

Manne, A.S. (2024), 'Global Climate Change: An Opponent's Notes', in *Global Crises, Global Solutions*, B. Lomborg (ed.), Cambridge University Press, Cambridge University.

Marten, A.L. (2011), 'Transient Temperature Response Modeling in IAMs: The Effect of Over Simplification on the SCC', *Economics – the Open-Access, Open-Assessment E-Journal*, **5**, (18), pp. 1–44.

Mendelsohn, R.O. (2004), 'Global Climate Change: An Opponent's Notes', in *Global Crises, Global Solutions*, B. Lomborg (ed.), Cambridge University Press, Cambridge University.

Narita, D., D.Anthoff, and R.S.J.Tol (2009), 'Damage Costs of Climate Change through Intensification of Tropical Cyclone Activities: An Application of FUND', *Climate Research*, **39**, pp. 87–97.

Narita, D., D.Anthoff, and R.S.J.Tol (2010), 'Economic Costs of Extratropical Storms under Climate Change: An Application of FUND', *Journal of Environmental Planning and Management*, **53**, (3), pp. 371–384.

Newell, R.G. and W.A.Pizer (2003), 'Discounting the distant future: how much do uncertain rates increase valuations?', *Journal of Environmental Economics and Management*, **46**, 52–71.

Nordhaus, W.D. (2010), 'Economic aspects of global warming in a post-Copenhagen environment', *Proceedings of the National Academy of Sciences of the United States of America*, **107**, (26), pp. 11721–11726.

Nordhaus, W.D. (1982), 'How Fast Should We Graze the Global Commons?', *American Economic Review*, **72**, (2), 242–246.

Nordhaus, W.D. (1991), 'To Slow or Not to Slow: The Economics of the Greenhouse Effect', *Economic Journal*, **101**, (444), 920–937.

Nordhaus, W.D. (1993), 'Rolling the 'DICE': An Optimal Transition Path for Controlling Greenhouse Gases', *Resource and Energy Economics*, **15**, (1), 27–50.

Nordhaus, W.D. (1994), *Managing the Global Commons: The Economics of Climate Change* The MIT Press, Cambridge.

Nordhaus, W.D. (2008), *A Question of Balance – Weighing the Options on Global Warming Policies* Yale University Press, New Haven.

Nordhaus, W.D. and J.G.Boyer (2000), *Warming the World: Economic Models of Global Warming* The MIT Press, Cambridge, Massachusetts — London, England.

Nordhaus, W.D. and D.Popp (1997), 'What is the Value of Scientific Knowledge? An Application to Global Warming Using the PRICE Model', *Energy Journal*, **18**, (1), 1–45.

Nordhaus, W.D. and Z.Yang (1996), 'RICE: A Regional Dynamic General Equilibrium Model of Optimal Climate-Change Policy', *American Economic Review*, **86**, (4), 741–765.

Parry, I.W.H. (1993), 'Some Estimates of the Insurance Value against Climate Change from Reducing Greenhouse Gas Emissions', *Resource and Energy Economics*, **15**, 99–115.

Pearce, D.W. (2003), 'The Social Cost of Carbon and its Policy Implications', *Oxford Review of Economic Policy*, **19**, (3), 1–32.

Peck, S.C. and T.J.Teisberg (1993), 'Global Warming Uncertainties and the Value of Information: An Analysis using CETA', *Resource and Energy Economics*, **15**, 71–97.

Penner, S.S., J.Haraden, and S.Mates (1992), 'Long-term global energy supplies with acceptable environmental impacts', *Energy*, **17**, (10), pp. 883–899.

Perrissin Fabert, B., P.Dumas, and J.-C.Hourcade (2012), *What Social Cost of Carbon? A Mapping of the Climate Debate*, Nota di Lavoro **34.2012**, Fondazione Eni Enrico Mattei, Milan.

Plambeck, E.L. and C.W.Hope (1996), 'PAGE95 — An Updated Valuation of the Impacts of Global Warming', *Energy Policy*, **24**, (9), 783–793.

Pycroft, J., L.Vergano, C.W.Hope, D.Paci, and J.C.Ciscar (2012), 'A tale of tails: Uncertainty and the social cost of carbon dioxide', *Economics – the Open-Access, Open-Assessment E-Journal*, **5**, (22), pp. 1–31.

Reilly, J.M. and K.R.Richards (1993), 'Climate Change Damage and the Trace Gas Index Issue', *Environmental and Resource Economics*, **3**, 41–61.

Roughgarden, T. and S.H.Schneider (1999), 'Climate change policy: quantifying uncertainties for damages and optimal carbon taxes', *Energy Policy*, **27**, 415–429.

Schauer, M.J. (1995), 'Estimation of the Greenhouse Gas Externality with Uncertainty', *Environmental and Resource Economics*, **5**, (1), 71–82.

Sohngen, B.L. (2010), 'Forestry Carbon Sequestration', in *Smart Solutions to Climate Change*, B. Lomborg (ed.), Cambridge University Press, Cambridge, pp. 114–132.

Stern, N.H., S.Peters, V.Bakhski, A.Bowen, C.Cameron, S.Catovsky, D.Crane, S.Cruickshank, S.Dietz, N.Edmondson, S.-L.Garbett, L.Hamid, G.Hoffman, D.Ingram, B.Jones, N.Patmore, H.Radcliffe, R.Sathiyarajah, M.Stock, C.Taylor, T.Vernon, H.Wanjie, and D.Zenghelis (2006), *Stern Review: The Economics of Climate Change* Cambridge University Press, Cambridge.

Stern, N.H. and C.Taylor (2007), 'Climate Change: Risks, Ethics and the Stern Review', *Science*, **317**, (5835), 203–204.

Tol, R.S.J. (1999), 'The Marginal Costs of Greenhouse Gas Emissions', *Energy Journal*, **20**, (1), 61–81.

Tol, R.S.J. (2005), 'Emission Abatement versus Development as Strategies to Reduce Vulnerability to Climate Change: An Application of FUND', *Environment and Development Economics*, **10**, (5), 615–629.

Tol, R.S.J. (2010), 'Carbon Dioxide Mitigation', in *Smart Solutions to Climate Change*, B. Lomborg (ed.), Cambridge University Press, Cambridge.

Tol, R.S.J. (2012), 'The Uncertainty about the Total Economic Impact of Climate Change', *Environmental and Resource Economics*.

Uzawa, H. (2003), *Economic Theory and Global Warming* Cambridge University Press, Cambridge, UK.

Wahba, M. and C.W.Hope (2006), 'The Marginal Impact of Carbon Dioxide under Two Scenarios of Future Emissions', *Energy Policy*, **34**, 3305–3316.

Waldhoff, S., D.Anthoff, S.K.Rose, and R.S.J.Tol (2011), *The marginal damage costs of different greenhouse gases: An application of FUND*, Working Paper **380**, Economic and Social Research Institute, Dublin.

PART III

TECHNOLOGY AND ENERGY POLICIES

CHAPTER 14

CLIMATE-FRIENDLY TECHNOLOGICAL CHANGE FOR DEVELOPING COUNTRIES

DAVID POPP

14.1 Introduction

Recent rapid economic growth of countries such as China and India brings the promise of a better life to much of the world's population. However, with growth often comes more pollution, particularly emissions of greenhouse gases (GHGs) such as carbon dioxide (CO_2) that lead to climate change. This raises a global policy challenge, as the need to reduce global CO_2 emissions occurs at a time when the share of emissions coming from developing countries is growing. In 2010, 75% of the growth in CO_2 emissions came from non-Organisation for Economic Co-operation and Development (OECD) countries.[1] CO_2 emissions from non-OECD countries are projected to be nearly double of those from OECD countries by 2035 (Energy Information Administration, 2010). This rapid growth in emissions from developing countries comes at a

This chapter is based on a report originally prepared for the Environment and Energy Team of the World Bank. I thank Michael Toman, Marianne Fay, and Stephane Hallegatte for helpful comments on earlier drafts of that report. The discussion in this chapter has also been informed by my work with various colleagues on other projects related to technological change and the environment, including Richard Newell, Adam Jaffe, Nick Johnstone, and Jung Eun Kim. Their implicit contributions to this work are duly noted. Any remaining errors are solely my responsibility. Views and errors remain mine alone, and should not be attributed to the World Bank Group or its member countries.

time when developed countries, particularly in Europe, are beginning to rein in CO_2 emissions.

Owing to the growth in emissions from developing countries, designing policy that increases the prevalence of clean technologies in developing countries has been a major discussion point in climate negotiations. This issue is complicated by the fact that most technological innovation currently takes place within a few highly developed economies. Thus, the transfer of climate-friendly technologies from developed to developing countries will be of prime importance, as will advancing technologies that cater to the specific needs of developing countries, such as off-grid electric applications and improved cook stoves. This chapter reviews the growing literature examining the links between technological change, environmental policy, and economic performance, focusing on technologies relevant for combatting climate change.

Technological change proceeds in three stages. At each stage, incentives, in the form of prices or regulations, affect the development and adoption of new technologies:

Invention: An idea must be born.

Innovation: New ideas are then developed into commercially viable products. Often, these two stages of technological change are lumped together under the rubric of research and development (R&D).

Diffusion: To have an effect on the economy, individuals must choose to make use of the innovation.

I begin with a discussion of where environmental innovation comes from. Given that most innovation is concentrated in a few rich countries, this leads to a discussion of the remaining role for lower-income countries, such as (1) the development of technologies with limited markets in high-income countries, (2) adaptive research and development (R&D), and (3) the potential for emerging economies to meet the green technology needs of high-income countries.

I continue with a discussion of technology transfer. Beginning with diffusion across countries, differences among countries raise important questions, such as (1) understanding how the technological distance between countries affects the transfer of green technologies, and (2) whether lessons learned from the recent successes of India and China are generalizable to smaller countries. Similarly, within countries, diffusion of green technologies can be affected by characteristics that are unique to developing countries. For instance, limited access to credit markets may make financing green technology difficult.

Because of the importance of market failures, I then discuss the role of both technology policy and environmental policy for promoting environmentally friendly technological change. The review concludes with a discussion of more general technology issues, such as what environmental economists can learn from other fields. While not emphasized here, other technologies will also be important for low-income countries, particularly pertaining to resource use (such as water) and agricultural

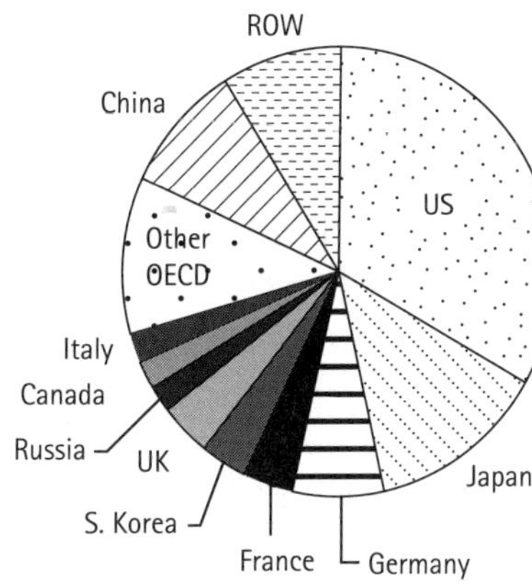

FIGURE 14.1 Share of global R&D by country, 2007.

Source: Author's calculations using data from National Science Board (2010).

productivity. As noted in the concluding section, future work should explore the differences that emerge among various technological fields.

14.2 Who Innovates?

As shown in Figure 14.1, most of the world's R&D occurs in a few high-income countries. In 2007, global R&D expenditures were an estimated $1.107 trillion, with OECD nations accounting for 80%, and the United States and Japan together accounting for 46%. Among non-OECD countries, China performs 9% of global R&D. Estimates of R&D from India and Brazil also place them among the top 15 R&D performers worldwide (National Science Board, 2010).

The dominance of high-income countries among the top R&D performers holds true for environmental innovation as well. Using patent data from the United States, Japan, Germany, and 14 low- and middle-income countries, Lanjouw and Mody (1996) study technological change for a variety of environmentally friendly technologies. They find that such innovation increases as pollution abatement expenditures in the country increase. For the United States, Japan, and Germany, patents on these innovations are typically domestic patents. In contrast, for developing countries, the majority of these patents come from other countries. This is especially true of air pollution control technologies, which tend to be complex. Water pollution control technologies, on the other hand, are more frequently local innovations, as local conditions shape the requirements of these technologies, and are less likely to be patented elsewhere.

Dechezleprêtre et al. (2011) examine climate-friendly innovation using patent data from 1978–2005 for 76 countries and covering a broad range of technologies, including renewable energy technologies, carbon capture and storage, and energy efficiency technologies for buildings, lighting, and cement manufacture. Like Lanjouw and Mody (1996), they find that most climate-friendly innovation occurs in developed countries. In fact, the United States, Japan, and Germany together account for two-thirds of the innovations in their sample. Reflecting the role and impact of policy, innovation increases after the Kyoto Protocol in all Annex I countries except the United States, which had not ratified Kyoto.[2]

Dechezleprêtre et al. (2011) do find some evidence of innovation in emerging economies. In particular, China, South Korea, Russia, and Brazil together accounted for 18.5% of climate-friendly innovations from 2000–2005. However, innovation in emerging economies is often of a different nature. For example, the most prevalent innovations in China, South Korea, Russia, and Brazil include technologies designed primarily for local markets, such as geothermal and cement manufacture. As a result, the share of high-value patents (defined as patent applications filed in multiple countries) from these four countries is just 7.2%. Consistent with Lanjouw and Mody (1996), Dechezleprêtre et al. (2011) find that technologies of wider use globally, measured by the percentage of patents that have corresponding applications in other countries, are nearly all from developed economies.[3]

Because so much green innovation occurs in high income countries, their environmental policies usually shape the development of environmentally friendly technologies worldwide. This is partially because these countries are typically the first to enact environmental regulations. Because most environmental innovations help to reduce externalities, there is little market for such innovations without policy incentives. By increasing the relative price of pollution, environmental polices provide incentive for green innovation. Drawing on the notion of induced innovation (Hicks, 1932; Binswanger and Ruttan, 1978; Acemoglu, 2002), which recognizes that R&D is a profit-motivated investment activity and that the direction of innovation likely responds positively in the direction of increased relative prices, there is a broad literature demonstrating the links between environmental policy and innovation in developed countries (see Popp et al., 2010 for a review of this literature).

In contrast, there is less work exploring the potential for additional R&D from developing countries. The technologies needed in developing country markets may differ from those created in high-income countries. Developing countries, particularly emerging economies with demonstrated existing R&D capacity, such as the BRICS (Brazil, Russia, India, China, and South Africa) may be able to play a role filling this gap. This suggests three key roles for developing countries.

14.2.1 Development of Technologies with Limited Markets in High-Income Countries

Given that the technologies needed in developing country markets may differ, developing countries must play a role encouraging innovation on technologies with limited markets in high-income countries. For example, technologies for use off of the main electric grid, such as improved cooking stoves, typically have limited markets in developed countries. However, nearly three billion people in developing nations use indoor stoves burning crop waste, wood, coal, or dung. Indoor air pollution from the burning of these fuels kills 1.9 million people per year (Broder, 2010). Moreover, recent research highlights the potential for improved cookstoves not only to reduce indoor air pollution, but also to mitigate climate emissions. Smoke from these stoves produces black carbon, which recent reports list as the second most important pollutant contributing to climate change, responsible for 18% of global warming (compared to 40% for CO_2). Ramanathan and Carmichael (2008) first noted the climate change potential of black carbon. They note in particular that China and India alone account for 25–35% of global black carbon emissions. Providing energy efficient and smoke-free cookers, along with reducing soot emissions from coal combustion in small industries, could reduce warming from black carbon in East Asia by 70–80%.

To illustrate the role of developing countries for such off-grid technologies, Table 14.1 presents total patent counts based on inventor country for four types of cooking stoves whose primary applications are in developing country markets.[4] In all four cases, China is the leading source of patents, ranging from 46% to 89% of the total for each technology. Among developing countries, we also include data for India and South Africa, as these countries are important sources of scientific publications, to be discussed later. However, neither is an important source of patenting. This may be because these countries are doing less commercial work on these technologies, or because intellectual property rights are not seen as valuable in India and South Africa.

Because developed country research on indoor cooking stoves may be led by noncommercial entities such as universities or nonprofit foundations, which are less likely to patent successful research outcomes, Table 14.1 also includes counts of scientific

Table 14.1 Patent and Publication Counts for Indoor Cooking Stoves

	China	India	South Africa	Japan	US	Germany	France	UK	Korea	Total
			Patents:							
Solar stoves	483	0	0	69	56	8	12	8	2	665
Biomass stoves	273	2	0	5	16	3	0	0	0	307
LPG stoves	304	1	0	10	8	0	0	1	5	358
Kerosene or butane stoves	143	0	1	112	21	2	4	2	18	313
			Publications:							
Solar stoves	7	86	12	6	17	9	4	7	0	215
Biomass stoves	40	61	3	7	101	8	7	17	4	319
LPG stoves	1	26	2	2	18	2	0	2	2	68
Kerosene or butane stoves	3	50	2	3	41	4	0	4	1	132

Source: Author's calculations. Both data sets include patents and publications through 2010. Patent counts start as early as 1963, although data availability for some countries, such as China, begins later. Publication counts begin in 1990.

LPG, liquefied petroleum gas.

publications. Even here, a developing country is the leading source of articles for three of the four stove technologies. However, in this case, it is India, rather than China, that is the leading source.[5]

14.2.2 Adaptive R&D

Because policies in developed countries have encouraged innovation of emissions-reducing technologies, in many cases technologies are readily available for developing markets. However, even technology transfer may require some investment in R&D. When adjustments are necessary to fit new technologies to local market conditions, it is the recipient countries that will be best positioned to do this research. Popp (2006) finds evidence of innovation even in countries that are late to adopt regulations, suggesting that these countries do not simply take advantage of "off the shelf" technologies that have been developed elsewhere. Rather, late adopters often undertake adaptive R&D to fit the technology to local markets, as evidence by the increased likelihood of these later patents to cite earlier foreign rather than earlier domestic inventions. Lanjouw and Mody (1996) find similar evidence that the environmentally friendly innovations that occur in developing countries are smaller inventive steps, typically done to modify existing technologies to local conditions.

Both studies suggest that foreign knowledge serves as a blueprint for further improvements, rather than as a direct source of technology. This suggests that when policymakers consider the potential for technological change to reduce environmental impacts in developing countries, they must make allowances for adaptive R&D to fit technologies to local conditions, or else be prepared for less successful results. As an example of such concerns, Wang (2010) finds that when evaluating potential Clean Development Mechanism (CDM) projects, the Chinese government does not encourage the use of technologies that are new to the Chinese market because of concern that technologies from abroad may not adapt well to local conditions. The risk of poor adaptation to local conditions would increase the risk to credits generated from the CDM project, thus lowering their value. Similarly, as prevailing wind speeds are lower in India than in Europe, wind turbines need to be adapted to generate electricity at these lower wind speeds to be effective (Kristinsson and Rao, 2007).

14.2.3 Innovation in Emerging Economies to Meet Demands of High-Income Countries

A third role of particular importance for emerging economies is whether such adaptive innovation can help them meet the demands of high-income countries. That is, can they be suppliers of advanced green technologies for global markets? A few recent studies provide evidence for emerging economies. Medhi (2009) finds that Korean automotive manufacturers first incorporated advanced emission controls into their vehicles to satisfy regulatory requirements in the US and Japanese markets. Only later did the Korean government pass domestic regulations requiring advanced emission controls. Similarly, Sawhney and Kahn (2012) find that imports of wind and solar equipment from poorer countries have grown faster than those from rich countries, and that emerging economies such as China and India have become important sources of wind and solar equipment, helping to reduce the costs of such equipment.

Adapting production processes to fit local conditions can play an important role in meeting global demand. The Chinese photovoltaic (PV) industry produced 35% of worldwide capacity in 2008, of which 98% was exported (de la Tour et al., 2011). de la Tour et al. (2011) note that Chinese PV manufacturers adapt production processes by replacing capital with labor, which is less expensive in China. Such innovations should require fewer resources than developing processes from scratch.

The potential influence of high-income demand raises several questions. First, will the development of such industries via adaptive innovation eventually provide spillover benefits to the environment in countries? For example, will domestic production of solar and wind equipment hasten the deployment of these technologies in China and India? The Korean automobile case provides a positive example. Can such spillovers to the domestic environment be achieved elsewhere? Second, although nearly the entire current production of solar PV cells from China is exported, and thus has limited impact on emissions in China, these imports also lower the cost of PV electricity in the global market. These price decreases may reduce emissions elsewhere. Thus, adaptive process innovations may also have important implications for global markets by making green technologies available at lower cost.

14.3 Technology Transfer and the Environment

As the previous section suggests, promoting clean technologies within developing countries will often be about the diffusion and adaptation of technology, rather than the creation of new technologies. Having discussed adaptation, we now turn to diffusion. Here two issues are relevant. First is the flow of technology across borders, which is important for getting green technologies to developing countries. Second, even when technologies are introduced in an economy, their spread within the country may be uneven. Moreover, uneven diffusion is often more of an issue in a developing country context. This section discusses both issues in turn.

14.3.1 International Technology Transfer and the Environment

While international technology transfer has received much attention in the broader economic literature, research focused specifically on environmental technologies has primarily been recent in nature.[6] Nonetheless, diffusion of environmental technologies, particularly to developing countries, is currently one of the most pressing environmental concerns. Technology transfer may include the exchange of products, equipment, experience, and knowledge. The benefits of the transfer to the recipient developing country, and thus the potential for technology transfer to improve well-being in the recipient country, depend on the type of transfer.

Embodied technology transfer comes through the importation of equipment into a country (e.g., flows of equipment). In such cases, the technology is *embodied* in the imported equipment.

Disembodied technology transfer involves the flow of know-how or experience. Examples include demonstration projects, training local staff, and local firms hiring away staff from multinational firms operating in a developing country. Disembodied transfers provide additional benefits to recipients, as they enable the recipient to develop skills that can be used in later projects initiated by the recipient country. At the same time, disembodied technology transfers are a concern for private firms, as such benefits may come in the form of knowledge spillovers for which technology suppliers are not fully compensated.

Knowledge spillovers provide benefit to the public as a whole, but not to the innovator. As a result, private firms do not have incentives to provide the socially optimal level of technology transfer. The transfers of disembodied knowledge will typically include knowledge spillovers, as it is nearly impossible for the firm transferring a technology to be fully compensated for the enhanced productivity the recipient will enjoy when employing the newly received skills in future projects. Indeed, encouraging knowledge spillovers is often a goal of developing country policy. For example, in 2011 China ruled that the Chevrolet Volt electric vehicle would not be eligible for the same tax subsidies available to other hybrid and electric vehicles in China unless General Motors transfers the knowledge necessary for building the Volt to a joint venture with a Chinese partner (Bradsher, 2011).

Technology transfer may come from public or private sources. Public funding includes aid from governments or nongovernmental organizations (NGOs), typically in the form of official developmental assistance (ODA). Compared to private investment, ODA flows are low, but are important in areas of the world that receive little foreign investment (Gupta et al., 2007). Technology transfer from private sources may come via international trade, foreign direct investment, or licensing. Spillovers are possible through private transfers, but depend both on the nature of technology flow (e.g., spillovers are often less likely via foreign direct investment [FDI], which allows multinational firms to maintain control over their technology) and the absorptive capacity of the country. Absorptive capacity describes a country's ability to do research to understand, implement, and adapt technologies arriving in the country. Absorptive capacity influences the speed at which a newly arriving technology diffuses through a developing country. It depends on the technological literacy and skills of the workforce, and is influenced by education, the strength of governing institutions, and financial markets.[7]

FDI is important for environmental technology transfer, as multinationals are usually the first to bring new environmental technologies to a country (see, e.g., Dasgupta et al., 2002). In many cases, it is easier for a multinational firm to use the same equipment and processes that it uses at home, rather than develop a dirtier process for use in developing countries.

14.3.2 Literature on Environmental Technology Transfer

In the broadest sense, environmental technological change is addressed in literature on trade and the environment. There, economists decompose the effect of international trade on environmental quality in developing countries into three components. First, scale effects account for increased pollution levels owing to the greater wealth and increased economic activity that follows international trade. Second, composition effects refer to reductions in pollution resulting from a preference for cleaner goods that develops as countries become richer. Third, technique effects refer to emission reductions that occur because trade expands access to cleaner technologies (Esty, 2001; Copeland and Taylor, 2003). Attempts to identify this technique effect can be seen as examples of technology transfer.

Fisher-Vanden and Ho (2010) consider the interaction of scale and technique effects in a simulation of increased science and technology (S&T) capabilities and energy use in China. They note that improving S&T capabilities has two offsetting effects. While technological development can lead to the use of cleaner technologies (the technique effect), increases in S&T also lead to larger energy intensive industries (the scale effect). Their paper simulates the effect of S&T growth in China, with R&D intensity reaching 2.5% by 2020, as stated in China's long-term policy goals. They note that China's R&D intensity has already increased from 0.6% in 1996 to 1.3% in 2003. Calibrating their model based on econometric results from 1500 industrial enterprises, they find that the S&T takeoff should have an energy-saving bias, resulting in lower energy prices. However, this leads to more economic growth and greater energy consumption by households, so that the net effect of the S&T takeoff is greater energy use and more carbon emissions. Fisher-Vanden and Sue Wing (2008) develop an analytical model that finds similar results.

Khanna and Zilberman (2001) illustrate the importance of trade to diffusion in a study of the adoption of energy efficient technologies at electric power plants in India. As is typical in adoption models, variations in the adoption of these technologies occur due to differences across heterogeneous plants. Emissions could be reduced by the adoption of high-quality coal. However, such coal would need to be imported. In an effort to protect the domestic coal industry, such imports were virtually banned by the Indian government. Khanna and Zilberman find that while an emissions tax is necessary to achieve optimal levels of abatement, simply removing domestic and trade policy distortions would increase adoption of energy efficient technology and potentially decrease carbon emissions. Thus, policies designed to protect specific sectors may have unintended consequences that increase environmental harm, raising political challenges to lowering carbon emissions.

Dechezleprêtre et al. (2008) provide a detailed look at technology transfer coming from the CDM. The CDM allows polluters in industrialized countries with emission constraints to receive credit for financing projects that reduce emissions in developing countries, which do not face emission constraints under the Kyoto Protocol.[8] Dechezleprêtre et al. reviewed 644 CDM projects registered by the Executive Board of the UNFCCC to determine how many projects transfer "hardware," such as equipment or machinery, as opposed to "software," which they define as knowledge, skills, or know-how. Spillovers of software exemplify disembodied technology transfer. Thus, their research helps to identify the settings under which such transfers are likely.

Dechezleprêtre et al. (2008) find that 279 projects, or 43%, involve technology transfer. However, these projects are among the most significant CDM projects, accounting for 84% of the expected emissions reductions from registered CDM projects. Of these projects, 57 transfer equipment, 101 transfer knowledge, and 121 transfer both equipment and knowledge. Dechezleprêtre et al. find that a project is more likely to include technology transfer if it is larger, if the project developer is a subsidiary of a company in a developed country, and if the project includes one or more carbon credit buyers. Before credits for a project can be sold, the emissions reductions must be certified. Because they have an interest in obtaining emissions credits, credit buyers help to facilitate this process. Dechezleprêtre et al. (2008) find that technology transfer is more likely if the country is more open to trade. They also find that technology transfer is less likely if there are other similar projects in the country. For instance, countries with greater technological capacity are better able to develop their own innovations in agriculture, reducing the need for technology transfer from abroad for agricultural projects.

Several recent studies explore the role of technology transfer, both through joint ventures with multinational firms and supported by policy, in the development of renewable energy industries in developing countries. Lewis (2007) explores the development of the wind energy in India and China. Both India and China went from having no wind turbine manufacturing capacity to almost complete local production of turbines in less than 10 years' time. In both cases, a combination of local energy policy that created demand for wind energy and efforts of the leading local firms to gain new skills were important. For example, Suzlon, the leading Indian wind turbine manufacturer, established R&D facilities in the Netherlands and Germany to take advantage of the expertise from these countries. In contrast, Goldwind, the leading Chinese wind turbine manufacturer, sends employees abroad for training, but has no overseas facilities. Both firms used licensing agreements with European manufacturers to gain initial access to turbine technology, which they then built upon through their own R&D efforts. In both cases, domestic policies encouraged licensing. India used customs and excise taxes to favor importing wind turbine components over complete turbines, thus providing a market for domestic firms to assemble turbines.

China requires that 70% of the content of a wind turbine used in China be produced domestically.

Lewis (2007) also provides examples of the potential constraints faced by developing countries when the promote technology transfer. For example, while foreign-owned wind turbine companies operating in China use China-based manufacturing facilities, they have typically chosen not to transfer intellectual property through licensing agreements. Moreover, in both India and China, the licensing agreements that have been reached have been with smaller companies that had little international presence. In contrast, larger companies avoided licensing agreements so as to avoid helping the development of international competitors.

de la Tour et al. (2011) provide a similar analysis of the development of the Chinese PV industry. This industry primarily serves international demand, as 98% of output is exported. However, these firms are not involved with all facets of PV production. Rather, Chinese production capacity is strongest in downstream segments such as cell production, rather than upstream segments such as silicon purification. These downstream processes require little previous experience, so that Chinese manufacturers are able to take advantage of the low cost of energy to provide PV cells for a global market. As in Lewis (2007), international mobility of workers was a more important source of information than FDI or licensing. Of the top 9 PV producers, only three receive FDI, and all three are late entrants into the market. Chinese firms do exchange knowledge with equipment suppliers. Training sessions of engineers and technicians also allow Chinese firms to adopt the manufacturing process to local conditions, such as substituting cheap labor for equipment. Indeed, to the extent that Chinese PV firms innovate, their innovations appear adaptive. For example, only 1% of Chinese PV patents are also filed abroad, suggesting they primarily target the specific features of the Chinese market.

Extending beyond the BRICs nations, Pueyo et al. (2011) examine the role of technology transfer in the development of the wind industry in Chile. The case examines Fibrovent Wind, a start-up company that produces wind turbine blades. The firm was created as a partnership with a Spanish turbine manufacturer. Interestingly, in this case, South–South transfer proved essential, as the firm hired a Brazilian wind turbine expert who helped set up the company. Indeed, the authors conclude that successful technology transfer in this case consisted not only of acquisition of foreign equipment and knowledge, but also extended to knowledge about management, which helped the firm to assimilate foreign technologies. Moreover, Fibrovent was able to transfer knowledge about composite materials used in the Chilean mining industry to blade production. Both examples further illustrate the importance of absorptive capacity in technology transfer.

Particularly in emerging economies, technology transfer has been a motivating factor in the development of green energy industries. Potential spillovers from technology transfer can enhance the domestic capabilities of recipient countries, thus promoting growth. Technology transfer can also influence innovation, as knowledge spillovers may enhance the recipient country's ability to develop future innovations. Each of the cases discussed in the preceding text provides examples of successful technology transfer. However, questions remain when considering the connections between technology transfer and green growth.

14.3.2.1 How Will the Technological Distance between Countries Affect Green Technologies?

The potential for successful technology transfer depends on a good match between the needs of the recipient and the technologies available from source countries. Using patent citation data to assess the flow of knowledge across borders, Verdolini and Galeotti (2011) test whether knowledge spillovers from foreign innovations influence domestic energy R&D. They show that increases in foreign knowledge have a larger impact on domestic R&D than increases in domestic knowledge, suggesting that knowledge spillovers across countries are an important driver of innovation. Although primarily focused on developed countries, Verdolini and Galeotti include data from emerging economies such as Brazil and China in their initial analysis of patent citation data. Importantly for developing countries, they find that greater technological distance, an index measuring the similarity of the patent portfolios of two countries, reduces the flow of knowledge across borders, and that technological distance is more important than geographic distance. Given that technological distance will be greatest between countries of disparate income levels, this further emphasizes the need to focus on technology transfer and adaptation of existing technologies, rather than innovation, for developing countries.

Concerns over technological distance also suggest a potential role for technology transfer *among* developing countries. For instance, one might expect emerging economies to be better positioned to provide technologies specific to developing country needs, as the technological distances will be smaller. The evidence on patents and publications pertaining to cooking stoves presented in Section 14.2 is an example. However, it is important to consider not only on the potential of emerging economies to create such technologies, but also on the potential for these economies to supply needed technologies to lower income countries.

Two papers consider flows of technology transfer among developing countries. Brewer (2008) suggests that policy should consider the possibility of South–South or even South–North technology transfers. He gives examples where developing countries play roles as technology leaders, such as biofuels in Brazil and subsidiaries of General Electric developing wind turbines in China. Doranova et al. (2010) provide further evidence in a study of 497 CDM projects. They ask whether existing knowledge in the host country shapes technology sourcing patterns, focusing on projects using local technologies. Of the 497 projects studied, 56% use technologies of local origin. Moreover, some technology transfer is South–South. China, Malaysia, Taiwan, and South Africa all provided technologies in other developing countries. They use data on patents and publications related to climate-friendly technologies to measure the knowledge base of a country. Countries with more publications more likely to use local technologies, but more those with more patents are more likely to use foreign technologies, either alone or combined with local technologies. Countries with more experience with a technology are more likely to use local or combined technologies. While these studies suggest that emerging countries can play a role meeting the research needs of developing country markets for environmental technologies, further research, such as on the incentives needed to encourage transfer of green technologies among developing countries, would be beneficial.

14.3.2.2 Are the Lessons from India and China Generalizable?

Much of the literature focuses on successful examples from China and India. For instance, Lewis notes the very different strategies used by India and China. Understanding where these strategies work is important. China offers multinational investors the opportunity to access a market of one billion people. Thus, firms may be willing to accept restrictions on technology transfer to enter the Chinese market that they would not accept to enter smaller markets. Smaller countries may face additional hurdles when attracting technology transfer. Should such countries focus their attention elsewhere? Could a group of smaller countries form partnerships to increase their bargaining power with multinational firms? Finally, while countries such as India and China may have the absorptive capacity to benefit from the spillovers provided via technology transfer, countries with a greater technological distance may find using technology transfer and adaptive R&D less valuable, either because they lack the skills necessary to adapt the technology or because even an adapted technology would not be appropriate for their market. More comparative studies would thus be of great value to policymakers interested in promoting green technology transfer.

14.3.3 Diffusion within Countries

The aforementioned studies focus on the flow of knowledge across countries. Also important is the flow of knowledge within countries. The diffusion of a new technology is a gradual, dynamic process. New technologies are not adopted en masse. Rather, adoption usually begins with a few early adopters, followed by a more rapid period of adoption, with the rate of adoption leveling off once most potential users have adopted the technology. This process generates the well-known S-shaped diffusion curve: the rate of adoption rises slowly at first, speeds up, and then levels off as market saturation approaches.

The role of information is important for diffusion in both developed and developing country settings. In one recent developing country example, Rebane and Barham (2011) survey households in Nicaragua about their knowledge and adoption of solar home systems for electricity. These systems are at an early stage of market penetration and are rarely seen in some poorer areas of the country. Rebane and Barham estimate a biprobit model where they first estimate determinants of knowledge about solar home systems and then estimate determinants of adoption of such systems. Not surprisingly, awareness of the technology is important for adoption. Among non-adopters, half were unaware of solar home systems. Of those aware of the systems, most learned about them from a family, friend, or neighbor. The importance of learning from others exemplifies how adoption provides a positive externality to others by increasing awareness of the technology. Rebane and Barham suggest that demonstration projects (e.g., on public buildings) or subsidies for early adopters can thus help spread technology within a market. Moreover, early adopters may also benefit future users by reducing uncertainty about the quality of new technologies.

Recent work also suggests that important differences can be found adoption rates in developed and developing countries. World Bank (2008a) notes that in industrialized countries, once technologies reach the country, they almost always achieve mass-market scale. In contrast, there is more disparity in developing countries. Of 67 technologies studied by World Bank (2008a) that reached 5% penetration in developing countries, only 6 reached a 50% market share. Similarly, Winkler et al. (2011) note that simply providing access to grid electricity is not sufficient to ensure its use in low-income countries. Affordability is an important constraint. Even after on-grid infrastructure is in place, poor households may be unable to afford appliances that use electricity. Thus, income disparities within countries will lead to uneven diffusion of new technologies.

Two studies by Allan Blackman illustrate differences in adoption of green technologies between developing and developed countries. Blackman and Kildegaard (2003) study the adoption of three clean leather tanning technologies in Mexico. They use original survey data on a cluster of small- and medium-scale leather tanneries in León, Guanajuato, noting that small- and medium-scale enterprises often dominate pollution intensive industries in developing countries. To explain the adoption of each tanning technique, they estimate a system of multivariate probit models. They find that a firm's human capital and stock of technical information influence adoption. They also find that private-sector trade associations and input suppliers are important sources of technical information about clean technologies. In contrast to results typically found in developed countries, neither firm size nor regulatory pressure is correlated with adoption. In addition to economic incentives, direct regulation, and information provision, some research has emphasized the role that "informal regulation" or community pressure can play in encouraging the adoption of environmentally clean technologies. For example, in an analysis of fuel adoption decisions for traditional brick kilns in Mexico, Blackman and Bannister (1998) suggest that community pressure applied by competing firms and local NGOs was associated with increased adoption of cleaner fuels, even when those fuels had relatively high variable costs.

Several recent case studies note the importance of maintenance and access to finance for successful technology adoption in developing countries. Barry et al. (2011) study the adoption of efficient stoves, small biogas plants, and efficient tobacco barns for commercial farmers in Rwanda, Tanzania and Malawi. They conclude that maintenance must be planned for (including funding) at the outset of the project, and must be kept simple, so that it does not require much additional training. If not, users will abandon a technology as soon as something goes wrong. Because information is spread by word of mouth, having a local champion for a technology is also important. Because of high start-up costs, financing was cited as the main stumbling block for all projects. Thus, providing aid for financing is also important. Reviewing the success of China's Renewable Energy Development Project, D'Agostino et al. (2011) also cite access to financial credit and quality of after-sales service as important barriers to the adoption of solar home systems in China. Finally, Romijn and Caniëls (2011) find that inadequate on-site technical support holds back adoption of small-scale biomass gasification in India.

Exploring the role of financing further, Brunnschweiler (2010) explores the importance of financial sector development in the adoption of renewable energy. Investment in renewable capacity often requires long-term loans. In low-income countries, access to such credit is limited, particularly for small and medium-sized companies. Brunnschweiler finds that a one-standard deviation increase in her measure of financial intermediation leads to a 0.3 standard deviation increase in non-hydro renewable energy generation per capita. As such, improving the financial infrastructure of a nation may not only lead to macroeconomic benefits, but also encourage green growth by providing easier funding for green infrastructure. This is particularly important for efficiency-enhancing technologies. Such technologies require up-front investments, but can provide cost savings that allow the investment to pay for itself over the life of the technology. However, because investors cannot typically borrow on the promise of future cost savings, other forms of financing need to be available to facilitate these investments.

14.4 The Role of Policy

Public policy plays an important role encouraging both the development and diffusion of green technologies. Market forces provide insufficient incentives for investment in either the development or diffusion of environmentally friendly technologies. Economists point to two market failures as the explanations for underinvestment in environmental R&D. These market failures provide the motivation for government policy designed to increase such research. In addition, other market failures, such as imperfect credit markets or incomplete information, may slow the diffusion of technology.

One market failure affecting environmental innovation is the traditional problem of environmental externalities. Because pollution is not priced by the market, firms and consumers have little incentive to reduce emissions without policy intervention. Thus, without appropriate policy interventions, the market for technologies that reduce emissions will be limited, reducing incentives to develop such technologies. Similarly, once green technologies are available, diffusion will be slow if market incentives do not properly reflect the environmental benefits offered by such technologies. It is true that there will likely be some incentives to develop clean technologies even without policy interventions, as private benefits may exist. For example, improving energy efficiency in industrial processes not only reduces emissions, but also lowers the costs of production. The market failure problem simply means that individuals do not consider the social benefits of using technologies that reduce emissions, so that not all socially beneficial opportunities for technological change are pursued.

The second market failure pertaining to technological change is the public goods nature of knowledge (see, e.g., Geroski 1995). In most cases, new technologies must be made available to the public for the inventor to reap the rewards of invention. However, by making new inventions available, some (if not all) of the knowledge embodied in the invention becomes public knowledge. This public knowledge may lead to additional innovations, or even to copies of the current innovations.[9] As noted earlier, such knowledge spillovers provide benefit to the public as a whole, but not to the innovator. As a result, private firms do not have incentives to provide the socially optimal level of research activity. Because inventors cannot be fully compensated for knowledge spillovers, environmentally friendly R&D will be underprovided by market forces even if environmental policies to correct the environmental externalities of pollution are in place. Similarly, when transferring technologies, multinational firms will attempt to do so in ways that minimize the spillovers that may occur.

As with R&D investments, market failures may affect the diffusion of technology. Externalities are still a concern, so that without appropriate accounting for the external benefits from reducing pollution, individual decisions to adopt environmental technologies will be suboptimal. Environmental regulation is particularly important for adoption of end-of-pipe solutions to pollution (e.g., Kemp, 1997; Kerr and Newell, 2003; Snyder et al., 2003; and Popp, 2010). For efficiency-enhancing investments, such as energy efficiency improvements, there are private incentives to adopt, but even then, adopters will undervalue the social benefits, such as reduced pollution, that come from improving efficiency.

Uncertainty is another factor that may limit the adoption of new technology (Geroski, 2000). Potential adopters may be uncertain both about the quality of a technology and about future market conditions. For example, investing in energy saving technology is less valuable if energy prices fall in the future. As suggested in the previous section, facilitating the provision of information can help to alleviate some concerns about uncertainty.

Because of these market failures, both technology policy and environmental policy will play a role promoting technology transfer of green technologies. Technology policy helps to reward innovators for the public benefits that result from knowledge spillovers. Environmental policy makes polluters accountable for the damages they cause, thus increasing demand for green technologies. This section discusses the role of each of these policy options.

14.4.1 Technology Policy

Policy plays a role throughout the innovation process. R&D subsidies and tax credits help promote the development of new technologies. Intellectual property rights protection helps to reward inventors by providing temporary monopoly protection for their invention. However, for developing countries, the goal of technology policy will typically be to attract technology transfer or to encourage adaptive R&D on existing technologies, rather than to promote the development of new technologies. As noted earlier, knowledge spillovers from international technology transfer are important for recipient countries. However, these same spillovers may discourage innovators who wish to avoid developing competitors for their own products. For technology transfer, policy must manage a careful balancing act, so as promote knowledge spillovers from technology transfer to the extent possible without discouraging investors from coming into the country at all. Indeed, the literature on technology transfer suggests that a one size fits all policy is not desirable. As a country's own innovative capacity grows, so should the strength of its intellectual property protection (e.g., Maskus, 2002).

Developing country policies can help to promote spillovers. First, policies that improve the absorptive capacity of a country increase the potential of benefiting from knowledge spillovers. Using patent applications as a measure of technology transfer, Hascic and Johnstone (2011) find that absorptive capacity increases wind energy patent applications filed in developing countries by developed country inventors. Indeed, in their study, absorptive capacity proves to be more important than traditional technology transfer policies such as CDM.

By providing access to technology, trade policy can also help to promote spillovers from technology transfer. World Bank (2008b) includes a study of the effect of tariff and non-tariff trade barriers on trade flows of four clean energy technologies: clean coal, wind energy, solar PV systems, and energy-efficient lighting. Examining imports to the top 18 developing countries ranked by GHG emissions, they find that eliminating tariff and non-tariff barriers would increase trade volumes by 4.6% for clean coal to 63.6% for energy-efficient lighting.

Enhancing absorptive capacity or improving access to trade promotes spillovers in a way that offers little cost to innovators deciding whether or not to transfer a technology. In contrast, efforts to require technology transfer require a careful balancing act, so as to not discourage multinationals from participating at all. Wang (2010) illustrates this balancing act in a study on China's policy toward CDM projects. While the Chinese government often acts as a broker to bring parties together when technology transfer is desired, its policies often hamper technology transfer from CDM. Most importantly, China has local content requirements. For example, by 2004, new wind farms had to have 70% local content. Moreover, regulations on CDM project ownership restrict potential of technology transfer through CDM. Only Chinese companies or Chinese holding companies (requires at least 51% Chinese ownership) are eligible for CDM projects in China. While such restrictions encourage the development of local industry, they limit the ability of local industry to benefit from spillovers from technology transfer partnerships. Certified Emission Reductions (CERs) are viewed as a national asset from which private foreign companies should not profit. Thus, while foreign companies may end up as buyers of CERs, they have limited incentives to finance CDM projects, since they cannot profit from the sale of emission credits. This limits the success of projects where the only benefits are emissions reductions (e.g., reducing landfill gases), as these projects are more likely to need foreign financial support to be viable.

Intellectual property rights (IPR) provide another example of balancing the need to promote innovation with the need to promote beneficial spillovers. IPR provide a tradeoff to both inventors and to society as a whole. The goal of IPR is to reward inventors for the fixed costs of innovation. For environmental technologies, patents are the relevant form of IPR. Successful patent applicants receive a temporary monopoly, lasting 20 years from the initial application date, in return for disclosing information on the innovation in the patent document, which is part of the public record. By granting this market power, IPR helps to mitigate potential losses from knowledge spillovers and encourage innovation. Thus, while it is certainly true that, *conditional on an innovation having taken place*, one would expect technology transfer to be slower when IPR is in place. However, one cannot assume that the level of innovation would be the same if IPR were not available.

There is rising interest in broader sharing of intellectual property pertaining to environmental technologies. For example, in 2008, the World Business Council for Sustainable Development (WBCSD) created the Eco-Patent Commons to allow free access to patents with environmental benefits. However, there has been little work directly studying the effect of intellectual property rights on technology transfer of eco-innovations. A Copenhagen Economics (2009) study on climate change concludes that IPR are not a barrier to the transfer of carbon emission–reducing technologies, and that the high costs of these technologies are due more to the immaturity of the technologies, rather than IPR. Hall and Helmers (2010) provide an extensive review of the literature on patent protection. While they find evidence that stronger IPR encourages innovation in general, this effect is strongest in chemical-related sectors such as pharmaceuticals. Regarding technology transfer, they cite the work by Copenhagen Economics (2009), as well as by Barton (2007), which suggests developing country policies such as tariffs on renewable energy technology and subsidies for fossil fuels do more to limit technology transfer of clean technologies than do IPR. IPR does seem to encourage technology transfer to middle income countries with the appropriate absorptive capacity. They caution that Copenhagen Economics' finding of few climate-related patents in developing countries need not imply that IPR are not a barrier to technology transfer. Rather, it may simply mean that those countries are not yet viewed as favorable markets for climate-related technologies. Moreover, they note that because climate protection is a global public good, wide diffusion of climate-friendly innovations is desirable. Thus, they conclude that additional research is needed to assess the specific implications of IPR for green technologies.

While there is still room for more research on the question of IPR and eco-innovation, the role of demand for clean technologies cannot be overstated, and is consistent with results found elsewhere. In an oft-cited study on the role of intellectual property on pharmaceuticals, Attaran and Gillespie-White (2001) ask whether patents constrain access to AIDS treatments in Africa. They find that, even in African countries where patent protection is possible, few AIDS drugs are patented, as the markets for such drugs are too small to be of interest to multinational pharmaceutical companies. Rather than patents, they conclude that a lack of income, national regulatory requirements, and insufficient international aid are the main barriers to the spread of AIDS treatments in Africa. Similarly, with green technologies, one would expect demand (or the lack thereof) for clean technologies to be a primary constraint on international technology transfer. The spread of environmental regulation across developing countries is an important pre-condition to the diffusion of eco-innovations. Calls to weaken IPR for eco-innovations will have little impact unless they are packaged in international agreements leading to stronger environmental regulation within the developing world.

14.4.2 Environmental Policy

Without environmental policy, polluters do not have incentives to adopt costly technologies that reduce emissions but provide no additional cost savings to the polluter. For instance, because regulations limiting particulate matter were enacted several years before regulations covering sulfur dioxide (SO_2) and nitrogen oxides (NO_X), most power plants in China have controls for particulate matter, while only the newest plants control NO_X and SO_2 (Lovely and Popp, 2011). Similarly, in a study of joint ventures between US and Chinese automobile firms, Gallagher (2006) finds that the emission control technologies transferred to China are not advanced, and, in most cases, the emissions control technologies used on autos in China would not meet standards in developed countries. She notes that "(t)he main reason cleaner and more energy-efficient technologies were not transferred is that there simply were no compelling policy incentives for the US firms to do so, and the foreign firms did not voluntarily transfer better technologies" (Gallagher, 2006, p. 387).

This is important not only for diffusion, but also for innovation, as inventors will not develop technologies for which there is little demand. As noted earlier, there is a broad literature, linking environmental policy to innovation in the developed world. Because high-income countries are typically the first to enact strict environmental regulations, they also take the lead in developing green technologies. Thus, when focusing on links between environmental policy and technological change in developing countries, much of the focus is on the links between policy and diffusion of technology.

Using the CDM as a policy example, two papers take a qualitative approach to evaluate the potential of CDM for enhancing technology transfer. For example, Schneider et al. (2008) suggest four barriers to transfer of environmentally sustainable technology: (1) lack of commercial availability, (2) lack of information, (3), lack of access to capital, and (4) lack of institutional framework (e.g., rule of law, IPR). Using existing empirical studies and expert interviews, they conclude that CDM addresses the first two barriers by creating a market for clean technologies in developing countries and by encouraging sharing of knowledge, such as through the project design process. However, improved access to capital varies depending on how a CDM project is financed. Many unilateral projects must find funds to start a project, with the hope of recouping these costs once CERs are sold. Finally, CDM does nothing to change institutional settings within host countries.

Doukas et al. (2009) provide an exploratory analysis of the current developed country status and developing country prospects for five renewable energy technologies: hydropower, wind, solar, geothermal, and ocean energy. Regarding solar energy, they find that it is only economically competitive where grid connection or fuel transport is difficult, costly or impossible, such as remote rural locations. Echoing the emphasis of Schneider et al. (2008, p. 1141) on institutional framework, they find that "the nonexistence of the required regulatory framework in most of the developing countries and the very high capital costs usually strangles the interest for (solar energy) projects in developing countries."

Not only do environmental regulations encourage both innovation and adoption of environmental technologies, but also the availability of technology itself may help shape regulation. This is important, as most pollution control technologies are first developed in industrialized countries, and because environmental regulations are needed to provide incentives to adopt these technologies, the decision to enact environmental regulation in developing countries is a key first step in the diffusion of environmental technologies. While the adoption of pollution control technologies within a country responds quickly to environmental regulation, the initial adoption of environmental regulations across countries follows the typical S-shaped pattern noted in studies of technology diffusion, in which a few early adopters, typically technology leaders, are followed by a period of more rapid adoption. A period of slower adoption by the remaining stragglers follows (Jänicke and Jacob, 2004; Lovely and Popp, 2011).

As a result of these diffusion patterns, over time, countries adopt environmental regulation at lower levels of per capita income. Lovely and Popp (2011) study the adoption of regulations limiting emissions of SO_2 and NO_X at coal-fired power plants in 39 developed and developing countries. They identify access to technology as an important factor influencing the adoption of regulations and find that as pollution control technologies improve, the costs of abatement, and thus the costs of adopting environmental regulation, fall. This enables countries that adopt environmental regulations at later dates to adopt them at lower levels of per capita income than early adopters who enacted similar regulations first. Lovely and Popp suggest that this trend shows that the availability of technologies (produced by those countries that chose to adopt SO_2 regulations first) lowered adoption costs to the point where more countries were able to afford to reduce SO_2 emissions. Moreover, they find that countries that are more open to international trade gain access to new abatement technologies sooner, and thus are able to regulate SO_2 emissions sooner.

14.4.2.1 The Role of Secondary Benefits from Green Innovation

Environmental policy encourages the development and deployment of green technologies by making consumers and producers consider the external effects of their actions. However, some green technologies provide benefits that are not externalities. For example, while technologies that increase energy efficiency reduce pollution, thus benefiting the public as a whole, they also provide cost savings to the user.

Such secondary benefits will be particularly important for efforts to foster the adoption of technologies that reduce global pollutants. A willingness to "leapfrog" over dirty technologies to a clean energy system depends not only on the availability of technology, but also on the political will to enact policies supporting more costly forms of energy (Perkins, 2003). For many lower-income countries, such support seems unlikely and undesirable. Making connections between global emissions reductions and activities that provide local benefits can help win support for emissions reduction efforts. For instance, electrification reduces the need to burn wood or waste for heating or cooking, reducing indoor air pollution. It also increases opportunities for economic development (Sathaye et al., 2007). Improved cooking stoves could reduce indoor air pollution by as much as 95% (Smith et al., 2000, cited in Sathaye et al., 2007). Improved energy efficiency brings local economic benefits through lower costs (Sathaye et al., 2007). PV cells are more costly than traditional electricity sources, but of great value to remote developing regions that are not connected to the electric grid. While the costs of PV energy are typically higher than other forms of electricity, solar PV can be economically competitive where grid connection or fuel transport is difficult, costly or impossible, such as remote rural locations (Doukas et al., 2009). As the primary focus of the environmental innovation literature has been on pollution control, these secondary benefits have received less attention. However, they will be important for encouraging expansion of green technologies to low-income markets.

The links between resource usage and technological change provide another example of secondary benefits worth further study. The focus of the papers cited here, and of much of the research in environmental economics, is on pollution control. However, concerns about access to energy and promoting secure and stable energy supplies often take priority among policymakers. Whether the goal of promoting energy security complements or competes with the goal of providing clean energy depends on the resources available to a country. Lovely and Popp (2011) find that countries producing larger amounts of coal per capita are less likely to adopt regulations on SO_2 and NO_x emissions at coal-fired power plants. Cragg and Kahn (2009) show that members of the US Congress representing districts with greater carbon emissions are less likely to support legislation reducing emissions. Relating such findings to innovation, Kim (2014) examines the effect of fossil fuel endowment on the patterns of technology innovation in automobile sector. She finds that countries with larger fossil fuel endowments are less likely to develop alternative fueled vehicle technologies such as electric vehicles or fuel cells. As emerging economies such as China and India increase energy consumption while they grow, more focus on the links between resource endowments and incentives for technological change in such economies is needed. Policies to promote green growth are likely to be most successful when they complement the resource endowments of a country.

A focus on pollution control also ignores the important role of coping with a changing environment. For developing countries, innovation will be particularly important when considering adaptation to climate change. Whereas mitigation of GHGs is a global public good, the benefits of adaptation are local public goods. In some cases, these local public goods may be provided publicly, such as flood control or irrigation projects. In other cases, private actors will undertake adaptive behavior (such as farmers switching to drought-resistant crops). However, while investments in adaptive infrastructure may only have local benefits, knowledge developed research and development that improves adaptive technologies will also have the spillover benefits that result from knowledge being a public good. Given that the types of technologies needed to adapt to climate change are likely to vary depending on local conditions, this suggests a role for developing countries and/or international aid to support R&D designed to improve adaptation options for developing countries.

14.5 Implications for Developing Countries

This literature review on environmental technological change suggests several lessons for promoting climate friendly technologies in developing countries. I highlight five of the most important here. First, the fact that high-income countries dominate R&D activities, both for green technologies and more generally, suggests that technology transfer is important. In many cases, the technologies needed to reduce GHG emissions will already be available. Second, even when technologies are available, adaptive R&D can improve the fit of new technologies to local market conditions. For example, production processes can be adapted to take advantage of cost savings in local markets. Third, technology transfer will be most likely to promote cleaner growth when it promotes knowledge spillovers. Fourth, financial constraints and ease of use play important roles determining diffusion of green technologies within developing countries. Fifth, policy incentives are important for creating markets for clean technologies, as market forces typically do not reward pollution prevention completely.

Although not emphasized here, other technologies will also be important for low-income countries, particularly pertaining to resource use (such as water) and agricultural productivity. For instance, advances in agriculture, such as drought resistant crops and more efficient irrigation, are of particular importance to developing countries. In health care, neglected tropical diseases are a prominent issue.[10] These diseases, primarily of an infectious or parasitic nature, occur almost exclusively in developing countries, so that for-profit pharmaceutical companies have had little incentive to invest in new medicines to combat these diseases (Ridley et al., 2006). Thus, the same problems of creating demand for innovations needed in developing countries that green technologies face occurs in other fields as well, such as agricultural economics and health economics.[11] Advance purchase commitments for medicines (Barder et al., 2006) provide an example of how researchers in the health care community propose creating demand for innovation on medicines for neglected diseases. Moving forward, environmental economists can learn from existing work in these fields to gain new insights on creating demand for green technology. At the same time, the additional market failure of environmental externalities suggests that simply applying the lessons from other sectors will not be sufficient.

APPENDIX

Indoor Cooking Stove Search Terms

Patent Searches

kerosene or butane stoves

((A47J 027<or>A47J 027??<or>A47J 027???<or>A47J 027????<or>A47J 037<or> A47J 037??<or>A47J 037???<or>A47J 037????<or>F24B*<or>F24C*) <in>IC) <AND>((kerosene<OR>butane) <in>AB))

liquefied petroleum gas stoves

(((A47J 027<or>A47J 027??<or>A47J 027???<or>A47J 027????<or>A47J 037<or> A47J 037??<or>A47J 037???<or>A47J 037????<or>F24B*<or>F24C*) <in>IC) <AND>(((LPG<OR>"liquefied petroleum gas") <in>AB))

biomass stoves

(((A47J 027<or>A47J 027??<or>A47J 027???<or>A47J 027????<or>A47J 037 <or>A47J 037??<or>A47J 037???<or>A47J 037????<or>F24B*<or>F24C*) <in>IC) <AND>(biomass <in>AB))

solar stoves

((solar AND (cooker OR oven OR stove)) <in>AB)

Publication Searches

solar stoves

TS=("solar cooker" OR "solar oven" OR "solar stove" OR "solar cookers" OR "solar ovens" OR "solar stoves" OR "solar cooking").[12]

biomass stoves

TS=(biomass SAME (stove OR stoves OR oven OR ovens OR cooker OR cooking))

LPG stoves

TS=((LPG OR "liquefied petroleum gas") SAME (stove OR stoves OR oven OR ovens OR cooker OR cooking))

kerosene or butane stoves

TS=((kerosene OR butane) SAME (stove OR stoves OR oven OR ovens OR cooker OR cooking))

NOTES: AB = abstract, IC = International Patent Classification, TS = topic search (includes title, abstract, and keywords)

Notes

1. http://www.iea.org/index_info.asp?id=1959
2. Annex I countries include all Annex B countries plus Belarus and Turkey. These are the developed and transitioning economies required to reduce emissions under the Kyoto Protocol. A list of Annex B countries can be found at http://unfccc.int/kyoto_protocol/items/3145.php
3. Because patents are valid only in the country granting the patent, an inventor must file a patent application in each country for which protection is desired. These related applications are called *patent families.* Economists use these patent families to indicate the importance of an invention (e.g., Lanjouw and Schankerman, 2004).
4. These patents were identified using a combination of keyword and patent classification searches using the Delphion on-line patent database. Countries are identified using the first inventor listed on the patent. If no inventor country is limited, the first priority country (e.g., the country where the application was first filed) is taken as the source of the invention. Scientific publication data are collected using a keyword search of abstracts and titles in the Web of Knowledge database. Here, the source country comes from author affiliations. For multiple authored papers, affiliations are counted for each country, so that the total number of affiliations may exceed the total number of articles. The Appendix lists the search terms used for each stove type. Note that the use of keyword searches may bias downward counts from countries whose patent abstracts may appear in other languages, such as France and Germany. However, that Chinese patent counts are larger than even the United States and Japan, who do the bulk of global R&D, is still notable.
5. While illustrative of differences in research trends across income levels (particularly given India's lead over the United States in most categories), English language bias is definitely an issue when using publication data, as seen by the large advantage of US publications over those of countries such as Japan or Germany.
6. For a general review of the literature on international technology transfer, see Keller (2004).
7. World Bank (2008a) provides a discussion of the role of absorptive capacity in technology transfer. They use data on education, governance and macroeconomic stability to construct an index of absorptive capacity. In addition to the importance of an educated workforce, they provide evidence that a stable economy and strong business environment improve adaptive capacity.

8. Lecocq and Ambrosi (2007) provide a description of the CDM.
9. Intellectual property rights, such as patents, are designed to protect inventors from such copies. However, their effectiveness varies depending on the ease in which inventors may "invent around" the patent by making minor modifications to an invention. See, for example, Levin et al. (1987).
10. See, for example, http://www.who.int/neglected_diseases/en/
11. For an example pertaining to pharmaceutical markets in developing countries, see Kremer (2002).
12. "TS" represents a "topic search" that looks for the search terms in the title, abstract, or keywords of the article.

References

Acemoglu, D. (2002). Directed technical change. *Review of Economic Studies, 69*, 781–809.

Attaran, A., and Gillespie-White, L. (2001). Do patents for antiretroviral drugs constrain access to AIDS treatment in Africa? *Journal of the American Medical Association, 286*(15), 1886–1892.

Barder, O., Kremer, M., and Williams, H. (2006). Advance market commitments: A policy to stimulate investment in vaccines for neglected diseases. *The Economists' Voice*, 3(1), Article 1. doi: 10.2202/1553-3832.1144. http://www.bepress.com/ev/vol3/iss3/art1.

Barry, M.-L., Steyn, H., and Brent, A. (2011). Selection of renewable energy technologies for Africa: Eight case studies in Rwanda, Tanzania and Malawi. *Renewable Energy, 36*, 2845–2852.

Barton, J. H. (2007). Intellectual property and access to clean energy technologies in developing countries. International Centre for Trade and Sustainable Development Issue Paper No. 2.

Binswanger, H., and Ruttan, V. (1978). *Induced Innovation: Technology Institutions and Development.* Baltimore: Johns Hopkins University Press.

Blackman, A., and Bannister, G. J. (1998). Community pressure and clean technology in the informal sector: An econometric analysis of the adoption of propane by traditional Mexican brickmakers. *Journal of Environmental Economics and Management, 35*(1), 1–21.

Blackman, A., and Kildegaard, A. (2003). Clean technological change in developing-country industrial clusters: Mexican leather tanning. Discussion Paper 03-12. Washington, DC: Resources for the Future.

Bradsher, K. (2011). Hybrid in a trade squeeze. *The New York Times*, September 6, 2011, p. B1.

Brewer, T. L. (2008). Climate change technology transfer: A new paradigm and policy agenda. *Climate Policy, 8*, 516–526.

Broder, J. M. (2010). Developing nations to get clean-burning cookstoves. *The New York Times*, September 21, 2010, A8.

Brunnschweiler, C. N. (2010). Finance for renewable energy: An empirical analysis of developing and transition economies. *Environment and Development Economics, 15*, 241–274.

Copeland, B. R., and Taylor, M. S. (2003). *Trade and the Environment: Theory and Evidence.* Princeton, NJ: Princeton University Press.

Copenhagen Economics (2009). Are IPR a barrier to the transfer of climate change technology? Report prepared by Copenhagen Economics and the IPR Company.

Cragg, M. I., and Kahn, M. E. (2009). Carbon geography: The political economy of congressional support for legislation intended to mitigate greenhouse gas production. NBER Working Paper 14963. Cambridge, MA: National Bureau of Economic Research.

D'Agostino, A. L., Sovacool, B. K., and Bambawale, M. J. (2011). And then what happened? A retrospective appraisal of China's Renewable Energy Development Project (REDP). *Renewable Energy, 36*, 3154–3165.

Dasgupta, S., Laplante, B., Wang, H., and Wheeler, D. (2002). Confronting the environmental Kuznets curve. *Journal of Economic Perspectives, 16*, 147–168.

Dechezleprêtre, A., Glachant, M., Hascic, I., Johnstone, N., and Ménière, Y. (2011). Invention and transfer of climate change mitigation technologies on a global scale: A study drawing on patent data. *Review of Environmental Economics and Policy, 5*(1), 109–130.

Dechezleprêtre, A., Glachant, M., and Ménière, Y. (2008). The Clean Development Mechanism and the international diffusion of technologies: An empirical study. *Energy Policy, 36*, 1273–1283.

de la Tour, A., Glachant, M., and Ménière, Y. (2011). Innovation and international technology transfer: The case of the Chinese photovoltaic industry. *Energy Policy, 39*, 761–770.

Doranova, A., Costa, I., and Duysters, G. (2010). Knowledge base determinants of technology sourcing in the Clean Development Mechanism projects. *Energy Policy, 38*(10), 5550–5559.

Doukas, H., Karakosta, C., and Psarras, J. (2009). RES technology transfer within the new climate regime: A 'helicopter' view under the CDM. *Renewable and Sustainable Energy Reviews, 13*, 1138–1143.

Energy Information Administration. (2010). *International Energy Outlook 2010*. Washington, DC: US Department of Energy.

Esty, D. C. (2001). Bridging the trade-environment divide. *Journal of Economic Perspectives, 15*(3), 113–130.

Fisher-Vanden, K., and Ho, M. S. (2010). Technology, development, and the environment. *Journal of Environmental Economics and Management, 59*(1), 94–108.

Fisher-Vanden, K., and Wing, I. S. (2008). Accounting for quality: Issues with modeling the impact of R&D on economic growth and carbon emissions in developing countries. *Energy Economics, 30*(6), 2771–2784.

Gallagher, K. S. (2006). Limits to leapfrogging in energy technologies? Evidence from the Chinese automobile industry. *Energy Policy, 34*, 383–394.

Geroski, P. (1995). Markets for technology: Knowledge, innovation, and appropriability, In P. Stoneman (ed.), pp. 90–131. *Handbook of the Economics of Innovation and Technological Change*. Oxford: Wiley-Blackwell.

Geroski, P. (2000). Models of technology diffusion. *Research Policy, 29*, 603–626.

Gupta, S., Tirpak, D. A., Burger, N., Gupta, J. Höhne, N., Boncheva, A. I., Kanoan, G. M., Kolstad, C., Kruger, J. A., Michaelowa, A., Murase, S., Pershing, J., Saijo, T., and Sari, A. (2007). Policies, Instruments and Co-operative Arrangements. In *Climate Change 2007: Mitigation. Contribution of Working Group III to the Fourth Assessment Report of the Intergovernmental Panel on Climate Change*. [B. Metz, O. R. Davidson, P. R. Bosch, R. Dave, and L. A. Meyer (eds.)]. Cambridge University Press, Cambridge, United Kingdom and New York, NY, USA, pp. 745–807.

Hall, B. H., and Helmers, C. (2010). The role of patent protection in (clean/green) technology transfer. *Santa Clara High Technology Law Journal, 26*, 487–565.

Hascic, I., and Johnstone, N. (2011). The Clean Development Mechanism and international technology transfer: Empirical evidence on wind power. *Climate Policy, 11*(6), 1303–1314.

Hicks, J. (1932). *The Theory of Wages.* London: Macmillan.

Jänicke, M., and Jacob, K. (2004). Lead markets for environmental innovations: A new role for the nation state. *Global Environmental Politics, 4,* 29–46.

Keller, W. (2004). International technology diffusion. *Journal of Economic Literature, 42,* 752–782.

Kemp, R. (1997). *Environmental Policy and Technical Change.* Cheltenham, UK: Edward Elgar.

Kerr, S., and Newell, R. G. (2003). Policy-induced technology adoption: Evidence from the U.S. lead phasedown. *Journal of Industrial Economics, 51*(3), 317–343.

Khanna, M., and Zilberman, D. (2001). Adoption of energy efficient technologies and carbon abatement: The electricity generating sector in India. *Energy Economics, 23,* 637–658.

Kim, J. E. (2014). Energy security and climate change: How oil endowment influences alternative vehicle innovation? *Energy Policy, 66,* 400–410.

Kremer, M. (2002). Pharmaceuticals and the developing world. *Journal of Economic Perspectives, 16*(4), 67–90.

Kristinsson, K. and Rao, R. (2007). Learning to grow: A comparative analysis of the wind energy sector in Denmark and India. DRUID Working Paper 07-18. Danish Research Unit for Industrial Dynamics. Aalborg, Denmark: Aalborg University.

Lanjouw, J. O., and Mody, A. (1996). Innovation and the international diffusion of environmentally responsive technology. *Research Policy, 25,* 549–571.

Lanjouw, J. O., and Shankerman, M. (2004). The quality of ideas: Measuring innovation with multiple indicators. *Economic Journal, 114*(495), 441–465.

Lecocq, F., and Ambrosi, P. (2007). The clean development mechanism: History, status, and prospects. *Review of Environmental Economics and Policy, 1*(1), 134–151.

Levin, R. C., Klevorick, A. K., Nelson, R. R., and Winter, S. G. (1987). Appropriating the returns from industrial research and development. *Brookings Papers on Economic Activity, 3,* 783–820.

Lewis, J. I. (2007). Technology acquisition and innovation in the developing world: Wind turbine development in China and India. *Studies in Comparative International Development, 42*(3–4), 208–232.

Lovely, M. and Popp, D. (2011). Trade, technology and the environment: Does access to technology promote environmental regulation? *Journal of Environmental Economics and Management, 61*(1), 16–35.

Maskus, K. E. (2002). Lessons from studying the international economics of intellectual property rights. *Vanderbilt Law Review, 53*(6), 2219–2239.

Medhi, N. (2009). *Adoption of Environmental Regulations and Diffusion of Environmentally Sound Technologies in Developing Countries.* PhD dissertation, Syracuse University.

National Science Board. (2010). Research and Development: Funds and Technology Linkages. In *Science and Engineering Indicators 2010,* pp. 4-1–4-66. Arlington, VA: National Science Foundation.

Perkins, R. (2003). Environmental leapfrogging in developing countries: A critical assessment and reconstruction. *Natural Resources Forum, 27,* 177–188.

Popp, D. (2006). International innovation and diffusion of air pollution control technologies: The effects of NO_X and SO_2 regulation in the U.S., Japan, and Germany. *Journal of Environmental Economics and Management, 51*(1), 46–71.

Popp D. (2010). Exploring the links between innovation and diffusion: Adoption of NO_X control technologies at U.S. coal-fired power plants. *Environmental and Resource Economics, 45*(3), 319–352.

Popp, D., Newell, R. G., and Jaffe, A. B. (2010). Energy, the environment, and technological change. In B. Hall and N. Rosenberg (eds.), *Handbook of the Economics of Innovation*, Vol. 2, pp. 873–937. San Diego: Academic Press/Elsevier.

Pueyo, A., García, R., Mendiluce, M., and Morales, D. (2011). The role of technology transfer for the development of a local wind component industry in Chile. *Energy Policy, 39*, 4274–4283.

Ramanathan, V., and Carmichael, G. (2008). Global and regional climate changes due to black carbon. *Nature Geoscience, 1*, 221–227.

Rebane, K., and Barham, B. L. (2011). Knowledge and adoption of solar home systems in rural Nicaragua. *Energy Policy, 39*, 3064–3075.

Ridley, D. B., Grabowski, H. G., and Moe, J. L. (2006). Developing drugs for developing countries. *Health Affairs, 25*(2), 313–324.

Romjin, H. A., and Caniëls, M. C. J. (2011). Pathways of technological change in developing countries: Review and new agenda. *Development Policy Review, 29*(3), 359–380.

Sathaye, J., Najam, A., Cocklin, C., Heller, T., Lecocq, F., Llanes-Regueiro, J., Pan, J., Petschel-Held, G., Rayner, S., Robinson, J., Schaeffer, R., Sokona, Y., Swart, R., and Winkler, H. (2007). Sustainable development and mitigation. In *Climate Change 2007: Mitigation. Contribution of Working Group III to the Fourth Assessment Report of the Intergovernmental Panel on Climate Change* [B. Metz, O. R. Davidson, P. R. Bosch, R. Dave, L. A. Meyer (eds.)]. Cambridge University Press, Cambridge, United Kingdom and New York, NY, USA, pp. 691–743.

Sawhney, A., and Kahn, M. E. (2012). Understanding cross-national trends in high-tech renewable power equipment exports to the United States. *Energy Policy, 46*, 308–318.

Schneider, M., Holzer, A., and Hoffmann, V. (2008). Understanding the CDM's contribution to technology transfer. *Energy Policy, 36*, 2930–2938.

Smith, K. R., Samet, J. M., Romieu, I., and Bruce, N. (2000). Indoor air pollution in developing countries and acute lower respiratory infections in children. *Thorax, 55*, 518–532.

Snyder, L. D., Miller, N. H., and Stavins, R. N. (2003). The effects of environmental regulation on technology diffusion: The case of chlorine manufacturing. *American Economic Review, 93*(2), 431–435.

Verdolini, E., and Galeotti, M. (2011). At home and abroad: An empirical analysis of innovation and diffusion in energy technologies. *Journal of Environmental Economics and Management, 61*(2), 119–134.

Wang, B. (2010). Can CDM bring technology transfer to China?—An empirical study of technology transfer in China's CDM projects. *Energy Policy, 38*, 2572–2585.

Winkler, H., Simões, A. F., La Rovere, E. L., Alam, M., Rahman, A., and Mwakasonda, S. (2011). Access and affordability of electricity in developing countries. *World Development, 39*(6), 1037–1050.

World Bank. (2008a). *Global Economic Prospects: Technology Diffusion in the Developing World.* Washington, DC: World Bank.

World Bank. (2008b). *International Trade and Climate Change: Economic, Legal, and Institutional Perspectives.* Washington, DC: World Bank.

CHAPTER 15

RENEWABLE ENERGY

Models, Implications, and Prospects

FRANZ WIRL AND YURI YEGOROV

15.1 Introduction

This chapter investigates the prospects of renewable energy from an economic perspective. Given the overall praise of renewable energy and the surrounding promises, this assessment focuses on the problems. Let us start with an uncontroversial statement. One cannot overemphasize the importance of renewable energy to reduce greenhouse gas (GHG) emissions and to solve hard resource constraints for fossil fuels. Of course one cannot ignore the physical (this applies in particular to biofuels but also solar and wind energy), but the apparently soft constraints from economics and politics must also be taken into consideration. Unfortunately, the latter constraints are ignored by most proponents of renewable energy and therefore this survey focuses on them as well.

A basic presumption that includes many economic models is that the large-scale availability of renewable energy can be taken for granted to meet all kinds of demands if only sufficient resources are dedicated to research and development (R&D). This assumption that sufficient input will deliver the required output may be naïve, particularly in light of the fact that many of the savior technologies (the electric car, photovoltaic) are old, have enjoyed substantial efforts including billions of subsidies, but show at best meager improvements over time that fall short by far for solving resource and environmental problems. Another point is ignorance of demand and supply interactions. Any breakthrough in renewable energy technology will induce energy suppliers to undercut the costs of renewable rather than to leave huge volumes of fossil energy in the ground. This can even lead to the "green paradox" (see Hans Werner Sinn, 2008), that advanced availability of renewable substitutes increases, at least transiently, carbon emissions and thus global warming, unless simultaneously a globally binding greenhouse mitigation compact is enacted. Yet such binding commitments of governments are very unlikely in general and in particular in this case, because poor developing countries will not eschew the use of cheap fossil energy.

This chapter is organized as follows. Section 15.2 reviews renewable energy, its importance, myths, and limits, and forecasts of renewable energy with emphasis on their (in-) efficiency. Section 15.3 presents economic models focusing on efficient policies. In contrast, Section 15.4 discusses the inability of real-world governments to commit to future actions and the consequences thereof. Final remarks complete this analysis.

15.2 Renewable Energy

15.2.1 Importance

Availability and costs of renewable energy are crucial in determining whether global warming will be mitigated by reduced carbon emissions. The reason is that significant mitigation of global warming by conservation will work only if severe cutbacks in consumption and individual benefits are accepted by the population (whether allowed to vote or not). While the costs of global warming are very high, especially for future generations (*The Economist*, 2010), people have high discount of future and are unlikely to accept a lot of sacrifices today. Therefore, given the absence of the availability of cheap renewable energy substitutes on a large scale, global warming mitigation strategies will most likely fail, because neither the costs nor the required huge changes in lifestyles will be accepted given the incentives to free ride. These incentives for free riding are too strong to resist at an individual level (being just one among 7 billion), but also nationally, in particular for small and poor developing countries. The only options are then either to do nothing (or little, more or less as tokens) or to experiment with relatively cheap geophysical techniques (spraying sulfur into the stratosphere, sea mist in the troposphere, trillion disks in space, etc.). Actually this cheapness is a potential problem, because country A may influence the climate to the detriment of B (Barrett, 2009). In addition, if these methods are removed or have to be removed because of unintended consequences, then global mean temperature will jump upward immediately, with obvious severe negative effects on people, animal species, and harvests. Therefore, the availability of renewable energy on a large scale and at affordable prices is the crucial point if we are to succeed in mitigating global warming in the politically correct way, that is, by lowering GHG emissions instead of applying the brute force of geo-engineering. Of course, unintended consequences are not confined to geo-engineering but to renewable energy too, as the increased demand for rare earths for new battery technologies and more efficient lighting is documenting.

15.2.2 Myths and Limits

In spite of the small share in current energy use, many conceive renewable energy as the magic bullet that will solve the world's energy problems including global warming, and at low costs. For example, Jacobson and Delucchi (2011) claim that the technologies for full shift to wind, water, and solar (WWS) power to combat climate change are already available. According to their plan, a full shift to renewable electricity (mostly from wind and the sun) will reduce world power demand by 30% and will require only 1% of world land. Similar claims are made for efficiency improvements, which, however, will not wash because of an additional consideration, the rebound effect. Although this effect has been known at least since Jevons's book on the coal question, it has been ignored until recently by famous conservationists.

Given this optimism it is important to keep the following in mind. The issue of alternative energy has been high on the political agenda at least since the early 1970s due to the second report to the Club of Rome, *Limit to Growth* by Meadows et al., and the quadrupling of oil prices in autumn 1973 following the Yom Kippur War. Since that time many different efforts, research funding, and most notably Carter's Project *Independence* have produced relatively low output. The spending on this major project initiated by the Carter administration on the premise of the "moral equivalent of war" turned out to be a pure waste of money and the related research funding produced very little. Just for the record, the costs of alternatives—no one dared to speak of renewable energy at that time—were in the range of $20–40 (when oil was above $10/barrel). Indeed it seems that their costs are far above the oil prices no matter how high the latter climb (with few exceptions such as coal liquefaction but that is not renewable). After all, who dared to predict oil prices above and around $100/barrel say in 2004–2005, when the International Energy Agency (IEA) and US Department of Energy were claiming that we have lots of oil at high prices. More precisely, given past cost estimates, a large number of alternatives should be highly profitable at these high prices, but very little is coming forward.

Despite much price variation (oil price is very volatile), overall buildup of renewable energy stock is not growing quickly. According to Eurostat,[1] the share of renewable energy in gross final energy consumption of EU27 grew from 9% in 2006 to only 11.9% in 2009, while the target is 20% by 2020. The country data are provided in Table 15.1. Moreover, those 20% seem to be quite a moderate goal given the growing scarcity of fossil fuels and rapid climate change.

One reason is the simple economics of no arbitrage: with the final product so dear feed stocks become equally expensive. All this disappointment with too slow substitution of fossil fuels by renewable is not so surprising if one accounts for the following issues.

Table 15.1 Shares of Primary Energies in Different EU Countries

Country \ Year	2006	2009	2012
European Union (28 c.)	9.3	11.9	14.1
Belgium	2.7	4.6	6.8
Bulgaria	9.7	12.4	16.3
Czech Republic	6.4	8.5	11.2
Denmark	15.9	20.4	26.0
Germany	7.7	9.9	12.4
Estonia	16.1	23.0	25.8
Ireland	3.1	5.2	7.2
Greece	7.2	8.5	13.8
Spain	9.2	13.0	14.3
France	9.5	12.2	13.4
Croatia	12.8	13.1	16.8
Italy	6.4	9.3	13.5
Cyprus	3.3	5.6	6.8
Latvia	31.1	34.3	35.8
Lithuania	17.0	20.0	21.7
Luxembourg	1.5	2.9	3.1
Hungary	5.1	8.0	9.6
Malta	0.4	0.4	1.4
Netherlands	2.6	4.1	4.5
Austria	25.6	30.4	32.1
Poland	7.0	8.8	11.0
Portugal	20.7	24.5	24.6
Romania	17.1	22.6	22.9
Slovenia	15.6	18.9	20.2
Slovakia	5.9	9.3	10.4
Finland	30.1	31.2	34.3
Sweden	42.6	48.2	51.0
United Kingdom	1.6	3.0	4.2
Norway	60.2	64.8	64.5

Source: http://appsso.eurostat.ec.europa.eu/nui/show.do?dataset=nrg_ind_335a&lang=en

15.2.2.1 Physical Limits

MacKay (2009) stated that the potential contribution of biofuels can be approximated from just three numbers: the intensity of sunlight, the efficiency with which plants turn that sunlight into stored energy, and the available land area. Meeting Britain's energy needs from onshore wind power would require covering literally the entire country in turbines, even assuming that the wind was guaranteed to blow. If only 10% of

Britain were covered, then wind could provide roughly a tenth of total demand. Switching every piece of agricultural land to biofuel production would provide just 12% of the requisite juice. It is a similar story for offshore wind, tidal, and wave energy: To make a dent in fossil fuel consumption without using nuclear power, renewable energy facilities will have to be "country-sized," with offshore wind farms bigger than Wales and huge solar power arrays in sunny deserts piping power to cloudier nations. Even recent attempts by Craig Venter and others to design bacteria-produced hydrocarbons efficiently requires feed stocks (say sugar) that face problems similar to the direct conversion say into alcohol. To quote Richard Feynman, "nature cannot be fooled" and something similar holds for economic laws, at least in the long run.

However, not all looks so dull. Indeed, global use of biofuels is limited to probably 10% of world arable land; at larger use there is a threat of famine. Wind and solar power also require land but to a less extent. Here countries with lower population density have an advantage to use land for such production that has low economic value. For example, not only the Sahara Desert (for which a solar energy project is already planned) but also most of Australia are unpopulated, and thus there is little physical limitation to substituting all fossil fuels by renewable (solar, wind, and wave energy) sources. It is worthwhile mentioning another effect of transition toward renewable energy: dispersion force that counterbalances the force of agglomeration, currently dominant in most of the countries.

15.2.2.2 Technologies Are Old

The major technologies under investigation are old. For example, the electric car predates the combustion engine yet the battery problem is unsolved to this very day, let alone that replacing petrol (and diesel) by complete reliance on electrically powered engines saves, if at all, relatively little compared with efficient cars. The photovoltaic (PV) effect has been known for about 170 years, and as an old technology it shows continuous improvements (its first use was in the space programs) but hardly significant breakthroughs. Delucchi and Jacobson (2011) present a forecast of fast cost reduction for solar PV systems, from above \$0.20 in 2010 to an already economic level of \$0.10 in 2020. But it is far from clear if this can be implemented. A further disadvantage of PV systems is that their design mixes up cause and effect of global warming: its dark material coupled with the low efficiency actually contributes to global warming, at least in gross terms, although it saves CO_2 emissions.[2] Wind energy is even older and as a result of modern technology has seen a substantial improvement of its efficiency (at least compared to millennia old windmills) but today faces strong opposition even from environmentalists and the physical limits as outlined previously. In short, given these highly favored but old technologies we doubt that they will deliver the required magic bullet. However, they certainly have a scope as niche players in future energy supply.

15.2.2.3 *Beliefs in R&D*

The preceding cases of PV and battery technologies for electric cars demonstrate that the common assumption that more R&D will "guarantee" a positive outcome is naïve. First, there is the possibility that there is no solution given the constraints such as physics and our current knowledge. Researchers often observe that no result is obtained because either no solution exists for a conjecture or that we are not able to find one even spending enormous efforts. Think about the very simple famous conjecture of Fermat, which took the work of thousands of the most talented mathematicians several centuries to prove. The final proof had to rely on very recent results from a field that is quite apart from number theory, which suggests that earlier proof has been highly unlikely. One can imagine living in the 15th century and proposing launch of an R&D program against the Black Death. It would have had no chance to succeed within decades and even a century given the resources and knowledge at the time (e.g., bacteria were discovered more than 400 years after the epidemic, as the microscope had not yet been invented). To return to electric cars, there may be no economic solution to the problem of batteries that hinder the success of this technology since its inception, which predated its competitor, the combustion engine.

15.2.2.4 *Socioeconomic and Scientific Barriers*

There are both socioeconomic and purely scientific barriers to new and truly more efficient technologies. Renewable energy would live up to its promise if it were not inhibited by barriers and conspiring industries (oil and car manufacturers). Of all myths, this often mentioned one is outright wrong. To prove how little such barriers matter one can consider mobile phone technology. First, this was not a big breakthrough (actually we even doubt whether it is indeed an achievement), at least with respect to industrialized countries. Everyone has a phone in his or her home and office, and public phones were available in practically every village, no matter how small, and also distributed throughout cities. The gain provided by mobile phones to developed economies was not a very large one, but the story is presumably different for many developing countries. Furthermore, entries of mobile companies had faced highly cost-efficient and well established networks of companies doing traditional telephony, and thus the availability of mobile phones was restricted at the beginning to centers (as the fixed cost of covering rural areas had been prohibitively high). Against all this, a meager gain, large and tough incumbents with established networks, the need to build a network structure, physical coverage, and then establishing a user base, this very profane technology swept the market, reaching almost saturation (with more than 5 billion mobile phones worldwide; even we have clumsy phones) within a decade. Therefore, the claim that an efficient, clean, and cheap energy technology faces an uphill battle and therefore needs public nurturing is untenable. Indeed there is even a counterexample with respect to energy in how diesel-powered cars penetrated the market quickly once the technology was available, and this against its very negative image in such an image-sensitive (at least this is what marketing wants us to believe) product like the car (e.g., diesel is equated rather to a tractor than to a car, but nowadays even a Porsche Cayenne uses diesel engines).

15.2.2.5 *Optimism about Low Costs*

An over-optimism about progress and an underestimation of the costs of all kinds of backstops has existed since the mid 1970s. For example, Ericsson and Morgan (1978) argue that 15 million barrels per day or three quarters of present US consumption can be profitably produced from shale oil for an oil price of 1975: US$18 per barrel. In fact, many alternatives seem to have a tendency to remain above the oil price no matter what the oil price level is. A survey in *The Economist* (2006) lists the costs of backstops at US$40 for tar sands, coal to liquids, and for the Brazilian ethanol program, US$50 for shale oil, US$60 US corn-based ethanol, and US$80 for biodiesel. However, the case of ethanol and other related alternatives neglects the feedback on prices for feedstock. For example, during the record high oil prices during 2008 it was impossible to break even for making diesel from disposed cooking oil as the price of the feedstock rose. This interdependence between prices for oil and its renewable substitutes is ignored (see later); in addition, the predictions are inefficient on statistical grounds.

A nice theoretical model about barriers for new technologies is Acemoglu et al. (2012) about directed technical change. The crucial point is the positive feedback on R&D on the existing stock of knowledge. This can deter investment into new areas. For example, car manufacturers have much more knowledge about improving the combustion engine than for solving the battery problems for electric cars and therefore focus on the first. The upshot is that subsidies are indeed necessary to direct technical change from fossil to renewable fuels.

15.2.2.6 *Uncertainty of the Development Path*

It is also important to mention such economic effects as uncertainty in the development path for substitution technologies and the network effects related to them. Both bring nonconvexities that repudiate classical theorems about market efficiency. The last four decades of the 20th century have been filled with optimism about nuclear fusion,[3] or nuclear synthesis. The advantage of this reaction versus nuclear fission (division of uranium or plutonium) is in a virtually unlimited stock of water on the Earth that can be used as the source of atoms for reactions (in contrast to a limited stock of uranium). The optimism has been also supported by the fact that this reaction is natural and takes place in all stars. Any success here could end energy scarcity. However, the problem became purely technological: the optimal temperature for this reaction is many million degrees, and the only way is to keep plasma stable in a magnetic field. Despite the construction of quite expensive devices it was impossible to get this reaction to last a sufficiently long time to be profitable economically. After the 1990s both the enthusiasm and financing declined, and now there is little hope for a fast breakthrough here. Another effect is purely economical, and is related to network industries. For any alternative fuel for cars (biodiesel, ethanol, electricity, etc.)

we need a dense network of stations where this fueling can be done. And here we have a vicious circle suggesting the existence of some threshold for network development. If initially alternative fuel has a cost disadvantage, there will be too little investment in such a network that will reinforce such a disadvantage even further owing to a network effect.[4] Hence, the development path of the network industry (associated with servicing cars by alternative fuel) will be one typical for a convex production function, with slow initial development requiring subsidies and fast breakthrough, but in uncertain moment.

The example of fast development of a mobile phone network (which has two types of network effects, population of users and physical coverage) shows that sometimes market forces can overcome network effects. As the example of mobile phones demonstrates, this network effect may pose less critical problems. Indeed, this has happened already in the past in the energy industry with electricity, natural gas, petrol stations, and more recently liquefied petroleum gas (before a corresponding petrol tax killed this market; see also discussion later). However, in the case of solar power the past indicates that obstacles linked to network effects and costs seem much more serious.

There also exists well developed nuclear energy technology. But random shocks also have had an important influence on its development path. The catastrophes of Chernobyl in 1986 and Fukushima in 2011 have undermined public support for it, despite the fact that nuclear energy is a remedy for both green gas emission and fossil fuel scarcity. Figure 15.9 shows a plot for nuclear energy production in EU27 and public belief in it. Interestingly, there exists a positive correlation between both variables, that is, public support is higher in countries with a large share of nuclear energy in their portfolio of primary energies.

15.2.3 Forecasts

Here we have to take into account both market interaction within an industry (network effects, considered earlier) and between industries. The typical renewable energy forecast takes the future evolution of the oil price as a given (typically with the moving average increasing at a constant rate) and assumes cost reductions for the renewable energy as a result of learning by doing, and technological progress to arrive at its profitability and consequently its availability. Yet this argument ignores foresight and market interactions between industries because a significant breakthrough in alternative fuel technologies will definitely affect the price of oil, which has been assumed to prove the economics of the alternative in the first place. To highlight the point, assume that the oil price is US$100 per barrel and we come up with an alternative at a cost of US$50 per barrel of oil equivalent. Furthermore, assume that this technology is available on a large scale. A naïve consequence would be that the super-rich of the world will have to blush from the money that we are going to make. However, a more realistic consequence is the likely consequence of bankruptcy because the oil price ex post our invention and product launch will be US$49 per barrel. Only resource constraints can render profitability to such premature innovations and their implementation.

The second point considers the efficiency of past renewable energy supply forecasts from a technical and statistical point of view. A seminal paper of Nordhaus (1987) demonstrates that the efficient revisions of forecasts concerning a fixed future event, say energy demand 2030, should be purely random. Yet professional forecasters like the IEA were continuously revising their forecast in the same direction, namely downwards. This pattern of inefficiency continues in the case of nuclear energy in spite of Nordhaus's criticism decades ago but this time continuously upward revising (see Figure 15.1). Wind energy shows an even stronger pattern of continuous upward revisions (see Figure 15.2). In all fairness, the predictions for solar (thermal as well as PV) power and biofuels look more efficient. Yet the total shows over-optimism around the turn of the century (in particular in 2000, the forecast was revised by 50%) followed by necessary and continuous downward revisions (see Figure 15.3). Over-optimistic predictions are played again in the context of renewables.

15.2.4 Challenges

As we can see, transition to renewable energies is inevitable but faces many challenges that are difficult to tackle by market forces.

First, it is clear that using a finite stock of fossil fuels is inconsistent not only with unbounded economic growth, but even with an unbounded existence of civilization. One of the models that follows will prove this formally. It is not quite clear (requires more geophysical studies) whether the threat of global warming (via burning of fossil fuels) to a nonacceptable level (change by 3–5° C) comes before or after exhaustion of the global stock of hydrocarbons. But both threats work for the same policy: to replace

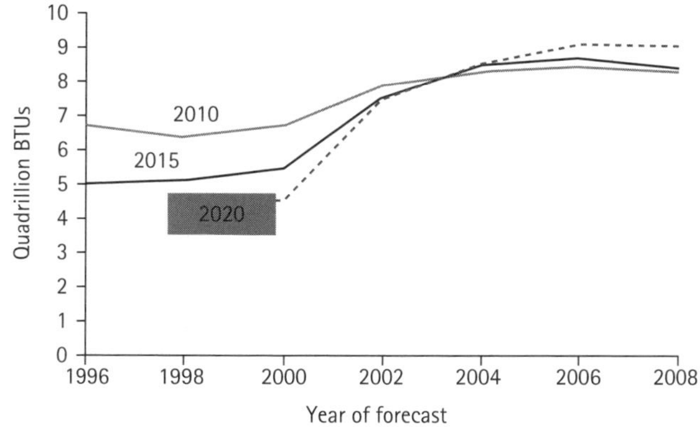

FIGURE 15.1 Past forecasts (IEA) of nuclear energy for indicated horizons (2010, 2015, and 2020) made at different dates (1998–2008).

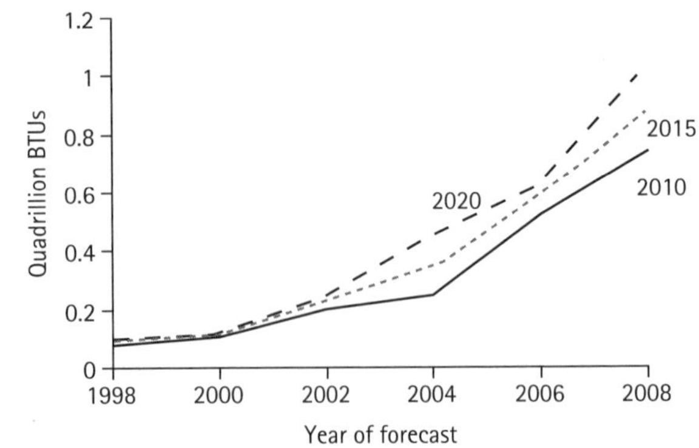

FIGURE 15.2 Past forecasts (IEA) of wind energy for indicated horizons (2010, 2015, 2020) made at different dates (1998–2008).

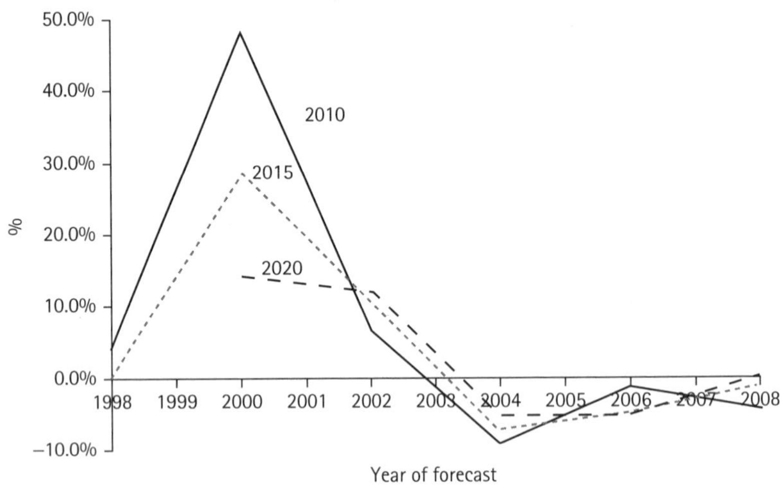

FIGURE 15.3 Revisions of forecasts about availability of total renewable energy for indicated horizons (2010, 2015, 2020) over previous one (two years earlier).

nonrenewable energy resources by renewable and to make all possible savings in energy consumption.

Both energy saving and shift to renewable energies require a great deal of R&D as well as proper public policies to create incentives and to avoid externalities. Here the free market often fails to work properly and even governments can have interests confronting global optimization. Thus, international institutions should develop proper policies and conduct monitoring.

Now we come to the core problem: Do we already have proper technologies at hand? Let us survey the known sources of renewable energies. With regard to biofuels, there is a strict limitation imposed by arable land that is not sufficient for full replacement of hydrocarbons. Here two potential ways out exist. First, next generation of biofuels should be produced, from wood. Second, oil used for automobile transport should be replaced by other sources (including natural gas in the middle run, but mostly of electricity, hydrogen, and not yet invented substitutes). If all biofuels are used only for air transport (where liquid fuel substitutes have not yet been invented), then it may require only marginal use of land with no severe consequences on reduction of the global food supply.

As for wind, perspectives are heterogeneous across countries. Denmark claims a possibility to use wind for half of all energy production by 2050, while the United Kingdom cannot. Countries with lower population density have a potential advantage here. But a global trade in electricity is problematic because no trans-ocean transportation of it is possible.

There are also institutional risks linked to the development of wind energy. Gennaioli and Tavoni (2011) have found that for weak institutions, efficient market-based policies can have an adverse impact. They suggested both a corruption model and an empirical test for the case of wind energy in Italian provinces for the period 1990–2007. Because the Italian government guaranteed a fixed price for wind energy with implicit subsidy, there was overinvestment in this sector, with politicians receiving bribes for issuing extra permits.

Solar energy has other problems. PV probably has a limited future, not only due to high production cost so far, but also because of a positive contribution to global warming. Still, it can be efficiently used for an autonomous electricity supply in isolated regions. Solar towers have more perspective, and the plan to use such a network in the Sahara to supply Europe has mostly political constraints, also linked to the emerging power of supplying countries and thus the security of the energy supply for Europe.

15.3 Economic Models: Efficient Policies and Thresholds

The standard model of renewable resources within the resource economic literature assumes a renewable backstop technology that is available at unlimited capacity but at high costs (c), possibly requiring prior R&D. Therefore, $p \leq c$, where p is price of non-renewable resource (oil).This assumption of immediate and unconstrained supply is of course ridiculous, because any technological transition is slow and even more so with fuels given the capital stock and equipment in place. Note also the historically slow replacement of coal by oil and the slow market penetration of natural gas. Nevertheless, very few models, for example, Wirl (1991b, 2008), investigate the interactions accounting for sluggish buildup of renewable energy capacity, resource prices, and government interventions. These models show that a resource cartel will undercut marginally the supply costs of renewables to deter entry, as outlined in the preceding green paradox. This aspect is sketched in the first subsection within a very simple framework.

It is also important to mention two working papers with modeling renewable energy based economy that appeared quite recently. Greiner et al. (2012) study an optimal dynamic path for transition to renewable energy also taking into account a negative externality from carbon emissions. They assume two sectors for energy production: the first uses fossil fuel and the second uses capital to produce renewable energy. They found that depending on fossil fuel stock it might become either fully or partly depleted before the transition is complete. We think that this approach is too optimistic because there are no constraints on renewable energy (other than available capital).

Cruz and Taylor (2012) present a dynamic macroeconomic model that incorporates the renewable energy sector. One of their crucial assumptions is about two-dimensional geographical space, where the sources of renewable energy are dispersed and have to be collected. The transportation cost of energy to cities (where scale economies fuel economic growth) is quite substantial, and this can limit growth.

A common thread concerning renewable energy is that it needs subsidies to overcome all these barriers, which are in my opinion not plausible as outlined in the introduction, with one exception: fossil energy was and still is partially subsidized in particular in developing countries. However, there are at least two motives for interventions:

- Environmental—Pigouvian to account for externalities.
- IO & regulatory—to mitigate monopoly power. This objective led in 1974 to the creation of the IEA to counter OPEC's cartel supply strategy.

The other objective, to collect revenues from Pigouvian taxes that allow for change in the tax system, is here ignored although it is hotly debated, in particular the questionable double dividend associated with environmental and especially energy taxes (see Bovenberg and de Mooij, 1994). Available instruments for interventions are taxing fossil fuel, subsidizing renewable energy, and issuing permits.

Although subsidies are inefficient at least relative to taxing fossil fuels, the first subsection considers how far and under what circumstances does it make sense to subsidize a currently heavily unprofitable technology, say PV, accounting for uncertainty. Under what conditions, good or bad, should subsidies stop and under what unfavorable prospect should the project be stopped entirely? This is addressed in Subsection 15.3.3.

Only very few approaches to a renewable energy model explicitly address the underlying (biological) production process of say biofuel, as is common in forestry and fishery models. Therefore, this question is addressed in the first subsection.

15.3.1 Timing of Investments (for Conservation and Synthetic Fuels)

Even considering only partial replacement of the finite resource must account for retaliation by suppliers. To fix ideas, assume that the level of demand A following a geometric Brownian motion at the rate a and relative standard error s and that offending suppliers have the option to invest at the cost (c) into alternative fuels delivering a volume q; alternatively, consumers can invest into a conservation project that lowers their demand by the amount q. The question is at what level of demand and resource prices one should undertake this investment. Applying a real option along the lines sketched in Section 15.3.2, one yields the crucial thresholds when to invest, that is, at which level of demand. Now, consider three scenarios:

1. Myopic consumers (indicated by superscript m), that is, consumers who assume that the current price remains forever (at least in terms of expectation) and use this price to evaluate their investment.
2. Consumers are aware of the expected growth demand and the resulting growth in prices and use this price expectation to evaluate their investment option; identified by superscript i.
3. Rational consumers (superscript r) include the growing demand pressure over time as in (2) but realize that if an investment pays off individually it will do so for all others. Yet if all others invest simultaneously, a resource monopoly will have to lower its price (this happens even under competition).

The expectation in (1) makes two opposite errors: on the one hand it ignores the drift in future prices and thus underestimates the profitability of conservation, and on the other hand it is ignorant of other consumers' actions and the price decline associated with any significant action. In scenario (2) consumers are less ignorant because they account for the drift but ignore that other consumers will act alike and that these aggregate reactions will bring fuel prices down. Only rational consumers under (3) take this feedback from the supply side into account. Therefore, conservation investments must pay off after accounting for this (expected) price reduction. Figure 15.4 compares the outcomes and highlights how rational expectations delay optimal investment substantially, a point that is ignored in almost all studies proclaiming that the profitability of renewable energy is just around the corner. A side effect is that the price decline triggered by the aggregate conservation efforts reduces actual conservation (in the example in Wirl [2008] to 50% of the potential). The reason is that conservation results in lower fuel prices, which induce higher service demands such that half of the money saved on fuel costs is spent again on fuel consumption. Accounting for option to delay, higher demand growth results in only a very moderate reduction of the threshold.

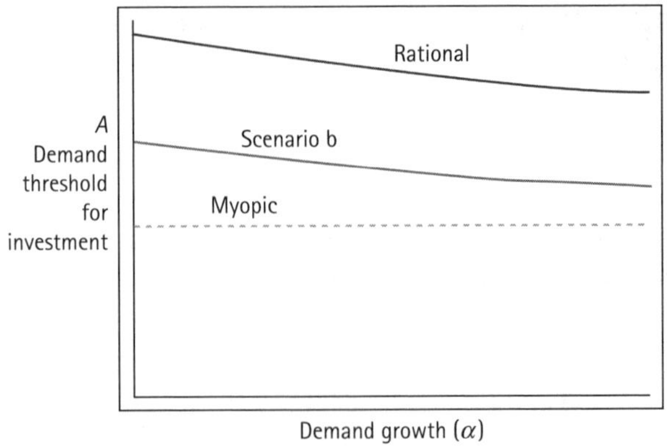

FIGURE 15.4 Comparing demand thresholds for conservation investments versus expected demand growth (α) under the three scenarios (a, b, and c).

15.3.2 Subsidizing Renewable Energy (PV) under Uncertain Future Profitability

To make matters simple, consider investment subsidies to say, PV, although the basic framework applies to renewable energy more broadly. The reasons are that PV has received not only considerable attention but also substantial public funding during the last decades, first owing to the conceived shortage of fossil fuels (in particular of oil, but also gas, less so coal) during the 1970s and 1980s and during the recent decades due to the threat of global warming caused by ongoing burning of fossil fuels. This funding involves subsidies for R&D, subsidies (e.g., tax incentives) for investment and subsidies for PV-generated electricity delivered to the grid (feed-in tariffs). Last but not least the again high oil prices add a topical flavor and the associated volatility of oil prices captures the volatility of potential returns on PV investments.

The United Nations Environment Program reported that investment in renewable energy leapt to US$100 billion in 2006, higher than most previous forecasts had suggested. Most of the capital went to the United States and Europe, but China accounted for 9% of the total. The UN said the figures proved that renewables had shed their "fringe image." An alternative is to look at IPOs of solar panel producers. In Germany 4 out 13 IPOs in the last two years had to do with solar energy. Two already made (Interhyp, HCI Capital) were vastly oversubscribed (*The Economist*, October 8, 2005, p. 82).

The following argument introduces a simple arithmetical model complementary to the so far verbal arguments. Let $X(t)$ denote a current measure of the profitability of PV technology at period t, for example, the difference between costs of 1 kWh from a PV plant compared with fossil fuel plants (possibly accounting for grid and external costs). Clearly this measure depends on technological breakthroughs, the scale of PV operations, and so on, which all are affected (positively) by investments. By and large, these investments are all directly or indirectly triggered by subsidies $u(t)$ costing $k(u)$ due to the conceived lack of profitability (at least at commercial rates of interest and without the associated reduction of externalities) because otherwise no subsidies would be needed. Of course, this measure X depends not only on the historical investments but also on random events inside (say a major breakthrough in waffle technologies) and outside (say cheap fossil fuels, a breakthrough in fuel cell technology) the solar energy industry. This second effect is described by a Brownian motion with the variance σ^2 (dz is the increment of a normalized Wiener process):

$$dX(t) = u(t)dt + \sigma\, dz(t), \quad X(0) = X_0. \tag{15.1}$$

The neglect of depreciation[5] allows for explicit analytical solutions and moreover is quite plausible because knowledge hardly deteriorates (at least compared with physical capital). To simplify further, assume that this investment can take only two values: a large and constant subsidy, $u = I$, or no subsidy, $u = 0$.

State X induces an instantaneous payoff $F(X)$, $F' > 0$, $F'' \leq 0$, such that F maps the profitability index X into the current flow of benefits or profits. These "profits" are presumably negative over a large domain, $F < 0$, that is, a cost, in particular for X small. Clearly, a higher index of profitability increases the benefits, and as is common, the benefits F satisfy the law of diminishing returns. The objective is to maximize the expected net present value of "benefits" F over investment costs $k(u)$,

$$V(X_0) := \max_{u(t)} E\left\{\int_0^\infty e^{-rt}[F(X(t)) - k(u(t))]dt\right\} \text{ subject to equation (15.1).} \tag{15.2}$$

To apply the standard real option approach, investment (or subsidy) u can take only two values, to invest (at a fixed level I) or to leave it:

$$u = I \text{ or } 0, \tag{15.3}$$

and thus

$$k(u) = \begin{cases} C \\ 0 \end{cases} \mathit{if}\ u = \begin{cases} I \\ 0 \end{cases} \tag{15.4}$$

This binary choice implies the two Hamilton–Jacobi–Bellman equations

$$rV(X) = \begin{cases} F(X) - C - IV' + \frac{\sigma^2}{2}V'' \\ F(X) + \frac{\sigma^2}{2}V'' \end{cases} \mathit{if}\ u = \begin{cases} I \\ 0 \end{cases} \tag{15.5}$$

for the value function defined in (15.2), see for example, Dixit and Pindyck (1994), depending on whether it is optimal to invest or not.

In addition we consider the following specification of the benefits

$$F(X) = A(1 - e^{-aX}), \tag{15.6}$$

which implies a constant absolute risk aversion of a, and satisfies the following plausible requirements: a negative domain, more precisely, $F(0) = 0$, provides threshold for benefits, increasing and satisfying the law of diminishing returns. This specification is not only plausible but also allows for a closed form analytical solutions.

The solution consists of subsidizing, $u = I$, and of no subsidies, $u = 0$. The latter case of no subsidies, $u = 0$, can occur, in principle, in three different circumstances and thus for quite different levels of X (see Figure 15.5):

1. Exiting or abandoning PV entirely. This saves fixed costs (if $F < 0$ in this domain) but destroys future uses of solar energy. Hence, $V = S = 0$. This is clearly, if at all, associated with low realizations of X and $\underline{X}$ denotes the corresponding threshold. That is, costs associated with the process X can be avoided for the entire future at the price of sacrificing all potential future gains.
2. The opposite case is that X is very large so that further subsidies are not justified. This upper threshold is denoted $\bar{X}$ and a fall below it again triggers subsidization (i.e., this kind of stopping as the one below is perfectly reversible in contrast to the irreversible exit under point 1).
3. X is small (as in 1) but not so small to justify scrapping the technology entirely. $\tilde{X}$ denotes this threshold. That is, it could be optimal to suspend all subsidies, $u = 0$, temporarily owing to the uncertain and poor prospects but avoid exiting because that would be irreversible. This keeps the option of future benefits alive and saves subsidies but requires bearing the associated fixed costs (if $F < 0$). This is probably a good account of the present state of nuclear power.

Therefore, the optimal strategies are:

- Exiting, that is, to give up PV with no possibility to enter and to use this technology in the future
- Stopping (or better, suspending) investments, $u = 0$, but with the possibility to invest in the future
- Investing, $u = I$, the interior part

The major contrast between exit and stop is that the first is irreversible, while any stop is reversible in the future (i.e., future investment is feasible and actually optimal if the process X improves on its own). Of course, the option to exit is valuable only because maintaining PV even at no further investments incurs costs (here captured by F). The basic feature is shown in Figure 15.5 and Figure 15.6 shows a numerical example.

Below we sketch two examples differing only with respect to flat or steep benefits associated with the profitability of PV. In the case of flat benefits, subsidies are confined to already profitable PV to push it even further. In contrast, the prospects of steep benefits (at the origin) suggests that subsidizing unprofitable PV technology does make sense, yet the subsidy strategy should terminate much earlier as incremental benefits get smaller. The point of sacking the technology entirely is relatively similar in both examples.

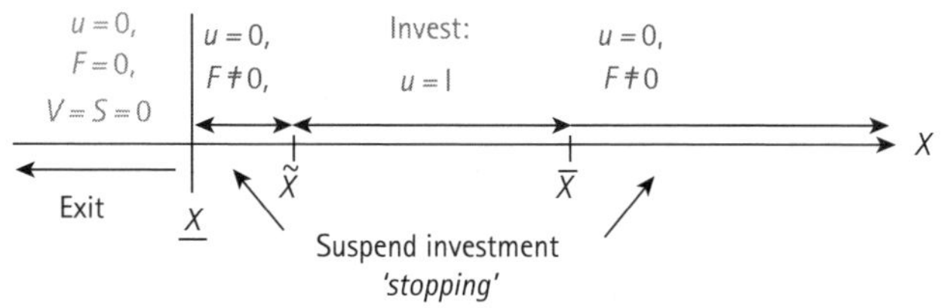

FIGURE 15.5 Possible strategies and their domains.

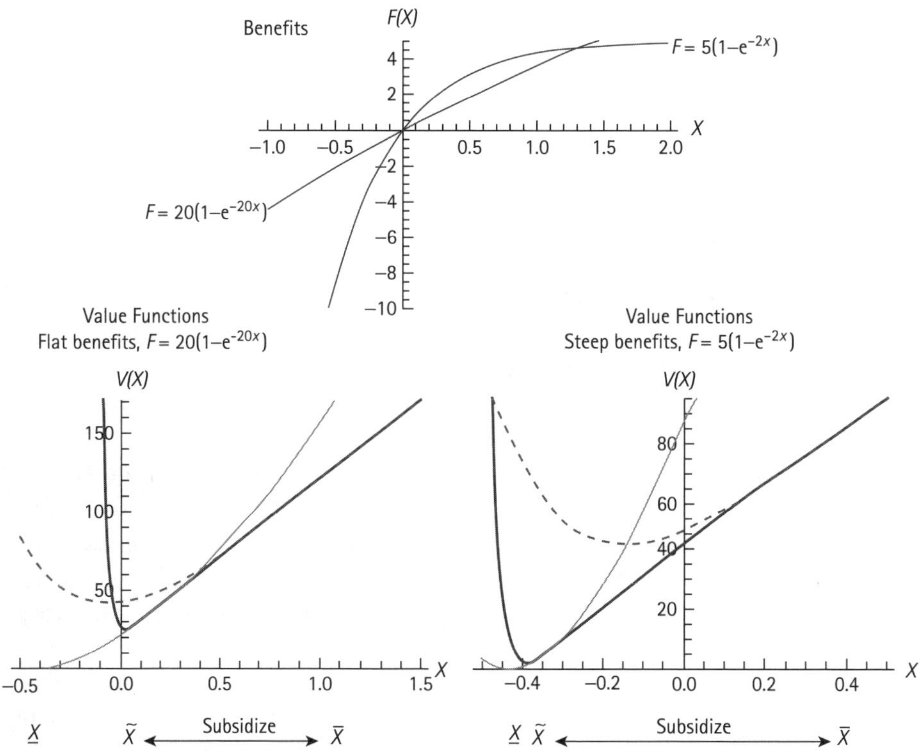

FIGURE 15.6 Value functions, thresholds and implied strategies domains for the example $r = 0.03$, $u = 0.2$, $c = 20$, $\sigma = 0.1$ and benefits shown in the figure.

15.3.3 Harvesting Renewable Resources: Sustainability

A number of papers, for example, starting probably with Lewis and Schmalensee (1982), ranging over Tahvonen and Salo (1996) and Tahvonen and Withagen (1996), to recent papers, Brock and Starrett (1999), Brock and Dechert (2003), Mäler (2000), and Mäler et al. (2000), and Rondeau (2001), emphasize the possibility of multiple equilibriums and associated thresholds in models of optimal renewable resource extraction. The common feature of all these papers is that they link the existence of thresholds and

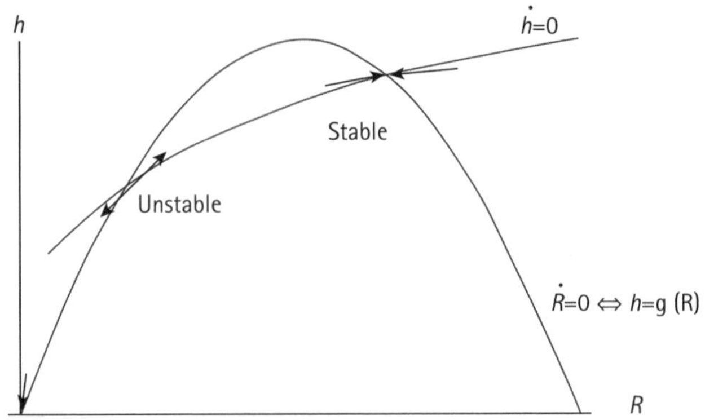

FIGURE 15.7 A potential outcome (e.g., for setting $\alpha = 3$, $r = 2$, $w = \frac{3}{4}$) with unstable steady state. All initial conditions below the unstable steady state render ultimate exploitation of the resource, i.e., an unsustainable outcome, optimal.

of multiple equilibriums to "nonconcavities" (i.e., the Hamiltonian of the associated optimal control problem is not jointly concave with respect to state and control so that the sufficient optimality conditions are violated).[6] This approach is based on the seminal, theoretical analysis of convex–concave dynamic optimization problems in Skiba (1978) and Dechert and Nishimura (1983); see also the recent and novel treatment by bifurcation techniques in Wagener (2003). The purpose is to show that unstable steady states and the ecologically important threshold property can occur in concave renewable resource models too.[7] As a consequence, the sensitivity of ecological management with respect to initial conditions extends beyond the familiar models characterized by convex–concave relations, which obviously has important consequences for the design of sustainable ecosystems.

Thresholds are critical levels of natural capital that separate multiple equilibria, one of which involves a collapse of the ecosystem as in the shallow lake models (Brock and Dechert, 2003; Brock and Starrett, 1999; Mäler, 2000; Mäler et al., 2000). This provides one way to characterize sustainability, which has been considered as vague from its very beginning, in precise terms. Heal (2001) suggests that sustainability can be linked to optimality. The following approach extends Heal (2001) for stability concerns. This approach of optimality and stability analysis allows applying rigorous and well-established analytical tools, highlights that optimality is not sufficient for sustainability, and can provide some policy guidance, in particular if one of the multiple equilibriums implies extinction.

The objective of the following formal framework is twofold: (1) to introduce the standard harvesting model and (2) to show that multiple equilibria can arise under concave biological growth. This complements the multiple equilibria in the much discussed shallow lake model due to convex regeneration functions. The argument follows Wirl (2004).

Consider the following optimal control problem that describes efficient renewable resource extraction:

$$\max_{\{h(t)\geq 0\}} \int_0^\infty \exp(-rt)u(h(t), R(t))dt, \tag{15.7}$$

$$\dot{R}(t) = g(R(t)) - h(t), R(0) = R_0, R(t) \geq 0. \tag{15.8}$$

Instantaneous utility (u) consists of two parts: consumption utility (or profits) due to harvesting (h) and nonconsumption uses (bird watching, forests for recreation and as a protection against landslides, etc.) provided by the resource stock (R). The resource grows according to the biological growth function $g(.)$ that is positive over $[0, \bar{R}]$, and where $\bar{R}$ corresponds to the carrying capacity (= nonharvested steady state), $\lim_{t\to\infty} R(t) = \bar{R}$ for $h(t) = 0$ and $R_0 > 0$. As the emphasis of this chapter is on "concave" renewable resource models, the following assumptions are made: (1) The benefit function $u(h, R)$ is C^2, increasing in both arguments and concave in (h, R) and strongly concave in the harvest h (u_{hh} <0). (2) The growth function $g(.)$ is C^2, positive and concave over the open interval $(0, \bar{R})$, and has two roots, $g(0) = g(\bar{R}) = 0$, and satisfies $g'(0) > r$.

Variants of this renewable resource extraction model have been studied in literally hundreds of papers, and Bach (2001) is a special application to tropical forests. Berck (1981) is the first that allows explicitly for nonconsumption benefits (but of a separable nature, $u(h, R) = u_1(h) + u_2(R)$, and overlooks the multiple equilibriums); Clark et al. (1979) include the resource stock in (1) but to account for its impact on the catch rate and in a way that the resulting objective is not jointly concave. The other recent examples, which account for stock effects, investigate the following: Heal (1998) concentrates on different intertemporal welfare objectives; Li and Löfgren (2000) focus on the consequences of declining discount rates (hyperbolic discounting) on socially optimal, intertemporal environmental policymaking; Rondeau (2001) considers utility functions u that are nonconcave with respect to R; and Ayong Le Kama (2001) combine (15.1)–(15.2) with a Ramsey model of optimal saving leading to two states (capital and resource). The previously mentioned recent applications to (shallow) lakes emphasize the convex–concave shape of g but neglect nonconsumption benefits from the resource stock. Wirl (1995, 1999) considers two-dimensional frameworks to study limit cycles.

Using very simple examples, for example, linear-quadratic and separable benefits u and the familiar logistic growth g:

$$u(h, R) = h - \frac{1}{2}\alpha h^2 + wR, \tag{15.9}$$

$$g(R) = R(1 - R), \tag{15.10}$$

allows for the overlooked phenomenon of multiple equilibria even if saturation is ruled out, as in assumption (1) that requires $u_h > 0 \Leftrightarrow h < 1/\alpha$, which is satisfied for $\alpha < 4$, because the maximum sustainable yield equals $\frac{1}{4} = \max\{R(1 - R),\ R \in [0, 1]\}$ for the logistic growth (15.5). The resource stock provides direct and according to (15.4) linear benefits (wR); this linearity is not crucial and similar results can be obtained for a concave relation, for example, for $w(R - \frac{1}{2}R^2)$ that induces satiation of nonconsumption uses at the carrying capacity $\bar{R} = 1$.

15.3.4 About Scale Economies

The story about the role of subsidies for the development of renewable energy sources can also go in a way opposite to that described in Subsection 15.3.2. While the model there accounts for uncertainty, it still has continuity in profitability along any path. This situation becomes different when we have scale economies. Suppose that the output of a particular renewable industry, $Y = F(K)$, depends on the capital invested in it in such a way that the function F is convex, that is, $F'(K) > 0$, $F''(K) > 0$, at least for a range of $0 < K < K^*$. Then the average cost, $AC(K) = K/Y(K)$, will be a function declining with the growth of K, that is, $AC' < 0$. Suppose that a competitor (oil sector, for example) has cost c, and thus cannot drop the price below this level. It might well happen that renewable industry can reach $AC = c$ only for rather large level of investment in it, K_1. This means that for all levels of $K < K_1$, the industry remains unprofitable and thus needs subsidy. However, above this threshold, that is, for $K < K_1$, it becomes profitable and can compete with the incumbent in the nonrenewable sector.

Which of the known industries are likely to be in this position? Biofuels cannot have scale economies, as the growth of production will be accompanied by fiercer competition with agriculture for land. Wind energy after expansion will face the increasing costs arising from the necessity to balance random output of this sector at a particular time. Consider electricity production from solar towers. Engineers and economists argue that this sector can produce a substantial effect of learning by doing, leading to scale economies. The other source of scale economies comes from infrastructure. Consider a large project of producing electricity in the Sahara Desert using solar towers with further export to Europe (Figure 15.8). Building a corresponding network of high-voltage lines definitely has scale economies in it, and thus this project can produce energy at competitive prices only if a substantial volume of capacities will be installed. However, even if this sector will be profitable in the long run, one problem still remains. It is linked to supply security and has a geopolitical origin. Still, such considerations give us some hope.

We have to recognize socioeconomic problems related to implementation of such a project, even if technological breakthroughs would allow for its profitability in the competitive electricity market. Given scale economies, the profitability threshold is likely to take place for a certain project size, let's say, requiring investment of several billions of euros. It will also require a certain amount of land, as technology is land consuming. What will happen if the project is located outside the European Union (Sahara Desert)? If its profitability were marginal, scale modest, and EU energy dependence on

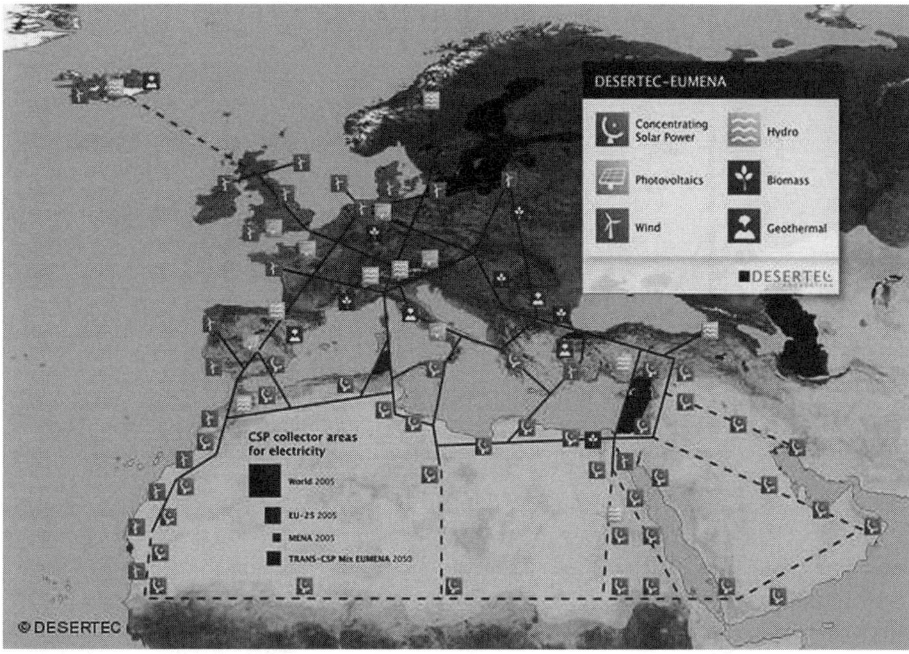

FIGURE 15.8 Plan of building solar and wind stations for generation of renewable electricity. DESERTEC EU-MENA Map: Sketch of possible infrastructure for a sustainable supply of power to Europe, the Middle East and North Africa (EU-MENA).

Source: http://en.wikipedia.org/wiki/File:DESERTEC-Map_large.jpg

it not too high, there will be no geopolitical problem. But suppose that in some distant future, given the scarcity of traditional electricity, this project will produce energy at half of the average European costs? Would the European Union be able to enjoy this cheap electricity, without a risk that land-holding countries would sack the profits or cut the supply? On the other hand, if the expected profit would be low (and thus the project will have little geopolitical risk), who would invest in it, given all technological risks?

There might be an intermediate solution on the table. It is project realization on EU territory, say, in southern Spain, Italy, and Greece, on the land with low opportunity cost. If the European Union will have enough free land to reach a profitability threshold, it might be an optimal strategy, as there are no geopolitical risks.

15.3.5 Energy-Saving Technologies

An important EU objective is to improve energy saving by 20% until 2020. Suppose that all energy is still produced from nonrenewables. At the same time, there is investment in R&D to make energy use more efficient. Will it be a consistent long-term plan?

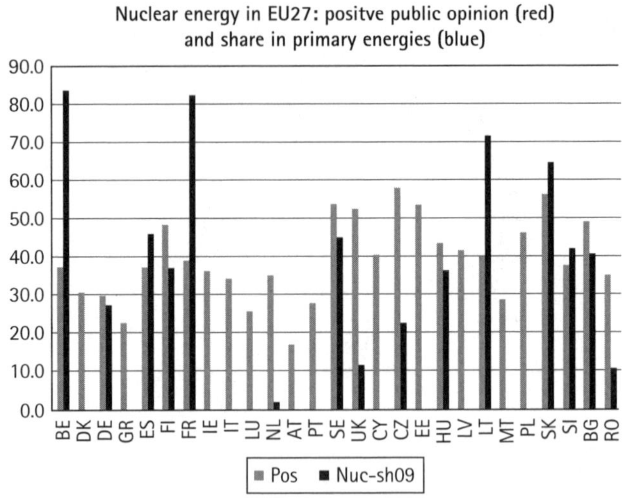

FIGURE 15.9 Share of nuclear energy in gross final energy consumption (Authors' calculation based on Eurostat data(Source: Eurostat, tsdcc110) and public opinion about positive effect of nuclear energy in the next 20 years (Source: Eurobaromer 2010, p. 132). There exists a positive correlation between both variables, with a regression line $y = -20.02 + 1.005x$, explaining 19% of the varaince.)

Not, because the basic source (fossil fuels) will become increasingly scarce. Even if we use this energy more efficiently (and this efficiency growth may require more than proportional increase of investments in R&D), we cannot solve the problem. However, such activity can have a temporary effect, and this time should be used for more R&D in renewable energies.

We can conclude that such activity can give only temporary effect, since the problem of global finite stock and thus permanently increasing cost of non-renewable energy still remains.

15.4 Real-World Governments

Suppose one disagrees with all the preceding sketched problems and thinks that given sufficient R&D and the right incentives, renewables will provide the much needed magic bullet. Even getting all engineering and business propositions right, potential entrepreneurs still have to face real-world governments. They are, however, unable to provide the right incentives. More precisely, a crucial, albeit (deliberately) ignored, fact is that governments, even benevolent ones, cannot tie their hands and commit to future policies. This is not only a consequence of democracy with its possibility to change the government every four years. Examples are manifold and not restricted to developing countries with poor governance. Most topical seems to be the financial crisis in the European Union and in particular in the euro area, where it turned out that governments have been unable to stick to their no-bailout commitment when facing the first casualties—initially Greece, then Ireland and Portugal. The United States is considered to offer the best protection of property rights. Therefore its government strongly defended the patents of its pharmaceutical industry against copying anti-HIV medicine by Brazil and South Africa. However, the same government was quite quick to suspend the patents of Bayer when facing the anthrax threat. Examples from the energy market are the renegotiation of contracts recently by Venezuela and Russia, and in the early 1980s by Algeria when oil prices were high. Such examples are not confined to countries with a poor legal structure but include mature and even common law countries like the United Kingdom. UK governments and regulators changed ex post contractual price guarantees (even Stephen Littlechild lowered price caps) or introduced ex post windfall profits as the following Labor government under Tony Blair did. Spain cut its "guaranteed" subsidies to PV after facing serious budgetary problems.

This impossibility to commit has far-reaching consequences not only for industries but for small consumers as well. Consider the topical example of electric cars, which are just appearing from different manufacturers such as GM, Nissan, and Renault. What is the basic incentive to buy such expensive cars? The major objective, green posturing and signaling aside, is to escape legally the high (at least in Europe) petrol tax and to enjoy a cheap ride. GM's Volt enter the market on the implicit promise to be exempted from petrol tax. But how long will it last? If many take this action, the treasuries will not remain passive and will ex post impose a levy on electricity used for cars, and they will find a way for sure. Therefore, the individual profitability consideration based on current electricity prices relative to petrol prices is naïve. Moreover, the outcome depends on how many decide to switch. If only a few do, the few will indeed enjoy the cheap ride, but definitely not if many decide to switch. Thus again, a strong tendency in society to use electric cars will deter their purchase owing to, as usual, an unintended consequence.

Related to this lack of commitment is the even greater temptation that governments will face. Will governments indeed honor important discoveries and associated patents given the vital importance of saving the planet? Probably not; given that they are for the sake of the planet, governments (at least many) will expropriate patents. And there are many precedents involving much less drastic cases. For example, the US government violated international patents of a German company during the threat of anthrax-related terror, which was a small one compared with all those related to global warming. Developing countries ignore patents for antiviral drugs against HIV; in passing this behavior may hamper the pharmaceutical firms to engage in R&D against malaria because they expect similar actions. Finally, the oil price regulation in the United States between 1974 and 1981 by the Nixon administration expropriated the windfall profit of US oil producers from OPEC's energy price hike; so did the United Kingdom's labor government with an ex post tax on regulated industries to correct windfall profits due to supposed too weak regulation (of course, viewed ex post). In short, even the much acclaimed common law countries do not honor property rights, so what can one expect from China? Therefore, firms anticipating the aforementioned retaliation may be reluctant to search for the magic bullet. This raises the question of whether emission taxes or permits are better suited to provide incentives to a monopolistic firm to expand and speed up the share of the clean technology knowing that the government is unable to commit to future policies.

15.5 Conclusions and Final Remarks

The unambiguous common denominator in this debate is that the availability of cheap renewable energy at a large scale is crucial for achieving both economical and sustainable development without exposing the planet and in particular climate to risk. There exists an urgent need to use more renewable energies, especially for Europe, with its growing dependence on imported fossil fuels. Apart from reducing GHG emissions this also solves the problem of global scarcity of fossil fuels that is becoming a reality for oil nowadays and will occur for natural gas in few decades. However, the shift to renewable energy sources might not be as simple and fast as assumed in many economic models. Moreover, market forces may not lead to the desired outcome, while governments might have the wrong incentives and their policies might not work.

Unfortunately, the picture does not seem rosy for a number of reasons. While there are several different renewable energies, none of them have seen major breakthroughs so far. And there are physical limits for those that have been proven competitive. For example, wind energy can nowadays be produced at competitive costs, but it requires vast land use. The same situation with biofuels: they will compete fiercely for arable land with agriculture well before the time of substantial substitution of oil. As for PV, it is a potentially vast source of energy, but despite huge investment in R&D there is too little progress in making this source price competitive.

Despite beliefs in automatic substitution of fossil fuels for alternatives (renewable energies) and very volatile oil prices in recent decades, the share of renewable energies in the European Union grows very slowly. The major technologies of renewable energy production are old. However, the cost of their production does not move down fast enough to make free market substitution a reality.

The first model of the chapter investigates the potential dynamic path of the development of a particular renewable industry (let's say PV) in a random environment. It appears that a higher rate of demand growth results only in a moderate reduction of the threshold that determines investment decision. This means that such an industry will not respond in time to economic incentives for faster development (emerging, for example, from negative shocks in beliefs about undiscovered fossil fuel stock or faster than expected climate change). It also suggests that government intervention (or better, some global agreements) into market for R&D and investment into renewable energies might become highly desirable.

The second model shows that multiplicity of equilibria might exist for harvesting renewable resources. There exists a danger of resource extinction. In some other cases, when economic and technological prospects are positive, political and geopolitical issues might be a problem. Governments' lack of commitment provides a serious obstacle for future private investments and arrive for this as well as a few constraints—physical, retaliation and entry deterrence by fossil energy suppliers, the uncertainty of R&D—at quite pessimistic conclusions. Reasons for optimism are that there is no alternative (conservation will not do the trick) and this is well understood as well as the threats from global warming (some Republicans notwithstanding). Moreover, ultimately renewable energy must prove its use in the market without the need for subsidies. Here, the energy poverty of a large share of the world population without access to electricity grids provides a huge market for renewables, solar and wind energy, in particular. Investing in these renewables in sunny Third World regions is much more efficient than in Germany, "a country where summers are just mild winters," according to Heinrich Heine.

Notes

1. See http://epp.eurostat.ec.europa.eu ; Data code: tsdcc110
2. *Business Week Online*, June 14, 2007, http://www.genuineideas.com/ArticlesIndex/blackAndWhite.htm.
3. See, for example, http://en.wikipedia.org/wiki/Nuclear_fusion. Fusion of deuterium and tritium creates an atom of helium and releases a substantial amount of energy.
4. Such a situation occurred with the initial distribution of fax machines: low usage was due to initially high cost, but it also had created a low incentive to buy a fax because one had few connections (see Varian, "Intermediate Microeconomics").
5. Depreciation introduces a multiplicative term, which complicates the analysis because the mixture of additive and multiplicative terms does not allow for simple analytical solutions.
6. Clark (1990) mentions multiple equilibria without this linkage, but the corresponding objective lacks joint concavity.
7. A formally similar point has been made in the context of economic growth in Kurz (1968), which is ignored in the literature on thresholds.

References

Acemoglu, D., Aghion P., Bursztyn L., and Hemous, D. (2012). The environment and directed technical change. *American Economic Review, 102*(1), 131–166.

Ayong Le Kama, A. D. (2001). Sustainable growth, renewable resources and pollution. *Journal of Economic Dynamics and Control, 25*, 1911–1918.

Bach, C. F. (2001). Economic incentives for sustainable management: A small optimal control model for tropical forestry. *Ecological Economics, 30*, 251–265.

Barrett, S. (2009). The coming global climate-technology revolution. *Journal of Economic Perspectives, 23*(2), 53–75.

Berck, P. (1981). Optimal management of renewable resources with growing demand and stock externalities. *Journal of Environmental Economics and Management, 11*, 101–118.

Bovenberg, L. A., and de Mooij, R. A. (1994). Environmental levies and distortionary taxation. *American Economic Review, 84*, 1085–1089.

Brock, W. A., and Dechert, D. W. (2003). *Lake Game.* Madison: University of Wisconsin-Madison

Brock, W. A., and Starrett, D. (1999). Nonconvexities in ecological problems. Mimeo, University of Wisconsin.

Clark, C. W. (1990). *Mathematical Bioeconomics: The Optimal Management of Renewable Resources.* New York: John Wiley & Sons.

Clark, C. W., Clarke, F. H., and Munro, G. R. (1979). The optimal exploitation of renewable resource stocks: Problems of irreversible investment. *Econometrica, 47*, 25–47.

Cruz, J. M., and Taylor, M. S. (2012). Back to the future of green powered economies. NBER WP 18236. http://www.nber.org/papers/w18236

Dechert, D. W., and Nishimura, K. (1983). Complete characterization of optimal growth paths in an aggregative model with a non-concave production function. *Journal of Economic Theory, 31*, 332–354.

Delucchi, M. A., and Jacobson, M. Z. (2011). Providing all global energy with wind, water, and solar power. Part I: Reliability, system and transmission costs, and policies. *Energy Policy, 39*, 1170–1190.

Dixit, A. K., and Pindyck, R. S. (1994). *Investment under Uncertainty.* Princeton: Princeton University Press, 476 pp.

EIA. *Annual Energy Outlook* (various years from 1996 to 2008, biannually).

Ekins, P., Folke, C., and De Groot, R. (2003). Identifying critical natural capital. *Ecological Economics, 44*, 159–163.

Ericsson, N. R., and Morgan, P. (1978). The economic feasibility of shale oil: An activity analysis. *Bell Journal of Economics, 9*, 457–487.

Eurobarometer. (2010). Europeans and Biotechnology in 2010. Winds of change? European Commission Directorate-General for Research. ISBN 978-92-79-16878-9.

Gennaioli, C., and Massimo, T. (2011). Clean or dirty energy: Evidence on a renewable energy resource curse. Working Paper No. 63. Milan, Italy: Fondazione Eni Enrico Mattei.

Greiner, A., Gruene, L., and Willi, S. (2012). Economic growth and the transition from non-renewable to renewable energy. http://ssrn.com/abstract=2098707

Heal, G. (2001). Optimality or sustainability. Presented at the Eleventh Annual Conference of the European Association of Environmental and Resource Economists, Southampton, June 28–30. http://www.soton.ac.uk/~eaere/conf2001/conf2001.html

Heal, G. (1998). *Valuing the Future.* New York: Columbia University Press.

Jacobson, M. Z., and Delucchi, M. A. (2011). Providing all global energy with wind, water, and solar power. Part I: Technologies, energy resources, quantities and areas of infrastructure, and materials. *Energy Policy, 39*, 1154–1169.

Lewis, T. R., and Schmalensee, R. (1982). Optimal use of renewable resources with nonconvexities in production. In L. J. Mirman and D. F. Spulber (eds.), *Essays in the Economics of Renewable Resources*, pp. 95–111. Amsterdam: North Holland.

Li, C.-Z.,-Zhong and Löfgren, K.-G. (2000). Renewable resources and economic sustainability: A dynamic analysis with heterogeneous time preferences. *Journal of Environmental Economics and Management, 40*, 236–250.

Limburg, K. E., O'Neill, R. V., Costanza, R., and Farber, S. (2002). Complex systems and valuation. *Ecological Economics, 41,* 409–420.

MacKay, D. J. C. (2009). *Sustainable Energy without the Hot Air.* Cambridge, UK: Cambridge University Press.

Mäler, K. G. (2000). Development, ecological resources and their management: A study of complex dynamic systems: Joseph Schumpeter Lecture. *European Economic Review, 44,* 645–665.

Mäler, K.-G., Xepapadeas, A., and de Zeeuw, A. (2003). The economics of shallow lakes. *Environmental and Resource Economics, 26,* 603–624.

Nordhaus, W. D. (1987). Forecasting efficiency concepts and applications. *The Review of Economics and Statistics, LXIX*(4), 667–674.

Phillis, Y. A., and Andriantiatsaholiniaina, L. A. (2001). Sustainability: An ill-defined concept and its assessment using fuzzy logic. *Ecological Economics, 37,* 435–456.

Rondeau, D. (2001). Along the way back from the brink. *Journal of Environmental Economics and Management, 42,* 156–182.

Sinn, H.-W. (2008). Public policies against global warming. *International Tax and Public Finance, 15,* 360–394.

Skiba, A. K. Optimal growth with a convex-concave production function. *Econometrica, 46,* 527–539.

Sorger, G. (1992). On the minimal rate of impatience for complicated economic growth paths. *Journal of Economic Theory, 56,* 160–179.

Tahvonen, O., and Salo, A. (1996). Nonconvexities in optimal pollution accumulation. *Journal of Environmental Economics and Management, 31,* 160–177.

Tahvonen, O., and Withagen, C. (1996). Optimality of irreversible pollution accumulation. *Journal of Economic Dynamics and Control, 20,* 1775–1795.

The Economist. (2005). IPOs in Germany. Solar flares. October 8, p. 82.

The Economist. (2006). The oil industry. Steady as she goes. April 22, pp. 65–67.

The Economist. (2010). Adapting the climate change. Facing the consequences. November 25, pp. 51–53.

Wagener F. O. O. (2003). Skiba points and heteroclinic bifurcations, with applications to the shallow lake system. *Journal of Economic Dynamics and Control, 27,* 1533–1561.

WCED (World Commission on Environment and Development). (1987). *Our Common Future.* New York: Oxford University Press.

Wirl, F. (1991a). Energy demand and consumer price expectations: An empirical investigation of the consequences from the recent oil price collapse. *Resources and Energy, 13,* 241–262.

Wirl, F. (1991b). Monopolistic resource extraction and limit pricing: The market penetration of competitively produced synfuels. *Environmental and Resource Economics, 1,* 157–178.

Wirl, F. (1995). The cyclical exploitation of renewable resource stocks may be optimal. *Journal of Environmental Economics and Management, 29,* 252–261.

Wirl, F. (1999). Complex dynamic environmental policies. *Resource and Energy Economics, 21,* 19–41.

Wirl, F. (2004). Thresholds in concave renewable resource models. *Ecological Economics, 48,* 259–267.

Wirl, F. (2008). Intertemporal investments into synfuels. *Natural Resource Modeling, 21,* 466–488.

CHAPTER 16

EMISSION TRADING SYSTEMS AND TECHNOLOGICAL INNOVATION

A Random Matching Model

ANGELO ANTOCI, SIMONE BORGHESI, AND MAURO SODINI

16.1 INTRODUCTION

EMISSIONS trading has gained increasing importance in the last years as policy instrument to reduce several different environmental problems.

While the theoretical foundations of the instrument are due to the seminal contributions by several authors in the 1960s (e.g., Coase, 1960; Dales, 1968; Montgomery, 1972), the first examples of applications of emission trading systems (henceforth ETS) date back to 1995 when they were succesfully implemented in the context of the US Acid Rain Program to cut nitrogen oxides (NO_X) and sulfur dioxide (SO_2) emissions (Coniff, 2009). More recent applications include water tradable permits to lower pollution and consumption of hydric resources, with different results in different countries and hydrological basins (see Borghesi, 2014).

Among recent applications of ETS, a particularly important role is played by the European Emission Trading Scheme (EU-ETS) for the reduction of carbon dioxide emissions. As Ellerman (2009) has argued, this scheme, which is the first world's multinational cap-and-trade system for greenhouse gases (GHGs) and has created the largest emissions trading market, represents a benchmark for the global GHG ETS that is currently proposed as the main policy instrument to combact climate change in the future (Aldy and Stavins, 2008).

Given the crucial role that the ETS is likely to play in the future international policy agenda, several works have recently investigated its functioning and implications from different perspectives (e.g., Ellerman and Buchner, 2007; Clò, 2008; Ellerman and Joskov, 2008; Convery, 2009; Ellerman, 2009; Carraro et al., 2010; Ellerman et al., 2010; Costantini et al., 2011; Grull and Taschini, 2011). In particular, among these studies a few contributions (e.g., Brauneis et al., 2011; Moreno-Bromberg and Taschini, 2011; Rogge et al., 2011; Borghesi et al., 2012; Calel and Dechezlepretre, 2012) have examined whether and to what extent the ETS contributes to induce technological innovation and diffusion in the regulated sectors. Several authors have analyzed the possible existence of strategic behaviors in the emissions trading market (e.g., Hahn, 1984; Hagem and Westkog, 1998; Smith and Swierzbinski; 2007; Wirl, 2009), while others have pointed out the possible emerging of moral hazard behaviors generated from the sanction system in the EU-ETS context (see, e.g., Borghesi, 2011) or the optimal environmental policy when firms are not compliant (see, e.g., Ino, 2011).

The present chapter aims at contributing to the increasing literature on this issue by investigating the functioning of an ETS and its impact on the diffusion of environmentally friendly technological innovations in the presence of strategic behaviors of firms, bounded rationality, and sanctions to non compliant firms.

Differently from all previous contributions in the EU-ETS literature, the present chapter adopts a random matching model to analyze the issue described before. The random matching framework is increasingly adopted in game theory to model markets in which frictions and bounded rationality prevent instantaneous adjustment of the level of economic activity. In particular, following the seminal contribution by Maynard Smith (1982) (see Hofbauer and Sigmund, 1988; Weibull, 1995; Samuelson, 1997 for an introduction to evolutionary game theory), several papers have adopted evolutionary game models in which individuals interact with each other during pairwise random matchings. Such a framework seems to fit and has therefore been applied to many different economic contexts and fields, such as labor economics (to describe the matching of unemployed workers and firms' vacancies), public economics (e.g., to analyze the evolution of cooperation), monetary economics (e.g., to analyze the allocation of loans from banks to entrepreneurs, or the role of money in facilitating sales when sellers and buyers meet), and so on. In the present context, the random matching structure of the game is employed to describe the potential emission trading between heterogeneous firms that can decide whether to adopt a clean technology or keep on using an old polluting technology. The former firms can sell their own permits to the latter, who need them to keep on producing to meet the requirements of the ETS and thus avoid the penalty to noncompliant firms.

To the best of our knowledge, the possible existence of path dependency in ETS and the analysis of its dynamic features has been mainly ignored in the existing literature.

To investigate this issue, the structure of the chapter will be as follows. Section 16.2 describes the model, distinguishing two possible payoff matrices according to the kind of firms that interact in random pairwise matchings. Section 16.3 investigates the dynamics emerging under each of the two possible cases and analyzes the corresponding Pareto ranking among the equilibria of the model. Section 16.4 contains some concluding remarks on the main results that descend from the model.

16.2 The Model

Let us consider a large population of firms that interact among themselves through pairwise random matchings. Each firm has to choose ex ante between two possible strategies: (1) keep on using an old, polluting technology (with production cost C_P) and buy the corresponding pollution permits (at price p) or (2) shift to a new, environmental-friendly technology that implies higher production costs ($C_{NP} > C_P$) but requires no pollution permits to operate.

To fix ideas, let us suppose that each firm initially has one permit at disposal and that the firms that use the polluting technology (henceforth firms *P*) need two permits to operate, while the firms that adopt the clean technology (firms *NP*) need no permit for the activity. If so, firms *P* need to buy one more permit to keep on producing, whereas firms *NP* can sell its permit, so that the conditions for their exchange are obviously satisfied.

Let us indicate with T the sanction that a noncompliant firm *P* has to pay if is discovered by the regulatory authority, namely, if it produces with the old technology without purchasing the additional permit that is needed for this purpose. We will denote with $\theta \in (0,1)$ the probability of being discovered by the regulatory authority; therefore θT indicates the expected fee for the noncompliant firms *P*.

Given the random matching structure of the game, we can obviously distinguish three possible cases depending on the kind of firms that meet up in pairwise matchings.

(a) If two firms *P* meet, then in principle they both have to pay the fee, since none of them has enough permits to operate. However, they can decide to exchange their permits (i.e., one firm *P* sells its permit to the other that has thus the two permits that it needs to operate) and share the expected penalty. In this case, the exchange price is $p = \theta T/2$ and the payoffs π_P of the two firms will be:

$$\pi_P = -C_P - \theta T/2$$

so that both firms are better off with respect to the no exchange case (in which they both have the "full" expected penalty θT).

(b) If two firms *NP* meet, the permits are useless for both of them so no permit trade will occur. In this case, the payoffs π_{NP} of the two firms will be:

$$\pi_{NP} = -C_{NP} + \delta$$

where $\delta \geq 0$ denotes the possible positive spillover deriving to each firm *NP* from the diffusion of the new technology (e.g., the positive externality in terms of reduction cost for the new technology that is allowed by the network effects emphasized by much of the empirical literature on this issue).[1]

(c) If a firm *P* meets a firm *NP*, the former can buy from the latter the permit that it needs to avoid the penalty; however, the permit exchange may not take place for different reasons. For instance, firm *P* might decide not to buy the permit and run the risk to be sanctioned by the regulatory authority since it regards the expected penalty to be sufficiently low. Alternatively, firm *NP* could decide not to sell the permit to damage and/or eliminate firm *P* as it may represent a potential competitor on the market.[2]

We can, therefore, distinguish two possible subcases within case c:

(c.1) No permit exchange occurs between firm *P* and *NP* (because *P* does not buy the permit and/or *NP* does not sell it). In this case, if firm *P* is not discovered (which occurs with probability $1 - \theta$), the payoffs of the two firms are simply represented by the costs of their respective technologies (C_P and C_{NP}). If, on the contrary, firm *P* is discovered (which occurs with probability θ) it will also have to pay the penalty T, while firm *NP* may possibly derive a competitive gain γ from the "punishment" suffered from its competitor *P*.[3] In this case, therefore, the expected payoff of firms *P* and *NP* are given by the probability that *P* is actually discovered/not discovered times the corresponding payoffs for each firm as described above, that is, respectively:

$$\pi_P = \theta(-C_P - T) + (1-\theta)(-C_P) = -C_P - \theta T$$

$$\pi_{NP} = \theta(-C_P + \gamma) + (1-\theta)(-C_{NP}) = -C_{NP} + \theta\gamma$$

where $\gamma \geq 0$ is the competitive gain for *NP* from "punishing" firm P.

(c.2) The permit exchange does take place and firms *P* buys the permit from firm *NP*. In this case, the payoffs of the two firms will simply be, respectively:

$$\pi_P = -C_P - p$$

$$\pi_{NP} = -C_{NP} + p$$

where p is the price of the tradable permit.

Notice that firm *P* will obviously be willing to buy the permit only if its corresponding payoff is higher than the expected payoff from not buying the permit, namely if:

$$-C_P - p > -C_P - \theta T$$

or, equivalently, if $p < \theta T$.

Similarly, firm *NP* will be willing to sell its permit only if the payoff that it derives from the exchange is higher or at least equal to the expected payoff from not selling the permit, namely if:

$$-C_{NP} + p > -C_{NP} + \theta\gamma$$

that is, if $p > \theta\gamma$.

For the permit exchange to actually take place, therefore, the equilibrium price must range between the minimum willingness to accept of firm *NP* and the maximum willingness to pay of firm *P*, that is $\theta\gamma < p < \theta T$.

We can, therefore, distinguish two possible cases that encompass all the possible situations described above:

Case 1: If $\gamma\theta \geq \theta T$, i.e., $\gamma \geq T$, there cannot exist any equilibrium price that satisfies the conditions above so that no trade will take place between firms *P* and *NP*. In this case (which encompasses cases a, b, and c.1 discussed above), the payoff matrix is as follows:

$$A: \begin{array}{c} \\ P \\ NP \end{array} \begin{array}{c} \begin{array}{cc} P & NP \end{array} \\ \begin{pmatrix} -C_P - \frac{\theta T}{2} & -C_P - \theta T \\ -C_{NP} + \gamma\theta & -C_{NP} + \delta \end{pmatrix} \end{array}$$

Case 2: If $\theta\gamma < \theta T$, i.e., $\gamma < T$, the permit exchange is mutually convenient for any $p \in (\theta\gamma, \theta T)$. In this case, therefore, summarizing the cases a, b, and c.2 above, the payoff matrix is given by:

$$B: \begin{array}{c} \\ P \\ NP \end{array} \begin{array}{c} \begin{array}{cc} P & NP \end{array} \\ \begin{pmatrix} -C_P - \frac{\theta T}{2} & -C_P - p \\ -C_{NP} + p & -C_{NP} + \delta \end{pmatrix} \end{array}$$

For the sake of simplicity, we will assume that the equilibrium price sets half way between the minimum willingness to accept of firm *NP* and the maximum willingness to pay of firm *P*, that is:[4]

$$p = \frac{\theta\gamma + \theta T}{2} = \theta\frac{\gamma + T}{2}$$

If so, the payoff matrix *B* becomes:

$$C: \begin{array}{c} \\ P \\ NP \end{array} \begin{array}{c} \begin{array}{cc} P & NP \end{array} \\ \begin{pmatrix} -C_P - \frac{\theta T}{2} & -C_P - \theta\frac{\gamma+T}{2} \\ -C_{NP} + \theta\frac{\gamma+T}{2} & -C_{NP} + \delta \end{pmatrix} \end{array}$$

In what follows we will examine the dynamics and the equilibria that emerge under each payoff matrix and the possible shifts in the dynamic regimes from one case to the other (i.e., from matrix *A* to matrix *C*) that may derive from changes in the parameter values of T and γ.

16.3 Dynamics of the Game

Let us indicate with $x(t) \in [0,1]$ the share of firms that adopt strategy P at time $t \in [0,+\infty)$. As a consequence, $1 - x(t)$ denotes the share of firms adopting the alternative strategy *NP*. Variable x represents, therefore, the distribution of the two strategies in the population of firms; if $x = 1$ (respectively, $x = 0$) then all firms adopt strategy *P*, that is, they all keep on using the polluting technology (respectively, all firms adopt strategy *NP*, i.e., they all shift to the clean technology).

At any time t a large number of pairwise matchings occur between firms that randomly interact.

Given the random maching structure of the game, x (respectively, $1-x$) measures the probability of "meeting" a firm that has adopted strategy P (respectively, NP).

Let us assume, for the sake of simplicity, that the adoption process of the two strategies can be described by the well-known *replicator dynamics* (see Weibull, 1995):

$$\dot{x} = x(1-x)\,[\Pi_P(x) - \Pi_{NP}(x)] \tag{16.1}$$

where $\Pi_P(x)$ and $\Pi_{NP}(x)$ indicate the expected payoffs of strategies P and NP, while $\dot{x}$ denotes the time derivative of $x(t)$, namely, $\dot{x} = dx(t)/dt$. According to replicator dynamics, the strategy whose expected payoff is greater than the average payoff spreads within the populations at the expense of the alternative strategy, namely:

$$\dot{x} \gtreqless 0 \text{ iff } \Pi_P(x) - \Pi_{NP}(x) \gtreqless 0, \forall x \in (0,1) \tag{16.2}$$

16.3.1 Dynamics of the Game When the Payoff Matrix A Applies

If $\gamma \geq T$, the payoff matrix A applies (i.e., tradable permits are exchanged only between firms P but not between heterogeneous firms, P and NP). In this case, the expected payoffs for the two strategies are as follows:

$$\Pi_P(x) = \left(-C_P - \frac{\theta T}{2}\right)x + (-C_P - \theta T)(1-x) = -C_P - \theta T + \frac{\theta T}{2}x$$

$$\Pi_{NP}(x) = (-C_{NP} + \gamma\theta)x + (-C_{NP} + \delta)(1-x) = -C_{NP} + \delta + (\gamma\theta - \delta)x$$

so that the replicator dynamics become:

$$\begin{aligned} \dot{x} &= x(1-x)\,[\Pi_P(x) - \Pi_{NP}(x)] \\ &= x(1-x)\left[C_{NP} - C_P - \theta T - \delta + \left[\left(\frac{T}{2} - \gamma\right)\theta + \delta\right]x\right] \end{aligned} \tag{16.3}$$

where $\frac{T}{2} - \gamma < 0$, since $\gamma \geq T$.

Notice that the payoff $\Pi_P(x)$ is a strictly increasing function of the share of polluting firms x: in fact, the higher is the share of polluting firms, the higher the probability for a firm P to meet a similar firm and thus share the expected penalty ($\frac{\theta T}{2}$) rather than having to pay it all (θT) as it occurs when it meets a firm NP.

Also observe that the payoff $\Pi_{NP}(x)$ is a strictly increasing function of x if $\gamma\theta - \delta > 0$, while it is strictly decreasing if $\gamma\theta - \delta < 0$. This is also consistent with what one would reasonably expect: if for a firm NP the expected gain from meeting a firm P ($\gamma\theta$) is higher than the gain from meeting another firm NP (δ), then its payoff will increase with the number of firms P. The opposite obviously occurs if the sign of the relationship between $\gamma\theta$ and δ is reversed. Notice that if $\delta = 0$, that is, the meeting of two firms *NP* does not generate any positive spillover for each of them, then only the former condition can apply and the payoff $\Pi_{NP}(x)$ is always strictly increasing in the share of polluting firms x.

As one easily observe from equation (16.3), the payoff differential $\Pi_P(x) - \Pi_{NP}(x)$ is strictly increasing (decreasing) in x if $\left(\frac{T}{2} - \gamma\right)\theta + \delta$ is positive (negative). As shown below, we will therefore distinguish two possible cases in the description of the dynamics of the model according to the sign of the previous expression.

The following Proposition illustrates the taxonomy of the dynamic regimes that may occur in the context $\gamma \geq T$.

Proposition 1. *When $\gamma \geq T$, dynamics (16.3) can lead to the following possible dynamic regimes:*

(1) *If $C_{NP} - C_P \geq \max\{\theta T + \delta, \theta(\frac{T}{2} + \gamma)\}$, then whatever the initial distribution of strategies $x(0) \in (0,1)$, x will always converge to the steady state $x = 1$ (see Figure 16.1).*
(2) *If $C_{NP} - C_P \leq \min\{\theta T + \delta, \theta(\frac{T}{2} + \gamma)\}$, then whatever the initial distribution of strategies $x(0) \in (0,1)$, x will always converge to the steady state $x = 0$ (see Figure 16.2).*
(3) *If $\theta(\frac{T}{2} + \gamma) < C_{NP} - C_P < \theta T + \delta$ and $(\frac{T}{2} - \gamma)\theta + \delta > 0$, then there exists a repulsive inner steady state:*

$$\overline{x} := (C_P - C_{NP} + \theta T + \delta) \Big/ \left[\left(\frac{T}{2} - \gamma\right)\theta + \delta\right] \in (0,1)$$

If $x(0) \in [0, \overline{x})$, then x converges to the steady state $x = 0$, while if $x(0) \in (\overline{x}, 1]$, then it converges to the steady state $x = 1$ (see Figure 16.3).
(4) *If $\theta T + \delta < C_{NP} - C_P < \theta\left(\frac{T}{2} + \gamma\right)$ and $\left(\frac{T}{2} - \gamma\right)\theta + \delta < 0$, then whatever the initial distribution of strategies $x(0) \in (0,1)$, x will always converge to the inner steady state $\overline{x} \in (0,1)$ in which the alternative strategies P and NP coexist (see Figure 16.4).*

The Proposition above suggests that there can be multiple equilibria of the game: two extreme equilibria ($x = 0$ and $x = 1$) in which all firms adopt the same (clean and dirty, respectively) technology and an inner equilibrium that can be either repulsive or attracting. In the former case, the system is path-dependent: the trajectories of the economy may lead to one extreme or the other depending on the initial distribution of polluting firms in the population so that the technolgical adoption strategy is self-enforcing. In the latter case the trajectories will lead to an attracting equilibrium in which both technological adoption strategies coexist.

Notice that the bi-stable dynamics characterizing case 3 above can occur if and only if $\left(\frac{T}{2} - \gamma\right)\theta + \delta > 0$, namely, only if the payoff differential $\Pi_P(x) - \Pi_{NP}(x)$ is strictly increasing in x, which generates a self-enforcing mechanism leading to extreme equilibria.[5] On the contrary, the coexistence regime characterizing case 4 above can

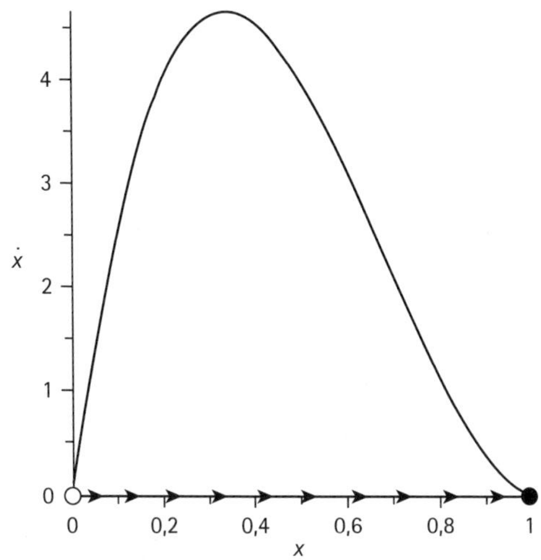

FIGURE 16.1 Whatever the initial distribution of strategies $x(0) \in (0, 1)$, x converges to the steady state $x = 1$. Parameter values: $\delta = 2$, $\gamma = 130$, $\theta = .4$, $C_{NP} = 115$, $C_P = 42$, $T = 100$.

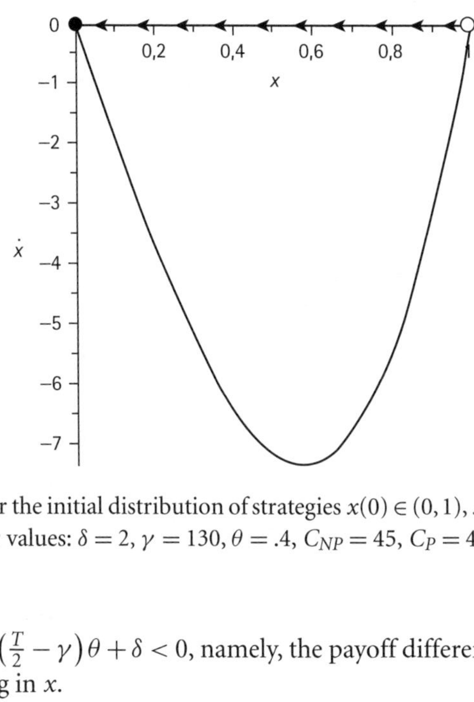

FIGURE 16.2 Whatever the initial distribution of strategies $x(0) \in (0, 1)$, x converges to the steady state $x = 0$. Parameter values: $\delta = 2$, $\gamma = 130$, $\theta = .4$, $C_{NP} = 45$, $C_P = 42$, $T = 100$.

occur if and only if $\left(\frac{T}{2} - \gamma\right)\theta + \delta < 0$, namely, the payoff differential $\Pi_P(x) - \Pi_{NP}(x)$ is downward sloping in x.

The following Proposition describes how a change in θ and/or T modifies the inner equilibrium value $\overline{x}$.

Proposition 2. *In the context* $\gamma \geq T$, *if* $\theta\left(\frac{T}{2} + \gamma\right) < C_{NP} - C_P < \theta T + \delta$ *and* $\left(\frac{T}{2} - \gamma\right)\theta + \delta > 0$ *(bi-stable regime), then* $\frac{\partial \overline{x}}{\partial T} > 0$ *and* $\frac{\partial \overline{x}}{\partial \theta} > 0$.

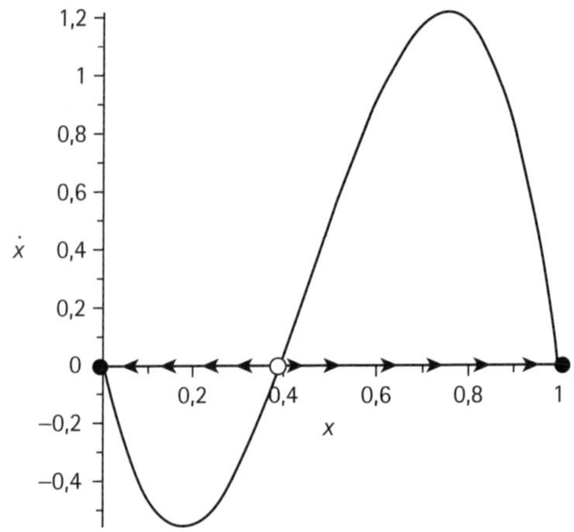

FIGURE 16.3 Bi stable dynamic regime ($x = 0$ and $x = 1$ locally attracting). Parameter values: $\delta = 50$, $\gamma = 130$, $\theta = .4$, $C_{NP} = 125$, $C_P = 42$, $T = 100$.

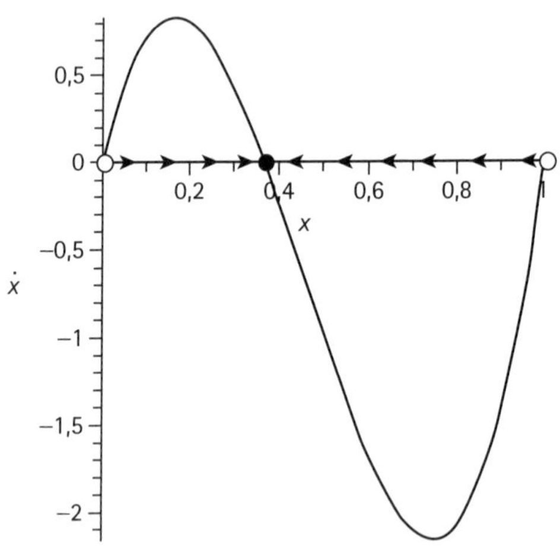

FIGURE 16.4 Coexistence dynamic regime: whatever the initial distribution of strategies $x(0) \in (0,1)$, x always converges to the inner steady state $\bar{x} \in (0,1)$. Parameter values: $\delta = 2$, $\gamma = 130$, $\theta = .4$, $C_{NP} = 95$, $C_P = 42$, $T = 100$.

If $\theta T + \delta < C_{NP} - C_P < \theta\left(\frac{T}{2} + \gamma\right)$ *and* $\left(\frac{T}{2} - \gamma\right)\theta + \delta < 0$ *(coexistence regime), then* $\frac{\partial \bar{x}}{\partial T} < 0$ *and* $\frac{\partial \bar{x}}{\partial \theta} < 0$.

The above Proposition suggests that an increase in θ and/or T shifts the repulsive inner equilibrium $\bar{x}$ to the right, thus enlarging the attraction basin of the "virtuous" equilibrium $x = 0$ in which no firm pollutes any longer. The opposite applies when the inner equilibrium $\bar{x}$ is an attractor: in this case an increase in the expected penalty (due to higher penalty level T and/or higher probability of being discovered θ by the regulatory authority for noncompliant firms) shifts $\bar{x}$ to the left, thus increasing the share of nonpolluting firms at the equilibrium.

In what follows, we intend to point out the possible Pareto dominance relationships between the stationary states of the dynamic system analyzed earlier. For this purpose, let us consider that the average payoff of the population of firms is given by:

$$\overline{\Pi}(x) = x \cdot \Pi_P(x) + (1-x) \cdot \Pi_{NP}(x)$$

Therefore $\overline{\Pi}(1) = \Pi_P(1)$ and $\overline{\Pi}(0) = \Pi_{NP}(0)$ hold. When the two extreme equilibria $x = 0$ and $x = 1$ are both attractors, it seems important to emphasize under which conditions the firms' payoffs are higher in $x = 0$ than in $x = 1$. This occurs when:

$$\Pi_{NP}(0) > \Pi_P(1)$$

That is,

$$-C_{NP} + \delta > -C_P - \frac{\theta T}{2}$$

which can be rewritten as follows:

$$\frac{\theta T}{2} + \delta > C_{NP} - C_P$$

Therefore if the cost differential $C_{NP} - C_P$ between the clean and the dirty technologies is sufficiently low, then both the firms and the citizens are better off in $x = 0$ than in $x = 1$: the former because they get a higher payoff, while the latter because they live in a nonpolluted environment. Notice that the condition above requires that the expected penalty θT and/or the spillover effect δ are sufficiently high so that all firms are highly motivated to shift to the clean technology.

If, on the contrary, the condition above does not apply, then the firms' payoffs are higher in $x = 1$ than in $x = 0$, while the opposite applies for the citizens, at least in terms of their benefits from a clean environment.[6]

16.3.2 Dynamics of the Game When the Payoff Matrix C Applies

If $\gamma < T$, the payoff matrix C applies (i.e., tradable permits are exchanged not only between homogeneous firms P, but also between heterogeneous firms, P and NP). In this case the expected payoffs are:

$$\Pi_P(x) = (-C_P - \frac{\theta T}{2})x + (-C_P - \overline{p})(1-x) = -C_P - E\overline{p} + \left(E\overline{p} - \frac{\theta T}{2}\right)x =$$

$$= -C_P - \theta\frac{\gamma + T}{2} + \theta\frac{\gamma}{2}x$$

$$\Pi_{NP}(x) = (-C_{NP} + \overline{p})x + (-C_{NP} + \delta)(1-x) = -C_{NP} + \delta + (E\overline{p} - \delta)x =$$
$$= -C_{NP} + \delta + \left(\theta\frac{\gamma + T}{2} - \delta\right)x$$

and the replicator dynamics become:

$$\dot{x} = x(1-x)\left[\Pi_P(x) - \Pi_{NP}(x)\right] = x(1-x)\left[C_{NP} - C_P - \delta - E\overline{p} + \left(\delta - \frac{\theta T}{2}\right)x\right] =$$
$$= x(1-x)\left[C_{NP} - C_P - \delta - \theta\frac{\gamma + T}{2} + \left(\delta - \frac{\theta T}{2}\right)x\right] \qquad (16.4)$$

Notice that the payoff function $\Pi_P(x)$ is always strictly increasing in x.[7] The payoff of the nonpolluting technology $\Pi_{NP}(x)$ is, instead, strictly increasing in x if $\theta\frac{\gamma+T}{2} - \delta > 0$, namely, if the price of the tradable permits ($\theta\frac{\gamma+T}{2}$) sold to firm P is higher than the benefit gained from meeting a firm NP (δ). Stated differently, in this case the payoff of firm NP increases with x since the firm NP is more likely to meet a firm P that makes it better off. The opposite obviously applies if the price of the tradable permits sold to firm P is lower than the spillover effect from meeting a firm NP.

The payoff differential $\Pi_P(x) - \Pi_{NP}(x)$ is strictly increasing in x if $\delta - \frac{\theta T}{2} > 0$, strictly decreasing if $\delta - \frac{\theta T}{2} < 0$. This is consistent with our apriori intuition: if the benefit obtained by the matching of two firms NP (δ) is higher than that from the meeting of two firms P ($\frac{\theta T}{2}$), then the payoff of the former firms grows faster than that of the latter as firms NP spread through the population. The opposite obviously applies if δ is lower than $\frac{\theta T}{2}$.

The following Proposition illustrates the taxonomy of the dynamic regimes that may occur in the context $\gamma < T$.

Proposition 3. *When $\gamma < T$, dynamics (16.4) can lead to the following possible dynamic regimes:*

(1) *If $C_{NP} - C_P \geq \max\left\{\theta\frac{\gamma+T}{2} + \delta, \theta\left(T + \frac{\gamma}{2}\right)\right\}$, then whatever the initial distribution of strategies $x(0) \in (0,1)$, x will always converge to the steady state $x = 1$ (see[8] Figure 16.1).*

(2) *If $C_{NP} - C_P \leq \min\left\{\theta\frac{\gamma+T}{2} + \delta, \theta\left(T + \frac{\gamma}{2}\right)\right\}$, then whatever the initial distribution of strategies $x(0) \in (0,1)$, x will always converge to the steady state $x = 0$ (see[8] Figure 16.2).*

(3) *If $\theta\left(T + \frac{\gamma}{2}\right) < C_{NP} - C_P < \theta\frac{\gamma+T}{2} + \delta$ and $\delta - \frac{\theta T}{2} > 0$, then there exists a repulsive inner steady state:*

$$\overline{x} = \left(C_P - C_{NP} + \delta + \theta\frac{\gamma + T}{2}\right) / \left(\delta - \frac{\theta T}{2}\right) \in (0,1)$$

If $x(0) \in [0, \overline{x})$, then x converges to the steady state $x = 0$, while if $x(0) \in (\overline{x}, 1]$, then it converges to the steady state $x = 1$ (see[8] Figure 16.3).

(4) *If* $\theta\frac{\gamma+T}{2}+\delta < C_{NP}-C_P < \theta\left(T+\frac{\gamma}{2}\right)$ *and* $\delta-\frac{\theta T}{2}<0$, *then whatever the initial distribution of strategies* $x(0)\in(0,1)$, x *will always converge to the inner steady state* $\overline{x}\in(0,1)$ *in which the alternative strategies P and NP coexist (see*[8] *Figure 16.4).*

Notice that, as occurred under matrix A, even in the present context a bi-stable (path-dependent) dynamic regime takes place only if the spillover parameter δ is sufficiently high (more precisely, $\delta > \frac{\theta T}{2}$, see case 3 above).

As it clearly emerges from the Proposition above, the dynamic regimes that may occur with matrix C (when permits are traded between heterogeneous firms) are similar to those that result from matrix A (when permits are traded only between polluting firms), although under different parameter values. In both cases (in particular under cases 3 of Propositions 1 and 3), we can have a bi-stable dynamics so that hysteresis takes place in the model. This implies that two economies that take part to the same ETS and undergo the same legislation in terms of sanctions to noncompliant firms may lead to two opposite outcomes ($x=0$ where none pollutes or $x=1$ where everyone pollutes) depending on the share of firms $x(0)$ that initially adopt the new technology *NP*. On the contrary, when cases 4 of Propositions 1 and 3 apply, the dynamics emerging from the payoff matrices A and C are independent of the initial conditions and there always exists a unique steady state that is globally attractive ($x=0$, $x=1$, or $x=\overline{x}$).

It is important to emphasize that—ceteris paribus—a rise in the penalty level T shifts the economy from the regime analyzed in Proposition 1 (case $\gamma \geq T$) to that of Proposition 3 (case $\gamma < T$), thus increasing the overall number of transactions in the ETS as it induces also firms P and NP to exchange permits.

The following Proposition describes how the inner equilibrium identified in Proposition 3 is modified by a change in the penalty level and/or in the monitoring capacity of the regulatory authority that affects the probability to discover noncompliant firms.

Proposition 4. *In the context* $\gamma < T$, *if* $\theta\left(T+\frac{\gamma}{2}\right) < C_{NP}-C_P < \theta\frac{\gamma+T}{2}+\delta$ *and* $\delta-\frac{\theta T}{2}>0$ *(bi-stable regime), then* $\frac{\partial\overline{x}}{\partial T}>0$ *and* $\frac{\partial\overline{x}}{\partial\theta}>0$.

If $\theta\frac{\gamma+T}{2}+\delta < C_{NP}-C_P < \theta\left(T+\frac{\gamma}{2}\right)$ *and* $\delta-\frac{\theta T}{2}<0$ *(coexistence regime), then* $\frac{\partial\overline{x}}{\partial T}<0$ *and* $\frac{\partial\overline{x}}{\partial\theta}<0$.

When a bi-stable dynamics regime applies (case 3 of Proposition 3 above), an increase of T raises the value of the repulsive inner steady state $\overline{x}$; therefore it increases the basin of attraction of $x=0$ with respect to that of $x=1$. Stated differently, when the system is path-dependent an increase of T raises the likelihood that the system may converge to the steady state $x=0$ (where all firms adopt the nonpolluting technology *NP*).

When the inner steady state $\overline{x}$ is globally attracting (case 4 of Proposition 3 above), an increase in T reduces the value of $\overline{x}$. In other words, in this case a rise in the penalty level (that shifts the system from matrix A to matrix C) increases the share of nonpolluting firms *NP* at the equilibrium.

In both cases, therefore, a rise in the penalty level implemented by the regulatory authority that increases permits trade tends to promote the diffusion of the new non polluting technology, as it increases either the basin of attraction of the totally clean outcome ($x = 0$) or the share of clean firms at the equilibrium.[9]

The same applies to an increase in the monitoring effort/ability of the regulator that raises the value of θ, thus making more difficult for noncompliant firms to escape the sanction.

Finally, it is important to underline that the dynamics of the economy may lock the system into a "poverty-trap." As a matter of fact, in some cases the dynamic regime may lead the system toward the "dirty" steady state $x = 1$, although the firms' profits would be higher in the "clean" steady state $x = 0$, in which also the overall collectivity would most likely be better off. To show that this may be the case, consider Proposition 3. In this context, we have:

$$\Pi_{NP}(0) > \Pi_P(1)$$

for:

$$-C_{NP} + \delta > -C_P - \theta\frac{T}{2} + \theta\gamma$$

or equivalently when:

$$\theta\left(\frac{T}{2} - \gamma\right) + \delta > C_{NP} - C_P \tag{16.5}$$

Recalling that the condition for a bi-stable dynamics under Proposition 3 is:

$$\theta\left(T + \frac{\gamma}{2}\right) < C_{NP} - C_P < \theta\frac{\gamma + T}{2} + \delta \tag{16.6}$$

it turns out that the two conditions (16.5) and (16.6) can simultaneously apply if:

$$\theta\left(T + \frac{\gamma}{2}\right) < \theta\left(\frac{T}{2} - \gamma\right) + \delta$$

that is, if:

$$\theta\left(\frac{T}{2} + \frac{3}{2}\gamma\right) < \delta$$

This condition suggests that if the positive spillover effect δ that firms *NP* enjoy when they meet on the market is sufficiently large, then all firms would be better off by adopting the new technology but the bi-stable dynamics may still lead the economy in the opposite direction if many firms are initially reluctant to change technology and keep on using the old one (i.e., if $x(0)$ is above the repulsive inner equilibrium $\overline{x}$).[10] In other words, in this case the economy may end up in a situation that is Pareto-dominated for the firms and most likely also for the society as whole.

16.3.3 Dynamics of the Game When θ is Endogenous

So far, we have assumed that the monitoring capacity of the regulatory authority and thus the probability θ of noncompliant firms of being discovered is exogenously given. However, this may not be the case. In fact, the monitoring capacity and effort of the regulatory authority in discovering and sanctioning noncompliant firms can actually be endogenously determined by the number of polluting firms that the authority has to control. In this section we intend to analyse how results may change if we account for this possibility by endogenising the probability θ. For this purpose, we focus on the case in which heterogeneous firms can exchange emission permits (matrix C above).[11]

Let us assume, for the sake of simplicity, that the probability that a noncompliant firm P is actually discovered by the regulatory authority is a linear function of the overall share of polluting firms, that is:

$$\theta(x) := a + bx$$

where: $a \geq 0$, $b \gtrless 0$ and $0 \leq a + bx \leq 1\ \forall x$.

Notice that we intentionally imposed no apriori condition on the sign of the parameter b. In fact, an increase in the share x of polluting firms may have conflicting effects on the monitoring capacity of the regulatory authority, so that the sign of b is apriori ambiguous. On the one hand, the higher is the share of polluting firms, the lower is the probability for each of them of being discovered if it keeps producing without purchasing the additional emission permit that is requested by law ($b < 0$). On the other hand, the higher is the share of polluting firms, the higher is likely to be the monitoring effort of the regulatory authority and thus also the probability for noncompliant firms of being discovered ($b > 0$).

Assuming $\theta(x) = a + bx$, the expected payoffs become:

$$\begin{aligned}
\Pi_P(x) &= -C_P - \frac{\gamma + T}{2}(a + bx) + \frac{\gamma}{2}x(a + bx) \\
&= -C_P - a\frac{\gamma + T}{2} + \frac{1}{2}(a\gamma - b(\gamma + T))\,x + b\frac{\gamma}{2}x^2 \\
\Pi_{NP}(x) &= -C_{NP} + \delta + \left(\frac{\gamma + T}{2}(a + bx) - \delta\right)x \\
&= -C_{NP} + \delta + \left(a\frac{\gamma + T}{2} - \delta\right)x + b\frac{\gamma + T}{2}x^2
\end{aligned}$$

Therefore, the following replicator dynamics apply:

$$\dot{x} = x(1 - x)\left[C_{NP} - C_P - \delta - a\frac{\gamma + T}{2} + \left(\delta - b\frac{\gamma + T}{2} - a\frac{T}{2}\right)x - b\frac{T}{2}x^2\right] \tag{16.7}$$

Observe that the graphs of the payoff functions $\Pi_P(x)$ and $\Pi_{NP}(x)$ are given by two convex (U-shaped) parabola if $b > 0$, while they can be represented as two concave (bell-shaped) parabola if $b < 0$. Both parabola, therefore, have a minimum (respectively, maximum) that may lie or not within the interval $(0,1)$. The payoff differential:

$$f(x) := C_{NP} - C_P - \delta - a\frac{\gamma+T}{2} + \left(\delta - b\frac{\gamma+T}{2} - a\frac{T}{2}\right)x - b\frac{T}{2}x^2$$

is a concave parabola if $b > 0$, whereas is a convex parabola if $b < 0$.

It follows that we can have two steady states in $(0,1)$, $\overline{x}_1$ and $\overline{x}_2$, with $\overline{x}_1 < \overline{x}_2$. In such case, if $b > 0$, we have four steady states, $x = 0$ and $\overline{x}_2$ being attractive, while $x = 1$ and $\overline{x}_1$ are repulsive (see Figure 16.5); if, on the contrary, $b < 0$ we still have the same four steady states but with opposite stability properties: $x = 0$ are $\overline{x}_2$ repulsive, while $x = 1$ and $\overline{x}_1$ are attractive (see Figure 16.6).

Observe that it is:

$$f(0) = C_{NP} - C_P - \delta - a\frac{\gamma+T}{2} < 0 \tag{16.8}$$

for $C_{NP} - C_P < \delta + a\frac{\gamma+T}{2}$ and:

$$f(1) = C_{NP} - C_P - (a+b)\left(\frac{\gamma}{2} + T\right) < 0 \tag{16.9}$$

for $C_{NP} - C_P < (a+b)\left(\frac{\gamma}{2} + T\right)$.

Also notice that the value of x that maximizes $f(x)$ (if $b > 0$) or minimizes $f(x)$ (if $b < 0$) is the solution of the following equation:

$$f'(x) = \delta - b\frac{\gamma+T}{2} - a\frac{T}{2} - bTx = 0$$

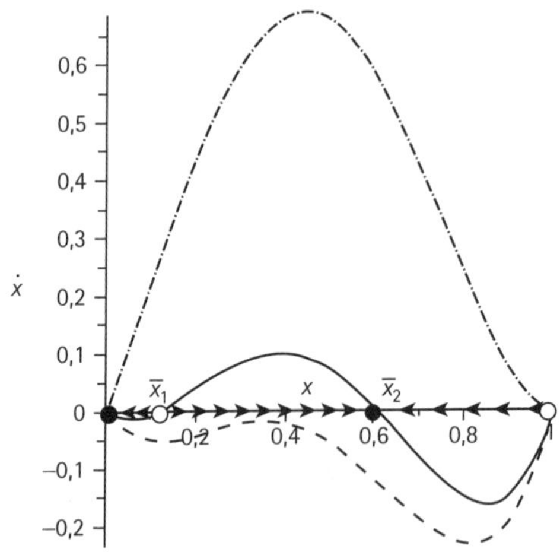

FIGURE 16.5 Graphs of $\dot{x}$ at different values of the cost differential. Dashed line: $C_{NP} - C_P = 31$, $x = 0$ globally attracting; continuous line: $C_{NP} - C_P = 31.5$, $x = 0$ and $\bar{x}_2$ locally attracting; dashdotted line: $C_{NP} - C_P = 33.9$, $x = 1$ globally attracting. The other parameter values: $a = 0.4$, $b = 0.3$, $T = 47$, $\delta = 22$, $\gamma = 3$.

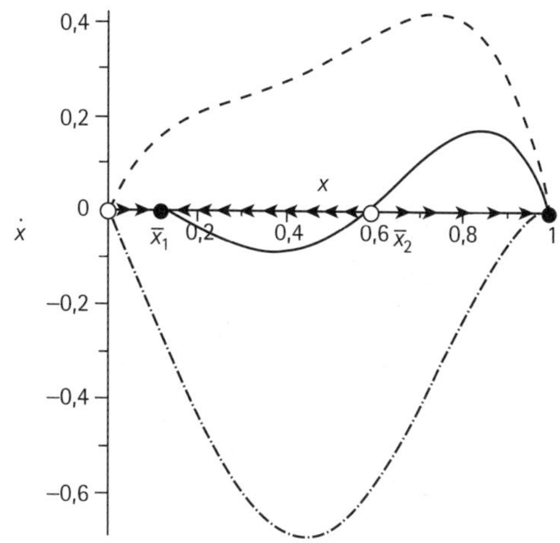

FIGURE 16.6 Graphs of $\dot{x}$ at different values of the cost differential. Dashed line: $C_{NP} - C_P = 23.5$, $x = 1$ globally attracting; continuous line: $C_{NP} - C_P = 22$, $\bar{x}_1$ and $x = 1$ locally attracting; dashdotted line: $C_{NP} - C_P = 19.5$, $x = 0$ globally attracting. The other parameter values: $a = 0.7$, $b = -0.3$, $T = 47$, $\delta = 4$, $\gamma = 3$.

namely:

$$x_e = \frac{\delta - b\frac{\gamma+T}{2} - a\frac{T}{2}}{bT}$$

where $x_e > 0$ when:

$$\delta - b\frac{\gamma + T}{2} - a\frac{T}{2} \gtrless 0 \text{ if } b \gtrless 0 \tag{16.10}$$

while $x_e < 1$ when:

$$\delta - b\frac{\gamma + T}{2} - a\frac{T}{2} \gtrless bT \text{ if } b \gtrless 0 \tag{16.11}$$

16.3.3.1 *Case $b > 0$*

When $b > 0$, the necessary and sufficient condition to have four steady states is that conditions (16.8)–(16.11) are simultaneously satisfied and that $f(x_e) > 0$ also holds.

Among this set of conditions, (16.10)–(16.11) jointly ensure that the value of x that maximizes $f(x)$ lies in the interval $(0, 1)$, namely $x_e \in (0, 1)$, iff:

$$b\frac{\gamma}{2} + (a+b)\frac{T}{2} < \delta < b\frac{\gamma}{2} + (a+3b)\frac{T}{2}$$

which can also be expressed in terms of the penalty T as follows:

$$\frac{2\delta - b\gamma}{a+3b} < T < \frac{2\delta - b\gamma}{a+b} \tag{16.12}$$

provided $a + b \neq 0$.[12]

The remaining conditions (16.8), (16.9) and $f(x_e) > 0$, that are needed to have four steady states, are all dependent on the cost difference between the two technologies $C_{NP} - C_P$. More precisely, as can be clearly seen from conditions (16.8)–(16.9), the cost difference between the clean and the dirty technology must be sufficiently low to have the dynamic regime with four equilibria described above. In fact, an increase in the difference $C_{NP} - C_P$ shifts upward the concave parabola $f(x)$. A relatively low increase in the cost of the two technologies moves the attracting equilibrium $\overline{x}_2$ to the right (thus raising the number of polluting firms at the equilibrium) and the repulsive equilibrium $\overline{x}_1$ to the left (which reduces the attraction basin of the "virtuous" equilibrium $x = 0$), which is consistent with what one would reasonably expect. But if the increase in the difference $C_{NP} - C_P$ is very high, the parabola may shift above the horizontal axis, so that there is no longer any inner equilibrium. Figure 16.5 shows three graphes of $\dot{x}$, corresponding to different values of $C_{NP} - C_P$, that give rise to three different dynamic regimes; in one regime, the steady states $\overline{x}_2$ and $x = 0$ are locally attracting, in the others the steady states $x = 0$ and $x = 1$ are globally attracting.

Summing up, when $b > 0$, if the difference in the technological costs is sufficiently low and the penalty level has intermediate values as described above, then we can have four steady states, that is, a path-dependent economy with one inner equilibrium $\overline{x}_2$ in which the two strategies P and NP coexist.

16.3.3.2 *Case $b < 0$*

A similar reasoning applies in the case $b < 0$. When $b < 0$, we have four steady states iff: $f(0) > 0, f(1) > 0, f(x_e) < 0$ and $x_e \in (0,1)$. The former three conditions crucially depend on the difference $C_{NP} - C_P$ (that has to be sufficiently high for the vertical intercept of the curve to be positive as well as its value at $x = 1$). As to the latter condition $x_e \in (0,1)$, it is easy to check that it holds iff:

$$a + 3b > 0 \text{ and } \frac{2\delta - b\gamma}{a+b} < T < \frac{2\delta - b\gamma}{a+3b}$$

Thus, when $b < 0$, if the difference in the technological costs is sufficiently high and the penalty level has intermediate values as described above, we have 4 steady states with opposite stability features with respect to the case $b > 0$, namely: $x = 0$ and $\overline{x}_2$ repulsive, while $x = 1$ and $\overline{x}_1$ are attractive.

Observe that an increase in the cost difference $C_{NP} - C_P$ shifts the attracting equilibrium $\overline{x}_1$ to the right (thus increasing the share of polluting firms P at the equilibrium) and the repulsive equilibrium $\overline{x}_2$ to the left (which extends the attraction basin of $x = 1$ where pollution is maximum). This seems consistent with our intuition: the higher is the cost of the clean technology with respect to the polluting technology, the lower is the number of firms that decide to invest in the new technology and the more attractive is the "business-as-usual" solution in which firms prefer to keep on using the traditional polluting technology.

Even in this case, however, if the increase in the cost difference $C_{NP} - C_P$ is remarkably high, the parabola will shift above the horizontal axis, so that the inner coexistence equilibria $\overline{x}_1$ and $\overline{x}_2$ cease to exist and there remains only one attracting equilibrium, $x = 1$. Figure 16.6 shows three graphes of $\dot{x}$, corresponding to different values of $C_{NP} - C_P$, that give rise to three different dynamic regimes; in one regime, the steady states $\overline{x}_1$ and $x = 1$ are locally attracting, in the others the steady states $x = 0$ and $x = 1$ are globally attracting.

16.4 Conclusions

The present chapter has examined how the implementation of an ETS may affect the diffusion of new environmentally friendly technologies, taking into account both the penalty to noncompliant firms established in the ETS and the possible strategic behavior of single firms. For this purpose, we have set up and analyzed an evolutionary game model with random matching. While this framework does not aim to be necessarily realistic (although it fits many contexts, possibly including also the pairwise meetings in local ETS), it allows to explain learning processes and to emphasize specific mechanisms that may derive from strategic interaction among economic agents.

As shown in the chapter, we can have two alternative payoff matrixes depending on the relationship between two crucial parameters, T and γ, that capture the penalty level and the incentive of clean firms to act strategically, respectively. In one case, only polluting firms exchange permits among themselves, whereas in the other case permits can be traded between heterogeneous firms (polluting and nonpolluting). We have shown that by properly increasing the penalty level the regulatory authority can shift from one dynamic regime to the other (i.e., we can pass from the former to the latter case) and that an increase in permits trade promotes the diffusion of innovative pollution-free technologies at the equilibrium.

In both cases, morever, multiple equilibria emerge from the model, with dynamics leading either to extreme equilibria or to inner equilibria. When the dynamics lead to extreme equilibria, all firms imitate the others and select the same (polluting or nonpolluting) strategy. When they converge to an inner attracting equilibrium, then there coexist heterogeneous choices in the population of firms, with some firms that adopt the clean technology and others that remain with the old polluting technology. When the inner equilibrium is, instead, a repulsive steady state, the system is characterized by path-dependency. This suggests that in a context characterized by bounded rationality and imitative behaviors as the one described in this chapter, the initial share of innovative firms that adopt the new nonpolluting technology may play a key role in determining the final outcome of the ETS. If the dynamics are path-dependent, in fact, two economies that take part to the same ETS and undergo the same penalty system (as it occurs, for instance, in the European ETS) might end up in opposite situations as to the diffusion of the new technology depending on the initial share of nonpolluting firms.

Finally, the number of possible equilibria can further increase (up to four alternative steady states) if we assume that the probability of discovering non-compliant firms is not exogenously given, but rather a function of the number of polluting firms. In any case, whatever the number of possible equilibria, it is also possible to rank them and analyze which one Pareto-dominates the others.

Further research will be needed in the future to deepen the present analysis. In particular, it would be desirable to extend the evolutionary game proposed here from pairwise random matchings to the case of *n* firms possible meetings, so that each firm can simultaneously match up and exchange permits with any other firm in the market rather than with a single firm. This would strengthen the realism of the model, potentially adding further complexity to the possible dynamics that derive from it.

Acknowledgments

The research of Angelo Antoci is financed by Regione Autonoma della Sardegna (L.R. 7/2007) under the project '*Capitale sociale e divari economici regionali*'. Simone Borghesi gratefully acknowledges financial support from the European Commission Directorate-General for Research & Innovation (FP7 project on "Financialisation, economy, society and sustainable development", Grant Agreement Number 266800) and the Italian Ministry of Education, University and Research (Scientific Research Program of National Relevance PRIN 2010-11, project code: 2010S2LHSE).

Notes

1. See, for instance, Borghesi et al. (2012) and the literature cited therein.
2. A similar use of emissions permits for strategic purposes has actually occurred in some applications of ETS. For instance, when a system of water pollution permits was implemented on the Fox River in Wisconsin, the largest firms that possessed most of the permits refused to sell them to the smaller firms to hinder the growth in the production activity of the latter ('O Neill et al., 1983).
3. One can interpret γ, for instance, as the increase in the revenues and/or in the market share accruing to firm *NP* from the closing of the noncompliant firm *P* or from the acquisition by *NP* of some green labeling that increases the number of its consumers who are concerned with the environmental consequences of the dirty production process used by firm *P*.
4. This is equivalent to assuming that firms *P* and *NP* have the same bargaining power. If this is not the case, the equilibrium price will obviously tend toward one extreme or the other of the range of values $(\theta\gamma, \theta T)$ according to the respective importance and bargaining power of the two firms.

5. Since $\gamma \geq T$, observe that for the condition above to apply it must be $\delta > 0$, that is, a positive spillover must derive from diffusion of the new technology.
6. Notice that in the present model we focus attention on the firms' profit rather than on the welfare of the whole collectivity. However, given the many and well-documented health damages provoked by environmental degradation (cf. WHO, 2005), it seems reasonable to argue that citizens would be better off in a perfectly clean world ($x = 0$) than in an extremely polluted one ($x = 1$). The opposite result will obviously emerge when the firms' profits are higher in $x = 1$ than in $x = 0$ (i.e., $\Pi_{NP}(0) < \Pi_P(1)$). In that case, the firms' interests are likely to conflict with the welfare of society as a whole. The welfare analysis of the whole collectivity, however, goes beyond the scope of the present chapter. We therefore leave it for future extensions of the present work.
7. This occurs because, if $\gamma > 0$, the price that a firm P pays when it buys the pollution permit from another firm P ($\frac{\theta T}{2}$) is higher than what it pays when it buys it from a firm NP ($\theta \frac{\gamma + T}{2}$).
8. Please note that although the referred figures in the statement are related to the matrix A, from a qualitative point of view they can fit also for the cases under scrutiny.
9. Notice that, when $\gamma = T$, the two matrices A and C coincide so that they have the same inner equilibrium $\overline{x}$. As a consequence, the comparative statics results concerning $\overline{x}$ described in the previous Propositions hold true even when an increase in T shifts the regime from matrix A to matrix C.
10. Notice that a positive technological spillover δ is a necessary but not a sufficient condition to satisfy the condition above, since such a spillover has to be sufficiently high for this to occur.
11. A similar analysis can obviously be performed also in the case of matrix A. We omit it for space reasons and prefer to focus on matrix C since in this latter case the permit market is more extended as it includes also the trade between firms P and NP.
12. Notice that it is always $a + b \geq 0$ since we have: $0 \leq a + bx \leq 1\ \forall x$.

References

Aldy, J. E., and Stavins, R. N. (2008). Introduction: International policy architecture for global climate change. In J. E. Aldy and Stavins R. N. (eds.), *Architectures for Agreement: Addressing Global Climate Change in the Post-Kyoto World*, pp. 1–27. Cambridge and New York: Cambridge University Press.

Borghesi, S. (2011). The European emission trading scheme and renewable energy policies: Credible targets for incredible results? *International journal of sustainable economy*, 3, 312–327.

Borghesi, S. (2014). Water tradable permits: a review of theoretical and case studies. Journal of Environmental Planning and Management forthcoming. DOI: 10.1080/09640568.2013.820175.

Borghesi, S., Cainelli, G., and Mazzanti, M. (2012). Brown sunsets and green dawns in the industrial sector: Environmental innovations, firm behavior and the European emission trading. Working Paper FEEM 3.2012, Milan: Fondazione ENI Enrico Mattei.

Brauneis, A., Loretz, M., Mestel, R., and Palan, S. (2011). Inducing low-carbon investment in the electric power industry through a price floor for emission trading. Working Paper FEEM 74.2011, Milan: Fondazione ENI Enrico Mattei.

Carraro, C., De Cian, E., Massetti, E., Nicita, L., and Verdolini, E. (2010). Environmental policy and technical change: A survey. *International review of environmental and resource economics*, 4, 163–219.

Calel, R., and Dechezlepretre, A. (2012). Environmental policy and directed technological change: Evidence from the European carbon market. Working Paper FEEM No.22.2012, Milan: Fondazione ENi Enrico Mattei.

Clò, S. (2008). Assessing the European emissions trading scheme effectiveness in reaching the Kyoto target: An analysis of the cap stringency, Institute of Law and Economics (RILE). Rotterdam: Working Paper Series No. 2008/14.

Coase, R. H. (1960). The problem of social cost. *Journal of law and economics*, 3, 1–44.

Coniff, R. (2009). The political history of cap and trade. Smithsonian magazine, August. http://www.smithsonianmag.com/air/the-political-history-of-cap-and-trade-34711212/?c=y?no-ist.

Convery, F. J. (2009). Origins and development of the EU ETS. *Environmental and Resource Economics*, 43, 391–412.

Costantini, V., D.'Amato, A., Martini, C., Tommasinoc., Valentini E. and Zoli M. (2013). Taxing International Emissions Trading. Energy Economics, 40, 609–621.

Dales, J. H. (1968). Land, water, and ownership. *The canadian journal of economics*, 1, 791–804.

Ellerman, A. D., and Buchner, B. K. (2007). The European Union emissions trading scheme: Origins. allocation, and early results. *Review of environmental economics and policy*, 1, 66–87.

Ellerman, A. D., and Joskov, P. L. (2008). The European Union's emissions trading system in perspective, Arlington, VA: Pew Center on Global Climate Change.

Ellerman, A. D. (2009). The EU's emissions trading scheme: A proto-type global system? Cambridge, MA: MIT Joint Programme on the Science and Policy of Global Change, Report No. 170, MIT.

Ellerman, A. D., Convery, F. J., and de Perthuis, C. (2010). Pricing Carbon: The European Union Emissions Trading Scheme. Cambridge, UK: Cambridge University Press.

Grull, G., and Taschini, L. (2011). Cap-and-trade properties under different hybrid scheme designs. *Journal of Environmental Economics and Management*, 61, 107–118.

Hagem, C., and Westkog, H. (1998). The design of a dynamic tradeable quota system under market imperfections. *Journal of Environmental Economics and Management*, 36, 89–107.

Hahn, R .W. (1984). Market power and transferable property rights. *Quarterly journal of economics*, 99, 753–765.

Hofbauer, J., and Sigmund, K. (1988). The Theory of Evolution and Dynamical Systems, Cambridge, UK: Cambridge University Press.

Ino, H. (2011). Optimal environmental policy for waste disposal and recycling when firms are not compliant. *Journal of Environmental Economics and Management*, 62, 290–308.

O'Neill, W., Martin, D., Moore, C., and Joeres, E. (1983). Transferable discharge permits and economic efficiency: The Fox river. *Journal of Environmental Economics and Management*, 10, 346–355.

Maynard Smith, J. (1982). Evolution and the Theory of Games, Cambridge, UK: Cambridge University Press.

Montgomery, W. D. (1972). Markets in licenses and efficient pollution control programs. *Journal of economic theory*, 5, 395–418.

Moreno-Bromberg, S., and Taschini, L. (2011). Pollution permits, strategic trading and dynamic technology adoption, Working Paper 45. London: Grantham Research Institute, LSE.

Rogge K. S., M. Schneider, and V. H. Hoffmann (2011). The innovation impact of the EU Emission Trading System—Findings of company case studies in the German power sector, *Ecological Economics*, 70, 513–523.

Samuelson L. (1997). Evolutionary games and equilibrium selection, The MIT Press, Cambridge, Mass.

Weibull J. W. (1995). Evolutionary game theory, The MIT Press, Cambridge, Mass.

WHO - World Health Organisation, 2005. Preventing disease through healthy environments: Towards an estimate of the environmental burden of disease, WHO, Geneva.

Wirl F. (2009). Oligopoly meets oligopsony: the case of permits, *Journal of Environmental Economics and Management*, 58, 329–337.

CHAPTER 17

THE REALITY OF NUCLEAR POWER

The Fukushima Experience and Its Impact

KOZO MAYUMI AND JOHN M. POLIMENI

17.1 Introduction: Fukushima Nuclear Power Accident and Its Time Course (March 3, 2011–March 10, 2012)

The main purpose of this chapter is to discuss several fundamental issues associated with nuclear power generation plants, with a particular focus on the case of Japan. These issues are critical components of any discussion on environmental sustainability. Before going into the core of the discussion, it is useful to review the course of development that led to the Fukushima nuclear accident in Japan.

Nuclear power generation remains controversial. Some countries, such as China, have decided to pursue the development of nuclear energy, while others, such as Germany, have decided to phase out production (Bunn and Heinonen, 2011). Countries in need of a steady supply of electricity have turned to nuclear power to satisfy their needs, while others have used the low carbon dioxide (CO_2) emissions to justify their use. In addition, operating costs have declined considerably while capacity has increased (Holt, 2009). Countries that have a moratorium on the construction of new nuclear power plants or are stopping production have largely done so owing to the high capital costs, regulatory compliance costs, and public pressure due to concerns over safety and nuclear waste disposal (Holt, 2009). Elliot (2009) provides a detailed examination of the controversies that surround nuclear energy and why countries decide to use or not use this source of electricity.

The Fukushima incident left an indelible mark on the world. Governments and regulators are reviewing their nuclear energy safety policies and whether to continue nuclear energy production. Not surprisingly, this has led to a considerable amount of literature on the subject covering a variety of topics. Davies (2011) explores the issues leading up to the Fukushima incident and then details the reactions of several countries to the disaster to explore how disasters help to transform energy law. Wittneben (2012) examines the European response to the Fukushima incident, in particular the reaction of Germany and the United Kingdom. She found that these two countries have divergent responses, the United Kingdom seeking to increase nuclear power generation while the Germans instituted a temporary moratorium on all nuclear power facilities, owing to political elections, media reporting of the disaster, trust in renewable technologies, a history of nuclear resistance, and a feeling of cultural closeness to the Japanese. Mayumi and Polimeni (2012) examine the disaster from the perspective of whether nuclear energy is needed in Japan and whether nuclear power generation is environmentally friendly because of a reduction in CO_2 emissions. They found that nuclear power generation is unnecessary for Japanese energy security and that nuclear energy does not deliver on its promise of reduced CO_2 emissions. As a result, nuclear power generation in Japan can stop and any future nuclear disasters can be avoided. Hayashi and Hughes (2013) build upon the preceding findings to examine the Japanese policy response to the Fukushima incident and its effect on energy security in the country. They detail the changes in Japanese energy policies and explore various energy futures for the country. They find that restricting energy generation to non-nuclear sources impacted Asian liquid natural gas and oil supplies. Furthermore, they conclude that nuclear energy will remain an important source of Japanese electricity and exports. Other literature on the Fukushima accident exists and we encourage readers to follow their own curiosity on the topic.

The Great Tohoku–Kanto Earthquake that struck Japan on March 11, 2011 and the huge tsunami that followed put the Fukushima nuclear power generation plants in peril. Units 1, 2, 3, and 4 of the Fukushima Nuclear Station 1 were severely damaged largely as a result of the hydrogen explosion that occurred soon after the earthquake. A month later on April 12, 2011 Japanese authorities notified the International Atomic Energy Agency (IAEA) of their decision to upgrade the accident from INES 5 to INES 7 on the International Nuclear and Radiological Event Scale. As a result of this reevaluation, the total amount of discharged iodine-131 is estimated to be 1.3×10^{17} becquerels, and caesium-137 is estimated to be 6.1×10^{15} becquerels according to the Nuclear and Industrial Safety Agency in Japan (Yomiuri Online, 2011a). A becquerel is the quantity of radioactive material in which one nucleus decays per second. The scale of INES is mainly based on the amount of discharged iodine-131 *per second*, so the scale of INES does not help us to evaluate the long-term effects of cumulative radioactive materials released from the Fukushima nuclear power plants onto the land and into the sea. In fact, much of the radionuclides released into the environment around the Fukushima plant have been a result of water leakages that were flushed into the ocean, rather than from those attached to carbon and other aerosols from a burning reactor moderator and released into the atmosphere. Thus, the situation of the Fukushima nuclear power plants is entirely different from that of the Chernobyl accident, which had the same INES 7 rating almost exactly 25 years earlier in 1986.

Despite the plausible serious long-term environmental and health problems associated with the Fukushima accident, Sergei Kirienko the Director General of the Russian state corporation Rosatom and well known advocate of the nuclear industry as an economic development tool, strongly questioned the decision of the Japanese government to upgrade the disaster from INES 5 to INES 7 (Asahi.com., 2011a).

However, the incident was significantly worse as a report, based on updated data analysis, released on May 24, 2011 by the Tokyo Electric Power Company (TEPCO). The new analysis found that in addition to a meltdown of Unit 1 on May 12, the nuclear fuels in Units 2 and 3 also melted down through the reactor vessels (Yomiuri Online, 2011b). For meltdown to occur, the temperature of uranium dioxide (UO_2) must reach a temperature of approximately 2800°C. TEPCO also acknowledged that the 3 cm thick steel containment structure of these three units (the temperature to melt steel is approximately 1600°C) must have been breached. Therefore, radioactive nuclear fuel is believed to have reached deep within the concrete situated under the containment structures.

The most dangerous nuclear unit was Fukushima Unit 4 because the wall supporting the spent fuel pool located in the reactor building was severely destroyed by a hydrogen explosion on March 15, 2011. This explosion caused serious damage to the top part of the reactor building of Unit 4 where the fuel pool is housed, as well as creating a large hole in a wall supporting the pool. Making the situation more dangerous was that the pool contains 1535 fuel rods, almost three times as many as usually held in one reactor. To support the pool, TEPCO "completed" the construction of a structure of steel beams beneath the pool on June 20, 2011. TEPCO's emergency measure for the pool is far from satisfactory and safe; another big earthquake would destroy the pool, potentially causing a serious release of radioactive substances from the fuel rods to the environment.

Given these circumstances, it is very sad to see that a report created by the International Atomic Energy Agency (IAEA) stated that the nuclear power generation accident could have been prevented if tsunami prevention measures had been properly prepared (Asahi.com. mini., 2011). The findings of the report prepared by the IAEA were perfectly echoed in a proposal made by approximately 20 Japanese politicians, including several former prime ministers, saying that nuclear power generation plants should be constructed underground (Sankei, 2011). Unfortunately, their claims and recommendations have no validity because the high-pressure coolant injection system within the reactor building in the Fukushima station was destroyed *immediately after the earthquake itself.* The IAEA and some Japanese politicians misunderstand the nature and characteristic of nuclear power generation technology, attributing the cause of the Fukushima accident to the tsunami, not to the huge earthquake that caused the tsunami and happen frequently in Japan. Furthermore, the Ministry of Education, Culture, Sports, Science and Technology, who is supposed to protect children from radioactive contamination as much as possible, raised the minimum allowable contamination level for children up to 20 mSv per year. This level is the maximum contamination legally allowed for a professional radiologist, a totally unacceptable decision.

Japan started nuclear power generation in 1970. The reactors were designed to last about 30 years for PWR and 40 years for BWR. Therefore, the reactors have exceeded their life expectancies. Because neutrons are used as a moderator for these reactors, once the quantity of neutron radiation within the reactor vessel exceeds a certain threshold the reactor becomes extremely fragile. According to H. Ino's study (2011), Japan has seven nuclear power units that have considerably high ductile brittle transition temperatures (DBTTs). The initial DBTT of high-strength steel is about –20°C. The Genkai Unit 1 in Saga Prefecture, Kyushu is reported to have reached a DBTT of 95°C. If the temperature of the reactor vessel is cooled below the DBTT, then there might be a high probability that the reactor will shatter on impact, especially in the case of a cold shutdown operation, without bending or deforming increases. In addition to these major problems, the aging of nuclear power plants is a serious threat for the Japanese people.

At a news conference (Environmental News Service, 2011), Prime Minister Noda said that the nuclear reactors have reached "a state" of cold shutdown, the end of the accident phase of the actual reactors. Yet the reality is that the *nuclear fuels of Unit 1, 2, and 3 are not in the pressure vessels because the nuclear fuels leaked through the containment structures.* It appears he intentionally distorted the technological meaning of cold shutdown because after the nuclear fuels in the three units of the Fukushima nuclear power station leaked through the containment structure a cold shutdown became impossible to accomplish. The only plausible, temporary remedy would be to contain all three units completely. One should remember that the containment strategy is nothing more than leaving nuclear fuels in the facility without putting the fuel into a cold shutdown state. However, immediate action toward the construction of a new containment structure is absolutely necessary to prevent radioactive waste from leaking into the ocean. Furthermore, there is a large amount of radioactively contaminated water within Fukushima Station 1. According to Tokyo Shimbun (2012), the radioactive water stored in Fukushima Station 1 amounts to more than 20,000 m^3, enough to fill 10,000 drums. If Japan is not successful in building a new containment structure, serious irreversible biological effects will result, heavily damaging marine ecosystems and adversely affecting human health. Unfortunately, during the construction process of these containment facilities a vast number of workers must go through serious radiation exposure, an exposure level similar to those experienced by workers at Chernobyl.

Recently a new estimate on the amount of cesium that was released has been found to be far greater than previously believed. Michio Aoyama, a senior researcher at the Meteorological Research Institute, released the finding at a scientific symposium in Tsukuba, Ibaraki Prefecture, on February 28, 2012, stating that a mind-boggling 40,000 trillion becquerels of radioactive cesium, or twice the amount previously thought, may have spewed from Fukushima Station 1 after the March 11 disaster (The Asahi Shimbun, 2101). The figure, which represents about 20% of the discharge during the 1986 Chernobyl nuclear disaster, is twice as large as previous estimates by research institutions in Japan and overseas. The estimate was calculated on the basis of radioactive content of seawater sampled at 79 locations in the north Pacific and is thought to reflect reality more accurately than previous simulation results. Scientists believe that around 30% of the radioactive substances discharged during the crisis ended up on land, while the remaining 70% flowed into the sea.

Another serious problem is how to compensate the people impacted by the disaster. TEPCO was recently informed by the Japan Atomic Energy Insurance Pool, which is composed of Japan's leading 23 insurance companies, that they would not be renewing TEPCO's liability insurance. It will be due for renewal this coming January (Majirox News, 2011).

Adding further instability to the situation, shareholders in TEPCO have sued the firm's directors over their role in the Fukushima nuclear plant disaster (BBC, 2012). The plaintiffs want the directors to pay damages of 5.5 trillion yen (US$68 billion) to the firm, claiming they failed to prepare for such an incident. It should be noted that the maximum amount guaranteed by the Act on Compensation for Nuclear Damage is only 120 billion yen (US$1.5 billion), 2.2% of the claim made by the shareholders. Therefore, TEPCO would face US$100 billion in scale compensation claims from those affected.

According to the Japanese police authority, as of March 8, 2012[1] the number of deaths is 15,854, 26,992 injured people and 3203 missing. The number of evacuees from Fukushima prefecture is 62,674.

The remainder of this chapter is organized as follows. The main focus is on the Japanese nuclear power situation, as there are various crucial factors associated with nuclear power generation that can be useful for public policy in any country that could face similar problems. Section 17.2 examines the stock of uranium-235, a fissile type of exhaustible primary energy. The proven reserve of uranium-235 has been shown to be limited. As a result, nuclear power generation supporters tried to establish a so-called nuclear fuel cycle, attempting to invent and construct a fast breeder reactor (FBR) that uses mixed oxide (MOX) fuel consisting of plutonium dioxide (PuO_2) and uranium dioxide (UO_2). Section 17.3 shows that, to date, the nuclear fuel cycle is not possible. Section 17.4 examines the issue of CO_2 emissions resulting from sea water evaporation caused by increased sea water temperatures triggered by hot water released from the nuclear power plants into the sea. This negative aspect of nuclear power generation is rarely examined. Thus, approximations of CO_2 emissions from evaporated sea water are calculated in this section. The estimates provided are dependent on many factors, but we believe that the values are within the negligible range of the most reliable values that have been calculated elsewhere. Section 17.5 discusses the capacity utilization of various electricity generation plants in Japan, showing that it is possible to supply electricity, in particular during peak demand, without resorting to the nuclear power plants in Japan. Section 17.6 deals with the economic and legal aspects associated with Japanese nuclear power generation policies. Specifically, this section examines how the electric service rate is determined and scrutinizes several forms of the government subsidies to promote nuclear power generation. Section 17.7 concludes the chapter.

17.2 The Reserves of U-235: An Exhaustible Primary Energy Source

Uranium is an exhaustible primary energy source like oil and coal. The total estimated amount of proven reserves of any type of exhaustible primary energy source has to be updated regularly to account for changes in technological and economic factors. However, *the relative size* of the estimated amount of several different *proven reserves*, such as coal and oil, has not changed much. Therefore, examining the relative size of proven reserves of uranium in comparison with those of coal, crude oil, and natural gas based on data provided by the World Energy Council (2010) is instructive. There are three types of energy (electricity, fuel, and heat) used for different tasks and goals produced from various forms of primary energy sources. As a first approximation, the proven reserves of each one of these primary energy sources must be converted into joules. Then, the number of years that each type of primary energy source can last is estimated and compared with the amount of total primary energy used in the year 2010, 502 exajoules (5.02×10^{20} J) shown in Table 17.1. The data are obtained from the BP Statistical Review of World Energy (2011) and the World Nuclear Association (2009, 2010).

Table 17.1 "Guestimated" Life Span of Four Primary Energy Sources in Terms of the Year 2010 Total Primary Energy Use in the World

	Proven reserves	Joules	Lifespan (years)
Coal	861 trillion tonnes[a]	2.52×10^{22}	50.2
Crude oil	1.383 trillion barrels[a]	8.46×10^{21}	16.9
Natural gas	187 trillion cubic feet[a]	1.97×10^{20}	0.4
Uranium	5.4 million tonnes[b]	2.36×10^{21}	4.7

[a]BP Statistical Review of World Energy, June 2011.
[b]World Nuclear Association.
http://www.world-nuclear.org/info/inf75.html
The total primary energy use in the year 2010 in the world $1 = 5.02 \times 10^{20}$ J.

The estimates of life span for four common primary energy sources—coal, crude oil, natural gas, and uranium—are calculated as follows:

1. Coal: 1 ton of coal equivalent = 2.93×10^7 kJ
2. Crude oil: 1 barrel = 42 gallons = 6.1×10^6 kJ
3. Natural gas: 1 cubic foot = 1055.06 kJ
4. Uranium-235; 1 ton of U-235 = 7.4×10^{13} kJ

Triuranium octaoxide (U_3O_8), often used in nuclear power generation because it is readily available in nature and kinetically and thermodynamically stable, is not directly usable as a fuel for a nuclear reactor without additional processing. This additional processing is necessary to obtain usable nuclear fuel. Only 0.7% of natural uranium is the fissile, or capable of undergoing fission, U-235 necessary to produce energy in a nuclear reactor while the remaining 99.3% is uranium-238 (U-238). So the average weight of U_3O_8 is 841. Only 0.59% of the total U_3O_8 is U-235. The energy equivalent of 1 ton of U-235 is 7.4×10^{16} kJ. So the total energy from the proven reserves of uranium is equal to $(7.4 \times 10^{16}\ \text{J}) \times (5.4 \times 10^6) \times 0.0059 = 2.36 \times 10^{21}$ J.

Table 17.1 illustrates how small the proven reserves of uranium are in comparison with other exhaustible primary energy sources. Judging from this preliminary examination of uranium reserves we are not surprised to see that "starting in 1991, the production of uranium, in terms of contained uranium, had been less than the reactor requirement of uranium up until now" (WEC, 2010, p. 204, Fig. 6.3).

If the following two points are taken into consideration, the low proven reserve levels of uranium are clear:

1. According to an estimate for 2030, primary energy demand in Asia reaches a level that is double (6.2 billion t.o.e.) the year 2004 level (3.1 billion t.o.e.), based on the expected high economic growth rate (Ito, 2007). This projected energy demand would be almost 40% of the total projected energy demand in the world by 2030.
2. There are three uses of energy for final consumption, fuels, heat, and electricity. Electricity that is partially produced from nuclear power generation plants using U-235 is only a small fraction of that used in final consumption. Moreover, of the three uses of energy, electricity is only 23% of the final energy consumption in Japan (EDMC, 2011).

17.3 Nuclear Fuel Cycle: A Delusion

The left part of Figure 17.1 is a schematic representation of the process of mining, milling, enriching, and fabricating for a thermal neutron reactor. Spent fuel usually contains 1% of plutonium. The current stock of separated plutonium stored for Japan

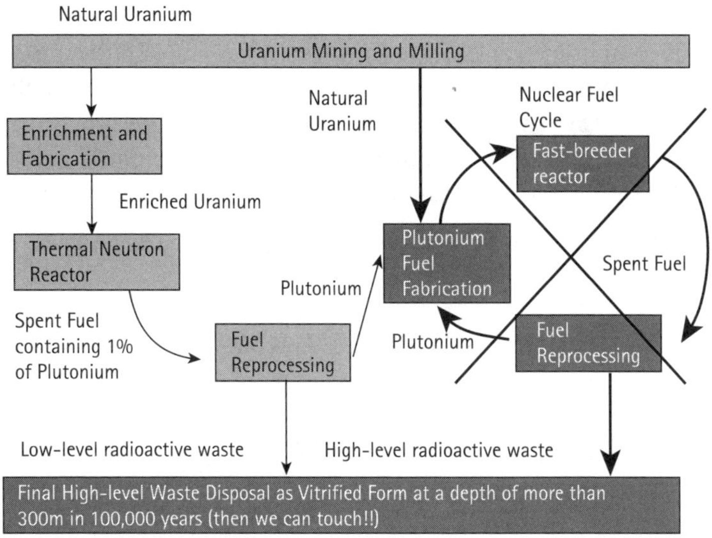

FIGURE 17.1 Nuclear fuel cycle. (Based on a slide prepared by Prof. Koide.)

amounts to more than 45 metric tons, equivalent to the potential production of about 4000 atomic bombs of the type dropped on Nagasaki in WWII. Plutonium is easily transformed into nuclear weapons. Therefore, under the nuclear nonproliferation treaty, Japan is prohibited from possessing plutonium in a pure form. The only law-abiding way for Japan to possess plutonium is to create a MOX form consisting of PuO_2 and UO_2.

As examined in Section 17.2, natural uranium consists of 0.7% of the fissile U-235 and 99.3% of U-238 that is not fissile and cannot be used directly in a light water reactor as fuel. Pu-239 and U-238 are supposed to be disposed of as radioactive nuclear waste. However, if U-238 is successfully transformed into plutonium within a FBR, almost 60% of the uranium (both U-235 and U-238) could theoretically be utilized as nuclear fuels. Thus, the actual stock of proven uranium reserves would be more than 60 times as much as the current stock of U-235! This imaginative idea is the basis of establishing the nuclear fuel cycle, depicted schematically on the right part of Figure 17.1. There are four phases leading to the construction of a commercially operated FBR: (1) experimental reactor, (2) prototype reactor, (3) demonstration reactor, and (4) commercial reactor. Japan has reached only the second phase and is now planning to construct a commercial reactor by 2050. In our view, establishing a nuclear fuel cycle based on a FBR is perhaps a delusion, a serious misconception that hampers the proper planning for energy safely in the long term. Because it might be impossible to establish a nuclear fuel cycle based on an FBR, MOX is now being used in the thermal-neutron reactor (not in a FBR) such as the Fukushima Unit 3, the fuel of which has reportedly melted down. It should be noted, however, that no nuclear power plants in Japan are currently operating right now with MOX fuels except the Ikata nuclear power generation station located in Shikoku Island, only 210 km away from Tokushima.

Making mistakes is the only way for humans to acquire a proper understanding of nature and the rationale behind any technology. In the case of nuclear power generation, the learning process mechanism seems to be very difficult to establish, perhaps beyond the reach of humans. This section concludes with Soichro Honda's famous quote to understand the nature and characteristics of nuclear power generation technology, "technology that does not take people seriously into account is not technology at all" (Honda, 2009).

17.4 CO_2 Emissions from the Sea: The Hidden Truth of Nuclear Power Generation

Light water reactors are the most common type of thermal neutron reactor. Currently, two types of light water reactors are widely used: the pressurized water reactor (PWR) and the boiling water reactor (BWR). More than 80% of nuclear power generation units in the world in 1999 were light water reactors (JA.Wikipedia, 2011). The United States and Japan are the two countries that intensively use light water reactors. In 2008, all 103 nuclear power generation units in the United States were light water reactors (Settle, 2011) and in the year 2007 all 55 commercial nuclear power generation units in Japan were light water reactors (JA.Wikipedia, 2011). Currently, all commercially operating nuclear power plants in Japan are either PWRs or BWRs. These types of reactors are constructed near the sea because they require a large amount of water for their operation, as water is used for the neutron moderator. All three units of the Fukushima power generation station that melted down are BWRs.

Only one-third of the total heat generated by light water reactors is transformed into electricity because of their low level of thermal efficiency. Therefore, boiling water from a light water reactor must be discarded into the sea, resulting in the sea water temperature in the surrounding marine ecosystems to rise. Yet, scientists concerned with the issue of climate change have not paid due attention to this highly plausible reason for rising sea water temperatures. The IPCC (2011), for example, has never mentioned this type of mechanism for rising sea water temperatures, instead focusing only on the absorption capacity of the ocean. Therefore, *as a first approximation*, an exercise aimed at investigating the order of magnitude of this temperature increase mechanism in terms of CO_2 emissions is provided. The numbers used in the exercise are dependent on many factors, but any discrepancy from the most reliable values is believed to be within the negligible range. Readers are encouraged to investigate further on this problem.

In the year 1998 the amount of electricity generation was 331.35 billion kWh. As already mentioned, the average thermal efficiency of light water reactors in Japan is one-third. Therefore, the total heat discarded into the surrounding sea is (2) $\times$ (331.35

$\times 10^6$kWh) $\times$ (3.6MJ) = 2.39 $\times 10^{12}$ MJ. The specific heat of 1 g of water is equivalent to 4.2 J. Thus, the amount of water that can be raised by 1°Celsius is (2.39 $\times 10^{12}$ MJ $\times 10^6$ J)/(4.2 J/g) = 0.569 $\times 10^{18}$ g = 0.569 $\times 10^{12}$ ton.

We can also examine how the amount of CO_2 in 1 liter of water (mol/kg) varies with the temperature. A 1°C increase in the surface sea water induces a 2% increase in CO_2 released from the sea[2]. Suppose that the average sea water temperature around Japan is 20°C. According to the Japanese Meteorological Agency (2011), the CO_2 concentration within the sea area around Japan is approximately 340 ppm. Therefore, the total amount of CO_2 that could be released from the sea is (0.569 $\times 10^{18}$) $\times$ (340 $\times 10^{-6}$) $\times$ (0.02) = 3.87 million tons.

According to the Kyoto Protocol, Japan is supposed to reduce CO_2 emissions by 6% of their 1990 level, which was 1144 million tons. Therefore, the required CO_2 reduction is 68.6 million tons. The total amount of CO_2 emissions *due to the operation process of electricity generation* from nuclear power generation plants in Japan is 5.6% of the required reduction of CO_2. This amount is not negligible and it must be emphasized that these CO_2 emissions come only from the operation process of electricity generation. There are many other possible sources of CO_2 emissions if we take other processes of nuclear power generation and radioactive waste, already suggested in Section 17.3, into consideration: (1) mining and milling, (2) enrichment and fabrication, (3) dealing with depleted uranium ore, (4) low-level radioactive waste management, and (5) the final disposal process. In addition to the issue of CO_2 emissions, there are, of course, other biological hazards, including human health problems that could ensue for an incredibly long period of time.

The following statement by Georgescu-Roegen in 1975 deserves special attention with respect to the threat of heat pollution created by nuclear power generation: "The *additional* heat into which all energy of terrestrial origin is ultimately transformed when used by man is apt to upset the delicate thermodynamic balance of the globe in two ways. First, the islands of heat created by power plants not only disturb the local fauna and flora of rivers, lakes, and even coastal seas, but they may also alter climatic patters. One nuclear plant alone may heat up the water in the Hudson River by as much as 7°F. Then again the sorry plight of where to build the next plant, and the next, is a formidable problem. Second, the additional global heat at the site of the plant and at the place where power is used may increase the temperature of the earth to the point at which the icecaps would melt—an event of cataclysmic consequences. Since *the Entropy Law allows no way to cool a continuously heated planet, thermal pollution could prove to be a more crucial obstacle to growth than the finiteness of accessible resources*" (the second italics part is added, Georgescu-Roegen, 1975, p. 358). This quote is very valuable for our debate on sustainability. Georgescu-Roegen argues that nuclear power plants could be a real threat to global warming. We must recall that some countries such as China and Russia are planning to launch the construction of many more nuclear power plants as a result of high oil prices, the need for additional energy supply, and, ironically, to fight global warming.

17.5 Electricity Supply and Peak Demand in Japan

Readers of this chapter might suspect that if Japan were to stop nuclear power generation the country would not be able to produce a sufficient supply of electricity, particularly because the country obtains 29% of its electricity from nuclear power (*The Economist*, 2011). Surprisingly, it is in fact possible for Japan to supply enough electricity to meet demand without relying on nuclear power plants. Figure 17.2 shows the full capacity and the operation ratio for each type of electricity generation method together with private electricity generation in the year 2005 in Japan. (Compiled by Prof. Koide from the date at Federation of Electric Power Companies of Japan 2011.) Japan can safely secure the necessary electricity demand without nuclear power generation plants if the idle capacity of other types of electricity generation plants were used more intensively, in particular, thermal electric power generation plants. It is also possible to supply peak electricity demand in summer evenings without any difficulty. According to Asahi.com (2011b), the Hirono Thermal Plants (five units with a capacity of 3.8 million kW) in the Fukushima Prefecture, shut down after the earthquake. However, these five units and a new unit of Hirono Thermal Plants are operating as of May 2014. So the peak electricity demand (55 million kW) can be supplied without any problem. Furthermore, according to Nikkei.com (2011), in the year 2011, for example, the full capacity of private electricity generation amounts to 60 million kW. Out of this amount, 16.4 million kW of electricity can be supplied to the district operated by TEPCO. At this time, the present maximum capacity of TEPCO is 56.2 million kW. So, if electricity is properly distributed there would be no electricity shortage. If this is the

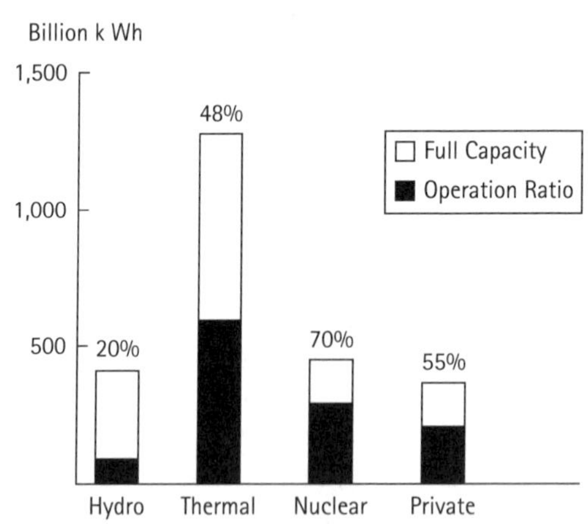

FIGURE 17.2 Full capacity and operation ratio for electricity generation in Japan in the year 2005. (Compiled by Prof. Koide from the date at Federation of Electric Power Companies of Japan 2011.)

case, then why are TEPCO and other Japanese electric power companies not relying on the possible electricity supply that could come from private electricity generation? The answer is that they are afraid of the possible separation between the generation and distribution of electricity, which will cause TEPCO and other Japanese electric power companies to lose their monopolistic power over the electricity market.

As shown in this section, the peak electricity demand in Japan can be met without resorting to nuclear power generation. Furthermore, to reduce the need for additional capital investments in power generation to fulfill the peak demand during the summer months, Japanese consumers could shift or average out their peak electricity demand. Moreover, Japanese industries could also be encouraged to average out their peak electricity demand. For example, after the earthquake and tsunami the Japanese people responded by turning off lights, turning down the air conditioning, and working from home; in addition, factories moved shifts to nights and weekends when demand for electricity was lower. As a result, peak electricity in the Tokyo region decreased by almost 20% from the previous year (*The Economist*, 2011). This policy is also very useful to reduce wasteful energy use by pumped-storage hydroelectricity generation plants that have more than 30% loss of electricity due to the rising and dropping of water during the periods of demand shortages. The cost of pumped-storage hydroelectricity is 10 times as much as that of thermal and normal hydroelectricity generation plants. Price-oriented policies could also be used to make demand management more flexible. For example, a peak electricity price scheme for summer evenings could be instituted. A more sophisticated way of demand management using market mechanisms can be useful.

Concerning peak demand, the Japanese government officially acknowledged that it was possible to supply the predicted summer peak electricity demand, in fact 6% more, for the summer of 2012 based on the actual electricity demand of 2010 (a very hot summer) with no operation of nuclear power plants (Mainichi Shimbun, 2012).

17.6 Electric Service Rate and Subsidy: Economic and Legal Aspects of Nuclear Power Generation

17.6.1 Electric Service Rate

There are two important works on the issue of electric service rate, Murota (1986) and Oshima (2010). This section examines the legal aspects associated with the determination of electric service rate.

The 10 general electric utilities, including TEPCO, have been given a very favorable position as a "natural form" of regional monopoly under Article 21 of the Anti-monopoly Act (AMA) and treated as exceptions to AMA regulation. However, in the 1990s the Japanese government, strongly influenced by the contemporary worldwide trend of the deregulation of the barriers to free market operations, introduced more market-oriented regulations associated with electricity generation so that the high electric service rates in Japan could be reduced to the international level under more efficient management of the general electric utilities. There are two economic and technological reasons behind this movement: (1) the issue of economies of scale associated with the size of electric utilities has become of minor importance; and (2) the more decentralized form of power generation has become more advantageous as a result of rapid development of communication and information technology. Under these circumstances, the general electric utilities became regulated under AMA in the year 2000. However, it should be noted that the electricity supply network is still monopolized by these general electric utilities even now. In addition to this electricity supply network monopoly, the general electric utilities still enjoy a privileged status associated with the determination of the electric service rate under the Electricity Utilities Industry Law (EUIL) and Provisions for Rules and Rate for Electric Service (PRRES). The most crucial article within the EUIL is Article 19. Article 19 stipulates that "a general electric utility shall set supply stipulations concerning power rates or other conditions for supply of electricity to correspond to general electric demand (excluding specific-scale demand), and shall obtain the approval of the Minister of Economy Trade and Industry (METI) in accordance with Provisions for Rules and Rate for Electric Service." Therefore, the electric service rates are determined not by the actual supply of electricity, but the general electricity demand, mainly based on the peak demand (hourly and daily peak demand in summer and winter) (Article 9 of PRRES). Furthermore, Article 19 stipulates that electric service rates "correspond to an appropriate rate of profit added to an appropriate cost under efficient management." It is very difficult for anybody to determine what "an appropriate rate of profit" and "an appropriate cost" are. The details of how to determine a set of the electric service rates are left to the PRRES. For each type of electricity supply the service rate is determined as follows: Sales and General Administration Expense plus Business Reward is divided by General Electric Demand.

Business Reward is derived from the multiplication of two terms, rate base items and business return rate (Article 4 of PRRES). Rate Base Items consist of (1) property, plant, and equipment; (2) property, plant, and equipment under construction; (3) nuclear fuels asset; (4) specific investment for research and development for long-term electricity supply; (5) working capital; and (6) deferred charges for depreciable asset. The business return rate is a weighted average of 30% of the owned capital rate and 70% of the debt capital rate.

There are several problematic issues associated with the actual process of determining the electric service rate:

1. The general electricity demand is based mainly on the peak demand of electricity, which tends to be significantly overvalued.
2. Several items such as nuclear damage compensation insurance, the general compensation charge to the Nuclear Damage Liability Facilitation Fund, and decommissioning costs of nuclear power units are included in the Sales and General Administration Expense.
3. Nuclear fuels assets include spent nuclear fuels, as well as nuclear fuel in the process of fabrication. Spent nuclear fuel is counted as an asset, even though no spent nuclear cycle is established.
4. When determining the business return rate, the interest rate of public bonds is adopted as *the lower bound* of the owned capital rate, and *the weighted average of interest for all types of debt loans that the general electric utilities owe* is adopted as the debt capital rate. Therefore, the general electric utilities are authorized by the PPRES to obtain a sufficient profit that is available after paying all the necessary interest for debt loans, and the Sales and General Administration Expense is automatically covered. In fact, according to a report of the Cabinet Secretariat (2011), the total amount of TEPCO's Business Reward for the 10-year period 2000–2009 was US$44. 94 billion (from now on, assuming that 1 US dollar is 80 yen), more than 11% higher than the total amount of interest and dividends paid out during the same period.

Another issue should also be examined. Because the construction costs of the nuclear power plants are generally much higher than those of other types of plants, the monetary value included in the rate base items within property, plant, and equipment (and those under construction) is much higher than those of other types of plants, given a business return rate. For example, if we adopt construction costs per electricity generation as a proxy for capital asset, we can obtain the following sampling result: (1) Tomari nuclear power unit 3 (320 billion yen/million kW = 292.6/0.912); (2) Kazunogawa hydroelectric plant, a pumped storage power plant (237 billion yen/million kW = 380/1.6); (3) Ichihara power plant, a natural gas plant (90 billion yen/million kW = 10/0.11); and (4) Tsuruga thermal power plant that uses coal (182 billion yen/million kW = 127.5/0.7). Therefore, as a general principle, it is more profitable for the general electric utilities to construct nuclear power generation plants.

17.6.2 Various Forms of Subsidies: Another Taxation Form

Other public policy in Japan also affects the method of energy production. For example, a variety of public policies exist that subsidize nuclear power generation. One such policy is the Power Source Siting Laws (Dengen-sanpoh) that consist of three legal regulations: (1) the Act on Tax for Promotion of Power-Resources Development (ATP-PRD); (2) the Energy Measures Special Account, Chapter 2 Section 6 within the Act on

Special Accounts (ASA); and (3) the Act on the Development of Areas Adjacent to Electric Power Generating Facilities (ADAAEPGF). These three regulations were enacted for the smooth siting of power plants, in particular nuclear power stations. These regulations provide subsidies to local governments that allow the construction of nuclear power generation plants in their jurisdiction. Article 6 of ATPPRD stipulates a tax rate of 0.375 yen (about US$0.0047) per kilowatt-hour. To give the reader some perspective, the typical Japanese household, using up to 90 kWh, pays 21.87 yen for each 1 kW consumed[3].

It is reported that an average Japanese household pays only about 110 yen (US$1.4),[4] so the tax payment for each individual household is very low. However, under this law, the total amount of tax revenue amounted to 355 billion yen (US$4.44 billion) in the year 2005 (Ministry of Finance Japan, 2005). It should be noted that the total national tax for the year 2005 was about 54 trillion yen, so the percentage share of the Tax for Promotion of Power-Resources Development was 0.66%. This share is not a negligible value at all. Of 448 billion yen (355 plus 941 that is retained as surplus), 162 billion yen (US$2.03 billion) is allotted to the Ministry of Education, Culture, Sports, Science and Technology (MEXT), all of which is for nuclear power, including FBR development and reprocessing research. Two hundred and eighty-seven287 billion yen (US$3.59 billion) is allotted to Ministry of Economy, Trade and Industry (METI). Of this 287 billion yen, only 46 billion yen (US$0.58 billion) is allocated to the development of alternative energy, and the other budget items (241 billion yen) seem to be all allocated to nuclear power and given to the local governments. According to the Asahi Newspaper (2005), approximately 82.4 billion yen (US$1.03 billion) in subsidies are provided based on the Power Source Siting Laws. These subsidies are appropriated as follows: (1) 13 billion yen (US$0.163 billion) for the Fukushima prefecture, which has Fukushima Nuclear Stations 1 and 2; (2) 12.1 billion yen (US$0.16 billion) for the Niigata prefecture, which has the Kashiwazakikariha Nuclear Station; (3) 11.3 billion yen (US$0.14 billion) for the Fukui prefecture, which has the Tsuruga Nuclear Station, Mihama Nuclear Station, Ooi Nuclear Station, and the Takahama Nuclear Station; (4) 10 billion yen (US$0.13 billion) for the Saga prefecture; and (5) 8.9 billion yen US$0.11 billion) for the Aomori prefecture, where the nuclear fuel reprocessing facilities are located in Rokkasho Village.

There also exist bureaucratic networks and political interest groups that facilitate electric power companies to take advantage of the Electric Utilities Industry Law. For example, some of the top ranking officers of METI can take Amakudari jobs for the electric power companies, where "Amakudari" is the practice of bureaucrats retiring into lucrative posts for corporations in industries they had overseen. The electric power companies are no exception for this very bad practice of Amakudari. In fact, a considerable amount of tax money is allocated to reinforce this bureaucratic system. A study by Tokyo Shimbun (2011) shows that in the year 2008 more than 50% (equivalent to 170 billion yen = US$2.13 billion) of the total amount of the Tax for Promotion of Power-Resources Development was appropriated to a set of independent administrative agencies and incorporated foundations where some retired bureaucrats, mainly from METI and MEXT, are working. Of these governmental agencies and foundations, the Japan Atomic Energy Agency is the one that received the most money, 122.6 billion yen (US$1.53 billion). Because this bureaucratic network with business leaders and researchers associated with the nuclear power industry is so influential, these bureaucrats can make secrete dealings without parliamentary control by simply issuing a ministerial ordinance or even a notice. In the year 2007, METI issued Notice 109, by which a prefecture can obtain 6 billion yen (US$0.75 billion) of subsidies if it authorizes the use of MOX fuel in the thermal reactor. Ten prefectures (Hokkaidou, Aomori, Miyagi, Fukushima, Shizuoka, Fukui, Shimane, Ehime, Ehime, Saga) agreed to this provision and received the money. This special subsidy was temporarily terminated in March 2009, but started again in the 2010 (the amount of subsidy was reduced to 3 billion yen).

17.7 Conclusion: Our Energy Future and Energy "Granfaloons"

We must emphasize three points associated with nuclear waste. First, there is no safe level of exposure to radiation; even very low doses can cause cancer (National Research Council, 2006). Second, it is almost impossible to safely operate large commercial plutonium plants for reprocessing spent fuels. For example, there is only one such place in Japan, Rokkasho-Mura (Rokkasho Village) of the Aomori Prefecture, and this plant is not in operation as of yet. Every year about 1000 tons of spent fuel is produced in Japan, and the stock of spent fuel that has not been processed properly is accumulating. Finally, concerning high-level radioactive waste, final disposal sites, located underground, where the vitrified wastes are supposed to be buried for 100,000 years, have not been determined. Given this information and, as we have shown, the fact that nuclear power is not needed to produce a sufficient supply of energy in Japan, any serious discussion of sustainability in Japan must be void of any argument for building additional nuclear power plants. Furthermore, the exercise performed in this chapter for Japan should be carried out for other countries before they entertain any discussion of building new nuclear power plants. Only then can serious sustainability discussions occur.

Yet, there is another deep theoretical and practical challenge associated with the quality and quantity of a primary energy source. That is, the metabolic pattern with the technological development of society based on the massive use of fossil fuels can be described in terms of an acceleration of energy and material consumption together with the dramatic reallocation of the distribution of age classes, the human time profile of activities, and the land use patterns in various sectors of the modern economy, *resulting in time and land savings in the energy and agricultural sectors* (Mayumi, 1991). Furthermore, fossil fuels are "optimal" in terms of the amount of bulk matter required for energy extraction, transformation, and transportation to support modern industrial society. The conclusion that fossil fuels are superior in terms of a material flow requirement is sometimes called Georgescu-Roegen's Fundamental Proposition (Kawamiya, 1983; Mayumi, 2001). Therefore, solar energy cannot easily support current fossil fuel–based manufacturing and consumption activities. As Georgescu-Roegen argues (1979, p. 1050), "It [the necessary amount of matter for a technology] is high for weak-intensity energy (as is the solar radiation at the ground level) because such energy must be concentrated into a much higher intensity if it is to support the intensive industrial processes as those now supported by fossil fuels." Therefore, large scale agro-biofuel production from corn or sugarcane is not viable (Giampietro and Mayumi, 2009). Concerning the feasibility of nuclear power generation, Georgescu-Roegen also argues that a large amount of matter is necessary for high-intensity energy, such as thermonuclear energy, because high-intensity energy must be contained and controlled within a stable boundary.

As one can see from the previous discussion in this chapter examining the Fukushima incident, nuclear power generation remains controversial, and many ideas and approaches exist on the topic. Even in Japan there is debate on how to approach nuclear power. After the Fukushima nuclear accident the Japanese people started to reconsider the need of rearranging the energy allocation profile of the various compartments of society. This energy allocation profile change would bring about the need of also rearranging the existing profile of political power among social actors (i.e., changing the status quo of the political power structure). A similar debate is occurring in the United States with regard to hydraulic fracturing, "fracking," to secure additional supplies of natural gas and the potential contamination of the water supply in regions where this occurs. All of these debates center on the issue of energy security and environmental sustainability.

However, many of the follies in the ongoing discussions over sustainability are strongly influenced by politically correct scientific discussions about the predicament of "energy, society and environment" and have led to a series of granfalloons. The term granfalloon was originally introduced by Kurt Vonnegut (1963) to indicate a proud and meaningless association of human beings. Granfalloons can be seen as "social crusades" to save the world based on wishful thinking rather than on solid analysis. In this context, the discussion of "energy, society and environment" fits perfectly.

Granfalloons in the field of sustainability are easy to spot; the chosen narrative is always focused on "solutions" aimed at fixing the external world, which is invariably perceived as harboring the problem. The granfalloon blissfully ignores that the problem may reside with ourselves, let alone that we might have to change ourselves to adjust to new boundary conditions. The typical definition of sustainability problems adopted by the granfalloon excludes, by default, the role of the storyteller (i.e., the power structure choosing the narrative) from the analysis. The definition is never considered among the things that might be changed within the chosen narrative and model. If we are running out of fossil energy then do we need liquid fuels? Then the solution is to make agro-biofuels, no matter what it costs, and keep consuming liquid fuels as before, or perhaps more. Are we generating too much CO_2 in the atmosphere? Then the solution is to sequestrate CO_2 under the sea and keep emitting. Are we altering the habitat of wildlife and thus causing mass extinctions of species? Then the solution is to clone those species and continue destroying habitats. And the list could go on . . . These examples are the same situation as with nuclear power generation.

However, if we look at things in a different (probably in a politically incorrect) way we can frame the discussion of energy and sustainability along either of the following two lines: (1) energy and sustainability seen as fixing the external world according to the needs and the narrative chosen by a given storyteller (considering only the inside view); or (2) energy and sustainability seen as an adaptation of the identity of the storyteller and of the narrative used to define the problem to "inconvenient" perceptions of the external world (considering also the outside view). We strongly believe that simultaneously following both lines is the more suitable approach when addressing sustainability issues. However, it certainly is not the most popular approach. This is nicely exemplified by an episode of *The Daily Show* of June 16, 2010,[5] showing a hilarious but at the same time frightening set of videos starring the last eight presidents of the United States, all presidencies since the first energy crisis of the 1970s, talking to the nation about the energy crisis. The episode shows that over these four decades, the essence of their speech with regard to the "energy issue" has not changed: "very soon, the USA will move beyond the petroleum dependence and dependence on imports." Despite the fact that dependence on petroleum in the United States has not ended but has actually increased in these four decades, all the presidential talks shown in the videos share the assumptions that: (1) it would be better for the US economy to produce alternative energy; and (2) it is possible to do so in a decade or two (they all define very close deadlines for achieving the promised results). Unfortunately, granfalloons are always with us.

ACKNOWLEDGMENTS

We would like to thank the following people. Prof. Hiroaki Koide of Kyoto University Reactor Research Institute generously allowed the senior author access to many important works he accomplished thus far, in particular a detailed study he presented in Saga Prefecture in 2005, Japan. Prof. Koide also allowed the senior author to use any of his materials. We are indebted to him for writing Sections 17.3 and Section 17.5. Without his generosity and benevolence this chapter would never been completed. Prof. Hiromitsu Ino of Tokyo University, Emeritus, provided us with information on neutron irradiation-induced embrittlement and ductile brittle transition temperature. A part of this chapter was presented by the senior author at ICTA Monday Seminar series—"Chernobyl, Fukushima and Beyond: Reflecting on the Future of Nuclear Energy," May 9, 2011, at the Autonomous University of Barcelona, Barcelona, Spain. Comments on the presentation by Louis Lemkow, Kate Farrell, Mario Giampietro,

Francois Diaz Maurin, Jesus Ramos-Martin, Sybille van den Hove, and other people at the seminar are very much appreciated. Parts of this chapter were an elaborated version of two presentations made by the senior author at The Bottom Line on Climate Change: Transitioning to Renewable Energy held at New School of Social Research in New York City on September 23–24, 2011. Constructive criticisms are given by the conference participants. We would like to emphasize that all responsibility for the writing of this chapter remains only with us. Any conceivable error in our commentary must not be attributed in any way to Prof. Koide or to Prof. Ino. We truly appreciate their scholarship and friendship.

Notes

1. http://ja.wikipedia.org/wiki/%E6%9D%B1%E6%97%A5%E6%9C%AC%E5%A4%A7%E9%9C%87%E7%81%BD
2. According to Henry's Law a 1°C increase in the surface sea water would result in a 4% increase in CO_2 released. However, because there are many factors that contribute to the release of CO_2 from the sea, such as pH level and plant life, that are not accounted for in Henry's Law, we use 2% as a conservative estimate of the CO_2 released into the atmosphere.
3. http://www.tepco.co.jp/e-rates/individual/data/chargelist/chargelist03-j.html
4. http://ja.wikipedia.org/wiki/%E9%9B%BB%E6%BA%90%E9%96%8B%E7%99%BA%E4%BF%83%E9%80%B2%E7%A8%8E
5. http://www.thedailyshow.com/watch/wed-june-16-2010/an-energy-independent-future

References

Asahi.com. (2011a). INES 7 is an overstatement. http://www.asahi.com/special/10005/TKY201104130698.html

Asahi. com. (2011b).http://www.asahi.com/business/update/0512/TKY201105120331.html

Asahi. com. mini. (2011). http://mini.asahi.com/1103eq/TKY201105310707.html

Asahi Shimbun Aomori Branch (2005). *Kakunen manei* (Money with Nuclear Power). Tokyo: Iwanami.

Asahi Shimbun. (2012). http://ajw.asahi.com/article/0311disaster/fukushima/AJ201202290025

BBC. (2012). http://www.bbc.co.uk/news/business-17268326

Bunn, M., and Heinonen, O. (2011). Preventing the next Fukushima. *Science, 333*(September 16), 1580–1581.

Cabinet Secretariat Japan. (2011). Summary of Commission Report on Management and Finance of TEPCO. http://www.cas.go.jp/jp/seisaku/keieizaimutyousa/dai10/siryou2.pdf

Davies, L. (2011). Beyond Fukushima: Disasters, nuclear energy, and energy law. *Brigham Young University Law Review, 11*, 1937–1989.

Elliot, D. (2009). *Nuclear Or Not?* London: Palgrave Macmillan.

Environmental News Service. (2011). http://www.ens-newswire.com/ens/dec2011/2011-12-16-02.html

Federation of Electric Power Companies of Japan. (2011). http://www.fepc.or.jp/library/data/index.html

Georgescu-Roegen, N. (1975). Energy and economic myths. *Southern Economic Journal, 41*, 347–381.

Georgescu-Roegen, N. (1979). Energy analysis and economic valuation. *Southern Economic Journal, 45*, 1023–1058.

Giampietro, M., and Mayumi, K. (2009). *The Biofuel Delusion: The Fallacy of Large Scale Agro-Biofuel Production.* London: The Earthscan.

Hayashi, M., and Hughes, L. (2013). The Fukushima nuclear accident and its effect on global energy securities. *Energy Policy, 59*, 102–111.

Holt, M. (2009). Nuclear energy policy. Working Paper 7-5700. Washington, DC: Congressional Research Policy, Congressional Research Service.

Honda, S. (2009). Heart moving quote by S. Honda. http://www.youtube.com/watch?v=CqYS4CrSO3A&feature=related

Ino, H. (2011). Roukyuka suru genpatsu (Aging nuclear power plants). *Kagaku* (*Science*), *81*(7): 658–669.

IPCC. (2011). Ocean storage. In *Special Report on Renewable Energy Sources and Climate Change Mitigation.* http://www.ipcc.ch/pdf/special-reports/srccs/srccs_chapter6.pdf

Ito, K. (2007). Setting goals and action plan for energy efficiency improvement., Paper presented at the EAS Energy Efficiency and Conservation Conference, Tokyo, June 19, 2007.

Japan Meteorological Agency. (2011). http://www.data.kishou.go.jp/shindan/a_2/co2_trend/co2_trend.html

JA.Wikipedia (2011). http://ja.wikipedia.org/wiki/%E8%BB%BD%E6%B0%B4%E7%82%89

Kawamiya, N. (1983). *Entropii to kougyoushakai no sentaku* (in Japanese) (Entropy and Future Choices for the Industrial Society). Tokyo: Kaimei.

Mainichi Shimbun. (2012). http://mainichi.jp/select/weathernews/20110311/konokunitogenpatsu/archive/news/20120123mog00m010999000c.html

Majirox News (2011). http://www.majiroxnews.com/2011/12/11/whos-afraid-of-tepco-japans-atomic-energy-insurance-pool/

Mayumi, K. (1991). Temporary emancipation from land: From the Industrial Revolution to the present time. *Ecological Economics, 4*, 35–56.

Mayumi, K. (2001). *The Origins of Ecological Economics: The Bioeconomics of Georgescu-Roegen.* London: Routledge.

Mayumi, K., and Polimeni, J. M. (2012). Uranium reserve, nuclear fuel cycle delusion, CO_2 emissions from the sea, and electricity supply: Reflections after the fuel meltdown of the Fukushima nuclear power units. *Ecological Economics, 73*, 1–6.

Murota, T. (1986). *Genshiryoku no keizaigaku* (The Economics of Nuclear Power). Tokyo: Nihonhyoron-Sha.

National Research Council. (2006). *Health Risks from Exposure to Low Levels of Ionizing Radiation. BEIR VII PHASE 2.* Washington, D.C.: The National Academies Press.

Nikkei.Com. (2011). http://www.nikkei.com/news/article/g=96958A9C93819488E3E3E2E3968DE3E3E2E7E0E2E3E399E3E6EBE2E2

Oshima, K. (2010). *Saisekanou enerugi no seijikeizaigaku* (Political Economics of Renewable Energy). Tokyo: Toyokeizai.

Sankei.Com. (2011). http://sankei.jp.msn.com/politics/news/110531/stt11053117580006-n1.htm

Settle, F. (2011). Nuclear reactors. *General Chemistry Case Studies.* http://www.chemcases.com/nuclear/nc-10.html
The Economist. (2011). Energy in Japan: Out with the old. September 17–23, p. 14.
The Institute of Energy Economics, Japan. (2011). *EDMC Handbook of Energy & Economic Statistics in Japan.* Tokyo: The Energy Conservation Center.
Tokyo Shimbun. (2011). More than 50% of nuclear power budget in Measures for Energy Special Account is spent on Amakudari agencies (in Japanese). September 30, 2011.
Vonnegut, K. (1963). *Cat's Cradle.* New York: Delacorte Press.
Wittneben, B. B. F. (2012). The impact of the Fukushima nuclear accident on European Energy policy. *Environmental Science & Policy, 15*(1), 1–3.
World Energy Council. (2010). Survey of Energy Resources. London: Regency House. http://www.worldenergy.org/documents/ser_2010_report_1.pdf
World Nuclear Association. (2009). Uranium. In *The Encyclopedia of Earth.* http://www.eoearth.org/article/Uranium?topic=49557
World Nuclear Association. (2010). The nuclear fuel cycle. http://large.stanford.edu/courses/2010/ph240/sagatov1/docs/nfc.pdf
Yomiuri Online. (2011a). http://www.yomiuri.co.jp/science/news/20110412-OYT1T00367.htm
Yomiuri Online. (2011b). http://www.yomiuri.co.jp/feature/20110316-866921/news/20110524-OYT1T00086.htm

PART IV

ECONOMIC EFFECTS OF MITIGATION AND ADAPTATION

CHAPTER 18

FORECAST-BASED PRICING OF WEATHER DERIVATIVES

WOLFGANG KARL HÄRDLE, BRENDA LÓPEZ-CABRERA, AND MATTHIAS RITTER

18.1 Introduction

Weather derivatives (WDs) are financial instruments to hedge against the random nature of weather variations that constitute weather risk (the uncertainty in cash flows caused by weather events). Two years after the first over the counter (OTC) trade of a WD in 1997, the formal exchange Chicago Mercantile Exchange (CME) introduced derivative contracts on weather indices in 1999. Both exchange traded and OTC derivatives are now written on a range of weather indices, including temperature, hurricanes, frost and precipitation. WDs differ from insurances, first because insurances cover low probability extreme events, whereas WDs cover lower risk high probability events such as winters colder than expected. Second, a buyer of a WD will receive the payoff at settlement period no matter the loss caused by weather conditions. For insurances, the payoff depends on the proof of damages. Third, from the seller's point of view, WDs eliminate moral hazard and avoid the higher administrative and the loss adjustment expenses of insurance contracts. The WD market is a typical example of an incomplete market in the sense that the underlying weather indexes are nontradeable assets and cannot be replicated by other underyling instruments, like there are in the equity market. Furthermore, the market is relatively illiquid. Campbell and Diebold (2005) argued that this illiquidity is due to nonstandardization of the weather. Given this, one might expect some inefficiencies in the WD market. The protection is achieved, when two counterparties in the transaction of a WD meet: a hedger (e.g., a farmer) who wants to hedge his weather risk exposure and a speculator, to whom the risk has been transferred in return for a reward.

The pricing of WDs is challenging because in contrast to complete markets, the assumption of no arbitrage does not assure the existence of a unique risk neutral measure. Many valuation techniques of WDs have overcome this problem: under an equilibrium representative framework (Cao and Wei, 2004), under the equivalent martingale approach (EMM) (Alaton et al., 2002; Benth, 2003), using marginal utility approach (Davis, 2001), or, more generally, with the principle of equivalent utility (Brockett et al., 2010). Standard pricing approaches for WDs are based on historical weather data, estimating the physical measure by time series analysis and then calibrating the market price of risk (MPR) in such a way that the traded WDs are martingales under the risk neutral measure. Forward-looking information such as meteorological forecasts or the MPR are often not incorporated in usual pricing approaches. Hence, important market information is not considered in an informational efficient markets, where futures prices reflect all publicly available information.

The literature on how to calibrate the MPR or how to incorporate meteorological weather forecast into the price of weather derivatives is limited. From one side, we have the studies from Härdle and López-Cabrera (2011) and Benth et al. (2011), who use statistical inverse techniques to imply the MPR from the temperature futures traded at CME and suggest a seasonal stochastic behavior of the nonzero MPR. On the other side, the work from Jewson and Caballero (2003) describes how probabilistic weather forecasts, via single and ensemble forecasts up to 12 days in advance, can be used for the pricing of weather derivatives. Yoo (2003) incorporates seasonal meteorological forecasts into a temperature model, which predicts one of three possible future temperature states. A new perspective on the commodities pricing literature is given in Benth and Meyer-Brandis (2009), who suggest the enlargement of the filtration information set and argue that the stochasticity behaviour of the MPR is due to the misspecified information set in the model. Dorfleitner and Wimmer (2010) include meteorological forecast in the context of WD-based index modeling. Ritter et al. (2011) combine historical data with meteorological forecast in a daily basis to price WDs. In this chapter, we adopt the risk-neutral approach (for each location) that allows the incorporation of meteorological forecasts in the framework of WD pricing and compare it with the information gained by the calibrated MPR. The aim is to study weather risk premiums (RPs), a central issue in empirical finance, implied from either the information MPR gain or the meteorological forecasts. The size of RPs is interesting for investors and issuers of weather contracts to take advantages of geographic diversification, hedging effects and price determinations. We quantify the RPs of weather risk by looking at the risk factor under different pricing measures and under different filtration information sets.

We analyze the RPs for temperature derivatives with reference stations London and Rome. Our main goal is to determine the nature of the risk factor embedded in temperature future prices. We find that the seasonal variance of temperature explains a significant proportion of the variation in RPs. The estimated forecast based prices reflect market prices much better than prices without the use of forecast. In both approaches, the RPs of futures are different from zero, negative in winters and positive in summers.

The findings of this chapter are presented as follows. In Section 18.2, we present the fundamentals of temperature index derivatives (futures and options) traded at the CME and review the stochastic pricing model for average daily temperature and study its properties. Section 18.3 introduces the concept of RPs across different risk measures and under different filtration information set. In the latter approach, meteorological weather forecasts are incorporated into the WD pricing. In Section 18.4, we conduct the empirical analysis to temperature futures referring to London and Rome, with meteorological forecast data for London 13 days in advance. Despite this relatively short forecast horizon, the models using meteorological forecasts outperform the classical approach and more accurately forecast the market prices of the temperature futures traded at the CME. Section 18.5 concludes the chapter. All computations were carried out in Matlab version 7.6 and R.

18.2 Weather Derivatives

The most commonly weather instruments traded at the CME are futures and call and put options written on weather indices. The CME traded futures can be thought as a swap, such that one party gets paid if the realized index value is greater than a predetermined strike level and the other party benefits if the index value is below. Typically, futures are entered without a payment of premium. In exchange for the payment of the premium, the call option gives the buyer a linear payoff based on the difference between the realized index value and the strike level. Below this level there is no payoff. On the other hand, the put option gives the buyer a linear payoff based upon the difference between the strike level and the realized index value.

The most popular underlying weather indices are temperature related. The reason is the abundance of historical temperature data and the demand for a weather product coming from end-users with temperature exposure. The weather indices most commonly used in the market are the heating degree days (HDDs), cooling degree days (CDDs), cumulative average temperature (CAT), and the cumulative total of 24-hour average temperatures (C24AT). The HDD index is computed as the maximum of zero and 65°F (or 18°C) minus the daily average temperature (average of maximal and minimal temperature), accumulated over every day of the corresponding contract period. Hence, the HDD index measures the deviation of the daily average temperature from the threshold, when the temperature is underneath and heating is needed. Equivalently, the CDD index is the accumulation of the maximum of zero and the average temperature minus 65°F (or 18°C), that is, the deviation if the temperature is above the threshold and cooling is needed. CAT and C24AT cumulate the daily average temperature and the 24-hour average temperature of each day, respectively. The corresponding trading months for CDD and CAT contracts are April to October, for HDD October to April, and for C24AT contracts all months of the year. Temperature derivatives are offered for 24 cities in the United States, 11 in Europe, 6 in Canada, 3 in Japan, and 3 in Australia. The notional value of a temperature contract, according to the product specification, is 20 USD, 20 AUD, 20 EUR, 20 GBP, or 2500 JPY per index point. In addition to monthly HDD, CAT and HDD futures and options, there are also HDD and CDD seasonal strips futures for multiple months. This study focuses only on monthly temperature futures contracts.

18.2.1 Pricing Temperature Derivatives

The weather market is an example of an incomplete market, that is, temperature cannot be hedged by other tradeable assets. However, the dynamics of temperature futures should be free of arbitrage. Therefore, a unique equivalent martingale measure does not exist and standard pricing approaches cannot be applied. We assume that a pricing measure $Q = Q_{\theta(t)}$ exists and can be parametrized via the Girsanov transform, where $\theta(t)$ denotes the market price of risk. Then, the arbitrage free temperature futures price is:

$$F_{(t,\tau_1,\tau_2)} = \mathsf{E}^{Q_\theta}\left[Y_T\{T(t)\}\,|\mathcal{F}_t\right] \tag{18.1}$$

with $0 \leq t \leq T$. $Y_T\{T(t)\}$ refers to the payoff at $T > t$ from the (CAT/HDD/CDD) temperature index with measurement period $[\tau_1, \tau_2]$ and $\mathcal{F}_t$ refers to the filtration information set at time t.

The price of a put option P_t or call option C_t written on temperature futures $F_{(t,\tau_1,\tau_2)}$ with strike K and exercise time $\tau < \tau_1$ is:

$$\begin{aligned} C_{(t,\tau_1,\tau_2)} &= \mathsf{E}^{Q_\theta}\left[\max\left\{F_{(t,\tau_1,\tau_2)} - K, 0\right\}\right] \\ P_{(t,\tau_1,\tau_2)} &= \mathsf{E}^{Q_\theta}\left[\max\left\{K - F_{(t,\tau_1,\tau_2)}, 0\right\}\right] \end{aligned} \tag{18.2}$$

Observe that although the payoff is not linked directly to the temperature but to a temperature index, one needs first to model the temperature dynamics $T(t)$ to solve equation (18.1).

18.2.1.1 Temperature Dynamics in Discrete Time

Most of the models for the daily average temperature discussed in the literature capture a linear trend and mean reversion with pronounced cyclical dynamics and strong correlations (long memory). Daily average temperature reflects not only a seasonal pattern from calendar effects (peaks in cooler winter and warmer summers) but also a variation that varies seasonally.

For a particular location, we propose the following model that captures seasonality effects in mean and variations, as well as intertemporal correlations:

1. Let T_t be the average temperature in discrete time with $t = 1, \dots M$. A conventional model for T_t is a model with linear trend and a seasonal pattern $T_t = \Lambda_t + X_t$.
2. Λ_t is a bounded and deterministic function denoting the seasonal effect and it is the mean reversion level of temperature at day t. The seasonality function might be modeled by using the next least squares fitted seasonal function with trend:

$$\Lambda_t = a + bt + \sum_{k=1}^{K} c_k \cos\left\{\frac{2k\pi(t - d_k)}{365}\right\} \tag{18.3}$$

where the coefficients a and b indicate the average temperature and the effect of global warming, urban heating, or air pollution (Campbell and Diebold, 2005). The series expansion in (18.3) with more and more periodic terms provides a fine tuning, but this increases the number of parameters. An alternative is modeling Λ_t by means of a local smoothing approach:

$$\arg\min_{e,f} \sum_{t=365}^{1} \left\{\bar{T}_s - e_s - f_s(t-s)\right\}^2 K\left(\frac{t-s}{h}\right) \tag{18.4}$$

where $\bar{T}_s$ is the mean of average daily temperature in J years and $K(\cdot)$ is a kernel. Asymptotically, they can be approximated by Fourier series estimators.
3. X_t is a stationary process $I(0)$ that can be checked by using the well known Augmented Dickey-Fuller test (ADF) or the Kwiatkowski–Phillips–Schmidt–Shin (KPSS) test. Empirical analysis of the partial autocorrelation function (PACF) in Diebold and Inoue (2001), Granger and Hyung (2004), and Benth et al. (2011) reveal that the persistence (pronounced cyclical dynamics and strong intertemporal correlation) of daily average can be captured by autoregressive processes of higher order AR(p):

$$X_t = \sum_{i=1}^{p} \beta_i X_{t-i} + \varepsilon_t,\ \varepsilon_t = \sigma_t e_t,\ e_t \sim \mathrm{N}(0,1) \tag{18.5}$$

The order of the appropriate AR(p) is chosen via the Box-Jenkins analysis. Empirical evidence shows that a simple AR(3), suggested by Benth et al. (2007), holds for many cities and explains well the stylised facts of average daily temperature.
4. σ_t is a bounded and deterministic function, representing the smooth seasonal variation of daily average temperature at time t. This can be calibrated with the two-step GARCH(1,1) model of Campbell and Diebold (2005) ($\hat{\sigma}^2_{t,\mathrm{FTSG}}$):

$$\hat{\sigma}^2_{t,\mathrm{FTSG}} = c_1 + \sum_{l=1}^{L} \left\{c_{2l} \cos\left(\frac{2l\pi t}{365}\right) + c_{2l+1} \sin\left(\frac{2l\pi t}{365}\right)\right\}$$
$$+ \alpha_1(\sigma^2_{t-1} e_{t-1})^2 + \beta_1 \sigma^2_{t-1}, e_t \sim \mathrm{N}(0,1) \tag{18.6}$$

or via Local Linear Regression $\hat{\sigma}^2_{t,\mathrm{LLR}}$:

$$\arg\min_{g,h} \sum_{t=1}^{365} \left\{\hat{\varepsilon}_t^2 - g_s - h_s(t-s)\right\}^2 K\left(\frac{t-s}{h}\right) \tag{18.7}$$

with $K(\cdot)$ being a kernel.

18.2.1.2 *Temperature Dynamics in Continuous Time*

Since pricing is done in continuous time, it is convenient to switch to modeling in continuous time. The literature in the last years has focused on the modeling and forecasting of time series trend and seasonal and noisy components, which are exactly the elements that characterize weather risk. Brody et al. (2002) suppose that the process T_t is modeled by a fractional Brownian Motion (fBM). It is not a semi-martingale, however, which is a requirement to work under the incomplete market setting. Alaton et al. (2002) show that an Ornstein-Uhlenbeck Model driven by a Brownian motion is enough to capture the stylized facts of temperature. Benth et al. (2007) and Härdle and López-Cabrera (2011) demonstrate that the dynamics of temperature X_t in (18.5) can be approximated in continuous time with a Continuous-time AutoRegressive process of order p (CAR(p)) for $p \geq 1$:

$$d\mathbf{X}_t = \mathbf{A}\mathbf{X}_t dt + \mathbf{e}_p \sigma_t dB_t \tag{18.8}$$

where $\mathbf{e}_k$ denotes the k'th unit vector in $\mathbb{R}^p$ for $k = 1, \dots p$, $\sigma_t > 0$ states the volatility, B_t is a Brownian motion and $\mathbf{A}$ is a $p \times p$-matrix:

$$\mathbf{A} = \begin{pmatrix} 0 & 1 & 0 & \dots & 0 & 0 \\ 0 & 0 & 1 & \dots & 0 & 0 \\ \vdots & & \ddots & & 0 & \vdots \\ 0 & \dots & \dots & 0 & 0 & 1 \\ -\alpha_p & -\alpha_{p-1} & \dots & & -\alpha_2 & -\alpha_1 \end{pmatrix} \tag{18.9}$$

with positive constants α_k. The proof is by linking the states $X_{1(t)}, X_{2(t)}, \dots, X_{p(t)}$ with the lagged temperatures up to time $t - p$. Thus, for $p = 3$ and $dt = 1$ we get:

$$\begin{aligned} X_{1(t+3)} \approx{}& (3-\alpha_1)X_{1(t+2)} + (2\alpha_1 - \alpha_2 - 3)X_{1(t+1)} \\ &+(-\alpha_1 + \alpha_2 - \alpha_3 + 1)X_{1(t)} \end{aligned} \tag{18.10}$$

18.2.1.3 *Pricing Temperature Models*

Several authors have dealt with the pricing problem. Davis (2001) models HDD indices $Y_T\{T(t)\}$ with a geometric Brownian motion and then prices by utility maximization theory. Alaton et al. (2002) price WDs as in (18.1) but with a constant MPR. Benth (2003) derived no arbitrage prices of FBM using quasi-conditional expectations and fractional stochastic calculus. However, there is a discussion in the literature about the arbitrage opportunities of this model. Others such as Benth and Saltyte-Benth (2005) assume that the process X_t follows a Lévy process, rather than a Brownian process, and get non-arbitrage prices under a martingale measures determined via the Esscher transform.

Following Benth et al. (2007), by considering the CAR(p) model (18.8) for the deseasonalised temperatures and by inserting the temperature indices (CAT/HDD/CDD) in (18.1), the risk neutral futures prices are:

$$F_{\mathrm{HDD}(t,\tau_1,\tau_2)} = \int_{\tau_1}^{\tau_2} \upsilon_{t,s}\psi\left[\frac{c - m_{\{t,s,\mathbf{e}_1^\top \exp\{\mathbf{A}(s-t)\}\mathbf{X}_t\}}}{\upsilon_{t,s}}\right] ds \tag{18.11}$$

$$F_{\mathrm{CDD}(t,\tau_1,\tau_2)} = \int_{\tau_1}^{\tau_2} \upsilon_{t,s}\psi\left[\frac{m_{\{t,s,\mathbf{e}_1^\top \exp\{\mathbf{A}(s-t)\}\mathbf{X}_t\}} - c}{\upsilon_{t,s}}\right] ds \tag{18.12}$$

$$\begin{aligned} F_{\mathrm{CAT}(t,\tau_1,\tau_2)} = & \int_{\tau_1}^{\tau_2} \Lambda_u du + \mathbf{a}_{t,\tau_1,\tau_2}\mathbf{X}_t + \int_t^{\tau_1} \theta_u\sigma_u \mathbf{a}_{t,\tau_1,\tau_2}\mathbf{e}_p du \\ & + \int_{\tau_1}^{\tau_2} \theta_u\sigma_u \mathbf{e}_1^\top \mathbf{A}^{-1}\left[\exp\{\mathbf{A}(\tau_2 - u)\} - I_p\right]\mathbf{e}_p du \end{aligned} \tag{18.13}$$

with $\mathbf{a}_{t,\tau_1,\tau_2} = \mathbf{e}_1^\top \mathbf{A}^{-1}\left[\exp\{\mathbf{A}(\tau_2 - t)\} - \exp\{\mathbf{A}(\tau_1 - t)\}\right]$, the $p\times p$ identity matrix I_p,

$$\begin{aligned} m_{\{t,s,x\}} &= \Lambda_s + \int_t^s \sigma_u\theta_u \mathbf{e}_1^\top \exp\{\mathbf{A}(s-t)\}\mathbf{e}_p du + x, \\ \upsilon_{t,s}^2 &= \int_t^s \sigma_u^2\left[\mathbf{e}_1^\top \exp\{\mathbf{A}(s-t)\}\mathbf{e}_p\right]^2 du \end{aligned} \tag{18.14}$$

and $\psi(x) = x\Phi(x) + \varphi(x)$ with $x = \mathbf{e}_1^\top \exp\{\mathbf{A}(s-t)\}\mathbf{X}_t$.

The explicit formulae for the CAT call option written on a CAT future with strike K at exercise time $\tau < \tau_1$ during the period $[\tau_1, \tau_2]$ is given by:

$$\begin{aligned} C_{\mathrm{CAT}(t,\tau,\tau_1,\tau_2)} = & \exp\{-r(\tau - t)\} \times \Big[\left(F_{\mathrm{CAT}(t,\tau_1,\tau_2)} - K\right)\Phi\{d(t,\tau,\tau_1,\tau_2)\} \\ & + \int_t^\tau \Sigma^2_{\mathrm{CAT}(s,\tau_1,\tau_2)} ds \phi\{d(t,\tau,\tau_1,\tau_2)\}\Big] \end{aligned} \tag{18.15}$$

where $d(t,\tau,\tau_1,\tau_2) = \frac{F_{\mathrm{CAT}(t,\tau_1,\tau_2)} - K}{\sqrt{\int_t^\tau \Sigma^2_{\mathrm{CAT}(s,\tau_1,\tau_2)} ds}}$ and $\Sigma_{\mathrm{CAT}(s,\tau_1,\tau_2)} = \sigma_t \mathbf{a}_{t,\tau_1,\tau_2}\mathbf{e}_p$ and Φ denotes the standard normal cdf. The option can be perfectly hedged once the specification of the risk neutral probability Q^θ determines the complete market of futures and options. Then, the option price will be the unique cost of replication.

To replicate the call option with CAT futures, one should compute the number of CAT futures held in the portfolio, which is simply computed by the option's delta:

$$\Phi\{d(t,T,\tau_1,\tau_2)\} = \frac{\partial C_{\mathrm{CAT}(t,\tau,\tau_1,\tau_2)}}{\partial F_{\mathrm{CAT}(t,\tau_1,\tau_2)}} \tag{18.16}$$

The strategy holds close to zero CAT futures when the option is far out of the money, close to 1 otherwise.

18.2.1.4 *Calibrating the Implied Market Price of Risk*

Note that the advantage of the latter pricing approach is that it provides a closed form solution for temperature futures. Hence, the calibration of the MPR θ_t from market data turns out to be an inverse problem. Härdle and López-Cabrera (2011) infer the MPR from temperature futures. From a parametric specification of the MPR, one checks consistency with different contracts every single date. One finds the MPR by fitting the data:

$$\arg\min_{\hat{\theta}} \Sigma_{i=1}^{I} \left(F_{(\theta,t,\tau_1^i,\tau_2^i)} - F_{(t,\tau_1^i,\tau_2^i)} \right)^2 \tag{18.17}$$

with $t \le \tau_1^i < \tau_2^i$, $i = 1,\cdots,I$ contracts, $F_{(\theta,t,\tau_1^i,\tau_2^i)}$ denote the observed market prices and $F_{(t,\tau_1^i,\tau_2^i)}$ are the model specified prices given in (18.11), (18.12) and (18.13).

18.2.1.5 *Meteorological Weather Forecasts*

Equation (18.1) prices temperature futures based on the filtration $\mathcal{F}_t$, which contains the historical temperature evolution until time t. Benth and Meyer-Brandis (2009) state that the main reason for the irregular pattern of the market price of risk is an inappropriate choice of $\mathcal{F}_t$. There is more information available in the market, such as forward-looking information. Hence, $\mathcal{F}_t$ may be enlarged to a filtration $\mathcal{G}_t$, which contains all relevant information available at time t.

Ritter et al. (2011) enlarge the filtration by adding meteorological forecast values up to k days in advance. These new filtrations are denoted by $\mathcal{G}_t^{\mathrm{MF}k}$ with $k = 0,1,2,\ldots$ being the number of days in advance where meteorological forecast data are available. It follows:

$$\mathcal{F}_t \subset \mathcal{G}_t^{\mathrm{MF0}} \subset \mathcal{G}_t^{\mathrm{MF1}} \subset \mathcal{G}_t^{\mathrm{MF2}} \subset \ldots \subset \mathcal{G}_t$$

In an extended model, these meteorological forecast values are added to the historical temperature data as if they were actually realized temperature observations. Then, a discrete-time temperature model (see Section 18.2.1.1) is fitted to the "future" extended time series. The orders K and L of the Fourier series of the seasonality and seasonal variance, see (18.3) and (18.6), as well as the lag p of the autoregressive process (18.5) are set beforehand. All other parameters, however, are estimated newly for every day t, according to the data available on that day (historical temperatures up to day $t-1$, meteorological forecasts calculated on day t for the days t, $t+1$, ...). By using Monte Carlo simulation and the simplifying assumption of an MPR $= 0$, theoretical futures prices with no meteorological forecast data (NMF) and theoretical prices including meteorological forecasts k days in advance (MFk) can be calculated:

$$\hat{F}^{\text{NMF}}_{(t;\tau_1,\tau_2)} = \mathsf{E}[Y_T(T(t))|\mathcal{F}_t],$$
$$\hat{F}^{\text{MF}k}_{(t;\tau_1,\tau_2)} = \mathsf{E}[Y_T(T(t))|\mathcal{G}^{\text{MF}k}_t] \tag{18.18}$$

where $\mathsf{E}(\cdot)$ is the objective or physical risk measure. For every day t in the trading period, these theoretical prices can be calculated and then compared with the actual market prices to find out if the models using meteorological forecasts predict market prices better than the standard model.

18.3 Risk Premium

Another way to think about future prices is in terms of risk premiums (RPs). RP effects are important in practice since issuers of weather contracts like to take advantages of geographic diversification, hedging effects and price determination. We adopt two ways for measuring the RP of weather risk. One is by looking at the risk factor under different pricing measures and the other one is by considering different filtrations.

18.3.1 Different Pricing Measures

The RPs in future markets are defined as the difference between the future prices computed with respect to the risk neutral measure and with respect to the objective measure (Geman, 2005):

$$\text{RP}(t,\tau) = \mathsf{E}^{Q_\theta}[Y_T\{T(t)\}|\mathcal{F}_t] - \mathsf{E}[Y_T\{T(t)\}|\mathcal{F}_t] \tag{18.19}$$

The first term denotes the future price calculated from the risk neutral dynamics and the second one is calculated from the objective dynamics. In other words, the RP is defined as a drift of the temperature dynamics or a Girsanov type change of probability. Putting (18.13) in (18.19) we obtain an expression for the RP for CAT temperature derivatives:

$$\text{RP}_{\text{CAT}(t,\tau_1,\tau_2)} = \int_t^{\tau_1} \theta_u\sigma_u \mathbf{a}_{t,\tau_1,\tau_2}\mathbf{e}_p du + \int_{\tau_1}^{\tau_2} \theta_u\sigma_u \mathbf{e}_1^\top \mathbf{A}^{-1}\left[\exp\{\mathbf{A}(\tau_2-u)\} - I_p\right]\mathbf{e}_p du$$

18.3.2 Information Premium

In the previous section, the pricing measure was changed. Incorporating meteorological forecasts, however, changes the filtration. To measure the influence the enlargement of the filtration has on the theoretical prices, Benth and Meyer-Brandis (2009) introduce the term "information premium (IP)." They define it as the difference between the theoretical prices calculated with and without using additional information such as meteorological weather forecasts:

$$\mathrm{IP}_t^{\mathcal{G}} = \hat{F}^{\mathcal{G}}_{(t;\tau_1,\tau_2)} - \hat{F}^{\mathcal{F}}_{(t;\tau_1,\tau_2)} = \mathsf{E}[Y_T\{T(t)\}|\mathcal{G}_t] - \mathsf{E}[Y_T\{T(t)\}|\mathcal{F}_t]. \qquad (18.20)$$

The IP measures how theoretical prices change over time when meteorological forecasts are considered. A nonzero information premium indicates that the meteorological forecasts differ on average from the predictions made by the temperature model without meteorological forecasts. The information premium is positive (negative) if the prices based on $\mathcal{G}_t$ are higher (lower) than those based on the filtration $\mathcal{F}_t$.

18.4 Empirical Analysis

18.4.1 Data

The temperature data used in this study for London and Rome are the daily average temperatures from 19730101 (yyyymmdd) to 20100201 and are provided by Bloomberg. To obtain years of equal length, February 29 is removed from the data.

Meteorological forecast data are derived from WeatherOnline. These data consist of point forecasts of the minimal and maximal temperatures for London from 0 to 13 days in advance, calculated every day between 20081229 and 20100201. The forecasts of the daily average temperature are calculated as the average of the forecasted minimal and maximal temperature.

The prices used in this study are the market prices of the London and Rome HDD and CAT futures contracts reported at CME as "last price" for every weekday in the trading period as well as the daily traded volume "last volume". The futures temperature data was extracted from Bloomberg. A detailed description of the HDD and CAT contracts for London can be found in Table 18.1.

18.4.2 Results

We first conduct an empirical analysis of the average daily temperature data for London and Rome. Figure 18.1 displays the seasonality Λ_t modeled with Fourier truncated

Table 18.1 Futures contracts for London used in this study overlapping with the period of the meteorological forecast data; the number of trading days, the traded volume (number of cleared trades), the number of days with volume > 0 and the payoffs (in index points) are shown. If two numbers are depicted, this indicates that less data than available were used because of missing meteorological forecast data.

London		Trading days	Traded volume	Days with vol>0	Payoff
Feb09	HDD	38/247	1430	11/12	366.0
Mar09	HDD	61/217	13800	18	300.0
Apr09	CAT	82/143	0	0	313.0
May09	CAT	102/249	200	4	441.0
Jun09	CAT	124/185	0	0	518.7
Jul09	CAT	145/206	250	4	570.0
Aug09	CAT	166/228	50	1	589.1
Sep09	CAT	187/249	0	0	487.1
Oct09	HDD	66/68	1270	5	160.4
Nov09	HDD	172/177	1650	1	241.3
Dec09	HDD	185/189	3250	10/11	429.5
Jan10	HDD	205/209	250	3	493.5

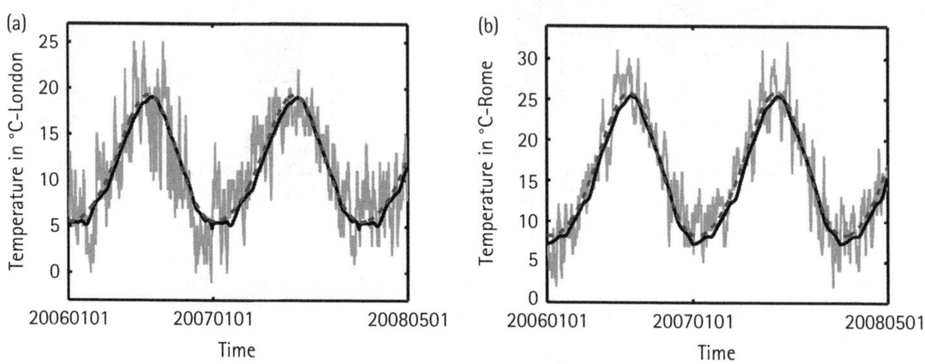

FIGURE 18.1 A stretch of eight years plot of the average daily temperatures (gray line), the seasonal component modelled with a Fourier truncated series (dashed line) and the local linear regression (black line) using Epanechnikov Kernel.

series and the Local linear regression. The latter estimator smooths the seasonal curve and captures peak seasons. The intercorrelations of the detrended temperature are well modeled with a simple autoregressive model of order $p = 3$. However, there is still seasonality remained in the residuals, as the ACFs of detrended (squared) residuals show in Figure 18.2. The empirical FTSG and LLR seasonal variations are displayed in Figure 18.3, which reveal high variations for both cities in winter times. After removing the seasonal variation of the residuals (corrected residuals), the ACFs of (squared)

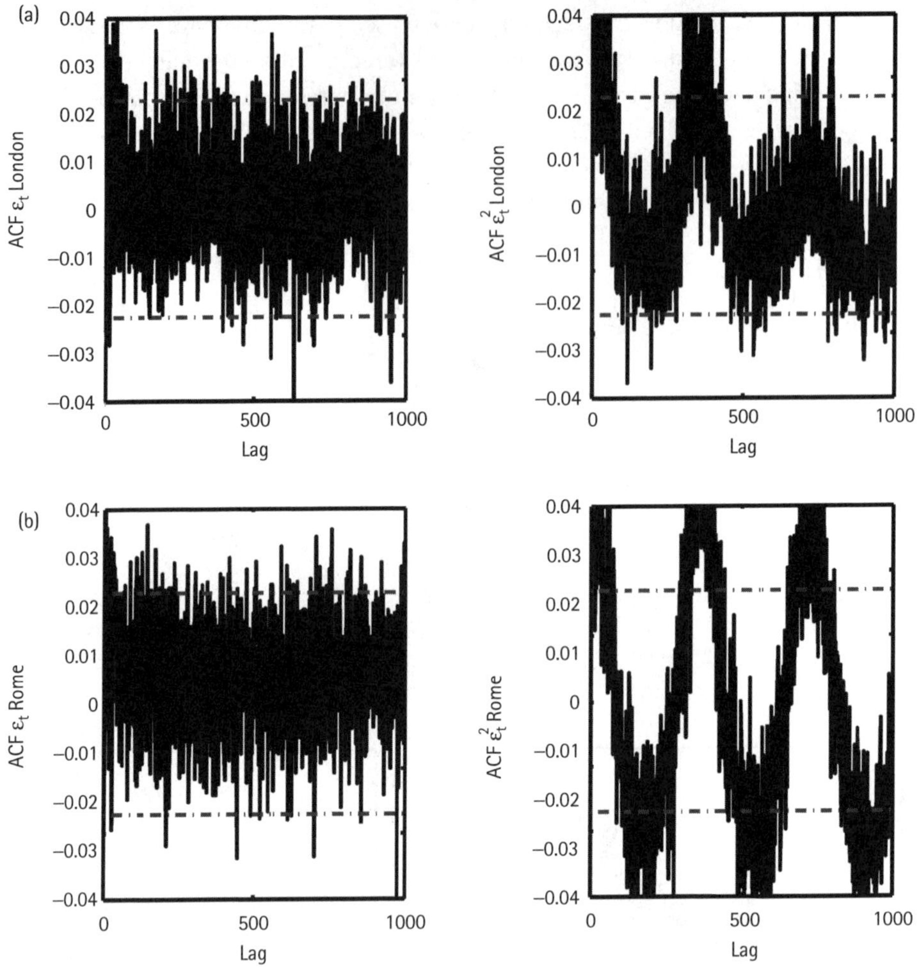

FIGURE 18.2 The ACF of Residuals of daily temperatures ϵ_t (left panels) and squared residuals ϵ_t^2 (right panels) of detrend daily temperatures for London (left) and Rome (right).

residuals in Figure 18.4 are close to zero indicating that we sufficiently reduced the seasonal effect. The result is displayed with the log of a normal density in Figure 18.5 (adequate for the Ornstein-Uhlenbeck pricing discussed in Section 18.2.1.3). The descriptive statistics given in Table 18.2 indicate the goodness of fit of the Local Linear (LLR) over the Fourier Truncated Series-GARCH (FTS-GARCH) estimator.

18.4.2.1 Implied Market Price of Risk

In Rome and London, HDD futures are traded from November–April (i.e., $i = 7$ calendar months) and CAT futures from April–November ($i = 7$). Our results for the implied MPR are given in Table 18.3 and 18.4. Table 18.3 presents the descriptive

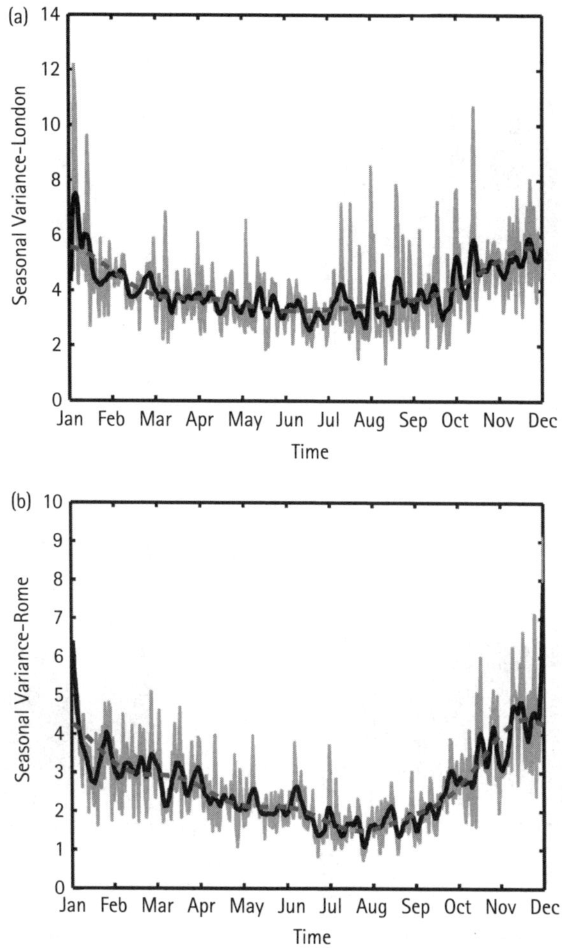

FIGURE 18.3 The daily empirical variance (black line), the Fourier truncated (dashed line) and the local linear smoother seasonal variation using Epanechnikov kernel (gray line) for London (left) and Rome (right).

statistics of different MPR specifications for London-CAT and Rome-CAT daily futures contracts traded before measurement period $t \leq \tau_1^i < \tau_2^i$ during 20031006-20101118 (6247 contracts in 1335 trading dates and 38 measurement periods) and 20050617-20090731 (2976 contracts corresponding to 891 trading dates and 22 measurement periods) respectively. The ranges for the MPR specifications values of London-CAT and Rome-CAT futures are $[-69.13, 43.93]$ and $[-64.55, 284.99]$, whereas the MPR averages are $(0.06, 0.0232)$ for constant MPR for different contracts, $(0.66, -0.23)$ for one piecewise constant, $(0.05, -0.31)$ for two piecewise constant, $(0.06, 0.02)$ for spline and $(0.08, 0.00)$ when bootstrapping the MPR.

We conduct the Wald statistical test to check whether the MPR derived from CAT/HDD futures is different from zero. We reject $H_0 : \hat{\theta}_t = 0$ under the Wald statistic

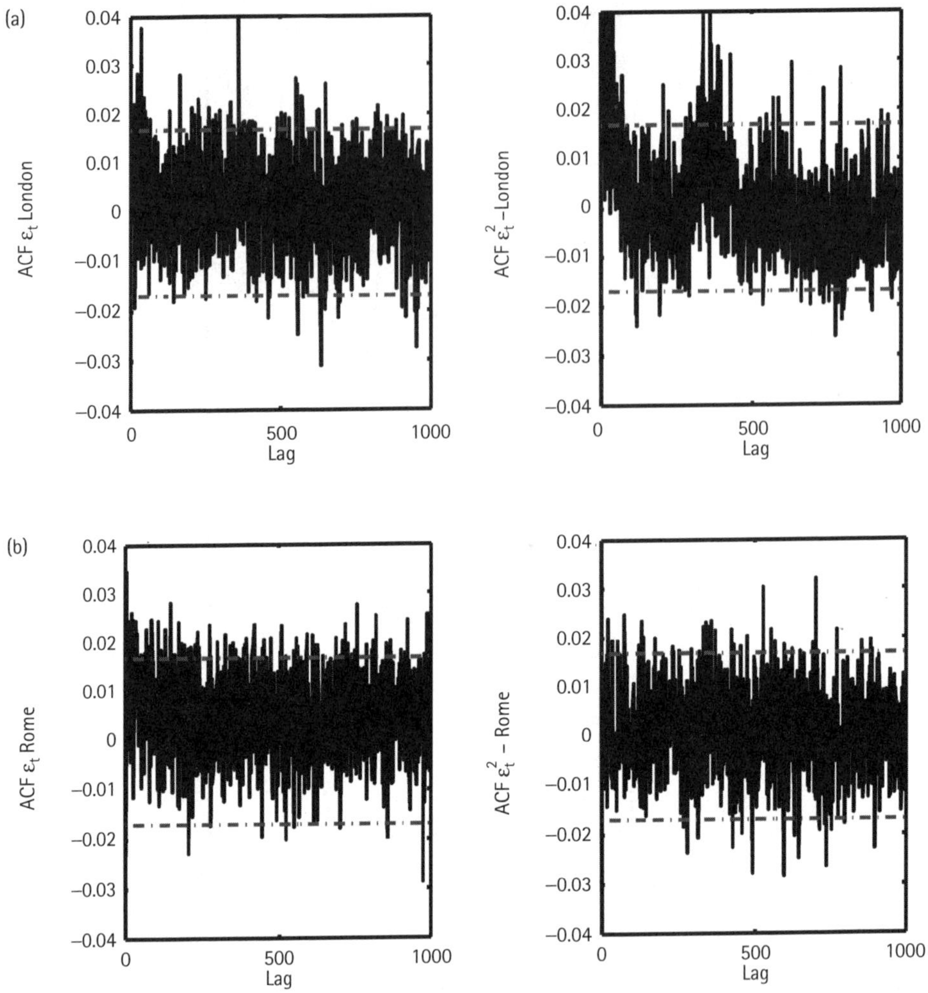

FIGURE 18.4 The ACF of Residuals e_t (left panels) and Squared residuals e_t^2 (right panels) of detrended daily temperatures after dividing out the local linear seasonal variance for London (left) and Rome (right).

that the MPR is different from zero for Rome and London-CAT futures, see Table 18.3, it changes over time and changes signs. These results suggest us that the weather market offers the possibility to have different risk adjustments for different times of the year.

Table 18.4 describes the root mean squared errors (RMSE) of the differences between market prices and the estimated futures prices with implied MPR values. Similar to Härdle and López-Cabrera (2011), the RMSE estimates in the case of the constant MPR for different CAT futures contracts are statistically significant enough to know CAT futures prices. When the MPR is equal to zero, we speak about the existence

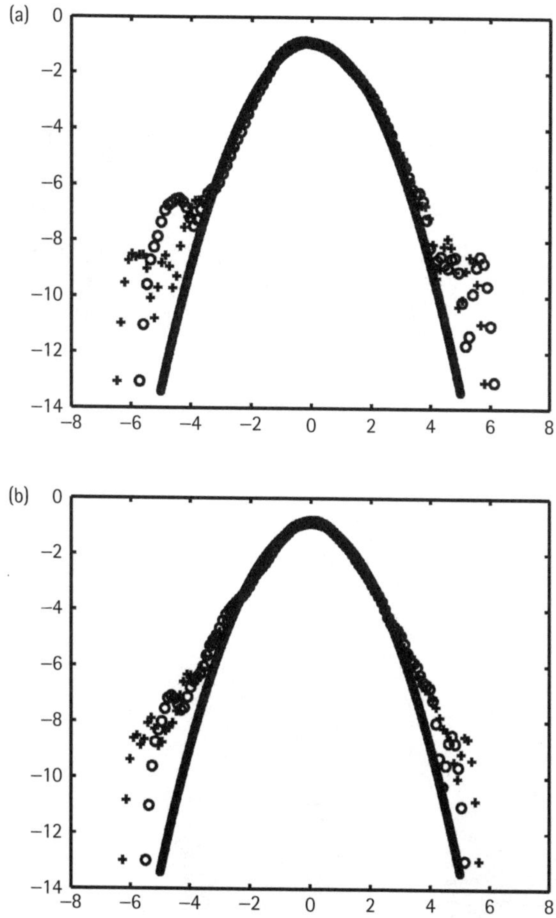

FIGURE 18.5 The log of Normal Kernel (*) and log of Kernel smoothing density estimate of residuals after correcting FTS (+) and local linear (o) seasonal variance for London (left) and Rome (right).

of additional risk premium revealing the evidence of buyers willing to pay for price protection.

18.4.2.2 Meteorological Forecasts

Section 18.2.1.5 argues that additional forward-looking information should be included in the pricing model. First, we compare the meteorological forecast data for 2009 and predictions from the statistical model without any meteorological forecast data with the realized temperatures in London in 2009. Figure 18.6 depicts the deviation in dependence of the number of days in advance the forecasts were calculated. The short-term meteorological forecasts clearly outperform those from the statistical model. The longer the forecast horizon gets, however, the smaller the difference

Table 18.2 Coefficients of the Fourier Truncated Seasonal series (FTS), ADF and KPSS-Statistics, the autoregressive process AR(3), continuous autoregressive model CAR(3), eigenvalues $\lambda_{1,2,3}$ of the matrix A of the CAR(3) model, seasonal variance $\{c_i\}_{i=1}^{9}$ fitted with a FTS, Skewness (Skew), kurtosis (Kurt), JarqueBera (JB) test statistics of the corrected residuals with seasonal variances fitted with FTS-GARCH and with local linear regression (LLR) for Rome and London. Confidence Intervals (CI) are given in parenthesis. Dates given in yyymmdd format. Coefficients are significant at 1% level. $+0.01$ critical values, * 0.1 critical value, **0.05 critical value, ***0.01 critical value.

Period		London 19730101-20091019	Rome 19730101-20091019
Seasonality	$\hat{a}$(CI)	10.75(10.62,10.89)	14.74(14.63,14.86)
	$\hat{b}$(CI)	0.0001(0.00005,0.00009)	0.0001(0.00010,0.00013)
	$\hat{c}_1$ (CI)	7.88(7.87,7.89)	8.81(8.80,8.82)
	$\hat{d}_1$ (CI)	−157.27(157.26,157.28)	−154.24(154.23,154.25)
ADF	$\hat{\tau}$	−33.41*	−37.62*
KPSS	$\hat{k}$	0.17***	0.06***
AR(3)	β_1	0.75	0.82
	β_2	−0.07	−0.08
	β_3	0.04	0.03
CAR(3)	α_1	−2.24	−2, 17
	α_2	−1.55	−1.44
	α_3	−0.26	−0.22
	λ_1	−0.25	−0.22
	$\lambda_{2,3}$	−0.99	−0.97
Coefficients of the FTS	$\hat{c}_1$	4.02	2.64
	$\hat{c}_2$	0.94	1.07
	$\hat{c}_3$	−0.07	0.21
	$\hat{c}_4$	0.34	0.35
	$\hat{c}_5$	−0.11	−0.25
	$\hat{c}_6$	0.21	0.07
	$\hat{c}_7$	−0.06	−0.14
	$\hat{c}_8$	0.04	0.11
	$\hat{c}_9$	0.01	−0.12
$\frac{\hat{e}_t}{\hat{\sigma}_t}$ with FTS	JB	190.60	637.26
	Kurt	3.50	4.04
	Skew	0.14	−0.10
$\frac{\hat{e}_t}{\hat{\sigma}_t}$ with LLR	JB	274.05	461.51
	Kurt	3.67	3.88
	Skew	0.09	−0.11

becomes, and for more than 10 days ahead, the meteorological forecasts get worse than the statistical model. This supports the assumption that meteorological forecasts contain additional information which can be used for pricing weather derivatives.

Table 18.3 Statistics of MPR specifications for London-CAT, Rome-CAT futures contracts traded during 20031006-20090529 (6247 observations corresponding to 1335 trading dates and 38 measurement periods), (20050617-20090731) respectively with trading date before measurement period $\tau \leq \tau_1^i < \tau_2^i$, $i = 1, \ldots I$, (where $i = 1$ (30 days), $i = 2$ (60 days),..., $i = 1$ (210 days)):the Wald statistics (WS), the WS probabilities (Prob), Minimum (Min), Maximum (Max), Median (Med) and Standard deviation (Std). MPR specifications: Constant for different contracts per trading date (Constant), one piecewise constant, 2 piecewise constant ($\xi = 150$ days), Bootstrap and Spline.

Type	Nr. contracts	Statistic	Constant	1 piecewise	2 piecewise	Bootstrap	Spline
London-CAT		WS(Prob)	0.44(0.49)	0.12(0.27)	0.00(0.02)	0.44(0.49)	1.32(0.75)
30days	589	Min(Max)	−0.49(0.54)	−4.52(4.43)	−4.52(4.48)	−0.49(0.54)	0.02(0.23)
(i=1)		Med(Std)	0.05(0.16)	0.12(1.41)	0.12(1.64)	0.05(0.16)	0.15(0.06)
60days	1215	Min(Max)	−1.70(0.86)	−10.92(16.83)	−69.13(43.93)	−1.70(0.86)	−0.00(0.03)
(i=2)		Med(Std)	0.07(0.19)	0.28(2.02)	0.13(5.71)	−0.07(5.03))	0.00(0.01)
90days	1168	Min(Max)	−0.40(0.12)	−20.63(27.39)	−1.42(0.12)	−0.40(0.12)	0.01(0.23)
(i=3)		Med(Std)	0.02(0.06)	−0.11(29.97)	−0.00(0.08)	0.07(0.19)	0.06(0.06)
120days	979	Min(Max)	−2.34(0.85)	−10.92(16.83)	−69.13(43.93)	−2.34(0.85)	0.00(0.23)
(i=4)		Med(Std)	0.07(0.22)	0.29(2.11)	0.14(5.84)	0.07(80.22)	0.13(0.07)
150days	876	Min(Max)	−2.89(0.84)	−10.92(16.83)	−18.26(36.78)	−2.89(0.84)	0.01(0.23)
(i=5)		Med(Std)	0.06(0.32)	0.48(2.14)	0.47(3.71)	0.06(0.32)	0.13(0.09)
180days	815	Min(Max)	−0.61(0.86)	−4.52(11.84)	−65.95(36.78)	−0.61(0.86)	−0.00(0.22)
(i=6)		Med(Std)	0.14(0.09)	0.52(1.76)	0.44(4.60)	0.14(0.09)	0.02(0.08)
210days	605	Min(Max)	−0.61(0.84)	−2.39(11.84)	−63.12(36.78)	−0.61(0.84)	−0.02(0.03)
(i=7)		Med(Std)	0.06(0.08)	0.84(1.55)	0.12(3.26)	0.06(0.08)	−0.01(0.01)
Rome-CAT		WS(Prob)	0.06(0.20)	0.00(0.01)	0.00(0.02)	0.00(0.06)	0.28(0.04)
30days	281	Min(Max)	−1.66(0.89)	−5.86(11.74)	−7.90(11.74)	−1.66(0.89)	0.00(0.01)
(i=1)		Med(Std)	0.02(0.76)	−0.66(2.52)	−0.66(2.88)	0.02(0.76)	0.00(0.02)
60days	583	Min(Max)	−2.38(1.39)	−64.55(284.99)	−64.55(284.99)	−2.38(1.39)	0.02(0.01)
(i=2)		Med(Std)	0.11(0.30)	−0.06(13.66)	−0.06(13.86)	0.11(0.30)	0.00(0.02)
90days	641	Min(Max)	−3.20(1.07)	−64.55(284.99)	−64.55(284.99)	−3.20(1.07)	0.00(0.43)
(i=3)		Med(Std)	0.17(0.36)	0.29(13.11)	0.18(13.25)	0.17(0.36)	0.00(0.05)
120days	476	Min(Max)	−3.40(1.09)	−11.32(45.78)	−11.32(3.33)	−3.40(1.09)	0.00(0.00)
(i=4)		Med(Std)	0.05(0.42)	0.50(3.67)	0.53(2.90)	0.05(0.42)	0.00(0.00)
150days	413	Min(Max)	−0.59(0.93)	−19.96(3.03)	−19.96(56.90)	−0.59(0.93)	0.01(0.02)
(i=5)		Med(Std)	0.08(0.08)	0.69(2.74)	0.71(4.30)	0.08(0.08)	0.00(0.02)
180days	373	Min(Max)	−0.95(0.18)	−19.96(3.03)	−19.96(56.90)	−0.95(0.18)	0.01(0.02)
(i=6)		Med(Std)	0.01(0.07)	0.91(2.96)	0.71(4.37)	0.01(0.07)	0.00(0.01)
210days	208	Min(Max)	−0.03(1.07)	−19.96(3.03)	−19.96(3.03)	−0.03(1.07)	0.02(0.01)
(i=7)		Med(Std)	0.17(0.10)	0.91(1.64)	0.91(1.68)	0.17(0.10)	0.00(0.00)

The extended model from Section 18.2.1.5 computes theoretical prices for every contract on every day t based on different filtrations, from not using any meteorological forecasts to using forecasts 13 days in advance. As an example, Figure 18.7 shows the results for an HDD contract for December 2009 with reference station London. This contract is offered starting April 2009, but all prices remain constant for a long

Table 18.4 Root mean squared error (RMSE) of the differences between observed CAT/HDD/CDD futures prices with $\tau \leq \tau_1^i < \tau_2^i$ and the estimated futures with extracted MPR from different MPR parametrizations (MPR=0, constant MPR for different contracts (Constant), 1 piecewise constant MPR, 2 piecewise constant MPR , bootstrap MPR and spline MPR). Computations with MPR implied directly from specific futures contract types (+) and through the parity HDD/CDD/CAT parity method(*).

Contract type	Measurement Period			RMSE between estimated with MPR (θ_t) and CME prices					
	τ_1	τ_2	No. contracts	MPR=0	Constant	1 piecewise	2 piecewise	Bootstrap	Spline
London-CAT+	20080501	20080531	22	28.39	10.37	196.09	196.09	10.37	27.67
London-CAT+	20080601	20080630	43	5.51	27.93	102.23	102.23	27.93	4.91
London-CAT+	20080701	20080731	64	12.85	61.41	688.99	688.99	61.41	12.44
London-CAT+	20080801	20080831	86	29.94	4.72	99.59	99.59	0.00	29.76
London-CAT+	20080901	20080930	107	41.57	45.97	646.49	646.49	45.97	41.18
London-CAT+	20090401	20090430	120	73.59	77.83	156.44	156.44	77.83	73.75
London-CAT+	20090501	20090531	141	93.51	96.77	96.74	96.747	96.77	93.60
London-CAT+	20090601	20090630	161	100.32	103.56	103.98	103.56	103.56	101.31
Rome-CAT+	20080501	20080531	22	19.10	8.92	103.55	103.55	8.92	18.58
Rome-CAT+	20080601	20080630	43	26.88	16.13	141.82	141.82	16.13	26.18
Rome-CAT+	20080701	20080731	64	13.46	17.27	324.18	324.18	17.27	13.22
Rome-CAT+	20080801	20080831	86	23.66	36.21	761.63	761.63	36.21	23.26
Rome-CAT+	20080901	20080930	107	18.53	45.43	718.83	718.83	45.43	18.51
Rome-CAT+	20090401	20090430	120	97.99	127.62	575.88	575.88	127.62	98.31
Rome-CAT+	20090501	20090531	141	117.13	121.90	117.17	117.17	121.91	117.49
Rome-CAT+	20090601	20090630	141	117.07	120.21	102.34	123.49	120.21	112.95

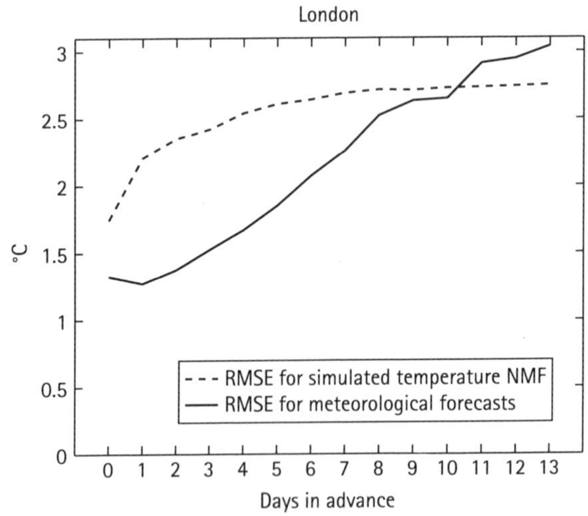

FIGURE 18.6 RMSE of the meteorological forecasts and the statistical model (NMF) compared with the observed temperature in London in 2009

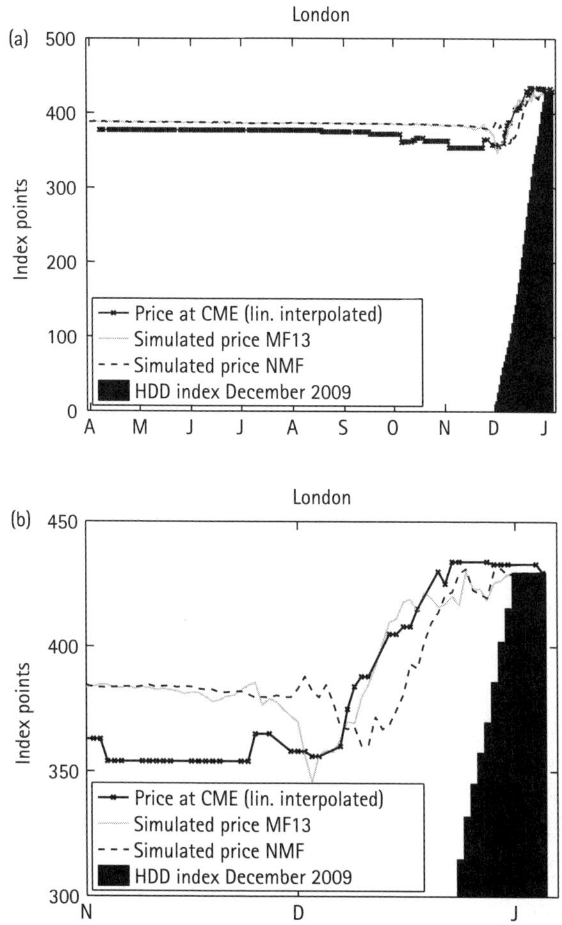

FIGURE 18.7 Observed and simulated prices of an HDD contract for December, 2009 in London

period. The theoretical prices with and without meteorological forecasts equal as the accumulation period is too far away for an influence of the forecasts on the expected temperature. This changes in the last two months where there are higher fluctuations in all prices and bigger differences between the theoretical prices. In this example, the theoretical prices with meteorological forecasts seem to predict the market prices much better than the theoretical price without using any forecast data.

The IP defined in (18.20) measures the influence the additional information has on the theoretical prices. Figure 18.8 shows the IP for the same example as above, the London HDD contract for December 2009. It can be seen that it is zero for a long time, but then it fluctuates and changes its sign several times. Figure 18.8 also depicts the average IP for all twelve contracts used in this study in absolute value. As expected, the meteorological forecasts have the biggest influence in the last two months before maturity.

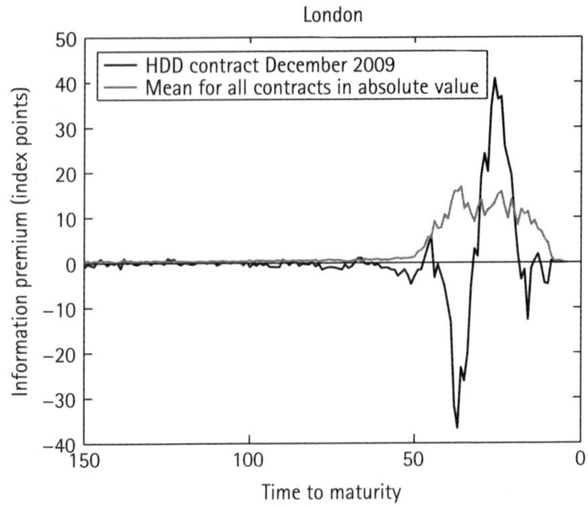

FIGURE 18.8 Information premium for the HDD contract for December 2009 in London and the mean in absolute value for all twelve London contracts

The RP (18.19) describes the difference between the prices under the risk-neutral measure and the physical measure. Hence, it can be calculated as the difference between the observed market prices and the theoretical prices with an MPR $= 0$. Figure 18.9 shows the RP for the HDD contract for December 2009 with reference station London, where the theoretical prices are calculated with and without using meteorological forecasts. The RP stays almost constant and is equal for both filtrations for the major part of the trading period. When approaching the measurement period, however, the RP with meteorological forecasts differs and is fluctuating closer around zero. This means that the RP declines in absolute value when incorporating meteorological forecasts. Similar results are obtained when depicting the average RP for all contracts in absolute value (Figure 18.9). For the major part of the trading period, there is no difference between the models. In the last two months, however, the RP is generally lower in absolute value with meteorological forecasts. Consequently, enlarging the filtration helps to better control the RP.

To compare the difference between the models, the RMSE between the theoretical and the observed market prices is calculated for every model and every contract separately. The results in Table 18.5 show that the error decreases for most of the contracts if a model with meteorological forecasts is used. The mean of the RMSE decreases from 19.1 to about 18 index points when meteorological forecasts are used. On average, the prediction of the market prices with forecasts is much better for the winter months with the HDD contracts. The normalized RMSE (i.e., the RMSE for the model without forecasts is set to 1) is shown in Figure 18.10.

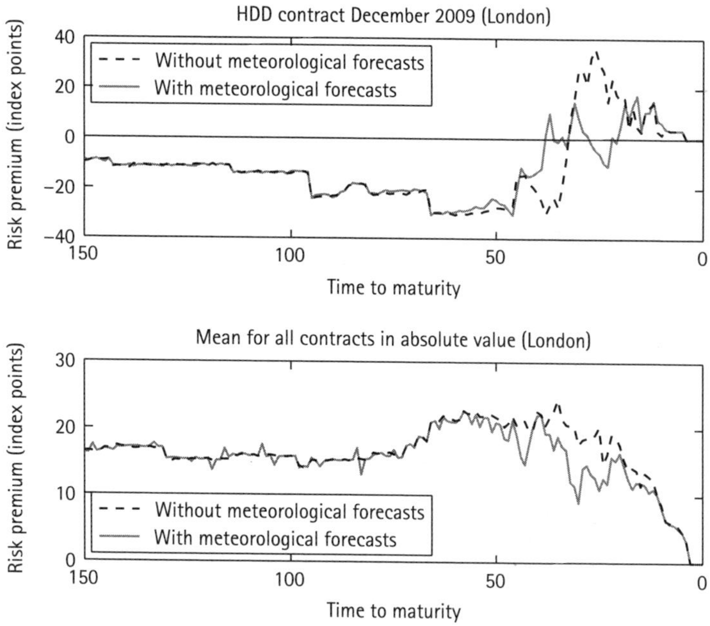

FIGURE 18.9 Risk premium for the HDD contract for December 2009 (top) and the mean in absolute value for all twelve London contracts (bottom) without and with including meteorological forecasts (MF13)

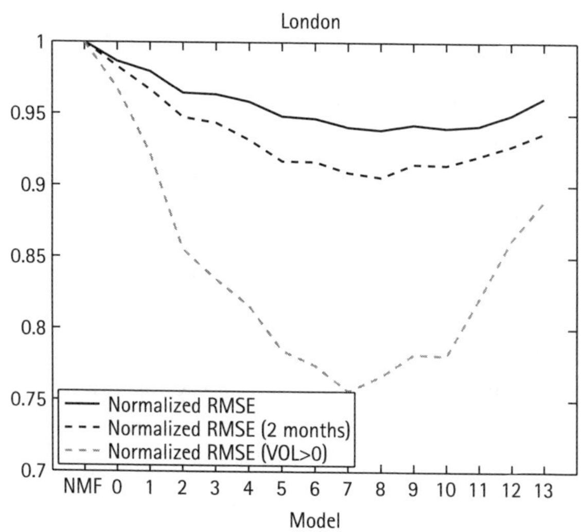

FIGURE 18.10 Average nRMSE (whole period, last 2 months, days with volume>0) for London for different models (NMF, MF0-MF13)

Table 18.5 RMSE in index points for monthly contracts and different models for London (whole trading period)

RMSE	Model														
	NMF	MF0	MF1	MF2	MF3	MF4	MF5	MF6	MF7	MF8	MF9	MF10	MF11	MF12	MF13
Feb09	27.9	26.9	26.1	23.7	23.6	23.7	22.1	21.2	20.9	20.0	20.3	19.4	18.4	18.6	18.9
Mar09	6.7	6.1	6.2	5.8	5.5	5.1	5.5	6.3	6.5	6.5	6.9	6.7	7.7	9.0	10.7
Apr09	16.2	16.1	16.7	16.7	16.8	17.0	17.1	17.1	16.9	17.0	17.2	17.4	17.6	18.0	18.6
May09	17.3	17.4	17.1	17.1	17.2	17.2	17.1	17.0	17.0	16.8	16.9	16.7	16.9	17.0	17.0
Jun09	14.8	15.0	15.3	15.6	16.0	16.0	16.1	16.1	16.3	16.5	16.5	16.6	16.5	16.7	16.7
Jul09	14.7	15.0	15.1	15.2	15.2	15.3	15.1	15.0	15.4	15.6	15.7	15.8	16.2	16.4	16.6
Aug09	18.4	18.5	18.4	18.3	18.5	18.5	18.3	18.3	18.3	18.4	18.6	18.6	18.8	18.8	19.1
Sep09	17.1	17.0	17.1	17.3	17.0	16.8	16.6	16.4	16.3	16.2	16.1	15.7	15.5	15.5	15.6
Oct09	35.6	34.3	33.8	33.6	33.7	33.2	32.7	32.8	31.8	32.2	31.9	32.3	31.8	31.3	31.3
Nov09	28.3	28.1	27.6	27.3	27.1	26.9	26.9	26.9	26.6	26.3	26.2	26.2	26.1	25.9	25.9
Dec09	15.8	15.4	15.1	14.8	14.7	14.5	14.3	14.2	13.9	13.8	13.7	13.8	13.9	13.8	13.8
Jan10	16.2	15.9	15.7	15.5	15.3	15.3	15.4	15.4	15.6	15.7	15.8	16.0	16.1	16.1	16.0
Mean	19.1	18.8	18.7	18.4	18.4	18.3	18.1	18.1	17.9	17.9	18.0	17.9	18.0	18.1	18.3
Mean HDD	21.8	21.1	20.8	20.1	20.0	19.8	19.5	19.5	19.2	19.1	19.1	19.1	19.0	19.1	19.4
Mean CAT	16.4	16.5	16.6	16.7	16.8	16.8	16.7	16.6	16.7	16.7	16.8	16.8	16.9	17.1	17.3

So far, the RMSE was calculated for the whole trading period of each contract. The results of the information premium, however, show that the influence of the forecasts on the theoretical prices is almost zero for a long time of the trading period and increases significantly for the last two months until maturity. The RMSE restricted on the last two months of the trading period of each contract shows that the meteorological forecasts stronger influence the pricing in that period (see Figure 18.10).

Although market prices are reported by the CME for every weekday in the trading period, actual trading takes place only on a few days in the trading period (compare Table 18.1). Only if the contract was actually traded on that day, however, the reported price is a real market price and can be assumed to capture all relevant information. The RMSE restricted on those days where the trading volume is larger than zero is also shown in Figure 18.10. It shows a clear decline of up to 25 % for those models, where meteorological forecasts are included.

All graphs in Figure 18.10 have in common that they decrease in the beginning, but turn upwards in the end. This means that including all forecast data into the pricing is worse than using just forecasts a few days ahead. A possible reason could be that the market participants are aware of the unreliability of long-term forecasts, which could also be seen in Figure 18.6.

18.5 Conclusions

In this chapter, we examine a forecasting based pricing approach for weather derivatives(WDs). The latter approach is incorporating weather forecast into the pricing model. We imply weather risk premiums (RPs) for Rome and London temperature futures traded at the CME. The goal was to determine the nature of the risk factor embedded in temperature option and future prices. Two ways for measuring these RPs are proposed: one is by studying the stochastic behavior of the temperature underlying under different risk pricing measures and the second one is by using different filtration information sets (IP). In both approaches, the RPs and IPs of futures contracts are different from zero, negative or positive. We find that the seasonal variance of temperature explains a significant proportion of the RP variation. The impact of forecast increases as the time to measurement period arises.

Acknowledgments

The financial support from the Deutsche Forschungsgemeinschaft via SFB 649 Ökonomisches Risiko, Humboldt-Universität zu Berlin is gratefully acknowledged.

References

Alaton, P., Djehiche, B., and Stillberger, D. (2002). On modelling and pricing weather derivatives. *Applied Mathematical Finance*, *9*(1), 1–20.

Benth, F. (2003). On arbitrage-free pricing of weather derivatives based on fractional Brownian motion. *Applied Mathematical Finance*, *10*(4), 303–324.

Benth, F., Härdle, W. K., and López-Cabrera, B. (2011). Pricing of Asian Temperature Risk. In P. Cizek, W. K. H'andle, and R.Weron (eds.), *Statistical Tools for Finance and Insurance*, Heidelberg: Springer Verlag. pp. 163–199.

Benth, F., and Meyer-Brandis, T. (2009). The information premium for non-storable commodities. *Journal of Energy Markets*, *2*(3), 111–140.

Benth, F., and Saltyte-Benth, J. (2005). Stochastic modelling of temperature variations with a view towards weather derivatives. *Applied Mathematical Finance*, *12*(1), 53–85.

Benth, F., Saltyte-Benth, J., and Koekebakker, S. (2007). Putting a price on temperature. *Scandinavian Journal of Statistics*, *34*, 746–767.

Brockett, P., Golden, L. L., Wen, M., and Yang, C. (2010). Pricing weather derivatives using the indifference pricing approach. *North American Actuarial Journal*, *13*(3), 303–315.

Brody, D., Syroka, J., and Zervos, M. (2002). Dynamical pricing of weather derivatives. *Quantitative Finance*, *3*, 189–198.

Campbell, S. D., and Diebold, F. X. (2005). Weather forecasting for weather derivatives. *Journal of the American Statistical Association*, *100*(469), 6–16.

Cao, M., and Wei, J. (2004). Weather derivatives valuation and market price of weather risk. *The Journal of Future Markets, 24*(11), 1065–1089.

Davis, M. (2001). Pricing weather derivatives by marginal value. *Quantitive Finance, 1*, 305–308.

Diebold, F., and Inoue, A. (2001). Long memory and regime switching. *Journal of Econometrics, 105*, 131–159.

Dorfleitner, G., and Wimmer, M. (2010). The pricing of temperature futures at the Chicago Mercantile Exchange. *Journal of Banking and Finance, 34*(6), 1360–1370.

Geman, H. (2005). *Commodities and Commodity Derivatives.* Chichester: Wiley-Finance, John Wiley & Sons.

Granger, C., and Hyung, N. (2004). Occasional structural breaks and long memory with an application to the S&P 500 absolute stock returns. *Journal of Empirical Finance, 11*, 399–421.

Härdle, W. K., and López-Cabrera, B. (2011). The implied market price of weather risk. *Applied Mathematical Finance, 5*, 1–37.

Jewson, S., and Caballero, R. (2003). The use of weather forecasts in the pricing of weather derivatives. *Meteorological Applications, 10*, 377–389.

Ritter, M., Mußhoff, O., and Odening, M. (2011). Meteorological forecasts and the pricing of weather derivatives. *The Journal of Derivatives, 19*(2), 45–60.

Yoo, S. (2003). Weather derivatives and seasonal forecast. Department of Applied Economics and Management, Cornell University, Working paper.

CHAPTER 19

EMPLOYMENT AND OUTPUT EFFECTS OF CLIMATE POLICIES

MIKA KATO, STEFAN MITTNIK, DANIEL SAMAAN, AND WILLI SEMMLER

19.1 Introduction

It is now well recognized that global warming results from economic activities that create carbon dioxide (CO_2) emissions. Academic work has thus been put forward that argues for a great urgency to implement effective climate policies to control global warming. Concrete policy proposals for reducing CO_2 emissions have been developed by the Intergovernmental Panel on Climate Change (see, IPCC, 2007, 2013, 2014). Given this recently published scientific evidence on global warming and its damages, the importance of climate change mitigation policies has been sufficiently demonstrated.

On the other hand, it has been recognized by the IPCC and other studies that climate change is not only an environmental problem but also that over the long run global warming is likely to have drastic effects on economic activity. Economic growth and climate change are increasingly seen as interdependent issues (see Uzawa, 2003; Stern, 2007; Greiner and Semmler, 2008; Nordhaus, 2008; and Weitzmann, 2008). Different approaches exist to analyze these interdependencies, to measure the cost and to derive appropriate policy recommendations. Based on the assumptions used and the respective climate or economic model employed the degree of urgency for action differs. Hansen (2008), or Greiner et al. (2010), for example, argue that due to the possibility of self-enforcing feedback effects, a much faster and stronger policy response is required than most other models suggest. Greiner et al. (2010) also provide a brief review about differing modeling approaches and their conclusions. Despite these differences in the analysis of the problem, there is wide agreement among scholars that some policy measures need to be implemented to stop or to slow down the anthropogenic climate change.

Correspondingly, a recent report by the IPCC (Fourth Assessment Report) has urgently suggested a broad range of mitigation policy measures, such as integrating climate policies, broader development policies, regulations and standards, voluntary agreements, information instruments, and financial incentives to control and reduce greenhouse gas (GHG) emissions.[1] It also emphasizes the role of technology policies to achieve lower CO_2 stabilization levels, a greater need for more efficient research and development (R&D) efforts, and higher investment in new technologies during the next few decades (for achieving stabilization and reducing costs). Further recommendations include government initiatives for funding or subsidizing alternative energy sources (solar energy, ocean power, windmills, biomass, and nuclear fusion). Overall, the IPCC stresses the fact that the effectiveness of such policies ultimately depends on national circumstances, their design, interaction, stringency, and implementation.

Yet, the major instruments that the IPCC and numerous well-respected economists propose are two specific tools to reduce GHG to fulfill the agreements of the Kyoto Protocol. These two tools are decentralized market trading of emission rights and carbon taxation—in the public discussion often called "cap-and-trade" and "carbon tax" (see Uzawa, 2003; Mankiw, 2007; Nordhaus, 2008 and also the IPCC). A tax on carbon as a means to reduce CO_2 emissions has been suggested by economists for quite some time (see Pearce, 1991). Both measures have a long-standing history in economic theory originating in the works of Pigou (1920), and Dales (1968). Independently of how these measures may look in detail, it is obvious that such policies will have an impact on economic activity and employment.

This chapter analyzes the effects of a carbon tax on output and employment. A carbon tax incentivitizes the avoidance of carbon-intensive production schemes and penalizes the consumption of carbon-intensive goods and services. Over the long term a carbon tax thus leads to some form of structural change in the economy. This structural change may cause costs in terms of unemployment and in terms of reduced consumption possibilities today or in the future. In neoclassical growth models with immediate clearing markets, the adjustment costs within an economy in terms of employment fluctuations are assumed to be zero. However, it seems reasonable to expect that different sectors in an economy would react differently to a carbon tax in terms of output and employment. We can expect that some sectors in the economy will increase in size, or that even new sectors emerge, while other sectors will decrease or even disappear. The net effect on employment may be positive or negative.

Structural change is usually understood as the massive reallocation of labor from the primary sector (agriculture) into the secondary (manufacturing) and tertiary (services) sectors. Many economists, for example, Fisher (1935), Clark (1940), Kuznets (1957), Kaldor (1957) or Cherney (1960) have well documented such a transition and have developed models that allow for the study of growth and structural change simultaneously. In Pasinetti (1981), for example, structural change occurs through a change in final demand driven by the income elasticity of demand (Engel curves).

These ideas principally also apply for the structural change required to cope with global climate change. However, instead of focusing on types of goods or sectors (agriculture, manufacturing, services) to describe the structure of an economy, the transition toward a sustainable ("low-carbon") economy can be analyzed based on the criterion of *carbon-intensity* of goods, sectors, and activities. Whatever climate policies will be implemented by policymakers in the future (regulations, carbon tax, emission trading systems, or others), their economic effect will be to strengthen the relative position of low-carbon industries in the economy, i.e., industries that emit low amounts of CO_2 during the production process. In addition, incentives are created for industries to develop techniques and products that allow for a low-carbon production of output. A three-sector growth model in which the economy experiences structural change on a balanced growth path has been developed in Samaan (2014). The high-carbon–intensive sector decreases in relative size while the relative size of the low-carbon sector increases. The main mechanism of the model is sketched in the appendix.

Thus, similar to the more traditional idea of structural change, a transition toward a low-carbon economy could be characterized by focusing on the structure of output and employment in the economy. In particular, a re-allocation of labor from the more traditional sectors ("high-carbon–intensive sector") to the "low-carbon–intensive" would mean that future jobs are created in the low-carbon–intensive sector while jobs would disappear in the high-carbon–intensive sector. Theoretically, structural economic change can occur by itself (and often does), that is, without government intervention. Changing relative prices, changing consumer preferences, new technological developments, or other factors can be the cause for a structural change. For example, government intervention was neither to induce a structural change from an industrial economy to a more service-oriented economy nor was this a goal. Fuchs (1968) identifies three factors as driving forces for structural change in the traditional sense:

First, the income elasticity of the demand for services is greater than 1. Second, as income rises it becomes more efficient to contract out services that were once produced in the household or firm. Third, productivity growth is slower in the service sector. For a more recent discussion of structural change in a theoretical growth model, see also Kongsamut et al. (2001).

In the case of a structural change toward a low-carbon economy, the situation is somewhat different since some form of government activity is required. From an economic point of view, pollution such as CO_2 emissions constitute a negative externality that needs to be internalized. Therefore, the government has to play an active role in this process, for example, through implementation of a Pigou tax in the form of a carbon tax.

It has been quite controversial what the employment effects of such a policy would be. Pearce (1991) already pointed out that a carbon tax could yield a double dividend, if it replaces a distorting tax like a labor tax. His conclusion is in line with the hypothesis that Porter (1990) makes in a broader context, namely that the economy would gain competitiveness through implemented environmental policies. For Porter and van der Linde (1993), it is accelerated technical change, and higher innovativeness of enterprises that leads to increased competitiveness in the long run. Others have challenged this view on theoretical grounds (see, e.g., Palmer et al., 1995). Overall, the question about employment and competitive effects remains unresolved and subject to debate. Anderson and Ekins (2009) and Ekins and Speck (2011) provide recent evidence on economic effects of environmental tax reforms (ETRs) in European countries.

In this chapter, we focus on the short-term employment dynamics that could be triggered by a carbon tax, ignoring long-term technical change. In particular, we are interested in the effects of a budget-neutral carbon tax scheme in which the collected tax revenue is reinjected into the economy, similar to ETR schemes that have been implemented in several European countries. We argue that even without considering technological change, positive or negative employment effects can occur in a two-sector model, depending on the growth and employment dynamics in the sectors. We analyze a tax scheme in which the carbon tax is imposed only on the the high-carbon–intensive sector of the economy and in which revenue is shifted toward the low-carbon sector. We assume that, in the short run, tax increases lead to a negative output growth shock while subsidies lead to a boost in output growth. The rationale behind this assumption is that technical change and innovation take time. In the short run a tax has a depressing effect on output while a tax decrease or subsidy encourages economic activity.

A review of the debate on the double dividend, a discussion of different versions of it, and evidence for and against it are provided in the following section.

19.2 The Double Dividend in the Literature

In the case of a carbon tax, or more generally, environmental taxes, the academic literature discusses possible positive employment effects in the context of the so-called double-dividend hypothesis. Different notions of a double dividend exist and following Goulder (1995b) we review different concepts of the double dividend on theoretical as well as on empirical grounds.

Economists have even been wondering if correcting for environmental externalities can at the same time generate a positive effect ("double-dividend hypothesis"). At least three versions of the double-dividend hypothesis exist (see Goulder, 1995b). The first dividend would be an increase of environmental quality. Emission of CO_2 constitutes an externality if it leads to damages in the environment, which in economic terms means that these damages cause a decrease in production, decreased profits, or some other form of welfare losses. The market solution therefore provides an inefficient allocation. Correcting this externality with a Pigou tax is welfare improving and results in efficiency gains.

Dealing with this kind of externality (CO_2 emission) is a very complex problem: First, polluters have been polluting in the present and in the past while most of the damages gross domestic product (GDP) will occur in the future. Second, the aggrieved parties are to a large extent unborn future generations. Third, since the damages occur mainly in the future and because the climate system is very complex and not fully understood, the magnitude of future damages is highly uncertain. In other words, the cost of the externality is difficult to quantify. Finally, the greenhouse effect is a global problem and polluters and aggrieved parties therefore need not reside in the same country or even the same region of the world.

The previous points make an internalization of such an external effect extremely difficult from a political perspective. However, considering the world population as a whole and looking at world gdp, the current allocation, that is, mostly unregulated CO_2 emissions, is inefficient and it is generally recognized that removing the externality leads to a Pareto improvement. Thus, it is possible to move to a world GDP growth path on which no one is worse off but some people may be better off. Internalizing the external effect is the first dividend. We refer to this first dividend as environmental benefits even though we emphasize that these benefits can very well be translated into tangible economic terms.

The problem with this first dividend, which justifies by itself the implementation of a tax or other correcting instrument, is that the magnitude of the benefits are uncertain and may lie far in the future (see Goulder, 1995b). The implementation of the tax does, however, cause gross costs in the form of behavioral changes compared to the status quo which are very certain, quantifiable and occur in the present. In other words, although the net cost of a properly designed CO_2 tax has to be negative, that is, produce global welfare gains, there is a gross cost to the tax, which is imposed on those who currently over-emit CO_2. This gross cost is usually expressed in terms of reductions in current GDP growth for some countries including possible employment losses. The implementation of such an instrument (carbon tax) constitutes therefore a rather unattractive situation for policy makers.

Out of this dilemma, policymakers have developed a preference for the double-dividend hypothesis, which claims that the gross cost of a carbon tax (environmental tax) be zero or even negative. Under these circumstances, the implementation of the tax would be either costless or beneficial no matter what the magnitude of the environmental benefits is (as long as they are still positive). If costs are zero (or negative), this guarantees positive net benefits. On the other hand, if one cannot be assured that the costs are zero, then before one can recommend an environmental tax swap on efficiency grounds one has to be involved in the messy business of comparing (uncertain) environmental benefits with abatement costs (Goulder, 1995b). The main mechanism that can reduce gross costs of a carbon tax is revenue recycling. If the raised revenue is used to reduce distortionary taxes the total cost of the tax can be reduced or even become zero or negative. It is important to keep in mind that we are talking about the gross cost, that is, excluding the environmental benefits, which, if included, would always lead to a net negative cost or welfare improvement.

Goulder (1995b) distinguishes three versions of the double-dividend hypothesis that depend on the size of the cost reduction of the implemented carbon tax (environmental tax). The weak form claims that one achieves cost savings relative to the case where the tax revenues are returned to taxpayers in lump-sum fashion if the tax revenues are instead used to reduce marginal tax rates of a distortionary tax. The intermediate form claims that it is possible to find a distortionary tax such that the revenue-neutral substitution of the carbon tax (environmental tax) for this tax involves a zero or negative gross cost. The strong form claims that the revenue-neutral substitution for typical or representative distortionary taxes involves a zero or negative cost.

The terms "cost reduction" or "zero or negative cost" have to be understood here in a general way for a number of welfare gains. Often these welfare gains are specified in concrete economic terms such as reduced unemployment or increased profits (see, e.g., Nielsen et al., 1995; Carraro et al., 1996; Ploeg, 2002). Thus, in our context of employment effects, the second dividend concerns the question of reduced unemployment caused by a reduction of distortionary taxes that is financed through a carbon tax (environmental tax). Typical candidates for distortionary taxes to be reduced are all kinds of labor costs such as wage taxes or social security contributions.

On theoretical grounds, the claims of the weak double dividend are widely accepted and are considered relatively uncontroversial (see Goulder, 1995b). Bovenberg and de Mooij (1994) develop a general equilibrium model to study the strong version of the double-dividend claim in the labor market context. The only tax in their model is a labor income tax. They find that the strong claim is substantiated if and only if the uncompensated wage elasticity of labor supply is negative. Empirical studies tend to find positive values for the uncompensated elasticity so that the Bovenberg-de-Mooij model suggests a rejection of the double-dividend hypothesis in its strong form.

Both conclusions, the general acceptance of the weak form and the rejection of the strong form in the Bovenberg-de-Mooij model, depend crucially on the assumptions about the tax system in place when the carbon tax (environmental tax) is implemented as well as the mechanisms in place on the labor market. Under idealized market conditions with perfect competition, a commodity tax and a tax on wages can be designed equivalently in terms of costs (see Kaplow, 2008). In other words, distortions in the labor and commodity markets are interrelated. An environmental tax on the commodity markets can therefore have distorting effects on the labor market as well, thereby reducing the potential of a strong double dividend. As Goulder (1995b) points out, a main insight of the Bovenberg de Mooij analysis is that partial equilibrium analyzes of the gross costs of environmental taxes can be highly misleading and that the question of a possible double dividend in the real world is very complex: In Bovenberg and de Mooij (1994), the authors use a dynamic model and then find that double-dividend may be possible if ETRs lead to lower regulatory pressure on companies.

Nielsen et al. (1995) analyze the double-dividend hypothesis with a model that allows for involuntary unemployment and show that unemployment can be reduced through the implementation of a pollution tax.

Despite the complexity of the mechanisms that may or may not lead to a double dividend, one can draw some general conclusions on the theoretical conditions under which a strong double dividend is likely to occur. The gross costs of revenue-neutral environmental tax will be lower to the extent that (Goulder, 1995b):

1. In the initial tax system, the difference in the marginal efficiency costs (marginal excess burdens) is large.
2. The burden of the environmental tax falls primarily on the factor with relatively low marginal efficiency cost.
3. The base of the environmental tax is relatively broad, so that the distortions it generates in intermediate good and consumer good markets are small.
4. Revenues from the tax are devoted to reducing tax rates on the factor with relatively high marginal efficiency cost.

Other aspects to be taken into account in the theoretical analysis concern the question of whether capital is considered, of whether involuntary unemployment exists, whether markets clear, or if the environment is treated as a capital good. Another important dimension is the question whether one deals with an open or a closed economy.

Several reviews about the employment effects of environmental policies have been prepared by the Organisation for Economic Co-operation and Development (OECD) over the last decades (OECD, 1978, 1997, 2004), and Chateau et al. (2011), who employ the OECD ENV-linkages model to simulate the effects of climate change policies on employment. In its 2004 report, the OECD also reviews the evidence of employment effects related to climate policies of OECD countries and draws some conclusions on the double-dividend hypothesis. Generally, the extent to which a double-dividend may be earned through environmental taxes depends largely on the already existing tax system of an economy. The interaction of environmentally related taxes with other taxes (e.g., replacement or reduction of taxes on labor through energy taxes) may then in total have a positive effect on employment. The OECD also points out that the current state of the labor market has to be considered before a meaningful evaluation of the double-dividend hypothesis can be undertaken.

Some studies on the employment effects of environmental or climate policies disregard economic feedback effects and mainly just determine if a number of jobs have directly been created in a particular (environmentally related) sector. More comprehensive studies employ some kind of theoretical model. Different models make different assumptions about the labor markets and the economic mechanisms at work; for example, just with respect to the processes at the labor market, one could employ a wage bargaining model, an efficiency wage model, or a job-matching model. In Chateau et al. (2011), OECD uses a computable general equilibrium model to estimate employment effects and finds evidence for the double dividend in its strong version for several OECD countries.

OECD (2004) roughly groups the economic models into (1) econometric models that are usually demand driven and allow for disequilibrium markets, (2) general equilibrium models that are based on simultaneous equilibria on all involved markets, and (3) partial equilibrium models. Most models assume exogenous technical change and exogenous and fixed preferences. Owing to the variety of assumptions that may still be altered, different results arise. However, the OECD can identify some general tendencies regarding the potential occurrence of a double dividend (OECD, 2004): "A strong double dividend cannot occur if the existing tax structure is revenue-optimal. If, as is likely in practice, the existing tax structure is not revenue-optimal, a strong double dividend will occur if the environmental tax reform moves the tax structure in the direction of revenue-optimality. In a situation with involuntary unemployment, employment will only increase if the use of environmental taxes to partially replace existing taxes results in an increased demand for labor. If the labor market is in equilibrium, additional employment could only be caused by increasing labor supply."

On a general level, no necessary or sufficient conditions can be found for when an increase in environmentally related taxes combined with a reduction in, for example, payroll taxes will increase employment—in addition to the first dividend stemming from the reduced externality and the improvement of the quality of life. Based on the study by Heady et al. (2000), OECD (2004) identifies the following factors that make the occurrence of a double dividend more likely. When there is involuntary unemployment, the prospects of increased employment are higher if:

1. The environmental tax can be passed on to factors that are inelastically supplied and relatively under-taxed.
2. Non-working households are large enough in numbers, and are significant as consumers of goods produced with the environmentally intensive inputs that are taxed.
3. Through international market power, the environmental tax can raise the price of goods produced with a relatively intensive use of the taxed environmental input.
4. Capital is relatively immobile internationally. In this case it can absorb some of the environmental tax and less of the tax burden falls on factors such as labor.
5. The elasticity of substitution between the environmental input and labor is greater than the elasticity of substitution between energy and capital.
6. The real wage rises little when unemployment falls, so that the reduction in the taxes on labor are not offset by wage rises.

When there is only voluntary unemployment, conclusions (1) to (4) still hold, but conclusions (5) and (6) are replaced by: The environmental tax is levied on goods that are more complementary to leisure in consumption than the goods whose taxes are reduced.

A very broad spectrum of econometric based literature on environmental policies and their employment effects exists. We concentrate here on major studies that discuss environmental policies that are or can be considered climate policies.

Several empirical studies have been conducted to analyze the double-dividend hypothesis for the US economy. Shackleton et al. (1992) make use of the DRI and LINK econometric macroeconomic models for the United States as well as of the Goulder and Jorgenson-Wilcoxen intertemporal general equilibrium model to answer this question. In all three modeling frameworks, they introduce a phased-in carbon tax accompanied by a cut in the personal income tax. In the framework of the Jorgenson-Wilcoxen model the revenue is recycled through a cut in the labor tax instead of a personal income tax reduction. In terms of welfare changes, the authors look only at the gross costs of the tax, that is, exclude the welfare gains that we have previously labeled environmental benefits. In the DRI and the LINK model, Shackleton et al. (1992) find positive gross costs of the tax, that is, welfare losses. These results do therefore not support the strong dividend claim. However, in the Jorgensen-Wilcoxen model, they find negative gross costs of the tax if the revenue is used to reduce labor taxes, hence supporting the strong dividend claim.

The reasons for the difference in these results are not entirely clear. Goulder (1995b) suspects that differences in the considerably higher marginal excess burden of capital taxation and the assumption of perfect capital mobility in the Jorgenson-Wilcoxen model are the causes for the different results.

The studies conducted by Goulder (1995a), Goulder (1994), and Shah and Larsen (1992) introduce a constant carbon tax or fossil fuel tax accompanied by reductions in the personal income tax rate. All three studies find positive gross costs of the implemented tax, casting further doubt on the strong double-dividend hypothesis in its strong form. Although these simulation results for the United States tend to not support the strong dividend claim there is no agreement on this issue, in particular because the sources of differences in the models are not entirely understood. Simulation results based on data of European economies tend to be a little bit more optimistic about the strong double-dividend.

Significant research on climate change has been done by the MIT Joint Program on the Science and Policy of Global Change. The Program integrates multidisciplinary expertise from the Center for Energy and Environmental Policy Research and the Center for Global Change Science and collaborates with other major research groups within and outside MIT.[2] At the heart of the Joint Program's work lies the MIT Integrated Global System Model (IGSM). This comprehensive tool analyzes interactions among humans and the climate system. The Emissions Prediction and Policy Analysis (EPPA) model is a component of the IGSM (see Babiker et al., 2001), which is also designed to evaluate the economic impacts of policies designed to limit GHG emissions. EPPA belongs to a class of economic simulation models known as computable general equilibrium (CGE) models. Babiker and Eckaus (2007) use the EPPA model to theoretically study the unemployment effects of restrictions on GHG emissions. A variety of research chapters focussing on different economic aspects of the climate change have been produced by the MIT Joint Program.[3]

Babiker and Eckaus (2007) allow for labor market rigidities, for example, limited mobility of labor among sectors, and thus include scenarios in which involuntary unemployment occurs. The authors simulate three different scenarios for the following labor market environments: (1) mobile labor and flexible wages; (2) sector specific labor, but flexible wages; (3) mobile labor, but rigid wages; and (4) sector specific labor and rigid wages. The three climate policy scenarios are: (1) no GHG policy restrictions (reference solution); (2) Kyoto-like emissions restrictions imposed, without any offsetting policies; and (3) Kyoto emissions restrictions, but with labor subsidies to offset the unemployment and economically depressing effects of those restrictions. These cases are similar to the first and second case in our chapter (carbon tax and carbon tax with wage subsidies).

Babiker and Eckaus (2007) are hesitant to give exact measures of the effects due to the limits of data and the EPPA model. However, they find similar but not identical empirical results as we do. Their analysis indicates that "there would be a real, direct depressing effect from the imposition of emissions restrictions." The employment effects they anticipate are expected to be only small but negative. The negative effects are caused mainly by a reduction in GDP growth under the implemented climate policies. Thus, in their modeling framework they cannot find support for the double-dividend hypothesis. They recommend that other policy measures, for example, wage subsidies, be implemented to mitigate negative employment effects of climate policies.

Several EU countries have introduced environmental tax reforms in the past years (see also Ekins and Speck, 2011). Most notably, Germany implemented its so called "ecological tax reform" in 1998, through which an energy tax was introduced and the tax revenue was used to subsidize wage cost. The reform gave reason to conduct several studies on the employment effects of the implemented policy measures. The most comprehensive studies were carried out by Bach et al. (2001) and Frohn, Chen, Hillebrand, Lemke, Lutz, Meyer, and Pullen (2003). The first study was conducted by the German Institute for Economic Research (DIW) on behalf of the German Federal Ministry of Finance ("Bundesministerium für Finanzen"). Both studies employ simulation models (PANTA RHEI, model system of RWI). The PANTA RHEI model is an econometric model for the German economy. It is a detailed multisectoral model covering 58 industrial branches. In PANTA RHEI, all parameters are estimated by econometric methods using time series of the input–output tables of the German economy. The model has a disaggregated energy and air pollution module. It is built for medium-term forecasts up to 2020. The methodology of PANTA RHEI, including empirical results, is also discussed in detail by Meyer et al. (1999) and Meyer (2005). Lutz and Meyer (2008) provide an overview of empirical studies about the effects of the German tax reform that have been conducted over the last years.

Strictly speaking, the German ecological tax reform was not targeted exclusively at achieving climate goals but, it was thought, to serving environmental and energy efficiency goals in general. Consequently, the cited studies analyze a broad variety of economic effects, not only employment. Nevertheless, we can gain some valuable insights on the employment effects of the policy measures, in particular since the tax reform was heavily promoted under the double-dividend hypothesis. Germany's ecological tax reform basically boils down to the introduction of energy taxes and an annualy increase of the already existing petroleum tax. The tax revenue has been used to subsidize social security contributions which are levied on labor, thereby reducing the effective wage cost. However, large exceptions from the energy tax exist for energy-intensive industries and air traffic.

The study by Bach et al. (2001) concludes that the eco tax will reduce Germany's growth only slightly (−0.1%) but will have a positive effect on employment and reduce CO_2 emissions. However, the latter two effects were also rather small and by no means sufficient to solve either the problem of climate change or the problem of high unemployment in Germany at that time. Due to these relative small effects, some economists have titled the German reform as an "eco-political fig leaf" (see Boehringer and Schwager, 2003).

The simulation of different scenarios in Frohn et al. (2003) confirm the results of Bach et al. (2001). All scenarios resulted in slightly positive employment effects and a small reduction of emissions. While the employment increase did not react very strongly to an increase in the tax rates and the abolishment of the eco tax exceptions, CO_2 emissions fell stronger in scenarios with higher tax rates and no exceptions from the eco tax. The highest reduction of CO_2 emissions was achieved in a scenario with a hypothetical CO_2 tax (as opposed to an energy tax). However, in this scenario, the still positive employment effect was the weakest and the decelerating effect on macroeconomic activity was the strongest. A switch from the current energy taxation to a CO_2 tax is endorsed by most authors. Besides different findings and criticism about the size of the "double-dividend" in the case of the German experiment, we can at least conclude that no cumulative negative effects on employment were found.

The Cambridge Econometric E3ME model uses a top-down, macroeconomic approach to study the competitiveness effects of a carbon tax at the European level (see Barker et al., 2009). The model focuses competitiveness effects and analyzes short- and long-term effects of price and wage rate changes in the six EU countries that formally implemented ETRs (Denmark, Germany, Netherlands, Finland, Sweden, and United Kingdom). Under the assumption of a carbon tax leading to an increase in energy prices, the model illustrates that such a policy would lead to a reduction in the demand for energy and ultimately to a reduction in carbon emissions. The largest emission reductions occur in countries with the highest tax rate. Moreover, all six countries witness an increase in GDP and national employment, despite some negative short-term transition effects. In some countries, employment even increases by as much as 0.5%.

Departing from the aforementioned literature on structural change, we propose in the following an econometric model with which we analyze the double-dividend hypothesis in its strong form. We suggest a multivariate time series approach utilizing data on employment, output, and CO_2 emissions of nine industrialized countries.

19.3 Data Description

In our model of structural change, we employ a German data set to identify high and low-carbon–intensive industries. Based on the German industry classification, we use employment and output data from the EU KLEMS database (http://www.euklems.net/index.html) to estimate in the form of a vector autoregression (VAR) a linear dynamic model of employment in high- and low-carbon industries.

The EU KLEMS database is the outcome of the EU KLEMS project which aims to create a database on measures of economic growth, productivity, employment creation, capital formation, and technological change at the industry level for all European Union member states from 1970 onwards and provides a systematic collection of industry-specific data. A detailed description of the contents and the construction of the EU KLEMS database can be found in O'Mahony and Timmer (2009). For the most part, data are comparable among countries. Mainly European countries are covered by the database but several other non-European economies such as the United States, Japan, or South Korea are also included.

Unfortunately, no data on environmental impacts of industries are included in EU KLEMS and these data (in particular data on CO_2 emissions) have to be taken from alternative sources. The level of disaggregation in EU KLEMS is for many countries by and large similar to common input–output tables and are therefore more or less compatible with information from input–output tables. However, no coefficients are provided by EU KLEMS so that computations that involve input–output coefficients have to be made on the basis of I/O tables and EU KLEMS together. This is not always possible or requires adjustment of data, in particular if the industries in one database do not match exactly with the industries in the other database.

We use data from German input-output tables (2005) to exemplarily generate the two sectors, a high carbon-intensive sector (HCIS), and a low carbon intensive sector (LCIS). German input-output tables are provided by the Federal Statistical Office ("Statistisches Bundesamt") and are available at a 71 sector level. In addition to traditional input–output tables, the German Federal Statistical Office provides industry-specific data on CO_2 emission in kilotonnes.

With these data, we calculate the CO_2-intensity of each industry measured in kilotons over gross output in million euros (direct CO_2 intensity). This ratio describes how many kilotons of CO_2 emissions a specific sector in the economy requires to generate €1 million of gross output. With the help of these key figures, we rank different industries according to their CO_2 intensity and classify industries in the two sectors (HCIS and LCIS). Industries whose carbon intensity per unit of output is above (below) the median are classified as belonging to the high–carbon intensity (low–carbon intensity) sector. Note that this grouping has been done on basis of the German CO_2 intensity data (2005), that is, the ranking of industries is identical for all countries analyzed.

The absolute level of CO_2 emissions as well as the absolute CO_2 intensity in a particular sector may of course differ among countries. This depends on the size of the industry, the technology used, the energy mix, and possibly on other factors. However, the relative position of an industry within a country can be expected to be roughly the same, especially among industrialized countries. Thus, energy-intensive manufacturing industries such as metals, coke, and mechanical wood and can be expected to be relatively high carbon intensive in any country. Since we have just two sectors (HCIS and LCIS), only changes in CO_2 intensities of industries around the median have an effect on the composition of the HCIS and LCIS in a country. Following an input–output modeling approach by Proops et al. (1993), we also calculated total CO_2 intensity. This method takes also the carbon intensity of inputs into account and produces therefore more accurate results on CO_2 productivity of certain industries. This alternative calculation did not, however, affect the industry composition of the two sectors, HCIS and LCIS.

As a next step, we use the industry time series data from EU KLEMS to determine the past growth of output and employment in the HCIS and the LCIS for nine industrialized countries. The countries examined are Germany, Australia, France, Hungary, Japan, South Korea, Sweden, the United Kingdom, and the United States. Table 19.1 summarizes the obtained sample.

19.3.1 Model

We specify a first-order, four-variable VAR model comprising high-carbon–intensity output, denoted by $OUT_{hi,t}$,low-carbon–intensity output ($OUT_{lo,t}$), high-carbon–

Table 19.1 Time Series: Employment and Output of HCIS and LCIS

No.	Country	Years	Observations
1	Germany	1992–2005	14
2	Australia	1989–2005	17
3	France	1978–2005	28
4	Hungary	1992–2005	14
5	Japan	1973–2005	33
6	South Korea	1970–2005	36
7	Sweden	1970–2005	36
8	United Kingdom	1970–2005	36
9	USA	1970–2005	36

intensive employment ($EMP_{hi,t}$) and low-carbon–intensive employment ($EMP_{lo,t}$). All variables in the VAR are specified in terms of annual growth rates (i.e., log–differences) and collected in a vector y_t, defined by

$$y_t = \begin{bmatrix} out_{hi,t} \\ out_{lo,t} \\ emp_{hi,t} \\ emp_{lo,t} \end{bmatrix} = \begin{bmatrix} \log OUT_{hi,t} - \log OUT_{hi,t-1} \\ \log OUT_{lo,t} - \log OUT_{lo,t-1} \\ \log EMP_{hi,t} - \log EMP_{hi,t-1} \\ \log EMP_{lo,t} - \log EMP_{lo,t-1} \end{bmatrix} \times 100$$

The first-order VAR is of the form

$$y_t = c + Ay_{t-1} + \varepsilon_t, \tag{19.1}$$

with disturbances ε_t satisfying $\mathrm{E}(\varepsilon_t) = 0$, and

$$\mathrm{Cov}(\varepsilon_t, \varepsilon_s) = \begin{cases} \Sigma, & t = s, \\ 0, & t \neq s, \end{cases} \tag{19.2}$$

with c and A being a constant parameter vector and matrix, respectively, and ε_t denoting the one-step-ahead prediction error. Table 19.2 shows summary statistics of the dataset for the United States with which we continue our discussion.

Multivariate least squares (MLS) estimation of the parameters yields the following results:

$$\hat{c}_{USA} = \begin{bmatrix} 1.25 \\ 3.25 \\ 0.54 \\ 0.58 \end{bmatrix}, \hat{A}_{USA} = \begin{bmatrix} 0.37 & 0.52 & 0.20 & -0.92 \\ 0.47 & 0.76 & -0.23 & -0.54 \\ -0.02 & 0.23 & 0.50 & -0.26 \\ -0.06 & 0.51 & 0.27 & -0.33 \end{bmatrix}, \hat{\Sigma}_{USA}$$

$$= \begin{bmatrix} 5.67 & 2.45 & 1.80 & 2.89 \\ 2.45 & 7.40 & 1.74 & 3.57 \\ 1.80 & 1.74 & 1.11 & 1.57 \\ 2.89 & 3.57 & 1.57 & 2.91 \end{bmatrix}.$$

Table 19.2 Summary Statistics (USA)

	$out_{hi,t}$	$out_{lo,t}$	$emp_{hi,t}$	$emp_{lo,t}$
Mean	2.47	3.09	1.39	1.72
$out_{hi,t}$	16.32	3.32	2.02	3.61
$out_{lo,t}$	0.39	11.00	2.11	5.04
$emp_{hi,t}$	0.65	0.51	1.52	2.30
$emp_{lo,t}$	0.68	0.72	0.89	4.39

Bottom panel: Variances (diagonal elements), covariances (above-diagonal elements), and correlations (below-diagonal elements)

With the eigenvalues of $\hat{A}_{USA}$ being $0.2164 \pm 0.5489i$, 0.5322, and 0.3444, and the moduli being 0.59, 0.5322 and 0.3444, the estimated system is stable.

For the t-ratios, we obtain:

$$T_{USA} = \begin{bmatrix} 1.58 & 1.64 & 2.50 & 0.24 & -1.39 \\ 3.59 & -1.82 & 3.20 & -0.24 & -0.72 \\ 1.55 & -0.24 & 2.53 & 1.36 & -0.90 \\ 1.03 & -0.38 & 3.41 & 0.45 & -0.71 \end{bmatrix}$$

We have the choice between d.f. $= KT - K^2p - K$ and d.f. $= T - Kp - 1$ for the number of degrees of freedom, whereby K denotes the number of variables and T the sample size. In the case of the United States, we have d.f. $= 116$ or d.f. $= 29$. For a two-tailed t-test at the 5% level, we get critical values between 2.048 and 2.365, indicating that several coefficients are not significant under this criterion.

The coefficients of the variable $out_{lo,t}$ are all significant at the 5% level for d.f. $= 29$.

Clearly, in view of the the data limitations, higher than first-order VARs cannot be estimated. However, given that we work with annual data, a first-order VAR should be sufficient for a principal approximation of the employment–output dynamics.

We continue the analysis here with the U.S. data. The estimatation results for all other countries are provided in the conclusion.

19.4 Policy Response Analysis

To investigate dynamic dependencies among the variables and to assess the consequences of policy measures we conduct a response analysis with the estimated model. Specifically, we derive impulse responses as well the responses to specific policy measures. The policy measures at hand are a tax on the consumption of high-carbon–intensive goods and a subsidy on the consumption of low-carbon–intensive goods.

Impulse response functions generally indicate how the endogenous variables respond to external influences. In a VAR model, where all variables are endogenous, the only external inputs are the disturbances, which amount to one-step-ahead prediction errors. They are "innovations" or "surprises," such as "policy shocks," that cannot by explained by the model and past data. We translate the instrument of a carbon tax into a negative growth shock for the HCIS while a subsidy for the LCIS is interpreted as a positive growth shock to all industries in this sector.

Using the lag operator, L, defined by $Ly_t = y_{t-1}$, we can express the VAR process (19.1) as $A(L)y_t = \varepsilon_t$,[4] with $A(L) = I - AL$. The infinite moving average representation, given by

$$y_t = A^{-1}(L)\varepsilon_t = \tilde{C}(L)\varepsilon_t, \qquad \mathrm{Cov}(\varepsilon_t) = \Sigma,$$

captures the responses of the y–variables with respect to the prediction errors, ε_t. Here, $\tilde{C}(L) = \tilde{C}_0 + \tilde{C}_1 L + \tilde{C}_2 L^2 + \ldots$ is, in general, a matrix polynomial of infinite order.[5] The i, j-element of $\tilde{C}_k$, $\tilde{c}_{k,ij}$, can be interpreted as the change in the ith component in y_{t+k} due to a unit shock in the jth innovation in vector ε_t at time t.

However, the prediction error ε_{jt} is not necessarily uniquely associated with a shock to y_{jt} in the same period. To have a unique association we have to make sure that the shocks are uncorrelated. In linear VAR analysis, this can be achieved by regarding ε_t as being some linear combination of "structural" shocks, denoted by u_t, such that

$$\varepsilon_t = R u_t. \tag{19.3}$$

A common strategy is to obtain the Choleski decomposition of the covariance matrix of the prediction errors, Σ, that is,

$$\Sigma = RR',$$

where R is a lower triangular matrix with positive diagonal elements. Transformation $u_t = R^{-1}\varepsilon_t$ is also called an *orthogonalization* of the prediction errors, because the components of u_t are uncorrelated and have unit variance, that is, $\text{Cov}(u_t) = I$, since

$$\text{E}(u_t u_t') = \text{E}[R^{-1}\varepsilon_t \varepsilon_t'^{-1})'] = R^{-1}\Sigma(R^{-1})' = I.$$

Interpreting vector u_t as the structural innovations driving the process, that is,

$$y_t = \tilde{C}(L)\varepsilon_t = \tilde{C}(L)Ru_t = C(L)u_t.$$

the *structural impulse response function* can be derived from the moving average coefficients by

$$C_k = \tilde{C}_k R. \tag{19.4}$$

Note that the derivation of the structural shocks, u_t, via Choleski decomposition places specific assumptions on the contemporaneous influence of the structural shocks on the endogenous variables. In our specification, with ordering $y_t = (out_{hi,t}, out_{lo,t}, emp_{hi,t}, emp_{lo,t})'$, a lower-triangular R implies that structural shocks to high-carbon–intensive output immediately affects hight-carbon–intensive output, low-carbon–intensive output, high-carbon–intensive employment, and low-carbon–intensive employment. A shock to the low-carbon–intensive sector output has, however, no simultaneous impact on the high-carbon–intensive sector, which reacts only with a delay of one period, but has an immediate effect on high-carbon–intensive and low-carbon–intensive employment.

Our estimates for VAR–coefficient matrix A, given above, and R,

$$\hat{R}_{USA} = \begin{bmatrix} 2.3817 & 0 & 0 & 0 \\ 1.0317 & 2.5179 & 0 & 0 \\ 0.7559 & 0.3836 & 0.6283 & 0 \\ 1.2145 & 0.9203 & 0.4872 & 0.5982 \end{bmatrix}$$

give rise to the impulse responses, $\hat{C}, k = 0, 1, \ldots 10$, shown in Figure 19.1. Clearly, in view of the small sample size, the results reported here can only be indicative. Interval estimation and significance testing, prevented by sample-size limitations, would be required for more definite conclusions. However, rather than producing erratic responses, as is often the case if the number estimated parameters is very high relative to the number of observations, response analysis discussed below yields smooth and plausible response estimates.

The plots indicate that all endogenous variables respond to impulses over a period of about five years at most, after which they decay to zero. In the following, we briefly discuss the point estimates of the unit-impulse responses, that is, the responses due to positive growth shocks with a size of 1%.

For a 1% shock to output of the high-carbon–intensive sector we have the following responses. It has only an immediate impact on the sector itself; there is almost no effect after 1 year and beyond. The low-carbon–intensive sector also experiences a simultaneous benefit in that it grows by about 0.2%, an effect that becomes negative after 1 year and then decays after 2 to 3 years. Employment in both sectors increases

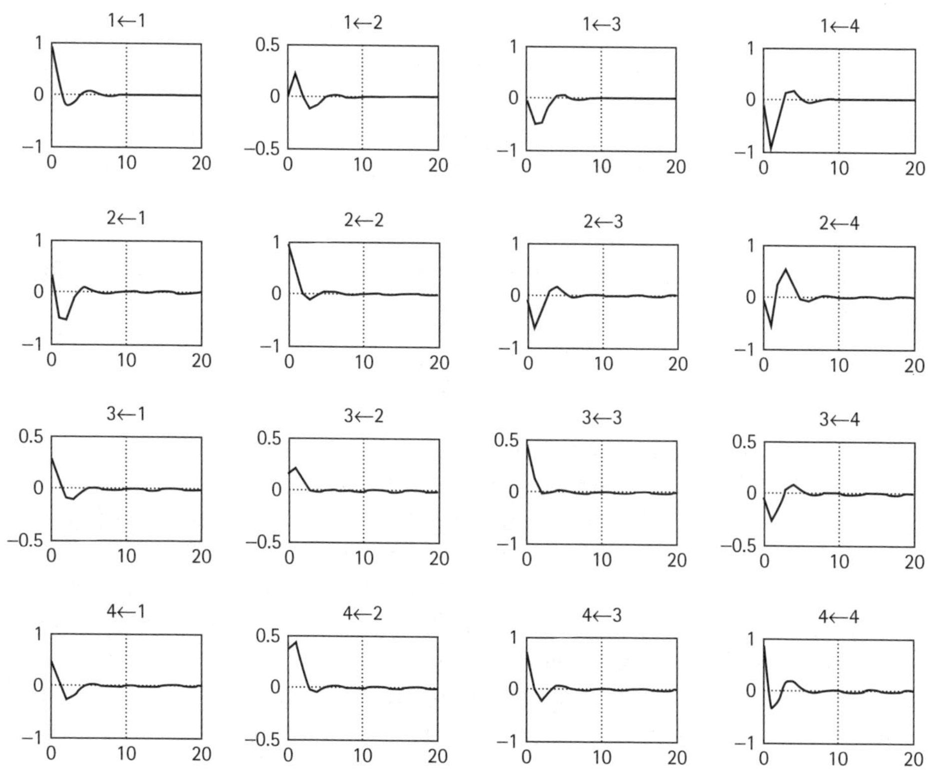

FIGURE 19.1 Impulse-response functions from the estimated VAR model (1) with $y_t = (out_{hi,t}, out_{lo,t}, emp_{hi,t}, emp_{lo,t})'$. The graph with heading "$i \longleftarrow j$" shows the response of the ith variable in y_t due to an unit impulse to structural shock j.

after 1 year by 0.3% in the HCIS and by 0.5% in the LCIS; this effect vanishes after three to five years.

A shock to the output in the LCIS has, due the identification restrictions in place, no immediate impact on the high-carbon–intensive sector, but causes the high-carbon–intensive sector to grow by about 0.21% after 1 year, by 0% after 2 years, by −0.12% after 2 years, and virtually no effect after that. The impact on the low-carbon–intensive sector itself remains positive for the first 2 years, after which it vanishes. Employment in the HCIS sector increases slightly by 0.15% in the year of the shock and then increases to 0.21% in the second year. The positive response drops to zero at year four and thereafter. The effect of the shock on employment in the LCIS is similar but with an increased growth of 0.36% in the first year and 0.42% increase in the second year slightly stronger.

A shock to employment in the HCIS lowers output growth in the high-carbon–intensive (low-carbon–intensive) sector by about 0.5% (0.65%) after 1 year. The negative consequences disappear after approximately 4 to 5 years. After the initial shock, high-carbon–intensive employment growth quickly returns to zero after 2 years.the second year and zero thereafter. The impact on employment in the LCIS is quite strong, with 0.77% in the first year but the decays to zero after.

A shock to employment in the LCIS lowers output growth in the high-carbon–intensive (low-carbon–intensive) sector by about 0.92% (0.54%) after 1 year. The negative consequences disappear after 2 years in both sectors. After the initial shock, high-carbon–intensive employment growth becomes slightly negative and then positive before the effect dies out after 2 to 3 years. The low-carbon–intensive employment growth becomes slightly negative after the initial shock and then positive before it decays to zero after 4 to 5 years.

To assess the cumulative effects, Figure 19.2 shows the cumulative-response functions, computed by

$$\bar{C}_k = \sum_{i=0}^{k} C_i.$$

The cumulative long-term effect of a 1% shock to high-carbon–intensive sector growth are as follows. The cumulative response of the high-carbon–intensive sector itself remains virtually at the initial shock level (0.94%); the low-carbon–intensive sector experiences a decrease of about 0.6%; and employment in both sectors reacts with positive growth of about 0.2% (HCIS) and 0.14% (LCIS) cumulatively. Thus, the effect on employment growth is slightly stronger in the high-carbon-intensive sector. A shock to the low-carbon–intensive growth induces basically no cumulative high-carbon–intensive growth; the low-carbon–intensive sector itself responds with an increase of about 1.49%; and employment in both sectors responds positively, with growth of about 0.5% (HCIS) and 0.94% (LCIS).

The cumulative long-term effects of an employment shock to the HCIS are negative on output in both sectors with about −1.0% and −0.7%. In terms of employment, the initial 1% shock increases to 1.4% employment growth in the high-carbon–intensive

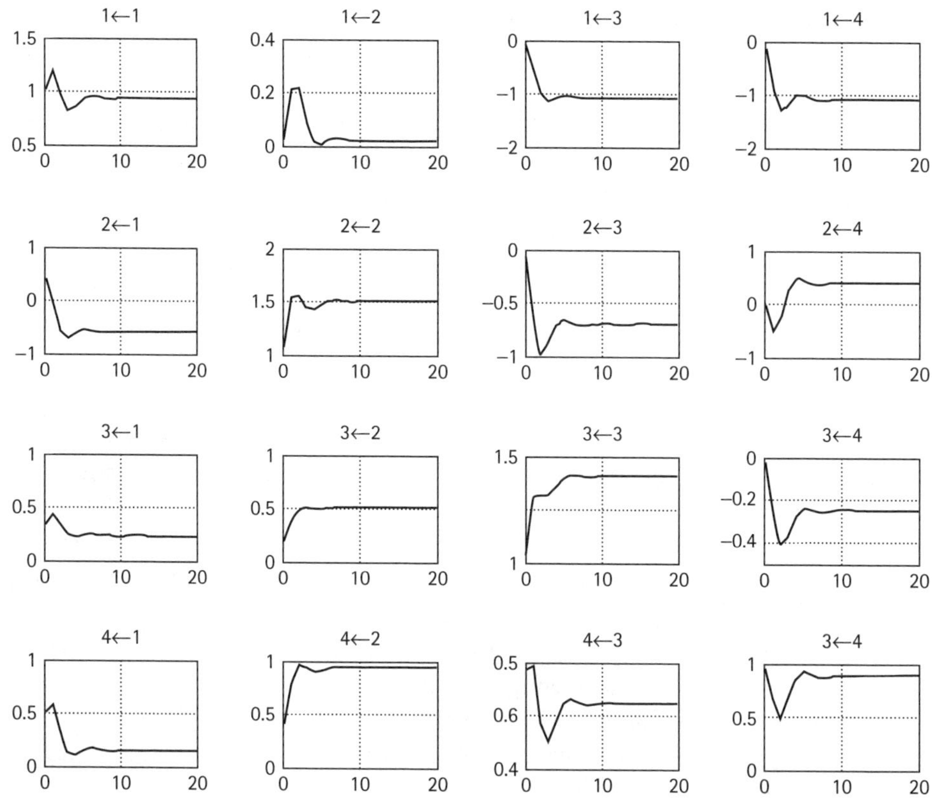

FIGURE 19.2 Cumulative-response functions from estimated VAR model (1) with $y_t = (out_{hi,t}, out_{lo,t}, emp_{hi,t}, emp_{lo,t})'$. The graph with heading "$i \longleftarrow j$" shows the response of the ith variable in y_t due to an unit impulse to structural shock j.

sector and to 0.6% in the low-carbon–intensive sector. Finally, a shock to employment in the LCIS results in cumulative responses of −1.0% output growth in the high-carbon–intensive sector and 0.37% in the low-carbon–intensive sector. Employment in the HCIS is negatively affected by this shock (− 0.25%). Cumulative employment growth in the LCIS itself is about 0.9%.

19.4.1 Policy Experiments

19.4.1.1 Carbon Tax and Subsidy

We start with the case in which a tax is levied on the goods of the high-carbon–intensive sector and a subsidy is paid on the consumption of low-carbon–intensive goods. We are interested in the effects of such a policy on employment and output.

Within the scope of impulse-response analysis, we model such a policy as a particular policy shock which combines a positive shock to the LCIS sector by granting, for example, some form of subsidies or tax relief, with a negative shock to the high-carbon–intensive sector by a reduction of existing subsidies or by imposing additional taxes, such that the latter finances the former. Specifically, we calculate the cumulative effects on employment in both sectors by shifting the amount equivalent to 1% of the gross output (base year 2005) of the HCIS from the HCIS to the LCIS. In the case of the United States, this amounts to a tax or subsidy cut in the amount of EUR 86.5 billion (in real 1995 US$) which is imposed on the HCIS and immediately transferred to the LCIS. The relief of the LCIS could come in the form of a tax cut, a direct subsidy, or some other type of direct or indirect support to the low-carbon–intensive sector. We cannot distinguish specific policy instruments with our method.

Technically, we impose a simultaneous one-time growth shock on both sectors: The output growth of the HCIS is reduced by 1% in the period of the shock and the output growth rate of the LCIS is boosted with a growth rate equivalent to the collected tax revenue from the HCIS (generally not 1%). In level terms, such a nonrecurring growth shock results in a permanent increase (decrease) of output in the LCIS (HCIS). Thus, our policy experiment assumes that the policy is upheld for all years after the shock, that, for example, the tax on the HCIS and the corresponding subsidy to the LCIS is permanent, and not abolished after the first year.

The cumulative effect of such a combined shock on employment, as shown in Figure 19.3, is positive. Employment growth is negative in the first year in both sectors but becomes positive quickly with about 0.75% in the LCIS and close to 0.25% in the HCIS. The growth effect on total employment lies at roughly 0.47% and is reached in less than 5 years.

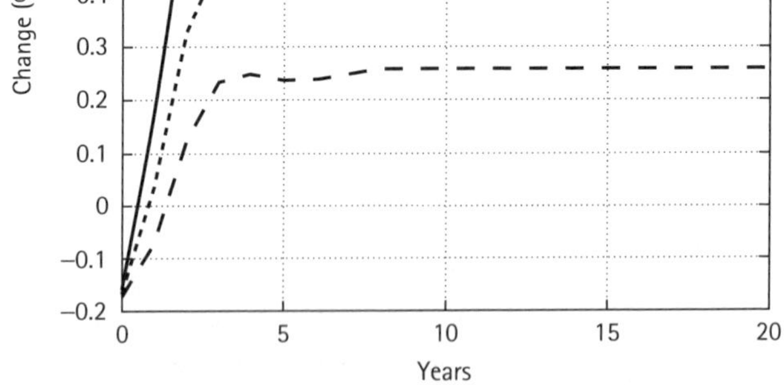

FIGURE 19.3 Cumulative response of aggregate employment and sector employment due to an instantaneously budget-neutral policy shock.

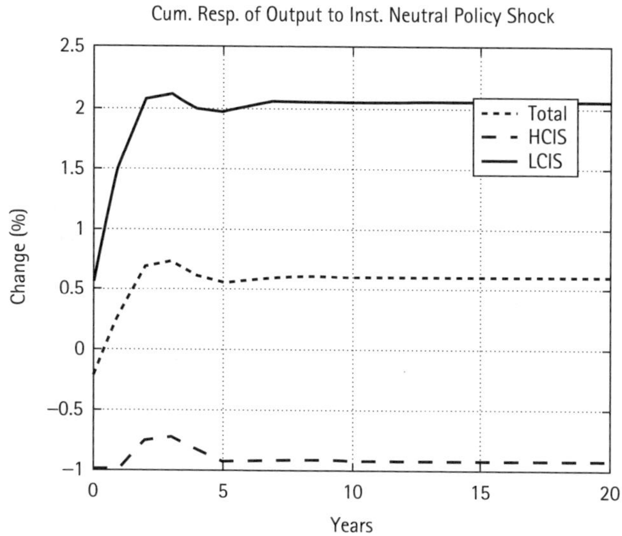

FIGURE 19.4 Cumulative response of aggregate output and sector due to an instantaneously growth–neutral policy shock.

Another question is whether the positive effect on employment is accompanied by a long–run drop in gross output. This, however, is not the case, as the cumulative joint response estimates (shown in Figure 19.4) indicates. Total gross output drops initially by about 0.2%, but increases within two years to over 0.5%. As one may expect, the output growth of the HCIS remains negatively affected by our policy while the additional output growth of the LCIS is more than 2% higher after 5 years than in the business-as-usual (BAU) scenario. Thus, the policy promotes or accelerates a structural change toward a low-carbon–intensive economy.

It should be emphasized that these cumulative growth effects are relative to the BAU: A reduction of growth by 1% in the HCIS after 5 years means that the total output growth in the HCIS after 5 years is approximately 1% lower than in a scenario in which no policy is implemented. A 1% reduction after 5 years translates into an annual reduction of growth of about 0.2%. The actual annual growth rate in the HCIS can still be positive but would be 0.2% lower if the policy is introduced.

In summary, our response analysis suggest that green policies, which favor the US low-carbon–intensive sector at the expense of the high-carbon–intensive sector, result in both, employment and output growth. Note again that the policy is strictly budget-neutral and finances itself. The results for the other countries are presented at the end of the appendix and in Section 19.4.2. We can, however, not observe the positive effects on total output and total employment for all countries.

19.4.1.2 Carbon Tax—No Subsidy

As a next case, we discuss the scenario of a carbon tax that is levied on the HCIS. This time, no subsidy is given to the LCIS. Technically, we shock the system by imposing a negative growth shock on output of the HCIS. The cumulative response of employment is given in Figure 19.5. We can see that the positive impact on employment that we could observe in the previous case disappears. Employment in both sectors decreases. In total, we estimate a reduction of employment of roughly 0.4% as compared to the BAU.

Figure 19.6 shows the cumulative joint response estimates on gross output in both sectors as well as on total output. As in the case of employment, the effects on output vary. In the HCIS, output is reduced by almost 1% as compared to the BAU but output increases by approximately 0.6% in the LCIS. Total gross output can be expected to be almost 0.4% lower than in the BAU.

It is essential to keep in mind that in this policy scenario of an isolated negative growth shock to the HCIS, we have burdened one sector without injecting anything back into the system. This explains the negative results compared to the previous policy experiment. In case of a tax, one may expect that the government uses the collected tax revenues for some purpose. This activity by the government may be stimulating growth in one or the other sector. This aspect is neglected here. However, these results also stress the importance of additional mitigating policies as an implemented carbon tax by itself—even if only imposed on one sector—has negative effects on output and employment.

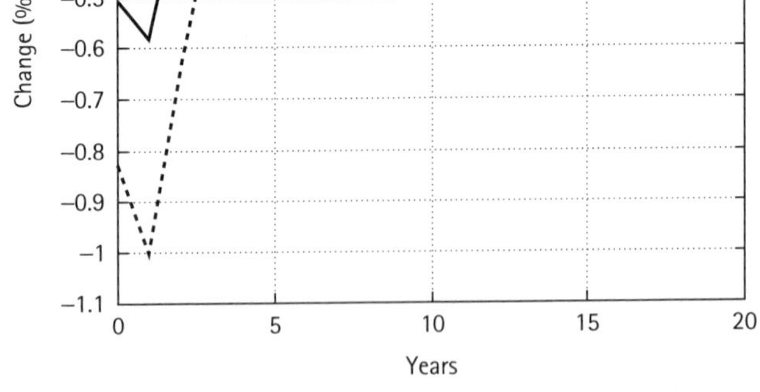

FIGURE 19.5 Cumulative response of aggregate employment and sector employment due to a an isolated policy shock on the HCIS only.

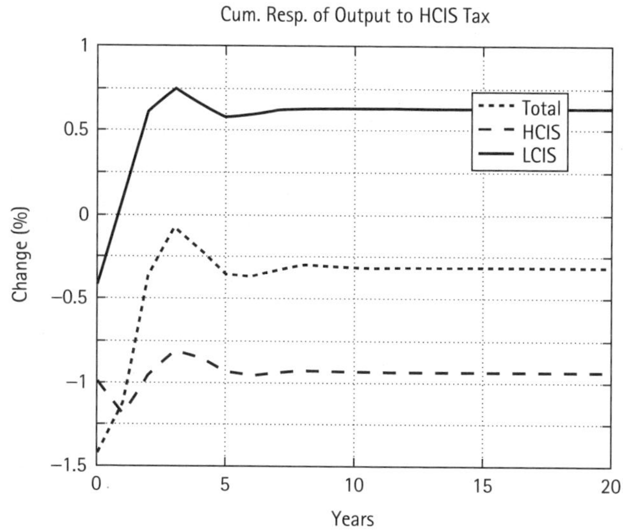

FIGURE 19.6 Cumulative response of aggregate output and sector output due to a an isolated policy shock on the HCIS only.

19.4.1.3 Carbon Tax and Wage Subsidy

Finally, we estimate the effects of a shock on the HCIS if a wage subsidy is given to both sectors. As noted previously, our method does not allow for an estimation of effects of *specific* policy instruments as, for example, a wage subsidy. We can, however, account for a general wage subsidy by adjusting the shock size for both sectors. We assume that the wage subsidies are entirely financed through the tax levied on the HCIS. Furthermore, we assume that the subsidy is distributed between the two sectors according to the relative size of the two sectors in terms of employment. Thus, in addition to the 1% negative output growth shock on the HCIS, we impose two simultaneous positive growth shocks on both sectors that correspond in total size to the negative shock (budget neutrality) and are allocated according to the relative size of employment in the two sectors. Thus, some portion of the 1% negative shock on the HCIS is mitigated and the positive shock on the LCIS depends on the relative size of LCIS employment.

We depict the cumulative response of employment in Figure 19.7 and output in Figure 19.8. One can clearly see in both graphs that this budget-neutral policy scenario is just a linear transformation of case 1 whereby the strength of the shock vector is scaled down. The effects are therefore similar to case 1 but are less strong.

19.4.2 Overview of Country Results

In the following, we present an overview of the results of our impulse response analysis for all nine countries examined. Detailed statistics for all countries can be found in

Table 19.3 Employment and Output Data on the Industry Level

No.	Country	Years	Observations
1	Germany	1992–2005	14
2	Australia	1989–2005	17
3	France	1978–2005	28
4	Hungary	1992–2005	14
5	Japan	1973–2005	33
6	South Korea	1970–2005	36
7	Sweden	1970–2005	36
8	United Kingdom	1970–2005	36
9	USA	1970–2005	36

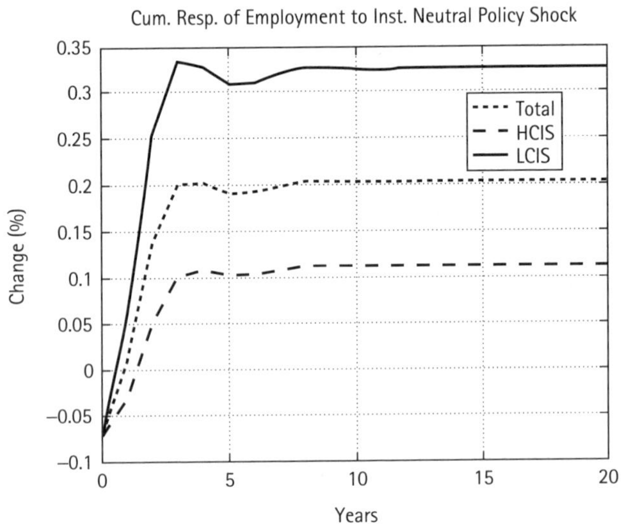

FIGURE 19.7 Cumulative response of employment due to a tax on the HCIS and wage subsidies to both sectors.

the appendix. We focus on case 1 (carbon tax and a subsidy) because it is a budget-neutral policy and the skimmed tax revenues are reinjected back into the economy. Table 19.5 shows the effects on total real gross output and employment *relative* to the BAU scenario after 5 years and Table 19.5 summarizes the effects after 10 years. We note that the results basically do not change anymore after 5 years. Our policy has no further impact on output and employment. In the discussion, we therefore refer only to Table 19.5.

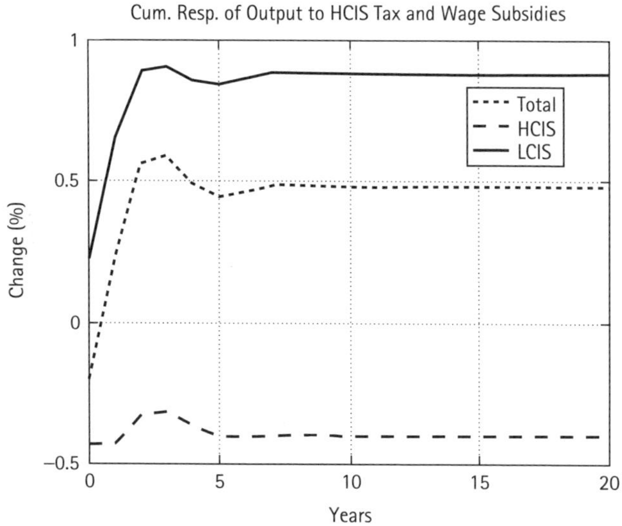

FIGURE 19.8 Cumulative response of output due to a a tax on the HCIS and wage subsidies to both sectors.

We can see that the results of the policy differ among countries. Consistently, output growth is boosted in the LCIS while it is slowed down in the LCIS. At this point, we remind ourselves that the growth rates given in tables are to be interpreted as deviations from the total growth of the BAU scenario. The actual growth rates can be positive or negative (For output at least, we would usually assume to have positive growth rates over 5 years.) We observe slight total output growth for some countries and slight negative total output growth for others. Overall, the imposed climate policiy does not have a huge effect on total gross output and total employment. Exceptions are Australia and Hungary. In Australia, the policy leads to a decrease of output growth in the amout of approximately 1% (corresponds to an annual gross output decrease of about 0.2%) and decrease in employment of about 1.6%. (annual decrease of about 0.32%). An opposite situation is found in Hungary, where the climate policy boosts the economy by 2.31% in terms of gross output (annual increase of about 0.46%) and an increase of employment growth of more than 0.9% (annual increase of about 0.18%).

In general, we can also oberve that additional output growth and additional employment growth usually move into the same direction, that is, these growth rates are either both positive or both negative. This is, however, not true for individual sector output and employment growth. Here we can see that sometimes positive gross output growth is accompanied by negative employment growth. This occurs in both the HCIS and the LCIS. In most countries, a 1% change of output growth in LCIS has a less strong effect on employment than a 1% change of output growth in the HCIS, suggesting that the average labor productivity in the LCIS sector is higher than in the HCIS. We can see

Table 19.4 Real Employment and Output Effects (%) Relative to BAU after 5 Years—Carbon Tax and Subsidy

No.	Country	HCIS employm. growth	LCIS employm. growth	Total employm. growth	HCIS output growth	LCIS output growth	Total output growth
1	Germany	0.29	0.08	0.19	−0.36	0.90	0.36
2	Australia	−1.41	−2.26	−1.63	−1.79	0.42	−0.98
3	France	0.00	0.32	0.15	−1.02	1.08	0.09
4	Hungary	1.20	2.83	1.90	−0.11	4.52	2.31
5	Japan	−0.18	−0.56	−0.35	−1.04	0.20	−0.40
6	South Korea	−0.19	−0.44	−0.27	−0.73	0.69	−0.12
7	Sweden	−0.48	−0.13	−0.33	−0.34	0.99	0.35
8	United Kingdom	−0.12	−0.03	−0.08	−1.19	0.24	−0.45
9	United States	0.24	0.72	0.45	−0.93	1.97	0.55

Table 19.5 Real Employment and Output Effects after 10 Years (%) Relative to BAU—Carbon Tax and Subsidy

No.	Country	HCIS employm. growth	LCIS employm. growth	Total employm. growth	HCIS output growth	LCIS output growth	Total output growth
1	Germany	0.28	0.07	0.18	−0.37	0.88	0.34
2	Australia	−1.41	−2.26	−1.63	−1.79	0.42	−0.99
3	France	0.01	0.26	0.11	−1.03	0.96	0.02
4	Hungary	1.25	2.81	1.92	−0.09	4.53	2.33
5	Japan	−0.18	−0.56	−0.35	−1.05	0.21	−0.40
6	South Korea	−0.19	−0.45	−0.27	−0.74	0.69	−0.12
7	Sweden	−0.48	−0.13	−0.33	−0.35	0.98	0.34
8	United Kingdom	−0.12	−0.03	−0.08	−1.19	0.24	−0.45
9	United States	0.26	0.75	0.47	−0.92	2.04	0.59

this nicely in the cases of France and South Korea, where the absolute value of the output growth effect in the HCIS and the LCIS are approximately the same. In France, the policy shock leads to an additional +1.08% of output growth in the LCIS and −1.02% in HCIS. Yet, employment in HCIS remains unaffected while employment growth in the LCIS is increased by only 0.32%. This means that labor productivity must have increased in the LCIS while it decreased in the HCIS.[6] In South Korea, the situation is similar, with almost identical changes of output in absolute terms for both sectors (HCIS −0.73%, LCIS +0.69%). Again, employment in the LCIS, responds not very strongly to the output increase in LCIS, resulting again in a higher labor productivity increase in the LCIS. In the HCIS, the decrease of output of 0.73% is accompanied by an employment decrease of "only" 0.19%, implying a decrease of average labor productivity in the HCIS. The same phenomenon can be observed for the HCIS and LCIS in all other countries. Such a decrease of labor productivity in the HCIS could occur if highly productive industries reduce their output strongly and lay off workers who then work in less productive industries within the HCIS.

We must keep in mind that we are dealing with gross output and not value added or GDP. So, the ratio output over labor might not serve well as a good indicator for labor productivity. Value added would be more appropriate. However, an estimation of average labor productivity in the HCIS and the LCIS by taking value added over engaged workers confirms the above results: The LCIS is on average more productive than the HCIS. The positive total employment effects that we found for several countries (Germany, France, Hungary, and the United States) must therefore come from the higher growth dynamics of the LCIS that are triggered by the policy shock. In all cases with positive employment growth, the shock kicked off a much stronger positive growth dynamic in the LCIS than it slowed down growth in the HCIS. This effect overcompensates the effect of higher labor productivity on total employment and results in a positive net effect on employment. Implementing policies that support the LCIS obviously support the more productive sector in the economy.

In summary, we find that the chosen double shock does not have a huge impact on the total level of output and employment. For the most part, structural adjustments are triggered and not reductions of economic activity as a whole. In several countries, like the United States or Hungary, we can see positive effects on total economic activity that are a little stronger than being closely around zero. For Australia, the effects are also somewhat stronger but on the negative side. The reasons for these differences on an individual country level not quite clear at this point. It is such asly that also the initial condititions (for example, sizes of the HCIS and LCIS in terms of output and employment) at the time of the shock or the differing sample sizes play a role.

19.5 Conclusion

Given the great urgency to implement effective climate policies to reduce global warming, a dynamic model with structural change and, related to that, concrete policy proposals of CO_2 emissions have been developed in this contribution. We consider three types of policies: (1) imposing a carbon tax on carbon-intensive industries, (2) imposing a carbon tax and subsidizing labor (or reducing overhead cost for labor), and (3) imposing a carbon tax and subsidizing the less carbon-intensive industries. We study the dynamics of output and employment resulting from each of these policy measures and their effects on structural change. To do so the carbon intensities of industries are computed and the empirical effects of policy measures are studied. The actual empirical evaluation of the carbon tax policies is undertaken by a double-sided VAR. As intuition might suggest, the least favorable outcome is obtained when only a carbon tax rate is imposed on carbon-intensive industries and the revenue not used for other purposes such as reducing other tax rates, subsidizing a wage or payroll tax, or the development of other (less carbon intensive) products. Since our our proposed double-sided VAR allows us to permit budgetary neutrality we study the cases when the revenue is used for other purposes. The empirical results show that in particular the third policy measure where carbon taxes are used to subsidize the development of other products has the greatest net gains in terms of output and employment.

Appendix

Samaan (2014) discusses a three-sector growth model that allows for structural change on a balanced growth path. Consumption goods are either high-carbon–intensive and are produced by the high-carbon–intensive sector (H), or they are low-carbon–intensive and are produced by the low-carbon–intensive sector (L). The third sector is the capital goods sector, whose carbon intensity is not further considered. In the baseline version of the model, that is, without climate change policies, a representative household chooses an optimal consumption path according to its preferences described by a CRRA (constant relative risk aversion) utility function:

$$U_t = \int_0^{\infty} e^{-\rho t} \frac{\left[H_t^{\beta} L_t^{\theta}\right]^{1-\sigma} - 1}{1-\sigma} dt \qquad (19.5)$$

where the parameters $\rho, \beta, \theta, \sigma$ are all strictly positive.

The three sectors have identical, neoclassical production functions with constant returns to scale. Two production factors (capital and labor) exist and technical change is assumed to be labor augmenting. Under the conditions of perfect competition, it can then be shown that the per-efficiency labor budget constraint is equal to:

$$\dot{k}_t + \left(g_t + \delta\right) k_t + P_H h_t + P_L l_t = B_K F(k_t, 1). \qquad (19.6)$$

The household consumption choice can be transformed into a dynamic constrained optimization problem: Maximization of (19.5) subject to (19.6), after rewriting the utility function using per-efficiency-labor variables.

Solving this problem gives us the time paths of output and employment of the three sectors. It is shown in the chapter, that the implementation of different climate change policies (the three policy scenarios corresponding to the ones in this chapter) lead to balanced growth paths in which the relative sizes of the two sectors H and L change. Output and employment shares in the H sector decrease over time while output and employment in the L sector increase.

Acknowledgments

Earlier versions of this chapter were presented at the International Institute for Labour Studies at ILO, Geneva, at the 36th Annual Meetings of the Eastern Economic Association, Philadelpia, February 2010, "The Economics of Climate Change" conference at the the New School hosted by SCEPA, New York, April 2010 and at Manchester University in July 2010. The paper was also discussed at the Meeting of the Task Force on Global Warming organized by Joe Stiglitz in July 2010. We thank all participants for the comments provided.

Notes

1. We limit the discussion to the reduction of CO_2 emissions because CO_2 emissions account by far for the largest portion of GHG and most other GHG are accounted for in terms of CO_2 equivalents in available statistics.
2. See http://globalchange.mit.edu/index.html
3. See http://globalchange.mit.edu/pubs/reports.php
4. To simplify the notation, we omit the constant term, c, as it does not enter the dynamics of the process.
5. We use superscript ε to refer to response coefficients and with respect to the prediction error.
6. We are loosely interpreting the ratio of gross output over employment as "labor productivity" here.

References

Anderson, S., and Ekins, P. eds. (2009). *Carbon Energy Taxation—Lessons from Europe.* Oxford: Oxford University Press.

Babiker, M., and Eckaus R. S. (2007). Unemployment effects of climate policy. *Environmental Science and Policy, 10,* 600–609.

Babiker, M. H., Reilly J. M., Mayer, M., Eckaus, R. S., Wing, I. S., and Hyman, R. C. (2001). The MIT emissions prediction and policy analysis (EPPA) model: Revisions, Sensitivities, and comparisons of results. Report No. 71, MIT Joint Program on the Science and Policy of Global Change.

Bach, S., Bork, C., Kohlhaas, M., Lutz, C., Meyer, B., Praetorius, B., and Welsch H. (2001). *Die oekologische Steuerreform in Deutschland–Eine modellgestuetzte Analyse ihrer Wirkungen auf Wirtschaft und Umwelt.* Heidelberg: Springer Verlag.

Barker, T., Junankar, S., Pollitt, H., and Summerton P. (2009). The effects of environmental tax reform on international competitiveness in the European Union: Modelling with E3ME, In *Carbon Energy Taxation–Lessons from Europe,* pp. 147–215. Oxford: Oxford University Press.

Boehringer, C., and Schwager, R. (2003). Die Oekologische Steuerreform in Deutschland: Ein umweltpolitisches Feigenblatt. *Perspektiven der Wirtschaftspolitik, 4*(2), 211–222.

Bovenberg, L., and de Mooij, R. (1994). Environmental levies and distortionary taxation. *The American Economic Review, 84*, 1085–1089.

Bovenberg, L., and van der Ploeg, F. (2002). Consequences of environmental tax reform for involuntary unemployment and welfare. In *Handbook of Public Economics*, Vol. 3, pp. 1471–1545. Amsterdam: Elsevier.

Carraro, C., Galeotti, M., and Gallo, M. (1996). Environmental taxation and unemployment: Some evidence on the double dividend hypothesis in Europe. *Journal of Public Economics, 62*(1–2), 141–181.

Chateau, J., Saint-Martin, A., and Manfredi, T. (2011). Employment impacts of climate change mitigation policies in the OECD—A general equilibrium perspective," Discussion paper. Paris: Organisation for Co-operation and Development.

Cherney, H. (1960). Patterns of industrial growth. *American Economic Review, 50*, 624–654.

Clark, C. G. (1940). *The Conditions of Economic Progress.* London: MacMillan.

Dales, J. (1968). *Pollution, Property and Prices.* Toronto: University of Toronto Press.

Ekins, P., and Speck, S., eds. (2011). *Environmental Tax Reform—A Policy for Green Growth.* Oxford: Oxford University Press.

Fisher, A. G. (1935). *The Clash of Progress and Security.* London: MacMillan.

Frohn, J., Chen, P., Hillebrand, B., Lemke, W., Lutz, C., Meyer, B., and Pullen, M. (2003). *Wirkungen umweltpolitischer Massnahmen—Abschaetzung mit zwei oekonometrischen Modellen.* Heidelberg: Physica-Verlag.

Fuchs, V. (1968). *The Service Economy.* New York: Columbia University Press.

Goulder, L. H. (1994). Energy taxes: Traditional efficiency effects and environmental implications. In *Tax Policy and the Economy 8*, pp. 105–158. Cambridge, MA: MIT Press.

Goulder, L. H. (1995a). Effects of carbon taxes in an economy with prior tax distortions: An intertemporal general equilibrium analysis. *Journal of Environmental Economics and Management, 29*, 271–297.

Goulder, L. H. (1995b). Environmental Taxation and the "double dividend": A reader's guide. *International Tax and Public Finance, 2*(2), 157–183.

Greiner, A., and Semmler, W. (2008). *The Global environment, natural resources and economic growth.* Oxford: Oxford University Press.

Greiner, A., Gruene, L., and Semmler, W. (2010). Growth and climate change: Thresholds and multiple equilibria. *Dynamic Modeling and Econometrics in Economics and Finance, 12*, 63–77.

Hansen, J. (2008). Tipping point: Perspective of a climatologist. In *In State of the Wild 2008–2009: A Global Portrait of Wildlife, Wildlands, and Oceans*, pp. 6–15. Washington, DC: Island Press.

Heady, C. J., Markandya, A., Blyth, W., Collingwood, J., and Taylor, P. G. (2000). Study on the Relationship between Environmental/Energy Taxation and Employment Creation. Final Report, Prepared for The European Commission, Directorate General XI.

IPCC (2007). *IPCC Fourth Assessment Report: Climate Change 2007.* In B. Metz, O. Davidson, P. Bosch, R. Dave, and L. Meyer (eds.). Intergovernmental Panel on Climate Change, United Nations. Cambridge, UK, and New York: Cambridge University Press.

IPCC (2013). *IPCC Fifth Assessment Report: Climate Change 2013.* Intergovermental Panel on Climate Change, United Nations.

IPCC (2014). *Climate Change 2014: Mitigation of Climate Change.* Contribution of Working Group III to the Fifth Assessment Report of the Intergovernmental Panel on Climate Change. In Edenhofer, O., R. Pichs-Madruga, Y. Sokona, E. Farahani, S. Kadner, K. Seyboth, A. Adler, I. Baum, S. Brunner, P. Eickemeier, B. Kriemann, J. Savolainen, S. Schlömer, C. von Stechow, T. Zwickel and J.C. Minx (eds.). Cambridge University Press, Cambridge, United Kingdom and New York, NY, USA.

Kaldor, N. (1957). A model of economic growth. *The Economic Journal, 67*, 591–624.

Kaplow, L. (2008). *The Theory of Taxation and Public Economics.* Princeton, NJ: Princeton University Press.

Kuznets, S. (1957). Quantitative aspects of the economic growth of nations: II. *Economic Development and Cultural Change, 5*, 3–111.

Lutz, C., and Meyer, B. (2008). Modellgestuetzte Simulationsrechnungen der GWS zu Energie- und Klimaschutzfragen. GWS Discussion Paper 2001/1 ISS 1867-7290.

Mankiw, N. G. (2007). One answer to global warming: A new tax. *The New York Times*, July 16, 2007.

Meyer, B. (2005). The Economic-Environmental model PANTA RHEI and its application. Paper presented at the Congress "Environment and Science–Concepts and Strategic Goals for the Future", April 9–11, 2005, Tokyo. GWS Discussion Paper 2005/3, Osnabrück.

Meyer, B., Bockermann, A., Ewerhard, G., and Lutz, C. (1999). *Marktkonforme Umweltpolitik–Wirkungen auf Luftschadstoffemissionen, Wachstum und Struktur der Wirtschaft.* Heidelberg: Physica-Verlag.

Nielsen, S., Pedersen, L., and Sorensen, P. (1995). Green tax reform, unemployment and endogenous growth. *International Tax and Public Finance, 2*, 185–205.

Nordhaus, W. (2008). *A Question of Balance—Weighing the Options on Global Warming Policies*, pp. 148–165. New Haven & London: Yale University Press.

OECD (1978). *Employment and Environment.* Paris: Organisation for Economic Co-operation and Development.

OECD (1997). *Environmental Policies and Employment.* Paris: Organisation for Economic Co-operation and Development.

OECD (2004). *Environment and Employment—An Assessment.* Paris: Organisation for Economic Co-operation and Development.

O'Mahony, M., and Timmer, M. P. (2009). Output, input and productivity measures at the industry level: The EU KLEMS database. *The Economic Journal, 119*, 374–409.

Palmer, K., Oates, W., and Portney, P. (1995). Tightening environmental standards: The benefit-cost paradigm or the no-cost paradigm. *Journal of Economic Perspectives, 9*, 119–132.

Pasinetti, L. (1981). *Structural Change and Economic Growth: A Theoretical Essay on the Dynamics of the Wealth of Nations.* Cambridge, UK: Cambridge University Press.

Pearce, D. (1991). The role of carbon tax in adjusting to global warming. *The Economic Journal, 101*(407), 938–948.

Pigou, A. C. (1920). *The Economics of Welfare.* London: Macmillan.

Porter, M. E. (1990). *The Competitive Advantage of Nations.* London: Macmillan.

Proops, J. L., Faber, M., and Wagenhals, G. (1993). *Reducing CO_2 Emissions—A Comparative Input-Output Study for Germany and the UK.* Berlin, Heidelberg, New York: Springer Verlag.

Samaan, D. (2014). *Climate Change Policies and Structural Change—An Empirical Analysis of Employment Impacts*, pp. 77–99. Saarbrücken, Germany: Scholar's Press.

Shackleton, R., Shelby, M., Cristofaro, A., Brinner, R., Yanchar, J., Goulder, L., Jorgenson, D., Wilcoxen, P., Shackleton, P. P., Shelby, M., and Cristofaro, A. (1992). The efficiency value of carbon tax revenues. Discussion Paper. U.S. Environmental Protection Agency.

Shah, A., and Larsen, B. (1992). Carbon taxes, the greenhouse effect and developing countries. Discussion Paper. Washington, DC: The World Bank.

Stern, N. (2007). *The Economics of Climate Change: The Stern Review.* Cambridge, UK: Cambridge University Press.

Uzawa, H. (2003). *Economic Theory and Global Warming.* Cambridge, UK: Cambridge University Press.

van der Linde, C. (1993). The micro-economic implications of environmental regulation: A preliminary framework. Discussion paper. Paris: Organisation for Economic Co-operation and Development.

Weitzman, M. L. (2009). On modeling and interpreting the economics of catastrophic climate change. *Review of Economics and Statistics, 91*(1): 1–19.

CHAPTER 20

MACROECONOMIC EFFECTS OF RENEWABLE ENERGY AND ENERGY EFFICIENCY POLICIES WITH A FOCUS ON GERMANY

CHRISTIAN LUTZ AND ULRIKE LEHR

20.1 INTRODUCTION AND BACKGROUND

ENERGY efficiency measures and the promotion of renewable energy (RE) sources are two of the main pillars of the German and European Union (EU) energy concept. The German government decided in autumn 2010 on its new energy concept (BMU, BMWi, 2010). Key components have been 8–14 year lifetime extension for nuclear power plants and the need for further measures to foster RE and energy efficiency. On the demand side, insulation of buildings is the most important of a number of measures. For the electricity sector, the continued expansion of partly fluctuating RE sources, such as wind and photovoltaic (PV) power generation, calls for new market design. Feed-in tariffs for RE sources will remain at least until 2020, but have to be adjusted to enforce the market entry of renewables.

The central targets of the new energy concept are to reduce greenhouse gas (GHG) emissions by 40% by 2020, 55% by 2030, 70% by 2040 and 80–95% by 2050 (compared with 1990 levels). By 2020, the share of renewables in final energy consumption is projected to reach 18%, and then gradually increase further to 30% by 2030 and 60% by 2050. The share in electricity production is targeted to reach 80% by 2050. Concerning energy efficiency, the new energy concept aims to reduce primary energy consumption by 20% by 2020 and 50% by 2050 compared to 2008. The building renovation rate has doubled from the current 1% to 2%. It is planned to cut energy consumption in the transport sector by around 10% by 2020 and around 40% by 2050 (BMU, BMWi, 2010).

In light of the nuclear disaster in Japan in March 2011, the German government defined higher security standards for nuclear power plants. As eight older reactors could not be retrofitted to meet these higher standards, they were shut down in the spring of 2011. The remaining nine reactors will be closed step by step until 2022. Additional measures for RE generation and energy efficiency will have to fill the gap. But the changes made in 2011 are marginal in the long term and in the overall economic perspective of the new German energy concept. The major decisions were made in 2010.

Europe has committed to a 20% reduction of total primary energy supply (TPES) by 2020 compared to a business-as-usual development (COM, 2008b). This efficiency target is part of a comprehensive energy concept (COM, 2008a). In January 2008 the commission passed a note to the EU parliament with the title "20, 20 and 20 by 2020," which includes the commitment for a reduction of GHGs to 20% below the 1990 level and a 20% share of RE in total energy consumption by 2020. These targets are intertwined, as the share of RE depends on the denominator and the reduction of GHGs is strongly dependent on energy consumption. Therefore, energy efficiency is a key to reach these goals, as has been pointed out by the Communication by the Commission to the European Parliament "Energy 2020" (COM, 2010). Though the political agenda seems set, the effectiveness of policy incentives for efficiency measures is still well disputed.

Energy efficiency plays a very important role in the development and potential reduction of final energy use. Taylor et al. (2010) show the historic development in International Energy Agency (IEA) countries. For the future, the IEA (Jollands et al., 2010) recommends energy efficiency policies in 25 fields as part of the G8 Gleneagles Plan of Action, which could make a very significant contribution to energy savings and global carbon emission reductions. The authors highlight key barriers that prevent the implementation of economic, that is, cost-effective measures and necessary conditions to fully exploit them. The barriers to exploit these potentials have been traced to lack of information, lack of financing instruments, transactions costs, low priority of energy issues, incomplete markets for energy efficiency, and other factors (IEA, 2012). National studies show positive economy-wide effects of energy efficiency measures (see, e.g., Wei et al., 2010 for the United States and Kuckshinrichs et al., 2010 for Germany).

In the literature, several attempts have been made to estimate the potential for energy saving. The Intergovernmental Panel on Climate Change (IPCC, 2001) found that cost-effective energy efficiency, that is, efficiency measures with payback periods smaller or equal to the lifetime of the equipment, could halve GHG emissions by 2020. A wide range of technologies and options has been identified: for instance, the general use of fluorescent lamps could save approximately 2880 PJ and 470 Mt CO_2 emissions in 2010. For heating and cooling of buildings, the potential cost-effective savings are estimated at 20 EJ on a global level per year by 2030. The IEA (2012) frequently highlights the importance of energy efficiency improvements to reach the 2°C target.

However, the economy-wide perspective of energy efficiency measures is still an open question (Guerra and Sancho, 2010). Could the so-called rebound effect work partly or fully against the energy savings? Computable general equilibrium (CGE), modeling experiments have been undertaken for several countries such as Sweden, China, Kenya, Sudan, Scotland, the United Kingdom, and Japan. Rather recent findings for Scotland are presented by Hanley et al. (2009), who apply a CGE model and find high rebound effects growing into backfire. Guerra and Sancho (2010) propose an unbiased measure for the economy-wide rebound effect combining input–output analysis and CGE modeling. Barker et al. (2007) present results for United Kingdom. They use a times-series econometric model and find moderate rebound effects. Our findings show similar effects for the German case study using a comparable modeling approach.

The positive impacts of an increasing share of RE on the mitigation of climate change as well as on reduced energy import dependency are indisputable. However, such are currently still the additional costs of heat and electricity generation from most renewable energy sources (RES). Additional investment in RES will obviously induce economic activity and employment. Recent studies often focus on these gross employment impacts. They show the importance of the RE industries concerning employment and other economic factors. Wei et al. (2010) apply a spreadsheet-based model for the United States that synthesizes data from 15 job studies. Cetin and Egrican (2011) find positive job impacts of solar energy in Turkey. They build their analysis on international literature, which is also positive about job impacts. Situational analyses, such as Delphi (2007), account for the past development of employment in the RE sector. The annual publication of the RE status report (REN 21, 2011) or the annual update by O'Sullivan et al. (2010, 2011) fall under this category.

Another type of paper applies econometric methods to analyze the past relation between the RE industry or the use of RES and economic development. A cross-country econometric study by Apergis and Payne (2010) reveals a possible correlation between RES investment and economic growth for a panel of Organisation for Economic Co-operation and Development (OECD) countries for the years 1985 to 2005. Fang (2011) also reports a positive correlation between RES and GDP growth for China in the period 1978 to 2008 based on econometric analysis. Mathiesen et al. (2011) analyze a long-term shift of the Danish energy system toward RES and find a positive impact on economic growth.

Frondel et al. (2010), however, doubt positive employment impacts of RES increase driven by the German feed-in-tariff in the long run. They argue that higher cost for RES will be "counterproductive to net job creation." They highlight the importance of international market developments. Especially for PV, they conclude that because of high import shares the net employment impact of German PV promotion will be negative. They build on earlier studies such as Hillebrand et al. (2006), who concluded that RES promotion will have positive net employment impacts in the short run due to RES installations, which will turn negative in the long run because of the long-term costs of the feed-in tariff, which guarantees fixed tariffs for up to 20 years.

Studies on the net employment impacts of the promotion of RES take also negative impacts into account. The comprehensive EMLPOY-RES study (ISI, 2009) for the EU Commission applies two complex models, ASTRA and NEMESIS, for calculating the net impacts. Though showing some differences in detail, both models report positive GDP and employment net effects of advanced RES deployment of the EU in comparison to a no policy reference scenario. These net impacts are significantly smaller than the gross impacts.

A study for Germany based on the econometric model SEEEM suggests overall positive net economic and employment effects of the expansion of RES in Germany (Blazejczak et al., 2011). The German feed-in tariff under the regime of which the share of RES in electricity consumption increased from below 5% in 1998 to 20% in 2011 will still play a major role in this development, but it is intended to make the future expansion of renewables more cost efficient. The further integration of more and more RES is challenging, as the electricity market design has to be adapted to cope with the growing share of fluctuating RES and to give the right price signals for non-fuel–based electricity generation.

Therefore, the overall balance of positive and negative effects under different possible future development pathways of fossil fuel prices, global climate policies, and global trade is of interest. To account for all effects in a consistent framework, the econometric input–output model PANTA RHEI is used. The economic impact of RES expansion and energy efficiency is measured via the comparison of economic indicators such as gross domestic product (GDP) and employment from different simulation runs. Overall positive net effects can be seen for instance as higher employment in one simulation run compared with the other. The model consistently links energy balance data to economic development on the sector level. It is enlarged by detailed data on 10 RES technologies based on comprehensive survey data. Based on bottom-up models economic energy efficiency measures have been identified. They are included in the model in the ambitious efficiency scenario.

This chapter presents recent results of economy-wide impact of energy efficiency and RE measures in Germany, which both build on the economy–energy–environment model PANTA RHEI. This contribution is organized as follows: First the concept of net economic impacts as a result of economy–energy–environment models is discussed. The model is introduced in Section 20.3. Results for energy efficiency scenarios are presented in Section 20.4, while Section 20.5 reports results for RE. In Section 20.6 results are discussed and some conclusions drawn. It also includes some methodological aspects and differences of measuring economic impacts of energy efficiency and RE.

20.2 Net Economic Effects

Macroeconomic impacts of energy and climate policy are often derived from complex model simulations. Examples include the EU decision on the 20–20–20 package in 2008 (COM, 2008a) as well as the German energy concept, which also builds on scenario analyses. Model results show the net economic impacts in form of changes of major economic indicators such as GDP, investment, and employment. In the discussion about employment effects of the increase of RE, gross and net impacts are not always precisely defined. Gross employment measures the overall importance of RE for the labor market, which obviously increases with growing investment in RE. For policy analysis net effects should be taken into account.

Production, installation, operation, and maintenance of windmills, solar modules, biomass power plants, or heating systems as well as biogas and solar thermal applications have a positive short-term investment effect on the respective industries (Figure 20.1). Operation and maintenance have a smaller long-term effect. International demand for RE technologies increases employment in these sectors. The German wind industry, for instance, makes up to 70% of its 2009 turnover from exports. Hydro energy and solar modules also exhibit high export shares in their respective turnover.

Negative impacts on the economy stem from two different sources: first, investment in RE technologies substitutes investment in fossil fuel technologies such as coal fired power plants, oil-fired heating systems and maybe at some future point gasoline-driven cars. This crowding-out or substitution effect leads to lower production in the respective economic sectors.

The second negative effect is larger than the substitution effect and is induced by the additional costs of RE systems. As most RE systems are still more expensive than conventional systems, feed-in tariffs, quota systems, or tax cuts are applied in many countries, which increase either electricity prices or are financed via public budgets.

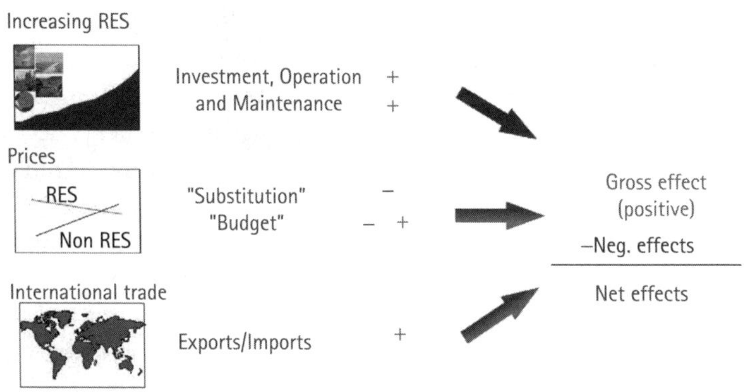

FIGURE 20.1 Economic effects of an RES increase on the labor market. Source: Lehr et al. (2011, p. 195).

This so-called budget effect (Figure 20.1) reduces the available budget for other expenditures, resulting in job losses in the respective sectors. The effects on employment of different scenarios for RE expansion have been analyzed in Lehr et al. (2008, 2012). The budget effect can work in either direction, as high PV electricity production during midday already avoids price peaks. With the further reduction of production costs and the better integration of RES into the electricity system, the average of future budget effects will tend to become less negative or even turn positive in the long run. As higher electricity prices may endanger international competitiveness of electricity intensive companies, those companies are widely exempt from the feed-in tariff in Germany.

Positive and negative impacts can induce additional indirect impacts throughout the economy (so-called second round effects): additional employment results in additional expenditure on consumption and additional jobs in the respective sectors as well as additional taxes and therefore increases in the governmental budget. Negative impacts affect the economy through the same channels. For calculation of the net effects a model of the total economy has to be applied.

Although the debate about net and gross impacts of energy efficiency measures is less vivid than for RE, the same arguments have to be taken into account in principle.

20.3 Model PANTA RHEI

The economy–energy–environment model PANTA RHEI is at the core of our methodological approach. PANTA RHEI (Lutz et al., 2005; Lehr et al., 2008; Meyer et al., 2012) is an environmentally extended version of the econometric simulation and forecasting model INFORGE (Meyer et al., 2007; Ahlert et al., 2009). A detailed description of the economic part of the model is presented in Maier et al. (2012). For a description of the whole model see Lutz (2011). Among others it has been used for economic evaluation of different energy scenarios that have been the basis for the German energy concept in 2010 (Lindenberger et al., 2010; Nagl et al., 2011). Recent applications include an evaluation of green ICT (Welfens and Lutz, 2012), and employment impacts of RE promotion (Lehr et al., 2012). A similar model with the same structure for Austria (Stocker et al., 2011) has recently been applied to the case of sustainable energy development in Austria until 2020. The paper gives very detailed insight into the model philosophy and structure.

The behavioral equations reflect bounded rationality rather than optimizing behavior of agents. All parameters are estimated econometrically from time series data (1991–2008). Producer prices are the result of mark-up calculations of firms. Output decisions follow observable historic developments, including observed inefficiencies rather than optimal choices. The use of econometrically estimated equations means that agents have only myopic expectations. They follow routines developed in the past. This implies, in contrast to optimization models, that markets will not necessarily be in an optimum and nonmarket (energy) policy interventions can have positive economic impacts.

The core of PANTA RHEI is the economic module, which calculates final demand (consumption, investment, exports) and intermediate demand (domestic and imported) for goods, capital stocks, and employment, wages, unit costs, and producer as well as consumer prices in deep disaggregation of 59 industries. The disaggregated system also calculates taxes on goods and taxes on production. The corresponding equations are integrated into the balance equations of the input–output system.

Value added of the different branches is aggregated and gives the base for the system of national accounts (SNA) that calculates distribution and redistribution of income, use of disposable income, capital account, and financial account for financial enterprises, nonfinancial enterprises, private households, the government, and the rest of the world. Macro variables such as disposable income of private households and disposable income of the government as well as demographic variables represent important determinants of sectoral final demand for goods. Another important outcome of the macro SNA system is net savings and governmental debt as its stock. Both are important indicators for the evaluation of policies. The demand side of the labor market is modeled on industry level. Wages per head are explained using Philips curve specifications. The aggregate labor supply is driven by demographic developments.

An integral element of input–output modeling is the determination of intermediate demand between industries. Input coefficients represent the relation of intermediate demand to total production. In the economic part technological change is identified by applying variable input coefficients. They are endogenously determined with relative prices and time trend. The Leontief-inverse $(I-A)^{-1}$—with A as input coefficient matrix and I as identity matrix—multiplied with final demand fd gives gross production y by 59 industries. In the following equations the notations are as follows: lowercase letters are vectors, and uppercase letters are either time series or matrices. The dimension of vectors and matrices are indicated with subscripts. The subscript t indicates time dependency.

$$y_t = (I - A_t)^{-1} \cdot fd_t \tag{20.1}$$

Private consumption patterns by 41 purposes of use c as a function of real disposable income Y/P and relative prices p/P are estimated. For some consumption purposes, trends t as proxy for long-term change in consumption behavior or the number of private households HH is used as an explanatory variable.

$$c_{l,t} = c_{i,t}\left(\frac{Y_t}{P_t}, \frac{p_{l,t}}{P_t}, t, HH_t\right) \quad l \in [1, \ldots, 41] \tag{20.2}$$

Gross fixed capital formation is separately modeled for equipment and construction investment. Equipment investments by 59 industries are determined by estimating capital stock k, which again is a function of production y of the previous year, costs of production factor labor l, autonomic technological change t, and real interest rates IR.

$$k_{i,t} = k_{i,t}\left(y_{i,t-1}, l_{i,t}, t, IR_t\right) \quad i \in [1,\ldots,59] \tag{20.3}$$

Export demand is kept constant in current prices, as similar energy and climate policy developments are assumed for the main competitors.

Prices are estimated econometrically. Basic prices p, which are decisive for entrepreneurs, are the result of unit costs uc and markup pricing. The extent to which markup pricing can be realized depends on the market form prevailing in specific industrial sectors. In industries with monopolistic structures, markup pricing is easier to realize than in competitive industrial structures. Industries will also consider import prices pim if they are exposed to foreign competitors as well.

$$p_{i,t} = p_{i,t}\left(uc_{i,t}, pim_{i,t}\right) \quad i \in [1,\ldots,59] \tag{20.4}$$

The labor demand functions depend on the number of hours employees work (volume of work). This approach builds on two important observations: first, a volume-based approach to labor demand considers the growing importance of part-time employees; second, labor policy instruments such as short-time work, for example, can be explicitly addressed. Working hours h are determined by sector-specific production y. In some industries real wages ae/p are also influential.

$$h_{i,t} = h_{i,t}\left(\frac{ae_{i,t}}{p_{i,t}}, y_{i,t}\right) \quad i \in [1,\ldots,59] \tag{20.5}$$

Average earnings are determined by using a Phillips curve approach (a graphic description of the inverse relationship between wages and unemployment levels). Accordingly, average earnings by industry ae depend on the one hand on tariff wages AE (e.g., in machinery) and on the other hand on sector-specific productivity y/h.

$$ae_{i,t} = ae_{i,t}\left(AE_t, \frac{y_{i,t}}{h_t}\right) \quad i \in [1,\ldots,59] \tag{20.6}$$

The number of employees e is derived by definition, dividing the number of working hours h by working time per year and head hy. The latter is preset exogenously.

$$e_{i,t} = \frac{h_{i,t}}{hy_{i,t}} \cdot 1000 \quad i \in [1,\ldots,59] \tag{20.7}$$

The energy module describes the interrelations between economic developments, energy consumption, and related emissions. The relations are interdependent. Economic activity such as gross production of industries or final consumer demand influence respective energy demand. Vice versa, the expenditure for energy consumption has a direct influence on economic variables.

The energy module contains the full energy balance with primary energy input, transformation, and final energy consumption for 20 energy consumption sectors,

27 fossil energy carriers, and the satellite balance for RE (AGEB, 2011). All together, the energy balances divide energy consumption into 30 energy carriers. Prices, also in euro per energy unit, are modeled for different energy users such as industry, services, and private households for all energy carriers. The energy module is fully integrated into the economic part of the model.

Final energy consumption of industries *fe* is explained by sector output *y*, the relation of the aggregate energy price *pe*—an average of the different carrier prices weighted with their shares in the energy consumption of that sector—and the sector price *p* and time trends, which mirror exogenous technological progress.

$$fe_{i,t} = fe_{i,t}\left(y_{i,t}, \frac{pe_{i,t}}{p_{i,t}}, t\right) \quad i \in [1,\ldots,59] \tag{20.8}$$

For services, the number of employees turned out to be a better proxy for economic activity than gross output. Average temperatures also play a role for the energy consumption of the service sector. For private households, consumption by purpose as heating or fuels is already calculated in the economic part of the model in monetary terms. Additional information can be taken from stock models for transport and heating from the specific modules, as only new investments in cars or houses, or expensive insulation measures will gradually change average efficiency parameters over time.

Final demand fed of energy carrier k for industries can be calculated by definition, multiplying the share of the carrier *sfe* with overall final energy demand of the sector. For the shares, the influence of relative prices, the price of energy carrier *k* in relation to the weighted price of all energy inputs of the sector, and of time trends are econometrically tested.

$$sfe_{k,t} = sfe_{k,t}\left(\frac{pe_{k,t}}{p_{k,t}}, t\right) \quad i \in [1,\ldots,59] \tag{20.9}$$

$$fed_{k,t} = sfe_{k,t} \cdot fe_{k,t} \quad k \in [1,\ldots,30] \tag{20.10}$$

Energy carrier prices *pe* depend on exogenous world market prices *pw* for coal, oil and gas, and specific other price components such as tax rates *tr* and margins *mr*. For electricity different cost components such as the assignment of the feed-in tariff for electricity are explicitly modeled.

$$pe_{k,t} = pe_{k,t}\left(pw_t, tr_{k,t,}, mr_{k,t}\right) \quad k \in [1,\ldots,30] \tag{20.11}$$

For services, households and transport specific prices are calculated, as, for example, tax rates partly differ between end users.

For energy-related carbon emissions *ce*, fix carbon emission factors *cef* from the German reporting (UBA, 2011) to the United Nations Framework Convention on Climate Change (UNFCCC) are applied. Multiplication with final energy demand *fe* gives sector and energy carrier specific emissions.

$$ce_{i,k,t} = cef_{i,k,t} \cdot fe_{i,k,t} \quad i \in [1,\ldots,59]; k \in [1,\ldots,30] \tag{20.12}$$

All detailed information in the energy balance for 30 energy carriers is consistently aggregated and linked to the corresponding four industries of the input–output table. For RES additional cost structure detail is used (see Lehr et al., 2008, 2012). This ensures that changes of international energy prices or tax rate changes and associated changes in energy volumes are fully accounted for in the economic part of the model.

To examine the economic effects of additional efficiency measures and increasing shares of RE in Germany our analysis applies PANTA RHEI to a set of scenarios and compares the resulting economic outcomes. The reference scenario is taken from the energy scenarios for the German energy concept (Prognos, EWI, GWS, 2010), which also made use of the PANTA RHEI model.

20.4 Energy Efficiency in Germany

The case study analyzes the impact of additional efficiency measures on the German economy. For this purpose, a set of efficiency measures and their additional costs have been identified. They are compared to a reference scenario (Lindenberger el al., 2010), which also assumes substantial energy efficiency increase (see Figure 20.2). The ambitious efficiency scenario includes a set of 43 additional measures accounting for about 12% of final energy consumption in 2030. These measures consist of a combination of attainable energy reduction and the necessary investment in more efficiency (for a similar approach see Sorrell, 2009 and Jollands et al., 2010).

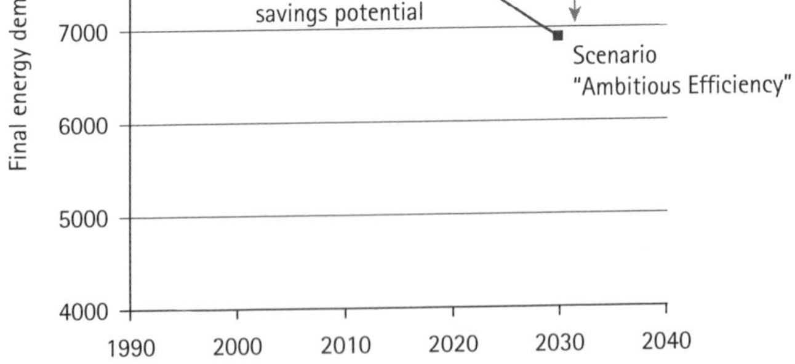

FIGURE 20.2 Final energy demand in different scenarios. Source: Ifeu et al. (2011, p. 20).

In the following we focus on economic efficiency potentials, that is, no-regret measures, which are cost-effective over the lifespan of the equipment. This definition includes the necessary investment for fuel-efficient technologies, new motors, etc. The ambitious efficiency scenario is constructed bottom up for households, trade and services, industry, and transport (see Ifeu et al., 2011 for technical details).

Additional investment of €301 billion until 2030 is necessary to tap the outlined potentials (see Table 20.1). The largest part of this sum will be necessary for insulation and other improvements of buildings as well as other energy savings in the household and transport sector (€120 billion each). Again, households contribute to this potential, but more than 50% of new vehicles, and especially the expensive ones, are bought as company cars or official cars.

To evaluate the impacts of political instruments or of certain measures, the results of the reference scenario are compared to the results of the ambitious efficiency scenario including additional efficiency measures. Effects on prices and quantities are taken into account. Here the additional measures consist of all cost-effective measures described in Ifeu et al. (2011). The ambitious efficiency scenario is characterized by investment in improved efficiency and savings on the energy bill. The additional spending enters the model as investment in equipment and buildings as well as consumption expenditures. Depreciation, annual interest payments, and savings reductions to finance the investment are fully included in the model. Owing to the cost-efficiency of measures, additional expenditure and investment will not crowd out other investments or consumption. Energy savings and the decrease in energy costs are fully accounted for in the model.

The sum of the economy-wide net effects is positive (see Table 20.2). Gross production and GDP, and its components consumption, investment, and trade, are higher in the efficiency scenario owing to the efficiency measures over the whole simulation period up to 2030. Obviously, higher production does not directly translate into higher value added, because it is partly imported and also increases imported inputs according to the German trade structure. A large share of the additional GDP (€22.8 billion in 2030) stems from private consumption (€16.2 billion). Overall imports are €3.8

Table 20.1 Additional Investment Compared to Reference Scenario

	Investment until 2030 in billion Euro
Total	**301**
Private households	120
Tertiary sector	54
Industry	8
Transport	120

Source: Ifeu et al. (2011), p. 22.

Table 20.2 Economic Impacts of "Ambitious Efficiency" against "Reference"

	Deviation		Percentage deviation	
	2020	2030	2020	2030
GDP in billion €constant pr.	17.4	22.8	0.7	0.8
Consumption	10.3	15.6	0.8	1.1
Investment	10.5	10.7	2.2	1.9
Exports	0.4	0.6	0.0	0.0
Imports	3.8	4.1	0.3	0.3
Deflators of pr. consumption	−0.20	−0.43	−0.16	−0.32
Employment in 1000	122.0	127.0	0.3	0.3

billion higher than in the reference in 2030, although energy imports are reduced significantly. The direct effect comes from consumption of durable energy efficient goods, but there is a large indirect effect from additional consumption due to energy savings. The reallocation from energy expenditure to other consumption expenditures leads to more employment. Employment rises significantly in the construction sector and in industry, adding to the consumption effect.

Figure 20.3 shows the differences in final energy demand between the scenarios. The reduction of final energy demand in the ambitious efficiency scenario yields considerable CO_2 reductions (−15% against the reference in 2030). Additional employment in the ambitious efficiency scenario reaches 127,000 in 2030. The positive employment effects are the results of different impacts:

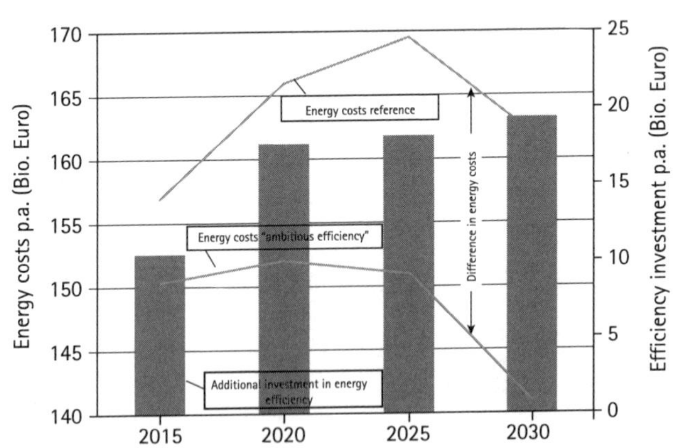

FIGURE 20.3 Additional investment (annual) and energy costs for the reference and the efficiency scenario. Source: Own calculations.

- Additional investment yields additional production and therefore additional employment.
- Energy is replaced by capital.
- Imports (e.g., crude oil, gas) are replaced by domestic value added.
- Construction, trade, and services are more labor intensive than the energy industry.
- Energy efficiency improves economic productivity and thus competitiveness.
- Short-term higher demand for (efficient) investment goods and equipment improves private budgets and induces additional incomes.

The main impact comes from additional investment, especially in the construction sector, where labor intensity is rather high. The long-term effects are driven by energy savings and reductions of the energy bill.

Figure 20.3 shows the long-term development of the energy costs for the two scenarios and contrasts investments and savings. Annual total savings in 2030 will be around €20 billion.

20.5 Renewable Energy

For the technical specification of our scenarios we make use of the official scenario for the development of new RE installations, the so-called "Lead Scenario" (Nitsch et al., 2010). This scenario includes bottom-up modeled cost structures of RE technologies, based on the learning curves for 10 RE technologies. It is a policy target oriented scenario, in which 84.7% RE will be reached in electricity generation, 49.4% in heat generation, and 49.5% in primary energy supply in 2050. A scenario with zero investment in RE since 2000 serves as the respective (hypothetical) reference development.

The scenario technique is often applied when future development depends on the development of some crucial quantities, whose development is highly uncertain. Future employment effects from expanding RE, for instance, critically depend on the relative costs of RE compared to fossil fuels, on national policies for the support of RE, and on international climate regimes and RE strategies.

Thus we constructed the following scenarios for the development of each of these decisive factors (see Lehr et al., 2012):

- Two different price paths for international energy prices
- Three different scenarios for the domestic RE investment
- Four different RE export scenarios, which vary by the share of imports and domestic production in 10 world regions and 10 technologies and with respect to the trade shares of Germany

International energy prices determine the reference price for the additional costs of RE systems in Germany, because large shares of fossil fuels are imported. The future development path of import prices for fossil fuels is highly uncertain considering the large fluctuations in the past couple of years. Therefore we implement a lower price scenario and a higher price scenario with the respective consequences for RE diffusion. The price scenarios follow essentially the projections of the IEA. The higher price level coincides with the projections in the World Energy Outlook (IEA, 2009). The lower price level is lower than the more recent projections in IEA (2010), but the upper price level exceeds the assumptions there. To keep the analysis on the safe side, in the following we report the findings for the lower price level, which is less favorable for the cost-effectiveness of RE installations. It assumes oil prices in constant 2005 prices of US$79/bbl in 2020 and US$94/bbl in 2030.

Germany has experienced a boom in the installation of PV panels in 2010. Though the German government annually updates its "Lead Scenario" (Nitsch and Wenzel, 2009) for the future development of electricity and heat from RE, the latest update in 2009 did not include this rapid increase. Therefore, we included two more scenarios in our analysis, which differ concerning domestic RE investment taking the likely PV development into account. It turned out that the higher path of this set was over-achieved by 10% in 2010, so that only the results of the original scenario and the highest sensitivity are reported here.

Currently, the additional costs of RE systems are the main driver of negative economic effects. They spur the budget effect through increases in the electricity prices from the burden sharing mechanism of the German feed-in tariff and through additional expenditure for hot water and heat generation. From the cost development observable in the past and industry information estimates for future cost development in Germany are obtained (Nitsch and Wenzel, 2009).

Export is a major driver of the economic performance in Germany. This holds for the economy as such as well as for the sector of the production of facilities for the use of RE. Earlier studies (Lehr et al., 2008) have shown that net employment strongly depends on assumptions on export levels. Therefore, RE technology exports have been modeled in great detail. Our analysis follows an idea developed by Blazejczak and Edler (2008) for "green" goods. They analyze the world market for green goods and derive German export quantities from shares of traded goods in this market and shares of German producers in world trade. We follow a similar logic and determine the trade volume of RE technologies in the year 2007 as a calibration for our projections of future exports. For this year, the trade shares of German producers can be estimated from statistical data and additional structural knowledge. For the future we develop four scenarios, all of them based on the energy [r]evolution scenario for global installations RE systems (Krewitt et al., 2008).

The minimum case for exports is defined by holding the volume of German exports constant until 2030. This translates into a high loss of German trade shares. The maximum case is determined by holding the trade shares constant on a rapidly expanding world market, which can be seen as an almost 10-fold increase of export volumes. Both scenarios serve as an upper and lower boundary to the more likely developments. One of them, the more optimistic scenario, assumes that Germany maintains significant shares in global trade of RE systems. The slower scenario can either be seen as a slowdown in German competitiveness or as a tendency to wall off markets in the future.

Instead of a business-as-usual reference, which in many studies describes a development under which no further measures are taken (e.g., ISI et al., 2009), this study uses a zero scenario. The same approach has been applied in Lehr et al. (2008). It describes a consistent hypothetical development of German energy generation without RE promotion from 2000 onwards and includes the additional fossil power plants and heat generation plants that would then be necessary along with the associated investment[1]. In this scenario, RE makes only a very limited contribution to the heat and electricity supply, for the latter predominantly from large-scale hydropower, which was already competitive even before the Renewable Energy Sources Act came into force.

In the following analysis results are reported for the low price path and the high domestic investment path. All export scenarios are included in the reported results.

All other things are equal across the scenarios; that is, regulations, taxes, and so on are taken as given. The PANTA RHEI model calculates endogenously economic development and labor market effects in the different scenarios. The zero scenario based on the low price path is now compared to a development with differing degrees of domestic investment in RE and differing export trends based on the same price path. The comparison of simulation results shows macroeconomic effects such as net employment effects, which can be traced back to the different scenario assumptions. To gain an overview of selected results in all the simulation runs, Table 20.3 shows the results for net employment over time. Absolute deviations from the zero scenario with the low price path are shown. Positive values should be seen as positive net employment by comparison with a development without expansion of RE. Negative values indicate that employment lags behind the value it would have had without the expansion of RE.

The increase of RE leads in most of the scenarios studied to positive net employment, rising steadily, particularly from 2020 onward, when global RE markets are expected to increase strongly according to Krewitt et al. (2008). The net effects are negative in

Table 20.3 Net Employment Impacts of Different Export Scenarios

Export scenario	Min		Slow		Opt		Max	
	2020	2030	2020	2030	2020	2030	2020	2030
	7.1	7.1	19.9	32.7	32.9	47.8	41.3	59.1
	-24.9	60.1	34.3	143.1	99.4	181.7	135.5	216.1

the scenarios with minimal exports (i.e., remaining constant at today's level), although this should be seen here more as a notional lower limit. In this case, for the two expansion paths (Lead Scenario and High PV) lower values for employment are observed by comparison with the zero scenario. However, at the end of the observation period there is a reversal in these cases: the net employment effects become slightly positive or are neutral. The influence of exports on the domestic employment level also becomes very evident in the scenarios studied: using the optimistic expectations, the positive net employment effect rises by 2030 to values in excess of 150,000. In combination with cautious export expectations, there are less positive deviations from the zero scenario up to 2015. After that the positive employment effects of exports become apparent.

Because we are showing only the low price path here, the higher additional costs of RES, brought about by low prices for fossil energy sources, attenuate the positive net employment effects in comparison to a scenario with a higher energy price path.

Overall, the highest net employment stems from maximal export in combination with high PV expansion. In this case, net employment in 2030 is a little more than 200,000 people higher than it would have been without expansion of RE in Germany.

Gross employment in the RE industries may increase to around 500–600,000 people compared to more than 370,000 today (O'Sullivan et al., 2011).

20.6 Conclusions and Outlook

Macroeconomic effects of mitigation policies have been described for Germany. The results clearly show that improved energy efficiency results in a variety of positive effects on the economy and the environment. These range from reduced GHG emissions to improved competitiveness of firms and budget savings for consumers to economy-wide impacts such as additional employment and economic growth. Thus, exploiting the huge potential stemming from cost-effective efficiency measures should have high priority for the design of energy and climate policies.

However, although the overall energy efficiency potential is large, it stems from completely different technologies and technology users. Consequently, also the pattern of barriers to invest in energy-efficient technologies is manifold and will need a broad mix of sector- and technology-specific policies.

Our analysis shows possible positive impacts of the expansion of RE in Germany—and the conditions and policy implication for a positive development. Positive net employment effects strongly depend on further growth of global markets and German RE exports. When relating the results to studies that report negative impacts of RES promotion, the treatment of international market developments in the studies can explain at least part of the differences. Another important factor for employment impacts are expectations of future cost reductions of different RES technologies.

The definition of a reference to mirror impacts of RES and energy efficiency development is difficult and will influence the magnitude of impacts. RES increase is still mainly driven by policy support, which makes it easier to apportion the overall impacts to policy. But this is about to change. Energy efficiency improvement is partly autonomous, which makes it very difficult to assign the policy-driven share.

The current discussion about the German energy concept, which builds on RE promotion and energy-efficiency improvement, should be opened to related issues such as external costs of energy consumption, energy security, the "green" technology race, and new export markets, and the more general discussion about green economy and welfare. Their inclusion in a comprehensive analysis makes the evaluation of the German "Energiewende" even more positive.

Economic impacts of energy-efficiency measures are less dependent on global market development. The construction sector plays a major role. But companies specialized on energy efficiency products can also profit from cost degression on international markets and focus on growing markets abroad. The German energy concept builds on RES development and on energy-efficiency deployment. Taken the structure and the competitiveness of the German industry into account, it looks like the energy concept will yield a double dividend of lower fossil energy use and GHG emissions on the one hand and additional jobs in the RES and efficiency industries on the other. Obviously, this has to be related to higher investment and costs such as electricity prices in the medium term.

Notes

1. Total investment in coal and gas fired plants and fossil fuel–based heat systems amounts to €52 billion until 2030. Details can be found in Lehr et al. (2011, p. 138 ff).

References

AGEB (2011). Energy balances for the Federal Republic of Germany. Berlin and Köln: Arbeitsgemeinschaft Energiebilanzen.

Ahlert, G., Distelkamp, M., Lutz, C., Meyer, B., Mönnig, A., and Wolter, M. I. (2009). Das IAB/INFORGE-Modell. In P. Schnur and G. Zika (eds.), *Das IAB/INFORGE-Modell. Ein sektorales makroökonometrisches Projektions- und Simulationsmodell zur Vorausschätzung des längerfristigen Arbeitskräftebedarfs*, pp. 15–175. Nürnberg: IAB-Bibliothek 318.

Apergis, N., and Payne, J. E. (2010). Renewable energy consumption and economic growth: Evidence from a panel of OECD countries. *Energy Policy, 38*, 656–660.

Barker, T., Ekins, P., and Foxon, T. (2007). The macroeconomic rebound effect and the UK economy. *Energy Policy, 35*, 4935–4946.

Blazejczak, J., and Edler, D. (2008). Szenarien zur Entwicklung des Weltmarktes für Umwelt- und Klimaschutzgüter. Forschungsprojekt im Auftrag des Umweltbundesamtes (Förderkennzeichen 204 14 107), Umwelt, Innovation, Beschäftigung 04/08. Hrsg. BMU, UBA, Dessau.

Blazejczak, J., Braun, F. G., Edler, D., and Schill, W.-P. (2011). Economic effects of renewable energy expansion: A model-based analysis for Germany. DIW Berlin Discussion Papers No. 1156.

BMU, BMWi. (2010). Federal Ministry for the Environment, Nature Conservation and Nuclear Safety (BMU), Federal Ministry of Economics and Technology (BMWi). Berlin: Energy Concept.

Cetin, M., and Egrican, N. (2011). Employment impacts of solar energy in Turkey. *Energy Policy, 39,* 7184–7190.

COM. (2008a). 30: 20 20 20 by 2020. Europe's climate change opportunity. Communication from the Commission to the European Parliament, the Council, the European Economic and Social Committee, and the Committee of the Regions, Brussels, January 23, 2008.

COM. (2008b). 772. Energy efficiency: Delivering the 20% target. Communication from the Commission, Brussels, November 13, 2008.

COM (2010). 639 Final Energy 2020: A strategy for competitive, sustainable and secure energy, Communication from the Commission to the European Parliament, the Council, the European Economic and Social Committee, and the Committee of the Regions, Brussels, November 10, 2010.

Delphi (2007). Situational Analysis of the Canadian Renewable Energy Sector with a Focus on Human Resource Issues, Final Report. The Delphi Group for the Human Resources and Social Development Canada.

Fang, Y. (2011). Economic welfare impacts from renewable energy consumption: The China experience. *Renewable and Sustainable Energy Reviews,* doi:10.1016/j.rser.2011.07.044.

Frondel, M., Ritter, N., Schmidt, C., and Vance, C. (2010). Economic impacts from the promotion of renewable energy technologies: The German experience. *Energy Policy, 38,* 4048–4056.

Guerra, A., and Sancho, F. (2010). Rethinking economy-wide rebound measures: An unbiased proposal. *Energy Policy, 38,* 6684–6694.

Hanley, N., McGregor, P., Swales, K., and Turner, K. (2009). Do increases in energy efficiency improve environmental quality and sustainability? *Ecological Economics, 68,* 692–709.

Hillebrand, B., Buttermann, H. G., Behringer, J. M., and Bleuel, M. (2006). The expansion of renewable energies and employment effects in Germany. *Energy Policy, 34,* 3884–3494.

IEA. (2009). *World Energy Outlook 2009.* Paris: International Energy Agency.

IEA. (2012). *World Energy Outlook 2012.* Paris: International Energy Agency.IEA (2010).*Energy Technology Perspectives 2010.* Paris: International Energy Agency.

Ifeu, Fraunhofer ISI, Prognos, GWS et al. (2011). Energieeffizienz: Potenziale, volkswirtschaftliche Effekte und innovative Handlungs- und Förderfelder für die Nationale Klimaschutzinitiative. Endbericht des Projektes "Wissenschaftliche Begleitforschung zu übergreifenden technischen, ökologischen, ökonomischen und strategischen Aspekten des nationalen Teils der Klimaschutzinitiative," Heidelberg, Karlsruhe, Berlin, Osnabrück, Freiburg.

IPCC. (2001). *Climate Change 2007: Mitigation. Contribution of Working Group III to the Fourth Assessment Report of the Intergovernmental Panel on Climate Change.* [B. Metz, O. R. Davidson, P. R. Bosch, R. Dave, and L. A. Meyer (eds.)]. Cambridge University Press, Cambridge, United Kingdom and New York, NY, USA.

ISI (2009). ISI, Ecofys, EEG, Rütter + Partner Socioeconomic Research + Consulting, LEI, SEURECO. EMPLOY-RES. Employment and growth impacts of sustainable energies in the European Union, Karlsruhe.

Jollands, N., Waide, P., Ellis, M., Onoda, T., Laustsen, J., Tanaka, K., de T'Serclaes, P., Barnsley, I., Bradley, R., and Meier, A. (2010). The 25 IEA energy efficiency policy recommendations to the G8 Gleneagles Plan of Action. *Energy Policy, 38*, 6409–6418.

Krewitt, W., Teske, S., Pregger, T., Naegler, T., Simon, S., Graus, W., Blomen, E., et al. (2008). "Energy (R)evolution—a Sustainable World Energy Outlook." Study commissioned by Greenpeace Int. and the European Renewable Energy Council (EREC), Stuttgart, Utrecht, 2nd ed. 2008.

Kuckshinrichs, W., Kronenberg, T., and Hansen, P. (2010). The social return on investment in the energy efficiency of buildings in Germany. *Energy Policy, 38*, 4317–4329.

Lehr, U., Lutz, C., and Edler, D. (2012). Green jobs? Economic impacts of renewable energy in Germany. *Energy Policy, 47*, 358–364.

Lehr, U., Lutz, C., Edler, D., O´Sullivan, M., Nienhaus, K., Simon, S., Nitsch, J., Breitschopf, B., Bickel, P., and Ottmüller, M. (2011). Kurz und langfristige Auswirkungen des Ausbaus der erneuerbaren Energien auf den deutschen Arbeitsmarkt. Study for the Federal Ministry of the Environment, Berlin.

Lehr, U., Nitsch, J., Kratzat, M., Lutz, C., and Edler, D., (2008). Renewable energy and employment in Germany. *Energy Policy, 36*, 108–117.

Lindenberger, D., Lutz, C., and Schlesinger, M. (2010). Szenarien für ein Energiekonzept der Bundesregierung. *Energiewirtschaftliche Tagesfragen, 60*, 32–35.

Lutz, C. (2011). Energy scenarios for Germany: Simulations with the model PANTA RHEI. In D. Mullins, J. Viljoen, and H. Leeuwner (eds.), *Interindustry Based Analysis of Macroeconomic Forecasting*. Proceedings from the 19th INFORUM World Conference, Pretoria, 203–224.

Lutz, C., Meyer, B., Nathani, C., and Schleich, J. (2005). Endogenous technological change and emissions: The case of the German steel industry. *Energy Policy, 33*, 1143–1154.

Maier, T., Mönnig, A., and Zika, G. (2014). Labour demand by industrial sector, occupational field and qualification until 2025—Model calculations using the IAB/INFORGE model. *Economic Systems Research* forthcoming.

Mathiesen, B.V., Lund, H., and Karlsson K. (2011). 100% Renewable energy systems, climate mitigation and economic growth. *Applied Energy, 88*, 488–501.

Meyer, B., Lutz, C., Schnur, P., and Zika, G. (2007). Economic policy simulations with global interdependencies: A sensitivity analysis for Germany. *Economic Systems Research, 19*(1), 37–55.

Meyer, B., Meyer, M., and Distelkamp, M. (2012). Modeling green growth and resource efficiency: New results. *Mineral Economics, 24*, 145–154.

Nagl, S., Fürsch, M., Paulus, M., Richter, J., Trüby, J., and Lindenberger, D. (2011). Energy policy scenarios to reach challenging climate protection targets in the German electricity sector until 2050. *Utilities Policy, 19*, 185–192.

Nitsch, J., Pregger, T., Scholz, Y., Naegler, T., Sterner, M., von Oehsen, A., Pape, C., Saint-Drenan, Y., and Wenzel, B. (2010). *Langfristszenarien und Strategien für den Ausbau der erneuerbaren Energien in Deutschland bei Berücksichtigung der Entwicklung in Europa und global.* Stuttgart and Berlin: Federal Ministry for the Environment, Nature Conservation and Nuclear Safety.

Nitsch, J., Wenzel, B., Leitszenario 2009—Langfristszenarien und Strategien für den Ausbau erneuerbarer Energien in Deutschland unter Berücksichtigung der europäischen und globalen Entwicklung. Stuttgart and Berlin: Federal Ministry for the Environment, Nature Conservation and Nuclear Safety.

O'Sullivan, M., Edler, D., Ottmüller, M., and Lehr, U. (2010). Gross employment from renewable energy in Germany in 2009—a first estimate. Stuttgart and Berlin: Federal Ministry for the Environment, Nature Conservation and Nuclear Safety.

O'Sullivan, M., Edler, D., van Mark, K., Nieder, T., and Lehr, U. (2011). Gross employment from renewable energy in Germany in 2010—a first estimate. Stuttgart and Berlin: Federal Ministry for the Environment, Nature Conservation and Nuclear Safety.

Prognos, EWI, GWS (2010). Energieszenarien für ein Energiekonzept der Bundesregierung. Study commissioned by the Federal Ministry of Economics and Technology (BMWi), Basel, Köln, Osnabrück.

REN 21. (2011). Renewables 2011. Global status report. Paris: Renewable Energy Policy Network for the 21 Century.

Sorrell, S. (2009). Jevon's Paradox revisited: The evidence for backfire from improved energy efficiency. *Energy Policy, 37*, 1456–1469.

Stocker, A., Großmann, A., Madlener, R., and Wolter, M. I. (2011). Sustainable energy development in Austria until 2020: Insights from applying the integrated model "e3.at". *Energy Policy, 39*, 6082–6099.

Taylor, P.G., Lavagne d'Ortigue, O., Francoeur, M., and Trudeau, N. (2010). Final energy use in IEA countries: The role of energy efficiency. *Energy Policy, 38*, 6463–6474.

UBA (2011). *National Inventory Report for the German Greenhouse Gas Inventory 1990–2009, Dessau-Roßlau.* Umweltbundesamt: Federal Environmental Agency.

Wei, M., Patadia, S., and Kammen, D. M. (2010). Putting renewables and energy efficiency to work: How many jobs can the clean energy industry generate in the US? *Energy Policy, 38*, 919–931.

Welfens, P. J. J., and Lutz, C. (2012). Green ICT dynamics: Key issues and findings for Germany. *Mineral Economics, 24*, 55–163.

PART V

INTERNATIONAL PERSPECTIVES

CHAPTER 21

STABILIZATION OF EARTH'S CLIMATE IN THE 21ST CENTURY BY THE STABILIZATION OF PER CAPITA CONSUMPTION

ASKAR AKAEV

21.1 Introduction

In this chapter, the scenario method of long-term forecasting of climate change and global warming is considered. Today it is taken as a given that the global warming taking place before our eyes is caused mainly by the anthropogenic growth of carbon dioxide (CO_2) in Earth's atmosphere. For the last 150 years, as a result of human industrial activity, CO_2 concentration has increased in the atmosphere from a preindustrial natural stationary level of 280 ppm (parts per million) to 390 ppm now, that is, by 40%. It has led to an increase of average global temperatures of approximately 0.6°C and, taking into account natural factors, by 1°C as compared to preindustrial levels. What are the admissible limits of global warming? As recommended by prominent climatologists as early as 1996, the European Council has made the decision that "global average preindustrial level of temperature should not be exceeded by more than 2°C and, therefore the global efforts aimed at the restriction or reduction of emissions should be directed by concentration of in atmosphere CO_2 not exceeding 550 ppm" (Rat der Europaischen Union, 1996, p. 27). The limit of warming equal to 2°C was confirmed by the United Nations in a declaration and accepted at the International Conference on Climate Change in Copenhagen in 2009; in addition, it was emphasized that the concentration of CO_2 in the atmosphere should not exceed 450–550 ppm, which can be achieved by the reduction of an average annual increase of carbon emissions to at least 3.3 Gt or by factor of 2, as compared with the 2000 level (6.61 Gt).

Because emissions of huge amounts of carbon in the form of CO_2 occur from burning organic fossil fuels (coal, oil, and natural gas) with the purpose of obtaining various kinds of energy, it is clear that one needs to consider development scenarios of low carbon energy industry or energy-ecological development with a minimum volume of emissions. The International Energy Agency (IEA) has considered a set of scenarios of energy industry development and has produced, in particular, a "Blue Map" scenario, which is targeted at a 50% decrease of emissions by 2050 as compared with 2005, on the basis of wide development of low-carbon technologies.

Among the variety of scenarios of energy development, we have selected the one that conforms to the new paradigm of power consumption, consisting of per capita energy consumption stabilization for the population of developed countries in the 21st century at a lower, but a comfortable enough, level. It is shown that this level of per capita energy consumption for the whole world comprises approximately 2.5 tonnes of conditional fuel (t.c.e.) per year. Transition to a new energy consumption paradigm began in the 1970s, after the energy shock caused by the oil crisis. Whereas before the oil crisis the demand for energy grew in proportion to a square of world population of the world ($E \sim N^2$), at full transition to the new power paradigm, it will grow in linear proportion to the population ($E \sim N$), which, as expected, will also stabilize at a certain stationary value. In addition, various scientists estimate the stationary Earth population in different ways. We will consider the following forecasted values in our calculations: 1–5.2 billion people, 2–6.2 billion people, 3–7.4 billion people, and 4–9.1 billion people. The new energy consumption paradigm is essentially targeted at a practical implementation of the IEA "Blue Map" energy consumption scenario.

In accordance with the selected scenario of energy development, we suggest a mathematical model for the description of the process of transition to the new paradigm of energy consumption, both for developed and developing countries. This mathematical model, developed by the author, describing demographic dynamics with stabilization near a stationary population is provided. Making use of these models, calculations are performed for various scenarios of demographic dynamics for the whole world and for leading countries, as well as the corresponding dynamics of their energy consumption, on the basis of a new power paradigm. Standards of per capita consumption for different groups of countries in the 21st century are listed.

Further, the structure of energy consumption for different kinds of energy sources (coal, oil, gas, renewable energy sources [RES], atomic energy, and water-power engineering) and a forecast of consumption dynamics for organic fossil types of fuel (coal, oil, and gas) are provided. It is shown that in the 21st century these kinds of fuel will play a dominant role and, by the end of century, their share in the balance of world energy consumption will decrease approximately twofold from the present 86.5% to 43%. Because different kinds of organic fuel produce various volumes of CO_2 at burning, by calculation of CO_2 emission dynamics, the structure of organic fuels and relative shares of coal, oil, and gas are taken into account. A calculation technique for a general carbon intensity coefficient for organic fossil fuels is suggested. The author has also suggested a calculation method for decreasing coefficients in the application of carbon capture and storage CO_2(CCS) techniques. As a result, the approximation formula for the calculation of dynamics of CO_2 emission and accumulation in the atmosphere for the 21st century, as well as for corresponding scenarios of energy-ecological development, is obtained.

Thus, a forecast of dynamics of CO_2 emission and accumulation in the atmosphere allows for direct transition to a calculation of the dynamics of climatic change, deviations of average global temperature from the present level, with confidence. Calculations show that, by stabilization of per capita energy consumption with differentiated standards, as set forth for both developed and developing countries, one can stabilize climate and avoid exceeding the limiting temperature excess of 2°C, as compared to the preindustrial era, by stabilization of the world population at the level of 5.2 billion people. If the stationary level is higher, standards for per capita consumption should be lowered.

Also, we considered the influence of energy-ecological development on economic growth. Because diversion of some investment resources for the purpose of using low-carbon energy technologies will reduce the rates of economic growth, it is important to estimate the value of this slowdown. We demonstrated that though at present this factor reduces the average rate of world economic growth by 0.5% for an average 4% growth rate during the previous decade, by 2030 it will be closer to 2.5%, that is, will cause an essential slowdown of economic growth. We have to deal with that as the risk of global warming abruptly decreases and stabilization of the climate is achieved.

21.2 Global Warming and Measures Taken by the International Community for Climate Stabilization

It is an established fact that large-scale changes are taking place on our planet (Tarko, 2005; Rahmstorf and Schellenhuber, 2007). The majority of experts, including the author of the present chapter, claim that global warming caused by anthropogenic human influence is taking place. To be fair, we should also note that there are few supporters of the scenario of an approaching next natural global cooling (Klimenko et al., 1997).

The main reason for global warming is also established. It is growth of CO_2 and other greenhouse gas (GHG) concentrations in the atmosphere, owing to their accruing emission at burning of fossil organic fuel—coal, oil, and gas—that is responsible for the growth. GHGs absorb infrared radiation emitted by Earth and heat up the atmosphere near Earth. Thus, energy consumption is the key factor in climate change and global warming. On the other hand, energy serves as a major factor of modern economic development and creation of comfortable conditions for life and people's activities; therefore energy consumption in the world grows in ever increasing quantity. Thus, within the 150 years after the beginning of Industrial Revolution dated to 1860, as a result of human industrial activity, the atmosphere received about 230 additional Gt of carbon (Gigatonne = 1 of billion tonnes), which has raised the temperature of the ground-level atmosphere by approximately 0.6°C. As a whole, at the expense of natural and anthropogenic factors, the average air temperature at ground level has increased by 0.8°C as compared with 1900 (Rahmstorf and Schellenhuber, 2007).

During the preindustrial era the atmosphere contained approximately 575 GtC, which was almost constant for several hundred thousand years, which proves the balance of the carbon cycle in nature (Budyko, 1974). Thus, the carbon content maintenance in the atmosphere to 805 Gt by 2010, that is, essentially a disorder of the carbon cycle, is observed. In fact, atmospheric carbon is present in the form of carbonic gas CO_2. The CO_2 weight in atmosphere is obtained by recalculation of carbon weight with a factor of 3.664. Therefore, the modern atmosphere contains approximately $2.95 \cdot 10^{12}$ t or $2.95 \cdot 10^3$ Gt of carbonic gas.

It is customary to measure volume concentration of CO_2in the atmosphere in parts per million. It is present in the atmosphere in very small quantities; today's volume concentration comprises 390 mln^{-1} or 390 ppm (parts per million) or 0.039%. In the stable atmosphere of interglacial ages (about 120–140,000 years ago the CO_2 content was measured at a concentration 280 ppm, which is equivalent to 575 GtC). Moreover, in the course of the last several hundreds years it experienced small fluctuations around some average value (275 ± 10 ppm), which is naturally considered the "preindustrial level" (Budyko, 1980). It means that the balance between absorption of $CO_2$by oceans and land ecosystems and its emission in the atmosphere in the preindustrial epoch was maintained with high accuracy. Most researchers today consider the preindustrial concentration level equal to 280 ppm. It can be seen that anthropogenic human activity has led to a considerable imbalance of the carbon cycle, and as a consequence over the last 150 years the volume concentration of CO_2 has increased in the atmosphere up to 390 ppm (0.039%), that is, almost by 40%.

It is common knowledge that the greenhouse effect mechanism lies in the difference between the absorbing ability of the atmosphere for sun radiation arriving at Earth and radiation emitted by Earth back into space. Visible short-wave radiation with an average wavelength about 0.5 microns that is emitted by the sun goes through the atmosphere almost completely. Earth releases energy received in this way almost absolutely as a black body in a long-wave infrared range with an average wavelength of about 10 microns. Carbonic gas, along with other gases (methane (CH_4), nitrous oxide (N_2O), and chlorofluorocarbons), absorb long-wave infrared radiation going from Earth in a range 12–18 microns at a high rate, and as a result, emits heat that warms up the atmosphere. Therefore it is one of major factors in causing the greenhouse effect. It has been proved that 57% of the anthropogenic greenhouse effect is caused by extraction and burning of organic fuel, 9% by disappearance of woods, and 14% by industrial production not related to the energy cycle (Isaev, 2003). $CO_2$is a main combustion product of fossil organic fuel. Slightly more than a half of the CO_2exhausted in the atmosphere remains there (about 56%), as only 44% is absorbed by oceans and the Earth biosphere (Budyko, 1980).

How seriously do anthropogenic emissions influence Earth's climate? To answer this question, climatologists use a special measure called climate sensitivity. As a unit of measure of climate sensitivity one uses the equilibrium of the ground-level temperature of air when the CO_2 concentration doubles (from 280 to 560 ppm). In 1896 the Swedish scientist and Nobel Prize winner Svante Arrhenius calculated for the first time that the increase of CO_2 concentration in the atmosphere by factor of two times would result in an increase of the Earth's temperature by 4–6°C. In the 1970s the National Academy of Sciences of the USA estimated the temperature effect of doubling of CO_2 concentration to be 1.5–4.5°C (Ramstorf and Schellnhuber, 2007). This estimation has been checked and further confirmed by many independent researchers, for example, Schlesinger (1983).

However important it is to restrict the aforementioned range, it has so far been impossible: according to modern estimates the temperature is from 2 to 4.5°C. The source of indeterminacy is the lack of data on the effect of claudage. The problem is that as CO_2concentration increases, the heating of the atmosphere is smoothed by the concurrently grows, that is, claudage to an extent smooths the thermal effect. According to S. Schneider (Schneider, 1972) the increase (reduction) of the amount of claudage by one point can lead to reduction (increase) in air temperature at the Earth surface by 1.5–2°C.

As the most probable value of climate sensitivity one should consider values close to 3°C (Budyko, 1974; Manabe and Wetherald, 1975). It is important that quite similar results have been obtained with application of various climate theories. In the first work (Budyko, 1974) a semi-empirical theory of a thermal mode of the atmosphere, based on the power balance of a terrestrial surface and atmosphere, was developed. In the second work (Manabe and Wetherald, 1975) the numerical model of the climate theory was developed, based on a model of the general circulation of the atmosphere, which takes into account circulation of waters at oceans. Besides, the sensitivity of a climate equal to 3°C is in good agreement with the data from the Ice Age. Therefore in the work of Rahmstorf and Schellnhuber (2007) the following conclusion is made: sensitivity of a climate should be estimated in 3 ± 1°C. In the same paper they formulated five basic theses that for the last few decades have received such convincing proof that their correctness is recognized by the overwhelming majority of actively working climatologists and does not lead to any further discussions—they are axioms. They are as follows:

1. Starting from about 1850, the CO_2 concentration in the atmosphere has grown considerably, as shown in Figure 21.1: from 280 ppm—typical for interglacial periods for the last 400,000 years up to 390 ppm at present.

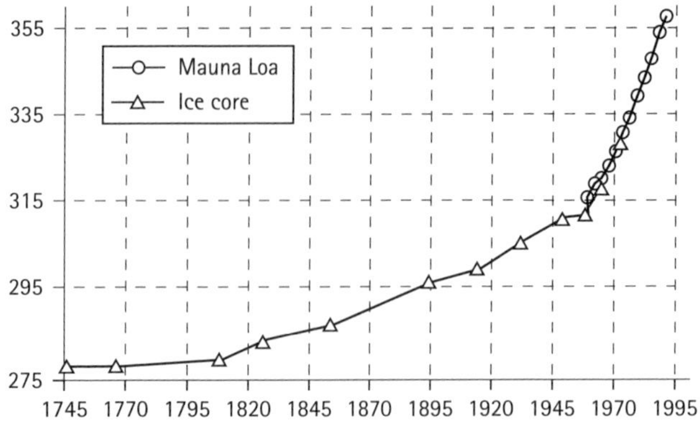

FIGURE 21.1 The growth of CO_2 concentration (million^{-1}) in the atmosphere according to an ice core of Antarctica in 1745–1973 and measurements at Mauna Loa station in 1959–1992 (according to Trends 93).

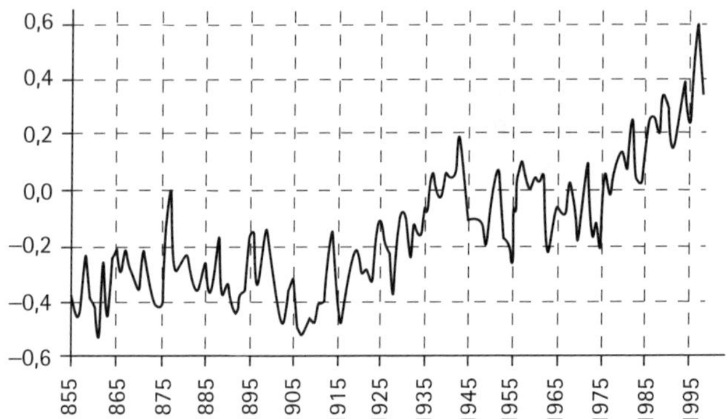

FIGURE 21.2 Anomalies of ground global temperature of atmosphere (°C) in 1856–1999 (after Jones et al., 1994).

2. The reasons for this change are human economic activities: burning of fossil organic fuel in the first place, and cutting of forests in the second place.
3. CO_2influences climate, changing the radiation balance of Earth: the growth of concentration of this gas results in an increase of the ground temperature of the atmosphere. As likely as not, the doubling of its concentration (from 280 to 560 ppm) will result in growth of the average global temperature by $3 \pm 1°C$.
4. Considerable warming of climate (on a global scale—by approximately 0.8°C, and in Europe—by 1°C) took place in the 20th century; temperatures of the last 10 years were on a global scale the highest since the beginning of observations in the 19th century, as observed in Figure 21.2.
5. The larger part of this warming, $\approx$0.6°C, is caused by the growth of concentrations of CO_2 and other anthropogenic gases; the smaller part has natural causes, in particular fluctuations of solar activity.

Air temperature is the prime climatic factor that defines quality and life conditions of humans and their economic activities. Changes of atmospheric temperature result in changes in intensities of biological processes on land and in the oceans and cause infringements of the established bio-geochemical cycles. Therefore the consequences of global warming can be rather destructive. There are proven data confirming a global growth of the world's ocean level and reduction of a snow and ice blanket. Scientists have shown that even partial meltdown of the continental ice shield can lead to growth of the world's ocean level equal to several meters that will lead to a radical change of coastal lines and flooding of hundreds of the largest cities of the world that are its industrial, trading, and cultural centers. Just a single Greenland glacier contains such a quantity of water that as a result of its complete meltdown the level of world oceans would rise by 7 meters. We do not dwell on these aspects of global warming here, referring interested readers to the numerous books written on this topic (Budyko, 1980; Rahmstorf and Schellnhuber, 2007), and also to other articles of the given review.

Under the statement of the e the Intergovernmental Panel on Climate Change (IPCC), until 1976 the variability of a climate did not exceed the natural variations estimated over a time interval of about 1000 years, but for the period after this time the amplitude of temperature fluctuations has exceeded this threshold, and it became possible to speak about anthropogenic global warming owing to the increased greenhouse effect (IPCC, 2001). Thus, it is not the greenhouse effect that poses the danger, but the exceeding of the stable level, because it is as a result of the greenhouse effect that the Earth climate became suitable for life. The reason for concern regarding global warming is that the natural mechanism is artificially aggravated by human activities. Without the greenhouse effect our entire planet inevitably would be covered by ice. The temperature fluctuation during the last millennium, according to the third IPCC report (IPCC, 2001), is represented in Figure 21.3, which clearly shows an almost stepped increase in global average temperature of air by approximately 0.8°C as compared with 1900.

According to IPCC (2001), the contribution of anthropogenic factors (GHGs and aerosols) to climate warming in the 20th century is estimated to be approximately equal to 0.6°C. It should be noted that aerosols in the atmosphere have little impact on the long-wave radiation leaving Earth. However, it can bring a significant change to the

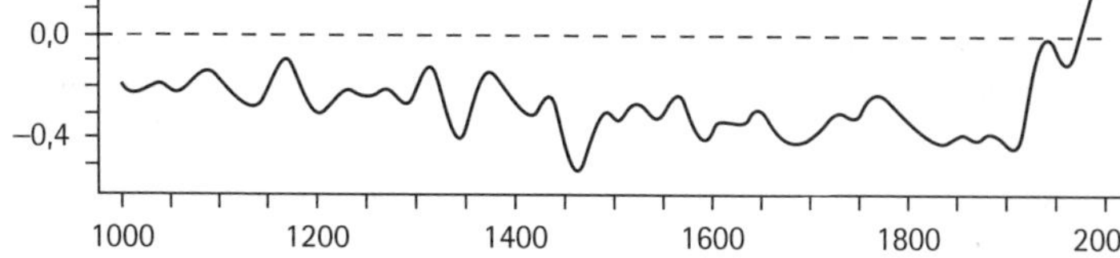

FIGURE 21.3 Anomalies of average global atmosphere temperature (°C) during the last millennium according to IPCC (2001). Horizontal axis = years, C.E.

stream of the short-wave radiation going from the sun, as a result of return radiation scattering on aerosol particles and its absorption by these particles, the size of which ranges from 0.1 to 1 micron. It is estimated that the cloud of aerosol particles reduces total radiation by approximately 1%, thereby reducing the average global temperature of the atmosphere. Though the question of the influence of anthropogenic aerosols on global climate has not been studied sufficiently well, experts believe that there is a high probability that such an influence is rather insignificant (Budyko, 1980).

Thus, we have accepted a hypothesis that modern global warming is directly connected with growth of industrial emissions. For the sake of impartiality it is necessary to stress that this hypothesis has not until now received a strict and complete demonstration. The existence of the detected empirical relationship between the two specified processes does not mean that it is strictly a cause-and-effect relationship. Modern climatic models of the general atmosphere and ocean circulation based on the accounting of the greenhouse effect of CO_2 industrial emissions and aerosols action describe the temperature chart in the 20th century well enough (Manabe and Wetherald, 1975; Tarko, 2005). However, as justly remarked by one of the pioneers in developing these models, A. Tarko (2005), the mathematical model also cannot serve as the proof of the presence of a causal relationship. The heads of states and governments participating in the United Nations conference on environment and development in Rio de Janeiro in 1992 knew both about an absence of proof of anthropogenic origin of global warming and about possible serious consequences of a CO_2 increase in atmosphere. Nevertheless, they have demonstrated wisdom and have accepted the UN Framework Convention on Climate Change (UNFCCC), providing a considerable reduction of atmospheric emissions of GHGs, and first of all, carbonic gas (CO_2) by burning of mineral organic fuels (coal, oil, gas).

It was truly a historical decision, as for the first time the majority of the heads of state had recognized the need for a global change of human economic activities associated with self-restriction. The specified decision was confirmed by them at the conference through the Declaration of Fundamental Principle of Precaution. According to this principle "when there is a threat of a serious or irreversible damage, lack of full scientific confidence is not used as the reason to delay the acceptance of economically effective measures as the prevention of deterioration of the state of environment" (the Report of Conference of the United Nations on Environment and Development, 1992, p. 92). Following this, in 1997 the Kyoto Protocol was accepted, specifying the conditions of emissions reductions for different countries. Later, with the new arguments in favor of anthropogenic increase of air temperature due to the growth of CO_2 concentration in atmosphere, IPCC in its fourth report advised on the presence of a causal relationship of warming and emissions of carbonic gas, confirming the aforementioned five theses on global warming (IPCC, 2007).

Once the UN Framework Convention on Climate Change was accepted in Rio de Janeiro in 1992, the question of admissible limits of global warming arose. According to the majority of climatologists the limit of temperature rise in should not exceed 2–3°C as compared with the temperature of preindustrial epoch. In 1996 at the meeting of European Council in Luxembourg the decision was made that "the global average temperature of preindustrial level should not be exceeded by more than 2°C and therefore global efforts directed on restriction or reduction of emissions should be guided by CO_2 concentration in the atmosphere, not exceeding 550 ppm" (Rat Ker Europaischen Union, 1996). Later on, the limit of warming equal to 2°C has been repeatedly confirmed by various decisions of council of EU Ecology Ministers and became a reference point guiding all European programs on restriction of influence on climate. By doing so, the European Union for the first time has accounted for the long-time discussion on the climate policy.

From that moment on, then the question about obligatory "limits of climate warming" on numerous occasions became a topic of various scientific conferences, among which one should point out scientific forum "Avoiding dangerous climate change," organized by the British prime minister Tony Blair in Exeter in 2005 (Avoiding dangerous climate change, 2006). At the forum it was, first, established, that global warming of the Earth climate by more than 2–3°C in comparison with a preindustrial epoch is unacceptable and is highly irresponsible, and second, is was established that the limit in 2°C can be kept only in case, if CO_2 concentration in atmosphere does not exceed the level in 450 ppm, and, to achieve that the global volume of CO_2 emissions should by 2050 be halved, as compared with 1990. The results have been obtained from the assumption that sensitivity of a climate lies in a range of 2.5–3°C. Moreover the Exeter forum has established that global rise in temperature by 1.5–2°C can already lead to full-scale destruction of nature and cultural heritage of humanity, and exceeding a 2°C level will give rise to a set of unpredictable consequences in climate. It was pointed out that hurricanes, flooding, droughts, and other disasters that have become more frequent recently are all consequences of global warming. To keep global warming within the specified permissible limits, worldwide transition to low-carbon energy is recommended, as well as the reduction of the average annual growth of CO_2 emissions to 12.1 Gt or by a factor of 2 with respect to year 2000 (24.2 Gt). As the first step scientists have suggested reducing emissions in the developed countries by 25–40% from this value by 2020. Recent studies show that climatic changes take place at such a high rate that the attainment of the 50% emission reduction by 2050 (80% of which will already be contributed by developing countries, owing to the accelerated industrialization of their economy) turns out to be insufficient to prevent dangerous consequences of global warming. Everyone is concerned today about feasibility of achievement of the specified goal, and the most important question is: What should be a scenario of energy development that is able to accomplish this goal?

It should be noted that even though international efforts in developing a long-term framework policy in the field of climatic changes are in progress, the 15th Conference of the Parties (Conference of the Parties [COP15]) to the UN Framework Convention on Climate Change in Copenhagen (2009) has revealed difficulty in achieving general agreement on the basis of legally obligatory goals. In this regard, boldness, resoluteness, and responsibility of climatologists, ecologists, and politicians elicits great respect, as 20 years ago in Rio de Janeiro they managed to begin on a global level the process of GHG emission limitation even though there was much less scientific knowledge regarding anthropogenic influences on climatic changes than there is today. During this period the political elite of many states, beginning with the EU countries, realized the severity of the climate change problem and the need for low-carbon energy growth but no radical steps to reduce GHG emissions to a safe level were taken. Our scientific knowledge today is already sufficient for implementation of preventive measures coinciding with priorities of national development, but not enough to give priority to a policy of emission reduction relative to goals of social-economic development, which was well observed at the UN Conference on Preservation of Environment in December, 2009 in Copenhagen.

The result of the conference in Copenhagen was a declaration that has no UN status as it was, developed by small group of political leaders. However, the important thing is that it was signed by leaders of the largest countries of the world—the United States and BRICS (Brazil, Russia, India, China, South Africa), which are also the largest pollutants of the atmosphere. China is the foremost atmospheric pollutant (26% of world level), and second is the United States (22%). Next follows the European Union (12%), India (6%), Russia (6%), the countries of the Near East (6%), and Japan (5%). The Copenhagen declaration is actually a political platform for future actions, at global, multilateral, and national levels. The declaration admits that anthropogenic climate change is a major problem today and it is necessary to restrict global warming to the 2°C level. The declaration also highlights the important role of low-carbon technologies in achieving this goal and the need for additional financing for developing countries for practical use of these technologies. For breakthroughs in this field the developed countries need to make active transfer of low-carbon technologies to developing countries on the basis of joint use with an effective funding scheme.

The countries that agreed with the Copenhagen declaration have sacrificed its legally obliging character in exchange for voluntary obligations on actions on the part of large developed and developing countries. Indeed, many of the largest countries have declared aspirations either to limit or to lower essentially CO_2 emissions per unit of gross national product. Thus, for example, China intends to reduce carbon capacity in the economy (emissions per unit of gross national product) by 40–45% by 2020 as compared to 2005; India has declared a corresponding decrease by 20–25%. Russia plans to lower the emissions level until 2020 by 25% as compared with 1990. These are rather hard-to-achieve goals considering that with the increased well-being of the population of these countries a manifold growth of energy consumption and, respectively, CO_2 emissions is inevitable.

The developed countries also have accepted corresponding obligations. The United States has committed to reduction of emissions of GHGs by 17% by 2020 as compared to 2007 and by 83% by 2050, and also to provide not less than 15% of all electric power in the country from renewable energy sources (RES). The European Union intends to achieve an increase in the portion of RES in the general balance of power manufacture by 2020 to 20% and to reduce emissions of hotbed gases to 20%. However, it is obvious that for the practical realization of all these obligations it is necessary to accept the basic international document, for example, the Convention on Climate of the United Nations. Such a document of long-term character should contain norms of international legal settlements of all aspects of global climate change, including mechanisms for monitoring and control of performance of the assumed obligations.

The situation around UNFCCC and the Kyoto Protocol has only become more complicated since the recent conference in South African Durban (November 28–December 9, 2011). At this conference once again, the community failed to get any fixed liabilities on lowering CO_2 emissions into the atmosphere from vanguard countries—the United States, China, and India. In addition, one of the largest CO_2 pollutants —Canada—has announced that it no longer intends to take part in Kyoto Protocol. It is a great concern that humanity is at risk of being left without any valid obligations of world countries to lower CO_2 emissions and ensure environmental care. What is reassuring is that the roadmap for a new universal international treaty has been approved.

21.3 Research Problem Statement

To estimate the possible consequences of the further increase of GHGs concentration on climate change in the future, researchers have performed modeling and computer calculations simulating various scenarios of world economic development. The problems of climate change directly impact economical ones in the energy field: the major part of anthropogenic emissions (approximately 60%) are linked to economic activity. Therefore the policy of the states and interstate associations relating to their reduction will be a major factor in decision making in this sphere. As shown previously, going forward, the energy strategy of the world's leading countries needs to be directed to lowering emissions of GHGs, which are considered the reason for anthropogenic climate change. Analysis and comparison of various scenarios of world energy development are carried out on a regular basis by the IEA.

The IEA report "Energy Technology Perspectives 2010" (ETP, 2010) lies within this framework, representing the IEA position on how low-carbon energy technologies (low-carbon future) can encourage the lowering of carbonic gas emission and, at the same time, serve as a powerful tool for increasing energy safety and providing economic development. Special attention is paid to problems of financial provision of energy safety and accelerating the development of energy technologies with low-carbon emissions in leading developing countries. Authors of the report pay attention to the fact that next decade (2012–2020) is crucial in this context. They believe that if emissions do not reach the peak by approximately 2020 and then do not start to decrease steadily, the achievement of the global goal—reduction of emissions by 2050 by 50%—will be much more costly to humanity.

The ETP 2010 report compares various scenarios of energy development, as shown in Figure 21.4. The basis scenario originates from the reference scenario (the Reference scenario to 2030), the energy forecast until 2030 (IEA, 2009), and extrapolates it to 2050. The scenario assumes that the governments of leading countries do not are not influenced by any special political decisions in the field of energy development and climate change. According to the basis scenario, by 2050 the level will comprise about 57 GtC (see Figure 21.4), which is absolutely unacceptable.

In contrast, various versions of the Blue Map scenario are focused on achievement of certain goals: it aims at twofold (to the level 14 GtC) decrease of emissions by 2050 with respect to 2005 and considers the least expensive implementation methods on the basis of development of existing and new low-carbon technologies.

As shown in Figure 21.4, a decrease of CO_2 emissions according to the Blue Map scenario can be achieved by making use of various technologies: (1) application of carbon capture and storage system (CCS) will reduce emissions by 19%; (2) use of RES by 17%; (3) expansion of atomic power stations use by 6%; (4) increased generation efficiency by 5%; (5) use of hybrid engines and installations in the consumption sector by 15%; (6) increase of efficiency of fuel and the electric power consumption use by 38%. Hence it follows that the best prospects of decrease in carbonic gas emissions are connected with an increase of efficiency of consumption energy use. Therefore an increase of energy efficiency should be of the highest priority in the short-term outlook.

Thus, as shown in the Blue Map scenario, by making use of the combinations of existing and new technologies, by 2050 one can provide a twofold reduction of global CO_2 emissions related to energy industry. It will require large investments; however, benefits connected with good environmental conditions, increase of energy safety, and depreciation of power resources will be substantial. For example, according to this scenario, the oil price in 2050 will be as low as US$70/barrel (in 2008 prices) whereas under the basis scenario it can reach US$120/barrel (in 2008 prices).

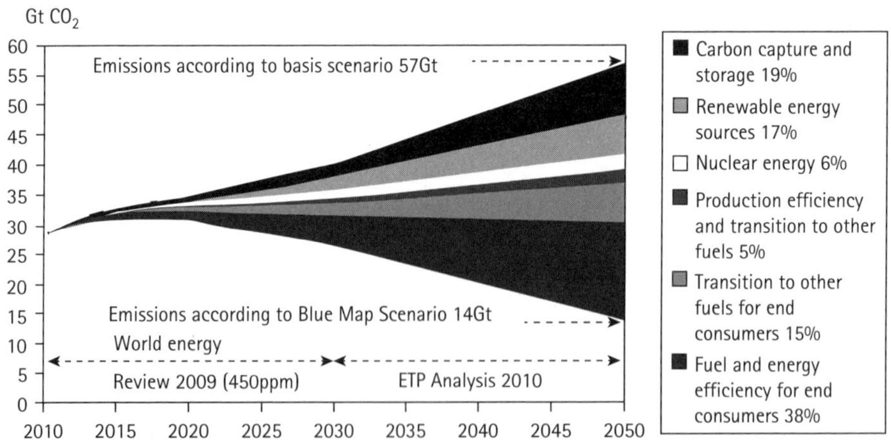

FIGURE 21.4 The basic technologies of emission reduction, according to the Blue Map scenario.

According to the estimate of the authors of the ETP 2010 report, to achieve 50% reduction of CO_2 emission, state funding for the research, development, and demonstration stage (RD&D) in the field of low-carbon technologies should be two to five times higher than at present. At the request of the ministers of G-8 countries, the IAE develops roadmaps for accelerated development and deployment of the most important low-carbon technologies. The ETP 2010 report demonstrates meeting world energy demand requires considerable investments. According to an estimate, in the basis scenario they might comprise US$270 trillion over the interval 2010–2050. Most of this amount (about 90%) falls on investments from the demand side, which will be carried by consumers in buying energy-consuming capacity machinery.

To achieve the goal of a 50% reduction of CO_2 emissions, more serious investments are required: according to the Blue Map scenario the demand for investment is forecast at the level of US$316 trillion. In recent years investments in low-carbon technologies comprised about US$165 billion per year. The implementation of the Blue Map scenario requires an increase in investments to US$750 billion per year by 2030 and to more than US$1.6 trillion per year in the period from 2030 to 2050. On the other hand, a technological revolution in energy production has a high potential of investment return. For example, low-carbon economics will give rise to considerable fuel savings at the expense of efficiency increase and lower prices. It was calculated in the ETP 2010 report that additional investments in the amount of US$46 trillion, required by the Blue Map scenario, will give in the period from 2010 to 2050 total fuel savings equivalent to US$112 trillion.

If we calculate the present value of investment and fuel savings in monetary terms, the net positive effect of fuel savings will comprise US$8 trillion. Besides, the revolution in the energy industry opens new possibilities for business, connected with development and promotion of new technologies, including in developing countries.

The aforementioned scenarios of the energy industry are not forecasts. They allow an estimate of the climate consequences of this or that action. Thus, for the calculation of climate scenario, we first need an exhaust scenario, that is, an estimate of future emission dynamics of carbonic gas and other GHGs and aerosols. Thus, between 1996 and 2000 a group of economists compiled a set of 40 such scenarios and described them in a special report of the IPCC on emission scenarios (IPCC, 2000). These scenarios cover the whole spectrum of economically plausible scenarios for how the situation may develop in the future. According to the most pessimistic scenario, CO_2 emissions will grow fourfold by 2100, while according to the optimistic scenario we should expect moderate emission growth, followed by its gradual decline to a fraction of today's volumes of emissions. According to this scenario, the CO_2 concentration will increase to 540–970 ppm by 2100, that is, by 90–250% with respect to preindustrial level of 280 ppm, provided that the fraction of emissions absorbed by the oceans and biosphere remains unchanged. When taking into account that climate change can influence the ability of oceans and the biosphere to absorb carbon, the range of possible values will increase to 490–1260 ppm. Thus, we can see that the IPCC scenarios cover a wide spectrum of possible developments.

Later, IPCC members used climatic models to calculate all possible consequences of the aforementioned scenario relating to global average temperature. The result of this calculation was warming by 1.1–6.4°C over the period from 1990 to 2100. This means that unless special measures on mitigation of climate change are undertaken, the anthropogenic warming may by 2100 comprise approximately 2–7°C and more as compared with the preindustrial level. Scientists from the University of South California have recently demonstrated that if average global temperature on Earth increases by 5°C, the planet awaits the repetition of the tragedy of the Permian period, when mass extinction of life occurred. According to their calculations, up to 90% of creatures living in the oceans will perish, as most of the excessive CO_2 is absorbed by oceans. Obviously it is expedient to limit the number of scenarios under consideration to a few in order to choose the most appropriate scenario of energy industry development.

The scenario approach also lies at the base of our model, which allows the calculation of the dynamics of CO_2 emission in the atmosphere for selected scenarios, and thereby incurred dynamics of average global atmosphere temperature variation. The key statement is the concept that many modern climate changes are, to a large extent, determined by anthropogenic factors. The main anthropogenic factor that may lead to the change of global temperature in the near future is energy industry. Among many scenarios of energy development, discussed earlier in the text, we selected the one that conforms to a new paradigm of energy consumption, which, in turn, consists in stabilization of per capita energy consumption at a certain quite comfortable level. This process started in the 1970s after the energy shock caused by the oil crisis. As a result of the process of development and widespread introduction of energy-saving technologies that began at that time, as well as an increase in energy efficiency on the part of the end users, developed countries had experienced a decrease and stabilization of per capita energy consumption at a lower level.

Whereas before the oil crisis energy demand grew proportionally to the square of the world population ($E \sim N^2$), under the transition to the new energy paradigm, it will grow proportionally to population size ($E \sim N$). The new energy consumption paradigm is aimed at practical implementation of the "Blue Map" scenario, using mainly technologies listed in paragraphs 4 and 6, that is, at the expense of huge and still largely unused energy saving potential and an increase in the level of energy efficiency. The effect of technologies directed at lowering CO_2 emissions should be taken into account at the stage of calculation of emission dynamics into the atmosphere. As far as the technologies of replacement of hydrocarbon fuels are concerned, they should be taken into account in consideration of the structure of energy consumption according to sources.

Thus, we suggest the following algorithm of calculation of climate forecast:

1. Development of a mathematical model for the description of the transition process to a new paradigm of energy consumption
2. Calculation of a different scenario of population growth of the world and of individual countries (demographic dynamics)

3. Calculation of a corresponding scenario of the dynamics of energy demand, based on a new paradigm of energy consumption
4. Forecast of the dynamics of the structure of energy consumption according to energy sources (coal, oil, gas, RES, nuclear energy, hydropower)
5. Forecast of the dynamics of demand in organic fossil fuels (coal, oil, gas)
6. Forecast of the dynamics of changes in the structure of hydrocarbon fuel (coal, oil, gas)
7. Calculation of CO_2 atmosphere emission dynamics by burning hydrocarbon fuels with an allowance for structural changes in the consumption of organic fossil fuels (coal, oil, gas) and application of carbon capture and storage technology (CCS)
8. Calculation of the dynamics of CO_2 accumulation in the atmosphere with allowance for nonindustrial CO_2 emissions (due to deforestation and soil erosion) and partial absorption of emissions by the oceans and land ecosystems
9. Forecast of climate change dynamics and calculation of average global ground atmosphere
10. Analysis of results and preparation of practical advice

All calculation have been carried out by making use of approximate mathematical models, presented in the following sections of this chapter. As a rule, for climate forecasting the forecasts for 50–100 years are used. We stick to general practice and limit the forecasting horizon to 90 years, to the year 2100. This methodology for the calculation of a climate change scenario is a simple alternative to forecasting based on a climate simulation model (Manabe and Wetherald, 1975; Tarko, 2005). The climate models allow calculation of forecast values for atmosphere temperature in space distribution and provide the possibility of predicting local changes in any region of interest of the planet. Our methodology provides information on changes in global temperature averaged over the space only. The advantage of the proposed methodology is the relative simplicity of its implementation and the ability to determine scenario parameters of energy development, meeting criteria that put forward the emission of carbon to the Earth atmosphere in the near future and long-term perspectives.

21.4 Dynamics of Energy Consumption in the 20th and 21st Centuries

21.4.1 Transition to a New Paradigm

Let us proceed with implementation of the aforementioned forecasting methodology of climate change. We first consider the dynamics of energy consumption in the 20th century and the trends of development in the 21st century.

The leading role of the energy industry in world economics will certainly remain in the 21st century. In the 20th century world GDP (Y) grew proportional to the amount of energy produced by humanity (E), that is, $Y \sim E$, which can be easily shown. Most developed countries have a similar structure of the production and consumption of primary energy. Approximately 40% of total energy production is used for manufacturing output; 25% for transport facilities of all kinds; and the remaining 35% for heating, illumination, and food production. The division of the world into developed and developing countries has a noticeable impact on the amount of the produced energy and the character of its distribution. At present two thirds of the energy produced is consumed in industrially developed countries with a population of just over 1 billion people; one third falls within the rest, just below 6 billion of the Earth population.

In the 20th century there was 15-fold increase in consumption of energy resources with a 3.8-fold growth of Earth's population. The comparison of population growth and the growth of consumption of energy, the main resource of development, is of great interest. A study establishing functional dependence of global energy consumption and world population growth was undertaken by J. Holdren (1991). He showed that total energy consumption E was proportional to the square of the Earth population N throughout the 20th century:

$$E \sim N^2. \tag{21.1}$$

Virtually all aspects of human life and activities are connected with use of certain types of energy. Therefore, growth of energy consumption by humans resulted in improvement of comfort of their life activities, which in turn has a positive influence on population increase. Both factors gave rise to a growth of world energy production and consumption in the 20th century. The growing population causes a further increase in demand for fuel and energy resources, leading to modern industrial development and expansion of food production.

Naturally, in this connection a question of whether the square law dependence (21.1) of energy consumption that took place in the 20th century will remain in the 21st century. Before answering this question, let us consider the main characteristics of energy consumption.

The most general criteria indicating the level of demand and consumption is per capita energy consumption. Without reaching some critical level of energy consumption, the achievement of the required level of productive power and prosperity is impossible. Taking into account that different countries have unequal levels of energy consumption, we can point out considerable regional difference of per capita energy consumption as shown in Table 21.1.

Thus, developed countries have per capita energy consumption that is 2.5 times higher than the world average. On the other hand, developing countries have per capita energy consumption that is 2.5 times lower than the world average. The gap in per capita energy consumption reaches a 10-fold level.

Table 21.1 Levels of Per Capita Energy Consumption of Leading World Countries in the 21st Century

Countries	Per capita energy consumption, t.c.e./person	
	Present	Mid-century
World average	2.4	2.5
Countries with per capita consumption above world average	6.9	4.0
USA	9.5	5.5
Russia	6.2	4.5
EU-Japan	5	3.5
Countries with per capita consumption below world average	1	2.5
Democratic People's Republic of Korea	1.2	2.5
India	0.8	2.5

Table 21.2 The Ratio of Per Capita Energy Consumption in Developed and Developing Countries

Years	Ratio of per capita consumption, units	
	Developed to developing countries	World average to developing countries
1930	52	22.5
1930	27	10.9
1950	19.7	7.5
1980	17.9	6.1
2000	7.1	2.5

At the same time, the estimate of world energy consumption over the last 100 years indicates that the gap between per capita energy consumption in developed and developing countries is constantly decreasing. For example, while at the beginning of the 20th century the gap was 52-fold, by the end of the century it was equal to the 7-fold level (see Table 21.2). Moreover, the developing countries have a typical trend of a quickly shortening gap between actual per capita consumption with respect to that of the world. Thus, while in the beginning of the 20th century the gap was more than 22-fold, at the end of the century it was 2.5-fold (see Table 21.2).

Over the last 30 years considerable changes were taking place in world energy production, connected first of all with the transition from extensive ways of development, from energy euphoria to a pragmatic energy policy, based on an increase of efficiency of energy use and its saving. The causes of these changes were the energy crises of

1973 and 1979, considerable depletion of fossil fuels and appreciation of their mining, and not least concern about worsening of the ecological situation both on land and in the Earth atmosphere. Thus, starting from the 1980s, the importance of per capita consumption growth started to decline, being gradually replaced by the importance of energy consumption efficiency. Consequently, the logic of development of energy consumption in the 21st century required minimization of the interregional gap, and, first of all, at the expense of a considerable decrease of per capita energy consumption in developed countries and considerable increase of energy consumption in developing countries. Obviously vanguard countries with dynamically developing markets, such as China and India, will considerably increase their per capita energy consumption in the 21st century. Generally, the increase of per capita energy consumption to the world average level of 2.5 t.c.e., providing industrialization of economics, is expected. After the energy crisis, developed countries drastically increased the efficiency of energy consumption by using energy-saving technologies on a large scale. Actual decrease of per capita energy consumption started in developed countries as early as the 1990s. This decrease will continue throughout the 21st century. Yet by the middle of the 21st century, by the end of implementation of the sixth technological stage (2015–2050), per capita energy consumption in developed countries will decrease to 40–45% and then will stabilize at a stationary level, given in Table 21.1. The latter should become a standard for developed countries. They also conform to the obligations assumed by developed countries at the UN Conference on Environment in Copenhagen in 2009. Besides, experts believe, that per capita energy consumption level of 3.5 t.c.e./year is quite comfortable for citizens of developed countries. Studying the aforementioned trends in per capita energy consumption in different countries of the world, the authors (Klimenko et al., 1997) have came to the conclusion that in the 21st century world average per capita energy consumption will stabilize at the level 2.6÷2.5 t.c.e. per person per year, as shown in Figure 21.5.

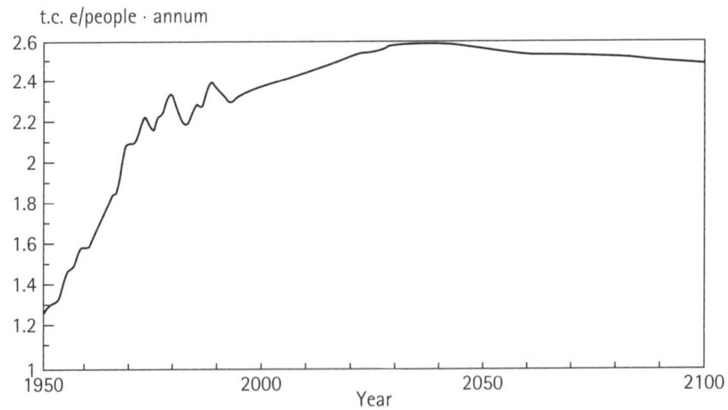

FIGURE 21.5 Forecast of world per capita energy consumption.

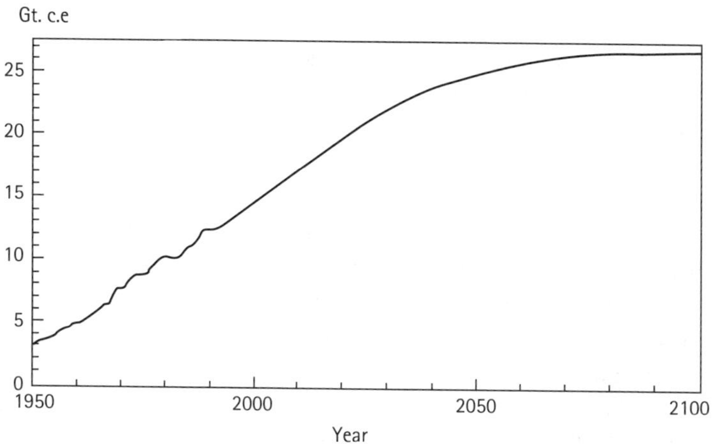

FIGURE 21.6 Forecast of world energy consumption.

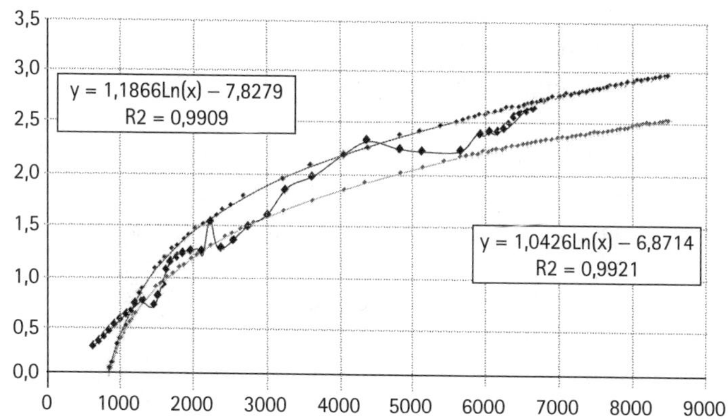

FIGURE 21.7 Dependence of world per capita energy consumption (t.c.e./person) on world population (billion people).

Multiplying this value by the forecast of world population growth in the 21st century they provided a forecast of total world energy consumption (E) (see Figure 21.6).

On the other hand, studying the dependence of world per capita energy consumption, Yu. A. Plakitkin (2006) has also come to the conclusion that in the 21st century world per capita energy consumption will stabilize at a "plateau" of 2.5–2.8 t.c.e. per year per person, as shown in Figure 21.7.

We should point out that the stabilization of per capita energy consumption at 2.5 t.c.e. per year level is possible only when three conditions are met simultaneously:

1. Per capita energy consumption in the developed countries decreases by 40% from 6.9 t.c.e. per annum to 4 t.c.e. per annum
2. A 150% increase of per capita energy consumption in developing countries from 1 t.c.e./year today to the world average of 1 t.c.e./year
3. Outstripping growth rate of energy consumption efficiency

We call the transition to the mode of per capita energy consumption stabilization in the 21st century the new energy consumption paradigm. Assuming the trend of stabilization of per capita energy consumption, valid without exception for all countries of the world, we note that the level of stabilization and terms of achievement are substantially different for different countries. Thus, according to the new energy consumption paradigm in the 21st century, the volume of world energy production will increase proportionally to the Earth population:

$$E_w = 2.5N.(\text{t.c.e. per annum}) \tag{21.2}$$

Thus, with the long-term population growth forecast at hand, using formula (21.2) we can readily calculate world energy consumption in the 21st century.

Based on the new energy consumption paradigm, Yu. Plakitkin suggested a model of per capita energy consumption for the 21st century, which is shown in graphic form in Figure 21.8.

The per capita energy consumption will fit the aforementioned model only if developing energy use efficiency as stated in the preceding will outstrip the growth rate. It is expected that the energy consumption coefficient will increase by a logistic curve, as shown in Figure 21.9. The energy use coefficient reflects the level of technological

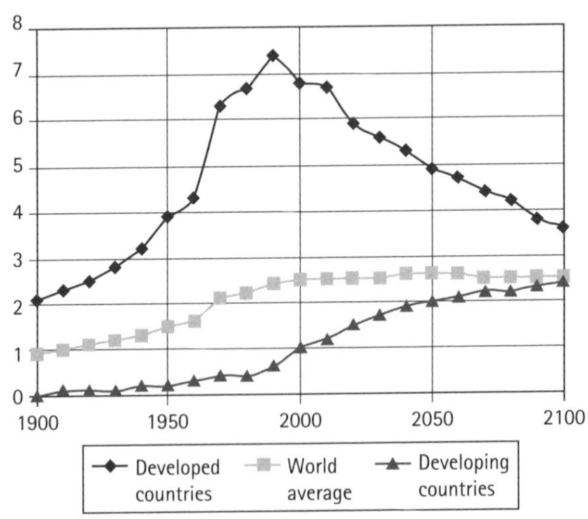

FIGURE 21.8 Forecast of per capita energy consumption (per capita t.c.e.) both in developed and developing countries.

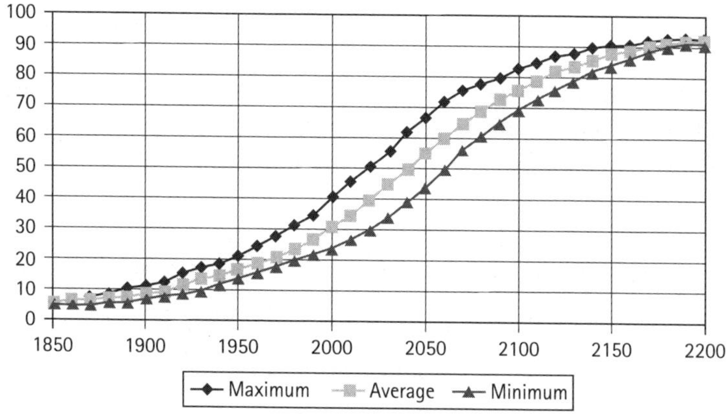

FIGURE 21.9 Forecast of energy use coefficient in developed countries.

development of power engineering. It holds true with regard to both the developed and the developing countries except for a certain time lag, which will decrease gradually. As a result, the per capita energy consumption will stabilize and be 2.5 t.c.e. It is quite sufficient to provide the current population with comfortable and up-to-date living conditions.

The preceding models of per capita energy consumption for developed and developing countries in the 21st century can be described by logistic curves with satisfactory accuracy, describing the transition to a new energy consumption paradigm:

1. Energy consumption dynamics E_d in the developing countries (China, India, Brazil, etc.) is described by an ascending logistic curve:

$$E_d = e_d N_d(T) = \frac{e_d^{(0)}(1+\rho)N_d(T)}{1+\rho\exp[-\vartheta(T-T_0]}, \tag{21.3}$$

where e^d = per capita energy consumption, indicated in t.c.e.; $N_d(T)$ = population at T; ρ and ϑ = constant parameters. With regard to $e_d^{\max} = e_d^{(0)}(1+\rho) = 2.5$ t.c.e. and $e_d^{(0)} \cong 1$ t.c.e., we get: $\rho = 1.5$ and $\vartheta = 0.044$; $T_0 = 2010$. For instance, for China, $e_d^{(0)} \cong 1.2$ t.c.e.; $\rho = 1.08$; $\vartheta = 0.031$, and for India, $e_d^{(0)} \cong 0{,}8$ t.c.e.; $\rho = 2.12$; $\vartheta = 0.037$.

2. For the developed countries (United States, European Union, Japan, etc.) energy consumption dynamics E_{hd} is described by a descending logistic curve:

$$E_{hd} = e_{hd}^{(0)} N_{hd}(T) \frac{1+\rho\left\{2\exp[-\vartheta(T-T_0)]-1\right\}}{1+\rho\exp[-\vartheta(T-T_0)]}. \tag{21.4}$$

Using data from Table 21.1 we can easily find certain values of parameters ρ and ϑ, assuming $T_0 = 2010$: for the United States $e_{hd}^{(0)} = 9.5$t.c.e.; $\rho = 0.42$; $\vartheta = 0.03$; for the

European Union and Japan, $e_{hd}^{(0)} = 5$t.c.e.; $\rho = 0.3$; $\vartheta = 0.032$; and for Russia, $e_{hd}^{(0)} = 6.2$ t.c.e.; $\rho = 0.274$; $\vartheta = 0.023$.

Thus, for the calculation of energy consumption dynamic in the 21st century for the world (21.2), developing countries (21.3), and developed countries (21.4), long-term forecasts of the corresponding demographic dynamics will be sufficient.

21.5 Mathematical Models for the Calculation of Demographic Dynamics

The unprecedented economic growth and geopolitical changes in the 20th century were caused by a record population explosion, when during only one century the world population grew almost four times: from 1656 billion in 1900 to 6055 billion people in 2000. Such explosive growth of the Earth population is usually connected with epoch-making achievements of science and technology, which, first, allow for a relatively affluent existence in Europe and North America, and, then—during the 20th century—spreading out to developing countries. Indeed, the achievements of science and technology have resulted in a manifold increase labor efficiency, the main factor of economic growth. Gradually, at the expense of industrialization and modernization of agriculture, people's lives were becoming ever more comfortable and stable, independent of the whims of nature. By the end of the 20th century even perpetually starving overpopulated countries such as China and India have managed to feed their huge fast-growing population. At the same time, starting from the 1960s humankind has been making a global demographic transition, essentially by replacement of the explosive growth by with stabilization of the population by a simultaneous decrease of birth and death rates.

There was a break in the demographic trend and the rate of population growth started to decrease slowly; the demographic explosion receded. By the end of the 21st century a demographic stabilization throughout the world can be expected. In either case, the natural population movement on the whole has a self-regulatory ability. The length of these fuel and energy balance transition processes, as shown by S. P. Kapitsa (2008), is defined by the doubled characteristic lifespan of a human, equal to 40–45 years, that is, a demographic transition lasts only for 80–90 years, until 2040. Most developed countries have already made the demographic transition, while in developing countries it is only now unfolding.

On the other hand, a large-scale and intensive use of Earth's resources, caused by the extreme growth of the world population, is leading to the destruction of the biosphere, climate change, human-caused environmental pollution, depletion of vital resources, and eventually to such radical change of environmental conditions as to pose a serious threat to the survival of mankind. Trying to live and act reasonably, while accounting for the limited capacity of the biosphere, we at the same time should be aware of the real influence of anthropogenic factors, as compared with natural ones, in destabilizing the atmosphere.

Because of this problem, the development of mathematical models capable of showing by computer simulation the limits of human expansion to the biosphere and the global and local limitations imposed by the environmental state on the Earth population becomes a vital need. The models of demographic dynamics comprise the basis of such macro-models.

Different models describe various development scenarios of demographic dynamics. In the general case world (country) population continues to grow by inertia and reaches a certain maximum level, exceeding an ecologically admissible one, and then either slowly decreases to a stationary level N_c, determined by the permissible carrying capacity of the Earth biosphere, or stabilizes at this level by diminishing oscillations after a sharp decrease. The important thing is that the whole process is governed by a demographic imperative (Kapitsa, 2008), which lies in the fact that that population growth is determined by the population of the world system itself, the process of social development, and scientific and technical progress, in contrast to the Malthusian population principle, in which limits of growth are set by external resources—earth, energy, food.

Indeed, it was pointed out as early as the mid-20th century that Earth population growth obeys a universal development trend along a hyperbolic trajectory. Thus, a number of authors, in particular, von Foerster, Mora, and Amiot (von Foerster et al., 1960; von Hoerner, 1975) have clearly demonstrated that the world population data for several centuries up to the 1970s are surprisingly well described by a hyperbolic function:

$$N = \frac{C}{T_0 - T} = \frac{200}{2025 - T} \text{ (billion people)}, \tag{21.5}$$

where T is the time in years, C.E.; T_0 is the singularity point, and$C$ is a constant. According to Hoerner $T_0 = 2025$ and $C = 200 \cdot 10^9$people$\times$years. Formula (21.5) as the power function has scale invariance or an absence of its own time scale, which indicates a self-similarity of growth.

21.5.1 Kapitsa's Phenomenological Model: Demographic Imperative

The analysis of hyperbolic population growth, binding population, and human development suggested a cooperative development mechanism, with the square of the population as a measure. Therefore Kapitsa (1992) suggested the use of a square law dependence of population growth:

$$\frac{dN}{dt} = \frac{N^2}{C}, \tag{21.6}$$

where C is a constant. The solution of this equation is a hyperbolic function (21.5). S. Kapitsa proceeded from the hypothesis according to which "...human development is fundamentally different by the fact, that due to intelligence and consciousness, culture and developed information transfer system, both vertically—from generation to generation—and spatially, humankind develops sustainably, following statistically determined self-similar growth. It continues until demographic revolution, when population growth ceases" (Kapitsa, 2008, p. 17). Thus the interpretation of development is based on the assumption that collective interaction takes place through the mechanism of information distribution and multiplication within humanity as a global network information society. Equations of the (21.6) type are well studied and their solutions (21.5) are known as blow-up regimes. The characteristic feature of such equations is that in a certain finite moment of time T_0, called the singularity point, the solution converges to infinity. What takes place in real life is the substitution of blow-up growth with limited reproducibility. This phenomena was discovered for the first time by French demographer Adolphe Landry in connection with France, and he called it the "demographic revolution" (Kapitsa, 2008, p. 17). Today, this phenomenon is given the name global demographic transition.

To describe the demographic transition, S. Kapitsa proposed taking into account time τ and such internal processes as lifespan and reproductive time—factors, limiting growth rate when it approaches the limit during demographic transition.

First, after differentiating (21.5) we obtain the dependence of the growth rate on time:

$$\frac{dN}{dt} = \frac{C}{(T_0 - T)^2}. \tag{21.7}$$

S. Kapitsa regularized the equation by introduction of characteristic time τ, limiting growth rate:

$$\frac{dN}{dt} = \frac{C}{(T_1 - T)^2 + \tau^2} \tag{21.8}$$

The modified equation obtained (21.8) does not provide a blow-up mode—the convergence of solution into infinity. Moreover, it can be easily integrated and provides a simple symbolic formula for the description of population dynamics:

$$N = K\text{arcctg}\left(\frac{T_1 - T}{\tau}\right). \tag{21.9}$$

We will call it Kapitsa's formula and also introduce Kapitsa's number: $K = \sqrt{\frac{C}{\tau}}$. Based on world demographic statistic data S. Kapitsa calculated constant numerical values in (21.5): $C = 163 \cdot 10^9$; $K = 60100$; $\tau = 45$; $T_1 = 1995$. Furthermore, he demonstrated that given the above values of parameters and constants, $N_{\max} = \pi K^2 \cong 11{,}36$ billion people, which follows from (21.5) at $T \to \infty$. This is, after Kapitsa, the upper estimate of Earth population in foreseeable future (Kapitsa, 2008). The graph of Earth population growth, calculated after Kapitsa's formula (21.9), is presented in Figure 21.10, where actual (observed) Earth population data are also presented,

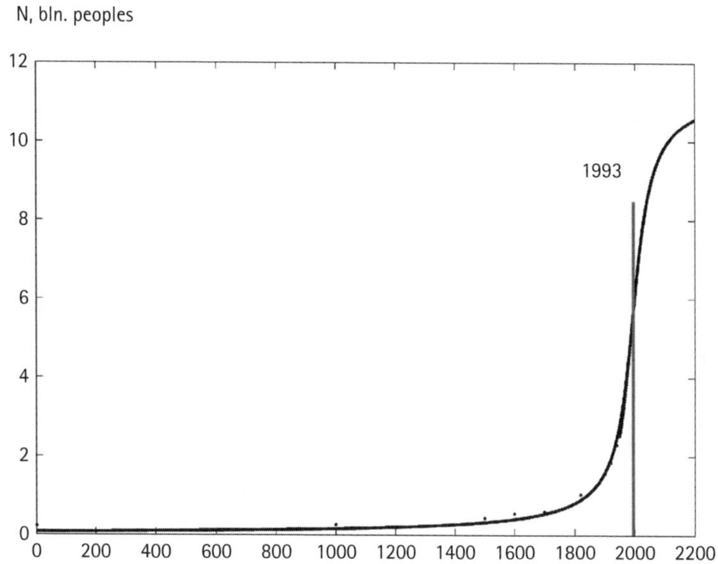

FIGURE 21.10 Evolution model of world population (billion people).

denoted with dots. It is important to note that the Earth population growth rate $\left(q_N = \frac{dN}{Ndt}\right)$ has already crossed maximum (1963, $q_N = 2{,}2\%$) and in the future it will only decrease, approaching zero. Thus, the global demographic transition is due to occurrence in the intensification mode the limit of world population growth rate. As the growth rate decreases, Earth population reaches a plateau and stabilizes at $N_{\max} = 11{,}36$ billion people. It should be noted that such a growth scenario is implemented only with sustainable development of humanity. From the analysis of Figure 21.10, one can see that Kapitsa's formula makes a perfect fit of world system demographic dynamics, particularly for the demographic transition period.

Kapitsa's model (21.9) can be successfully used for the calculation of demographic dynamics of individual countries, capable of providing robust development when population grows according to the stabilization scenario without a noticeable decrease. An indispensable condition is the absence of compulsory birth control measures and a substantial influence of migration flows on the social and economic processes in the country. As an example, Figure 21.11 shows population growth in the United States, Germany, and Great Britain after Kapitsa's model (21.9). One can observe good agreement of the theoretical demographic trajectory with actual data. The chart of demographic dynamics in Japan was obtained with a cusp growth model, described later, because the population of Japan, after reaching a maximum, decreases and demographers forecast that it will stabilize at 120 million.

Thus, S. Kapitsa demonstrated that the Earth population growth can be described mathematically (21.8), without introduction of additional variables besides N, that is, essentially, without attraction of any additional factors. This property served the basis

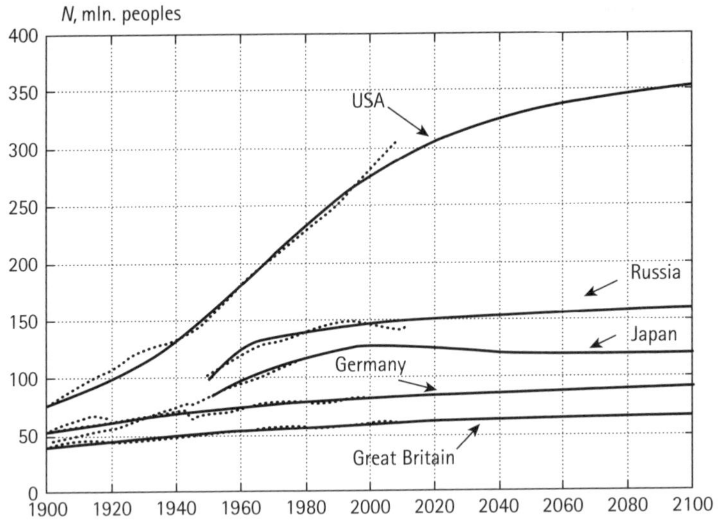

FIGURE 21.11 Population dynamics of developed countries in the 21st century (million people). (USA: $T_1 = 1967$, $\tau = 46.7$, $K = 354.9$; Japan: $T_1 = 1963$, $\tau = 60.7$, $K = 247$; Germany: $T_1 = 1896$, $\tau = 78.8$, $K = 181$; UK: $T_1 = 1893$, $\tau = 93.6$, $K = 156$).

for S. Kapitsa to formulate a demographic imperative, according to which global social, historical, economical, and cultural processes are subject to a change of the Earth population. This value plays the part of the leading slow variable, called rank parameter in synergetic, which brings under control all other variables (Haken, 1985). This implies that demographic dynamics plays a primary and decisive role in the history of development of human society.

On the other hand, the character of creation of global demographic dynamics reveals that humankind possesses an inherent, genetic ability for controlling its development, which is the essence of the demographic imperative.

21.5.2 Demographic Dynamics in Cusp Growth Model

The works of Akimov (2008) and Dolgonosov (2009) convincingly showed that the most probable scenario of growth of the Earth population dynamics is the cusp regime, with growth and subsequent stabilization at stationary levels. This fact is in agreement with J. Smail's (2002) consideration that there is population limit, to be reached soon, and its further stabilization with a significant decrease is most likely unavoidable. The expected significant decrease in population will be the result of explosive growth for more than century, after which, according to many indicators, the carrying capacity of Earth biosphere has been seriously exceeded. At present, according to expert estimates, the human population consumes more than 20% of planetary biomass in energy equivalents, while acceptable harvesting that is nondestructive to the biosphere does not exceed 1% (Gorshkov, 1995). Therefore, human population exceeded the permissible economic limit more than 20-fold and crossed the sustainability limit of the biosphere. From the paper by Wackernagel et al. (2002) it follows that the human population was at a sustainability level for the last time in the 1980s. According to J. Smail's estimates, the time-independence of the environment is below 2–3 billion people, and it will be reached no sooner than in two centuries. Naturally, in the course of time, biologic and social mechanisms of falling birth rates should appear, which are still inactive in many developing countries. But this process will take at least half a century (approximately two generations), while population will grow by inertia up to 9–10 billion people (Smail, 2002), and only then will population decline start.

For formal presentation of the population growth model with cusp, one should first build a function describing the instant capacity of environment $K(T)$, that is, maximum population size, achieved at given level of knowledge and technology. B. M. Dolgonosov (2009) connected instant capacity of environment directly with the level of knowledge (Q), using information priority, which required additional study of information production modes and made forecasts more complex. In our paper (Akaev and Sadovnichij, 2010), we demonstrated that one can limit oneself by a demographic imperative when constructing a function for description of the instant capacity of environment, that is, $K = K(N)$. It can be done as follows.

M. Kremer (1993) showed that at any given time interval there is a certain threshold population level, equal to $K(A)$, that cannot be exceeded at the given level of technological development ?. The quantity K is the current environmental capacity. Thus, the momentary environmental capacity is determined by the level of technological development and expands as the level of technological development goes higher. Kremer also supposed, following S. Kuznets (1960), that the rates of technological growth are proportional to the current population:

$$\frac{dA}{Adt} = cN. \tag{21.10}$$

This equation, called the Kuznets–Kremer equation (Korotayev 2005, 2007), is the equation of technological development. Empirical verification of the equation (21.10), presented in the monograph by Korotayev et al. (2006), showed that it completely corresponds with the available data until the 1980s. It also results from equation (21.10) that the momentary capacity K can expand proportionally to the rates of growth of technological development. Therefore,

$$K(A) \sim N. \tag{21.11}$$

On the other hand, as the world population with its uncontrollable economic activities grows, anthropogenic stress on the biosphere grows as well, causing degradation of ecosystems worldwide, and as a result, the momentary environmental capacity declines. The rates of the momentary capacity reduction are evidently proportional to the rates of population growth:

$$\frac{dK}{Kdt} = \kappa \frac{dN}{dt}, \kappa = \text{const.} \tag{21.12}$$

It follows that

$$K \sim \exp(-\kappa N). \tag{21.13}$$

Combining (21.11) and (21.13) we obtain:

$$K \sim N \exp(-\kappa N). \tag{21.14}$$

Thus, the given formula of instant capacity of the Earth biosphere includes, on one hand, extension of natural capacity by using new technologies, and, on the other hand, its concurrent shrinkage caused by limitations due to growing anthropogenic pressure on the environment.

Adding to (21.14) the stationary world (country's) population level we obtain the final formula of the momentary environmental capacity, which is determined exclusively by the population, that is, by the demographic imperative:

$$K = N_c + \gamma N \exp(-\kappa N), \gamma = \text{const.} \tag{21.15}$$

The problem of the permissible world population at a stationary level is one of the fundamental modern problems. Various methods of estimating the stationary world population N_C are presented in the paper by Fedotov (2002). Let us accept a stable population of 7.7 billion people as the permissible world population in the resource model of D. Meadows and his colleagues (2008). The academician V. M. Morozov, developing the resource model of Meadows, determined the permissible world population equal to 6.5 billion people (Fedotov, 2002). B. Dolgonosov has given an estimate for $N_C = 5.2$ billion. people (Dolgonosov, 2009). We earlier provided an estimate by the respected expert J. Smail of stabilization at a level not higher than 2–3 billion (Smail, 2002).

According to the data on world population growth, on the basis of the theory of critical levels of growth of biological populations (Zhirmunski and Kuzmin, 1994), limiting population values, which lead to changes in growth trends after they are reached, were also calculated. The theory of critical phenomena singles out levels of 6.2, 7.4, and 9.1 billion people as critical levels. It is stated that every time it crosses a critical population, a biological community lives through crisis phenomena. The possibility of achievement of the next critical population is determined by how successfully previous critical levels have been overcome. The lower border of 6.2 billion people was successfully crossed in 2000. The next critical level of 7.4 billion people after the Kapitsa model (21.9) will be crossed in 2015. If it is successfully crossed, then humankind will have to overcome the level of 9.1 billion people around the 2050s. The authors of this paper (Jermunsky and Kuzmin, 1994) insist that it is a critical population, which rules out any possibility of further growth, because it is limited by the limiting critical mass of the population. Thus, a stationary world population equal 9.1 billion people is the most optimistic forecast. It is in good agreement with the most probable average long-term UN Forecast (World population in 2300, 2003), according to which Earth population will reach a maximum by 2075 and then stabilize at a level of around 9 billion people.

Thus, we can speak about the fact that the most probable, scientifically proved value of the Earth population lies within the range of 2 to 10 billion people. In our model calculations we assume $N_C = 5.2$ billion people, which is a stationary level that can be found in recent forecast calculations (Akimov, 2008; Dolgonosov, 2009). Furthermore, when making use of demographic dynamics for the calculation of energy consumption dynamics, we think it is expedient to consider four major scenarios of demographic development with stabilization at the main stationary level: $N_C = 5.2$, 6.2, 7.4, and 9.1 billion people. It should be pointed out that there is an exigency in development of reliable and precise methods of estimation of the stationary population level for the whole world as well as for separate countries. In this connection we cannot miss the historical fact related to the prediction by Charles Fourier (1772–1837), one of the founders of utopian socialism. He believed that it is expedient to "set up population equilibrium, a ratio between the number of consumers and productive power," and "to reduce the number of residents of Earth globe to exact proportionality of power and demand, i.e. to approximately 5bln.people" (Fourier 1939: 138). By the way, at the beginning of the 19th century, when C. Fourier made his calculations, the Earth population comprised about 1 billion people, that is, it hardly exceeded the acceptable level of biological consumption.

V. G. Gorshkov (1995) has answered the fundamental question: he discovered that the biota is capable of regulation and stabilization of the environment if the amount of consumption of primary biological products by humanity does not exceed 1% of total production by the biosphere. He also calculated that the value of admissible biological consumption corresponds to the Earth population of 1 billion people, which was achieved by the 1820s. At present, according to estimates by Gorshkov, humanity consumes about 22–23% of planetary biomass. Thus, humans have exceeded more than 20-fold the acceptable level of natural stability of the biosphere. So, the practical influence of life-supporting technologies on the instant capacity of media started at the beginning of the 19th century and exceeded the natural limit of biological consumption. To take this factor into account we will write (21.15) as follows:

$$K = N_c + \gamma(N - N_0)\exp[-\kappa(N - N_0)], \qquad (21.16)$$

where $N_0 = 1$ billion people.

We can now write a demographic dynamics equation in the following form, making use of the well-known population model describing dynamics of a thinned population, where reproduction is limited by the creation of married couples (Svirijev, 1987):

$$\frac{dN}{dt} = rN^2 \left\{ 1 - \frac{N}{N_c + \gamma(N - N_0)\exp[-\kappa(N - N_0)]} \right\}. \qquad (21.17)$$

This model is described by hyperbolic growth at $N << N_c$, with subsequent slowdown, when the values of N are of the same magnitude as N_c, and transition to the stationary level $N \to N_c$ at $T \to \infty$.

Introducing typical lateness we finally obtain (Akaev and Sadovnichiy, 2010):

$$\frac{dN}{dt} = rN^2(t-\tau_1)\left\{1 - \frac{N(t)}{K(N,\tau_2,\tau_3)}\right\}, K(N,\tau_2,\tau_3)$$
$$= N_c + \gamma\,[N(t-\tau_2) - N_0]\exp\{-\kappa\,[N(t-\tau_3) - N_0]\}, \qquad (21.18)$$

where

$\tau_1 =$ average age of start of reproductive ability;
$\tau_2 =$ diffusion time of basis technologies;
$\tau_3 =$ reaction lag of biosphere on anthropogenic load

The average age of the start of reproductive ability is 25 years. The diffusion time of basis technologies nowadays equals 25–30 years. The reaction lag of biosphere on anthropogenic load exceeds 100 years.

The fitting of parameters r, κ, γ, τ_1, τ_2, τ_3 for nonlinear differential equations of demographic dynamics with three lags (21.18) was done numerically by the least squares technique over available data on the population of the world as a whole and of the countries under consideration (t_k, N_k). The studies revealed that the objective function of the least squares technique can be written as

$$\Phi(r,\kappa,\gamma,\tau_1,\tau_2,\tau_3) = \sum_k (N_k - N(t_k; r,\kappa,\gamma,\tau_1,\tau_2,\tau_3))^2, \qquad (21.19)$$

where $N(t_k; r,\kappa,\gamma,\tau_1,\tau_2,\tau_3)$ is the solution of (21.18), which has many local minima; therefore we selected hypercube $(r,\kappa,\gamma,\tau_1,\tau_2,\tau_3)$ in six-dimensional space

$$(r,\kappa,\gamma,\tau_1,\tau_2,\tau_3) \in [0, r_{\max}] \times [0,\kappa_{\max}] \times [0,\gamma_{\max}] \times$$
$$\times [0,\tau_{1,\max}] \times [0,\tau_{2,\max}] \times [0,\tau_{3,\max}],$$

which was divided by grids with constant step in every direction. In every grid node we solved the numerically differential equation (21.18) for $T > t_0 = 1950$ and calculated the objective function (21.19). Further we selected several nodes with the smallest value (21.19); then in their vicinities the grid with the smaller step was selected, where minimum (21.19) was found again. This procedure was repeated several times, and then the resulting values r, κ, γ were taken as initial ones for the least squares technique. After minimizing functional (21.19) with given sets of initial parameter values, we selected a minimum value, and the corresponding set of parameters was assumed to be optimal.

For numerical solution of differential equation (21.18) one needs to set the prehistory $N_h(T)$ at no more than 100 years because it is assumed that the lag of biospheric reaction after anthropogenic load does not exceed 100 years.

The two scenarios of world population dynamics, obtained with the use of the lag model (21.18) and their comparison with the S. P. Kapitsa model are presented in

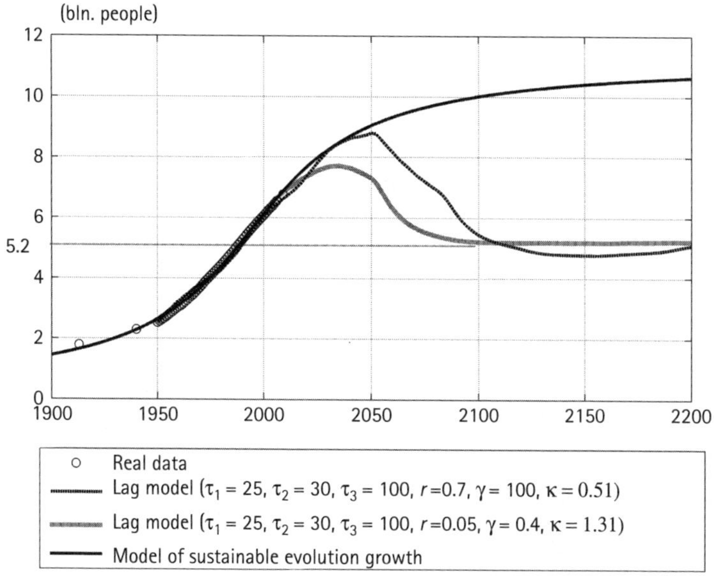

FIGURE 21.12 World population in the 20th–22nd centuries.

Figure 21.12, with real data. The first scenario corresponds to the following set of parameters: $r = 0.0257$, $\gamma = 1.623$, $\kappa = 0.566$, $\tau_1 = 25$, $\tau_2 = 30$, $\tau_3 = 100$, the second to $r = 0.0242$, $\gamma = 1.978$, $\kappa = 1.357$, $\tau_1 = 25$, $\tau_2 = 30$, $\tau_3 = 100$. Both scenarios correspond to the solutions, deviating from real data from 1950 up to now within a 3–5% limit. The first scenario predicts a maximum population of 9 billion people in 2050 with subsequent decline, with pronounced oscillation behavior, down to 5.2 billion people. The second scenario gives a maximum population around 7.7 billion people in 2030 with subsequent stabilization at 5.2 billion people by 2100.

By analyzing Figure 21.12, one can see that the proposed model (21.18) allows simulation of various scenarios of population dynamics: growth with aperiodic return to stationary level (lower dashed line) and growth and stabilization around the stationary level by means of diminishing oscillations (upper dashed line). The model (21.18), due to introduction of time lags τ_1, τ_2, and τ_3, allows efficient use of demographic dynamics prehistory over a 100-year period and therefore provides perfect agreement with actual data with hindsight. From Figure 21.12 it follows that sustainable growth with the stabilization scenario described by the Kapitsa equation can hardly be implemented in life, as the stationary level after Kapitsa exceeds by almost twofold the stationary level obtained by a number of authors (Fedotov, 2002; Dolgonosov, 2009).

Forecasts of demographic dynamics of the growth model with cusp (21.18) corresponding to different stationary stabilization levels are presented in Figure 21.13. For the sake of comparison, the models of unlimited growth by Kapitsa (Figure 21.10) and UN (Population Division Database, 2010) models are presented. As can be seen

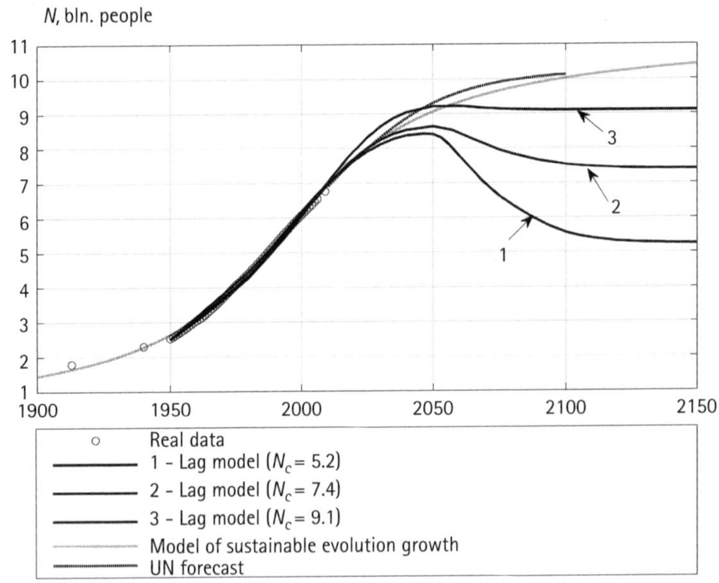

FIGURE 21.13 Different scenarios of world population dynamics in the 20th–22nd centuries (billion people).

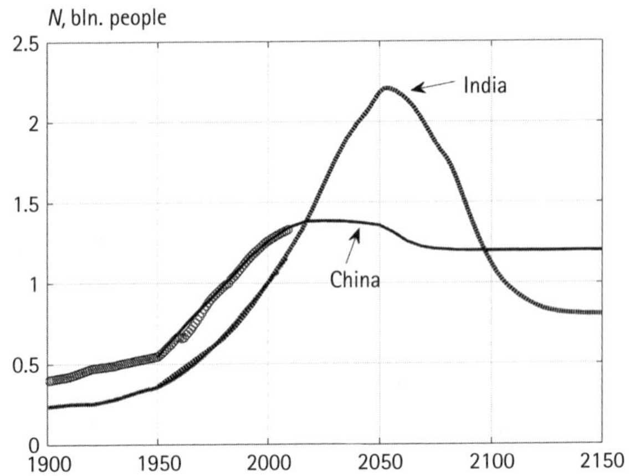

FIGURE 21.14 Forecast of population dynamics of China and India (billion people) in the 21st–22nd centuries.

from this figure, the UN forecast coincides with the trajectory of unlimited sustainable growth by Kapitsa.

To show the stabilization process, forecast trajectories of China and India demographic dynamics in the 21st–22nd centuries are presented in Figure 21.14. The stationary population of a country can be found by dividing the stationary world population by the anthropogenic load index of the country of interest, derived from special reference tables (Fedotov, 2002). For example, if we take the world population $N_c = 5.2$ billion people, then $N_{cc} = 1.2$ billion people for China and $N_{ci} = 0.98$ billion people for India. Forecasts in Figure 21.14 are compiled with the account for stabilization of the population at the indicated stationary level.

As can be seen from Figure 21.14, owing to the introduction of a strict birth control mechanism, the demographic dynamic in China represents a smooth growth trajectory with aperiodic return to a stationary level. However, unless similar measures are taken, India most likely will confront a full-scale ecological crisis. As a result, a sharp population decline will start, which later, after serious losses, will stabilize in a diminishing oscillation mode. In both cases we observe perfect agreement of the calculated population with factual data until 2010. Besides, the maximum deviation does not exceed 70 million people, and the root-mean-square does not exceed 30 million people. The China and India population dynamic forecast for the 21st century, along with corresponding UN forecasts (UN Population Division Database, 2010) are presented in Figure 21.15. One can see that our model provides an overrated forecast, as compared with the one by the UN, which shows the need for further clarification of mathematical cusp growth models.

It should be noted that China demonstrates an approach to sustainable growth typical for developing countries. China has developed a strategy of sustainable development called "China's Agenda XXI"—The White Book about population, environment, and development of China in the 21st century (China's Agenda 21, 1994). Whereas the

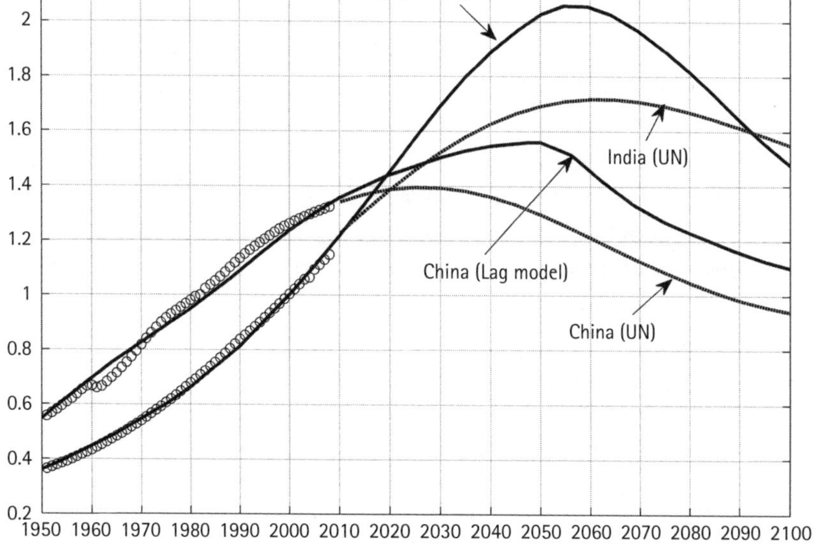

FIGURE 21.15 Population dynamics of China and India in the 21st century.

goals of sustainable development in most developed countries are shifted toward environmental protection (Brown, 2003), China puts emphasis on economical growth in its program. It is in economic growth that China sees the possibility of finding funds and technologies for environmental protection. If this program is implemented completely, then undoubtedly China can ensure sustainable development and carry out forecast scenarios of demographic dynamics (see Figure 21.14).

Thus, as we have seen in the preceding text, after demographic transition, different scenarios of demographic dynamics came into existence, ranging from the most desirable of sustainable growth with stabilization after the Kapitsa model (e.g., for the United States, many countries of Western Europe, Brazil, and others "well-off" countries) to a growth scenario with aperiodic mode (as for China) or in the cusp oscillation mode (as, possibly, will be in India). Therefore, the above development scenarios should be taken into account when developing forecast models for the 21st century.

21.6 Examples of Calculating the Dynamics of Energy Consumption for Developed and Developing Countries in the 21st Century in Energy -Ecological Development

Using the resulting parities in Section 21.3 describing the dynamics of per capita energy consumption for the world as a whole (21.2) and separately for the developing (21.3) and also developed (21.4) countries, and knowing the demographic dynamics both for the world as a whole (21.18) and for developed and developing countries separately (21.9, 21.18), we can now calculate the dynamics of the total energy consumption in the 21st century within the conditions of energy-ecological development.

The dynamics of world energy consumption are shown in Figure 21.16. It is seen that the peak of total energy consumption is projected for the years 2040—2050 and is about 21–23 billion t.c.e.; it then begins a gradual decline and stabilization at various levels by the end of the 21st century. The resulting estimates of world energy consumption correspond well with existing data of the IEA forecast (IEA, 2010) until 2035. The relevant comparison is presented in Table 21.3.

Figure 21.17 shows the energy consumption forecast of developed countries: the United States, Russia, the United Kingdom, Japan, and Germany. The peak of energy consumption is projected for the years 1960–1980; for the United States it is 2.7 billion t.c.e. For other countries, the maximum energy consumption is four to six times lower,

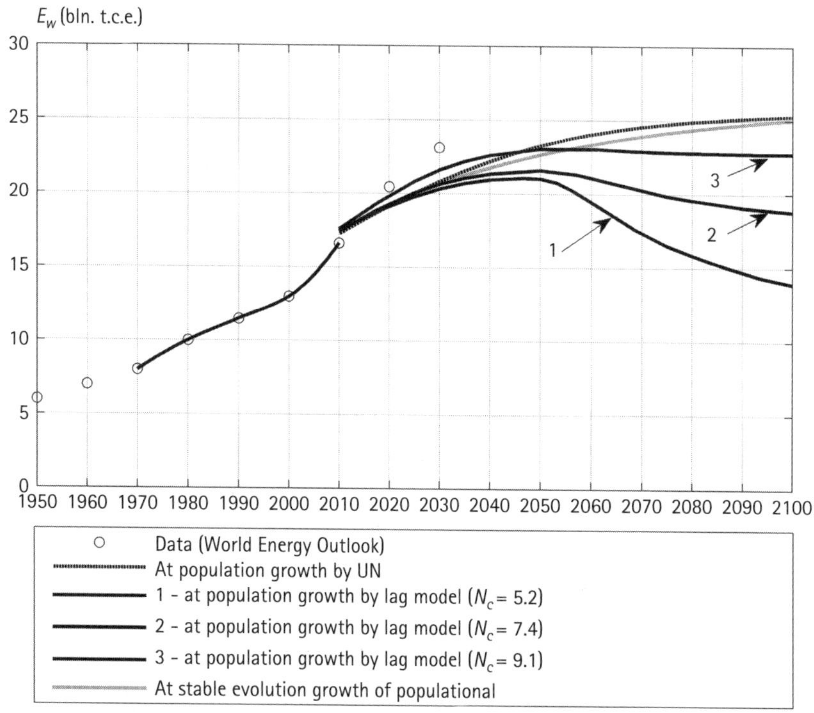

FIGURE 21.16 The dynamics of world energy consumption.

Table 21.3 Comparison of the Calculation Results for World Energy Consumption

Year	World energy consumption (billion t.c.e.)		
	IEA forecast	The result of calculation for different scenarios of demographic dynamics	
		$N_C = 5.2$ billion people	$N_C = 9.1$ billion people
2010	16.6	17.5	17.6
2015	18.3	18.4	18.8
2020	20.4	19.1	19.8
2025	21.4	19.8	20.8
2030	22.4	20.3	21.6
2035	23.4	20.7	22.2

so for the United Kingdom it is at 0.4 billion t.c.e., for Japan at 0.7 billion t.c.e., and for Germany at 0.5 billion t.c.e. Gradual decline and stabilization of energy consumption for developed countries is expected after 2050. US energy consumption will be about 2 billion t.c.e.; in the United Kingdom, 0.25 billion t.c.e.; in Japan, 0.45 billion t.c.e.; and Germany, 0.35 billion t.c.e.

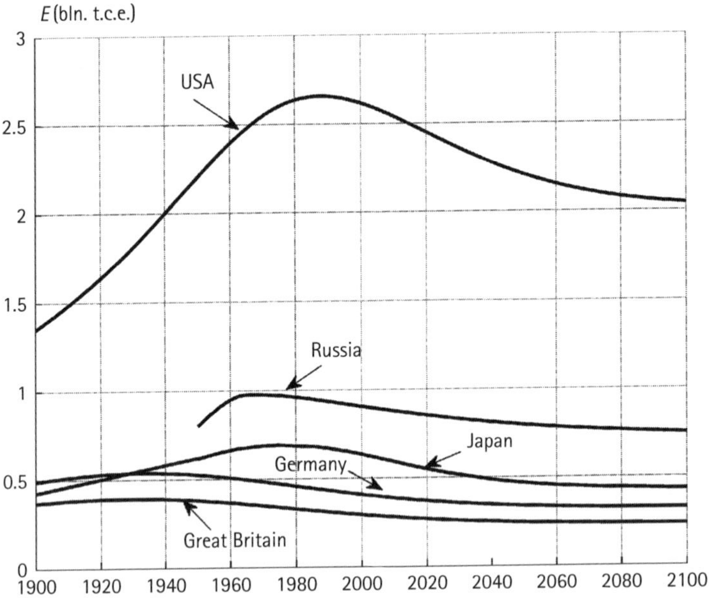

FIGURE 21.17 Energy consumption in developed countries.

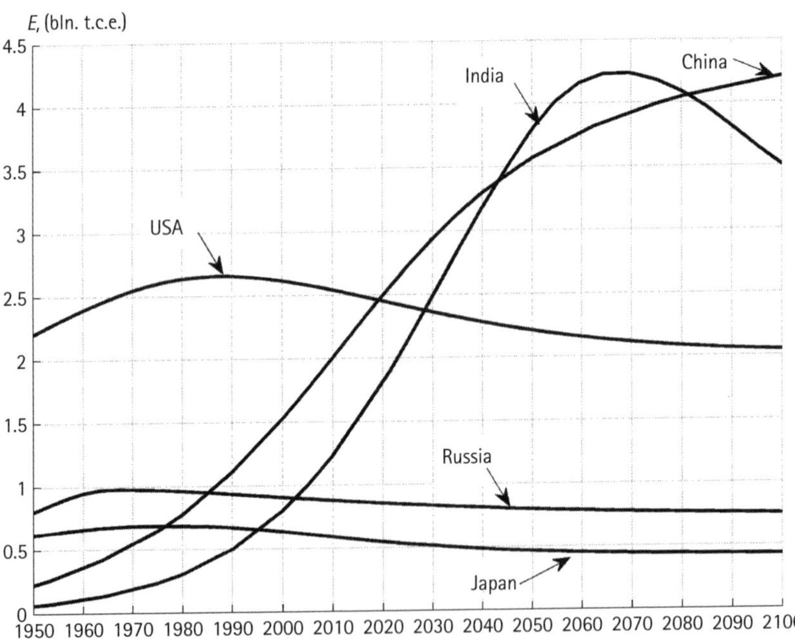

FIGURE 21.18 Energy consumption in developing countries.

The significant contribution to world energy consumption is made by developing countries. The energy consumption dynamics of the largest of them—China and India—are shown in Figure 21.18. Energy consumption of China will increase monotonically over the entire century, asymptotically approaching the level of 4.25 billion t.c.e. The peak of India's energy consumption is projected, approximately, for the year 2065 and is 4.25 billion t.c.e., followed by a recession. As seen from Figure 21.18, with a gradual reduction of energy consumption in developed countries there is rapid growth of consumption in developing and transitional countries undergoing a period of industrialization of the economy.

21.7 The Structure of the Modern World Fuel and Energy Balance

In Section 21.6, we calculated the dynamics of the total energy requirement that is necessary for sustainable development in the 21st century. It will be provided from various energy sources: coal, oil, natural gas, hydropower (HPS), nuclear energy (NPS), and renewable energy sources (RES). We mainly are interested in the hydrocarbon fuel resources—coal, oil, and gas, the combustion of which releases huge amounts of carbon, which is mainly in the form of CO_2 emitted into the atmosphere.

Currently, about 87% of all primary energy is made from fossil fuel resources—coal, oil, and natural gas. In recent years great efforts have been made to replace hydrocarbon fuel resources by dint of nuclear energy, renewable energy, and other alternative energy sources, such as hydrogen power. Many experts believe that by the middle of the 21st century (by the year 2050) the share of the latter will exceed 50% and become prevalent by respect to hydrocarbon energy sources. We think that this estimate is highly exaggerated. Actually, as will be shown later, we believe that in 21st century hydrocarbon fossil fuels will remain the foundation of world energy, and its share by the end of the 21st century will still be close to half of the world energy balance. The dynamics of changes in the world energy balance for the last half century, according to the IEA (IEA, 2010), and also forecast until 2030 (IEA, 2010) are presented in Table 21.4. IEA predicts further growth of energy consumption. As seen from Table 21.4, according to IEA estimates, the total primary energy consumption in the period from 2010 to 2030 will increase on the average on 1.6% per annum and will increase from 11.86 billion t.o.e. (oil equivalent) to 16.52 billion t.o.e. These data are easily translated to t.c.e., by multiplying to a factor equal 1.4 (as 1 oil t. = 1.4 t.c.e.). Let us consider the application prospects for each of the specified in Table. 21.4 main energy sources.

Table 21.4 World Fuel and Energy Balance

Sources of energy	1950	1960	1970	1980	1990	2000	2005	2010	2015	2020	2025	2030
World energy consumption, million toe					8194	9277	10,678	11,863	13,371	14,600	15,558	16,518
Coal (%)	51.8	35.3	23.4	16.5	27.4	24.3	27.0	29.5	30.2	29.5	28.2	27.1
Oil (%)	31.8	41.5	50.3	50.8	38.9	38.8	36.5	32.9	30.7	29.2	28.2	26.0
Gas (%)	10.2	15.8	18.3	19.3	21.8	23.5	23.6	24.1	24.5	25.2	25.7	26.2
HPS (%)	6.2	7.4	7.2	6.2	5.9	6.5	6.2	6.5	6.4	6.6	6.7	6.9
NPS (%)	–	–	0.8	7.2	5.6	6.3	5.8	5.2	5.4	5.6	6.0	6.6
RES (%)	–	–	–	–	0.4	0.5	0.7	1.3	2.1	3.0	4.0	4.8
Biofuels (%)	–	–	–	–	0.1	0.1	0.2	0.5	0.7	0.9	1.2	1.4
Fossil fuels (%)	93.8	92.6	92.0	86.6	88.1	86.6	87.1	86.5	85.4	83.9	82.1	79.3
Fossil fuels, million toe					7219	8034	9300	10,102	11,419	12,249	12,873	13,098

Data source: World Energy Outlook 2010–Annexes.

21.7.1 Oil

In the first third of the 21st century oil remains the dominant type of fuel, and then gradually will start to give this position to gas. Resulted in Table 21.4. data show that the maximum share of oil in the fuel and energy balance was reached during the world energy crisis of the last century in the late 1970–1980s. As a result, since the share of coal and gas has become a steadily increasing. According to various forecasts variants (Plakitkin, 2006), the decline of oil production will begin in 2015–2020. Consequently, the oil mode begins to give way to gas mode in 2030, as mentioned previously. However, oil will play a significant role until the end of the 21st century, because replacing liquid fuels will be extremely difficult from an economic point of view. The share of oil in the fuel and energy balance will decrease slowly and monotonically, and by the end of the 21st century is projected that its share will decrease approximately in four times in comparison with today's and will be equal 9–10%.

21.7.2 Gas

Total detected and forecast natural gas reserves will suffice for more than 100 years, with annual production 3–6.5 trillion cubicmeter. Currently, global demand for natural gas has a more rapid growth than oil and equal 1.8% per year. Gas consumption will grow steadily and in 2030 the share of gas (26.2%) will reach and exceed the share of liquid fuels (26%), and by 2050 the value of gas also will be great as the value of oil at present. By then the gas will become the dominant energy source, having reached a peak in 2035–2040 years. The share of gas in the fuel and energy balance by the end of the 21st century is projected at the level of 4–5%.

21.7.3 Coal

In absolute terms demand for coal will grow more than for any other type of fuel. Average demand for coal according to the IEA (2010) estimates will grow by 2% per year, although its share of global energy demand will decrease from the current 29.5% to 27.1% (see Table 21.4). Coal will continue to play an important role in the global economy, and its share in the world fuel and energy balance will remain at about 30% by the end of the 21st century. The world's known coal reserves are much greater than the total reserves of oil and gas and are able to provide the current level of production (about 5 billion tonnes) within 200 years. An extremely important factor in favor of coal is that it is processed into diesel fuel and gasoline by means of the chemical process called Fischer-Tropp synthesis. However, despite the fact that this technology was well mastered more than 70 years ago, the reactors required for its use are still quite expensive. It is predicted that in period until 2030 will be developed more committed and cost technology of production from gas synthetic coal and liquid fuel on an industrial scale. This is substantially enhance the possibility of using coal in energetic, communal and household sector and in transport. In the same period will become to the level of practical application the technologies of hydrogen production from coal. Also begins a broad introduction at the coal-fired power units of different technologies for catching, fastening and disposal of CO_2, what will contribute to sustainable and energy-ecological development.

Thus, until the end of the 21st century oil, gas, and coal will remain the basic components of global energy and their share in the fuel and energy balance will be slightly less than half of the world's energy balance, even to the end of the century. In addition, it is projected that by the middle of the 21st century the chemical industry will use up to 10% of extracted hydrocarbons, and by the end of the 21st century up to 30%, whereas at present oil, gas, and coal are used primarily as fuel, and only 5% of their volume is delivered to the chemical industry. It is important to note that since in the 21st century the value and volume of coal used for energy and chemical industry purposes, emissions of CO_2 into the atmosphere will also increase, as almost all are attributable to coal.

21.7.4 Hydropower

It is predicted by most experts that the share of HPS energy in the global energy balance in the 21st century will be remain relatively constant—about 6% (see Table 21.4). Hydropower will be developed due to the construction of large HPS in China, Brazil and other major developing countries, as well as small and medium-sized HPS in the rest of the developing world. However, it is hard to expect in the future a significant growth of hydropower's role in the world energy balance.

21.7.5 Nuclear Energy

After a period of rapid growth in the 1960–1970s and early 1980s, nuclear energetic is experiencing a severe crisis, which caused a surge of social conflict arising from such accidents as Chernobyl in the USSR in 1986 and the NPS Fukushima in Japan in 2010, and the remaining technical difficulties in providing the increased security requirements and disposal problems of radioactive waste. In the intermediate term period until 2030 it is necessary to expect decrease in the share of nuclear energy in the balance of world energy production to a level of 5%. But further more likely, the share of nuclear energy by the middle of the 21st century will double, if are not found a safer alternative sources such as thermonuclear reaction or etc., and will grow further in order to increase in four times by the end of the century.

21.7.6 Renewable Energy Sources

Despite considerable progress, RES (wind energy, solar and geothermal energy, tidal and wave energy) are only on the way to scale development and now their total contribution to the global energy balance is measured by units of percent (1.3% in 2010; see Table 21.4). Their proportion will rise to a tangible 5% only by 2030 and only from this point on it will be possible to talk about the beginning of the practical substitution of hydrocarbon fossil fuels by means of RES and NPS; as shown earlier, the share of hydropower will remain almost unchanged throughout the 21st century.

It is well known that substitution of one technology for another occurs according to the logistic law (Sahal, 1985). Therefore, the dynamics of change in share fossil fuels in global fuel and energy balance at the 21st century can be described by a decreasing logistic function of the form:

$$e_c(T) = 0.866 \cdot \left(1 - \frac{r\exp\left(k(T - T_0)\right)}{1 + r\left\{\exp\left(k(T - T_0) - 1\right)\right\}}\right) \tag{21.20}$$

The coefficient 0.866 corresponds to the share of fossil fuels in the fuel and energy balance which will be equal 86.6% in 2000 (see the Table 21.4). To determine the r and k use the following considerations. In the work (Akimov, 2008) was conducted a thorough calculation of the total installed coal reserves, oil and gas in the world at the beginning of the 21st century (until 2006), as well as total energy demand, based on average energy consumption per capita of a 5 t.c.e. (the current standard in the European Union and Japan). As a result, it was shown that the established reserves will suffice for 75–80 years. As we have adopted standard for per capita consumption in the 21st century of 2.5 t.c.e., the specified period will increase to 160 years. Thus, we can assume that fossil fuels will be used in 2160 at the level of exhaustion, that is, 5%. On the other hand, from an examination of Table 21.3, we see that the substitution of fossil fuels is carried out mainly with the use of RES. As regards nuclear energy, it is just as hydropower will have a nearly constant proportion up to foreseeable 2030-s years. Consequently, 5% replacement of fossil fuels, taking into account the average share of HPS in 6.5% and NPS in 5.5%, will come about in 2020, when the share of fossil fuels will equal approximately 84%. Thus, the parameters of the logistic function (21.20) can be determined based on the fact. Thus, the parameters of the logistic function (21.20) can be determined based on the fact that the 95th percentile level of fossil fuels use coincides with 2020, and of 5th percentile with 2160. Hence, the inflection point coincides with 2090, when the share of fossil fuels in the fuel and energy balance will be about 42%. They are as follows: $r = 0{,}05$, $k = 0{,}0421$. For comparison with actual data and partly with IEA forecasts until 2030 (Table 21.4), for the total share of hydrocarbon fuels in the global fuel and energy balance, the latter is presented in a separate Table 21.5, since 2000, when started the steady decline of this share. To them have been added forecasts for 2050, 2070, and 2100, borrowed from the work of Edwards (1997). A graph of the function (21.20), describing the dynamics of change the share of hydrocarbon fuels in the global fuel and energy balance in the 21st century is shown in Figure 21.19. In the same place, points are noted the data from Table 21.5, it is easy to see that all forecasts are quite close to each other, indicating their viability. One can immediately see from the figure, that the share of hydrocarbon fuels will be considerable throughout the 21st century and only by the end of the century will go down to 35%.

Thus, for the calculation of an aggregate amount of hydrocarbon fuels (coal, oil, and gas), required for the provision of energy-ecological development, the value of

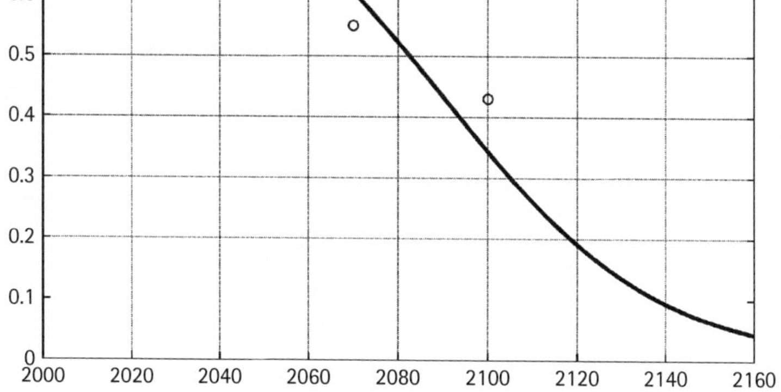

FIGURE 21.19 Dynamics of the share of organic fuel world energy balance in the 21st century.

Table 21.5 Total Share of Hydrocarbon Energy Sources in the Global Fuel and Energy Balance for the Period from 2000 to 2030

Year	2000	2005	2010	2015	2020	2025	2030	2050	2070	2100
Share	0.866	0.871	0.865	0.854	0.839	0.821	0.793	0.72	0.55	0.43

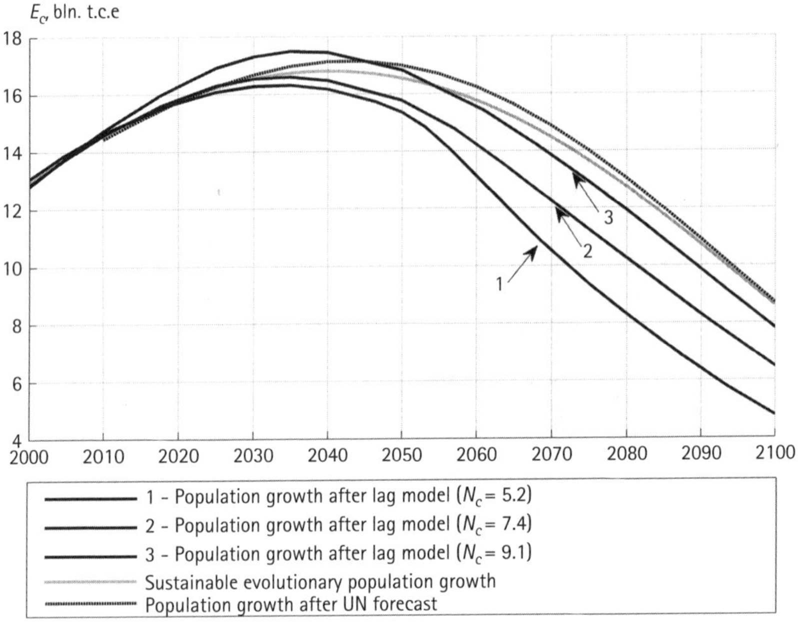

FIGURE 21.20 Forecast of world energy consumption in the 21st century.

total energy consumption E_W (21.2) should be multiplied by the coefficient e_c(21.20), presented in Figure 21.19:

$$E_c = e_c E_W. \qquad (21.21)$$

Forecasts E_c, corresponding to different scenario of demographic development (Figure 21.16), are presented in Figure 21.20.

21.8 Calculation of CO_2 Emissions and Accumulation in the Atmosphere

In Section 21. we have showed how one can calculate the dynamics of total amount of hydrocarbon fuels (coal, oil, and gas), necessary to meet world demand in energy resources, required for sustainable development. However, different types of fossil fuel

Table 21.6 Carbon Emission per Unit of Fuel, Used for Energy Production

Fossil fuel (coal) – 0.733 T. C/t.c.e.
Liquid fuel (oil) – 0.586 T. C/t.c.e.
Natural gas – 0.398 T. C/t.c.e.

emit different volumes of CO_2 at burning. Therefore, when calculating CO_2 emission dynamics it is important, to take into account not only total amount of hydrocarbon fuels, but its structure as well. The most suitable for the purpose is the Marland–Rotti technique, developed on the basis of fundamental analysis of carbon content in numerous samples of organic fuels, studies of burning technology and energy flows in various countries of the world (Marland and Rotty, 1984). The authors of paper (Klimenko et al., 1997) have made the modification of Marland–Rotti technique in adaptation of carbon emissions per unit of thermal energy to the data on energy consumption. They have obtained estimations of coefficients, defining carbon emissions per unit of conditional fuel used in energy production purposes, with allowance for transportation and distribution losses (Klimenko et al., 1997). The coefficients are given in Table 21.6. Some amount of CO_2, emitted by burning biomass, because it is equal to its absorption by plant growth (wood, etc.) Small amount of CO_2 is also emitted in the atmosphere at burning of oil gas and by cement production. The total emission from this sources is relatively small and comprises no more than 3%. Naturally, we don't take them into account in our calculations.

For a given dynamics of hydrocarbon energy resources (21.21) carbon emissions (C) from their combustion can be determined by using the gross carbon intensity coefficient, which characterizes the magnitude of carbon emissions per unit of carbon fuels, measured in tonnes of standard fuel. Thus, when calculating the carbon emissions from burning coal, oil, and gas on the modified Marlanda–Rott methodology, the overall coefficient of carbon intensity is defined as (Klimenko et al., 1997):

$$c_c = \frac{0,733E_s + 0,586E_l + 0,398E_g}{E_c}, \tag{21.22}$$

where E_c is the total amount of hydrocarbon fuels, subject to the consumption of a given time (in t.c.e); E_s, E_l, E_g of solid, liquid and gaseous fuels (all in t.c.e.). As we don't know the dynamics of changes in the internal structure of hydrocarbon fuels is, it is proposed to use the following approximate method (Klimenko et al., 1997). Consider the behavior of the coefficient c_c (N.7.1) in retrospect (Figure 21.21) and extrapolate it into the future.

It is well known, that in 1900, when the dominant energy source was coal, coefficient c_c exceeded the value of 0.7, specific for coal. After that it monotonically decreased to a value of 0.57 in 2000, which is specific for oil—the dominant energy source of the second half of the 20th century. If we analyze Table 21.4, we can see that starting from

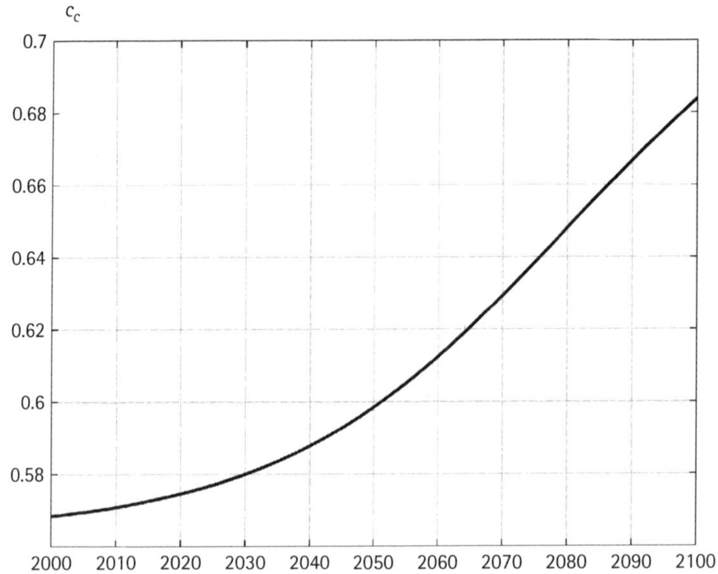

FIGURE 21.21 World average carbon efficiency coefficient c_c.

2000, the share of coal increases, while the cumulative share of oil and gas drops, while before 2000 the situation was the opposite. It means, that around 2000, the coefficient c_c takes minimal value, approximately equal to 0.57. Naturally, in the future, throughout the 21st century, the coefficient will monotonically increase, because, as noted in Section 21.7, the share of coal in the hydrocarbon fuels will continue to grow. Moreover, significant growth is expected in the 2050s, when gas as the dominant fuel, will reach the peak and then will go on a slow decline. In the future, the pace of growth of the share of coal in energy–fuel balance also will go on a steady decline.

This behavior of the coal's share in the supply–demand balance will be the determining factor for the behavior of c_c coefficient, so it can be reasonably well approximated by a logistic function with initial value $c_c^0 = 0.57$ in 2000, with an inflection point in the 2160s, when $c_c = 0,99 \cdot 0,733 \cong 0,726$. In the limit, by the 2160s, when oil and gas will be virtually depleted and the only remaining among the hydrocarbon fuel will be coal, the rate of coefficient will tend to the corresponding value for the coefficient for coal = 0.733 tC/t.c.e. Considering these data for describing the behavior of the coefficient for the whole 21st century we have the following logistic function:

$$c_c = c_{-\infty} + \frac{a}{1 + r\exp\left[-k(T - 2000)\right]}, \tag{21.23}$$

where $c_c^0 = 0{,}57$ for $T_0 = 2000$; $c_{-\infty} = 0{,}564 = 0{,}99 c_c^0$; $a = 0{,}169$; $r = 3{,}7$ and $k = 0{,}045$.

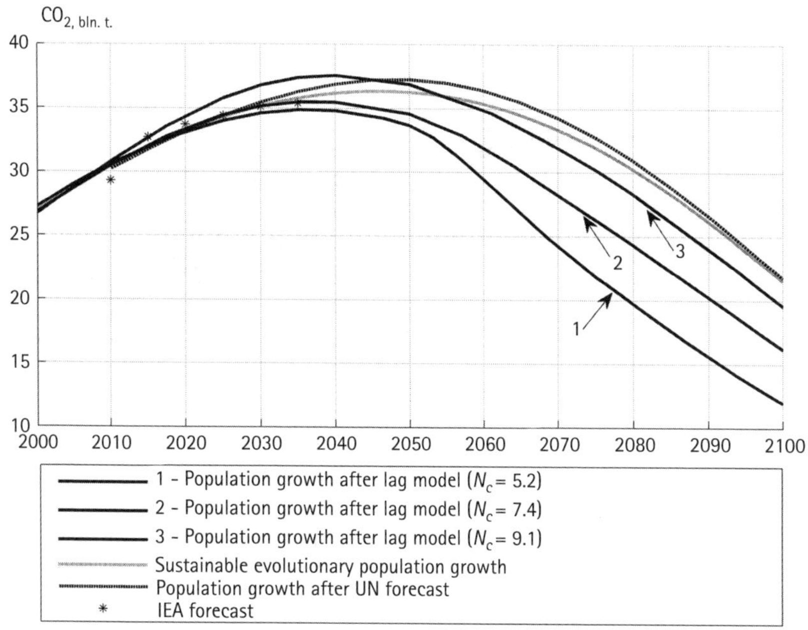

FIGURE 21.22 Dynamics of industrial ĐąĐđ$_2$ emissions in the 21st century (billion tonnes).

Hence we can calculate the value $c_c^* = 0.683$ in 2100. Graphic representation of coefficient c_c over the interval 2000 to 2100 in presented in Figure 21.21.

Thus, the dynamics of the total amount of CO_2 emitted to the atmosphere by burning of organic fossil fuels (coal, oil, and gas) can be calculated as follows:

$$C = c_c \cdot E_c = \left\{ c_{-\infty} + \frac{a}{1 + r\exp\left[-k(T - 2000)\right]} \right\} E_c, \tag{21.24}$$

where E_c is determined by formula (21.21) and is presented in graphic form in Figure 21.20. The mass of carbon produced by the formula (21.24) can be easily converted into a mass of CO_2 by multiplying by a constant coefficient, equal to 3.664. Graphs describing the dynamics of industrial carbon emissions in the form of CO_2 in the course of the 21st century are presented in Figure 21.22. It can be seen from the chart that under transition to a new energy consumption paradigm the emission of carbonic gas (CO_2) to the atmosphere that achieves the maximum between 2035 and 2045 and then declines, decreasing by the end of the century by a factor of 1.5–2 as compared with 2010.

Assume that the part of CO_2 produced during combustion of hydrocarbon fuels is captured and bound by special technology (CCS) for further disposal to reduce emissions into the atmosphere. So, if we start today to implement actively CCS technology in accordance with the "Blue Card" scenario, then a decrease of emissions by 19% in 2050 is forecast (ETP, 2010). The dynamics of the emission reductions through using

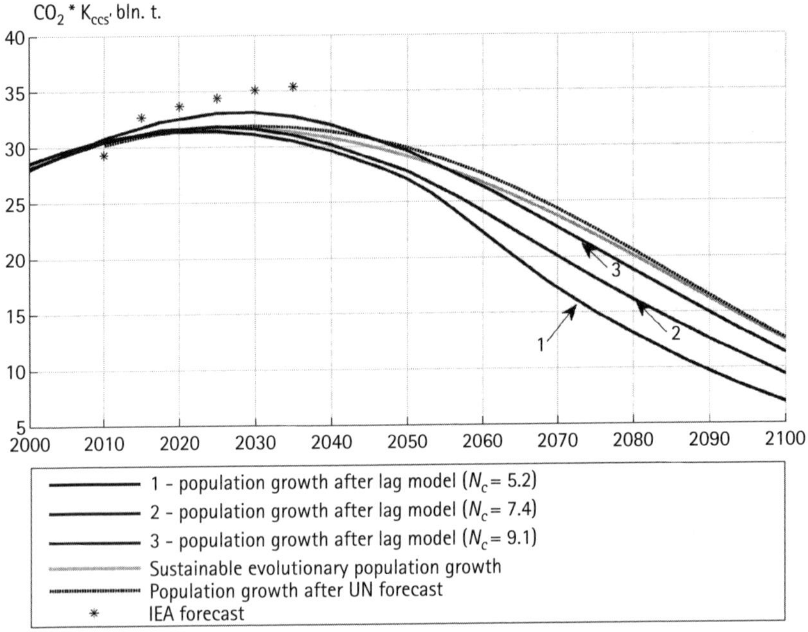

FIGURE 21.23 Dynamics of industrial CO_2 emissions in the 21st century (billion tonnes) by using CCS technology for capture and storage of part of the CO_2 emissions.

CCS could also be described by the logistic function. Therefore, to account for this effect the mass of carbon emitted to the atmosphere (21.24) should be multiplied by the following coefficient:

$$k_{CCS} = \frac{2\exp[-\vartheta(T - T_0)]}{1 + \exp[-\vartheta(T - T_0)]}. \tag{21.25}$$

where $T_0 = 2010$; $\vartheta = 0.01$. It can be easily calculated that by $T = T_0$, $k_{CCS} = 1$, by $T = 2050$, $k_{CCS} = 0.81$, that is, decreased exactly by 19%. Thus, we have:

$$C_{CCS} = k_{CCS} \cdot C. \tag{21.26}$$

Graphs describing the carbon emissions with allowance for the application of CCS technology for capture and burial of part of carbon (21.26) are presented in Figure 21.23. As can be seen from the figure, by using carbon capture and storage technology for part of the CO_2 the maximum of industrial CO_2 emissions falls in the mid-2020s, and by the end of the century the CO_2 emissions will decrease threefold and more. The results presented in Figures 21.22 and 21.23 show that is virtually impossible to halve CO_2 emissions by 2050, as foreseen by a number of scenarios. We will see later that there is no need for such a demand.

Anthropogenic inflow of CO_2 in the atmosphere is the result not only of industrial emissions, but also of deforestation and soil erosion. The main effect of deforestation is revealed in tropical forests.

The cut phytomass decomposes and with some delay goes to the atmosphere in the form of CO_2. Soil erosion is related to inappropriate agricultural land use. We assume that the mass of tropical forests is reduced by 0.6% every year and erosion comprises 0.15% per year, after work (Tarko, 2005). At the same time oceans and terrestrial ecosystems absorb part of the CO_2, and an extremely important role in absorbing excessive CO_2 volume belongs to the forest areas. Therefore, the preservation of existing and planting of new forests are crucial for maintaining a stable climate. Let us consider the balance of CO_2 flows, for example, in 1995, corresponding to measurement data given in Trends 93 (1994):

Industrial emissions: 6.41 GtC/year
Deforestation: 1.08 GtC/year
Soil erosion: 0.91 GtC/year
Absorption by oceans: 1.05 GtC/year
Absorption by terrestrial ecosystems: 4.05 GtC/year
Remain in the atmosphere: 3.30 GtC/year

This implies that approximately 52% of industrial emissions of CO_2 remain in the atmosphere. It is quite characteristic that for a long period in the second half of the 20th century about half of the industrial emissions of CO_2 permanently remained in the atmosphere (Tarko, 2005). Thus, the continuous accumulation of anthropogenic carbon in the atmosphere is in progress, which can be described by the formula:

$$C_{\Sigma} = \int_{2000}^{T} C(t)dt - 3{,}1\,(T - 2000), \tag{21.27}$$

where $2000 \leq T \leq 2100$. Industrial emissions of carbon $C(t)$ into the atmosphere should be used in this formula in the form of (21.24) and (21.26). The latter variant corresponds to the capture of emissions of carbon and their disposal, which reduces emissions into the atmosphere. The formula (21.27) obtained under the assumption of stability of nonindustrial anthropogenic emissions and constant absorption by the oceans and terrestrial ecosystems throughout the 21st century. This assumption certainly can be accepted very approximately. Figures 21.24 and 21.25 are graphs of the accumulation of the mass of carbon in the atmosphere for the two aforementioned variants.

The charts in Figure 21.25, illustrating the dynamics of accumulation of carbon in the atmosphere in the 21st century under the transition to the new paradigm of energy consumption, with wide application of carbon capture and storage technology for part of the CO_2, indicate that the amount of carbon accumulated in the atmosphere

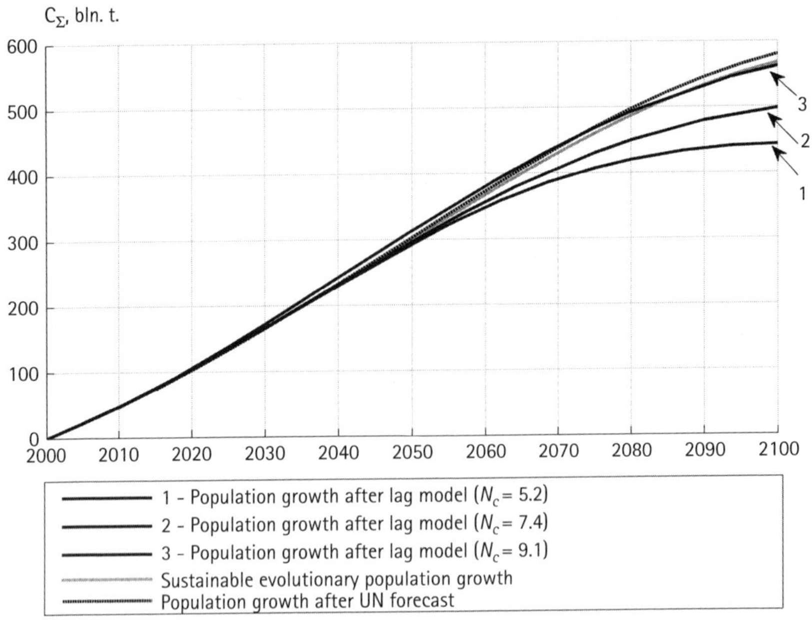

FIGURE 21.24 Dynamics of carbon accumulation in the atmosphere in the 21st century.

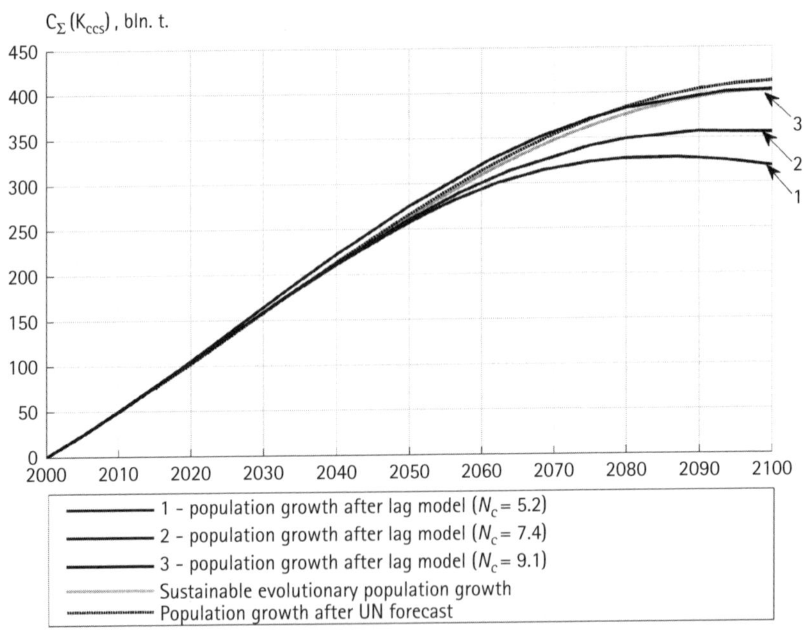

FIGURE 21.25 Dynamics of carbon accumulation in the atmosphere by using CCS technology for capture and storage of part of the CO_2 emissions.

achieves a maximum value of 330–410 Gt and is then stabilized at the general level of 1097–1177 Gt (in 2000: 767 Gt). The important fact is that it does not increase.

For practical usage it is more convenient to deal with relative values of the mass of carbon accumulated in the atmosphere (z):

$$z = \frac{C_0 + C_\Sigma}{\tilde{C}_0} = 1 + \frac{C_\Sigma}{\tilde{C}_0}, \tag{21.28}$$

where $\tilde{C}_0$ = total mass of carbon in the atmosphere in 2000, $\tilde{C}_0 \cong 767$ Gt, given that in 2000 $z = 1$.

21.9 Forecast of Changes of Earth Ground Atmosphere

The character of temperature dependence on CO_2 content in the atmosphere was determined by means of approximation of empirical data by various model representations (Budyko, 1980). We use an approximate formula presented in work of Tarko (2005):

$$T_g = \begin{cases} 2,5\{1 - \exp[-0,82(z-1)]\}, z \geq 1; \\ -5,25z^2 + 12,55z - 7,3, z < 1, \end{cases} \tag{21.29}$$

where T_g is the deviation of average global atmospheric temperature at the Earth surface from the current value, which is due only to the greenhouse effect caused by industrial CO_2 emissions into the atmosphere; z is the increase of relative CO_2 (or Ðą) content in the atmosphere (21.28). Hence, real (actual) deviation of ground atmosphere $\Delta T = T_g + T_e$, where T_e is the deviation of temperature caused by natural factors. Charts illustrating deviations of global Earth average ground temperature T_g in the course of the whole 21st century are presented in Figures 21.26 and 21.27.

From the analysis of Figures 21.26 and 21.27 one can see that the deviation of average global temperature over the 21st century will not exceed 0.9–1.2°C, while by using CCS technology for capture and storage of part of the CO_2 on an ever increasing scale, the global temperature will increase by 0.7–0.9°C and will stabilize at the corresponding level. If we take into account that during the next 150 years the global average temperature grew by approximately 1°C as compared with preindustrial temperature levels, it becomes obvious that the transition to a new paradigm of energy consumption, along with wide application of CCS technology, allows stabilization of deviations of average global temperature at a level not exceeding the permissible 2°C.

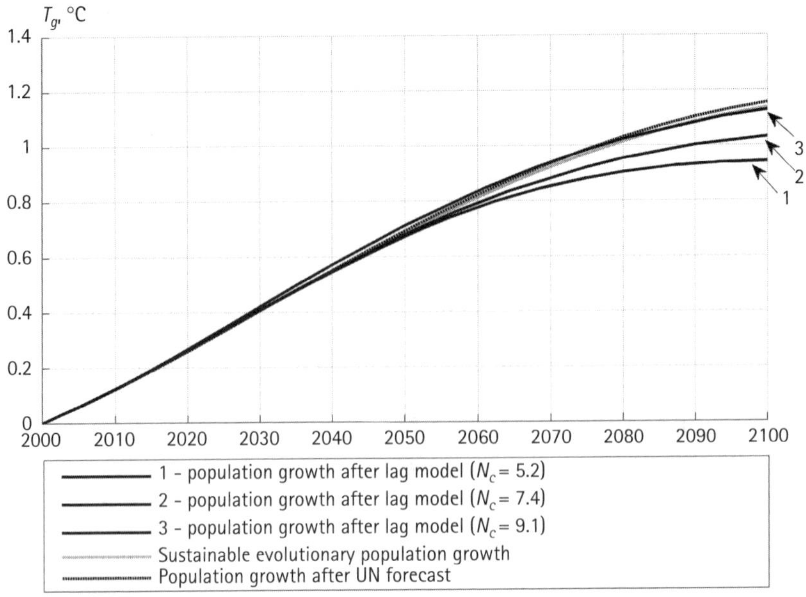

FIGURE 21.26 Deviations of world global average ground temperature in the 21st century from the value in the year 2000.

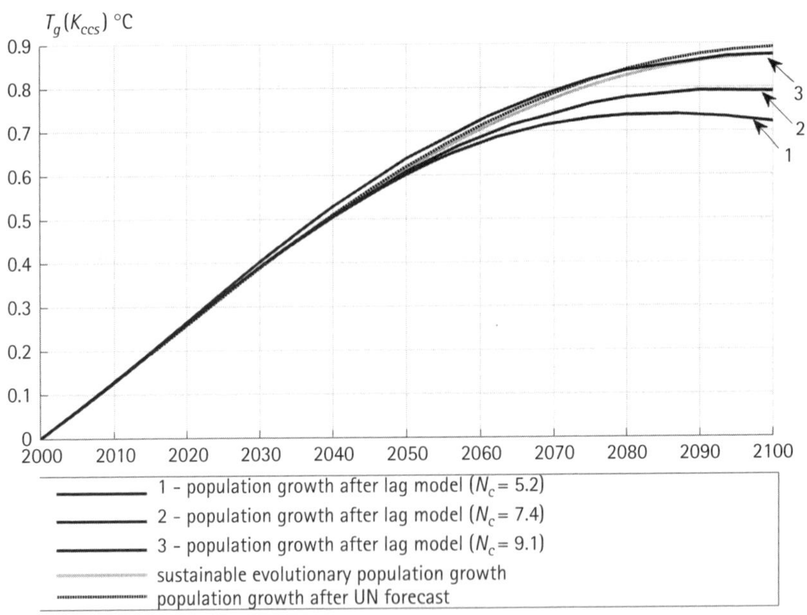

FIGURE 21.27 Deviations of world global average ground temperature in the 21st century from the value in the year 2000 by using CCS technology for capture and storage of part of the CO_2 emissions.

21.10 Energy-Ecological Development and Its Influence on Economical Growth

Energy-ecological development, the essence of which in this chapter is defined as a transition to a new paradigm of energy consumption associated with the stabilization of per capita energy consumption (Section), requires ever increasing amounts of investment in the development, improvement, and practical use of energy-saving technologies and increase of energy efficiency, as well as capture, binding, and burial of the part of the GHGs emitted into the atmosphere. We have already cited data from the IEA presented in the report (ETP, 2010) and characterizing the investment costs of the "Blue Card" scenario: up to US\$750 billion per year by 2030 and more than US\$1.6 trillion per year from 2030 to 2050 (Section 21.3), whereas in recent years, investment in low-carbon energy technologies averaged approximately US\$165 billion per year. In the famous Stern report, commissioned by the UK Treasury, the amount of annual investment in measures to mitigate climate change and adaptation is estimated at 1% of GDP, while the price of "climate inaction" is at least 5% of global GDP (Stern, 2006). In the Human Development Report 2007/2008 (UNDP, 2008) the cost of stabilizing GHGs emissions at the 450 ppm level is estimated at 1.6% of annual world GDP before 2030, roughly two thirds of annual military spending, whereas the damage could reach up to 5–10% of global GDP, if stabilization of the climate is not achieved.

We can approximately estimate the slowdown in economic growth resulting from diverting part of the investment resources for purposes connected with the provision of energy-ecological development. In the first decade of this century, average global economic growth was approximately 4%. To estimate the possible economic slowdown, we use the imperfect Harrod–Domar model optimized for long-term growth and showing a direct relationship between the investment growth (I) and growth rate of GDP (Y):

$$\frac{\Delta Y}{Y} = \frac{1}{m}\frac{\Delta I}{I}, m = \text{const.} \tag{21.30}$$

This relation holds true under conditions of equilibrium growth, constant capital/labor ratio ($\frac{K}{Y}$), and constant savings ratio (s). It was verified and confirmed by numerous econometric studies. For instance, Hayami (1997) showed that under today's conditions the value of the coefficient $m \cong 2$. Assuming that part of the investments are allocated for assimilation of low-carbon energy technologies, equal to I_{EE}, the right part of equation (21.30) can be expressed in the following form:

$$\frac{\Delta I - I_{EE}}{mI} = \frac{\Delta I}{mI} - \frac{I_{EE}}{mI} = \frac{\Delta Y}{Y} - \frac{\varepsilon Y}{msY} = \frac{\Delta Y}{Y} - \frac{\varepsilon}{ms}, \tag{21.31}$$

where ε is the share of GDP allocated to the development of low-carbon energy production. It was noted earlier that in recent years about US\$165 billion, that is, approximately 0.25% of world GDP, is allocated for this purpose. Given that $s \cong 0.25$

from (21.31) we obtain an estimate of slowdown of economic growth, equal to $\frac{0.0025}{2 \cdot 0.25} \cong 0.005$ or 5%. As we can see, the slowdown is insignificant. What will be the economic slowdown when the amount of investment increases to US$750 billion? Substituting into the right part of (21.31) the corresponding value of investments as a percentage ($\cong$ 1.12% of GDP), we obtain $\frac{0.012}{2 \cdot 0.25} \cong 0.025$ (or 2.5%), which is a significant slowdown. Thus, if the amount of annual investment into implementation of low-carbon energy technologies increases approximately fivefold, average global economic growth will slow down to 2% per year. The economical losses, as we can see, will be significant, but the risk of global warming declines dramatically.

One should keep in mind that the given estimates describe the upper border of limitations, attributable to climate stabilization measures. The limit can be significantly decreased by an optimal policy of economic regulation of CO_2 emissions. For example, most economists agree that a tax on carbon emissions is preferred as compared with the system of limitations and trading with emissions quota. Mittnik et al. (2010), in the context of a model of economic growth with structural changes, showed that the policy of carbon taxation and subsidizing low-carbon products lowers the impact of decreasing output and employment.

21.11 Conclusion

1. By making use of a long-term scenario forecast of global warming we showed that stabilization of the Earth climate is possible by means of a transition to a new paradigm of energy consumption. The new paradigm of energy consumption is reduced to the stabilization of per capita energy consumption in all countries of the world with various factors differentiated for different countries. The developed countries, in compliance with the assumed obligations, will gradually reduce existing limitations by 40%. Developing countries provide moderate growth of energy consumption to the world average level.

Calculations show that by stabilization of the world average per capita energy consumption to the minimum acceptable level of 2.5 t.c.e. by 2030, it is possible to achieve climate stability and prevent the global warming temperature limit from exceeding 2°C as compared to the atmospheric temperature in the preindustrial epoch. Moreover, this statement holds true if a stationary level of the world's population is achieved, up to the maximum level of 9.1 billion people.

2. While in the 20th century the energy demand of humanity grew in proportion to the square of the world population ($E \sim N^2$), with complete transition to the new energy paradigm, it will grow in direct proportion to the population size ($E \sim N$). It is shown that in the second half of the 21st century, in turn, the population of the world will stabilize around the stationary value, determined by the capacity of the Earth biosphere. In our forecast calculations, we considered four stationary world population

levels, corresponding to various groups of world scientists: 1–5.2 billion people; 2–6.2 billion people; 3–7.4 billion people; and 4–9.1 billion people.

For the stabilization of the global energy consumption in the 20th century the simultaneous fulfillment of the following three conditions is required:

a. The reduction of per capita energy consumption in developed countries by 40%, from 6.9 t.c.e./year to 4 t.c.e./year
b. Moderate growth of per capita energy consumption in developing countries to the world average of 2.5 t.c.e./year from the present 1 t.c.e./year
c. Priority rates of energy consumption efficiency

As the total energy consumption of developing countries will only grow and eventually significantly exceed the energy consumption of the developed countries, the latter must actively transmit low-carbon technologies to developing countries on the basis of joint use of the effective financing scheme. Otherwise, stabilization of energy consumption will not be possible, as about 100 developing countries will most likely continue the development of their industry, without regard to any limitations, because they have no other way to avoid poverty and hunger.

3. The study of the structure of energy consumption for the main types of energy sources (coal, oil, gas, RES, nuclear energy, and hydropower) showed the inconsistency of optimistic forecasts concerning the replacement of hydrocarbon fossil fuels (coal, oil, and gas) by RES already by 2050. In the 21st century organic fossil fuels will play a dominant role as well, and by the end of the century, their share in the balance of global energy consumption will decrease by a factor of 2.5 from the current level of 86.5% to a level of 35%, that is, it will remain one of the basic components of world energy. Therefore, urgent and wide-scale development of new highly effective technologies for the limitation and reduction of industrial CO_2 emissions in the atmosphere still remains a priority.

4. The diversion of a significant part of investment resources for the development and implementation of low-carbon energy technologies will naturally reduce the rate of world economic growth. Estimates made using the simplest Harrod–Domar model show that by today's level of investment in low-carbon technologies, the decrease in rates of economic growth equals 0.5%, and by 2030, with the implementation of the full program of energy-ecological development, it will reach 2.5%. We have to deal with it, because it sharply reduces the risk of global warming, stabilization of the climate is achieved, and sustainable development of humanity is ensured. On the other hand, the negative impact of measures to lower CO_2 emissions on rates of economical growth can be smoothed and even substantially lowered by an optimal policy of regulation of CO_2 emissions by economical measures.

5. The current decade (2012–2020) plays a key role in the launch of a large-scale program of development of low-carbon energy technologies to ensure minimum CO_2 emissions into the atmosphere, as well as technologies for the capture and disposal of a part of CO_2 (CCS). This is due to the fact that we should achieve a situation

such that the CO_2 emissions reach a peak in the 2020–2030s and then begin to decline steadily, to a reduction of two to threefold by 2100. Only through these conditions will it be possible to stabilize the Earth climate and prevent an increase of global average temperature of the atmosphere by greater than 2°C as compared with the preindustrial value, which is suitable and comfortable for human life on Earth.

References

Akaev, A., and Sadovnichii, V. A. (2010). Mathematical model of population dynamics with stabilization of the world population is around a stationary level. *Doklady Akademii Nauk, 435*(3), 317–321.

Akimov, A. V. (2008). 2300 year: Global challenges and Russia. Moscow: Eastern University.

Brown, L. R. (2003). *Ecoeconomics: How to Build the Economy, Protecting the Planet.* Moscow: Izd-vo, the Whole World.

Budyko, M. I. (1974). *Of Climate Change.* Leningrad: Gidrometeoizdat.

Budyko, M. I. (1980). *The Climate in the Past and the Future.* Leningrad: Gidrometeoizdat.

China's Agenda 21. (1994). *China's Agenda 21.* Beijing: China Environment Science Press.

Dolgonosov, V. M. (2009). *Nonlinear Dynamics of Ecological and Hydrological Processes.* Moscow: LYBROCOM.

Edwards, J. D. (1997). Crude oil and alternate energy production forecasts for the twenty-first century: The end of the hydrocarbon era. *American Association of Petroleum Geologists Bulletin, 81*(8), 1292–1305.

Energy Technology Perspectives 2010. (2010). *Scenarios & Strategies to 2050.* Paris: International Energy Agency.

Fedotov, A. P. (2002). Global studies: The beginning of the science of the modern world. Moscow: Aspect Press.

Foerster H. von, Mora, P., and Amiot, L. (1960). Doomsday: Friday, 13 November, A.D. 2026. *Science, 132*, 1291–1295.

Fourier, W. (1939). *Selected Works*, Vol. 2, p. 138. Moscow: Politizdat.

Gorshkov, V. G. (1995). *Physical and Biological Bases of Life Stability.* Moscow: Viniti.

Haken, H. (1985). Synergetics. Moscow: The World.

Hayami, Y., and Godo, Y. (1997). *Development Economics from the Poverty to Wealth of Nations*, p. 37. Oxford: Oxford University Press.

Hoerner, S. J. von (1975). Population explosion and interstellar expansion. *Journal of the British Interplanetary Society, 28*, 691–712.

Holdren, J. (1991). Population and the energy problem. *Population and Environment, 12*, 231–255.

IEA. (2009). *World Energy Outlook 2009.* Paris: International Energy Agency.

IEA. (2010). *World Energy Outlook 2010*—Annexes. Paris: International Energy Agency.

IPCC. (2000). *Special Report on Emissions Scenarios. A Special Report of Working Group III of the IPCC.* Cambridge, UK: Cambridge University Press.

IPCC. (2001). *Climate Change 2001: The Scientific Basis. Contribution of Working Group II to the Third Assessment Report of the Intergovernmental Panel on Climate Change* [T. Houghton, Y. Ding, D. J. Griggs, M. Noquer, P. J. van der Linden, X. Dai, K. Maskell and

C. A. Johnson (eds.)]. Cambridge University Press, Cambridge, United Kingdom and New York, NY, USA.

IPCC. (2007). *Climate Change 2007: The Physical Science Basis. Contribution of Working Group III to the Fourth Assessment Report of the Intergovernmental Panel on Climate Change* [Solomon, S., D. Qin, M. Manning, Z. Chen, M. Marquis, K. B. Averyt, M. Tignor and H. L. Miller (eds.)] Cambridge University Press, Cambridge, United Kingdom and New York, NY, USA.

Isaev, A. A. (2003). *Ecological Climatology.* Moscow: The World of Science.

Jones, P. D., Parker, D. E., Osborn, T. J., and Briffa, K. R. (1994). Global temperature anomalies in 1856–1999 In *Trends 93: A Compendium of Data on Global Change.* Oak Ridge, Tenn.: Carbon Dioxide Informational Analysis Center.

Kapitsa, S. P. (1992). Mathematical model of population growth of the world. *Mathematical Modeling, 4*(6), 65–79.

Kapitsa, S. P. (2008). *Essay on the theory of the growth of humanity: The demographic revolution and information society.* Moscow: Nikitsky Club.

Klimenko, V. V., Klimenko, A. V, Andreichenko, T. N., Dovgalyck, V. V., Mikyshina, O. V., Tereshin, A. G., and Fedorov, M. V. (1997). *Energy, Nature and Climate.* Moscow: Publishing house of the Moscow Power Engineering Institute.

Korotayev, A. (2005). A compact macromodel of World System evolution. *Journal of World-Systems Research, 11*(1): 79–93.

Korotayev, A. (2007). Compact mathematical models of World System development, and how they can help us to clarify our understanding of globalization processes. In: G. Modelski, T. Devezas, and W. R. Thompson (eds.), *Globalization as Evolutionary Process: Modeling Global Change*, pp. 133–160. London: Routledge.

Korotayev, A., Malkov, A., and Khaltourina, D. (2006). *Introduction to Social Macrodynamics: Secular Cycles and Millennial Trends.* Moscow: KomKniga/URSS.

Kremer, M. (1993). Population growth and technological change: One million B.C. to 1990. *The Quarterly Journal of Economics, 108*(3), 684–716.

Kuznets, S. (1960). Population change and aggregate output. In: National Bureau of Economic Research (ed.), *Demographic and Economic Change in Developed Countries*, pp. 324–340. New York, NY: Columbia University Press/Princeton, N.J.: Princeton University Press.

Manabe, S., and Wetherald, R. T. (1975). The effect of doubling the CO_2 concentration on the climate of a general circulation model. *Journal of the Atmospheric Sciences, 32*(1), 3–15.

Marland, G., and Rotty, R. M. (1984). Carbon dioxide emission from fossil fuels: A procedure for estimation and results for 1950–1982. *Tellus, 36B*(4), 232–261.

Meadows, D. H., Randers, Th., Meadows, D. L., (2008). *The Limits of Growth: 30 Years Later.* Moscow: Akademkniga.

Mittnik, S., Semmler, W., Kato, M., and Samaan, D. (2010). Employment and output effects of climate policies. In *The Economics of Climate Change* conference at the New School hosted by SCEPA, New York, April.

Plakitkin, Y. U. (2006). *Regularities of the Development of the World Energy Sector and their Impact on the Power Industry of Russia.* Moscow: IT Energy.

Rahmstorf, S., and Schellnhuber, H. J. (2007). *Der Klimavandel: Diagnose, prognose, therapie.* Munchen: Verlag C.H. Beck OHG.

Rat der Europaischen Union. (1996). Pressemitteilung zur 1939. Ratssitzung Umwelt vom 25.6.1996, Nr.8518/96.

Report of the Forum United Nations on Environment and Development. (1992). Rio de Janeiro, June 3–14. Vol. 1: Resolution adopted by the Conference. Appendix, A/conr.151/26//REV.1.

Sahal, D. (1985). *Technical progress: Concepts, models, assessment.* Moscow: Finances and Statistics.

Schellnhuber, H. J., ed. (2006). *Avoiding Dangerous Climate Change.* Cambridge, UK: Cambridge University Press.

Schlesinger, M. E. (1983). A review of climate models and their simulation of CO_2-induced warming. *International Journal of Environmental Studies, 20,* 103–114.

Schneider, S. H. (1972). Cloudiness as a global climatic feedback mechanism: The effects on the radiation balance and surface temperature of variations in cloudiness. *Journal of Atmospheric Science, 29*(8), 1413–1422.

Smail, J. K. (2002). Confronting a surfeit of people: Reducing global human numbers to sustainable levels. *Environment, Development and Sustainability, 4,* 21–50.

Stern, N. (2006). *The Economics of Climate Change: The Stern Review.* Cambridge, UK: Cambridge University Press.

Svirijev, Y. U. (1987). *Nonlinear Waves, Dissipative Structures and Catastrophes in Ecology.* Moscow: Nauka.

Tarko, A. M. (2005). *Anthropogenic Changes of the Global Biosphere Processes.* Moscow: FIZMATLIT.

Trends 93 (1994). *Compendium of Data on Global Change,* edited by T. A. Boden D. P. Kaiser, R. J. Sepanski, and F. W. Stoss. Oak Ridge, Tenn.: Carbon Dioxide Informational Analysis Center, Oak Ridge National Laboratory.

UNDP. (2008). *Human Development Report 2007/2008.* New York: United Nations Development Programme.

UN Population Division Database (2010). United Nations Department of Economic and Social Affairs, Population Division Database. New York: United Nations. http://www.un.org/esa/population

Wackernagel, M., Schulz, N. B., Deumling, D., Callejas Linares, A., Jenkins, M., Kapos, V., Monfreda, C., Loh, J., Myers, N., Norgaards, R., and Randers, J. (2002). Tracking the ecological overshoot of the human economy. *Proceedings of the National Academy of Sciences of the USA, 99*(14), 9266–9271.

World Population in 2300. (2003). Highlights. ESA/P/WP. 187, Draft. New York: United Nations.

Zhirmunsky, A. V., and Kuz'min, V. L. (1994). The critical levels of population growth of the world. *Izvestiya RAN: Biological series,* (5), 839–842.

CHAPTER 22

DOES THE KYOTO PROTOCOL INTENSIFY CARBON LEAKAGE TO CHINA?

ZHONG MAOCHU AND SHI YADONG

22.1 INTRODUCTION

THE Kyoto Protocol is the only international climate agreement with legally binding force at present. As it only required industrialized countries (Annex I) to reduce greenhouse gas (GHG) emissions by about 5% compared to 1990 levels in the period 2008–2012, while allowing other nations to make voluntary abatements, it was thought at least by those countries as an embodiment of the Common but Differentiated Responsibilities Principle. However, numerous criticisms have been voiced on its environmental effects since it was signed. According to IEA's report (2011), although carbon dioxide (CO_2) emissions of Annex I countries were 6.4% below their 1990 collective level in 2009, the emissions of developing countries (non-Annex I) increased by more than 3%, and the prospect of limiting temperature increase to 2°C is bleak. What makes a seemingly fair agreement on control of GHGs unsatisfactory? Contrary to some researchers' arguments that the unilateral climate policy is the main reason, we think the leading cause of carbon leakage is the current accounting principle for CO_2 emissions. As the accounting method in the United Nations Framework Convention on Climate Change (UNFCCC) and other climate agreements is based on the territorial principle (Eder and Narodoslawsky, 1999), which means a nation is responsible only for emissions within its political boundaries, countries have incentives to transfer emissions abroad when facing strict legal agreements. One way of transfer is to import from other countries, which saves domestic energy consumption and reduces CO_2 emissions in producing those goods and services. The method to reflect the extent of carbon leakage through international trade is by calculating embodied emissions in exports. In this chapter, it refers to the direct and indirect CO_2 emitted in the manufacturing process of goods and services that are demanded by foreign nations and produced by domestic inputs.

Calculating embodied emissions in exports has special meaning for a country like China, which has experienced fast economic growth and rapid increase in energy consumption since it adopted an "open and reform" policy. According to some authorities' reports (IEA, 2010, BP, 2010), China has became the largest energy consumer and CO_2 emitter in the world since 2009. However, some Chinese researchers found that China was a net exporter of emissions embodied in trade. For example, Qi Ye et al. (2008) calculated embodied carbon in international trade for China in 1997–2006 and found that it was a carbon export nation during that period and the proportion of net carbon export in total carbon emissions was increasing rapidly. Peng Shuijun and Liu (2010) computed levels of four other kinds of pollutions including industrial sulfur dioxide, and found that China was also the net exporter of those pollutions. Other similar recent research includes Zhang Youguo (2010), Zhou Xin (2010), Zhang and Du (2011), and Wang and Xiang (2011). Those results implicated that China's high emissions can be explained by carbon leakage. Some researchers analyzed the factors influencing carbon emissions embodied in exports and thought the primary drivers were the growth of export volume and the trade structure (Huang Min et al., 2010; Yan and Yang 2010; Zhang Youguo 2010); however, few of them performed analyses from the aspect of carbon accounting method and carbon leakage. In terms of carbon transfer, most domestic researchers focused on the relationship between international trade or foreign direct investment (FDI) and pollution emissions, which actually empirically tested the hypothesis of a pollution haven (Walter and Ugelow, 1979), and there is controversy over the conclusions (He Jie, 2010; Li and Lu, 2010; Xue and Song 2010).

The Chinese government has been aware of the problem of increasing emissions embodied in exports. In the eleventh five-year plan, China has implemented energy saving and emission reduction policies. In 2006, it brought forward restriction measures, including adjusting export rebate rates and limiting exports of "two high a capital"[1] products. However, the measure of limiting international trade is not the ultimate way to deal with carbon leakage. If the accounting method and responsibility allocation principle are not changed, countries still have incentives to transfer emissions abroad when they are facing strict abatement policies. Therefore, it is urgent to change the territorial responsibility principle; otherwise the fair and strict climate agreements are destined to lead to failure in control of GHGs.

The rest of the chapter is organized as follows. Section 22.2 describes the methodology to analyze this issue, including the base model to compute emissions embodied in exports, the data procedures, and the empirical model. Section 22.3 presents the estimation results, and Section 22.4 concludes the chapter.

22.2 Methodology

The analysis framework of this chapter is first calculating CO_2 emissions embodied in exports of China using an environmental input–output (IO) model and the extrapolation technology, and then setting the empirical model to test the effect of the Kyoto Protocol on emissions embodied in exports.

22.2.1 The Base Model to Calculate Emissions Embodied in Exports

Considering the standard form of the IO model set by Leontief in 1930s, the economy of n sectors can be represented by

$$x = Ax + y \tag{22.1}$$

where$x$is the gross output vector over sectors, A is direct consumption coefficient matrix with its interior elements $a_{ij} = \frac{x_{ij}}{x_j}$, and y is the vector of final demands. This model means that in an economy with n sectors, the gross output equals the intermediate input together with the final demands.

equation (22.1) is usually written in the form of solving x.

$$x = (I - A)^{-1} y \tag{22.2}$$

In equation (22.2), I is the identity matrix, and $(I - A)^{-1}$ is called the Leontief inverse matrix. This equation is the base of the environmental IO model. Let F represent the row vector of environmental impact per unit industry output, and then the direct and indirect environmental effects to obtain industry output can be valued as

$$f = F(I - A)^{-1} y \tag{22.3}$$

In terms of the climate change problem, this equation can be used to calculate the direct and indirect CO_2 emissions if F represents the row vector of emissions per unit output.

This environmental IO model does not distinguish international trade. In order to calculate emissions embodied in international trade, we use Peters' model (2008), which rewrites equation (22.1) as

$$x + m = Ax + y + e \tag{22.4}$$

where m and e represent the imports and exports vector. Suppose m is the linear function of Ax and y; and then m can be written as,

$$m = M_1 Ax + M_2 y \tag{22.5}$$

There is something to say about imports m. As the imported goods are mainly used for domestic intermediate production and domestic final consumption for China, the imports m can be decomposed into a part for intermediate input M_1Ax and a part for final demands M_2y. Thus, the total intermediate input Ax and the final demands y can be divided into two parts. One is from domestic output and the other is from output abroad. Equations (22.6) and (22.7) show the described relationships as follows:

$$Ax = A^{rr}x + M_1Ax \tag{22.6}$$

$$y = y^{rr} + M_2y \tag{22.7}$$

m can be removed by putting equations (22.5), (22.6), and (22.7) into (22.4), and the industry output can be written as

$$x = [I - A^{rr}]^{-1}(y^{rr} + e) \tag{22.8}$$

Therefore, the equation to calculate direct and indirect CO_2 emissions is

$$\begin{aligned} f &= F[I - A^{rr}]^{-1}(y^{rr} + e) \\ &= F[I - A^{rr}]^{-1}y^{rr} + F[I - A^{rr}]^{-1}e \end{aligned} \tag{22.9}$$

As equation (22.9) is a linear form about domestic demands y^{rr} and exports e, the CO_2 emissions can be decomposed into components of domestic demands and overseas demands on domestic output. Therefore, the equation to calculate emissions embodied in exports according to its definition can be written as

$$EC = F[I - A^{rr}]^{-1}e \tag{22.10}$$

Equation (22.10) can also be used to compute emissions embodied in exports to some fixed countries, if we let e represent exports to those countries.

22.2.2 Procedures to Obtain Time Series Data

It seems easily to compute any years' emissions embodied in exports using equation (22.10), if relative variables are known, including the annual data of total output, CO_2 emissions, and exports. However, these data are hard to find, and certain procedures are needed to deal with them. For example calculating matrices A^{rr} is a bit difficult. As the IO tables compiled by National Bureau of Statistics of China are discontinuous and do not separate the imports share from intermediate production, we need to use the Organisation for Economic Co-operation and Development (OECD) edition's IO tables and obtain relative data from the domestic parts. To get the time series data of matrices A^{rr}, the extrapolation technology is also used.

The common method to extrapolating IO tables is the RAS approach (Stone and Brown, 1962). Its basic idea is supposing the change of direct consumption coefficient matrix is composed of two sides. One side reflects the absorption effect, which uses a positive diagonal matrix R to represent the substitute extent of intermediate input for other goods. The other side is called the fabrication effect, which uses a positive diagonal matrix S to represent the proportion's change of intermediate input to total input induced by fabrication technology's change. Knowing two years' direct consumption coefficient matrices A_t and A_T, matrices R and S can be obtained by adjusting A_t to A_T. Namely let the column sum and row sum of matrix RA_tS equal the column sum and row sum of matrix A_T, and then compute matrices R and S by multi-iteration. Suppose the changing rates of direct consumption coefficient matrices are invariable; the average changing rates can be written as $\sqrt[T-t]{R}$ and $\sqrt[T-t]{S}$. Therefore, the matrix A of any years can be obtained through the equation $A_{t+1} = \sqrt[T-t]{R}A_t \sqrt[T-t]{S}$.

The solutions using this simple RAS approach have the characteristics of existence, uniqueness, and iterative convergence. As it assumes that the changing rate of matrices A is unchanged, which means no structural variations occurred during the updating period, this method is suitable for estimating for short time interval. When the time interval is relatively long, applying the RAS method may have errors in adjusting some sectors' direct consumption coefficients. In this chapter, we applied blocked the RAS method (Li and Liu, 2002) when extrapolating IO tables. This method first separates matrices A according to different types of changes into blocks, and then applies the RAS approach to each block. Using this technique can capture different structural changes of input and demand from one sector to other sectors. To avoid estimating results overly dependent on the base year's information, we use A_t and A_T separately as the base year, and put weights on two sets of matrices R and S.

Solving the problem to extrapolating IO tables is the first step to obtaining time series data that are needed to calculate embodied emissions. There are still the other two main variables to deal with. One is calculating annual CO_2 emissions per unit industry output; the other is getting relative data about annual exports.

To acquire the emissions per unit output, it is necessary to make sure the annual emissions of each sector. As carbon dioxide emissions mainly come from combustion of fossil fuels combustion, the common approach to get these data is to multiply the final quantity of fossil fuels that each sector consumed by the corresponding coefficients. The annual data of final energy consumption by each industry come from the China Energy Statistical Yearbook. As the agriculture and service industries are not energy transformation sectors, we use those sectors' energy consumption data from the China Statistical Yearbook. Considering the possibility to get data and the status that coal, oil, and gas are the major energy sources for China, the combusted energies we studied in this chapter include 10 fossil fuels: coal, coke, coke oven gas, crude oil, gasoline, kerosene, diesel oil, fuel oil, liquefied petroleum gases, and natural gas. The reference approach to compute CO_2 emissions from fuel combustion is from the 2006

IPCC Guidelines for National Greenhouse Gas Inventories. The computing equation is expressed as

$$CO_2 = \sum_{i}^{n} E_i \times NCV_i \times CEF_i \times COF_i \times \frac{44}{12}$$

Where E represents energy consumption, NCV is the net calorific value, CEF is the CO_2 emission factor, and COF is the carbon oxidation factor. The parameters used in this equation come from IPCC Guidelines and China Energy Statistical Yearbook.

After obtaining the data of total emissions, we estimated annual industry output of each sector. Using the output data from IO tables that the National Statistical Bureau has published, we set up an empirical model, which is written as $x_i = \exp(a_i t)$, to estimate the missing years' output. To make these data comparable with each other, we also valued these data at a constant price.

As the data about international merchandise trade are classified by their categories, to obtain annual exports data by sectors one needs to convert the international trade classification to industrial classification. Some researchers' and authorities' work provides references for our study. When aggregating export data of agriculture, hunting, forestry, fishing, and industries, we used the converter file offered by UN Statistics Division, and the approach used by Sheng Bin (2002), and Muendler (2009). The original data come from UN comtrade database. In term of service industries' exports, the World Trade Organization (WTO)'s classification was corresponded with sectors in our chapter. The annual data come from the United Nations Conference on Trade and Development (UNCTAD) database.

22.2.3 Empirical Analysis of the Effect of the Kyoto Protocol on China's Embodied Emissions in Exports

The Kyoto Protocol is the strictest climate agreement in the history of addressing climate change problem. It took effect in 2005, and has more than 190 signatory countries. Because of this protocol, the activities to abate GHG emissions became a reality, especially for the Annex I countries. However, although most of those countries accomplished their commissions well, the protocol's total environmental effects are not satisfactory. As the emissions of non-Annex I nations rose greatly since it came into force, the total emissions worldwide increased instead of decreased. Unlike some researchers who thought the reason leading to this phenomenon is unilateral abatement policies, we ascribe the increased emissions of non-Annex I nations to the accounting principle. The territorial responsibility principle makes a country (or a region) responsible only for the emissions within its boundaries, so it has the incentive to transfer its emissions abroad when facing strict policies. When it does so through international trade, a country transfers its emissions by importing energy-intensive goods and let its trade partners' emissions rise.

Recently, China's CO_2 emissions have grown rapidly; however, many scholars found that the emissions were caused mainly by foreign countries' demands. In other words, they were caused by carbon leakage from foreign countries. With the Annex I nations facing the strict agreement Kyoto Protocol, we suspect that the carbon leakage through international trade is intensified in China.

To be specific, the hypothesis tested in this chapter is expressed as: the enactment of the Kyoto Protocol has a positive impact on China's CO_2 emissions embodied in exports to Annex I nations.

Generally speaking, the common approaches to analyze effects of policies include the difference-in-difference method, Chow test or Bai and Perron test in regression models, and structural breaks analysis in time series models. As we have already obtained the panel time series data of embodied emissions, in this chapter we use the latter way to set up empirical model and test whether these time series data had structural breaks when the Kyoto Protocol came into force. The model is established as follows:

$$\ln ec_{it} = \beta_0 + \beta_1 \ln ec_{it-1} + \beta_2 dk_t + \beta_3 D_t + \varepsilon_{it} \tag{22.11}$$

where $\ln ec_{it}$ denotes the logarithmic form of embodied emissions in exports of sector i in period t, dk_t is the dummy variable indicating whether the Kyoto Protocol is becoming effective, and D_t denotes the dummy variables representing other polices' effects if they exist. As there are first-order lags of dependent variables, we use the generalized method of moments (GMM) (Arellano and Bond, 1991) instead of ordinary least squares (OLS) approach.

22.3 Estimation Results and Analysis

22.3.1 Calculation Results of Embodied Emissions

Figure 22.1 illustrates time series data of emissions embodied in exports of several main sectors from 1991–2009. The data of total emissions embodied in exports exhibits an upwards trend. In 2009, the total embodied emissions were 216 MT, almost six times as large as in 1991, with an annual growth of 10.3%. In terms of sectors, the secondary industries have the most embodied emissions, and the next are tertiary industries. Manufacturing is the main source of emissions in secondary industries, predominantly iron and steel and nonferrous metals. The embodied emissions of pollution-intensive industries obviously increase during the research period, while those of other industries, such as agriculture, are relatively stable.

Observing the changing trend, we find that embodied emissions remained at a stable level before 2002. However, since then, they began to rise significantly, especially after the year 2005. In 2009, they dropped slightly. We think there are three exogenous factors that can explain this phenomenon. One is the WTO effect. As China joined WTO

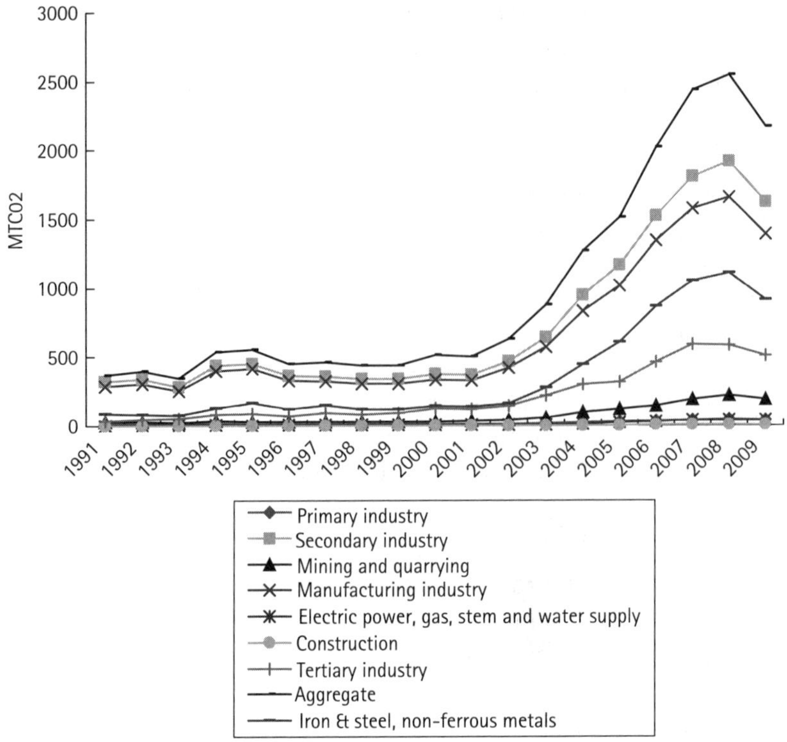

FIGURE 22.1 Time-series data of emissions embodied in exports by sectors.

in 2001, embodied emissions increased in association with an increase in export trade. Another one may be the effect of the Kyoto Protocol, which is our research objective waiting to be tested. The reason why the emissions dropped in 2009 probably is that the international financial crisis occurred and export trade declined.

The impacts of WTO and the international financial crisis may weaken the influence of the Kyoto Protocol. To better reveal the changing trend, we also calculated the emissions embodied in exports to Annex I nations.[2] Figure 22.2 illustrates the ratio of emissions embodied in exports to Annex I nations to total emissions embodied in exports. From this figure we can see that the ratio remained at a level of 30% to 40% before 2005. However, after that time, this ratio rose quickly and was close to 60% in 2009. Observing the ratios grouped by industries, we find that the ratios of all industries show an upward trend. However, the change of the primary industries with lower emissions is less evident compared with that of the secondary and tertiary industries. Based on our hypothesis, we guess that after the Kyoto Protocol came into force, Annex I countries intensified the energy-intensive industries' imports from China. So the current accounting principle of CO_2 emissions needs to be revised urgently; otherwise the stricter the policy, the more serious the carbon leakage.

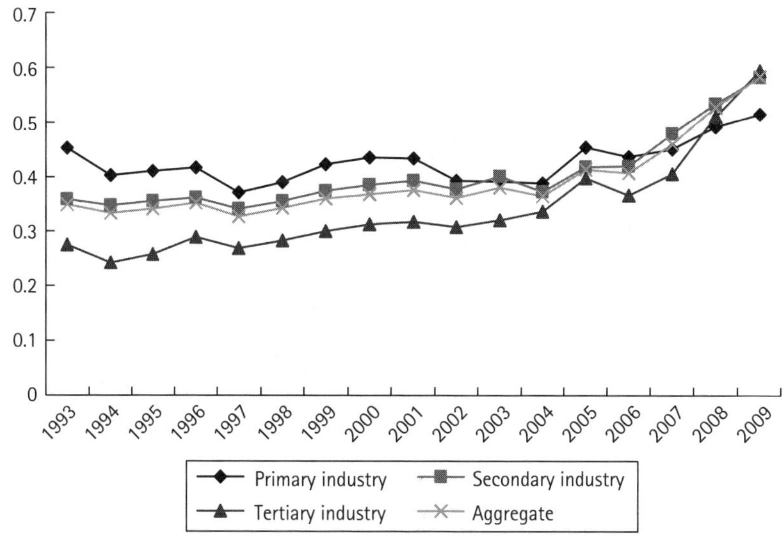

FIGURE 22.2 The ratio of emissions embodied in exports to Annex I nations to total emissions embodied in exports.

22.3.2 Empirical Analysis of the Effect of the Kyoto Protocol

Using the panel time series data of emissions embodied in exports to Annex I countries from 1991–2009, we estimate the model (22.11). The results are described in Table 22.1. The first and the second column are the results of two-step GMM and fixed effect estimation separately, when considering only the Kyoto Protocol's effect. It can be seen that the coefficients of the dummy variable are positive and significant, which means that there is an upwards break in the level when the Kyoto Protocol is becoming effective. Based on the preceding analysis, we know that there may be other influencing factors including the WTO and international financial crisis, besides the Kyoto Protocol. So we add other dummy variables indicating these effects in this model. The third to sixth columns are the results when considering those effects. It is obvious to see that the coefficients of the dummy variable denoting the effect of the Kyoto Protocol are still positive, whether one adds other influencing factors or not. And they are significant regardless of using GMM or fixed effect estimation. Furthermore, the coefficients of the WTO are positive and those of the international financial crisis are negative. So, it means that joining the WTO also brings an upward break to embodied emissions, while the occurrence of the crisis creates a downwards impulse. To verify that the GMM estimation is valid, we performed the Wald test of model coefficients and Sargan test to check over-identifying restrictions. The results show that the coefficients are significant and the instruments are valid. The model also passes the Arellano–Bond AR (2) test, which means that there is no second-order autocorrelation in residual series.

Table 22.1 Estimation of the Effect of the Kyoto Protocol

Independent variables	1	2	3	4	5	6
	GMM	FE	GMM	FE	GMM	FE
$\ln ec_{it-1}$	0.840	0.846	0.743	0.783	0.747	0.789
	(184.22)**	(22.00)**	(110.60)**	(20.44)**	(64.45)**	(19.50)**
dk	0.208	0.212	0.166	0.127	0.167	0.134
	(82.84)**	(3.41)**	(51.00)**	(2.07)*	(33.61)**	(2.13)*
dw			0.259	0.258	0.257	0.256
			(28.10)**	(5.63)**	(19.82)**	(5.55)**
df					-0.012	-0.035
					(-2.43)**	(-0.52)
constant	1.072	1.038	1.559	1.324	1.534	1.285
	(27.36)**	(4.47)**	(28.10)**	(5.83)**	(17.79)**	(5.36)**
Tests of the model						
wald chi^2	78835.82		47560.17		48520.96	
	(0.00)		(0.00)		(0.00)	
F-stat		753.96(0.00)		565.02(0.00)		422.78(0.00)
sargan test	19.913		19.855		19.854	
	(1.00)		(1.00)		(1.00)	
ar(1)	-2.65(0.01)		-2.71(0.01)		-2.71(0.01)	
ar(2)	0.22(0.82)		0.12(0.91)		0.13(0.90)	

Notes: Figures in parentheses of panel A are *Z*-statistics or *T*-statistics. P-statistics are given in parentheses of tests part. *Significance at 5% level. **Significance at 1% level.

Comparing the coefficients of the dummy variables, we find that the coefficients indicating the WTO effect are greater than those denoting the Kyoto Protocol effect. We think it is because carbon leakage occurs on the premise of an open economy and the calculation is dependent on the trade volume. However, it is not the point. In other words, the purpose of analyzing embodied emissions in exports is not to restrict international trade. What we think is important is to change the current accounting principle of CO_2 emissions. If countries are held responsible only for emissions within its boundaries and ignoring the consumers' responsibilities, strict and fair climate polices will intensify emissions transfer. What is more, the public will pay attention to the negative impact of a climate agreement, and doubt whether countries should implement such a fair protocol.

22.4 Conclusions and Remarks

Using environmental input–output model and the extrapolating technology, we obtain embodied emissions in exports of 20 sectors from 1991 to 2009. Through establishing a panel autoregression model, we empirically test whether the Kyoto Protocol intensifies CO_2 leakage to China. We find that the enactment of the Protocol produces a positive impulse on the change of embodied emissions in exports to Annex I nations. So, we conclude that when facing strict climate policy, Annex I countries intensified transferring emissions to China through international trade.

Recently, China has borne a great deal of pressure from the international community in terms of its huge CO_2 emissions. However, a large portion of those emissions were produced to satisfy overseas demands. According to the theory of the ecological footprint, the final driving factor inducing environmental damage is consumers' demands. Therefore, requiring China to be responsible for the entirety of its emissions is not fair and reasonable. Furthermore, neither the unilateral abatement policy nor the legal restriction is the reason for carbon leakage. To prevent emissions transfer, the most pressing need currently is changing the principle of the CO_2 accounting method. It is the key point in controlling global GHG emissions and promoting international climate cooperation.

Notes

1. "Two high" refers to industries with high energy consumption and high pollution. "A capital" refers to resource-related industries.
2. Here Annex I countries refers to the signatory countries in the Kyoto Protocol Annex I list, excluding the United States, Croatia, Lithuania, Slovenia, Ukraine, Liechtenstein, and Monaco.

References

Arellano, M., and Bond, S. R. (1991). Some tests of specification for panel data: Monte Carlo evidence and an application to employment equations." *Review of Economic Studies, 58*, 277–297.

BP. (2010). Statistical Review of World Energy. http://www.bp.com/

Eder, P., and Narodoslawsky, M. (1999). What environmental pressures are a region's industries responsible for? A method of analysis with descriptive indices and input-output models. *Ecological Economics, 29*, 359–374.

Huang, M., and Jiang, Q. (2010). Accounting embodied carbon in foreign trade and the analysis of influential factors. *Shanghai Economic Review, 3*, 68–76.

He, J. (2010). Environmental impacts of international trade: The case of industrial emission of sulfur dioxide in Chinese provinces. *China Economic Quarterly, 9*, 416–446.

International Energy Agency. (2010). *World Energy Outlook 2010*. http://www.iea.org/Textbase/npsum/weo2010sum.pdf

International Energy Agency. (2011). CO_2 emissions from fuel combustion highlights. http://www.iea.org/co2highlights/co2highlights.pdf

IPCC. (2006). *2006 IPCC Guidelines for National Greenhouse Gas Inventories*. http://www.ipcc-nggip.iges.or.jp/public/2006gl/vol2.html

Li, B., and Liu, L. (2002). A study of input-output tables in series. *Journal of Beijing Institute of Technology, 22,* 258–261.

Li, X., and Lu, X. (2010). International trade pollution industry transfer and Chinese industries' CO_2 emissions. *Economic Research Journal, 1,* 17–26.

Muendler, M. (2009). Converter from SITC to ISIC. CESifo and NBER. http://dss.ucsd.edu/~muendler/docs/conc/sitc2isic.pdf

Peng, S. and Liu, A. (2010). Environmental impact of China foreign trade. *The Journal of World Economy, 5,* 141–160.

Peters, G. P. (2008). From production-based to consumption-based national emission inventories. *Ecological Economics, 65,* 13–23.

Qi, Y., Li, H., and Xu, M. (2008). Accounting embodied carbon in import and export in China. *China Population, Resources and Environment, 18,* 8–13.

Sheng, B. (2002). *Political Economic Analysis on China's Foreign Trade Policies.* Shanghai: Shanghai Sanlian Press.

Stone, R., and Brown, A. (1962). *A Computable Model of Economic Growth: A Programme for Growth.* London: Chapman and Hall.

Walter, I., and Ugelow, J. (1979). Environmental policies in developing countries. *Ambio, 8*(2, 3), 102–109.

Wang, W., and Xiang, Q. (2011). Accounting and responsibility analysis on carbon emissions embodied in international trade. *China Industrial Economics, 10,* 56–68.

Xue, G., and Song, D. (2010). An empirical research on the relationship of export trade, economic growth and carbon emissions. *Journal of International Trade, 1,* 74–79.

Yan, Y., and Yang, L. (2010). China's foreign trade and climate change: A case study of CO_2 emissions. *Energy Policy, 38,* 350–356.

Zhang, W., and Du, Y. (2011). On the misalignment of the CO_2 emissions embodied in China's foreign trade. *China Industrial Economics, 4,* 138–147.

Zhang, Y. (2010). Carbon contents of the Chinese trade and their determinants: An analysis based on non-competitive (import) input-output tables. *China Economic Quarterly, 9*(4), 1287–1310.

Zhou, X. (2010). Emissions embodied in international trade and trade adjustment to national GHG inventory. *Management Review, 22,* 17–24.

CHAPTER 23

CLIMATE THRESHOLDS, WEATHER EXTREMES, AND CATASTROPHIC LOSSES

LOPAMUDRA BANERJEE

23.1 Introduction

This chapter reviews our existing state of knowledge on threshold behavior of Earth's climate system and examines fluctuations in the weather system attributed to climate change. The focus here is on abrupt rather than gradual change in Earth's atmospheric system. Drawing evidence from the existing literature, the chapter makes the following two points: First, abrupt changes are not entirely unlikely in complex systems exhibiting threshold behavior such as Earth's atmospheric system. Second, chances of effective coping and adaptation to the changes are lowered if the changes are abrupt rather than being gradual. Evidence of abrupt changes in Earth's atmospheric system in the historic and recent past can be found in paleoanthropologic and instrumentally recorded data on hydrometeorological variables. Though abrupt regime changes may occur spontaneously in a complex system, their likelihood increases with anthropogenic forcings, including increased emission of greenhouse gases (GHGs) such as carbon dioxide (CO_2), methane (CH_4), and nitrous oxide (N_2O). Abrupt climate changes are likely to be accompanied with extreme perturbations in the weather system. This may entail, among other things, extreme fluctuations in seasonal diurnal temperatures, extreme fluctuations in precipitation cycles, and increased frequency of extreme storms. When these changes occur abruptly, ecosystems and social systems may fail to cope and adapt. In case of such failures, cataclysmic losses may result. The chapter posits that if there is a nonzero probability of such catastrophic ecological and social losses, regardless of how small the probability is, circumspection is called for.

Since the early 1990s, climate models that analyze effects of global warming on mean and trend behaviors of atmospheric system have been supplemented with models that analyze future changes in extreme behaviors of weather systems. "Weak indicators," or early warnings of catastrophic outcomes, that are likely from these extreme weather perturbations are provided by nontrivial losses that are observed in times of natural disasters (e.g., violent storms, extreme rise in temperature, and critical decline in precipitation). Even when conclusive scientific proof of the precise extent and nature of losses from abrupt climate change may be patchy at best and missing at worst, the "weak indicators" may provide the sufficient conditions for strong interventions and regulations. The chapter invokes the notion of the "precautionary principle" in this regard.

The chapter is organized as follows: Section 23.2 explores threshold behavior exhibited by Earth's climate system and examines the plausibility of abrupt climate changes. Section 23.3 discusses past episodes of abrupt climate change and their effects on the ecosystem and the social system. Section 23.4 discusses certain model predictions regarding extreme perturbations in the weather system (in terms of deviations and fluctuations) that are likely to accompany abrupt changes in climate systems (in terms of mean and trend behaviors). "Weak indicators" (or early warnings) of potential catastrophic outcomes of these extreme perturbations are then gauged in terms of disaster outcomes currently observed. Section 23.5 examines distribution of potential outcomes of abrupt climate change across regions of the world and economic sectors of production. The analysis highlights, on one hand, that there are uncertainties regarding the frequency distribution of extreme weather events; and on the other, there are asymmetries in distribution of potential outcomes if and when they occur. In the presence of these uncertainties and asymmetries, standard risk analysis and cost–benefit analysis are less effective to guide appropriate preventive policies. Section 23.6 concludes the chapter by arguing that it is the precautionary principle that may be the more desirable judgment criterion to inform policy choice under these circumstances.

23.2 Thresholds and Abrupt Changes in the Climate System

It is now widely recognized that threshold behavior is key to our knowledge of dynamics and stability of Earth's climate system (Claussen et al., 1999; Pitman and Stouffer, 2006; Greiner et al., 2010). Threshold behavior is regarded as an extreme form of nonlinear dynamics that involves a rapid qualitative change of a regime or a process or the response of a system (Zehe and Sivapalan, 2009). A formal definition, presented by authors like Bloschl and Zehe (2005) McGrath et al. (2007), and Alley et al. (2003), state that threshold behavior is exhibited by complex systems with unstable dynamic modes where the state variables (or ?uxes) can potentially switch from zero to nonzero values over a short time or space increment. When the switch occurs, the associated processes or responses occur at a rate much greater than the typical time scales of the system, and at a rate much faster than that of the external forcing conditions (or boundary conditions) that caused the switch in regime in the first place. Two illustrative examples are often cited to explain this behavior. The first one, presented in Alley et al. (2003), describes tipping of canoes, where leaning slightly over the side of a canoe would cause only a small tilt, but leaning slightly more may cause breaching of a gradient threshold, tipping the craft into the lake. The second example, presented in Zehe and Sivapalan (2009), describes water boiling in a kettle, where an initial increase in temperature gradient leads to formation of convection cells, but with further increase a threshold is eventually breached and turbulent eddies form as the water begins to boil.

Regime transitions are smooth if the system is forced slowly, keeping it in quasi-equilibrium. Regime transitions are abrupt when the system is forced to change quickly. These abrupt changes are of serious concern, as, on one hand, they cannot be predicted in entirety in advance, and on the other, ecosystems and social systems may be unprepared or incapable of adapting when disturbances exceed resilience.

An earlier generation of climate models, including atmospheric dynamical models exhibiting spontaneous regime changes (Lorenz, 1963), atmospheric energy-balance models (Sellers, 1969), and oceanic thermohaline circulation models (Stommel, 1961) (with more recent application to the Atlantic thermohaline circulation (THC; Rahmstorf and Ganopolski, 1999), provided initial evidence of possibilities of large and rapid threshold transitions between distinct states of nature at a subcontinental level. A more recent generation of models, including models of decay of the Greenland ice sheet (Huybrechts and de Wolde, 1999) and Arctic sea melt (Lindsay and Zhang, 2005), have focused on "tipping points," or a critical value of the parameters controlling a subsystem of the Earth system, a slight but continued deviation from which will inevitably lead to qualitative change. Lenton et al. (2008) present the following formal definition in this regard. A system E is a tipping element if the parameters controlling the system can be transparently combined into a single control ρ, and there exists a critical control value ρ_{crit}, from which any significant variation by $\delta\rho > 0$ leads to a qualitative change ($\hat{F}$) in a crucial system feature F, after some observation time $T > 0$, measured with respect to a reference feature at the critical value, that is, $|F(\rho \geq \rho_{crit} + \delta\rho|T) - F(\rho_{crit}|T)| \geq \hat{F}$. Although the critical condition may be reached autonomously (without human interference), human activities have the potential to push components of the system past critical states. Greiner et al. (2009), for example, examined how increased emissions of GHGs such as CO_2 and CH_4 through increased production activities in a social system may trigger a qualitative change in the atmospheric system.

In these models, thresholds are theorized in terms of bifurcations (most commonly, saddle-node and Hopf bifurcations). Instability and randomness exist in close proximity to thresholds, and existing models are usually not accurate enough to predict reliably where critical thresholds may occur. Nevertheless, certain generic properties are observed when the dynamics of the systems approach ρ_{crit} (Carpenter and Brock, 2006; Scheffer et al., 2009). These properties provide early signals of impending regime change. For one, autocorrelations and amplitude of fluctuations (indicated by variances) of the state variable of the system increase closer to the threshold. Accordingly, recovery from even a small perturbation near the threshold is slow. In their study on eight examples of abrupt climate change phenomena, Dakos et al. (2008), for example, showed significant increases in autocorrelations preceding sudden regime changes. In addition, when the dynamics of the system approach an unstable equilibrium point, asymmetry of fluctuations increases and flickering is often observed. The asymmetry is indicated by skewness of distribution of states around ρ_{crit}, while flickering is indicated by increased variance and skewness as well as bimodality (reflecting the two alternative regimes) in this distribution. Studies on rapid oceanic and atmospheric changes, for instance, suggest flickering precedes abrupt regime changes (Bakke et al., 2009).

More recent studies on climate change have thus focused on detection of these "early signals" of abrupt regime change in climate system in terms of fluctuation patterns of state variables in the weather system (including temperature variability, precipitation variability, and variability in wind flow patterns). Some of these models are discussed later in this chapter.

Through what process are the thresholds crossed? Four critical conditions are acknowledged (Alley et al., 2003): triggers, amplifiers, globalizers, and sources of persistence. A trigger (or a combination of triggers) sets off the initial perturbations in a system with unstable dynamic modes. These perturbations get blown up in scale in the presence of an amplifier, which pushes the system closer to a threshold. Globalizers spread local anomalies across large regions or even the whole Earth. In presence of a source of persistence, the perturbations continue to go on. Eventually, a critical state or boundary condition is breached, and qualitative changes are observed in systemic conditions. Usually positive feedbacks from within the system provide the source of this persistence and prevent the system from flipping over to its original stable state. The feedbacks are often between biotic and abiotic components of the system, and may be multiple in number (Zehe and Sivapalan, 2009).

Abrupt changes pose extraordinary challenges, because, though their potential impacts may be catastrophic, predictions of qualitative changes are difficult for several reasons. For instance, though triggers, amplifiers, and sources of persistence are relatively easy to identify, globalizers are not (Alley et al., 2003). As mentioned earlier, globalizers indicate how perturbation and anomaly patterns spread across the system. Climate scientists have aimed to predict this spread by forcing on hypothesized causes of abrupt climate changes on General Circulation Models (GCMs). There are, however, epistemic and aleatory uncertainties involved in the process. Epistemic uncertainty arises, as, it is difficult to conceive of all forms of natural forcings and include them in the model. There are always the risks of omitting a potentially important globalizer from the numerical experiments. Aleatory uncertainty arises, as the models often underestimate the size and extent of climate response to threshold crossings. Thus, limited success is achieved in predicting patterns of abrupt changes. Even as the GCMs are successful in simulating certain regional changes, they habitually underestimate other changes, or altogether fail to generate sufficiently widespread anomaly patterns in certain other cases (Alley et al., 2003).

The second set of problems with prediction arises as modes of dynamic behavior at the "macro-scale" of the system are qualitatively different from those exhibited at the "micro-scale." As a result, it is difficult to extrapolate from the behavior of individual elements of a system the threshold values that determine qualitative changes in system behavior (Zehe and Sivapalan, 2009). Further, in the presence of multiple feedbacks it is difficult to determine internal states and boundary conditions at larger scales (Zehe et al., 2007). Thus, threshold behavior of climate system drastically reduces the ability to make predictions at the level of (1) an individual process and (2) the response of larger units that involve interactions of many processes.

Finally, multiple and mutually interacting sources of persistence of perturbations within the system pose additional problems for prediction. With multiple feedbacks, it is difficult to separate out the role played by natural variability in the complex system in generating an outcome from that of anthropogenic forcing as a source of the outcome. In particular, it is difficult to separate out the role of endogenous tendencies from that of exogenous drivers in triggering regime shifts in complex systems.

To address at least some of these problems, the "degenerate fingerprinting" method was developed (Lenton et al., 2008). The method aims at "fractional risk attribution" to distinguish natural vis-à-vis anthropogenic sources of perturbations using complexity models. Analysis is based on time series data on prehistorical climate conditions (generated from paleoclimatic records) and more recent historical weather conditions (generated from instrumental records). In lay terms, fingerprints are changes in the atmospheric system exhibiting certain patterns that are unique to a specific climate change driver. Once the unique pattern is observed, it is relatively easier to attribute climate variations to particular sources.

The "degenerate fingerprinting" method has been applied to examine the relative roles of natural driving factors (e.g., solar radiation and volcanic eruptions) and anthropogenic driving factors (e.g., GHGs, ozone, and sulfate aerosols) in changing global surface temperature over the 20th century (Meehl et al., 2005). Simulation results attributed global surface warming during the first few decades of the 20th century to changes in solar energy and volcanic activity, but indicated anthropogenic GHGs were by far the most important contributor to global surface warming during the last half of the 20th century.

Another prominent study (Barnett et al., 2005) applied the method to examine warming of six of the Earth's major oceans (namely, North Atlantic, South Atlantic, North Indian, South Indian, North Pacific, and South Pacific). The study carried out physical simulation of heat penetration to examine relative roles of internal variability and external forcing. Internal variability of ocean temperature implies natural variations in ocean temperatures that occur at different times, often in direct opposite patterns, as heat is transported from one place to another, without adding new heat to the system. In contrast, external forcing of ocean temperature indicates additions of new heat into the system. Simulation results showed there has been simultaneous warming of the six oceans since the 1950s. Though internal variability was an important driving force behind this phenomenon, simulation results attributed external forcing induced by GHGs to drive up the process.

23.3 Evidence of Abrupt Changes

Alley et al. (2003) remind us that large, abrupt, and widespread climate changes with major impacts have occurred repeatedly in the past. The collapse of North Mesopotamian civilization in the third millennium is a case in point (Weiss et al., 1993). In many cases, anthropogenic drivers played a critical role in exacerbating the catastrophic outcomes of these changes. Three such instances are now discussed. The first model examines drying of the Sahara during the latter part of the Holocene. The second model examines extended periods of drought in the 1930s in the United States, popularly known as the Dust Bowl, or the Dirty Thirties. The third model examines recent episodes of extreme droughts in Sahel and resulting famine conditions. The model on drying of Sahara is based on paleoclimatic records, while the models on Dust Bowl and Sahel drought are based on instrumental records of climate shifts. Each of the models demonstrates how threshold changes in hydrometeorological cycles have led to droughts with catastrophic social consequences. The first model emphasizes the role of natural driving factors in triggering the changes. The second model emphasizes how changes once triggered by natural factors may be amplified by anthropogenic factors. The third model emphasizes the interplay of natural and anthropogenic driving factors in generating spiraling of catastrophic consequences in the environmental system and the social system.

In the mid-Holocene (approximately 8000 B.C.E. to 6000 B.C.E.), regions that are now known as Egypt, Chad, Libya, and Sudan experienced a sudden onset of humid conditions (Markey, 2006), likely triggered by Bölling–Allerod warming and formation of low-pressure areas over the collapsing ice sheets to the north. In the late Holocene (approximately around 5300 B.C.E.), however, the region started drying up, leading to the formation of the current Sahara. Desertification of Sahara is cited as a threshold-crossing climate change phenomenon and modeled in terms of bistable states that are maintained by climate–vegetation feedbacks (Brovkin et al., 1998; Claussen et al., 1999). It is argued that the process of desertification was triggered by a stronger tilting in Earth's axis of orbit, or "orbital forcing," which caused a decline in summertime incoming solar radiation, and eventually weakened the African monsoon (Kutzbach et al., 1996). The desertification process was amplified and globalized as vegetation cover in the region shriveled and soil moisture content was lost. Because evapotranspiration of soil moisture is a significant source of precipitation, rainfall in the region declined further. The climate–vegetation feedbacks provided their own source of persistence. As vegetation died or became dormant due to lack of rainfall, the ability of roots to trap water declined. Thus, even when there was rainfall, the precipitation was not retained in the soil, but ran off to streams and ocean. Soil moisture content thus declined further, leading to further desertification.

Desertification of the Sahara proved to be socially disruptive for the prehistoric hunter-gatherer society settled in the region. Mass migration resulted, either to the east into the Nile Valley, or to the south into the African Great Lakes region. Skilled members of this migrant human population that settled near the Nile River gave rise to the first pharaonic cultures in Egypt (Markey, 2006). The relatively slow pace of decline in environmental abundance driven by climate change in Sahara allowed for social adaptation and adjustment. Mobility of the prehistoric human population, and relative abundance of land for relocation and resettlement, facilitated this adaptation. The process would have been far more disruptive for a stationary population, or if the system was unmanaged. The case of the Dust Bowl, or the Dirty Thirties, in the United States provides an example.

The 1930s Dust Bowl in the United States is considered as a major drought of the 20th century in terms of duration and spatial extent (NOAA, 2003; Science Daily, 2004). The drought came in three waves—1934, 1936, and 1939–1940 in the Great Plains (extending over Texas and Oklahoma panhandles, and the adjacent parts of New Mexico, Colorado, and Kansas)—but in some regions of the High Plains drought conditions continued for as many as eight years. Schubert et al. (2004) used ensembles of long-term (1930–1999) simulations and NASA's Seasonal-to-Interannual Prediction Project (NSIPP) Atmospheric General Circulation Model (AGCM) to examine this climatic event. It is argued that abnormal cooling of the tropical Pacific Ocean and abnormal warming of the tropical Atlantic Ocean triggered the onset of this drought. Abnormal changes in sea surface temperatures caused rapid changes in large-scale weather patterns and low-level wind patterns. The process was amplified and globalized as the low-level jet stream weakened. Though the jet stream normally flows westward over the Gulf of Mexico and then turns northward, bringing abundant rainfall to the Great Plains, with abnormal changes in sea surface temperature it changed its course to travel farther south than normal. This reduced the normal supply of moisture from the Gulf of Mexico, holding back rainfall throughout the Great Plains (extending over Texas and Oklahoma panhandles, and the adjacent parts of New Mexico, Colorado, and Kansas). As a result, soil in the Great Plains dried up, vegetation became sparse, and dust storms formed. As in the case of Sahara, with decline in evapotranspiration of soil moisture, the climate–vegetation feedbacks provided a source of persistence of the drought conditions.

The relatively fast pace of decline in environmental abundance in the Great Plains, triggered by abrupt climate shift and the resultant North Atlantic warming, was further aggravated by anthropogenic forcing. In this case, anthropogenic forcing came in the form of over-extraction of land resources and mismanagement of land use practices. Decades of deep plowing of the virgin topsoil in the Great Plains, displacement of the natural deep-rooted grasses that normally kept the soil in place and trapped moisture, extensive farming of land in the region without crop rotation, and similar other extractive farming techniques aggravated wind erosion (NOAA, 2003). Immense dust storms (popularly known as "black blizzards" and "black rollers") formed, and extensive areas of farmland became barren and crop-less. The droughts forced the largest migration in American history within a short period of time, and by 1940, 2.5 million people moved out of the Great Plains (James, 1991). The catastrophe intensified unemployment in the region and deepened the economic impact of the Great Depression (Worster, 1979).

Past experiences show that consequences of environmental catastrophes are particularly acute for the poor and the marginalized population. The Sahel drought experiences underscore this issue. The decreasing rainfall and devastating droughts in the Sahel region in the late 20th century are one of the largest and most undisputed abrupt climate change phenomena recognized by the climate research community. Several possible mechanisms to explain rainfall decline in the region have been proposed (Dai et al., 2004). These include local land–atmosphere interactions models, tropical Atlantic and global sea-surface temperature influences, and atmospheric wave disturbances.

Recently, an influential climate modeling study carried out at National Oceanic and Atmospheric Administration (NOAA)/Geophysical Fluid Dynamics Laboratory has intimately linked the late 20th century Sahel drought to natural variability in climatic conditions with an anthropogenic forcing of regional drying trend (Held et al., 2005). It is argued increased aerosol loading that cooled the Northern Hemisphere and changed sea surface temperature patterns, affecting the West African Monsoon (WAM) circulation, triggered the drought. The drought effects were further exacerbated with gradual decimation of vegetation covers and decline in agricultural productivity of land. The natural response of the local grass ecosystem to the initial forcing of the dry conditions played a critical role in maintaining the drought through the following decades (Wang and Eltahir, 2000). Decline in rainfall and rapid withering of regional flora caused droughts as farmlands became parched and desertification occurred. The Sahara was pushed further southward.

The droughts caused severe decline in food production and triggered famine situations in the region. With further anthropogenic hindrance, including failure of a welfare state to provide relief and food aid, government apathy, export regulations on agriculture, and dismal responses from international communities, famine intensified into a critical humanitarian crisis. United Nations Environment Programme (UNEP, 2002) reports that the famines triggered by droughts have affected generations of Sahel's population, with 100,000 people dying from starvation, disease, and malnutrition between the late 1960s to early 1980s. The droughts have severely affected economies and livestock and human populations of much of Mauritania, Mali, Chad, Niger, and Burkina Faso. Approximately 750,000 people of the region continue to be dependent on food aid.

23.4 Abrupt Climate Change and Weather Extremes

The abrupt changes that have occurred in the past may also occur in future. The first and the second assessment reports of the Intergovernmental Panel on Climate Change (IPCC) (Houghton et al., 1996; Zhang et al., 1998) emphasize this point. The reports, together with a series of five papers entitled "Understanding Changes in Weather and Climate Extremes," published in 2000 in *Bulletin of the American Meteorological Society* predict abrupt regime changes in Earth's atmospheric system are likely to be accompanied by extreme behaviors of climate and weather systems (Changnon et al., 2000; Easterling et al., 2000; Meehl et al., 2000a, 2000b; Parmesan et al., 2000). With a rise in mean and trend global temperatures, greater fluctuations and deviations in temperature (Hansen and Lebedeff, 1988; Hansen et al., 2010), rainfall, and storms (McGuffie, 1998; Oouchi et al., 2006) are predicted. The frequency of extreme warm days and lower frequency of extreme cold days are now likely to increase. In mid-latitude areas of the Northern Hemisphere, the diurnal temperature range is expected to tighten in winter but stretch in summer. These changes are likely to be associated with increased aridness during summer, increasing chances of drought in the region.

The other area of active research is the effect of rise in mean landmass and ocean surface temperatures on precipitation patterns and storm occurrences. In topical regions of the Earth, global temperature rise is likely to be accompanied with extreme variability in precipitation patterns. The effects on Indian Ocean Summer Monsoon (ISM) occurrences are an area of particular concern (Bhaskharan and Mitchell, 1998; Trenberth et al., 2000; Zickfeld, 2005). In addition, tropical storms are likely to increase in frequency and intensity. In two extremely influential studies, Emanuel (2005) and Webster et al. (2005) independently found tropical cyclone in the North Atlantic and Northeast Pacific oceans are becoming more intense over recent decades, and this trend is observed in all of the Earth's oceans where tropical cyclones develop. Other studies highlight increased tropical cyclone activity in the Asia–Pacific region.

A brief discussion on disastrous outcomes of hydrometeorological extremes is now presented in the following three contexts: rise in temperature, fluctuations in ISM patterns, and rise in frequency of hurricanes.

Extreme temperature conditions can have potentially life-threatening effects on the animal and human world. Two such effects are now examined. Recent research by Pounds et al. (2006) attributed widespread mass amphibian extinctions in the tropics to abrupt climate change events associated with ocean surface and atmospheric temperatures. An unusual warming and moistening trend in tropical mountain environments led to disease outbreaks in the amphibian population. The effects were amplified as the extraordinary warming and moistening conditions caused migrations of disease-causing organisms such as chytrids (a type of fungus) to new habitats, especially mountainsides. Abnormal onslaught of these organisms led to threshold crossings in the regional ecosystems. As the disturbances exceeded resilience, amphibian species loss ensued.

For human beings, rising morbidity and mortality rates have been associated with extreme variations in temperature (Gouveia et al., 2003). Estimates by the World Health Organization (WHO) relate more than 150,000 annual deaths across the world over the past 30 years to extreme warming conditions associated with anthropogenic climate change (Patz et al., 2005). The effect of extremely high temperature on health was studied extensively for the 2003 European heat wave, when the average temperature rose 3.5°C above the normal expected level. An estimated 22,000–45,000 deaths in the first two weeks of August of that year were attributed to extreme temperature (Kosatsky, 2005; IFRC, 2004). These effects provide "early warnings" of catastrophic outcomes likely in case of abrupt climate change. Stott et al. (2004) found the risk of a future heat wave of a magnitude similar to the 2003 Europe heat wave more than doubles with anthropogenic forcing of global warming.

Rises in mean landmass and ocean surface temperatures are also likely to cause fluctuations in ISM patterns. The fluctuations are likely to increase drought and deluge cycles in South Asia. These increases have potential catastrophic effects for the South Asian economy and society. Agriculture is the main source of livelihood in the region, and agricultural productivity remains largely dependent on natural variability in precipitation cycles. Estimates of crop loss attributed to abrupt climate change for India alone are staggering. Shifting in crop cycle due to change in precipitation patterns may cause as much as a 40% decline in crop production (Kumar and Parikh, 2001). An increase in the intensity of deluges and droughts would affect agricultural production, and may even lead to famines (Alagmir, 1980). Furthermore, South Asia is at the same time the most populous and most densely populated geographical region in the world. In 2008, the income of approximately 40% of this population was below the International Poverty Line of $1.25 per day (World Bank, 2012). Increasing incidences of a deluge are likely to displace tens of millions of people. The number will rise substantially if global warming leads to a sea level rise.

CO_2-induced global warming is also predicted to increase hurricane intensities (Knutson and Tuleya, 1999; Landsea, 2005). Not unlike changes in monsoon circulation patterns, rises in the incidence and severity of tropical storms have potential catastrophic effects. "Weak indications" of the probable effects are provided by our current experiences. For instance, many commentators are now treating the 2005 hurricane season in North America as an indicator of what may follow if abrupt changes do occur and if such changes increase the intensity and frequency of extreme weather phenomena. The year 2005 may go down in history as the one in which a maximum number of storms (27 in number), maximum number of hurricanes (13 in number), most strong landfalling hurricanes in United States (4 in number), and 3 of the strongest storms (namely, Hurricanes Wilma, Rita, and Katrina) ever recorded instrumentally have occurred (Dlugolecki, 2006). More than 1300 people died that year from direct exposures to the storms, and many times that number were displaced and traumatized. Hurricanes Rita and Katrina triggered a major global energy crisis. Massive costs were involved in repairing, public works, and long-term relief payments.

Historical loss data in the United States assembled since the late 1940s from records kept by the property insurance industry show financial losses (adjusted for inflation) from weather and climate extremes have been steadily increasing, and between the 1950s and the past decade they increased by a factor close to 100 (Changnon et al., 2000). A significant proportion of these losses have been associated with violent storms, specifically hurricanes (Grenier, 2006). The hurricane season of the year 2005 was the costliest in terms of financial losses for the country. The hurricane season is estimated to cost insurers US$60 billion (approximately 0.005% of US GDP for the year), which is more than double that of any previous year. The true economic costs (which include uninsured losses and property blight) were estimated at US$250 billion (approximately 0.02% of US GDP for the year). The insurance industry is increasingly becoming cognizant of the escalating threats of catastrophic losses. Repeat occurrences of the 2005 hurricane season in North America are deemed unacceptable, both to insurers and insurees, for the following reasons. First, any increases in frequency of extreme weather related events have critical implications for health and life insurance (Kunreuther and Michel-Kerjan, 2007). Second, these increases may also affect premiums and available coverage for property damage and business interruption losses.

But questions remain as to whether hurricane losses are driven by an abnormally high intensity of storms (measured in terms of wind speed), or by greater exposure of vulnerable assets to storm. Societal shifts, including demographic shifts to hazard-prone zones, increasing density of valuable property, and increasing urbanization in coastal areas and storm-prone areas, are exposing communities and valuable assets to these extreme phenomena and increasing their susceptibility to harm (Changnon et al., 2000). In addition, the general population growth is increasing pressure on land and making safe relocations and readjustments difficult.

Irrespective of the specific sources of financial loss, it is, however, apparent that if frequency and/or intensity of natural extremes indeed do increase in the future, the losses would only multiply manifold. An example is the following: if the more active hurricane seasons in the 1940s and 1950s were to occur today, societal impacts would be substantially greater than in earlier decades (Meehl et al., 2000b). In light of this evidence, it seems if there is a nonzero probability of extreme weather conditions, regardless of how small the probability is, caution is required. The issue is not so much whether anthropogenic forcing is already inducing abrupt climate change, or when climate thresholds will be crossed. Rather, the issue is if abrupt climate change is likely, and if it is likely to be tied in with increased occurrences of disasters, then a genuine basis for apprehension is present by now.

23.5 Regional Spread and Probable Outcomes of Weather Extremes

If extreme weather conditions accompany abrupt climate change, how will their impact be experienced? This issue is now examined, focusing on distribution of probable outcomes of extreme temperature and precipitation variations along two axes: different regions of the world and different sectors of economic production.

On a global scale, the largest changes in the hydrological cycle (e.g., snowmelt and river flow) due to global warming are predicted for the snow-dominated basins of mid to higher latitudes (Barnett et al., 2005); while the largest changes in hydrometeorological cycles (i.e., rainfall and storm formation) are predicted for tropical regions (Patz et al., 2005). As a result, seasonal runoff patterns of surface water in mid to higher latitudes are expected to change, and precipitation predictions for tropical regions are likely to become more uncertain. These changes in temperature and precipitation patterns are likely to affect the biota of a region, as distribution and reproductive generation patterns of species change over time. The resulting effects on regional biota may intensify further with alteration in the solar radiation period and extreme weather events (McCarthy, 2001).

A large number of models predict that if near-surface air temperature increases at a modest but a steady rate, there would be a serious reduction in dry-season water availability in many regions of the Earth within the next few decades (Barnett et al., 2005). These changes are likely to generate considerable impacts on water availability for irrigation, industry, and household consumption. The model-predicted changes are already being captured by recorded data.

In agriculture, the decline in water availability for irrigation will be particularly severe for those regions of the world where changes in snow melt patterns trigger seasonal shifts in stream flows. In Canadian prairies and the western United States, for example, agricultural production and aquatic habitat are likely to be endangered as a result of these changes (Barnett et al., 2005). In the Himalaya–Hindu Kush region, extending over China, India, and other parts of Asia, vanishing glaciers will disrupt the flow of mighty rivers such as the Ganges and Yangtze. As the agrosystem of the region is dependent more on surface irrigation from rivers than on irrigation from rainfall, agrarian distress may result in the region. Similar effects are likely to occur in the South American Andes (Thompson et al., 2003).

Atmospheric regime changes will also directly affect plant productivity and crop cycles. The effects are, however, predicted to be quite different across various regions of the world. In temperate regions of northern Europe, the changes may produce positive effects on agriculture through introduction of new crop species and varieties, higher crop production, and expansion of suitable areas for crop cultivation (Olesen and Bindi, 2002). In southern Europe, especially in regions with a Mediterranean climate, the changes are expected to produce negative effects with lower harvestable yields, higher variability in yield rate, and shrinkage of suitable areas of traditional crops (Maracchi et al., 2005). These effects are likely to intensify agriculture in northern and western Europe, and reduce its concentration in the Mediterranean and southeastern parts of Europe (Olesen, 2006). In tropical regions, the changes in temperature and rainfall patterns are likely to change crop cycles and reduce yield rates (McCarthy, 2001). The plantation-to-harvest ratio may decline further with increased incidences of natural disasters. In addition, warmer temperatures are likely to indirectly affect agricultural productivity by speeding up growth rates of plant pests, pathogens, and weeds (Cerri et al., 2007).

Productivity changes in agrosystems are likely to produce cascading effects in the economy. With decline in agricultural output, commodity trade flows would be adversely affected, sectoral contribution of agriculture to national income would decline, and personal income of households employed in the agricultural sector would decline. More importantly, decline in agricultural output may have critical implications for food security in countries of the adversely affected region, many of which are already plagued by consumption poverty and hunger (Weitzman, 2009).

The effect of global warming on forestry is another area of intense research. In temperate regions of northern Europe, rise in rainfall is expected to compensate for the decline in surface water availability, and increase forest production (Maracchi et al., 2005). Rise in rainfall, cloudiness, and rain days may, however, also negatively affect labor productivity, by disrupting forest work and timber logging. The flow of recreational services from forestry is also likely to be disrupted with increased precipitation, and the reduced duration of snow cover and soil frost. In Mediterranean regions, forestry may be mainly affected by increases in drought and forest fires. Model predictions for the timber industry in United States, however, show a rise in temperature is expected to expand timber supplies and benefit the timber market (Sohngen and Mendelsohn, 1998).

Changes in hydrological regimes are projected to threaten hydroelectric power production. An influential study on the Columbia River system, for instance, predicts that by 2050 there may be a significant decline (by 10–20%) in hydroelectricity generation capacity of the river (Payne et al., 2004). With a decline in snowfall and advancing snow melting periods, the Columbia River system cannot be managed to accommodate all of its needs, and there would be a conflict in use of water stored in reservoirs. In particular, a choice would be forced between water releases in summer and autumn to produce hydroelectricity, or water releases in spring and summer for salmon runs. A similar decline in hydropower generation is also predicted in some parts of Rhine River basins in Europe and along snow-fed river systems of the South American Andes (Barnett et al., 2005).

Atmospheric regime changes may also affect the supply of other energy sources. For instance, changes in river flow patterns in response to changes in hydrological system would reduce availability of water as coolants for thermal power plants; and changes in wind speed in response to changes in atmospheric temperature and air pressure systems are likely to critically affect generation of wind power (Aaheim et al., 2009). The former effects may intensify as abrupt regime changes bring about droughts and sudden sharp increases in summertime surface temperature.

Changes in energy production are likely to have reverberating effects on industrial production. In the European Union regions, the energy sectors contribute 2–6% of GDP, with the highest contributions in the Baltics and in central Europe, followed by the Nordic countries and on the British islands (Aaheim et al., 2009). Any changes in energy production are thus likely to have relatively more severe effects for these economies.

Extreme variations in atmospheric conditions are also related to increasing health risks, including higher incidences of cardiovascular mortality and respiratory illnesses due to thermal stress, and altered transmission of infectious diseases (Patz et al., 2005). Changes in temperature and humidity are also projected to increase prevalence of vector-borne diseases. For example, the epidemic potential of malaria is projected to increase by twofold in tropical regions and by a hundred-fold in temperate regions by the year 2100 (Martens et al., 1995). In tropical regions where the disease is currently endemic, the number of years of healthy life lost due to malaria is likely to increase. The subtropical regions, where the disease currently has lower endemicity, the spread of infection is even more sensitive to abrupt changes in temperature and humidity conditions. In traditionally nonmalarial regions, including parts of Australia, the United States, and southern Europe, the risk of introducing the disease is now high. Whereas preventive and curative measures for the disease are more readily accessible to developed nations of temperate regions, they may not be economically feasible in underdeveloped nations in the tropics and subtropics. This, with regime changes in climate and atmospheric systems, distribution of the incidence of malaria and other such vector-borne diseases is expected to be grossly disproportionate across regions of the world. Under the threat of declining regional food yields and malnutrition, the effects are likely to be exacerbated.

Declining health conditions may bring about a wide spectrum of social, demographic, and economic disruptions (Kalkstein and Smoyer, 1993). Increased mortality will reduce the labor supply and increased morbidity will reduce labor productivity. Models further predict that in regions where net health impacts are likely to be negative, decline in GDP and investments is likely (Bosello et al., 2006). Prices, production, and terms of trade, however, show a mixed pattern. For households, on the one hand, income losses due to labor days lost from ill health are predicted; on the other, expenditures on health care are likely to increase.

Though there may be uncertainties regarding the precise nature of macroeconomic impacts of atmospheric perturbations, there are no uncertainties regarding the distribution of these impacts at a microeconomic scale. Households that are relatively poor are likely to be more adversely affected by the changes. On one hand, resource deficits would increase the chance of exposure to extreme environmental conditions for households; on the other, these deficits may lead to a failure to smooth out the disruption in consumption flows caused by extreme conditions. The effects of abrupt changes are more severe than those of gradual changes, as there is less scope to prepare, adapt, and cope.

23.6 Summary, Conclusions, and an Appeal to the "Precautionary Principle"

This chapter draws attention to the fact that abrupt threshold crossing of the climate system is possible, and anthropogenic forcing may hasten the process. Abrupt climate changes would be accompanied by extreme perturbations in the weather system. Existing evidence suggests that impacts of extreme weather events are, on one hand, distributed unevenly across exposed population groups, while, on the other, they generate domino effects across sectors of the economy. A rise in frequency or severity of extreme events in the atmospheric system raises the chances of inconsequential losses in the ecological and socioeconomic systems. These losses provide "early warnings" of potential effects of abrupt climate change, and are at least "weak indicators" of the likely nature of their adverse outcomes.

Most current policy research on climate change phenomena addresses the impacts of slow and gradual changes on ecosystems and society. Nordhaus (2000) and Stern (2006), for example, have suggested that efficient economic responses for slow and gradual changes should include modest but increasing emissions reductions and increased carbon taxes. Abrupt changes, with potentially catastrophic effects, are, however, difficult to analyze in this framework. As abrupt changes involve potential discontinuities and strong nonlinear effects on the social and economic systems, the abatement costs are likely to be much larger (Keller et al., 2000). Accordingly, standard application of cost–benefit analysis is likely to be unsuitable in guiding policymakers.

Furthermore, abrupt changes across thresholds involve uncertainties. Conventional analysis of choice under risk cannot be applied in these cases. In the standard application of risk analysis, weighted averages of outcomes associated with different states of nature are quantified to yield a single reductive indicator of risk, the weights being the respective probabilities of outcomes. When outcomes are unknown or ambiguous, and/or their probability distribution is unknown, as is possible in the case of threshold changes, derivation of risk indicators is no longer feasible.

The main argument in favor of timely stringent intervention is that real risks of highly detrimental consequences cannot be ignored because the available evidence for the threats has not fulfilled the strict criteria of scientific knowledge (Ahteensuu, 2007). Thus, even if the exact nature or timetable of future losses from greenhouse-induced climate change are speculative, it is always more desirable to avoid false negatives than false positives (Peterson, 2007) when it comes to catastrophic risks. Risk aversion is justified in the face of non-inconsequential losses.

Indeed, policy prescriptions based on the application of the current generation of Energy Balance Climate Models (EBCMs) show that, in the presence of nonlinearities, rapid mitigation policies are more desirable than any gradualist policy (Brock et al., this volume). Similarly, the climate-economy models that incorporate nonlinearities predict that with delayed policy decisions, an undesirable steady state may result for the economic system in which the amount of output produced (and the stock of capital accumulated) is low but thermal stress is high (Greiner et al., 2009). In contrast, with a timely policy intervention that prevents GHG concentration levels from reaching a critical threshold, a more desirable steady state may result in an economic system with higher growth rate and lower rise in atmospheric temperature. The latter scenario is all the more desirable as it yields a higher level of social welfare. The arguments for immediate intervention, rather than slow and gradual changes, are further strengthened when one considers the mitigating efforts that have actually been made by countries of the world. The gradualist "cap and trade" mechanism inherent in the Kyoto Protocol has now proven to be an ineffective policy instrument for providing sufficient incentives to countries to reduce their carbon emissions (Hansen, this volume).

In the presence of strong prima facie evidence of threshold behavior of Earth's climate and weather systems, caution is called for. Although traditional guiding principles of policy making, such as cost–benefit and risk analysis, may be ineffective in this regard, the "precautionary approach" may be more appropriate. The "precautionary principle" calls attention to the need for anticipatory policy intervention (as against reactionary actions) when there is an expectation of loss, even if there is no complete certainty (Miller and Conko, 2000; Conko, 2003; Hahn and Sunstein, 2005; Stirling, 2007). These tenets are particularly attractive when expected losses are catastrophic and irreversible, and when intervention may maximize net social benefit. The principle draws inspiration from the "foresight principle" (*vorsorgeprinzip* in German) (Kriebel et al., 2001; Iverson and Perrings, 2009) and "prudent avoidance" principles (Aasen et al., 1996) that form the cornerstones of German and Scandinavian environmental policies, and is enshrined in Article 3.3 of the United Nations Framework Convention on Climate Change (UNFCCC, 1992). The principle highlights that although conclusive and irrefutable scientific proofs may not be available, even in their absence, stringent regulations may be implemented, as "weak indicators" may provide sufficient conditions for choosing such policies. In the present chapter, "weak indicators" of potential nontrivial damages from climate change have been discussed in terms of the resulting effects of weather extremes on ecology, economy, and society. When probabilities of catastrophic losses are nonzero, no matter how small the probabilities, it is sensible to err on the side of caution. Even if the precise nature and extent of losses in the future may be patchy, and may fall short of providing the necessary conditions for justifying strong interventions, these "weak indicators" provide sufficient conditions for regulation.

References

Aaheim, A., Amundsen, H., Dokken, T., Ericson, T., and Wie, T. (2009). A macroeconomic assessment of impacts and adaptation to climate change in Europe. ADAM Project DA 1.

Aasen, S., Johnsson, A., Bratlid, D., and Christensen, T. (1996). Fifty-hertz magnetic field exposures of premature infants in a neonatal intensive care unit. *Biology of the Neonate*, *70*, 249–264.

Ahteensuu, M.(2007). Defending the precautionary principle against three criticisms. *Trames, 4*, 366–381.

Alagmir, M. (1980). *Famine in South Asia: Political Economy of Mass Starvation.* Cambridge, MA: Oelgeschlager, Gunn and Hain.

Alley, R. B., Marotzke, J., Nordhaus, W. D., Overpeck, J. T., Peteet, D. M., Pielke Jr, Pierrehumbert, R. T., Rhines, P. B., Stocker, T. F., Talley, L. D., and Wallace, J. M. (2003). Abrupt climate change. *Science, 299*(5615), 2005–2010.

Bakke, J, Lie, Ø., Heegaard, E., Dokken, T., Haug, G. H., Birks, H. H., Dulski, P., and Nilsen, T. (2009). Rapid oceanic and atmospheric changes during the Younger Dryas cold period. *Nature Geoscience, 2*(3), 202–205.

Barnett, T. P., Pierce, D. W., AchutaRao, K. M., Gleckler, P. J., Santer, B. D., Gregory, J. M., and Washington, W. M. (2005). Penetration of human-induced warming into the world's oceans. *Science, 309*(5732), 284–287.

Bhaskharan, B., and Mitchell, J. F. B. (1998). Simulated changes in Southeast Asian monsoon precipitation resulting from anthropogenic emissions. *International Journal of Climatology, 18*, 1455–1462.

Bloschl, G., and Zehe, E. (2005). On hydrological predictability. *Hydrological Processes, 19*(19), 3923–3929.

Bosello, F., Roson, R., and Tol, R. S. J. (2006). Economy-wide estimates of the implications of climate change: Human health. *Ecological Economics, 58*(3), 579–591.

Brovkin, V., Claussen, M., Petoukhov, V., and Ganopolski, A. (1998). On the stability of the atmosphere-vegetation system in the Sahara/Sahel region. *Journal of Geophysical Research, 103*, 31613–31624.

Carpenter, S. R., and Brock, W. A. (2006). Rising variance: A leading indicator of ecological transition. *Ecology Letters, 9*(3), 311–318.

Cerri, C. E. P., Sparovek, G., Bernoux, M., Easterling, W. E., Melillo, J. M., and Cerri, C. C. (2007). Tropical agriculture and global warming: impacts and mitigation options. *Scientia Agricola, 64*(1), 83–99.

Changnon, S. A., Jr., Pielke, R. A., Changnon, D., Sylves, R. T., and Pulwarty, R. (2000). Human factors explain the increased losses from weather and climate extremes. *Bulletin of the American Meteorological Society, 81*(3), 437–442.

Claussen, M., Kubatzki, C., Brovkin, V., Ganopolski, A., Heolzmann, P., and Pachur, H-J. (1999). Simulation of an abrupt change in Saharan vegetation in the mid-Holocene. *Geophysical Research Letters, 26*(14), 2037–2040.

Conko, G. (2003). Safety, risk and the precautionary principle: rethinking precautionary approaches to the regulation of transgenic plants. *Transgenic Research, 12*, 639–647.

Dai, A., Lamb, P. J., Trenberth, K. E., Hulme, M., Jones, P. D., and Xie, P. (2004). The recent Sahel drought is real. *International Journal of Climatology, 24*, 1323–1331.

Dakos, V., Scheffer, M., van Nes, E. H., Brovkin, V., Petoukhov, V., and Held, H. (2008). Slowing down as an early warning signal for abrupt climate change. *Proceedings of the National Academy of Sciences, 105*(38), 14308–14312.

Dlugolecki, A. (2006). Thoughts about the impact of climate change on insurance claims. Paper presented at Climate Change and Disaster Losses Workshop, Hohenkammer, Germany, May 25–26, 2006.

Easterling, D. R., Evans, J. L., Groisman, P. Y., Karl, T. R., Kunkel, K. E., and Ambenje, P. (2000). Observed variability and trends in extreme climate events: A brief review. *Bulletin of the American Meteorological Society, 81*(3), 417–426.

Emanuel, K. (2005). Increasing destructiveness of tropical cyclones over the past 30 years. *Nature, 46*, 686–688.

Giorgi, F., Mearns, L., Shields, S., and McDaniel, L. (1998). Regional nested model simulations of present day and $2XCO_2$ climate change over the central Great Plains of the United States. *Climate Change, 40*, 457–493.

Gouveia, N., Hajat, S., and Armstrong, B. (2003). Socioeconomic differentials in the temperature-mortality relationship in Sao Paulo, Brazil. *International Journal of Epidemiology, 32*, 390–397.

Greiner, A., Gruene, L., and Semmler, W. (2010). Growth and Climate Change: Threshold and Multiple Equilibria. In *Dynamic Systems, Economic Growth, and the Environment*, edited by J. Crespo Cuaresma, T. Palokangas, and A. Tarasyev, pp. 63–78. Heidelberg and New York: Springer Science+Business Media.

Grenier, H. Climate change and disaster losses: Understanding and attributing losses and projections. Paper presented at Climate Change and Disaster Losses Workshop, Hohenkammer, Germany, May 25–26, 2006.

Greiner, R., Patterson, L., and Miller, O. (2009). Motivations, risk perceptions and adoption of conservation practices by farmers. *Agricultural Systems, 99*(2), 86–104.

Hahn, R.W., and Sunstein, C. R. (2005). The precautionary principle as a basis for decision making. *The Economists' Voice, 2*(2), 1–9.

Hansen, J., and Lebedeff, S. (1988). Global surface air temperatures: Update through 1987. *Geophysical Research Letters, 15*(4), 323–326.

Hansen, J., Ruedy, R., Sato, M., and Lo, K. (2010). Global surface temperature change. *Reviews of Geophysics, 48*(4), RG4004.

Held, I. M., Delworth, T. L., Lu, J., Findell, K. L., and Knutson, T. R. (2005). Simulation of Sahel drought in the 20th and 21st centuries. *Proceedings of the National Academy of Sciences of the USA, 102*(50), 17891–17896.

Hodell, D. A., Curtis, J. H., and Brenner, M. (1995). Possible role of climate in the collapse of Classic Maya civilization. *Nature, 375*, 391–394.

Houghton, J. T., Meira Filho, L. G., Callandar, B. A., Harris, N., Kattenberg, A., and Maskel, K. *Climate Change 1995: The Science of Climate Change.* Cambridge, UK: Cambridge University Press, 1996.

Huybrechts, P., and de Wolde, J. (1999). The dynamic response of the Greenland and Antarctic ice sheets to multiple-century climatic warming. *Journal of Climate, 12*(8), 2169–2188.

IFRC. World Disaster Report. International Federation of Red Cross and Red Crescent Societies, 2004.

Iverson, T., and Perrings, C. (2009). The precautionary principle and global environmental change. Ecosystem Services Economics. UNEP Policy Brief. Nairobi, Kenya: United Nations Environment Programme.

James, G. N. (1991). *American Exodus: The Dust Bowl Migration and Okie Culture in California.* New York: Oxford University Press.

Kalkstein, L. S., and Smoyer, K. E. (1993). The impact of climate change on human health: Some international perspectives. *Experientia, 49*, 969–979.

Keller, K., Tan, K., Morel, F. M. M., and Bradford, D. F. (2000). Preserving the ocean circulation: Implications for climate policy. Working Paper No. w7476. Cambridge, MA: National Bureau of Economic Research.

Knutson, T. R., and Tuleya, R. E. (1999). Increased hurricane intensities with CO_2-induced warming as simulated using the GFDL hurricane prediction system. *Climate Dynamics, 15*, 503–519.

Kosatsky, T. (2005). The 2003 European heat waves. *European Communicable Disease Journal*, 10(7), 148–149.

Kriebel, D., Tickner, J., Epstein, P., Lemons, J., Levins, R., Loechler, E. L., Quinn, M., Rudel, R., Schettler, T., and Stoto, M. (2001). The precautionary principle in environmental science. *Environmental Health Perspectives, 109*(9), 871–876.

Kumar, K. S., and Parikh, J. (2001). Indian agriculture and climate sensitivity. *Global Environmental Change, 11*(2), 147–154.

Kunreuther, H. C., and Michel-Kerjan, E. O. (2007). *Climate change, insurability of large-scale disasters and the emerging liability challenge (No. w12821)*. National Bureau of Economic Research.

Kutzbach, J. E., Bonan, G., Foley, J., and Harrison, S. P. (1996). Vegetation and soil feedbacks on the response of the African monsoon to orbital forcing in the early to middle Holocene. *Nature, 384*, 623–626.

Landsea, C. W. (2005). Hurricanes and global warming. *Nature, 438*, E11–E13.

Lindsay, R. W., and Zhang, J. (2005). The thinning of Arctic sea ice, 1988-2003: Have we passed a tipping point? *Journal of Climate, 18*(22), 4879–4894.

Lorenz, E. N. (1963). Deterministic nonperiodic flow. *Journal of the Atmospheric Sciences, 20*(2), 130–141.

Maracchi, G., Sirotenko, O., and Bindi, M. (2005). Impacts of present and future climate variability on agriculture and forestry in the temperate regions: Europe. In *Increasing Climate Variability and Change*, edited by James Salinger, M. V. K. Sivakumar, and Raymond P. Motha, pp. 117–135. Dordrecht, The Netherlands: Springer.

Markey, S. (2006, July 20). Exodus from drying Sahara gave rise to pharaohs, study says. *National Geographic News*.

Martens, W. J., Niessen, L. W., Rotmans, J., Jetten, T. H., and McMichael, A. J. (1995). Potential impact of global climate change on malaria risk. *Environmental Health Perspectives, 103*(5), 458–464.

McCarthy, J. J. (Ed.). (2001). *Climate change 2001: impacts, adaptation, and vulnerability: contribution of Working Group II to the third assessment report of the Intergovernmental Panel on Climate Change*. Cambridge: Cambridge University Press.

McGrath, G. S., Hinz, C., and Sivapalan, M. (2007). Temporal dynamics of hydrological threshold events. *Hydrology and Earth System Sciences Discussions, 11*(2), 923–938.

McGuffie, K. (1998). Tropical cyclones and global climate change: A post-IPCC assessment. *Bulletin of American Meteorological Society, 79*(1), 19–38.

Meehl, G. A., Karl, T., Easterling, D. R., Changnon, S. A., Pielke, R. A., Changnon, D., Evans, J., Groisman, P. Y., Knutson, T. R., Kunkel, K. E., Mearns, L.O., Parmesan, C., Pulwarty, R., Root, T., Sylves, R.T., Whetton, P., and Zwiers, F. (2000a). An introduction to trends in extreme weather and climate events: Observations, socioeconomic impacts, terrestrial ecological impacts, and model projections. *Bulletin of the American Meteorological Society, 81*, 413–416.

Meehl, G. A., Washington, W. M., Collins, W. D., Arblaster, J. M., Hu, A., Buja, L.E., Warren, L. E., Strand, G., and Teng, H. (2005). How much more global warming and sea level rise? *Science, 307*, 1767–1772.

Meehl, G. A., Zwiers, F., Evans, J., Knutson, T., Mearns, L., and Whetton, P. (2000b). Trends in extreme weather and climate events: Issues related to modeling extremes in projections of future climate change. *Bulletin of the American Meteorological Society, 81*(3), 427–436.

Miller, H. I., and Conko, G. (2000). Genetically modified fear and the international regulation of biotechnology. In *Rethinking Risk and the Precautionary Principle*, edited by J. Morris, pp. 84–104. Oxford: Butterworth-Heinemann.

NOAA. (2003). Drought: A paleo perspective. National Climatic Data Center. http://www.ncdc.noaa.gov/paleo/drought/drght_history.html.

Nordhaus, W. D., and Boyer, J. (2000). *Warming the World: Economic Modeling of Global Warming*. Cambridge, MA: MIT Press.

Olesen, J. E. (2006). Climate change as a driver for European agriculture. SCAR-Foresight in the field of agricultural research in Europe, Expert paper. Danish Institute of Agricultural Sciences. SCAR Standing Committee on Agriculture Research portal.

Olesen, J. E., and Bindi, M. (2002). Consequences of climate change for European agricultural productivity, land use and policy. *European Journal of Agronomy, 16*(4), 239–262.

Oouchi, K., Yoshimura, J., Yoshimura, H., Mizuta, R., Kusunoki, S., and Noda, A. (2006). Tropical cyclone climatology in a global-warming climate as simulated in a 20 km-mesh global atmospheric model: Frequency and wind intensity analyses. *Journal of the Meteorological Society of Japan, 84*(2), 259–276.

Parmesan, C., Root, T. L., and Willig, M. R. (2000). Impacts of extreme weather and climate on terrestrial biota. *Bulletin of the American Meteorological Society, 81*(3), 443–450.

Patz, J. A., Campbell-Lendrum, D., Holloway, T., and Foley, J. A. (2005). Impact of regional climate change on human health. *Nature, 438*(17), 310–317.

Payne, J. T., Wood, A. W., Hamlet, A. F., Palmer, R. N., and Lettenmaier, D. P. (2004). Mitigating the effects of climate change on the water resources of the Columbia River basin. *Climatic Change, 62*(1), 233–256.

Peterson, M. (2007). The precautionary principle should not be used as a basis for decision-making. *EMBO Reports (European Molecular Biology Organization), 8*(4), 305–308.

Pitman, A. J., and Stouffer, R. J. (2006). Abrupt change in climate and climate models. *Hydrology and Earth System Sciences Discussions, 10*(6), 903–912.

Pounds, J. A., Bustamante, M. R., Coloma, L. A., Consuegra, J. A., Fogden, Foster, P. N., La Marca, E., Masters, K. L., Merino-Viteri, A., Puschendorf, R., Ron, S. R., Sánchez-Azofeifa, G. A., Still, C. J., and Young, B. E. (2006). Widespread amphibian extinctions from epidemic disease driven by global warming. *Nature, 439*(7073), 161–167.

Rahmstorf, S., and Ganopolski, A. (1999). Long-term global warming scenarios computed with an efficient coupled climate model. *Climate Change, 43*, 353–367.

Scheffer, M., Bascompte, J., Brock, W. A., Brovkin, V., Carpenter, S. R., Dakos, V., Held, H., Van Nes, E. H., Rietkerk, M., and Sugihara, G. (2009). Early-warning signals for critical transitions. *Nature, 461*(7260), 53–59.

Schubert, M. J., Siegfried, D., and Pegion, P. J. (2004). On the cause of the 1930s Dust Bowl. *Science, 303*(19), 1855–1859.

Science Daily. (2004, March 19). NASA explains "Dust Bowl" drought. *Science Daily*.

Sellers, W. D. (1969). A global climatic model based on the energy balance of the Earth-atmosphere system. *Journal of Applied Meteorology, 8*(3), 392–400.

Sen, A. (1982). *Poverty and Famines: An Essay and Entitlement and Deprivation.* Oxford: Clarendon.

Sohngen, B., and Mendelsohn, R. (1998). Valuing the impact of large-scale ecological change in a market: The effect of climate change on U.S. timber. *The American Economic Review, 88*(4), 686–710.

Stern, N. (2006). *Stern Review on the Economics of Climate Change.* United Kingdom Treasury.

Stirling, A. (2007). Risk, precaution and science: Towards a more constructive policy debate. *EMBO Reports (European Molecular Biology Organization), 8*(4), 309–315.

Stommel, H. (1961). Thermohaline convection with two stable regimes of flow. *Tellus, 13*(2), 224–230.

Stott, P. A., Stone, D. A., and Allen, M. R. (2004). Human contribution to the European heatwave of 2003. *Nature, 432*, 610–614.

Thompson, L. G., Mosley-Thompson, E., Davis, M. E., Lin, P. N., Henderson, K., and Mashiotta, T. A. (2003). Tropical glacier and ice core evidence of climate change on annual to millennial time scales. *Climatic Change, 59*(1), 137–155.

Lenton, T. M., Held, H., Kriegler, E., Hall, J. W., Lucht, W., Rahmstor, S., and Schellnhuber, H. J. (2008). Tipping elements in the Earth's climate system. *Proceedings of the National Academy of Sciences of the USA, 105*(6), 1786–1793.

Trenberth, K. E., Stepaniak, D. P., and Caron, J. M. (2000). The global monsoon as seen through the divergent atmospheric circulation. *Journal of Climate, 13*, 3969–3993.

UNEP. (2002). Africa environment outlook. Past, present and future perspectives. Nairobi, Kenya: United Nations Environment Programme.

UNFCCC. (1992). United Nations Framework Convention on Climate Change. Bonn, Germany: United Nations.

Wang, G., and Eltahir, E. A. B. (2000). Ecosystem dynamics and the Sahel drought. *Geophysical Research Letters, 27*(6), 795–798.

Webster, P. J., Holland, G. J., Curry, J. A., and Chang, H. R. 2005. Changes in tropical cyclone number, duration and intensity in a warming environment. *Science, 309*, 1844–1846.

Weiss, H., Courty, M. A., Wetterstrom, W., Guichard, F., Senior, L., Meadow, R., and Curnow, A. (1993). The genesis and collapse of third millennium north Mesopotamian civilization. *Science, 261*(5124), 995–1004.

Weitzman, M. L. (2009, February 19). Some basic economics of extreme climate change. Mimeo. World Bank, 2012. World Bank data. Iresearch.worldbank.org. http://iresearch.worldbank.org/PovcalNet/index.html

Worster, D. *Dust Bowl: The Southern Plains in the 1930s.* New York: Oxford University Press, 1979.

Zehe, E., and Sivapalan, M. (2009). Threshold behaviour in hydrological systems as (human) geo-ecosystems: Manifestations, controls, implications. *Hydrology and Earth System Sciences Discussions, 13*, 1273–1297.

Zehe, E., Elsenbeer, H., Lindenmaier, F., Schulz, K., and Bloschl, G. (2007). Patterns of predictability in hydrological threshold systems. *Water Resources Research, 43*, W07343–W07445.

Zhang, H., Berz, G., Emanuel, K., Gray, W., Landsea, C., Holland, Lighthill, J., Shieh, S. L., Webster, P., and McGuffie, K. (1998). Tropical cyclones and global climate change: A post-IPCC assessment. *Bulletin of the American Meteorological Society, 79*, 19–38.

Zickfeld, K., Knopf, B., Petoukhov, V., and Schellnhuber, H. J. (2005). Is the Indian summer monsoon stable against global change? *Geophysical Research Letters, 32*, L15707–L15707.

CHAPTER 24

CLIMATE IMPACTS ON AGRICULTURE

A Challenge to Complacency?

FRANK ACKERMAN AND ELIZABETH A. STANTON

A new paradigm is emerging in recent research on climate and agriculture. Its findings are not yet well known outside of specialized academic journals—but they deserve much wider attention. Taken seriously, this new standard constitutes a challenge to the complacency of most countries' climate policies. A warming world may experience food crises in the not-so-distant future, a threat that should inspire immediate responses.

This chapter draws on our recent book, *Climate Economics: The State of the Art* (Ackerman and Stanton, 2013) and on our other research, including a major study of climate impacts on the US Southwest (Ackerman and Stanton, 2011), to attempt a synthesis of recent findings on climate and agriculture and their implications for public policy.

24.1 Background: The Foundations of Inaction

Climate policies rely, explicitly or implicitly, on estimates of the damages that will be caused by climate change. This dependence is explicit when policy recommendations draw on the results of formal economic models. Such models typically weigh the costs of policy initiatives against the benefits. The costs of emission reduction are the incremental expenditures for renewable electricity generation, low-emission vehicles, and the like, compared to more conventional investments in the same industries. The benefits are the future climate damages that can be avoided by emission reduction.

The greater the expected damages, the more it is "worth" spending to avoid them. As explained later, many of the best-known and most widely used models are significantly out of date in their damage estimates, in agriculture among other areas.

Often, of course, policy decisions are not based on formal models or explicit economic analysis. Yet even when politicians and voters decide that climate action is simply too expensive, they may be relying on implicit estimates of damages. Declaring something to be too expensive is not solely a statement of objective fact; it is also a judgment that a proposed expenditure is not particularly urgent. Protection against threats of incalculable magnitude—such as military defense of a nation's borders, or airport screening to keep terrorists off of planes—is rarely described as "too expensive."

The conclusion that climate policy is too expensive thus implies that it is an option we can do without, rather than a response to an existential threat to our way of life. Can we muddle along without expensive climate initiatives, and go on living—and eating—in the same way as in the past? Not for long, according to some of the new research on climate and agriculture.

24.2 What We Used to Know About Agriculture

Agriculture is one of the most climate-sensitive industries, with outdoor production processes that depend on particular levels of temperature and precipitation. Although only a small part of the world economy, it has always played a large role in estimates of overall economic impacts of climate change. In monetary terms, agriculture represents less than 2% of gross domestic product (GDP) in high-income countries, and 2.9% for the world as a whole.[1] It is more important to the economies of low-income countries, amounting to almost one-fourth of GDP in the least developed countries. And its product is an absolute necessity of life, with virtually no substitutes.[2]

In the 1990s, it was common to project that the initial stages of climate change would bring net benefits to global agriculture (e.g., Mendelsohn et al., 1994). As late as 2001, the US Global Change Research Program still anticipated that US agriculture would experience yield increases due to climate change throughout this century (Reilly et al., 2001).Warmer weather was expected to bring longer growing seasons in northern areas, and plants everywhere were expected to benefit from carbon fertilization. Because plants grow by absorbing carbon dioxide (CO_2) from the air, higher CO_2 concentrations might act as a fertilizer, speeding the growth process.

Simple and dated interpretations of climate impacts on agriculture continue to shape relatively recent economic assessments of climate damages. Widely used integrated assessment models such as DICE (Dynamic Integrated model of Climate and the

Economy) and FUND (Climate Framework for Uncertainty, Negotiation and Distribution) are still calibrated to relatively old and optimistic agricultural analyses.[3] Even the more sophisticated and detailed PESETA (Projection of Economic impacts of climate change in Sectors of the European Union based on bottom-up Analysis) project, analyzing climate impacts throughout Europe, assumed linear relationships between average temperatures and crop yields.[4] It projected that temperature changes through the end of this century would cause yield declines in Mediterranean and southern Atlantic Europe, and yield increases elsewhere (Iglesias et al., 2011). For Europe as a whole, PESETA estimated little change in crop yields for average European temperature increases up to 4.1°C, with a 10% yield decline at 5.4°C, the highest temperature analyzed in the study (Ciscar et al., 2011).

Such estimates have fallen well behind the state of the art in the research literature. There are three major areas in which recent results and models suggest a more complex relationship between climate and agriculture: the revised understanding of carbon fertilization; the threshold model of temperature effects on crop yields; and the emerging analyses of climate and regional precipitation changes.

24.3 Reduced Estimates of Carbon Fertilization

The best-known of the new areas of research is the empirical evidence that carbon fertilization benefits are smaller than previously believed. Plants grow by photosynthesis, a process that absorbs carbon dioxide (CO_2) from the air and converts it into organic compounds such as sugars. If the limiting factor in this process is the amount of CO_2 available to the plant, then an increase in the atmospheric concentration of CO_2 could act as a fertilizer, providing additional nutrients and allowing faster growth.

Almost all plants use one of two styles of photosynthesis.[5] The majority of food crops and other plants are C_3 plants (so named because a crucial molecule contains three carbon atoms), in which growth is limited by the availability of CO_2, so that carbon fertilization could be beneficial to them. In contrast, C_4 plants have evolved a different photosynthetic pathway that uses atmospheric CO_2 more efficiently. C_4 plants, which include maize, sugarcane, sorghum, and millet (as well as switchgrass, a potentially important biofuel feedstock), do not benefit from increased CO_2 concentrations except in drought conditions (Leakey, 2009).

Initial experimental studies conducted in greenhouses or other enclosures found substantial carbon fertilization effects. The 2001 US National Assessment summarized the experimental evidence available at that time as implying yield gains of 30% in C_3 crops and 7% in C_4 crops from a doubling of CO_2 concentrations (Reilly et al., 2001). More recently, Free-Air CO_2 Enrichment (FACE) experiments have allowed crops to be grown in outdoor environments with a greater resemblance to the actual conditions of production. According to a widely cited summary, the effects of CO_2 on yields for major grain crops are roughly 50% lower in FACE experiments than in enclosure studies (Long et al., 2004).[6] Another literature review reaches similar conclusions, offering "important lessons from FACE," one of which is that "the [CO_2] 'fertilization' effect in FACE studies on crop plants is less than expected" (Leakey, 2009).

One summary of the results of FACE experiments reports that an increase in atmospheric CO_2 from 385 ppm (the actual level a few years ago) to 550 ppm would increase yields of the leading C_3 crops, wheat, soybeans, and rice, by 13% and would have no effect on yields of maize and sorghum, the leading C_4 grains (Ainsworth and McGrath, 2010). Cline (2007) develops a similar estimate; because C_4 crops represent about one-fourth of world agricultural output, he projects a weighted average of 9% increase in global yields from 550 ppm.

While research on carbon fertilization has advanced in recent years, there are at least three unanswered questions in this area that are important for economic analysis. First, there is little information about the effects of very high CO_2 concentrations; many studies have only examined yields up to 550 ppm, and few have gone above 700 ppm. Long-term projections of business-as-usual emissions scenarios, however, frequently reach even higher concentrations. Does CO_2 fertilization continue to raise yields indefinitely, or does it reach an upper bound?

Second, most studies to date have focused on the leading grains and cotton; other plants may have different responses to increases in CO_2. For at least one important food crop, the response is negative: Cassava (manioc), a dietary staple for 750 million people in developing countries, shows sharply reduced yields at elevated CO_2 levels, with tuber mass reduced by an order of magnitude when CO_2 concentrations rise from 360 ppm to 710 ppm (Gleadow et al., 2009; Ghini et al., 2011). This result appears to be based on the unique biochemistry of cassava, and does not directly generalize to other plants. It is, nonetheless, a cautionary tale about extrapolation from studies of a few plants to food crops as a whole.

Third, carbon fertilization may interact with other environmental influences. Fossil fuel combustion, the principal source of atmospheric CO_2, also produces tropospheric (ground-level) ozone, which reduces yields of many plants (Ainsworth and McGrath, 2010). The net effect of carbon fertilization plus increased ozone is uncertain, but it is very likely to be less than the experimental estimates for carbon fertilization alone.

24.4 Temperature Thresholds for Crop Yields

Describing climate change by the increase in average temperatures is inescapably useful, but at the same time often misleading. Increases in global average temperature of only a few degrees, comparable to normal month-to-month changes in many parts of the world, will have drastic and disruptive effects. A recent study suggests that it may be easier for people to perceive climate change as reflected in temperature extremes, such as the marked increase in the frequency of temperatures more than three standard deviations above historical summer averages (Hansen et al., 2012).

An important new wave of research shows that crops, too, are often more sensitive to temperature extremes than to averages. In many cases, yields rise gradually up to a temperature threshold, then collapse rapidly as temperatures increase above the threshold. This threshold model often fits the empirical data better than the earlier models of temperature effects on yields.

It is obvious that most crops have an optimum temperature, at which their yields per hectare are greater than at either higher or lower temperatures. A simple and widely used model of this effect assumes that yields are a quadratic function of average temperatures.[7] The quadratic model, however, imposes symmetry and gradualism on the temperature-yield relationship: yields rise smoothly on the way up to the optimum temperature, and then decline at the same smooth rate as temperatures rise beyond the optimum.

The threshold model makes two innovations: it allows different relationships between temperature and yield above and below the optimum; and it measures temperatures above the optimum in terms of the growing-season total of degree-days above a threshold, rather than average seasonal or annual temperatures.[8] Perhaps the first use of this model in recent agricultural economics was Schlenker et al. (2006), drawing on earlier agronomic literature. This approach has a solid grounding in plant biology: many crops are known to have temperature thresholds, in some cases at varying temperatures for different stages of development (Luo, 2011).

The threshold model has been widely used in the last few years. For instance, temperature effects on maize, soybean, and cotton yields in the United States are strongly asymmetric, with optimum temperatures of 29–32°C and rapid drops in yields for degree-days beyond the optimum. For maize, replacing 24 hours of the growing season at 29°C with 24 hours at 40°C would cause a 7% decline in yields (Schlenker and Roberts, 2009).

A very similar pattern was found in a study of temperature effects on maize yields in Africa, with a threshold of 30°C (Lobell et al., 2011). Under ordinary conditions, the effects on yields of temperatures above the threshold were similar to those found in the United States; under drought conditions, yields declined even faster with temperature increases. Limited data on wheat in northern India also suggest that temperature increases above 34°C are more harmful than similar increases at lower levels (Lobell et al., 2012).

A study of five leading food crops in sub-Saharan Africa found strong relationships of yields to temperatures (Schlenker and Lobell, 2010). By mid-century, under the A1B climate scenario, yields are projected to drop by 17–22% for maize, sorghum, millet, and groundnuts (peanuts) and by 8% for cassava. These estimates exclude carbon fertilization, but maize, sorghum, and millet are C_4 crops, while cassava has a negative response to increased CO_2, as noted above. Negative impacts are expected for a number of crops in developing countries by 2030. Among the crops most vulnerable to temperature increases are millet, groundnut, and rapeseed in South Asia; sorghum in the Sahel; and maize in Southern Africa (Lobell et al., 2008).

Other crops exhibit different, but related, patterns of temperature dependence. Some perennials require a certain amount of "chill time," or annual hours below a low temperature threshold such as 7°C. In a study of the projected loss of winter chilling conditions in California, Germany, and Oman, fruit and nut trees showed large decreases in yield due to climate change (Luedeling et al. 2011). In this case, as with high-temperature yield losses, the relevant temperature variable is measured in terms of threshold effects, not year-round or even seasonal averages. Small changes in averages can imply large changes in the hours above or below thresholds, and hence large agricultural impacts.

Studies of temperatures and yields based on recent experience, including those described here, are limited in their ability to project the extent of adaptation to changing temperatures. Such adaptation has been important in the past: as North American wheat production expanded into colder, drier regions, farmers adapted by selecting different cultivars that could thrive in the new conditions; most of the adaptation occurred before 1930 (Olmstead and Rhode, 2010). On the other hand, regions of the United States that are well above the optimum temperatures for maize, soybeans, and other major crops have grown these crops for many years, without any evidence of a large-scale shift to more heat-resistant crops or cultivars; temperature-yield relationships are quite similar in northern and southern states (Schlenker and Roberts, 2009). Thus adaptation is an important possibility, but far from automatic.

24.5 Climate Change, Water, and Agriculture

A third area of research on climate and agriculture has reached less definite global conclusions, but it will be of increasing local importance. As the world warms, precipitation patterns will change, with some areas becoming wetter, but some leading agricultural areas becoming drier. These patterns are difficult to forecast; climate model predictions are more uncertain for precipitation than for temperature, and "downscaling" global models to yield regional projections is only beginning to be feasible. Yet recent droughts in many parts of the world underscore the crucial role of changes in rainfall. Even if total annual precipitation is unchanged, agriculture may be harmed by changes in the seasonality or intensity of rainfall.

Overall, warming is increasing the atmosphere's capacity to hold water, resulting in increases in extreme precipitation events (Min et al., 2011). Both observational data and modeling projections show that with climate change, wet regions will generally (but not universally) become wetter, and dry regions will become drier (John et al. 2009; Sanderson et al., 2011). Perceptible changes in annual precipitation are likely to appear in many areas within this century. While different climate models disagree about some parts of the world, there is general agreement that boreal (far-northern) areas will become wetter, and the Mediterranean will become drier (Mahlstein et al., 2012).

With 2°C of warming, dry-season precipitation is expected to decrease by 20% in northern Africa, southern Europe, and western Australia, and by 10% in the southwestern United States and Mexico, eastern South America, and northern Africa by 2100 (Giorgi and Bi, 2009).[9] In the Sahel area of Africa, the timing of critical rains will shift, shortening the growing season (Biasutti and Sobel, 2009), and more extensive periods of drought may result as temperatures rise (Lu, 2009).[10] In the Haihe River basin of northern China, projections call for less total rainfall but more extreme weather events (Chu et al., 2009). Indian monsoon rainfall has already become less frequent but more intense, part of a pattern of climate change that is reducing wet-season rice yields (Auffhammer et al., 2011).

The relationship of crop yields to precipitation is markedly different in irrigated areas than in rain-fed farming; it has even been suggested that mistakes in analysis of irrigation may have accounted for some of the optimism about climate and agriculture in the 1990s literature (Schlenker et al., 2005). In California, by far the leading agricultural state in the United States, the availability of water for irrigation is crucial to yields; variations in temperature and precipitation are much less important, as long as access to irrigation can be assumed (Schlenker et al., 2007). Yet there is a growing scarcity of water and competition over available supplies in the state, leading some researchers to project a drop in irrigated acreage and a shift toward higher-value, less water-intensive crops (Howitt et al., 2009). An analysis of potential water scarcity due to climate change in California estimates that there will be substantial costs in dry years, in the form of both higher water prices and supply shortfalls, to California's Central Valley agriculture (Hanemann et al., 2006).

In our study of climate change and water in the southwestern United States, we found that climate change is worsening the already unsustainable pattern of water use in agriculture (Ackerman and Stanton, 2011).[11] Nearly four-fifths of the region's water is used for agriculture, often to grow surprisingly water-intensive, low-value crops; a tangled system of legal restrictions and entitlements prevents operation of a market in water. If there were a market for water in the Southwest, municipal water systems and power plants would easily outbid many agricultural users. Yet one-fifth of US agricultural output comes from this region, virtually all of it dependent on irrigation.

More than half of the water used in the region is drawn from the Colorado River and from groundwater, neither of which can meet projected demand. The Colorado River is infamously oversubscribed, and is the subject of frequent, contentious negotiations over the allocation of its water. Climate change is projected to cause a decrease in precipitation, runoff, and streamflow in the Colorado River basin, leading to frequent water shortages and decreases in energy production (Christensen and Lettenmaier, 2007).[12]

Groundwater supplies are difficult to measure, and there are two very different estimates of California's groundwater reserves. Even assuming the higher estimate, the state's current patterns of water use are unsustainable, leading to massive shortfalls of groundwater within a few decades.

In California, projections of changes in annual precipitation are not consistent across climate models. Even if annual precipitation remains constant, however, climate change can worsen the state's water crisis in at least two ways. On the demand side, higher temperatures increase the need for water for irrigation, and for municipal and other uses. On the supply side, rising temperatures mean that winter snows will be replaced by rain, or will melt earlier in the year—which can have the effect of reducing the available quantity of water.

The mountain regions of the western United States are experiencing reduced snowpack, warmer winters, and stream flows coming earlier in the calendar year. Since the mid-1980s, these trends have been outside the past range of natural variation, but consistent with the expected effects of anthropogenic (human-caused) climate change (Barnett et al., 2008). In the past, snowmelt gradually released the previous winter's precipitation, with significant flows in the summer when demand is highest. The climate-related shift means that water arrives, in large volume, earlier in the year than it is needed—and the peak runoff may overflow existing reservoir capacity, leading some of it to flow directly to the ocean without opportunity for human use (Barnett et al., 2005).

We developed a model of the interactions of climate, water, and agriculture in California and in the five-state region, assuming constant annual precipitation but modeling temperature-driven increases in demand as well as changes in seasonal streamflows (Stanton and Fitzgerald, 2011). We found that climate change makes a bad situation much worse, intensifying the expected gap between water supply and demand. Under one estimate of the cost of supplying water, we found that climate change is transforming the region's $4 trillion water deficit over the next century into a $5 trillion shortfall (Ackerman and Stanton, 2011). If we had also modeled a decline in annual precipitation, of course, the problem would have been even worse.

To those unfamiliar with the southwestern United States, this may sound like an excursion into hydrology and water management rather than an analysis of agriculture. No one who lives there could miss the connection: most of the region's water is used for agriculture; virtually all of the region's agriculture is completely dependent on a reliable flow of water for irrigation. As climate change presses down on western water, it will start to squeeze a crucial sector of the US food supply. This is a far cry from the optimism of earlier decades about what climate change will mean for agriculture.

24.6 Conclusion

The extraordinary proliferation of recent research on climate change has moved far beyond an earlier complacency about agricultural impacts. With better empirical studies, estimates of carbon fertilization benefits have shrunk for C_3 crops (most of the world's food) in general—as well as being roughly zero for maize and other C_4 crops, and negative for cassava. With a better explanatory framework, focused on temperature extremes rather than averages, judgments about temperature impacts on crop yields have become more ominous. With more detailed local research, the regionally specific interactions of climate, water, and agriculture are beginning to be understood, often implying additional grounds for concern.

It should not be surprising that even a little climate change is bad for agriculture. The standard models and intuition of economic theory emphasize options for substitution in production—less steel can be used in making cars, if it is replaced by aluminum or plastic—but agriculture is fundamentally different. It involves natural processes that frequently require fixed proportions of nutrients, temperatures, precipitation, and other conditions. Ecosystems do not make bargains with their suppliers, and do not generally switch to making the same plants out of different inputs.

Around the world, agriculture has been optimized to the local climate through decades of trial and error. The conditions needed to allow crops to flourish include not only their preferred ranges of average temperature and precipitation, but also more fine-grained details of timing and extreme values. This is true for temperatures, as shown by the existence of thresholds and the sensitivity of yields to brief periods of extreme temperatures beyond the thresholds. It is also true for precipitation, as shown by the harm to Indian rice yields from less frequent but more intense monsoon rains, or by the sensitivity of California agriculture to the delicate timing of snowmelt.

Global warming is now causing an unprecedented pace of change in the climate conditions that affect agriculture—much faster than crops can evolve on their own, and probably too fast for the traditional processes of trial-and-error adaptation by farmers. At the same time, the world's population will likely continue to grow through mid-century or later, increasing the demand for food just as climate change begins to depress yields. To adapt to the inescapable early states of climate change, it is essential to apply the rapidly developing resources of plant genetics and biotechnology to the creation of new heat-resistant, and perhaps drought-resistant, crops and cultivars.

Adaptation to climate change is necessary but not sufficient. If warming continues unabated, it will, in a matter of decades, reach levels at which adaptation is no longer possible. Any long-run solution must involve rapid reduction of emissions, to limit the future extent of climate change. The arguments against active climate policies, based on formal or informal economic reasoning, have been propped up by a dated and inaccurate picture of climate impacts on agriculture, which lives on in the background of recent models and studies. Updating that picture, recognizing and accepting the implications of new research on climate threats to agriculture, is part of the process of creating climate policies that rest soundly on the latest scientific research.

Acknowledgments

This article was written while we were at the Stockholm Environment Institute-US Center, and was funded by a grant from the Stockholm Environment Institute. A different version of this article appears in our recent book, *Climate and Global Equity* (Anthem Press, 2014).

Notes

1. World Bank data on agricultural value added as a share of GDP in 2008, http://data.worldbank.org.
2. In economic terms, the fact that food is a necessity means that it has a very low price elasticity of demand, implying that it has a very large consumer surplus. If contributions to well-being are measured by consumer surplus rather than shares of GDP, as economic theory suggests, then agriculture looms much larger in importance.
3. For the damage estimates used in DICE, including a projection of virtually no net global losses in agriculture from the first few degrees of warming, see Nordhaus and Boyer (2000); this earlier analysis is still a principal source for damages estimates in newer versions of DICE (Nordhaus, 2007, 2008). On the dated and problematical treatment of agricultural impacts in FUND, see Ackerman and Munitz (2012).
4. Using historical data from 1961–1990, PESETA modeled yields at nine locations, as linear functions of annual and monthly average temperatures (as well as precipitation). In three locations, there was a negative coefficient on a summer month's temperature as well as positive coefficients on springtime and/or annual average temperatures—perhaps a rough approximation of the threshold model discussed later in this chapter (Iglesias et al., 2011).
5. A third photosynthetic pathway exists in some plants subject to extreme water stress, such as cacti and succulents; it is not important in agriculture.
6. This article has been criticized by Tubiello et al. (2007); the original authors respond in Ainsworth et al. (2008).
7. That is, the equation for yields has both temperature (with a positive coefficient) and temperature squared (with a negative coefficient) on the right-hand side.
8. Degree-days are the product of the number of days and the number of degrees above a threshold. Relative to a 32°C threshold, one day at 35°C and three days at 33°C would each represent three degree-days.
9. End-of-century (2081–2100) precipitation under A1B relative to 1981–2000.
10. Lu (2009) notes that there is significant uncertainty regarding future Sahel drying, because it is influenced by (1) sea surface temperature changes over all the world's oceans;

and (2) the radiative effects of greenhouse gas forcing on increased land warming, which can lead to monsoon-like conditions.

11. We studied a five-state region: California, Nevada, Utah, Arizona, and New Mexico. California accounts for most of the population, agriculture, and water use of the region.
12. The Colorado River basin includes most of the four inland states in our study region, but only a small part of California. Nonetheless, California is legally entitled to, and uses, a significant quantity of Colorado River water. Other rivers are also important to water supply in California, but much less so in the inland states.

References

Ackerman, F., and Munitz, C. (2012). Climate damages in the FUND model: A disaggregated analysis. *Ecological Economics, 77*, 219–224.

Ackerman, F., and Stanton, E. A. (2011). *The Last Drop: Climate Change and the Southwest Water Crisis.* Somerville, MA: Stockholm Environment Institute-U.S. Center. http://frankackerman.com/publications/climatechange/Last_Drop_Water_Crisis.pdf.

Ackerman, F., and Stanton, E. A. (2013). *Climate Economics: The State of the Art.* London: Routledge.

Ainsworth, E. A., and McGrath, J. M. (2010). Direct effects of rising atmospheric carbon dioxide and ozone on crop yields. *Climate Change and Food Security. Advances in Global Change Research, 37*(Part II), 109–130.

Ainsworth, E. A., Leakey, A. D. B., Ort, D. R., and Long, S. P. (2008). FACE-ing the facts: Inconsistencies and interdependence among field, chamber and modeling studies of elevated CO2 impacts on crop yield and food supply. *New Phytologist, 179*(1), 5–9.

Auffhammer, M., Ramanathan, V., and Vincent, J. R. (2011). Climate change, the monsoon, and rice yield in India. *Climatic Change, 111*(2), 411–424.

Barnett, T. P., Adam, J. C., and Lettenmaier, D. P. (2005). Potential impacts of a warming climate on water availability in snow-dominated regions. *Nature, 438*, 303–309.

Barnett, T. P., Pierce, D. W., Hidalgo, H. G., Barnett, T. P., Pierce, D. W., Hidalgo, H. G., Bonfils, C., Santer, B. D., Das, T., Bala, G., Wood, A. W., Nozawa, T., Mirin, A. A., Cayan, D. R., and Dettinger, M. D. (2008). Human-induced changes in the hydrology of the western United States. *Science, 319*(5866), 1080–1083.

Biasutti, M., and Sobel, A. H. (2009). Delayed Sahel rainfall and global seasonal cycle in a warmer climate. *Geophysical Research Letters, 36*(23). DOI:10.1029/2009GL041303.

Christensen, N. S., and Lettenmaier, D. P. (2007). A multimodel ensemble approach to assessment of climate change impacts on the hydrology and water resources of the Colorado River Basin. *Hydrology and Earth System Sciences Discussions, 11*(4), 1417–1434.

Chu, J. T., Xia, J., Xu, C.-Y., and Singh, V. P. (2009). Statistical downscaling of daily mean temperature, pan evaporation and precipitation for climate change scenarios in Haihe River, China. *Theoretical and Applied Climatology, 99*(1–2), 149–161.

Ciscar, J.-C., Iglesias, A., Feyen, L., Ciscar, J.-C., Iglesias, A., Feyen, L., Szabó, L., Van Regemorter, D., Amelung, B., Nicholls, R., Watkiss, P., Christensen, O. B., Dankers, R., Garrote, L., Goodess, C. M., Hunt, A., Moreno, A., Richards, J., and Soria, A. (2011). Physical and economic consequences of climate change in Europe. *Proceedings of the National Academy of Sciences of the USA, 108*(7), 2678–2683.

Cline, W. R. (2007). *Global Warming and Agriculture: Impact Estimates by Country*. Washington, DC: Center for Global Development & Peterson Institute for International Economics. http://www.cgdev.org/content/publications/detail/14090.

Ghini, R., Bettiol, W., and Hamada, E. (2011). Diseases in tropical and plantation crops as affected by climate changes: Current knowledge and perspectives. *Plant Pathology, 60*(1), 122–132.

Giorgi, F., and Bi, X. (2009). Time of emergence (TOE) of GHG-forced precipitation change hot-spots. *Geophysical Research Letters, 36*(6). DOI:10.1029/2009GL037593.

Gleadow, R. M., Evans, J. R., McCaffery, S., and Cavagnaro, T. R. (2009). Growth and nutritive value of cassava (Manihot esculenta Cranz.) are reduced when grown in elevated CO_2. *Plant Biology, 11*, 76–82.

Hanemann, M., Dale, L., Vicuña, S., Bickett, D., and Dyckman, C. (2006). *The Economic Cost of Climate Change Impact on California Water: A Scenario Analysis*. CEC-500-2006-003. Prepared for the California Energy Commission, Public Interest Energy Research Program. http://www.energy.ca.gov/2006publications/CEC-500-2006-003/CEC-500-2006-003.PDF.

Hansen, J., Sato, M., and Ruedy, R. (2012). Perception of climate change. *Proceedings of the National Academy of Sciences of the USA*. DOI:10.1073/pnas.1205276109.

Howitt, R., Medellín-Azuara, J., and MacEwan, D. (2009). *Estimating the Economic Impacts of Agricultural Yield Related Changes for California*. CEC-500-2009-042-F. California Climate Change Center. http://www.energy.ca.gov/2009publications/CEC-500-2009-042/CEC-500-2009-042-F.PDF.

Iglesias, A., Garrote, L., Quiroga, S., and Moneo, M. (2011). A regional comparison of the effects of climate change on agricultural crops in Europe. *Climatic Change, 112*(1), 29–46.

John, V. O., Allan, R. P., and Soden, B. J. (2009). How robust are observed and simulated precipitation responses to tropical ocean warming? *Geophysical Research Letters, 36*(14). DOI:10.1029/2009GL038276.

Leakey, A. D. B. (2009). Rising atmospheric carbon dioxide concentration and the future of C4 crops for food and fuel. *Proceedings of the Royal Society B: Biological Sciences, 276*(1666), 2333–2343.

Lobell, D. B., Bänziger, M., Magorokosho, C., and Vivek, B. (2011). Nonlinear heat effects on African maize as evidenced by historical yield trials. *Nature Climate Change, 1*(1), 42–45.

Lobell, D. B., Burke, M. B., Tebaldi, C., Mastrandrea, M. D., Falcon, W. P., and Naylor, R. L. (2008). Prioritizing climate change adaptation needs for food security in 2030. *Science, 319*(5863), 607–610.

Lobell, D. B., Sibley, A. and Ivan Ortiz-Monasterio, J. (2012). Extreme heat effects on wheat senescence in India. *Nature Climate Change, 2*(3), 186–189.

Long, S. P., Ainsworth, E. A., Rogers, A., and Ort, D. R. (2004). Rising atmospheric carbon dioxide: Plants FACE the future. *Annual Review of Plant Biology, 55*, 591–628.

Lu, J. (2009). The dynamics of the Indian Ocean sea surface temperature forcing of Sahel drought. *Climate Dynamics, 33*(4), 445–460.

Luedeling, E., Girvetz, E. H., Semenov, M. A., and Brown, P. H. (2011). Climate change affects winter chill for temperate fruit and nut trees. *PLoS ONE, 6*(5), e20155.

Luo, Q. (2011). Temperature thresholds and crop production: a review. *Climatic Change, 109*(3–4), 583–598.

Mahlstein, I., Portmann, R. W., Daniel, J. S., Solomon, S., and Knutti, R. (2012). Perceptible changes in regional precipitation in a future climate. *Geophysical Research Letters, 39*(5). DOI:10.1029/2011GL050738.

Mendelsohn, R., Nordhaus, W. D., and Shaw, D. (1994). The impact of global warming on agriculture: A Ricardian analysis. *The American Economic Review, 84*(4), 753–771.

Min, S.-K., Zhang, X., Zwiers, F. W., and Hegerl, G. C. (2011). Human contribution to more-intense precipitation extremes. *Nature, 470*(7334), 378–381.

Nordhaus, W. D. (2007). *Accompanying Notes and Documentation on Development of DICE-2007 Model: Notes on DICE-2007.v8 of September 21, 2007.* New Haven, CT: Yale University. http://nordhaus.econ.yale.edu/Accom_Notes_100507.pdf.

Nordhaus, W. D. (2008). *A Question of Balance: Economic Modeling of Global Warming.* New Haven, CT: Yale University Press.

Nordhaus, W. D., and Boyer, J. (2000). *Warming the World: Economic Models of Global Warming.* Cambridge, MA: MIT Press.

Olmstead, A. L., and Rhode, P. W. (2010). Adapting North American wheat production to climatic challenges, 1839-2009. *Proceedings of the National Academy of Sciences of the USA, 108*(2), 480–485.

Reilly, J. M., Graham, J., and Hrubovcak, J. (2001). *Agriculture: The Potential Consequences of Climate Variability and Change for the United States.* U.S. National Assessment of the Potential Consequences of Climate Variability and Change, U.S. Global Change Research Program. New York: Cambridge University Press.

Sanderson, M. G., Hemming, D. L., and Betts, R. A. (2011). Regional temperature and precipitation changes under high-end ($\geq$4°C) global warming. *Philosophical Transactions of the Royal Society A: Mathematical, Physical and Engineering Sciences, 369*(1934), 85–98.

Schlenker, W., and Lobell, D. B. (2010). Robust negative impacts of climate change on African agriculture. *Environmental Research Letters, 5*(1), 014010.

Schlenker, W., and Roberts, M. J. (2009). Nonlinear temperature effects indicate severe damages to U.S. crop yields under climate change. *Proceedings of the National Academy of Sciences of the USA, 106*(37), 15594–15598.

Schlenker, W., Hanemann, W. M., and Fisher, A. C. (2005). Will U.S. agriculture really benefit from global warming? Accounting for irrigation in the hedonic approach. *The American Economic Review, 88*(1), 113–125.

Schlenker, W., Hanemann, W. M., and Fisher, A. C. (2006). The impact of global warming on U.S. agriculture: An econometric analysis of optimal growing conditions. *The Review of Economics and Statistics, 88*(1), 113–125.

Schlenker, W., Hanemann, W. M., and Fisher, A. C. (2007). Water availability, degree days, and the potential impact of climate change on irrigated agriculture in California. *Climatic Change, 81*(1), 19–38.

Stanton, E. A., and Fitzgerald, E. (2011). *California Water Supply and Demand: Technical Report.* Somerville, MA: Stockholm Environment Institute-U.S. Center. http://sei-us.org/publications/id/369.

Tubiello, F. N., Amthor, J. S., Boote, K. J., Tubiello, F. N., Amthor, J. S., Boote, K. J., Donatelli, M., Easterling, W., Fischer, G., Gifford, R. M., Howden, M., Reilly, J., and Rosenzwei, C. (2007). Crop response to elevated CO_2 and world food supply: A comment on 'Food for Thought . . . ' by Long et al., *Science, 312*, 1918–1921, 2006. *European Journal of Agronomy, 26*(3), 215–223.

PART VI

DIRECTIONS IN MITIGATION POLICY DESIGN

CHAPTER 25

THE LEGAL FRAMEWORK OF GLOBAL ENVIRONMENT GOVERNANCE ON CLIMATE CHANGE

A Critical Survey

RAPHAËLE CHAPPE

25.1 Introduction

The Stockholm Conference in 1972 marks the emergence of the awareness of the need for international global cooperation on environmental matters. The decades that followed led to significant achievements, with the creation of environmental treaties addressing the issue of climate change, the challenge being fundamentally one of effective global environmental governance. In a 1995 report, the Commission on Global Governance defined global governance as "the sum of the many ways individuals and institutions, public and private, manage their common affairs" (Commission on Global Governance, 1995, pp. 2–3). This includes formal institutions, legal regimes, informal arrangements, intergovernmental relationships, nongovernmental organizations (NGOs), global capital markets, and multinational corporations. Focusing on the legal framework for international environmental governance, this chapter reviews the different sources of international law on global warming and provides an overview of global environmental governance as developed through a series of major global conferences and treaties. The chapter also assesses how to measure the accomplishments and effectiveness of international environmental law, as well as enforcement and compliance issues.

Governments can adopt unilateral measures to attempt to resolve global environmental problems, or coordinate with other governments through bilateral or multilateral actions taken in concert with other nations that have a stake in the outcome. There are clear limitations of unilateral measures (one major issue being that countries rarely take actions that may place them at an economic competitive disadvantage), while multilateral actions raise issues of equity and negotiation. Unilateral, bilateral, and multilateral actions have led to the development of international environmental law, which consists primarily of "hard law," such as treaties (or agreements, protocols, covenants, conventions), and "soft law" (such as nonbinding policy declarations). This framework is useful in thinking about the various sources and enforceability of international environmental law.

A treaty is a legally binding agreement between participating nations that creates legal obligations for the signatory states. Treaties can be bilateral (between two states only) or multilateral (with many parties). Ratification is the process whereby a country's legislature approves a treaty (in the United States, for instance, a two-thirds majority vote in the Senate is required). Though ratification is purely voluntary (each nation-state is independent and sovereign), and nations can leave treaties at any time, treaty commitments are legally binding on parties while a treaty is in effect (a nation that fails to live up to its obligations under the treaty can be held liable under international law).

Once ratified by governments, some treaties are self-executing, meaning that ratification immediately creates domestically enforceable rules (self-executing treaties are automatically part of domestic law), while others are non-self-executing and need to be implemented domestically with legislation that provides for their enforcement (and therefore do not create any domestically enforceable obligations until such implementing legislation has been adopted). In the United States, courts typically determine whether a treaty is self-executing or not depending on the intent of contracting nations and the language of the treaty itself.[1] With multilateral treaties, typically a minimum number of ratifying states are required for the treaty to enter into force.

In the United States treaties are considered part of the "supreme law of the land" under the Constitution (Article VI), which means that they take precedence over conflicting state laws. Further, the Supreme Court has applied two important principles: first, that treaties are legally equivalent to federal law (in the event of a conflict, the most recent will prevail), and second, that if there is ambiguity federal statutes are to be interpreted so as to conform to existing treaty obligations.[2] If there is a breach of a treaty obligation, there is an immediate obligation to cease the breach and conform conduct to the treaty (see *LaGrand* Case[3]).

Soft law, on the other hand, consists of commitments or declarations entered into to reflect the will of the international community, or specific international organizations that do not have the capacity to enter into binding decisions on the part of their member states. Though there is often desire to bring "soft law" into the lawmaking process, these commitments are not legally binding. In some circumstances, nonbinding instruments are more appropriate than formal treaties to the extent that they allow for the formulation of general policy goals and guidelines in situations where crafting detailed rules (as would be required for legally binding obligations susceptible of being implemented) is premature or difficult. The guiding principles in Agenda 21 adopted in 1992 at the Earth Summit are a good example of such situation. The advantage of "soft law" is that nonbinding texts do not require formal national ratification and as such are typically much easier to adopt than treaties, which allows pressing matters to be brought quickly to public awareness. Further, soft law allows for the participation of a wider range of actors and organizations (international institutions, nongovernmental actors), while treaties typically need to be negotiated by state delegates only.

The rest of the chapter is organized as follows. Section 25.2 describes the major conferences relevant to climate change, and the "soft law" instruments they produced (non-legally binding declaration and principles). Section 25.3 reviews the major treaties regarding climate change: the Vienna Convention on the Protection of the Ozone Layer, the UN Framework Convention on Climate Change (the "Framework Convention"), and the Kyoto Protocol. Note that we have limited ourselves to the specific issue of global warming and climate change, and have not reviewed all existing treaties on environmental matters (for a list of such treaties, see Annex I).[4] Section 25.4 examines whether the existing treaty framework and other soft-law agreements have successfully addressed climate change issues. This discussion includes issues of treaty compliance, efficacy of established regime rules, and what climate change policies may be needed to successfully address climate change and produce results.

25.2 Global Environmental Governance—The Major Global Conferences

25.2.1 The Stockholm Conference on the Human Environment in 1972

The General Assembly of the United Nations convened the World Conference on the Human Environment in Stockholm in June 5–16, 1972 shortly after the 1967 "black tide" disaster of the Torrey Canyon incident along the coasts of France, England, and Belgium. The conference brought together delegations from 113 states, as well as 400 nongovernmental organizations. It led to the first comprehensive statements and principles on environmental protection by adopting a set of Principles of lasting importance, the Stockholm Declaration on the Human Environment, as well as an Action Plan with 109 recommendations. Principles 2 to 7 contain "the ecological heart"[5] of the Declaration: the acknowledgment that the protection of the environment is a major issue and that growing evidence of man-made harm exists in many regions of the earth, and the identification of natural resources (water, air, earth, wildlife, living beings, and the biosphere) as worthy of being protected and rationally managed.

Of particular interest to the development of international environmental law are the set of last principles. Principle 21 (later to be reformulated in the Rio Declaration, Principle 2) acknowledges the sovereign right of nations to exploit their own natural resources subject to state responsibility for transboundary environmental harm, that is, the responsibility to ensure that activities under their jurisdiction do not cause environmental damage to other states:

> States have, in accordance with the Charter of the United Nations and the principles of international law, the sovereign right to exploit their own resources pursuant to their own environmental policies, and the responsibility to ensure that activities within their jurisdiction or control do not cause damage to the environment of other States or of areas beyond the limits of national jurisdiction. (Principle 21)

This would seem to impose automatic state responsibility for any transfrontier damage to the environment (strict liability). Yet this has never been invoked for unintentional accidents. The case in point is the Chernobyl nuclear accident in 1986 that released radioactive material into the air throughout Europe—the affected states never filed claims of any sorts.

Principle 22 refers to the needed cooperation between states to develop international law ensuring responsibility for transfrontier pollution (liability and compensation). Principle 24 clearly articulates the need for international cooperation on environmental matters, through multilateral or bilateral arrangements. The role to be played by international organizations is specifically acknowledged in Principle 25. Finally, Principle 26 contemplates the elimination of nuclear weapons.

The Stockholm Conference played a significant role in raising awareness of environmental issues, and advocating for a global perspective and international cooperation on these matters. This said, the basic principles outlined in the Declarations are very general in nature and did not specifically aim to regulate the specific sources of environmental deterioration. New problems emerged in the 1980s, such as the depletion of the ozone layer, the Chernobyl nuclear accident, and the dumping of toxic waste in developing countries. The response in international law shifted to the specific regulation of industrial processes leading to environmental degradation during their entire lifetime, and waste disposal. For example, the Convention for the Protection of the Ozone Layer led to an effective system reducing ozone-depleting substances (further discussion in Section 25.3).

In addition, the Stockholm Conference led to the creation of the United Nations Environment Programme (UNEP), an international organization in charge of coordinating the environmental work of the United Nations. Some of its key tasks included developing environmental information and assessment programs, promoting environmental science, preparing reports on environmental matters, bringing environmental concerns to the forefront of global thinking, and furthering international cooperation and government action. The UNEP, together with the World Meteorological Organization, would later establish the Intergovernmental Panel on Climate Change (IPCC) in 1988.

25.2.2 The UN Conference on Environment and Development in Rio de Janeiro (the "Earth Summit") in 1992

Attended by 178 nations, the United Nations Conference on Environment and Development (UNCED) was held in Rio de Janeiro June 5 to June 18, 1992. The Earth Summit dealt extensively with many global environmental concerns, with a strong focus on the relations between industrialized and developing nations regarding environmental matters. Two texts were produced: the Declaration on Environment and Development (also known as the Rio Declaration), which elaborated 27 guiding principles, and an action program known as Agenda 21, a detailed blueprint for implementing sustainable development in everyday life. Though both the Rio Declaration and Agenda 21 are soft law with no legally binding power on nations, conceptually they can be thought of as an emerging body of international environmental law, and are reviewed in the text that follows.

In addition to the Rio Declaration and Agenda 21, an important treaty was signed at the Earth Summit, the UN Framework Convention on Climate Change (UNFCCC). The Framework Convention was the result of new political awareness of anthropogenic interference with the climate system following the IPCC First Assessment Report in 1990. There was, for the first time, the realization that the increase in the planet's temperature was due to the accumulation of greenhouse gases (GHGs) attributable to human activity (mainly the combustion of fossil fuels and deforestation). The objective of the Framework Convention was to stabilize GHG concentrations in the atmosphere. The parties to the Framework Convention have been meeting annually in Conferences of the Parties (COP) to negotiate further legally binding amendments to the Framework Convention (including the Kyoto Protocol), and assess climate change issues. See Section 25.3 for a further discussion of the Framework Convention and the Kyoto Protocol. The meetings continue to date, and are numbered accordingly (e.g., negotiations in Copenhagen are the 15th session of the parties, COP 15). Note that starting in 2005, these Conferences have met in conjunction with Meetings of Parties of the Kyoto Protocol (MOP). See later for a discussion of Copenhagen (COP 15/MOP 5), Cancún (COP 16/MOP 6), and Durban (COP 17/MOP 7).

25.2.2.1 The Rio Declaration

The Rio Declaration reaffirmed the Stockholm Declaration, but with a philosophy focused on sustainable development. We review here some of the Principles of the Rio Declaration.

Principle 2 acknowledged the sovereign right of states to exploit resources, but also identified the states' responsibility to not pollute or damage areas beyond their national jurisdiction.

> States have . . . the sovereign right to exploit their own resources pursuant to their own environmental and developmental policies, and the responsibility to ensure that activities within their jurisdiction or control do not cause damage to the environment of other States or of areas beyond the limits of national jurisdiction. (Principle 2)

Note that Principle 2 asserts state sovereignty to exploit resources pursuant to both environmental and developmental policies, while the Stockholm Declaration made reference to environmental policies only (Principle 21 of the Stockholm Declaration).

Principle 7 introduced the concept of a "global partnership" among nations to protect the environment and the Earth's ecosystem, resulting in a shared responsibility, while acknowledging the special responsibility of developed countries due to the strain that the industrialization process has placed on the environment.

> States shall cooperate in a spirit of global partnership to conserve, protect and restore the health and integrity of the Earth's ecosystem. In view of the different contributions to global environmental degradation, States have common but differentiated responsibilities. The developed countries acknowledge the responsibility that they bear in the international pursuit of sustainable development in view of the pressures their societies place on the global environment and of the technologies and financial resources they command. (Principle 7)

In the developing world, one fundamental question is whether the growth will be consistent with the principles of sustainable development, and whether developing countries will cooperate to achieve the sustainable development goals of the major treaties. A related issue is that of the fairness of the cost-sharing between developing and industrialized nations. Many developing countries need assistance to improve their policymaking capabilities, technical skills, transparency, and NGO involvement so as to improve domestic enforcement. Principle 5 of the Rio Declaration calls for cooperation to eradicate poverty, while Principle 27 further clarifies that cooperation is to be conducted in good faith and focused on sustainable development. Finally, Principle 22 provides that the full participation of women and indigenous people will be essential to achieve sustainable development.

Another key concept in the Rio Declaration is the precautionary principle. States are to apply the precautionary approach according to their capabilities. The precautionary approach is defined as "where there are threats of serious or irreversible damage, lack of full scientific certainty shall not be used as a reason for postponing cost-effective measures to prevent environmental degradation" (Principle 15).

25.2.2.2 Agenda 21

Agenda 21 contained 40 chapters covering four broad areas: social and economic development, conservation and management of resources, strengthening the role of actors other than governments, and the organization of international and national support. The UN General Assembly created the Commission on Sustainable Development to monitor the implementation of Agenda 21. This Commission meets annually in New York at the UN headquarters. The approach was highly dependent on strong country leadership to meet the goals.

> Although *Agenda 21* was impressive, its scope and comprehensiveness resulted in a very ambitious agenda for governments that made the whole enterprise heavily dependent on strong leadership from major countries, adequate financing, and effective institutional arrangements for follow-up. Unfortunately, as we shall see, none of these materialized in the years after Rio. (Speth and Haas, 2006, p. 72)

Martin Khor, director of the Third World Network, assesses that Agenda 21 and other agreements reached at the Rio Earth Summit have largely failed due to lack of implementation:

> The reason for failure is not to be found in the sustainable development paradigm [forged in Rio]; rather, the paradigm was not given the chance to be implemented. Instead, intense competition came from a rival—the countervailing paradigm of globalization, driven by the industrialized North and its corporations, that has swept the world in recent years. This is perhaps the most basic factor causing the failure to realize the [Rio] objectives. (Khor, 2001)

The Earth Summit defined in general terms what needs to be done to meet global environmental challenges and resulted in an increased awareness of such challenges. Many conventions and treaties focusing on environmental protection were signed after the Earth Summit, and environmental protection was included in virtually every major international convention, in the areas of human right, trade protection, and so forth. Most states accepted that global efforts were needed, and that cooperation between developing and industrialized nations was required.

Yet progress has been slow in terms of actual results, and the environmental outlook has worsened in terms of loss of biological diversity, depletion of fish stocks, tropical forest destruction and desertification, air and water pollution, and climate change. It has become generally accepted that the Rio agreements have not been effectively implemented. The organizer of the Earth Summit, Maurice Strong, has assessed that the Summit's failure is due to a cooperation failure—higher income countries should be ready to make initial commitments, and be prepared to compensate developing nations for managing resources sustainably. That simply has not happened, and there have not been transfers of funds going into the right areas (Luck-Baker, 2002).

25.2.3 The World Summit on Sustainable Development in Johannesburg in 2002

Attended by 190 nations, the World Summit for Sustainable Development took place in September 2002 in Johannesburg, to mark the 10th anniversary of the Earth Summit. The Johannesburg World Summit was an opportunity to reaffirm the commitment to the Rio Principles and the full implementation of Agenda 21. The participating governments reached fairly general agreements, including the Declaration on Sustainable Development. This Declaration reaffirmed broad principles, such as the acknowledgment of the problem of environmental deterioration:

> The global environment continues to suffer. Loss of biodiversity continues, fish stocks continue to be depleted, desertification claims more and more fertile land, the adverse effects of climate change are already evident, natural disasters are more frequent and more devastating, and developing countries more vulnerable, and air, water and marine pollution continue to rob millions of a decent life. (Johannesburg Declaration on Sustainable Development, Paragraph 13)

Generally speaking, the Johannesburg World Summit mainly endorsed the Millennium Development Goals (MDGs) adopted in 2000 by the Millennium Assembly of the United Nations. The MDGs were developed out of several global conferences sponsored by the United Nations in the 1990s and the work of the Organisation for Economic Co-operation and Development (OECD)'s Development Assistance Committee, and consisted in quantitative targets designed to improve social and economic conditions in poor countries. Regarding environmental matters, these targets included reducing biodiversity loss, restoring fish stocks by 2012, and achieving a reduction in the number of species threatened with extinction by 2010. The Johannesburg World Summit also placed an emphasis on the notion of "partnerships" between different actors. "Type II initiatives" for sustainable development involved the participation of national actors, international businesses, as well as NGOs, thus leaving a role to play for various counterparts on development projects.

25.2.4 The Bali Conference (COP 13/MOP 3) and the Bali Action Plan

Negotiations in Bali, Indonesia held in December 2007 led to the adoption of the Bali Roadmap, an agreement on a two-year process to finalize a binding agreement in Copenhagen in December 2009. This included the Bali Action Plan (BAP), a process focusing on key elements of long-term cooperation to further the implementation of the Convention past the expiry date of the Kyoto Protocol, including mitigation, adaptation, finance and technology transfer. For this purpose, the BAP established the Ad

Hoc Working Group on Long-term Cooperative Action, an official body with the task of organizing workshops and reports to work on these very issues.

25.2.5 United Nations Climate Change Conference in Copenhagen (also known as the Copenhagen Summit) in 2009 (COP 15/MOP 5)

The Copenhagen climate talks were held December 7–18, 2009 in Copenhagen, Denmark. This was the 15th session of the parties to the UNFCCC, and the 5th session of the parties to the Kyoto Protocol. The outcome of the conference was the Copenhagen Accord, a non-legally binding document that was not formally adopted by all participating countries (with the parties merely agreeing to "take note" of the Accord).

One key feature of this document was the embracement of the scientific view that in order to prevent anthropogenic interference with the climate system, a long-term goal of limiting the global average temperature increase to no more than 2° Celsius above preindustrial levels should be adopted. The Copenhagen Accord also included a reference to possibly limiting the temperature increase to below 1.5° Celsius, in response to a demand made by vulnerable developing countries. Unfortunately Copenhagen did not reach a consensus as to how to achieve this goal in practical terms. With the first commitment period under the Kyoto Protocol coming to an end in 2012, any long-term goal of keeping temperature increases below a 2° Celsius threshold required individual commitments on the part of nations to reduce GHG emissions worldwide. The Copenhagen Accord provided for no such targeted emission reductions.

Developed countries agreed to help poorer nations to adapt to climate impacts and transition to sustainable economies, with a promise to provide $30 billion for the period 2010–2012, with a further long-term financing goal of US$100 billion a year by 2020. A significant portion of such funding is to flow through the Green Climate Fund, established as "an operating entity of the financial mechanism of the Convention to support projects, programme, policies and other activities in developing countries related to mitigation including REDD-plus, adaptation, capacity-building, technology development and transfer" (Copenhagen Accord, Paragraph 10). Further, this funding is to come from "a wide variety of sources, public and private, bilateral and multilateral, including alternative sources of finance" (Copenhagen Accord, Paragraph 8).

To study the potential sources of revenue to meet the goal of mobilizing US$100 billion per year by 2020, including alternative sources of finance, the Copenhagen Accord established a High Level Panel. Further, on February 12, 2010, Ban Ki-moon announced the creation of a High Level Advisory Group on Climate Change Finance, with a very similar mandate (to study potential sources of revenue to mobilize the funds pledged in Copenhagen). Headed by Meles Zenawi, Gordon Brown, Bharrat Jagdeo, and Jens Stoltenberg, this Group also included academics and private sector investors such as Lawrence Summers, George Soros and Nicholas Stern.[6] The High

Level Advisory Group on Climate Change Finance issued its report in November 2010. The report examined a wide range of potential sources of funds, including existing public finance sources, new public instruments based on carbon pricing, international private investment flows, carbon-related instrument coordinated internationally (for example on international transportation), and a global financial transaction tax (High Level Advisory Group on Climate Change Finance, 2010, pp. 10–11). The report also identified a carbon price in the range of US$20 to US$25 per ton of carbon dioxide (CO_2) equivalent in 2020 as a key element of reaching the US$100 billion goal.

The Framework Convention and the Kyoto Protocol do not specifically contemplate forest management as a mitigation policy.[7] Largely through the efforts of a group of developing countries, the Copenhagen Accord gives priority to the immediate establishment of a mechanism for forest protection including REDD-plus,[8] with recognition of the crucial role of reducing emission from deforestation and forest degradation and the need to enhance removals of GHG emission by forests (Copenhagen Accord, Paragraph 6).

The failure of the Copenhagen climate talks to result in binding commitments to reduce emissions is likely to have a high economic cost. The International Energy Agency (IEA) has developed a plan (the "450 Scenario") to limit the long-term concentration of GHGs in the Earth's atmosphere to 450 parts per million of CO_2 equivalent. In 2010, the IEA estimated that assuming even the most environmentally ambitious interpretation of the Copenhagen Accord, the prospective costs of the global energy investment in the 450 Scenario have increased by US$1 trillion (International Energy Agency, 2010, p. 379) as compared with 2009 projections. This increase is attributable to two factors: first, a shift in energy demand projections, and second, the Copenhagen pledges falling short of what is necessary to achieve the goal of the 450 Scenario.

25.2.6 The UN Climate Summit in Cancún, Mexico in 2010 (COP 16/MOP 6)

The Cancún climate talks were held November 29–December 11, 2010 in Cancún, Mexico. This was the 16th session of the parties to the UNFCCC, and the 6th session of the parties to the Kyoto Protocol. Though many countries favored a single binding comprehensive agreement on emission reductions, expectations were relatively modest in terms of reaching a legally binding outcome in Cancún. The Japanese government had announced at one of the opening plenary sessions that Japan would not renew pledges under the Kyoto Protocol for the post-2012 period, unless the biggest carbon polluters also made firm commitments:

> The Kyoto protocol presents a first step to change. It does not make sense to set a second commitment period. [Signatories] to Kyoto only represent 15% of global emissions, but the countries who have signed up to the Copenhagen accord cause 80% of emissions. We want a single binding treaty. (Vidal, 2010).

Hence, the expectation was that the Summit would be a stepping stone toward a future agreement. The stakes were high in terms of renewing with a process toward climate change cooperation. The parties reached the Cancún Agreement, which did not really add much to the Copenhagen Accord, and in substance reiterated and accepted the content of this earlier agreement, including the agreed on threshold of an overall temperature increase of 2° Celsius above preindustrial levels, without the backing of concrete commitments for the reduction of GHG emissions.

This said, items achieved at the Cancún talks include developing countries agreeing for the first time to look into cutting emissions (though no specific pledges were made); industrialized countries reaffirming the promise made at Copenhagen to raise US$100 billion by 2020 to help developing countries mitigate climate change; a framework for paying countries in exchange for refraining from cutting down forests; the Cancún Adaptation Framework, designed to enhance action on adaptation, including through international cooperation; a Technology Mechanism (comprised of a Technology Executive Committee[9] and a Climate Technology Centre and Network) expected to facilitate the implementation of enhanced action on technology development and transfer to support action on mitigation and adaptation to climate change; and the launching of the Green Climate Fund, designed to support projects, programs, policies, and other activities in developing countries. The setup of the Green Climate Fund had been agreed to in principle in the Copenhagen Accord. Its actual launching is one of the major accomplishments of the Cancún talks, which secured informal commitments for a "fast track" US$30 billion line of financing by 2012 (e.g., the UK Government agreed to provide £1.5 billion, approximately US$2.4 billion).

25.2.7 Durban in 2011 (COP 17)

The 2011 United Nations Climate Change Conference was held in Durban, South Africa, from November 28 to December 11, 2011. The agenda was very much to establish a new treaty to limit carbon emissions. The outcome of the negotiations showed that participating nations differ in their attitude and expectations. Developing countries invoked their right to development and the issue of equity, stressing the importance of a leadership from industrialized countries in the form of further reduction commitments. The European Union showed its commitment to a second Kyoto period and pledged to extend the Kyoto targets to 2017–2020 (Krukowska, 2011), as consistent with its internal policy—the European Union has an internal target to reduce emissions by 20% in 2020 compared with 1990 levels (Bakewell, 2011).[10] But Japan, Russia, and Canada have refused to join the second commitment period and renew their pledge. Canada has actually invoked its legal right to withdraw from the Kyoto Protocol altogether, on the basis of the lack of participation from the United States and China (Ljunggren and Palmer, 2011). As discussed, the Japanese government had already announced at one of the opening plenary sessions in Cancún that Japan would not renew pledges under the Kyoto Protocol for the post-2012 period, unless the biggest carbon polluters also made firm commitments. The United States, of course, has still not ratified the Kyoto Protocol, and has made clear that it also wants a single binding commitment on all nations.

The Durban Conference closed with some kind of a compromise, an agreement to launch a process to develop such a legally binding agreement to keep average temperature increase below the 2° or 1.5° Celsius threshold. The roadmap is outlined in a draft decision adopted on December 11, 2011, the "Outcome of the work of the Ad Hoc Working Group on Further Commitments for Annex I Parties under the Kyoto Protocol at its sixteenth session." This new text proposal establishes a second commitment for five years (until 2017), and sets set a clear target of reductions of 25–40% below 1990 levels for Annex I countries. Note that yet again the document is very weak and only "takes note" of these reduced emission targets and proposed amendments to the Kyoto Protocol (Paragraphs 3 and 4).

Finally, it was also decided to launch the Green Climate Fund to help channel up to US$100 billion a year in aid to poor countries by 2020. There have been some delays in getting the Fund up and running, including some disagreements between countries regarding the board composition. The Fund's inaugural meeting, originally scheduled for April 10, 2012, has been rescheduled for May 31, 2012.

Overall, Durban received a mixed reception. The European Union has hailed the talks as a "historic breakthrough" (Hood and Ingham, 2011), but in light of the absence of concrete emission reduction commitment from the biggest emitters, we can only conclude that the future of the second commitment period remains uncertain.

25.3 Global Environmental Governance on Climate Change—The Major Treaties

25.3.1 Ozone Depletion—The Vienna Convention on the Protection of the Ozone Layer (1985)

One of the first successful global governance efforts was that the regulation of the emission of chemical substances, mainly chlorofluorocarbons (CFCs) contained in aerosol sprays, leading to the depletion of the ozone layer (the scientific evidence became apparent in the late 1970s). The Vienna Convention on the Protection of the Ozone Layer (1985) and its Protocol (Montreal, 1987) were aimed at preventing the depletion of the ozone layer, and for this purpose, provided a general framework for cooperation in the legal, scientific, and technical fields to protect the ozone layer. The Montreal Protocol provided for some very specific targets to eliminate CFCs progressively: industrial countries agreed to cut production and use of CFCs in half by 1998, and to freeze production and use of halons by 1992 (these phase-out dates were later advanced to 1996 for CFCs and 1994 for halons). The ozone treaty regime also regulates many other ozone-depleting chemicals such as hydrobromofluorocarbons (HBFCs), hydrochlorofluorocarbons (HCFCs), bromomethane (CH_3Br), Bromochloromethane (BCM), and so forth. To provide incentives to join the treaty, the Montreal Protocol also restricted trade between members and non-members.

All of these efforts were very successful. Global production of these substances was reduced by 76% between 1988 and 1995. For this reason, the Montreal Protocol is often hailed as an example of one of the "best developed and most effective global environmental regimes" (Downie, 2005, p. 71).

25.3.2 The UN Framework Convention on Climate Change (1992)

The UNFCCC, adopted after hard bargaining and signed at the Rio Earth Summit in 1992 by 194 nations, was the starting point to addressing climate change at an international level, and entered into force in March 1994. The stated purpose of the Framework Convention is the "stabilization of greenhouse gas concentrations in the atmosphere at a level that would prevent dangerous anthropogenic interference with the climate system".[11] Climate change is defined as "a change of climate which is attributed directly or indirectly to human activity that alters the composition of the global atmosphere and which is in addition to natural climate variability observed over comparable time periods."[12] GHGs are defined as "those gaseous constituents of the atmosphere, both natural and anthropogenic, that absorb and re-emit infrared radiation."[13]

The Framework Convention outlines a number of commitments for all member states.[14] These include measuring (and publishing national inventories) anthropogenic emissions, formulating and implementing measures to mitigate climate change, promoting the application of processes that control emissions including transfer of technologies, promoting sustainable management of sinks and reservoirs of all GHGs, and elaborating integrated plans for coastal zone management and cooperation in research.[15] There is a stated goal of transparency, as all member states are to provide detailed information on national policies and measures. For this purpose, developed countries are expected to provide financial assistance for developing countries to comply with their obligations—specifically, to provide information regarding their national inventory of anthropogenic emissions by sources, a description of steps taken or envisaged to implement the Convention, and any other relevant information for the calculations of global emission trends.

A significant omission is that although recognizing the necessity of returning to earlier levels of anthropogenic emissions of GHGs,[16] the Convention sets no specific timetables or targets for reducing emissions. It also does not dictate any specific policies or measures to be adopted to reduce emissions. Although all member states are required to coordinate with other states to reduce emissions, developed countries are to take the lead in modifying long-term trends in anthropogenic emission.[17] The Convention explicitly provides that the extent to which developing countries will implement their commitments depends on the effective implementation by developed countries of their commitments related to financial resources and transfer of technology.[18] Acknowledgment is also made of the priorities of economic and social development of developing countries.

Though the Convention did not set any mandatory limits on emissions, instead it contemplated the possibility of updates (called protocols—the Kyoto Protocol would become more famous than the Convention itself) to evaluate the necessity of introducing such limitations.

25.3.3 The Kyoto Protocol and the First Commitment Period (1997)

The Kyoto Protocol, an amendment to the UNFCCC, was negotiated in December 1997 and came into force on February 16, 2005. The reason for this delay was that in order to take effect, the Kyoto Protocol required as a first condition ratification by 55 states, and as a second condition that ratifying countries account for at least 55% of total CO_2 emissions in 1990. The first condition was met in 2002 (Iceland became the 55th ratifying country), the second in 2005 when the Kyoto Protocol finally entered into force.

The goal of the agreement was to call for individual commitments by industrial nations to reduce GHG emissions worldwide, with a focus on six specific gases: CO_2, methane, nitrous oxide, sulfur hexafluoride, hydrofluorocarbons (HFCs) and perfluorocarbons (PFCs). The targeted emission reduction was 5% below 1990 levels to be achieved by 2008–2012 (the first commitment period). This represented a 29% cut from projected emissions level for 2010. For this purpose, only developed industrialized countries ("Annex I countries") had commitments to reduce emissions, with differing national targets on the part of various participating nations: 8% reduction for most members of the European Union, 7% for the United States, 6% for Japan, 0% for Russia, and permitted increases of 10% for Iceland, 8% for Australia, and 1% for Norway. Emission targets are expressed as amounts of allowable CO_2 emissions (informally known as Kyoto units).

The emissions of developing countries were not limited,[19] under the principle of "common but differentiated responsibility"—the idea being that developing countries did not account for the largest share of emission, and still had to meet social and development needs (the assumption being that any commitment to restrict emission would interfere with the need to grow rapidly to improve the quality of life of their citizens). Developing countries still had the obligation to formulate, where relevant, cost effective national and regional programs to mitigate climate change.

The allowable emission amounts are to be tracked through national registry systems. The Kyoto Protocol provides for some flexibility in terms of the variety of methods that may be used to achieve the emission reduction goals,[20] including carbon-trading schemes. Annex I countries may also use International Emissions Trading (IET), which allows nations that have exceeded their emission reduction goal to sell Kyoto units to nations that exceed their quota. As such, the national registry systems also "settle" emission trades in the carbon-trading markets, delivering emission units from buyers to sellers. Another flexibility mechanism is the Clean Development Mechanism (CDM), designed to allow Annex I countries to meet their emission goals by collaborating with Non-Annex I countries (developing countries).[21] Annex I countries can be given credit for projects that reduce emissions in developing countries. There are some implementation difficulties, including the actual computation of the amount of emission reduction associated with the project,[22] with the possible perverse effect that firms raise their emissions in the short-term to increase credits for emission reduction, and the requirement that CDM emission savings be additional to reductions that would have occurred otherwise. The additionality of individual projects is difficult to prove. Ultimately, the CDM has been more effective in reducing climate change mitigation costs than in advancing sustainable development (World Bank, 2010, p. 265), and has brought little transformational change in developing countries' overall development strategies (World Bank, 2010, p. 233).

The outcome of Kyoto is mitigated. One positive outcome is that the European Union and other individual countries have adopted carbon-trading schemes, such as cap-and-trade program designed to push major corporations to reduce emissions. The World Bank has summarized that helping create these carbon-trading schemes, as well as placing emission reduction at the forefront of policy agendas are amongst the main achievements of the Kyoto Protocol:

> Kyoto set binding international limits on the greenhouse gas emissions of developed countries. It created a carbon market to drive private investment and lower the cost of emission reductions. And it prompted countries to prepare national climate-change strategies. (Word Bank, 2010, p. 233)

However, the Kyoto Protocol has not had a big impact on global emissions, which have increased by 25% since Kyoto was negotiated (World Bank, 2010, p. 233). Kyoto was weakened by the missing participation of some key players, including the biggest emitters. China and India had no legally binding obligations under Kyoto (not Annex I countries). The United States never ratified Kyoto, though it had originally signed the agreement. The US Senate was opposed to signing the Kyoto Protocol precisely because it failed to include binding commitments for developing nations. The Bush administration was also opposed to Kyoto for the same reasons, because the lack of participation of developing nations would be at the expense of the US economy. The United States proceeded with a different approach, proposing to reduce CO_2 emissions by 4.5% (against a current benchmark rather than the Kyoto 1990 benchmark) by 2010. This was to be achieved by giving incentives to businesses to reduce emissions. Though at the state level some states have shown leadership in the matter (Governor Schwarzenegger calling for an 80% cut in GHG emissions in California by 2050), at the national level the United States did not come close to meeting the Kyoto targets for carbon emission. The absence of positive leadership from the world's biggest per capita polluter has not been helpful.

Another issue is that participating nations have accounted for an ever-decreasing share of global emission (e.g., in 2008, Kyoto participation nations accounted for only 27% of global emissions). For this very reason, among participating nations the Japanese government has been the most vocal critic of the Kyoto Protocol, arguing that Kyoto has not been effective in reducing total emission of energy-related CO_2.

25.3.4 The Kyoto Protocol and the Second Commitment Period

The expectation had been that the parties to the Kyoto Protocol would eventually agree to renew their pledge to reduce emissions after the 2012 deadline—the second commitment period. In 2005, MOP 1 was held in Montreal, Canada, and established the Ad Hoc Working Group on Further Commitments for Annex I Parties under the Kyoto Protocol, mandated to consider further commitments for the Annex I countries.[23] The hope had been that at this point participating states would be in a position to commit to more ambitious targets for reducing emissions. Following Copenhagen, the scientific community (including the IPCC) is now in general agreement that the most feasible target would be to reduce emissions so as to stabilize temperature increase at 2° Celsius over preindustrial levels.

Negotiation on this second commitment period recently took place in the Durban Climate Change Conference, as discussed in Section 25.2. While the European Union showed its commitment to a second Kyoto period, and pledged to extend the Kyoto targets to 2017–2020, Japan, Russia, and Canada refused to renew their pledge under the Kyoto Protocol. These nations argue (along with the United States, which has yet to ratify the Kyoto Protocol), that a second commitment period does not make sense unless it is achieved with a single binding commitment on all nations. Yet developing countries such as China, India, and Brazil have not yet committed to specific reduction targets.

The Durban Conference closed with a draft decision (i.e., a document that does not create legally binding obligations) outlining a roadmap to launch a process to develop such single agreement to keep the average temperature increase below the 2° or 1.5° Celsius threshold. As discussed in Section 25.2, this roadmap establishes a second commitment for five years (until 2017), and sets set a clear target of reductions of 25–40% below 1990 levels for Annex I countries. At present, in light of the absence of concrete emission reduction commitment from the biggest emitters, we can only conclude that the future of the second commitment period remains uncertain.

25.4 Compliance, Enforceability, and Effectiveness Issues in International Environmental Law

There are three related issues associated with the implementation and enforcement of international environmental law: first, the issue of what formal steps must be taken to implement a state's legal obligations; second, the issue of what legal or natural person may enforce environmental law and hold a state accountable for environmental obligations; and third, the issue of what procedures and institutions exist to provide a framework to resolve disputes related to the non-compliance of environmental obligations (Sands, 2003, p. 173). We review these three issues in the text that follows: the possible enforcement of treaty obligations in national and international courts; the issue of standing for state and non-state claimants; and conflict resolution mechanisms. We then provide an overview of possible remedies. Finally, we comment on the overall effectiveness of international environmental law.

25.4.1 Framework for International Disputes: Procedure, Standing, and Conflict Resolution

25.4.1.1 Enforcement in National and International Courts

Treaties are designed to result in self-imposed limit on the sovereignty (i.e., the exclusive jurisdiction over its own territory) of participating countries. There are very few treaties that actually provide for strict liability for any harm that occurs in another state's territory as a result of a treaty breach.[24] As discussed in Section 25.2, though Stockholm Principle 21 (and its later reformulations)[25] would seem to impose strict liability for any transfrontier damage to the environment, this has never been invoked for unintentional accidents. This means that in general responsibility is based on fault: under international law, states bear responsibility for international law violations that can be attributed to them, including treaty violations. In August 2001, the International Law Commission (a commission set up by the United Nations in 1949 to produce research on various aspects of public international law) completed Draft Articles on the Responsibility of States for Internationally Wrongful Acts. According to Articles 2 and 3, an act or omission attributable to a state that violates a treaty (or international) obligation constitutes an international wrong governed by international law.

Environmental obligations may be enforced before national courts. As previously mentioned, Principle 10 of the Rio Declaration highlights that "environmental issues are best handled with the participation of all concerned citizens, at the relevant level" and specifically contemplates access to judicial and administrative proceedings at the national level. Here there are opportunities for non-state actors to challenge violations of international environmental law. Several treaties contemplate an enforcement role for individuals and provide for international rules on civil liability. There are two broad categories, mainly treaties requiring victims to bring proceedings in the state where the treaty violation (e.g., transboundary pollution) originated, and treaties allowing victims to choose to bring proceedings either in the state where the pollution originated, or the state where the damage was suffered (Sands, 2003, p. 197). This latter category typically allocates jurisdiction to national courts over a wide variety of matters, including civil disputes, with a choice of courts for the victims.

At the European level, a violation of European law can be challenged before the European Court of Justice. There is a vast case law concerning environmental issues. At the international level, disputes can be presented to the International Court of Justice (ICJ) for a determination of rights arising under bilateral treaties. Here opportunities for non-state actors are more limited, and states play a primary role in enforcing treaty obligations. The ICJ is the principal judicial organ of the United Nations, established in June 1945 by the Charter of the United Nations, charged with resolving disputes between states upon consideration of a variety of legal sources, including international conventions (treaties) and international custom. In 1993, the ICJ established a Chamber for Environmental Matters as a framework for dispute settlement. This Chamber is a panel of seven judges empowered to hear environmental cases with the consent of the parties to the case.

Disputes have also come up regarding the right for countries to violate obligations under international trade agreements (e.g., banning the import of a product), to the extent such violation is motivated by environmental protection efforts (if the banned product is not manufactured in an environmentally friendly manner). Old environmental disputes involving trade agreements have been handled under the old General Agreement on Tariffs and Trade (GATT) dispute settlement procedure. For example, in a famous case the United States tried to ban the import of Mexican tuna on the ground that the tuna was not caught in a manner safe to dolphins.[26] In 1991, the ban was declared illegal under GATT,[27] on the ground that the United States was seeking to apply national law (its own national standards for dolphin protection under the US Marine Mammal Protection Act) extraterritorially. Subsequent disputes have been handled by the World Trade Organization (WTO) system. WTO decisions have allowed for greater recognition for a government's environmental protection agenda through the interpretation of the concept of "like goods"—if foreign goods produced in environmentally damaging conditions are not comparable with domestic products, they are not subject to the disallowance of discrimination (discrimination solely on the basis of the production process) between comparable domestic and imported goods ("like goods"). Under this interpretation, imports may be restricted. The dispute settlement procedures have also been made more transparent (for instance, members of arbitration panels are publicly announced).

Under the North American Free Trade Agreement (NAFTA), any NGOs and other non-state actors can formally challenge governments if environmental laws are not properly implemented, by petitioning the NAFTA Commission on Environmental

Cooperation. Though few of these challenges have actually produced results, the procedure is quite unique in international law in that civil society actors typically cannot thus challenge environmental legal violations.

25.4.1.2 Standing Issues for State and Non-State Claimants

Once evidence is available that a party to a treaty has not complied with an international environmental obligation, the right to enforce this obligation internationally (i.e., take measures to enforce the obligation, for instance by obtaining a ruling by an appropriate international court) is referred to as having proper "standing." Depending on the nature and legal basis of the violation, states, international organization or other non-state actors (businesses, individuals) may or may not have adequate standing to bring international claims. For breaches of treaty obligations, the terms of the treaty will typically determine standing issues, and the right of a state or non-state actor to enforce obligations.

States, of course, have a primary role in enforcing treaty obligations because they are the principal subjects of international law (and parties to treaties). A state does not necessarily have standing if it has not itself suffered some kind of damage. This said, even if it has not suffered material damage, a state may bring an action under a treaty on the basis of obligations owed *erga omnes*. Treaties typically explicitly settle this issue of standing. Under the European Community (EC) Treaty, for example, a member state may bring an action against another member state for an alleged infringement of an obligation under the EC Treaty before the European Court of Justice.[28] In this case, the breach of a treaty obligation is sufficient to grant standing, and there is no need to show that the member state bringing the claim has suffered any kind of damage.

In the absence of a specific treaty right, a state will not have standing, as there is no general legal interest in the protection of the environment on behalf of the international community (*actio popularis*), except in rare cases where the activities of a state may cause environmental damage to global commons (Sands, 2003, p. 187). Though it would seem that this issue would have come up a lot in practice, since the global commons (oceans, Antarctica, biomass, etc.) have significantly deteriorated in the past few decades, the ICJ has considered this issue on only two occasions.[29] Only once did the Court recognize the possibility of an *actio popularis* under international law where an obligation exists *erga omnes* (owed to all the states).[30] In traditional international law, this is the case when the matter is of common concern to the international community. The possibility of an *actio popularis* is more likely to be successful in cases involving significant damage to the environment (Sands, 2003, p. 189).

There is also the possibility of *private* enforcement of national environmental obligations, with non-state actors (e.g., individuals or businesses) filing suit to enforce environmental obligation in the public interest. Environmental organizations have played a key role in the enforcement process of international environmental law. International organizations are international legal persons capable of enforcing international law, though in practice their involvement has been limited.

Principle 10 of the Rio Declaration provides that individuals are to have access from information concerning the environment and that "effective access to judicial and administrative proceedings, including redress and remedy, shall be provided." In the European Union, the European Commission has acknowledged that individuals and public interest groups should have access to courts to that effect.[31] The European Court of Justice has allowed individuals to challenge the failure by member states to adopt measures to implement European environmental law, but not challenge European legislative and administrative acts.[32]

Some conventions specifically provide standing to non-state actors for purposes of enforcing specific provisions. For instance, the Lugano Convention (1993 Convention on Civil Liability for Damage Resulting from Activities Dangerous to the Environment) allows for the recovery of damages in respect of "environmental impairment" (Article 7), and allows standing for environmental interest groups to seek injunctive relief before national courts (Article 18). The Aarhus Convention (1998 Convention on Access to Information, Public Participation In Decision-Making and Access to Justice in Environmental Matters) establishes that members of the public with a "sufficient interest" or with an "impairment of a right" are to "have access to a review procedure before a court of law and/or another independent and impartial body established by law, to challenge the substantive and procedural legality of any decision, act or omission" (Article 9.2).

25.4.1.3 *Arbitration and Conflict Resolution*

Before making use of a formal enforcement mechanism before a court, environmental disputes can be settled through a range of dispute resolution mechanisms outside the courts, such as negotiation, international arbitrage, mediation, or other diplomatic means. These methods typically involve a third person to facilitate the process (investigate the facts, moderate the exchange of proposals in the negotiation process, etc.). Mediation and conciliation do not produce decisions that are legally binding. International arbitration, on the other hand, does result in binding and final decisions.

Many environmental treaties encourage the use of such dispute resolution mechanisms to avoid more formal disputes between states. The Framework Convention, for instance, contemplates three mechanisms to assist in dispute resolution: a Subsidiary Body for Implementation, a multilateral consultative process, and the settlement of remaining disputes by negotiation, arbitration, or international conciliation.[33]

Many multilateral treaties provide their own non-compliance procedures. The Kyoto Protocol provides in its Article 18:

> The Conference of the Parties serving as the meeting of the Parties to this Protocol shall, at its first session, approve appropriate and effective procedures and mechanisms to determine and to address cases of non-compliance with the

provisions of this Protocol, including through the development of an indicative list of consequences, taking into account the cause, type, degree and frequency of non-compliance. Any procedures and mechanisms under this Article entailing binding consequences shall be adopted by means of an amendment to this Protocol. (Kyoto Protocol, Article 18)

In 2001, at the seventh conference of the parties to the Kyoto Protocol, a very comprehensive compliance regime was adopted, consisting of a Compliance Committee with two branches, a Facilitative Branch, designed to provide advice and assistance to promote compliance, and an Enforcement Branch, designed to make final determinations regarding noncompliance. However, we note that this Branch has no power of sanction over noncompliant parties. This is one of the failures of the Kyoto Protocol, its lack of any real enforcement mechanism.

25.4.2 Remedies for Breach of Treaty

The normal sanction for a treaty violation consists in other treaty states withholding treaty benefits from the breaching state. The large majority of multilateral environmental treaties focus on the conduct of a delinquent state (duties of comportment, for instance) rather than repairing any damage suffered by other states. For example, if a party to the Kyoto Protocol is found to be noncompliant, its access to the IET transaction registry, or other flexibility mechanisms, can be denied.

States can also file claims for reparation for any harm suffered (claim for damages). Yet harm can be difficult to measure as an economic matter, because the environment is typically outside of the marketplace. Establishing that a state has directly suffered actual damage as a result of a treaty violation is difficult as a practical matter, especially in situations where the noncompliance arises strictly within the limits of national jurisdiction. In these situations, claims for reparations can only be successful if obligations are owed to all states (*erga omnes*). In traditional international law, this is the case when the matter is of common concern to the international community.

In July 2004, the International Law Commission adopted in draft form a set of "Principles on Allocation of Loss in the Case of Transboundary Harm Arising Out of Hazardous Activities" (finally adopted in May 2006). These principles provide a framework for treaties to ensure compensation for victims of transboundary damage, and support the establishment of state-funded compensation schemes as well as industry-wide funds to ensure that financial resources are available.

Fines can also be imposed. The European Court of Justice, for instance, can fine countries that violate EU law. For example, the European Commission took legal action against 12 European states on July 12, 2005 for failing to carry out EU law regarding proper environmental impact assessments of land use, road construction, and waste management schemes.

25.4.3 The Effectiveness of International Environmental Law

Has global environmental governance successfully addressed climate change issues? Whether the existing treaty framework, with the Framework Convention and the Kyoto Protocol, as well as other softlaw guidelines and principles developed in Stockholm, Rio, Copenhagen, Cancún, Durban are adequate to meet the major climate change challenges, can be broken down into two related but distinct questions. First is the issue of international treaty compliance, that is, whether nations are respecting treaty obligations. Second is the issue of whether the existing treaty framework, as it stands, is able to meet the major environmental challenges of climate change. This latter question is more difficult, and entails underlying issues such as what measures and commitments are required to produce actual results and reverse negative trends, and how to actually incorporate those measures in an international legal framework (issues of what level of political will, international cooperation, and negotiation processes are needed to result in international agreements).

25.4.3.1 International Compliance

International compliance is one of the main issues in environmental law. There are many reasons for this. First, the mechanisms of liability under international law are far less defined than domestic mechanisms to enforce laws within each nation-state. This is because no supranational legislature exists with the power to enforce laws at an international level. Second, to the extent treaty violations originate in actions committed by non-state actors (e.g., corporations, individuals), compliance will be difficult if there is a political cost associated with enforcing international law obligations (if, for example, non-state actors play a powerful role in domestic politics, or even legislation). And third, dealing with environmental matters raises specific causality issues that challenge the traditional concept of responsibility. For instance, there may not be a clear link between polluting activities and their effects, because of the distance separating the source of pollution and the place of damage, or timing disconnect (e.g., an increase in the rate of cancer can be undetected for many years, or manifest itself many years after the international violation). It can also be difficult the identify the specific causes when there are a plurality of factors involved, complex production processes, potential cumulative nonlinear effects (tipping points, etc.), and variations in physical circumstances (making it difficult to identify the specific effects of a pollutant).[34]

For all these reasons, the effectiveness of a treaty framework in terms of compliance has not been guaranteed by the existence of a formal enforcement mechanism, either because treaties do not provide for strong sanctions, or because formal enforcement initiatives are difficult and rarely initiated. Hence, it is suggested that environmental treaties will be effective only to the extent participating states view that compliance is in their self-interest:

> Curiously, few international environmental treaties contain strong sanctions or compliance mechanisms. While most treaties include legal language for arbitration, arbitration proceedings are rarely initiated. To the extent that environmental treaties are effective, it is through nations' own calculations of their self-interest, rather than through fears of consequences of noncompliance. (Speth and Haas, 2006, p. 130)

Recently, states' compliance with international environmental obligations has been analyzed mainly as an economic issue, since noncompliance tends to be perceived as an attempt to gain economic advantage (Sands, 2003, p. 172). To the extent international agreements ultimately cannot be enforced against nations, key to successful implementation is the realization that compliance is in a country's self-interest. This is one of the factors in support of the cap-and-trade approach (Keohane and Raustiala, 2008).

25.4.3.2 The Efficiency of Global Environment Governance

We find that ozone depletion being a notable exception, all the effort at international governance in climate change (the Framework Convention, the Kyoto Protocol, the various conferences of the parties) have not reversed the disturbing trends in CO_2 emissions and global warming. It has led many legal scholars to conclude that the past 20 years of international environmental negotiations have been deeply disappointing, the issue not being one of noncompliance, but rather weak treaties that do not go far enough:

> It is not that what has been agreed upon, for example, in the framework conventions on climate, desertification, biodiversity or the Law of the Sea is wrong or useless. Those conventions have raised awareness, provided frameworks for action, and stimulated useful national planning exercises. But the bottom line is that these treaties and their associated agreements and protocols do not drive the changes that are needed. In general, the issue with these treaties is not weak enforcement or noncompliance; the issue is weak treaties. (Speth, 2004)

Therefore we can flag that the main issue is not one of noncompliance, but rather the inefficacy of established regime rules. Weak treaties, for example, might simply match the status quo so that they do little to produce actual change in the behavior of polluters. Another problem is the issue of ambitious rules that are too vague for actual implementation, and therefore encourage widespread noncompliance with no real possibility of enforceability. As we will discuss, this is the main issue with the Stockholm Declaration, the Rio Declaration, and Agenda 21.

Environmental policy analyst David Leonard Downie has developed a helpful framework to understand the inefficiency of treaties to meet the major environmental challenges, classifying all contributing factors into four main types: systemic obstacles, procedural obstacles, lack of critical preconditions, and the very complexity of environmental issues (Downie, 2005).

First are "systemic obstacles" to the cooperation amongst nation states required to tackle the complexity of environmental issues. The interdependence of different sectors (with, for example, complex causal chains linking atmospheric pollution to soil contamination to marine pollution to biodiversity, etc.) requires a holistic approach, but while environmental issues are large-scale in nature, transcending national boundaries, nation-states only have legal sovereignty within their borders, resulting in coordination issues:

> Such interrelationships necessarily have international consequences, because the transfer of pollution from one milieu to another will frequently result in transboundary impacts. Yet, there is no comprehensive international environmental agreement addressing these matters in a holistic manner nor is there a single agency addressing the problems. The lack of coordination among different agencies and treaty bodies has had some negative effect on the success of environmental laws and policies and is a priority issue for the future. (Kiss and Shelton, 2007, p. 45)

The resolution of environmental issues thus requires some level of cooperation among nation-states. This cooperation is inherently difficult for political, legal, and economic reasons. Here we might identify some underlying dynamics analyzed by economists, such as the free rider problem, the tragedy of the commons, or game-theoretical accounts of the types of strategic interactions between nation-states. The free-rider problem is the temptation on the part of some treaty members to ignore treaty obligations in the hope that treaty objectives will be met through the actions of other treaty parties—in other words, reap the benefits of collective actions without sharing the costs. We find that treaties that specifically address the free-rider issue, such as the Montreal Protocol to the Convention for the Protection of the Ozone Layer, by providing states with an incentive to join the treaty and encourage compliance, are typically more successful in reaching their stated goals. Economists have also extensively analyzed environmental issues from a game-theoretical standpoint (see Finus, 2001). For example, the negotiations in Copenhagen, Cancún and Durban to reach a consensus (a Pareto-optimal single binding commitment) regarding a Kyoto second commitment period illustrate a prisoner dilemma type of game-theoretic dynamic at play. The United States has been opposed to Kyoto because of the lack of participation of developing nations, and developing nations feel that industrialized countries need to take the lead.

Second are procedural obstacles. International agreements are difficult to reach and typically require a lengthy negotiation process. Important countries with more bargaining power typically have more influence to shape agreements to fit their interests. Further, countries most interested in addressing a problem need to gain the cooperation of countries that have little vested interest in the problem. This, according to Downie, results in "lowest common denominator agreements." We see this today in climate change politics, with the negotiations over the Kyoto second commitment period requiring concerted efforts by all the major emitters of GHGs, but big emitters such as the United States and China being reluctant to curb their emission. In Downie's analysis, this explains the failure of the Kyoto Protocol due to its lowest-denominator policy:

> This has limited the ability of Europe and other countries to move forward with aggressive global policies. They could create an agreement without U.S., Chinese, and Indian participation, or act on their own domestically, as the European Union has done, but effective global policy will require the eventual participation of the least willing but necessary actors. Such actors, the necessary but least willing, are thus in position to have a lowest-common-denominator impact on global policy. (Downie, 2005, p. 80)

Third is the lack of critical necessary conditions, such as the level of public concern of participating governments and the overall state capacity to understand and negotiate the issues, at a scientific, political and administrative level. Capacity can be thought of as the ability of states to adopt environmental policies that may run counter to short-term economic interests, and the ability to make decisions in a context of uncertainty and complexity. This can be a very serious obstacle to effective environmental policy:

> Because the global challenges tend to have weak domestic constituencies, politicians tend not to give them priority when it comes to funds, nor are they willing to take on powerful corporate interests (for example, in the energy, transportation, and chemical industries) often vested in the status quo. Meanwhile, the treaty-making process is allowed to plunge ahead because both governments and businesses understand the many weaknesses of international environmental law and know that they can almost always ensure toothless treaties if they like. (Speth and Haas, 2006, p. 79)

Finally, global environmental problems are difficult to solve due to the very nature of the issues at hand. Environmental issues are complex, costly and uncertain in nature, with potentially unequal distributions of costs and benefits among nations. As a factual matter, the greater the economic implications of a problem, the greater the probability of failure of a treaty-based approach. When economic costs are important, companies do not have financial incentives to comply with treaty restrictions and tend to find ways around them. As an added problem, such issues may not be suitable to be handled by political leaders, or even international businesses, which tend to be constrained by short-term objectives (this point, of course, is connected to the lack of critical necessary conditions).

As a general matter, we find that when goals are targeted and more specific, a treaty framework has a higher likelihood of effective implementation and actual results. For instance, the Convention for the Protection of the Ozone Layer led to an effective system to reduce ozone-depleting substances to the extent the Montreal Protocol provided for some very specific targets and phase-out dates to eliminate CFCs progressively. On the other hand, broad, general goals tend to be less effective. The set of principles outlined in the Stockholm Declaration on the Human Environment, the Rio Declaration, and Agenda 21 constitute an ambitious agenda, yet not specific enough to generate actual results. Urging to protect and manage natural resources, calling for state responsibility for damage to the environment resulting from activities within the state's jurisdiction, and for shared responsibility among nations to protect the environment and the Earth's ecosystem are all worthy goals, but they lack concrete measures. In this case implementation is heavily dependent on institutional arrangements, financial resources and strong leadership from major countries to further these goals.

The Kyoto Protocol also contained differing national targets on the part of various participating nations, with a tracking system through national registries. The mitigated outcome of the Kyoto Protocol, in terms of its limited impact on global emissions, can be explained as a result of the failure to include all big emitting countries. As we discussed, the missing participation of the United States, and the lack of emission targets for developing countries (combined with a trend for these countries to account for larger shares of worldwide emissions), significantly undermined Kyoto. This shows that the effectiveness of global environmental law also depends on its comprehensiveness, that is, its ability to target all countries that contribute to a given problem. This is the reason that many parties to the Kyoto Protocol insist that a single binding agreement is needed to meet the long-term goal of keeping temperature increases below a 2° Celsius threshold. This, in turn, is dependent upon the degree of political commitment in the negotiation process, and the ability to overcome all the obstacles outlined previously.

We can conclude with a general overview of the various factors linked to successful international environmental law. First, there is a need for a clear scientific consensus regarding the existence of a particular problem. This ensures some level of public concern and facilitates governments' ability to understand and negotiate the issues. Further, a scientific consensus increases the likelihood that states take a long-term view of their best interest and adopt environmental policies that may run counter to short-term economic interests. Since the IPCC process began in the late 1980s, a great deal of attention has been focused on the study of the sensitivity of climate to enhanced levels of GHGs. There is now a general view that emissions of GHGs will have to be reduced by at least 60% in the industrialized world to avoid severe consequences to climate and ecosystems (IPCC, 2001). The failure of the Copenhagen climate talks (and subsequent negotiations in Cancún and Durban) to result in binding commitments to reduce emissions is indicative that there are many obstacles to a successful legal regime, even when a scientific consensus exists.

Second, a successful regime must have an understandable and legitimate dispute resolution process, with consensus-building mechanisms and an ongoing forum to manage issues (Speth and Haas, 2006, p. 133). As discussed, the Kyoto Protocol has set up a comprehensive compliance regime with two branches, a Facilitative Branch to provide advice and assistance to promote compliance, and an Enforcement Branch to make final determinations regarding non-compliance. This said, Kyoto is weakened by the lack of any real enforcement mechanism, with the Enforcement Branch lacking any power of sanction over noncompliant parties.

Third, successful regimes have specific clear-cut quantifiable targets, as is apparent with the success of the Convention for the Protection of the Ozone Layer and the Montreal Protocol. Therefore, it is essential that emission reduction targets be established to renew pledges for the second commitment period under the Kyoto Protocol.

Fourth, any successful regime must give itself the financial means to meet stated goals. Here we can applaud the set up of a Green Climate Fund with a further long-term financing goal of mobilizing US$100 billion per year by 2020 to help poorer countries implement mitigation policies. The variety of sources (both public and private) under consideration means that there is the added possibility of attracting industry support.

Finally, a successful regime should give incentives for nations to join the treaty. It has been suggested that cap-and-trade systems can be used to give reluctant nations some incentive to join, with for example the attribution of permits in excess of likely future emission (Keohane and Raustiala, 2008). The strategy here for the post-2012 Kyoto negotiations would be to induce governments that have refused to cap their emissions to participate in a single binding comprehensive framework with the possibility of gaining from the sale of emission permits.

25.4.3.3 Economic Modeling for Successful Climate Change Policies

Climate change can also be thought of as an economic problem that requires reducing emissions of GHGs today, at the cost of current consumption of goods and services, to avoid the future potential drastic consequences of climate change (including future adverse economic consequences). Economic models have been developed to help with this analysis. The interactions between climate change and economic growth are extremely complex. Modeling can help unravel this complexity, understand the major tradeoffs involved in climate-change policy, and evaluate the relative efficiency of different policies.

One of the earliest dynamic economic models of climate change was the DICE model (a Dynamic Integrated model of Climate and the Economy)—see, for instance, the full model described in Nordhaus (1994). A regionalized version, known as RICE (a Regional dynamic Integrated model of Climate and the Economy), was subsequently developed (see, e.g., Nordhaus and Yang, 1996). Following the new endogenous growth literature, most leading climate-economy models now feature endogenous technical change (for a summary of different results and different models, see Edenhofer et al., 2006). There is a strong belief that endogenous technical change is vital to climate change economic modeling given that a long-term horizon is involved. In these models, technical change is typically driven by the development of knowledge capital. Many climate economy models incorporate knowledge through learning using experience curves (such curves relate investment and/or R&D expenditures to cost reductions) and spillover effects.

Some of the central issues relevant for policy include estimating the cost of business as usual, how sharply and quickly should countries reduce GHG emissions, and the cost of mitigation policies. More specific policy questions might include whether reductions should be equally distributed across countries, how emission reductions should be imposed (through taxes, emission limits, or subsidies to low-carbon intensive energy). Economic models of climate change allow for the simulation and assessment of the economic and environmental impacts of alternative approaches to climate change policy. The link between GHG emissions and global temperatures is typically modeled by the so-called relative forcing, which the IPCC has described as "a measure of the influence a factor has in altering the balance of incoming and outgoing energy in the Earth-atmosphere system" and "an index of the importance of the factor as a potential climate change mechanism" (IPCC, 2007, p. 36).

In terms of estimating economic costs of mitigation policies, RICE and DICE models, for instance, show a net economic impact of 2,414 and 4,396 billions (respectively) of 1990 US dollars to keep global temperature limited to a 2.5 degrees increase (Nordhaus and Boyer, 2000). This net economic impact increases to 26,555 and 20,931 billions to limit temperatures to a 1.5° Celsius increase. The Stern Report (Stern, 2006) estimates that the annual costs of keeping global average temperature rise from exceeding 2° Celsius (achieving stabilization between 500 and 550 ppm CO_2-eq[35]) are around 1% of global GDP in 2050 (with an error range of plus or minus 3%).[36] In June 2008, Stern increased this estimate to 2% of GDP.

Though the urgency of immediate action to reduce emissions was not stressed initially, there is now growing evidence supporting the need for early government intervention. In the RICE model, delaying action by 10 years led to a relatively trivial loss of US$6 billion, leading the authors to conclude that "the loss from waiting and gathering more information is relatively small, assuming that action is appropriately taken in the future" (Nordhaus and Boyer, 2000, p. 127). On the other hand, the Stern report highlights the dangers of business-as-usual,[37] and stresses that the benefits of strong, early action considerably outweigh the costs (Stern, 2006). Though Weitzman (2007) has criticized the Stern Report on the basis that the results are highly dependent on the low 1.4% discount rate used in for modeling purposes,[38] the need for early government intervention can also be established through transition dynamics. For example, Greiner et al. (2010) also support the need for early government intervention before GHG concentration rises above a critical threshold, in order for the economy to stabilize at the socially optimum steady state (where the long-run temperature is smaller and production is higher).

Although the urgency of immediate action might be established, there is no clear consensus regarding design of specific optimal policies and the conditions for their success (as well as the added problem of technical feasibility). Stern (2006) advocates for government support for specific low-emission technologies[39] to be brought to commercial viability. Models with endogenous technical change display a wide range of outcomes owing to parameter and structural uncertainty. Policy implications are difficult to assess in this context, when there are still many uncertainties about what model structure is the most appropriate, and with so many discrepancies in predicted outcomes. There are still many open modeling issues.[40] Further, although scientists have improved their understanding of climate, estimating the probability of abrupt catastrophic climate change is very difficult, owing to nonlinear changes and threshold effects at higher temperatures. The exact threshold for what levels of GHG concentrations may be dangerous is difficult to ascertain. Accordingly, there are still many reservations regarding the exact structure, data, parameters, and overall reliability of different modeling approaches.

All of these uncertainties (combined with complex interactions between different sectors and complex feedback effects) mean that any damage cost assessments and policy recommendations must be with interpreted with caution. This said, a gradual approach that slowly (but surely) imposes restraints on carbon emissions is probably a safe fallback approach:

> In the author's view, the best approach is one that gradually introduces restraints on carbon emissions. One particularly efficient approach is internationally harmonized carbon taxes—ones that quickly become global and universal in scope and harmonized in effect. A sure and steady increase in harmonized carbon taxes may not have the swashbuckling romance of a crash program, but it is also less likely to be smashed on the rocks of political opposition and compromise. Slow, steady, universal, predictable, and boring—those are probably the secrets to success for policies to combat global warming. (Nordhaus, 2007, p. 181)

The Copenhagen Accord embraces a temperature constraint (the long-term goal of limiting the global average temperature increase to no more than 2° Celsius above preindustrial levels), as is consistent with scientific evidence (IPCC, 2001). Though specific threshold for dangerous levels of GHG concentrations are difficult to establish, most economic models validate the Kyoto approach of emission reductions as a mitigation measure. In light of the urgency of immediate action, the speed with which a single binding agreement can be negotiated, post Cancún and Durban, to carve the path to emission reductions, is of critical importance.

25.5 Conclusions

There is now a general consensus in the scientific community that emissions of GHGs will have to be reduced by at least 60% in the industrialized world to prevent anthropogenic interference with the climate system. Though this view was adopted in Copenhagen, with a long-term goal of limiting global temperature increase to no more than 2° Celsius above preindustrial levels, it is not captured in a legally binding agreement. At this stage, in light of the urgency of immediate action to reverse emission and temperature trends, this "soft law" approach is evidently insufficient. There is currently little doubt that any successful policy will require binding commitments with clear-cut quantifiable targets. Most economic models validate the Kyoto approach of emission reductions as a mitigation measure. Though the Kyoto Protocol did establish targets for emission reductions, it has had a limited impact on global emissions, owing to the missing participation of big emitters such as the United States, China, and India. We argue that any successful environmental legal framework will require the participation of all big emitters. As such, many parties to the Kyoto Protocol rightfully insist that a single binding agreement is needed to meet the long-term goal of keeping temperature increases below a 2° Celsius threshold.

There is no doubt it will be very difficult to negotiate such comprehensive agreement. The recent failures of negotiations in Cancún and Durban to reach further binding commitments (post-2012) under the Kyoto Protocol illustrate the limitations of a treaty-based approach. The resolution of environmental issues requires cooperation amongst nation states, yet as we outlined this cooperation is inherently difficult for political, legal, and economic reasons—this creates a serious limitation on the international community's ability to pursue aggressive global climate policies. The treaty-based approach has a high probability of failure when a given problem has major economic implications. We see today big emitters such as the United States, China, and India reluctant to curb their emission for this very reason, with a perceived high economic cost for their economies, resulting in a "lowest-denominator policy." The issue of how reductions should be distributed across countries is of course a major negotiation point.

Environmental treaties are more successful to the extent participating states view that compliance is in their self-interest. The speed with which a single binding agreement can be negotiated, post Cancún and Durban, will depend on broad public support in developed nations for mitigation actions, and on the ability of political leaders to consider that emission reductions is in their long-term interest. Keohane and Raustiala (2008) suggest that politicians' desire for public recognition should be manipulated to that effect through an "economy of esteem." They argue that incentives can be used to encourage climate-related actions, such as prizes for climate leadership.

A single binding agreement should provide incentives for countries to join and encourage compliance. For this reason, flexibility in terms of the variety of methods that may be used to achieve the emission reduction goals (taxes, emission limits, or subsidies to low-carbon-intensive energy) is desirable. Flexibility mechanisms under the Kyoto Protocol were broadly successful, helping, among other thing, to create carbon-trading schemes. It is suggested that an international cap-and-trade system where buyers are liable for the validity of their emissions permits is the only international architecture that is likely to encourage participation and compliance by many nations, and ultimately produce results:

> The best chance of securing their participation [China and India] is a combination of persuasion—that climate change will be bad for them as well as for others—and material inducements in the form of valuable (because tradable) hot air. (Keohane and Raustiala, 2008, p. 6)

In summary, the post-Kyoto era requires a comprehensive working system not doomed by enforcement problems, with solid political and popular support, accompanied by technological innovation to drive economic growth.

Annex I: A Timeline of Major International Environmental Agreements

1972 United Nations Conference on the Human Environment (UNCHE), Stockholm. Stockholm Declaration adopted.
1973 United Nations Environment Programme (UNEP) created.
1973 Convention on International Trade in Endangered Species (CITES). Entered into force 1975.
1979 Convention on Long Range Transboundary Air Pollution (CLRTAP). Entered into force 1983.
1982 United Nations Convention on the Law of the Sea (UNCLOS). Entered into force 1994.
1985 Vienna Convention for the Protection of the Ozone Layer. Entered into force 1988.
1987 Montreal Protocol on Substances that Deplete the Ozone Layer. Entered into force 1989.
1987 World Commission on Environment and Development (WCED). Publication of the Brundtland Report.
1989 Basel Convention on the Control of Transboundary Movements of Hazardous Wastes and Their Disposal. Entered into force 1992.
1991 Establishment of the Global Environmental Facility (GEF).
1992 United Nations Conference on Environment and Development (UNCED), Rio de Janeiro (The Earth Summit). Rio Declaration adopted. Agenda 21 adopted.
1992 United Nations Framework Convention on Climate Change (UNFCCC). Entered into force 1994.
1992 United Nations Commission on Sustainable Development (CSD) created.
1992 United Nations Convention on Biological Diversity. Entered into force 1993.
1994 International Convention to Combat Desertification. Entered into force 1996.
1997 Kyoto Protocol on Climate Change adopted. Entered into force 2005.
1998 Rotterdam Convention on the Prior Informed Consent Procedure for Certain Hazardous Chemicals and Pesticides in International Trade. Entered into force 2004.
2000 Cartagena Protocol on Biosafety adopted. Entered into force 2003.
2001 Stockholm Convention for the Elimination of the Persistent Organic Pollutants (POPs) adopted. Entered into force 2004.
2002 World Summit on Sustainable Development (WSSD) held in Johannesburg Johannesburg Declaration adopted. Johannesburg Plan of Implementation adopted.

2007 United Nations Climate Change Conference, Bali. Bali Roadmap adopted.
2009 United Nations Climate Change Conference, Copenhagen (The Copenhagen Summit). Copenhagen Accord adopted.
2010. United Nations Climate Summit, Cancún. Cancún Agreement adopted.
2011 United Nations Climate Change Conference, Durban. "Outcome of the work of the Ad Hoc Working Group on Further Commitments for Annex I Parties under the Kyoto Protocol at its sixteenth session" adopted.

Notes

1. See Foster v. Nielson, 27 U.S. (2 Pet.) 253, 314 (1829).
2. Murray v. The Schooner Charming Betsy, 6 U.S. (2 Cranch) 64, 118 (1804).
3. LaGrand Case (Ger. v. U.S.), 2001 ICJ (June 27), 40 ILM 1069 (2001).
4. Though strictly speaking the Vienna Convention does not deal with climate change, it is one of the earliest examples of international cooperation to protect the environment against detrimental effects resulting from industrial activities (the production and consumption of ozone-depleting substances). As such, it did not seem appropriate to omit it.
5. The expression is found in Kiss and Shelton (2007, p. 36).
6. See the UN Press Release at http://www.un.org/News/Press/docs/2010/sga1223.doc.htm
7. For instance, reduced deforestation is not included as a Clean Development Mechanism.
8. REDD (Reducing Emissions from Deforestation and Forest Degradation) is a series of measures designed to use a market-based approach to reduce the emissions of GHGs from deforestation and forest degradation. REDD-plus includes Reducing Emissions from Deforestation and Forest Degradation in Developing Countries; and the role of Conservation, Sustainable Management of Forests and Enhancement of Forest Carbon Stocks.
9. 20 high level expert members, elected by the Conference of the Parties.
10. We also note that the United Kingdom has put in place a national policy to reduce emissions by 60% by midcentury, and that Germany has become the world leader in renewable energy.
11. Article 2 of the Framework Convention.
12. Article 1(2) of the Framework Convention.
13. Article 1(5) of the Framework Convention.
14. Articles 4 and 12 of the Framework Convention.
15. Article 4 of the Framework Convention.
16. Article 4(2)(a) of the Framework Convention.
17. Article 3(1) of the Framework Convention.
18. Article 4(7) of the Framework Convention.
19. Articles 10 and 11 of the Kyoto Protocol.
20. Article 2 lists the various methods that may be used: enhancement of energy efficiency, protection and enhancement of sinks and reservoirs of GHGs, promotion of sustainable forms of agriculture, research on and increased use of new and renewable forms of energy, progressive reduction of market imperfections, the use of tax incentives and

subsidies, limitation and reduction of emissions of GHGs in the transport sector, and limitation and/or reduction of methane through recovery and use in waste management.

21. Article 12 of the Kyoto Protocol.
22. The methodology used to establish the baseline, that is, the emission amount that would have occurred but for the project, must be approved by the CDM Executive Board.
23. The Ad Hoc Working Group was mandated on the basis of Article 3.9 of the Kyoto Protocol, which mandates consideration of further commitments for Annex I countries at least seven years before the end of the first commitment period.
24. Strict liability is liability in the absence of fault or negligence, and arising strictly on evidence of damage caused.
25. The principle of "polluter pays," meaning that the party responsible for pollution should be automatically responsible to pay for any environmental damage, is a key principle in the Framework Convention.
26. See Tuna/Dolphin I, 30 ILM 1594 (1991) 953, 955, 960–961 and Tuna/Dolphin II, 33 ILM 839 (1991) 953, 958–961.
27. The only acceptable practice was a dolphin-safe labeling mechanism (and the denial of the label to products that did not meet the safety requirement), rather than an outright ban.
28. Article 170—EC Treaty (Maastricht consolidated version).
29. The South West Africa case (1966), and the Barcelona Traction Company case (Belgium v. Spain) (1970).
30. In the Barcelona Traction Company case (Belgium v. Spain) (1970).
31. See EC Commission, Fifth Environmental Action Programme (1992), chapter 15, n. 107.
32. See for instance Case C-321/95P, Greenpeace v. EC Commission 1998 ECR I-6151.
33. Articles 10, 13, and 14 of the Framework Convention.
34. The idea that society is now confronted by risks that are not accountable according to the prevailing rules of causality, guilt, and liability has been developed in the sociological literature on risk (see, e.g., Beck, 1992, 1995), with a clear focus on environmental issues. Beck's famous term "organized irresponsibility" describes the fact though some destructive consequences of risk might clearly originate in human or organizational decisions, no individual responsibility can be identified. This is the result of the increasing complexity of production processes, the "systemic interdependence of the highly specialized agents of modernization," where causal links are difficult to establish (Beck, 1992, p. 32).
35. CO_2 is the most important anthropogenic GHG. A CO_2-equivalent emission is the amount of CO_2 emission that would cause the same time-integrated radiative forcing, over a given time horizon, as an emitted amount of a long-lived GHG or a mixture of GHGs (IPCC, 2007, p. 36).
36. The Stern Report estimated that the stock of greenhouse gases in the atmosphere would reach 550 ppm CO_2-eq by 2050 (double preindustrial levels). To the extent the annual flow of emissions is accelerating to meet the development needs of fast-growing economies, the level of 550 ppm CO_2-eq could be reached as early as 2035. Depending on the climate model used, at this level there is at least a 77% chance (and perhaps near certainty) of a global average temperature rise exceeding 2° Celsius.

37. Under a business as usual scenario, the stock of GHGs by the end of the century could result in a 50% risk of exceeding 5° Celsius global average temperature change during the following decades.
38. Indeed, adding 1% age point to the discount rates reduces the damage cost estimates by more than half.
39. Such as potentially energy storage, photovoltaics, biofuel conversion, fusion, material science, and carbon capture and storage.
40. For instance, the damage function is poorly understood, particularly the response of developing countries and natural ecosystems to climate change (Nordhaus and Boyer, 2000, p. 172). The issue of what discount rate to use to value future outcomes is also problematic—as it may involve decision criteria that are not strictly economic (e.g., ethical judgments about intergenerational equity).

References

Bakewell, S. (2011). Second Kyoto commitment period should be eight years, Huhne Says. *Bloomberg News*, December 13, 2011. http://www.bloomberg.com/news/2011-12-13/second-kyoto-commitment-period-should-be-eight-years-huhne-says.html

Beck, U. (1992). *Risk Society*. London: SAGE.

Beck, U. (1995). *Ecological Enlightenment: Essays on the Politics of the Risk Society*. Atlantic Highlands, N.J.: Humanities Press International.

Commission on Global Governance. (1995). *Our Global Neighborhood*. Oxford: Oxford University Press.

Downie, D. L. (2005). Global environmental policy: Governance through regimes. In R. S. Axelrod and N. J. Vig (eds.), *The Global Environment: Institutions, Law and Policy*, p. 64/, Washington, DC: CQ Press.

Edenhofer, O., Lessman, K., Kemfert, C., Grubb, M., and Köhler, J. (2006). Induced technological change: Exploring its implications for the economics of atmospheric stabilization." *The Energy Journal Special Issue*, Endogenous Technological Change and the Economics of Atmospheric Stabilization.

Finus, M. (2001). *Game Theory and International Environmental Cooperation*. Northampton, MA: Elgar.

Greiner, A., Grune, L., and Semmler, W. (2010). Growth and climate change: Threshold and multiple equilibria. *Dynamic Modeling and Econometrics in Economics and Finance 12*, 63–78.

High Level Advisory Group on Climate Change Finance. (2010). *Report of the Secretary-General's High-Level Advisory Group on Climate Change Financing*. New York: United Nations.

Hood, M., and Ingham, R. (2011). "Nations set course for 2015 global climate pact." AFP, December 10, 2011. http://www.google.com/hostednews/afp/article/ALeqM5gH-FzzDQ0s8Ised7mZUbg0R4hTb1w

International Energy Agency (2010). *World Energy Outlook 2010*. Paris: Economic Co-operation and Development/International Energy Agency.

IPCC (2001). *Climate Change 2001: The Scientific Basis. Contribution of Working Group I to the Third Assessment Report of the Intergovernmental Panel on Climate Change* [T. Houghton, Y. Ding, D. J. Griggs, M. Noquer, P. J. van der Linden, X. Dai, K. Maskell and C. A. Johnson (eds.)]. Cambridge University Press, Cambridge, United Kingdom and New York, NY, USA.

IPCC (2007). Climate Change 2007: Synthesis Report. http://www.ipcc.ch/pdf/assessment-report/ar4/syr/ar4_syr.pdf

Keohane, R. O. and K. Raustiala (2008). Toward a post-Kyoto climate change architecture: A political analysis. Discussion Paper 2008-01. Cambridge, MA: Harvard Project on International Climate Agreements, July 2008.

Khor, M. (2001). Globalization and sustainable development. *International Review for Environmental Strategies, 2*(2), 210.

Kiss, A., and Shelton, D. (2007). Guide to International Environmental Law. Leiden, The Netherlands and Boston: Martinus Nijhoff.

Krukowska, E. (2011). EU agrees to extend Kyoto emission-reduction goals beyond 2012. *Bloomberg News.* http://www.bloomberg.com/news/2011-12-11/eu-agrees-to-extend-kyoto-emission-reduction-goals-beyond-2012.html

Ljunggren, D., and Palmer, R. (2011). Canada to pull out of Kyoto protocol. Reuters. http://business.financialpost.com/2011/12/13/canada-to-pull-out-of-kyoto-protocol/?__lsa=c13b575b

Luck-Baker, A. (2002, January 4). Earth summit: Decade of failure. *BBC News.* http://news.bbc.co.uk/2/hi/americas/1741164.stm

Nordhaus, W. (1994). *Managing the Global Commons: The Economics of Climate Change.* Cambridge, MA: MIT Press.

Nordhaus, W. (2007). The Challenges of Global Warming: Economic Models and Environmental Policy. Yale University. http://www.climatechangeecon.net/index.php?option=com_mtree&task=viewlink&link_id=1147&Itemid

Nordhaus, W., and Boyer, J. (2000). *Warming the World: Economic Models of Global Warming.* Cambridge, MA: MIT Press.

Nordhaus, W., and Yang, Z. (1996). A regional dynamic general-equilibrium model of alternative climate-change strategies. *American Economic Review, 86*(4), pp. 741–765.

Sands, P. (2003). *Principles of International Environmental Law,* 2nd ed. New York: Cambridge University Press.

Speth, J. G. (2004). International environmental law: Can it deal with the big issues? *Vermont Law Review, 28*(3), 780.

Speth, J. G., and Haas, P. (2006). *Global Environmental Governance.* Washington, DC: Island Press.

Stern, N. (2006). What is the economic impact of climate change? Stern Review on the Economics of Climate Change, Final Report. http://webarchive.nationalarchives.gov.uk/+/http://www.hmtreasury.gov.uk/independent_reviews/stern_review_economics_climate_change/stern_review_report.cfm

Vidal, J. (2010, December 2). Cancún climate change summit: Japan accused of threatening Kyoto Protocol. *The Guardian.*http://www.guardian.co.uk/environment/2010/dec/02/japan-stance-kyoto-protocol

Weitzman, M. (2007). The Stern Review of the Economics of Climate Change. *Journal of Economic Literature, 45*, 703–724.

World Bank. (2010). World Development Report 2010: Development and Climate Change. Washington, DC: The International Bank for Reconstruction and Development / The World Bank.

CHAPTER 26

ENVIRONMENT AND DEVELOPMENT CHALLENGES

The Imperative of A Carbon Fee and Dividend

JAMES E. HANSEN

MOST governments have paid little attention to the threat of human-made climate change. They have acknowledged its likely existence, notably in the United Nations Framework Convention on Climate Change (UNFCCC, 1992), in which 195 nations agreed to avoid "dangerous anthropogenic interference" with climate. However, the instrument chosen to implement the Framework Convention, the Kyoto Protocol, is so ineffectual that global fossil fuel carbon dioxide (CO_2) emissions have increased by about 3% per year since its adoption in 1997, as opposed to a growth rate of 1.5% per year in the decades preceding the Kyoto Protocol [http://www.columbia.edu/~mhs119/Emissions/, which is an update of a graph in Hansen and Sato (2001)].

This feckless path cannot continue much longer, if there is to be hope of preserving a planet resembling the one on which civilization developed, a world that avoids the economic devastation of continually receding shorelines and the moral nightmare of having exterminated a large fraction of the species on Earth. The science is clear enough: burning most fossil fuels would invoke such consequences (Hansen et al., 2013).

At least a moderate overshoot of climate change into the dangerous zone is unavoidable now, but, fortunately, prompt actions initiating a change of directions this decade could minimize the impacts on humanity and nature. The policies needed to produce a rapid phase-out of fossil fuel emissions would have a wide range of other benefits for the public, especially in those nations that recognize the advantages in being early adopters of effective policies. So there is some basis for optimism that the political will necessary to enact effective policies could be marshaled.

However, for this to happen it is essential that the next approach not repeat the fundamental mistakes that doomed the Kyoto Protocol. If another 15 years is wasted on an ineffectual approach, it will be too late to avoid catastrophic consequences for today's young people and future generations. Therefore it is important to clarify the principal flaws in the Kyoto approach from the standpoint of climate science.

26.1 Kyoto Protocol

A fundamental flaw of the Kyoto approach is that it was based on a "cap" mechanism. This approach embodies two ineluctable problems. First, it made it impossible to find a formula for emission caps that was equitable among nations and also reduced carbon emissions at the rate required to stabilize climate. Second, it failed to provide clear price signals that would reward businesses, individuals and nations that led the way in reducing emissions.

The validity of the first assertion can be proven by comparing national responsibilities for climate change, which are proportional to cumulative historical emissions (Hansen et al., 2007; Hansen, 2009). The United Kingdom, United States, and Germany have per capita responsibilities exceeding the responsibilities of China and India by almost a factor of ten (Hansen et al., 2007). Even if the United Kingdom, United States, and Germany terminated emissions tomorrow, by the time China, India and other developing nations reached comparable responsibility for climate change the world would be on a course headed to certain climate disasters.

26.2 Key Points: Why a Carbon Fee and Dividend Is Imperative

1. There is a limit on fossil fuel carbon dioxide that we can pour into the atmosphere without guaranteeing unacceptably tragic, immoral climatic consequences for young people and nature.
2. It is clear that we will soon pass the limit on carbon emissions, because it requires decades to replace fossil fuel energy infrastructure with carbon-neutral and carbon-negative energies.
3. Climate system inertia, which delays full climate response to human-made changes of atmospheric composition, is both our friend and foe. The delay

allows moderate overshoot of the sustainable carbon load, but it also brings the danger of passing a climatic point of no return that sets in motion a series of catastrophic events out of humanity's control.

4. The ineffectual paradigm of prior efforts to reign in carbon emissions must be replaced by one in which an across-the-board rising carbon fee is collected from fossil fuel companies at the place where the fossil fuel enters a domestic market, that is, at the domestic mine or port-of-entry.
5. All funds collected from fossil fuel companies should be distributed to the public. This is needed for the public to endorse a substantial continually rising carbon price and to provide individuals the wherewithal to phase in needed changes in energy-use choices.

It is unrealistic to think that a "cap" approach can be made global or near-global. Nations less responsible for the world's climate predicament believe, with considerable justification, that they should not have to adhere to caps on CO_2 emissions (much less steadily shrinking caps) that are comparable to caps on industrialized countries. At the same time, some industrialized countries, including the United States, refuse to bind themselves to caps that are more stringent than those imposed on developing countries. This impasse cannot be resolved under a cap approach. Indeed, the targets adopted to date with a cap approach have been but a drop in the bucket compared to the reductions required to stabilize climate.

A secondary, but important, flaw of the Kyoto approach is its introduction of "offsets." Nations are allowed to limit reduction of fossil fuel emissions by means of alternative actions such as tree planting or reduced emissions of non-CO_2 climate forcings such as methane or chlorofluorocarbons. However, these offsets are not equivalent to fossil fuel emissions, because the fossil fuel carbon will stay in surface carbon reservoirs (atmosphere, ocean, soil, biosphere) for millennia. Rapid phase-out of fossil fuel emissions, as required to stabilize climate, becomes implausible if leakage is permitted via offsets. Leakage is avoided via the flat across-the-board carbon fee on fossil fuels in the fee-and-dividend approach. Incentives to reduce non-CO_2 climate forcings will be useful, but such programs should not be allowed to interfere with the more fundamental requirement of phasing out fossil fuel CO_2 emissions.

26.3 Fee and Dividend

Fee-and-dividend (Hansen, 2009) has a flat fee (a single number specified in US$ per tonne of CO_2) collected from fossil fuel companies covering domestic sales of all fossil fuels. Collection cost is trivial, as there are only a small number of collection points: the first sale at domestic mines and at the port-of-entry for imported fossil fuels. All funds collected from the fee are distributed electronically (to bank account or debit card) monthly to legal residents of the country in equal per capita amounts. Citizens using less than average fossil fuels (more than 60% of the public with current distribution of energy use) will therefore receive more in their monthly dividend than they pay in increased prices. But all individuals will have a strong incentive to reduce their carbon footprint in order to stay on the positive side of the ledger or improve their position.

The carbon fee would start small and rise at a rate that sows benefits of economic stimulation while minimizing economic disruptions from sudden change. Economic efficiency requires the price of fossil fuels to rise toward a level that matches their cost to society. At present fossil fuels are the dominant energy only because the environmental and social costs are externalized onto society as a whole rather than being internalized into their prices (G-20 Summit Team, 2010). Human health costs due to air and water pollution from mining and burning of fossil fuels are borne by the public, as are costs of climate change that have been estimated at US$100–1000/t$CO_2$ (Ackerman et al., 2009).

26.4 International Implementation

When the reality and consequences of the climate threat become clear enough the international community should recognize that all nations are in the same boat and that the fruitless cap-and-trade-with-offsets approach must be abandoned. The reality is that the Kyoto Protocol and proposed replacements are "indulgences" schemes Hansen (Hansen, 2009), which allow aggressive development of fossil fuels to continue worldwide. Developing countries acquiesce if sufficient payments for offsets and adaptation are provided. This works fine for adults in developed and developing countries today, but this abuse of young people and future generations must eventually end as the facts become widely apparent.

A fundamental fact is that as long as fossil fuels are allowed to be cheap, via subsidies and failure to pay their costs to society, they will be burned. Even ostensibly successful caps have no significant benefit. They simply reduce demand for the fuel, thus lowering its price and creating incentives for it to be burned somewhere by somebody. What is required is an approach that results in economically efficient phase-out of fossil fuels, with replacement by energy efficiency and carbon-free energy sources such as renewable energy and nuclear power.

Specifically, there must be a flat (across-the-board) rising fee (tax) on carbon emissions. With such a flat fee, collected by the energy-using nation at its domestic mines and ports of entry, there is no need for trading carbon permits or financial derivatives based on them. Indeed the price oscillations inherent in carbon trading drown out the price signals. The required rapid phase-out of fossil fuels and phase-in of alternatives requires that businesses and consumers be confident that the fee will continue to rise. Another flaw of trading is the fact that it necessarily brings big banks into the matter—and all of the bank profits are extracted from the public via increased energy prices.

A carbon fee (tax) approach can be made global much more readily than cap-and-trade (Hsu, 2011). For example, say a substantial economic block (e.g., Europe and the United States or Europe and China) agrees to have a carbon tax. They would place border duties on products from nations without an equivalent carbon tax, based on a standard estimates of fossil fuels used in production of the product. Such a border tax is allowed by rules of the World Trade Organization, with the proviso that exporters who can document that their production uses less fossil fuels than the standard will be assigned an appropriately adjusted border duty. Border duties will create a strong incentive for exporting nations to impose their own carbon tax, so they can collect the funds rather than have them collected by the importing country.

Once the inevitability of a rising carbon price is recognized, the economic advantages of being an early adopter of fee-and-dividend will spur its implementation. These include improved economic efficiency of honest energy pricing and a head-start in development of energy-efficient and low-carbon products. The potential economic gains to middle and lower income citizens who minimize their carbon footprint will address concerns of people in many nations where citizens are becoming restive about growing wealth disparities. Note that the effect of a carbon price on upper class citizens is modest and nonthreatening except to a handful of fossil fuel moguls who extract obscene profits from the public's dependence on fossil fuels. An added social benefit of fee-and-dividend is its impact on illegal immigration—by providing a strong economic incentive for immigrants to become legal, it provides an approach for slowing and even reversing illegal immigration that will be more effective than border patrols.

26.5 National Implementation

The greatest barriers to solution of fossil fuel addiction in most nations are the influence of the fossil fuel industry on politicians and the media and the short-term view of politicians. Thus it is possible that leadership moving the world to sustainable energy policies may arise in China (Hansen, 2010), where the leaders are rich in technical and scientific training and rule a nation that has a history of taking the long view. Although China's CO_2 emissions have skyrocketed above those of other nations, China has reasons to move off the fossil fuel track as rapidly as practical. China has several hundred million people living within a 25-meter elevation of sea level, and the country stands to suffer grievously from intensification of droughts, floods, and storms that will accompany continued global warming (IPCC, 2007; Hansen, 2009; Hansen et al., 2013). China also recognizes the merits of avoiding a fossil fuel addiction comparable to that of the United States. Thus China has already become the global leader in development of energy efficiency, renewable energies, and nuclear power.

Conceivably the threat of impending second-class economic status could stir the United States into action, but it is imperative that the action contain no remnant of prior cap-and-trade fiascos, which were loaded with giveaways to big banks, big utilities, big coal and big oil. The approach must be simple and clear, with the fee rising steadily and 100% of the collected revenue distributed to legal residents on a per capita basis.

The fee-and-dividend approach allows the market place to select technology winners. The government should not choose favorites, that is, subsidies should be eliminated for all energies, not just fossil fuels. This approach will spur innovation, stimulating the economy as price signals encourage the public to adopt energy efficiency and clean energies. All materials and services will naturally incorporate fossil fuel costs. For example, sustainable food products from nearby farms will gain an advantage over highly fertilized products from halfway around the world.

The carbon price will need to start small, growing as the public gains confidence that they are receiving 100% of the proceeds. If the fee begins at US\$15/tCO_2 and rises \$10 per year, the rate after 10 years would be equivalent to about US\$1 per gallon of gasoline. Given today's fossil fuel use in the United States, that tax rate would generate about US\$600 billion per year, thus providing dividends of about US\$2000 per legal adult resident or about US\$6000 per year for a family with two or more children, with half a share for each child up to two children per family.

The proposal for a gradually rising fee on carbon emissions collected from fossil fuel companies with proceeds fully distributed to the public was praised in the United States by the policy director of Republicans for Environmental Protection (Dipeso, 2010) as: "Transparent. Market-based. Does not enlarge government. Leaves energy decisions to individual choices ... Sounds like a conservative climate plan."

A grassroots organization, Citizens Climate Lobby, has been formed in the United States and Canada with the objective of promoting fee-and-dividend. My advice to this organization is adoption of a motto "100% or fight," because politicians are certain to try to tap such a large revenue stream. Already there are suggestions that part of the proceeds should be used "to pay down the national debt," a euphemism for the fact that it would become just another tax thrown into the pot. Supporters of young people and climate stabilization will need to have the determination and discipline shown by the "Tea Party" movement if they are to successfully overcome the forces for fossil fuel business-as-usual.

26.6 Global Strategic Situation

Europe is the region where citizens and political leaders have been most aware of the urgency of slowing fossil fuel emissions. Given the stranglehold that the fossil fuel industry has achieved on energy policies in the United States, it is natural to look to Europe for leadership. Yet Europe, despite dismal experience with cap-and-trade-with-offsets, continues to push this feckless approach, perhaps because of bureaucratic inertia and vested interests of individuals. China, at least in the short run, likely would be only too happy to continue such a framework, as the "offsets" have proven to be a cash cow for China.

The cap-and-trade-with-offsets framework, set up with the best of intentions, fails to make fossil fuels pay their costs to society, thus allowing fossil fuel addiction to continue and encouraging "drill, baby, drill" policies to extract every fossil fuel that can be found. There is a desperate need for global political leaders who can see through special financial interests and understand the actions required to achieve a bright future for young people and the planet. Perhaps such leaders exist—the problem is really not *that* difficult.

Acknowledgments

I thank Shi-Ling Hsu and Charles Komanoff for useful reviews and suggestions.

References

Ackerman, F., DeCanio, S., Howarth, R., and Sheeran, K. (2009). Limitations of integrated assessment models of climate change. *Climatic Change, 95*, 297–315.

Citizens Climate Lobby: http://citizensclimatelobby.org/

Dipeso, J., 2010: Jim Hansen's conservative climate plan, blog post at Republican's for Environmental Protection, October 11, 2010. http://www.rep.org/opinions/weblog/weblog10-10-11.html

G-20 Summit Team (2010). *Analysis of the Scope of Energy Subsidies and Suggestions for the G-20 Initiative.* Library of Official G-20 Documents and Related Reports, http://www.iisd.org/gsi/library-official-g-20-documents-and-related-reports-0

Hansen, J. (2009). *Storms of My Grandchildren.* New York: Bloomsbury.

Hansen, J., and Sato, M. (2001). Trends of measured climate forcing agents. *Proceedings of the National Academy of Sciences of the USA, 98*, 14778–14783.

Hansen, J., Kharecha, P, Sato, M., Masson-Delmotte, V., Ackerman, F., Beerling, D.J., Hearty, P.J., Hoegh-Guldberg, O., Hsu, S.L., Parmesan, C., Rockstrom, J., Rohling, E.J., Sachs, J., Smith, P., Steffen, K., Van Susteren, L., von Schuckmann, K., and Zachos, J.C. (2013). Assessing "dangerous climate change": Required reduction of carbon emissions to protect young people, future generations and nature. *PLoS ONE, 8*(12), e81648.

Hansen, J., Sato, M., Ruedy, R., Kharecha, P., Lacis, A., Miller, R., Nazarenko, L., Lo, K., Schmidt, G.A., Russell, G., Aleinov, I., Bauer, S., Baum, E., Cairns, B., Canuto, V., Chandler, M., Cheng, Y. Cohen, A., Del Genio, A. Faluvegi, G., Fleming, E., Friend, A., Hall, T., Jackman, C., Jonas, J., Kelley, M., Kiang, N.Y., Koch, D., Labow, G., Lerner, J., Menon, S., Novakov, T., Oinas, V., Perlwitz, Ja., Perlwitz, Ju., Rind, D., Romanou, A., Schmunk, R., Shindell, D., Stone, P., Sun, S., Streets, D., Tausnev, N., Thresher, D., Unger, N., Yao, M., and Shang, S. (2007). Dangerous human-made interference with climate: A GISS modelE study. *Atmospheric Chemistry and Physics, 7,* 2287–2312.

Hansen, J. E. (2010). China and the barbarians: Part 1. http://www.columbia.edu/~jeh1/mailings/20101124_ChinaBarbarians1.pdf

Hsu, S.-L. (2011). *The Case for a Carbon Tax.* Washington, DC: Island Press.

IPCC. 2007: *Climate Change 2007, Impacts, Adaptation and Vulnerability. Contribution of Working Group II to the Fourth Assessment Report of the Intergovernmental Panel on Climate Change (IPCC).* [Parry, M. L., Canziani, O. F., Palutikof, J. P., Van Der Linden, P. J., and Hanson, C. E. eds.]. Cambridge University Press, Cambridge, United Kingdom and New York, NY, USA.

UNFCCC. (1992). United Nations. http://www.unfccc.int.

CHAPTER 27

THE NEED FOR SUSTAINABLE DEVELOPMENT AND A CARBON MARKET

Avoiding Extinction

GRACIELA CHICHILNISKY

27.1 Introduction

For the first time ever, humans dominate planet Earth. We are changing the basic metabolism of the planet: the composition of gases in the atmosphere, the integrity of its bodies of water, and the complex web of species that makes life on Earth. Geologists recognize that we have entered a new period that can be read in rock formations, called the Anthropocene. What comes next?

The changes we are precipitating in the atmosphere are fundamental and can lead to disruptions in climate and global warming. Signals abound: in the Southern Hemisphere alpine glaciers and Antarctic ice sheets are melting; in the Northern Hemisphere Alaska's permafrost is melting, sinking entire towns whose inhabitants are being relocated at a cost of $140,000 per person. Greenland's ice sheet is gone, creating hostile climate conditions for a number of species that are now close to extinction such as the polar bear. In Patagonia and the Alps we observe mountains without ice or glaciers, reducing the ability of these regions to store water needed for human consumption. In the Caribbean seas 50% of corals are already extinct. Desertification has overtaken 25% of China's land mass. Climatic instability has led to Australia's longest draught on record, followed by the worst floods in that continent's history. We observe disappearing summer ice in the Arctic Seas and soil erosion and storm surges in Alaska. Where is all of this coming from? The rapid industrialization of wealthy nations during the last century since the end of WWII is responsible for most of the changes and for the risks they entail. Historically the industrialized nations in the Organisation of Economic Cooperation and Development (OECD) originated 70% (now still 60%) of all global emissions of carbon, emissions that most scientists in the world, including those in the United Nations Intergovernmental Panel on Climate Change (IPCC), believe to cause climate change. China's relentless industrial growth over the last two decades is a sign of things to come: it accelerates the risk of climate change and underscores the fact that in 20 or 30 years into the future most emissions could come from today's poor nations as they assume their turn to industrialize.

Water expands when it warms. Because the seas are warming they are rising all over the world. This irrevocable upward trend is well documented: slowly but surely the rising waters will sink the Maldives and most other island states—there are 43 island states in the United Nations representing about 20% of the global vote, and most or all could disappear soon under the warming seas.

The current shift in climate patterns has led to habitat changes for many insect species and therefore vector illnesses, for example, new outbreaks of malaria in Africa. Twenty-five million people are reportedly migrating because of drought and other climate change conditions, and the numbers are increasing rapidly.

In the United States the consequences are less extreme but they stack up: the mighty Colorado River is drying up, its basin under stress prompts orders to turn off farm water. In Nevada, Lake Mead's waters exhibit record lows, threatening the main supply of water to Las Vegas, and arid areas are spreading quickly as Vegas' new sites double water use. Wild fires from drought conditions have multiplied and spread rapidly around the region, including California since 2006. Miami is the lead US city at risk from the raising seas.

The world is aware of the connection that scientists postulate between climate change and the use of fossil energy. Even in the United States the majority of the population now recognizes this link (Pew Poll January 2013). The largest segment of carbon emissions, 45% of all global emissions of carbon dioxide (CO_2), originate in the world's power plant infrastructure, 87% of which are fossil fuel plants that produce the overwhelming majority of the world's electricity. This power plant infrastructure is worth US$55 trillion according to the International Energy Agency (IEA), about the size of the world's economic output. New forms of clean energy are emerging such as wind farms in Scotland and solar farms in Spain and elsewhere in an attempt to forestall carbon emissions. But the process is slow because the world's fossil power plant infrastructure is comparable to the world's entire gross domestic product (GDP), and changing this infrastructure will take decades. This time frame—several decades—is too slow to avert the potential catastrophes that are anticipated in the next 10–20 years. What, then, is the solution?

Below we propose a realistic plan that involves market solutions in both industrial and developing nations, simultaneously resolving the problems of economic development and climate change, and their implementation within the UN global climate negotiations. Critical in this plan is the Carbon Market of the Kyoto Protocol that I designed and wrote into the Kyoto Protocol in December 1997 and became international law in 2005. The Carbon Market, we show, can change the value of all goods and services in the world economy, since everything is made with energy and with the Carbon Market clean energy is more profitable and attractive while fossil energy becomes more expensive and less profitable. The Carbon Market was designed and negotiated by the author with the US Treasury, the US State Department, and US Congress, and its creation was announced at a key note presentation to the World Bank Annual Meetings in December 1996 by the author, through participation within the United Nations as a whole and from a position as US Lead Author in the IPCC (Chichilnisky and Sheeran, 2009). The words that made it a reality were written into the Kyoto Protocol by the author in the United Nations Framework Convention on Climate Change Convention of the Parties (COP) at the 1997 meetings in Kyoto Japan working with the French Delegation and the Lead Negotiator of the Kyoto Protocol, Ambassador Raul Estrada-Oyuela (Chichilnisky and Sheeran, 2009). In the text that follows we discuss two official proposals made by the author since the Carbon Market became international law in 2005, to fully utilize its potential, both introduced in 2009 at the Copenhagen Convention of the Parties (COP 15). These have become or are becoming international law and have the potential to change the entire climate regime for the better: one is to incorporate carbon-negative technologies into the Clean Development Mechanism of the UN Carbon Market and the second is the creation of a US$200 billion/year Green Power Fund using the Carbon Market $250 billion that is traded annually (the World Bank, 2012), a fund that would build carbon-negative power plants in developing nations and particularly in Latin America, Africa and the Small Island States.

The climate change issue is just one of several global environmental areas that are in crisis today. Biodiversity is another: industrialization and climate warming threaten ecosystems. Endangered species include sea mammals; birds such as cockatoos; polar bears; and marine life such as coral, sawfish, whales, sharks, dogfish, sea turtles, skates, grouper, seals, rays, and bass; even the survival of primates, our cousins in evolution is at risk. Scientists know that in the Anthropocene we are in the midst of the sixth largest extinction of biodiversity in the history of Planet Earth, and that the scope of extinction is so large that 75% of all known species are at risk today. The UN Millennium Report documents rates of extinction 1,000 times higher than is found in fossil records. The current sixth largest extinction event follows the dinosaurs' extinction, which took place 65 million years ago. But today's extinction event is unique in that it is caused, created, by human activity. It puts our own species at risk. There is a warning signal worth bringing up: all major recorded planetary extinctions were related to changes in climate conditions. Through industrialization and our first global economic institutions—the Bretton Woods Institutions—we have created environmental conditions that could put our own species' survival at risk. This is the reason for an official proposal made to the United Nations Economic and Social Commission for Asia and the Pacific (UNESCAP) by the author for the creation of global markets that emulate the Carbon Market for biodiversity and for water bodies (Chichilnisky, 2012).

99.9% of all species that ever existed are now extinct. Are we to be next? Will humans survive? The issue now is how to avoid extinction.

27.2 Survival and Avoiding Extinction

To avoid extinction we have to develop social survival skills. This seems reasonable and natural—yet the social skills that are needed are not here and are not obvious either. They could be quite different from what human societies recognize as individual survival skills. A simple but somewhat unexpected experimental finding involves colonies of bacteria, microorganisms that are the world's oldest living species. They have been around for billions of years and biologists agree that they have shaped the planet's geology and atmosphere to suit their needs. Bacteria are champions of survival. They have developed some unexpected skills based on "altruism." Since bacteria are some of the longest lived species in the planet, many times longer lived than the relatively recent humanoids, we need to take their survival skills seriously as a model of survival. Bacterial colonies know how to avoid extinction. New findings indicate that *Escherichia coli*—and indeed most known bacterial colonies—when exposed to a pathogen or stressor such as antibiotics—not only evolve to develop resistance but the evolved members also produce specific resistance tools that they do not need themselves in order to share them with the rest of the (nonevolved) members of the colony that are still at risk (Hyun Youk and Alexander van Oudenaarden, 2010). In other words—when exposed to stress, mutant bacteria use some of their own energy—"altruistically"—to create a chemical called indole that protects nonmutants from the pathogen. This way the entire group survives. A way to summarize this finding is to say that *altruism* is an effective survival tool and bacteria—those champions of survival—have developed and mastered altruism for this task.

This finding is quite different from what we believe to be effective survival skills in human colonies or societies. Until now human survival skills have focused on avoiding natural risks and confronting successfully the threats posed by other humans or other species that preyed on us, species that are dangerous to us. Altruism is often considered a weakness in human societies; it is thought of as a desirable trait rather than a survival skill. Yet, it is a survival skill. Aggressive and individualistic behavior may have been a useful survival tool until now. The war society that humans have created has become an efficient killing machine. But when things change, as they are changing right now, what used to be a strength can become a weakness. And things have fundamentally changed and they continue to evolve quickly. Indeed physical strength and aggression matter much less today for human survival than intelligence does. This may have been true all along but has not been seriously recognized. Some of the worst risks we face today are caused not by other species that prey on us, but by traits that evolved to succeed against our predators—for example, extracting energy and burning fossil fuel to dominate nature and other species. In other words, we are now at risk due to the impact of human dominance on the planet. Our success as a species has become the source of our main risks. Humans are causing some of the worst risks humans face. The situation is somewhat unusual and is new for our species; it is also new for the planet itself. As the situation changes, the rules we used to follow for survival must change too.

Let's start from basic principles. Survival is about protecting life, not just about fighting against others and inducing death. Life may be difficult to define, but we all agree that it is a phenomenon characterized by reproduction. Only those systems that incorporate reproduction are said to be alive. Life forms are able to reproduce. To be alive means to be part of a time series of reproductive activities. Reproduction characterizes life. Destruction does not. Asteroids destroy very effectively, and so do volcanoes. But they are not alive, because they do not reproduce. We humans are alive because we do.

Reproduction fundamentally requires altruism rather than dominance and aggression. How so? This is simple. We must donate our energy and even our bodily resources and substance to be able to reproduce, sometimes at the cost of our own.

Survival is often viewed as the ability to conquer, dominate, and kill. War is an example. Ask any man what characterizes life: a common answer would be "the survival of the fittest" and "dog eats dog," which is a typical view of life that reflects the evolutionary role that males originally had in human societies, a role that is now somewhat outdated. The reality is that humans could not be alive and indeed we could not be part of the chain of life on Earth, unless we successfully reproduce. Women understand that reproduction means life, and that it requires altruism. They donate their physical substance such as eggs, blood, and milk—and they do so voluntarily—for the sake of reproduction. All living beings—animals and plants—do the same. They donate their substance voluntarily to the next generation, sometimes at the cost of their own welfare and their own lives. Observe that donating voluntarily one's own substance, one's flesh and body fluids, is the very essence of altruism, and that this altruistic donation is the key to the survival of the species. The great British author and social commentator Jonathan Swift once satirically suggested, as a "modest proposal" to the problem of famines in Ireland, that humans should eat their own children (Swift, 1729). If the essence of life was the survival of the fittest, then humans would eat their children who are totally powerless at birth—nothing is less fit than new born infants.

The question is: why don't we follow Swift's "modest proposal"? Why not eat our own children?

No species that ate its children would survive—it may not even get started as a species. Survival depends crucially on reproduction and this means protecting the weakest of all—the small children. This is quite different from the blanket policy of survival of the fittest, which are the adult members of the species. Indeed, I venture to say that survival is more than anything about altruism and cooperation, and about the protection of the weakest. It is not about "dog eat dog"—it is not about dominance and survival of the fittest. It is about the nurturing and protection of new generations; it is about voluntary donations, about protection and nurturing of the weakest, sometimes at the expense of our own survival. These are facts of life, facts that women understand well. The precise features of this point can be disputed, but the general drift of the argument—that our society is more aggressive and violent than would be desirable and that it gives relative little importance to nurturing and altruism—is not contested. In the United States the recent Newton, Connecticut incident where 22 small school children and 6 adults were tragically killed touched a raw nerve, and based on this the Obama Administration is now attempting to decrease the availability of arms that is guaranteed in the US constitution "the right to bear arms" in an attempt to decrease the consequences of mindless violence. And in his acceptance speech in January 2013, President Obama paraphrased the points made here about the need to nurture and support each other in order to improve our lives and our society.

Women are critical to human survival, as they are key to reproduction and they provide voluntarily their substance and energy to give birth and protect the weakest as needed for the survival of the human species. Yet their role and importance in society is minimized and indeed there is endemic and persistent violence and abuse of women that even the US Congress recognizes and is trying to correct in "Violence against Women" legislation. It is true that there have been changes in the role of women, most of all their rapid entrance in the market for labor in industrial societies. But this change has not been fast enough. Modern societies like the United States have enormously high rates of abuse of women at home and elsewhere, both physical and economic abuse. For example, the United States has a 30% gender difference in salaries, which is not budging. These are the salaries that are paid to men and women even when comparing men and women with equal training, same age and experience, with everything other than gender being equal. The gender inequality is prevailing, persistent, and systematic. In any given society, there is a deep connection statistically between the amount of housework a woman does at home and the difference between male and female salaries in the economy as a whole. These are two different statistics that are apparently unrelated—two indices of abuse—but they are indeed related, because when women are overworked and underpaid at home this leads them to be overworked and underpaid in the marketplace (Chichilnisky, 2011). Gender inequality in salaries is in reality legally sanctioned—for example, the United States still does not have an Equal Pay Act. Unequal pay is legal in the United States. Why? Is there a reason to pay women less than men? If so, what is it?

The deepest suspicion created by sexism to explain the persistent unequal situation is based on a rationale of the "genetic inferiority" of women. Even a former president of the oldest University in the United States, Harvard University, Larry Summers, presented this suspicion in public as a plausible hypothesis to explain the persistent 30% difference in salaries between women and men in our economy, explicitly mentioning the genetic interiority or women in the sciences. Furthermore, when he was subsequently fired by the Harvard University faculty he served, he went on to become the lead economic advisor of President Barack Obama. One wonders whether Mr. Summers would have been selected as an economic advisor of the president of the United

States—the first black president—if he had presented in public suspicions about the genetic inferiority of blacks. I venture to say that he may not have been selected by Barack Obama if he had said in public that blacks were genetically inferior. But saying this about women is acceptable, and indeed he was rewarded despite his unfortunate public statements about women. This was an amazing and very discouraging event for some of us, but not for the many US men who secretly or openly believe that women are indeed genetically inferior to men.

Raising in public the hypothesis of the genetically inferiority of women is not an innocent remark. The issue of genetic inferiority is often raised in racial contexts; it is an argument used to justify ideology and a systematic way in which our societies perpetrate economic and cultural abuse, violence and brutality against women, pornography, sexual slavery, torture of women and rape, which is sufficiently acknowledged that US Congress is currently voting policies to outlaw violence against women. Ultimately this represents a form of control and intimidation and reveals a deep social instinct against the altruism, protection of the weak, and reproductive sensibility that women bring to society and that is a necessary precondition for the survival of the human species. Until we change the current male-dominated culture of abuse and its barbaric treatment of women, as US Congress is attempting to do, until we revolt against the seeming acceptance of electronic games that the US Supreme Court found acceptable for children in their recent 2011 decision, games involving the systematic torture and killing of women as entertainment, and until we develop altruism and nurturing as efficient survival skills, our society will not be well prepared to avoid extinction and to survive.

The role of women extends to a critical issue of sustainable development: the provision of abundant energy that is the immediate source of economic growth in all societies. Survival in poor and in rich nations depends on the availability of energy, and in poor nations—which house 80% of the world's population—women are often the providers of energy in fetching wood and dung for heat and cooking, providing water and food supplies for human consumption. In explaining how we can develop a sustainable form of energy production, this chapter will explain how the current role of women can evolve from beast of burden that are the main providers of energy, and how these societies can replace women's physical labor by clean and abundant forms of energy that provide the foundation for sustainable development the world over.

The future of humankind will be played out in the rest of this 21st century. Here is a summary of the situation and what to do about it.

First let's take stock of the world today: in a nutshell we see energy limits confronting enormous global needs for energy today and in the future. Energy use is supposed to double in the next 20–30 years, most of which will occur in developing nations. The problem of overuse of natural resources, more generally, continues to be a clash of civilizations: it is a North/South impasse in using the world's resources. The North includes the rich OECD nations that inhabit mostly the Northern Hemisphere of Earth, while the South represents the poor. The former have about 20% of the world population, and the latter, about 80%. We will examine the market's role in getting us here and in finding a solution, and define building blocks that are needed for a solution going forward. We will discuss the next generation of green markets: how to bridge the global wealth gap and to transform capitalism as needed for this purpose—and finally, we will examine whether and how what we envision is possible. We will examine the role of the United Nations Kyoto Protocol and its Carbon Market in this global transformation process—by itself and in conjunction with other global markets for environmental resources that are critical for our survival, water and biodiversity. We will examine the critical role of women and how the global financial crisis fits into all this, what is the light it throws onto our future, and what lessons we have learned. It can be said that avoiding extinction is the ultimate goal of Sustainable Development.

27.3 Green Capitalism and the Financial and Global Environmental Crisis

While we try to climb up from the depths of a global financial crisis that started its deadliest stages in 2008, the world knows that the game is not over yet. Judging by the threats from the Eurozone, it could all re-start next year. The recent downgrading of the United States as a debtor nation—for the first time in history—and its financial markets' shocks underscore these points. At the same time, within a larger historical context, the financial crisis takes a second place. We have seen such a crisis before. What we have never seen before is the global threat to human survival that is developing in front of our own startled eyes (Vivek and Montenegro, 2011). We are in the midst of a global environmental crisis that started with the dawn of industrialization but was accelerated and exacerbated by globalization, ever since the Bretton Woods Institutions were created after World War II to provide a financial infrastructure for international markets and to expand the role of markets and industrialization across the world economy. In both cases financial mechanisms are at work, and financial markets are implicated. Both the financial crisis and the environmental crisis are essentially two aspects of the same problem. How so?

Examples are available through the media and read by the average person on the street. The urgency of the situation has become clear. For example, on Tuesday, June 21, 2011, *The Times* newspaper in London wrote, "Marine life is facing mass extinction," and explained: "The effects of overfishing, pollution and climate change are far worse than we thought." The assessment of the International Program on the State of the Oceans (IPSO) suggests that a "deadly trio" of factors—climate change, pollution, and overfishing—are acting together in ways that exacerbate individual impacts, and that "the health of the oceans is deteriorating far more rapidly than expected. Scientists predict that marine life could be on the brink of mass extinction." Observe that *all the three causes* of extinction just mentioned—overfishing, pollution, and climate change—are attributable to the industrialized world, which consumes the majority of the marine life used as sea food, which generates more than 60% of the global emissions of carbon dioxide and which uses 70% of the world's energy, all this while housing only 20% of the world's population. Economic factors such as international trade in biodiversity resources (Chichilnisky, 1994), economic policies focused on natural resource exports—petroleum, raw materials—that have been strongly encouraged in the developing nations by the Bretton Woods Institutions such as the International Monetary Fund and the World Bank, and their financial policies in debt and trade, all have been at work in the impending destruction and mass extinction in the earth's seas, the origin of life as we know it (Chichilnisky, 1994, 2011, 2012; Peters et al., 2011; Lenzen et al., 2012). Economics as a science has been slow in recognizing the situation, which is relegated to the new area of environmental economics. Mainstream economists are starting to recognize the issues, but the transition is slow and may not get there on a timescale that matters. Nicholas Stern (2006) has called the situation with carbon emissions "the largest externality in the history of humankind" to indicate the difficulty of current market structures in recognizing and valuing the costs to the environment and the benefits of environmentally sound policies. It is baffling for economic science as we know it.

The complexity of the problem is also baffling scientists. Normally the Earth self-regulates, but now we are tying the Earth's hands, preventing it from self-regulating and therefore rescuing itself from the problem industrialization has created. There is no quick fix. The standard way that the planet regulates carbon, by sucking carbon from the atmosphere to maintain a balance, is by using its vegetation mass in land and seas, which breathes CO_2 and emits oxygen. Animals—humans included—do exactly the opposite. Animals breathe in oxygen and emit CO_2. In balance, the two sets of species—vegetation mass and animals—maintain a stable mix of CO_2 and oxygen, and therefore since CO_2 in the atmosphere regulates its temperature, a stable climate. But the enormous use of energy by industrial societies is tipping the scales, preventing the planet from readjusting.[1]

Observe that it is not the developing nations with 80% of the world's population that are causing this problem. This is because more than 70% of the energy used in the world today is used by 20% of the world population that lives in industrial nations, who emit 60% of the CO_2. These are the same industrial nations that created the Bretton Woods Institutions in 1945 and have consumed since then the overwhelming amount of all the Earth's resources (Chichilnisky, 1995, 1998).

For these reasons I say that the financial crisis and the environmental crisis are two sides of the same coin. They are at the foundation of the current model of economic growth in industrial nations and of its voracious use of the Earth's resources. The world's financial crisis and the global environmental crisis—the two sides of the same coin—both require a new model of economic growth.

This opinion is not just mine. Indeed, the newly created international group G-20, the first world leading group of nations that includes developing countries, met in Pittsburgh, Pennsylvania on September 24–25, 2009. Their Leader's Statement declares:

> As we commit to implement a new, sustainable growth model, we should encourage work on measurement methods so as to better take into account the social and environmental dimensions of economic development . . . Modernizing the international financial institutions and global development architecture is essential to our efforts to promote global financial stability, foster sustainable development, and lift the lives of the poorest. . . . Increasing clean and renewable energy supplies, improving energy efficiency, and promoting conservation are critical steps to protect our environment, promote sustainable growth and address the threat of climate change. Accelerated adoption of economically sound clean and renewable energy technology and energy efficiency measures diversifies our energy supplies and strengthens our energy security. We commit to:—Stimulate investment in clean energy, renewables, and energy efficiency and provide financial and technical support for such projects in developing countries. Take steps to facilitate the diffusion or transfer of clean energy technology including by conducting joint research and building capacity. The reduction or elimination of barriers to trade and investment in this area are being discussed and should be pursued on a voluntary basis and in appropriate fora.

The statement continues:

> Each of our countries will need, through its own national policies, to strengthen the ability of our workers to adapt to changing market demands and to benefit from innovation and investments in new technologies, clean energy, environment, health, and infrastructure. It is no longer sufficient to train workers to meet their specific current needs; we should ensure access to training programs that support lifelong skills development and focus on future market needs. Developed countries should support developing countries to build and strengthen their capacities in this area. These steps will help to assure that the gains from new inventions and lifting existing impediments to growth are broadly shared.

And it concludes:

> We share the overarching goal to promote a broader prosperity for our people through balanced growth within and across nations; through coherent economic, social, and environmental strategies; and through robust financial systems and effective international collaboration, and we have a responsibility to secure our future through sustainable consumption, production and use of resources that conserve our environment and address the challenge of climate change. (G-20 Leader's Statement, September 2009)

I could not have written this better myself. The G-20 nations know the problem alright. What they may not know is the solutions. For this, read on.

The task in front of us is nothing less than building the human future. In the midst of the sixth largest extinction on planet Earth, facing potentially catastrophic climate change and extinction of marine life in the world's seas—the basis of life on Earth—we can fairly say that this qualifies as a global emergency. And with the adult humans in charge we came so close to the brink that it would appear right now that only the young can help.

A green future is about sharing the wealth and saving the planet. Is this an impossible mandate? We need to stave off biodiversity extinction and reduce carbon emissions, while rebuilding the world economy and supporting the needs of developing nations. Is this possible?

It is, but to understand the solutions we need to look closer at the root of the problem so we can change it.

Rapid expansion of international markets since World War II led by the Bretton Woods Institutions led to enormous consumption of resources. Industrialization is resource intensive, fueled by cheap resources from developing nations—forests, minerals, biodiversity.

These resources were and continue to be exported at very low prices. As a result, poverty in resource-exporting regions has grown to constitute a false "competitive advantage" in the form of cheap labor and cheap resources, an advantage that has exacerbated and amplified resource overconsumption in the North. Resources were over-extracted in poor nations that were desperate for export revenues, and they were over-consumed in industrial nations, thus leading to an ever expanding global wealth divide. Globalization since WWII increased together with an increasing global divide between the rich and the poor nations, the North and the South (Chichilnisky, 1994). Indeed the difference in wealth between the industrial and the developing nations grew threefold over this period of record industrialization and globalization. This is how the global financial system that was created by the Bretton Woods Institutions in 1945, which is tied up with the financial crisis of the day, is also tied up with the global environmental problems we face, and with the global divide between the North and the South (Chichilnisky, 1994).

Since energy use goes hand in hand with economic progress, and most of the energy used in the world today is fossil (87% IEA, 2012a, b), GDP growth remains closely tied with carbon emissions. Industrial nations consume about 70% of the world's energy, and the North/South divide is therefore inexorably connected to the carbon emissions that are destroying the stability of our global climate.

Of course the same North/South divide is the stumbling block in the UN Climate Negotiation as it was clear in the global United Nations negotiations on climate issues in Copenhagen 2009 and also at the Durban 2010 and the Cancún 2011 annual meetings of the Convention of the Parties of the United Nations Framework Convention on Climate Change (UNFCCC), COP 15, 16, and 17 respectively. The problem is: Who should use the world resources? Or, otherwise put, who should abate carbon emissions (Chichilnisky and Heal, 1994)?

It can be said that we are re-living last century's Cold War conflict, but this time it is a conflict between China and the United States (Chichilnisky, *Time* magazine, 2009). Each party could destroy the world as they are the largest emitters and by themselves they can change the world's climate. Each wants the other to "disarm," that is, to reduce carbon emissions, first. This time the conflict is between the rich nations represented by the United States and the poor nations represented by China. This time it has become clear that the solution requires that we overcome the North/South divide, along with the imbalanced use of the use of the world's resources among the rich and the poor nations. Stated otherwise, global justice and the environment are two sides of the same coin. Poverty is caused by cheap resources in a world where developing nations are the main seller into the international market of natural resources, resources that are consumed by the rich nations. This perverse economic dynamics is destroying the stability of the atmosphere of the planet, undermining climate patterns and causing the sixth largest extinction in the history of the planet.

Humans are part of the complex web of species that makes life on Earth. How long will it take until this situation reaches its logical limits and victimizes our own species?

How to avoid extinction?

The Gordian knot that must be cut is the link between natural resources, fossil energy, and economic progress. Only clean energy can achieve this. But this requires changing a $US55 trillion power plant infrastructure, the power plants that produce electrical power around the world (see IEA, 2012a, b), because 87% of world's energy is driven by fossil fuels, and power plants produce 45% of the global carbon emissions (IEA, 2012a, b).

In short—how to make a swift transition to renewable energy?

27.4 The Need for a Carbon Market

Energy is the mother of all markets. Everything is made with energy. Our food, our homes and ours car, the toothpaste and the roads we use, the clothes we wear, the heating of our offices, our medicines: everything. Changing the cost of energy, making dirty energy more expensive and undesirable and clean energy more profitable and desirable—changes everything.

It makes the transition to clean energy possible. We have the technologies—we just have to get the prices right. Is it possible to thus change the price of energy?

Yes, it is. And it has been already done, although it requires more input at present to continue this process after 2015, as discussed in the text that follows. This is what my life is all about now. This is what this chapter is all about.

Here is the background and a summary of the current situation. In 1997, the Carbon Market of the United Nations Kyoto Protocol was signed by 160 nations. In it, and after a long period of lobbying and designing the Carbon Market, I was able to write the structure of the Carbon Market (Chichilnisky and Sheeran, 2009) into the Kyoto Protocol that became international law in 2005 when ratified by nations representing 55% of the world's emissions. The Kyoto Protocol and its Carbon Market have now been adopted as law by 195 nations, and four continents now have a Carbon Market. The United States is excluded from the Kyoto Protocol, because it signed it but did not ratify it, but its most populated state, California, introduced a similar Carbon Market which is law since 2012. In creating the Carbon Market I helped change the value of all goods and services in the world economy because the Carbon Market changes the cost of energy the world over: it makes clean energy more profitable and desirable and dirty energy unprofitable. This changes the prices of products and services in the world—since everything is made with energy—and drives the economy to use cleaner rather than dirty energy sources. It is more profitable and less costly to use clean energy that reduces emissions of carbon; this is precisely the role of the Carbon Market as designed and into the United Nations Kyoto Protocol in December 1997.

The Carbon Market written is now trading carbon credits at the EU Emissions Trading System EU ETS, and as already stated, has been international law since 2005. The World Bank reports on its progress in its report "Status and Trends of the Carbon Market" which has been published annually since the Carbon Market became international law in 2005. The World Bank report documents that by 2010 the European Union Emissions Trading System (EU ETS) was trading about $250 billion per year, and decreased the equivalent of over 30% of EU's emissions of CO_2. Through the Carbon Market, those nations who over-emit compensate those who under emit,—and throughout the entire KP process the world emissions' remains always under a fixed emissions limit that are documented in the protocol for Annex 1 nations, providing nation by nation emissions limits for OECD nations. A "carbon price" emerges from trading the "carbon credits" or rights to emit, which represents the monetary value of the damage caused by each ton of CO_2. The Carbon Market therefore introduces a "carbon price" that corrects what has been called the biggest externality in the history of humankind (cf. Stern, 2006).

The Carbon Market cuts the Gordian knot and makes change possible. It does so because it makes clean energy more profitable and dirty energy less profitable, and it therefore encourages economic growth without environmental destruction: it fosters green development. The market itself costs nothing to run, and requires no subsidies except for minimal logistics costs. In net terms the world economy is exactly in the same position before and after—there are no additional costs from running the Carbon Market, nor from its extremely important global services. The over-emitter nations are worse off, since they have to pay. But every payment they make goes to an under-emitter, so some nations pay and some receive, and in net terms the world economy is exactly in the same position before and after the Carbon Market is introduced. There are no costs to the world economy from introducing a Carbon Market, nor from the limits on carbon emissions and environmental improvement that it produces. It is all gain.

What is the status of the Carbon Market of the Kyoto Protocol today? Initially its nation by nation carbon limits were to expire in 2012 but the Kyoto Protocol itself—its overall structure and the structure of the Carbon Market—do not expire; they are and continue to be international law. Furthermore in Durban South Africa at the United

Nations Convention of the Parties COP 17, it was agreed to continue the Kyoto Protocol provisions to 2015 and to enlarge them to include the whole world by 2020. In any case, all we have to do to keep the Carbon Market's benefits is to define new emissions limits nation by nation for the OECD nations, something that we should be doing in any case since they are the major emitters and without limiting their emissions there is no solution to the global climate issue.

What is the current status of the Carbon Market in the United States, which is the single industrial nation that has not yet ratified the United Nations Kyoto Protocol? There are cross-currents since the United States is a politically divided nation. But the United States already has a Carbon Market in California, US, largest state, and in 10 northeastern US states, called RGGI, which is operating timidly, for its limits on emissions are small and so are therefore the prices for carbon credits. Yet the economic incentives of the Kyoto Protocol's Carbon Market are enormous and many want them. China, for example, created reportedly 1 million new jobs and became the world's main exporter of clean technology equipment (sun and wind) since 2005, namely after signing and ratifying the Kyoto Protocol in 2005 and benefitting from US$40 billion from its Carbon Market and Clean Development Mechanism (World Bank, 2011). China is right now introducing its own Carbon Market. Many in the United States want part of the Carbon Market advantages. President Obama said he wishes to ratify the Kyoto Protocol, and by now 22 US states are planning to create a Carbon Market of their own in addition to California, which created its mandatory Carbon Market in 2012. Hundreds of cities and towns support the Carbon Market in the United States. In the fall of 2007 the US Supreme Court agreed that the federal government and the Environmental Protection Agency (EPA) can enforce carbon emissions limits without requiring Congressional approval. Every effort to deem this regulation illegal by Republican representatives has failed so far. It is generally accepted that global businesses (e.g., the automobile industry) will benefit from the Kyoto Protocol's guidelines, and could suffer economic losses without the benefit of Kyoto Protocol economic incentives at home. This is because the automobile industry is global, and cars that do not sell in other OECD nations create huge losses and lead to bankruptcies. Since all OECD nations are buying carbon-efficient cars, because they ratified the Kyoto Protocol, the US car industry is commercially isolated. For these reasons, in 2010 the EPA imposed automobile emission limits (36.7 miles per gallon), an efficiency requirement that has been increased further by the Obama administration in 2011. The automobile industry voluntarily supported a rise to 54 MPH in 2011. The Republican presidential candidate Mitt Romney, formerly the governor of Massachusetts, himself endorsed the creation a "cap-and-trade" system or a Carbon Market in his state. In December 2011, the EPA announced that it would impose limits on stationery sources like power plants, which is the beginning of a US Carbon Market. These limits were placed on new power plants by the Environmental Protection Agency and the US government executive branch, in March 27, 2012, becoming US federal law as part of the Clean Air Act that was created by President Richard Nixan. The emission limits on power plants are indeed the likely beginning of a federal Carbon Market in the United States: a similar sequence of events took place when the sulfur dioxide (SO_2) market was created at the Chicago Board of Trade (CBOT) 21 years ago. First it was quite controversial, but when the SO_2 emission limits were passed for US power plants they started trading in the SO_2 market at the CBOT, which is now widely considered to have been very successful in eradicating acid rain in the United States.

Are the new EPA carbon limits the beginning of the US Carbon Market, as the SO_2 limits were 21 years ago? Will the mandatory Carbon Market in California extend to a Federal Carbon Market in the United States?

History is being written right now.

The United States is a critical for the success of global climate policies because it is the source of about 25% of the global carbon emissions. Though the United States signed the Kyoto Protocol in 1997, its Congress did not ratify it, and has maintained a critical position toward the Kyoto Protocol since then. Nevertheless, in his second term acceptance speech of January 2012, President Obama singled out climate change as the area that will measure his success for future generations. This seems to set a difficult, perhaps unachievable standard. The United States is divided; there is skepticism about human influence on the environment, and passing a law, budget, or even a national appointment can encounter toxic battlefields in Congress.

It may therefore come as a surprise to many that with a single stroke of the pen, a pen that the US Supreme Court has already handed out to the Executive Office in 2007 and again in 2014, climate change issues can be neatly resolved in the United States. No need to battle Congress.

With the same stroke of the pen, in addition, the United States can provide leadership in the global climate negotiations, showing the way to resolve the issue globally while helping the global economy. This is possible because we have a number of "levers" in place, all ready to be activated by President Obama and the EPA with a stroke of the pen. They can keep a "domino" from falling that makes all the rest follow, enhancing economic performance, accelerating innovation, and creating jobs in the United States and in developing nations, all while improving the environment. The way we measure economic progress the world over—the GDP—can in addition be made to reflect the value of a clean environment. My suggestion is simple: it consists of enhancing in a very simple and legally sanctioned way a piece of a 2012 legislation. On March 27, 2012 President Obama and the EPA, with the support of a 2007 US Supreme Court resolution, set carbon emission limits on newly built power plants under the US Clean Air Act. My proposal was to extend this law to encompass not just newly built but also existing power plants. It is in Obama's power to do what the same he did in 2012, and it is equally within his power to do the simple extension that I required when this article was first written in 2013 now. That is it. To prove this point, in the spring of 2014 President Obama and the EPA (Environmental Protection Agency) passed a law that decreases by 30% carbon emissions for all power plants in the US, existing and now ones, this law was subsequently ratified by the US Supreme Court in June 2014, based on the Clean Air Act. This is the stroke of the few required and anticipated—It happened, and it was ratified by the US Supreme Court in 2014, this is also the foundation for a federal Carbon Market in the US, and is now in place. And this is my proposal.

A skeptical reader may wonder how such a simple step—one that is already in the power of the executive branch of government, the US president and the EPA—can achieve so much with so little. Let me explain how this works. We all know that what is needed to decrease the risk of Climate Change is to reduce the carbon emissions caused by from burning fossil fuels. The largest source of carbon emissions in the United States and globally—about 45% of all emissions—are power plants that burn fossil fuels to produce electricity. Once carbon emissions limits are placed on the main source of emissions—the power plants—these plants will naturally wish to establish a flexible way to comply—such as the so called "Carbon Market." Others call it "cap-and-trade." Power plants took this same action 20 years ago when limits were placed on their SO_2 emissions, and the SO_2 market in the Chicago Board of Trade was created, which is widely credited with eliminating in a very efficient way the worst of acid rain in the United States. The US government only sets the emissions limits—private enterprise does the rest. The process works because the carbon limits reduce the emissions from the largest source of CO_2 emissions—the power plants. Without reducing power plants emissions, the climate change problem cannot be solved. This is why the solution proposed works. It may be the only solution that works. It is clear that the Carbon Market is not a way to escape emissions limits—it is only a way to rearrange who emits more and who emits less, as the overall lower limits remain in place. Now dirty power plants have to pay cleaner power plants for the rights to emit, creating an economic incentive that we all know we need for cleaner plants. It creates also an economic incentive for technology innovation and for investment in the crucial energy infrastructure. We all know that US infrastructure needs renovation. More jobs are created in the process of rebuilding our power plants and building more of them, the most important source of energy that feeds the US economy. Under this proposal there are no taxes to pay to the government. The net cost can be zero—as we are simply redistributing gains from the dirty power plants to the cleaner ones. The latter receive money and the former pay money—the net cost is zero. There is a period of transition where today's market cost of electricity could go up, but we all know that the low costs of dirty power can be illusory. A recent MIT study shows that the real cost of gasoline paid by the US tax payer is about $15 per gallon, more than three times of what we pay at the pump. Similarly the US taxpayer is paying today much more for dirty electricity than we appear to do, including health costs of coal plants, the scary risks of "fracking" for natural gas plants that contaminate drinking water, the defense costs and the political costs from importing gasoline from unstable regions, not to mention the environmental and health risks that are widely accepted from climate change damages such as increased frequency and violence of hurricanes and typhoons, increased costs of food from droughts that scorch the earth, and floods that destroy entire communities. The difference between illusory and real costs is exactly what the Carbon Market captures; the price of "carbon credits" evens up the computations. In any case, transitional costs of new technologies are just that—transitional. Our innovation-bent society understands that, and we invest enormous amounts of money on innovation in education and in risk capital every year for that reason. Transitional costs can also be covered by using the current subsidies to the fossil fuels to ease the transition thus avoiding all the risks and costs of fossil fuels already described. Finally, at the end of the day, as the scope of the clean technologies increases, when the built capacity of clean plants increases, the laws of innovation such as "learning curves" and increasing returns to scale kick in, and clean energy costs can emulate or even improve on existing ones. For full disclosure, the author is working on and has patented a technology that captures carbon very economically from ambient air and from industrial sources, showing that one can make money from the sale of useful CO_2 from this process. This technology—called Global Thermostat™—can make power plants carbon negative and its cost is low enough that it creates profits from the sales of the CO_2 captured. At the end of the day we all know that transition to new technologies can be made to pay and pay very well. The result is innovation, new jobs, and a cleaner economy.

Does the Carbon Market work to reduce emissions? Yes, the European Union that was able to decrease its carbon emissions by about 37% since the Kyoto Protocol emission limits were imposed and the EU Emissions Trading System became international law in 2005. For full disclosure, the author designed and wrote the Carbon Market into the Kyoto Protocol in 1997, the same Carbon Market that became international law in 2005. This market requires no external funding—it is self-financing—and it works well in economic terms, creating incentives for cleaner technology in industrial and developing nations. For example, China received about US$30 billion from the Kyoto Clean Development Mechanism to invest in clean technology, becoming since then the largest exporter of wind and solar power equipment in the world (World Bank, 2011). The EU Emissions Trading System Carbon Market is now trading about US$250 billion annually, and Carbon Markets now exist in four continents, including Australia, Asia, and the European Union and in 2012 a mandatory Carbon Market started to trade in the largest state of the Union, California, a state that leads the rest of the nation in presenting a positive example by fully balancing its budget in 2012.

The United States cannot solve the global climate change problem alone. At its core, climate change is a global problem. By burning its own coal reserves, for example, Africa can produce enough carbon emissions to cause trillions of dollars of damage to the rest of the world—according to the OECD. Yet with the same stroke of the pen the United States can also become a world leader in the climate negotiations. This is because the United States emits 25% of the global emissions, and all Carbon Markets will eventually converge. Therefore the US Carbon Market will enhance the Carbon Market of the Kyoto Protocol globally. Why? This is because markets have a very interesting feature that Wall Street calls "no arbitrage": it means that two markets side to side will end up trading at the same prices for the same commodity. Therefore the price of carbon emitted in the US Carbon Market will soon converge to that of the EU Carbon Market, the Australian, and the Asian carbon markets—and all these markets will be strengthened in their mission of making money while cleaning the environment. Since US markets dominate the world economy, the

United States can enhance the performance of this crucial new market: the global Carbon Market.

A global Carbon Market will change the way we measure economic progress in ways that many clamor for, including the Group of 20. It will create a new global system of economic values. With the Carbon Market, cleaner nations become richer and their economies grow faster than dirty nations, which have to pay the former and can be left behind. A new stick is created to measure economic progress—the GDP now measures the value of all goods and services at market value but now market value includes the value of a clean atmosphere and a stable climate for humankind. We know that we must provide a cleaner environment for future generations—and President Obama has made his contribution to avert climate change the measuring stick of success of his second administration. The simple solution I propose is already available to him; it is legally supported by the US Supreme Court and is independent from the vagaries of bipartisan politics. There seems to be no excuse for not implementing it.

What is a Green Market and why does it matter? A shining example of a Green Market is of course the Kyoto Protocol Carbon Market just discussed, which as we pointed out, became international law in 2005. Another successful example of a Green Market is the SO_2 Market in Chicago Board of Trade. This is quite different from the Carbon Market because SO_2 concentration is not a "global commons" since it varies city by city—while CO_2 is the same uniformly all over the planet. There are more green markets in the works. Today the UN is exploring markets mechanisms for biodiversity and for watersheds proposed officially in Chichilnisky (2011). As in the case of the Kyoto Protocol Carbon Market, these are markets that would trade rights to use the global commons—the use of the world's atmosphere, of its bodies of water, and its biodiversity—and therefore have a deep built-in link between efficiency and equity (Chichilnisky and Heal, 2000). In the Carbon Market of the Kyoto Protocol, by design, the poor nations are preferentially treated, having in practical terms more access and more user rights to the global commons (in that case the planet's atmosphere). This is not the case with SO_2, which is a simple "cap-and-trade" approach because SO_2 is not a public good, as was discussed previously.

Efficiency with equity is what it's all about. They are really two sides of the same coin. One is equity and the other is efficiency, and both matter. The Carbon Market provides efficiency with equity. How? Through its Clean Development Mechanism (CDM), the Kyoto Protocol provides a link between rich and poor nations—the only such link within the Kyoto Protocol—as poor nations do not have emissions limits under the Kyoto Protocol and therefore cannot trade in the Carbon Market. But developing nations face steep opportunity costs if they do not reduce emissions, which strongly encourages reducing emissions—through the CDM of the Carbon Market—how so?

Developing nations have benefitted from the Kyoto Protocol. Since 2005, when it became international law, the Kyoto Protocol Carbon Market funded US$50 billion in clean technology (CDM) projects in poor nations (World Bank, 2005–2012). Its CDM projects have decreased so far the equivalent of more than 30% of EU emissions. The CDM works as follows. Private clean technology projects in the soil of a developing nation—China, Brazil, India—that are proven to decrease the emissions of carbon from this nation below its given "UN agreed baseline" are awarded "carbon credits" for the amount of carbon that is reduced that are themselves tradable for cash in the Carbon Market—so as to recognize in monetary terms the amount of carbon avoided in those projects and fill the role of shifting prices in favor of clean technologies. These CDM carbon credits—by law—can be transformed into cash in the Kyoto Protocol's Carbon Market. This is the role of the Carbon Market in the CDM and this is how the Kyoto Protocol has provided over US$50billion in funding to developing nations since 2005 (World Bank, 2005–2012).

The North/South conflict—namely, who should abate first—puts all this at risk. To move forward in the global negotiations we must overcome the China–United States impasse, which is an intense form of the same conflict that prevails between rich nations and poor nations as a whole—the North and the South (Chichilnisky, 2009). Is it possible to overcome the North/South divide? Yes, it is. But the interests of the industrial and developing nations are so opposed that once again, we need a two-sided coin. This is the same dual role that the Carbon Market played in the Kyoto 1997 global negotiations, where it provided market efficiency that the United States and the OECD wanted, while limiting only OECD nations' emissions, which is what poor nations wanted. This was what I saw then, and this is how, by introducing the Carbon Market into the wording of the Kyoto Protocol, I saved the negotiations and the Kyoto Protocol was voted by 160 nations. Equity and efficiency are the two sides of the coin (Chichilnisky and Heal, 2000). We need both.

27.5 Organizing Principles for Green Capitalism

Readers may think that this chapter offers few details about how to fix the problem. Yet I will show how green capitalism is the solution—it remains to be explained how this works.

Green capitalism is a transformation of capitalism as we know it, by the introduction of new types of markets and market values that change fundamentally how we measure economic performance and in doing so induce a sustainable way forward. Green capitalism is consistent with making more energy available to the world, both for the rich and the poor nations: this is about clean energy that benefits from US technological leadership, and economic growth that brings emissions reductions in developing nations, such as China, Brazil, and India. The basis for green capitalism was explained in Chichilnisky (2009), where it was shown that the Kyoto Protocol CDM can play a critical role as a foundation for a major technology-driven global financial strategy that propels economic progress and is driven by the renovation of the Kyoto targets post 2012. There are three building blocks for green capitalism: (1) efficient US carbon negative technologies, (2) The Kyoto Protocol Carbon Market and its CDM, and (3) innovation in global capital markets.

27.5.1 Carbon-Negative Power Plants for Developing Nations

Cost efficient technologies exist today that capture CO_2 from the atmosphere, directly from ambient air. For example, Global Thermostat LLC (http://www. globalthermostat.com)is commercializing a technology that takes CO_2 out of air and uses low-cost residual heat to drive the capture process, making the entire process of capturing CO_2 from the atmosphere very inexpensive and the activity of selling CO_2 for safe use profitable (Chichilnisky and Eisenberger, 2011). Indeed, there is enough residual heat in a coal power plant that it can be used to capture twice as much CO_2 as the plant emits, thus transforming the power plant into a "carbon sink." For example, a coal plant that emits 1 million tons of CO_2 per year can become a sink absorbing a net amount of 1 million tons of CO_2 instead. This is what is meant by "carbon negative power plants" (Chichilnisky and Eisenberger, 2012) and "carbon-negative technologies^{TM}" (IEA, 2012, IPCC Policy Report, 2014). Carbon capture from air can be done anywhere and at any time, and so inexpensively that the CO_2 can be sold for industrial uses or enhanced oil recovery, a very profitable opportunity (Chichilnisky and Eisenberger, 2009). Any source of low (85°C) heat, lower than needed to boil a cup of tea, will drive this technology, requiring very little energy to function otherwise. In particular, renewable (solar) technology can power the process of carbon capture. This can help advance solar technology and make it more cost efficient. This means more energy and more jobs, and it also means economic growth in developing nations, all with less CO_2 in the atmosphere. Carbon-negative technologies are now needed to forestall the worse climate change scenarios, since we have procrastinated too long and reducing emissions will no longer do—carbon-negative technologies are needed that take off the existing carbon in the atmosphere (Chichilnisky, 2009, 2011; IEA 2012, IPCC Policy Report, 2014).

27.5.2 The Kyoto Protocol Carbon Market

The role of the Kyoto Protocol Carbon Market and its CDM is critical, as it can provide funding and financial incentives to build carbon-negative power plants in developing nations as described previously (Chichilnisky and Eisenberger, 2011; IEA, 2012). The Carbon Market is trading already US$250 billion annually at the EU Emissions Trading System in Brussels (EU ETS) (World Bank, 2005–2012), and each of these dollars goes to decrease carbon emissions. In addition the CDM has transferred US$50 billion for clean energy projects in developing nations since 2005, and it can be used to provide "offsets," such as contracts that promise to buy the electricity that is provided by carbon-negative power plants for a number of years at agreed prices. This unlocks financial resources for investment in carbon-negative power plants. The scheme covers fixed costs and greatly amplifies private profits.

27.5.3 A "Green Power Fund" to Build Carbon-Negative Power Plants in Latin America, Africa, and Small Island States

A US$200 billion/year Green Power Fund was named and proposed by the author in writing to the US Department of State in Copenhagen COP on December 15, 2009, and it was published in the *Financial Times* in 2009 (Chichilnisky, 2009). The concept was accepted and two days later was publicly offered by US Secretary of State Hillary Clinton in the global negotiations at Copenhagen COP 15, and subsequently partially voted by the nations at COP 16 and 17 in Cancún, Mexico and in Durban, South Africa as the "Green Climate Fund." It is making the rounds in the negotiations, where it has received substantial support, although as yet the entire scheme has not been incorporated, in particular its positive connection with the Kyoto Protocol that can provide funding for this US$200 billion/year fund, has was not made explicit. The scheme proposed is a private/public fund that raises funding from global capital markets to invest in investment grade firms that build carbon-negative power plants in developing nations, attracting CDM funding to provide off-takes to buy the ensuing electricity, thus ensuring a market for the electricity they produce, as mentioned previously.

Existing technologies can efficiently and profitably transform existing coal power plants into "carbon sinks" that *reduce* atmospheric carbon concentration (www.globalthermostat.com). Concentrated solar plants (CSPs) that emit no CO_2 can also become carbon negative, by using their residual heat to power carbon capture from air (Chichilnisky and Eisenberger, 2011). Investment is needed to build carbon-negative power plants in developing nations and elsewhere, to renovate the US$55 trillion power plant industry infrastructure worldwide (IEA), which is 87% fossil today. What is required is about US$200 billion a year for about 15–20 years. This amount of money will go to investment in investment-grade power plant builders (General Electric, SSE, Siemens, etc.) to build carbon-negative power plants in developing nations, which is less than what the Carbon Market is trading today per year (US$250 billion; see World Bank's "Status and Trends of the Carbon Market," 2012). Therefore the financial target proposed here is eminently achievable once the connection is made between the Green Power Fund and the Kyoto Protocol Carbon Market and its CDM.

27.6 Blueprint for Sustainable Development

From the organizing principles presented in the preceding text a blueprint emerges for sustainable development, one that is based on generally accepted aims:

1. Clean and abundant energy available worldwide
2. Sustainable growth in developing nations

3. Accelerating transition to solar energy
4. Transformation of fossil energy into a clean alternative

New types of markets are needed to transform capitalism, providing incentives that make green economic projects more profitable than their alternatives, fostering conservation of biodiversity, clean water, and a safe atmosphere. Some of these markets already exist and have been described previously—while some are yet to be created. Green markets change the measurement of GDP as required by the G-20 by creating a measurable market value for the Global Commons, such as a clean atmosphere, biodiversity, and clean water. Because these are markets for global public goods that are privately produced, they link equity with efficiency (Chichilnisky and Heal, 2000) thus helping resolve the North/South wealth divide. Examples of existing green markets are:

1. Carbon Market—international law since 2005
2. SO_2 market in the United States—trading at the CBOT since 1991
3. Markets for biodiversity markets for water—to emerge, proposed officially by the author and under UN consideration (Chichilnisky, 2012)

Green markets provide the missing signal of scarcity that is normally provided by standard market prices when a good or service becomes very scarce. When a resource that humans need for survival becomes scarce (water, oxygen in the atmosphere, biodiversity, and a stable climate) price signals can be tantamount to "traffic lights" for human survival. In Copenhagen COP December 15, 2009 the author was able to insert wording into the CDM allowing carbon negative technologies to be compensated as part of the CDM, working as part of the Papua New Guinea delegation to COP 15. This means that the CDM can now fund properly certified carbon negative technologies. An opportunity to implement the above strategies going forward falls within the UNFCCC Global Climate Negotiations at the annual COP meetings.

27.7 Short and Long Term Strategies

There is a major difference between long- and short-run strategies. Long-run strategies do not work in the short run. In the short run we must actually reduce carbon in the atmosphere and do so quickly—taking a carbon-negative approach—while using renewable energy is the long-run solution. Using renewable energy is, however, too slow for the short run, since replacing a US$55 trillion power plant infrastructure that is based on fossil fuels today with renewable power plants could take many decades. Action is needed sooner than that (IEA, 2012). For the short run we need *carbon-negative technologies,* namely technologies that capture more carbon than what is emitted. Trees do that—and they must be conserved to help preserve biodiversity.

Biochar does that. But trees and other natural sinks are too slow for what we need today, as was validated earlier (Chichilnisky, 2012).

Carbon negative technologies are therefore needed now as part of a blueprint for transformation, a blueprint for sustainable development. While in the long run only renewable sources of energy will do, wind, biofuels, nuclear, geothermal, and hydroelectric energy are in limited supply and therefore cannot replace fossil fuels. Global energy today is divided as follows: 87% fossil, namely gas coal, oil; 10% is nuclear, geothermal, and hydroelectric; and less than 1% is solar power—photovoltaic and solar thermal. Nuclear fuel is very scarce and nuclear technology can be dangerous, as shown in the Japanese nuclear reactor at the Fukushima plant in 2011. Therefore it seems unrealistic to seek a global energy solution in the nuclear direction. Only solar energy can provide a realistic solution because costs are nearly competitive with those of fossil fuels, and less than 1% of the solar energy the planet receives can be transformed into 10 times the fossil fuel energy used in the world today with technologies we know and use today (Chichilnisky and Eisenberger, 2011).

The short run is the next 10 years. It was already mentioned that there is no time in this period to transform the entire fossil fuel infrastructure, which would cost US$55 trillion (International Energy Agency, www.IEA.com) to replace. We need to directly reduce carbon in the atmosphere. Carbon capture and sequestration (CCS) may works but it does not suffice because it captures only what power plants emit. And any amount of new carbon emissions adds to the stable and high concentration we have today in the atmosphere. We need to reduce the carbon already in the atmosphere (Chichilnisky and Eisenberger, 2011, IEA, 2012). But we need a short-term strategy that accelerates long-run renewable energy, or we will defeat our long-term goals. The solution is to combine air capture of CO_2 with storage into biochar, plastics, or other materials, and to use it to produce renewable gasoline through algae or from CO_2 separated from air added to hydrogen separated from water. Air and water can produce a clean substance that is identical to currently used gasoline: if the CO_2 comes from air burning this gasoline simply closes the carbon cycle, it does not put more CO_2 into the atmosphere. This technique is already feasible at commercial and competitive rates whenever there is an inexpensive source of energy. In addition air capture of CO_2 may be combined with solar thermal electricity using the residual heat from a concentrated solar plant (CSP) to drive the carbon capture process, making a solar plant more productive and efficient so it can out-compete coal as a source of energy.

This technology strategy blends the short and the long term. Air capture technology is indeed a transition to the future.

The blueprint offered here follows a private/public approach, it is based on industrial technology and financial markets' leadership, it is self-funded and uses profitable derivative markets—carbon credits as the "underlying" assets, based on the Kyoto Protocol CDM, alongside with markets for biodiversity and water (Chichilnisky, 2011)—all of this providing abundant clean energy to stave off impending and actual energy crisis in developing nations and fostering mutually beneficial cooperation for industrial and developing nations.

The blueprint proposed for sustainable development provides the two sides of the coin, equity and efficiency, and it assigns a critical role as stewards for human survival and sustainable development (Chichilnisky and Heal, 2000). In reality, as was already pointed out, women are today the main source of energy in poor nations, used as beasts of burden in fetching and producing clean water and food for the family as well as sources of energy as wood and dung. Our vision is to replace women by clean energy in poor nations. This agrees with existing policies and encourages a much faster transformation. Indeed, the education of women has been identified by the World Bank as critical for economic development and for the reduction of fertility that goes along with it.

27.8 Conclusions

Avoiding extinction is about the survival of the human species. Survival is not about violent competition and struggle; it is about life, not death. Women are the stewards of a new economic system based on public goods rather than increasing resource exploitation for private gain, and are key for sustainable development. Carbon-negative solutions are the future of energy, replacing the role of women in the poorest nations, and creating green markets that change global value systems and lead the way to green capitalism, helping resolve the global climate negotiations overcome the global wealth divide, providing clean energy and economic growth that fosters the satisfaction of basic needs that is the foundation of sustainable development, economic progress that is harmonious with the Earth's resources and with nurturing life on Earth.

Note

1. On the same date, *The Times* finds: "Planting trees does little to reduce global warming" (p. 17) and it is explained how in a recent Canadian report: "Even if we were to plant trees in all the planet's arable land—an impossible scenario with the global population expected to rise to 9 billion this century—it would cancel out less than 10% of the warming predicted for this century from continuing to burn fossil fuels" (*The Times*, June 21, 2011).

References

Arora, Vivek K., and Montenegro, A. (2011). Small temperature benefits provided by realistic afforestation efforts. *Nature Geoscience, 4*, 514–518.

Chichilnisky, G. (1994). North–South trade and the global environment. *American Economic Review, 84* (4), 851–874

Chichilnisky, G. (1995). Biodiversity as knowledge. *Proceedings of the National Academy of Sciences of the USA*, 1995.

Chichilnisky, G. (1998). The economic value of the Earth resources. In E. Futter (ed.), *Scientists on Biodiversity*. New York: American Museum of Natural History.

Chichilnisky, G. (2009, December). Forward trading: A proposal to end the stalemate between the US and China on climate change. *Time* magazine, Special Issue of Heroes of the Environment, p. 109.

Chichilnisky, G. (2012). The missing signal. Prepared for the Summit of Ministers of the United Nations Economic and Social Commission for Asia and the Pacific (UNESCAP). www.chichilnisky.com

Chichilnisky, G., and Eisenberger, P. (2011). Carbon negative power plants. *Cryogas International*, US. May, p. 36.

Chichilnisky, G., and Heal, G. (1994). Who should abate: An international perspective. *Economic Letters 44*, 443–449.

Chichilnisky, G., and Heal, G. M., eds. (2000). *Environmental Markets: Equity and Efficiency*. New York: Columbia University Press.

Chichilnisky, G., and Sheeran, K. (2009). *Saving Kyoto*. London: New Holland.

G-20 Leaders' Statement from Meeting in Pittsburgh, PA, September 24–25, 2009. http://www.pittsburghsummit.gov/mediacenter/129639.htm

Hyun Youk, and van Oudenaarden, A. (2010, September 2). Microbiology: Altruistic defense needed for survival. *Nature, 467* (7311).

IEA. (2012a). *Global Energy Sources by Type of Power Plants, and Global Sources of* CO_2 *Emissions*. Paris: International Energy Agency. www.IEA.com

IEA. (2012b). *Electricity in a Climate Constrained World – Data and Analysis*. Paris: International Energy Agency.

Lenzen, M., Moran, D., Kanemoto, K., Foran, B., Lobefaro, L., and Geschke, A. (2012, June 7). International trade drives biodiversity threats in developing nations. *Nature, 486*, 109–111.

Peters, G. P., Minx, J. C., Weber, C. L., and Edenhofer, O. (2011). Growth in emission transfers via international trade from 1990 to 2008. *Proceedings of the National Academy of Sciences of the USA, 108*(21), 8903–8908.

Stern, N. (2006). *The Economics of Climate Change: The Stern Report*. Oxford: Oxford University Press.

Swift, J. (1729). A Modest Proposal for preventing the Children of Poor People in Ireland from Being a Burden on their Parents or Country, and for Making them Beneficial to the Publick. London: Sarah Harding.

The Times, London (2011, June 21). Marine life facing mass extinction. page 15.

World Bank. (2005–2012). Status and trends of the carbon market. Annual Reports. Washington, DC: The World Bank.

Name Index

Subject Index

Figures and tables are indicated by "*f*" and "*t*" following page numbers.